COLLINS
POCKET
GREEK
DICTIONARY

A
B
Γ
Δ
E
Z
H
Θ
I
K
Λ
M
N
Ξ
O
Π
P
Σ
T
Y
Φ
X
Ψ
Ω

Αντωνης
1 - 1 - 1986

I wish you, this dictionary
helps your wishes to leen Greek

COLLINS POCKET GREEK DICTIONARY

GREEK·ENGLISH ENGLISH·GREEK

Harry T. Hionides B.S., M.A. (Oxon)
Athens College

Collins
London and Glasgow

First published as Collins Contemporary Greek Dictionary 1977
First published in this edition 1982
© William Collins Sons and Company Limited 1977, 1982
ISBN 0 00 433205 9
Latest reprint 1983

To Marjorie and Homer W. Davis

ISBN 0 00 433206 7 Special edition for Greece and Cyprus

Filmset by Oliver Burridge Filmsetting Limited, Crawley, Sussex
Printed and bound in Great Britain by William Collins Sons and
Company Limited

CONTENTS

Foreword	page	vii
Pronunciation of Modern Greek		viii
Key to Pronunciation of English		ix
Abbreviations		xi
Greek-English Dictionary		1
English-Greek Dictionary		201
English Strong and Irregular Verbs		425
Numerals		429

Πρόλογος

Ἡ εὐρεῖα χρῆσις τῆς ἀγγλικῆς γλώσσης εἰς ὅλον τόν κόσμον κατέστησε λίαν αἰσθητήν τήν ἀνάγκην τῆς γνώσεως τῆς ἀκριβοῦς σημασίας τῆς ἀγγλικῆς ὁρολογίας. Τήν ἀνάγκην αὐτήν ζητεῖ νά πληρώση τό νέον ἀνά χεῖρας Ἀγγλοελληνικόν καί Ἑλληνοαγγλικόν Λεξικόν, τό ὁποῖον προορίζεται κυρίως διά τούς, ἕλληνας μαθητάς τῆς ἀγγλικῆς καί διά τούς ἀγγλοφώνους ἐπισκέπτας τῆς Ἑλλάδος. Κατά τήν σύνταξιν τοῦ ἐπιτόμου Λεξικοῦ δύο στοιχεῖα ἐλήφθησαν ὑπ'ὄψιν, ἡ περιεκτικότης καί ἡ σαφήνεια. Κατά τήν περιεκτικότητα τό Λεξικόν εἶναι πλουσιώτατον διότι περιλαμβάνει τάς μᾶλλον προχείρους καί συνήθεις λέξεις καί φράσεις τῆς ἀγγλικῆς καί τῆς ἑλληνικῆς. Ὡς πρός τήν σαφήνειαν μεγάλη προσοχή κατεβλήθη εἰς τήν ἀπόδοσιν τῆς ἀκριβοῦς σημασίας ἑκάστης λέξεως. Ὅπου τυχόν μία λέξις ἔχει πλείονας σημασίας, ἀναγράφονται αὗται κατά σειράν συχνότητος χρησιμοποιήσεως. Ἐκτός τούτου προσεπάθησα νά ἀποδώσω εἰς τήν ἑλληνικήν πλείστας ὅσας λαϊκάς καί ἰδιωματικάς ἐκφράσεις τῆς ἀγγλικῆς.

Περιλαμβάνει ὅλας τάς ἐν χρήσει λέξεις τῆς ἀγγλικῆς καί τῆς ἑλληνικῆς γλώσσης μέ τάς κυριωτέρας σημασίας ἑκάστης, ὅσον ἐπιτρέπει ὁ χῶρος, ὡς καί τούς πλέον συνήθεις τεχνικούς καί ἐπιστημονικούς ὅρους τῶν δύο γλωσσῶν. Πλεῖσται νέαι λέξεις ἔχουν περιληφθῆ τάς ὁποίας δέν θά εὕρη τις εἰς ἄλλα ὀγκωδέστερα λεξικά.

Οὕτω τό Ἀγγλοελληνικόν καί Ἑλληνοαγγλικόν Λεξικόν ἀποτελεῖ δύο κεχωρισμένα μέν ἀλλά ἀλληλοσυμπληρούμενα τμήματα ἑνός ἀρτίου συνόλου, τό ὁποῖον τίθεται εἰς τήν διάθεσιν τῶν μαθητῶν καί τῶν γνωριζώντων τήν ἀγγλικήν.

Χάρης Χιονίδης

Foreword

Of all publications issuing from the press, a dictionary is certainly the last to require a long preface. The user has only to glance at a few pages to find out the system followed and to gauge the value of the work as a whole.

The aim of this Greek-English, English-Greek dictionary is to be a work of practical utility within convenient size in which are met the needs of Greek students of English and of English-speaking travellers in Greece. Completeness, as far as practicable, conciseness and accuracy have been the guide lines for the compilation. The vocabularies have been carefully sifted and compiled to embrace most words in current use including many scientific and technical terms which have become a part of everyday speech. Idiomatic and slang expressions as well as Americanisms are also included.

That bane of the Greek language, 'diglossia', has been resolved by preference for the popular and colloquial rather than the learned usage whenever this has been practicable. Every effort has been made not to give a mere string of terms on the chance of hitting the right one among them, but to find the exact and generally received equivalent of the word or phrase under consideration. And no effort has been spared to produce a comprehensive, yet concise, lucid and safe guide for those users of the dictionary whether they be students or travellers.

I wish here to express my gratitude to the numerous friends and colleagues who have in one way or another encouraged me to undertake this compilation. Among these I mention W. Lee Pierson, E. Glassmeyer, G. Savvides, Richard Thomas, Carol Purdon, and Iseabail Macleod.

Harry T. Hionides

Pronunciation of Modern Greek

Greek has nineteen consonant sounds and only five vowel sounds. Some of them are exactly as in English, some resemble their English counterparts very closely, and there are two for which no English equivalent exists. The system adopted here is to transcribe simply into Latin letters the sounds of Greek. The pronunciation is very simple. Each letter has the same phonetic sound with few exceptions. There are no variations in the pronunciation of Greek letters as in English, no silent characters or long or short vowel sounds. And there are only two letters without English equivalents—γ and χ.

Modern Greeks pronounce the following consonants like the English:

β, ζ, κ, λ, μ, ν, ξ, π, ρ, σ, τ, φ, ψ
v z k l m n ks p r s t f ps

Other consonant sounds:

Greek letter(s)	Symbols	
μπ	b (when initial)	b as in boy
	mb, mp (when medial)	
ντ	d	d as in day, do
	nd (when medial)	
	nt	
γκ or γγ	ng	g as in go and
		ng as in England
θ	th	as in thin
δ	δ	as in this
γ	γ	as in yes

The following three sounds are the most troublesome:

ρ	r	as in roll (rolled like the Scottish r)
γ	γ	To produce this sound make a continuous g sound without withdrawing the tongue.
χ	h	There are two h sounds. One resembles the ch of the Scottish loch and it is how χ is generally pronounced. The other is like the ch sound of the German ich.

The υ of the groups αυ, ευ, ηυ is generally pronounced v. Before ϑ, κ, ξ, π, σ, τ, φ, χ, ψ it is pronounced f.

The three genders of nouns only are distinguished by the articles ὁ (masculine), ἡ (feminine) and τό (neuter).

Ἐπεξήγησις Προφορᾶς

Key to Pronunciation of English

Δέν ἀναφέρομεν παραδείγματα διὰ τὰ ἀκόλουθα φωνητικὰ σύμβολα, διότι εἶναι γνωστὰ ὡς γράμματα τοῦ ἀλφαβήτου

p, b, d, t, k, m, n, l, r, f, v, s, z, h.

Ἐφιστῶμεν τὴν προσοχὴν τοῦ μαθητοῦ ἐπὶ τῶν κάτωθι συμβόλων, τὰ ὁποῖα εἴτε δὲν ἀπαντοῦν εἰς τὸ ἀλφάβητον, εἴτε χρησιμοποιοῦνται πρὸς δήλωσιν φθόγγου ὁ ὁποῖος συχνὰ διαφέρει ἀπὸ τὴν φωνὴν τοῦ γράμματος τοῦ ἀλφαβήτου.

Ι Σύμφωνα

1.	g	leg	6. ʒ	régime
2.	ŋ	finger	7. j	your
3.	θ	thumb	8. w	water
4.	ð	this	9. tʃ	chest
5.	ʃ	ship	10. dʒ	danger

Κατάταξις τῶν Συμφώνων ἀναλόγως τῆς φωνῆς των καὶ τρόπου προφορᾶς

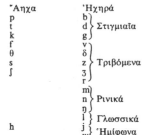

```
        Ἄηχα          Ἠχηρά
         p            b ⎫
         t            d ⎬ Στιγμιαῖα
         k            g ⎭
         f            v ⎫
         θ            ð ⎪
         s            z ⎬ Τριβόμενα
         ʃ            ʒ ⎪
                      r ⎭
                      m ⎫
                      n ⎬ Ρινικά
                      ŋ ⎭
                      l ⎫ Γλωσσικά
         h            j ⎬
                      w ⎭ Ἡμίφωνα
```

Τὰ 24 Σύμφωνα κατὰ σειράν

b, d, f, g, h, k, l, m, n, p, r, s, t, v, w, z

θ, ð, ŋ, j, ʃ, ʒ, tʃ, dʒ

II Φωνήεντα

'Οπίσθια

1	2	3	4		5	6	7	8	9
i:	i	e	æ		ɑ:	ɔ	ɔ:	u	u:
see	chin	leg	hand		arm	on	your	foot	food

Κεντρικά

10	11	12
ʌ	ə:	ə
thumb	girl	bitter

III Δίφθογγοι

13	14	15	16	17	18	19	20	21	22
ei	ou	ai	au	ɔi	iə	ɛə	uə	aiə	auə
face	nose	eye	mouth	boy	ear	there	poor	fire	power

English and Greek Abbreviations

a	adjective	ἐπίθετον
abbr	abbreviation	σύντμησις
ad	adverb	ἐπίρρημα
agr	agriculture	γεωργία
anat	anatomy	ἀνατομία
arch	archeology	ἀρχαιολογία
archit	architecture	ἀρχιτεκτονική
art	art	τέχνη
astr	astronomy	ἀστρονομία
attr	attributive	ἐπίθετον
aut	automobile	αὐτοκίνητον
aviat	aviation	ἀεροπορία
bibl	biblical	βιβλικός
biol	biology	βιολογία
bot	botany	βοτανική
Brit	British usage	Ἀγγλισμός
carp	carpentry	ξυλουργική
chem	chemistry	χημεία
cine	cinema	κινηματογράφος
col	colloquial	κοινός
collect	collective	περιληπτικός
comm	commercial	ἐμπορικός
comp	comparative	συγκριτικός
compd	compound, compound element	σύνθετος
cj	conjunction	σύνδεσμος
dim	diminutive	ὑποκοριστικός
dip	diplomacy	διπλωματική
eccl	ecclesiastical	ἐκκλησιαστικόν
econ	economics	οἰκονομία
elec	electricity	ἠλεκτρισμός
esp	especially	εἰδικῶς
excl	exclamation	ἐπιφώνημα
f	feminine noun	θηλυκόν
fig	figuratively	μεταφορικῶς
fin	finance	οἰκονομία
geog	geography	γεωγραφία
geol	geology	γεωλογία
gram	grammar	γραμματική
hunt	hunting	κυνήγι
impers	impersonal	ἀπρόσωπον
infin	infinitive	ἀπαρέμφατος

interj	interjection	ἐπιφώνημα
irreg	irregular	ἀνώμαλον
law	law	νομική
ling	linguistics	γλωσσολογία
lit	literal	κυριολεκτικός
liter	literature	λογοτεχνία
m	masculine noun	ἀρσενικόν
math	mathematics	μαθηματικά
mech	mechanism	μηχανισμός
med	medicine	ἰατρική
mil	military	στρατιωτικός
mus	music	μουσική
n	(neuter) noun	οὐδέτερον
naut	nautical, naval	ναυτικός
num	numeral	ἀριθμός
old	old-fashioned	ἀπηρχαιωμένος
o.s.	oneself	ἑαυτόν
parl	Parliament	κοινοβούλιον
part	participle	μετοχή
pej	pejorative	ὑποτιμητικός
pers	personal	προσωπικός
phil	philosophy	φιλοσοφία
phon	phonetics	φωνητική, φωνολογία
phot	photography	φωτογραφία
phys	physics	φυσική
pl	plural	πληθυντικός
poet	poetry	ποίησις
pol	politics	πολιτική
poss	possessive	κτητικός
pp	past participle	παθητική μετοχή, μετοχή ἀορίστου
pred	predicative	κατηγορούμενον
prep	preposition	πρόθεσις
print	printing/typography	τυπογραφία
pron	pronoun	ἀντωνυμία
pt	past tense	ἀόριστον, παρατατικόν
rad	radio	ραδιοφωνία
rail	railways	σιδηρόδρομος
rel	religion	θρησκεία
sch	school	σχολεῖον
sing	singular	ἑνικός
sl	slang	λαϊκός
s.o.	someone, somebody	κάποιος
sport	sport	ἀθλητικά
sth	something	κάτι
sup	superlative	ὑπερθετικός
tech	technical	τεχνικός
tel	telephone	τηλέφωνον
tex	textiles	ὑφαντά
theat	theatre	θέατρον
TV	television	τηλεόρασις
univ	university	πανεπιστήμιον
US	American usage	Ἀμερικανισμός
v	verb	ρῆμα

vi	intransitive verb	ρῆμα ἀμετάβατον
vt	transitive verb	ρῆμα μεταβατικόν
vti	transitive and intransitive verb	ρῆμα μεταβατικόν καί ἀμετάβατον
zool	zoology	ζωολογία

ἀθλητ	ἀθλητικά	athletics, sport
ἀερο	ἀεροπορία	aviation
ἀμ, ἀμετ, ἀμετάβ	ρῆμα ἀμετάβατον	intransitive verb
ἀνατ	ἀνατομία	anatomy
ἀρχιτεκ	ἀρχιτεκτονική	architecture
ἀστρον	ἀστρονομία	astronomy
βλ	βλέπε	see (cross-reference)
βοτ	βοτανική	botany
γεωγρ	γεωγραφία	geography
γεωμ	γεωμετρία	geometry
γραμμ	γραμματική	grammar
ἐκκλ	θρησκεία	religion
ἐμπορ	ἐμπόριον	commerce
ἐπίθ	ἐπίθετον	adjective
ἐπίρ	ἐπίρρημα	adverb
ἐπιφ	ἐπιφώνημα	exclamation
ζωολ	ζωολογία	zoology
ἠλεκ, ἠλεκτ	ἠλεκτρισμός	electricity
ἰατρ	ἰατρική	medicine
κτλ	καί τά λοιπά	et cetera
μαθημ	μαθηματικά	mathematics
μηχαν	μηχανισμός	mechanism
μεταφ	μεταφορικῶς	figuratively
μουσ	μουσική	music
ναυτ	ναυτικόν	nautical, naval
νομ	νομική	law
οἰκ, οἰκον, οἰκονομ	οἰκονομικά	economics
ὄνομ, οὐσ	ὄνομα, οὐσιαστικόν	noun
πλ	πληθυντικός	plural
πολιτ	πολιτική	politics
προθ	πρόθεσις	preposition
π.χ.	παραδείγματος χάριν	e.g. (for example)
στρατ	στρατιωτικός	military
σύνδ	σύνδεσμος	conjunction
τεχν	τεχνολογία	technical
τηλεφ	τηλέφωνον	telephony
τυπογρ	τυπογραφία	printing, typography
φιλοσ	φιλοσοφία	philosophy
φωτογρ	φωτογραφική	photography
χημ	χημεία	chemistry

Greek—English

A, α

ἀ-, ἀν- (negative particle) in-, un-, il-, ir-, -less.

ἀβαθής [avathees] shallow.

ἀβάντα, ἡ [avanta] advantage.

ἀβάπτιστος [avapteestos] unbaptised.

ἀβασίλευτος [avaseeleftos] without a king ‖ (ἥλιος κτλ) not set.

ἀβάσιμος [avaseemos] groundless ‖ unfounded.

ἀβάστακτος [avastaktos] unbearable ‖ (δύναμις) uncontrollable.

ἄβατος [avatos] inaccessible ‖ untrodden.

ἀβγαλτος [avyaltos] inexperienced.

ἀβγό, τό [avyo] egg.

ἀβγολέμονο, τό [avyolemono] sauce or soup with eggs and lemon.

ἀβέβαιος [aveveos] doubtful ‖ uncertain.

ἀβίαστος [aveeastos] unforced, natural.

ἀβίωτος [aveeotos] unbearable, intolerable.

ἀβλαβής [avlavees] unhurt, unharmed.

ἀβλεψία, ἡ [avlepseea] inadvertence.

ἀβοήθητος [avoeetheetos] without help, helpless.

ἄβολος [avolos] inconvenient ‖ (κάθισμα κτλ) uncomfortable.

ἄβραστος [avrastos] unboiled ‖ undercooked.

ἄβυσσος, ἡ [aveesos] abyss.

ἀγαθός [ayathos] good, kind ‖ (ἀφελής) naive ‖ (τίμιος) honest.

ἀγάλια [ayaleea] slowly, softly, gently.

ἄγαλμα, τό [ayalma] statue.

ἄγαμος [ayamos] unmarried, single.

ἀγανακτῶ [ayanakto] be indignant, be angry.

ἀγανάκτησις, ἡ [ayanakteesees] indignation, anger.

ἀγάπη, ἡ [ayapee] love, affection.

ἀγαπημένος [ayapeemenos] dear, beloved ‖ favourite.

ἀγαπητικός, ὁ [ayapeeteekos] lover, sweetheart.

ἀγαπητός [ayapeetos] βλ ἀγαπημένος.

ἀγαπῶ [ayapo] love ‖ (μοῦ ἀρέσει) like.

ἀγγαρεία, ἡ [angareea] chore ‖ drudgery.

ἀγγεῖον, τό [angeeon] vase ‖ pot ‖ (ἀνατ) blood vessel.

ἀγγειοπλαστική, ἡ [angeeoplasteekee] pottery.

ἀγγελία, ἡ [angeleea] announcement ‖ (ἐμπορ) advertisement.

ἀγγελιαφόρος, ὁ, ἡ [angeleeaforos] messenger ‖ orderly.

ἀγγελικός [angeleekos] angelic(al).

ἀγγέλω [angello] announce, declare.

ἄγγελμα, τό [angelma] message, notice.

ἄγγελος, ὁ [angelos] angel.

ἀγγίζω [angeezo] touch.

ἄγγιχτος [angeehtos] untouched ‖ (ἄθικτος) intact.

Ἀγγλία, ἡ [angleea] England.

ἀγγλικά, τά [angleeka] English (language).

ἀγγλικός [angleekos] English.

Ἀγγλίς, ἡ [anglees] Englishwoman.

Ἄγγλος, ὁ [anglos] Englishman.

ἀγγούρι, τό [angouree] cucumber.

ἀγελάδα, ἡ [ayelaδa] cow ‖ (μεταφ). big fat woman, old cow (col).

ἀγέλαστος [ayelastos] morose, sullen ‖ undeceived.

ἀγέλη, ἡ [ayelee] herd ‖ (προβάτων) flock ‖ (λύκων) pack.

ἀγέμιστος [ayemeestos] empty ‖ (στρῶμα κτλ) unstuffed.

ἀγένεια, ἡ [ayeneea] impoliteness.

ἀγενής [ayenees] rude, impolite.

ἀγέραστος [ayerastos] ever young.

ἀγέρωχος [ayerohos] haughty, arrogant.

ἀγιάζι [ayeeazi] hoarfrost, cold.

ἀγιάζω [ayeeazo] (γίνομαι ἅγιος) become a saint.

ἁγιασμός, ὁ [ayeeasmos] blessing of holy water.

ἀγιάτρευτος [ayeeatreftos] incurable ‖ (μή γιατρευθείς) uncured.

ἀγίνωτος [ayeenotos] (φροῦτο) unripe, raw ‖ (φαγητό) uncooked.

ἁγιογραφία, ἡ [ayeeoyrafeea] icon, hagiography.

ἅγιος [ayeeos] holy ‖ (πρόσωπον) saint.

ἀγκαζάρω [angazaro] reserve, book ‖ hire.

ἀγκαζέ [angaze] arm in arm ‖ (πιασμένο) engaged, taken, occupied.

ἀγκάθι, τό [angathee] thorn, prickle.

ἀγκαλιά, ἡ [angalia] embrace ‖ (ἐπιρ) armful.

ἀγκαλιάζω [angaliazo] embrace, hug.

ἀγκίδα, ἡ [angeeδa] splinter, thorn.

ἀγκινάρα, ἡ [angeenara] artichoke.

ἀγκίστρι, τό [angeestri] hook.

ἀγκομαχῶ [angomaho] gasp, pant.

ἀγκύλαι, αἱ [angeele] brackets.

ἀγκυλωτός [angeelotos] crooked, bent.

άγκυρα, ή [angeera] anchor ‖ σηκώνω ~ weigh anchor.

άγκυροβολία, ή [angeerovoleea] anchoring, mooring.

άγκυροβολώ [angeerovolo] anchor, drop anchor.

άγκών, ό [angon] elbow.

άγλαΐζω [aylaeezo] embellish, adorn, decorate.

άγναντεύω [aynantevo] see from a distance.

άγνοια, ή [ayneea] ignorance.

άγνός [aynos] chaste, modest.

άγνοώ [aynoo] be ignorant of ‖ (περιφρονώ) ignore.

άγνωμοσύνη, ή [aynomoseenee] ungratefulness.

άγνώμων [aynomon] ungrateful, unthankful.

άγνώριστος [aynoreestos] unrecognizable.

άγνωστος [aynostos] not known, obscure.

άγονος [ayonos] infertile, barren ‖ (μεταφ) vain ‖ ~ γραμμή unprofitable shipping line.

άγορά, ή [ayora] (τό μέρος) market ‖ (ή πράξις) purchase.

άγοράζω [ayorazo] purchase, buy.

άγοραίος [ayoreos] for hire ‖ (μεταφ) vulgar, common.

άγορανομία, ή [ayoranomeea] market inspection police.

άγοραπωλησία, ή [ayorapoleeseea] buying and selling.

άγοραστής, ό [ayorastees] buyer, purchaser.

άγορεύω [ayorevo] make a speech, harangue.

άγόρι, τό [ayoree] boy, lad.

άγουρίδα, ή [ayouriδa] sour grape.

άγουρος [ayouros] unripe, green, sour.

άγρα, ή [ayra] chase, hunting.

άγράμματος [ayrammatos] illiterate, ignorant.

άγραφος [ayrafos] unwritten.

άγριάδα, ή [ayriaδa] fierceness, savageness.

άγριάνθρωπος, ό [ayrianthropos] savage.

άγριεύω [ayrievo] be infuriated, become angry.

άγρίμι, τό [ayreemee] wild animal ‖ (μεταφ) rude fellow.

άγριος [ayreeos] wild, furious, harsh.

άγροίκος [ayreekos] coarse, unrefined, ill-bred.

άγρόκτημα, τό [ayrokteema] farmland.

άγρός, ό [ayros] field ‖ country.

άγρότης, ό [ayrotees] farmer, peasant.

άγροφυλακή, ή [ayrofeelakee] agrarian police.

άγρυπνώ [ayreepno] keep awake, lie awake ‖ be watchful.

άγυάλιστος [ayeealistos] unpolished, tarnished.

άγύμναστος [ayeemnastos] untrained, unexercised.

άγύρτης, ό [ayeertees] charlatan, impostor.

άγχιστεία, ή [anghisteea] affinity by marriage.

άγχόνη, ή [anghonee] gallows, hanging.

άγχος, τό [anghos] anxiety.

άγω [ayo] lead, conduct, guide.

άγωγή, ή [ayoyee] breeding, conduct ‖ (νομ) lawsuit.

άγώγι, τό [ayoyee] fare, carriage.

άγωγιάτης, ό [ayoyeeatees] driver, guide.

άγωγός, ό [ayoyos] conductor ‖ pipe, conduit.

άγών, ό [ayon] struggle, fight ‖ (άθλητ) game, contest ‖ ~ ες πλ games, sports events.

άγωνία, ή [ayoneea] agony, anxiety.

άγωνίζομαι [ayoneezome] struggle, fight, strive.

άγωνιστής, ό [ayoneestees] contestant, fighter ‖ war veteran.

άγωνιώ [ayoneeo] be in agony, be anxious.

άγωνιώδης [ayoneeoδees] anxious, troubled.

άδαής [aδaees] inexperienced, unfamiliar (with).

άδαμάντινος [aδamanteenos] diamond ‖ (χαρακτήρ) indomitable.

άδάμας, ό [aδamas] diamond.

άδάμαστος [aδamastos] untamed ‖ (λαός) unconquered ‖ (θάρρος) unbroken.

άδάπανος [aδapanos] free, inexpensive.

άδεια, ή [aδeea] leave, permission ‖ (γάμου κτλ) licence, permit.

άδειάζω [aδeeazo] empty ‖ (εύκαιρώ) have time, have leisure.

άδειος [aδeeos] empty, unoccupied ‖ at leisure.

άδέκαστος [aδekastos] incorruptible ‖ (άμερόληπτος) equitable, unbiased.

άδελφή, ή [aδelfee] sister.

άδέλφια, τά [aδelfeea] πλ brothers, brother and sister.

άδελφικός [aδelfeekos] brotherly, dear.

άδελφός, ό [aδelfos] brother.

άδενδρος [aδenδros] treeless.

άδέξιος [aδekseeos] awkward, clumsy.

άδέσμευτος [aδesmeftos] (μεταφ) under no obligation.

άδέσποτος [aδespotos] stray, without owner.

άδετος [aδetos] (βιβλίο) unbound ‖ (λυμένος) loose, untied.

άδηλος [aδeelos] uncertain, doubtful ‖ άδηλοι πόροι invisible income.

άδήλωτος [aδeelotos] undeclared.

άδημονώ [aδeemono] be anxious, fret.

άδήν, ό [aδeen] gland.

Άδης, ό [aδees] Hell ‖ Hades.

άδηφάγος [aδeefayos] voracious ‖ greedy.

άδιάβαστος [aδeeavastos] (βιβλίο) unread ‖ (μαθητής) unprepared.

άδιάβατος [aδeeavatos] impassable, impenetrable.

άδιάβροχον, τό [aδeeavrohon] raincoat.

ἀδιάϑετος [aðeeathetos] (ὑγεία) unwell ‖ (κεφάλαιον) unspent.
ἀδιαίρετος [aðieretos] indivisible ‖ undivided.
ἀδιάκοπος [aðeeakopos]· uninterrupted, ceaseless.·
ἀδιάκριτος [aðeeakreetos] imperceptible ‖ (χαρακτήρ) indiscreet.
ἀδιάλλακτος [aðeealaktos] irreconcilable, uncompromising.
ἀδιάλυτος [aðeealeetos] indissoluble, undissolved.
ἀδιάντροπος [aðeeantropos] brazen ‖ (ἐνέργεια) impudent.
ἀδιαπέραστος [aðeeaperastos] impenetrable, impermeable.
ἀδιάρρηκτος [aðeeareektos] unbreakable ‖ (μεταφ) indissoluble.
ἀδιάσπαστος [aðeeaspastos] unbroken, inseparable.
ἀδιάφορος [aðeeaforos] apathetic ‖ of no interest.
ἀδιαχώριστος [aðeeahoreestos] inseparable.
ἀδίδακτος [aðeeðaktos] untaught.
ἀδιέξοδος, ἡ [aðieksoðos] impasse ‖ (δρόμος) cul-de-sac, dead end.
ἀδικία, ἡ [aðeekeea] injustice, wrongdoing, offence.
ἄδικος [aðeekos] unjust, unfair ‖ ἔχω ἄδικον I'm in the wrong.
ἀδικῶ [aðeeko] do wrong, be-unjust.
ἀδιόρατος [aðeeoratos] imperceptible.
ἀδιόρϑωτος [aðeeorthotos] irreparable ‖ (χαρακτήρ) incorrigible.·
ἀδίσταχτος [aðeestahtos] unhesitating, resolute.
ἄδολος [aðolos] guileless, innocent.
ἄδοξος [aðoksos] inglorious.
ἀδούλευτος [aðouleftos] unwrought, raw ‖ (ἀγρός) uncultivated.
ἀδράνεια, ἡ [aðraneea] inertness ‖ (μεταφ) inactivity, apathy.
ἀδράχτι, τό [aðrahtee] spindle.
ἀδρός [aðros] plentiful, generous.
ἀδύνατος [aðeenatos] feeble, thin ‖ (δέν γίνεται) impossible.
ἀδυναμία, ἡ [aðeenameea] (πνεύματος) deficiency ‖ (σώματος) weakness.
ἀδυνατῶ [aðeenato] be unable to, cannot.
ἀδυσώπητος [aðeesopeetos] relentless, implacable.
ἄδυτον, τό [aðeeton] (ἐκκλ) sanctuary.
ἄδω [aðo] sing.
ἀεί [aee] always ‖ ἐς~ forever.
ἀειϑαλής [aeethalees] evergreen.
ἀεικίνητος [aeekeeneetos] of perpetual motion.
ἀείμνηστος [aeemneestos] of blessed memory.
ἀεράμυνα, ἡ [aerameena] air defence.
ἀεράγημα, τό [aerayeema] airborne troops.
ἀεραγωγός, ἡ [aerayogos] air duct.
ἀέρας, ὁ [aeras] air, wind.

ἄεργος [aeryos] unemployed, idle.
ἀερίζω [aereezo] ventilate, fan.
ἀερισμός, ὁ [aereesmos] ventilation, airing.
ἀέριον, τό [aereeon] gas.
ἀεριοῦχος [aereeouhos] aerated, gaseous.
ἀεριστήρ, ὁ [aereesteer] ventilator.
ἀεροδρόμιον, τό [aeroðromeeon] aerodrome.
ἀερόλιϑος, ὁ [aeroleethos] meteorite.
ἀερολιμήν, ὁ [aeroleemeen] airport.
ἀεροπλάνον, τό [aeroplanon] aeroplane.
ἀεροπορία, ἡ [aeroporeea] air force.
ἀεροπορικῶς [aeroporeekos] by air.
ἀερόστατον, τό [aerostaton] balloon.
ἀετός, ὁ [aetos] eagle ‖ (μεταφ) clever person ‖ (χαρταετός) kite.
ἀζήτητος [azeeteetos] unclaimed ‖ (ἐμπορ) not sought after, not demanded.
ἄζυμος [azeemos] unleavened.
ἄζωτον, τό [azoton] nitrogen.
ἀηδής [aeeðees] loathsome, sickening.
ἀηδία, ἡ [aeeðeea] disgust, loathing, odiousness.
ἀηδιάζω [aeeðeeazo] feel disgust for, loathe.
ἀηδόνι, τό [aeeðonee] nightingale.
ἀήρ, ὁ [aeer] air.·
ἀήττητος [aeeteetos] undefeated, unbeatable.
ἀϑανασία, ἡ [athanaseea] immortality, eternity.
ἀϑάνατος [athanatos] immortal, deathless.
ἀϑέατος [atheatos] invisible, unseen.
ἀϑελα [athela] unintentionally.
ἀϑέμιτος [athemeetos] illegal, unlawful.
ἄϑεος [atheos] godless ‖ (οὐσ) atheist.
ἀϑεόφοβος [atheofovos] impious ‖ (οὐσ) rogue.
ἀϑεράπευτος [atharapevtos] incurable, incorrigible.
ἀϑετῶ [atheto] break one's word, violate.
ἄϑικτος [atheektos] untouched, unharmed.
ἀϑλητής, ὁ [athleetees] athlete.
ἀϑλητικός [athleeteekos] athletic, robust.
ἀϑλητισμός, ὁ [athleeteesmos] athletics.
ἄϑλιος [athleeos] wretched, miserable.
ἄϑλος, ὁ [athlos] feat, exploit.
ἀϑόρυβος [athoreevos] quiet, silent.
ἄϑραυστος [athravstos] unbroken ‖ unbreakable.
ἄϑρησκος [athreeskos] irreligious.
ἀϑροίζω [athreezo] add up, count ‖ (στρατ) gather, assemble.
ἄϑροισμα, τό [athreesma] sum, total.
ἀϑυμία, ἡ [atheemeea] dejection, depression.
ἀϑυρόστομος [atheerostomos] indiscreet, impertinent.
ἀϑῶος [athoos] innocent, guileless.
ἀϑωώνω [athoono] acquit, exonerate.
αἰγιαλός, ὁ [eyeealos] seashore, coast.
αἴγλη, ἡ [eylee] splendour ‖ (ὀνόματος κτλ) grandeur, glory.

αἰγόκλημα, τό [eγokleema] honeysuckle.

αἰδέσιμος [eδeseemos] reverend, venerable.

αἰδήμων [eδeemon] modest, chaste.

αἰθέριος [ethereeos] ethereal, essential.

αἰθήρ, ὁ [etheer] ether, air.

αἴθουσα, ἡ [ethousa] room, hall || (σχολική) schoolroom.

αἴθριος [ethreeos] clear, bright, fair.

αἷμα, τό [ema] blood.

αἱματηρός [emateeros] bloody, bloodstained.

αἱματοχυσία, ἡ [ematoheeseea] bloodshed.

αἱματώνω [ematono] besmear with blood || bleed.

αἱμοβόρος [emovoros] bloodthirsty || (μεταφ) ferocious, cruel.

αἱμοδοσία, ἡ [emoδoseea] blood donation.

αἱμομιξία, ἡ [emomeekseea] incest.

αἱμορραγία, ἡ [emoraγeea] haemorrhage.

αἱμοσφαίριον, τό [emosfereeon] blood corpuscle.

αἴνιγμα, τό [eneeγma] enigma, riddle.

ἄιντε [aeede] (ἔπιφ) come now!, come on!

αἴξ, ἡ [eks] goat.

αἵρεσις, ἡ [ereses] heresy.

αἱρετικός [ereteekos] heretical.

αἴρω [erro] lift || raise.

αἰσθάνομαι [esthanome] feel.

αἴσθημα, τό [estheema] sensation, feeling || ~ τα feelings.

αἰσθηματικός [estheemateekos] sentimental.

αἴσθησις, ἡ [estheesees] sense, sensation.

αἰσθητικός [estheeteekos] aesthetic, sensitive.

αἰσθητός [estheetos] perceivable, noticeable.

αἰσιόδοξος [eseeoδoksos] optimistic.

αἶσχος, τό [eshos] shame, disgrace.

αἰσχροκέρδεια, ἡ [eshrokerδeea] profiteering, sordid gain.

αἰσχρολογία, ἡ [eshroloγeea] obscenity, filthy talk.

αἰσχρός [eshros] shameful, infamous.

αἰσχύνη, ἡ [esheenee] shame, infamy.

αἴτησις, ἡ [eteesees] application, petition, request.

αἰτία, ἡ [eteea] cause, reason, motive.

αἰτιατική, ἡ [eteeateekee] (γραμμ) accusative (case).

αἰτιολογία, ἡ [eteeoloγeea] explanation || (οἴκον) particulars.

αἴτιον, τό [eteeon] cause || motive.

αἴτιος [eteeos] responsible, causing.

αἰτῶ [eto] request (κάτι) || αἰτοῦμαι beg (κάτι).

αἰφνης [efnees] suddenly || (π.χ.) for example.

αἰφνιδιασμός, ὁ [efneeδeeasmos] surprise.

αἰχμαλωτίζω [ehmaloteezo] capture || (μεταφ) captivate.

αἰχμάλωτος, ὁ [ehmalotos] captive, prisoner.

αἰχμή, ἡ [ehmee] (βελόνης) point || (βέλους) head.

αἰών, ὁ [eon] age, century.

αἰώνιος [eoneeos] eternal || perpetual.

ἀκαδημία, ἡ [akaδeemeea] academy.

ἀκαθαρσία, ἡ [akatharseea] filth, dirt.

ἀκάθαρτος [akathartos] dirty, filthy.

ἀκάθεκτος [akathektos] unbridled, impetuous, unchecked.

ἀκαθόριστος [akathoreestos] undefined.

ἄκαιρος [akeros] inopportune, untimely, unseasonable.

ἀκακία, ἡ [akakeea] (δένδρον) acacia.

ἄκακος [akakos] harmless, innocent.

ἀκαλαισθησία, ἡ [akalestheeseea] lack of taste.

ἀκάλεστος [akalestos] uninvited.

ἀκαλλιέργητος [akalierγeetos] uncultivated || (ἄνθρωπος) uncultured.

ἀκαμάτης, ὁ [akamatees] lazy fellow, loafer.

ἄκαμπτος [akamptos] unbending.

ἀκάμωτος [akamotos] undone || unripe.

ἄκανθα, ἡ [akantha] thorn, thistle.

ἀκανθώδης [akanthoδees] thorny, prickly.

ἀκανόνιστος [akanoneestos] unregulated || (σχήμα) irregular || (σφυγμός) uneven.

ἀκαριαῖος [akareeayos] in an instant, momentary.

ἄκαρπος [akarpos] unfruitful || (μεταφ) fruitless.

ἀκατάβλητος [akatavleetos] indomitable || (χρέη) unsettled, unpaid.

ἀκατάδεκτος [akataδektos] disdainful, snobbish.

ἀκατάληπτος [akataleeptos] incomprehensible.

ἀκατάλληλος [akataleelos] unsuitable, unfit.

ἀκαταλόγιστος [akataloγeestos] not responsible (for) || incalculable.

ἀκατανόητος [akatanoeetos] inconceivable, unintelligible.

ἀκατάπαυστος [akatapavstos] unceasing, endless.

ἀκατάστατος [akatastatos] untidy || (καιρός) unstable, unsettled.

ἀκατέργαστος [akaterγastos] unwrought, raw.

ἀκατοίκητος [akateekeetos] uninhabited.

ἀκατόρθωτος [akatorthotos] infeasible, impossible.

ἀκέραιος [akereos] integral, whole || (τίμιος) upright || ~ ἀριθμός integer.

ἀκεφιά, ἡ [akefia] dejection, gloom.

ἀκίνδυνος [akeenδeenos] safe, harmless.

ἀκίνητος [akeeneetos] immovable || (περιουσία) estate, property.

ἀκλείδωτος [akleeδotos] unlocked.

ἄκληρος [akleeros] childless, without an heir.

ἄκλιτος [akleetos] indeclinable.

ἀκμάζω [akmazo] flourish, thrive, be in full bloom.

ἀκμαῖος [akmeos] vigorous, sturdy ‖ (γερός) robust.

ἀκμή, ἡ [akmee] height, peak, edge.

ἄκμων, ὁ [akmon] anvil.

ἀκοή, ἡ [akoee] hearing ‖ ἐξ ἀκουῆς by hearsay.

ἀκοινώνητος [akeenoneetos] unsociable ‖ (ἐκκλ) not having taken first communion.

ἀκολασία, ἡ [akolaseea] debauchery, excess.

ἀκόλαστος [akolastos] licentious ‖ (διαγωγή) unprincipled, lawless.

ἀκολουθία, ἡ [akoloutheea] retinue, suite ‖ (ἐκκλ) church service ‖ κατ' ~ν in consequence.

ἀκόλουθος [akolouthos] (οὐσ) attendant ‖ (στρατ) attaché ‖ (ἐπίθ) following, next.

ἀκολουθῶ [akoloutho] follow ‖ attend.

ἀκολούθως [akolouthos] consequently, afterwards ‖ ὡς ~ as follows.

ἀκόμα [akoma] yet, more ‖ ~ καί even if.

ἀκονίζω [akoneezo] sharpen, whet.

ἀκόντιον, τό [akonteeon] javelin, dart.

ἄκοπος [akopos] not cut ‖ (εὔκολος) easy ‖ (ξεκούραστα) untiring.

ἀκόρεστος [akorestos] insatiable, greedy.

ἄκοσμος [akosmos] indecent, improper.

ἀκουμπῶ [akoumbo] lean, stand ‖ (ρ.ἀ.) rest.

ἀκούμπωτος [akoumbotos] unbuttoned.

ἀκούραστος [akourastos] indefatigable, unwearied.

ἀκούρδιστος [akourdeestos] not tuned, not wound up.

ἀκούσιος [akouseeos] unintentional ‖ involuntary.

ἀκουστικόν, τό [akousteekon] (τηλεφ) receiver.

ἀκουστικός [akousteekos] acoustic.

ἀκουστός [akoustos] famous, celebrated.

ἀκούω [akouo] hear, listen to, learn ‖ (εἰσακούω) obey.

ἄκρα, ἡ [akra] end, tip, extremity.

ἀκραιφνής [akrefnees] sincere, pure.

ἀκρατής [akratees] intemperate, incontinent.

ἀκράτητος [akrateetos] impetuous, rash, unrestrained.

ἄκρη, ἡ [akree] βλ ἄκρα.

ἀκριβά [akreeva] dearly.

ἀκρίβεια, ἡ [akreeveea] (ὡρολογίου) accuracy, precision ‖ (μεταφράσεως κτλ) exactness ‖ (τιμῆς) costliness, dearness.

ἀκριβής [akreevees] exact ‖ (ὡρολόγιον κτλ) accurate ‖ (ὑπολογισμός) correct ‖ (σέ ραντεβοῦ) punctual.

ἀκριβός [akreevos] dear ‖ expensive.

ἀκριβῶς [akreevos] precisely, accurately.

ἀκρίδα, ἡ [akreeda] locust, grasshopper.

ἄκριτος [akreetos] thoughtless.

ἀκρόασις, ἡ [akroasees] hearing, listening ‖ (συνάντησις) audience, interview.

ἀκροατήριον, τό [akroateereeon] audience ‖ auditorium.

ἀκροατής, ὁ [akroatees] listener ‖ (πανεπιστημίου) auditor.

ἀκροβάτης, ὁ [akrovatees] acrobat.

ἀκρογιάλι, τό [akroyeealee] seashore.

ἄκρον, τό [akron] extremity, end, tip.

ἀκρόπολις, ἡ [akropolees] acropolis ‖ citadel.

ἄκρος [akros] extreme, utmost, excessive, outermost.

ἀκροσφαλής [akrosfalees] precarious, dangerous.

ἀκρωτηριάζω [akroteereeazo] maim ‖ amputate.

ἀκρωτήριον, τό [akroteereeon] cape, promontory.

ἀκτή, ἡ [aktee] shore, beach, coast.

ἀκτινοβολία, ἡ [akteenovoleea] radiation, brilliancy.

ἀκτινογραφία, ἡ [akteenoyrafeea] X-ray.

ἀκτινοθεραπεία, ἡ [akteenotherapeea] radiotherapy.

ἀκτίς, ἡ [aktees] ray, beam ‖ (ἐλπίδος) gleam ‖ (ἐνεργείας) range ‖ (τροχοῦ) spoke ‖ (κύκλου) radius.

ἀκτοπλοΐα, ἡ [aktoploeea] coastal shipping, coasting.

ἄκυρος [akeeros] invalid, void, null.

ἀκυρώνω [akeerono] nullify, invalidate, cancel.

ἀλάβαστρον, τό [alavastron] alabaster.

ἀλάδωτος [aladotos] unanointed with oil ‖ (μεταφ) not bribed.

ἀλαζονεία, ἡ [alazoneea] arrogance, boastfulness.

ἀλάθευτος [alathevtos] infallible, unerring.

ἀλάθητος [alatheetos] certain, sure, infallible.

ἄλαλος [alalos] speechless, dumb, mute.

ἀλάνθαστος [alanthastos] infallible, certain.

ἀλάργα [alarya] afar, apart, off.

ἅλας [alas] βλ ἁλάτι.

ἁλάτι, τό [alatee] salt ‖ ἁλατιέρα saltcellar.

ἁλατίζω [alateezo] salt.

ἄλγεβρα, ἡ [alyevra] algebra.

ἄλγος, τό [alyos] pain, grief, suffering.

ἀλέθω [aletho] grind.

ἀλείβω [aleevo] coat, smear, rub.

ἀλείφω [aleefo] βλ ἀλείβω.

ἀλέκτωρ, ὁ [alektor] cock, rooster.

ἀλεξίβροχον, τό [alekseevrohon] umbrella.

ἀλεξικέραυνον, τό [alekseekeravnon] lightning conductor.

ἀλεξιπτωτιστής, ὁ [alekseeptoteestees] parachutist.

ἀλεξίπτωτον, τό [alekseeptoton] parachute.

ἀλεποῦ, ἡ [alepou] fox ‖ (μεταφ) sly person.

ἄλεσμα, τό [alesma] grinding.

ἀλέστα [alesta] quickly.
ἀλέτρι, τό [aletree] plough.
ἀλεύρι, τό [alevri] flour.
ἀλήθεια, ἡ [aleetheea] truth ‖ (ἐπιρ) really, indeed.
ἀληθεύω [aleethevo] be true, be right.
ἀληθινός [aleetheenos] true, truthful ‖ real, genuine.
ἀλησμόνητος [aleesmoneetos] unforgettable.
ἀλήτης, ὁ [aleetees] vagabond, vagrant.
ἁλιεία, ἡ [alieea] fishing, fishery.
ἁλιεύς, ὁ [alievs] fisherman.
ἁλιεύω [alievo] fish (for).
ἀλισίβα, ἡ [aleeseeva] lye.
ἄλκιμος [alkeemos] strong, sturdy, robust.
ἀλκοολικός [alkooleekos] alcoholic.
ἀλκυών, ἡ [alkeeon] kingfisher, halcyon.
ἀλλά [alla] but, however, yet.
ἀλλαγή, ἡ [allayee] change ‖ variation.
ἀλλάζω [allazo] change, alter.
ἀλλαντικά, τά [allanteeka] πλ sausages.
ἀλλαχοῦ [allahou] elsewhere.
ἀλλεπάλληλος [allepaleelos] repeated, successive.
ἀλλεργία, ἡ [alleryeea] allergy.
ἀλληλεγγύη, ἡ [alleelengiee] mutual help, solidarity.
ἀλληλένδετος [alleelendetos] interdependent, bound together.
ἀλληλογραφία, ἡ [alleeloyrafeea] correspondence.
ἀλλοδαπή, ἡ [allodapee] foreign country.
ἀλλοδαπός, ὁ [allodapos] foreigner, alien.
ἀλλοίθωρος [alleethoros] cross-eyed.
ἀλλοίμονο [alleemono] (ἐπιφ) alas!, oh dear!
ἀλλοιώνω [alleeono] alter, change.
ἀλλοιῶς [aleeos] otherwise, in a different way.
ἀλλοίωσις, ἡ [aleeosees] change, alteration ‖ (τροφίμων) adulteration.
ἀλλοιώτικος [aleeoteekos] different, unlike ‖ (πρόσωπον) odd, strange.
ἀλλόκοτος [alokotos] queer, strange, odd.
ἄλλος [allos] (an)other, else ‖ (ἐπόμενος) next ‖ (διαφορετικός) different ‖ (ἐπί πλέον) more ‖ κάθε ἄλλο! anything but!
ἄλλοτε [allote] formerly ‖ sometime.
ἀλλοῦ [allou] elsewhere.
ἀλλόφρων [allofron] beside o.s., mad, frantic.
ἄλλως [allos] otherwise, else, differently, in other words ‖ οὕτως ἤ ~ anyway.
ἄλλωστε [alloste] besides, on the other hand.
ἅλμα, τό [alma] jump, leap ‖ ~ τώδης by leaps and bounds.
ἅλμη, ἡ [almee] brine, pickle.
ἁλμυρός [almeeros] salty ‖ (μεταφ) costly.
ἀλόγιστος [aloyeestos] thoughtless, inconsiderate, irrational.

ἄλογο, τό [aloyo] horse ‖ ἀλογόμυγα horsefly.
ἄλογος [aloyos] irrational, unreasoned.
ἀλόη, ἡ [aloee] aloe.
ἀλοιφή, ἡ [aleefee] ointment.
ἀλουμίνιον, τό [aloumeeneeon] aluminium.
ἄλουστος [aloustos] unwashed, unbathed.
ἄλσος, τό [alsos] grove, thicket.
ἅλτης, ὁ [altees] (ἀθλητ) jumper.
ἀλύγιστος [aleeyeestos] inflexible.
ἀλύπητος [aleepeetos] pitiless, cruel, unmerciful.
ἁλυσίδα, ἡ [aleeseeδa] chain.
ἄλυτος [aleetos] (πού δέν ἐλύθη) unsolved ‖ (δέν μπορεῖ νά λυθῆ) unsolvable.
ἄλφα, τό [alfa] the letter A.
ἀλφαβητάριον, τό [alfaveetareeon] primer, ABC-book.
ἀλφάβητον, τό [alfaveeton] alphabet.
ἀλφάδι, τό [alfaδee] level, plumbline.
ἁλώνι, τό [allonee] threshing floor ‖ ἁλωνίζω thresh ‖ (σκορπῶ) scatter.
ἀλώπηξ, ἡ [alopeeks] fox.
ἅλωσις, ἡ [alosees] fall, capture, conquest.
ἅμα [ama] as soon as ‖ (ἐάν) if ‖ ~ ἔπος ἅμ' ἔργον no sooner said than done.
ἀμαζών, ἡ [amazon] amazon.
ἀμάθεια, ἡ [amatheea] ignorance, illiteracy.
ἀμαθής [amathees] ignorant, illiterate.
ἀμάν [aman] (ἐπιφ) for heaven's sake!
ἀμανάτι, τό [amanatee] pawn, security, pledge.
ἅμαξα, ἡ [amaksa] coach, carriage ‖ (μέ ἄλογο) horse cab.
ἁμαξᾶς, ὁ [amaksas] coachman, cab driver.
ἁμάξι, τό [amaksee] horse cab ‖ (αὐτοκίνητο) car.
ἁμαξοστοιχία, ἡ [amaksosteeheea] train.
ἁμαρτάνω [amartano] sin.
ἁμαρτία, ἡ [amarteea] sin ‖ εἶναι ~ ἀπ' τό Θεό it's a pity!
ἀμαυρώνω [amavrono] darken, obscure ‖ (μεταφ) sully.
ἄμαχος [amahos] non-combatant.
ἀμβλύς [amvlees] blunt ‖ (γεωμ) obtuse.
ἄμβων, ὁ [amvon] pulpit.
ἀμέ [amme] (ἐπιφ) why not? ‖ of course!
ἀμείβω [ameevo] reward, compensate.
ἀμείλικτος [ameeleektos] implacable, inexorable.
ἀμείωτος [ameeotos] undiminished.
ἀμέλγω [amelyo] milk.
ἀμέλεια, ἡ [ameleea] negligence, carelessness.
ἀμελέτητα [ameleteeta] πλ testicles.
ἀμελής [amelees] negligent ‖ (μαθητής) lazy.
ἀμελῶ [amelo] neglect.
ἄμεμπτος [amemptos] irreproachable, blameless.
ἀμερικάνικος [amereekaneekos] American.
Ἀμερικανός, ὁ [amereekanos] American.
ἀμέριμνος [amereemnos] carefree, heedless.

ἀμέριστος [amereestos] indivisible ‖ undivided.

ἀμερόληπτος [ameroleeptos] impartial.

ἄμεσος [amesos] direct, immediate.

ἀμέσως [amesos] at once, immediately.

ἀμετάβλητος [ametavleetos] unchanged ‖ immutable.

ἀμετάκλητος [ametakleetos] irrevocable.

ἀμεταχείριστος [ametaheereestos] unused, new.

ἀμέτοχος [ametohos] exempt, not participating in.

ἀμέτρητος [ametreetos] countless, immeasurable.

ἀμήχανος [ameehanos] perplexed, embarrassed.

ἀμηχανία [ameehaneea] perplexity, confusion.

ἀμίαντος [ameeantos] undefiled ‖ (οὐσ) asbestos.

ἀμίλητος [ameeleetos] silent, quiet.

ἅμιλλα, ἡ [ameela] emulation, rivalry.

ἀμίμητος [ameemeetos] inimitable.

ἄμισθος [ameesthos] unsalaried, without pay.

ἀμμοκονία, ἡ [ammokoneea] cement, mortar.

ἄμμος, ἡ [ammos] sand.

ἀμμουδιά, ἡ [amoudia] sandy beach.

ἀμμώδης [amodees] sandy.

ἀμμωνία, ἡ [amoneea] ammonia.

ἀμνάς, ἡ [amnas] ewe, lamb.

ἀμνημόνευτος [amneemonevtos] immemorial ‖ unmentioned.

ἀμνησία, ἡ [amneeseea] amnesia.

ἀμνηστία, ἡ [amneesteea] amnesty.

ἀμνός, ὁ [amnos] lamb.

ἀμοιβάδες, αἱ [ameevades] πλ amoebic dysentery.

ἀμοιβαῖος [ameeveyos] mutual, reciprocal.

ἀμοιβή, ἡ [ameevee] reward, recompense.

ἄμοιρος [ameeros] unfortunate, destitute.

ἀμόνι, τό [amonee] anvil.

ἄμορφος [amorfos] shapeless.

ἀμόρφωτος [amorfotos] uneducated, unrefined.

ἀμπαζούρ, τό [ambazour] lampshade.

ἀμπάρα, ἡ [ambara] bolt, bar.

ἀμπάρι, τό [ambari] storeroom ‖ (ναυτ) hold.

ἀμπέλι, τό [ambelee] vine ‖ vineyard.

ἀμπελών, ὁ [ambelon] vineyard.

ἄμποτε(ς) [ambote(s)] (ἐπιφ) would that! ‖ would to God!

ἀμπραγιάζ, τό [ambrayeeaz] clutch.

ἄμπωτις, ἡ [ambotees] ebb tide.

ἀμυγδαλές, αἱ [ameeɣdales] πλ tonsils.

ἀμύγδαλο, τό [ameeɣdalo] almond.

ἀμυδρός [ameeðros] dim, faint.

ἄμυλον, τό [ameelon] starch.

ἄμυνα, ἡ [ameena] defence.

ἄμφια, τά [amfeea] πλ vestments.

ἀμφιβάλλω [amfeevalo] doubt.

ἀμφίβιος [amfeeveeos] amphibious.

ἀμφίβολος [amfeevolos] doubtful, dubious.

ἀμφίεσις, ἡ [amfiesees] dress, attire, clothing.

ἀμφιθέατρον, τό [amfeetheatron] amphitheatre.

ἀμφίρροπος [amfeeropos] undecided, in the balance, wavering.

ἀμφισβητῶ [amfeesveeto] dispute.

ἀμφορεύς, ὁ [amforevs] amphora, pitcher.

ἀμφότεροι [amfoteree] πλ both.

ἄν [an] if, whether ‖ ~ καί although, though.

ἀνά [ana] along, over ‖ ~ εἰς one by one ‖ ~ τήν πόλιν through the city.

ἀναβαίνω [anaveno] ascend, climb, go up.

ἀναβάλλω [anavalo] put off, postpone, delay.

ἀνάβασις, ἡ [anavasees] going up, ascension.

ἀναβολή, ἡ [anavolee] postponement, adjournment.

ἀναβρασμός, ὁ [anavrasmos] agitation, excitement ‖ fermentation.

ἀνάβω [anavo] light ‖ (φῶς κτλ) turn on, switch on ‖ (θυμώνω) get provoked.

ἀναγγέλλω [anangelo] announce, make known.

ἀναγγελία, ἡ [anangeleea] announcement, notice.

ἀναγέννησις, ἡ [anayeneesees] revival, renaissance.

ἀναγινώσκω [anayeenosko] read.

ἀναγκάζω [anangazo] force, compel.

ἀναγκαῖος [anangeyos] necessary, essential, needed.

ἀναγκασμός, ὁ [anangasmos] constraint, necessity.

ἀναγκαστικός [anangasteekos] compulsory ‖ (προσγείωσις κτλ) forced.

ἀνάγκη, ἡ [anangee] need, necessity, want.

ἀνάγλυφον, τό [anayleefon] bas-relief.

ἀναγνώρισις, ἡ [anaynoreesees] recognition, acknowledgement.

ἀναγνωρίζω [anaynoreezo] recognize ‖ (παραδέχομαι) admit.

ἀνάγνωσις, ἡ [anaynosees] reading.

ἀναγνώστης, ὁ [anaynostees] reader.

ἀναγνωστικόν, τό [anaynosteekon] primer, reader.

ἀναγούλα, ἡ [anayoula] nausea, disgust.

ἀνάγω [anaɣo] raise ‖ (μετατρέπω) reduce, convert.

ἀνάγωγος [anaɣoɣos] ill-bred, ill-mannered.

ἀναδάσωσις, ἡ [anaðasosees] reafforestation.

ἀναδεικνύομαι [anaðeekneeome] be distinguished.

ἀναδιοργανώνω [anaðeeorɣanono] re-organize.

ἀναδιπλασιασμός, ὁ [anaðeeplaseeasmos] (γραμμ) reduplication.

ἀνάδοχος, ὁ [anadohos] godparent, sponsor.

ἀναδρομικός [anadromeekos] retroactive, retrospective.

ἀναδύομαι [anadeeome] emerge.

ἀναζητῶ [anazeeto] search for, seek.

ἀναζωογονῶ [anazooyono] revive, invigorate.

ἀναζωπυρῶ [anazopeero] relight, rekindle ‖ (μεταφ) revive.

ἀναθαρρεύω [anatharevo] regain courage, cheer up.

ἀνάθεμα, τό [anathema] curse ‖ (ἐκκλ) excommunication.

ἀναθέτω [anatheto] commission, entrust ‖ (ἀφιερώνω) dedicate.

ἀναθεώρησις, ἡ [anatheoreesees] revision, review.

ἀναθυμίασις, ἡ [anatheemeeasees] stench, exhalation, fumes.

ἀναίδεια, ἡ [anedeea] impudence.

ἀναιδής [anedees] impudent, shameless.

ἀναίμακτος [anemaktos] bloodless.

ἀναιμία, ἡ [anemeea] anaemia.

ἀναίρεσις, ἡ [aneresees] refutation ‖ (ἐπί ἀνθρωποκτονία) manslaughter.

ἀναισθησία, ἡ [anestheeseea] unconsciousness ‖ (μεταφ) insensibility.

ἀναισθητικόν, τό [anestheeteekon] anaesthetic.

ἀναίσθητος [anestheetos] insensitive ‖ (στούς πόνους) unconscious, insensible ‖ (ἀσυγκίνητος) unmoved.

ἀναίσχυντος [anesheentos] shameless, impudent.

ἀναίτιος [aneteeos] innocent, blameless.

ἀνακαινίζω [anakeneezo] renovate, renew.

ἀνακαλύπτω [anakaleepto] discover, detect.

ἀνακαλῶ [anakalo] recall ‖ (ἄδεια, διάταγμα) repeal, abrogate ‖ (διαταγήν κτλ) cancel, withdraw ‖ (ὑπόσχεσιν) retract.

ἀνακατώνω [anakatono] mix, stir ‖ (συγχέω) confuse.

ἀνακάτωμα, τό [anakatoma] mixing ‖ (φασαρία) confusion ‖ (στομάχου) nausea.

ἀνακεφαλαίωσις, ἡ [anakefaleosees] recapitulation.

ἀνακηρύσσω [anakeereeso] proclaim, declare.

ἀνακινῶ [anakeeno] stir up ‖ (μεταφ) bring up, raise.

ἀνάκλησις, ἡ [anakleesees] revocation, recalling.

ἀνάκλιντρον, τό [anakleentron] reclining chair.

ἀνακοινῶ [anakeeno] announce.

ἀνακοινωθέν, τό [anakeenothen] communiqué, notification.

ἀνακολουθία, ἡ [anakoloutheea] incoherence, inconsistency.

ἀνακοπή, ἡ [anakopee] checking ‖ (νομ) reprieve.

ἀνακουφίζω [anakoufeezo] relieve, alleviate, lighten.

ἀνακριβής [anakreevees] inaccurate.

ἀνάκρισις, ἡ [anakreesees] interrogation, inquiry.

ἀνακριτής, ὁ [anakreetees] examining magistrate.

ἀνάκτορον, τό [anaktoron] palace ‖ πλ palace.

ἀνακωχή, ἡ [anakohee] armistice, truce.

ἀναλαμβάνω [analamvano] undertake ‖ recover.

ἀναλαμπή, ἡ [analambee] flash, glare.

ἀνάλατος [analatos] without salt ‖ (μεταφ) dull.

ἀνάληψις, ἡ [analeepsees] (ἐργασίας) resumption, undertaking ‖ (τοῦ Χριστοῦ) ascension.

ἀναλλοίωτος [analeeotos] unchanging, constant, unaltered.

ἀναλογία, ἡ [analoyeea] relation, proportion, ratio ‖ portion.

ἀναλογίζομαι [analoyeezome] call to mind, reflect on.

ἀναλογικός [analoyeekos] proportionate.

ἀνάλογος [analoyos] proportionate ‖ (μαθημ) proportional.

ἀναλόγως [analoyos] proportionately, according to.

ἀνάλυσις, ἡ [analeesees] analysis.

ἀναλυτικός [analeeteekos] analytical ‖ detailed.

ἀναλφάβητος [analfaveetos] illiterate, ignorant.

ἀναμένω [anameno] wait for, expect.

ἀνάμεσα [anamesa] in between, among.

ἀναμεταξύ [anametaksee] between, among ‖ στό ~ in the meantime, meanwhile.

ἀναμετρῶ [anametro] weigh up, estimate, consider.

ἀναμιγνύω [anameeyneeo] mix, blend ‖ implicate.

ἀνάμικτος [anameektos] mixed.

ἀνάμιξις, ἡ [anameeksees] mixing, interfering.

ἄναμμα, τό [anama] lighting ‖ (προσώπου) inflammation ‖ (ἔξαψις) excitement ‖ (μοτέρ κτλ) ignition.

ἀναμμένος [anamenos] alight, burning.

ἀνάμνησις, ἡ [anamneesees] recollection, remembrance.

ἀναμονή, ἡ [anamonee] expectation, waiting.

ἀναμφισβήτητος [anamfeesveeteetos] indisputable, unquestionable.

ἀνανᾶς, ὁ [ananas] pineapple.

ἀνανεώνω [ananeono] renew, renovate.

ἀνανέωσις, ἡ [ananeosees] renewal, renovation.

ἀναντίρρητος [ananteereetos] incontrovertible, incontestable.

ἄναξ, ὁ [anaks] sovereign, king, ruler.

ἀναξιοπρεπής [anakseeoprepees] (συμπεριφορά) unseemly ‖ (ἄτομον) ill-bred, uncouth ‖ (βίος) disreputable.

ἀνάξιος [anakseeos] unworthy, unfit, inefficient.

ἀνάπαλιν [anapaleen] conversely, vice versa.

ἀναπαράστασις, ἡ [anaparastasees] representation ‖ (ἐγκλήματος) reconstruction.

ἀνάπαυλα, ἡ [anapavla] respite, rest.

ἀνάπαυσις, ἡ [anapavsees] rest, repose ‖ (στρατ) stand easy!

ἀναπαυτικός [anapavteekos] comfortable, restful.

ἀναπαύομαι [anapavome] rest, relax.

ἀναπέμπω [anapembo] give forth, emit.

ἀναπηδῶ [anapeedo] jump up, leap up, start.

ἀνάπηρος [anapeeros] disabled ‖ (διανοητικῶς) deficient.

ἀνάπλασις, ἡ [anaplasees] reforming, remodelling.

ἀναπληρώνω [anapleerono] replace ‖ substitute ‖ refill.

ἀναπνέω [anapneo] breathe.

ἀναπνοή, ἡ [anapnoee] breath, breathing, respiration.

ἀνάποδα [anapoda] backwards ‖ (μέσα ἔξω) inside out, topsy-turvy.

ἀνάποδη, ἡ [anapodee] wrong side ‖ inside out.

ἀναποδιά, ἡ [anapodia] reverse, bad luck ‖ contrariness.

ἀναποδογυρίζω [anapodoyeereezo] turn upside down.

ἀνάποδος [anapodos] reversed ‖ (ἄνθρωπος) difficult, cantankerous.

ἀναπολῶ [anapolo] recollect, remember.

ἀναπόφευκτος [anapofevktos] inevitable, unavoidable.

ἀναπτήρ, ὁ [anapteer] cigarette lighter.

ἀνάπτυξις, ἡ [anapteeksees] development ‖ (ἐξήγησις) explanation.

ἀναπτύσσω [anapteeso] unfold, develop ‖ (λόγον) expound, explain.

ἀνάπτω [anapto] βλ ἀνάβω.

ἀναρίθμητος [anareethmeetos] countless, innumerable.

ἀναρμόδιος [anarmodeeos] not competent, unqualified.

ἀνάρμοστος [anarmostos] (διαγωγή) improper, unbecoming ‖ (γλῶσσα) unsuitable.

ἀνάρπαστος [anarpastos] quickly bought up.

ἀναρριχῶμαι [anareehome] climb up, mount.

ἀνάρρωσις, ἡ [anarrosees] convalescence, recovery.

ἀναρτῶ [anarto] hang up, suspend.

ἀναρχία, ἡ [anarheea] anarchy.

ἀναρχικός [anarheekos] anarchical ‖ (οὐσ) anarchist.

ἀναρωτιέμαι [anarotieme] ask o.s., wonder.

ἀνάσα, ἡ [anasa] breath, breathing ‖ rest, respite.

ἀνασηκώνω [anaseekono] lift up, raise.

ἀνασκάπτω [anaskapto] dig, excavate.

ἀνασκαφή, ἡ [anaskafee] excavation.

ἀνάσκελα [anaskela] on one's back.

ἀνασκευάζω [anaskevazo] refute, disprove.

ἀνασκόπησις, ἡ [anaskopeesees] review, weighing up.

ἀνασταίνω [anasteno] revive, restore to life.

ἀνασταλτικός [anastalteekos] restraining, holding back.

ἀνάστασις, ἡ [anastasees] resurrection, rising.

ἀνάστατος [anastatos] in disorder, agitated, excited.

ἀναστατώνω [anastatono] disturb, upset.

ἀναστέλλω [anastelo] stop, stay, suspend.

ἀναστενάζω [anastenazo] sigh, groan.

ἀναστηλώνω [anasteelono] restore, erect.

ἀναστήλωσις, ἡ [anasteelosees] restoration, erection.

ἀνάστημα, τό [anasteema] height, stature.

ἀναστολή, ἡ [anastolee] reprieve ‖ suspension ‖ restraint.

ἀναστρέφω [anastrefo] turn back, reverse, invert.

ἀνασυγκρότησις, ἡ [anaseengroteesees] rehabilitation.

ἀνασύρω [anaseero] raise, pull out, pull up, draw up.

ἀνασφάλιστος [anasfaleestos] uninsured.

ἀναταράσσω [anataraso] stir up, upset.

ἀνατείνω [anateeno] extend, hold up, lift up, stretch up.

ἀνατέλλω [anatelo] rise ‖ appear.

ἀνατέμνω [anatemno] dissect, cut.

ἀνατίμησις, ἡ [anateemeesees] rise in price ‖ revaluation.

ἀνατινάζω [anateenazo] blow up ‖ spring up.

ἀνατίναξις, ἡ [anateenaksees] explosion, blowing up.

ἀνατοκισμός, ὁ [anatokeesmos] compound interest.

ἀνατολή, ἡ [anatolee] east ‖ Ἄπω Ἀ~ Far East ‖ Μέση Ἀ~ Middle East.

ἀνατολικός [anatoleekos] eastern ‖ oriental.

ἀνατομία, ἡ [anatomeea] anatomy.

ἀνατρέπω [anatrepo] upset ‖ (βάρκα κτλ) overturn, capsize.

ἀνατρέφω [anatrefo] rear, bring up, raise.

ἀνατρέχω [anatreho] refer back to, go back to.

ἀνατριχιάζω [anatreeheeazo] shiver, shudder.

ἀνατριχιαστικός [anatreeheeasteekos] terrifying, hair-raising.

ἀνατροπή, ἡ [anatropee] upset, overthrow ‖ (νομ) refutation, reversal.

ἀνατροφή, ἡ [anatrofee] upbringing, breeding.

ἀνάτυπον, τό [anateepon] offprint, reprint.

ἄναυδος [anavðos] speechless, dumbfounded.

ἀναφαίνομαι [anafenome] appear, rise, emerge.

ἀναφανδόν [anafanðon] manifestly, openly.

ἀναφέρω [anafero] mention, cite || report || relate.

ἀναφλέγω [anafleγo] inflame, ignite.

ἀνάφλεξις, ἡ [anafleksees] combustion conflagration, ignition.

ἀναφορά, ἡ [anafora] report, relation | (αἴτησις) petition.

ἀναφορικός [anaforeekos] relative to || referring to.

ἀναφωνῶ [anafono] cry out, exclaim.

ἀναχαιτίζω [anaheteezo] check, restrain.

ἀναχρονισμός, ὁ [anahroneesmos] anachronism.

ἀνάχωμα, τό [anahoma] mound, bank, dyke.

ἀναχώρησις, ἡ [anahoreesees] departure.

ἀναχωρῶ [anahoro] leave, depart, go.

ἀναψυκτικά, τά [anapseekteeka] πλ refreshments.

ἀναψυχή, ἡ [anapseehee] recreation.

ἀνδραγάθημα, τό [anðra'γatheema] heroic feat, exploit.

ἀνδράποδον, τό [anðrapoðon] slave.

ἀνδρεία, ἡ [anðreea] bravery, valour.

ἀνδρείκελον, τό [anðreekelon] puppet, manikin.

ἀνδρεῖος [anðreeos] brave, courageous.

ἀνδριάς, ὁ [anðrias] statue.

ἀνδρικός [anðreekos] manly, virile, male.

ἀνεβάζω [anevazo] carry up, lift up || (θέατρον) put on || (οἰκονομία) raise, put up.

ἀνεβαίνω [aneveno] βλ ἀναβαίνω.

ἀνέβασμα, τό [anevasma] going up || lifting || (ἔργου) production.

ἀνεβοκατεβαίνω [anevokateveno] go up and down || (τιμές) fluctuate.

ἀνέγγιχτος [anengeehtos] untouched, new.

ἀνεγείρω [aneγeero] raise, erect, build.

ἀνέγερσις, ἡ [aneγersees] erection || (σήκωμα) getting up.

ἀνεγνωρισμένος [aneγnoreesmenos] recognized.

ἀνειλικρινής [aneeleekreenees] insincere || false.

ἀνέκαθεν [anekathen] always, ever, from the beginning.

ἀνεκδιήγητος [anekðieeγeetos] defying description, ineffable.

ἀνέκδοτον, τό [anekðoton] anecdote, story.

ἀνεκμετάλλευτος [anekmetalevtos] not exploited.

ἀνεκπλήρωτος [anekpleerotos] unfulfilled.

ἀνεκτικός [anekteekos] tolerant, patient, indulgent.

ἀνεκτίμητος [anekteemeetos] priceless, inestimable.

ἀνεκτός [anektos] bearable, tolerable.

ἀνέκφραστος [anekfrastos] inexpressible, indescribable || (ἠθοποιός) expressionless || (βλέμμα) vacant.

ἀνελεύθερος [aneleftheros] servile, illiberal.

ἀνελκυστήρ, ὁ [anelkeesteer] lift, elevator.

ἀνελλιπής [aneleepees] flawless || (ὀργάνωσις) complete || (φοίτησις) continuous.

ἀνέλπιστος [anelpeestos] unexpected || (γεγονός) unforeseen.

ἀνεμίζω [anemeezo] ventilate, air || (σῖτον) winnow.

ἀνεμιστήρ, ὁ [anemeesteer] fan, ventilator.

ἀνεμοβλογιά, ἡ [anemovloγia] chickenpox.

ἀνεμοδείκτης, ὁ [anemoðeektees] weathercock, wind indicator.

ἀνεμόμυλος, ὁ [anemomeelos] windmill.

ἄνεμος, ὁ [anemos] wind.

ἀνεμοστρόβιλος, ὁ [anemostroveelos] whirlwind.

ἀνεμπόδιστος [anemboðeestos] unhindered, unimpeded.

ἀνεμώδης [anemoðees] windy.

ἀνεμώνη, ἡ [anemonee] anemone.

ἀνενδοίαστος [anenðeeastos] unhesitating, unhesitant.

ἀνένδοτος [anenðotos] unyielding, inflexible.

ἀνενόχλητος [anenohleetos] undisturbed.

ἀνεξαίρετος [anekseretos] without exception || not exempted.

ἀνεξάντλητος [aneksantleetos] inexhaustible.

ἀνεξαρτησία, ἡ [aneksarteeseea] independence.

ἀνεξάρτητος [aneksarteetos] independent.

ἀνεξέλεγκτος [anekselengtos] not confirmed, unchecked || (δαπάνη κτλ) unexamined.

ἀνεξήγητος [anekseeγeetos] inexplicable.

ἀνεξίκακος [anekseekakos] forbearing, meek.

ἀνεξίτηλος [anekseeteelos] indelible.

ἀνέξοδος [aneksoðos] inexpensive, cheap.

ἀνεξόφλητος [aneksofleetos] unpaid.

ἀνεπαίσθητος [anepestheetos] imperceptible, slight.

ἀνεπαρκής [aneparkees] insufficient, inadequate.

ἀνέπαφος [anepafos] untouched, intact.

ἀνεπηρέαστος [anepeereastos] unaffected, uninfluenced.

ἀνεπιθύμητος [anepeetheemeetos] undesirable.

ἀνεπίσημος [anepeeseemos] unofficial.

ἀνεπιτήδειος [anepeeteeðeeos] unskilful, unfit.

ἀνεπιτυχής [anepeeteehees] unsuccessful.

ἀνεπιφύλακτος [anepeefeelaktos] unreserved.

ἀνεπτυγμένος [anepteeɣmenos] (ἄνθρωπος) cultured || (σωματικῶς) developed.

ἄνεργος [aneryos] unemployed, idle.

ἀνέρχομαι [anerhome] ascend, climb || (λογαριασμός) amount to.

ἄνεσις, ἡ [annesees] ease, comfort || μὲ ἄνεσιν at leisure.

ἀνεστραμμένος [anestramenos] reversed, inverted.

ἀνέτοιμος [aneteemos] unprepared, not ready.

ἄνετος [anetos] comfortable, easy.

ἄνευ [anev] without.

ἀνεύθυνος [anevtheenos] not accountable, not responsible.

ἀνευλαβής [anevlavees] disrespectful, irreverent.

ἀνευρίσκω [anevreesko] find out, discover, recover.

ἀνεφάρμοστος [anefarmostos] inapplicable || (μὴ ἐφαρμοσθείς) unapplied.

ἀνέφικτος [anefeektos] unattainable, impossible.

ἀνεφοδιάζω [anefoδeeazo] provision, restock.

ἀνέχεια [aneheea] poverty, want.

ἀνέχομαι [anehome] tolerate.

ἀνεψιά, ἡ [anepsia] niece.

ἀνεψιός, ὁ [anepsios] nephew.

ἀνήθικος [aneetheekos] immoral, corrupt.

ἄνηθο, τό [aneetho] dill, anise.

ἀνήκουστος [aneekoustos] unheard of, incredible.

ἀνήκω [aneeko] belong (to), pertain.

ἀνηλεής [aneeleyees] pitiless, cruel.

ἀνήλικος [aneeleekos] under age || minor.

ἀνήμερα [aneemera] on the same day.

ἀνήμπορος [aneemboros] indisposed.

ἀνήρ, ὁ [aneer] man.

ἀνησυχία, ἡ [aneeseeheea] uneasiness, concern.

ἀνήσυχος [aneeseehos] uneasy, anxious.

ἀνησυχῶ [aneeseeho] be anxious, be worried.

ἀνήφορος, ὁ [aneeforos] uphill road || ascent.

ἀνθεκτικός [anthekteekos] endurable, resistant.

ἀνθηρός [antheeros] flourishing, blooming.

ἄνθησις, ἡ [antheesees] flowering, blossoming.

ἀνθίζω [antheezo] blossom, flourish.

ἀνθίσταμαι [antheestame] resist, oppose.

ἀνθοδέσμη, ἡ [anthoδesmee] bouquet, nosegay.

ἀνθοδοχεῖον, τό [anthoδoheeon] flowerpot, vase.

ἀνθολογία, ἡ [antholoɣeea] anthology.

ἀνθόνερο, τό [anthonero] orange-flower water, rose water.

ἀνθοπώλης, ὁ [anthopolees] florist.

ἄνθος, τό [anthos] flower.

ἀνθρακιά, ἡ [anthrakia] glowing embers.

ἀνθρακικός [anthrakeekos] carbonic.

ἀνθρακωρυχεῖον, τό [anthrakorreeheeon] coalmine.

ἄνθραξ, ὁ [anthraks] coal || (ἰατρ) anthrax.

ἀνθρωπιά, ἡ [anthropia] civility || good breeding.

ἀνθρώπινος [anthropeenos] human.

ἀνθρωπιστής, ὁ [anthropeestees] humanist.

ἀνθρωποκτονία, ἡ [anthropoktoneea] homicide.

ἀνθρωπολόγος, ὁ [anthropoloɣos] anthropologist.

ἄνθρωπος, ὁ [anthropos] man, person.

ἀνθρωπότης, ἡ [anthropotees] mankind, humanity.

ἀνθυγιεινός [antheeɣieinos] unhealthy, unwholesome.

ἀνθυπασπιστής, ὁ [antheepaspeestees] warrant officer || sergeant-major.

ἀνθυπολοχαγός, ὁ [antheepolohaɣos] second lieutenant.

ἀνθυποσμηναγός, ὁ [antheeposmeenaɣos] pilot officer.

ἀνθυποπλοίαρχος, ὁ [antheepopleearhos] sub-lieutenant.

ἀνθῶ [antho] βλ ἀνθίζω.

ἀνία, ἡ [aneea] boredom, weariness, ennui.

ἀνίατος [aneeatos] incurable.

ἀνίδεος [aneeδeos] unsuspecting || ignorant.

ἀνιδιοτελής [aneeδeeotelees] disinterested.

ἀνικανοποίητος [aneekanopieetos] unsatisfied.

ἀνίκανος [aneekanos] incapable, unable, unfit || impotent.

ἀνισόρροπος [aneesoropos] unbalanced.

ἄνισος [aneesos] unequal, uneven.

ἀνιστορῶ [aneestoro] relate, recollect.

ἀνίσχυρος [aneesheeros] powerless, weak, feeble.

ἀνίχνευσις, ἡ [aneehnevsees] tracking, searching.

ἄνοδος, ἡ [anoδos] ascent, accession.

ἀνοησία, ἡ [anoeeseea] folly, foolishness, nonsense.

ἀνόητος [anoeetos] foolish, silly, absurd.

ἀνόθευτος [anothevtos] unadulterated, pure.

ἄνοιγμα, τό [aneeɣma] opening, aperture.

ἀνοίγω [aneeɣo] open || (βρύση) turn on || (σύρτη) draw || (ὀμπρέλλα) put up || (φῶτα κτλ) turn on, switch on || (συζήτησις) open, broach || (χάρτη) unfold || (χορό) lead, open || (πηγάδι) dig || (κουρτίνες) draw back || (γιά χρῶμα) fade.

ἀνοίκειος [aneekeeos] unbecoming, improper.

ἀνοίκιαστος [aneekeeastos] unlet, unrented.

ἀνοικοδομῶ [aneekoδomo] rebuild.

ἀνοικονόμητος [aneekonomeetos] intractable, unmanageable.

ἀνοικτός [aneektos] open || (ἐπί χρωμάτων) light.

ἀνοιξιάτικος [aneekseeateekos] spring.

άνοιξις, ή [aneeksees] spring, springtime.

άνοιχτόκαρδος [aneehtokarðos] open-hearted, cheerful.

άνοιχτοχέρης [aneehtoherees] open-handed, magnanimous.

άνομβρία, ή [anomvreea] drought, scarcity of rain.

άνόμοιος [anomeeos] dissimilar, unlike.

άνοξείδωτος [anokseeðotos] stainless, rust-proof.

άνοργάνωτος [anoryanotos] unorganized.

άνορεξία, ή [anorekseea] loss of appetite || (μεταφ) half-heartedness.

άνορθογραφία, ή [anorthoyrafeea] mis-spelling.

άνορθώνω [anorthono] raise, stand upright || restore.

άνοσία, ή [anoseea] immunity from disease.

άνοστος [anostos] insipid, unsavoury || (μεταφ) ugly, disagreeable.

άνοχή, ή [anohee] forbearance, tolerance || οίκος ~ς brothel.

άνταγωνίζομαι [antayoneezome] compete, vie with.

άνταγωνισμός, ό [antayoneesmos] competition, contest, rivalry.

άνταλλαγή, ή [antallayee] exchange, barter.

άντάλλαγμα, τό [antallayma] thing exchanged, recompense.

άνταλλακτικόν, τό [antallakteekon] spare part, refill.

άνταλλάξιμος [antalakseemos] exchangeable.

άνταλλάσσω [antalaso] exchange.

άντάμα [antama] together.

άνταμείβω [antameevo] reward, recompense.

άνταμώνω [antamono] meet, join.

άντάμωση [antamosee]: **καλή ~** goodbye, farewell.

άντανάκλασις, ή [antanaklasees] reflection.

άντανακλῶ [antanaklo] reflect.

άντάξιος [antakseeos] worthy, deserving.

άνταποδίδω [antapoðeeðo] return, repay.

άνταποκρίνομαι [antapokreenome] be like, correspond to, respond, suit.

άνταπόκρισις, ή [antapokreesees] correspondence || (έφημερίδος) dispatch.

άνταποκριτής, ό [antapokreetees] correspondent, reporter.

άντάρα, ή [antara] tumult, uproar, storm.

άνταρσία, ή [antarseea] rebellion, revolt, mutiny.

άντάρτης, ό [antartees] rebel, insurgent, guerrilla.

άντε [annte] (έπιφ) come on!, get a move on!

άντένα, ή [antena] aerial, antenna.

άντεπανάστασις, ή [antepanastasees] counter-revolution.

άντεπίθεσις, ή [antepeethesees] counter-attack.

άντεπιτίθεμαι [antepeeteetheme] counter-attack.

άντεραστής, ό [anterastees] rival.

άντερο, τό [antero] intestine.

άντέχω [anteho] endure, hold firm, last.

άντζούγια, ή [antzouyeea] anchovy.

άντηλιά, ή [anteelia] glare, reflected sunlight.

άντηχῶ [anteeho] resound, re-echo.

άντί [antee] instead of, in exchange for || (τιμή) for || **~ γιά** instead of || **~ νά** instead of.

άντιαεροπορικός [anteeaeroporeekos] anti-aircraft.

άντιβαίνω [anteeveno] be against, be contrary to, be opposed to.

άντιβασιλεύς [anteevaseelevs] regent, viceroy.

άντιγραφή, ή [anteeyrafee] copy, copying.

άντίγραφον, τό [anteeyrafon] copy, transcript.

άντιγράφω [anteeyrafo] copy, imitate || . (στό σχολείο) crib.

άντίδι, τό [anteeðee] endive.

άντίδικος, ό [anteeðeekos] opponent.

άντίδοτον, τό [anteeðoton] antidote.

άντίδρασις, ή [anteeðrasees] reaction, opposition.

άντιδραστικός [anteeðrasteekos] reactionary, reactive.

άντιδρῶ [anteeðro] react, counteract, oppose.

άντίδωρον [anteeðoron] (έκκλ) holy bread.

άντίζηλος [anteezeelos] rival.

άντίθεσις, ή [anteethesees] contrast || opposition.

άντίθετος [anteethetos] contrary, opposite.

άντίκα, ή [anteeka] antique.

άντικαθιστῶ [anteekatheesto] replace, substitute || relieve.

άντικανονικός [anteekanoneekos] irregular, not according to rules.

άντικατάστασις [anteekatastasees] replacement || substitution.

άντικαταστάτης, ό [anteekatastatees] substitute || successor.

άντίκειμαι [anteekeeme] be opposed to.

άντικειμενικός [anteekeemeneekos] objective.

άντικείμενον, τό [anteekeemenon] object, thing || topic.

άντικλείδι, τό [anteekleeðee] passkey.

άντικοινωνικός [anteekeenoneekos] unsocial.

άντικρούω [anteekrouo] oppose, refute.

άντίκρυ [anteekree] opposite, face to face.

άντικρύζω [anteekreezo] face, front || meet.

άντικρυνός [anteekreenos] opposite, facing.

άντίκτυπος, ό [anteekteepos] repercussion, effect, result.

άντίλαλος, ό [anteelalos] echo.

άντιλαμβάνομαι [anteelamvanome] understand || perceive, notice.

άντιλέγω [anteeleyo] object, contradict.

ἀντιληπτός [anteeleeptos] perceptible ‖ understandable.

ἀντίληψις, ἡ [anteeleepsees] understanding, opinion ‖ quickness of mind.

ἀντιλυσσικός [anteeleeseekos] anti-rabies.

ἀντιμετωπίζω [anteemetopeezo] confront, face.

ἀντιμέτωπος [anteemetopos] face to face, facing.

ἀντιμισθία, ἡ [anteemeestheea] reward ‖ (ἐργάτου) daily wage.

ἀντιμόνιον, τό [anteemoneeon] antimony.

ἀντιναύαρχος, ὁ [anteenavarhos] vice-admiral.

ἀντίο [anteeo] (ἐπίφ) goodbye!

ἀντιπάθεια, ἡ [anteepatheea] antipathy, aversion.

ἀντιπαθητικός [anteepatheeteekos] repulsive, repugnant.

ἀντιπαθῶ [anteepatho] dislike, feel aversion for.

ἀντίπαλος, ὁ [anteepalos] adversary, opponent ‖ (στρατ) enemy.

ἀντιπαρέρχομαι [anteeparerhome] go by, pass ‖ (μεταφ) escape, elude.

ἀντιπειθαρχικός [anteepeetharheekos] undisciplined.

ἀντίπερα [anteepera] on the other side, opposite.

ἀντιπερισπασμός, ὁ [anteepereespasmos] distraction ‖ (στρατ) diversion.

ἀντιπλοίαρχος, ὁ [anteepleearhos] commander.

ἀντίποινα, τά [anteepeena] πλ reprisals.

ἀντιπολίτευσις, ἡ [anteepoleetevsees] opposition.

ἀντίπραξις, ἡ [anteepraksees] opposition, thwarting.

ἀντιπρόεδρος, ὁ [anteeproedros] vice-president, deputy chairman.

ἀντιπροσωπεία, ἡ [anteeprosopeea] representation ‖ delegation.

ἀντιπροσωπεύω [anteeprosopevo] represent, stand for.

ἀντιπρόσωπος, ὁ [anteeprosopos] representative ‖ (ἐμπορικός) agent.

ἀντίρρησις, ἡ [anteerreesees] objection, contradiction.

ἀντισηπτικός [anteeseepteekos] antiseptic.

ἀντίσκηνον, τό [anteeskeenon] army tent.

ἀντισμήναρχος, ὁ [anteesmeenarhos] wing commander.

ἀντισταθμίζω [anteestathmeezo] balance ‖ (μηχανική) compensate.

ἀντίστασις, ἡ [anteestasees] resistance, opposition.

ἀντιστέκομαι [anteestekome] resist, oppose.

ἀντίστοιχος [anteesteehos] corresponding, equivalent.

ἀντιστράτηγος, ὁ [anteestrateeyos] lieutenant-general.

ἀντιστρέφω [anteestrefo] invert, reverse.

ἀντίστροφος [anteestrofos] reverse, inverse.

ἀντισυνταγματάρχης, ὁ [anteeseentaymatarhees] lieutenant-colonel.

ἀντισυνταγματικός [anteeseentaymateekos] unconstitutional.

ἀντιτάσσω [anteetaso] oppose ‖ array (against).

ἀντιτίθεμαι [anteeteetheme] be opposed.

ἀντίτιμον, τό [anteeteemon] value, price.

ἀντιτορπιλλικόν, τό [anteetorpeeleekon] destroyer.

ἀντίτυπον, τό [anteeteepon] copy.

ἀντίφασις, ἡ [anteefasees] contradiction, discrepancy.

ἀντιφάσκω [anteefasko] contradict o.s.

ἀντίχειρ, ὁ [anteeheer] thumb.

ἄντλησις, ἡ [antleesees] pumping, drawing up of water.

ἀντλία, ἡ [antleea] pump.

ἀντλῶ [antlo] pump, draw up water ‖ derive.

ἀντοχή, ἡ [antohee] endurance, strength, resistance.

ἄντρας, ὁ [antras] man ‖ husband.

ἀντρίκιος [antreekeeos] βλ ἀνδρικός.

ἀντρόγυνο, τό [antroyeeno] married couple.

ἄντρον, τό [antron] cave, cavern, grotto.

ἀντωνυμία, ἡ [antoneemeea] pronoun.

ἄνυδρος [aneedros] waterless, dry, arid.

ἀνύμφευτος [aneemfevtos] unmarried.

ἀνύπανδρος [aneepandros] unmarried, single.

ἀνύπαρκτος [aneeparktos] non-existent.

ἀνυπαρξία, ἡ [aneeparkseea] non-existence, lack.

ἀνυπέρβλητος [aneepervleetos] insuperable ‖ incomparable.

ἀνυπόληπτος [aneepoleeptos] not esteemed, not respected.

ἀνυπολόγιστος [aneepoloyeestos] incalculable.

ἀνυπόμονος [aneepomonos] impatient, anxious.

ἀνύποπτος [aneepoptos] not suspecting ‖ not suspect.

ἀνυπόστατος [aneepostatos] groundless, unfounded ‖ unsubstantial.

ἀνυπότακτος [aneepotaktos] insubordinate ‖ (λαός) not subdued ‖ (παιδί) disobedient.

ἀνυπόφορος [aneepoforos] intolerable.

ἀνυψώνω [aneepsono] raise ‖ (μεταφ) praise, elevate, extol.

ἄνω [ano] up, above ‖ ~ κάτω in confusion, upset ‖ (μέ γεν) above, over.

ἀνώγι, τό [anoyee] upper floor, upper storey.

ἀνώδυνος [anodeenos] painless.

ἀνωμαλία, ἡ [anomaleea] irregularity, unevenness ‖ anomaly.

ἀνώμαλος [anomalos] (ἐπιφάνεια) irregular, uneven ‖ (ἄνθρωπος) erratic, eccentric.

ἀνώνυμος [anoneemos] anonymous ‖ ~ ἐταιρεία limited company.

ἀνώτατος [anotatos] supreme, uppermost ‖ ~ ὄροφος top floor.

ἀνώτερος [anoteros] superior, higher, upper ‖ ~ χρημάτων above money ‖ ἀνωτέρα κοινωνία upper class.

ἀνωφελής [anofelees] fruitless, futile, vain.

ἄξαφνα [aksafna] βλ. ἔξαφνα.

ἀξέγνοιαστος [akseyneeastos] unconcerned ‖ without worries.

ἄξενος [aksenos] inhospitable.

ἄξεστος [aksestos] uncouth, rough, unpolished.

ἀξέχαστος [aksehastos] unforgotten ‖ unforgettable.

ἀξία, ἡ [akseea] worth, value, price.

ἀξιαγάπητος [akseeayapeetos] amiable, lovable.

ἀξιέπαινος [aksiepenos] praiseworthy, laudable.

ἀξίζω [akseezo] be worth, cost ‖ merit ‖ ἀξίζει νά τιμωρηθῇ he deserves to be punished.

ἀξίνα, ἡ [akseena] pickaxe.

ἀξιοθαύμαστος [akseeothavmastos] wonderful, admirable.

ἀξιοθέατος [akseeotheatos] worth seeing ‖ τά ἀξιοθέατα the sights.

ἀξιοθρήνητος [akseeothreeneetos] lamentable, deplorable.

ἀξιόλογος [akseeoloyos] remarkable ‖ distinguished.

ἀξιόπιστος [akseeopeestos] trustworthy, reliable.

ἀξιοπρεπής [akseeoprepees] dignified, decent.

ἄξιος [akseeos] capable ‖ deserving ‖ worthy, worth.

ἀξιοσημείωτος [akseeoseemeeotos] noteworthy, notable, remarkable.

ἀξιότιμος [akseeoteemos] estimable, honourable.

ἀξιῶ [akseeo] claim, expect.

ἀξιωματικός, ὁ [akseeomateekos] officer.

ἀξιώνομαι [akseeonome] manage.

ἀξίωσις, ἡ [akseeosees] claim, pretension.

ἀξύριστος [akseereestos] unshaven.

ἄξων, ὁ [akson] axis ‖ axle, pivot, shaft.

ἄοκνος [aoknos] tireless ‖ indefatigable.

ἀόμματος [aomatos] blind.

ἄοπλος [aoplos] unarmed.

ἀόριστος [aoreestos] invisible, indefinite ‖ (γραμμ) aorist.

ἄοσμος [aosmos] odourless, scentless.

ἀπαγγελία, ἡ [apangeleea] recitation, declamation ‖ diction.

ἀπαγόρευσις, ἡ [arayorevsees] prohibition.

ἀπαγορεύω [arayorevo] prohibit, forbid.

ἀπαγχονίζω [apanghoneezo] hang.

ἀπαγωγή, ἡ [arayoyee] abduction ‖ (παιδιοῦ) kidnapping.

ἀπάθεια, ἡ [apatheea] indifference, apathy.

ἀπαίδευτος [apeδevtos] uneducated, unskilled, illiterate.

ἀπαισιόδοξος [apeseeoδoksos] pessimist.

ἀπαίσιος [apeseeos] frightful, sinister, horrible.

ἀπαίτησις, ἡ [apeteesees] claim ‖ demand.

ἀπαιτητικός [apeteeteekos] demanding, exacting, importunate.

ἀπαιτῶ [apeto] claim, demand, require.

ἀπαλλαγή, ἡ [apallayee] deliverance ‖ release ‖ dismissal.

ἀπαλλάσσω [apallasso] deliver, free ‖ (καθήκοντα) relieve.

ἀπαλλοτριῶ [apallotreeo] expropriate, alienate.

ἁπαλός [apalos] soft ‖ gentle.

ἀπάνθρωπος [apanthropos] inhuman, cruel.

ἅπαντα, τά [apanta] πλ. complete works.

ἀπάντημα, τό [apanteema] encounter.

ἀπάντησις, ἡ [apanteesees] reply, answer, response.

ἀπαντῶ [apanto] answer, reply ‖ meet.

ἀπάνω [apano] up, above ‖ upstairs ‖ ~ κάτω approximately ‖ ἀπό πάνω on top, from above ‖ ἕως ~ to the top ‖ ~ πού at the moment when ‖ ~ ἀπό above, more than ‖ ~ σέ at the moment of.

ἅπαξ [apaks] once, inasmuch as.

ἀπαξίωσις, ἡ [apakseeosees] disdain, contempt.

ἀπαράβατος [aparavatos] inviolable ‖ inviolate.

ἀπαράδεκτος [aparaδektos] unacceptable, inadmissible.

ἀπαραίτητος [apareeteetos] indispensable.

ἀπαράλλακτος [aparalaktos] identical ‖ unchanged.

ἀπαράμιλλος [aparameelos] unrivalled, incomparable, peerless.

ἀπαρατήρητος [aparateereetos] unnoticed, unobserved.

ἀπαρέμφατον, τό [aparemfaton] (γραμμ) infinitive.

ἀπαρηγόρητος [apareeyoreetos] inconsolable.

ἀπαριθμῶ [apareethmo] enumerate, count.

ἀπαρνοῦμαι [aparnoume] renounce, deny, disavow, disown.

ἀπαρτίζω [aparteezo] form, constitute.

ἀπαρχή, ἡ [aparhee] beginning, outset.

ἅπας [apas] all, whole, entire ‖ ἐξ ἅπαντος without fail.

ἀπασχόλησις, ἡ [apasholeesees] occupation.

ἀπασχολῶ [apasholo] occupy, busy.

ἀπατεών, ὁ [apateon] cheat, deceiver, swindler.

ἀπάτη, ἡ [apatee] deceit, fraud ‖ illusion.

ἀπατηλός [apateelos] deceptive, false, fraudulent.

ἀπάτητος [apateetos] untrodden.

ἀπατῶ [apato] deceive, cheat, defraud.

ἀπαυδῶ [apavδo] tire, become tired.

ἀπεγνωσμένος [apeynosmenos] desperate.

απειθαρχία, ή [apeetharheea] insubordination, lack of discipline.

απειθής [apeethees] disobedient.

απεικονίζω [apeekoneezo] represent, portray, depict.

απειλή, ή [apeelee] threat, menace.

απειλητικός [apeeleeteekos] threatening.

απείραχτος [apeerahtos] untouched, untroubled.

απειρία, ή [apeereea] inexperience || (μέτρου) infinity, immensity.

άπειρος [apeeros] inexperienced || (αριθμός) infinite, boundless.

απέλασις, ή [apelasees] deportation, expulsion.

απελευθερώνω [apeleftherono] set free, emancipate.

απελευθέρωσις, ή [apeleftherosees] liberation, emancipation.

απελπίζομαι [apelpeezome] despair.

απελπισία, ή [apelpeeseea] despair || είναι ~ it's hopeless!

απέναντι [apenantee] opposite, across the way || (πληρωμή) towards, against.

απεναντίας [apenanteeas] on the contrary.

απένταρος [apentaros] penniless, broke.

απέραντος [aperantos] immense, boundless, endless.

απέραστος [aperastos] impassable, unbeatable || (κλωστή) not threaded.

απεργία, ή [aperyeea] strike.

απερίγραπτος [apereeyraptos] indescribable.

απεριόριστος [apereeoreestos] unlimited.

απεριποίητος [apereepieetos] neglected, untidy.

απερίσκεπτος [apereeskeptos] thoughtless, foolish, heedless.

απερίσπαστος [apereespastos] undistracted.

απέριττος [apereetos] simple, plain, concise.

απέρχομαι [aperhome] depart, go away, leave.

απεσταλμένος, ό [apestalmenos] envoy, minister, delegate.

απευθύνομαι [apeftheenome] apply, appeal, address.

απεύχομαι [apevhome] do not wish, deprecate.

απεχθάνομαι [apehthanome] detest, abhor.

απεχθής [apehthees] odious, repulsive, detestable.

απέχω [apeho] abstain || be distant, be far from.

απηγορευμένος [apeeyorevmenos] forbidden, prohibited.

απηνής [apeenees] merciless, cruel, ferocious.

απήχησις, ή [apeeheesees] effect || echo.

απηχώ [apeeho] echo, resound.

άπιαστος [apeeastos] not caught || intact, intangible.

απίδι, τό [apeedee] pear.

απίθανος [apeethanos] unlikely, improbable.

απίστευτος [apeestevtos] unbelievable, incredible.

απιστία, ή [apeesteea] infidelity || incredulity.

άπιστος [apeestos] unbelieving, unfaithful || faithless, infidel.

απιστώ [apeesto] disbelieve || be unfaithful.

άπλα, ή [apla] spaciousness.

απλά [apla] simply.

απλανής [aplanees] fixed.

άπλετος [apletos] abundant.

απλήρωτος [apleerotos] unfilled || unpaid.

απλησίαστος [apleeseeastos] unapproachable.

άπληστος [apleestos] insatiable, greedy, avid.

απλοϊκός [aploeekos] naive, simple.

απλός [aplos] simple || (εισητήριον) single || (ντύσιμο) plain.

απλότης, ή [aplotees] simplicity, naïvety, plainness.

απλούστατα [aploustata] simply.

απλοχέρης [aploherees] open-handed, liberal.

απλόχωρος [aplohoros] spacious, roomy.

άπλυτος [apleetos] unwashed || τά άπλυτα dirty linen.

άπλωμα, τό [aploma] spreading, unfolding || (χεριών) stretching || (ρούχων) hanging out.

απλώνω [aplono] spread, stretch || (ρούχα) hang out.

απλώς [aplos] simply, merely, plainly.

άπνοια, ή [apneea] lack of wind.

άπνους [apnous] lifeless, breathless.

από [apo] from, of || ~ καιρού εις καιρόν from time to time || ~ φόβο out of fear || by || ~ μνήμης by heart || ~ τόν ίδιο δρόμο by the same road || through || ~ τό παράθυρο through the window || than || ξέρω περισσότερα ~ σένα I know more than you || (προ9) μέσα ~ out of || πρίν ~ before.

αποβάθρα, ή [apovathra] pier, wharf || (σιδηροδρομική) platform.

αποβάλλω [apovalo] reject, expel, dismiss || (μωρό) miscarry.

απόβασις, ή [apovasees] disembarkation, landing.

αποβιβάζω [apoveevazo] disembark, unload.

αποβλέπω [apovlepo] consider || aim at, look forward to || regard.

αποβολή, ή [apovolee] dismissal, turning out || (μωρού) miscarriage, abortion.

αποβραδίς [apovradees] yesterday evening, since last night.

απόβρασμα, τό [apovrasma] scum, refuse, dregs.

απόγειος [apoyeeos] offshore, land.

απογειούμαι [apoyeeoume] take off.

ἀπογείωσις, ἡ [apogeeosees] takeoff.
ἀπόγεμα, τό [apoyema] afternoon.
ἀπογίνομαι [apoyeenome] become, happen.
ἀπόγνωσις, ἡ [apoynosees] despair, desperation.
ἀπογοήτευσις [apoyoeetevsees] disappointment, disillusionment.
ἀπογοητεύω [apoyoeetevo] disappoint, disillusion.
ἀπόγονος, ὁ [apoyonos] offspring, descendant.
ἀπογραφή, ἡ [apoyrafee] (πληθυσμοῦ) census ‖ (ἐμπορ) inventory.
ἀπογυμνώνω [apoyeemnono] strip, plunder ‖ unclothe.
ἀποδεικνύω [apodeekneeo] prove, demonstrate.
ἀποδεικτικόν, τό [apodeekteekon] certificate.
ἀπόδειξις, ἡ [apodeeksees] proof ‖ receipt.
ἀποδεκατίζω [apodekateezo] decimate.
ἀποδέκτης, ὁ [apodektees] addressee, receiver, consignee.
ἀποδεκτός [apodektos] acceptable ‖ accepted.
ἀποδέχομαι [apodehome] accept ‖ admit.
ἀποδημία, ἡ [apodeemeea] migration, travel.
ἀπόδημος [apodeemos] living abroad.
ἀποδίδω [apodeedo] give back, return ‖ (τιμάς) grant, award ‖ (κάτι σέ κάτι) attribute ‖ (ἐλευθερίαν) restore ‖ (μετάφρασιν) express ‖ (ἔργον) produce.
ἀποδοκιμάζω [apodokeemazo] disapprove of ‖ demonstrate against.
ἀποδοκιμασία, ἡ [apodokeemaseea] disapproval, rejection ‖ booing.
ἀπόδοσις, ἡ [apodosees] (ἐπιστροφή) return, repaying ‖ (μηχανῆς κτλ) efficiency, capacity ‖ (ἐργοστασίου) output ‖ (τῆς γῆς) yield, produce ‖ (ἔργου) rendering.
ἀποδοχή, ἡ [apodohee] acceptance ‖ acceptation ‖ ἀποδοχαί πλ salary, fees.
ἀπόδρασις, ἡ [apodrasees] escape.
ἀποδύομαι [apodeeome] undress ‖ (μεταφ) ~ στόν ἀγῶνα roll up one's sleeves.
ἀποδυτήριον, τό [apodeeteereeon] changing room.
ἀποζημιώνω [apozeemeeono] compensate, indemnify.
ἀποζημίωσις, ἡ [apozeemeeosees] compensation, indemnity.
ἀποθανών [apothanon] deceased, late.
ἀποθαρρύνω [apothareeno] discourage.
ἀπόθεμα, τό [apothema] deposit ‖ stock, reserve.
ἀποθέωσις, ἡ [apotheosees] apotheosis ‖ (μεταφ) rousing reception.
ἀποθηκάριος, ὁ [apotheekareeos] storehouse keeper.
ἀποθηκεύω [apotheekevo] store up.
ἀποθήκη, ἡ [apotheekee] storage room, storehouse, warehouse.

ἀποθνήσκω [apothneesko] die, pass away.
ἀποθρασύνομαι [apothraseenome] become arrogant.
ἀποθυμῶ [apotheemo] miss ‖ wish for.
ἀποικία, ἡ [apeekeea] colony, settlement.
ἀποκαθιστῶ [apokatheesto] rehabilitate, restore ‖ (κόρη) marry.
ἀποκαλύπτω [apokaleepto] disclose, unveil, reveal.
ἀποκάλυψις, ἡ [apokaleepsees] revelation ‖ (θρησκεία) Apocalypse.
ἀποκάμω [apokamo] get tired ‖ (τελειώνω) finish off.
ἀποκαρδιωτικός [apokarδeeoteekos] disheartening.
ἀποκατάστασις, ἡ [apokatastasees] restoration, resettlement ‖ (κόρης) marriage.
ἀποκατινός [apokateenos] underneath, below.
ἀπόκειμαι [apokeeme] it is up to, it depends on ‖ σέ σένα ἀπόκειται it's up to you.
ἀπόκεντρος [apokentros] outlying, remote, out-of-the-way.
ἀποκέντρωσις, ἡ [apokentrosees] decentralization.
ἀποκεφαλίζω [apokefaleezo] decapitate, behead.
ἀποκήρυξις, ἡ [apokeereeksees] denunciation, proscription.
ἀποκηρύσσω [apokeereeso] renounce, disavow ‖ proscribe, outlaw.
ἀποκλεισμός, ὁ [apokleesmos] exclusion, blockade, boycott.
ἀποκλειστικός [apokleesteekos] exclusive.
ἀποκλείω [apokleeo] exclude ‖ debar ‖ boycott ‖ ἀποκλείεται it's out of the question.
ἀποκληρώνω [apokleerono] disinherit.
ἀποκλίνω [apokleeno] lean, diverge, incline.
ἀποκοιμίζω [apokeemeezo] lull to sleep.
ἀποκοιμοῦμαι [apokeemoume] fall asleep.
ἀποκομίζω [apokomeezo] carry away ‖ derive.
ἀπόκομμα, τό [apokoma] press cutting ‖ (κομμάτι) bit.
ἀποκοπή, ἡ [apokopee] cutting off ‖ amputation.
ἀπόκοτος [apokotos] bold.
ἀποκούμπι, τό [apokoumbee] prop.
ἀπόκρημνος [apokreemnos] precipitous, steep, abrupt.
ἀποκριές, οἱ [apokries] πλ carnival.
ἀποκρίνομαι [apokreenome] answer, reply.
ἀπόκρισις, ἡ [apokreesees] reply, answer.
ἀπόκρουσις, ἡ [apokrousees] repulsion ‖ (κατηγορίας) refutation.
ἀποκρούω [apokrouo] repulse ‖ reject.
ἀποκρύπτω [apokreepto] conceal, hide, cover.
ἀπόκρυφος [apokreefos] secret ‖ (ἐκκλ) apocryphal.
ἀπόκτησις, ἡ [apokteesees] acquisition.

ἀποκτῶ [apokto] obtain, get ‖ (παιδί) have (a child).

ἀπολαβή, ἡ [apolavee] gain, profit, income.

ἀπολαμβάνω [apolamvano] gain, earn ‖ (διασκεδάζω) enjoy.

ἀπόλαυσις, ἡ [apolavsees] enjoyment.

ἀπολήγω [apoleego] terminate, finish, end up in.

ἀπολίθωμα, τό [apoleethoma] fossil.

ἀπολλύω [apoleeo] lose.

ἀπολογία, ἡ [apologeea] defence, plea, excuse.

ἀπολογισμός, ὁ [apologeesmos] financial statement, account, report.

ἀπολογοῦμαι [apologoume] justify o.s., apologize.

ἀπολύμανσις, ἡ [apoleemansees] disinfection.

ἀπόλυσις, ἡ [apoleesees] release ‖ dismissal.

ἀπολυτήριον, τό [apoleeteereeon] discharge certificate ‖ (σχολείου) school leaving certificate, diploma.

ἀπόλυτος [apoleetos] absolute ‖ (ἀριθμός) cardinal.

ἀπολυτρώνω [apoleetrono] ransom ‖ redeem.

ἀπολύτως [apoleetos] absolutely ‖ entirely.

ἀπολύω [apoleeo] untie ‖ release ‖ (διώχνω) dismiss.

ἀπομακρύνω [apomakreeno] remove, send away, keep off.

ἀπόμαχος [apomahos] veteran, pensioner.

ἀπομεινάρια [apomeenaria] πλ remains, left-overs, remnants.

ἀπομένω [apomeno] remain, be left ‖ (κατάπληκτος) be left speechless.

ἀπομίμησις, ἡ [apomeemeesees] imitation, copy.

ἀπομνημονεύματα, τά [apomneemonev-mata] πλ memoirs.

ἀπομονώνω [apomonono] isolate ‖ (ἡλεκτ) insulate.

ἀπονέμω [aponemo] bestow, allot ‖ confer, award.

ἀπονομή, ἡ [aponomee] award, bestowal.

ἀποξενώνω [apoksenono] alienate, estrange.

ἀποξήρανσις, ἡ [apokseeransees] draining, drying.

ἀπόπατος, ὁ [apopatos] W.C., toilet.

ἀπόπειρα, ἡ [apopeera] attempt, trial.

ἀποπεράτωσις, ἡ [apoperatosees] completion.

ἀποπλάνησις, ἡ [apoplaneesees] seduction ‖ (φωτός) aberration.

ἀποπλέω [apopleo] set sail, sail away.

ἀποπλύνω [apopleeno] wash, rinse.

ἀπορία, ἡ [aporeea] doubt ‖ uncertainty, perplexity.

ἄπορος [aporos] needy, poor.

ἀπορρέω [aporeo] flow, stem (from), emanate.

ἀπόρρητος [aporeetos] secret.

ἀπορρίματα, τά [aporeemata] πλ rubbish, refuse.

ἀπορρίπτω [aporeepto] cast off ‖ (προσφο-ράν κτλ) reject, refuse ‖ (στίς ἐξετάσεις) fail.

ἀπορροφητικός [aporofeeteekos] absorbent, sucking.

ἀπορροφῶ [aporofo] absorb.

ἀπορρυπαντικόν, τό [aporeepanteekon] detergent.

ἀπορῶ [aporo] be at a loss, wonder, be surprised.

ἀπόσβεσις, ἡ [aposvesees] extinguishing ‖ (χρέους) liquidation (of debt).

ἀποσείω [aposeeo] shake off.

ἀποσιωπητικά, τά [aposeeopeeteeka] πλ points of omission.

ἀποσιωπῶ [aposeeopo] hush up, pass in silence.

ἀποσκοπῶ [aposkopo] aim, have in view.

ἀπόσπασμα, τό [apospasma] extract, excerpt ‖ (στρατ) detachment.

ἀποσπῶ [apospo] detach, tear out ‖ (στρατ) detach.

ἀπόσταξις, ἡ [apostaksees] distillation ‖ trickling.

ἀποστασία, ἡ [apostaseea] revolt, defection ‖ apostasy.

ἀπόστασις, ἡ [apostasees] distance ‖ remoteness.

ἀποστειρῶ [aposteero] sterilize.

ἀποστέλλω [apostelo] dispatch, send, transmit.

ἀποστεροῦμαι [aposteroume] be deprived of, lose.

ἀποστερῶ [apostero] deprive.

ἀποστηθίζω [aposteetheezo] learn by heart.

ἀπόστημα, τό [aposteema] abscess.

ἀποστολεύς, ὁ [apostolevs] sender, shipper.

ἀποστολή, ἡ [apostolee] sending, consignment ‖ (ἐμπορική κτλ) mission.

ἀποστομώνω [apostomono] silence.

ἀποστράτευσις, ἡ [apostratevsees] demobilization.

ἀπόστρατος, ὁ [apostratos] retired officer, ex-serviceman, veteran.

ἀποστρέφομαι [apostrefome] detest, abhor, despise.

ἀποστρέφω [apostrefo] avert, turn away.

ἀποστροφή, ἡ [apostrofee] repugnance, aversion, abhorrence.

ἀπόστροφος, ὁ [apostrofos] apostrophe.

ἀποσύνθεσις, ἡ [aposeenthesees] decay, decomposition ‖ disorganization.

ἀποσύρω [aposeero] withdraw ‖ retract.

ἀποσώνω [aposono] complete, finish off.

ἀπότακτος [apotaktos] discharged (dishonourably).

ἀποταμιεύω [apotamievo] save, put aside ‖ (τρόφιμα) lay up.

ἀποτείνομαι [apoteenome] apply, inquire.

ἀποτελειώνω [apoteleeono] complete ‖ finish off.

ἀποτέλεσμα [apotelesma] result, effect ‖ ἀποτελεσματικός effective.

ἀποτελοῦμαι [apoteloume] consist of, be composed of.

ἀποτεφρώνω [apotefrono] reduce to ashes, burn down.

ἀποτίνω [apoteeno] pay off ‖ (ποινήν) serve ‖ (εὐγνωμοσύνην) repay.

ἀπότομος [apotomos] sudden, abrupt ‖ (στροφή)· steep, sheer ‖ (τρόπος) curt, gruff.

ἀποτραβιέμαι [apotravieme] withdraw, give up.

ἀποτρέπω [apotrepo] avert, turn aside, ward off.

ἀποτρόπαιος [apotropeos] abominable, hideous, horrible.

ἀποτροπή [apotropee] averting, warding off, dissuasion.

ἀποτρώγω [apotroyo] finish eating.

ἀποτσίγαρο, τό [apotseeyaro] cigarette end, stub, fag end.

ἀποτυγχάνω [apoteenghano] fail, fall through, miss.

ἀποτυπώνω [apoteepono] impress, imprint.

ἀποτυφλώνω [apoteeflono] blind.

ἀποτυχία, ἡ [apoteeheea] failure, reverse.

ἀπουσία, ἡ [apouseea] absence ‖ ἀπουσιάζω be absent.

ἀποφάγια, τά [apofayeea] πλ scraps of food, remnants of a meal.

ἀποφασίζω [apofaseezo] decide, resolve, determine.

ἀπόφασις, ἡ [apofasees] decision, resolution ‖ (νομ) verdict ‖ τό παίρνω ~ν make up one's mind.

ἀποφασιστικός [apofaseesteekos] decisive, determined.

ἀποφέρω [apofero] yield, bring in ‖ produce.

ἀποφεύγω [apofevyo] avoid, keep clear of ‖ (κάπνισμα κτλ) abstain from.

ἀπόφθεγμα, τό [apoftheyma] maxim, apothegm.

ἀπόφοιτος [apofeetos] school leaver ‖ university graduate.

ἀποφορά, ἡ [apofora] stink, emanation.

ἀποφυγή, ἡ [apofeeyee] avoidance, evasion.

ἀποφυλακίζω [apofeelakeezo] release from prison.

ἀπόφυσις, ἡ [apofeesees] excrescence ‖ protuberance.

ἀποχαιρετίζω [apohereteezo] wish goodbye, bid farewell.

ἀποχαιρετισμός, ὁ [apohereteesmos] farewell, goodbye.

ἀποχέτευσις, ἡ [apohetevsees] draining, drainage.

ἀπόχρωσις, ἡ [apohrosees] shade, tone ‖ (χρώματος) fading.

ἀποχώρησις, ἡ [apohoreesees] withdrawal, retirement, departure.

ἀποχωρητήριον, τό [apohoreeteerion]

W.C., lavatory ‖ (στρατ) latrine.

ἀποχωρίζομαι [apohoreezome] part with, be separated.

ἀποχωρισμός, ὁ [apohorreesmos] separation, parting.

ἀποχωρῶ [apohoro] withdraw, retire, lèave.

ἀπόψε [apopse] tonight, this evening.

ἀποψινός [apopseenos] tonight's.

ἄποψις, ἡ [apopsees] view, sight ‖ (μεταφ) view, idea.

ἀπραγματοποίητος [apraymatopieetos] unrealizable ‖ unfulfilled.

ἄπρακτος [apraktos] unsuccessful ‖ unachieved.

ἀπραξία, ἡ [aprakseea] inactivity ‖ (οἰκ) stagnation, standstill.

ἀπρέπεια, ἡ [aprepeea] indecency, bad manners.

ἀπρεπής [aprepees] indecent, improper, unbecoming.

Ἀπρίλης, ὁ [apreelees] April.

ἀπρόβλεπτος [aprovleptos] unforeseen, unexpected.

ἀπροετοίμαστος [aproeteemastos] unprepared, unready.

ἀποθυμία, ἡ [aprotheemeea] reluctance, hesitancy.

ἀπρόθυμος [aprotheemos] unwilling, reluctant, hesitant.

ἀποκάλυπτος [aprokaleeptos] undisguised, unfeigned, frank.

ἀπρόκλητος [aprokleetos] unprovoked, uncalled-for, unchallenged.

ἀπρομελέτητος [apromeleteetos] unpremeditated.

ἀπρονοησία, ἡ [apronoeeseea] improvidence, imprudence.

ἀπρόοπτος [aprooptos] unforeseen, unexpected.

ἀπρόσβλητος [aprosvleetos] unassailable ‖ invulnerable.

ἀπροσδόκητος [aprosdokeetos] unexpected, unforeseen, sudden.

ἀπρόσεκτος [aprosektos] inattentive, careless, remiss.

ἀπροσεξία, ἡ [aprosekseea] inattention, inadvertence.

ἀπρόσιτος [aproseetos] inaccessible, unapproachable.

ἀπροσποίητος [aprospieetos] frank, unaffected, open, sincere.

ἀποστάτευτος [aprostatevtos] unprotected ‖ forlorn.

ἀπρόσωπος [aprosopos] impersonal.

ἀπροχώρητον, τό [aprohoreeton] limit, dead end.

ἄπταιστος [aptestos] faultless, perfect, correct.

ἄπτερος [apteros] wingless.

ἀπτόητος [aptoeetos] undaunted, intrepid.

ἄπτομαι [aptome] touch, feel, finger.

ἁπτός [aptos] tangible, palpable, evident.

ἀπύθμενος [apeethmenos] bottomless.

ἀπωθῶ [apotho] repel, repulse, thrust back ‖ (μεταφ) reject.

ἀπώλεια, ἡ [apoleea] loss ‖ (θάνατος) bereavement.

ἀπώλητος [apoleetos] unsold.

ἀπών [apon] absent, missing.

ἀπώτατος [apotatos] furthest, remotest, most distant.

ἀπώτερος [apoteros] farther, further ‖ ~ σκοπός ulterior motive.

ἄρα [ara] so, thus, therefore, consequently.

ἆρα [ara] I wonder if, can it be that?

ἀρά [ara] curse, imprecation.

ἀραβικός [araveekos] Arabian, Arabic.

ἀραβόσιτος, ὁ [aravoseetos] maize, corn.

ἄραγε [araγe] is it?, can it be?, I wonder if.

ἄραγμα, τό [araγma] anchoring, mooring.

ἀράδα, ἡ [araδa] line, row, file, rank ‖ (ἐπίρ) continuously ‖ τῆς ~ς common.

ἀραδιάζω [araδeazo] put in a row, line up ‖ (ὀνόματα κτλ) enumerate.

ἀράζω [arazo] moor, anchor, drop anchor.

ἀράθυμος [aratheemos] irascible, irritable, testy.

ἀραιός [areos] sparse, scattered ‖ (ἐπισκέψεις) infrequent, rare.

ἀραιώνω [areono] (σάλτσα κτλ) thin down ‖ (γραμμές κτλ) spread out ‖ (ἐπισκέψεις) lessen, cut down.

ἀρακᾶς, ὁ [arakas] common pea.

ἀραμπᾶς, ὁ [arambas] two-wheeled cart.

ἀράπης, ὁ [arapees] negro, dark person ‖ (φόβητρον) bogey.

ἀραπίνα, ἡ [arapeena] negress, dark woman.

ἀράχνη, ἡ [arahnee] spider ‖ cobweb.

Ἄραψ, ὁ [araps] Arab.

ἀρβύλα, ἡ [arveela] boot.

ἀργά [arγa] slowly ‖ late.

ἀργαλειός, ὁ [arγalios] loom.

ἄργητα, ἡ [arγeeta] delay.

ἀργία, ἡ [arγeea] holiday, closing day ‖ idleness.

ἄργιλλος, ἡ [arγeelos] clay.

ἀργοκίνητος [arγokeeneetos] slow-moving, sluggish.

ἀργομισθία, ἡ [arγomeestheea] sinecure.

ἀργοπορία, ἡ [arγoporeea] slowness, delay.

ἀργός [arγos] slow ‖ idle, inactive.

ἀργόσχολος [arγosholos] idle, unoccupied.

ἀργότερα [arγotera] later, then.

ἀργυραμοιβός, ὁ [arγerameevos] money-changer.

ἄργυρος, ὁ [arγeeros] silver.

ἀργῶ [arγo] be late ‖ (μαγαζί) be closed.

ἄρδευσις, ἡ [arδevsees] irrigation.

ἄρδην [arδeen] entirely, from top to bottom, wholly.

ἀρειμάνιος [areemaneeos] bellicose, pugnacious.

Ἄρειος [areeos]: ~ Πάγος Supreme Court.

ἀρέσκεια, ἡ [areskeea] taste, pleasure ‖ κατ' ~ν as much as I like.

ἀρεστός [arestos] agreeable, pleasing, gratifying.

ἀρέσω [areso] please, delight, like ‖ μοῦ ἀρέσει I like it.

ἀρετή, ἡ [aretee] virtue.

ἀρετσίνωτος [aretseenotos] unresinated.

ἀρθρῖτις, ἡ [arthreetees] arthritis.

ἀρθρογράφος, ὁ [arthroγrafos] journalist.

ἄρθρον, τό [arthron] article, clause, term.

ἄρθρωσις, ἡ [arthrosees] articulation, joint ‖ pronouncing distinctly.

ἀρίθμησις, ἡ [areethmeesees] numbering, counting, pagination.

ἀριθμητής, ὁ [areethmeetees] numerator ‖ (μηχάνημα) adding machine.

ἀριθμητική, ἡ [areethmeeteekee] arithmetic.

ἀριθμός, ὁ [areethmos] number.

ἀριθμῶ [areethmo] count, enumerate.

ἄριστα [areesta] very well ‖ (βαθμολογία) excellent.

ἀριστεῖον, τό [areesteeon] first prize, medal.

ἀριστερά [areestera] left hand ‖ (ἐπιρ) on the left, to the left.

ἀριστερός [areesteros] left, left-handed ‖ (σπόρ) left-wing.

ἀριστοκρατία, ἡ [areestokrateea] aristocracy.

ἀριστούργημα, τό [areestouryeema] masterpiece.

ἀρκετά [arketa] enough, sufficiently.

ἀρκετός [arketos] enough, sufficient, adequate.

ἀρκούδα, ἡ [arkouδa] bear.

ἀρκούντως [arkountos] βλ ἀρκετά.

ἀρκτικός [arkteekos] Arctic, northern.

ἄρκτος, ἡ [arktos] bear.

ἀρκῶ [arko] be enough, suffice ‖ ἀρκεῖ νά as long as.

ἀρλούμπα, ἡ [arloumba] foolish talk, nonsense.

ἅρμα, τό [arma] chariot ‖ (στρατ) ~ μάχης tank.

ἁρμαθιά, ἡ [armathia] bunch ‖ string.

ἀρμάρι, τό [armaree] cupboard ‖ wardrobe.

ἄρματα, τά [armata] πλ weapons.

ἁρματώνω [armatono] arm ‖ equip.

ἀρμέγω [armeγo] milk ‖ (μεταφ) fleece.

Ἀρμένης, ὁ [armenees] Armenian.

ἁρμενίζω [armeneezo] set sail, sail.

ἄρμη, ἡ [armee] brine, pickling brine.

ἁρμόδιος [armoδeeos] qualified, competent ‖ propitious.

ἁρμοδιότης, ἡ [armoδeeotees] competency, province, jurisdiction.

ἁρμόζω [armozo] fit ‖ befit, be becoming, be proper.

ἁρμονία, ἡ [armoneea] harmony, concord.

ἁρμός, ὁ [armos] joint.

ἁρμοστής, ὁ [armostees] high commisioner, governor.

ἁρμύρα, ἡ [armeera] saltiness.

ἁρμυρός [armeeros] salty.

ἀρνάκι, τό [arnakee] baby lamb.

ἀρνησίθρησκος [arneeseethreeskos] renegade, apostate.

ἄρνησις, ἡ [arneesees] refusal ‖ denial ‖ negation.

ἀρνί, τό [arnee] lamb ‖ (μεταφ) docile person.

ἀρνοῦμαι [arnoume] refuse, deny, decline ‖ disown.

ἄροτρον, τό [arotron] plough.

ἀρουραῖος, ὁ [aroureos] field mouse, rat.

ἄρπα, ἡ [arpa] harp.

ἀρπαγή, ἡ [arpayee] rapine ‖ rape ‖ stealing.

ἁρπάγη, ἡ [arpayee] hook, harpoon, grapnel.

ἁρπάζω [arpazo] grab, snatch ‖ steal, pinch ‖ (εὐκαιρία) seize ‖ (λέξεις) catch, pick up.

ἁρπάζομαι [arpazome] take hold of ‖ come to blows.

ἁρπακτικός [arpakteekos] greedy ‖ (ζῶον) rapacious, predatory.

ἅρπαξ, ὁ [arpaks] plunderer ‖ (σφετεριστής) usurper.

ἀρραβῶνες, οἱ [aravones] engagement, betrothal (old).

ἀρραβωνιάζω [arravoneeazo] betroth (old), engage.

ἀρραβωνιαστικιά, ἡ [aravoneeasteekia] fiancée.

ἀρραβωνιαστικός, ὁ [aravoneeasteekos] fiancé.

ἀρράγιστος [arrayeestos] uncracked ‖ (φιλία) strong, firm.

ἄρρεν, τό [aren] son, boy.

ἀρρενωπός [arrenopos] manly, masculine.

ἄρρηκτος [areektos] unbreakable ‖ unbroken.

ἄρρην [arreen] male.

ἄρρητος [arreetos] unsaid ‖ unspeakable ‖ indescribable.

ἀρρωσταίνω [arrosteno] make sick ‖ fall ill.

ἀρρώστια, ἡ [arrosteea] illness, sickness.

ἄρρωστος [arrostos] ill, sick, unwell.

ἀρσενικός [arseneekos] male ‖ (γραμμ) masculine.

ἄρσις, ἡ [arsees] removal, lifting ‖ (μεταφ) raising, abrogation.

ἀρτηρία, ἡ [arteereea] artery ‖ (ὁδός) thoroughfare.

ἄρτι [artee] recently, lately, just now.

ἀρτιγενής [arteeyenees] newborn.

ἄρτιος [arteeos] whole, entire ‖ (ἀριθμός) even.

ἀρτοποιεῖον, τό [artopieeon] bakery, baker's shop.

ἀρτοπωλεῖον, τό [artopoleeon] baker's shop.

ἄρτος, ὁ [artos] bread.

ἄρτυμα, τό [arteema] seasoning, sauce.

ἀρτύ(ν)ω [artee(n)o] season.

ἀρχαιοκαπηλία, ἡ [arheokapeeleea] illicit trade in antiquities.

ἀρχαιολόγος, ὁ [arheoloyos] archeologist.

ἀρχαιολογία, ἡ [arheoloyeea] archeology.

ἀρχαῖος [arheos] ancient ‖ antiquated.

ἀρχαιότης, ἡ [arheotees] antiquity ‖ (στά γραφεῖα) seniority.

ἀρχαιρεσίαι, αἱ [arheresie] πλ election.

ἀρχάριος [arhareeos] beginner, novice, apprentice.

ἀρχέγονος [arheyonos] primitive, primordial, original.

ἀρχεῖον, τό [arheeon] archives, records.

ἀρχέτυπον, τό [arheteepon] archetype, original.

ἀρχή, ἡ [arhee] beginning, start ‖ (φιλοσ) principle ‖ (διοίκ) authority ‖ κατ' ἀρχήν in principle.

ἀρχηγεῖον, τό [arheeyeeon] headquarters.

ἀρχηγία, ἡ [arheeyeea] command, leadership.

ἀρχηγός, ὁ [arheeyos] commander, leader, chief ‖ (οἰκογενείας) head.

ἀρχιεπίσκοπος, ὁ [arhiepeeskopos] archbishop.

ἀρχιεργάτης, ὁ [arhieryates] leading workman, foreman.

ἀρχιερεύς, ὁ [arhierevs] prelate, high priest.

ἀρχίζω [arheezo] begin, start, commence.

ἀρχικός [arheekos] initial, first, original.

ἀρχινῶ [arheeno] begin, start.

ἀρχιστράτηγος, ὁ [arheestrateeyos] commander-in-chief, generalissimo.

ἀρχισυντάκτης, ὁ [arheeseentaktees] chief editor.

ἀρχιτέκτων, ὁ [arheetekton] architect.

ἄρχοντας, ὁ [arhontas] notable, lord, master, elder.

ἀρχοντιά, ἡ [arhontia] distinction, nobility ‖ wealth.

ἀρχοντικός [arhonteekos] fine, of distinction, lordly.

ἄρχων, ὁ [arhon] chief, lord, prince ‖ (στήν ἀρχαιότητα) archon.

ἀρωγή, ἡ [aroyee] help, assistance, aid.

ἄρωμα, τό [aroma] aroma, perfume, odour ‖ ἀρωματικός scented.

ἄς [as] let, may ‖ ~ εἶναι be it so, let it be.

ἀσανσέρ, τό [asanser] lift, elevator.

ἀσαφής [asafees] obscure, vague.

ἀσβέστης, ὁ [asvestees] lime.

ἀσβεστώνω [asvestono] whitewash.

ἀσέβεια, ἡ [aseveea] disrespect ‖ impiety.

ἀσεβής [asevees] disrespectful ‖ impious.

ἀσέλγεια, ἡ [aselyeea] lewdness, debauchery.

ἀσελγής [aselyees] licentious, lewd.

ἄσεμνος [asemnos] indecent, obscene, immodest.

ἀσήκωτος [aseekotos] unraised ‖ (βαρύς) impossible to lift.

ἀσήμαντος [aseemantos] insignificant, unimportant.

ἀσημένιος [aseemeneeos] silver(y).

ἀσήμι, τό [aseemee] silver ‖ ~ κά πλ silver-ware.

ἄσημος [aseemos] obscure, insignificant, unimportant.

ἀσθένεια, ἡ [astheneea] sickness, illness ‖ (θελήσεως) weakness.

ἀσθενής [asthenees] ill, weak ‖ (ὁ ἄρρωστος) patient.

ἀσθενικός [astheneekos] sickly.

ἀσθενῶ [astheno] be ill, fall sick, get sick.

ἄσθμα, τό [asthma] asthma.

ἀσθμαίνω [asthmeno] pant, gasp, be out of breath.

ἀσιτία, ἡ [aseeteea] undernourishment, fasting.

ἀσκεπής [askepees] uncovered, bareheaded.

ἀσκέρι, τό [askeree] army, crowd.

ἄσκησις, ἡ [askeesees] exercise, practice ‖ drill.

ἀσκητής, ὁ [askeetees] hermit.

ἄσκοπος [askopos] pointless, aimless, purposeless.

ἀσκός, ὁ [askos] (skin) bag ‖ wineskin.

ἀσκοῦμαι [askoume] exercise, practise.

ἀσκῶ [asko] exercise, practise.

ἄσμα, τό [asma] song, air.

ἀσμένος [asmenos] gladly.

ἀσπάζομαι [aspazome] kiss, embrace ‖ (μεταφ) adopt, espouse.

ἀσπασμός, ὁ [aspasmos] embrace, kiss ‖ greeting.

ἄσπαστος [aspastos] unbroken ‖ unbreakable.

ἄσπιλος [aspeelos] immaculate, spotless.

ἀσπιρίνη, ἡ [aspeereenee] aspirin.

ἀσπίς, ἡ [aspees] shield ‖ (ὄφις) asp.

ἄσπλαγχνος [asplanghnos] hard-hearted, pitiless, unmerciful.

ἄσπονδος [aspondos] irreconcilable, relentless.

ἀσπούδαστος [aspoudastos] uneducated, ignorant.

ἀσπράδα, ἡ [asprada] whiteness.

ἀσπράδι, τό [aspradee] white spot ‖ (ματιοῦ, αὐγοῦ) white.

ἀσπρειδερός [aspreederos] whitish.

ἀσπρίζω [aspreezo] whiten, bleach ‖ (γίνομαι ἄσπρος) turn white.

ἀσπρομάλλης [aspromalees] white-haired.

ἀσπροπρόσωπος [asproprosopos] clean-faced, uncorrupted ‖ successful.

ἀσπρόρουχα, τά [asprorouha] πλ underclothes, linen.

ἄσπρος [aspros] white.

ἀσπρόχωμα, τό [asprohoma] white clay.

ἄσσος, ὁ [assos] ace.

ἀστάθεια, ἡ [astatheea] instability, inconstancy, fickleness.

ἀσταθής [astathees] unsteady, fickle, unstable.

ἀστακός, ὁ [astakos] lobster.

ἄστατος [astatos] fickle, unstable.

ἄστεγος [asteyos] homeless ‖ roofless.

ἀστειεύομαι [astievome] joke, jest.

ἀστεῖο, τό [asteeo] joke, pleasantry.

ἀστεῖος [asteeos] humorous, funny.

ἀστείρευτος [asteerevtos] inexhaustible, limitless.

ἀστέρι, τό [asteree] star.

ἀστερισμός, ὁ [astereesmos] constellation.

ἀστεροσκοπεῖον, τό [asteroskopeeon] observatory.

ἀστήρικτος [asteereektos] unsupported ‖ (μεταφ) untenable.

ἀστιγματισμός, ὁ [asteeymateesmos] astigmatism.

ἀστικός [asteekos] urban ‖ civic ‖ ~ κῶδιξ civil code.

ἄστικτος [asteektos] unspotted, unblemished.

ἀστοιχείωτος [asteeheeotos] unlearned, ignorant.

ἀστοργία, ἡ [astoryeea] lack of affection.

ἀστόχαστος [astohastos] thoughtless, imprudent.

ἀστοχία, ἡ [astoheea] failure ‖ carelessness.

ἀστοχῶ [astoho] miss the mark, fail ‖ (λησμονῶ) forget.

ἀστράγαλος, ὁ [astrayalos] anklebone ‖ (παιγνίδι) knucklebone.

ἀστραπή, ἡ [astrapee] lightning.

ἀστραπιαῖος [astrapieos] lightning, quick.

ἀστράπτω [astrapto] lighten ‖ flash, glitter.

ἀστρικός [astreekos] stellar, astral.

ἄστριφτος [astreeftos] not twisted.

ἄστρο, τό [astro] star.

ἀστρολογία, ἡ [astroloyeea] astrology.

ἀστρολόγος, ὁ [astroloyos] astrologer.

ἀστρονομία, ἡ [astronomeea] astronomy.

ἀστρονόμος, ὁ [astronomos] astronomer.

ἀστροπελέκι, τό [astropelekee] thunderbolt.

ἀστροφεγγιά, ἡ [astrofengia] starlight.

ἄστρωτος [astrotos] (κρεββάτι) not made ‖ (τραπέζι) unlaid ‖ (πάτωμα) bare ‖ (δρόμος) unpaved.

ἄστυ, τό [astee] city.

ἀστυνομία, ἡ [asteenomeea] police.

ἀστυνομικός [asteenomeekos] policeman, of the police.

ἀστυνόμος, ὁ [asteenomos] police officer.

ἀστυφύλαξ, ὁ [asteefeelaks] police constable.

ἀσυγκίνητος [aseengkeeneetos] unmoved, unfeeling.

ἀσυγκράτητος [aseengkrateetos] unsuppressible.

ἀσύγκριτος [aseengkreetos] incomparable.

ἀσυγύριστος [aseeyeereestos] untidy, disarranged.

ἀσυγχώρητος [aseenghoreetos] inexcusable, unforgivable.

ἀσυδοσία, ἡ [aseedoseea] immunity, exemption.

ἀσύδοτος [aseedotos] enjoying immunity.

ἀσυζήτητος [aseezeeteetos] unquestionable, incontrovertible.

ἀσυλία, ἡ [aseeleea] asylum, immunity, inviolability.

ἀσύλληπτος [aseeleeptos] elusive, not caught ‖ (μεταφ) inconceivable.

ἀσυλλόγιστος [aseeloyeestos] rash, thoughtless.

ἄσυλον, τό [aseelon] shelter, refuge, asylum.

ἀσυμβίβαστος [aseemveevastos] irreconcilable, incompatible.

ἀσύμμετρος [aseemetros] disproportionate.

ἀσυμπλήρωτος [aseembleerotos] uncompleted, incomplete.

ἀσύμφορος [aseemforos] disadvantageous, not profitable.

ἀσυναγώνιστος [aseenayoneestos] unbeatable, unrivalled.

ἀσυναίσθητος [aseenestheetos] unconscious, inconsiderate.

ἀσυναρτησία, ἡ [aseenarteeseea] incoherence, inconsistency.

ἀσυνάρτητος [aseenarteetos] incoherent ‖ inconsistent.

ἀσυνείδητος [aseeneedeetos] unscrupulous, unconscionable.

ἀσυνέπεια, ἡ [aseenepeea] inconsequence, inconsistency.

ἀσυνεπής [aseenepees] inconsistent.

ἀσύνετος [aseenetos] imprudent, unwise.

ἀσυνήθιστος [aseeneetheestos] unusual, uncommon.

ἀσυνταξία, ἡ [aseentakseea] (γραμμ) grammatical fault.

ἀσυρματιστής, ὁ [aseermateestees] wireless operator.

ἀσύρματος, ὁ [aseermatos] wireless ‖ σταθμός ἀσυρμάτου wireless station.

ἀσύστατος [aseestatos] not recommended ‖ (ἰσχυρισμός) groundless, unsupported.

ἀσύστολος [aseestolos] impudent, brazen.

ἄσφαιρος [asferos] blank.

ἀσφάλεια, ἡ [asfaleea] security, safety ‖ (ζωῆς κτλ) insurance ‖ (ἀστυνομία) police ‖ (ἤλεκτ) fuse ‖ (ὅπλου) safety catch.

ἀσφαλής [asfalees] safe, secure, sure.

ἀσφαλίζω [asfaleezo] secure, assure ‖ (ζωήν κτλ) insure.

ἀσφαλιστήριον, τό [asfaleesteereeon] insurance policy.

ἀσφάλιστρον, τό [asfaleestron] insurance premium.

ἄσφαλτος, ἡ [asfaltos] asphalt ‖ (δρόμος) tarred road.

ἀσφαλῶς [asfalos] surely, certainly ‖ safely.

ἀσφυκτικός [asfeekteekos] suffocating.

ἀσφυξία, ἡ [asfeekseea] suffocation, asphyxia.

ἄσχετος [ashetos] irrelevant, unrelated, unconnected.

ἀσχημία, ἡ [asheemeea] ugliness, deformity.

ἀσχημίζω [asheemeezo] make ugly ‖ (μεταφ) spoil, mar.

ἀσχημονῶ [asheemono] offend modesty, misbehave.

ἄσχημος [asheemos] ugly ‖ unsightly ‖ bad.

ἀσχολία, ἡ [asholeea] occupation, business, job.

ἀσχολοῦμαι [asholoume] be occupied with, keep busy.

ἀσώματος [asomatos] incorporeal.

ἀσωτία, ἡ [asoteea] dissipation, prodigality.

ἄσωτος [asotos] dissolute ‖ prodigal, wasteful.

ἀταίριαστος [atereeastos] incompatible ‖ dissimilar.

ἄτακτος [ataktos] irregular ‖ disorderly ‖ (παιδί) naughty, unruly.

ἀταξία, ἡ [atakseea] confusion, disorder ‖ unruliness.

ἀτάραχος [atarahos] calm, composed, quiet.

ἀταραξία, ἡ [atarakseea] composure, calmness, serenity.

ἀτάσθαλος [atasthalos] disorderly ‖ improper, rude.

ἄταφος [atafos] unburied.

ἄτεκνος [ateknos] childless.

ἀτέλεια, ἡ [ateleea] defect ‖ (δασμοῦ) exemption ‖ (χαρακτῆρος) imperfection.

ἀτελείωτος [ateleeotos] endless ‖ unfinished, incomplete.

ἀτελεσφόρητος [atelesforeetos] ineffectual, fruitless.

ἀτελεύτητος [atelevteetos] endless, interminable.

ἀτελής [atelees] incomplete ‖ defective ‖ (φόρου) tax-free.

ἀτελώνιστος [ateloneestos] duty-free ‖ not cleared through customs.

ἀτενής [atenees] fixed, steadfast.

ἀτενίζω [ateneezo] gaze, stare at, look fixedly on.

ἄτεχνος [atehnos] unskilful, badly made.

ἀτζαμής [atzamees] unskilled ‖ awkward, clumsy.

ἀτζέμ-πιλάφι, τό [atzempeelafee] lamb with rice.

ἄτι, τό [atee] steed, horse.

ἀτίθασος [ateethasos] stubborn ‖ (ἄλογο) difficult to tame.

ἀτιμάζω [ateemazo] dishonour, disgrace ‖ (βιάζω) defile, ravish.

ἀτίμητος [ateemeetos] inestimable, priceless, invaluable.

ἀτιμία, ἡ [ateemeea] dishonour, disgrace, infamy.

ἄτιμος [ateemos] dishonest, infamous, disreputable ‖ (συμπεριφορά) disgraceful.

ἀτιμώρητος [ateemoreetos] unpunished.

ἀτλάζι, τό [atlazee] satin.

ἀτμάκατος, ἡ [atmakatos] small steamboat.

ἀτμάμαξα, ἡ [atmamaksa] locomotive.

ἀτμοκίνητος [atmokeeneetos] steam-driven.

ἀτμομηχανή, ἡ [atmomeehanee] steam engine, locomotive.

ἀτμοπλοΐα, ἡ [atmoploeea] steam navigation.

ἀτμόπλοιον, τό [atmoploeon] steamship.

ἀτμός, ὁ [atmos] steam, vapour ‖ (κρασιοῦ) fume.

ἀτμόσφαιρα, ἡ [atmosfera] atmosphere.

ἄτοκος [atokos] without interest.

ἄτολμος [atolmos] timid, faint-hearted.

ἀτομικιστής [atomeekeestees] egoist.

ἀτομικός [atomeekos] personal ‖ (ἐνέργεια κτλ) atomic.

ἀτομικότης, ἡ [atomeekotees] individuality.

ἄτομον, τό [atomon] (Φυσική) atom ‖ (ἄνθρωπος) individual, person.

ἀτονία, ἡ [atoneea] languor, weakness, dejection.

ἄτονος [atonos] languid, dull ‖ (γραμμ) unaccented.

ἄτοπος [atopos] improper, unbecoming, indecent ‖ ridiculous.

ἀτοῦ, τό [atoo] trump.

ἀτόφυος [atofeeos] solid, massive.

ἀτραπός, ἡ [atrapos] path, track.

ἄτριφτος [atreeftos] not rubbed, not grated.

ἀτρόμητος [atromeetos] bold, dauntless, daring.

ἀτροφία, ἡ [atrofeea] atrophy.

ἀτροφικός [atrofeekos] atrophied, emaciated.

ἀτρύγητος [atreeγeetos] ungathered, unharvested.

ἄτρωτος [atrotos] unwounded, unhurt ‖ invulnerable.

ἀτσαλένιος [atsaleneeos] of steel, steely.

ἀτσάλι, τό [atsalee] steel.

ἄτσαλος [atsalos] untidy, disorderly, unkempt ‖ (ζωή) riotous, lawless.

ἀτσίγγανος, ὁ [atseenganos] gypsy.

ἀτσίδα, ἡ [atseeδa] alert person, wideawake person.

ἀτύχημα, τό [ateeheema] mishap, accident, misfortune, injury.

ἀτυχής [ateehees] unfortunate, unlucky, wretched.

ἄτυχος [ateehos] βλ ἀτυχής.

ἀτυχία, ἡ [ateeheea] misfortune, bad luck.

ἀτυχῶ [ateeho] fail, have bad luck, meet with misfortune.

αὐγερινός, ὁ [avγereenos] morning star.

αὐγή, ἡ [avγee] dawn, daybreak.

αὐγό, τό [avγo] egg.

αὐγολέμονο, τό [avγolemono] lemon and egg sauce or soup.

αὐγοτάραχο, τό [avγotaraho] botargo.

αὐγουλιέρα, ἡ [avγouliera] eggcup.

Αὔγουστος, ὁ [avγoustos] August.

αὐθάδεια, ἡ [avthaδeea] audacity, insolence.

αὐθάδης [avthaδees] impertinent, saucy.

αὐθαιρεσία, ἡ [avthereseea] high-handed act.

αὐθαίρετος [avtheretos] arbitrary, high-handed.

αὐθεντία, ἡ [avthenteea] authority, authenticity.

αὐθεντικός [avthenteekos] authentic, authoritative.

αὐθημερόν [avtheemeron] on the very same day.

αὖθις [avthees] once more, again.

αὐθόρμητος [avthormeetos] spontaneous.

αὐθυποβολή, ἡ [avtheepovolee] autosuggestion.

αὐθωρεί [avthoree] immediately, instantly, at once.

αὐλαία, ἡ [avlea] curtain.

αὐλάκι, τό [avlakee] channel, ditch, trench ‖ (ξύλου κτλ) groove.

αὐλακωτός [avlakotos] grooved, furrowed, scored.

αὐλάρχης, ὁ [avlarhees] Lord High Chamberlain.

αὐλή, ἡ [avlee] yard, courtyard ‖ (βασιλέως) court.

αὐλικός [avleekos] of the court.

αὐλόγυρος, ὁ [avloγeeros] enclosure, surrounding wall.

αὐλός, ὁ [avlos] pipe, flute, reed.

ἄϋλος [aeelos] immaterial, incorporeal.

αὐξάνω [avksano] increase, augment ‖ (ταχύτητα) accelerate.

αὔξησις, ἡ [avkseesees] increase ‖ (γραμμ) augment.

αὐξομείωσις, ἡ [avksomeeosees] fluctuation, variation.

αὔξων [avkson] increasing ‖ ~ ἀριθμός serial number.

ἀϋπνία, ἡ [aeepneea] sleeplessness, insomnia.

ἄϋπνος [aeepnos] sleepless, wakeful.

αὔρα, ἡ [avra] breeze.

αὐριανός [avreeanos] of tomorrow.

αὔριον [avreeon] tomorrow.

αὐστηρός [avsteeros] severe, rigorous, austere.

αὐστηρότης, ἡ [avsteerotees] severity, strictness, austerity.

αὔτανδρος [avtanδros] with all hands.

αὐταπάρνησις, ἡ [avtaparneesees] self-abnegation.

αὐταπάτη, ἡ [avtapatee] self-delusion, self-deception.

αὐταρέσκεια, ἡ [avtareskeea] complacency.

αὐτάρκεια, ἡ [avtarkeea] contentment, self-content.

αὐτάρκης [avtarkees] self-sufficient, satisfied.

αὐταρχικός [avtarheekos] authoritative, dictatorial.

αὐτεξούσιος [avteksouseeos] independent, free.

αὐτί, τό [avtee] ear.

αὐτοβιογραφία, ἡ [avtoveeoγrafeea] autobiography.

αὐτόβουλος [avtovoulos] of one's own free will, unconstrained.

αὐτόγραφον, τό [avtoγrafon] autograph.

αὐτόδηλος [avtoδeelos] self-evident.

αὐτοδημιούργητος [avtoδeemeeouryeetos] self-made.

αὐτοδιάθεσις, ἡ [avtoδeeathesees] self-determination.

αὐτοδικαίως [avtoδeekeos] of right, de jure.

αὐτοδιοίκησις, ἡ [avtoδieekeesees] self-government.

αὐτόθι [avtothee] in the same place, there.

αὐτοθυσία, ἡ [avtotheeseea] self-sacrifice.

αὐτοκαλούμενος [avtokaloumenos] self-styled.

αὐτοκέφαλος [avtokefalos] independent ‖ (ἐκκλ) autocephalous.

αὐτοκινητάμαξα, ἡ [avtokeeneetamaksa] railcar.

αὐτοκινητιστής, ὁ [avtokeeneeteestees] motorist, rallyist.

αὐτοκίνητο, τό [avtokeeneeto] car ‖ (US) automobile.

αὐτοκρατορία, ἡ [avtokratoreea] empire.

αὐτοκράτωρ, ὁ [avtokrator] emperor.

αὐτοκτονία, ἡ [avtoktoneea] suicide.

αὐτοκτονῶ [avtoktono] commit suicide.

αὐτολεξεί [avtoleksee] word for word, verbatim.

αὐτόματος [avtomatos] automatic.

αὐτονόητος [avtonoeetos] self-explanatory, obvious.

αὐτοπεποίθησις, ἡ [avtopepeetheesees] self-confidence, self-reliance.

αὐτοπροαίρετος [avtoproeretos] voluntary.

αὐτοπροσώπως [avtoprosopos] personally.

αὐτόπτης, ὁ [avtoptees] eyewitness.

αὐτός [avtos] he ‖ ὁ ~ the same.

αὐτοστιγμεί [avtosteeΥmee] instantly, immediately.

αὐτοσυντήρησις [avtoseenteereesees] self-preservation.

αὐτοσυντήρητος [avtoseenteereetos] self-supporting.

αὐτοσχεδιάζω [avtosheδeeazo] improvise, extemporize.

αὐτοσχέδιος [avtosheδeeos] improvised, impromptu, makeshift.

αὐτοτελής [avtotelees] self-sufficient ‖ independent.

αὐτοῦ [avtou] there.

αὐτουργός, ὁ [avtouryos] perpetrator.

αὐτοφυής [avtofiees] indigenous, self-growing, natural.

αὐτόφωρος [avtoforos] in the very act, red-handed.

αὐτόχειρ, ὁ [avtoheer] suicide.

αὐτόχθων, ὁ [avtohthon] indigenous, aboriginal, native.

αὐτόχρημα [avtohreema] wholly, entirely, indeed.

αὐτοψία, ἡ [avtopseea] (ἰατρ) autopsy ‖ (νομ) local inspection.

αὐχήν, ὁ [avheen] nape (of neck) ‖ (μεταφ) neck, pass.

αὐχμηρός [avhmeeros] dry, arid, barren.

ἀφάγωτος [afaγotos] uneaten ‖ not having eaten ‖ untouched.

ἀφαίμαξις, ἡ [afemaksees] bloodletting.

ἀφαίρεσις, ἡ [aferesees] deduction, subtraction ‖ (φιλοσ) abstraction.

ἀφαιροῦμαι [aferoume] be absent-minded.

ἀφαιρῶ [afero] deduct, subtract ‖ (κλέβω) steal, rob.

ἀφαλός, ὁ [afalos] navel.

ἀφάνεια, ἡ [afaneea] obscurity, oblivion.

ἀφανής [afanees] obscure, unknown ‖ invisible.

ἀφανίζω [afaneezo] ruin, destroy.

ἀφάνταστος [afantastos] unimaginable.

ἄφαντος [afantos] invisible, unseen.

ἀφαρπάζομαι [afarpazome] lose one's temper.

ἀφασία, ἡ [afaseea] muteness, aphasia.

ἄφατος [afatos] inexpressible, unspeakable.

ἀφειδής [afeeδees] lavish, extravagant.

ἀφελής [afelees] simple, ingenuous, guileless.

ἀφέντης, ὁ [afentees] master, boss ‖ owner.

ἀφεντικό, τό [afenteeko] governor, boss, employer.

ἀφερέγγυος [aferengeeos] insolvent.

ἄφεσις, ἡ [afesees] remission ‖ discharge.

ἀφετηρία, ἡ [afeteereea] starting point ‖ beginning.

ἄφευκτος [afevktos] inevitable, unavoidable.

ἀφή, ἡ [afee] sense of touch ‖ (αἴσθησις) feeling.

ἀφήγησις, ἡ [afeeγeesees] narration, account.

ἀφηγοῦμαι [afeeγoume] narrate, relate, tell.

ἀφηνιάζω [afeeneeazo] bolt ‖ (ἐπὶ ἀνθρώπων) run amok.

ἀφήνω [afeeno] let, permit ‖ (μόνος) let alone ‖ (ἐλευθερώνω) let go of ‖ (ἐγκαταλείπω) abandon.

ἀφηρημάδα, ἡ [afeereemaδa] absent-mindedness.

ἀφηρημένος [afeereemenos] absent-minded ‖ (φιλοσ) abstract.

ἀφθαρσία, ἡ [aftharseea] indestructibility, incorruptibility.

ἄφθαρτος [afthartos] incorruptible, indestructible.

ἄφθαστος [afthastos] unsurpassed, incomparable, unexcelled.

ἀφθονία, ἡ [afthoneea] abundance, profusion.

ἄφθονος [afthonos] abundant, plentiful, profuse.

ἀφθονῶ [afthono] abound with, teem with, be plentiful.

αφιέρωμα, τό [afieroma] offering, dedication.

αφιερώνω [afierono] dedicate, devote ‖ (βιβλίο κτλ) inscribe.

αφιέρωσις, ή [afierosees] dedication, devotion.

αφικνούμαι [afeeknoume] arrive, come.

αφιλοκερδής [afeelokerdees] disinterested, selfless.

αφιλότιμος [afeeloteemos] wanting in self-respect, mean.

αφίνω [afeeno] βλ **αφήνω.**

άφιξις, ή [afeeksees] arrival, coming.

αφιόνι, τό [afeeonee] poppy ‖ opium.

αφίσταμαι [afeestame] stand away from ‖ (διαφέρω) differ, vary.

άφλεκτος [aflektos] non-inflammable.

άφοβος [afovos] intrepid, fearless, bold.

αφομοιώνω [afomeeono] assimilate.

αφομοίωσις, ή [afomeeosees] assimilation.

αφοπλίζω [afopleezo] disarm ‖ (φρούριο κτλ) dismantle.

αφοπλισμός, ό [afopleesmos] disarmament.

αφόρετος [aforetos] unworn, new.

αφόρητος [aforeetos] intolerable, insufferable.

αφορίζω [aforeezo] excommunicate.

αφορισμός, ό [aforeesmos] excommunication.

αφορμή, ή [aformee] motive, pretext, cause.

αφορολόγητος [aforoloyeetos] untaxed, free from taxation.

αφορώ [aforo] concern ‖ regard ‖ **όσον αφορά** as regards.

αφοσιούμαι [afoseeoume] devote o.s., be attached to.

αφοσίωσις, ή [afoseeosees] devotion, attachment, affection.

αφότου [afotou] since, as long as.

αφού [afou] since, after.

άφρακτος [afraktos] without a fence or wall.

αφράτος [afratos] light and crisp ‖ frothy, foamy ‖ (δέρμα) soft.

αφρίζω [afreezo] foam ‖ (μεταφ) be furious.

αφρόγαλα, τό [afroyala] cream.

αφροδισιολόγος, ό [afrodeesioloyos] venereal disease specialist.

αφροδίσιος [afrodeesios] venereal.

αφρόντιστος [afronteestos] neglected, uncared for.

αφρός, ό [afros] foam ‖ (κοινωνίας) cream ‖ (σαπουνιού) lather.

αφροσύνη, ή [afroseenee] foolishness, rashness.

αφρώδης [afrodees] frothy, foamy.

άφρων [afron] foolish, thoughtless, rash.

αφυδάτωσις, ή [afeedatosees] dehydration.

αφύπνισις, ή [afeepneesees] awakening ‖ (μεταφ) dawning.

αφύσικος [afeeseekos] unnatural ‖ (προσποιητός) affected.

άφωνος [afonos] mute, speechless, silent.

αφώτιστος [afoteestos] dark ‖ (άνθρωπος) unenlightened.

άχ [ah] (επιφ) ah!, oh!, alas!

αχαΐρευτος [ahaeerevtos] scoundrel.

αχάλαστος [ahalastos] unspoilt ‖ indestructible, intact.

αχαλίνωτος [ahaleenotos] unbridled ‖ (μεταφ) unmanageable.

αχαμνός [ahamnos] skinny, thin, lean.

αχανής [ahanees] immense, enormous, vast.

αχαρακτήριστος [aharakteereestos] unprincipled, hard to describe.

άχαρις [aharees] ungraceful, awkward, unsightly.

αχαριστία, ή [ahareesteea] ingratitude.

αχάριστος [ahareestos] ungrateful.

άχαρος [aharos] unsightly ‖ unpleasant.

αχηβάδα, ή [aheevaδa] cockle, sea shell, shellfish.

άχθος, τό [ahthos] weight, burden, load.

αχθοφόρος, ό [ahthoforos] porter.

αχινός, ό [aheenos] sea urchin.

αχλάδι, τό [ahlaδee] pear.

άχνα, ή [ahna] βλ **αχνός.**

αχνάρι, τό [ahnaree] footprint ‖ (μεταφ) pattern.

άχνη, ή [ahnee] mist, evaporation ‖ (χημ) corrosive sublimate.

αχνίζω [ahneezo] evaporate ‖ steam.

αχνός, ό [ahnos] vapour, steam ‖ (χρώμα) pale, colourless.

αχόρταγος [ahortayos] insatiable, greedy ‖ (ζώον) voracious.

άχου [ahoo] (επιφ) oh!, damn it!

αχούρι, τό [ahouree] stable, stall.

αχρείαστος [ahreeastos] unnecessary, needless.

αχρείος [ahreeos] wicked, vile.

αχρησιμοποίητος [ahreeseemopieetos] unused.

αχρηστεύω [ahreestevo] make useless.

αχρηστία, ή [ahreesteea] obsoleteness, uselessness.

άχρηστος [ahreestos] useless, worthless.

άχρι [ahree] till, until.

αχρονολόγητος [ahronoloyeetos] undated.

άχρους [ahrous] colourless, uncoloured.

αχρωμάτιστος [ahromateestos] unpainted, uncoloured, plain.

άχτι, τό [ahtee] yearning, longing.

αχτίδα, ή [ahteeδa] ray, beam.

αχτένιστος [ahteneestos] uncombed, unkempt ‖ (λόγος κτλ) unpolished.

άχυρον, τό [aheeron] straw, hay.

αχυρών, ό [aheeron] barn, hayloft.

αχώνευτος [ahonevtos] undigested ‖ indigestible.

αχώριστος [ahoreestos] inseparable.

άψητος [apseetos] not cooked, underdone.

αψηφώ [apseefo] disregard, disdain, scorn.

αψιδωτός [apseeδotos] arched, vaulted.

άψιμαχία, ή [apseemaheea] skirmish.

αψίς, ή [apsees] arch, vault ‖ apse.

άψογος [apsoyos] faultless, irreproachable.

αψυχολόγητος [apseeholoγeetos] ill-considered, impolitic.

άψυχος [apseehos] lifeless ‖ (δειλός) cowardly, timid.

άωρος [aoros] (καρπός) unripe ‖ (σκέψις) premature.

άωτον, τό [aoton]: άκρον ~ acme, height of.

Β, β

Βαβυλωνία, ή [vaveeloneea] Babylonia ‖ (μεταφ) chaos, confusion.

βαγένι, τό [vaγenee] βλ βαρέλι.

βαγόνι, τό [vaγonee] carriage ‖ (έμπορικόν) wagon, truck ‖ (βαγκόν-λί) sleeping car.

βάδην [vaδeen] at a walking pace.

βαδίζω [vaδeezo] walk ‖ (στρατ) march ‖ (πηγαίνω) go.

βάδισμα, τό [vaδeesma] step, walk, gait.

βαζελίνη, ή [vazeleenee] vaseline.

βάζο, τό [vazo] vase.

βάζω [vazo] put, set, place ‖ (φορώ) put on ‖ (φόρους κτλ) impose, lay ‖ ~ έμπρός start, begin ‖ ~ χέρι lay hands on ‖ ~ τά δυνατά μου do my best.

βαθαίνω [vatheno] deepen ‖ βλ καί βαθύνω.

βαθειά [vatheea] deep(ly), profoundly.

βαθμηδόν [vathmeedon] by degrees, gradually.

βαθμιαίος [vathmieos] gradual, progressive.

βαθμίς, ή [vathmees] step, stair ‖ (μεταφ) rank.

βαθμολογία, ή [vathmoloγeea] (όργάνου) graduation ‖ (μαθήματος) grades, marks.

βαθμός, ό [vathmos] degree ‖ (στρατ) grade, rank ‖ (μαθήματος) mark.

βάθος, τό [vathos] depth, bottom ‖ (φόντο) back, background.

βαθούλωμα, τό [vathouloma] hollow, depression.

βαθουλώνω [vathoulono] hollow out ‖ become hollow.

βάθρον, τό [vathron] (βάσις) basis, foundation ‖ (άγάλματος κτλ) pedestal ‖ (γεφύρας) pillar ‖ έκ βάθρων radically, entirely.

βαθύνους [vatheenous] sagacious, perspicacious.

βαθύνω [vatheeno] deepen, hollow out, become deeper.

βαθύπλουτος [vatheeploutos] opulent.

βαθύς [vathees] deep ‖ (σκότος κτλ) heavy, deep ‖ (ύπνος) sound ‖ (αίσθημα) profound ‖ (πνεύμα) penetrating, sagacious.

βαθύτης, ή [vatheetees] depth, profundity, deepness.

βαθύφωνος [vatheefonos] bass, deep-voiced.

βαίνω [veno] (βαδίζω) walk, go ‖ (στηρί-

ζομαι) rest on ‖ (μεταφ) be on the way, progress.

βάϊον, τό [vaeeon] palm branch.

βακαλάος, ό [vakalaos] cod.

βάκιλλος, ό [vakeelos] bacillus.

βακτηρία, ή [vakteereea] walking stick ‖ (δεκανίκι) crutch.

βακτηρίδιον, τό [vakteereedeeon] bacillus.

βαλανίδι, τό [valaneedee] acorn ‖ βαλανιδιά oak tree.

βάλανος, ό [valanos] acorn.

βαλάντιον, τό [valanteeon] purse.

βαλβίς, ή [valvees] valve.

βαλές, ό [vales] knave (in cards).

βαλίτσα, ή [valeetsa] suitcase, (hand)bag.

βαλκάνια, τά [valkaneea] πλ the Balkans.

βάλλω [valo] fire, shoot, hurl ‖ (μεταφ) launch an attack.

βάλς, τό [vals] waltz.

βάλσαμον, τό [valsamon] balsam, balm ‖ (μεταφ) consolation.

βαλσαμώνω [valsamono] embalm ‖ (μεταφ) console, comfort.

βάλσιμο, τό [valseemo] placing, setting, laying.

βάλτος, ό [valtos] marsh, fen, bog.

βαλτός [valtos] instigated, planted.

βαμβακερός [vamvakeros] of cotton.

βαμβάκι, τό [vamvakee] cotton.

βάμβαξ, ό [vamvaks] cotton.

βάμμα, τό [vamma] tincture, dye.

βαμμένος [vamenos] dyed, painted.

βανάνα, ή [vanana] βλ μπανάνα.

βάναυσος [vanavsos] rough, coarse, rude.

βάνδαλος, ό [vandalos] vandal.

βανίλ(λ)ια, ή [vaneeleea] vanilla.

βάνω [vano] βλ βάλλω.

βαπόρι, τό [vapori] steamship.

βαπτίζω [vapteezo] baptize, christen ‖ dip, plunge.

βάπτισις, ή [vapteesees] βλ βάπτισμα.

βάπτισμα, τό [vapteesma] baptism, christening.

βαπτιστικός [vapteesteekos] baptismal ‖ (ούσ) godchild.

βάπτω [vapto] (χάλυψ) temper ‖ (μπογιά) paint ‖ (παπούτσια) polish.

βάραθρον, τό [varathron] abyss, gulf, chasm.

βαραίνω [vareno] weigh down, make heavier ‖ (κουράζω) weary ‖ (αίσθάνομαι βάρος) feel heavy ‖ (μεταφ) carry weight.

βαράω [varao] βλ βαρώ.

βαρβαρικός [varvareekos] barbaric.

βάρβαρος [varvaros] barbarous, brutal, savage.

βαρβάτος [varvatos] (άλογο) stallion ‖ (μεταφ) robust, vigorous.

βάρδια, ή [varδeea] watch, duty, shift.

βαρεία, ή [vareea] (γραμμ) grave accent.

βαρέλι, τό [varelee] barrel, cask.

βαρετός [varetos] annoying, boring, tedious.

βαρέως [vareos] badly, severely ‖ (φορτωμένος) heavily.

βαρήκοος [vareekoos] hard of hearing.

βαριά, ἡ [varia] (σφυρί) hammer ‖ (ἐπιρ) seriously.

βαρίδι, τό [vareedee] (counter)weight.

βαριέμαι [varieme] be bored, be tired (of) ‖ (δέν θέλω) not want (to) ‖ δέν βαριέσαι never mind!, don't bother!

βάρκα, ἡ [varka] small boat, rowing boat, dinghy.

βαρκάρης, ὁ [varkarees] boatman.

βαρόμετρον, τό [varometron] barometer.

βάρος, τό [varos] weight, load, burden ‖ εἰς ~ του at his expense.

βαρούλκον, τό [varoulkon] winch, windlass.

βαρύθυμος [vareetheemos] sad, depressed.

βαρύνω [vareeno] weigh down, lie heavy ‖ βλ καί βαραίνω.

βαρύς [varees] heavy ‖ (ποινή) severe, harsh ‖ (σφάλμα) serious ‖ (ὕπνος) deep, heavy ‖ (ζυγός) oppressive ‖ (εὐθύνη) grave ‖ (ἄνθρωπος) slow, dull-witted.

βαρυσήμαντος [vareeseemantos] significant, grave, momentous.

βαρύτιμος [vareeteemos] precious, costly, valuable.

βαρύτονος [vareetonos] baritone ‖ (γραμμ) with a grave accent.

βαρύφωνος [vareefonos] deep-voiced, bass.

βαρῶ [varo] beat, hit, shoot ‖ (σάλπιγγα) sound ‖ (καμπάνα) toll.

βασανίζω [vasaneezo] torture, torment ‖ (ἕνα θέμα κτλ) examine thoroughly, go into ‖ (τό μυαλό) rack.

βασανιστήριον, τό [vasaneesteereeon] torture rack, torture chamber.

βάσανο, τό [vasano] pain, trial, ordeal ‖ (μεταφ) nuisance.

βάσανος, ἡ [vasanos] torture ‖ scrutiny, proof.

βασίζω [vaseezo] base.

βασικός [vaseekos] primary, basic, fundamental.

βασιλεία, ἡ [vaseeleea] kingdom ‖ reign.

βασίλειον, τό [vaseeleeon] kingdom.

βασιλεύς, ὁ [vaseelevs] king.

βασιλεύω [vaseelevo] reign, rule.

βασιλιᾶς, ὁ [vaseelias] βλ βασιλεύς.

βασιλική, ἡ [vaseeleekee] basilica.

βασιλικός [vaseeleekos] royal, royalist ‖ (οὐσ) basil.

βασίλισσα, ἡ [vaseeleesa] queen.

βασιλομήτωρ, ἡ [vaseelomeetor] queen mother.

βασιλόπηττα, ἡ [vaseelopeeta] New Year's cake.

βασιλόφρων [vaseelofron] royalist.

βάσιμος [vaseemos] sound, trustworthy.

βάσις, ἡ [vasees] base, foundation ‖ (βαθμῶν) pass mark.

βασκανία, ἡ [vaskaneea] evil eye.

βαστάζω [vastazo] βλ βαστῶ.

βαστῶ [vasto] (φέρω) bear, hold, support ‖ (συγκρατῶ) hold, control ‖ (ὕφασμα κτλ) keep, wear ‖ (κρατῶ) carry, hold.

βάτ(τ), τό [vat] watt.

βατόμουρο, τό [vatomouro] blackberry.

βάτος, ὁ [vatos] bush, bramble.

βατός [vatos] (δρόμος) passable ‖ (ποτάμι) fordable ‖ (ὕψωμα) accessible.

βάτραχος, ὁ [vatrahos] frog, toad.

βαυκαλίζω [vavkaleezo] lull to sleep ‖ (μεταφ) lull.

βαφή, ἡ [vafee] dyeing ‖ shoe polish ‖ dye.

βάφομαι [vafome] make up.

βαφτίσια, τά [vafteeseea] πλ christening.

βαφτισιμιός, ὁ [vafteeseemios] godson.

βάφω [vafo] βλ βάπτω.

βάψιμο, τό [vapseemo] painting, make-up.

βγάζω [vγazo] take off, raise, draw out ‖ (ἐξαλείφω) get out, wash out ‖ (λάδι, χυμό κτλ) press out of, squeeze ‖ (πόδι, χέρι) dislocate ‖ (καπνό κτλ) give off ‖ (παράγω) produce ‖ (χρήματα) make, earn ‖ (βουλευτάς κτλ) elect ‖ (διακρίνω) make out, read ‖ (δίδω ὄνομα) name, call ‖ (ἀποδεικνύω) prove ‖ (ἀφαιρῶ) take from ‖ (ἐφημερίδα κτλ) publish ‖ ·(περίπατο) take for a walk.

βγαίνω [vγeno] go out, come out, get out ‖ (ἀνατέλλω) rise ‖ (κυκλοφορῶ) be out ‖ (ἐκλέγομαι) be elected ‖ (ἐξαλείφομαι) fade, come out ‖ (ἄγω) lead.

βγαλμένος [vγalmenos] taken off, removed.

βγάλσιμο, τό [vγalseemo] extraction, removal ‖ (κοκκάλου) dislocation.

βδέλλα, ἡ [vδella] leech.

βδέλυγμα, τό [vδeleeγma] abomination, detestable object.

βδελυρός [vδeleeros] repugnant, loathsome.

βέβαιος [veveos] certain, sure, convinced.

βεβαιώνω [veveono] confirm, affirm, assure ‖ certify.

βεβαίως [veveos] certainly, surely.

βεβαίωσις, ἡ [veveosees] confirmation ‖ (χαρτί) certificate.

βεβαρημένος [vevareemenos] marked ‖ (συνείδησις) heavy.

βέβηλος [veveelos] profane, sacrilegious, impious.

βεβιασμένος [veviasmenos] forced.

βεζίρης, ὁ [vezerees] vizier.

βέης, ὁ [vayees] bey.

βελάζω [velazo] bleat.

βελανίδι, τό [velaneeδee] acorn.

βέλο, τό [velo] veil.

βελόνα, ἡ [velona] needle.

βελονιά, ἡ [velonia] stitch.

βέλος, τό [velos] arrow; dart.

βελοῦδο [velouδo] velvet.

βέλτιστος [velteestos] the best.

βελτίων [velteeon] better.

βελτιώνω [velteeono] improve, better.

βελτίωσις, ἡ [velteeosees] improvement.

βενζινάκατος, ἡ [venzeenakatos] small motorboat.

βενζίνη, ἡ [venzeenee] petrol.

βεντάλια, ἡ [ventaleea] fan.

βεντέττα, ἡ [venteta] vendetta || (ἠθοποιός) star.

βεντούζα, ἡ [ventouza] cupping glass.

βέρα, ἡ [vera] wedding ring.

βεράντα, ἡ [veranta] veranda, porch.

βερβερίτσα, ἡ [ververeetza] squirrel.

βέργα, ἡ [verγa] stick, rod, switch, twig.

βερεσέ [verese] on credit, on trust.

βερίκοκκο, τό [vereekoko] apricot.

βερμούτ, τό [vermout] vermouth.

βερνίκι, τό [verneekee] varnish, polish || (μεταφ) veneer.

βέρος [veros] genuine, true, real.

βέτο, τό [veto] veto.

βῆμα, τό [veema] step, pace || (βίδας) pitch, thread || (ἕλικος) twist || (ἕδρα) rostrum, tribune.

βηματίζω [veemateezo] step, pace, walk.

βῆτα, τό [veeta] the letter B.

βήχας, ὁ [veehas] cough.

βήχω [veeho] cough.

βία, ἡ [veea] force, violence || hurry || μετά ~ς with difficulty.

βιάζομαι [veeazome] be in haste, be rushed.

βιάζω [veeazo] force, compel || (παραβιάζω) break open || (παραβαίνω) violate || (ἀσελγῶ) rape, ravish.

βιαιοπραγία, ἡ [vieopraγeea] bodily assault, outrage.

βίαιος [vieos] violent, forcible || fiery, passionate.

βιαιότητες [vieoteetes] πλ acts of violence.

βιαίως [vieos] violently, forcibly.

βιασμός, ὁ [veeasmos] rape, violation.

βιαστής, ὁ [veeastees] ravisher.

βιαστικός [veeasteekos] urgent, pressing, hurried.

βιασύνη, ἡ [veeaseenee] haste, urgency.

βιβλιάριον, τό [veevleeareeon] booklet, card, bank-book.

βιβλικός [veevleekos] biblical.

βιβλιογραφία, ἡ [veevleeoγrafeea] bibliography.

βιβλιοδέτης, ὁ [veevleeodetees] bookbinder.

βιβλιοθηκάριος, ὁ [veevleeotheekareeos] librarian.

βιβλιοθήκη, ἡ [veevleeotheekee] bookcase || library.

βιβλιοκρισία, ἡ [veevleeokreeseea] book review.

βιβλίον, τό [veevleeon] book.

βιβλιοπώλης, ὁ [veevleeopolees] bookseller.

βίβλος, ἡ [veevlos] Bible.

βίγλα, ἡ [veeγla] lookout post, watch.

βίδα, ἡ [veeda] screw || (μεταφ) whim, caprice.

βιδέλο, τό [veedelo] calf || veal.

βιδολόγος, ὁ [veedoloγos] screwdriver, turn-screw.

βιδώνω [veedono] screw.

βίζα, ἡ [veeza] visa.

βίζιτα, ἡ [veezeeta] visit, call || visitor.

βίλλα, ἡ [veela] villa.

βιογραφία, ἡ [veeoγrafeea] biography.

βιολέττα, ἡ [veeoleta] violet.

βιολί, τό [veeolee] violin, fiddle || ἀλλάζω ~ change one's tune.

βιολιτζῆς, ὁ [veeoleetzees] fiddler, violinist.

βιολόγος, ὁ [veeoloγos] biologist.

βιομηχανία, ἡ [veeomeehaneea] industry || manufacture.

βιομηχανικός [veeomeehaneekos] industrial.

βιοπαλαιστής, ὁ [veeopalestees] breadwinner, toiler.

βιοπάλη, ἡ [veeopalee] working hard to make a living.

βίος, ὁ [veeos] life || διά βίου for life.

βιός, τό [veeos] wealth, property.

βιοτεχνία, ἡ [veeotehneea] handicraft.

βιοχημεία, ἡ [veeoheemeea] biochemistry.

βιταμίνη, ἡ [veetameenee] vitamin.

βιτρίνα, ἡ [veetreena] shop window, showcase.

βίτσιο, τό [veetseeo] bad habit.

βιώσιμος [veeoseemos] viable, feasible.

βλαβερός [vlaveros] harmful || (ἔντομον) noxious || (ἐνέργεια) injurious.

βλάβη, ἡ [vlavee] harm, damage || (μηχανῆς) motor trouble, breakdown.

βλάκας, ὁ [vlakas] βλ βλάξ.

βλακεία, ἡ [vlakeea] nonsense, silliness.

βλακώδης [vlakodees] stupid, silly.

βλάξ, ὁ, ἡ [vlaks] blockhead, fool, idiot.

βλάπτω [vlapto] harm, injure, damage.

βλαστάρι, τό [vlastaree] sprout, bud || (οἰκογενείας) scion.

βλάστησις, ἡ [vlasteesees] sprouting || (φυτεία) vegetation.

βλαστός, ὁ [vlastos] shoot, sprout || (μεταφ) scion, offspring.

βλασφημία, ἡ [vlasfeemeea] blasphemy, curse.

βλασφημῶ [vlasfeemo] curse, revile.

βλάφτω [vlafto] βλ βλάπτω.

βλάχος, ὁ [vlahos] (μεταφ) rustic fellow, boor.

βλέμμα, τό [vlemma] look, glance, eye.

βλεννόρροια, ἡ [vlenoreea] gonorrhoea.

βλέπω [vlepo] see, look at || (ἐπί ἀψύχων) face, command.

βλεφαρίς, ἡ [vlefarees] eyelash.

βλέφαρον, τό [vlefaron] eyelid.

βλέψις, ἡ [vlepses] aim, purpose || πλ aspirations, designs, intentions.

βλῆμα, τό [vleema] projectile.

βλητική, ἡ [vleeteekee] ballistics.

βλογιά, ἡ [vloγia] smallpox.

βλοσυρός [vloseeros] fierce, stern, grim.

βόας, ὁ [voas] boa.

βογγητό, τό [vongeeto] groan, moan.

βογγῶ [vongo] moan, groan || roar.

βόδι, τό [vodee] ox.
βοδινό, τό [vodeeno] beef.
βοή, ή [voee] shout, cry, humming, roaring ‖ (ὄχλου) clamour.
βοήθεια, ή [voeetheea] help, aid, assistance.
βοήθημα, τό [voeetheema] help, assistance, relief.
βοηθητικός [voeetheeteekos] auxiliary ‖ (ἄνεμος) favourable, fair.
βοηθός, ὁ [voeethos] assistant, helper, collaborator.
βοηθῶ [voeetho] help, aid, relieve, give a hand.
βόθρος, ὁ [vothros] cesspool, ditch.
βολά, ή [vola] (upon a) time.
βολάν, τό [volan] steering wheel, driving wheel.
βολβός, ὁ [volvos] bulb, kind of onion ‖ (ματιοῦ) eyeball.
βολετός [voletos] possible, convenient.
βολεύομαι [volevome] get comfortable ‖ get fixed up.
βολεύω [volevo] accommodate, fit in, suit ‖ τά ~ get along, do well.
βολή, ή [volee] throw, blow, stroke, shot ‖ (ἀπόστασις) range.
βόλι, τό [volee] ball, bullet.
βολιδοσκοπῶ [voleedoskopo] sound.
βολικός [voleekos] convenient, easy, handy.
βολίς, ή [volees] sounding lead ‖ (ἄστρον) meteor ‖ (σφαίρα) bullet, ball.
βόλτα, ή [volta] walk ‖ (στροφή) revolution ‖ (κοχλίου) thread ‖ κόβω βόλτες I stroll about.
βόμβα, ή [vomva] bomb.
βομβαρδίζω [vomvardeezo] bomb, bombard ‖ (μεταφ) assail.
βομβαρδισμός, ὁ [vomvardeesmos] bombing.
βομβαρδιστικόν, τό [vomvardeesteekon] (ἀέρο) bomber.
βόμβος, ὁ [vomvos] hum, buzz, buzzing noise.
βόμβυξ, ὁ [vomveeks] silkworm.
βομβῶ [vomvo] buzz, hum.
βορά, ή [vora] prey ‖ (μεταφ) food.
βόρβορος, ὁ [vorvoros] mire, mud, dirt.
βορειοανατολικός [voreeoanatoleekos] north-east(ern).
βορειοδυτικός [voreeodeeteekos] north-west(ern).
βόρειος [voreeos] north(ern).
βορείως [voreeos] northwards, to the north, on the north.
βοριάς, ὁ [vorias] βλ βορρᾶς.
βορρᾶς, ὁ [vorras] north (wind).
βοσκή, ή [voskee] pasture, pasturage.
βοσκοπούλα, ή [voskopoula] shepherdess.
βοσκός, ὁ [voskos] shepherd.
βοσκότόπι, τό [voskotopee] pasture land.
βόσκω [vosko] graze ‖ (μεταφ) drift.
βόστρυχος, ὁ [vostreehos] curl, lock of hair.
βοτάνι, τό [votanee] plant, herb.

βοτανικός [votaneekos] botanic(al).
βότανο, τό [votano] herb, plant.
βοτανολόγος, ὁ [votanoloyos] botanist.
βότρυς, ὁ [votrees] bunch of grapes.
βότσαλο, τό [votsalo] pebble.
βουβαίνω [vouveno] make mute.
βουβάλι, τό [vouvalee] buffalo.
βουβός [vouvos] dumb, mute.
βουβών, ὁ [vouvon] groin.
βουδδιστής, ὁ [vouδeestees] Buddhist.
βουερός [voueros] noisy.
βουή, ή [vouee] βλ βοή.
βουΐζω [voueezo] buzz, hum.
βουκόλος, ὁ [voukolos] cowherd, herdsman.
βούλευμα, τό [voulevma] decision, ordinance, decree.
βουλεύομαι [voulevome] deliberate.
βουλευτήριον, τό [voulevteereeon] parliament, chamber (of deputies).
βουλευτής, ὁ [voulevtees] member of parliament, deputy.
βουλή, ή [voulee] parliament, chamber ‖ (θέλησις) will, volition.
βούλησις, ή [vouleesees] desire, will ‖ κατά βούλησιν at will.
βούλιαγμα, τό [vouleeayma] sinking, submergence ‖ collapse.
βουλιάζω [vouleeazo] sink ‖ (μεταφ) ruin, be ruined.
βουλιμία, ή [vouleemeea] insatiable appetite.
βούλλα, ή [voula] seal, stamp.
βουλλοκέρι, τό [voulokeree] sealing wax.
βούλλωμα, τό [vouloma] sealing, stamping ‖ (τό ἀντικείμενον) cork, stopper.
βουλλώνω [voulono] seal ‖ (πωματίζω) stop, choke up, fill.
βούλομαι [voulome] will, wish, intend.
βουνήσιος [vouneeseeos] mountainous ‖ (οὐσ) highlander.
βουνό, τό [vouno] mountain.
βούρδουλας, ὁ [vourδoulas] whip, lash.
βόρκος, ὁ [vourkos] mud, mire ‖ (μεταφ) mire, gutter.
βουρκώνω [vourkono] fill with tears ‖ (ὁ οὐρανός) become overcast.
βοῦρλο, τό [vourlo] (bul)rush.
βούρτσα, ή [vourtsa] (hair)brush ‖ (ρούχων) clothes brush ‖ (ὀδόντων) toothbrush.
βουρτσίζω [vourtseezo] brush, brush down.
βοῦς, ὁ [vous] ox, bullock.
βουστάσιον, τό [voustaseeon] ox stall, cowshed.
βούτηγμα, τό [vouteeyma] plunging, dipping ‖ (μεταφ) plundering, stealing.
βούτημα, τό [vouteema] hard biscuit.
βουτηχτής, ὁ [vouteehtees] diver ‖ (μεταφ) thief.
βουτιά, ή [voutia] dive ‖ (μεταφ) snatching, stealing.
βουτσί, τό [voutsee] cask, barrel.
βούτυρο, τό [vouteero] butter.

βουτῶ [vouto] plunge, dip ‖ (κλέβω) steal, snatch.
βοῶ [voo] yell, cry out.
βραβεῖον, τό [vraveeon] prize.
βραβεύω [vravevo] award, reward.
βράγχια, τά [vrangheea] πλ gills ‖ (ἰατρ) branchiae.
βραδέως [vradeos] slowly, gradually.
βραδιά, ἡ [vradia] evening.
βραδιάζω [vradeeazo]: βραδιάζει it's getting dark.
βραδινός [vradeenos] evening.
βράδυ, τό [vradee] evening.
βραδύνω [vradeeno] be late, be slow.
βραδύς [vradees] slow, sluggish, tardy.
βραδύτης, ἡ [vradeetees] slowness, tardiness.
βράζω [vrazo] boil, ferment, seethe.
βράκα, ἡ [vraka] large breeches.
βρακί, τό [vrakee] trousers ‖ underpants.
βράσιμο, τό [vraseemo] boiling, fermentation.
βράσις, ἡ [vrasees] boiling ‖ (μούστου κτλ) fermentation.
βρασμός, ὁ [vrasmos] boiling ‖ (μεταφ) agitation, excitement.
βραστός [vrastos] boiled ‖ boiling, hot.
βραχιόλι, τό [vraheeolee] bracelet.
βραχίων, ὁ [vraheeon] arm, forearm ‖ branch.
βραχνάδα, ἡ [vrahnada] hoarseness.
βραχνᾶς, ὁ [vrahnas] nightmare.
βραχνιάζω [vrahneeazo] become hoarse.
βραχνός [vrahnos] hoarse.
βράχος, ὁ [vrahos] rock.
βραχυκύκλωμα, τό [vraheekeekloma] short circuit.
βραχύνω [vraheeno] shorten ‖ (βῆμα) slow down.
βραχυπρόθεσμος [vraheeprothesmos] short-dated ‖ short-termed.
βραχύτης, ἡ [vraheetees] shortness, brevity, conciseness.
βραχώδης [vrahodees] rocky.
βρέ [vre] (ἐπιφ) you there!, hey, you!
βρεγμένος [vreymenos] wet, moist.
βρέξιμο, τό [vrekseemo] wetting, watering, moistening.
βρεφοκομεῖον, τό [vrefokomeeon] foundling hospital, public nursery.
βρέφος, τό [vrefos] baby, infant.
βρέχω [vreho] water, wet, dampen, rain.
βρίζω [vreezo] abuse, swear at, insult ‖ outrage.
βρίθω [vreetho] teem with, swarm with.
βρισιά, ἡ [vreesia] abuse, insult, outrage.
βρισίδι, τό [vreeseedee] stream of abuse.
βρίσκομαι [vreeskome] be, find o.s.
βρίσκω [vreesko] find ‖ (τυχαίως) come across, discover ‖ (σκέπτομαι) think, deem ‖ (παίρνω) get, procure ‖ (μαντεύω) guess.
βρογχῖτις, ἡ [vrongheetees] bronchitis.

βροντερός [vronteros] thundering, noisy.
βροντή, ἡ [vrontee] thunder.
βρόντος, ὁ [vrontos] noise, roar ‖ heavy fall ‖ στὸ βρόντο in vain.
βροντῶ [vronto] (μεταφ) knock, make a noise.
βροντώδης [vrontodees] thundering, loud.
βροχερός [vroheros] wet, rainy.
βροχή, ἡ [vrohee] rain ‖ ~ ψιλή drizzle.
βρόχι, τό [vrohee] net, snare.
βρόχος, ὁ [vrohos] noose, loop, lasso.
βρυκόλακας, ὁ [vreekolakas] vampire, ghost.
βρύον, τό [vreeon] moss ‖ seaweed.
βρύση, ἡ [vreesee] fountain, spring ‖ (μεταλλικὴ) tap.
βρυχῶμαι [vreehome] roar, bellow.
βρύω [vreeo] teem with.
βρῶμα, ἡ [vroma] filth, stink ‖ (γιά πρόσωπο) hussy, bitch, slut.
βρωμερός [vromeros] stinky, smelly ‖ (ὑπόθεσις) nasty, odious, vile ‖ (ἄτομον) stinking, dirty, slovenly.
βρώμη, ἡ [vromee] oats.
βρωμιά, ἡ [vromia] filth, dirt ‖ (μεταφ) nasty business, corruption.
βρωμίζω [vromeezo] stink, dirty, sully.
βρώμικος [vromeekos] dirty, grubby ‖ (μεταφ) nasty, odious, vile.
βρωμῶ [vromo] give off a stench, smell badly, stink.
βύζαγμα, τό [veezaɣma] nursing, lactation ‖ sucking.
βυζαίνω [veezeno] suckle ‖ (μεταφ) suck.
βυζαντινός [veezanteenos] Byzantine.
βυζί, τό [veezee] breast.
βυθίζω [veetheezo] sink, plunge, dip.
βύθισις, ἡ [veetheesees] sinking, submersion.
βύθισμα, τό [veetheesma] (ναυτ) draught ‖ sinking.
βυθοκόρος, ἡ [veethokoros] dredger, dredge.
βυθός, ὁ [veethos] bottom of the sea.
βυρσοδεψεῖον, τό [veersodepseeon] tannery.
βύσσινο, τό [veeseeno] sour cherry.
βυτίον, τό [veeteeon] cask, barrel.
βωβός [vovos] dumb, mute, silent.
βωλοκοπῶ [volokopo] harrow.
βῶλος, ὁ [volos] clod ‖ βῶλοι πλ marbles.
βωμολοχία, ἡ [vomoloheea] obscenity, scurrility.
βωμός, ὁ [vomos] altar.
βώτριδα, ἡ [votreeda] moth.

Γ, γ

γαβάθα, ἡ [ɣavatha] earthenware vessel ‖ wooden bowl.
γάγγλιον, τό [ɣangleeon] ganglion.
γάγγραινα, ἡ [ɣangrena] gangrene ‖ (μεταφ) canker.

γάδος, ὁ [yaδos] cod(fish).

γάζα, ἡ [yaza] gauze.

γαζί, τό [yazee] stitch ‖ (τῆς χειρός) hand-stitch ‖ (τῆς μηχανῆς) machine-stitch.

γάζωμα, τό [yazoma] stitching.

γαῖα, ἡ [yea] earth, land.

γαιανθρακωρυχεῖον, τό [yeanthrakoreeheeon] coalmine, coalpit.

γαιάνθραξ, ὁ [yeanthraks] coal.

γάϊδαρος, ὁ [yaeeδaros] ass, donkey ‖ (μεταφ) boor, ass.

γαϊδουράγκαθο, τό [yaeeδourangatho] thistle.

γαϊδουριά, ἡ [yaeeδouria] rudeness.

γαιοκτήμων, ὁ [yeokteemon] landowner.

γάλα, τό [yala] milk.

γαλάζιος [yalazeeos] azure, blue.

γαλαζοαίματος [yalazoematos] blue-blooded.

γαλαζόπετρα, ἡ [yalazopetra] turquoise.

γαλακτερός [yalakteros] milky, of milk.

γαλακτικός [yalakteekos] lactic.

γαλακτοκομεῖον, τό [yalaktokomeeon] dairy farm.

γαλακτοπωλεῖον, τό [yalaktopoleeon] dairy.

γαλακτοπώλης, ὁ [yalaktopolees] milkman.

γαλακτώδης [yalaktodees] milky, milk-white.

γαλάκτωμα, τό [yalaktoma] emulsion.

γαλανόλευκος, ἡ [yalanolevkos] the Greek flag.

γαλανομμάτης [yalanomatees] blue-eyed.

γαλανός [yalanos] blue.

Γαλαξίας, ὁ [yalakseeas] Milky Way.

γαλαρία, ἡ [yalareea] gallery.

γαλατᾶς, ὁ [yalatas] milkman.

γαλβανίζω [yalvaneezo] galvanize ‖ (μεταφ) electrify, rouse, stimulate.

γαλέρα, ἡ [yalera] galley.

γαλέττα, ἡ [yaleta] hard tack.

γαληνεύω [yaleenevo] calm, quieten down.

γαλήνη, ἡ [yaleenee] calm, peace, serenity.

γαλήνιος [yaleeneeos] calm, composed, serene.

γαληνός [yaleenos] βλ γαλήνιος.

γαλιφίζω [yaleefeezo] flatter, fawn.

Γαλλία, ἡ [yaleea] France.

γαλλικός [yaleekos] French.

γαλλοπούλα, ἡ [yalopoula] turkey hen.

Γάλλος, ὁ [yalos] Frenchman.

γαλόνι, τό [yalonee] (μέτρον) gallon ‖ (στρατ) stripe, pip.

γαλούχημα, τό [yalouheema] suckling ‖ (μεταφ) education, upbringing.

γαλουχῶ [yalouho] suckle, nurse ‖ (μεταφ) bring up.

γάμα, τό [yama] the letter Γ.

γαμβρός, ὁ [yamvros] bridegroom ‖ son-in-law ‖ brother-in-law.

γαμήλιος [yameeleeos] nuptial, bridal ‖ γαμήλιον ταξίδι honeymoon.

γάμπα, ἡ [yamba] calf, leg.

γαμψός [yampsos] hooked, crooked.

γάντζος, ὁ [yantzos] hook, grapple.

γαντζώνω [yantzono] hook.

γάντι, τό [yantee] glove.

γανώνω [yanono] tin, pewter.

γαργαλίζω [yaryalizo] tickle ‖ (μεταφ) tempt, allure.

γαργάρα, ἡ [yaryara] gargle.

γαργαρίζω [yaryareezo] gargle.

γαρδένια, ἡ [yarδeneea] gardenia.

γαρίδα, ἡ [yareeδa] shrimp, prawn.

γαρνίρισμα, τό [yarneereesma] adornment, garnishing, decoration.

γαρνίρω [yarniro] garnish, trim.

γαρνιτούρα, ἡ [yarneetoura] garniture, trimming.

γαρυφαλλιά, ἡ [yareefalia] carnation ‖ (μπαχαρικοῦ) clove tree.

γαρύφαλλο, τό [yareefalo] carnation ‖ (μπαχαρικό) clove.

γαστήρ, ἡ [yasteer] belly.

γαστραλγία, ἡ [yastralyeea] stomach ache.

γαστρικός [yastreekos] gastric.

γαστρίτις, ἡ [yastreetees] gastritis.

γαστροεντερικός [yastroentereekos] gastro-intestinal.

γαστρονομία, ἡ [yastronomeea] gastronomy.

γάτα, ἡ [yata] cat.

γαυγίζω [yavyeezo] bark.

γαύγισμα, τό [yavyeesma] barking, baying.

γδάρσιμο, τό [yδarseemo] (πρᾶξις) flaying ‖ (ἀποτέλεσμα) scratch.

γδέρνω [yδerno] flay, skin ‖ (μεταφ) fleece.

γδύνομαι [yδeenome] get undressed, strip.

γδύνω [yδeeno] undress ‖ (μεταφ) rob.

γεγονός, τό [yeyonos] event, fact.

γειά, ἡ [yia] health ‖ ~σας hello ‖ so long, goodbye.

γεῖσον, τό [yeeson] (ἀρχιτεκ) eaves ‖ cornice ‖ (κασκέτου) peak.

γειτνιάζω [yeetneeazo] βλ γειτονεύω.

γειτονεύω [yeetonevo] be close to, be adjoining.

γειτονιά, ἡ [yeetonia] neighbourhood, vicinity.

γελάσμα, τό [yelasma] (ἀπάτη) deceit ‖ laughing stock.

γελαστός [yelastos] smiling, pleasant, cheerful.

γελάω [yelao] βλ γελῶ.

γελέκι, τό [yelekee] waistcoat.

γελιέμαι [yelieme] be deceived, be mistaken.

γέλιο, τό [yeleeo] laugh, laughter.

γελοιογραφία, ἡ [yeleeoyrafeea] caricature, cartoon.

γελοιοποίησις, ἡ [yeleeopieesees] ridicule, derision.

γελοιοποιοῦμαι [yeleeopeeoume] make o.s. ridiculous.

γελοιοποιῶ [yeleeopeeo] make ridiculous, ridicule.

γελοῖος [yeleeos] ludicrous, ridiculous.

γελῶ [yelo] laugh ‖ (μάτια κτλ) smile, twinkle ‖ (ἐξαπατῶ) deceive, take in.

γέλως, ὁ [yelos] βλ γέλιο.

γεμᾶτος [yematos] full ‖ (δρόμος κτλ) crowded, swarming ‖ (ὅπλο, δένδρο κτλ) loaded ‖ (δωμάτιος κτλ) packed, crammed ‖ (παχύς) stout, plump.

γεμίζω [yemeezo] fill up ‖ (πλοῖο) load ‖ (μαξιλάρι κτλ) stuff ‖ (συμπληρώνω) fill out.

γέμισμα, τό [yemeesma] filling ‖ (στρώματος) stuffing ‖ (φεγγαριοῦ) waxing ‖ (ὅπλου) charging, loading.

γεμιστός [yemeestos] stuffed.

γέμω [yemo] be full (of), abound.

γενάκι, τό [yenaki] small beard.

Γενάρης [yenarees] βλ Γεννάρης.

γενεά, ἡ [yenea] race, generation, breed.

γενεαλογία, ἡ [yenealoyeea] genealogy, lineage, pedigree.

γενέθλια, τά [yenethleea] πλ birthday, anniversary.

γενειάς, ἡ [yenias] beard.

γενειοφόρος, ὁ [yeneeoforos] bearded.

γενεσιουργία, ἡ [yeneseeouryeea] creation.

γένεσις, ἡ [yenesees] origin, birth ‖ (ἐκκλ) Genesis.

γενέτειρα, ἡ [yeneteera] native country, birthplace.

γενετή, ἡ [yenetee]: ἐκ ~ς from birth.

γενετήσιος [yeneteeseeos] productive, generative, sexual.

γενίκευσις, ἡ [yeneekevsees] generalization.

γενικεύω [yeneekevo] generalize.

γενική [yeneekee] general, universal, wide ‖ (γραμμ) genitive (case) ‖ βλ καί γενικός.

γενικός [yeneekos] general ‖ βλ καί γενική.

γενικότης, ἡ [yeneekotees] generality.

γέννα, ἡ [yenna] birth, childbirth ‖ (μεταφ) breed.

γενναιοδωρία, ἡ [yenneodoreea] generosity.

γενναιόδωρος [yenneodoros] generous, magnanimous.

γενναῖος [yenneos] courageous, brave.

γενναιότης, ἡ [yenneotees] courage, bravery.

γενναίως [yenneos] bravely.

γενναιοφροσύνη, ἡ [yenneofroseenee] generosity, liberality.

γενναιόφρων, ὁ [yenneofron] magnanimous, liberal.

γενναιόψυχος [yenneopsyhos] generous, brave.

Γεννάρης, ὁ [yennarees] January.

γέννημα, τό [yenneema] offspring, product ‖ (μωρό) progeny ‖ ~ τα cereals.

γέννησις, ἡ [yenneesees] birth.

γεννητικός [yenneeteekos] genital, sexual.

γεννήτρια, ἡ [yenneetreea] generator.

γεννήτωρ, ὁ [yenneetor] father.

γεννῶ [yenno] (γιά γυναῖκα) give birth to,

bring forth ‖ (γιά ἄλογα) drop a foal ‖ (γιά κουνέλια, γουρούνια) litter ‖ (γιά πτηνά) lay ‖ (μεταφ) create, breed, cause.

γεννῶμαι [yennome] be born.

γένος, τό [yenos] race, family, line ‖ τό ἀνθρώπινον ~ mankind ‖ (ζώων, φυτῶν) kind, species ‖ (γραμμ) gender.

γερά [yera] strongly, hard, vigorously.

γεράκι, τό [yerakee] hawk.

γεράματα, τά [yeramata] πλ old age.

γεράνιον, τό [yeraneeon] geranium.

γερανός, ὁ [yeranos] (πτηνό) crane ‖ (μηχάνημα) crane, winch.

γέρας, τό [yeras] prize, reward.

γερατειά [yeratia] βλ γεράματα.

Γερμανία, ἡ [yermaneea] Germany.

γερμανικός [yermaneekos] German.

Γερμανός, ὁ [yermanos] German.

γέρνω [yerno] lean, bend ‖ (γιά βάρκα κτλ) lean, tilt ‖ (γιά ἥλιο κτλ) go down, sink.

γερνῶ [yerno] βλ γηράσκω.

γεροντικός [yeronteekos] senile.

γεροντοκόρη, ἡ [yerontokoree] old maid, spinster.

γεροντοπαλήκαρο, τό [yerontopaleekaro] old bachelor.

γέρος, ὁ [yeros] old man.

γερός [yeros] (ἄνθρωπος) vigorous, sturdy ‖ (κράσις) sound, healthy ‖ (τροφή) solid, substantial, hearty ‖ (ξύλο) sound ‖ (πάτωμα) solid, firm ‖ (τοῖχος) strong ‖ (ἐπιχείρημα) strong, valid.

γερουσία, ἡ [yerouseea] senate.

γερουσιαστής, ὁ [yerouseeastees] senator.

γέρων, ὁ [yeron] old man.

γεῦμα, τό [yevma] meal, dinner.

γεύομαι [yevome] taste, try.

γεῦσις, ἡ [yevsees] taste, flavour.

γέφυρα, ἡ [yeffera] bridge.

γεφυρώνω [yefeerono] bridge ‖ build a bridge.

γεωγραφία, ἡ [yeoyrafeea] geography.

γεωγραφικός [yeoyrafeekos] geographic.

γεωγράφος, ὁ [yeoyrafos] geographer.

γεωδαισία, ἡ [yeodeseea] geodesy.

γεώδης [yeodees] earthy.

γεωλογία, ἡ [yeoloyeea] geology.

γεωλόγος, ὁ [yeoloyos] geologist.

γεωμετρία, ἡ [yeometreea] geometry.

γεωμετρικός [yeometreekos] geometric(al).

γεώμηλον, τό [yeomeelon] potato.

γεωπονία, ἡ [yeoponeea] agriculture.

γεωργία, ἡ [yeoryeea] agriculture, farming.

γεωργικός [yeoryeekos] agricultural.

γεωργός, ὁ [yeoryos] farmer.

γεώτρησις, ἡ [yeotreesees] drilling.

γεωτρύπανον, τό [yeotreepanon] drill.

γῆ, ἡ [yee] earth, land, ground.

γηγενής [yeeyenees] native, indigenous.

γήινος [yeeinos] earthly, terrestrial.

γήλοφος, ὁ [yeelofos] hillock, mound.

γήπεδον, τό [yeepeδon] ground, sportsground.

γήρας, τό [yeeras] old age.

γηράσκω [yeerasko] age, grow old.

γιά [yea] for, because of, on behalf of ‖ γι' αὐτό therefore ‖ ~ καλά for certain, for good ‖ ~ τήν ὥρα for the time being ‖ ~ ποῦ whither? ‖ ~ τό Θεό for God's sake ‖ (ἐπίρ) as, for ‖ (συνδ) ~ νά in order to ‖ ~ φαντάσου! fancy that! ‖ ~ πές μου tell me.

γιαγιά, ἡ [yeeayia] grandmother.

γιακᾶς, ὁ [yeekas] collar.

γιαλός, ὁ [yeealos] seashore.

γιαούρτι, τό [yeeaourtee] yoghurt.

γιασεμί, τό [yeeasemee] jasmine.

γιατί [yeeatee] why? ‖ (συνδ) because.

γιατρεύω [yeeatrevo] cure, heal, treat.

γιατρός, ὁ [yeeatros] doctor.

γιαχνί, τό [yeeahnee] ragout.

γιγάντιος [yeeyanteeos] gigantic.

γιγαντομαχία, ἡ [yeeyantomaheea] battle of the giants.

γιγαντόσωμος [yeeyantosomos] huge (in size).

γίγας, ὁ [yeeyas] giant.

γιγνώσκω [yeeynosko] βλ γνωρίζω.

γίδα, ἡ [yeeδa] goat.

γιδοβοσκός, ὁ [yeeδovoskos] goatherd.

γιλέκο, τό [yeeleko] waistcoat.

γινάτι, τό [yeenatee] obstinacy, stubbornness ‖ spite.

γίνομαι [yeenome] be done, become ‖ (μεγαλώνω) grow ‖ (στρέφω) turn ‖ (γεγονός κτλ) happen, occur ‖ (ὡριμάζω) ripen ‖ ~ καλά recover ‖ τί γίνεσαι; how are you?

γινόμενον, τό [yeenomenon] product.

γινώσκω [yeenosko] βλ γνωρίζω.

γιουβαρλάκια, τά [yeeouvarlakeea] πλ meatballs with rice.

γιούχα [yeeouha] boo.

γιουχαΐζω [yeeouhaeezo] hoot, jeer.

γιρλάντα, ἡ [yeerlanta] garland, wreath.

γιώτ, τό [yeeot] yacht.

γκαβός [ngavos] cross-eyed ‖ (κατ' ἐπέκτασιν) blind.

γκάζι, τό [ngazee] gas ‖ πατῶ ~ step on the gas.

γκαζιέρα, ἡ [ngaziera] cooking stove, primus stove.

γκαζόζα, ἡ [ngazoza] lemonade.

γκάϊδα, ἡ [ngaeeδa] bagpipe.

γκαρίζω [ngareezo] bray.

γκαρσόν, τό [ngarson] waiter.

γκαρσονιέρα, ἡ [ngarsoniera] bachelor flat.

γκάφα, ἡ [ngafa] blunder.

γκέμι, τό [ngemee] bridle, reins.

γκέττα, ἡ [ngetta] gaiter, legging.

γκίνια, ἡ [ngeeneea] bad luck.

γκιώνης, ὁ [ngeeonees] (scops) owl.

γκουβερνάντα, ἡ [ngouvernanta] governess.

γκρεμίζω [ngremeezo] βλ κρημνίζω.

γκρεμνός [ngremnos] βλ κρημνός.

γκρίζος [ngreezos] grey.

γκρίνια, ἡ [ngreeneea] grumble, murmur, nag.

γκρινιάζω [ngreeneeazo] complain, nag, grumble.

γλάρος, ὁ [ylaros] seagull.

γλάστρα, ἡ [ylastra] flowerpot.

γλαυκός [ylavkos] blue, azure.

γλαύκωμα, τό [ylavkoma] glaucoma.

γλαῦξ, ἡ [ylafks] owl.

γλαφυρός [ylafeeros] elegant, graceful.

γλαφυρότης, ἡ [ylafeerotees] smoothness, elegance.

γλείφω [yleefo] lick.

γλεντζές, ὁ [ylentzes] fun-loving person, reveller.

γλέντι, τό [ylentee] party, feast.

γλεντῶ [ylento] amuse ‖ (ἀπολαμβάνω) enjoy ‖ (ἐπί χρημάτων) squander.

γλεῦκος, τό [ylevkos] must.

γλιστερός [yleesteros] slippery.

γλίστρημα, τό [yleestreema] slide, slip ‖ (μεταφ) blunder, mistake.

γλιστρῶ [yleestro] slide, slip ‖ (μεταφ) slip away.

γλίσχρος [yleeshros] niggardly, paltry, meagre.

γλοιῶδες [yleeoδees] slimy, sticky ‖ (μεταφ) oily (person).

γλόμπος, ὁ [ylombos] globe.

γλουτός, ὁ [yloutos] buttock, rump.

γλύκα, ἡ [yleeka] sweetness.

γλυκά, τά [yleeka] πλ pastries, confectionery.

γλυκάδι, τό [yleekaδee] vinegar.

γλυκαίνω [yleekeno] sweeten, make mild, soften.

γλυκάνισον, τό [yleekaneeson] anise.

γλύκισμα, τό [yleekeesma] cake, pastry.

γλυκοκυττάζω [yleekokeetazo] look at tenderly.

γλυκομίλητος [yleekomeeleetos] softspoken, affable.

γλυκομιλῶ [yleekomeelo] speak tenderly, speak kindly.

γλυκόν, τό [yleekon] jam, sweetmeat.

γλυκόξινος [yleekokseenos] bitter-sweet.

γλυκοτραγουδῶ [yleekotrayouδo] sing sweetly.

γλυκοχάραγμα, τό [yleekoharayma] daybreak, twilight.

γλυκύς [yleekees] affable, sweet ‖ (καιρός) mild ‖ (φῶς) subdued, mellow ‖ (χρῶμα) delicate ‖ (ἦχος) soft, sweet ‖ (κρασί) sweet ‖ (ὄνειρα) pleasant.

γλύπτης, ὁ [yleeptees] sculptor.

γλυπτική, ἡ [yleepteekee] sculpture.

γλυπτός [yleeptos] sculptured, carved.

γλυτωμός, ὁ [yleetomos] deliverance, escape.

γλυτώνω [yleetono] save, deliver ‖ (ἀμεταβ) escape.

γλύφω [yleefo] βλ γλείφω.

γλῶσσα, ή [ylossa] tongue, language ‖ (ψάρι) sole.

γλωσσᾶς, ὁ [ylossas] chatterbox, gossip.

γλωσσίδι, τό [ylosseedee] tongue, clapper.

γλωσσικός [ylosseekos] lingual ‖ linguistic.

γλωσσολογία, ή [ylossoloyeea] linguistics.

γλωσσολόγος, ὁ [ylossoloyos] linguist.

γλωσσομαθής [ylossomathees] polyglot, linguist.

γλωσσοτρώγω [ylossotroyo] backbite, slander.

γνάθος, ὁ [ynathos] jaw.

γνέθω [ynetho] spin.

γνήσιος [yneeseeos] genuine, real ‖ (τέκνον) legitimate.

γνησίως [yneeseeos] genuinely, authentically.

γνωμάτευσις, ή [ynomatevsees] opinion, adjudication.

γνωματεύω [ynomatevo] express an opinion.

γνώμη, ή [ynomee] opinion, mind, view.

γνωμικόν, τό [ynomeekon] maxim, saying, adage.

γνωμοδότης, ὁ [ynomodotees] adviser, councillor.

γνωμοδοτῶ [ynomodoto] give one's opinion, judge.

γνώμων, ὁ [ynomon] set square, level ‖ (μεταφ) criterion, model.

γνωρίζω [ynoreezo] let it be known, inform ‖ (ἔχω γνῶσιν) know, be aware of ‖ (ἀναγνωρίζω) discern, distinguish ‖ (ἔχω σχέσεις) know, be acquainted with ‖ (παρουσιάζω κάποιον) introduce.

γνωριμία, ή [ynoreemeea] acquaintance, familiarity.

γνώριμος [ynoreemos] known, intimate.

γνώρισμα, τό [ynoreesma] sign, mark, indication.

γνῶσις, ή [ynosees] knowledge, notion ‖ πλ knowledge, learning.

γνώστης, ὁ [ynostees] expert, connoisseur, specialist.

γνωστικός [ynosteekos] prudent.

γνωστοποίησις, ή [ynostopieesees] notification, announcement.

γνωστοποιῶ [ynostopeeo] notify, inform, advise.

γνωστός [ynostos] known ‖ (φίλος) acquaintance.

γογγύζω [yongeezo] groan, grumble, moan, complain.

γογγυσμός, ὁ [yongeesmos] grumbling, groan.

γογγύλη, ή [yongeelee] turnip.

γοερός [yoeros] plaintive, woeful.

γόης, ὁ [yoees] charmer.

γοητεία, ή [yoeeteea] charm ‖ attractiveness.

γοητευτικός [yoeetevteekos] charming, captivating.

γοητεύω [yoeetevo] charm, attract.

γόητρον, τό [yoeetron] prestige, reputation.

γομάρι, τό [yomaree] load ‖ (μεταφ) simpleton, beast.

γόμμα, ή [yomma] gum ‖ (σβυσήματος) indiarubber, eraser.

γόμφος, ὁ [yomfos] peg, bolt, pin ‖ (κοκκάλων) joint.

γόμωσις, ή [yomosees] stuffing ‖ (ὅπλου) charge.

γονατίζω [yonateezo] (make to) kneel ‖ (μεταφ) humble ‖ (ἀμεταβ) kneel down ‖ (μεταφ) give way, yield.

γονατιστά [yonateesta] on the knees, kneeling.

γόνατο, τό [yonato] knee.

γονεύς, ὁ [yonevs] father ‖ πλ parents.

γονιμοποίησις, ή [yoneemopieesees] fertilization, impregnation.

γονιμοποιῶ [yoneemopeeo] fecundate, fertilize.

γόνιμος [yoneemos] fertile, prolific ‖ (μεταφ) inventive.

γονιμότης, ή [yoneemotees] fecundity, fertility.

γονίμως [yoneemos] fruitfully, productively.

γόνος, ὁ [yonos] child, offspring ‖ (σπέρμα) sperm, seed.

γόνυ, τό [yonee] knee.

γόπα, ή [yopa] bogue (fish).

γοργός [yoryos] rapid, quick.

γοργότης, ή [yoryotees] quickness, promptness.

γορίλλας, ὁ [yoreelas] gorilla.

γούβα, ή [youva] cavity, hole.

γουδί, τό [youdee] mortar.

γουδοχέρι, τό [youdoheree] pestle.

γουλί, τό [youlee] stalk, stump ‖ (μεταφ) bald.

γουλιά, ή [youlia] mouthful, drop.

γούμενα, ή [youmena] cable.

γούνα, ή [youna] fur.

γουναρικόν, τό [younareekon] fur.

γουργουρητό, τό [youryoureeto] rumbling, rumble.

γούρι, τό [youree] good luck.

γουρλομάτης, ὁ [yourlomatees] person with bulging eyes, goggle-eyed person.

γουρλώνω [yourlono] open wide, goggle.

γουρούνα, ή [yourouna] sow, piglet.

γουρούνι, τό [yourounee] pig, hog.

γουρσούζης, ὁ [yoursouzees] luckless person, unlucky person.

γουρσουζιά, ή [yoursoozia] bad luck.

γουστάρω [youstaro] desire, feel like ‖ (εὐχαριστοῦμαι) delight in, enjoy.

γουστέρα, ή [youstera] lizard.

γοῦστο, τό [yousto] taste ‖ (φιλοκαλία) good taste ‖ γιά ~ for the hell of it.

γοφός, ὁ [yofos] haunch, hip.

γραῖα, ή [yrea] old woman.

γραῖγος, ὁ [yreyos] north-east (wind).

Γραικός, ὁ [yrekos] Greek.

γράμμα, τό [yramma] letter, character.

γραμμάριον, τό [yrammareeon] gram(me).

γραμματεία, ἡ [yrammateea] secretariat, secretary's office.

γραμματεύς, ὁ [yrammatevs] secretary.

γραμματική, ἡ [yrammateekee] grammar.

γραμματικῶς [yrammateekos] grammatically.

γραμμάτιον, τό [yrammateeon] bill of exchange ‖ (χρεωστικόν) promissory note.

γραμματισμένος [yrammateesmenos] well-read, learned.

γραμματοκιβώτιον, τό [yrammatokeevoteeon] letterbox, postbox.

γραμματολογία, ἡ [yrammatoloyeea] literature.

γραμματόσημον, τό [yrammatoseemon] (postage) stamp.

γραμμένος [yrammenos] written ‖ (μεταφ) destined.

γραμμή, ἡ [yrammee] line, row ‖ (ἐπιρ) straight, in a row ‖ πρώτης ~ς first-class.

γραμμικός [yrameekos] linear.

γραμμόφωνον, τό [yrammofonon] gramophone.

γραμμοτός [yrammotos] lined, ruled ‖ (ὕφασμα) striped.

γρανίτης, ὁ [yraneetees] granite.

γραπτός [yraptos] written.

γραπτῶς [yraptos] in writing.

γραπώνω [yrapono] seize, snatch.

γρασίδι, τό [yraseeδee] grass.

γρατσουνίζω [yratsouneezo] scratch.

γρατσούνισμα, τό [yratsouneesma] scratch.

γραφειοκράτης, ὁ [yrafeeokratees] bureaucrat.

γραφειοκρατία, ἡ [yrafeeokrateea] bureaucracy.

γραφεῖον, τό [yrafeeon] desk, bureau ‖ (δωμάτιον) study ‖ (ἵδρυμα) office, bureau.

γραφεύς, ὁ [yrafevs] clerk, copyist.

γραφικός [yrafeekos] of writing, clerical ‖ (μεταφ) picturesque, colourful.

γραφικότης, ἡ [yrafeekotees] picturesqueness, vividness.

γραφίς, ἡ [yrafees] nib, pen.

γραφίτης, ὁ [yrafeetees] graphite.

γραφομηχανή, ἡ [yrafomeehanee] typewriter.

γράφω [yrafo] write, record, compose ‖ enrol.

γράψιμο, τό [yrapseemo] writing.

γρήγορα [yreeyora] quickly, promptly.

γρηγορῶ [yreeyoro] watch, be alert ‖ be awake.

γρίλλια, ἡ [yreeleea] grille.

γρῖπος, ὁ [yreepos] dragnet.

γρίππη, ἡ [yreepee] influenza.

γρῖφος, ὁ [yreefos] riddle, puzzle, enigma.

γριφώδης [yreefoδees] enigmatic(al), obscure.

γρονθοκόπημα, τό [yronthokopeema] boxing, punch.

γρονθοκοπῶ [yronthokopo] punch, pound on.

γρόνθος, ὁ [yronthos] fist ‖ punch.

γρουσούζης [yroosoozees] βλ γουρσούζης.

γρῦ [yree] not a word ‖ absolutely nothing.

γρυλισμός, ὁ [yreeleesmos] grunting, snorting.

γρυλλίζω [yreeleezo] grunt, squeal.

γρύλλος, ὁ [yreelos] piglet ‖ (ἔντομον) cricket ‖ (μηχάνημα) jack.

γρυπός [yreepos] hooked, crooked.

γρύψ, ὁ [yreeps] griffin.

γυάλα, ἡ [yeeala] glass, jar ‖ (ψαριῶν) bowl.

γυαλάδα, ἡ [yeealaδa] brilliance, shine, gloss.

γυαλάδικο, τό [yeealaδeeko] glassware ‖ glass works.

γυαλένιος [yeealeneeos] glass.

γυαλί, τό [yeealee] glass ‖ πλ spectacles, glasses.

γυαλίζω [yeealeezo] polish, shine.

γυάλισμα, τό [yeealeesma] polishing, glazing.

γυαλιστερός [yeealeesteros] polished, glossy.

γυαλόχαρτον, τό [yeealoharton] glasspaper, sandpaper.

γυιός, ὁ [yeeos] son.

γυλιός, ὁ [yeeleeos] knapsack ‖ (ἐργάτου) toolbag.

γυμνάζομαι [yeemnazome] train o.s., exercise, practise.

γυμνάζω [yeemnazo] exercise, train, drill.

γυμνασιάρχης, ὁ [yeemnaseearhees] director of a secondary school, headmaster.

γυμνάσια, τά [yeemnaseea] πλ manoeuvres.

γυμνάσιον, τό [yeemnaseeon] secondary school, high school.

γύμνασις, ἡ [yeemnasees] exercise, training.

γύμνασμα, τό [yeemnasma] exercise, task, theme.

γυμναστήριον, τό [yeemnasteereeon] gymnasium.

γυμναστής, ὁ [yeemnastees] P.T. instructor.

γυμναστική, ἡ [yeemnasteekee] πλ gymnastics ‖ exercise.

γύμνια, ἡ [yeemneea] nudity, nakedness ‖ poverty.

γυμνιστής, ὁ [yeemneestees] nudist.

γυμνός [yeemnos] naked, bare, nude.

γυμνώνω [yeemnono] bare, expose ‖ (μεταφ) strip.

γύμνωσις, ἡ [yeemnosees] disrobing ‖ denudation ‖ fleecing.

γυναῖκα, ἡ [yeeneka] woman ‖ (σύζυγος) wife.

γυναικαδέλφη, ἡ [yeenekaδelfee] sister-in-law.

γυναικάδελφος, ὁ [yeenekaδelfos] brother-in-law.

γυναικάρα, ἡ [yeenekara] virago.

γυναικᾶς, ὁ [yeenekas] woman-chaser, rake.

γυναικεῖος [yeenekeeos] womanly, feminine.

γυναικολογία, ἡ [yeenekoloyeea] gynaecology.

γυναικολόγος, ὁ [yeenekoloyos] gynaecologist.

γυναικόπαιδα, τά [yeenekopeða] πλ women and children.

γυναικοπρεπής [yeenekoprepees] womanly, effeminate, womanish.

γυναικωνίτης, ὁ [yeenekoneetees] harem.

γυνή [yeenee] βλ **γυναῖκα**.

γυρεύω [yeerevo] ask for, call for ‖ (ἐλεημοσύνη) beg for ‖ (νά εὕρω κάτι) look for, seek ‖ (ἀποζημίωσι κτλ) claim ‖ (διαζύγιο) apply for ‖ (βοήθεια) request.

γυρίζω [yeereezo] turn, rotate, revolve ‖ (σβοῦρα) spin ‖ (στρέφω) turn ‖ (ἀναστρέφω) turn ‖ (ἐπιστρέφω) return ‖ (ἀμετάβ) turn, rotate ‖ (ταινία) shoot ‖ (ὁ ἥλιος) sink.

γύρισμα, τό [yeereesma] turn, revolution ‖ (δρόμου, ποταμοῦ) turn, twist, winding ‖ (ἐπιστροφή) return.

γυρισμός, ὁ [yeereesmos] return, coming back.

γυριστός [yeereestos] curved, turned up, crooked.

γυρνάω [yeernao] βλ **γυρίζω**.

γυρολόγος, ὁ [yeeroloyos] hawker, pedlar.

γῦρος, ὁ [yeeros] circle, circumference ‖ (φορέματος) hem ‖ (περιστροφή) turn, revolution ‖ (περπάτημα) walk ‖ (βαρελιοῦ) hoop.

γυρτός [yeertos] bent, inclined, curved.

γύρω [yeero] round, around, about, round about.

γυφτιά, ἡ [yeeftia] stinginess, avarice, shabbiness.

γύφτος, ὁ [yeeftos] gipsy ‖ blacksmith.

γύψ, ὁ [yeeps] vulture.

γύψινος [yeepseenos] plaster.

γύψος, ὁ [yeepsos] plaster of Paris.

γυψώνω [yeepsono] plaster.

γύψωσις, ἡ [yeepsosees] plastering.

γωνία, ἡ [yoneea] angle, corner ‖ (ἐργαλεῖο) square, set square ‖ (ἀπόμερος τόπος) nook, den ‖ (ψωμιοῦ) crust of bread.

γωνιακός [yoneeakos] angular ‖ (τῆς γωνίας) corner.

γωνιόλιθος, ὁ [yoneeoleethos] cornerstone.

γωνιώδης [yoneeoðees] angular.

Δ, δ

δά [ða] (indeclinable particle) ὄχι ~ certainly not! ‖ τόσος ~ only so tall, so small.

δάγκωμα, τό [ðangoma] bite.

δαγκώνω [ðangono] bite.

δαδί, τό [ðaðee] pinewood, firewood.

δαίδαλος [ðeðalos] labyrinthine, intricate, complicated.

δαιμονίζω [ðemoneezo] enrage, infuriate.

δαιμονισμένος [ðemoneesmenos] (μεταφ) mischievous ‖ possessed.

δαιμόνιον, τό [ðemoneeon] genius ‖ (διάβολος) demon, fiend.

δαιμόνιος [ðemoneeos] very clever, marvellous, divine.

δαίμων, ὁ [ðemon] demon, devil, fiend.

δάκρυ, τό [ðakree] tear.

δακρύζω [ðakreezo] shed tears, weep ‖ (ἐπί φυτῶν) sweat ‖ (ἐπί ἀγγείων) ooze.

δακτυλήθρα, ἡ [ðakteeleethra] thimble.

δακτυλίδι, τό [ðakteeleeðee] ring.

δακτυλικός [ðakteeleekos] digital, dactylic.

δάκτυλο, τό [ðakteelo] βλ **δάκτυλος**.

δακτυλογράφος, ὁ, ἡ [ðakteeloyrafos] typist.

δάκτυλος, ὁ [ðakteelos] finger ‖ (ποδιοῦ) toe ‖ (μονάς μήκους) inch ‖ (ποίησις) dactyl.

δαμάζω [ðamazo] tame, subdue.

δαμαλίζω [ðamaleezo] vaccinate.

δαμαλισμός, ὁ [ðamaleesmos] vaccination.

δαμάσκηνον, τό [ðamaskeenon] plum ‖ (ξηρό) prune.

δανείζομαι [ðaneezome] borrow.

δανείζω [ðaneezo] lend, loan.

δάνειον, τό [ðaneeon] loan.

δανειστής, ὁ [ðaneestees] lender, creditor.

Δανία, ἡ [ðaneea] Denmark.

δαντέλλα, ἡ [ðantella] lace.

δαπάνη, ἡ [ðapanee] expenditure, expense, cost.

δαπανηρός [ðapaneeros] costly, expensive.

δαπανῶ [ðapano] spend, consume.

δάπεδον, τό [ðapeðon] floor ‖ ground.

δαρμός, ὁ [ðarmos] βλ **δάρσιμο**.

δάρσιμο, τό [ðarseemo] beating ‖ (γάλακτος) churning.

δασεῖα, ἡ [ðaseea] rough breathing (in Greek grammar).

δασκάλα, ἡ [ðaskala] βλ **διδασκάλισσα**.

δασκαλεύω [ðaskalevo] coach, teach.

δάσκαλος, ὁ [ðaskalos] βλ **διδάσκαλος**.

δασμολόγιον, τό [ðasmoloyeeon] tariff.

δασμός, ὁ [ðasmos] tax, (customs) duty.

δάσος, τό [ðasos] forest, woodland.

δασύλλιον, τό [ðaseeleeon] thicket, grove.

δασύς, ὁ [ðasees] thick, bushy, hairy.

δασύτης, ἡ [ðaseetees] thickness, density.

δασώδης [ðasoðees] wooded, woody.

δαυλί, τό [ðavlee] torch, firebrand.

δάφνη, ἡ [ðafnee] laurel, bay tree, bay.

δαψίλεια, ἡ [ðapseeleea] abundance.

δαψιλής [ðapseelees] abundant, profuse.

δέ [ðe]: ὁ μέν ... ὁ — the one ... the other ‖ and ‖ but ‖ on the other hand.

δεδομένα, τά [ðeðomena] πλ data, facts.

δεδουλεμένος [ðeðoulemenos]: ~ τόκος accrued interest.

δέησις, ή [deesees] prayer, supplication.

δεῖ [dee] there is need, it is necessary.

δεῖγμα, τό [deeyma] sample, specimen ‖ (ἔνδειξις) token, sign.

δειγματολόγιον, τό [deeymatoloyeeòn] sample, collection.

δεικνύω [deekneeo] show, point out ‖ (ἐπί ὀργάνων) mark, indicate.

δείκτης, ὁ [deektees] indicator ‖ (χειρός) forefinger ‖ (ὡρολογίου) hand ‖ (ζυγοῦ) index, cock ‖ (πυξίδος) needle.

δεικτικός [deekteekos] indicative ‖ (γραμμ) demonstrative.

δειλά [deela] timidly, faint-heartedly.

δείλι, τό [deelee] (late) afternoon.

δειλία, ή [deeleea] timidity, cowardice.

δειλιάζω [deeleeazo] lose courage, be afraid.

δειλινό, τό [deeleeno] afternoon.

δειλός [deelos] timid ‖ cowardly, faint-hearted.

δεινός [deenos] horrid ‖ (ἱκανός) able, clever, expert.

δεισιδαιμονία, ή [deeseedemoneea] super-stition.

δεισιδαίμων [deeseedemon] superstitious.

δείχνω [deehno] βλ δεικνύω.

δέκα [deka] ten.

δεκάγωνον, τό [dekayonon] decagon.

δεκαδικός [dekadeekos] decimal.

δεκαεννέα [dekaenea] nineteen.

δεκαέξ [dekaeks] sixteen.

δεκαεπτά [dekaepta] seventeen.

δεκαετηρίς, ή [dekaeteerees] decade ‖ (ἑορτή) tenth anniversary.

δεκαετής, ὁ, ή [dekaetees] ten-year-old.

δεκαετία, ή [dekaeteea] ten years, decade.

δεκάζω [dekazo] corrupt, bribe.

δεκάκις [dekakees] tenfold.

δεκάλογος, ὁ [dekaloyos] decalogue, Ten Commandments.

δεκανεύς, ὁ [dekanevs] corporal.

δεκανίκι, τό [dekaneekee] crutch.

δεκαπενθήμερον, τό [dekapentheemeron] fortnight.

δεκαπέντε [dekapente] fifteen.

δεκαπλάσιος [dekaplaseeos] tenfold.

δεκάρα [dekara] one tenth of a drachma.

δεκάρι, τό [dekaree] ten-drachma piece ‖ (στά χαρτιά) ten.

δεκάς, ή [dekas] set of ten.

δεκασμός, ὁ [dekasmos] bribery, corrup-tion.

δεκατέσσαρες [dekatessares] fourteen.

δέκατος [dekatos] tenth.

δεκατρείς [dekatrees] thirteen.

Δεκέμβριος, ὁ [dekemvreeos] December.

δέκτης, ὁ [dektees] receiver.

δεκτικός [dekteekos] capable of, suscep-tible to, receptive.

δεκτός [dektos] accepted ‖ (γνώμη) ad-missible.

δελεάζω [deleazo] tempt, entice, bait.

δέλεαρ, τό [delear] lure, bait.

δελεαστικός [deleasteekos] tempting, attractive.

δέλτα, τό [delta] (γράμμα) delta ‖ (ποταμοῦ) delta.

δελτάριον, τό [deltareeon] postcard, card ‖ bulletin.

δελτίον, τό [delteeon] bulletin ‖ (ὑγείας) report ‖ (ψηφοδέλτιον) ballot.

δελφίν, ὁ [delfeen] dolphin.

δέμα, τό [dema] (ἱμάς, κορδόνι) cord, ribbon ‖ (πάκο) bale, bundle ‖ (ταχυ-δρομικόν) parcel.

δεμάτι, τό [dematee] bundle ‖ (καρότων κτλ) bunch ‖ (φρυγάνων) faggot.

δέ(ν) [δe(n)] (negative particle) no, not.

δενδράκι, τό [dendrakee] small tree, shrub.

δενδρολίβανον, τό [dendroleevanon] rose-mary.

δένδρον, τό [dendron] tree.

δενδρόφυτος [dendrofeetos] full of trees, wooded.

δενδρύλλιον, τό [dendreeleeon] young tree, shrub.

δένω [deno] bind, tie ‖ (μέ ἁλυσίδα) chain, link ‖ (γραβάτα κτλ) tie ‖ (βιβλίο) bind ‖ (προσδένω) fasten, fix ‖ (καράβι) moor, berth ‖ (γλυκό κτλ) thicken ‖ (μεταφ) bind.

δεξαμενή, ή [deksamenee] tank, reservoir ‖ (ναυτ) dock, basin.

δεξιά, ή [deksia] right hand ‖ (σπόρ) right wing ‖ (ἐπιρ) to the right.

δεξιός [dekseeos] right ‖ right-handed ‖ (σπόρ) right-wing ‖ (ἐπιτήδειος) clever.

δεξιόστροφος [dekseeostrofos] clockwise (movement).

δεξιότης, ή [dekseeotees] skilfulness, cleverness.

δεξιόχειρ, ὁ [dekseeoheer] right-handed (person).

δεξιώνομαι [dekseeonome] receive, wel-come.

δεξίωσις, ή [dekseeosees] reception.

δέομαι [deome] have need of ‖ (προσ-εύχομαι) pray, beg, beseech.

δέον, τό [deon] what is needful.

δεόντως [deontos] suitably, fitly, properly.

δέος, τό [deos] awe, fear, fright.

δέρας, τό [deras]: τό χρυσόμαλλον ~ the golden fleece.

δέρμα, τό [derma] skin, pelt ‖ leather.

δερμάτινος [dermateenos] of leather.

δερματῖτις, ή [dermateetees] dermatitis.

δερματοπώλης, ὁ [dermatopolees] leather merchant.

δέρνω [derno] beat, flog ‖ (γάλα) churn.

δέσιμον, τό [deseemon] tying, binding ‖ bandage.

δεσμά, τά [desma] πλ chains, fetters, bonds.

δέσμευσις, ή [desmevsees] tying, binding.

δεσμεύω [desmevo] bind by a promise, pledge.

δέσμη, ή [desmee] bunch ‖ (φύλλων) bundle ‖ (παιγνιοχάρτων) pack.

δέσμιος, ό [desmeeos] prisoner, captive.

δεσμίς, ή [desmees] (χάρτου) ream of paper.

δεσμός, ό [desmos] tie, bond.

δεσμοφύλαξ, ό [desmofeelaks] prison warder.

δεσπόζω [despozo] dominate, rule ‖ (ὑπέρκειμαι) tower above, overlook ‖ (μεταφ) rise above.

δέσποινα, ή [despeena] mistress, madame.

δεσποινίς, ή [despeenees] young lady ‖ Miss.

δεσπότης, ό [despotees] ruler, master ‖ (ἐκκλ) (arch)bishop.

δεσποτικός [despoteekos] despotic.

δέστρα, ή [δestra] stake.

δετός [δetos] tied, bound.

δεῦτε [δevte] (ἐπιφ) come!

Δευτέρα, ή [δevtera] Monday.

δευτερεύων [δevterevon] secondary ‖ subordinate.

δευτέρι, τό [δevteree] account book.

δευτεροβάθμιος [δevterovathmeeos] second-degree.

δευτεροετής [δevteroetees] of the second year.

δευτερόλεπτον, τό [δevterolepton] second.

δεύτερος [δevteros] second ‖ (σέ ποιότητα) inferior.

δευτερότοκος [δevterotokos] second-born.

δέχομαι [δehome] accept, receive ‖ (παραδέχομαι) approve ‖ (δεξιοῦμαι) welcome, greet ‖ (ὑφίσταμαι) receive ‖ (ἀνέχομαι) tolerate.

δήγμα, τό [δeeγma] bite ‖ (ἑρπετοῦ) sting.

δῆθεν [δeethen] apparently, so-called, as if.

δηκτικός [δeekteekos] biting, scathing.

δηλαδή [δeelaδee] that is to say, namely, viz.

δηλητηριάζω [δeeleeteereeazo] poison ‖ (μεταφ) corrupt, taint.

δηλητηρίασις [δeeleeteereeasees] poisoning ‖ (μεταφ) corruption.

δηλητήριον, τό [δeeleeteereeon] poison, venom.

δηλοποιῶ [δeelopeeo] βλ δηλώνω.

δῆλος [δeelos] manifest, obvious.

δηλώνω [δeelono] declare, state ‖ (γέννησιν κτλ) register, give notice ‖ (ἐμπόρευμα) enter (goods).

δήλωσις, ή [δeelosees] declaration, statement ‖ (γέννησις κτλ) register.

δημαρχεῖον, τό [δeemarheeon] town hall ‖ (US) city hall.

δήμαρχος, ό [δeemarhos] mayor.

δήμευσις, ή [δeemevsees] confiscation.

δημεύω [δeemevo] confiscate, seize.

δημηγορία, ή [δeemeeγoreea] harangue.

δημητριακός [δeemeetreeakos]: τά δημητριακά cereals, crops.

δήμιος, ό [δeemeeos] executioner, hangman.

δημιουργία, ή [δeemeeourγeea] creation.

δημιουργικός [δeemeeourγeekos] creative.

δημιουργός, ό [δeemeeourγos] creator.

δημιουργῶ [δeemeeourγo] create ‖ establish.

δημογέρων, ό [δeemoγeron] elder.

δημοδιδάσκαλος, ό [δeemoδeeδaskalos] primary schoolteacher.

δημοκοπία, ή [δeemokopeea] demagogy.

δημοκράτης, ό [δeemokratees] democrat.

δημοκρατία, ή [δeemokrateea] democracy ‖ republic.

δημοκρατικός [δeemokrateekos] democratic, republican.

δημοπρασία, ή [δeemopraseea] auction.

δῆμος, ό [δeemos] municipality.

δημοσία [δeemoseea] (ἐπιρ) publicly.

δημοσίευμα, τό [δeemoseevma] newspaper article, publication.

δημοσίευσις, ή [δeemoseevsees] publication.

δημοσιεύω [δeemoseevo] publish, make known.

δημοσιογράφος, ό [δeemoseeoγrafos] journalist, reporter.

δημόσιον, τό [δeemoseeon] the state, the public.

δημόσιος [δeemoseeos] public ‖ (κρατικός) national.

δημοσιότης, ή [δeemoseeotees] publicity.

δημότης, ό [δeemotees] citizen.

δημοτική, ή [δeemoteekee] demotic (Greek).

δημοτικός [δeemoteekos] municipal ‖ (δημοφιλής) popular.

δημοτικότης, ή [δeemoteekotees] popularity.

δημοφιλής [δeemofeelees] popular, well-liked.

δημοψήφισμα, τό [δeemopseefeesma] plebiscite.

δημώδης [δeemoδees] popular, folk.

δηώνω [δeeono] ravage, plunder.

διά [δia] for, by, with, about ‖ (μετά γενικῆς) through, across, by means of ‖ ~ παντός forever ‖ ~ μιᾶς at one go ‖ ~ θαλάσσης by sea.

διαβάζω [δeeavazo] read, study ‖ (μετά προσοχῆς) peruse.

διαβάθμισις, ή [δeeavathmeesees] grading, graduation.

διαβαίνω [δeeaveno] pass, go across, pass through.

διαβάλλω [δeeavalo] slander, defame, calumniate.

διάβασις, ή [δeeavasees] crossing, passage ‖ (στενόν) pass, ford.

διάβασμα, τό [δeeavasma] reading, lecture ‖ studying.

διαβασμένος [δeeavasmenos] learned, prepared (for examination).

διαβατήριον, τό [δeeavateereeon] passport.

διαβάτης, ό [δeeavatees] passer-by.

διαβατικός [δeeavateekos] passing by, transient.

διαβατός [δeeavatos] passable ‖ (ποταμός) fordable.

διαβεβαιώνω [δeeaveveono] assure, assert, affirm.

διαβεβαίωσις, ἡ [δeeaveveosees] assurance, affirmation.

διάβημα, τό [δeeaveema] step, measure, move.

διαβήτης, ὁ [δeeaveetees] pair of compasses ‖ (ἰατρ) diabetes.

διαβιβάζω [δeeaveevazo] transmit, forward, convey.

διαβίβασις, ἡ [δeeaveevasees] transmission, forwarding.

διαβιβρώσκω [δeeaveevrosko] corrode ‖ (σκώληξ) eat into ‖ (θάλασσα κτλ) erode.

διαβίωσις, ἡ [δeeaveeosees] living.

διαβλέπω [δeeavlepo] discern, penetrate, foresee.

διαβόητος [δeeavoeetos] notorious.

διαβολάκι, τό [δeeavolakee] little devil.

διαβολεμένος [δeeavolemenos] shrewd, cunning ‖ (μεταφ) devilish.

διαβολή, ἡ [δeeavolee] slander, calumny.

διαβολικός [δeeavoleekos] satanic, diabolical.

διάβολος, ὁ [δeeavolos] devil, satan ‖ (φασαρίας) noisy, boisterous.

διαβουλεύομαι [δeeavoulevome] deliberate, confer ‖ (μηχανορραφῶ) plot.

διαβρέχω [δeeavreho] wet, soak, steep.

διάβροχος [δeeavrohos] drenched.

διάβρωσις, ἡ [δeeavrosees] corrosion.

διαγγέλλω [δeeangelo] announce, notify.

διαγινώσκω [δeeayeenosko] discern, distinguish ‖ (ἰατρ) diagnose.

διάγνωσις, ἡ [δeeaynosees] diagnosis.

διάγραμμα, τό [δeeayrama] diagram, drawing, plan.

διαγραφή, ἡ [δeeayrafee] cancellation.

διαγράφω [δeeayrafo] trace out ‖ (σβήνω) efface, cancel ‖ (περιγράφω) depict, picture.

διάγω [δeeayo] live, pass one's time.

διαγωγή, ἡ [δeeayoyee] behaviour, conduct, deportment.

διαγωνίζομαι [δeeayoneezome] compete, contend.

διαγώνιος [δeeayoneeos] diagonal.

διαγωνισμός, ὁ [δeeayoneesmos] competition ‖ (ἐξετάσεις) examination.

διαδέχομαι [δeeaδehome] succeed, follow.

διάδηλος [δeeaδeelos] manifest, evident.

διαδήλωσις, ἡ [δeeaδeelosees] demonstration, manifestation.

διάδημα, τό [δeeaδeema] crown, diadem.

διαδίδω [δeeaδeeδo] spread, circulate, propagate.

διαδικασία, ἡ [δeeaδeekaseea] procedure, legal inquiry.

διάδικος, ὁ, ἡ [δeeaδeekos] litigant.

διάδοσις, ἡ [δeeaδosees] spreading ‖ rumour.

διαδοχή, ἡ [δeeaδohee] succession.

διάδοχος, ὁ, ἡ [δeeaδohos] successor, crown prince.

διαδραματίζω [δeeaδramateezo] play (a role), act.

διαδρομή, ἡ [δeeaδromee] course, distance ‖ (ἐμβόλου) stroke.

διάδρομος, ὁ [δeeaδromos] passage, corridor, hall.

διαζευγνύω [δeeazevyneeo] separate ‖ (ξεζεύω) unyoke.

διαζευκτικός [δeeazevkteekos] (γραμμ) disjunctive.

διάζευξις, ἡ [δeeazevksees] separation, severance.

διαζύγιον, τό [δeeazeeyeeon] divorce.

διάζωμα, τό [δeeazoma] frieze.

διαθέσιμος [δeeatheseemos] available, free.

διάθεσις, ἡ [δeeathesees] arrangement, disposal ‖ (κέφι) mood, humour.

διαθέτω [δeeatheto] dispose, arrange ‖ (χρησιμοποιῶ) employ, use, make available ‖ (διανέμω) allot.

διαθήκη, ἡ [δeeatheekee] will, testament.

διάθλασις, ἡ [δeeathlasees] refraction.

διαίρεσις, ἡ [δieresees] division, separation ‖ (μεταφ) discord, difference.

διαιρέτης, ὁ [δieretees] divisor, divider.

διαιρῶ [δiero] divide, separate.

διαισθάνομαι [δiesthanome] feel, have a presentiment.

διαίσθησις, ἡ [δiestheesees] presentiment.

δίαιτα, ἡ [δieta] diet.

διαιτησία, ἡ [δieteseea] arbitration.

διαιτητής, ὁ [δieteetees] arbiter ‖ (ποδοσφαίρου) referee ‖ umpire.

διαιωνίζω [δieoneezo] perpetuate ‖ protract.

διαιώνισις, ἡ [δieoneesees] perpetuation.

διακαής [δeeakaees] ardent, fervent, eager.

διακανονίζω [δiakanoneezo] regulate, adjust, settle.

διακατέχω [δeeakateho] possess.

διακαῶς [δeeakaos] ardently.

διάκειμαι [δeeakeeme] be disposed, be inclined.

διακεκριμένος [δeeakekreemenos] distinguished, eminent.

διάκενος [δeeakenos] empty, hollow, vacant ‖ τό διάκενον void, vacuum.

διακήρυξις, ἡ [δeeakeereeksees] declaration, proclamation.

διακηρύττω [δeeakeereeto] declare, proclaim, announce.

διακινδυνεύω [δeeakeenδeenevo] risk, endanger, hazard.

διακλάδωσις, ἡ [δeeaklaδosees] branching off, fork ‖ (δρόμου κτλ) branch.

διακοίνωσις, ἡ [δeeakeenosees] communication, diplomatic note.

διακομίζω [δeeakomeezo] transport, carry.

διακονιάρης, ὁ [δeeakoneearees] beggar.

διάκονος, ὁ [δeeakonos] deacon.

διακοπή, ή [deeakopee] suspension, interruption, recess ‖ (ρεύματος) cut.

διακόπτης, ὁ [deeakoptees] switch, stopcock.

διακόπτω [deeakopto] suspend, cut off, interrupt, discontinue.

διακορεύω [deeakorevo] deflower.

διάκος, ὁ [deeakos] deacon.

διακόσια [deeakoseea] two hundred.

διακόσμησις, ἡ [deeakosmeesees] decoration, embellishment.

διακοσμητής, ὁ [deeakosmeetees] decorator.

διάκοσμος, ὁ [deeakosmos] ornamentation, decoration.

διακοσμῶ [deeakosmo] decorate, adorn.

διακρίνω [deeakreeno] discern, discriminate.

διάκρισις, ἡ [deeakreesees] distinction ‖ (κρίσις) discretion.

διακύμανσις, ἡ [deeakeemansees] fluctuation, undulation.

διακωμῳδῶ [deeakomoδo] ridicule, satirize.

διαλαλῶ [deealalo] proclaim, broadcast, cry out.

διαλαμβάνω [deealamvano] contain, include.

διαλάμπω [deealambo] shine, glitter.

διαλανθάνω [deealanthano] escape unnoticed.

διαλεγμένος [deealeymenos] selected, chosen.

διαλέγομαι [deealeyome] converse, hold a discourse.

διαλέγω [deealeyo] choose, select, pick out.

διάλειμμα, τό [deealeema] interval, recess ‖ intermission.

διάλειψις, ἡ [deealeepsees] irregularity.

διαλεκτική, ἡ [deealekteekee] dialectics.

διαλεκτός [deealektos] chosen, select.

διάλεκτος, ἡ [deealektos] dialect, idiom.

διάλεξις [deealeksees] lecture ‖ conversation.

διαλεύκανσις, ἡ [deealevkansees] elucidation.

διαλλακτικός [deealakteekos] conciliatory.

διαλογή, ἡ [deealoyee] sorting.

διαλογίζομαι [deealoyeezome] meditate, consider.

διαλογισμός, ὁ [deealoyeesmos] reflection, thought.

διάλογος, ὁ [deealoyós] dialogue, conversation.

διάλυμα, τό [deealeema] solution.

διάλυσις, ἡ [deealeesees] dissolution, decomposition ‖ (ἐντός ὑγροῦ) solution ‖ (ἑταιρείας κτλ) liquidation ‖ (στρατ) disbanding.

διαλυτός [deealeetos] soluble, dissolvable.

διαλύω [deealeeo] dissolve ‖ (ἑταιρείαν) liquidate ‖ (συμβόλαιον κτλ) annul, cancel ‖ (ἐχθρόν) disband, defeat, scatter ‖ (ἀμφιβολίαν κτλ) dispel.

διαμάντι, τό [deeamantee] diamond ‖

διαμαντικά πλ jewellery, gems.

διαμαρτύρομαι [deeamarteerome] protest.

διαμαρτυρόμενος [deeamarteeromenos] Protestant.

διαμαρτυρῶ [deeamarteero] protest.

διαμάχη, ἡ [deeamahee] dispute, fight.

διαμελίζω [deeameleezo] dismember.

διαμένω [deeameno] reside, live, stay.

διαμέρισμα, τό [deeamereesma] region, constituency, district ‖ (οἰκία) apartment, flat.

διάμεσος [deeamesos] intermediary, intermediate.

διαμετακομίζω [deeametakomizo] convey, transport, carry.

διαμέτρημα, τό [deeametreema] bore, calibre.

διάμετρος, ἡ [deeametros] diameter ‖ gauge.

διαμηνύω [deeameeneeo] inform, apprise.

διαμοιράζω [deeameerazo] distribute, share.

διαμονή, ἡ [deeamonee] stay, residence, sojourn.

διαμορφώνω [deeamorfono] model, shape, form.

διαμφισβήτησις, ἡ [deeamfeesveeteesees] contestation, calling into question.

διαμφισβητῶ [deeamfeesveeto] question, contest, dispute.

διανέμω [deeanemo] distribute ‖ divide.

διανόησις, ἡ [deeanoeesees] thought ‖ intelligence.

διανοητικῶς [deeanoeeteekos] intellectually.

διάνοια, ἡ [deeaneea] intellect, mind.

διανοίγω [deeaneeyo] open (up).

διανομεύς, ὁ [deeanomevs] distributor ‖ (ταχυδρομικός) postman.

διανομή, ἡ [deeanomee] distribution.

διανοούμενοι, οἱ [deeanooumenee] πλ intellectuals.

διανυκτερεύω [deeaneekterevo] spend the night ‖ stay open all night.

διανύω [deeaneeo] go through, cover, terminate.

διαξιφισμός, ὁ [deeakseefeesmos] sword thrust ‖ fencing.

διαπασῶν, ἡ, τό [deeapason] tuning fork ‖ (μουσ) octave.

διαπεραιώνω [deeapereono] ferry over.

διαπεραστικός [deeaperasteekos] piercing, sharp ‖ (βροχή) drenching.

διαπερῶ [deeapero] pierce, penetrate, pass through.

διαπιστευτήριον, τό [deeapeestevteereeon]: τά διαπιστευτήρια credentials.

διαπιστώνω [deeapeestono] ascertain, find out, confirm.

διαπίστωσις, ἡ [deeapeestosees] ascertainment.

διάπλασις, ἡ [deeaplasees] (con)formation ‖ moulding.

διαπλάσσω [deeaplaso] form, shape ‖ (μεταφ) educate, train.

διάπλατα [deeaplata] wide open.

διαπλάτυνσις, ή [δeeaplateensees] widening.
διάπλευσις, ή [δeeaplevsees] crossing.
διαπλέω [δeeapleo] cross over, sail through.
διαπληκτισμός, ό [δeeapleekteesmos] dispute, quarrel.
διαπνοή, ή [δeeapnoee] respiration.
διαποικίλλω [δeeapeekeelo] embellish, diversify, vary.
διαπόρθμευσις, ή [δeeaporthmevsees] ferrying across.
διαποτίζω [δeeapoteezo] soak, saturate.
διαπραγματεύομαι [δeeapraɣmatevome] negotiate ‖ discuss.
διαπραγμάτευσις, ή [δeeapraɣmatevsees] negotiation.
διαπράττω [δeeaprato] perpetrate, commit.
διαπρεπής [δeeaprepees] eminent, distinguished.
διαπρέπω [δeeaprepo] excel.
διάπυρος [δeeapeeros] red-hot ‖ (μεταφ) fervent, eager.
διάρθρωσις, ή [δeearthrosees] articulation, joint, structure.
διάρκεια, ή [δeearkeea] duration.
διαρκῶ [δeearko] last, endure ‖ continue.
διαρκῶς [δeearkos] continually, constantly, always.
διαρπάζω [δeearpazo] pillage, plunder, loot.
διαρρέω [δeeareo] traverse ‖ (δοχεῖον) leak ‖ (ὑγροῦ, νέα κτλ) leak out ‖ (χρόνος) elapse, pass.
διαρρηγνύω [δeeareeɣneeo] tear, burst open, break.
διαρρήδην [δeeareeδeen] flatly, frankly, categorically.
διάρρηξις, ή [δeeareeksees] breaking, rupture ‖ (κλοπή) burglary.
διαρροή, ή [δeearoee] flow ‖ (σωλῆνος) leakage.
διάρροια, ή [δeeareea] diarrhoea.
διαρρυθμίζω [δeeareethmeezo] arrange, regulate.
διαρρύθμισις, ή [δeeareethmeesees] arrangement, regulation.
διασάλευσις, ή [δeeasalevsees] disturbance, agitation.
διασαφηνίζω [δeeasafeeneezo] clarify, elucidate.
διασαφήνισις, ή [δeeasafeeneesees] clarification, elucidation.
διασάφησις, ή [δeeasafeesees] βλ διασαφήνισις.
διάσεισις, ή [δeeaseesees] concussion, shock.
διάσελο, τό [δeeaselo] pass, saddle (in hills).
διάσημον, τό [δeeaseemon]: τά διάσημα insignia.
διάσημος [δeeaseemos] famous, celebrated, renowned.
διασκεδάζω [δeeaskeδazo] scatter, dispel ‖ (ψυχαγωγῶ) divert, amuse ‖ (ἀμεταβ) amuse o.s.

διασκέδασις, ή [δeeaskeδasees] dispersion ‖ (ψυχαγωγία) entertainment.
διασκεδαστικός [δeeaskeδasteekos] diverting, entertaining.
διασκευάζω [δeeaskevazo] arrange, modify, alter.
διασκευή, ή [δeeaskevee] arrangement, adaptation, modification.
διάσκεψις, ή [δeeaskepsees] deliberation ‖ conference.
διασκορπίζω [δeeaskorpeezo] scatter, disperse ‖ (χρῆμα) waste.
διασπαθίζω [δeeaspatheezo] waste, squander.
διάσπασις, ή [δeeaspasees] distraction ‖ (ἀτόμου) splitting.
διασπείρω [δeeaspeero] disseminate, disperse, scatter ‖ (μεταφ) circulate.
διασπορά, ή [δeeaspora] dispersion, scattering.
διασπῶ [δeeaspo] sever, separate with violence, rupture.
διασταλτικός [δeeastalteekos] dilating, dilative.
διάστασις, ή [δeeastasees] separation, disagreement ‖ (μέτρον) dimension.
διασταυρώνω [δeeastavrono] cross ‖ meet.
διασταύρωσις, ή [δeeastavrosees] crossing ‖ (δρόμων) intersection.
διαστέλλω [δeeastelo] distinguish ‖ (διανοίγω) distend, expand.
διάστημα, τό [δeeasteema] space, interval, period ‖ κατά διαστήματα from time to time ‖ at intervals.
διάστικτος [δeeasteektos] spotted, stippled ‖ tattooed.
διαστολή, ή [δeeastolee] distinction ‖ (καρδιᾶς) diastole ‖ (γραμμ) comma.
διαστρεβλώνω [δeeastrevlono] twist, bend ‖ (μεταφ) alter, distort.
διαστρέφω [δeeastrefo] twist, bend ‖ (μεταφ) pervert, corrupt.
διαστροφή, ή [δeeastrofee] perversion, distortion.
διασύρω [δeeaseero] (μεταφ) defame, slander, backbite.
διασχίζω [δeeasheezo] tear ‖ (μεταφ) cross, travel through.
διάσχισις, ή [δeeasheesees] crossing, traversing.
διασώζω [δeeasozo] preserve, rescue, deliver.
διάσωσις, ή [δeeasosees] deliverance, rescue, preservation.
διαταγή, ή [δeeatayee] order, command, instruction.
διάταγμα, τό [δeeataɣma] order, decree, edict.
διάταξις, ή [δeeataksees] arrangement ‖ (νόμου κτλ) provision.
διαταραξις, ή [δeeataraksees] disturbance, upheaval.
διαταράσσω [δeeataraso] disturb, agitate.

διατάσσω [δeeataso] arrange ‖ order, command.
διατείνομαι [δeeateenome] maintain, declare.
διατείνω [δeeateeno] stretch, tighten.
διατελῶ [δeeatelo] be, stand.
διατέμνω [δeeatemno] intersect, split.
διατήρησις [δeeateereesees] maintenance, preservation, conservation.
διατηρῶ [δeeateero] hold, maintain ‖ preserve, conserve ‖ (ψυχραιμίαν) keep.
διατί [δeeatee] why? ‖ τό ~ cause, reason.
διατίμησις, ἡ [δeeateemeesees] tariff, rate, price list.
διατιμῶ [δeeateemo] fix the price of, regulate the sale of.
διατομή [δeeatomee] cross-cut, cut.
διατράνωσις, ἡ [δeeatranosees] manifestation.
διατρέφω [δeeatrefo] keep, feed, support.
διατρέχω [δeeatreho] run through ‖ (ἀπόστασιν) cover, traverse.
διάτρησις, ἡ [δeeatreesees] perforation, drilling, cutting.
διάτρητος [δeeatreetos] perforated, holed, drilled.
διατριβή, ἡ [δeeatreevee] stay ‖ (μελέτη) study, thesis ‖ (ἀσχολία) pastime.
διατροφή, ἡ [δeeatrofee] feeding, board ‖ (ἐπί διαζυγίου) alimony.
διατρυπῶ [δeeatreepo] pierce, bore through.
διάττων, ὁ [δeeaton] shooting star.
διατυμπανίζω [δeeateembaneezo] divulge, let out, give away.
διατυπώνω [δeeateepono] formulate, state.
διαύγεια, ἡ [δeeavyeea] clearness, transparency.
διαφαίνομαι [δeeafenome] show through, appear, come in sight.
διαφανής [δeeafanees] clear, transparent.
διαφέρω [δeeafero] be different from, differ.
διαφεύγω [δeeafevyo] escape, get away, evade.
διαφημίζω [δeeafeemeezo] advertise.
διαφήμισις, ἡ [δeeafeemeesees] advertisement, advertising.
διαφημιστής, ὁ [δeeafeemeestees] advertiser.
διαφθείρω [δeeaftheero] spoil, damage ‖ (μεταφ) corrupt ‖ (κορίτσι) deflower.
διαφθορά, ἡ [δeeafthora] corruption, depravity.
διαφιλονεικῶ [δeeafeeloneeko] dispute, quarrel.
διαφορά, ἡ [δeeafora] difference ‖ dissension, contention.
διαφορετικός [δeeaforeteekos] different, dissimilar.
διαφορικόν, τό [δeeaforeekon] differential.
διαφορικός [δeeaforeekos] differential.
διάφορο, τό [δeeaforo] profit, interest, gain.
διαφοροποίησις, ἡ [δeeaforopieesees] differentiation.

διάφορος [δeeaforos] different, · various, mixed ‖ τά διάφορα miscellaneous.
διαφοροτρόπως [δeeaforotropos] diversely, variously.
διάφραγμα, τό [δeeafraɣma] partition ‖ (ἀνατ) diaphragm.
διαφυγή, ἡ [δeeafeeyee] escape, evasion ‖ (ὑγροῦ κτλ) leak, leakage.
διαφύλαξις, ἡ [δeeafeelaksees] preservation, protection.
διαφυλάσσω [δeeafeelaso] preserve, protect, keep.
διαφωνία, ἡ [δeeafoneea] discord, disagreement.
διαφωνῶ [δeeafono] disagree, differ.
διαφωτίζω [δeeafoteezo] clear up ‖ enlighten.
διαφώτισις, ἡ [δeeafoteesees] enlightenment.
διαχαράσσω [δeeaharaso] trace, mark out.
διαχειρίζομαι [δeeaheereezome] administer, manage, handle.
διαχείρισις, ἡ [δeeaheereesees] management, handling, administration.
διαχειριστής, ὁ [δeeaheereestees] administrator ‖ (στρατ) pay corps officer.
διαχέω [δeeaheo] diffuse, give out.
διάχυσις, ἡ [δeeaheesees] diffusion ‖ (μεταφ) effusiveness, gaiety.
διαχυτικός [δeeaheeteekos] effusive, gushing, demonstrative.
διάχυτος [δeeaheetos] diffuse.
διαχωρίζω [δeeahoreezo] separate, divide.
διαχώρισις, ἡ [δeeahoreesees] separation.
διαψεύδομαι [δeeapsevδome] contradict o.s., fail.
διαψεύδω [δeeapsevδo] deny, give the lie to ‖ disappoint.
διάψευσις, ἡ [δeeapsevsees] denial, contradiction ‖ disappointment.
διγαμία, ἡ [δeeyameea] bigamy.
δίγαμος, ὁ [δeeyamos] bigamist.
δίγλωσσος [δeeɣlosos] bilingual.
δίδαγμα, τό [δeeδaɣma] teaching, moral ‖ (ἐκκλ) lesson.
διδακτήριον, τό [δeeδakteereeon] institute, school.
διδακτικός [δeeδakteekos] instructive, didactic.
διδακτορία, ἡ [δeeδaktoreea] doctorate.
δίδακτρα, τά [δeeδaktra] πλ tuition fees.
διδάκτωρ, ὁ [δeeδaktor] doctor.
διδασκαλεῖον, τό [δeeδaskaleeon] teacher's training college.
διδασκαλία, ἡ [δeeδaskeleea] teaching, instruction ‖ (θέατρον) production.
διδασκάλισσα, ἡ [δeeδaskaleesa] schoolmistress.
διδάσκαλος, ὁ [δeeδaskalos] teacher, schoolmaster.
διδάσκω [δeeδasko] teach, instruct.
διδαχή, ἡ [δeeδahee] teaching ‖ (ἐκκλ) sermon.

δίδυμος [deedeemos] twin.

δίδω [deedo] give, grant ‖ (τιμή) offer ‖ (παράγω) produce, yield ‖ (μάχην) give battle ‖ (γροθιάν) deal a blow to.

διεγείρω [dieyeero] excite, rouse, incite.

διέγερσις, ή [dieyersees] excitation, stimulation.

διεζευγμένος [diezevgmenos] divorced.

διεθνής [diethnees] international.

διείσδυσις, ή [dieesdeesees] penetration, piercing.

διεισδύω [dieesdeeo] penetrate, enter, advance.

διεκδίκησις, ή [diekdeekeesees] claim, vindication.

διεκδικῶ [diekdeeko] claim, contest.

διεκπεραιώνω [diekpereono] finish off, forward.

διεκπεραίωσις, ή [diekpereosees] forwarding, consignment.

διεκφεύγω [diekfevyo] slip away, escape.

διελαύνω [dielavno] drive through ‖ (μεταφ) run through.

διέλευσις, ή [dielevsees] crossing, passing.

διένεξις, ή [dieneksees] dispute, quarrel.

διενεργῶ [dieneryo] operate, effect, hold.

διεξάγω [dieksayo] conduct, accomplish, carry out.

διεξέρχομαι [diekserhome] traverse, travel through ‖ (μεταφ) look into.

διεξοδικός [dieksodeekos] lengthy, extensive, detailed.

διέξοδος, ή [dieksodos] issue, outlet ‖ (μεταφ) way out, alternative.

διέπω [diepo] govern, rule.

διερεθίζω [dieretheezo] irritate.

διερεύνησις, ή [dierevneesees] investigation, research.

διερευνητικός [dierevneeteekos] searching, exploratory.

διερευνῶ [dierevno] search, explore, examine.

διερμηνεύς, ό [diermeenevs] interpreter, translator.

διερμηνευτής, ό [diermeenevtees] interpreter, explainer.

διερμηνεύω [diermeenevo] interpret, translate.

διέρχομαι [dierhome] pass by, cross ‖ (χρόνον) spend.

διερωτῶμαι [dierotome] ask o.s., wonder.

διεσπαρμένος [diesparmenos] dispersed.

διεστραμμένος [diestramenos] perverse, wicked.

διετής [dietees] lasting two years ‖ (ἐπί φυτῶν) biennial.

διετία, ή [dieteea] (space of) two years.

διευθέτης, ό [dievthetees] adjuster.

διευθέτησις, ή [dievtheteesees] arrangement, settlement.

διευθετῶ [dievtheto] arrange, settle ‖ adjust.

διεύθυνσις, ή [dievtheensees] address ‖ direction ‖ (ἑταιρείας) management.

διευθυντής, ό [dievtheentees] director ‖ (σχολῆς) principal ‖ (μουσ) conductor ‖ (θεάτρου) manager ‖ (ἐφημερίδος) editor ‖ (φυλακῶν) governor, warden ‖ (σωματείου) president ‖ (προσωπικοῦ) personnel manager.

διευθύνω [dievtheeno] direct, guide ‖ (ἐπιχείρησιν) manage ‖ (ἐφημερίδα) edit ‖ (βιομηχανίαν) handle, manage, direct ‖ (ἔργα) superintend, oversee ‖ (ὀρχήστραν) lead, conduct.

διευκόλυνσις, ή [dievkoleensees] easing, help.

διευκολύνω [dievkoleeno] facilitate, help forward.

διευκρίνησις, ή [dievkreeneesees] elucidation, explanation.

διευκρινίζω [dievkreeneezo] clear up, explain.

διεύρυνσις, ή [dievreensees] widening, broadening, enlargement.

διεφθαρμένος [dieftharmenos] corrupt, immoral, dissolute.

δίζυγον, τό [deezeeyon] πλ parallel bars.

διήγημα, τό [dieeyeema] story, tale.

διήγησις, ή [dieeyeesees] narration.

διηγοῦμαι [dieeyoume] narrate, relate, tell.

διήθησις, ή [dieetheesees] filtration, percolation.

διηθῶ [dieetho] filter, percolate.

διημέρευσις, ή [dieemerevsees] spending the day, staying all day.

διηνεκής [dieenekees] unceasing, incessant.

διηνεκῶς [dieenekos] continually.

διηρημένος [dieereemenos] divided, separated.

διθύραμβος, ό [deetheeramvos] dithyramb ‖ (μεταφ) bombast.

διΐσταμαι [dieestame] (μεταφ) stand apart ‖ (μεταφ) disagree.

διϊσχυρίζομαι [dieesheereezome] maintain.

δικάζω [deekazo] try, judge.

δικαιόγραφον, τό [deekeoyrafon] title deed.

δικαιοδοσία, ή [deekeodoseea] jurisdiction, province.

δικαιολόγησις, ή [deekeoloyeesees] justification, excuse.

δικαιολογητικά, τά [deekeoloyeeteeka] πλ supporting vouchers.

δικαιολογία, ή [deekeoloyeea] justification, excuse.

δικαιολογῶ [deekeoloyo] justify, excuse, vindicate.

δίκαιον, τό [deekeon] justice, right ‖ law.

δίκαιος [deekeos] fair, just, righteous.

δικαιοσύνη, ή [deekeoseenee] justice, fairness.

δικαιοῦχος, ό [deekeouhos] beneficiary.

δικαιώνω [deekeono] side with ‖ justify, vindicate.

δικαίωμα, τό [deekeoma] right, claim.

δικαίωσις, ή [deekeosees] justification, vindication.

δίκανον, τό [δeekanon] double-barrelled shotgun.

δικάσιμος, ή [δeekaseemos] day of trial.

δικαστήριον, τό [δeekasteereeon] court of justice, tribunal.

δικαστής, ὁ [δeekastees] judge, justice, magistrate.

δικαστικός [δeekasteekos] judicial, judiciary.

δικέλλα, ή [δeekela] two-pronged fork.

δικέφαλος [δeekefálos] two-headed.

δίκη, ή [δeekee] trial, suit, lawsuit, case.

δικηγόρος, ὁ, ή [δeekeeyoros] lawyer, barrister, attorney.

δικηγορῶ [δeekeeyoro] practise as a lawyer, plead.

δίκην [δeekeen] (ἐπιρ) after the manner of, like.

δικλείς, ή [δeeklees] valve.

δικογραφία, ή [δeekoyrafeea] file of proceedings || (δικηγόρου) brief.

δικονομία, ή [δeekonomeea] procedure.

δίκοχον, τό [δeekohon] forage cap.

δίκρανον, τό [δeekranon] pitchfork.

δίκταμο, τό [δeektamo] dittany.

δικτατορία, ή [δeektatoreea] dictatorship.

δικτατορικός [δeektatoreekos] dictatorial.

δίκτυον, τό [δeekteeon] net, network || (μεταφ) snare, trap.

δικτυωτόν, τό [δeekteeoton] wire netting, lattice, grille, trellis.

δίλημμα, τό [δeeleema] dilemma.

διμερής [δeemerees] bipartite.

διμοιρία, ή [δeemeereea] platoon, section.

δίνη, ή [δeenee] whirlpool, whirlwind.

δίνω [δeeno] βλ δίδω.

διό [δio] therefore, hence.

διογκώνω [δeeongono] swell, inflate.

διόγκωσις, ή [δeeongosees] swelling, inflation.

διόδια, τά [δeeoδeea] πλ toll || (ναυτ) port toll.

δίοδος, ή [δeeoδos] passage, pass, defile.

διοίκησις, ή [δieekeesees] administration, command.

διοικητήριον, τό [δieekeeteereeon] prefecture, commissioner's office.

διοικητής, ὁ [δieekeetees] governor, commandant, commissioner.

διοικητικός [δieekeeteekos] administrative.

διοικῶ [δieeko] administer, govern, rule, command.

διολισθαίνω [δeeoleestheno] slip through.

διόλου [δeeolou] (ἐπιρ) not at all || ὅλως ~ entirely, quite.

διομολογῶ [δeeomoloyo] stipulate, agree.

διονυχίζω [δeeoneeheezo] scrutinize, sift.

διοξείδιον, τό [δeeokseeδeeon] dioxide.

διόπερ [δeeoper] wherefore, hence.

διοπτεύω [δeeoptevo] observe with field glasses || (ναυτ) take bearings of.

διόπτρα, τά [δeeoptra] πλ spectacles, glasses.

διόπτρα, ή [δeeoptra] binoculars.

διόρασις, ή [δeeorasees] perspicuity.

διορατικός [δeeorateekos] clear-sighted || (πνεῦμα) shrewd, keen.

διορατικότης, ή [δeeorateekotees] perspicacity.

διοργανώνω [δeeoryanono] organize, form, arrange.

διοργάνωσις, ή [δeeoryanosees] organization, arrangement.

διορθώνω [δeeorthono] correct, put straight || (πανταλόνι) patch, mend || (μεταφ) remedy, make good.

διόρθωσις, ή [δeeorthosees] correction, putting right.

διορθωτής, ὁ [δeeorthotees] (τυπογρ) proofreader.

διορία, ή [δeeoreea] time limit, term, delay.

διορίζω [δeeoreezo] appoint || order, fix.

διορισμός, ὁ [δeeoreesmos] appointment.

διόρυξις, ή [δeeoreeksees] digging, excavation.

διορρύσσω [δeeoreeso] dig out, scoop out, excavate.

διορῶ [δeeoro] βλ διαβλέπω.

διότι [δeeotee] because.

διουρητικός [δeeoureeteekos] diuretic.

διοχέτευσις, ή [δeeohetevsees] (ἠλεκ) conduct || (ὕδατος) conveyance.

διοχετεύω [δeeohetevo] conduct, convey || (μεταφ) transmit, divert.

δίπατος [δeepatos] two-storeyed.

δίπλα, ή [δeepla] fold, pleat, wrinkle.

δίπλα [δeepla] (ἐπιρ) by, near, next door, close.

διπλά [δeepla] twice as much.

διπλανός [δeeplanos] nearby, next-door, adjacent.

διπλαρώνω [δeeplarono] accost || (ναυτ) come alongside.

διπλασιάζω [δeeplaseeazo] double.

διπλασιασμός, ὁ [δeeplaseeasmos] reduplication.

διπλάσιος [δeeplaseeos] double, twice as much.

διπλόγραφον, τό [δeeployrafon] duplicate.

διπλότυπον, τό [δeeploteepon] duplicate, stub.

διπλοῦς [δeeplous] double.

δίπλωμα, τό [δeeploma] diploma, degree || (τύλιγμα) folding, wrapping.

διπλωμάτης, ὁ [δeeplomatees] diplomat.

διπλωματία, ή [δeeplomateea] diplomacy.

διπλωματικός [δeeplomateekos] diplomatic.

διπλωματοῦχος [δeeplomatouhos] possessing a diploma, holding a degree.

διπλώνω [δeeplono] fold.

δίπλωσις, ή [δeeplosees] folding, wrapping.

δίπους [δeepous] two-legged, two-footed.

διπρόσωπος [δeeprosopos] two-faced, deceitful.

δισυρίτης, ή [δeepeereetees] hard tack.

δίς [δees] twice.

δισάκκι, τό [δeesakee] saddlebag, travelling bag.

δισέγγονος, ὁ, ἡ [δeesengonos] great-grandchild.

δισεκατομμύριον, τό [δeesekatomeereeon] billion.

δίσεκτον, τό [δeesekton]: ~ ἔτος leap year.

δισκίον, τό [δeeskeeon] tray ‖ (ἰατρ) tablet.

δισκοβόλος, ὁ [δeeskovolos] discus thrower.

δισκοπότηρον, τό [δeeskopoteeron] chalice.

δίσκος, ὁ [δeeskos] tray ‖ (ζυγοῦ) pan, scale ‖ (ἀθλητ) discus ‖ (ἡλίου κτλ) disk ‖ (ἐκκλ) collection plate ‖ (φωνογράφου) record.

δισταγμός, ὁ [δeestaymos] hesitation, doubt.

διστάζω [δeestazo] hesitate, doubt.

διστακτικός [δeestakteekos] hesitant, irresolute.

δίστηλος [δeesteelos] two-columned.

δίστιχον, τό [δeesteehon] distich, couplet.

δισύλλαβος [δeeseelavos] of two syllables.

δισχιδής [δeesheeδees] bifurcated.

δισχίλιοι [δeesheeliee] two thousand.

δίτροχος [δeetrohos] two-wheeled.

διττανθρακικός [δeetanthrakeekos] bicarbonate.

διττῶς [δeetos] doubly.

διϋλίζω [δieeleezo] filter, distil, strain.

διϋλισις [δieeleesees] filtering, straining.

διϋλιστήριον, τό [δieeleesteereeon] filter, strainer ‖ (πετρελαίου) refinery.

διφθερῖτις, ἡ [δeefthereetees] diphtheria.

δίφθογγος, ἡ [δeefthongos] diphthong.

διφορούμενος [δeeforoumenos] ambiguous ‖ τό διφορούμενον ambiguity.

δίφραγκο, τό [δeefrango] two-drachma piece.

δίφυλλος [δeefeelos] two-leaved.

διχάζομαι [δeehazome] (μεταφ) become disunited, disagree.

διχάζω [δeehazo] divide, split ‖ (μεταφ) estrange, disunite.

διχάλη, ἡ [δeehalee] pitchfork.

διχαλωτός [δeehalotos] forked, cloven.

διχασμός, ὁ [δeehasmos] division ‖ disagreement.

διχογνωμία, ἡ [δeehoynomeea] dissent, disagreement.

διχόνοια, ἡ [δeehoneea] dissension, discord.

δίχορδος [δeehorδos] two-stringed.

διχοτομία, ἡ [δeehotomeea] bisection.

διχοτόμος [δeehotomos] bisector.

διχοτομώ [δeehotomo] bisect.

δίχρονος [δeehronos] (μηχανή) two-stroke (engine).

δίχως [δeehos] without ‖ ~ ἄλλο without fail.

δίψα, ἡ [δeepsa] thirst.

διψασμένος [δeepsasmenos] thirsty, eager (for).

διψῶ [δeepso] feel thirsty ‖ thirst for, be eager for.

διωγμός [δeeoymos] persecution.

διώκω [δeeoko] pursue, chase, expel, persecute ‖ (μεταφ) banish, dispel.

διώνυμον, τό [δeeoneemon] binomial.

δίωξις, ἡ [δeeoksees] persecution, hunting.

διωρισμένος [δeeoreesmenos] appointed.

διώροφος [δeeorofos] two-storeyed.

διῶρυξ, ἡ [δeeoreeks] canal.

διωστήρ, ὁ [δeeosteer] connecting rod.

διώχνω [δeeohno] βλ διώκω.

δόγμα, τό [δoyma] dogma, creed, doctrine.

δογματικός [δoymateekos] dogmatic(al).

δοθιήν, ὁ [δotheeen] boil.

δόκανον, τό [δokanon] trap ‖ (μεταφ) lure, snare.

δοκάρι, τό [δokaree] beam, rafter, girder.

δοκιμάζω [δokeemazo] taste, try out ‖ (αὐτοκίνητο) test, try ‖ (ἐνδυμασία) fit ‖ (ὑποφέρω) undergo, suffer.

δοκιμασία, ἡ [δokeemaseea] suffering.

δοκιμαστικός [δokeemasteekos] trial, test ‖ ~ σωλήν test tube.

δοκιμή, ἡ [δokeemee] trial, test, testing ‖ (θέατρον) rehearsal ‖ (ροῦχα) fitting.

δοκίμιον, τό [δokeemeeon] treatise ‖ (τυπογρ) printer's proof.

δόκιμος [δokeemos] esteemed, first-rate ‖ ὁ ~ cadet.

δοκός, ἡ [δokos] girder, beam.

δοκοῦν, τό [δokoon]: κατά τό ~ at pleasure, at will.

δόλιος [δoleeos] fraudulent, crafty.

δόλιος [δoleeos] wretched, unlucky, poor.

δολιότης, ἡ [δoleeotees] deceit, fraudulence, fraud.

δολοπλόκος [δoloplokos] treacherous, artful.

δόλος, ὁ [δolos] fraud, deceit, guile.

δολοφονία, ἡ [δolofoneea] murder.

δολοφονικός [δolofoneekos] murderous.

δολοφόνος, ὁ, ἡ [δolofonos] assassin, murderer.

δολοφονῶ [δolofono] murder, assassinate.

δόλωμα, τό [δoloma] bait, decoy.

δόνησις, ἡ [δoneesees] vibration ‖ (σεισμός) tremor, shock.

δόντι, τό [δontee] tooth ‖ (ἐλέφαντος) tusk ‖ (μηχαν) cog.

δοντιά, ἡ [δontia] bite.

δονῶ [δono] vibrate, shake.

δόξα, ἡ [δoksa] glory.

δοξάζω [δoksazo] glorify, celebrate, extol.

δοξάρι, τό [δoksaree] (μουσ) bow.

δοξασία, ἡ [δoksaseea] belief.

δοξολογία, ἡ [δoksoloyeea] doxology, Te Deum.

δοξομανής [δoksomanees] ambitious, pretentious.

δορά, ἡ [δora] skinning ‖ skin, hide.

δορκάς, ἡ [δorkas] roebuck.

δόρυ, τό [δoree] spear.

δορυφόρος, ὁ [δoreeforos] satellite.

δοσίλογος [δoseeloyos] quisling.

δόσις, ἡ [dosees] portion ‖ dose ‖ (πληρωμή) instalment.

δοσοληψία, ἡ [dosoleepseea] transaction.

δοτική, ἡ [doteekee] (γραμμ) dative (case).

δουκᾶτον, τό [doukaton] duchy ‖ (νόμισμα) ducat.

δούκισσα, ἡ [doukeesa] duchess.

δούλα, ἡ [doula] servant girl, maidservant.

δουλεία, ἡ [douleea] slavery, servitude.

δουλειά, ἡ [doulia] work, affair, business.

δούλεμα, τό [doulema] teasing.

δουλευτής, ὁ [doulevtees] hard worker, industrious worker.

δουλεύω [doulevo] work, operate ‖ (ἔχω δουλειά) have a job ‖ (ὡρολόγι κτλ) work, operate ‖ (περιπαίζω) tease.

δούλη, ἡ [doulee] slave.

δουλικός [douleekos] servile, slavish.

δουλοπάροικος, ὁ [doulopareekos] serf.

δουλοπρεπής [douloprepees] servile, mean.

δοῦλος, ὁ [doulos] slave ‖ servant.

δουλώνω [doulono] enslave, subjugate.

δοῦναι, τό [doune] (ἔμπορ) debit.

δούξ, ὁ [douks] duke.

δοῦπος, ὁ [doupos] thump, bump.

δοχεῖον, τό [doheeon] receptacle, vessel, pot.

δρακόντειος [drakonteeos] (μεταφ) severe, harsh.

δράκος, ὁ [drakos] ogre, dragon.

δρᾶμα, τό [drama] drama ‖ (μεταφ) trouble.

δραματική, ἡ [dramateekee] πλ dramatics.

δραματικός [dramateekos] dramatic, tragic.

δράμιον, τό [drameeon] dram ‖ (μεταφ) tiny amount.

δράξ, ἡ [draks] handful.

δραπετεύω [drapetevo] escape.

δραπέτης [drapetees] fugitive.

δράσις, ἡ [drasees] activity, action ‖ ἄμεσος ~ flying squad.

δραστήριος [drasteereeos] active, energetic, vigorous.

δραστηριότης, ἡ [drasteereeotees] activity, energy, effectiveness.

δράστης, ὁ [drastees] perpetrator, culprit.

δραστικός [drasteekos] efficacious, drastic, effective.

δράττομαι [dratome] seize, grasp ‖ (μεταφ) avail o.s. of ‖ ~ τῆς εὐκαιρίας take the opportunity.

δραχμή, ἡ [drahmee] drachma.

δρεπάνι, τό [drepanee] βλ δρέπανον.

δρέπανον, τό [drepanon] sickle.

δριμέως [dreemeos] acutely, harshly.

δριμύς [dreemees] sharp, bitter, severe, keen.

δρομαῖος [dromeos] precipitate, hasty.

δρομάς, ἡ [dromas] dromedary.

δρομεύς, ὁ [dromevs] runner.

δρομίσκος, ὁ [dromeeskos] narrow street, lane.

δρομολόγιον, τό [dromoloyeeon] itinerary ‖ timetable.

δρόμος, ὁ [dromos] road, street ‖ (ἀθλητ) race ‖ (ἀπόστασι) distance.

δροσερός [droseros] cool, fresh.

δροσερότης, ἡ [droserotees] coolness, freshness.

δροσιά, ἡ [drosia] freshness ‖ dew.

δροσίζομαι [droseezome] refresh o.s., cool down.

δροσίζω [droseezo] cool, refresh ‖ get cool.

δροσιστικός [droseesteekos] refreshing.

δρόσος, ἡ [drosos] dew.

δρύϊνος [drieenos] oak(en).

δρυμός, ὁ [dreemos] forest, wood.

δρυοκολάπτης, ὁ [dreeokolaptees] woodpecker.

δρῦς, ἡ [drees] oak.

δρύφρακτον, τό [dreefrakton] balustrade, barrier.

δρῶ [dro] act, do, take effect.

δυαδικός [deeadeekos] binary ‖ dual.

δυάρι, τό [deearee] (στά χαρτιά) deuce.

δυάς, ἡ [deeas] couple, pair.

δυϊκός [dieekos] (γραμμ) dual (number).

δύναμαι [deename] can, may ‖ be able to.

δυναμική, ἡ [deenameekee] dynamics.

δυναμικός [deenameekos] energetic, dynamic.

δύναμις, ἡ [deenamees] strength, might, power, force.

δυναμῖτις, ἡ [deenameetees] dynamite.

δυναμό, τό [deenamo] dynamo.

δυνάμωμα, τό [deenamoma] intensification, strengthening.

δυναμώνω [deenamono] strengthen, make stronger ‖ (ὑγείαν) become stronger.

δυναμωτικός [deenamoteekos] fortifying, strengthening ‖ (ἰατρ) tonic.

δυναστεία, ἡ [deenasteea] dynasty, regime, rule.

δυνάστης, ὁ [deenastees] ruler, potentate ‖ (μεταφ) oppressor, despot.

δυνατά [deenata] strongly, hard ‖ loudly.

δυνατός [deenatos] strong, powerful ‖ (κυβέρνησις) powerful ‖ (φωνή) loud ‖ (ἄνοδος) possible ‖ δυνατόν! possibly!, maybe!

δυνατότης, ἡ [deenatotees] possibility.

δυνητική, ἡ [deeneeteekee] (γραμμ) conditional (mood).

δύο [deeo] two.

δυόσμος, ὁ [deeosmos] mint, spearmint.

δυσανάγνωστος [deesanaynostos] illegible.

δυσανάλογος [deesanalogos] disproportionate.

δυσανασχετῶ [deesanasheto] be anxious, be indignant, get angry.

δυσαρέσκεια, ἡ [deesareskeea] displeasure, discontent.

δυσάρεστος [deesarestos] unpleasant, disagreeable.

δυσαρεστημένος [deeasaresteemenos] displeased, dissatisfied.

δυσαρεστῶ [δeesaresto] displease, dissatisfy.

δυσαρμονία, ἡ [δeesarmoneea] disharmony, discord.

δυσβάστακτος [δeesvastaktos] unbearable, heavy, overwhelming.

δύσβατος [δeesvatos] inaccessible, rough.

δυσειδής [δeeseeδees] ugly, unsightly.

δυσεντερία, ἡ [δeesentereea] dysentery.

δυσεξίτηλος [δeesekseeteelos] difficult to remove.

δισεπίλυτος [δeesepeeleetos] difficult to solve.

δισεύρετος [δeesevretos] difficult to find.

δυσήνιος [δeeseeneeos] insubordinate, refractory.

δυσθυμία, ἡ [δeestheemeea] sadness, depression.

δύσθυμος [δeestheemos] depressed, sad.

δύσις, ἡ [δeesees] west || (ἡλίου) setting || (μεταφ) decline.

δύσκαμπτος [δeeskamptos] rigid, stiff, hard to bend.

δυσκινησία, ἡ [δeeskeeneeseea] sluggishness.

δυσκοιλιότης, ἡ [δeeskeeleeotees] constipation.

δυσκολεύομαι [δeeskolevome] find difficult, find hard, be hard put.

δυσκολεύω [δeeskolevo] make difficult, make hard.

δυσκολία, ἡ [δeeskoleea] difficulty.

δυσκολο- [δeeskolo] (first component) difficult, hard.

δύσκολος [δeeskolos] difficult || (ἄνθρωπος) hard to please.

δυσκόλως [δeeskolos] with difficulty.

δύσληπτος [δeesleeptos] difficult to understand, hard to catch.

δυσμένεια, ἡ [δeesmeneea] disfavour, disgrace.

δυσμενής [δeesmenees] adverse, unfavourable.

δύσμοιρος [δeesmeeros] ill-fated, unlucky.

δύσμορφος [δeesmorfos] deformed, ugly.

δυσνόητος [δeesnoeetos] difficult to understand.

δυσοίωνος [δeeseeonos] inauspicious, ill-omened.

δυσοσμία, ἡ [δeesosmeea] bad smell, stench, offensive odour.

δύσπεπτος [δeespeptos] difficult to digest.

δυσπιστία [δeespeesteea] mistrust, incredulity.

δύσπιστος [δeespeestos] incredulous, distrustful, unbelieving.

δυσπιστῶ [δeespeesto] distrust, mistrust.

δύσπνοια, ἡ [δeespneea] difficult breathing.

δυσπρόσιτος [δeesproseetos] inaccessible.

δύστηνος [δeesteenos] wretched, unfortunate.

δυστοκία, ἡ [δeestokeea] difficult birth || (μεταφ) indecision.

δύστροπος [δeestropos] perverse, peevish.

δυστροπῶ [δeestropo] behave peevishly.

δυστύχημα, τό [δeesteeheema] accident, stroke of bad luck.

δυστυχής [δeesteehees] unhappy, unfortunate.

δυστυχία, ἡ [δeesteeheea] unhappiness, adversity, poverty.

δυστυχισμένος [δeesteeheesmenos] βλ δυστυχής.

δυστυχῶ [δeesteeho] be unhappy, be unfortunate, be poor.

δυσφημίζω [δeesfeemeezo] defame, slander.

δυσφήμισις, ἡ [δeesfeemesees] calumny, slander.

δυσφόρητος [δeesforeetos] hard to endure.

δυσφορῶ [δeesforo] be displeased || (μέ κάτι) be discontented.

δυσχεραίνω [δeeshereno] impede, make difficult.

δυσχέρεια, ἡ [δeeshereea] difficulty || hardship.

δυσχερής [δeesherees] difficult.

δύσχρηστος [δeeshreestos] unwieldy, inconvenient, awkward.

δυσώδης [δeesoδees] stinking, malodorous, fetid.

δυσωδία, ἡ [δeesoδeea] stench, stink.

δυσώνυμος [δeesoneemos] ill-famed, notorious.

δύτης, ὁ [δeetees] diver.

δυτικός [δeeteekos] west(ern).

δύω [δeeo] set || (μεταφ) decline, wane.

δυωδία, ἡ [δeeoδeea] duet.

δώδεκα [δoδeka] twelve.

δωδεκάγωνον, τό [δoδekaγonon] dodecagon.

δωδεκαδάκτυλον, τό [δoδekaδakteelon] duodenum.

δωδεκαετής [δoδekaetees] twelve years old.

δωδεκαπλάσιος [δoδekaplaseeos] twelvefold.

δωδεκάς, ἡ [δoδekas] dozen.

δωδέκατος [δoδekatos] twelfth.

δῶμα, τό [δoma] flat roof, terrace || apartment.

δωμάτιον, τό [δomateeon] room || (ὕπνου) bedroom.

δωρεά, ἡ [δorea] bequest, present, gift || ~ν (ἐπιρ) gratis, free, for nothing.

δωροδοκία, ἡ [δoroδokeea] bribery, corruption.

δωροδοκῶ [δoroδoko] bribe, corrupt.

δῶρον, τό [δoron] gift, present.

δωσίλογος [δoseeloγos] responsible, answerable.

E, ε

ἔ [e] (ἐπιφ) well!, hey!, hallo!

ἐάν [ean] βλ ἄν.

ἔαρ, τό [ear] spring.

ἑαυτός [eaftos] oneself ‖ καθ'ἑαυτοῦ really, exactly, precisely.
ἑβδομάδα, ἡ [evδomaδa] week.
ἑβδομαδιαῖος [evδomaδieos] weekly.
ἑβδομήντα [evδomeenta] seventy.
ἕβδομος [evδomos] seventh.
ἑβραϊκός [evraeekos] Jewish.
Ἑβραῖος, ὁ [evreos] Hebrew, Jew.
ἔγγαμος [engamos] married.
ἐγγίζω [engeezo] draw near ‖ (μεταφ) touch.
ἔγγιστα [engeesta]: ὡς ~ approximately, nearly.
ἐγγλέζικος [englezeekos] English.
Ἐγγλέζος, ὁ [englezos] Englishman.
ἐγγόνι, τό [engonee] grandchild.
ἐγγονός, ὁ [engonos] grandson.
ἐγγράμματος [engramatos] learned, lettered.
ἐγγραφή, ἡ [engrafee] registration, record, entry.
ἔγγραφον, τό [engrafon] document.
ἐγγράφω [engrafo] register, enrol ‖ (μάθημ) inscribe.
ἐγγύησις, ἡ [engieesees] security, guarantee, bail.
ἐγγύς [engees] near, at hand.
ἐγγυῶμαι [engeeome] guarantee, vouch for.
ἐγείρομαι [eyeerome] rise ‖ (ἐκ τοῦ ὕπνου) awake.
ἐγείρω [eyeero] raise, build.
ἔγερσις, ἡ [eyersees] raising, building ‖ (ἀπό ὕπνου) awakening.
ἐγκαθίσταμαι [engkatheestame] settle, put up, settle o.s.
ἐγκαθιστῶ [engkatheesto] set up, settle, establish.
ἐγκαίνια, τά [engkeneea] πλ inauguration, opening.
ἔγκαιρος [engkeros] timely, opportune.
ἐγκάρδιος [engkarδeeos] cordial, affectionate.
ἐγκάρσιος [engkarseeos] transversal, slanting, oblique.
ἐγκαταλείπω [engkataleepo] abandon, desert.
ἐγκατάστασις, ἡ [engkatastasees] installation, establishing.
ἔγκαυμα, τό [engkavma] burn.
ἔγκειται [engkeete]: εἰς ὑμᾶς ~ it rests with you.
ἐγκέφαλος, ὁ [engkefalos] brain.
ἐγκλείστως [engkleestos] enclosed (herein), herewith.
ἐγκλείω [engkleeo] enclose ‖ confine ‖ lock up.
ἔγκλημα, τό [engkleema] crime ‖ sin ‖ ~ τίας, ὁ criminal ‖ ~ τικός criminal ‖ ~ τικότης, ἡ delinquency, wrongdoing, crime.
ἔγκλισις, ἡ [engkleesees] inclination ‖ (γραμμ) mood.
ἐγκόλπιον, τό [engkolpeeon] (φυλακτό) amulet ‖ manual.

ἐγκοπή, ἡ [engkopee] incision, notch, groove.
ἐγκόσμιος [engkosmeeos] mundane, worldly ‖ social.
ἐγκράτεια, ἡ [engkrateea] sobriety, moderation, temperance.
ἐγκρίνω [engkreeno] approve, ratify.
ἔγκρισις, ἡ [engkreesees] approval, sanction.
ἐγκύκλιος, ἡ [engkeekleeos] circular letter.
ἐγκυκλοπαιδεία, ἡ [engkeeklopeδeea] encyclopaedia.
ἔγκυος [engkeeos] pregnant.
ἔγκυρος [engkeeros] valid, sound, well-grounded.
ἐγκώμιον, τό [engkomeeon] praise, encomium.
ἔγνοια, ἡ [eyneea] care, anxiety, concern.
ἐγχείρησις, ἡ [engheereesees] operation.
ἐγχειρίδιον, τό [engheereeδeeon] manual ‖ (στιλέττο) dagger.
ἔγχρωμος [enghromos] coloured.
ἐγχώριος [enghoreeos] local, native, domestic.
ἐγώ [eyo] I ‖ (οὐσ) τό ~ ego ‖ ἐγωισμός, ὁ pride, conceit, selfishness.
ἐδάφιον, τό [eδafeeon] paragraph, passage.
ἔδαφος, τό [eδafos] ground, earth, soil.
ἕδρα, ἡ [eδra] seat, chair ‖ (ἀνατ) bottom ‖ (ἐκκλ) see.
ἑδραιώνω [eδreono] establish, strengthen, make firm.
ἑδρεύω [eδrevo] reside, have one's seat.
ἐδῶ [eδo] here ‖ ~ καί τρία χρόνια three years ago.
ἐδώλιον, τό [eδoleeon] bench, seat.
ἐθελοντής, ὁ [ethelontees] volunteer.
ἐθελουσίως [ethelouseeos] voluntarily.
ἔθιμον, τό [etheemon] custom, tradition ‖ habit.
ἐθιμοτυπία, ἡ [etheemoteepeea] formality, etiquette.
ἐθνάρχης, ὁ [ethnarhees] national leader.
ἐθνικισμός, ὁ [ethneekeesmos] nationalism.
ἐθνικός [ethneekos] national.
ἐθνικότης, ἡ [ethneekotees] nationality.
ἐθνικόφρων [ethneekofron] patriotic, nationalistic.
ἔθνος, τό [ethnos] nation.
εἰ [ee] if ‖ ~ δέ if not ‖ ~ δέ μή otherwise.
εἰδάλλως [eeδalos] if not, otherwise.
εἰδεχθής [eeδehthees] hideous, horrible, repulsive.
εἰδήμων [eeδeemon] expert, skilled, well-informed.
εἰδήσεις, οἱ [eeδeesees] πλ news.
εἰδικός [eeδeekos] special, particular ‖ (ἄνθρωπος) specialist.
εἰδοποίησις, ἡ [eeδopieesees] notification, notice.
εἰδοποιῶ [eeδopeeo] notify, inform, advise.
εἶδος, τό [eeδos] sort, kind, type ‖ (βοτ) species ‖ τά εἴδη goods, wares ‖ kinds.

εἰδύλλιον, τό [eedeeleeon] love affair ‖ idyll.

εἰδωλολάτρης, ὁ [eedololatrees] pagan, heathen.

εἴδωλον, τό [eedolon] idol ‖ image.

εἰθισμένα, τά [eetheesmena]: κατά τά ~ as is the practice.

εἴθισται [eetheeste] it is the custom.

εἰκασία, ἡ [eekaseea] conjecture, guess.

εἰκαστικός [eekasteekos] conjectural ‖ εἰκαστικαί τέχναι fine arts.

εἰκόνα [eekona] βλ εἰκών.

εἰκονίζω [eekoneezo] portray, depict, represent.

εἰκονικός [eekoneekos] figurative ‖ (ἐπίθεσις) sham ‖ (πρᾶξις) bogus ‖ (τιμή) conventional.

εἰκόνισμα, τό [eekoneesma] portrait ‖ (ἁγιογραφία) icon.

εἰκονογραφία, ἡ [eekonoγrafeea] illustration ‖ (ἐκκλ) iconography.

εἰκονοστάσι(ον), τό [eekonostasee(on)] (ἐκκλ) shrine, screen.

εἴκοσι [eekosee] twenty.

εἰκοστός [eekostos] twentieth.

εἰκών, ἡ [eekon] image, picture ‖ (ἐκκλ) icon.

εἰλικρίνεια, ἡ [eeleekreeneea] sincerity, frankness.

εἰλικρινής [eeleekreenees] sincere, candid.

εἶμαι [eeme] I am, I'm.

εἰμή [eemee] unless, except, but.

εἶναι [eene] be, is, it is ‖ τό ~ being.

εἰρήνη, ἡ [eereenee] peace.

εἰρηνικός [eereeneekos] peaceful.

εἰρηνοδικεῖον, τό [eereenoδeekeeon] magistrate's court.

εἱρμός, ὁ [eermos] train of thought, continuity.

εἰρωνεύομαι [eeronevome] speak derisively, speak ironically.

εἰρωνεία, ἡ [eeroneea] irony, mockery.

εἷς [ees] one ‖ (ἄρθρον) a, an.

εἰς [ees] in, among, at ‖ (χρόνος) within ‖ to, into, on.

εἰσαγγελεύς, ὁ [eesangelevs] public prosecutor ‖ (US) district attorney.

εἰσάγω [eesaγo] import ‖ (νομοσχέδιον) introduce ‖ (φέρω πρῶτα) introduce for the first time ‖ (παρουσιάζω) present ‖ εἰσαγωγεύς, ὁ importer ‖ εἰσαγωγή, ἡ importation ‖ (παρουσίασις) introduction ‖ εἰσαγωγικά, τά inverted commas.

εἰσβάλλω [eesvalo] invade ‖ (ποταμός) flow into.

εἰσβολή, ἡ [eesvolee] invasion.

εἰσδύω [eesδeeo] penetrate, slip in.

εἰσέρχομαι [eeserhome] come in, enter, go in.

εἰσέτι [eesetee] still, (not) yet, up to now.

εἰσήγησις, ἡ [eeseeγeesees] report ‖ suggestion.

εἰσηγοῦμαι [eeseeγoume] propose, move ‖ introduce.

εἰσιτήριον, τό [eeseeteereeon] ticket.

εἰσιτήριος [eeseeteereeos] of entry, of admission.

εἰσόδημα, τό [eesoδeema] income, revenue.

εἴσοδος, ἡ [eesoδos] entry, entrance ‖ admission.

εἰσπνέω [eespneo] inhale, breathe in.

εἰσπράκτωρ, ὁ [eespraktor] conductor ‖ collector.

εἴσπραξις, ἡ [eespraksees] collection ‖ receipt.

εἰσπράττω [eesprato] collect.

εἰσφορά, ἡ [eesfora] contribution.

εἰσχωρῶ [eeshoro] penetrate, intrude, get in.

εἶτα [eeta] then ‖ afterwards.

εἴτε [eete]: ~...~ either ... or, whether ... or.

ἐκ [ek] from, out of, by, of ‖ ἐξ ἀνάγκης of necessity ‖ ~ νέου again ‖ ἐξ ἴσου equally.

ἐκ-, ἐξ- [ek, eks] out, off ‖ completely, wholly.

ἕκαστος [ekastos] each, every one ‖ καθ' ἑκάστην every day ‖ τά καθ' ἕκαστα the details.

ἑκάστοτε [ekastote] each time.

ἑκατέρωθεν [ekaterothen] on both sides, mutually.

ἑκατομμύριον, τό [ekatomeereeon] million.

ἑκατομμυριοῦχος, ὁ [ekatomeereeouhos] millionaire.

ἑκατό(ν) [ekato(n)] hundred ‖ τά ~ per cent.

ἑκατονταετηρίς, ἡ [ekatontaeteerees] century ‖ centenary.

ἑκατονταπλάσιος [ekatontaplaseeos] hundredfold.

ἑκατοντούτης, ὁ [ekatontoutees] centenarian.

ἑκατοστάρι, τό [ekatostaree] hundred-drachma note.

ἑκατοστόμετρον, τό [ekatostometron] centimetre.

ἑκατοστός [ekatostos] hundredth.

ἐκβάλλω [ekvalo] take out, extract ‖ (ἀπομακρύνω) repudiate ‖ (ἐχθρόν) drive out ‖ (ἐπί ποταμῶν) flow into.

ἔκβασις [ekvasees] issue, outcome, result.

ἐκβιάζω [ekveeazo] (κάποιον) force, compel ‖ blackmail ‖ (διάβασιν κτλ) force.

ἐκβολή, ἡ [ekvolee] ejection ‖ (ποταμοῦ) mouth, estuary.

ἐκγυμνάζω [ekγeemnazo] exercise, train, drill.

ἔκδηλος [ekδeelos] manifest, evident, obvious.

ἐκδηλώνω [ekδeelono] show, reveal, evince.

ἐκδίδω [ekδeeδo] issue, publish ‖ (ἀπόφασιν) pronounce ‖ (συναλλαγματικήν) draw ‖ (ἐγκληματίαν κτλ) extradite.

ἐκδίκησις, ἡ [ekdeekeesees] vengeance, revenge.

ἐκδικητικός [ekdeekeeteekos] revengeful, vindictive.

ἐκδικοῦμαι [ekdeekoume] take revenge on, get even with.

ἐκδιώκω [ekdeeeoko] expel, oust ‖ (στρατ) dislodge, drive out.

ἐκδορά, ἡ [ekdora] abrasion ‖ skinning.

ἔκδοσις, ἡ [ekdosees] publication, edition ‖ (χαρτονομίσματος) issue ‖ (παραλλαγή) version, story ‖ (ἐγκληματίου κτλ) extradition.

ἐκδότης, ὁ [ekdotees] publisher, editor.

ἐκδοτικός [ekdoteekos] publishing.

ἐκδοχή, ἡ [ekdohee] interpretation, version.

ἐκδρομή, ἡ [ekdromee] excursion, outing, trip.

ἐκεῖ [ekee] there ‖ ~ πού instead of, while, whereas ‖ ~ θεν thence, from there.

ἐκεῖνος [ekeenos] he, that one there.

ἐκεχειρία, ἡ [ekeheereea] truce, armistice.

ἔκθαμβος [ekthamvos] dazzled, astounded.

ἔκθεμα, τό [ekthema] exhibit.

ἔκθεσις, ἡ [ekthesees] (στό ὕπαιθρον) exposure ‖ (ἀνθέων κτλ) exhibition ‖ (ἐμπορευμάτων) display, exposition ‖ (γραπτή) composition.

ἐκθέτης, ὁ [ekthetees] exhibitor ‖ (μαθημ) exponent.

ἔκθετον, τό [ektheton] abandoned baby.

ἔκθετος [ekthetos] exposed.

ἐκθέτω [ektheto] expose, display, exhibit ‖ (τήν ζωήν) expose, imperil ‖ (τέκνον) abandon ‖ (σχέδια) state, expose, disclose ‖ (μεταφ) lay bare, expose.

ἐκθρονίζω [ekthroneezo] dethrone.

ἐκκαθαρίζω [ekathareezo] clear out, clean ‖ (λογαριασμόν) liquidate, settle.

ἐκκεντρικός [ekentreekos] eccentric.

ἐκκενῶ [ekeno] empty out, vacate ‖ (ποτήρι κτλ) drain ‖ (ὅπλον) fire ‖ (οἰκίαν) leave.

ἐκκένωσις, ἡ [ekeeneosees] evacuation, emptying ‖ (ἡλεκ) discharge.

ἐκκίνησις, ἡ [ekeeneesees] departure, starting off.

ἐκκλησία, ἡ [ekleeseea] church ‖ **ἐκκλησιαστικός** ecclesiastic(al).

ἔκκλησις, ἡ [ekleesees] appeal.

ἐκκλίνω [ekleeno] deviate ‖ (μεταφ) go astray, become corrupted.

ἐκκρεμής [ekremees] unsettled, pending.

ἐκκωφαντικός [ekofanteekos] deafening.

ἐκλαμβάνω [eklamvano] construe, interpret, take (for).

ἐκλέγω [eklego] choose, pick out ‖ elect.

ἔκλειψις, ἡ [ekleepsees] eclipse ‖ (μεταφ) disappearance.

ἐκλεκτικός [eklekteekos] choosy, selective.

ἐκλεκτός [eklektos] choice, select, picked ‖ **οἱ ἐκλεκτοί** élite.

ἐκλιπαρῶ [ekleeparo] entreat, implore.

ἐκλογεύς, ὁ [ekloyevs] elector, voter.

ἐκλογή, ἡ [ekloyee] choice, selection ‖ election.

ἐκλογές, οἱ [ekloyes] πλ elections.

ἐκλογικός [ekloyeekos] electoral.

ἐκμαγεῖον, τό [ekmayeeon] (plaster) cast.

ἐκμαιεύω [ekmeyevo] extract, elicit.

ἐκμεταλλεύομαι [ekmetalevome] exploit.

ἐκμηδενίζω [ekmeedeneezo] annihilate.

ἐκμίσθωσις, ἡ [ekmeesthosees] leasing, lease.

ἐκμισθωτής, ὁ [ekmeesthotees] lessor, hirer.

ἐκμυζῶ [ekmeezo] suck out, drain ‖ (μεταφ) exploit.

ἐκμυστηρεύομαι [ekmeesteerevome] confide a secret, confess.

ἐκνευρίζω [eknevreezo] annoy, exasperate.

ἐκούσιος [ekouseeos] voluntary ‖ willing.

ἐκπαίδευσις, ἡ [ekpeδevsees] education, training.

ἐκπαιδευτήριον, τό [ekpeδevteereeon] school, institute.

ἐκπαιδευτικός [ekpeδevteekos] educational ‖ (διδάσκων) schoolteacher.

ἐκπαιδεύω [ekpeδevo] educate, train, instruct.

ἔκπαλαι [ekpale] from time immemorial, long ago.

ἐκπατρίζω [ekpatreezo] expatriate.

ἐκπέμπω [ekpembo] send forth, emit ‖ (διά ραδιοφώνου) broadcast.

ἐκπίπτω [ekpeepto] decline, fall ‖ (μεταφ) deduct, reduce, lower.

ἐκπληκτικός [ekpleekteekos] astonishing, surprising.

ἔκπληξις, ἡ [ekpleeksees] surprise, astonishment.

ἐκπληρῶ [ekpleero] fulfil, perform.

ἐκπλήσσω [ekpleesso] surprise, astonish.

ἔκπλους, ὁ [ekplous] departure of ship.

ἐκπνέω [ekpneo] exhale ‖ (πεθαίνω) die ‖ (μεταφ) expire, terminate.

ἐκποιῶ [ekpeeo] sell, dispose of.

ἐκπομπή, ἡ [ekpombee] emission ‖ (ραδιοφώνου) broadcast.

ἐκπρόθεσμος [ekprothesmos] overdue.

ἐκπρόσωπος, ὁ [ekprosopos] representative.

ἐκπροσωπῶ [ekprosopo] represent.

ἔκπτωσις, ἡ [ekptosees] decline, fall ‖ (δικαιωμάτων) loss ‖ (τιμῆς κτλ) reduction, rebate, discount, deduction.

ἐκρήγνυμαι [ekreeyneeme] explode, erupt, burst.

ἐκρηκτικός [ekreekteekos] explosive.

ἔκρηξις, ἡ [ekreeksees] explosion, eruption, outburst.

ἔκρυθμος [ekreethmos] irregular, abnormal, unusual.

ἐκσκαφή, ἡ [ekskafee] excavation, cutting.

ἔκστασις, ἡ [ekstasees] ecstasy, rapture.

ἐκστομίζω [ekstomeezo] utter, launch.

ἐκστρατεία, ἡ [ekstrateea] expedition, campaign.

ἐκσφενδονίζω [eksfenδoneezo] fling, throw, hurl.

ἔκτακτος [ektaktos] temporary, emergency ‖ (εἰδικός) special, exceptional, excellent.

ἐκτάκτως [ektaktos] temporarily ‖ extraordinarily, unusually.

ἔκτασις, ἡ [ektasees] extent, stretch.

ἐκτεθειμένος [ektetheemenos] exposed ‖ compromised.

ἐκτείνω [ekteeno] stretch, extend, prolong.

ἐκτέλεσις, ἡ [ektelesees] execution ‖ performance, fulfilment.

ἐκτελεστικός [ektelesteekos] executive.

ἐκτελῶ [ektelo] execute ‖ perform, carry out.

ἐκτενής [ektenees] extensive, lengthy, prolix.

ἐκτεταμένος [ektetamenos] extensive, long.

ἐκτίθεμαι [ekteetheme] be embarrassed ‖ display ‖ (γιά ἐκλογές) run for office.

ἐκτίμησις, ἡ [ekteemeesees] esteem, estimation, appreciation.

ἐκτιμῶ [ekteemo] esteem, value, appreciate, estimate.

ἐκτοξεύω [ektoksevo] shoot, cast, hurl.

ἐκτοπίζω [ektopeezo] displace, dislodge ‖ (ἐξορίζω) exile.

ἐκτόπισμα, τό [ektopeesma] displacement.

ἕκτος [ektos] sixth.

ἐκτός [ektos] outside, save ‖ ~ τῆς πόλεως outside the city ‖ ~ ἀπό apart from, besides, except for ‖ ~ τοῦ Γεώργου except George ‖ ~ ἄν unless ‖ ~ κινδύνου out of danger.

ἔκτοτε [ektote] ever since, since then.

ἐκτρέπομαι [ektrepome] deviate from ‖ (μεταφ) go astray.

ἐκτρέπω [ektrepo] deflect, turn aside, divert.

ἔκτροπος [ektropos] improper, devious.

ἐκτροχιάζομαι [ektroheeazome] become derailed ‖ (μεταφ) go astray.

ἔκτρωμα, τό [ektroma] monster, freak.

ἔκτρωσις, ἡ [ektrosees] abortion, miscarriage.

ἐκτυλίσσομαι [ekteeleesome] develop, evolve.

ἐκτυπώνω [ekteepono] print ‖ engrave in relief.

ἐκτυφλωτικός [ekteéfloteekos] blinding.

ἐκφέρω [ekfero] express.

ἐκφοβίζω [ekfoveezo] intimidate, frighten.

ἐκφορά, ἡ [ekfora] funeral, burial.

ἐκφορτωτής, ὁ [ekfortotees] unloader, docker.

ἐκφράζω [ekfrazo] express, reveal.

ἔκφρασις, ἡ [ekfrasees] expression.

ἐκφραστικός [ekfrasteekos] expressive.

ἐκφυλισμός, ὁ [ekfeeleesmos] degeneration.

ἐκφωνῶ [ekfono] deliver a speech ‖ read aloud.

ἐκχύλισμα, τό [ekheeleesma] extract.

ἐκχωρῶ [ekhoro] transfer, assign, cede ‖ (θέσιν) make way.

ἑκών [ekon] willing ‖ voluntary ‖ ~ ἄκων willy-nilly.

ἔλα [ela] (ἐπιφ) come!, come now!

ἐλαία, ἡ [elea] olive tree.

ἐλαιογραφία, ἡ [eleoγrafeea] oil painting.

ἐλαιόλαδον, τό [eleolaδon] olive oil.

ἔλαιον, τό [eleon] olive oil, oil.

ἐλαιοτριβεῖον, τό [eleotreeveeon] olive press.

ἐλαιόχρωμα, τό [eleohroma] oil paint.

ἐλαιώνας, ὁ [eleonas] olive grove.

ἔλασμα, τό [elasma] metal plate, sheet iron.

ἐλάσσων [elason] less, smaller ‖ (μουσ) minor.

ἐλαστικόν, τό [elasteekon] tyre ‖ rubber, elastic.

ἐλαστικός [elasteekos] flexible, elastic.

ἐλατήριον, τό [elateereeon] spring ‖ (μεταφ) incentive, motive.

ἔλατο, τό [elato] fir, fir tree.

ἐλάττωμα, τό [elatoma] defect, fault.

ἐλαττώνω [elatono] diminish, lessen, decrease.

ἐλάττωσις, ἡ [elatosees] decrease, curtailment.

ἐλαύνω [elavno] drive, press on, push on.

ἔλαφι, τό [elafee] deer.

ἐλαφρόπετρα, ἡ [elafropetra] pumice stone.

ἐλαφρός [elafros] light, slight ‖ (καφές κτλ) mild, thin, weak.

ἐλαφρώνω [elafrono] reduce, lighten ‖ feel relieved.

ἐλάχιστα [elaheesta] very little.

ἐλάχιστος [elaheestos] least, very little ‖ τ' οὐλάχιστον at least.

Ἐλβετία, ἡ [elveteea] Switzerland.

Ἐλβετικός [elveteekos] Swiss.

Ἐλβετός, ὁ [elvetos] Swiss (person).

ἐλεγκτής, ὁ [elengtees] inspector, auditor.

ἔλεγχος, ὁ [elenghos] inspection, examination ‖ (λογαριασμοῦ) verification, control, auditing ‖ (μηχανῆς) testing, overhauling ‖ (μεταφ) censure, check, reproach.

ἐλέγχω [elengho] check, control, test.

ἐλεεινός [eleeenos] pitiful, wretched, vile.

ἐλεημοσύνη, ἡ [eleyeemoseenee] alms, charity.

ἔλεος, τό [eleos] mercy, pity.

ἐλευθερία, ἡ [eleftheereea] liberty, freedom.

ἐλεύθερος [eleftheros] free ‖ (ἐργένης) unmarried.

ἐλευθερώνω [eleftherono] redeem, set free, release, rid.

ἐλεφαντόδους, ὁ [elefantoδous] tusk ‖ ivory.

ἐλεφαντοστοῦν, τό [elefantostoun] ivory.

ἐλέφας, ὁ [elefas] elephant.

ἐλεῶ [eleo] give alms to, commiserate with ‖ Κύριε ἐλέησον (ἐπιφ) Lord have mercy!, for Heaven's sake!

ἐλιά, ἡ [elia] olive, olive tree ‖ (προσώπου κτλ) mole.

ἐλιγμός, ὁ [eleeymos] twisting, winding ‖ (στρατ) manoeuvre, movement.

ἑλικόπτερον, τό [eleekopteron] helicopter.

ἕλιξ, ἡ, ὁ [eleeks] coil, spiral ‖ (προπέλλα) screw, propeller ‖ (βοτ) tendril.

ἑλίσσομαι [eleesome] wind, coil, twist ‖ (στρατ) manoeuvre.

ἕλκηθρον, τό [elkeethron] sledge, sled.

ἑλκυστικός [elkeesteekos] attractive, winsome.

ἑλκύω [elkeeo] charm, attract ‖ draw, pull.

ἕλκω [elko] draw, pull, haul.

Ἑλλάδα, ἡ [elada] Greece.

ἑλλανοδίκης, ὁ [elanoδeekees] judge, referee.

Ἑλλάς, ἡ [elas] Greece.

ἔλλειμμα, τό [eleema] deficit, shortage.

ἔλλειψις, ἡ [eleepsees] lack, want, deficiency ‖ (μαθημ) ellipse.

Ἕλλην(ας), ὁ [eleen(as)] Greek (person).

ἑλληνικά, τά [eleeneeka] πλ Greek (language).

ἑλληνικός [eleeneekos] Greek.

ἑλληνισμός, ὁ [eleeneesmos] the Greek race.

ἑλληνιστί [eleeneestee] in Greek.

ἐλλιπής [eleepees] defective, wanting.

ἕλξις, ἡ [elksees] pull, traction, drawing, attraction.

ἑλονοσία, ἡ [elonoseea] malaria.

ἕλος, τό [elos] marsh, swamp, morass.

ἐλπίδα, ἡ [elpeeδa] hope, expectation ‖ παρ' ~ contrary to expectation.

ἐλπίς [elpees] βλ ἐλπίδα.

ἑλώδης [eloδees] marshy, swampy.

ἐμβαδόν, τό [emvaδon] area.

ἐμβαθύνω [emvatheeno] (μεταφ) examine thoroughly, probe deeply.

ἐμβάλλω [emvallo] insert, get into, put in.

ἔμβασμα, τό [emvasma] remittance of money.

ἐμβατήριον, τό [emvateereeon] march.

ἔμβλημα, τό [emvleema] emblem, crest, symbol.

ἐμβολιάζω [emvoleeazo] (φυτόν) graft ‖ (ἄνθρωπον) vaccinate, inoculate.

ἐμβόλιον, τό [emvoleeon] vaccine ‖ (φυτόν) graft.

ἔμβολον, τό [emvolon] piston, rod ‖ (πλοίου) ram.

ἐμβριθής [emvreethees] erudite ‖ grave, serious.

ἐμβρόντητος [emvronteetos] thunderstruck, stupefied.

ἔμβρυον, τό [emvreeon] embryo, foetus.

ἐμένα [emena] me.

ἐμεῖς [emees] we.

ἐμετικός [emeteekos] emetic.

ἐμετός, ὁ [emetos] vomiting.

ἐμμένω [emeno] adhere to ‖ persist, insist.

ἔμμεσος [emesos] indirect.

ἔμμετρος [emetros] in moderation ‖ (ποίησις) in verse, metrical.

ἔμμηνα, τά [emeena] πλ menstruation, monthlies.

ἔμμισθος [emeesthos] salaried, paid.

ἔμμονος [emonos] persistent, obstinate, persevering.

ἐμός [emos] my, mine.

ἐμπάθεια, ἡ [empatheea] animosity, ill feeling.

ἐμπαίζω [empezo] tease, mock, deceive.

ἐμπειρία, ἡ [embeereea] experience, skill.

ἐμπειρογνώμων, ὁ, ἡ [embeeroγnomon] expert, specialist.

ἔμπειρος [embeeros] experienced, skilled in, able.

ἐμπιστεύομαι [embeestevome] (en)trust, confide.

ἐμπιστευτικός [embeestevteekos] confidential.

ἔμπιστος [embeestos] trustworthy, reliable, faithful ‖ ἐμπιστοσύνη, ἡ trust, confidence.

ἔμπλαστρον, τό [emblastron] plaster.

ἐμπλοκή, ἡ [emblokee] (στρατ) engagement ‖ (μηχανῆς) jamming ‖ gear of car.

ἐμπλουτίζω [emblouteezo] enrich.

ἐμπνευσις, ἡ [embnevsees] inspiration.

ἐμπνέομαι [embneome] feel inspired.

ἐμπνέω [embneo] inspire.

ἐμποδίζω [emboδeezo] hinder, obstruct, prevent ‖ hold back, impede.

ἐμπόδιον, τό [emboδeeon] obstacle, impediment, obstruction.

ἐμπόλεμος [embolemos] belligerent.

ἐμπόρευμα, τό [emborevma] merchandise, article of commerce.

ἐμπορεύομαι [emborevome] engage in commerce ‖ deal in, trade in.

ἐμπορικόν, τό [emboreekon] shop, store, haberdashery.

ἐμπορικός [emboreekos] commercial, mercantile.

ἐμπόριον, τό [emboreeon] trade, commerce.

ἔμπορος, ὁ [emboros] merchant, trader, vendor.

ἐμπορουπάλληλος, ὁ, ἡ [emboroepaleelos] shop assistant, shopgirl ‖ (US) clerk.

ἐμπρησμός, ὁ [embreesmos] arson.

ἐμπρηστικός [embreesteekos] incendiary ‖ (μεταφ) fiery.

ἐμπρόθεσμος [embrothesmos] within the time limit.

ἐμπρός [embros] forward(s), before, in front of ‖ ~ σέ compared with ‖ πηγαίνω ~ succeed ‖ ~ ἀπό in front of ‖ τό ρολόϊ πάει ~ the clock is fast ‖ ~ μου in front of me ‖ ~! hallo!, come in! ‖ βάζω ~ start.

ἐμπροσθεν [embrosthen] in front ‖ (προηγουμένως) previously ‖ (ἐπίθ) in front, previous.

ἐμπρόσθιος [embrostheeos] front, fore, anterior.

έμπυο, τό [embeeo] pus, matter.
έμφανής [emfanees] apparent, obvious, clear.
έμφανίζομαι [emfaneezome] appear, present o.s., make an appearance.
έμφανίζω [emfaneezo] exhibit, reveal ‖ (φωτογρ) develop.
έμφάνισις, ή [emfaneesees] appearance, presentation ‖ (φωτογρ) development.
έμφασις, ή [emfasees] stress, emphasis.
έμφύλιος [emfeeleeos]: ~ πόλεμος civil war.
έμφυτον, τό [emfeeton] instinct, intuition.
έμφυτος [emfeetos] innate, inherent, intuitive.
έμψυχώνω [empseehono] encourage, stimulate.
έν [en] in, at, within ‖ ~ τούτοις however, nevertheless ‖ ~ τάξει all right.
έν(α), τό [en(a)] one ‖ a, an.
έναγκαλίζομαι [enangaleezome] embrace, hug.
έναγόμενος [enayomenos] defendant.
ένάγω [enayo] sue, bring action against.
έναγωνίως [enayoneeos] anxiously, with anguish.
έναέριος [enaereeos] aerial, overhead ‖ airy.
έναλλαγή, ή [enalayee] permutation, exchange, interchange.
έναλλάξ [enallaks] alternately, in turn.
έναλλάσσω [enalaso] alternate, exchange.
έναντι [enantee] towards, against ‖ βλ καί άπέναντι.
ένάντια [enanteea] adversely, contrarily ‖ ~ σέ against.
έναντίον [enanteeon] against ‖ contrary to.
έναντίον, τό [enanteeon] the contrary.
ένάντιος [enanteeos] adverse, contrary, opposite ‖ άπ' έναντίας on the contrary.
έναπόκειται [enapokeete]: σέ σένα ~ it's up to you.
έναργής [enaryees] clear, obvious, manifest.
ένάρετος [enaretos] virtuous, upright.
έναρθρος [enarthros] articulate, jointed.
έναρκτήριος [enarkteereeos] inaugural.
έναρμονίζω [enarmoneezo] harmonize.
έναρξις, ή [enarksees] opening, beginning, inauguration.
ένας, ό [enas] one ‖ a, an ‖ ~ ~ one by one ‖ ~ κι ~ especially good, very bad ‖ ό ~ τόν άλλον one another.
ένασχόλησις, ή [enasholeesees] occupation, employment.
ένατος [enatos] ninth.
ένδεια, ή [endeea] deficiency ‖ poverty.
ένδεικνύομαι [endeekneeome] be called for, be necessary.
ένδεικνύω [endeekneeo] indicate.
ένδεικτικόν, τό [endeekteekon] certificate.
ένδεικτικός [endeekteekos] indicative.
ένδειξις, ή [endeeksees] indication, sign.

ένδεκα [endeka] eleven.
ένδέχεται [endehete] it is possible, it is likely.
ένδεχόμενον, τό [endehomenon] eventuality, possibility.
ένδιάμεσος [endeeamesos] intermediate, in between.
ένδιαφέρομαι [endeeaferome] be interested in.
ένδιαφέρον, τό [endeeaferon] interest, concern.
ένδιαφέρω [endeeafero] concern, interest ‖ ~ν interesting.
ένδίδω [endeedo] give way to ‖ give way, bend.
ένδικος [endeekos] legal, judicial.
ένδοιάζω [endeeazo] hesitate, waver.
ένδόμυχος [endomeehos] intimate, inward, inmost, secret.
ένδον [endon] within, in.
ένδοξος [endoksos] celebrated, glorious, illustrious.
ένδότερος [endoteros] inner, interior.
ένδοχώρα, ή [endohora] hinterland.
ένδυμα, τό [endeema] dress, garment, clothes ‖ ~σία, ή suit, dress, garb.
ένδύομαι [endeeome] dress o.s., put on one's clothes.
ένέδρα, ή [enedra] ambush, ambuscade.
ένεκα [eneka] on account of, because of.
ένενήντα [enenenta] ninety.
ένέργεια, ή [eneryeea] energy, action ‖ (φαρμάκου) efficacy.
ένεργητικός [eneryeeteekos] energetic, active ‖ (φάρμακον) effective.
ένεργός [eneryos] active ‖ effective.
ένεργούμαι [eneryoume] move the bowels ‖ take place.
ένεργῶ [eneryo] act, take steps ‖ (φάρμακον κτλ) take effect, work ‖ (καθαρτικόν) purge.
ένεσις, ή [enesees] injection.
ένεστώς, ό [enestos] (γραμμ) present tense.
ένετικός [eneteekos] Venetian.
ένεχυροδανειστής, ό [eneheerodaneestees] pawnbroker.
ένηλικιούμαι [eneeleekeeoume] come of age, reach majority.
ένῆλιξ [eneeleeks] of age, adult.
ένήμερος [eneemeros] aware, inf :d.
ένημερώνω [eneemerono] inform, bring up to date.
ένθα [entha] where.
ένθάδε [enthaδe] here, hither.
ένθαρρύνσις, ή [enthareensees] encouragement, cheering up.
ένθαρρύνω [enthareeno] encourage, cheer up, hearten.
ένθεν [enthen] from here ‖ ~ καί ~ on each side.
ένθερμος [enthermos] ardent, warm, hearty.
ένθουσιάζομαι [enthouseeazome] be enthusiastic about.

ἐνθουσιασμός, ὁ [enthouseeasmos] enthusiasm.

ἐνθυμίζω [entheemeezo] call to mind ‖ remind.

ἐνθύμιον, τό [entheemeeon] keepsake, souvenir, memento.

ἐνθυμοῦμαι [entheemoume] recall, remember, recollect.

ἐνιαῖος [enieos] single, uniform.

ἐνικός [eneekos] (γραμμ) singular (number).

ἔνιοι [eniee] πλ some.

ἐνίοτε [eneeote] sometimes, now and then.

ἐνίσχυσις, ἡ [eneesheesees] reinforcement, strengthening ‖ (ἠλεκ) amplification.

ἐνισχύω [eneesheeo] support, reinforce, assist.

ἐννέα [ennea] nine ‖ ~ κόσιοι nine hundred.

ἐννιά [ennia] nine.

ἔννοια, ἡ [enneea] sense, concept, meaning, interpretation.

ἔννοια, ἡ [enyeea] concern, worry ‖ (σκοτούρα) anxiety ‖ ~ σου (ἐπιφ) take care!, don't worry!

ἔννομος [ennomos] lawful, legal, legitimate.

ἐννοεῖται [ennoeete] it is understood, certainly.

ἐννοῶ [ennoo] understand, mean, intend.

'ἐνοικιάζεται' [eneekeeazete] 'to let', 'for rent'.

ἐνοικιάζω [eneekeeazo] rent, let, hire.

ἐνοικιαστής, ὁ [eneekeeastees] tenant ‖ (νομ) lessee.

ἐνοίκιον, τό [eneekeeon] rent.

ἔνοικος, ὁ [eneekos] tenant, lodger.

ἔνοπλος [enoplos] armed, in arms.

ἐνόρασις, ἡ [enorasees] intuition.

ἐνορία, ἡ [enoreea] parish.

ἐνόρκως [enorkos] under oath, on oath.

ἐνόσω [enoso] as long as.

ἑνότης, ἡ [enotees] unity, concord.

ἐνοχή, ἡ [enohee] guilt, culpability.

ἐνόχλησις, ἡ [enohleesees] trouble, annoyance, inconvenience.

ἐνοχλητικός [enohleeteekos] troublesome, inconvenient, annoying.

ἐνοχλῶ [enohlo] trouble, annoy, pester, inconvenience.

ἐνσάρκωσις, ἡ [ensarkosees] incarnation, embodiment.

ἔνσημον, τό [enseemon] stamp.

ἐνσκήπτω [enskeepto] happen suddenly, break out ‖ break into.

ἐνσπείρω [espeero] sow, spread, inspire.

ἔνστασις, ἡ [enstasees] objection.

ἐνστερνίζομαι [esterneezome] embrace ‖ adopt, accept ‖ (μία ἰδέα) borrow.

ἔνστικτον, τό [ensteekton] instinct.

ἔνταλμα, τό [entalma] warrant, writ.

ἔντασις, ἡ [entasees] strain, tension ‖ intensity, intensification.

ἐντατικός [entateekos] intensive.

ἐνταῦθα [entavtha] here ‖ (ἔνδειξις ἐπιστολῆς) in town, local.

ἐντείνω [enteeno] stretch ‖ (τάς προσπαθείας) intensify ‖ (τάς σχέσεις) overstrain.

ἔντεκα [enteka] eleven.

ἐντέλεια, ἡ [enteleea] perfection.

ἐντέλλομαι [entelome] order, command, be ordered.

ἐντελῶς [entelos] completely, entirely, totally.

ἐντερικός [entereekos] intestinal.

ἔντερον, τό [enteron] intestine.

ἐντεταλμένος [entetalmenos] responsible for, charged with ‖ (οὐσ) delegate.

ἐντεῦθεν [entevthen] hence, from here.

ἔντεχνος [entehnos] skilful, artistic, ingenious.

ἔντιμος [enteemos] honest ‖ (οἰκογένεια κτλ) respectable, honourable.

ἔντοκος [entokos] with interest.

ἐντολή, ἡ [entolee] order, mandate ‖ authorization, commission.

ἐντομή [entomee] incision, groove.

ἐντομοκτόνον, τό [entomoktonon] insecticide.

ἔντομον, τό [entomon] insect.

ἔντονος [entonos] (προσπάθεια) strenuous, intense ‖ (φῶς) strong ‖ (χρῶμα) bright, deep.

ἐντοπίζω [entopeezo] localize ‖ (πυρκαϊάν) restrict, confine.

ἐντόπιος [entopeeos] local, native, indigenous.

ἐντός [entos] within, inside, in, into ‖ ~ ὀλίγου soon.

ἐντόσθια, τά [entostheea] πλ entrails, intestines.

ἐντριβή, ἡ [entreevee] massage ‖ (μηχανική) friction.

ἐντροπή, ἡ [entropee] shame, modesty.

ἔντυπον, τό [enteepon] printed matter.

ἔντυπος [enteepos] printed.

ἐντυπωσιακός [enteeposeeakos] impressive, striking.

ἐντύπωσις, ἡ [enteeposees] impression, sensation, feeling.

ἐνῶ [eno] while, whereas, since.

ἑνώνω [enono] unite, join, connect.

ἐνώπιον [enopeeon] in the presence of, in front of.

ἐνωρίς [enorees] early, in good time.

ἕνωσις, ἡ [enosees] union ‖ (ἠλεκτ) short circuit.

ἐξ [eks] βλ ἐκ.

ἐξαγοράζω [eksayorazo] buy off, redeem, ransom, obtain by bribery.

ἐξαγριώνω [eksayreeono] infuriate, enrage.

ἐξάγω [eksayo] take out, extract ‖ (ἐμπόριον) export ‖ (φιλοσ) deduce.

ἐξαγωγή, ἡ [eksayoyee] export ‖ (ὀδόντος) extraction.

ἐξάδελφος, ὁ [eksadelfos] cousin.

ἐξαερίζω [eksaereezo] ventilate, air.

ἐξαεριστήρ, ὁ [eksaereesteer] ventilator.

ἐξαίρεσις, ἡ [ekserésees] exception, exemption from, immunity (from).

ἐξαιρετικά [eksereteeka] exceptionally, unusually.

ἐξαιρετικός [eksereteekos] exceptional, unusual, excellent, remarkable.

ἐξαίρετος [ekseretos] excellent, remarkable.

ἐξαίρω [eksero] elevate, lift up ‖ (μεταφ) exalt, extol, praise.

ἐξαιρῶ [eksero] except, exempt ‖ (ἀποσπῶ) extract.

ἐξαίσιος [ekseseeos] excellent, splendid.

ἐξαίφνης [eksefnees] all of a sudden.

ἐξακολουθῶ [eksakoloutho] continue.

ἐξακόσιοι [eksakosiee] six hundred.

ἐξακριβώνω [eksakreevono] verify, ascertain, establish, clear up.

ἐξαλείφω [eksaleefo] efface, rub out, remove, obliterate.

ἔξαλλος [eksalos] beside o.s., frenzied.

ἐξάμβλωμα, τό [eksamvloma] monstrosity.

ἐξάμετρον, τό [eksametron] hexameter.

ἐξαμηνία, ἡ [eksameeneea] six months ‖ pay for such period.

ἐξαναγκάζω [eksanangazo] compel, force, coerce.

ἐξάνθημα, τό [eksantheema] rash, pimples.

ἐξανίσταμαι [eksaneestame] rebel, protest.

ἐξαντλῶ [eksantlo] exhaust.

ἐξάπαντος [eksapantos] without fail, by all means.

ἐξαπατῶ [eksapato] cheat, deceive, delude ‖ be unfaithful to.

ἐξαπίνης [eksapeenees] unexpectedly, suddenly.

ἐξάπλωσις, ἡ [eksaplosees] spreading out, extension.

ἐξαπολύω [eksapoleeo] let loose, hurl.

ἐξάπτω [eksapto] excite, provoke ‖ (περιέργειαν κτλ) rouse, stir.

ἐξαργυρώνω [eksaryeerono] cash, turn into money.

ἐξάρθρωσις, ἡ [eksarthrosees] dislocation.

ἔξαρσις, ἡ [eksarsees] (μεταφ) elevation, exaltation.

ἐξαρτήματα, τά [eksarteemata] πλ gear, tackle, rigging, accessories.

ἐξάρτησις, ἡ [eksarteesees] dependence.

ἐξαρτῶμαι [eksartome] depend on, turn on.

ἐξασθένησις, ἡ [eksastheneesees] weakening, enfeeblement.

ἐξάσκησις, ἡ [eksaskeesees] exercise, practice, training.

ἐξασκῶ [eksasko] exercise, practise ‖ (πίεσιν) exert.

ἐξασφαλίζω [eksasfaleezo] assure ‖ (θέσιν) book, reserve.

ἐξατμίζω [eksatmeezo] evaporate ‖ (μεταφ) vanish, melt away.

ἐξάτμισις, ἡ [eksatmeesees] evaporation ‖ (αὐτοκινήτου) exhaust.

ἐξαφανίζομαι [eksafaneezome] disappear, vanish.

ἐξαφανίζω [eksafaneezo] eliminate, wipe out, destroy.

ἔξαφνα [eksafna] all of a sudden ‖ (π.χ.) for instance.

ἔξαφνος [eksafnos] unexpected.

ἔξαψις, ἡ [eksapsees] fit of anger ‖ excitement, elation.

ἐξεγείρομαι [ekseyeerome] rise, rebel.

ἐξέδρα, ἡ [ekseðra] platform, stand ‖ (λιμανιοῦ) pier.

ἐξελιγμένος [ekseleeymenos] developed, evolved.

ἐξέλιξις, ἡ [ekseleeksees] evolution, development.

ἐξελίσσομαι [ekseleesome] unfold, evolve, develop.

ἐξεπίτηδες [eksepeeteeðes] deliberately.

ἐξερευνητής, ὁ [ekserevneetees] explorer.

ἐξερευνῶ [ekserevno] investigate, explore.

ἐξέρχομαι [ekserhome] go out, leave ‖ βλ καί βγαίνω.

ἐξετάζω [eksetazo] examine, interrogate, investigate.

ἐξέτασις, ἡ [eksetasees] examination, inspection.

ἐξεύρεσις, ἡ [eksevresees] discovery, finding out, invention.

ἐξευτελίζω [eksevteleezo] cheapen, lower, humiliate.

ἐξέχω [ekseho] stand out, project ‖ excel.

ἐξήγησις, ἡ [ekseeyeesees] explanation, interpretation.

ἐξηγοῦμαι [ekseeyoume] explain, make clear, give an explanation.

ἐξηγῶ [ekseeyo] explain ‖ interpret.

ἑξή(κο)ντα [eksee(ko)nta] sixty.

ἐξημερώνω [ekseemerono] tame.

ἐξηντλημένος [ekseentleemenos] exhausted, used up.

ἑξῆς [eksees]: ὡς ~ as follows ‖ τά ~ the following ‖ εἰς τό ~ henceforth ‖ καί οὕτω καθ' ~ and so on.

ἐξιλεώνω [ekseeleono] appease, pacify ‖ atone for.

ἕξις, ἡ [eksees] habit, custom, use.

ἐξίσταμαι [ekseestame] be astonished, wonder at.

ἐξίσωσις, ἡ [ekseesosees] balancing, equalizing ‖ (μαθημ) equation.

ἐξόγκωμα, τό [eksongoma] swelling, tumour, bulge.

ἐξογκώνω [eksongono] swell ‖ (μεταφ) exaggerate, overcolour.

ἐξόγκωσις, ἡ [eksongosees] swelling ‖ exaggeration.

ἐξοδεύω [eksoðevo] spend, use up, consume.

ἔξοδον, τό [eksoðon] expense.

ἔξοδος, ἡ [eksoðos] opening, emergence ‖ (πόρτα) exit ‖ (στρατ) sortie ‖ (ἐκκλ) exodus.

ἐξοικειώνω [ekseekeeono] familiarize, accustom.

ἐξοκέλλω [eksokelo] run aground, go astray.

ἐξολοθρεύω [eksolothrevo] exterminate, destroy.

ἐξομαλύνω [eksomaleeno] smooth down ‖ level.

ἐξομοιώνω [eksomeeono] assimilate to, liken to, rank together.

ἐξομολόγησις, ἡ [eksomoloyeesees] confession, acknowledgement.

ἐξομολογῶ [eksomoloyo] confess.

ἐξόν [ekson] besides, except ‖ ~ ἄν unless.

ἐξοντῶ [eksonto] annihilate, exterminate.

ἐξοπλίζω [eksopleezo] arm, equip.

ἐξοργίζω [eksoryeezo] enrage, make angry.

ἐξορία, ἡ [eksoreea] banishment, exile.

ἐξορίζω [eksoreezo] exile, banish.

ἐξορκίζω [eksorkeezo] conjure, exorcise.

ἐξουδετερώνω [eksoudeterono] neutralize.

ἐξουθενίζω [eksoutheneezo] debase, degrade.

ἐξουσία, ἡ [eksouseea] power, authority, government.

ἐξουσιοδοτῶ [eksouseeodoto] give authority to, authorize, empower.

ἐξόφθαλμος [eksofthalmos] obvious, plain.

ἐξοφλῶ [eksoflo] (λογαριασμόν) pay off, liquidate ‖ (μεταφ) fulfil.

ἐξοχή, ἡ [eksohee] countryside ‖ (ἐδαφική) eminence, protrusion ‖ κατ' ~ν pre-eminently, par excellence.

ἐξοχικός [eksoheekos] country, rural, rustic.

ἔξοχος [eksohos] excellent, eminent, notable.

ἐξοχότης, ἡ [eksohotees] excellence ‖ ἡ αὐτοῦ ~ His Excellency.

ἐξύβρισις, ἡ [ekseevreesees] abuse, insult, offence.

ἐξυμνῶ [ekseemno] praise, celebrate.

ἐξυπακούεται [ekseepakouete] it is understood, it follows.

ἐξυπηρέτησις, ἡ [ekseepeereeteesees] assistance, service, attendance.

ἐξυπηρετικός [ekseepeereeteekos] helpful, useful.

ἐξυπηρετῶ [ekseepeereeto] serve, assist, attend upon.

ἐξυπνάδα, ἡ [ekseepnaða] cleverness, shrewdness.

ἔξυπνος [ekseepnos] clever, intelligent, smart, witty.

ἐξυπνῶ [ekseepno] wake up, awake.

ἐξυφαίνω [ekseefeno] weave ‖ (κίνημα) hatch, plot, contrive.

ἐξυψώνω [ekseepsono] elevate, raise ‖ (μεταφ) exalt, extol, glorify.

ἔξω [ekso] out, outside, without, abroad ‖ ἀπ' ~ from outside ‖ (μάθημα) by heart ‖ ~ ἀπό outside, except for ‖ μιά καί ~ at one go.

ἐξώγαμος [eksoyamos] illegitimate, bastard.

ἔξωθεν [eksothen] from outside, from without.

ἐξώθυρα, ἡ [eksotheera] outside door, gateway.

ἐξωθῶ [eksotho] drive, push, force.

ἐξωκκλήσιον, τό [eksokleeseeon] chapel, country church.

ἐξωμότης, ὁ [eksomotees] renegade, apostate.

ἐξώπορτα, ἡ [eksoporta] βλ ἐξώθυρα.

ἐξωραΐζω [eksoraeezo] beautify, decorate, embellish.

ἔξωσις, ἡ [eksosees] eviction, expulsion.

ἐξώστης, ὁ [eksostees] balcony.

ἐξωτερικόν, τό [eksotereekon] exterior ‖ foreign country.

ἐξωτερικός [eksotereekos] external ‖ foreign.

ἐξωτικό, τό [eksoteeko] spook, spectre, wraith.

ἐξωτικός [eksoteekos] exotic ‖ outlandish.

ἐξωφρενικός [eksofreneekos] crazy ‖ maddening ‖ unreasonable, absurd.

ἐξώφυλλον, τό [eksofeelon] cover, flyleaf ‖ (παραθύρου) shutter.

ἑορτάζω [eortazo] celebrate.

ἑορτή, ἡ [eortee] holiday ‖ name day ‖ festival.

ἐπάγγελμα, τό [epangelma] profession, vocation ‖ ἐπαγγελματίας, ὁ craftsman, businessman.

ἐπαγγέλλομαι [epangelome] practise ‖ (παριστάνω) pretend.

ἔπαθλον, τό [epathlon] prize, trophy.

ἔπαινος, ὁ [epenos] praise.

ἐπαινῶ [epeno] praise, speak highly of.

ἐπαισθητός [epestheetos] perceptible, noticeable.

ἐπαίσχυντος [epesheentos] shameful.

ἐπαίτης, ὁ [epetees] beggar.

ἐπακόλουθα, τά [epakoloutha] πλ consequences.

ἐπακολουθῶ [epakoloutho] follow, come after.

ἔπακρον, τό [epakron]: εἰς τό ~ extremely, to the extreme.

ἐπαλείφω [epaleefo] smear, anoint (with).

ἐπαληθεύω [epaleethevo] establish, verify.

ἐπάλληλος [epaleelos] successive, one after another.

ἐπάναγκες [epananges] essential, necessary.

ἐπανάγω [epanayo] bring back (again).

ἐπανακάμπτω [epanakampto] return.

ἐπανακτῶ [epanakto] recover.

ἐπαναλαμβάνω [epanalamvano] repeat, resume.

ἐπανάληψις, ἡ [epanaleepsees] resumption, repetition.

ἐπανάστασις, ἡ [epanastasees] revolution.

ἐπαναστάτης, ὁ [epanastatees] revolutionary, rebel.

ἐπαναστατικός [epanastateekos] revolutionary.

ἐπαναστατῶ [epanastato] revolt, rebel.
ἐπαναφέρω [epanafero] restore, bring back.
ἐπανειλημμένος [epaneeleemenos] repeatedly.
ἐπανέρχομαι [epanerhome] return.
ἐπάνοδος, ἡ [epanodos] return.
ἐπανόρθωσις, ἡ [epanorthoses] reparation, restoration.
ἐπανωφόρι, τό [epanoforee] overcoat.
ἐπαξίως [epakseos] deservedly, worthily.
ἐπάρατος [eparatos] (μεταφ) hateful, abominable.
ἐπάρκεια, ἡ [eparkeea] sufficiency, adequacy.
ἔπαρσις, ἡ [eparsees] conceit, haughtiness.
ἐπαρχία, ἡ [eparheea] province, district.
ἐπαρχιώτης, ὁ [eparheeotees] provincial.
ἔπαυλις, ἡ [epavlees] villa || country house.
ἐπαύριον [epavreeon]: ἡ ~ the following day, tomorrow.
ἐπαφή, ἡ [epafee] contact, touch.
ἐπαχθής [epahthees] oppressive || tedious.
ἐπείγομαι [epeeyome] be in a hurry, make haste.
ἐπειγόντως [epeeyontos] urgently.
ἐπείγων [epeeyon] urgent, pressing.
ἐπειδή [epeedee] because, as, for, since.
ἐπεισόδιον, τό [epeesodeeon] episode, incident || (καυγᾶς) quarrel, dispute.
ἔπειτα [epeeta] next, then, afterwards || moreover || ~ ἀπό after.
ἐπέκτασις, ἡ [epektasees] extension.
ἐπεκτείνω [epekteeno] extend, prolong.
ἐπεμβαίνω [epemveno] interfere, intervene.
ἐπέμβασις, ἡ [epemvasees] intervention, interference || (ἰατρ) operation.
ἐπένδυσις, ἡ [endeesees] lining, covering || (οἴκον) investment.
ἐπεξεργασία, ἡ [epekseryaseea] processing, elaboration.
ἐπεξήγησις, ἡ [epekseeyeesees] explanation, elucidation.
ἐπέρχομαι [eperhome] come suddenly, occur, happen.
ἐπέτειος, ἡ [epeteeos] anniversary.
ἐπετηρίς, ἡ [epeteerees] anniversary.
ἐπευφημῶ [epefeemo] cheer, applaud.
ἐπηρεάζω [epeereazo] influence, affect.
ἐπί [epee] on, upon, over, above || (διαρκείας) for || ~ πλέον furthermore || ~ τέλους at last.
ἐπιβαίνω [epeeveno] go aboard || mount.
ἐπιβάλλομαι [epeevalome] assert o.s. || be indispensable.
ἐπιβάλλω [epeevalo] impose, inflict.
ἐπιβαρύνω [epeevareeno] burden.
ἐπιβατηγόν, τό [epeevateeyon] passenger ship.
ἐπιβάτης, ὁ [epeevatees] passenger.
ἐπιβατικόν, τό [epeevateekon] passenger vehicle, passenger ship.
ἐπιβεβαιώνω [epeeveveono] confirm, corroborate.

ἐπιβιβάζομαι [epeeveevazome] embark, go on board.
ἐπιβιβάζω [epeeveevazo] put aboard.
ἐπιβλαβής [epeevlavees] harmful.
ἐπιβλέπω [epeevlepo] supervise.
ἐπιβλητικός [epeevleeteekos] imposing.
ἐπιβολή, ἡ [epeevolee] imposition, infliction.
ἐπιβουλεύομαι [epeevoulevome] plot against.
ἐπίβουλος [epeevoulos] insidious, malicious.
ἐπιβραδύνω [epeevradeeno] retard, delay.
ἐπίγειος [epeeyeeos] earthly, worldly.
ἐπίγνωσις, ἡ [epeeynosees] knowledge, understanding.
ἐπίγονος, ὁ [epeeyonos] descendant.
ἐπίγραμμα, τό [epeeyrama] epigram.
ἐπιγραφή, ἡ [epeeyrafee] inscription || (βιβλίου) title.
ἐπιγραφική, ἡ [epeeyrafeekee] epigraphy.
ἐπιδεικνύομαι [epeedeekneeome] show off, be pompous.
ἐπιδεικνύω [epeedeekneeo] display || show off.
ἐπιδεικτικός [epeedeekteekos] showy.
ἐπιδείνωσις, ἡ [epeedeenosees] aggravation.
ἐπίδειξις, ἡ [epeedeeksees] display || showing off.
ἐπιδέξιος [epeedekseeos] skilful.
ἐπιδερμίδα, ἡ [epeedermeeða] complexion || epidermis.
ἐπίδεσμος, ὁ [epeedesmos] bandage.
ἐπιδέχομαι [epeedehome] allow, be susceptible, tolerate.
ἐπιδημία, ἡ [epeedeemeea] epidemic.
ἐπιδίδω [epeedeeðo] present || deliver || serve.
ἐπιδιόρθωσις, ἡ [epeedeeorthosees] repair, mending.
ἐπιδιώκω [epeedeeoko] aim at, pursue, seek.
ἐπιδοκιμάζω [epeedokeemazo] approve.
ἐπίδομα, τό [epeedoma] allowance, extra pay.
ἐπίδοσις, ἡ [epeedosees] presentation, delivery || (νομ) deposit || (μεταφ) progress, development || (ἀθλητ) record.
ἐπίδρασις, ἡ [epeedrasees] effect, influence.
ἐπιδρομή, ἡ [epeedromee] invasion, raid.
ἐπιδρῶ [epeedro] influence, act upon.
ἐπιεικής [epieekees] lenient, indulgent.
ἐπιζήμιος [epeezeemeeos] harmful, injurious.
ἐπιζῶ [epeezo] survive, outlive.
ἐπίθεσις, ἡ [epeethesees] attack || application.
ἐπιθετικός [epeetheteekos] aggressive || (γραμμ) adjectival.
ἐπίθετον, τό [epeetheton] adjective || surname.
ἐπιθανάτιος [epeethanateeos] of death, mortal.

ἐπιθεώρησις, ἡ [epeetheoreesees] inspection ‖ (περιοδικόν) review ‖ (θέατρον) revue.

ἐπιθυμία, ἡ [epeetheemeea] desire, wish.

ἐπιθυμῶ [epeetheemo] wish for, desire.

ἐπίκαιρος [epeekeros] timely, opportune ‖ topical.

ἐπικαλοῦμαι [epeekaloume] invoke.

ἐπίκειμαι [epeekeeme] be imminent ‖ impend.

ἐπικερδής [epeekerðees] profitable.

ἐπικεφαλίς, ἡ [epeekefalees] headline ‖ title.

ἐπικίνδυνος [epeekeenðeenos] dangerous, hazardous.

ἐπικλινής [epeekleenees] sloping, inclined.

ἐπικοινωνία, ἡ [epeekeenoneea] contact, communication.

ἐπικοινωνῶ [epeekeenono] communicate.

ἐπικός [epeekos] epic.

ἐπικουρία, ἡ [epeekoureea] help ‖ (στρατ) relief, reinforcements.

ἐπικράτεια, ἡ [epeekrateea] state, dominion.

ἐπικρατῶ [epeekrato] prevail, predominate.

ἐπικρίνω [epeekreeno] criticize, censure.

ἐπικροτῶ [epeekroto] approve.

ἐπικυρώνω [epeekeerono] ratify, confirm, sanction.

ἐπιλαχών, ὁ [epeelahon] runner-up.

ἐπίλεκτος [epeelektos] select, chosen.

ἐπιληψία, ἡ [epeeleepseea] epilepsy.

ἐπιλογή, ἡ [epeeloyee] selection, choice.

ἐπίλογος, ὁ [epeeloyos] epilogue ‖ conclusion.

ἐπιλοχίας, ὁ [epeeloheeas] sergeant-major.

ἐπίμαχος [epeemahos] disputed ‖ controversial.

ἐπιμελής [epeemelees] diligent, industrious, careful.

ἐπιμελητήριον, τό [epeemeleeteereeon] (ἐμπορικόν) chamber of commerce.

ἐπιμελητής, ὁ [epeemeleetees] superintendent ‖ (university) tutor.

ἐπιμελοῦμαι [epeemeloume] take care of.

ἐπιμένω [epeemeno] insist, persist.

ἐπιμήκης [epeemeekees] oblong, elongated.

ἐπιμονή, ἡ [epeemonee] insistence, perseverance.

ἐπίμονος [epeemonos] persistent, stubborn ‖ obstinate.

ἐπινοῶ [epeenoo] invent, contrive, devise.

ἐπιοῦσα, ἡ [epeeousa] the next day.

ἐπίπαγος, ὁ [epeepayos] crust.

ἐπίπεδον, τό [epeepeðon] plane.

ἐπίπεδος [epeepeðos] plane, level, flat ‖ even.

ἐπιπίπτω [epeepeepto] fall upon.

ἔπιπλα, τά [epeepla] πλ furniture.

ἐπίπλαστος [epeeplastos] feigned, fictitious.

ἐπιπλέω [epeepleo] float ‖ (μεταφ) keep afloat.

ἐπίπληξις, ἡ [epeepleeksees] reproach, rebuke.

ἐπιπλήττω [epeepleeto] reproach, chide.

ἐπιπλοκή, ἡ [epeeplokee] complication.

ἐπιπλώνω [epeeplono] furnish.

ἐπίπλωσις, ἡ [epeeplosees] furnishing.

ἐπιπόλαιος [epeepoleos] superficial ‖ frivolous.

ἐπίπονος [epeeponos] laborious, toilsome.

ἐπιπροσθέτως [epeeprosthetos] in addition, furthermore.

ἐπίρρημα, τό [epeereema] adverb.

ἐπιρροή, ἡ [epeeroee] influence.

ἐπίσημος [epeeseemos] official, formal.

ἐπίσης [epeesees] likewise, also, too.

ἐπισιτισμός, ὁ [epeeseeteesmos] provisioning, victualling, provisions.

ἐπισκεπτήριον, τό [epeeskepteereeon] visiting card.

ἐπισκέπτης, ὁ [epeeskeptees] visitor.

ἐπισκέπτομαι [epeeskeptome] visit, call upon.

ἐπισκευάζω [epeeskevazo] repair, mend.

ἐπισκευή, ἡ [epeeskevee] repairing, mending.

ἐπίσκεψις, ἡ [epeeskepsees] visit, call.

ἐπίσκοπος, ὁ [epeeskopos] bishop.

ἐπισμηναγός, ὁ [epeesmeenayos] squadron leader.

ἐπισπεύδω [epeespevðo] hasten, rush.

ἐπιστάτης, ὁ [epeestatees] supervisor ‖ overseer ‖ attendant.

ἐπιστήθιος [epeesteetheeos]: ~ φίλος bosom friend.

ἐπιστήμη, ἡ [epeesteemee] science.

ἐπιστημονικός [epeesteemoneekos] scientific.

ἐπιστήμων, ὁ, ἡ [epeesteemon] scientist, professional (man) ‖ expert.

ἐπιστολή, ἡ [epeestolee] letter.

ἐπιστόμιον, τό [epeestomeeon] mouthpiece ‖ valve, plug.

ἐπιστράτευσις, ἡ [epeestratevsees] mobilization, call-up.

ἐπιστρέφω [epeestrefo] return.

ἐπιστροφή, ἡ [epeestrofee] return.

ἐπίστρωμα, τό [epeestroma] covering ‖ (κρεββατιοῦ) blanket.

ἐπισύρω [epeeseero] attract, draw, catch one's eye.

ἐπισφαλής [epeesfalees] precarious, risky ‖ unstable.

ἐπισωρεύω [epeesorevo] accumulate, pile up.

ἐπιταγή, ἡ [epeetayee] order ‖ cheque.

ἐπιτακτικός [epeetakteekos] imperative.

ἐπίταξις, ἡ [epeetaksees] requisition.

ἐπιτάφιος, ὁ [epeetafeeos] Good Friday procession.

ἐπιταχύνω [epeetaheeno] accelerate, speed up.

ἐπιτελάρχης, ὁ [epeetelarhees] chief of staff.

ἐπιτελεῖον, τό [epeeteleeon] (general) staff.

ἐπιτετραμμένος, ὁ [epeetetramenos] chargé d'affaires.
ἐπίτευγμα, τό [epeetevyma] achievement.
ἐπίτευξις, ἡ [epeetevksees] attainment || obtaining.
ἐπιτήδειος [epeeteedeeos] suitable for || clever, skilful.
ἐπίτηδες [epeeteedes] on purpose, purposely.
ἐπιτηδευμένος [epeeteedevmenos] affected.
ἐπιτηρῶ [epeeteero] supervise, oversee, watch.
ἐπιτίθεμαι [epeeteetheme] attack, assail, assault.
ἐπίτιμος [epeeteemos] honorary.
ἐπιτόκιον, τό [epeetokeeon] compound interest.
ἐπιτομή, ἡ [epeetomee] summary, abridgement.
ἐπίτομος [epeetomos] abridged, shortened, condensed.
ἐπιτόπιος [epeetopeeos] local.
ἐπιτρέπω [epeetrepo] allow, permit.
ἐπιτροπή, ἡ [epeetropee] committee, commission.
ἐπίτροπος, ὁ [epeetropos] guardian, trustee || agent.
ἐπιτυγχάνω [epeeteenghano] attain, get || get right || (κατά τύχην) meet, find || (στήν δουλειά) succeed.
ἐπιτυχής [epeeteehees] successful.
ἐπιτυχία, ἡ [epeeteeheea] success.
ἐπιφάνεια [epeefaneea] surface.
ἐπιφανής [epeefanees] eminent, prominent.
Ἐπιφάνια, τά [epeefaneea] πλ Epiphany.
ἐπιφέρω [epeefero] bring about, cause.
ἐπίφοβος [epeefovos] dangerous, alarming.
ἐπιφυλακή, ἡ [epeefeelakee]: ἐν ~ at the ready, on the alert.
ἐπιφύλαξις, ἡ [epeefeelaksees] circumspection || reservation.
ἐπιφυλάσσομαι [epeefeelasome] reserve, intend.
ἐπιφώνημα, τό [epeefoneema] (γραμμ) interjection.
ἐπιχείρημα, τό [epeeheereema] argument || attempt.
ἐπιχειρηματίας, ὁ [epeeheereemateeas] businessman.
ἐπιχείρησις, ἡ [epeeheereesees] undertaking || (οἴκον) enterprise, business || (στρατ) operation.
ἐπιχρίω [epeehreeo] coat, paint, daub.
ἐπιχρυσώνω [epeehreesono] gild.
ἐποικοδομητικός [epeekoδomeeteekos] constructive, edifying.
ἔπομαι [epome] follow.
ἑπόμενος [epomenos] next, following.
ἑπομένως [epomenos] consequently, therefore.
ἐπονομάζω [eponomazo] surname, name.
ἐποπτεύω [epoptevo] supervise, oversee, inspect.

ἐπουλώνω [epoulono] heal.
ἐποφθαλμιῶ [epofthalmeeo] covet.
ἐποχή, ἡ [epohee] epoch, era || (τοῦ ἔτους) season.
ἑπτά [epta] seven.
ἑπτακόσιοι [eptakosiee] seven hundred.
ἐπώδυνος [eroδeenos] painful.
ἐπωμίζομαι [epomeezome] shoulder (a burden).
ἐπωμίς, ἡ [epomees] epaulette.
ἐπωνυμία, ἡ [eponeemeea] (nick)name || surname || (ἑταιρείας) title.
ἐπώνυμον, τό [eponeemon] surname, family name.
ἐπωφελής [epofelees] profitable, beneficial, useful.
ἐπωφελοῦμαι [epofeloume] take advantage, avail o.s., profit.
ἔρανος, ὁ [eranos] fund, collection.
ἐρασιτέχνης, ὁ [eraseetehnees] amateur.
ἐραστής, ὁ [erastees] lover.
ἐργάζομαι [eryazome] work || function.
ἐργαλεῖον, τό [eryaleeon] tool, implement.
ἐργασία, ἡ [eryaseea] work, job, business || (ἐπιδεξιότης) workmanship.
ἐργαστήριον, τό [eryasteereeon] laboratory || studio || workshop.
ἐργάτης, ὁ [eryatees] labourer, worker || (ναυτ) windlass.
ἐργατιά, ἡ [eryateea] working class.
ἐργατικός [eryateekos] industrious, of the working class.
ἐργένης, ὁ [eryenees] bachelor.
ἐργοδηγός, ὁ [eryoδeeyos] foreman.
ἐργοδότης, ὁ [eryoδotees] employer.
ἐργολάβος, ὁ [eryolavos] contractor || (γλυκό) macaroon.
ἔργον, τό [eryon] work || act, deed || (βιβλίον) book || (σινεμά) film.
ἐργοστάσιον, τό [eryostaseeon] factory || works.
ἐργόχειρον, τό [eryoheeron] handiwork || (κέντημα) embroidery.
ἐρεθίζω [eretheezo] irritate, excite.
ἐρεθισμός, ὁ [eretheesmos] irritation.
ἐρείπιον, τό [ereepeeon] ruin, wreck.
ἔρεισμα, τό [ereesma] prop, support.
ἔρευνα, ἡ [erevna] (re)search, investigation.
ἐρευνητής, ὁ [erevneetees] researcher || explorer.
ἐρευνῶ [erevno] search, investigate.
ἐρημία, ἡ [ereemeea] solitude || wilderness.
ἔρημος, ἡ [ereemos] desert || (ἐπίθ) desolate, deserted.
ἐρημώνω [ereemono] lay waste, devastate.
ἔριον, τό [ereeon] wool, fleece.
ἔρις, ἡ [erees] dispute, quarrel.
ἐρίφι, τό [ereefee] kid.
ἔρμαιον, τό [ermeon] prey || victim.
ἐρμάριον, τό [ermareeon] cupboard, closet.
ἑρμηνεία, ἡ [ermeeneea] interpretation.
ἑρμηνεύω [ermeenevo] interpret.
ἑρμητικός [ermeeteekos] hermetic.

ἑρπετόν, τό [erpeton] reptile.
ἕρπω [erpo] crawl, creep.
ἐρυθριῶ [ereethreeo] blush.
ἐρυθρόδερμος, ὁ [ereethroðermos] redskin.
ἐρυθρός [ereethros] red.
ἔρχομαι [erhome] come.
ἐρχόμενος [erhomenos] coming, next.
ἐρχομός, ὁ [erhomos] coming, arrival.
ἐρωμένη, ἡ [eromenee] mistress.
ἐρωμένος, ὁ [eromenos] lover.
ἔρωτας, ὁ [erotas] love, passion.
ἐρωτευμένος [erotevmenos] in love.
ἐρωτεύομαι [erotevome] fall in love.
ἐρώτημα, τό [eroteema] question, problem.
ἐρωτηματικόν, τό [eroteemateekon] question mark.
ἐρωτηματολόγιον, τό [eroteematoloyeeon] questionnaire.
ἐρώτησις, ἡ [eroteesees] question, query.
ἐρωτικός, ὁ [eroteekos] erotic ‖ amatory.
ἐρωτοτροπία, ἡ [erototropeea] flirtation.
ἐρωτύλος [eroteelos] amorous.
ἐρωτῶ [eroto] ask, inquire ‖ question.
ἐσκεμμένος [eskemenos] premeditated ‖ deliberately.
ἐσοδεία, ἡ [esoðeea] crop, harvest.
ἔσοδον, τό [esoðon] income, revenue, receipt.
ἐσοχή, ἡ [esohee] recess, indentation.
ἑσπέρα, ἡ [espera] evening.
ἐσπεριδοειδῆ, τά [espereeðoeeðee] πλ citrus fruits.
ἐσπερινός [espereenos] evening.
ἐσπερινός, ὁ [espereenos] vespers.
ἐσπευσμένος [espevsmenos] hasty, hurried.
ἑστία, ἡ [esteea] hearth, fireplace ‖ (σπίτι) home ‖ (λίκνος) cradle ‖ (σόμπας) burner.
ἑστιατόριον, τό [esteeatoreeon] restaurant.
ἔστω [esto] so be it ‖ ~ καί even, even if.
ἐσύ [esee] you.
ἐσχάρα, ἡ [eshara] grill, gridiron, grid.
ἔσχατος [eshatos] extreme, utmost, last.
ἐσχάτως [eshatos] recently, lately.
ἔσω [eso] within, inside.
ἐσωκλείω [esokleeo] enclose.
ἐσώρρουχα, τά [esorouha] πλ underclothes, underwear.
ἐσωτερικός [esotereekos] interior, inner, internal ‖ domestic.
ἑταιρεία, ἡ [etereea] company, society, firm, partnership.
ἑτερογενής [eteroyenees] heterogeneous.
ἕτερος [eteros] (an)other ‖ ἀφ᾽ ἑτέρου on the other hand.
ἐτήσιος [eteeseeos] annual, yearly.
ἔτι [etee] moreover, still, yet.
ἐτικέττα, ἡ [eteeketa] label, price tag.
ἑτοιμάζομαι [eteemazome] get ready, prepare.
ἑτοιμάζω [eteemazo] prepare, make ready.
ἑτοιμασία, ἡ [eteemaseea] preparation.
ἕτοιμος [eteemos] ready.
ἔτος, τό [etos] year.

ἔτσι [etsee] thus, so, like this, like that, in this way ‖ ~ κι᾽ ~ middling ‖ in any case ‖ ~ κι᾽ ἀλλοιῶς in any case, either way.
ἐτυμηγορία, ἡ [eteemeeyoreea] verdict.
ἐτυμολογία, ἡ [eteemoloyeea] etymology.
εὖ [ev] well.
εὖ— [ev] well, easily.
εὐαγγέλιον, τό [evangeleeon] gospel.
Εὐαγγελισμός, ὁ [evangeleesmos] Annunciation.
εὐάερος [evaeros] well-ventilated, airy.
εὐαισθησία, ἡ [evestheeseea] sensitivity.
εὐαίσθητος [evestheetos] sensitive.
εὐανάγνωστος [evanaynostos] legible.
εὐάρεστος [evarestos] agreeable, pleasant.
εὐαρεστοῦμαι [evarestoume] be pleased, be willing.
εὖγε [evye] (ἐπιφ) bravo!, good show!
εὐγένεια, ἡ [evyeneea] courtesy, politeness.
εὐγενικός [evyeneekos] polite, courteous.
εὐγενής [evyenees] βλ εὐγενικός.
εὔγευστος [evyevstos] palatable, tasty.
εὐγλωττία, ἡ [evyloteea] eloquence.
εὐγνωμοσύνη, ἡ [evynomoseenee] gratitude.
εὐγνώμων [evynomon] grateful, thankful.
εὐδαιμονία, ἡ [evðemoneea] prosperity ‖ happiness.
εὐδιάθετος [evðeeathetos] in good humour.
εὐδιάκριτος [evðeeakreetos] discernible, distinct.
εὐδοκιμῶ [evðokeemo] succeed ‖ thrive ‖ prosper.
εὐδοκῶ [evðoko] be pleased to, deign, consent.
εὔελπις [evelpees] hopeful, promising ‖ (στρατ) cadet.
εὐεξάπτος [eveksaptos] irritable, excitable.
εὐεργέτης, ὁ [everyetees] benefactor.
εὐεργετικός [everyeteekos] beneficial, beneficent, charitable.
εὔζωνας, ὁ [evzonas] evzone.
εὐήλιος [eveeleeos] sunny.
εὐημερῶ [eveemero] prosper.
εὔηχος [eveehos] melodious, tuneful.
εὐθεῖα, ἡ [evtheea] straight line ‖ κατ᾽ ~ direct, straight.
εὔθετος [evthetos] suitable, proper, convenient.
εὔθικτος [evtheektos] touchy, sensitive.
εὔθραυστος [evthravstos] fragile, brittle.
εὐθύγραμμος [evtheeyramos] straight, rectilinear.
εὐθυμία, ἡ [evtheemeea] gaiety, cheerfulness.
εὔθυμος [evtheemos] merry, gay, cheerful.
εὐθύνη, ἡ [evtheenee] responsibility.
εὐθύνομαι [evtheenome] be responsible, be accountable.
εὐθύς [evthees] (ἐπιρ) immediately, at once.
εὐθύς [evthees] straight, upright ‖ (τίμιος) honest, straightforward.

εὐκαιρία, ἡ [evkereea] opportunity, chance || (ἐμπόριον) bargain.

εὔκαιρος [evkeros] opportune || (ἐλεύθερος) available, free.

εὐκάλυπτος [evkaleeptos] eucalyptus.

εὔκαμπτος [evkamptos] flexible, pliable.

εὐκατάστατος [evkatastatos] well-to-do, well-off.

εὐκίνητος [evkeeneetos] agile, nimble.

εὐκοιλιότης, ἡ [evkeeleeotees] diarrhoea.

εὐκολία, ἡ [evkoleea] ease, convenience || (χάρις) favour.

εὔκολος [evkolos] easy || convenient.

εὐκολύνω [evkoleeno] facilitate.

εὐκρατής [evkratees] temperate, mild.

εὐκρινής [evkreenees] clear, distinct, lucid.

εὐκτική, ἡ [evkteekee] (γραμμ) optative (mood).

εὐλαβής [evlavees] devout, pious.

εὐλογία, ἡ [evloyeea] blessing, benediction.

εὐλογιά, ἡ [evloyia] smallpox.

εὔλογος [evloyos] reasonable, fair.

εὐλογῶ [evloyo] bless.

εὐλύγιστος [evleeyeestos] flexible, supple, pliant.

εὐμενής [evmenees] benevolent, kind, well-disposed.

εὐμετάβλητος [evmetavleetos] changeable, inconstant.

εὔμορφος [evmorfos] βλ ὄμορφος.

εὐνόητος [evnoeetos] easily understood || intelligible.

εὔνοια, ἡ [evneea] favour, goodwill.

εὐνοϊκός [evnoeekos] propitious, favourable.

εὐνοούμενος [evnooumenos] favourite.

εὐνοῶ [evnoo] favour.

εὐοδοῦμαι [evodoume] succeed, go well.

εὐοίωνος [eveeonos] auspicious.

εὐπαθής [evpathees] sensitive, delicate.

εὐπαρουσίαστος [evparouseeastos] presentable, imposing.

εὐπειθής [evpeethees] obedient.

εὔπιστος [evpeestos] credulous, gullible.

εὔπορος [evporos] well-off, prosperous.

εὐπρέπεια, ἡ [evprepeea] propriety || decency.

εὐπρεπίζω [evprepeezo] put in order || adorn, embellish.

εὐπρόσδεκτος [evprosdektos] welcome, acceptable.

εὐπρόσιτος [evproseetos] accessible, approachable.

εὕρεσις, ἡ [evresees] discovery.

εὑρετήριον, τό [evreteereeon] index, catalogue.

εὐρέως [evreos] widely, largely.

εὕρημα, τό [evreema] find, discovery.

εὑρίσκομαι [evreeskome] find o.s., be.

εὑρίσκω [evreesko] find, obtain || (τυχαίως) come across.

εὐρύνω [evreeno] widen, broaden, enlarge.

εὐρύς [evrees] wide, extended, broad.

εὐρύχωρος [evreehoros] spacious, roomy.

εὐρωπαϊκός [evropaeekos] European.

Εὐρώπη, ἡ [evropee] Europe.

εὔρωστος [evrostos] robust, vigorous.

εὐσέβεια, ἡ [evseveea] piety, devoutness.

εὐσεβής [evsevees] pious, devout.

εὐσπλαγχνία, ἡ [evsplanghneea] compassion, pity.

εὐστάθεια, ἡ [evstatheea] stability, firmness.

εὔστοχος [evstohos] well-aimed, proper.

εὔστροφος [evstrofos] agile, nimble, versatile.

εὐσυνείδητος [evseeneedeetos] conscientious || scrupulous.

εὔσωμος [evsomos] well-built, stout, sturdy.

εὐτέλεια, ἡ [evteleea] meanness, baseness, cheapness.

εὐτελής [evtelees] cheap, mean, worthless.

εὐτράπελος [evtrapelos] humorous, witty.

εὐτύχημα, τό [evteeheema] good luck, lucky thing.

εὐτυχής [evteehees] lucky, fortunate, happy.

εὐτυχία, ἡ [evteeheea] happiness, good fortune.

εὐτυχισμένος [evteeheesmenos] βλ εὐτυχής.

εὐτυχῶς [evteehos] luckily, happily, fortunately.

εὐυπόληπτος [eveepoleeptos] reputable, esteemed.

εὔφλεκτος [evflektos] inflammable.

εὐφορία, ἡ [evforeea] fruitfulness, fertility.

εὐφραδής [evfradees] fluent, eloquent.

εὐφραίνω [evfreno] delight, rejoice, gladden.

εὐφυής [evfiees] intelligent, witty, clever.

εὐφυΐα, ἡ [evfieea] intelligence, wit, ingenuity.

εὐχαρίστησις, ἡ [evhareesteesees] satisfaction, pleasure.

εὐχαριστίες, οἱ [evhareesties] πλ thanks.

εὐχάριστος [evhareestos] pleasant, agreeable.

εὐχαρίστως [evhareestos] gladly, with pleasure.

εὐχαριστῶ [evhareesto] thank || please, gratify.

εὐχέρεια, ἡ [evhereea] ease, facility.

εὐχή, ἡ [evhee] prayer || wish || blessing.

εὔχομαι [evhome] wish, hope.

εὔχρηστος [evhreestos] useful, handy || in general use.

εὐώδης [evodees] fragrant.

ἐφ'- [ef] βλ ἐπί.

ἐφάμιλλος [efameelos] equal to, on a par with, a match for.

ἐφάπαξ [efapaks] in a lump sum, once only.

ἐφαπτομένη, ἡ [efaptomenee] tangent.

ἐφαρμογή, ἡ [efarmoyee] application, fitting.

ἐφαρμόζω [efarmozo] fit || apply || enforce.

ἔφεδρος, ὁ [efedros] reservist.

ἐφεκτικός [efekteekos] reserved, guarded.

ἐφεξῆς [efeksees] henceforth, hereafter.

ἔφεσις, ἡ [efesees] (νομ) appeal.
ἐφετεῖον, τό [efeteeon] court of appeal.
ἐφετεινός [efeteenos] of this year.
ἐφέτος [efetos] this year.
ἐφεύρεσις, ἡ [efevresees] invention.
ἐφευρετικός [efevreteekos] inventive, ingenious.
ἔφηβος, ὁ [efeevos] youth, adolescent.
ἐφηβικός [efeeveekos] of youth, of puberty || ἐφηβική ἡλικία adolescence.
ἐφημερεύω [efeemerevo] be on duty.
ἐφημερίδα, ἡ [efeemereeδa] newspaper, journal, gazette.
ἐφιάλτης, ὁ [efeealtees] nightmare || bugbear.
ἐφικτός [efeektos] possible, attainable, feasible.
ἐφιστῶ [efeesto]: ~ τήν προσοχήν draw attention to.
ἐφόδια, τά [efoδeea] πλ supplies, equipment || ἐφοδιάζω supply, equip, furnish.
ἔφοδος [efoδos] charge, assault, attack.
ἐφοπλιστής, ὁ [efopleestees] shipowner.
ἐφορεία, ἡ [eforeea] tax office, revenue department || trustees.
ἐφορμῶ [eformo] attack, fall upon.
ἔφορος, ὁ [eforos] inspector, director, keeper, curator.
ἐφτά [efta] βλ ἑπτά.
ἐφτακόσιοι [eftakosiee] βλ ἑπτακόσιοι.
ἐχέγγυον, τό [ehengeeon] guarantee, pledge.
ἐχεμύθεια, ἡ [ehemeetheea] secrecy, discretion || ὑπό ~ν under pledge of secrecy.
ἐχθές [ehthes] yesterday.
ἔχθρα, ἡ [ehthra] enmity, hostility.
ἐχθρεύομαι [ehthrevome] hate, dislike.
ἐχθρικός [ehthreekos] hostile, (of the) enemy, inimical.
ἐχθρικότης, ἡ [ehthreekotees] hostility.
ἐχθροπραξίες, οἱ [ehthropraksies] πλ hostilities.
ἐχθρός, ὁ [ehthros] enemy, foe.
ἔχιδνα, ἡ [eheeδna] viper, adder.
ἐχῖνος, ὁ [eheenos] sea urchin.
ἔχω [eho] have, keep || consider || cost, be worth || ~ δίκιο I am right || τί ἔχεις; what's wrong?, what's the matter?
ἐψές [epses] yesterday.
ἔψιλον, τό [epseelon] the letter E.
ἑωθινός [eotheenos] morning.
ἕως [eos] till, until, to || as far as.
Ἑωσφόρος, ὁ [eosforos] Lucifer.

Z, ζ

ζαβολιά, ἡ [zavolia] cheating, trickery.
ζαβός [zavos] crooked, perverse || clumsy.
ζακέτα, ἡ [zaketa] jacket.
ζαλάδα, ἡ [zalaδa] giddiness, dizziness || headache.
ζάλη, ἡ [zalee] dizziness.

ζαλίζομαι [zaleezome] become dizzy, become confused.
ζαλίζω [zaleezo] make dizzy, confuse, daze, stun.
ζαμπόν, τό [zambon] ham.
ζάπλουτος [zaploutos] very rich, opulent.
ζάρα, ἡ [zara] crease, wrinkle.
ζάρια, τά [zareea] πλ dice.
ζαρκάδι, τό [zarkaδee] roe(buck).
ζάρωμα, τό [zaroma] creasing, wrinkling || crease, wrinkle.
ζαρώνω [zarono] crease, wrinkle || shrink.
ζαφείρι, τό [zafeeree] sapphire.
ζαχαρένιος [zahareneeos] sugary || (μεταφ) honeyed.
ζάχαρη, ἡ [zaharee] sugar.
ζαχαροκάλαμο, τό [zaharokalamo] sugar cane.
ζαχαροπλαστεῖο, τό [zaharoplasteeo] confectioner's shop, pastry shop.
ζαχαρωτά, τά [zaharota] πλ sweets.
ζεματίζω [zemateezo] scald || be very hot.
ζεματιστός [zemateestos] scalding, boiling.
ζεμπίλι, τό [zembeelee] straw basket, straw bag.
ζενίθ, τό [zeneeth] zenith.
ζερβά [zerva] on the left || (μεταφ) awry.
ζερβός [zervos] left-handed || left.
ζέσις, ἡ [zesees] boiling || (μεταφ) warmth, fervour.
ζεσταίνομαι [zestenome] get warm, feel hot.
ζεσταίνω [zesteno] heat up, warm.
ζεστασιά, ἡ [zestasia] warmth, heat.
ζέστη, ἡ [zestee] heat, warmth || κάνει ~ it's hot, it's warm.
ζεστός [zestos] hot, warm.
ζευγαράκι, τό [zevyarakee] pair (of lovers).
ζευγάρι, τό [zevyaree] pair, couple || (βοδιῶν) yoke || (ἄροσις) ploughing, tilling.
ζευγνύω [zevyneeo] yoke, harness, link.
ζεῦγος, τό [zevyos] pair, couple.
ζεῦξις, ἡ [zevksees] yoking || bridging, junction.
ζέφυρος, ὁ [zefeeros] light breeze.
ζέω [zeo] boil.
ζήλεια, ἡ [zeeleea] envy, jealousy.
ζηλευτός [zeelevtos] enviable, desirable || much desired.
ζηλεύω [zeelevo] envy, be jealous of.
ζηλιάρης [zeeleearees] envious, jealous.
ζῆλος, ὁ [zeelos] zeal, ardour, eagerness.
ζηλότυπος [zeeloteepos] βλ ζηλιάρης.
ζημία, ἡ [zeemeea] damage, loss, injury || harm.
ζημιώνω *[zeemeeono] damage, cause a loss, injure.
ζῆτα, τό [zeeta] the letter Z.
ζήτημα, τό [zeeteema] question, subject, matter || εἶναι ~ it's doubtful (whether).
ζήτησις, ἡ [zeeteesees] demand || search, pursuit.
ζητιανεύω [zeeteeanevo] beg, ask for alms.
ζητιάνος, ὁ [zeeteeanos] beggar.

ζήτω [zeeto] (ἐπιφ) long live!, up with!

ζητῶ [zeeto] seek, ask for, look for, demand ‖ beg.

ζητωκραυγή, ἡ [zeetokravyee] cheer.

ζιζάνιον, τό [zeezaneeon] (μεταφ) naughty person.

ζόρι, τό [zoree] force, violence ‖ difficulty ‖ μέ τό ~ against one's will.

ζορίζω [zoreezo] force, exert pressure on.

ζόρικος [zoreekos] hard, difficult ‖ (ἐπί ἀνθρώπων) hard to please, irksome.

ζούγκλα, ἡ [zoungla] jungle.

ζουζούνι, τό [zouzounee] insect.

ζούλισμα, τό [zouleesma] squeezing, crushing.

ζουμερός [zoumeros] juicy, succulent.

ζουμί, τό [zoumee] juice ‖ broth ‖ (ψητοῦ) gravy.

ζουμπούλι, τό [zoumboulee] hyacinth.

ζούρλα, ἡ [zourla] lunacy, folly.

ζουρλομανδύας, ὁ [zourlomandeeas] strait jacket.

ζουρλός [zourlos] crazy, insane.

ζοφερός [zoferos] dark, gloomy.

ζοχάδα, ἡ [zohada] peevishness, sourness, sullenness.

ζοχάδες, οἱ [zohades] πλ piles, haemorrhoids.

ζυγαριά, ἡ [zeeyaria] pair of scales, balance.

ζυγίζομαι [zeeyeezome] hover over.

ζυγίζω [zeeyeezo] weigh.

ζυγός, ὁ [zeeyos] yoke ‖ (παλάντζας) scale, beam.

ζυγός [zeeyos] even (number) ‖ μονά ζυγά odd or even.

ζυγώνω [zeeyono] draw near.

ζύθος, ὁ [zeethos] beer, ale.

ζυμάρι, τό [zeemaree] dough ‖ ζυμαρικά pastry, pies, cakes.

ζύμη, ἡ [zeemee] leaven, dough ‖ (μεταφ) quality, nature.

ζύμωμα, τό [zeemoma] kneading.

ζυμώνομαι [zeemonome] ferment.

ζυμώνω [zeemono] knead ‖ ferment.

ζύμωσις, ἡ [zeemosees] fermentation.

ζῶ [zo] live, experience ‖ lead a life.

ζωάριον, τό [zoareeon] small animal ‖ (μεταφ) worthless fellow.

ζωγραφιά, ἡ [zoyrafia] painting, drawing.

ζωγραφική, ἡ [zoyrafeekee] painting.

ζωγραφιστός [zoyrafeestos] painted ‖ (μεταφ) very beautiful.

ζωγράφος, ὁ [zoyrafos] painter, artist.

ζώδιον, τό [zodeeon] sign of the zodiac ‖ (μεταφ) fate, lot.

ζωέμπορος, ὁ [zoemboros] cattle dealer.

ζωή, ἡ [zoee] life, living ‖ lifetime.

ζωηρεύω [zoeerevo] become lively ‖ brighten up.

ζωηρός [zoeeros] lively, vivid ‖ (θερμός) warm, animated ‖ (χρώματος) bright ‖ (εὔθυμος) gay, full of life.

ζωηρότης, ἡ [zoeerotees] heat, warmth ‖

(κινήσεως) quickness, promptness ‖ (βλέμματος) vivacity, brightness.

ζωικός [zoeekos] animal ‖ vital, necessary.

ζωμός, ὁ [zomos] broth, soup.

ζωνάρι, τό [zonaree] belt, sash, girdle, waistband.

ζώνη, ἡ [zonee] zone ‖ βλ καί ζωνάρι.

ζώνομαι [zonome] put on.

ζωντανεύω [zontanevo] revive, return to life.

ζωντάνια, ἡ [zontaneea] liveliness, alertness.

ζωντανός [zontanos] living, live, vivid ‖ lively.

ζωντοχήρα, ἡ [zontoheera] divorced woman, divorcee.

ζωντοχήρος, ὁ [zontoheeros] divorced man, divorcee.

ζωογονῶ [zooyono] animate ‖ (μεταφ) stimulate, excite.

ζωοδόχος [zoodohos]: ~ πηγή source of life.

ζωοκλοπή, ἡ [zooklopee] cattle rustling, sheep stealing.

ζωολογία, ἡ [zooloyeea] zoology.

ζῶον, τό [zoon] animal ‖ (μεταφ) fool, ass.

ζωοτροφίες, οἱ [zootrofies] πλ animal fodder, provisions.

ζωόφιλος [zoofeelos] fond of animals.

ζωοφόρος, ἡ [zooforos] frieze.

ζωπυρῶ [zopeero] rekindle, revive.

ζωστήρ, ὁ [zosteer] belt, sash ‖ (ἰατρ) shingles.

ζωτικός [zoteekos] vital.

ζωτικότης, ἡ [zoteekotees] vitality ‖ (μεταφ) vital importance.

ζωύφιον, τό [zoeefeeon] insect, louse ‖ πλ vermin.

H, η

ἡ [ee] the.

ἤ [ee] or ‖ ~ . . . ~ either . . . or ‖ (συγκριτικός) than.

ἥβη, ἡ [eevee] puberty.

ἡγεμών, ὁ [eeyemon] prince, sovereign ‖ governor.

ἡγεσία, ἡ [eeyeseea] leadership.

ἡγέτης, ὁ [eeyetees] leader, chief.

ἡγοῦμαι [eeyoume] lead, command.

ἡγούμενος, ὁ [eeyoumenos] abbot.

ἡδέως [eedeos] sweetly, pleasingly.

ἤδη [eedee] already, even now.

ἡδονή, ἡ [eedonee] delight, sensual pleasure, lust.

ἡδονικός [eedoneekos] delightful ‖ sensual.

ἡδύς [eedees] sweet, agreeable, pleasant.

ἠθική, ἡ [eetheekee] ethics ‖ morality.

ἠθικόν, τό [eetheekon] morale ‖ morality, morals.

ἠθικός [eetheekos] ethical, moral ‖ virtuous, modest.

ἠθικότης, ἡ [eetheekotees] morality, modesty.

ἠθογραφία, ἡ [eethoγrafeea] folk customs, folklore.

ἠθοποιία, ἡ [eethopieea] acting.

ἠθοποιός, ὁ, ἡ [eethopeeos] actor, actress.

ἤθη, τά [eethee] πλ manners, habits, customs.

ἦθος, τό [eethos] character, nature, manner.

ἥκιστα [eekeesta] not at all, least || in the least.

ἠλεκτρίζω [eelektreezo] electrify.

ἠλεκτρικόν, τό [eelektreekon] electricity.

ἠλεκτρικός [eelektreekos] electric.

ἠλεκτρισμός, ὁ [eelektreesmos] electricity.

ἠλεκτρολόγος, ὁ [eelektroloγos] electrician.

ἠλεκτρονική, ἡ [eelektroneekee] πλ electronics.

ἠλεκτρόνιον, τό [eelektroneeon] electron.

ἠλεκτροπληξία, ἡ [eelektropleekseea] electric shock.

ἡλιακός [eeleeakos] of the sun, solar.

ἡλίασις, ἡ [eeleeasees] sunstroke.

ἠλίθιος [eeleetheeos] idiotic, stupid, silly.

ἡλικία, ἡ [eeleekeea] age.

ἡλικιωμένος [eeleekeeomenos] aged, advanced in years.

ἡλιοβασίλεμα, τό [eeleeovaseelema] sunset.

ἡλιοθεραπεία, ἡ [eeleeotherapeea] sunbathing.

ἡλιοκαμένος [eeleeokamenos] sunburnt, tanned.

ἥλιος, ὁ [eeleeos] sun || (φυτόν) sunflower.

ἧλος, ὁ [eelos] nail || (μεταφ) corn.

ἡμεῖς [eemees] we.

ἡμέρα, ἡ [eemera] day || τῆς ~ς fresh, today's.

ἡμερεύω [eemerevo] tame, domesticate || calm down, appease.

ἡμερήσιος [eemereeseeos] daily, everyday.

ἡμερολόγιον, τό [eemeroloγeeon] calendar, almanac || (πλοίου) logbook || (ἀτόμου) diary.

ἡμερομηνία, ἡ [eemeromeeneea] date.

ἡμερομίσθιον, τό [eemeromeestheeon] daily wage.

ἥμερος [eemeros] domesticated || tame, gentle.

ἡμερώνω [eemerono] tame || calm down, pacify.

ἡμέτερος [eemeteros] our, ours.

ἡμι- [eemee] half.

ἡμιαργία, ἡ [eemeearγeea] half-day (holiday).

ἡμιεπίσημος [eemiepeeseemos] semiofficial.

ἡμιθανής [eemeethanees] half-dead.

ἡμίθεος, ὁ [eemeetheos] demigod.

ἡμικύκλιον, τό [eemeekeekleeon] semicircle.

ἡμιμαθής [eemeemathees] half-learned (person), having a smattering of learning.

ἡμίμετρα, τά [eemeemetra] πλ half-measures.

ἡμίονος, ὁ, ἡ [eemeeonos] mule.

ἡμιπληγία, ἡ [eemeepleeγeea] stroke, paralysis.

ἡμισέληνος, ἡ [eemeeseleenos] crescent.

ἥμισυ, τό [eemeesee] half.

ἡμισφαίριον, τό [eemeesfereeon] hemisphere.

ἡμιτελής [eemeetelees] half-finished.

ἡμίφωνον, τό [eemeefonon] (γραμμ) semivowel.

ἡμίφως, τό [eemeefos] twilight || dim light.

ἡμιχρόνιον, τό [eemeehroneeon] (ἀθλητ) half-time.

ἡμίωρον, τό [eemeeoron] half-hour.

ἡμπορῶ [emboro] be able, be in a position to || may.

ἡνίον, τό [eeneeon] rein, bridle.

ἡνίοχος, ὁ [eeneeohos] charioteer.

ἡνωμένος [eenomenos] united, joint.

ἡξεύρω [eeksevro] βλ ξέρω.

ἧπαρ, τό [eepar] liver.

ἤπειρος, ἡ [eepeeros] continent || mainland, land.

ἠπειρωτικός [eepeeroteekos] continental.

ἤπιος [eepeeos] mild, indulgent || (ἀσθένεια) benign.

ἠρέμως [eeremos] quietly, calmly.

ἠρεμία, ἡ [eeremeea] quietness, tranquility, serenity.

ἤρεμος [eeremos] calm, tranquil, peaceful, still.

ἠρεμῶ [eeremo] be calm || keep quiet, keep still.

ἡρωικός [eeroeekos] heroic.

ἡρωίνη, ἡ [eeroeenee] heroin.

ἡρῷον, τό [eeroon] war memorial, hero's tomb.

ἥρωας, ὁ [eeroas] hero.

ἡρωίς, ἡ [eeroees] heroine.

ἡρωισμός, ὁ [eeroeesmos] heroism.

ἡσυχάζω [eeseehazo] grow quiet, rest, calm down.

ἡσυχία, ἡ [eeseeheea] quietness, peace, serenity.

ἥσυχος [eeseehos] quiet, peaceful, composed.

ἦτα, τό [eeta] the letter H.

ἤτοι [eetee] that is, namely.

ἦττα, ἡ [eeta] defeat, beating.

ἡττοπάθεια, ἡ [eetopatheea] defeatism.

ἧττον [eeton] less || οὐχ ~ nevertheless, nonetheless.

ἡττῶμαι [eetome] be defeated, succumb.

ἡφαίστειον, τό [eefesteeon] volcano.

ἠχηρός [eeheeros] loud, ringing, resonant.

ἠχητικός [eeheeteekos] producing sound, resounding.

ἦχος, ὁ [eehos] sound.

ἠχώ, ἡ [eeho] echo, sound || (μεταφ) repercussion.

ἠχῶ [eeho] ring, sound, strike, reverberate.

ἠώς, ἡ [eeos] dawn, daybreak.

Θ, ϑ

θά [tha] shall, will, should, would.
θάβω [thavo] βλ **θάπτω.**
θαλαμηγός, ή [thalameeyos] yacht.
θάλαμος, ό [thalamos] room ‖ (νοσοκομείου) ward ‖ (ποδηλάτου κτλ) inner tube ‖ (όπλου) chamber.
θάλασσα, ή [thalassa] sea ‖ τά κάνω ~ mess up, fail.
θαλασσινά, τά [thalaseena] πλ shellfish.
θαλασσοδέρνω [thalassoδerno] buffet ‖ (μεταφ) struggle against (adversity).
θαλασσόλυκος, ό [thalasoleekos] sea dog, mariner.
θαλασσοπόρος, ό [thalasoporos] navigator, seafarer.
θαλασσώνω [thalasono]: τά ~ turn things topsy-turvy, mess it up.
θαλερός [thaleros] green, in bloom ‖ (μεταφ) fresh, vigorous.
θάμβος, τό [thamvos] astonishment, wonder.
θάμνος, ό [thamnos] bush, shrub, scrub.
θαμπός [thambos] (χρώμα) lifeless, without lustre ‖ dim, cloudy.
θάμπωμα, τό [thamboma] dazzle ‖ astonishment ‖ (ματιού) dimness ‖ (μυαλού) confusion.
θαμπώνω [thambono] dazzle ‖ tarnish, blur, dim ‖ grow dim.
θαμών, ό [thamon] habitué, regular customer, frequent visitor.
θανάσιμος [thanaseemos] deadly, fatal.
θανατηφόρος [thanateeforos] deadly, murderous.
θανατικός [thanateekos] capital, of death.
θάνατος, ό [thanatos] death.
θανατώνω [thanatono] execute.
θανή, ή [thanee] death ‖ funeral.
θάπτω [thapto] bury, inter ‖ (μεταφ) hide.
θαρραλέος [tharaleos] plucky, daring, bold.
θαρρετός [tharetos] βλ **θαρραλέος.**
θαρρεύω [tharevo] venture, dare, hazard.
θάρρος, τό [tharos] daring, courage, spunk, mettle.
θαρρῶ [tharo] believe, think.
θαῦμα, τό [thavma] miracle, wonder.
θαυμάζω [thavmazo] wonder at, admire, be amazed.
θαυμάσιος [thavmaseeos] admirable, marvellous, superb.
θαυμασμός, ό [thavmasmos] wonder, admiration, astonishment.
θαυμαστής ό [thavmastees] admirer, fan.
θαυμαστικόν, τό [thavmasteekon] exclamation mark.
θαυμαστικός [thavmasteekos] admiring.
θαυμαστός [thavmastos] admirable, astonishing.
θαυματουργός [thavmatouryos] wondrous, miracle-making, miraculous.
θάψιμο, τό [thapseemo] burial.

θεά, ή [thea] goddess.
θέα, ή [thea] view, sight, aspect.
θέαμα, τό [theama] spectacle, show ‖ **θεαματικός** spectacular, wonderful.
θεάρεστος [thearestos] pleasing.
θεατής, ό [theatees] spectator, onlooker.
θεατός [theatos] visible, perceptible.
θεατρικός [theatreekos] theatrical ‖ (μεταφ) pompous, showy.
θεατρίνος, ό [theatreenos] actor.
θέατρο, τό [theatro] theatre, stage.
θεία, ή [theea] aunt.
θειάφι, τό [theeafee] sulphur.
θεϊκός [theyeekos] divine.
θεῖον, τό [theeon] βλ **θειάφι.**
θεῖος, ό [theeos] uncle.
θεῖος [theeos] divine, holy, sacred.
θέλγητρον, τό [thelyeetron] charm, enchantment, attraction.
θέλγω [thelyo] charm, enchant, fascinate.
θέλημα, τό [theleema] will, wish, desire ‖ **θεληματικός** voluntary ‖ willing.
θέλησις, ή [theleesees] will, volition, will power.
θελκτικός [thelkteekos] seductive, attractive, captivating.
θέλω [thelo] wish, want, require, need ‖ be willing ‖ ~ νά πῶ I mean to say ‖ θέλει δέν θέλει whether he likes it or not.
θέμα, τό [thema] subject, point, topic ‖ (γραμμ) stem, theme.
θεμέλιον, τό [themeleeon] foundation ‖ (μεταφ) basis, groundwork.
θεμιτός [themeetos] lawful, legal ‖ permissible.
θεόγυμνος [theoyeemnos] stark naked.
θεοκρατία, ή [theokrateea] theocracy.
θεολογία, ή [theoloyeea] theology.
θεολογικός [theoloyeekos] theological.
θεολόγος, ό [theoloyos] theologian.
θεομηνία, ή [theomeeneea] natural disaster, calamity.
θεοποιῶ [theopeeo] (μεταφ) idolize, praise, laud.
θεόρατος [theoratos] enormous, colossal.
θεός, ό [theos] god.
θεοσεβής [theosevees] pious, devout.
θεότης, ή [theotees] deity.
θεοτόκος, ή [theotokos] the Virgin Mary.
θεοφάνεια, τά [theofaneea] πλ the Epiphany.
θεοφοβούμενος [theofovoumenos] godly, pious.
θεραπεία, ή [therapeea] cure, treatment ‖ recovery.
θεραπευτήριον, τό [therapevteereeon] hospital, clinic ‖ (σχολῆς) infirmary.
θεραπευτικός [therapevteekos] curative.
θεραπεύω [therapevo] cure, treat ‖ (μεταφ) satisfy.
θεράπων, ό [therapon] servant ‖ attendant.
θέρετρον, τό [theretron] resort ‖ country house.

θ

θερίζω [thereezo] mow, cut ‖ reap ‖ (μεταφ) annihilate.

θερινός [thereenos] summer, summery.

θεριό, τό [therio] beast.

θερισμός, ὁ [thereesmos] reaping, mowing, cutting.

θεριστής, ὁ [thereestees] reaper, mower.

θεριστικός [thereesteekos] of reaping, for mowing ‖ sweeping.

θέρμαι, οἱ [therme] πλ hot springs.

θερμαίνομαι [thermenome] be feverish.

θερμαίνω [thermeno] heat up, warm up ‖ (μεταφ) revive.

θέρμανσις, ἡ [thermansees] heating, warming.

θερμαστής, ὁ [thermastees] stoker.

θερμάστρα, ἡ [thermastra] heating stove, furnace.

θέρμη, ἡ [thermee] fever ‖ (μεταφ) ardour, zeal.

θερμίς, ἡ [thermees] calorie.

θερμόαιμος [thermoemos] hot-blooded, irritable, touchy.

θερμοκήπιον, τό [thermokeepeeon] hot-house, greenhouse.

θερμοκρασία, ἡ [thermokraseea] temperature.

θερμόμετρον, τό [thermometron] thermometer.

θερμός [thermos] warm ‖ (μεταφ) passionate, fervent, heated.

θερμοσίφων, ὁ [thermoseefon] water heater.

θερμοστάτης, ὁ [thermostatees] thermostat.

θερμότης, ἡ [thermotees] heat, warmth ‖ (μεταφ) zeal, earnestness.

θερμοφόρος, ἡ [thermoforos] hot-water bottle.

θέρος, ὁ [theros] harvest.

θέρος, τό [theros] summer.

θέσις, ἡ [thesees] place, seat ‖ (τάξις) position ‖ (στρατ) emplacement, location ‖ (ἐργασίαν) employment, job, office ‖ (χῶρος) room, space ‖ (ταξιδιοῦ) class.

θεσμός, ὁ [thesmos] institution, law, decree.

θεσπίζω [thespeezo] decree, legislate, enact (laws).

θετικός [theteekos] positive, real, actual ‖ (πληροφορία) definite.

θετός [thetos] adopted ‖ foster.

θέτω [theto] put, set ‖ impose.

θεῶμαι [theome] see, behold ‖ be seen.

θεωρεῖον, τό [theoreeon] (θεάτρου) box ‖ (τύπου κτλ) gallery.

θεώρημα, τό [theoreema] theorem.

θεώρησις, ἡ [theoreesees] visa ‖ (ἐγγράφου) certification.

θεωρητικός [theoreeteekos] theoretical ‖ imposing.

θεωρία, ἡ [theoreea] theory ‖ (ὄψις) appearance, air.

θεωρῶ [theoro] consider, regard, look at ‖ certify, visa.

θηκάρι, τό [theekaree] scabbard, sheath.

θήκη, ἡ [theekee] box, case ‖ (ἐργαλείων) toolbag.

θηλάζω [theelazo] suckle, nurse.

θηλαστικόν, τό [theelasteekon] mammal.

θηλειά, ἡ [theelia] noose, loop, slipknot ‖ buttonhole.

θηλή, ἡ [theelee] nipple, teat.

θηλυκό, τό [theeleeko] female.

θηλυκός [theeleekos] female ‖ (γραμμ) feminine.

θηλυκότης, ἡ [theeleekotees] femininity.

θηλυκώνω [theeleekono] button up, fasten, clasp.

θηλυπρεπής [theeleeprepees] effeminate, womanish.

θῆλυς [theelees] female, feminine.

θημωνιά, ἡ [theemonia] stack, pile ‖ (σανοῦ) haystack.

θήρα, ἡ [theera] chase, hunt ‖ (κυνήγι) (hunting) game, quarry.

θήραμα, τό [theerama] game, prey.

θηρεύω [theerevo] hunt, shoot ‖ (μεταφ) seek, search.

θηρίον, τό [theereeon] wild beast, brute ‖ (μεταφ) monster, fiend.

θηριώδης [theereeodees] fierce, savage, brutal, bestial.

θησαυρίζω [theesavreezo] hoard up, accumulate ‖ become wealthy.

θησαυρός, ὁ [theesavros] treasure ‖ (μεταφ) storehouse, thesaurus.

θησαυροφυλάκειον, τό [theesavrofeelakeeon] treasury.

θῆτα, τό [theeta] the letter Θ.

θητεία, ἡ [theeteea] military service ‖ term of office.

θιασάρχης, ὁ [theeasarhees] manager, impressario.

θίασος, ὁ [theeasos] cast, troupe.

θιασώτης, ὁ [theeasotees] adherent, supporter, devotee.

θίγω [theeyo] touch (upon) ‖ (μεταφ) offend, insult.

θλάσις, ἡ [thlasees] breaking ‖ (ἰατρ) fracture, bruise.

θλιβερός [thleeveros] sad ‖ (γεγονότα) deplorable, painful.

θλίβω [thleevo] press, crush ‖ (μεταφ) afflict, distress.

θλιμμένος [thleemenos] distressed, afflicted ‖ in mourning.

θλίψις, ἡ [thleepsees] crushing ‖ (μεταφ) grief, sorrow.

θνησιμότης, ἡ [thneeseemotees] death rate, mortality.

θνήσκω [thneesko] βλ ἀποθνήσκω.

θνητός [thneetos] mortal.

θόλος, ὁ [tholos] (ἀρχιτεκ) vault, dome ‖ (οὐρανίσκου) roof.

θολός [tholos] dull, blurred ‖ (κρασί) turbid ‖ (κατάστασις) confused.

θολώνω [tholono] make dull ‖ (τό μυαλό)

confuse, disturb || (νερό κτλ) make muddy || (οὐρανός) get overcast.

θολωτός [tholotos] vaulted.

θόρυβος, ὁ [thoreevos] noise, turmoil, clamour.

θορυβοῦμαι [thoreevoume] worry, be uneasy.

θορυβῶ [thoreevo] create a disturbance || disturb.

θορυβώδης [thoreevodees] noisy, boisterous.

θρανίον, τό [thraneeon] (school) desk, bench, seat.

θράσος, τό [thrasos] impudence, insolence.

θρασύς [thrasees] impudent, brazen, saucy, bold.

θραῦσις, ἡ [thravsees] fracture || destruction, ruin.

θραῦσμα, τό [thravsma] fragment || (λίθου) splinter.

θραύω [thravo] break, smash, crack.

θρεμμένος [thremenos] well-fed.

θρεπτικός [threpteekos] nourishing, nutritious.

θρέφω [threfo] βλ **τρέφω.**

θρέψις, ἡ [threpsees] feeding, nourishing.

θρῆνος, ὁ [threenos] lamentation, wailing.

θρηνῶ [threeno] lament, mourn || complain.

θρησκεία, ἡ [threeskeea] religion.

θρησκευτικός [threeskevteekos] religious || (ἀκρίβεια) scrupulous.

θρησκόληπτος [threeskoleeptos] fanatically religious.

θρῆσκος [threeskos] religious.

θριαμβευτικός [threeamvefteekos] triumphant, triumphal.

θριαμβεύω [threeamvevo] triumph || (μεταφ) excel, prevail.

θρίαμβος, ὁ [threeamvos] triumph, victory.

θρίξ, ἡ [threeks] hair || (βούρτσας) bristle.

θρόϊσμα, τό [throeesma] rustle.

θρόμβωσις, ἡ [thromvosees] thrombosis.

θρόνος, ὁ [thronos] throne.

θρούμπα, ἡ [throumba] ripe olive.

θρυαλλίς, ἡ [threealees] wick.

θρυλεῖται [threeleete] people are saying.

θρυλικός [threeleekos] legendary.

θρῦλος, ὁ [threelos] legend || rumour.

θρύμμα, τό [threema] fragment, scrap || **θρυμματίζω** break to pieces, shatter.

θυγατέρα, ἡ [theeyatera] daughter.

θύελλα, ἡ [thiela] storm.

θυελλώδης [thielodees] stormy.

θυλάκιον, τό [theelakeeon] pocket.

θύλαξ, ὁ [theelaks] satchel, pouch.

θῦμα, τό [theema] victim.

θυμᾶμαι [theemame] βλ **θυμοῦμαι.**

θυμάρι, τό [theemaree] thyme.

θυμηδία, ἡ [theemeedeea] gaiety, levity.

θύμηση, ἡ [theemeesee] memory, remembrance.

θυμητικό, τό [theemeeteeko] memory.

θυμίαμα, τό [theemeeama] incense.

θυμιατό, τό [theemeeato] censer.

θυμίζω [theemeezo] remind, recall.

θυμός, ὁ [theemos] anger, rage.

θυμοῦμαι [theemoume] remember, recall.

θυμώνω [theemono] make angry, infuriate || get angry, flare up.

θύρα, ἡ [theera] door, gate, doorway.

θυρίς, ἡ [theerees] small window || (θεάτρου) box office || (τραπέζης) counter.

θυρόφυλλον, τό [theerofeelon] leaf of a door, shutter.

θυρωρός, ὁ [theeroros] hall porter, concierge.

θύσανος, ὁ [theesanos] crest, tuft || tassel.

θυσία, ἡ [theeseea] sacrifice || **θυσιάζω** sacrifice.

θύω [theeo] offer up a sacrifice.

θωπεία, ἡ [thopeea] petting, patting, stroking, caress(ing).

θωπεύω [thopevo] caress, fondle || (μεταφ) make much of, fawn upon.

θωρακίζω [thorakeezo] plate with steel.

θώραξ, ὁ [thoraks] cuirass, breastplate || thorax.

θωρηκτόν, τό [thoreekton] battleship.

θωριά, ἡ [thoria] air, appearance || colour, complexion.

θωρῶ [thoro] see, look.

Ι, ι

ιαματικός [eeamateekos] curative, medicinal.

ίαμβος, ὁ [eeamvos] iambus.

Ἰανουάριος, ὁ [eeanouareeos] January.

Ἰαπωνία, ἡ [eeaponeea] Japan.

Ἰάπων, ὁ [eeapon] Japanese (person).

ιαπωνικός [eeaponeekos] Japanese.

ιάσιμος [eeaseemos] curable.

ίασις, ἡ [eeasees] cure, healing, recovery.

ιατρεῖον, τό [eeatreeon] doctor's surgery, clinic || infirmary.

ιατρεύω [eeatrevo] βλ **θεραπεύω.**

ιατρική, ἡ [eeatreekee] medicine.

ιατρικόν, τό [eeatreekon] medicine || remedy.

ιατρικός [eeatreekos] medical.

ιατρός, ὁ, ἡ [eeatros] doctor, physician.

ιβίσκος, ὁ [eeveeskos] hibiscus.

ιδανικόν, τό [eedaneekon] ideal.

ιδανικός [eedaneekos] ideal.

ιδέα, ἡ [eedea] idea || notion, thought.

ιδεαλιστής, ὁ [eedealeestees] idealist.

ιδεολογία, ἡ [eedeoloyeea] ideology.

ιδεολόγος, ὁ, ἡ [eedeoloyos] idealist.

ιδεώδης [eedeodees] ideal.

ιδία [eedeea] specially, especially, chiefly, primarily.

ιδιάζων [eedeeazon] typical, singular.

ιδιαίτερος [eedieteros] special, characteristic || ὁ ~ private secretary || τά ιδιαίτερα private affairs.

ἰδιαιτέρως [eedieteros] in particular ‖ privately.

ἰδικός [eedeekos] my, my own, mine.

ἰδιοκτησία, ἡ [eedeeokteeseea] ownership ‖ property, estate.

ἰδιοκτήτης, ὁ [eedeeokteetees] owner, proprietor ‖ landlord.

ἰδιόκτητος [eedeeokteetos] privately owned.

ἰδιοποιοῦμαι [eedeeopeeoume] appropriate, usurp.

ἰδιόρρυθμος [eedeeoreethmos] peculiar, original, eccentric.

ἴδιος [eedeeos] same ‖ own, oneself ‖ particular ‖ ~ μέ same as ‖ ἐγώ ὁ ~ I myself.

ἰδιοσυγκρασία, ἡ [eedeeoseengkraseea] temperament, idiosyncrasy.

ἰδιοτελής [eedeeotelees] selfish, self-centred.

ἰδιότης, ἡ [eedeeotees] property, quality, characteristic.

ἰδιότροπος [eedeeotropos] peculiar, eccentric ‖ singular.

ἰδιοφυής [eedeeofiees] talented, gifted.

ἰδιόχειρος [eedeeoheeros] handwritten, with one's own hand.

ἰδίωμα, τό [eedeeoma] idiom, dialect ‖ property, characteristic ‖ ἰδιωματικός idiomatic.

ἰδιωματισμός, ὁ [eedeeomateesmos] idiom.

ἰδίως [eedeeos] specially, especially, particularly.

ἰδιωτεύω [eedeeotevo] lead a private life, live in retirement.

ἰδιωτικός [eedeeoteekos] private, particular.

ἰδιώτης, ὁ [eedeeotees] individual, layman.

ἰδού [eedou] (ἐπιφ) look!, behold!, here it is!

ἴδρυμα, τό [eedreema] institution, foundation ‖ establishment.

ἵδρυσις, ἡ [eedreesees] establishment, founding.

ἱδρυτής, ὁ [eedreetees] founder.

ἱδρύω [eedreeo] found, establish.

ἰδρώνω [eedrono] perspire, sweat.

ἱδρώτας, ὁ [eedrotas] sweat.

ἱέραξ, ὁ [ieraks] falcon, hawk.

ἱεραπόστολος, ὁ [ierapostolos] missionary.

ἱερεύς, ὁ [ierevs] priest.

ἱερόδουλος, ἡ [ierodoulos] prostitute.

ἱεροκήρυξ, ὁ [ierokeereeks] preacher, missionary.

ἱερόν, τό [ieron] sanctuary, holy of holies.

ἱερός [ieros] holy, sacred.

ἱεροσυλία, ἡ [ieroseeleea] sacrilege.

ἵζημα, τό [eezeema] sediment.

ἰθαγένεια, ἡ [eethayeneea] nationality, citizenship.

ἰθαγενής [eethayenees] native, indigenous.

ἰθύνω [eetheeno] direct, manage, rule ‖ (ἰσιώνω) straighten.

ἱκανοποίησις, ἡ [eekanopieesees] satisfaction, contentment.

ἱκανοποιητικός [eekanopieeteekos] satisfactory, satisfying.

ἱκανοποιῶ [eekanopeeo] satisfy, please ‖ (τά πάθη) satiate ‖ (πεῖνα) appease.

ἱκανός [eekanos] capable, able ‖ sufficient ‖ (ἐργάτης) skilful.

ἱκανότης, ἡ [eekanotees] capacity, competence, skill.

ἱκετεύω [eeketevo] implore, beg.

ἱκρίωμα, τό [eekreeoma] scaffold(ing) ‖ (γιά θεατάς) platform, stand.

ἴκτερος, ὁ [eekteros] jaundice.

ἱλαρά, ἡ [eelara] measles.

ἱλιγγιώδης [eeleengeeodees] giddy, dizzy.

ἴλιγγος, ὁ [eeleengos] giddiness, dizziness.

ἰλύς, ἡ [eelees] mud, sediment, deposit.

ἰμάμ μπαϊλντί [eemam mbaeelndee] aubergines with oil.

ἱμάς, ὁ [eemas] strap ‖ (μηχανῆς) belt, band.

ἱματιοθήκη, ἡ [eemateeotheekee] wardrobe ‖ cloakroom.

ἱμάτιον, τό [eemateeon] garment, dress.

ἴνα, ἡ [eena] fibre, filament.

ἵνα [eena] (in order) to, so that.

ἴνδαλμα, τό [eendalma] ideal ‖ illusion, fancy.

ἰνδιάνος, ὁ [eendeeanos] turkey.

ἰνδικός [eendeekos] Indian.

ἰνδοκάλαμος, ὁ [eendokalamos] bamboo.

ἰνστιτοῦτον, τό [eensteetouton] institute ‖ ~ καλλονῆς beauty salon.

ἴντσα, ἡ [eentsa] inch.

ἰνώδης [eenodees] fibrous ‖ (κρέας) stringy.

ἰξώδης [eeksodees] glutinous, sticky, gummy.

ἰοβόλος [eeovolos] venomous, poisonous.

ἴον, τό [eeon] violet.

ἰός, ὁ [eeos] venom ‖ (ἰατρ) virus ‖ (μεταφ) malice, spite.

Ἰουδαῖος, ὁ [eeoudeos] Jew.

Ἰούλιος, ὁ [eeouleeos] July.

Ἰούνιος, ὁ [eeouneeos] June.

ἱππασία, ἡ [eepaseea] horsemanship ‖ riding.

ἱππεύς, ὁ [eepevs] rider, horseman ‖ (σκακιοῦ) knight.

ἱππικόν, τό [eepeekon] cavalry.

ἱπποδρομίες, οἱ [eepodromies] πλ races.

ἱπποδρόμιον, τό [eepodromeeon] racecourse ‖ hippodrome.

ἱπποδύναμις, ἡ [eepodeenamees] horsepower.

ἱπποπόταμος, ὁ [eepopotamos] hippopotamus.

ἵππος, ὁ [eepos] horse ‖ ὀχτώ ἵππων eight horsepower.

ἱππότης, ὁ [eepotees] knight, chevalier.

ἵπταμαι [eeptame] fly, soar.

ἱπταμένη, ἡ [eeptamenee] air hostess.

ἱπτάμενος, ὁ [eeptamenos] flyer.

ἰριδισμός, ὁ [eereedeesmos] iridescence.

ἶρις, ἡ [eerees] rainbow ‖ (ματιοῦ) iris.

ἴς, ἡ [ees] fibre, sinew.

ἴσα [eesa] equally, as far as ‖ straight,

directly ‖ ~ ~ exactly, precisely ‖ ~ μέ up to, until.
ἰσάζω [eesazo] straighten ‖ adjust ‖ fix.
ἴσαμε [eesame] βλ **ἴσα μέ**.
ἰσάξιος [eesakseeos] equivalent (to).
ἰσάριθμος [eesareethmos] equal in number.
ἰσημερία, ἡ [eeseemereea] equinox.
ἰσημερινός [eeseemereenos] equinoctial ‖ (οὖσ) equator.
ἰσθμός, ὁ [eesthmos] isthmus.
ἴσια [eeseea] βλ **ἴσα**.
ἴσιο, τό [eeseeo] justice, right.
ἴσιος [eeseeos] straight, erect ‖ honest ‖ equal to.
ἰσ(ι)ώνω [ees(ee)ono] straighten ‖ make even, smooth.
ἴσκιος, ὁ [eeskeeos] shade, shadow.
ἰσόβιος [eesoveeos] for life, lifelong.
ἰσόγειον, τό [eesoγeeon] ground floor.
ἰσοδύναμος [eesoδeenamos] equivalent ‖ equal in force.
ἰσοδυναμῶ [eesoδeenamo] be equivalent to.
ἰσοζύγιον, τό [eesozeeγeeon] balancing, balance.
ἰσολογισμός, ὁ [eesoloγeesmos] balance sheet.
ἰσόπαλος [eesopalos] evenly matched, of equal strength.
ἰσοπεδώνω [eesopeδono] level up, level down, smooth.
ἰσόπλευρος [eesoplevros] equilateral.
ἰσορροπημένος [eesoropeemenos] well-balanced.
ἰσορροπία, ἡ [eesoropeea] balance, equilibrium.
ἰσορροπῶ [eesoropo] balance.
ἴσος [eesos] equal to, the same as ‖ ἐξ ἴσου likewise.
ἰσοσκελής [eesoskelees] (γεωμ) isosceles.
ἰσότης, ἡ [eesotees] equality.
ἰσότιμος [eesoteemos] equal in rank ‖ equal in value.
ἰσοφαρίζω [eesofareezo] equal, make equal ‖ be equal to.
Ἰσπανία, ἡ [eespaneea] Spain.
ἰσπανικός [eespaneekos] Spanish.
Ἰσπανός, ὁ [eespanos] Spaniard.
ἵσταμαι [eestame] stand.
ἱστίον, τό [eesteeon] sail.
ἱστιοπλοΐα, ἡ [eesteeoploeea] sailing.
ἱστιοφόρον, τό [eesteeoforon] sailing ship.
ἱστορία, ἡ [eestoreea] history ‖ story, tale.
ἱστορίες, οἱ [eestories] πλ trouble, scene, quarrel.
ἱστορικός [eestόreekos] historic(al) ‖ (οὖσ) historian.
ἱστός, ὁ [eestos] mast, pole ‖ (βιολ) tissue.
ἰσχιαλγία, ἡ [eesheealγeea] sciatica.
ἰσχίον, τό [eesheeon] hip.
ἰσχνός [eeshnos] lean, thin ‖ (βλάστησις) scanty, sparse.
ἰσχυρίζομαι [eesheereezome] assert, maintain, declare.

ἰσχυρισμός, ὁ [eesheereesmos] assertion, contention, allegation.
ἰσχυρογνώμων [eesheeroγnomon] stubborn, headstrong, obstinate.
ἰσχυρός [eesheeros] strong, sturdy ‖ (φωνή) loud ‖ (ἄνεμος) stiff, strong.
ἰσχύς, ἡ [eeshees] strength, power, force ‖ (νόμου κτλ) validity.
ἰσχύω [eesheeo] have validity ‖ be in force.
ἰσώνω [eesono] βλ **ἰσ(ι)ώνω**.
ἴσως [eesos] perhaps, probably, maybe.
Ἰταλία, ἡ [eetaleea] Italy.
ἰταλικός [eetaleekos] Italian.
Ἰταλός, ὁ [eetalos] Italian (person).
ἰταμός [eetamos] impudent, shameless.
ἰτιά, ἡ [eetia] willow tree.
ἰχθυοπωλεῖον, τό [eehtheeopoleeon] fishmonger's shop.
ἰχθύς, ὁ [eehthees] fish.
ἰχνογράφημα, τό [eehnoγrafeema] sketch, drawing, design.
ἰχνογραφία, ἡ [eehnoγrafeea] sketching, drawing.
ἴχνος, τό [eehnos] footprint, track ‖ trace, vestige ‖ (μεταφ) mark, sign.
ἰωβηλαῖον, τό [eeoveeleon] jubilee, anniversary.
ἰώδιον, τό [eeoδeeon] iodine.
ἰωνικός [eeoneekos] Ionic, Ionian.
ἰῶτα, τό [eeota] the letter I.

Κ, κ

κάβα, ἡ [kava] wine cellar.
καβαλιέρος, ὁ [kavalieros] escort, partner.
καβάλλα, ἡ [kavala] riding ‖ (ἐπιρ) on horseback ‖ (σέ τοῖχο κτλ) astride.
καβαλλάρης, ὁ [kavalarees] rider, horseman ‖ (ἐγχόρδου) bridge.
καβαλλέτο, τό [kavaleto] easel.
καβαλλικεύω [kavaleekevo] mount a horse ‖ (μεταφ) dominate.
καβαλλῶ [kavalo] βλ **καβαλλικεύω**.
καβγαδίζω [kavγaδeezo] quarrel, wrangle, squabble.
καβγᾶς, ὁ [kavγas] row, quarrel.
καβγατζῆς, ὁ [kavγatzees] grouch, wrangler.
κάβος, ὁ [kavos] cape, headland ‖ (ναυτ) cable.
καβούκι, τό [kavoukee] shell.
κάβουρας, ὁ [kavouras] crab ‖ crawfish.
καβουρδίζω [kavourδeezo] roast, brown ‖ scorch.
καβούρι, τό [kavouree] βλ **κάβουρας**.
καγκελάριος, ὁ [kangelareeos] chancellor.
κάγκελο, τό [kangelo] (παραθύρου κτλ) bar ‖ (σκάλας) balustrade ‖ (κήπου) railings ‖ (δικτυωτό) grille.
καγχάζω [kanghazo] guffaw.
καδής, ὁ [kaδees] Turkish judge.

Κ

κάδος, ὁ [kados] bucket, vat, tub, small barrel.

κάδρο, τό [kadro] (πλαίσιον) frame || (πίνακος) frame || (χάρτου) border || (φωτογραφία) framed picture.

καημένος [kaeemenos] (μεταφ) miserable, wretched.

καημός, ὁ [kaeemos] longing, yearning, mental anguish.

καθαίρεσις, ἡ [katheresees] dismissal, degradation.

καθαιρῶ [kathero] dismiss, discharge || (ἱερέα) unfrock.

καθαρεύουσα, ἡ [katharevousa] formal Greek (language).

καθαρίζω [kathareezo] clean, clear || (κουκιά, φροῦτα) peel, pare, shell || (μετάλλινα εἴδη) burnish || (ποτήρια) polish || (ἐξηγῶ) explain, clarify || (λογαριασμούς) settle, clear up.

καθαριότης, ἡ [kathareeotees] cleanness, cleanliness || brightness.

καθάρισμα, τό [kathareesma] cleaning || peeling || polishing.

καθαριστήριον, τό [kathareesteereeon] dry cleaner's.

καθαρίστρια, ἡ [kathareestria] charwoman, cleaning lady.

κάθαρμα, τό [katharma] (μεταφ) rogue, rascal, scamp.

καθαρόαιμος [katharoemos] thoroughbred.

καθαρός [katharos] (πρόσωπον κτλ) neat, tidy || (φωνή) clear, distinct || (χρυσός) pure || (οὐρανός) clear || (ἀπάντησις) plain, straightforward || (ἰδέα) clear, distinct || (κέρδος) clear, net || (ἔννοια) obvious, manifest, evident.

καθαρότης, ἡ [katharotees] cleanness, purity || clearness.

καθάρσιον, τό [katharseeon] cathartic, purge.

κάθαρσις, ἡ [katharsees] cleansing, refining || catharsis || quarantine.

καθαυτό [kathavto] exactly, precisely || really.

κάθε [kathe] each, every || ~ ἄλλο far from it || τό ~ τι everything.

κάθειρξις, ἡ [katheerksees] βλ φυλάκισις.

καθείς [kathees] everyone, each one, everybody.

καθέκαστα, τά [kathekasta] πλ details, particulars.

καθελκύω [kathelkeeo] (ναυτ) launch.

καθένας [kathenas] βλ καθείς.

καθεξῆς [katheksees] so forth, so on.

καθεστώς, τό [kathestos]: τό ~ regime, status quo.

κάθετος [kathetos] vertical, perpendicular, upright.

καθηγητής, ὁ [katheeyeetees] professor, teacher.

καθήκι, τό [katheekee] chamberpot || (μεταφ) rogue, vicious person.

καθῆκον, τό [katheekon] duty, task || ~ τα πλ functions, duties.

καθηλώνω [katheelono] pin down, fix || immobilize.

καθημερινός [katheemereenos] daily, everyday.

καθημερινῶς [katheemereenos] daily.

καθησυχάζω [katheeseehazo] (ἕνα φόβο) calm, reassure, pacify || become calm.

καθιερώνω [kathierono] consecrate, dedicate || establish, validate.

καθίζησις, ἡ [katheezeesees] subsidence, landslide.

καθίζω [katheezo] seat, place || (πλοῖον) run aground.

καθισιό, τό [katheesio] idleness, unemployment, inactivity.

κάθισμα, τό [katheesma] chair, seat || (πλοίου) stranding.

καθίσταμαι [katheestame] become, get, grow.

καθιστός [katheestos] sitting (down).

καθιστῶ [katheesto] (ἐγκαθιστῶ) establish, install || (κάποιον) make, render || (διορίζω) appoint.

καθό [katho] as, inasmuch as, insofar as.

καθοδηγῶ [kathodeeyo] instruct, guide, lead.

κάθοδος, ἡ [kathodos] descent || alighting || (ἐξ ἵππου) dismounting.

καθολικόν, τό [katholeekon] ledger || (ἐκκλ) nave.

καθολικός [katholeekos] catholic || (γνώμη) unanimous || universal.

καθόλου [katholou] generally || (διόλου) not at all, no way.

κάθομαι [kathome] be seated, sit down, sit.

καθομιλουμένη, ἡ [kathomeeloumenee] the spoken language.

καθορίζω [kathoreezo] determine, define, fix, decide.

καθορισμός, ὁ [kathoreesmos] defining, fixing, determination.

καθόσον [kathoson] as || according to what || being.

καθρέφτης, ὁ [kathreftees] mirror, looking-glass.

καθρεφτίζω [kathrefteezo] reflect, mirror.

καθυστερημένος [katheestereemenos] backward || late.

καθυστέρησις, ἡ [katheestereesees] delay, lateness.

καθυστερούμενα, τά [katheesteroumena] πλ arrears.

καθώς [kathos] as well as, like, as || ~ πρέπει proper.

καί [ke] and, also, too || ~ . . . ~ both . . . and || ~ νά even if.

καΐκι, τό [kaeekee] caique, sailing vessel.

καϊμάκι, τό [kaeemakee] cream || (τοῦ καφέ) froth.

καινοτομία, ἡ [kenotomeea] innovation.

καινούργιος [kenouryeos] new, fresh.

καίπερ [keper] though, although.
καιρικός [kereekos] of the weather.
καίριος [kereeos] timely ‖ (πλῆγμα) deadly, mortal ‖ (σημεῖον) vital, important.
καιρός, ὁ [keros] time, period ‖ weather ‖ μὲ τόν καιρό in course of time.
καιροσκοπῶ [keroskopo] wait for an opportunity, be an opportunist.
καισαρικός [kesareekos] Caesarean.
καίτοι [ketee] though, although.
καίομαι [keome] be on fire.
καίω [keo] burn.
κακά [kaka] badly, ill ‖ bad things.
κακάο, τό [kakao] cocoa.
κακαρίζω [kakareezo] cluck, gobble.
κακαρώνω [kakarono] perish from cold ‖ die, kick the bucket (col).
κακεντρέχεια, ἡ [kakentreheea] malevolence, spite.
κακία, ἡ [kakeea] wickedness, malice.
κακίζω [kakeezo] reproach, blame, reprimand.
κακοβαλμένος [kakovalmenos] untidy ‖ badly placed.
κακόβουλος [kakovoulos] malicious.
κακογλωσσιά, ἡ [kakoγloseea] slander, calumny ‖ gossip.
κακοδαιμονία, ἡ [kakoδemoneea] misfortune, adversity.
κακοήθης [kakoeethees] dishonest, vile ‖ (ἰατρ) malignant, serious.
κακόηχος [kakoeehos] dissonant, unpleasant to hear.
κακοκαιρία, ἡ [kakokereea] bad weather.
κακοκεφιά, ἡ [kakokefia] depression, bad mood.
κακομαθαίνω [kakomatheno] (μωρό κτλ) spoil ‖ acquire bad habits.
κακομαθημένος [kakomatheemenos] illbred, spoilt, rude.
κακομεταχειρίζομαι [kakometaheereezome] maltreat, abuse.
κακομοίρης [kakomeerees] hapless, wretched.
κακό(ν), τό [kako(n)] evil, harm, wrong, bad, mischief.
κακοπέραση, ἡ [kakoperasee] privation, hardship.
κακοπερνῶ [kakoperno] lead a hard life, suffer.
κακοπιστία, ἡ [kakopeesteea] perfidy, faithlessness.
κακοποιός [kakopeeos] criminal, ill-doer.
κακοποιῶ [kakopeeo] maltreat ‖ rape.
κακορρίζικος [kakoreezeekos] βλ **κακομοίρης.**
κακός [kakos] bad, wicked ‖ (παιδί) mischievous ‖ nasty, serious.
κακοσμία, ἡ [kakosmeea] stench, stink.
κακοσυνηθίζω [kakoseeneetheezo] βλ **κακομαθαίνω.**
κακοτυχία, ἡ [kakoteeheea] misfortune, bad luck.

κακούργημα, τό [kakourγeema] crime, villainy, felony.
κακουργιοδικεῖον, τό [kakourγeeoδeekeeon] criminal court.
κακοῦργος, ὁ [kakouryos] criminal ‖ (μεταφ) villain, rogue.
κακουχία, ἡ [kakouheea] hardship, privation.
κακοφαίνεται [kakofenete]: μοῦ ~ it displeases me, it offends me.
κακοφέρνομαι [kakofernome] behave badly.
κακοφτιαγμένος [kakofteeaγmenos] badly made, badly wrought.
κακόφωνος [kakofonos] discordant, dissonant.
κάκτος, ὁ [kaktos] cactus.
κακῶς [kakos] badly, wrongly.
κάκωσις, ἡ [kakosees] ill treatment ‖ (ἀποτέλεσμα) suffering, hardship.
καλά [kala] well, all right ‖ properly, thoroughly.
καλάθι, τό [kalathee] basket.
κάλαθος, ὁ [kalathos]: ~ ἀχρήστων wastepaper bin.
καλάι, τό [kalaee] solder, pewter.
καλαισθησία, ἡ [kalestheeseea] good taste, elegance.
καλαμαράς, ὁ [kalamaras] writer, scholar.
καλαμάρι, τό [kalamaree] inkstand, inkpot ‖ (ψάρι) cuttlefish, squid.
καλαματιανός [kalamateeanos] (dance) of Kalamata.
καλάμι, τό [kalamee] reed, cane ‖ (ψαρέματος) fishing rod ‖ (ἀνατ) shinbone.
κάλαμος, ὁ [kalamos] cane, reed ‖ pen.
καλαμοσάκχαρον, τό [kalamosakharon] cane sugar.
καλαμπόκι, τό [kalambokee] maize, corn.
καλαμπούρι, τό [kalambouree] pun.
κάλαντα, τά [kalanta] πλ carols.
καλαπόδι, τό [kalapoδee] (shoemaker's) last, shoe last.
καλαφατίζω [kalafateezo] caulk.
κάλεσμα, τό [kalesma] invitation.
καλεσμένος [kalesmenos] invited ‖ (οὐσ) guest.
καλημαύκι, τό [kaleemavkee] priest's high hat.
καλημέρα [kaleemera] (ἐπιφ) good morning.
καληνύχτα [kaleeneehta] (ἐπιφ) good night.
καληνυχτίζω [kaleeneehteezo] bid good night.
καλησπέρα [kaleespera] (ἐπιφ) good afternoon ‖ good evening.
καλησπερίζω [kaleespereezo] wish good evening.
κάλι, τό [kalee] potash.
καλιακούδα, ἡ [kaleeakouδa] crow.
καλλιέργεια, ἡ [kalierγeea] cultivation, tilling ‖ (μεταφ) cultivation.
καλλιεργῶ [kalierγo] cultivate, till, grow.

καλλικάντζαρος, ὁ [kaleekantzaros] sprite, spook, goblin.

κάλλιστα [kaleesta] very well.

καλλιστεῖα, τά [kaleesteea] πλ beauty competition.

κάλλιστος [kaleestos] best, perfect, exquisite, excellent.

καλλιτέχνης, ὁ [kaleetehnees] artist.

καλλιτεχνικός [kaleetehneekos] of art, of artists, artistic.

καλλονή, ἡ [kalonee] beauty.

κάλλος, τό [kalos] beauty, charm.

καλλυντικά, τά [kaleenteeka] πλ cosmetics, make-up.

καλλωπίζω [kalopeezo] beautify, decorate, adorn.

καλμάρω [kalmaro] become calm, relax.

καλντερίμι, τό [kalntereemee] cobbled street, paving stone.

καλοαναθρεμμένος [kaloanathremenos] well brought up.

καλοβαλμένος [kalovalmenos] well turned out, well-groomed, tidy.

καλόβολος [kalovolos] accommodating, easy-going, complaisant.

καλόγερος, ὁ [kaloyeros] monk ‖ (σπυρί) boil, carbuncle ‖ (παιχνίδι) hopscotch.

καλόγηρος, ὁ [kaloyeeros] βλ καλόγερος.

καλόγνωμος [kaloynomos] well-disposed, good-natured.

καλόγρια, ἡ [kaloyreea] nun.

καλοζῶ [kalozo] live well ‖ support comfortably.

καλοήθης [kaloeethees] moral, virtuous ‖ (ἐπί νόσου) benign.

καλοθρεμμένος [kalothremenos] well-nourished ‖ well-bred.

καλοκάγαθος [kalokayathos] kind-natured, good.

καλοκαίρι, τό [kalokeree] summer ‖ καλοκαιρία fine weather ‖ καλοκαιρινός summer, summery.

καλοκαμωμένος [kalokamomenos] well-made ‖ handsome.

καλόκαρδος [kalokardos] good-hearted, cheerful.

καλοκοιτάζω [kalokeetazo] look closely at ‖ look after well ‖ ogle.

καλομαθαίνω [kalomatheno] spoil, pamper, pet ‖ develop good habits.

καλομαθημένος [kalomatheemenos] pampered.

καλό(ν), τό [kalo(n)] good, benefit ‖ favour ‖ blessing ‖ στό ~! so long!

καλοντυμένος [kalonteemenos] well-dressed.

καλοπέραση, ἡ [kaloperasee] comfort, happy life, good life.

καλοπερνῶ [kaloperno] lead a pleasant life ‖ be well treated.

καλοπιάνω [kalopeeano] coax, treat gently.

καλοπροαίρετος [kaloproeretos] well-disposed, obliging.

καλοριφέρ, τό [kaloreefer] central heating ‖ radiator, heater.

καλορρίζικος [kaloreezeekos] lucky.

κάλος, ὁ [kalos] corn.

καλός [kalos] (ἄνθρωπος) kind, good ‖ (ἐργάτης) skilful ‖ (ὑπάλληλος) able, efficient ‖ (νέα) good, favourable ‖ (τροφή) wholesome ‖ (καρδιά) kind.

καλοσυνηθίζω [kaloseeneetheezo] βλ καλομαθαίνω.

καλούπι, τό [kaloupee] form, mould.

καλούτσικος [kaloutseekos] not bad, passable, adequate.

καλπάζω [kalpazo] gallop ‖ walk fast, run.

κάλπη, ἡ [kalpee] ballot box.

κάλπικος [kalpeekos] counterfeit, false ‖ (μεταφ) worthless.

κάλτσα, ἡ [kaltsa] sock, stocking.

καλύβι, τό [kaleevee] hut, cabin, hovel.

κάλυμμα, τό [kaleema] wrapper, cover ‖ (κρεββατιοῦ) blanket, coverlet ‖ (κεφαλῆς) cap, headdress ‖ (τραπεζιτικό) margin, cover.

κάλυξ, ὁ [kaleeks] (βοτ) calyx ‖ (στρατ) cartridge ‖ (ἀνατ) calix.

καλύπτω [kaleepto] cover, veil, hide ‖ (προθέσεις) cloak, mask, conceal.

καλύτερα [kaleetera] better.

καλυτερεύω [kaleeterevo] improve ‖ get better.

καλύτερος [kaleeteros] better.

κάλυψις, ἡ [kaleepsees] covering.

καλῶ [kalo] call, beckon, name ‖ (σέ δεῖπνο) invite ‖ (νομ) summon.

καλώδιον, τό [kalodeeon] rope ‖ cable.

καλῶς [kalos] well ‖ rightly, properly ‖ ἔχει ~ good, agreed ‖ ~ ὡρίσατε (ἐπιφ) welcome!

καλωσορίζω [kalosoreezo] welcome.

καλωσύνη, ἡ [kaloseenee] goodness, kindness ‖ (καιρός) fine weather.

καμάκι, τό [kamakee] harpoon, fish spear.

κάμαρα, ἡ [kamara] room.

καμάρα, ἡ [kamara] arch, archway, arcade ‖ (θόλου) vault.

καμάρι, τό [kamaree] pride, boast.

καμαριέρα, ἡ [kamariera] chambermaid, parlourmaid.

καμαρότος, ὁ [kamarotos] steward, cabin boy.

καμαρώνω [kamarono] take pride in, glory in.

καμαρωτά [kamarota] proudly, haughtily.

καμαρωτός [kamarotos] (ἀρχιτεκ) arched, vaulted ‖ (ὑπερηφάνεια) proud, haughty.

κάματος, ὁ [kamatos] fatigue ‖ (ἀροτρίασις) tilling.

καμέλια, ἡ [kameleea] camellia.

καμήλα, ἡ [kameela] camel.

καμηλοπάρδαλις, ἡ [kameeloparδalees] giraffe.

καμινάδα, ἡ [kameenaδa] chimney, smokestack ‖ funnel.

καμινέτο, τό [kameeneto] spirit lamp.
καμίνι, τό [kameenee] furnace, kiln.
καμιόνι, τό [kameeonee] lorry, truck.
καμμιά [kamia] βλ κανένας.
κάμνω [kamno] make, do, create, build.
καμουτσίκι, τό [kamoutseekee] whip.
καμουφλάζ, τό [kamouflaz] camouflage, disguise.
καμουφλάρω [kamouflaro] camouflage, disguise.
καμπάνα, ή [kambana] bell.
καμπαναρειό, τό [kambanario] belfry, steeple.
καμπανιά, ή [kambania] bell ringing.
καμπαρντίνα, ή [kambarndeena] gabardine.
καμπή, ή [kambee] bend, turn || (σωλήνος κτλ) elbow, knee.
κάμπια, ή [kambeea] caterpillar.
καμπίνα, ή [kambeena] cabin.
καμπινές, ό [kambeenes] toilet, rest room, W.C.
κάμπος, ό [kambos] plain, flat country.
καμπόσος [kambosos] considerable, some.
καμπούρα, ή [kamboura] hump, hunch.
καμπούρης, ό [kambourees] hunchback.
καμπουριάζω [kamboureeazo] hunch || stoop.
κάμπτομαι [kamptome] bow || yield, sag || (τιμές) go down.
κάμπτω [kampto] bend, turn, curve.
καμπύλη, ή [kambeelee] curve, bend.
καμπύλος [kambeelos] curved, rounded || crooked.
καμτσίκι, τό [kamtseekee] whip.
καμφορά, ή [kamfora] camphor.
κάμψις, ή [kampsees] bending, flexion || (τιμῶν) fall, drop.
καμώματα, τά [kamomata] πλ affected manners, antics.
καμωμένος [kamomenos] done, made || ripe.
καμώνομαι [kamonome] pretend, feign.
κἄν [kan] at least, even || οὔτε ~ not even || ~ ... ~ either ... or.
κανακάρης [kanakarees] petted, spoilt || (οὖ) only child.
κανάλι, τό [kanalee] channel, canal.
καναπές, ό [kanapes] sofa.
καναρίνι, τό [kanareenee] canary.
κανάτα, ή [kanata] jug, pitcher.
κανείς [kanees] someone, anyone || no one, nobody.
κανέλλα, ή [kanela] cinnamon.
κανένας [kanenas] anyone, one, some || no, no one.
κάνθαρος, ό [kantharos] beetle.
κανναβάτσο, τό [kanavatso] canvas, pack cloth.
κάνναβι, τό [kanavee] hemp.
κάννη, ή [kanee] barrel of a gun.
κανvίβαλος, ό [kaneevalos] cannibal.
κανόνας, ό [kanonas] rule.
κανόνι, τό [kanonee] cannon.

κανονίζω [kanoneezo] regulate || (ὑποθέσεις) settle, arrange || (λογαριασμούς) settle, close, pay off.
κανονικός [kanoneekos] regular, usual, ordinary || (ἐκκλ) canonical.
κανονισμός, ό [kanoneesmos] regulation, rule(s), by-laws.
κάνουλα, ή [kanoula] tap || (US) faucet.
καντάδα, ή [kantada] serenade.
καντήλι, τό [kanteelee] small olive-oil light, nightlight.
καντίνα, ή [kanteena] canteen.
κάνω [kano] do, make, create, build || (ὑποκρίνομαι) play, sham || τά ~ θάλασσα (ἤ σαλάτα) make a mess of it || ~ παιδί have a child || ~ νερά leak || (μεταφ) hedge || ~ πώς pretend that || τί κάνετε; how are you?
κανών, ό [kanon] rule || (ἐκκλ) canon.
κάπα, ή [kapa] peasant's cloak.
κάπακι, τό [kapakee] lid, cover.
κάπαρο, τό [kaparo] deposit.
καπαρώνω [kaparono] give a deposit || book, engage.
καπαρτίνα, ή [kaparteena] gabardine.
κάπελας, ό [kapelas] tavern-keeper.
καπέλλο, τό [kapelo] hat.
καπετάνιος, ό [kapetaneeos] captain, skipper, chief.
καπηλεία, ή [kapeeleea] (μεταφ) huckstering, exploiting.
καπηλειό, τό [kapeelio] wine shop, taverna.
καπίστρι, τό [kapeestree] bridle, halter.
καπλαμάς, ό [kaplamas] veneer.
καπνέμπορος, ό [kapnemboros] tobacco dealer, tobacconist.
καπνιά, ή [kapnia] soot, lampblack.
καπνίζω [kapneezo] smoke || cure.
κάπνισμα, τό [kapneesma] smoking.
καπνιστής, ό [kapneestees] smoker || (κρέατος) curer.
καπνιστός [kapneestos] smoked, smoke-cured.
καπνοδόχος, ή [kapnodohos] chimney || (πλοίου) funnel.
καπνοπώλης, ό [kapnopolees] tobacconist.
καπνός, ό [kapnos] smoke || tobacco || (μεταφ) ἔγινε ~ he vanished (into thin air).
κάποιος [kapeeos] someone || a certain.
καπόνι, τό [kaponee] capon.
καπότα, ή [kapota] shepherd's cloak || prophylactic, rubber.
κάποτε [kapote] from time to time, now and again, sometimes || once.
κάπου [kapou] somewhere || ~ ~ once in a while || ~ δέκα about ten.
κάππα, τό [kapa] the letter K.
κάππαρη, ή [kaparee] caper.
καπρίτσιο, τό [kapreetseeo] caprice, whim, fancy.
κάπρος, ό [kapros] wild boar.

κάπως [kapos] somehow, somewhat.
κάρα, ή [kara] head, skull.
καραβάνα, ή [karavana] mess tin || platter.
καραβάνι, τό [karavanee] caravan.
καράβι, τό [karavee] ship, boat, vessel.
καραβίδα, ή [karaveeδa] crawfish || crab.
καραβοκύρης, ό [karavokeerees] owner of a vessel || captain.
καραγκιόζης, ό [karangeeozees] (μεταφ) comical person, comedian.
καραδοκώ [karoδoko] watch for, look out for || waylay.
καρακάξα, ή [karakaksa] magpie.
καραμέλα, ή [karamela] sweet || caramel.
καραμούζα, ή [karamouza] toy flute || (αὐτοκινήτου) horn.
καραμπίνα, ή [karambeena] carbine.
καραντίνα, ή [karanteena] quarantine.
καράτι, τό [karatee] carat.
καρατομῶ [karatomo] behead, decapitate.
καράφα, ή [karafa] carafe || (κρασιοῦ) decanter.
καράφλα, ή [karafla] baldness.
καρβέλι, τό [karvelee] (round) loaf.
καρβουνιάρης, ό [karvouneearees] coal merchant || coalman.
κάρβουνο, τό [karvouno] coal, charcoal.
κάργα [karγa] quite full || tightly, closely.
κάρδαμον, τό [karδamon] cress.
καρδιά, ή [karδia] heart || (φρούτου) core, centre.
καρδιακός [karδiakos] affected with heart disease.
καρδιολόγος, ό [karδioloγos] heart specialist.
καρδιοχτύπι, τό [karδiohteepee] heartbeat || (μεταφ) anxiety.
καρέκλα, ή [karekla] chair, seat.
καρίνα, ή [kareena] keel.
καριοφίλι, τό [kareeofeelee] flintlock, carabine.
καρκινοβατῶ [karkeenovato] make no progress, get nowhere.
καρκίνος, ό [karkeenos] cancer || crab.
καρκίνωμα, τό [karkeenoma] carcinoma.
καρμανιόλα, ή [karmaneeola] guillotine || (στά χαρτιά) dishonest card game.
καρμπόν, τό [karbon] carbon paper.
καρναβάλι, τό [karnavalee] carnival.
καρότο, τό [karoto] carrot.
καρούλι, τό [karoulee] reel, spool || pulley.
καρούμπαλο, τό [karoumbalo] bump (on the head).
καρπαζιά, ή [karpazia] clout on the head.
καρπός, ό [karpos] fruit || (ἀνατ) wrist.
καρπούζι, τό [karpouzee] watermelon.
καρποῦμαι [karpoume] reap the fruits of || (μεταφ) benefit by.
καρποφόρος [karpoforos] fruitful || effective || lucrative.
καρποφορῶ [karpoforo] produce fruit || (μεταφ) succeed.
καρρέ, τό [karre] (στά χαρτιά) foursome ||

(φουστανιοῦ) open neck of dress.
καρρό, τό [karo] (στά χαρτιά) diamond || (σχεδίου) check.
κάρρο, τό [karo] cart, wagon.
καρροτσάκι, τό [karotsakee] handcart, barrow || (μωροῦ) pram.
καρσί [karsee] opposite.
κάρτα, ή [karta] postcard || visiting card.
καρτέρι, τό [karteree] βλ ἐνέδρα.
καρτερῶ [kartero] persevere, persist || wait for, expect.
καρύδι, τό [kareeδee] walnut || Adam's apple || καρυδιά, ή walnut tree, walnut (wood).
καρύκευμα, τό [kareekevma] seasoning || (τό μπαχαρικό) condiment, spice.
καρυοθραύστης, ό [kareeothravstees] nutcracker.
καρυοφύλλι, τό [kareeofeelee] clove || (ὅπλου) flintlock.
καρφί, τό [karfee] nail.
καρφίτσα, ή [karfeetsa] pin || (κόσμημα) brooch.
καρφώνω [karfono] nail, pin || (μεταφ) fix.
καρχαρίας, ό [karhareeas] shark.
κασετίνα, ή [kaseteena] (σχολική) pencil box || (κοσμημάτων) jewellery box.
κάσ(σ)α, ή [kasa] case, box || (χρηματοκιβώτιον) safe || (μεταφ) coffin, bier.
κασ(σ)έλα, ή [kasela] wooden chest, trunk.
κασκέτο, τό [kasketo] cap.
κασμίρι, τό [kasmeeree] cashmere.
κασ(σ)όνι, τό [kasonee] packing case.
κασσίτερος, ό [kaseeteros] tin.
καστανιά, ή [kastania] chestnut tree.
κάστανο, τό [kastano] chestnut.
καστανός [kastanos] chestnut-coloured, maroon.
καστόρι, τό [kastoree] beaver || felt.
κάστρο, τό [kastro] castle, fortress.
κατά [kata] against, upon, during, according to, by, about || ~ ξηράν by land || ~ τύχην by chance || ~ βάθος at bottom || καθ' ἑκάστην every day || ~ διαβόλου to the devil, to hell.
καταβαίνω [kataveno] βλ κατεβαίνω.
καταβάλλω [katavalo] overthrow, overcome, exhaust || (προσπαθείας) strive, endeavour || (χρήματα) pay, put down.
κατάβασις, ή [katavasees] descent, alighting, getting off.
καταβιβάζω [kataveevazo] let down, take down || (ὕψος) lower, reduce.
καταβολή, ή [katavolee] (χρημάτων) paying in, deposit.
καταβρέχω [katavreho] sprinkle, soak, water.
καταβροχθίζω [katavrohtheezo] devour, eat ravenously, gulp down.
καταγγελία, ή [katangeleea] denunciation, accusation || annulment, revocation.
καταγέλαστος [kataγelastos] ridiculous, ludicrous.

καταγῆς [katayees] on the ground, on the floor.

καταγίνομαι [katayeenome] busy o.s. with, see to.

κάταγμα, τό [katayma] fracture.

κατάγομαι [katayome] be descended from, come from.

καταγωγή, ἡ [katayoyee] descent, origin, lineage.

καταγώγιον, τό [katayoyeeon] hovel, hideout, den of vice.

καταδεικνύω [kataδeekneeo] demonstrate, show clearly.

καταδέχομαι [kataδehome] deign, condescend.

κατάδηλος [kataδeelos] evident, clear.

καταδίδω [kataδeeδo] denounce, betray.

καταδικάζω [kataδeekazo] condemn, sentence ‖ (μεταφ) doom, proscribe.

καταδίκη, ἡ [kataδeekee] sentence, conviction ‖ censure, blame.

κατάδικος, ὁ, ἡ [kataδeekos] prisoner, condemned person.

καταδιωκτικόν, τό [kataδeeokteekon] fighter (plane).

καταδιώκω [kataδeeoko] pursue, chase ‖ (πολιτικῶς) persecute, oppress.

κατάδοσις, ἡ [kataδosees] betrayal, denunciation.

καταδρομή, ἡ [kataδromee] pursuit ‖ (μεταφ) bad luck, bad streak.

καταδρομικόν, τό [kataδromeekon] cruiser.

καταδυναστεύω [kataδeenastevo] oppress.

καταδύομαι [kataδeeome] dive, plunge.

καταζητῶ [katazeeto] pursue, chase.

καταθέτω [katatheto] deposit, lay down ‖ (ὡς μάρτυρας) give evidence ‖ (ὅπλα) lay down ‖ (σχέδιον) introduce.

καταθλιπτικός [katathleepteekos] crushing, overwhelming.

καταιγίδα, ἡ [kateyeeδa] tempest, storm, hurricane.

καταῖφι, τό [kateefee] kind of oriental cake.

κατακάθι, τό [katakathee] residue, sediment, dregs.

κατάκειμαι [katakeeme] lie flat, lie down.

κατάκαρδα [katakarδa] deeply, seriously, profoundly, to heart.

κατακέφαλα [katakefala] headlong, on the head.

κατακλίνομαι [katakleenome] lie down, go to bed.

κατακλύζω [katakleezo] flood, inundate ‖ (μεταφ) invade, overrun.

κατακλυσμός, ὁ [katakleesmos] flood.

κατάκοιτος [katakeetos] bedridden.

κατάκοπος [katakopos] exhausted, deadbeat, dog-tired.

κατακόβω [katakovo] cut to pieces, cut up, lacerate.

κατακόρυφον, τό [katakoreefon] zenith ‖ (μεταφ) acme.

κατακόρυφος [katakoreefos] vertical, perpendicular.

κατακρατῶ [katakrato] withhold, keep illegally.

κατακραυγή, ἡ [katakravyee] outcry ‖ protestation.

κατακρεουργῶ [katakreouryo] butcher, massacre.

κατακρημνίζω [katakreemneezo] demolish, pull down.

κατακρίνω [katakreeno] blame, criticize, condemn.

κατάκτησις, ἡ [katakteesees] conquest, subjugation.

κατακτῶ [katakto] conquer, subjugate.

καταλαβαίνω [katalaveno] βλ καταλαμβάνω.

καταλαμβάνω [katalamvano] take, lay hold of, seize ‖ (χῶρο) take up ‖ (τό νόημα) understand.

καταλείπω [kataleepo] leave behind, abandon, forsake.

καταλεπτῶς [kataleptos] in detail, minutely.

καταλήγω [kataleeyo] end in, come to, result in, come to an end.

κατάληξις, ἡ [kataleeksees] termination, ending.

καταληπτός [kataleeptos] comprehensible, intelligible, clear.

κατάληψις, ἡ [kataleepsees] occupation, capture ‖ (ἰδέας) understanding, comprehension.

κατάλληλος [katalleelos] suitable, appropriate, fit, proper.

καταλογίζω [kataloyeezo] attribute, impute, ascribe.

κατάλογος, ὁ [kataloyos] catalogue, list ‖ (φαγητῶν) menu ‖ (τιμῶν) inventory, register, roll.

κατάλυμα, τό [kataleema] lodging, housing ‖ (στρατ) barracks, billeting.

κατάλυσις, ἡ [kataleesees] abolition ‖ (χημ) catalysis.

καταλύω [kataleeo] abolish, do away with ‖ take up lodging.

καταμερίζω [katamereezo] share out, distribute, apportion.

καταμεσῆς [katameses] in the very middle.

κατάμεστος [katamestos] quite full, crowded.

καταμετρῶ [katametro] measure, survey, gauge.

κατάμουτρα [katamoutra] point-blank.

καταναλίσκω [katanaleesko] consume, spend, use up ‖ (ποτά) drink.

κατανάλωσις, ἡ [katanalosees] consumption ‖ drinking.

καταναλωτής, ὁ [katanalotees] consumer, customer.

κατανέμω [katanemo] distribute ‖ (εὐθύνας) allot, assign, share.

κατανόησις, ἡ [katanoeesees] understanding, comprehension.

κατανοώ [katanoo] understand, comprehend.

κατάντημα, τό [katanteema] wretched state.

καταντώ [katanto] be reduced to, bring to, end up as.

κατάνυξις, ή [kataneeksees] compunction, piety.

καταπακτή, ή [katapaktee] trap, pitfall.

καταπατώ [katapato] violate, encroach upon.

κατάπαυσις, ή [katapavsees] cessation, stopping, halting.

καταπέλτης, ό [katapeltees] catapult.

καταπέτασμα, τό [katapetasma]: **τρώω τό ~** eat to bursting point.

καταπιάνομαι [katapeeanome] undertake, enter upon, engage upon.

καταπιέζω [katapiezo] oppress, crush, harass.

καταπίνω [katapeeno] swallow, gobble up || (ἐπί κυμάτων) engulf.

καταπίπτω [katapeepto] fall down, come down || collapse || (ὀλιγοστεύω) diminish.

καταπλακώνω [kataplakono] flatten, crush.

κατάπλασμα, τό [kataplasma] poultice.

καταπλέω [katapleo] sail in, sail down.

καταπληκτικός [katapleekteekos] amazing, wonderful, marvellous, astonishing.

κατάπληκτος [katapleektos] stupefied, amazed.

κατάπληξις, ή [katapleeksees] surprise, astonishment.

καταπλήσσω [katapleeso] astonish, surprise, amaze, stupefy.

καταπνίγω [katapneego] strangle, throttle, suffocate || (στάσιν) suppress, put down.

καταπονάω [kataponao] strain, weary, exhaust || (ἵππον) override.

καταποντίζομαι [kataponteezome] go down, sink.

καταπότιον, τό [katapoteeon] pill, tablet.

καταπραΰνω [katapraeeno] pacify, mollify, appease, calm, assuage.

κατάπτυστος [katapteestos] despicable, abject, low, villainous.

κατάπτωσις, ή [kataptosees] downfall || (ἐδάφους) landslide || (μεταφ) prostration, exhaustion || dejection, depression.

κατάρα, ή [katara] curse, imprecation || (μεταφ) hell, woe, damnation.

καταραμένος [kataramenos] cursed, damned.

καταργώ [katargo] abolish, annul, cancel || (κάπνισμα) cut out.

καταριέμαι [katarieme] curse, damn, call down curses on.

καταρράκτης, ό [kataraktees] cascade, waterfall || (τεχν) sluice.

καταρρέω [katarreo] collapse, fall down || (μεταφ) give out.

καταρρίπτω [katareepto] (κάποιον) knock down || (τοῖχον) pull down, demolish ||

(ἐπιχείρημα) prove to be wrong || (ρεκόρ) beat, break || (ἀερο) shoot down.

καταρροή, ή [kataroee] catarrh, head cold.

κατάρτι, τό [katartee] mast.

καταρτίζω [katarteezo] organize, establish, form, prepare, construct.

καταρῶμαι [katarome] βλ **καταριέμαι**.

κατάσβεσις, ή [katasvesees] extinction, blowing out || (μεταφ) suppression || (δίψας) slaking, quenching.

κατασκευάζω [kataskevazo] construct, make, erect, build || (ἱστορία κτλ) invent, concoct, fabricate || (ἔργον τέχνης) fashion, model.

κατασκεύασμα, τό [kataskevasma] fabrication, concoction || construction, creation.

κατασκευή, ή [kataskevee] making, construction || (ἔργον) structure, edifice, building || (ἐφεύρεσις) invention, fabrication.

κατασκήνωσις, ή [kataskeenosees] camp, encampment || camping.

κατάσκοπος, ό [kataskopos] spy, secret agent.

κατασκοτώνομαι [kataskotonome] make a great effort || overwork.

κάτασπρος [kataspros] pure white, white as a sheet.

κατασταλάζω [katastalazo] (μεταφ) end in, conclude, settle on.

κατάστασις, ή [katastasees] situation, condition, state || (περιουσία) wealth, property || (ὀνομαστική) register, list.

καταστατικόν, τό [katastateekon] (ἑταιρείας) statute.

καταστέλλω [katastelo] suppress, overcome || curb, control, contain.

κατάστημα, τό [katasteema] establishment, institution || shop, store || **καταστηματάρχης** shopkeeper.

κατάστικτος [katasteektos] spotted, dotted, speckled || tattooed.

κατάστιχον, τό [katasteehon] accounts book || register.

καταστολή, ή [katastolee] suppression || checking, bridling, controlling.

καταστρεπτικός [katastrepteekos] destructive, devastating, ruinous.

καταστρέφω [katastrefo] destroy, ruin, devastate || spoil, damage.

καταστροφή, ή [katastrofee] destruction, ruin, disaster, catastrophe.

κατάστρωμα, τό [katastroma] deck.

καταστρώνω [katastrono] draw up, make up, frame || lay down.

κατάσχεσις, ή [katashesees] seizure, confiscation || (λόγω χρέους) attachment.

κατάταξις, ή [katataksees] classification, sorting, grading || (στρατ) induction.

κατατάσσομαι [katatasome] enlist.

κατατομή, ή [katatomee] profile || vertical section, cutoff.

κατατόπια, τά [katatopeea] πλ locality, every nook and cranny.

κατατοπίζομαι [katatopeezome] find one's bearings.

κατατοπίζω [katatopeezo] direct, explain, inform.

κατατρέχω [katatreho] persecute, harass.

κατατρίβω [katatreevo] pulverize || abrade, powder.

καταφανής [katafanees] obvious, evident, manifest.

καταφατικός [katafateekos] affirmative, positive.

καταφέρνω [kataferno] persuade, convince, manage, accomplish, succeed || τά ~ succeed, manage.

καταφέρω [katafero] deal, strike || βλ καί **καταφέρνω**.

καταφθάνω [katafthano] arrive || overtake, catch up, overhaul.

κατάφορτος [katafortos] overloaded.

καταφρονώ [katafrono] scorn, despise.

καταφύγιον, τό [katafeeyeeon] refuge, hiding place.

κατάφυτος [katafeetos] covered with vegetation.

κατάφωρος [kataforos] manifest, flagrant, evident.

κατάφωτος [katafotos] profusely illuminated.

κατάχαμα [katahama] on the ground, on the floor.

καταχθόνιος [katahthoneeos] infernal, fiendish, devilish.

καταχνιά [katahneea] mist, fog.

καταχραστής, ὁ [katahrastees] embezzler, defaulter.

κατάχρεως [katahreos] deep in debt.

κατάχρησις, ἡ [katahreesees] abuse, misuse, breach of trust.

καταχρηστικῶς [katahreesteekos] abusively, excessively, unduly.

καταχρῶμαι [katahrome] abuse, take advantage of, presume upon.

καταχωρῶ [katahoro] enter in a register, insert, register, record.

καταψηφίζω [katapseefeezo] vote against, oppose.

κατάψυξις, ἡ [katapseeksees] refrigeration.

κατεβάζω [katevazo] let down || (ἀποσκευές) take or bring down || (θερμοκρασία κτλ) lower, reduce || (κόστος) lessen, decrease || (αὐλαίαν) drop.

κατεβαίνω [kateveno] come down, go down, descend.

κατέβασμα, τό [katevasma] descent, lowering, taking down.

κατεβασμένος [katevasmenos] (τιμή) reduced || (κατηφής) depressed.

κατεδαφίζω [kateðafeezo] demolish, pull down, raze.

κατειλημμένος [kateeleemenos] occupied, reserved.

κατέναντι [katenantee] right opposite.

κατεργάζομαι [kateryazome] elaborate, work out, shape, fashion.

κατεργάρης, ὁ [kateryarees] rascal, rogue || (ἐπίθ) cunning, tricky.

κατέρχομαι [katerhome] βλ **κατεβαίνω**.

κατεύθυνσις, ἡ [kateftheensees] direction, line, course.

κατευθύνομαι [kateftheenome] turn, head (for).

κατευθύνω [kateftheeno] direct, guide, aim, turn.

κατευνάζω [katevnazo] calm, pacify, appease, mollify.

κατευόδιον, τό [katevoðeeon] (a) good journey, (a) bon voyage.

κατέχω [kateho] possess, own, have, hold || (θέσιν) occupy || (γνωρίζω) know.

κατεψυγμένος [katepseeymenos] frozen, icy, frigid, polar.

κατηγορηματικός [kateeyoreemateekos] categorical, explicit.

κατηγορητήριον, τό [kateeyoreeteereeon] indictment.

κατηγορία, ἡ [kateeyoreea] accusation, charge || category, class, division.

κατήγορος, ὁ [kateeyoros] plaintiff, accuser || δημόσιος ~ public prosecutor.

κατηγορούμενον, τό [kateeyoroumenon] (γραμμ) complement || attribute.

κατηγορούμενος [kateeyoroumenos] the accused || defendant.

κατηγορῶ [kateeyoro] accuse, charge || blame, criticize.

κατηφής [kateefees] gloomy, depressed.

κατήφορος, ὁ [kateeforos] descent, slope.

κατηχῶ [kateeho] (ἐκκλ) catechize || (σὲ ὀργάνωσι) initiate.

κάτι [katee] something || some.

κατιών [kateeon] descending, falling.

κατοικία, ἡ [kateekeea] dwelling, residence, home.

κατοικίδιος [kateekeeðeeos] domesticated.

κατοικῶ [kateeko] live in, dwell in, inhabit, reside.

κατολίσθησις, ἡ [katoleestheesees] landslide.

κατόπιν [katopeen] after, close after || then || behind || ~ after.

κατοπτεύω [katoptevo] keep an eye on, observe, survey.

κατοπτρίζω [katoptreezo] reflect, mirror || (μεταφ) represent.

κάτοπτρον, τό [katoptron] mirror, looking-glass.

κατόρθωμα, τό [katorthoma] achievement, feat.

κατορθώνω [katorthono] succeed in, perform well.

κατορθωτός [katorthotos] feasible, possible, practicable.

κατουρλιό, τό [katourlio] urine, piss (col).

κατουρῶ [katouro] piss (col), urinate.

κατοχή, ή [katohee] possession ‖ (στρατ) occupation ‖ (νομ) detention.

κάτοχος, ὁ [katohos] possessor, occupier ‖ experienced person ‖ ~ τῆς Ἀγγλικῆς one whose English is good.

κατοχυρώνω [katoheerono] fortify ‖ (μεταφ) secure, safeguard.

κατρακυλῶ [katrakeelo] bring down, tumble down, come down.

κατράμι, τό [katramee] tar, asphalt.

κατσαβίδι, τό [katsaveedee] screwdriver.

κατσάδα, ή [katsaδa] scolding, dressing-down, reprimand.

κατσαρίδα, ή [katsareeδa] cockroach.

κατσαρόλα, ή [katsarola] saucepan.

κατσαρός [katsaros] curly, curled, fuzzy.

κατσίκα, ή [katseeka] goat.

κατσικήσιος [katseekeeseeos] of a goat.

κατσίκι, τό [katseekee] kid.

κατσουφιάζω [katsoufeeazo] look sour, look sullen, frown.

κάτω [kato] down, under, underneath, below ‖ on the ground ‖ στό ~ ~ after all ‖ ἀπάνω ~ approximately, about ‖ ἄνω ~ upset, in a turmoil.

κατώγειον, τό [katoyeeon] basement, cellar.

κάτωθεν [katothen] from below ‖ below.

κατώτατος [katotatos] lowest, least, undermost.

κατώτερος [katoteros] lower ‖ poorer (quality), inferior.

κατώφλι, τό [katoflee] threshold, doorstep ‖ (μεταφ) eve.

καυγάς, ὁ [kavyas] quarrel, wrangle, squabble, argument.

καύκαλο, τό [kavkalo] skull ‖ shell, carapace.

καῦμα, τό [kavma] burn ‖ burning heat.

καύσιμα, τά [kavseema] πλ fuel.

καύσιμος [kavseemos] combustible, inflammable.

καῦσις, ή [kavsees] burning ‖ (χημ) combustion.

καυστικός [kavsteekos] caustic.

καύσων, ὁ [kavson] heatwave.

καυτερός [kavteros] hot ‖ (ὑγρό) scalding ‖ (μεταφ) caustic, biting.

καυτηριάζω [kavteereeazo] cauterize ‖ (ζῶα) brand ‖ (μεταφ) stigmatize.

καυτός [kavtos] scalding, boiling, hot.

καύχημα, τό [kavheema] boast, pride, glory.

καυχηματίας, ὁ [kavheemateeas] braggart.

καυχιέμαι [kavhieme] boast of, be proud.

καφάσι, τό [kafasee] trellis, lattice ‖ (γιά φροῦτα) crate.

καφενεῖον, τό [kafeneeon] coffee house.

καφές, ὁ [kafes] coffee.

καφετζῆς, ὁ [kafetsees] coffee-house keeper.

καφετιέρα, ή [kafetiera] coffee pot.

καφετής [kafetees] coffee-coloured.

καχεκτικός [kahekteekos] sickly (person), weakly (person).

καχύποπτος [kaheepoptos] suspicious, distrustful.

κάψα, ή [kapsa] excessive heat.

καψαλίζω [kapsaleezo] singe, broil ‖ toast.

κάψιμο, τό [kapseemo] burning ‖ scald.

καψούλι, τό [kapsoulee] (ιατρ) capsule.

κέδρος, ή [keδros] cedar tree, cedar (wood).

κεῖμαι [keeme] lie ‖ be situated.

κείμενον, τό [keemenon] text.

κειμήλιον, τό [keemeeleeon] heirloom, treasure.

κέκτημαι [kekteeme] possess, own, occupy.

κελαϊδῶ [kelaeeδo] sing, warble, chirp.

κελεπούρι, τό [kelepouree] bargain ‖ windfall, godsend.

κελευστής, ὁ [kelevstees] petty officer.

κελλάρι, τό [kelaree] cellar ‖ larder.

κελλί(ον), τό [kelee(on)] cell ‖ honeycomb.

κέλυφος, ὁ [keleefos] shell, husk, bark.

κενόδοξος [kenoδoksos] conceited, self-satisfied, vainglorious.

κενόν, τό [kenon] void, empty space, vacuum ‖ (μεταφ) gap.

κενός [kenos] empty ‖ (οἰκία) unoccupied, vacant.

κέντημα, τό [kenteema] sting, bite ‖ embroidery ‖ (μεταφ) exhortation.

κεντητός [kenteetos] embroidered.

κεντρί, τό [kentree] sting ‖ thorn.

κεντρίζω [kentreezo] (βῶδι) prick, goad ‖ (ἄλογο) spur ‖ (δένδρον) graft ‖ (μεταφ) rouse, stir up.

κεντρικός [kentreekos] central, middle ‖ principal.

κεντρομόλος [kentromolos] centripetal.

κέντρον, τό [kentron] sting, goad, spur ‖ (πόλεως) centre ‖ (γεωμ) centre ‖ (διακεσκεδάσεως) (night) club, taverna ‖ τηλεφωνικόν ~ telephone exchange.

κεντρόφυξ [kentrofeeks] centrifugal.

κεντρώνω [kentrono] βλ **κεντρίζω**.

κεντῶ [kento] embroider ‖ (μεταφ) incite, rouse, awaken, stir up.

κενώνω [kenono] empty ‖ (δρόμο) drain ‖ (συρτάρι) clean out ‖ (σπίτι) evacuate.

κένωσις, ή [kenoses] emptying, clearing out ‖ bowel movement.

κεραία, ή [kerea] antenna, feeler ‖ (ἀσυρμάτου) aerial.

κεραμίδι, τό [kerameeδee] tile, slate ‖ πλ roof.

κεραμική, ή [kerameekee] ceramics.

κέρας, τό [keras] horn.

κεράσι, τό [kerasee] cherry ‖ **κερασιά, ή** cherry tree.

κέρασμα, τό [kerasma] treat.

κερατᾶς, ὁ [keratas] cuckold.

κέρατο, τό [kerato] horn ‖ (ἐπί ἀνθρώπου) obstinate, perverse.

κεραυνοβόλος [keravnovolos] blitzkrieg-like, like lightning.

κεραυνός, ὁ [keravnos] thunderbolt.

κερδίζω [kerdeezo] win, earn ‖ get, gain ‖ profit by.

κέρδος, τό [kerdos] earnings, winnings ‖ advantage.

κερδοσκοπῶ [kerdoskopo] speculate.

κερένιος [kereneeos] wax, waxen.

κερί, τό [keree] wax ‖ taper, wax candle.

κερκίδα, ἡ [kerkeeδa] tier of seats.

κέρμα, τό [kerma] fragment ‖ coin ‖ (διά μηχάνημα) token.

κερνῶ [kerno] treat ‖ stand or buy a drink.

κεσές, ὁ [keses] shallow dish.

κετσές, ὁ [ketses] felt.

κεφαλαιοκρατία, ἡ [kefaleokrateea] capitalism.

κεφάλαια, τά [kefalea] πλ funds, capital.

κεφάλαιον, τό [kefaleon] capital, funds ‖ (βιβλίου) chapter.

κεφαλαῖον, τό [kefaleon] capital (letter).

κεφαλαιώδης [kefaleoδees] essential, fundamental.

κεφαλαλγία, ἡ [kefalalyeea] headache.

κεφαλή, ἡ [kefalee] head ‖ leader, chief.

κεφάλι, τό [kefalee] head ‖ (μεταφ) brains.

κέφαλος, ὁ [kefalos] mullet.

κεφᾶτος [kefatos] well-disposed, merry, jovial.

κέφι, τό [kefee] good humour, gaiety ‖ στὸ ~ merry, mellow.

κεφτές, ὁ [keftes] meatball, rissole.

κεχρί, τό [kehree] millet.

κεχριμπάρι, τό [kehreembaree] amber.

κηδεία, ἡ [keeδeea] funeral (procession).

κηδεμών, ὁ [keeδemon] guardian ‖ curator.

κήλη, ἡ [keelee] hernia, rupture.

κηλιδώνω [keeleeδono] stain, dirty ‖ (μεταφ) sully, tarnish.

κηλίς, ἡ [keelees] spot, stain ‖ (μεταφ) slur, blemish.

κῆπος, ὁ [keepos] garden.

κηπουρική, ἡ [keepoureekee] gardening, horticulture.

κηπουρός, ὁ [keepouros] gardener.

κηρήθρα, ἡ [keereethra] honeycomb.

κηρίον, τό [keereeon] βλ **κερί**.

κηροπήγιον, τό [keeropeeyeeon] candlestick, taper-stand.

κηρός, ὁ [keeros] wax.

κήρυγμα, τό [keereeyma] proclamation ‖ (ἐκκλ) sermon, preaching.

κήρυξ, ὁ [keereeks] herald ‖ (ἐκκλ) preacher.

κηρύσσω [keereeso] proclaim, announce ‖ (ἐκκλ) preach.

κῆτος, τό [keetos] cetacean, whale.

κηφήν, ὁ [keefeen] drone ‖ (μεταφ) idler, loafer.

κιάλια, τά [kialeea] πλ binoculars, opera glasses.

κίβδηλος [keevδeelos] adulterated, counterfeit ‖ (μεταφ) fraudulent.

κιβώτιον, τό [keevoteeon] chest, box ‖ ~ ταχυτήτων gearbox.

κιγκλίδωμα, τό [keengleeδoma] (φράκτης) barrier, fence ‖ (σιδηροῦν) grating ‖ (ξύλινον) lattice work ‖ (παραθύρου) bar.

κιθάρα, ἡ [keethara] guitar.

κιλό, τό [keelo] kilogram.

κιμᾶς, ὁ [keemas] minced meat.

κιμωλία, ἡ [keemoleea] chalk.

Κίνα, ἡ [keena] China.

κινδυνεύω [keenδeenevo] endanger ‖ be in danger, risk, venture.

κίνδυνος, ὁ [keenδeenos] danger, peril, hazard, jeopardy.

κινέζικα, τά [keenezeeka] πλ Chinese language.

Κινέζος, ὁ [keenezos] Chinese, Chinaman.

κίνημα, τό [keeneema] movement ‖ (μεταφ) rebellion, revolt.

κινηματογράφος, ὁ [keeneematoyrafos] cinema.

κίνησις, ἡ [keeneesees] movement ‖ (κυκλοφορίας) flow of traffic ‖ (ἀξιῶν) transactions.

κινητήρ, ὁ [keeneeteer] motor.

κινητός [keeneetos] movable.

κίνητρον, τό [keeneetron] motive.

κινίνη, ἡ [keeneenee] quinine.

κινοῦμαι [keenoume] move.

κινῶ [keeno] set in motion, move, rouse, make go, set going.

κιόλα(ς) [keeola(s)] already, also, even.

κιονόκρανον, τό [keeonokranon] capital (archit).

κιονοστοιχία, ἡ [keeonosteeheea] colonnade.

κιόσκι, τό [keeoskee] kiosk.

κίσσα, ἡ [keesa] magpie.

κισσός, ὁ [keesos] ivy.

κιτρινάδα, ἡ [keetreenaδa] paleness ‖ (ἀρρώστεια) jaundice.

κιτρινίζω [keetreeneezo] go yellow, make yellow, pale.

κίτρινος [keetreenos] yellow ‖ sallow, pale.

κίτρον, τό [keetron] citron.

κίων, ὁ [keeon] pillar, column.

κλαγγή, ἡ [klangee] clanking of arms, clashing.

κλαδευτήρι, τό [klaδevteeree] pruning hook, pruning scissors.

κλαδεύω [klaδevo] prune, trim.

κλάδος, ὁ [klaδos] branch, arm.

κλαίομαι [kleome] complain, gripe.

κλαίω [kleo] cry, weep ‖ feel sorry for, weep for.

κλάμα, τό [klama] crying, wailing, weeping.

κλάνω [klano] break wind, fart (col).

κλαρί, τό [klaree] small branch.

κλάσις, ἡ [klasees] class, age group, category ‖ breaking.

κλάσμα, τό [klasma] fraction ‖ fragment.

κλασσικός [klaseekos] classic(al) ‖ (μεταφ) standard, standing.

κλαυθμηρός [klafthmeeros] tearful, mournful, plaintive.

κλαψιάρης [klapseearees] given to complaining ‖ tearful, plaintive.

κλαψιάρικος [klapseeareekos] always whining ‖ always beefing.

κλάψιμο, τό [klapseemo] crying, grumbling.

κλέβω [klevo] βλ κλέπτω.

κλειδαριά, ή [kleedaria] lock ‖ (ἀσφαλείας) safety lock ‖ (κρεμαστή) padlock.

κλειδαρότρυπα, ή [kleedarotreepa] keyhole.

κλειδί, τό [kleedee] key.

κλειδώνω [kleedono] lock up ‖ (περιορίζω) confine, coop up.

κλείδωσις, ή [kleedosees] joint.

κλεῖθρον, τό [kleethron] lock ‖ bar.

κλείνω [kleeno] close, shut, shut up, seal ‖ (μέ σύρτη) bolt ‖ (βρύση) turn off ‖ ~ τό μάτι wink ‖ ~ τά ἑξήντα I'm nearing sixty.

κλείς, ή [klees] key.

κλείσιμο, τό [kleeseemo] closing, locking up ‖ (μεταφ) conclusion.

κλεισούρα, ή [kleesoura] pass ‖ mustiness.

κλειστός [kleestos] shut, closed.

κλέπτης, ὁ [kleptees] thief, burglar ‖ (πορτοφολιῶν) pickpocket.

κλέπτω [klepto] (κάτι) steal ‖ (κάποιον) rob ‖ (μέ ἀπάτη) cheat, swindle.

κλεφτά [klefta] furtively, stealthily ‖ hurriedly.

κλέφτης, ὁ [kleftees] thief ‖ klepht.

κλεφτοπόλεμος, ὁ [kleftopolemos] guerrilla warfare.

κλεφτός [kleftos] stolen ‖ furtive, stealthy.

κλεψιά, ή [klepseea] βλ κλοπή.

κλέψιμο, τό [klepseemo] theft, robbery, burglary.

κλεψύδρα, ή [klepseedra] water clock, sandglass.

κλήθρα, ή [kleethra] alder.

κλῆμα, τό [kleema] vine ‖ κληματαριά, ή vine arbour, climbing vine ‖ bower ‖ κληματόφυλλο, τό vine leaf.

κληρικός [kleereekos] clerical, of the clergy.

κληροδότημα, τό [kleerodoteema] legacy, bequest.

κληρονομιά, ή [kleeronomeea] inheritance ‖ heritage, legacy.

κληρονομικός [kleeronomeekos] hereditary.

κληρονόμος, ὁ, ή [kleeronomos] heir, heiress.

κληρονομῶ [kleeronomo] inherit, come into an estate.

κλῆρος, ὁ [kleeros] lot, fate ‖ (ἐκκλ) clergy ‖ (μεταφ) lot, fortune.

κλήρωσις, ή [kleerosees] drawing of lottery, prize drawing.

κλῆσις, ή [kleesees] call, calling ‖ writ of summons.

κλητήρας, ὁ [kleeteeras] usher ‖ (δικαστικός) bailiff.

κλητική, ή [kleeteekee] (γραμμ) vocative (case).

κλίβανος, ὁ [kleevanos] oven, kiln, furnace.

κλίμα, τό [kleema] climate ‖ (μεταφ) atmosphere.

κλιμάκιον, τό [kleemakeeon] detachment, gang ‖ (στρατ) echelon ‖ small scale.

κλιμακωτός [kleemakotos] graduated.

κλίμαξ, ή [kleemaks] staircase, stairs, ladder ‖ scale ‖ (μουσ) gamut, scale.

κλιματισμός, ὁ [kleemateesmos] air conditioning.

κλινάμαξα, ή [kleenamaksa] sleeper (rail).

κλίνη, ή [kleenee] bed ‖ (ἐκστρατείας) campbed ‖ (μωροῦ) cot, crib.

κλινήρης [kleeneerees] bedridden.

κλινική, ή [kleeneekee] clinic, (private) hospital.

κλινοσκέπασμα, τό [kleenoskepasma] blanket, coverlet.

κλίνω [kleeno] lean, bend ‖ (ἔχω τάσιν πρός) tend ‖ (γραμμ) decline, conjugate.

κλίσις, ή [kleesees] inclination, slope ‖ proneness, tendency ‖ (γραμμῆς) slope ‖ (γραμμ) declension, conjugation ‖ (στέγης) slant.

κλιτύς, ή [kleetees] slope (of mountain), declivity.

κλονίζομαι [kloneezome] stagger ‖ (μεταφ) hesitate, falter, waver.

κλονίζω [kloneezo] shake, unsettle ‖ (ὑγείαν) damage, ruin.

κλονισμός, ὁ [kloneesmos] shaking, concussion ‖ (μεταφ) hesitation, wavering.

κλοπή, ή [klopee] theft, robbery, burglary.

κλοπιμαῖος [klopeemeos] stolen ‖ furtive, stealthy.

κλουβί, τό [klouvee] cage.

κλούβιος [klouveeos] bad, rotten ‖ (μεταφ) empty-headed, stupid.

κλύσμα, τό [kleesma] enema.

κλωβός, ὁ [klovos] cage.

κλώθω [klotho] spin.

κλωνάρι, τό [klonaree] branch (of tree) ‖ shoot.

κλώσιμο, τό [kloseemo] spinning.

κλῶσσα, ή [klosa] (brooding) hen.

κλωστή, ή [klostee] thread, string.

κλωτσιά, ή [klotsia] kick.

κλωτσῶ [klotso] kick.

κνήμη, ή [kneemee] shin ‖ leg.

κόβομαι [kovome] cut o.s.

κόβω [kovo] (ψωμί) cut, slice ‖ (μαλλιά) cut, trim ‖ (νύχια) pare ‖ (κρέας) carve ‖ (νομίσματα) coin, mint ‖ (νερό) turn off ‖ (καφέ, σιτάρι) grind, mill ‖ (κεφάλι) behead ‖ (ἐφόδια) cut off ‖ ~ μονέδα make money ‖ ~ εἰσιτήριο buy a ticket ‖ ~ δεξιά turn right.

κόγχη, ή [konghee] marine shell ‖ (ματιοῦ) eye socket ‖ (ἀρχιτεκ) niche.

κογχύλι, τό [kongheelee] sea shell ‖ shellfish.

κοιλάδα, ή [keelada] valley, vale.

κοιλαράς [keelaras] pot-bellied, portly.

κοιλιά, ή [keelia] belly, abdomen || (τοίχου) bulge.

κοιλόπονος, ὁ [keeloponos] stomach ache.

κοῖλος [keelos] hollow, sunken.

κοιλότης, ή [keelotees] hollowness || concavity.

κοιμᾶμαι [keemame] sleep, be asleep.

κοίμησις, ή [keemeesees] (ἐκκλ) Assumption || sleeping.

κοιμητήριον, τό [keemeeteereeon] cemetery, graveyard.

κοιμίζω [keemeezo] put to sleep || quiet, lull, beguile.

κοιμισμένος [keemeesmenos] (μεταφ) sluggish, stupid, dull.

κοιμοῦμαι [keemoume] βλ κοιμᾶμαι.

κοινοβουλευτικός [keenovoulevteekos] parliamentary, parliamentarian.

κοινοβούλιον, τό [keenovouleeon] parliament || (εἰς Ἀγγλίαν) Houses of Parliament.

κοινόν, τό [keenon] the public.

κοινοποιῶ [keenopeeo] notify, inform, announce || serve (a notice).

κοινοπολιτεία, ή [keenopoleeteea] commonwealth.

κοινός [keenos] common || ordinary, vulgar || (ἐργασία κτλ) collective || (γραμμ) common (noun) || κοινή γνώμη public opinion || ἀπό κοινοῦ in common, together.

κοινότης, ή [keenotees] community || parish || Βουλή τῶν Κοινοτήτων House of Commons.

κοινοτοπία, ή [keenotopeea] commonplace || banality.

κοινωνία, ή [keenoneea] society, community, association || (ἐκκλ) Holy Communion.

κοινωνικός [keenoneekos] social, sociable.

κοινωνῶ [keenono] receive Holy Communion || administer Holy Communion.

κοιτάζομαι [keetazome] look after o.s.

κοιτάζω [keetazo] look at, pay attention to || consider, see || attend.

κοίτασμα, τό [keetasma] layer, deposit, stratum.

κοίτη, ή [keetee] bed || (ζώων) lair || (πτηνῶν) nest.

κοιτίς, ή [keetees] cradle || (μεταφ) origin, birthplace.

κοιτών, ὁ [keeton] bedroom || dormitory.

κοκεταρία, ή [koketareea] smartness, coquetry, stylishness.

κόκκαλο, τό [kokalo] bone || (παπουτσιοῦ) shoehorn || ἔμεινε ~ he was astounded.

κοκκινάδι, τό [kokeenaðee] rouge.

κοκκινέλι, τό [kokeenelee] red wine.

κοκκινίζω [kokeeneezo] redden, blush, turn red.

κοκκινογούλι, τό [kokeenoɣoulee] beetroot, beet.

κοκκινομάλλης [kokeenomalees] redhaired.

κόκκινος [kokeenos] red, scarlet || (μάγουλα) ruddy, rosy.

κόκκος, ὁ [kokos] grain || (καφέ) bean || (σκόνης) speck.

κοκκύτης, ὁ [kokeetees] whooping cough.

κόκορας, ὁ [kokoras] cock, rooster.

κοκορέτσι, τό [kokoretsee] sheep's entrails.

κολάζω [kolazo] punish, chastise.

κολακεία, ή [kolakeea] flattery, softsoaping.

κολακευτικός [kolakevteekos] complimentary.

κολακεύω [kolakevo] flatter, fawn upon.

κόλακας, ὁ [kolakas] flatterer, wheedler.

κόλασις, ή [kolasees] hell.

κολατσίζω [kolatseezo] have a snack.

κολατσιό, τό [kolatsio] snack.

κολικός, ὁ [koleekos] colic.

κολιός, ὁ [kolios] kind of mackerel.

κόλλα, ή [kola] glue, gum, paste || (κολλαρίσματος) starch || (χαρτιοῦ) sheet of paper.

κολλάρο, τό [kolaro] collar.

κολλέγιον, τό [koleɣeeon] college.

κόλλημα, τό [koleema] glueing, sticking || soldering.

κολλητικός [koleeteekos] contagious, infectious.

κολλητός [koleetos] soldered || closefitting || (ἐφαπτόμενος) contiguous.

κολλητσίδα, ή [koleetseeða] burdock || (μεταφ) pest.

κολλιέ, τό [kolie] necklace.

κόλλυβα, ή [koleeva] boiled wheat.

κολλῶ [kolo] glue, stick, paste || solder, fuse || (ἀρρώστεια) get, catch || (σέ κάποιον) stick to, attach to.

κολοβός [kolovos] truncated, mutilated || deficient.

κολοκύθι, τό [kolokeethee] vegetable marrow, pumpkin.

κολόνα, ή [kolona] βλ κολώνα.

κολόνια, ή [koloneea] eau de Cologne.

κολοσσιαῖος [kolosieos] colossal, enormous.

κολοσσός, ὁ [kolosos] colossus, giant.

κολοφών, ὁ [kolofon] summit || (μεταφ) height, acme.

κόλπο, τό [kolpo] trick, artifice, deceit.

κόλπος, ὁ [kolpos] breast, bosom || (γεωγραφικός) gulf, bay.

κολυμβήθρα, ή [koleemveethra] font.

κολυμβητής, ὁ [koleemveetees] swimmer.

κολύμπι, τό [koleembee] swimming.

κολυμπῶ [koleembo] swim.

κολώνα, ή [kolona] pillar, column.

κομβίον, τό [komveeon] button.

κομβολόγιον, τό [komvoloɣeeon] string of beads, worry beads.

κόμβος, ὁ [komvos] knot || junction.

κόμη, ή [komee] hair.

κόμης, ὁ [komees] count, earl.
κομητεία, ἡ [komeeteea] county, shire.
κομήτης, ὁ [komeetees] comet.
κομίζω [komeezo] bring, carry, convey.
κομιστής, ὁ [komeestees] carrier, bearer.
κόμιστρα, τά [komeestra] πλ carriage fees.
κόμμα, τό [koma] (πολιτικόν) party ‖ (γραμμ) comma ‖ (μαθημ) decimal point.
κομματάρχης, ὁ [komatarhees] party leader.
κομμάτι, τό [komatee] piece ‖ (ψωμί) slice ‖ (ζάχαρις) lump ‖ fragment, chip ‖ (ὡς ἐπιρ) a bit.
κομματιάζομαι [komateeazome] try hard.
κομματιάζω [komateeazo] cut up, parcel out, tear, break.
κομμένος [komenos] sliced, cut ‖ (κουρασμένος) exhausted.
κομ(μ)ό, τό [komo] chest of drawers.
κομ(μ)οδίνο, τό [komoδeeno] bedside table.
κομμουνιστής, ὁ [komouneestees] communist.
κόμμωσις, ἡ [komosees] hairdressing, hair style.
κομμωτήριον, τό [komoteereeon] hairdressing salon.
κομπάζω [kombazo] brag of, boast (about).
κομπιάζω [kombeeazo] (μεταφ) hesitate.
κομπίνα, ἡ [kombeena] racket (col).
κομπιναιζόν, τό [kombeenezon] slip, petticoat.
κομπογιαννίτης, ὁ [komboyeeaneetees] impostor, charlatan.
κομπόδεμα, τό [komboδema] hoard of money, savings.
κόμπος, ὁ [kombos] βλ κόμβος.
κομπόστα, ἡ [kombosta] compote.
κομπρέσσα, ἡ [kombresa] compress.
κομφόρ, τά [komfor] πλ home comforts, necessities.
κομψός [kompsos] fashionable, stylish, smart.
κονδύλιον, τό [konδeeleeon] item, entry.
κονδυλοφόρος, ὁ [konδeeloforos] penholder.
κονιάκ, τό [koneeak] cognac, brandy.
κονίαμα, τό [koneeama] mortar ‖ plaster.
κόνικλος, ὁ [koneeklos] rabbit.
κονιορτός, ὁ [koneeortos] dust.
κόνις, ἡ [konees] powder, dust.
κονίστρα, ἡ [koneestra] arena ‖ (μεταφ) political lists.
κονσέρβα, ἡ [konserva] tinned food, canned food, preserve(s).
κονσέρτο, τό [konserto] concert.
κοντά [konta] close to, close by, near ‖ almost, nearly ‖ ~ σέ near, next to ‖ ~ στά ἄλλα moreover.
κονταίνω [konteno] shorten, curtail ‖ get shorter.
κοντάρι, τό [kontaree] pole ‖ (σημαίας) staff ‖ (ναυτ) mast.

κοντεύω [kontevo] be about to, be nearly finished, be on the verge (of) ‖ (πλησιάζω) approach, come near, draw near.
κόντημα, τό [konteema] shortening, shrinking.
κοντινός [konteenos] neighbouring, near-(by) ‖ (δρόμος) short, quick.
κοντοζυγώνω [kontozeeyono] approach, come near.
κοντολογής [kontoloyees] in short, in a few words.
κοντός [kontos] short ‖ (οὐσ) pole, post, stake.
κοντοστέκω [kontosteko] pause ‖ hesitate, waver.
κοντούλης [kontoulees] short.
κόντρα [kontra] against, opposite.
κοπάδι, τό [kopaδee] flock ‖ herd, drove ‖ (λύκων) pack ‖ (ἀνθρώπων) crowd, throng.
κοπάζω [kopazo] calm down, grow quiet, subside.
κοπανίζω [kopaneezo] beat, pound, grind ‖ (μεταφ) reprimand, rebuke.
κόπανος, ὁ [kopanos] pestle, crusher ‖ (μεταφ) fool, idiot.
κοπέλλα, ἡ [kopela] girl ‖ (ὑπηρεσίας) servant, maid.
κοπή, ἡ [kopee] cutting ‖ stoppage.
κόπια, ἡ [kopeea] copy, transcript.
κοπιάζω [kopeeazo] labour, toil ‖ take the trouble (to).
κοπιαστικός [kopeeasteekos] wearisome, hard, fatiguing, troublesome.
κοπίδι, τό [kopeeδee] chisel.
κοπιώδης [kopeeoδees] βλ κοπιαστικός.
κόπος, ὁ [kopos] fatigue, toil, labour, trouble, effort.
κόπρανα, τά [koprana] πλ excrement.
κοπριά, ἡ [kopreea] dung, manure.
κόπρος, ἡ [kopros] βλ κοπριά.
κοπρόσκυλο, τό [koproskeelo] (μεταφ) worthless person, scoundrel.
κοπτήρ, ὁ [kopteer] incisor ‖ (χαρτοκοπτήρ) cutter.
κοπτική, ἡ [kopteekee] cutting, tailoring.
κόπτω [kopto] βλ κόβω.
κόπωσις, ἡ [koposees] fatigue, weariness, toil.
κόρακας, ὁ [korakas] crow, raven.
κοράλλιον, τό [koraleeon] coral.
κόραξ, ὁ [koraks] βλ κόρακας.
κοράσιον, τό [koraseeon] little girl.
κορδέλλα, ἡ [korδela] ribbon, band, tape ‖ (μεταφ) zigzag, twist and turn.
κορδόνι, τό [korδonee] cord, string.
κορδώνομαι [korδonome] strut, swagger, put on airs.
κορδώνω [korδono] tighten, stretch, extend.
κορεσμός, ὁ [koresmos] satisfaction, satiety.
κόρη, ἡ [koree] girl ‖ (παρθένα) virgin ‖

(παιδί) daughter ‖ (ὀφθαλμοῦ) pupil.

κορινθιακός [koreentheeakos] Corinthian.

κοριός, ὁ [korios] bedbug.

κοριτσάκι, τό [koreetsakee] little girl.

κορίτσι, τό [koreetsee] girl ‖ virgin.

κορμί, τό [kormee] body ‖ trunk.

κορμός, ὁ [kormos] trunk.

κορμοστασιά, ἡ [kormostasia] stature, bearing, figure.

κορνάρω [kornaro] sound one's horn, hoot.

κορνίζα, ἡ [korneeza] frame ‖ cornice.

κοροϊδεύω [koroeedevo] scoff at, laugh at, ridicule ‖ deceive.

κορόϊδο, τό [koroeedo] laughing stock, butt, scapegoat.

κορόμηλο, τό [koromeelo] plum.

κόρος, ὁ [koros] satiety.

κορσές, ὁ [korses] corset.

κορτάρω [kortaro] flirt, court.

κορυδαλλός, ὁ [koreedalos] skylark, lark.

κορυφαῖος, ὁ [koreefeos] leader, chief.

κορυφή, ἡ [koreefee] top ‖ (ὄρους) top, peak ‖ (γωνίας) vertex ‖ (μεταφ) leading person, outstanding person.

κορφή, ἡ [korfee] βλ **κορυφή**.

κόρφος, ὁ [korfos] bosom ‖ (γεωγραφικός) bay, inlet.

κορώνα, ἡ [korona] crown, coronet ‖ ~ γράμματα heads or tails.

κοσκινίζω [koskeeneezo] sift, screen ‖ (μεταφ) sift carefully.

κόσκινο, τό [koskeeno] sieve, sifter.

κοσμάκης, ὁ [kosmakees] the man in the street.

κόσμημα, τό [kosmeema] decoration, jewel ‖ ~τα πλ jewellery.

κοσμήτωρ, ὁ [kosmeetor] dean (univ).

κοσμικός [kosmeekos] lay ‖ mundane ‖ (γεγονός) social.

κόσμιος [kosmeeos] decent, modest, proper.

κόσμος, ὁ [kosmos] universe, world ‖ (ἄνθρωποι) people ‖ (στόλισμα) embellishment.

κοσμῶ [kosmo] adorn, embellish.

κοστίζω [kosteezo] cost, be expensive.

κόστος, τό [kostos] cost (price).

κοστούμι, τό [kostoumee] suit.

κότερο, τό [kotero] sailboat ‖ (ναυτ) cutter.

κοτέτσι, τό [kotetsee] hen coop.

κοτολέττα, ἡ [kotoleta] cutlet.

κοτόπουλο, τό [kotopoulo] chicken.

κοτρώνι, τό [kotronee] large stone, boulder.

κοτσάνι, τό [kotsanee] stem, stalk.

κότσι, τό [kotsee] anklebone.

κότσια, τά [kotseea] πλ guts, strength.

κοτσίδα, ἡ [kotseeda] tress, braid, pig-tail.

κότσυφας, ὁ [kotseefas] blackbird.

κότ(τ)α, ἡ [kota] hen ‖ fowl.

κοτῶ [koto] dare, venture.

κουβαλῶ [kouvalo] carry, bring, transport.

κουβάρι, τό [kouvaree] ball.

κουβαριάζω [kouvareeazo] wind into a ball ‖ (μεταφ) crumple ‖ cheat.

κουβαρίστρα, ἡ [kouvareestra] bobbin, spool.

κουβᾶς, ὁ [kouvas] bucket, pail.

κουβέντα, ἡ [kouventa] conversation, chat.

κουβεντιάζω [kouventeeazo] converse, discuss, chat.

κουβέρ, τό [kouver] service charge, cover charge.

κουβερνάντα, ἡ [kouvernanta] governess.

κουβέρτα, ἡ [kouverta] blanket, coverlet ‖ (ναυτ) deck.

κουδούνι, τό [koudounee] bell ‖ (εἰσόδου) doorbell.

κουδουνίζω [koudouneezo] ring, tinkle, jingle.

κουδουνίστρα, ἡ [koudouneestra] rattle.

κουζίνα, ἡ [kouzeena] kitchen ‖ (γιά μαγείρευμα) stove.

κουκέτα, ἡ [kouketa] berth.

κουκί, τό [koukee] broad bean ‖ grain.

κούκλα, ἡ [koukla] doll ‖ (ράφτη) dummy ‖ (καλαμποκιοῦ) corn cob ‖ (μεταφ) lovely child ‖ pretty woman.

κούκ(κ)ος, ὁ [koukos] cuckoo ‖ bonnet, cap.

κουκουβάγια, ἡ [koukouvayeea] owl.

κουκούλα, ἡ [koukoula] cowl, hood ‖ (τσαϊοῦ) tea cosy.

κουκούλι, τό [koukoulee] cocoon.

κουκουλώνω [koukoulono] keep secret ‖ bury ‖ wrap warmly.

κουκουνάρι, τό [koukounaree] pine cone ‖ seed of pine cone.

κουκούτσι, τό [koukoutsee] stone, kernel, pip ‖ (μεταφ) morsel, scrap.

κουλούρα, ἡ [kouloura] roll, French roll ‖ (ναυτ) lifebuoy.

κουλούρι, τό [koulouree] ring-shaped biscuit.

κουλουριάζω [kouloureeazo] coil, roll up, fold.

κουμάντο, τό [koumanto] order, control, direct.

κουμάρι, τό [koumaree] jug, crock, pitcher.

κουμπάρα, ἡ [koumbara] godmother ‖ matron of honour.

κουμπαράς, ὁ [koumbaras] moneybox, piggy bank.

κουμπάρος, ὁ [koumbaros] godfather ‖ (σέ γάμο) best man.

κουμπί, τό [koumbee] button, stud ‖ (φώτων) switch.

κουμπότρυπα, ἡ [koumbotreepa] button-hole.

κουμπώνω [koumbono] button up, fasten.

κουνάβι, τό [kounavee] marten, ferret.

κουνέλι, τό [kounelee] rabbit.

κούνημα, τό [kouneema] shaking, swinging, wagging ‖ (μεταφ) swaying.

κούνια, ἡ [kouneea] cradle, cot, crib ‖ (κήπου) swing.

κουνιάδα, ή [kouneeaδa] sister-in-law.
κουνιάδος, ὁ [kouneeaδos] brother-in-law.
κουνιστός [kouneestos] rocking ‖ (μεταφ) swaying.
κουνούπι, τό [kounoupee] mosquito.
κουνουπίδι, τό [kounoupeeδee] cauliflower.
κουνουπιέρα, ή [kounoupiera] mosquito net.
κουνιέμαι [kounieme] move, shake ‖ get moving.
κουνῶ [kouno] move, shake ‖ (μαντήλι) wave ‖ (οὐράν) wag ‖ (μωρό) rock ‖ (κεφάλι) toss.
κούπα, ή [koupa] cup, bowl, glass ‖ (σέ χαρτιά) heart.
κουπί, τό [koupee] oar ‖ **τραβῶ** ~ row.
κουπόνι, τό [kouponee] coupon.
κούρα, ή [koura] cure ‖ medical attendance.
κουράγιο, τό [kouraγeeo] bravery, fearlessness.
κουράζομαι [kourazome] get tired, tire o.s.
κουράζω [kourazo] tire, weary ‖ bore ‖ (δρασιν) strain.
κουραμάνα, ή [kouramana] army bread.
κουραμπιές, ὁ [kourambies] bun.
κούραση, ή [kourasee] weariness, fatigue ‖ (μηχανῆς) wear and tear.
κουρασμένος [kourasmenos] tired, weary ‖ (πρόσωπον) drawn.
κουραστικός [kourasteekos] tiresome, trying, troublesome.
κουραφέξαλα, τά [kourafeksala] πλ bullshit (col), balls (col).
κουρδίζω [kourδeezo] wind up ‖ (βιολί) tune ‖ (μεταφ) stir up, incite.
κουρέας, ὁ [koureas] barber.
κουρεῖον, τό [koureeon] barber's shop.
κουρελιάρης, ὁ [koureleearees] person in rags ‖ vagabond.
κουρέλι, τό [kourelee] rag, tatter, shred.
κούρε(υ)μα, τό [koure(v)ma] haircut ‖ shearing, clipping.
κουρεύω [kourevo] cut the hair of, trim, clip ‖ (πρόβατον) shear ‖ (χλόη) mow.
κουρκούτι, τό [kourkoutee] batter ‖ pap.
κούρσα, ή [koursa] race ‖ (διαδρομή) ride ‖ (ἁμάξι) car.
κουρσάρος, ὁ [koursaros] pirate.
κουρσεύω [koursevo] plunder, raid.
κουρτίνα, ή [kourteena] curtain.
κουσούρι, τό [kousouree] defect, fault.
κουτάβι, τό [koutavee] puppy.
κουτάλι, τό [koutalee] spoon.
κουταμάρα, ή [koutamara] foolishness, nonsense.
κούτελο, τό [koutelo] forehead.
κουτί, τό [koutee] box, case ‖ (σπίρτων) matchbox ‖ (κονσέρβας) tin.
κουτός [koutos] silly, foolish, slow-witted.
κουτουλῶ [koutoulo] nod drowsily ‖ butt.
κουτουροῦ [koutourou]: **στά** ~ heedlessly, haphazardly, by chance.
κουτρουβάλα, ή [koutrouvala] somersault.

κουτρούλης [koutroulees] bald.
κούτσα, ή [koutsa] lameness.
κουτσαίνω [koutseno] limp ‖ cripple.
κουτσομπολεύω [koutsombolevo] gossip, spread reports, tittle-tattle.
κουτσομπολιό, τό [koutsombolio] gossip, tittle-tattle.
κουτσός [koutsos] crippled, limping.
κούτσουρο, τό [koutsouro] log, stump.
κουφαίνομαι [koufenome] go deaf.
κουφαίνω [koufeno] deafen, make deaf.
κουφαμάρα, ή [koufamara] deafness.
κουφάρι, τό [koufaree] body.
κουφέτο, τό [koufeto] sugared almond.
κούφιος [koufeeos] hollow, empty ‖ (δόντι) decayed ‖ (ἦχο) muffled ‖ (ἄνθρωπος) not serious, frivolous.
κουφόβραση, ή [koufovrasee] sweltering heat.
κοῦφος [koufos] lightweight.
κουφός [koufos] hard of hearing.
κούφωμα, τό [koufoma] hollow, cavity ‖ opening.
κοφίνι, τό [kofeenee] basket, hamper, pannier.
κοφτά [kofta]: **ὀρθά** ~ frankly, categorically.
κοφτερός [kofteros] sharp, cutting.
κόφτω [kofto] βλ **κόβω**.
κόχη, ή [kohee] βλ **κώχη**.
κοχλάζω [kohlazo] boil, bubble ‖ (μεταφ) seethe.
κοχλιάριον, τό [kohleeareeon] spoon.
κοχλίας, ὁ [kohleeas] snail ‖ (ἦλος) screw.
κοχύλι, τό [koheelee] sea shell.
κόψη, ή [kopsee] cutting, slicing, clipping ‖ edge.
κόψιμο, τό [kopseemo] cut, gash ‖ cutting ‖ (ἀσθένια) bellyache (col).
κραγιόν, τό [kraγion] crayon ‖ lipstick.
κραδαίνω [kraδeno] flourish, wave, vibrate.
κράζω [krazo] croak, caw ‖ cry out ‖ call.
κραιπάλη, ή [krepalee] riot, orgy ‖ drunkenness.
κρᾶμα, τό [krama] mixture, blend ‖ alloy, amalgam.
κράμβη, ή [kramvee] cabbage.
κρανίον, τό [kraneeon] cranium ‖ skull.
κράνος, τό [kranos] helmet ‖ (ἀποικιῶν) topee, sun helmet.
κράξιμο, τό [krakseemo] crowing, cawing.
κρασᾶτος [krasatos] cooked in wine.
κρασί, τό [krasee] wine.
κρᾶσις, ή [krasees] (σώματος) temperament, make-up.
κράσπεδον, τό [kraspeδon] (φορέματος) hem, border ‖ (λόφου) foot ‖ (πεζοδρομίου) kerb ‖ (US) curb.
κρατήρ, ὁ [krateer] crater.
κράτησις, ή [krateesees] confinement, arrest ‖ (μισθοῦ) deduction(s).
κρατιέμαι [kratieme] hold one's own, be well preserved.

κρατικοποίησις, ἡ [krateekopieesees] nationalization.

κρατικός [krateekos] national.

κράτος, τό [kratos] influence, power, authority || the state.

κρατῶ [krato] last, keep || (ἐπιβάλλομαι) hold in check, rule || (κατάγομαι) be descended from || (βαστῶ) have, hold || (ὑποβαστῶ) support.

κραυγάζω [kravgazo] cry, howl, shout, scream.

κραυγή, ἡ [kravyee] shout, cry, outcry.

κρέας, τό [kreas] meat, flesh.

κρεατόμυγα, ἡ [kreotomeeya] bluebottle.

κρεατόπηττα, ἡ [kreatopeeta] meat pie.

κρεββάτι, τό [krevatee] bed.

κρεββατοκάμαρα, ἡ [krevatokamara] bedroom.

κρεββατώνω [krevatono] confine to bed, lay up.

κρέμα, ἡ [krema] cream.

κρεμάζω [kremazo] hang, suspend.

κρεμάλα, ἡ [kremala] gallows, gibbet.

κρέμασμα, τό [kremasma] suspension, hooking on || hanging.

κρεμαστός [kremastos] suspended.

κρεμάστρα, ἡ [kremastra] hanger || hat rack || portmanteau.

κρεμιέμαι [kremieme] hang, be suspended.

κρεμμύδι, τό [kremeeδee] onion.

κρεμ(ν)ῶ [krem(n)o] hang, hook up, suspend.

κρεοπώλης, ὁ [kreopolees] butcher.

κρεουργῶ [kreouryo] butcher || massacre.

κρέπ, τό [krep] crêpe rubber || crape.

κρεπάρω [kreparo] split, burst || grieve, mourn.

κρημνίζομαι [kreemneezome] fall, crumble, collapse.

κρημνίζω [kreemneezo] hurl down, pull down, wreck.

κρημνός [kreemnos] sheer drop, crag.

κρήνη, ἡ [krenee] fountain.

κρηπίδωμα, τό [kreepeeδoma] foundation, base, groundwork || (ναυτ) breakwater || (σταθμοῦ) railway platform.

κρησφύγετον, τό [kreesfeeyeton] hideaway, retreat.

κριάρι, τό [kreearee] ram.

κριθαράκι, τό [kreetharakee] barley-shaped noodle || (ματιοῦ) sty.

κριθάρι, τό [kreetharee] barley.

κρίκος, ὁ [kreekos] link, buckle, ring || (ἀνυψώσεως) jack.

κρίμα, τό [kreema] sin, guilt || pity, misfortune || τί ~ ! what a pity!, what a shame!

κρίνος, ὁ [kreenos] lily.

κρίνω [kreeno] judge, consider || (ἀποφασίζω) decide.

κριός, ὁ [krios] ram.

κρίσιμος [kreeseemos] critical, grave, momentous || trying.

κρίσις, ἡ [kreesees] judgment, view || (οἰκο-

νομική) crisis, depression || (ἔλλειψις) deficiency, shortage || (πνεύματος) judgment.

κριτήριον, τό [kreeteereeon] criterion, test.

κριτής, ὁ [kreetees] judge.

κριτική, ἡ [kreeteekee] criticism, review.

κριτικός [kreeteekos] discerning, critical || (οὐσ) critic.

κροκάδι, τό [krokaδee] yolk.

κροκόδειλος, ὁ [krokoδeelos] crocodile.

κρόκος, ὁ [krokos] crocus || (αὐγοῦ) yolk.

κρομμύδι, τό [kromeeδee] onion.

κρόσσι, τό [krosee] fringe.

κρόταλον, τό [krotalon] rattle.

κρόταφος, ὁ [krotafos] temple (anat).

κρότος, ὁ [krotos] crash, bang, noise || (μεταφ) sensation.

κρουαζιέρα, ἡ [krouaziera] cruise.

κρουνός, ὁ [krounos] source, spring || tap, cock || (US) faucet.

κροῦσις, ἡ [krousees] striking, sounding || (στρατ) encounter.

κροῦσμα, τό [krousma] case (law, med).

κροῦστα, ἡ [krousta] crust, rind || scab.

κρούω [krouo] strike, sound || knock on || (κουδούνι) ring.

κρυάδα, ἡ [kreeaδa] cold, chill.

κρύβομαι [kreevome] go into hiding.

κρύβω [kreevo] βλ **κρύπτω.**

κρυμμένος [kreemenos] concealed.

κρύο, τό [kreeo] cold.

κρυολόγημα, τό [kreeoloyeema] cold (med).

κρυοπάγημα, τό [kreeopayeema] frostbite.

κρύος [kreeos] cold || indifferent, phlegmatic, cool.

κρύπτω [kreepto] hide, conceal || cover, screen || (μεταφ) withhold, hold back.

κρυστάλλινος [kreestaleenos] like crystal, very clear.

κρύσταλλον, τό [kreestalon] crystal (glass).

κρυφά [kreefa] secretly, clandestinely, stealthily.

κρύφιος [kreefeeos] βλ **κρυφός.**

κρυφός [kreefos] private, secluded || (χαρά) secret, inner || (ἄνθρωπος) discreet, reticent.

κρυφτός [kreeftos] hidden.

κρύψιμο, τό [kreepseemo] concealing, hiding.

κρυψίνους [kreepseenous] deceitful, underhand, sneaky.

κρυψώνας, ὁ [kreepsonas] hideout, lurking place.

κρυώνω [kreeono] grow cold, feel cold || cool down, chill.

κτένι, τό [ktenee] comb || (τσουγκράνα) rake || **κτενίζω** comb || (μεταφ) brush up, finish in detail || ~**σμα** combing || hairdressing.

κτῆμα, τό [kteema] estate, land || **κτηματίας, ὁ** landowner, proprietor.

κτηνίατρος, ὁ [kteeneeatros] veterinary surgeon.

κτῆνος, τό [kteenos] brute, beast, animal ‖ πλ cattle.

κτηνοτροφία, ἡ [kteenotrofeea] stock-breeding.

κτηνώδης [kteenodees] beastly, bestial ‖ (ὄρεξις) hoggish.

κτῆσις, ἡ [kteesees] acquisition, occupation, occupancy.

κτητικός [kteeteekos] (γραμμ) possessive ‖ acquisitive.

κτίζω [kteezo] construct, erect, build.

κτίριον, τό [kteereeon] building, edifice.

κτίσιμον, τό [kteeseemon] building, erection.

κτίστης, ὁ [kteestees] builder, mason.

κτυπῶ [kteepo] beat, strike, flog, thrash.

κύαμος, ὁ [keeamos] bean.

κυάνιον, τό [keeaneeon] cyanide.

κυανόλευκος [keeanolevkos] blue and white.

κυανοῦς [keeanous] blue, azure.

κυβέρνησις, ἡ [keeverneesees] government, management.

κυβερνήτης, ὁ [keeverneetees] governor ‖ (ναυτ) commander.

κυβερνητικός [keeverneeteekos] governmental.

κυβερνῶ [keeverno] govern ‖ (πλοῖο) steer ‖ (σπίτι) manage, direct.

κύβος, ὁ [keevos] cube ‖ die.

κυδώνι, τό [keedonee] quince ‖ (ὄστρακο) kind of shellfish.

κύησις, ἡ [kieesees] pregnancy ‖ gestation.

κυκεών, ὁ [keekeon] confusion, anarchy, chaos, disorder.

κυκλάμινο, τό [keeklameeno] cyclamen.

κυκλικός [keekleekos] circular.

κύκλος, ὁ [keeklos] circle ‖ (ἡλιακός κτλ) cycle, period ‖ (προσώπων) set.

κυκλοτερής [keekloterees] circular.

κυκλοφορία, ἡ [keekloforeea] circulation ‖ (αὐτοκινήτων) traffic flow.

κυκλοφορῶ [keekloforo] put into circulation, spread ‖ go about.

κύκλωμα, τό [keekloma] electric circuit ‖ encirclement.

κυκλών, ὁ [keeklon] cyclone.

κυκλώνω [keeklono] surround, encircle, envelop.

κύκνος, ὁ [keeknos] swan.

κυλάω [keelao] roll.

κυλιέμαι [keelieme] roll over ‖ (χοῖρος) wallow.

κυλικεῖον, τό [keeleekeeon] buffet, sideboard ‖ refreshment room.

κύλινδρος, ὁ [keeleenδros] cylinder ‖ roller, barrel.

κυλιῶ [keeleeo] roll, trundle, push.

κυλότα, ἡ [keelota] panties.

κῦμα, τό [keema] wave.

κυμαίνομαι [keemenome] undulate, wave, ripple ‖ (μεταφ) fluctuate, waver, hesitate.

κυματίζω [keemateezo] wave, flutter ‖ ripple.

κυματοθραύστης, ὁ [keematothravstees] breakwater.

κύμινον, τό [keemeenon] cumin.

κυνήγι, τό [keeneeyee] hunting, shooting, chase ‖ game.

κυνηγός, ὁ [keeneeyos] hunter, shooter.

κυνηγῶ [keeneeyo] hunt, chase, run after ‖ go shooting.

κυνικός [keeneekos] cynic(al).

κυοφορῶ [keeoforo] be pregnant.

κυπαρίσσι, τό [keepareesèe] cypress tree.

κύπελλον, τό [keepelon] cup, goblet, tumbler.

κυπρῖνος, ὁ [keepreenos] carp.

κύπτω [keepto] bend, bow ‖ slant ‖ (μεταφ) give way.

κυρά, ἡ [keera] missus (col).

κυρία, ἡ [keereea] lady, mistress ‖ Mrs.

κυριακάτικος [keereeakateekos] Sunday (attr).

Κυριακή, ἡ [keereeakee] Sunday.

κυριαρχία, ἡ [keereearheea] sovereignty, dominion.

κυριαρχῶ [keereearho] dominate, exercise authority ‖ be sovereign.

κυριεύω [keerievo] subjugate, capture, dominate ‖ (ἐπὶ πάθους) seize, possess.

κυριολεκτικῶς [keereeolekteekos] exactly, precisely, to the letter.

κύριος, ὁ [keereeos] master, sir, gentleman ‖ Mr.

κύριος [keereeos] essential, vital ‖ main, chief, leading.

κυριότης, ἡ [keereeotees] ownership.

κυρίως [keereeos] principally, chiefly, mainly, especially.

κῦρος, τό [keeros] authority, power ‖ validity, weight.

κυρτός [keertos] bent, crooked ‖ convex, bulging.

κυρώνω [keerono] confirm ‖ (νόμον) sanction, approve ‖ (ἀπόφασιν) ratify, validate.

κύρωσις, ἡ [keerosees] confirmation, sanction ‖ penalty.

κύστις, ἡ [keestees] bladder, cyst.

κυτίον, τό [keeteeon] small box, case.

κύτος, τό [keetos] (ναυτ) hold.

κυττάζω [keetazo] βλ κοιτάζω.

κύτταρον, τό [keetaron] cell.

κυφός [keefos] hunchbacked, humpbacked.

κυψέλη, ἡ [keepselee] swarm (of bees) ‖ beehive ‖ (αὐτιοῦ) earwax.

κύων, ὁ, ἡ [keeon] dog, bitch.

κῶδιξ, ὁ [koδeeks] code ‖ codex.

κώδων, ὁ [koδon] bell.

κωδωνοκρουσία, ἡ [koδonokrouseea] chiming, ringing, pealing.

κωδωνοστάσιον, τό [koδonostaseeon] belfry, church steeple.

κώκ, τό [kok] coke.

κῶλον, τό [kolon] (γραμμ) colon.

κῶλος, ὁ [kolos] arse (col), bottom, backside (col) ‖ ~ καί βρακί intimate.

κωλοφωτιά, ἡ [kolofotia] glow-worm.

κώλυμα, τό [koleema] obstacle, impediment.

κωλυσιεργῶ [koleesieryo] obstruct, hinder.

κωλύω [koleeo] stop, prevent, hinder.

κῶμα, τό [koma] coma.

κωματώδης [komatodees] comatose, lethargic.

κώμη, ἡ [komee] small market town, hamlet.

κωμικός [komeekos] comic(al), funny ‖ (οὐσ) comedian.

κωμόπολις, ἡ [komopolees] market town.

κωμωδία, ἡ [komodeea] comedy.

κώνειον, τό [koneeon] hemlock.

κῶνος, ὁ [konos] cone.

κώνωψ, ὁ [konops] mosquito.

κώπη, ἡ [kopee] oar.

κωπηλασία, ἡ [kopeelaseea] rowing.

κωπηλάτης, ὁ [kopeelatees] rower.

κωφάλαλος [kofalalos] deaf-and-dumb.

κωφός [kofos] deaf.

κώχη, · ἡ [kohee] corner, nook, recess ‖ (πανταλονιοῦ) crease.

Λ, λ

λάβα, ἡ [lava] lava.

λαβαίνω [laveno] βλ λαμβάνω.

λάβαρον, τό [lavaron] banner, standard.

λαβεῖν, τό [laveen] credit ‖ δοῦναι καί ~ debit and credit.

λαβή, ἡ [lavee] handle, grip ‖ pretext, excuse, reason.

λαβίς, ἡ [lavees] grip, nippers, hold ‖ (χειρουργική) forceps.

λάβρα, ἡ [lavra] excessive heat, suffocating heat.

λαβράκι, τό [lavrakee] bass fish.

λαβύρινθος, ὁ [laveereenthos] labyrinth.

λαβωματιά, ἡ [lavomatia] wound.

λαβώνω [lavono] wound.

λαγάνα, ἡ [layana] unleavened bread.

λαγήνι, τό [layeenee] pitcher, jug, crock.

λαγκάδι, τό [langadee] ravine, narrow valley, defile.

λάγνος [laynos] lewd, lascivious, wanton.

λαγόνες, οἱ [layones] πλ loins ‖ flanks.

λαγός, ὁ [layos] hare.

λαγωνικό, τό [layoneeko] hunting dog ‖ greyhound, pointer.

λαδερός [laderos] oily, greasy ‖ cooked with oil.

λάδι, τό [ladee] olive oil.

λαδομπογιά, ἡ [ladomboyia] oil paint.

λαδόχαρτο, τό [ladoharto] greaseproof paper.

λαδώνω [ladono] apply oil ‖ lubricate ‖ (μεταφ) bribe.

λαδωτήρι, τό [ladoteeree] cruet stand.

λάθος, τό [lathos] error, mistake, slip, fault ‖ κατά ~ by mistake.

λαθραῖος [lathreos] furtive, clandestine, secret.

λαθραίως [lathreos] secretly, furtively, stealthily.

λαθρεμπόριο, τό [lathremboreeo] smuggling ‖ contraband.

λαθρέμπορος, ὁ [lathremboros] smuggler, contrabandist.

λαθρεπιβάτης, ὁ [lathrepeevatees] stow-away.

λαΐδη, ἡ [leδee] lady.

λαϊκός [laeekos] popular, familiar, vulgar ‖ current, common ‖ lay.

λαῖλαψ, ἡ [lelaps] hurricane, tempest.

λαίμαργος [lemaryos] gluttonous, greedy ‖ (οὐσ) gourmand.

λαιμητόμος, ἡ [lemeetomos] guillotine.

λαιμοδέτης, ὁ [lemoδetees] necktie, cravat.

λαιμός, ὁ [lemos] neck, throat, gullet ‖ (μεταξύ βουνῶν) gorge, pass.

λακέρδα, ἡ [lakerδa] salted tunny fish.

λακές, ὁ [lakes] lackey, flunkey.

λακκάκι, τό [lakakee] dimple.

λάκκος, ὁ [lakos] hole, pit ‖ grave.

λακκούβα, ἡ [lakouva] βλ λάκκος.

λακτίζω [lakteezo] kick, boot, lash out.

λακωνικός [lakoneekos] laconic, terse, brief.

λαλιά, ἡ [lalia] voice ‖ speech ‖ (ἐπί πτηνῶν) singing, warbling.

λαλῶ [lalo] speak, talk ‖ crow ‖ sing.

λάμα, ἡ [lama] sheet, thin plate ‖ (μαχαιριοῦ) blade.

λαμαρίνα, ἡ [lamareena] sheet iron, iron plate.

λαμβάνω [lamvano] take hold of, take ‖ receive, obtain ‖ ~ τήν τιμήν I have the honour ‖ ~ χώραν take place, occur.

λάμδα, τό [lamδa] the letter Λ.

λάμια, ἡ [lameea] ogress ‖ (μεταφ) greedy eater, glutton.

λάμπα, ἡ [lamba] lamp ‖ (ἠλεκτρική) electric lamp, bulb.

λαμπάδα, ἡ [lambaδa] torch ‖ candle, taper.

λαμπίκος, ὁ [lambeekos] distilling apparatus ‖ (μεταφ) very clean, clear.

λαμποκοπῶ [lambokopo] shine, gleam.

Λαμπρή, ἡ [lambree] Easter.

λαμπρός [lambros] brilliant, splendid, excellent, superb.

λαμπρῶς [lambros] (ἐπιφ) splendid!, excellent! ‖ (ἐπίρ) brilliantly.

λαμπτήρ, ὁ [lambteer] βλ λάμπα.

λαμπυρίς, ἡ [lambeerees] glow-worm.

λάμπω [lambo] shine, glitter, gleam ‖ (μεταφ) excel.

λάμψις, ἡ [lampsees] brightness, brilliance ‖ glaze.

λανθάνομαι [lanthanome] deceive o.s., be mistaken, err.

Λ

λανθάνω [lanthano] be latent ‖ escape notice.

λανθασμένος [lanthasmenos] mistaken, wrong.

λανσάρω [lansaro] launch, advertise, present.

λαξεύω [laksevo] hew, chisel, carve.

λαογραφία, ή [laoɣrafeea] folklore.

λαός, ὁ [laos] people, multitude, masses.

λαοῦτο, τό [laouto] lute.

λαπᾶς, ὁ [lapas] pap, boiled rice ‖ poultice ‖ (μεταφ) indolent person.

λαρδί, τό [lardee] lard, fat.

λαρύγγι, τό [lareengee] throat, larynx, windpipe, gullet.

λαρυγγῖτις, ή [lareengeetees] laryngitis.

λαρυγγολόγος, ὁ [lareengoloɣos] throat specialist.

λάρυγξ, ὁ [lareenks] βλ λαρύγγι.

λασκάρω [laskaro] slacken, loosen ‖ (ναυτ) cast off.

λάσπη, ή [laspee] mud, mire ‖ mortar ‖ τὄκοψε ~ he escaped ‖ he disappeared.

λασπώνω [laspono] cover with mud, dirty, soil.

λαστιχένιος [lasteeheneeos] rubber ‖ elastic.

λάστιχο, τό [lasteeho] rubber ‖ elastic ‖ rubber band ‖ (αὐτοκινήτου) tyre ‖ (παιδιοῦ) catapult, sling.

λατέρνα, ή [laterna] barrel organ.

λατινικά, τά [lateeneeka] πλ Latin.

λατινικός [lateeneekos] Latin.

λατομεῖον, τό [latomeeon] quarry.

λατρεία, ή [latreea] adoration, worship ‖ (ἀγάπη) fervent love.

λατρευτός [latrevtos] adorable, adored.

λατρεύω [latrevo] adore ‖ idolize.

λάτρης, ὁ [latrees] worshipper ‖ fan.

λάφυρον, τό [lafeeron] booty, spoils, loot.

λαχαίνω [laheno] meet, come across ‖ (συμβαίνω) happen, occur ‖ (στό κλῆρο) fall to, win.

λαχαναγορά, ή [lahanaɣora] vegetable market.

λαχανιάζω [lahaneeazo] pant, gasp.

λαχανικόν, τό [lahaneekon] vegetable, green.

λάχανον, τό [lahanon] cabbage.

λαχεῖον, τό [laheeon] lottery, raffle.

λαχνός, ὁ [lahnos] lot, chance ‖ prize, share.

λαχτάρα, ή [lahtara] anxiety ‖ (ἐπιθυμία) yearning ‖ (φόβος) dread, fright.

λαχταρῶ [lahtaro] be impatient ‖ (ἐπιθυμῶ) yearn, desire ‖ (φοβᾶμαι) be frightened.

λέαινα, ή [layena] lioness.

λεβάντα, ή [levanta] lavender.

λεβαντίνος, ὁ [levanteenos] ·Levantine.

λεβέντης, ὁ [leventees] fine man, gentleman ‖ brave man.

λεβεντιά, ή [leventia] manliness.

λέβης, ὁ [levees] kettle, cauldron ‖ boiler.

λεβιές, ὁ [levies] lever.

λεγάμενος [leɣamenos]: ὁ ~ you know who ‖ the so-called.

λεγεών, ὁ, ή [leɣeon] legion ‖ great number.

λέγω [leɣo] say, tell, speak ‖ (πιστεύω) think ‖ (ἐννοῶ) mean ‖ δέν σοῦ ~ I do not deny it, but ‖ τί λές (ἐπιφ) you don't say!, fancy that! ‖ ποῦ λές well! ‖ λές καί as if.

λεηλασία, ή [leyeelaseea] plundering, looting, pillage.

λεηλατῶ [leyeelato] plunder, loot.

λεία, ή [leea] prey ‖ booty, loot.

λειαίνω [lieno] smooth, level, plane, polish.

λειβάδι, τό [leevadee] pasture land, meadow.

λειμών, ὁ [leemon] βλ λειβάδι.

λεῖος [leeos] smooth, even, level.

λείπω [leepo] be absent, be missing, want, lack ‖ μοῦ λείπει I am missing, I lack ‖ μᾶς ἔλειπες we missed you ‖ λίγο ἔλειψε νά he nearly, he almost.

λειρί, τό [leeree] cockscomb, crest.

λειτουργία, ή [leetourɣeea] function, operation ‖ (ἐκκλ) mass, liturgy.

λειτουργός, ὁ, ή [leetourɣos] officer, official, civil servant.

λειτουργῶ [leetourɣo] function, work ‖ (ἐκκλ) celebrate mass.

λειχήν, ὁ [leeheen] lichen.

λείχω [leeho] lick.

λείψανα, τά [leepsana] πλ remnants, remains ‖ (ἐκκλ) relics.

λειψός [leepsos] deficient, defective.

λειώνω [leeono] melt, liquefy ‖ (συνθλίβω) crush, smash ‖ (διαλύω) dissolve ‖ (παθαίνω φθορά) wear out, spoil.

λεκάνη, ή [lekanee] basin, washbowl ‖ pan.

λεκές, ὁ [lekes] stain, splash, spot ‖ (μελάνης) blot.

λεκιάζω [lekeeazo] stain, soil, spot.

λελέκι, τό [lelekee] stork.

λεμβοδρομία, ή [lemvodromeea] regatta, boat race.

λέμβος, ή [lemvos] rowboat ‖ launch.

λεμβοῦχος, ὁ [lemvouhos] boatman, rower.

λεμονάδα, ή [lemonada] lemonade.

λεμόνι, τό [lemonee] lemon ‖ λεμονιά lemon tree.

λεξικογραφία, ή [lekseekoɣrafeea] lexicography.

λεξικό(ν), τό [lekseeko(n)] lexicon, dictionary.

λεξιλόγιον, τό [lekseeloɣeeon] vocabulary ‖ glossary.

λέξις, ή [leksees] word.

λεοντάρι, τό [leontaree] lion.

λεοπάρδαλις, ή [leopardalees] leopard.

λέπι, τό [lepee] (ψαριοῦ) scale (of fish).

λεπίς, ή [lepees] blade.

λέπρα, ή [lepra] leprosy.

λεπρός [lepros] leprous.

λεπτά, τά [lepta] πλ money.

λεπταίνω [lepteno] thin, make slender ‖ refine.

λεπτοκαμωμένος [leptokamomenos] delicate, frail || thin, slim.
λεπτολογῶ [leptoloγo] scrutinize, examine carefully, sift.
λεπτομέρεια [leptomereea] detail, particular || λεπτομερειακός detailed, of detail.
λεπτομερής [leptomerees] detailed, minute, scrupulous, close.
λεπτομερῶς [leptomeros] minutely, closely, in detail.
λεπτόν, τό [lepton] (τῆς ὥρας) minute || (νόμισμα) lepton (one hundredth of a drachma).
λεπτός [leptos] thin, fine, slight, slim || (στήν σκέψιν) subtle || (ρουχισμόν) light || (τῶν αἰσθήσεων) keen.
λεπτότης, ἡ [leptotees] delicacy, weakness || tactfulness, tact || subtlety.
λεπτύνω [lepteeno] βλ λεπταίνω.
λέρα, ἡ [lera] dirt, filth || (ἄνθρωπος) rogue, rascal.
λερωμένος [leromenos] dirty, filthy, grubby, grimy.
λερώνομαι [leronome] get dirty.
λερώνω [lerono] dirty, soil, stain || (μεταφ) tarnish, taint.
λέσχη, ἡ [leshee] club || casino.
λεύκα, ἡ [levka] poplar.
λευκαίνω [levkeno] whiten || bleach || (τοῖχο) whitewash.
λευκόλιθος, ὁ [levkoleethos] magnesite.
λευκός [levkos] white, clean || blank.
λευκοσίδηρος [levkoseedeeros] tin.
λευκόχρυσος, ὁ [levkohreesos] platinum.
λεύκωμα, τό [levkoma] album || (ἰατρ) albumin.
λευτεριά, ἡ [levteria] freedom, liberty.
λευχαιμία, ἡ [levhemeea] leukaemia.
λεφτά [lefta] βλ λεπτά.
λεφτό [lefto] βλ λεπτόν.
λεχώνα, ἡ [lehona] woman who has just given birth.
λέω [leo] βλ λέγω.
λέων, ὁ [leon] lion.
λεωφορεῖον, τό [leoforeeon] bus, omnibus, coach.
λεωφόρος, ἡ [leoforos] avenue, boulevard.
λήγω [leeγo] come to an end, terminate || (οἶκον) mature, fall due.
λήθαργος, ὁ [leetharγos] lethargy, drowsiness, stupor.
λήθη, ἡ [lethee] forgetfulness, forgetting, oversight.
λημέρι, τό [leemeree] retreat, hiding place, hideout, den.
ληξιαρχεῖον, τό [leekseearheeon] registry office, parish register.
ληξιπρόθεσμος [leekseeprothesmos] falling due, expired (of terms).
λῆξις, ἡ [leeksees] termination, conclusion || expiration date.
λησμονῶ [leesmono] forget, neglect, omit.
ληστεία, ἡ [leesteea] holdup, robbery.

ληστεύω [leestevo] rob, hold up.
ληστής, ὁ [leestees] brigand, bandit, robber.
ληστρικός [leestreekos] predatory || pertaining to robbers.
λῆψις, ἡ [leepsees] receipt, receiving.
λιάζομαι [leeazome] sunbathe, lie in the sun.
λιακάδα, ἡ [leeakaδa] sunshine.
λίαν [leean] much, very much, too.
λιανίζω [leeaneezo] cut to pieces, mince.
λιανικός [leeaneekos] retail.
λιανός [leeanos] thin, slender.
λιβάδι, τό [leevaδee] βλ λειβάδι.
λιβάνι, τό [leevanee] incense, frankincense.
λιβανίζω [leevaneezo] burn incense || (μεταφ) flatter basely.
λίβελλος, ὁ [leevelos] libel || lampoon.
λίβρα, ἡ [leevra] pound.
λιγάκι [leeγakee] a little, a bit.
λίγδα, ἡ [leeγδa] fat, grease || dirt, stain.
λιγνίτης, ὁ [leeγneetees] lignite.
λιγνός [leeγnos] skinny, thin, slim.
λίγο [leeγo] a little, a bit || ~ πολύ more or less.
λίγος [leeγos] a little, a bit || παρά λίγο nearly, almost.
λιγοστεύω [leeγostevo] lessen, decrease.
λιγοστός [leeγostos] very little, hardly enough.
λιγότερος [leeγoteros] less.
λιγούρα, ἡ [leeγoura] nausea || faintness from hunger.
λιγοψυχία, ἡ [leeγopseeheea] faintheartedness || faintness.
λιγώνομαι [leeγonome] long for, be impatient || be faint from desire.
λιγώνω [leeγono] nauseate || make faint.
λιθάρι, τό [leetharee] stone.
λίθινος [leetheenos] of stone.
λιθοβολῶ [leethovolo] pelt with stones, stone.
λιθογραφία, ἡ [leethoγrafeea] lithography.
λιθοδομή, ἡ [leethoδomee] stonework, masonry.
λιθοκόπος, ὁ [leethokopos] stone-breaker.
λιθόκτιστος [leethokteestos] built in stone.
λιθοξόος, ὁ [leethoksoos] stone-cutter, marble worker.
λίθος, ὁ, ἡ [leethos] stone || (ἰατρ) calculus.
λιθόστρωτον, τό [leethostroton] pavement, paved way.
λιθόστρωτος [leethostrotos] paved with stones.
λικέρ, τό [leeker] liqueur.
λικνίζω [leekneezo] rock, lull to sleep || swing.
λίκνον, τό [leeknon] cradle, cot, crib.
λίμα, ἡ [leema] (ἐργαλεῖον) file || (μεταφ) talkativeness, tiresome chatter.
λιμάνι, τό [leemanee] port, harbour.
λιμάρω [leemaro] file || chatter, gossip.
λιμενάρχης, ὁ [leemenarhees] harbour master.

λιμενικός [leemeneekos] of the port, of the harbour.

λιμήν, ὁ [leemeen] βλ. **λιμάνι.**

λίμνη, ἡ [leemnee] lake.

λιμνοθάλασσα, ἡ [leemnothalasa] lagoon.

λιμοκτονῶ [leemoktono] starve, famish.

λιμός, ὁ [leemos] famine.

λινάρι, τό [leenaree] flax.

λινάτσα, ἡ [leenatsa] sacking.

λινέλαιον, τό [leeneleon] linseed oil.

λίνον, τό [leenon] βλ. **λινάρι.**

λινός [leenos] linen.

λιοντάρι, τό [leeontaree] lion.

λιπαίνω [leepeno] lubricate, grease ‖ (μέ λίπασμα) manure, fertilize.

λιπαρός [leeparos] greasy, fatty ‖ (γόνιμος) fat, rich.

λίπασμα, τό [leepasma] fertilizer, manure.

λιποθυμία, ἡ [leepotheemeea] faint(ing), swooning.

λιποθυμῶ [leepotheemo] faint, lose consciousness.

λίπος, τό [leepos] fat, lard ‖ grease.

λιποτάκτης, ὁ [leepotaktees] deserter.

λίρα, ἡ [leera] pound, sovereign.

λιρέττα, ἡ [leereta] Italian lira.

λίστα, ἡ [leesta] list, catalogue.

λιτανεία, ἡ [leetaneea] religious procession.

λιτός [leetos] temperate, frugal ‖ plain.

λιτότης, ἡ [leetotees] temperance, moderation.

λίτρα, ἡ [leetra] (βάρος) pound ‖ litre.

λίτρον, τό [leetron] βλ. **λίτρα.**

λιχνίζω [leehneezo] winnow, sift.

λιχουδιά, ἡ [leehoudia] titbit ‖ appetizer.

λοβός, ὁ [lovos] lobe ‖ husk ‖ (ἀρχιτεκ) foil.

λογαριάζω [loyareeazo] count, measure, compute ‖ rely on, look to ‖ (λαμβάνω ὑπ' ὄψιν) consider ‖ (πρόθεσις νά) count on, aim to, mean to.

λογαριασμός, ὁ [loyareeasmos] count, calculation, computation ‖ bill ‖ accounts.

λογάριθμος, ὁ [loyareethmos] logarithm.

λογάς, ὁ [loyas] gossip, babbler, long-winded talker.

λόγγος, ὁ [longos] thicket.

λόγια, τά [loya] πλ words.

λογιάζω [loyeeazo] take into consideration.

λογίζομαι [loyeezome] calculate, consider ‖ think o.s., deem o.s.

λογική, ἡ [loyeekee] logic.

λογικός [loyeekos] rational, logical, sensible ‖ right, fair.

λόγιος [loyeeos] scholar, man of letters.

λογισμός, ὁ [loyeesmos] reasoning, thought ‖ reckoning ‖ (μαθημ) calculus.

λογιστήριον, τό [loyeesteereeon] bursar's office ‖ bursary.

λογιστής, ὁ [loyeestees] accountant, bookkeeper ‖ (ναυτ) purser.

λογιστική, ἡ [loyeesteekee] accountancy.

λογοδιάρροια, ἡ [loyodeeareea] unrestrained talkativeness, chattering.

λογοδοτῶ [loyodoto] give an account, account for.

λογοκρισία, ἡ [loyokreeseea] censorship.

λογομαχία, ἡ [loyomaheea] dispute, wrangle, controversy.

λογοπαίχνιον, τό [loyopehneeon] pun.

λόγος, ὁ [loyos] (ὁμιλία) speech ‖ (φράσις κτλ) word, saying ‖ (μνεία) mention ‖ rumour ‖ (αἴτιον) cause, reason, purpose ‖ (παράδειγμα) instance, supposition ‖ (ἀγόρευσις) speech, discourse ‖ (λογοδοσία) explanation, account ‖ (ὑπόσχεσις) promise ‖ (ἀναλογία) ratio, proportion.

λογοτέχνης, ὁ [loyotehnees] author, writer.

λογοτεχνία, ἡ [loyotehneea] literature.

λόγχη, ἡ [longhee] bayonet ‖ spear, lance.

λοιδορῶ [leedoro] insult, abuse, outrage, ridicule.

λοιμός, ὁ [leemos] pestilence, pest, plague.

λοιμώδης [leemodees] pestilential.

λοιπόν [leepon] then, thus, and so ‖ well!, what then!

λοιπός [leepos] left, remaining ‖ **καί τά λοιπά** and so forth, and so on ‖ **τοῦ λοιποῦ** henceforth, from now on.

λόξα, ἡ [loksa] (γιά μόδα κτλ) whim, mania, fancy.

λοξά [loksa] on the slant, obliquely ‖ in an underhand way.

λοξοδρομῶ [loksodromo] shift course, deviate ‖ (ναυτ) tack ‖ (μεταφ) go astray.

λοξός [loksos] oblique, slanting, inclined.

λόξυγγας, ὁ [lokseengas] hiccup.

λόρδος, ὁ [lordos] lord.

λοσιόν, ἡ [losion] lotion.

λοστός, ὁ [lostos] crowbar, iron bar.

λοστρόμος, ὁ [lostromos] boatswain.

λούζομαι [louzome] have a bath.

λούζω [louzo] wash, bathe ‖ (μεταφ) reproach severely.

λουκάνικο, τό [loukaneeko] sausage, hot dog, frankfurter.

λουκέτο, τό [louketo] padlock.

λουκι, τό [loukee] pipe, conduit ‖ gutter.

λουκούμι, τό [loukoumee] Turkish delight ‖ (μεταφ) delicious (attr).

λουλάκι, τό [loulakee] indigo.

λουλούδι, τό [louloudee] flower, blossom.

λούξ [louks] luxurious, posh.

λουρί, τό [louree] strap ‖ (μηχανῆς) belt, band.

λουρίδα, ἡ [loureeda] strip, belt, band.

λούσιμο, τό [louseemo] bathing, washing ‖ (μεταφ) reprimanding.

λοῦσο, τό [louso] smart clothes ‖ sumptuousness, luxury.

λουστράρω [loustraro] gloss, glaze ‖ (παπούτσια) polish.

λουστρίνια, τά [loustreeneea] πλ patent leather shoes.

λοῦστρος, ὁ [loustros] shoeblack, bootblack.

λουτρά, τά [loutra] πλ baths, hot springs.
λουτρόν, τό [loutron] bath ‖ (δωμάτιον) bathroom.
λουτρόπολις, ή [loutropolees] bathing resort, spa.
λουφάζω [loufazo] remain silent ‖ cringe with fear.
λούω [louo] bathe, wash, give a bath to.
λοφίον, τό [lofeeon] plume ‖ (πτηνού) tuft, crest ‖ (στρατ) pompom.
λόφος, ὁ [lofos] hill, height.
λοχαγός, ὁ [lohagos] captain.
λοχίας, ὁ [loheeas] sergeant.
λόχος, ὁ [lohos] company.
λυγερός [leeyeros] slim, lithe, graceful.
λυγίζω [leeyeezo] bend, curve ‖ yield.
λυγμός, ὁ [leeymos] sob, sobbing.
λύγξ, ὁ [leenks] lynx.
λυθρίνι, τό [leethreenee] kind of red mullet, gurnard.
λυκαυγές, τό [leekavyes] daybreak, dawn.
λύκειον, τό [leekeeon] private secondary school, lyceum.
λύκος, ὁ [leekos] wolf.
λυκόσκυλον, τό [leekoskeelon] wolfhound.
λυκόφως, τό [leekofos] evening twilight, dusk.
λυμαίνομαι [leemenome] ravage, devastate, lay waste.
λυντσάρω [leentsaro] lynch.
λύνω [leeno] βλ λύω.
λύομαι [leeome] come undone.
λυπάμαι [leepame] be sorry, regret ‖ pity.
λύπη, ή [leepee] grief, chagrin, sorrow ‖ pity, commiseration.
λυπημένος [leepeemenos] sad, grieved, distressed.
λυπούμαι [leepoume] βλ λυπάμαι.
λύσιμο, τό [leeseemo] undoing, loosening ‖ solution, solving ‖ taking to pieces.
λύσις, ή [leesees] answer, solution ‖ untying ‖ dismantling.
λυσιτέλεια, ή [leeseeteleea] utility, usefulness, benefit.
λύσσα, ή [leesa] rabies ‖ (μεταφ) rage, fury, wrath.
λυσσάζω [leesazo] rage, go mad.
λυσσῶ [leeso] (μεταφ) be furious.
λυσσώδης [leesodees] rabid ‖ fierce, stubborn, desperate.
λυτός [leetos] loose, untied, unfastened.
λύτρα, τά [leetra] πλ ransom money.
λυτρώνω [leetrono] deliver, free, set free.
λυτρωτής, ὁ [leetrotees] liberator, redeemer, rescuer.
λυχνάρι, τό [leehnaree] small lamp, Chinese lantern.
λυχνία, ή [leehneea] lamp.
λύχνος, ὁ [leehnos] βλ λυχνάρι.
λύω [leeo] unloose ‖ (δεσμόν κτλ) untie, unfasten ‖ (διαλύω) dismantle ‖ (εὑρίσκω λύσιν) resolve ‖ (παύω) close, discharge ‖ (καταργῶ) annul, break off.

λυώνω [leeono] βλ λειώνω.
λώβα, ὁ [lova] leprosy.
λωβός [lovos] leprous.
λωλαίνω [loleno] drive mad, bewilder.
λωλός [lolos] foolish, crazy, mad.
λωποδύτης, ὁ [lopodeetees] thief, blackleg, sharper.
λωρίον [loreeon] βλ λουρί.
λωρίς, ή [lorees] strip, band, belt.
λωτός, ὁ [lotos] lotus.
λωφάζω [lofazo] βλ λουφάζω.

Μ, μ

μά [ma] but ‖ by ‖ ~ τόν Θεό! by God!, God be witness!
μαγαζί, τό [mayazee] shop, store.
μαγγάνι, τό [manganee] (ἐργαλεῖον) tool, vice ‖ (πηγαδιοῦ) wheel ‖ winch.
μαγγάνιον, τό [manganeeon] manganese.
μαγγανοπήγαδο, τό [manganopeeyado] wheel well (for water).
μαγγώνω [mangono] grip, squeeze, clip.
μαγεία, ή [mayeea] sorcery, witchcraft, magic ‖ charm, fascination.
μάγειρας, ὁ [mayeeras] cook.
μαγειρεῖον, τό [mayeereeon] kitchen.
μαγειρεύω [mayeerevo] cook ‖ (μεταφ) plot, manipulate.
μαγειρική, ή [mayeereekee] cooking, cookery.
μαγευτικός [mayevteekos] charming, enchanting, delightful.
μαγεύω [mayevo] charm, fascinate, delight, attract.
μάγια, τά [mayeea] πλ witchcraft, spell, charm.
μαγιά, ή [mayia] yeast, leaven.
μαγικός [mayeekos] magic(al), fascinating, bewitching.
μαγιό, τό [mayio] bathing suit, swimsuit.
μαγιονέζα, ή [mayeeoneza] mayonnaise.
μάγισσα, ή [mayeesa] witch, enchantress.
μαγκάλι, τό [mangalee] brazier, firepan.
μάγκας, ὁ [mangas] urchin, rascal, bum.
μαγκούρα, ή [mangoura] crook, heavy stick.
μαγκούφης, ὁ [mangoufees] lonely person ‖ miserable person.
μαγνήσιον, τό [mayneeseeon] magnesium.
μαγνήτης, ὁ [mayneetees] magnet.
μαγνητίζω [mayneeteezo] magnetize ‖ attract, captivate.
μαγνητικός [mayneeteekos] magnetic ‖ attractive.
μαγνητισμός, ὁ [mayneeteesmos] magnetism.
μαγνητόφωνον, τό [mayneetofonon] tape recorder.
μάγος, ὁ [mayos] magician, wizard.
μαγουλήθρα, ή [mayouleethra] mumps, parotitis.
μάγουλο, τό [mayoulo] cheek (of face).

μαδέρι, τό [maδeree] thick plank, joist, beam.

μάδημα, τό [maδeema] plucking, depilation || (μεταφ) fleecing.

μαδῶ [maδo] pluck, pluck off, remove the hair || (μεταφ) fleece.

μαέστρος, ὁ [maestros] conductor || (μεταφ) authority.

μάζα, ἡ [maza] paste || lump || (ἐπί ἀνθρώπων) mass, crowd.

μάζεμα, τό [mazema] collecting, gathering || (ὑφάσματος) shrinking.

μαζεμένος [mazemenos] good-mannered || snuggling.

μαζεύομαι [mazevome] collect || nestle || settle down.

μαζεύω [mazevo] gather, collect || (μαλλί) wind || (γιά ροῦχα) shrink.

μαζί [mazee] together, with, in one lot, jointly.

μαζικός [mazeekos] of the mass, collective.

μαζώνω [mazono] βλ **μαζεύω**.

Μάης, ὁ [maees] May.

μαθαίνω [matheno] learn || teach, train || (νέα) hear || learn.

μάθημα, τό [matheema] lesson.

μαθηματικά, τά [matheemateeka] πλ mathematics.

μαθηματικός [matheemateekos] mathematical || (οὐσ) mathematician.

μαθημένος [matheemenos] used to.

μάθησις, ἡ [matheesees] learning, education.

μαθητεία, ἡ [matheeteea] apprenticeship.

μαθητευόμενος [matheetevomenos] apprentice, novice.

μαθητεύω [matheetevo] be a student, be an apprentice.

μαθητής, ὁ [matheetees] student, pupil || (φιλοσόφου) disciple.

μαῖα, ἡ [mea] midwife.

μαίανδρος, ὁ [meanδros] meander, in-and-out.

μαιευτήρ, ὁ [mayevteer] obstetrician.

μαιευτήριον, τό [mayevteereeon] maternity hospital.

μαιευτική, ἡ [mayevteekee] obstetrics.

μαϊμοῦ, ἡ [maeemou] monkey, ape.

μαίνομαι [menome] rage, be furious.

μαϊντανός, ὁ [maeentanos] parsley.

Μάϊος, ὁ [maeeos] May.

μακάβριος [makavreeos] macabre, gruesome, ghastly.

μακάρι [makaree] (ἐπιφ) would to God!, may!

μακαρίζω [makareezo] regard as fortunate, envy.

μακάριος [makareeos] happy, fortunate, blessed || calm, serene.

μακαρίτης [makareetees] late, deceased.

μακαρόνια, τά [makaroneea] πλ macaroni.

μακελειό, τό [makelio] (μεταφ) slaughter, massacre.

μακέττα, ἡ [maketa] model, drawing, plan.

μακραίνω [makreno] make longer || grow taller.

μακράν [makran] (a)far, far off, at a distance.

μακριά [makria] βλ **μακράν**.

μακρινός [makreenos] far distant, far off || (ταξίδι) long.

μακρόβιος [makroveeos] long-lived.

μακρόθεν [makrothen] from a distance, from afar.

μάκρος, τό [makros] length || duration.

μακρός [makros] long, lengthy, extensive.

μακρύνω [makreeno] βλ **μακραίνω**.

μακρύς [makrees] βλ **μακρός**.

μάκτρον, τό [maktron] dishcloth || table napkin || rag.

μαλάζω [malazo] massage, knead || soften, mollify, pacify || (πόνον) alleviate.

μαλάκιον, τό [malakeeon] mollusc.

μαλακός [malakos] soft || mild, gentle || (κλίμα) genial.

μαλάκυνσις, ἡ [malakeensees] softening, enervation.

μαλακώνω [malakono] soften, get milder || assuage || become calmer.

μάλαμα, τό [malama] gold.

μαλάσσω [malaso] βλ **μαλάζω**.

μαλθακός [malthakos] soft, effeminate, delicate.

μάλιστα [maleesta] more especially, particularly || yes, indeed || even.

μαλλί, τό [malee] wool, fleece || hair.

μαλλιά, τά [malia] πλ hair (of the head) || ~ κουβάρια upside down.

μαλλιαρός [maleearos] hairy, long-haired || woolly.

μάλλινος [maleenos] woollen.

μᾶλλον [malon] more, better, rather || κατά τό ~ ἤ ἧττον more or less.

μαλώνω [malono] argue || chide, reprimand, rebuke.

μαμά, ἡ [mama] mother, mummy.

μάμμη, ἡ [mamee] grandmother.

μαμμή, ἡ [mamee] midwife.

μαμμούνι, τό [mamounee] small insect, grub.

μάνα [mana] βλ **μάννα**.

μάνδαλος, ὁ [manδalos] latch, bolt, bar.

μανδύας, ὁ [manδeeas] mantle, cloak || (στρατ) greatcoat.

μανθάνω [manthano] βλ **μαθαίνω**.

μάνι μάνι [maneemanee] quickly, in a jiffy.

μανία, ἡ [maneea] fury, passion, mania || whim, fancy || ἔχω ~ν μέ be crazy about.

μανιακός [maneeakos] raving, frenzied || (παίκτης) inveterate.

μανιβέλλα, ἡ [maneevela] starting handle || lever, bar.

μανικέτι, τό [maneeketee] cuff.

μανίκι, τό [maneekee] sleeve.

μανιτάρι, τό [maneetaree] mushroom.

μανιώδης [maneeoδees] passionate, inveterate || furious, raging.

μάν(ν)α, ή [mana] mother, mamma.

μαν(ν)ούλα, ή [manoula] mummy || (US) mom.

μανουάλιον, τό [manoualeeon] candelabrum.

μανούβρα, ή [manouvra] manoeuvre.

μανούρι, τό [manouree] kind of white cheese.

μανταλάκι, τό [mantalakee] clothes peg.

μάνταλο, τό [mantalo] βλ μάνδαλος.

μανταλώνω [mantalono] latch, lock up, bolt.

μανταρίνι, τό [mantareenee] tangerine.

μαντάρισμα, τό [mantareesma] darning || (ύφάσματος) mending.

μαντάρω [mantaro] darn, mend.

μαντάτο, τό [mantato] information, news.

μαντείον, τό [manteeon] oracle.

μαντεύω [mantevo] foretell || guess || find out, fathom.

μαντήλι, τό [manteelee] handkerchief.

μαντινάδα, ή [manteenaδa] rhyming couplet.

μάντις, ό [mantees] wizard, prophet.

μαντολάτο, τό [mantolato] nougat.

μάντρα, ή [mantra] pen, fold, sty || (περίφραγμα) enclosure, wall || yard.

μαντράχαλος, ό [mantrahalos] lanky fellow.

μαντρόσκυλο, τό [mantroskeelo] sheepdog.

μαξιλλάρι, τό [makseelaree] pillow, cushion.

μάπ(π)α, ή [mapa] cabbage.

μάππας, ό [mapas] stupid fellow, imbecile.

μαραγκός, ό [marangos] carpenter || joiner.

μαράζι, τό [marazee] pining, depression, languor.

μάραθ(ρ)ο, τό [marath(r)o] fennel.

μαραίνομαι [marenome] fade, wither away, shrivel || (μεταφ) waste away.

μαραίνω [mareno] wither, dry up, fade.

μαρασμός, ό [marasmos] withering, fading away || (μεταφ) decay.

μαργαρίνη, ή [margareenee] margarine.

μαργαρίτα, ή [margareeta] daisy.

μαργαριτάρι, τό [margareetaree] pearl.

μαργαρίτης, ό [margareetees] βλ μαργαριτάρι.

μαρίδα, ή [mareeδa] whitebait, small fry.

μάρκα, ή [marka] (έμπορ) trademark, make || (αύτοκινήτου) model || (νόμισμα) mark || (μεταφ) cunning fellow.

μαρμαρένιος [marmareneeos] of marble.

μάρμαρον, τό [marmaron] marble.

μαρμελάδα, ή [marmelaδa] marmalade.

μαρούλι, τό [maroulee] lettuce.

Μάρτης, ό [Martees] March.

μαρτυρία, ή [marteereea] deposition, giving of evidence || proof, token.

μαρτυρικός [marteereekos] insufferable, unbearable.

μαρτύριον, τό [marteereeon] torment, suffering.

μαρτυρῶ [marteero] give evidence, testify || (προδίδω) betray, inform against || (ένδεικνύω) show, indicate || (γίνομαι μάρτυς) suffer martyrdom (for Christ).

μάρτυς, ό [martees] witness || (έκκλ) martyr.

μᾶς, μας [mas] us || our.

μασέλλα, ή [masela] false teeth.

μασιά, ή [masia] πλ tongs, fire-tongs || pincers.

μάσκα, ή [maska] mask || μασκαράς, ό masquerader || (μεταφ) impostor, rascal, scoundrel.

μασόνος, ό [masonos] freemason.

μασουλῶ [masoulo] chew, munch.

μασούρι, τό [masouree] spool, bobbin || tube.

μαστάρι, τό [mastaree] udder.

μαστίγιον, τό [masteeyeeon] whip || switch.

μαστιγώνω [masteeyono] whip, lash, flog.

μαστίζω [masteezo] infest, devastate, desolate.

μάστιξ, ή [masteeks] whip || (μεταφ) curse, plague.

μαστίχα, ή [masteeha] mastic || (ποτόν) mastic brandy.

μάστορας, ό [mastoras] artisan, workman || (μεταφ) expert, skilful person.

μαστορεύω [mastorevo] work || mend, repair.

μαστός, ό [mastos] breast || (μεταφ) hillock.

μαστροπός, ό, ή [mastropos] procurer, procuress, pimp.

μασχάλη, ή [mashalee] armpit.

μασῶ [maso] chew, masticate || (τά λόγια) stammer.

ματαιόδοξος [mateoδoksos] vain, self-conceited.

ματαιοπονῶ [mateopono] work in vain, labour uselessly.

μάταιος [mateos] vain, useless, unavailing || conceited.

ματαιώνω [mateono] frustrate, foil, cancel, stop.

μάτην [mateen] to no purpose, uselessly, vainly.

μάτι, τό [matee] eye || (φύλλου κτλ) bud || αύγό ~ fried egg (sunny-side up) || βάζω στό ~ set one's heart on || έχω στό ~ covet || κλείνω τό ~ wink || ~ μου! my darling!

ματιά, ή [matia] glance, gaze, eye, look || ~ ζω cast an evil eye on, bewitch.

ματίζω [mateezo] splice || lengthen.

ματογυάλια, τά [matoyeealeea] πλ spectacles, glasses.

ματόκλαδο, τό [matoklaδo] eyelash, lash.

ματόφρυδο, τό [matofreeδo] eyebrow.

ματόφυλλο, τό [matofeelo] eyelid.

μάτσο, τό [matso] truss, bunch, bundle || (ξύλων) faggot.

ματσούκα, ή [matsouka] club, cudgel.

ματώνω [matono] bleed.

μαυραγορίτης, ὁ [mavrayoreetees] black marketeer.

μαυρειδερός [mavreederos] blackish ‖ brown.

μαυρίζω [mavreezo] blacken, darken ‖ (ἀπό ἥλιο) get sunburnt ‖ (μεταφ) blackball, vote against.

μαυρίλα, ἡ [mavreela] blackness, darkness, gloominess.

μαυροδάφνη, ἡ [mavroδafnee] kind of sweet wine.

μαυροπίναξ, ὁ [mavropeenaks] blackboard ‖ blacklist.

μαυροπούλι, τό [mavropoulee] starling.

μαῦρος [mavros] black ‖ brown ‖ (νέγρος) negro ‖ (μεταφ) miserable, luckless.

μαχαίρι, τό [maheree] knife ‖ στά ~α at loggerheads.

μαχαιριά, ἡ [maheria] stab.

μαχαιροβγάλτης, ὁ [maherovyaltees] cutthroat ‖ bully.

μαχαιροπήρουνα, τά [maheropeerouna] πλ cutlery.

μαχαιρώνω [maherono] stab.

μαχαλᾶς, ὁ [mahalas] quarter, district, neighbourhood.

μάχη, ἡ [mahee] battle, combat ‖ struggle, fight.

μαχητής, ὁ [maheetees] combatant, fighter, soldier.

μαχητικός [maheeteekos] warlike, martial ‖ combative, ready to fight.

μάχομαι [mahome] fight, combat, struggle ‖ hate, abhor.

μέ [me] with, by, through, by means of, on, of ‖ ~ τά πόδια on foot ‖ ~ τό καλό God willing ‖ ~ τό μῆνα by the month ‖ δύο ~ τρία two by three (feet etc) ‖ ~ τόν καιρό eventually, in the course of time ‖ δύο ~ τρεῖς between two and three o'clock ‖ ἔχω μανία ~ τό be mad on, be crazy about ‖ γελῶ ~ laugh at ‖ ~ τή σειρά in turn ‖ λίρες ~ δραχμές pounds for drachmas ‖ ἀναλόγως ~ according to whether.

μέ, με [me] me.

μεγάθυμος [meyatheemos] generous, magnanimous.

μεγαλεῖο [meyaleeo] first-rate!

μεγαλεῖον, τό [meyaleeon] splendour, grandeur ‖ (μεταφ) splendid.

μεγαλειότης, ἡ [meyaleeotees] majesty, grandeur ‖ ἡ Αὐτοῦ ~ His Majesty.

μεγαλειώδης [meyaleeoδees] magnificent, superb, majestic.

μεγαλέμπορος, ὁ [meyalemboros] wholesaler.

μεγαλεπήβολος [meyalepeevolos] grandiose, imposing.

μεγάλη [meyalee]: ~ Ἑβδομάδα Holy Week.

μεγαλόδωρος [meyaloδoros] munificent, generous, bounteous.

μεγαλοποιῶ [meyalopeeo] magnify, exaggerate, overdo.

μεγαλοπρεπής [meyaloprepees] majestic, stately, splendid, magnificent.

μεγάλος [meyalos] great, large, big, long.

μεγαλουργῶ [meyalouryo] achieve great things.

μεγαλόφρων [meyalofron] generous, magnanimous ‖ boastful, arrogant.

μεγαλοφυής [meyalofiees] gifted, ingenious.

μεγαλόψυχος [meyalopseehos] magnanimous, generous.

μεγαλύνω [meyaleeno] magnify, exalt.

μεγαλώνω [meyalono] increase, enlarge ‖ (ἀνατρέφω) bring up, raise ‖ (μεγαλοποιῶ) magnify, exaggerate ‖ grow up.

μέγαρον, τό [meyaron] mansion, palace, imposing building.

μέγας [meyas] βλ μεγάλος.

μεγάφωνον, τό [meyafonon] (ραδιοφώνου) loudspeaker ‖ megaphone.

μέγγενη, ἡ [mengenee] (ἐργαλεῖον) vice.

μέγεθος, τό [meyethos] size, greatness, height, magnitude, extent, length.

μεγέθυνσις, ἡ [meyetheensees] enlargement, increase, extension.

μεγιστάν, ὁ [meyeestan] magnate, seigneur.

μέγιστον, τό [meyeeston] maximum, greatest.

μέγιστος [meyeestos] greatest, largest ‖ enormous, colossal.

μεδούλι, τό [meδoulee] marrow.

μέδουσα, ἡ [meδousa] kind of jellyfish.

μεζές, ὁ [mezes] titbit, snack.

μεζούρα, ἡ [mezoura] tape measure.

μεθαύριον [methavreeon] the day after tomorrow.

μέθη, ἡ [methee] intoxication, drunkenness ‖ (μεταφ) enthusiasm.

μεθοδικός [methoδeekos] systematic, methodical.

μέθοδος, ἡ [methoδos] method, system, process.

μεθόριος, ἡ [methoreeos] boundary, frontier.

μεθύσι, τό [metheesee] βλ μέθη.

μεθύσκομαι [metheeskome] get drunk.

μεθύσκω [metheesko] intoxicate, make drunk.

μεθυσμένος [metheesmenos] drunk.

μεθύω [metheeo] βλ μεθύσκομαι.

μεθῶ [metho] make drunk ‖ get drunk.

μειδίαμα, τό [meeδeeama] smile.

μειδιῶ [meeδeeo] smile.

μείζων [meezon] larger, greater ‖ (μουσ) major.

μειλίχιος [meeleeheeos] mild, gentle, affable.

μειοδοτῶ [meeoδoto] bid the lowest price.

μεῖον [meeon] less, minus.

μειονέκτημα, τό [meeonekteema] disadvantage, inconvenience.

μειονότης, ή [meeonotees] minority.

μειοψηφία, ή [meeopseefeea] minority of votes.

μείων [meeon] lesser.

μειώνω [meeono] lesson, diminish, reduce, decrease.

μείωσις, ή [meeosees] decrease, reduction || (μεταφ) humiliation.

μελαγχολία, ή [melangholeea] melancholy, dejection, gloominess.

μελαγχολικός [melangholeekos] sad, depressed, gloomy.

μελαγχολώ [melangholo] become sad.

μελάνη, ή [melanee] ink.

μελανιά, ή [melania] inkstain || bruise || ~ζω bruise || turn blue with cold.

μελανοδοχείον, τό [melanoδoheeon] inkstand, inkpot.

μέλας [melas] black.

μελᾶτος [melatos] (αὐγό) soft-boiled (egg).

μελαχροινός [melahreenos] dark, brown, swarthy.

μελαψός [melapsos] dark-skinned, swarthy.

μέλει [melee]: δεν μέ ~ I don't care, I'm not interested.

μελέτη, ή [meletee] (πραγματεία) treatise || study || (κτιρίου) plan, design || meditation, contemplation.

μελετηρός [meleteeros] studious.

μελετῶ [meleto] study || (ἐρευνῶ) search, investigate || (σκοπεύω) have in mind, intend || (πιάνο) practise.

μέλημα, τό [meleema] concern, care, solicitude, duty.

μέλι, τό [melee] honey.

μελίγγι, τό [meleenghee] temple (anat).

μέλισσα, ή [meleesa] bee.

μελίσσι, τό [meleesee] beehive || swarm.

μελισσοκομία, ή [meleesokomeea] beekeeping.

μελιτζάνα, ή [meleetzana] eggplant.

μέλλον, τό [melon] future || outlook.

μελλόνυμφος, ὁ, ή [meloneemfos] husband-to-be, fiancé || fiancée.

μέλλω [melo] intend, be about to.

μέλλων [melon] future || ὁ ~ (γραμμ) future tense.

μελόδραμα, τό [meloδrama] melodrama.

μέλος, τό [melos] member || (μουσ) melody, air || (τοῦ σώματος) member, limb.

μελτέμι, τό [meltemee] north wind, trade wind.

μελωδία, ή [meloδeea] melody, tune.

μελωδικός [meloδeekos] melodious, tuneful.

μεμβράνη, ή [memvranee] membrane || (χαρτί) parchment.

μεμονωμένος [memonomenos] isolated, lonely, alone.

μέμφομαι [memfome] reproach, blame, censure, find fault with.

μέν [men] on the one hand || οἱ ~ ... οἱ δέ some ... others.

μενεξές, ὁ [menekses] violet.

μένος, τό [menos] fervour, zeal, eagerness || wrath, anger, fury.

μέντα, ή [menta] mint, peppermint.

μένω [meno] remain, stop, stay || (ἀπομένω) be left, survive || (διαμένω) reside, live || ~ ἀπό run out of, be short of.

μέρα, ή [mera] βλ ἡμέρα.

μεράκι, τό [merakee] ardent desire, yearning || (λύπη) regret, sorrow.

μεραρχία, ή [merarheea] division.

μερδικό, τό [merδeeko] portion, part, share.

μερί, τό [meree] thigh.

μεριά, ή [meria] place || side.

μερίδα, ή [mereeδa] ration, portion, helping.

μερίδιον, τό [mereeδeeon] share, portion.

μερικός [mereekos] partial, some, a few || μερικά πλ some, certain, a few.

μέριμνα, ή [mereemna] care, anxiety, solicitude, concern.

μεριμνῶ [mereemno] look after, care for, be anxious about.

μερίς, ή [merees] βλ μερίδα.

μέρισμα, τό [mereesma] dividend || allotment, part.

μερμήγκι, τό [mermeengee] ant.

μεροδούλι, τό [meroδoulee] day's wages.

μεροκάματο, τό [merokamato] day's wages.

μερροληπτῶ [meroleepto] take sides, be partial, be one-sided.

μέρος, τό [meros] part, party || (μερίς) portion, share || (τόπος) place, spot || (πλευρά) side || (ρόλος) role || (γραμμ) part of speech || (ἀποχωρητήριον) W.C. || κατά ~ aside, apart.

μέσα [mesa] in(to) || inside || within || among || (πολιτ) means || ~ σέ inside, within || in, into.

μεσάζω [mesazo] mediate, intercede.

μεσαῖος [meseos] middle.

μεσαίων, ὁ [meseon] Middle Ages || μεσαιωνικός medieval.

μεσάνυχτα, τά [mesaneehta] πλ midnight.

μέση, ή [mesee] middle || (σώματος) waist || ἀφίνω στή ~ leave incomplete, leave undone.

μεσῆλιξ [meseeleeks] middle-aged.

μεσημβρία, ή [meseemvreea] midday, noon || (νότος) south.

μεσημβρινός [meseemvreenos] of noon || (νότιος) southern || (οὐσ) meridian.

μεσημέρι, τό [meseemeree] noon || μέρα ~ in broad daylight || μεσημεριανός midday || μεσημεριανός ὕπνος siesta.

μεσίστιος [meseesteeos] half-mast.

μεσιτεία, ή [meseeteea] mediation, agency || (ἐμπορ) brokerage.

μεσιτεύω [meseetevo] intercede, intervene || be a broker.

μεσίτης, ὁ [meseetees] mediator ‖ agent, broker.

μεσιτικό [meseeteeko]: ~ γραφεῖο house agency.

μεσογειακός [mesoyeeakos] Mediterranean.

Μεσόγειος, ἡ [mesoyeeos] the Mediterranean.

μεσόκοπος [mesokopos] βλ μεσῆλιξ.

μεσολαβῶ [mesolavo] intercede, intervene ‖ (εἰς χρόνον) come between.

μέσον, τό [meson] middle, midst ‖ (τρόπος) method, means, way ‖ μέσα πλ influence, pull, power.

μέσος [mesos] middle ‖ medium ‖ (ὅρος) mean, average.

μεσοφόρι, τό [mesoforee] petticoat, underskirt.

μεστός [mestos] full, replete, crammed with ‖ (ὥριμος) ripe.

μεστώνω [mestono] mature, ripen, mellow.

μέσω [meso] through, via.

μετά [meta] with ‖ after, in ‖ (ἐπίρ) afterwards.

μεταβαίνω [metaveno] go, proceed.

μεταβάλλω [metavalo] change, convert, transform.

μετάβασις, ἡ [metavasees] going, passage, transference.

μεταβατικός [metavateekos] transitional, provisory ‖ (γραμμ) transitive (verb).

μεταβιβάζω [metaveevazo] (διαταγήν) transmit, hand on ‖ (μεταφέρω) transport ‖ (ἰδιοκτησίαν) transfer, hand over.

μεταβλητός [metavleetos] variable, unsettled, changeable.

μεταβολή, ἡ [metavolee] alteration, change ‖ (στρατ) about-turn, half-turn.

μετάγγισις, ἡ [metangeesees] transfusion, drawing off ‖ (κρασιοῦ κτλ) decanting.

μεταγενέστερος [metayenesteros] posterior, subsequent, later.

μεταγραφή, ἡ [metayrafee] transfer.

μεταγωγικόν, τό [metayoyeekon] (ναυτ) transport ship.

μεταγωγικός [metayoyeekos] of transport.

μεταδίδω [metadeedo] impart, transmit ‖ (ραδιοφωνία) broadcast ‖ (νόσον) infect.

μετάδοσις, ἡ [metadosees] transmission ‖ (νόσου) contagion, spreading ‖ ἁγία ~ Holy Communion.

μεταδοτικός [metadoteekos] contagious, infectious.

μετάθεσις, ἡ [metathesees] transfer, removal.

μεταθέτω [metatheto] transpose, transfer, remove, move.

μεταίχμιον, τό [metehmeeon] (μεταφ) halfway point ‖ turning point.

μετακινῶ [metakeeno] move, shift, displace.

μετακομίζω [metakomeezo] transport, transfer, remove ‖ (σπίτι) move, change residence, move out.

μεταλαμβάνω [metalamvano] take Holy Communion.

μεταλλεῖον, τό [metaleeon] mine.

μετάλλευμα, τό [metalevma] ore.

μεταλλικός [metaleekos] metallic ‖ mineral.

μετάλλινος [metaleenos] of metal.

μετάλλιον, τό [metaleeon] medal.

μέταλλον, τό [metalon] metal.

μεταμέλεια, ἡ [metameleea] repentance, regrets.

μεταμεσημβρινός [metameseemvreenos] afternoon.

μεταμόρφωσις, ἡ [metamorfosees] transformation, reformation ‖ (ἐκκλ) transfiguration.

μεταμόσχευσις, ἡ [metamoshevsees] transplantation.

μεταμφίεσις, ἡ [metamfiesees] disguise, masquerade.

μετανάστευσις, ἡ [metanastevsees] emigration, (im)migration.

μεταναστεύω [metanastevo] (e)migrate, immigrate.

μετανάστης, ὁ [metanastees] (e)migrant, immigrant.

μετάνοια, ἡ [metaneea] repentance, regret ‖ (ἐκκλ) penance ‖ (γονυκλισιά) genuflexion.

μετανοῶ [metanoo] repent, regret, be sorry (for).

μετάξι, τό [metaksee] silk.

μεταξοσκώληξ, ὁ [metaksoskoleeks] silkworm.

μεταξύ [metaksee] between, among, amongst, amid(st) ‖ ~ μας between ourselves, between you and me ‖ ἐν τῷ ~ meanwhile.

μεταξωτόν, τό [metaksoton] silk material, silk stuff.

μεταπείθω [metapeetho] dissuade, prevail upon.

μεταποιῶ [metapeeo] transform, alter, convert.

μεταπολεμικός [metapolemeekos] postwar.

μετάπτωσις, ἡ [metaptosees] change, relapse.

μεταπωλῶ [metapolo] resell, sell again.

μεταρρυθμίζω [metareethmeezo] reform, rearrange.

μεταστάς [metastas] deceased, late.

μετασχηματιστής, ὁ [metasheemateestees] transformer.

μετατοπίζω [metatopeezo] shift, displace.

μετατόπισις, ἡ [metatopeesees] shifting ‖ displacement.

μετατρέπω [metatrepo] transform, turn, change, alter ‖ (ἐπί ποινῶν) commute.

μεταφέρω [metafero] transport, carry, convey ‖ (οἶκον) transfer, carry over.

μεταφορά, ἡ [metafora] transportation, conveyance ‖ (γραμμ) metaphor.

μεταφορικά, τά [metaforeeka] πλ carriage fees.

μεταφορικός [metaforeekos] transporting, transport ‖ (γραμμ) metaphoric(al).

μεταφράζω [metafrazo] translate.

μετάφρασις, ἡ [metafrasees] translation.

μεταφραστής, ὁ [metafrastees] translator.

μεταφυτεύω [metafeetevo] transplant.

μεταχειρίζομαι [metaheereezome] use, employ ‖ treat, behave towards.

μεταχειρισμένος [metaheereesmenos] worn, used ‖ (δεύτερο χέρι) secondhand.

μετεκπαιδεύσις, ἡ [metekpedevsees] postgraduate study.

μετεξεταστέος [meteksetasteos] be re-examined (sch).

μετέπειτα [metepeeta] after, afterwards, subsequently ‖ οἱ ~ posterity, the descendants.

μετέχω [meteho] take part in, participate ‖ partake of.

μετέωρον, τό [meteoron] meteor, shooting star.

μετέωρος [meteoros] dangling, in the air ‖ (μεταφ) hesitant, undecided ‖ in suspense.

μετημφιεσμένος [meteemfiesmenos] disguised.

μετοικῶ [meteeko] emigrate ‖ (σπίτι) move house.

μετόπισθεν [metopeesthen]: τά ~ the rear.

μετοχή, ἡ [metohee] (οἶκον) stock, share ‖ (γραμμ) participle.

μετόχι, τό [metohee] dependency of a monastery.

μετοχικός [metoheekos] (οἶκον) of a share, of joint stock ‖ (γραμμ) participial.

μέτοχος, ὁ [metohos] participant, sharer ‖ (οἶκον) shareholder.

μέτρημα, τό [metreema] measuring, mensuration ‖ counting, numbering.

μετρημένος [metreemenos] measured, limited ‖ (ἄνθρωπος) temperate, discreet, moderate.

μετρητά, τά [metreeta] πλ: τά ~ cash, money ‖ τοῖς μετρητοῖς in cash, (for) ready money.

μετρητής, ὁ [metreetees] meter, counter, gauge.

μετρητός [metreetos] measurable, calculable.

μετριάζω [metreeazo] moderate, diminish, slacken, lessen.

μετρική, ἡ [metreekee] versification, prosody, metrics.

μετρικός [metreekos] metric(al).

μετριοπάθεια, ἡ [metreeopatheea] moderation, temperance.

μετριοπαθής [metreeopathees] moderate, sober, temperate.

μέτριος [metreeos] ordinary, moderate ‖ (καφές) medium ‖ mediocre.

μετριοφροσύνη, ἡ [metreeofroseenee] modesty, decency.

μετρόφρων [metreeofron] modest, unassuming, decent, retiring.

μέτρα, τά [metra] πλ measurements ‖ proceedings, steps ‖ λαμβάνω ~ take measures.

μέτρον, τό [metron] measure, metre ‖ (μεταφ) measure, step ‖ (μουσική) bar, measure ‖ (ποιητικό) metre, foot.

μετρῶ [metro] measure, count, number, gauge.

μέτωπον, τό [metopon] forehead, brow ‖ (πρόσοψις) face, front, façade ‖ (μάχη) front, battlefront.

μέχρι(ς) [mehree(s)] till, until, down to, up to ‖ as far as ‖ ~ ἑνός to the last man ‖ ~ τοῦδε until now.

μή [mee] don't ‖ not, no ‖ lest.

μηδαμινός [meeδameenos] worthless, of no account, insignificant, trivial.

μηδέ, μηδείς [meeδe, meeδees] βλ οὐδείς.

μηδέν, τό [meeδen] nothing ‖ zero ‖ cipher.

μηδενικό, τό [meeδeneeko] zero ‖ cipher.

μηδενίζω [meeδeneezo] nullify ‖ mark with a zero.

μηδενιστής [meeδeneestees] nihilist.

μῆκος, τό [meekos] length ‖ (γεωγραφικόν) longitude ‖ κατά ~ in length, lengthwise.

μηκύνω [meekeeno] lengthen, elongate ‖ protract, prolong.

μηκώμαι [meekome] roar ‖ bleat ‖ howl, yell.

μηλίγγι, τό [meeleengee] temple (anat).

μῆλον, τό [meelon] apple ‖ (τῶν παρειῶν) cheekbone ‖ μηλονίτης apple cider.

μηλόπηττα, ἡ [meelopeeta] apple pie.

μήν(ας), ὁ [meen(as)] month.

μηνιαῖος [meenieos] monthly ‖ month's.

μηνιάτικο, τό [meeniateeko] month's wages ‖ month's rent.

μηνίγγι, τό [meeneengee] βλ μηλίγγι.

μηνιγγῖτις, ἡ [meeneengeetees] meningitis.

μῆνις, ἡ [meenees] rage, anger, fury, wrath.

μήνυμα, τό [meeneema] message, notice, announcement.

μήνυσις, ἡ [meeneesees] summons, charge.

μηνυτής, ὁ [meeneetees] plaintiff, complainant.

μηνύω [meeneeo] give notice ‖ bring a charge against.

μηνῶ [meeno] send a message, send word, call for.

μήπως [meepos] lest in any way, in case ‖ I wonder if.

μηρός, ὁ [meeros] thigh, leg.

μηρυκάζω [meereekazo] chew the cud, ruminate.

μήτε [meete] βλ οὔτε.

μητέρα, ἡ [meetera] mother.

μήτρα, ἡ [meetra] uterus, womb ‖ (χυτηρίου) mould, matrix, form.

μητρική [meetreekee]: ~ γλῶσσα mother tongue, native language.

μητρόπολις, ἡ [meetropolees] metropolis, capital ‖ (ἐκκλ) cathedral.

μητροπολιτικός [meetropoleeteekos] metropolitan.

μητροπολίτης, ὁ [meetropoleetees] metropolitan bishop.

μητρότης, ἡ [meetrotees] motherhood.

μητρυιά, ἡ [meetria] stepmother.

μητρυιός, ὁ [meetrios] stepfather.

μητρῷον, τό [meetroon] register, roll, official list of names.

μηχανεύομαι [meehanevome] contrive, engineer, plot, bring about.

μηχανή, ἡ [meehanee] machine, engine, works || (μεταφ) typewriter || camera.

μηχάνημα, τό [meehaneema] machine, apparatus, contrivance.

μηχανική, ἡ [meehaneekee] engineering, mechanics.

μηχανικόν, τό [meehaneekon] corps of engineers.

μηχανικός [meehaneekos] mechanical || (οὐσ) engineer || mechanic || architect.

μηχανισμός, ὁ [meehaneesmos] mechanism, machinery.

μηχανοδηγός, ὁ [meehanodeeyos] engine driver.

μηχανοκίνητος [meehanokeeneetos] motorized || machine-operated.

μηχανοποιῶ [meehanopeeo] mechanize.

μηχανορραφία, ἡ [meehanorafeea] machination || intrigue.

μία, μιά [meea, mia] one || a, an || ~ καί since seeing that || ~ πού as, since.

μιαίνω [mieno] pollute, sully, soil || (ἱερόν) desecrate.

μιαρός [meearos] dirty, polluted || foul.

μίασμα, τό [meeasma] miasma, infection.

μιγάς, ὁ [meeyas] half-caste, mulatto || hybrid.

μίγμα, τό [meeyma] mixture, blend.

μίζα, ἡ [meeza] (μηχανῆς) self-starter || (στά χαρτιά) stake.

μιζέρια, ἡ [meezereea] misery, wretchedness || (τσιγγουνιά) meanness.

μικραίνω [meekreno] curtail, lessen || shorten, grow smaller.

μικρέμπορος, ὁ [meekremboros] retailer.

μικρόβιον, τό [meekroveeon] microbe.

μικρογραφία, ἡ [meekroyrafeea] miniature.

μικροπρά(γ)ματα, τά [meekropra(γ)mata] πλ trifles.

μικροπρεπής [meekroprepees] mean, base.

μικρός [meekros] small, little || short || young || (διαφορά) trivial.

μικροσκοπικός [meekroskopeekos] minute.

μικροσκόπιον, τό [meekroskopeeon] microscope.

μικρόφωνον, τό [meekrofonon] microphone.

μικρόψυχος [meekropseehos] faint-hearted.

μικρύνω [meekreeno] βλ μικραίνω.

μικτόν [meekton]: ~ βάρος gross weight.

μικτός [meektos] mixed, composite || (σχολεῖον) coeducational.

μιλιά, ἡ [meelia] speech, word.

μίλι(ον), τό [meelee(on)] mile.

μιλῶ [meelo] speak.

μίμησις, ἡ [meemeesees] imitation.

μιμητής, ὁ [meemeetees] imitator.

μιμητικός [meemeeteekos] imitative.

μιμόζα, ἡ [meemoza] mimosa.

μῖμος, ὁ [meemos] mimic, jester.

μιμοῦμαι [meemoume] imitate, copy, mimic.

μιναρές, ὁ [meenares] minaret.

μινιατούρα, ἡ [meeneeatoura] miniature.

μῖξις, ἡ [meeksees] mixing, mixture, blend.

μισαλλόδοξος [meesalodoksos] intolerant.

μισάνθρωπος, ὁ [meesanthropos] misanthrope.

μισεύω [meesevo] depart, leave.

μισητός [meeseetos] hated, hateful, odious.

μίσθαρνος [meestharnos] mercenary, venal.

μισθοδοτῶ [meesthodoto] pay a salary to, hire.

μισθολόγιον, τό [meestholoyeeon] payroll || rate of pay.

μισθός, ὁ [meesthos] salary, wages, pay.

μισθοφόρος, ὁ [meesthoforos] mercenary, hired man.

μισθώνω [meesthono] hire, rent || let out, hire out.

μισθωτής, ὁ [meesthotees] tenant || hirer.

μισθωτός [meesthotos] salaried, paid.

μισό, τό [meeso] half || στά μισά halfway, in the middle.

μισογύνης, ὁ [meesoyeenees] woman-hater, misogynist.

μῖσος, τό [meesos] hatred, aversion.

μισός [meesos] half.

μισοφέγγαρο, τό [meesofengaro] half-moon, crescent.

μίσχος, ὁ [meeshos] stalk (of leaf).

μισῶ [meeso] hate, detest, loathe.

μίτος, ὁ [meetos] thread, woof.

μίτρα, ἡ [meetra] mitre.

μνεία, ἡ [mneea] mention.

μνῆμα, τό [mneema] grave, tomb, sepulchre.

μνημεῖον, τό [mneemeeon] monument, cenotaph.

μνήμη, ἡ [mneemee] memory, mind, recollection.

μνημονεύω [mneemonevo] celebrate, commemorate || quote, mention || learn by heart.

μνημονικόν, τό [mneemoneekon] βλ μνήμη.

μνημόσυνον, τό [mneemoseenon] requiem.

μνήμων [mneemon] mindful.

μνησίκακος [mneeseekakos] spiteful, vindictive.

μνηστεία, ἡ [mneesteea] engagement.

μνηστεύομαι [mneestevome] get engaged.

μνηστεύω [mneestevo] affiance.

μνηστή, ἡ [mneestee] fiancée.

μνηστήρ, ὁ [mneesteer] fiancé || (μεταφ) claimant.

μόδα, ή [μοδα] fashion, custom, habit, way ‖ τῆς ~ς fashionable.
μοδίστρα, ή [μοδεεστρα] dressmaker, seamstress.
μοιάζω [μεεαζο] look like.
μοῖρα, ή [μεερα] fate, destiny, fortune ‖ (ἀερο) squadron ‖ (γεωμ) degree.
μοιράζομαι [μεεραζομε] share with.
μοιράζω [μεεραζο] share out, divide, distribute ‖ (ρόλους) allot, assign ‖ (διανέμω) deliver ‖ (χαρτιά) deal ‖ ~ τή διαφορά split the difference. ·
μοιραῖος [μεερεος] unavoidable ‖ fatal, deadly.
μοιραίως [μεερεος] inevitably, fatally.
μοίραρχος, ὁ [μεεραρχος] captain of the gendarmerie.
μοιρολατρία, ή [μεερολατρεεα] fatalism.
μοιρολόγι, τό [μεερολογεε] dirge, lamentation.
μοιρολογῶ [μεερολογο] lament, mourn.
μοιχεία, ή [μεεχεεα] adultery.
μολαταῦτα [μολαταυτα] nevertheless, yet, still.
μόλις [μολες] barely, hardly, scarcely ‖ as soon as.
μολονότι [μολονοτε] although, though.
μολοσσός, ὁ [μολοσος] large sheepdog.
μόλυβδος, ὁ [μολεευδος] lead.
μολύβι, τό [μολεεβε] lead ‖ pencil.
μόλυνσις, ή [μολεενσες] contamination, infection, pollution.
μολύνω [μολεενο] infect, contaminate, pollute.
μόλυσμα, τό [μολεεσμα] infection, contagion.
μομφή, ή [μομφεε] blame, reproach, reprimand.
μοναδικός [μοναδεεκος] unique, singular, only.
μοναξιά, ή [μοναξια] solitude, isolation, loneliness.
μονάρχης, ὁ [μοναρχες] monarch, sovereign.
μοναρχία, ή [μοναρχεεα] monarchy.
μοναρχικός, ὁ [μοναρχεεκος] monarchist.
μονάς, ή [μονας] unit.
μοναστήρι, τό [μοναστεερε] monastery.
μονάχα [μοναχα] only.
μοναχή, ή [μοναχεε] nun.
μοναχικός [μοναχεεκος] monastic ‖ (ἐρημικός) isolated, solitary, lonely.
μοναχοπαίδι, τό [μοναχοπεδε] only child.
μονάχος [μοναχος] alone, single, only, sole ‖ real, authentic.
μοναχός, ὁ [μοναχος] monk.
μονέδα, ή [μονεδα] money.
μονή, ή [μονεε] βλ **μοναστήρι**.
μονήρης [μονεερες] solitary, isolated, lonely.
μόνιμος [μονεεμος] permanent, lasting, durable, fixed.
μονογαμία, ή [μονογαμεεα] monogamy.

μονογενής [μονογενεες] one and only.
μονόγραμμα, τό [μονογραμα] monogram, initials.
μονογραφή, ή [μονογραφεε] initials.
μονογραφία, ή [μονογραφεεα] monograph, treatise.
μονόδρομος, ὁ [μονοδρομος] one-way street.
μονοιάζω [μονεεαζο] agree with, get on well with ‖ reconcile.
μονοκατοικία, ή [μονοκατεεκεεα] one-family house.
μονοκόμματος [μονοκοματος] in one piece ‖ stiff ‖ forthright ‖ massive.
μονομανία, ή [μονομανεεα] obsession ‖ whim, fancy.
μονομαχία, ή [μονομαχεεα] duel.
μονομερής [μονομερεες] one-sided, partial.
μονομιᾶς [μονομιας] all at once.
μόνο(ν) [μονο(ν)] only, alone, solely, merely, nothing but ‖ ~ πού except that ‖ ~ νά provided that.
μονοπάτι, τό [μονοπατε] footpath, pathway.
μονόπλευρος [μονοπλευρος] one-sided, partial.
μονοπώλιον, τό [μονοπολεεον] monopoly.
μονοπωλῶ [μονοπολο] monopolize.
μόνος [μονος] alone, single, by o.s., apart ‖ ~ μου of my own accord, by myself.
μονός [μονος] single ‖ simple ‖ (ἀριθμός) odd.
μονότονος [μονοτονος] monotonous, unvaried ‖ (μεταφ) wearisome.
μονόφθαλμος [μονοφθαλμος] one-eyed.
μοντέλο, τό [μοντελο] model.
μοντέρνος [μοντερνος] modern, up-to-date.
μονύελος, ὁ [μονιελος] monocle.
μονώνω [μονονο] set apart, cut off ‖ insulate.
μόνωσις, ή [μονοσες] insulation ‖ solitude, isolation.
μονωτικός [μονοτεεκος] insulating.
μορέα, ή [μορεα] mulberry tree.
μόριον, τό [μορεεον] particle ‖ molecule.
μόρτης, ὁ [μορτες] hooligan, blackguard.
μορφάζω [μορφαζο] grimace, make faces ‖ (ἀπό πόνο) wince.
μορφασμός, ὁ [μορφασμος] grimace ‖ wince.
μορφή, ή [μορφεε] shape, form ‖ look, face, aspect ‖ phase.
μορφίνη, ή [μορφεενε] morphine.
μορφολογία, ή [μορφολογεεα] morphology.
μορφώνω [μορφονο] shape, form ‖ (ἐκπαιδεύω) train, educate, teach.
μόρφωσις, ή [μορφοσες] education, learning.
μορφωτικός [μορφοτεεκος] cultural ‖ instructive.
μόστρα, ή [μοστρα] shop window, display ‖ specimen, sample.
μοσχάρι, τό [μοσχαρε] calf ‖ veal.

μοσχάτο, τό [moshato] muscatel.

μοσχοβολῶ [moshovolo] smell sweetly, be fragrant.

μοσχοκάρυδο, τό [moshokareedo] nutmeg.

μοσχοκάρφι, τό [moshokarfee] clove.

μοσχολίβανο, τό [mosholeevano] frankincense.

μόσχος, ὁ [moshos] βλ μοσχάρι.

μοτοσυκλέτα, ἡ [motoseekleta] motorbike, motorcycle.

μοῦ, μου [mou] me ‖ my.

μουγγός [moungos] dumb, mute.

μουγγρίζω [moungreezo] roar, bellow ‖ (ἄνεμος) howl, wail ‖ (ἀπό πόνο) moan, groan.

μουδιάζω [moudeeazo] become numb.

μουλάρι, τό [moularee] mule.

μοῦλος, ὁ [moulos] bastard, crossbreed.

μούμια, ἡ [moumeea] mummy ‖ shrivelled person.

μουνουχίζω [mounouheezo] castrate.

μουντζούρα, ἡ [mountzoura] smudge, stain, smear ‖ (μεταφ) blemish.

μουντός [mountos] dull, dim.

μούρη, ἡ [mouree] face ‖ snout.

μούρλια, ἡ [mourleea] madness ‖ εἶναι ~ it's perfect!, it's a dream!

μουρλός [mourlos] mad, insane ‖ bewildered.

μουρμουρητό, τό [mourmoureeto] murmuring ‖ grumbling.

μουρμουρίζω [mourmoureezo] mutter, murmur ‖ (μεταφ) whisper ‖ babble.

μοῦρο, τό [mouro] mulberry.

μουρούνα, ἡ [mourouna] codfish.

μοῦσα, ἡ [mousa] muse.

μουσακᾶς, ὁ [mousakas] moussaka, minced meat with vegetables.

μουσαμᾶς, ὁ [mousamas] oilcloth, linoleum ‖ mackintosh.

μουσαφίρης, ὁ [mousafeerees] guest, visitor.

μουσεῖον, τό [mouseeon] museum.

μούσι, τό [mousee] goatee.

μουσική, ἡ [mouseekee] music.

μουσικός [mouseekos] musical ‖ (οὐσ) musician.

μούσκεμα, τό [mouskema] wetting, soaking ‖ τά κάνω ~ make a mess of.

μουσκεύω [mouskevo] soak, wet, damp ‖ get wet.

μούσμουλο, τό [mousmoulo] loquat.

μουσουργός, ὁ, ἡ [mousouryos] composer.

μουστάκι, τό [moustakee] moustache.

μουσταλευριά, ἡ [moustalevria] must-jelly.

μουστάρδα, ἡ [moustarda] mustard.

μοῦστος, ὁ [moustos] must.

μούτρα, τά [moutra] πλ: ἔχω ~ νά I dare to ‖ πέφτω μέ τά ~ apply o.s. enthusiastically ‖ tuck in.

μοῦτρο [moutro]: εἶναι ~ he's a thief, he's deceitful.

μοῦτσος, ὁ [moutsos] cabin boy.

μούχλα, ἡ [mouhla] mould, mildew.

μουχλιάζω [mouhleeazo] make mouldy ‖ become mouldy.

μοχθηρός [mohtheeros] wicked, mischievous, malicious.

μόχθος, ὁ [mohthos] pains, fatigue, trouble.

μοχλός, ὁ [mohlos] lever, (crow)bar ‖ (μεταφ) promoter, instigator.

μπαγιάτικος [mbayeateekos] (ψωμί) stale ‖ rancid.

μπάγκος, ὁ [mbangos] bench ‖ counter.

μπάζ(ι)α, τά [mbaz(i)a] πλ debris, rubble.

μπάζω [mbazo] usher in, thrust ‖ (συμμαζεύομαι) shrink.

μπαίνω [mbeno] go into, get in, enter ‖ (ὑφάσματος) shrink ‖ (μεταφ) catch on, understand ‖ ~ μέσα fall into debt ‖ ~ σέ μιά σειρά settle down, fall into line.

μπακάλης, ὁ [mbakalees] grocer.

μπακάλικο, τό [mbakaleeko] grocer's shop ‖ (US) grocery.

μπακαλιάρος, ὁ [mbakaleearos] salted codfish.

μπακίρι, τό [mbakeeree] copper.

μπακλαβᾶς, ὁ [mbaklavas] pastry of almonds and honey.

μπαλαντέρ, ὁ [mbalander] (στά χαρτιά) joker.

μπαλάντζα, ἡ [mbalantza] balance, pair of scales.

μπαλκόνι, τό [mbalkonee] balcony.

μπάλλα, ἡ [mbala] ball ‖ bullet.

μπαλλέτο, τό [mbaleto] ballet.

μπαλλόνι, τό [mbalonee] balloon.

μπαλντᾶς, ὁ [mbalntas] axe, hatchet.

μπάλωμα, τό [mbaloma] mending, patching, repairing.

μπαλώνομαι [mbalonome] benefit, profit.

μπαλώνω [mbalono] patch, mend, repair ‖ τά ~ make excuses ‖ make up.

μπάμιες, οἱ [mbamies] πλ okra, gumbo, lady's fingers.

μπαμπάκι, τό [mbambakee] cotton.

μπαμπᾶς, ὁ [mbambas] daddy, papa.

μπαμπέσης [mbambesees] perfidious, treacherous, fraudulent.

μπάμπουρας, ὁ [mbambouras] hornet.

μπανάνα, ἡ [mbanana] banana.

μπανιέρα, ἡ [mbaniera] bathtub.

μπανιερό, τό [mbaniero] swimsuit, bathing suit.

μπάνιο, τό [mbaneeo] bath ‖ bathing, swimming ‖ (λεκάνη) tub ‖ (δωμάτιο) bathroom.

μπάντα, ἡ [mbanta] (ἥσυχη γωνιά) corner ‖ (πλευρά) side ‖ (μουσική) band ‖ (συμμορία) gang, band ‖ βάζω στή ~ save ‖ κάνε στή ~ make room, stand aside.

μπαντιέρα, ἡ [mbantiera] banner, standard.

μπαξές, ὁ [mbakses] garden.

μπαοῦλο, τό [mbaoulo] trunk, chest.

μπαρκάρω [mbarkaro] go on board ‖ ship.

μπάρμπας, ὁ [mbarbas] old man ‖ uncle.

μπαρμπούνι, τό [mbarbounee] red mullet.

μπαρούτι, τό [mbaroutee] gunpowder ‖ ἔγινε ~ he got furious.

μπάρρα, ἡ [mbara] bar, crowbar.

μπασμένος [mbasmenos] aware ‖ knowledgeable ‖ shrunk.

μπάσταρδος, ὁ [mbastarðos] bastard.

μπαστούνι, τό [mbastounee] walking stick, cane ‖ (χαρτιά) club.

μπαταρία, ἡ [mbatareea] battery.

μπατζανάκης, ὁ [mbatzanakees] brother-in-law.

μπάτσος, ὁ [mbatsos] slap, smack.

μπαχαρικό, τό [mbahareeko] spice.

μπέζ [mbez] beige.

μπεκάτσα, ἡ [mbekatsa] woodcock.

μπεκιάρης, ὁ [mbekiarees] bachelor.

μπεκρῆς, ὁ [mbekrees] drunkard, tippler, boozer.

μπελᾶς, ὁ [mbelas] trouble, embarrassment, annoyance.

μπελντές, ὁ [mbelntes] tomato purée ‖ (φρούτων) jelly.

μπέμπης, ὁ [mbembees] baby.

μπενζίνα, ἡ [mbenzeena] petrol ‖ (πλοιάριον) motorboat.

μπέρδεμα, τό [mberðema] tangle, entanglement, confusion, disorder.

μπερδεύομαι [mberðevome] get implicated, become entangled ‖ be confused.

μπερδεύω [mberðevo] involve ‖ confuse, make a muddle of ‖ entangle.

μπερμπάντης, ὁ [mbermbantees] rascal, scoundrel.

μπετόν, τό [mbeton] concrete.

μπετούγια, ἡ [mbetouyeea] latch, catch.

μπήζω [mbeezo] drive in, hammer in ‖ (βελόνην) stick in, thrust in.

μπιζέλι, τό [mbeezelee] pea.

μπιλιέτο, τό [mbeelieto] visiting card ‖ ticket.

μπίρα, ἡ [mbeera] beer.

μπισκότο, τό [mbeeskoto] biscuit.

μπίτ(ι) [mbeet(ee)] entirely ‖ not in the least.

μπιφτέκι, τό [mbeeftekee] steak.

μπλάστρι, τό [mblastree] plaster.

μπλέ [mble] blue.

μπλέκω [mbleko] complicate, perplex ‖ get implicated.

μπλέξιμο, τό [mblekseemo] entanglement, involvement, complication.

μπλοκάρω [mblokaro] blockade ‖ block.

μπλούζα, ἡ [mblouza] blouse.

μπλόφα, ἡ [mblofa] bluff, deception.

μπογιά, ἡ [mboyia] paint, dye ‖ (παπουτσιῶν) boot-polish.

μπόγιας, ὁ [mboyeas] dog-catcher ‖ hangman.

μπογιατζῆς, ὁ [mboyeeatzees] painter ‖ polisher.

μπογιατίζω [mboyeeateezo] paint, colour, coat ‖ polish.

μπόϊ, τό [mboee] height, size.

μπόλι, τό [mbolee] graft ‖ μπολιάζω vaccinate, inoculate ‖ graft.

μπόλικος [mboleekos] plentiful, abundant, numerous.

μπόμπα, ἡ [mbomba] bomb.

μπομπότα, ἡ [mbombota] maize flour, bread of maize.

μποναμᾶς, ὁ [mbonamas] New Year's gift ‖ present.

μποξᾶς, ὁ [mboksas] shawl.

μπόρα, ἡ [mbora] rain squall, shower, storm.

μπορετός [mboretos] possible, practicable.

μπορῶ [mboro] can, be able, may.

μπόσικος [mboseekos] loose, slack ‖ (μεταφ) trifling ‖ unreliable.

μποστάνι, τό [mbostanee] melon field.

μποτίλια, ἡ [mboteeleea] bottle ‖ μποτιλιάρω bottle ‖ (μεταφ) block up, jam.

μπόττα, ἡ [mbota] boot.

μπουγάδα, ἡ [mbouγaða] family wash, washing.

μπουζί, τό [mbouzee] spark plug.

μπουζούκι, τό [mbouzoukee] kind of mandolin, bouzouki.

μπούκα, ἡ [mbouka] hole, mouth, entrance ‖ muzzle.

μπουκάλα, ἡ [mboukala] big bottle ‖ ἔμεινε ~ he was left in the lurch.

μπουκάλι, τό [mboukalee] bottle.

μπουκιά, ἡ [mboukia] mouthful.

μπούκλα, ἡ [mboukla] curl, lock (of hair).

μπουκώνω [mboukono] fill the mouth ‖ (μεταφ) bribe.

μπουλούκι, τό [mbouloukee] crowd ‖ band, troop.

μπουμπούκι, τό [mboumboukee] bud, sprout.

μπουμπουνητό, τό [mboumbouneeto] thundering, roll of thunder, rumble.

μπουνάτσα, ἡ [mbounatsa] fine weather ‖ calm sea.

μπουνιά, ἡ [mbounia] punch, blow with the fist.

μπούρδα, ἡ [mbourða] rubbish, hot air.

μπουρμπουλήθρα, ἡ [mbourmbouleethra] bubble.

μπουσουλῶ [mbousoulo] crawl.

μποῦστος, ὁ [mboustos] bust.

μπούτι, τό [mboutee] thigh ‖ (ἀρνήσιο) leg of lamb.

μπουφές, ὁ [mboufes] sideboard ‖ buffet.

μποῦφος, ὁ [mboufos] horned owl ‖ (μεταφ) booby.

μπουχτίζω [mbouhteezo] have enough of ‖ eat one's fill.

μπόχα, ἡ [mboha] stink, foul smell.

μπράβο [mbravo] (ἐπιφ) good show!, bravo!, good for you!

μπράτσο, τό [mbratso] arm.

μπριγιαντίνη, ή [mbreeγeeanteenee] brilliantine.

μπριζόλα, ή [mbreezola] chop, cutlet.

μπρίκι, τό [mbreekee] coffee pot.

μπρός [mbros] forward(s), in front of || βλ καί ἔμπρός.

μπροστινός [mbrosteenos] in front || former.

μπρούμυτα [mbroumeeta] flat on one's face.

μπροῦντζος, ὁ [mbrountzos] bronze, brass.

μπύρα, ή [mbeera] βλ μπίρα.

μῦ, τό [mee] the letter M.

μυαλό, τό [meealo] brain(s) || (γνώση) mind, intellect.

μυαλωμένος [meealomenos] learned, wise.

μῦγα, ή [meeγa] fly.

μύδι, τό [meeδee] mussel.

μυδραλλιοβόλον, τό [meeδraleeovolon] machine gun.

μυελός, ὁ [mielos] marrow (of bone).

μυζήθρα, ή [meezeethra] kind of white soft cheese.

μυζῶ [meezo] suck.

μύησις, ή [mieesees] initiation.

μυθικός [meetheekos] mythical, legendary || incredible.

μυθιστόρημα, τό [meetheestoreema] novel, romance, story.

μυθιστοριογράφος, ὁ [meetheestoreeoγrafos] novelist.

μυθολογία, ή [meetholoγeea] mythology.

μῦθος, ὁ [meethos] fable || myth || legend.

μυθώδης [meethoδees] fabled, legendary || untrue || incredible.

μυῖα, ή [meea] fly.

μυϊκός [mieekos] muscular.

μυκηθμός, ὁ [meekeethmos] bellowing, howling || lowing.

μύκης, ὁ [meekees] fungus, mushroom.

μυκτηρίζω [meekteereezo] scoff, mock at, sneer.

μυκῶμαι [meekome] bellow, roar || low.

μῦλος, ὁ [meelos] mill || (ἀνεμόμυλος) windmill.

μυλωνᾶς, ὁ [meelonas] miller.

μύξα, ή [meeksa] snot || mucus.

μυριάκις [meereeakees] infinitely, often.

μυρίζω [meereezo] smell.

μύριοι [meeriee] ten thousand || (μεταφ) numberless.

μυρμήγκι, τό [meermeengee] ant.

μύρμηξ, ὁ [meermeeks] βλ μυρμήγκι.

μυροβόλος [meerovolos] fragrant, scented.

μύρον, τό [meeron] aromatic oil || perfume || ἅγιον ~ holy oil, unction.

μυροπωλεῖον, τό [meeropoleeon] perfumery.

μυρσίνη, ή [meerseenee] βλ μυρτιά.

μυρτιά, ή [meertia] myrtle.

μυρτόν, τό [meerton] myrtle bough.

μυρωδᾶτος [meeroδatos] aromatic, fragrant.

μυρωδιά, ή [meeroδia] smell, scent, odour

|| (ἀρωματικό) fragrance, perfume || παίρνω ~ get wind of.

μυρώνω [meerono] anoint, administer the holy oil.

μῦς, ὁ [mees] muscle || (ποντικός) mouse.

μυσαρός [meesaros] abominable, detestable, odious.

μυσταγωγία, ή [meestaγoγeea] initiation || holy ceremony.

μύσταξ, ὁ [meestaks] moustache || (γάτας) whiskers.

μυστήριον, τό [meesteereeon] mystery, secret.

μυστήριος [meesteereeos] mysterious, inexplicable.

μυστηριώδης [meesteereeoδees] mysterious, dark.

μύστης, ὁ [meestees] initiate || (μεταφ) adept, expert.

μυστικιστής, ὁ [meesteekeestees] mystic.

μυστικόν, τό [meesteekon] secret.

μυστικός [meesteekos] secret(ive) || reticent, discreet || (ἀστυνόμος) undercover man || ~ δεῖπνος Last Supper.

μυστικότης, ή [meesteekotees] secrecy, discretion.

μυστρί, τό [meestree] trowel.

μυτερός [meeteros] pointed.

μύτη, ή [meetee] nose || (ἄκρη) tip || (παπουτσιοῦ) toe || (πέννας) nib || (βελόνας) point.

μύχιος [meeheeos] intimate, secret, internal.

μυχός, ὁ [meehos] recess, corner || creek, bay.

μυῶ [meeo] initiate into, admit into.

μυώδης [meeoδees] muscular, brawny, powerful.

μυῶν, ὁ [meeon] muscle, muscular flesh.

μύωψ [meeops] near-sighted, short-sighted.

μωαμεθανός, ὁ [moamethanos] Mohammedan.

μώβ [mov] mauve.

μῶλος, ὁ [molos] mole, jetty, pier.

μωλωπίζω [molopeezo] bruise, contuse.

μώλωψ, ὁ [molops] bruise, contusion.

μωραίνω [moreno] make stupid, become dull, stupefy.

μωρέ [more] (ἐπιφ) hey you!, you!, I say!

μωρία, ή [moreea] stupidity, foolishness.

μωρό, τό [moro] baby, infant.

μωρολόγος, ὁ [moroloγos] babbler, dotard, driveller.

μωρός [moros] silly, stupid, idiotic.

μωσαϊκόν, τό [mosaeekon] mosaic.

N, ν

νά [na] that, to, in order to, so as to || here it is!

ναί [ne] yes, indeed, certainly.

νάϊλον, τό [naeelon] nylon.

ναΐσκος, ὁ [naeeskos] chapel, small church.

νάνος, ὁ [nanos] dwarf.

νανουρίζω [nanoureezo] lull to sleep ‖ (στήν κούνια) rock ‖ (στήν ἀγκάλη) nurse.

νανούρισμα, τό [nanoureesma] lullaby ‖ rocking to sleep.

ναός, ὁ [naos] church ‖ temple.

ναργιλές, ὁ [naryeeless] hubble-bubble, hookah.

νάρθηξ, ὁ [nartheeks] (ἐκκλ) nave, narthex ‖ (βοτ) fennel.

ναρκαλιευτικόν, τό [narkalievteekon] mine-sweeper.

νάρκη, ἡ [narkee] numbness, torpor ‖ (ναυτ) mine ‖ (πνεύματος) sluggishness.

νάρκισσος, ὁ [narkeesos] narcissus.

ναρκοθέτις, ἡ [narkothetees] minelayer.

ναρκώνω [narkono] numb ‖ (μεταφ) dull, stupefy.

νάρκωσις, ἡ [narkosees] numbness ‖ torpidity, sluggishness.

ναρκωτικά, τά [narkoteeka] πλ drugs, narcotics.

νάτριον, τό [natreeon] sodium.

ναυάγιον, τό [navayeeon] shipwreck ‖ (μεταφ) wreck.

ναυαγός, ὁ [navayos] shipwrecked person.

ναυαρχεῖον, τό [navarheeon] admiralty.

ναύαρχος, ὁ [navarhos] admiral.

ναύκληρος, ὁ [navkleeros] boatswain.

ναῦλα, τά [navla] πλ fare, passage money.

ναυλώνω [navlono] charter, freight.

ναυμαχία, ἡ [navmaheea] sea battle, naval action.

ναυπηγεῖον, τό [navpeeyeeon] shipyard, dockyard.

ναῦς, ἡ [navs] ship, vessel.

ναυσιπλοΐα, ἡ [navseeploeea] sailing, shipping ‖ navigation.

ναύσταθμος, ὁ [navstathmos] dockyard, naval arsenal.

ναύτης, ὁ [navtees] sailor, seaman, mariner.

ναυτία, ἡ [navteea] seasickness ‖ nausea.

ναυτική, ἡ [navteekee] seamanship, art of navigation.

ναυτικόν, τό [navteekon] navy.

ναυτικός [navteekos] maritime ‖ nautical ‖ (ἄνδρας) seafarer.

ναυτιλία, ἡ [navteeleea] navigation ‖ shipping ‖ ναυτιλιακός marine, naval, nautical.

ναυτολογῶ [navtoloyo] enlist a crew, muster seamen.

ναυτόπαις, ὁ [navtopes] ship's boy, cabin boy.

νέα, ἡ [nea] girl ‖ τά ~ news.

νεανίας, ὁ [neaneeas] young man, lad, youth.

νεανικός [neaneekos] youthful, juvenile.

νεᾶνις, ἡ [neanees] girl, lass.

νεαρός [nearos] young ‖ youthful, juvenile.

νέγρος, ὁ [neyros] negro.

νέκρα, ἡ [nekra] dead silence, stagnation.

νεκρικός [nekreekos] of death, funeral ‖ gloomy.

νεκροθάπτης, ὁ [nekrothaptees] grave-digger ‖ (μεταφ) killjoy.

νεκροκεφαλή, ἡ [nekrokefalee] skull.

νεκρολογία, ἡ [nekroloyeea] obituary.

νεκρός [nekros] dead, lifeless ‖ (οὐσ) ὁ ~ dead person.

νεκροταφεῖον, τό [nekrotafeeon] cemetery, graveyard.

νεκροτομεῖον, τό [nekrotomeeon] mortuary.

νεκροφόρα, ἡ [nekrofora] hearse.

νεκροψία, ἡ [nekropseea] autopsy, post-mortem.

νεκρώνω [nekrono] deaden ‖ (τά πάθη) subdue.

νεκρώσιμος [nekroseemos] funeral.

νέκρωσις, ἡ [nekrosees] stagnation.

νέκταρ, τό [nektar] nectar.

νέμομαι [nemome] enjoy something, reap the profit from.

νέμω [nemo] distribute, share.

νέο, τό [neo] piece of news.

νεογέννητος [neoyeneetos] newborn.

νεογνόν, τό [neoynon] newborn animal ‖ newborn baby. ·

νεόδμητος [neoðmeetos] newly constructed.

νεοελληνικά, τά [neoeleeneeka] πλ modern Greek (language).

νεοελληνικός [neoeleeneekos] of modern Greece.

νεόκτιστος [neokteestos] βλ νεόδμητος.

νεολαία, ἡ [neolea] youth.

νεόνυμφος, ὁ, ἡ [neoneemfos] recently married man or woman.

νεόπλουτος [neoploutos] nouveau riche, parvenu.

νέος [neos] young ‖ (καινούριο) new, fresh ‖ (ἐπιπρόσθετο) further, · additional ‖ (σύγχρονος) modern ‖ (οὐσ) ὁ ~ a young man.

νεοσσός, ὁ [neosos] nestling, chick.

νεοσύλλεκτος, ὁ [neoseelektos] recruit.

νεοσύστατος [neoseestatos] newly-established, newly-founded.

νεότης, ἡ [neotees] βλ νεολαία.

νεράϊδα, ἡ [neraeeða] fairy, Nereid.

νεράντζι, τό [nerantzee] bitter orange.

νερό, τό [nero] water ‖ urine.

νερόβραστος [nerovrastos] boiled in water ‖ (μεταφ) insipid, tasteless.

νερομπογιά, ἡ [neromboyia] watercolour.

νερόμυλος, ὁ [neromeelos] water mill.

νεροποντή, ἡ [neropontee] shower of rain, downpour.

νερουλός [neroulos] watery, thin.

νερόχιονο, τό [neroheeono] sleet.

νεροχύτης, ὁ [neroheetees] kitchen sink.

νερώνω [nerono] mix with water.

νέτα σκέτα [netasketa] frankly, flatly.

νέτος [netos] net ‖ (μεταφ) done, finished, completed.

νεῦμα, τό [nevma] sign, nod, wink, beckoning.

νευραλγία, ή [nevralyeea] neuralgia.

νευραλγικός [nevralyeekos]: νευραλγικὸν σημεῖον weak spot.

νευριάζω [nevreeazo] make angry, irritate, vex ‖ become angry.

νευρικός [nevreekos] nervous ‖ excitable, highly strung.

νεῦρον, τό [nevron] nerve ‖ muscle ‖ vigour.

νευρόσπαστον, τό [nevrospaston] marionette ‖ (μεταφ) weak-willed person.

νευρώδης [nevrodees] sinewy ‖ nervous ‖ (μεταφ) strong, spirited.

νευρωτικός [nevroteekos] neurotic.

νεύω [nevo] nod, make a sign, beckon, wink.

νεφέλη, ή [nefelee] cloud.

νεφελώδης [nefelodees] cloudy, nebulous ‖ (μεταφ) vague, hazy.

νέφος, τό [nefos] cloud ‖ (μεταφ) gloom, shadow.

νεφοσκεπής [nefoskepees] cloudy, overcast.

νεφρόν, τό [nefron] kidney.

νέφτι, τό [neftee] turpentine, turps.

νεωκόρος, ὁ [neokoros] sacristan, verger.

νεώριον, τό [neoreeon] dry dock, dockyard.

νεωστί [neostee] lately, recently, newly.

νεωτερισμός, ὁ [neotereesmos] innovation ‖ novelty, fashion.

νεώτερα, τά [neotera] πλ latest news.

νεώτερος [neoteros] younger ‖ (γεγονός) recent, later ‖ (νέα) fresh.

νῆμα, τό [neema] thread ‖ (βαμβακερόν) linen thread ‖ (μάλλινο) yarn.

νηνεμία, ή [neenemeea] calmness, stillness.

νηολόγιον, τό [neeoloyeeon] register of merchant shipping.

νηοπομπή, ή [neeopompee] convoy, escort of ships.

νηοψία, ή [neeopseea] inspection or searching of ship.

νηπιαγωγεῖον, τό [neepeeayoyeeon] kindergarten.

νήπιον, τό [neepeeon] infant, baby, new-born child.

νησί, τό [neesee] island.

νησιώτης, ὁ [neeseeotees] islander.

νῆσος, ή [neesos] βλ νησί.

νῆσσα, ή [neesa] duck.

νηστεία, ή [neesteea] fast, fasting ‖ Lent.

νηστεύω [neestevo] fast, keep Lent.

νηστήσιμος [neesteeseemos] Lenten (food).

νηστικός [neesteekos] hungry.

νηφάλιος [neefaleeos] sober ‖ (μεταφ) calm, cool, composed.

νιαουρίζω [neeaoureezo] miaow, mew.

νιάτα, τά [neeata] πλ youth.

νίβω [neevo] βλ νίπτω.

νικέλιον, τό [neekeleeon] nickel.

νίκη, ή [neekee] victory, triumph.

νικητής, ὁ [neekeetees] victor ‖ (σέ παιχνίδι) winner.

νικηφόρος [neekeeforos] victorious, triumphant.

νικῶ [neeko] (τόν ἐχθρόν) defeat, vanquish ‖ (ἀνταγωνιστήν) beat, surpass ‖ (ἐμπόδια κτλ) surmount, overcome.

νίλα, ή [neela] practical joke ‖ calamity, ruin.

νιπτήρ, ὁ [neepteer] washbasin, washstand.

νίπτω [neepto] wash ‖ (μεταφ) wash out.

νισάφι, τό [neesafee] mercy, compassion, pity.

νίτρον, τό [neetron] nitre, saltpetre.

νιφάς, ή [neefas] snowflake.

Νοέμβρης, ὁ [noemvrees] November.

νοερός [noeros] mental, intellectual.

νόημα, τό [noeema] reflection, thought ‖ (ἔννοια) sense, meaning ‖ (νεῦμα) sign, wink.

νοημοσύνη, ή [noeemoseenee] intelligence, intellect.

νοήμων [noeemon] intelligent, smart.

νόησις, ή [noeesees] understanding, intellect ‖ mind, wit.

νοητός [noeetos] comprehensible, conceivable.

νοθεία, ή [notheea] falsification, adulteration.

νόθευσις, ή [nothevsees] adulteration, forgery.

νοθεύω [nothevo] falsify, forge, adulterate.

νόθος [nothos] bastard ‖ (ἐπί ζώων κτλ) hybrid ‖ (μεταφ) unstable.

νοιάζει [neeazee]: μέ ~ I care, I am anxious about.

νοιάζομαι [neeazome] care about, look after ‖ be anxious about.

νοῖκι, τό [neekee] rent ‖ νοικιάζω rent, hire, let out ‖ νοικάρης, ὁ tenant.

νοικοκυρά, ή [neekokera] housewife, mistress of the house ‖ landlady.

νοικοκύρης, ὁ [neekokeerees] landlord ‖ owner ‖ (αὐτεξούσιος) independent ‖ wise.

νοικοκυριό, τό [neekokeerio] housekeeping.

νοιώθω [neeotho] understand ‖ feel, perceive ‖ know.

νομαδικός [nomadeekos] nomadic, roving.

νομαρχεῖον, τό [nomarheeon] prefecture.

νομάρχης, ὁ [nomarhees] prefect, governor.

νομάς, ὁ [nomas] nomad, rover.

νομή, ή [nomee] pasture.

νομίζω [nomeezo] believe, think ‖ suppose, presume.

νομικά, τά [nomeeka] πλ law studies, jurisprudence.

νομική, ή [nomeekee] law.

νομικός [nomeekos] of the law, legal, lawful.

νομιμοποιῶ [nomeemopeeo] legitimize, legalize, validate.

νόμιμος [nomeemos] legal, lawful, rightful.

νομιμότης, ή [nomeemotees] legitimacy, legality.

νομιμόφρων [nomeemofron] law-abiding, obedient, loyal.

νόμισμα, τό [nomeesma] money, coin, currency.

νομισματολογία, ή [nomeesmatoloγeea] numismatics.

νομοθεσία, ή [nomotheseea] legislation, law-making.

νομοθέτης, ὁ [nomothetees] legislator, lawgiver.

νομομαθής, ὁ [nomomathees] jurist, legist.

νομός, ὁ [nomos] prefecture, province.

νόμος, ὁ [nomos] law, act (of Parliament) enactment.

νομοσχέδιον, τό [nomoshedeeon] bill, draft of a law.

νομοταγής [nomotaγees] law-abiding, loyal.

νονά, ή [nona] godmother, sponsor.

νονός, ὁ [nonos] godfather, sponsor.

νοοτροπία, ή [nootropeea] mentality, mental character.

νοσηλεία, ή [noseeleea] nursing, treatment, care of the sick.

νοσηλεύω [noseelevo] treat, tend, nurse.

νόσημα, τό [noseema] sickness, illness, disease, malady.

νοσηρός [noseeros] unhealthy, sickly, weakly || (περιέργεια) morbid.

νοσοκομεῖον, τό [nosokomeeon] hospital, infirmary.

νοσοκόμος, ὁ, ἡ [nosokomos] nurse || (στρατ) hospital orderly.

νόσος, ἡ [nosos] illness, disease, sickness.

νοσταλγία, ἡ [nostalγeea] nostalgia || homesickness.

νοσταλγικός [nostalγeekos] nostalgic || homesick.

νοσταλγῶ [nostalγo] feel nostalgic for || crave for || be homesick.

νοστιμάδα, ἡ [nosteemaδa] tastiness || prettiness || piquancy.

νοστιμεύω [nosteemevo] flavour, make tasty || make attractive.

νόστιμος [nosteemos] tasty || attractive, charming.

νοσῶ [noso] be sick, be ill.

νότα, ἡ [nota] (διπλωματική) note || (μουσ) note (mus).

νοτιά, ἡ [notia] south || south wind.

νοτίζω [noteezo] moisten, dampen || become damp.

νοτιοανατολικός [noteeoanatoleekos] south-eastern.

νοτιοδυτικός [noteeoδeeteekos] south-western.

νότιος [noteeos] southern.

νότος, ὁ [notos] south.

νουθεσία, ἡ [noutheseea] admonition, advice, counsel.

νουθετῶ [noutheto] admonish, advise, give advice to.

νούμερο, τό [noumero] number || (θεάτρου) act || odd character.

νουνεχής [nounehees] prudent, careful, wary.

νουνός, ὁ [nounos] godfather, sponsor.

νοῦς, ὁ [nous] mind, wit, intelligence, sense.

νούφαρο, τό [noufaro] water lily.

νοῶ [noo] comprehend, understand || think, reflect.

νταβᾶς, ὁ [ndavas] kind of baking tin or tray.

ντάης, ὁ [ndaees] bully, hector, ruffian.

ντάλια, ἡ [ndaleea] dahlia.

ντάμα, ἡ [ndama] lady || partner || (στά χαρτιά) queen || (παιχνίδι) game of draughts.

νταμιτζάνα, ἡ [ndameetzana] demijohn.

νταμπλᾶς, ὁ [ndamblas] apoplexy || (μεταφ) amazement, stupefaction.

νταντά, ἡ [ndanda] child's nurse, nanny.

νταντέλλα, ἡ [ndantela] lace.

νταούλι, τό [ndaoulee] drum.

νταραβέρι, τό [ndaraveree] relation, dealing || (φασαρία) fuss, trouble.

ντέ [nde]: ἔλα ~ (ἐπιφ) come on!, hurry up!

ντεπόζιτο, τό [ndepozeeto] cistern || tank.

ντέρτι, τό [ndertee] regret, pain, sorrow || longing, yearning.

ντιβάνι, τό [ndeevanee] divan.

ντολμᾶς, ὁ [ndolmas] stuffed vine || stuffed cabbage.

ντομάτα, ἡ [ndomata] tomato.

ντόμπρος [ndombros] sincere, candid, frank, honest.

ντόπιος [ndopeeos] local, native.

ντόρος, ὁ [ndoros] trouble, din || (μεταφ) sensation.

ντουβάρι, τό [ndouvaree] wall || (μεταφ) fool.

ντουέτο, τό [ndoueto] duet.

ντουζίνα, ἡ [ndouzeena] dozen.

ντουλάπα, ἡ [ndoulapa] wardrobe.

ντουλάπι, τό [ndoulapee] cupboard.

ντουνιᾶς, ὁ [ndounias] people, mankind, humanity.

ντοῦρος [ndouros] hard, firm || obstinate.

ντούς, τό [ndous] shower bath.

ντρέπομαι [ndrepome] be bashful || be ashamed.

ντροπαλός [ndropalos] shy, modest, timid.

ντροπή, ἡ [ndropee] shame || modesty, bashfulness.

ντροπιάζω [ndropeeazo] shame.

ντυμένος [ndeemenos] dressed.

ντύνομαι [ndeenome] get dressed.

ντύνω [ndeeno] dress || (ἔπιπλα) upholster.

ντύσιμο, τό [ndeeseemo] dressing || attire, outfit, dress.

νῦ, τό [nee] the letter N.

νυγμός, ὁ [neeγmos] bite, prick || (μεταφ) hint, allusion.

νυκτερινός [neektereenos] of night, nocturnal.

νυκτόβιος [neektoveeos] living by night.

νυκτοφύλαξ, ὁ [neektofeelaks] night watchman.

νύκτωρ [neektor] by night.

νυμφεύω [neemfevo] marry, wed.

νύμφη, ἡ [neemfee] bride || (μυθολογία) nymph || (ζωολ) larva.

νῦν [neen] now, at present.

νύξ, ἡ [neeks] night, darkness.

νύξις, ἡ [neeksees] βλ νυγμός.

νύστα, ἡ [neesta] sleepiness, drowsiness.

νυστάζω [neestazo] be sleepy, feel sleepy.

νυσταλέος [neestaleos] sleepy || (μεταφ) dull, sluggish.

νύφη, ἡ [neefee] βλ νύμφη.

νυφικός [neefeekos] bridal, nuptial.

νυφίτσα, ἡ [neefeetsa] weasel.

νυχθημερόν [neehtheemerón] day and night.

νύχι, τό [neehee] nail || (ποδιῶν) toenail || (ζώου) claw, talon || ~α, τά clutches.

νυχιά, ἡ [neehia] scratch.

νύχτα, ἡ [neehta] night, darkness || (ἐπιρ) at night, by night.

νυχτερίδα, ἡ [neehtereeδa] bat.

νυχτικό, τό [neehteeko] nightgown.

νυχτώνω [neehtono]: νυχτώνει night falls.

νωθρός [nothros] sluggish, lazy, slothful.

νωματάρχης, ὁ [nomatarhees] sergeant.

νωπός [nopos] fresh, new, recent || (γιά ροῦχα) still damp.

νωρίς [norees] early.

νῶτα, τά [nota] πλ back || (στρατ) rear.

νωχελής [nohelees] indolent, idle, slothful.

Ξ, ξ

ξαγρυπνῶ [ksayreepno] stay awake || watch over || burn the midnight oil.

ξαδέρφη, ἡ [ksaδerfee] cousin.

ξάδερφος, ὁ [ksaδerfos] cousin.

ξαίρω [ksero] know, know how to.

ξακουστός [ksakoustos] renowned, celebrated, famous.

ξαλαφρώνω [ksalafrono] lighten the load of, help || (μεταφ) relieve || relieve one's mind.

ξανά [ksana] again, afresh, anew.

ξαναβάζω [ksanavazo] put back again, replace.

ξανάβω [ksanavo] irritate || become annoyed, get furious.

ξαναγυρίζω [ksanayeereezo] return, send back || turn again.

ξαναδίνω [ksanaδeeno] return, restore.

ξανακάνω [ksanakano] redo, remake, repeat.

ξαναλέω [ksanaleo] repeat, reiterate.

ξανανιώνω [ksananeeono] rejuvenate || become young again.

ξαναπαθαίνω [ksanapatheno] be taken in again || suffer again.

ξαναπαίρνω [ksanaperno] take again || (θάρρος) pluck up again || (ὑπάλληλος) take on again, rehire || (θέση) go back to.

ξαναπαντρεύομαι [ksanapandrevome] remarry.

ξαναρχῆς [ksanarhees] from the beginning, again.

ξανασαίνω [ksanaseno] recover, refresh o.s., relax.

ξαναφορτώνω [ksanafortono] reload.

ξανθίζω [ksantheezo] become fairer.

ξανθομάλλης [ksanthomalees] fair-haired.

ξανθός [ksanthos] blond, fair, light || (στάχυς) yellow, golden.

ξάνοιγμα, τό [ksaneeyma] clearing up, brightening || launching out.

ξανοίγομαι [ksaneeyome] confide one's secrets || spend freely.

ξανοίγω [ksaneeyo] (μεταφ) look, see || clear up.

ξάπλα, ἡ [ksapla] sprawling around || lying down.

ξάπλωμα, τό [ksaploma] lying down || stretching out, spreading.

ξαπλώνομαι [ksaplonome] spread || lie down.

ξαπλώνω [ksaplono] spread out || lie down.

ξαπλωτός [ksaplotos] reclining, lying down.

ξαποσταίνω [ksaposteno] rest, relax.

ξαποστέλνω [ksapostelno] send off, forward || dismiss.

ξασπρίζω [ksaspreezo] whiten || blanch, pale, fade.

ξάστερα [ksastera] frankly, flatly, categorically.

ξάστερος [ksasteros] cloudless, bright || (μεταφ) lucid, clear.

ξαφνιάζομαι [ksafneeazome] be taken by surprise, be frightened.

ξαφνιάζω [ksafneeazo] startle, surprise, frighten, scare.

ξαφνικά [ksafneeka] all of a sudden.

ξαφνικό, τό [ksafneeko] surprise || accident, mishap.

ξαφνικός [ksafneekos] unexpected.

ξάφνου [ksafnou] βλ ξαφνικά.

ξαφρίζω [ksafreezo] skim || (μεταφ) steal.

ξάφρισμα, τό [ksafreesma] skimming || frothing.

ξεβάφω [ksevafo] fade || lose colour, discolour.

ξεβγάζω [ksevyazo] wash out || (προπέμπω) show out, get rid of.

ξεβρακώνω [ksevrakono] take off the trousers.

ξεβράκωτος [ksevrakotos] trouserless || (μεταφ) penniless.

ξεβρωμίζω [ksevromeezo] disinfect || clean, remove the dirt.

ξεγελῶ [kseyelo] cheat, dupe, deceive.

ξεγεννώ [kseyeno] deliver a child ‖ be delivered of.

ξεγνοιάζω [kseyneeazo] be free from care.

ξεγράφω [kseyrafo] efface, strike out ‖ (μεταφ) wipe out ‖ write off.

ξεδιαλέγω [ksedeealeyo] select, choose, sort.

ξεδιαλύνω [ksedeealeeno] get to the bottom of, unravel.

ξεδιάντροπος [ksedeeantropos] immodest, brazen.

ξεδιπλώνω [ksedeeplono] unfurl, open out, spread.

ξεδιψώ [ksedeepso] quench one's thirst ‖ refresh.

ξεθαρρεύω [kstharevo] become too bold.

ξεθεώνω [kstheono] wear out, exhaust, harass, worry.

ξεθυμαίνω [kstheemeno] escape, leak out ‖ (μεταφ) calm down, abate.

ξεθωριάζω [ksthoreeazo] fade ‖ lose colour, discolour.

ξεκαθαρίζω [ksekathareezo] liquidate, settle accounts ‖ elucidate ‖ kill off.

ξεκάνω [ksekano] sell off ‖ kill, exterminate.

ξεκαρδίζομαι [ksekardeezome] burst out laughing.

ξεκάρφωτος [ksekarfotos] (μεταφ) unconnected, irrelevant.

ξεκινώ [ksekeeno] set off, start, depart ‖ drive off.

ξεκοκκαλίζω [ksekokaleezo] eat to the bone ‖ (μεταφ) spend foolishly.

ξεκομμένα [ksekomena] to the point, frankly.

ξεκομμένη [ksekomenee]: τιμή ~ fixed price.

ξεκούμπωτος [ksekoumbotos] unfastened, unbuttoned.

ξεκουμπώνω [ksekoumbono] unbutton, unfasten.

ξεκουράζομαι [ksekourazome] relax, rest.

ξεκουράζω [ksekourazo] rest, relieve, refresh, repose.

ξεκουφαίνω [ksekoufeno] deafen, stun.

ξελιγωμένος [kseleeyomenos] be hungry for, hunger for.

ξελιγώνω [kseleeyono] (μεταφ) wear o.s. out, tire.

ξελογιάζω [kseloyeeazo] seduce, lead astray, fascinate.

ξεμαλλιασμένος [ksemaleeasmenos] dishevelled.

ξεμοναχιάζω [ksemonaheeazo] take aside.

ξεμπαρκάρω [ksembarkaro] land ‖ unload.

ξεμπερδεύω [ksemberdevo] unravel, disentangle ‖ get clear of, get rid of.

ξεμπλέκω [ksembleko] free o.s. ‖ ~ από get free of.

ξεμυαλίζω [ksemeealeezo] infatuate, turn the head of, lead astray.

ξένα, τά [ksena] πλ foreign parts.

ξεναγός, ὁ, ἡ [ksenayos] tourist guide.

ξενητειά, ἡ [kseneetia] foreign parts, foreign country.

ξενητεύομαι [kseneetevome] live abroad.

ξενίζομαι [kseneezome] be astonished.

ξενίζω [kseneezo] surprise, astonish.

ξενικός [kseneekos] foreign, alien, outlandish.

ξεν(ν)οιάζω [kseneeazo] be free from cares.

ξενοδοχεῖον, τό [ksenodoheeon] hotel.

ξενοδόχος, ὁ [ksenodohos] hotelier, innkeeper.

ξενοικιάζομαι [kseneekeeazome] become vacant.

ξένος [ksenos] foreign, strange, unfamiliar ‖ (οὐσ) ὁ ~ foreigner, stranger ‖ visitor.

ξενοφοβία, ἡ [ksenofoveea] xenophobia.

ξενόφωνος [ksenofonos] foreign-speaking.

ξεντύνω [ksenteeno] undress, disrobe.

ξενυχτῶ [kseneehto] stay up late, stay out all night.

ξενών, ὁ [ksenon] spare room, guest room.

ξεπαγιάζω [ksepayeeazo] freeze ‖ get frozen.

ξεπαστρεύω [ksepastrevo] exterminate, wipe out.

ξεπατώνω [ksepatono] (μεταφ) exhaust, tire, overwork.

ξεπερασμένος [kseperasmenos] out-of-date, old-fashioned.

ξεπερνώ [kseperno] surpass, overtake ‖ (σέ δρόμο) outrun ‖ (σέ ὕψος) be taller.

ξεπεσμός, ὁ [ksepesmos] decay, decline ‖ (τιμῶν) fall ‖ (νομίσματος) depreciation.

ξεπετιέμαι [ksepetieme] jump up suddenly, shoot up.

ξεπέφτω [ksepefto] reduce, abate ‖ (ἐπί τιμῶν) fall ‖ (μεταφ) fall into disrepute.

ξεπηδῶ [ksepeedo] jump out suddenly.

ξεπλένω [ksepleno] rinse.

ξεπληρώνω [kspleerono] pay off, discharge (a debt).

ξέπλυμα, τό [kspleema] rinsing.

ξεπούλημα, τό [kspouleema] sale, sellout, liquidation ‖ (US) fire sale.

ξεπουλῶ [kspoulo] sell off ‖ sell out, liquidate.

ξεπροβοδίζω [kseprovodeezo] escort off, say goodbye to.

ξέρα, ἡ [ksera] (θαλάσσης) rock, reef ‖ (καιροῦ) drought, dryness.

ξεραΐλα, ἡ [kseraeela] aridity, dryness, drought.

ξεραίνομαι [kserenome] dry up, wither, get parched.

ξεραίνω [ksereno] dry up ‖ parch, bake ‖ (φυτά) wither.

ξερακιανός [kserakeeanos] thin, lean, skinny.

ξέρασμα, τό [kserasma] vomiting.

ξερνῶ [kserno] vomit, bring up ‖ belch out.

ξερόβηχας, ὁ [kseroveehas] dry cough.

ξεροβούνι, τό [kserovounee] bare mountain, naked mountain.

ξεροκαταπίνω [kserokatapeeno] swallow with embarrassment.

ξεροκέφαλος [kserokefalos] thickheaded ‖ obstinate, stubborn.

ξερονήσι, τό [kseroneesee] barren island, desert island.

ξερός [kseros] arid, dry, barren ‖ (γλώσσα) parched ‖ (ύφος) curt, snappish ‖ έμεινε ~ he was stumped ‖ he dropped dead ‖ έπεσε ~ στόν ύπνο he dropped off to sleep.

ξερ(ρ)ιζώνω [ksereezono] pull up, uproot ‖ root out, wipe out.

ξέρω [ksero] know how to, understand, be aware of.

ξεσηκώνω [kseseekono] rouse, excite ‖ (σχέδιο) transfer, copy.

ξεσκάζω [kseskazo] refresh o.s., relax.

ξεσκεπάζω [kseskepazo] unveil, uncover ‖ reveal, disclose, let out.

ξεσκίζω [kseskeezo] rip up.

ξεσκονίζω [kseskoneezo] dust, give a dusting to.

ξεσκονιστήρι, τό [kseskoneesteeree] feather duster.

ξεσκονόπανο, τό [kseskonopano] duster, dust rag.

ξεσκούφωτος [kseskoufotos] bare-headed.

ξεσπάζω [ksespazo] (μεταφ) burst into, burst out.

ξεσπαθώνω [ksespathono] unsheathe one's sword.

ξεστομίζω [ksestomeezo] utter, launch, hurl.

ξεστραβώνω [ksestravono] straighten out ‖ become straight.

ξεστρώνω [ksestrono] take up, remove ‖ (τραπέζι) clear away.

ξέστρωτος [ksestrotos] unmade ‖ unpaved.

ξεσχίζω [ksescheezo] tear to pieces, lacerate.

ξετινάζω [kseteenazo] toss, shake, beat ‖ (μεταφ) reduce to poverty.

ξετρελλαίνω [ksetreleno] drive mad, bewilder ‖ (άπό έρωτα) bewitch.

ξετρυπώνω [ksetreepono] appear suddenly, crop up.

ξετσίπωτος [ksetseepotos] shameless.

ξεύρω [ksevro] βλ ξέρω.

ξεφαντώνω [ksefantono] live fast, feast, revel.

ξεφεύγω [ksefevgo] elude ‖ slip out.

ξεφλουδίζω [ksefloudeezo] peel ‖ pare ‖ shell ‖ (τό δέρμα) lose the skin.

ξεφορτώνομαι [ksefortonome] get rid of, shake off.

ξεφορτώνω [ksefortono] unload ‖ (μεταφ) get rid of.

ξεφτέρι, τό [ksefteree] sharp person, witty person.

ξεφτίζω [ksefteezo] fray out ‖ (νήμα) pull out, unweave.

ξεφυλλίζω [ksefeeleezo] skim over, run through ‖ strip the leaves, pluck.

ξεφυτρώνω [ksefeetrono] sprout, shoot up ‖ appear suddenly.

ξεφωνητό, τό [ksefoneeto] yell, shout, outcry, scream.

ξεφωνίζω [ksefoneezo] shout, bawl, yell, scream.

ξεχαρβαλωμένος [kseharvalomenos] shaky, loose, falling apart.

ξεχασμένος [ksehasmenos] forgotten.

ξεχειλίζω [kseheeleezo] overflow, run over.

ξεχειμωνιάζω [kseheemoneeazo] pass the winter, winter.

ξεχνώ [ksehno] forget, leave out, neglect.

ξεχρεώνω [ksehreono] pay up, discharge ‖ settle, fulfil.

ξεχύνομαι [kseheenome] overflow.

ξεχύνω [kseheeno] pour out, overflow.

ξέχωρα [ksehora] apart, separately ‖ ~ άπό apart from.

ξεχωρίζω [ksehoreezo] separate ‖ single out ‖ distinguish, discern ‖ make one's mark.

ξεχωριστά [ksehoreesta] separately.

ξεχωριστός [ksehoreestos] separate ‖ distinct, peculiar ‖ distinguished, exceptional.

ξεψυχώ [ksepseeho] die, expire, give up the ghost.

ξέω [kseo] scratch, scrape ‖ erase.

ξηλώνω [kseelono] take apart, unstitch.

ξημερώματα [kseemeromata] πλ daybreak, dawn.

ξημερώνομαι [kseemeronome] stay awake till morning.

ξηρά, ή [kseera] dry land, mainland.

ξηραίνομαι [kseerenome] dry up, get parched, wither.

ξηραίνω [kseereno] dry, drain.

ξηραντήριον, τό [kseeranteereeon] drier.

ξηρασία, ή [kseeraseea] aridity ‖ drought.

ξηροί [kseeree]: ~ καρποί πλ dried fruit and nuts.

ξῖ, τό [ksee] the letter Ξ.

ξινάρι, τό [kseenaree] pickaxe.

ξινίζω [kseeneezo] turn sour, get sour.

ξινίλα, ή [kseeneela] bitterness, acidity, tartness, sharpness.

ξινό, τό [kseeno] citric acid.

ξινός [kseenos] sour, acid, sharp ‖ (έπί φρούτων) unripe, green.

ξιππασμένος [kseepasmenos] vain, conceited.

ξιππάζω [kseepazo] frighten ‖ impress.

ξιφασκία, ή [kseefaskia] fencing, swordplay.

ξιφίας, ό [kseefeeas] swordfish.

ξιφολόγχη, ή [kseefolonghee] bayonet.

ξιφομαχώ [kseefomaho] fence.

ξίφος, τό [kseefos] sword ‖ (ξιφομαχίας) foil.

ξόβεργα, ή [ksoverγa] lime twig.

ξοδεύομαι [ksodevome] spend, incur expenses.

ξοδεύω [ksoðevo] spend, use up, consume, expend.

ξόμπλι, τό [ksomblee] pattern for embroidery.

ξόρκι, τό [ksorkee] exorcism ‖ entreaty.

ξουρίζω [ksoureezo] βλ ξυρίζω.

ξύγκι, τό [kseengee] fat, lard, grease, tallow.

ξυδᾶτος [kseeðatos] pickled.

ξύδι, τό [kseeðee] vinegar.

ξυλάδικο, τό [kseelaðeeko] timberyard, woodyard.

ξυλάνθραξ, ὁ [kseelanthraks] charcoal.

ξυλεία, ἡ [kseeleea] timber, lumber.

ξύλινος [kseeleenos] wooden, wood.

ξύλο, τό [kseelo] wood ‖ τρώω ~ receive a beating ‖ ἔπεσε ~ there was a fight.

ξυλογράφημα, τό [kseeloyrafeema] woodcut, wood engraving.

ξυλοκάρβουνο, τό [kseelokarvouno] charcoal.

ξυλοκέρατο, τό [kseelokerato] carob.

ξυλοκόπος, ὁ [kseelokopos] woodcutter, lumberjack.

ξυλοκοπῶ [kseelokopo] thrash, beat soundly.

ξυλοκρέββατο, τό [kseelokrevato] wooden bedstead ‖ (μεταφ) coffin.

ξυλοπόδαρο, τό [kseeloroðaro] stilt.

ξυλοστάτης, ὁ [kseelostatees] jamb.

ξυλουργική, ἡ [kseelouryeekee] joinery, carpentry.

ξυλουργός, ὁ [kseelouryos] joiner, carpenter.

ξυλοφορτώνω [kseelofortono] thrash, leather, lick.

ξύνομαι [kseenome] scratch (o.s.).

ξύνω [kseeno] scratch, scrape ‖ (μολύβι) sharpen ‖ scrape off.

ξύπνημα, τό [kseepneema] awakening, waking up.

ξυπνητήρι, τό [kseepneeteeree] alarm clock.

ξύπνιος [kseepneeos] wakeful, awake ‖ (μεταφ) alert, clever, intelligent.

ξυπνῶ [kseepno] wake up, rouse.

ξυπόλυτος [kseepoleetos] barefooted, shoeless.

ξυράφι, τό [kseerafee] razor.

ξυραφάκι, τό [kseerafakee] razor blade.

ξυρίζομαι [kseereezome] shave, get shaved, have a shave.

ξυρίζω [kseereezo] shave.

ξύρισμα, τό [kseereesma] shave, shaving.

ξυριστική [kseereesteekee]: ~ μηχανή safety razor.

ξύσιμο, τό [kseeseemo] scratching, scraping ‖ rubbing, erasing ‖ sharpening.

ξυστήρ, ὁ [kseesteer] βλ ξύστρα.

ξυστός [kseestos] grated, scratched.

ξύστρα, ἡ [kseestra] grater, scraper, rasp ‖ pencil sharpener.

ξύω [kseeo] βλ ξύνω.

ξωκκλήσι, τό [ksokleesee] country chapel.

ξωτικιά, ἡ [ksoteekia] fairy, sprite.

ξωτικό, τό [ksoteeko] ghost, spirit, goblin.

ξώφυλλο, τό [ksofeelo] book cover ‖ (παραθύρου) outside shutter.

Ο, ο

ὁ [o] the.

ὄασις [oasees] oasis.

ὀβελίας, ὁ [oveleeas] lamb on the spit.

ὀβελίσκος, ὁ [oveleeskos] small spit ‖ (στήλη) obelisk.

ὀβίδα, ἡ [oveeða] shell.

ὀβίς, ἡ [ovees] βλ ὀβίδα.

ὀβολός, ὁ [ovolos] mite, contribution.

ὀγδοήκοντα [oyðoeekonta] eighty.

ὀγδοηκοστός, ὁ [oyðoeekostos] eightieth.

ὄγδοος [oyðoos] eighth.

ὀγκηθμός, ὁ [ongeethmos] braying.

ὀγκόλιθος, ὁ [ongoleethos] block of stone.

ὄγκος, ὁ [ongos] volume, mass, bulk, lump ‖ (ἰατρ) tumour.

ὀγκοῦμαι [ongoume] swell, grow fatter ‖ (μεταφ) increase, swell.

ὀγκώδης [ongoðees] voluminous, massive ‖ (ἄτομον) stout, portly.

ὀδαλίσκη, ἡ [oðaleeskee] odalisque.

ὅδε [oðe] this.

ὁδεύω [oðevo] walk, tramp, trudge ‖ accompany ‖ (πρός) proceed, advance.

ὁδηγητής, ὁ [oðeeyeetees] guide.

ὁδηγία, ἡ [oðeeyeea] direction, guidance ‖ instruction, directions, orders.

ὁδηγός, ὁ [oðeeyos] guide, conductor ‖ (αὐτοκινήτου) driver, chauffeur.

ὁδηγῶ [oðeeyo] guide, lead ‖ (αὐτοκίνητον κτλ) drive ‖ show how to, instruct.

ὁδογέφυρα, ἡ [oðoyefeera] viaduct.

ὁδοιπορία, ἡ [oðeeporeea] walk, journey ‖ march.

ὁδοιπορικά, τά [oðeeporeeka] πλ: ~ ἔξοδα travelling expenses.

ὁδοιπόρος, ὁ, ἡ [oðeeporos] traveller, voyager.

ὁδοιπορῶ [oðeeporo] walk, tramp ‖ march ‖ travel.

ὁδοκαθαριστής, ὁ [oðokatha̱reestees] street sweeper.

ὁδόμετρον, τό [oðometron] pedometer.

ὀδονταλγία, ἡ [oðontalyeea] toothache.

ὀδοντιατρεῖον, τό [oðonteeatreeon] dentist's surgery, dental clinic.

ὀδοντιατρική, ἡ [oðonteeatreekee] dentistry.

ὀδοντίατρος, ὁ, ἡ [oðonteeatros] dentist.

ὀδοντόβουρτσα, ἡ [oðontovourtsa] toothbrush.

ὀδοντογλυφίδα, ἡ [oðontoyleefeeða] toothpick.

ὀδοντόκονις, ἡ [oðontokonees] dentifrice, tooth powder.

ὀδοντόπονος, ὁ [odontoponos] toothache.
ὀδοντοστοιχία, ἡ [odontosteeheea] (set of) false teeth.
ὀδοντόφωνος [odontofonos] (γραμμ) dental.
ὀδοντωτός [odontotos] toothed, jagged, cogged ‖ ~ σιδηρόδρομος funicular railway.
ὀδοποιία, ἡ [odopieea] road construction, roadmaking.
ὀδός, ἡ [odos] street ‖ (εὐρεῖα) main street, thoroughfare ‖ (ἐθνική) state highway ‖ (ἐμπορική) trade route ‖ καθ' ὁδόν on the way, along the road.
ὀδόστρωμα, τό [odostroma] road surface.
ὀδοστρωτήρ, ὁ [odostroteer] steamroller.
ὀδούς [odous] βλ δόντι.
ὀδόφραγμα, τό [odofrayma] barricade, roadblock, barrier.
ὀδύνη, ἡ [odeenee] pain, suffering ‖ (ἠθική) grief ‖ affliction.
ὀδυνηρός [odeeneeros] (πληγή) painful ‖ (μέρος) sore ‖ (θέαμα) harrowing.
ὀδυρμός, ὁ [odeermos] lamentation, wailing.
ὀδύρομαι [odeerome] lament, complain, moan.
ὄζον, τό [ozon] ozone.
ὄζος, ὁ [ozos] knot ‖ (τῶν δακτύλων) knuckles.
ὀζώδης [ozodees] knotty, gnarled.
ὅθεν [othen] whence, thence, then, therefore.
ὁθενδήποτε [othendeepote] from any place, from anywhere.
ὀθόνη, ἡ [othonee] linen ‖ (τραπέζης) table linen ‖ (κλίνης) linen sheet ‖ (κινηματογράφου) screen.
Ὀθωμανός, ὁ [othomanos] Ottoman.
οἰακίζω [eeakeezo] steer, pilot.
οἴαξ, ὁ [eeaks] tiller, helm.
οἴδημα, τό [eedeema] swelling.
οἴκαδε [eekade] at home ‖ homeward.
οἰκειοθελῶς [eekeeothelos] (ὑπακούω) voluntarily ‖ (κάνω κάτι) purposely, wilfully.
οἰκειοποίησις, ἡ [eekeeopieesees] appropriation.
οἰκειοποιοῦμαι [eekeeopeeoume] appropriate to o.s., usurp.
οἰκεῖος [eekeeos] intimate, familiar ‖ sociable, affable ‖ οἱ οἰκεῖοι relatives, close relations.
οἰκειότης, ἡ [eekeeotees] familiarity, closeness.
οἰκείως [eekeeos] intimately, closely.
οἴκημα, τό [eekeema] dwelling, lodging, habitation.
οἴκησις, ἡ [eekeesees] inhabiting, habitation.
οἰκία, ἡ [eekeea] house, home.
οἰκιακός [eekeeakos] domestic, home ‖ (ζῷον) domesticated.
οἰκίζω [eekeezo] inhabit, colonize, settle.
οἰκίσκος, ὁ [eekeeskos] cottage ‖ (σκύλου)

dog kennel ‖ (ξυλοκόπου) cabin, hut ‖ (φύλακος) lodge.
οἰκισμός, ὁ [eekeesmos] settling, colonizing.
οἰκιστής, ὁ [eekeestees] settler, colonist.
οἰκογένεια, ἡ [eekoyeneea] family.
οἰκογενειακός [eekoyeneeakos] of the family.
οἰκογενειακῶς [eekoyeneeakos] with the entire family.
οἰκοδέσποινα, ἡ [eekoδespeena] lady of the house, hostess.
οἰκοδεσπότης, ὁ [eekoδespotees] master of the house, host.
οἰκοδομή, ἡ [eekoδomee] construction, act of building ‖ building under construction.
οἰκοδόμημα, τό [eekoδomeema] building, structure.
οἰκοδόμησις, ἡ [eekoδomeesees] construction, building, erection.
οἰκοδομική, ἡ [eekoδomeekee] building.
οἰκοδομικός [eekoδomeekos] constructive.
οἰκοδομῶ [eekoδomo] build, construct, raise.
οἴκοθεν [eekothen]: ~ ἐννοεῖται it is obvious.
οἴκοι [eekee] at home.
οἰκοκυρά [eekokeera] βλ νοικοκυρά.
οἰκοκύρης [eekokeerees] βλ νοικοκύρης.
οἰκονομία, ἡ [eekonomeea] economy, husbandry, thrift ‖ saving.
οἰκονομικά, τά [eekonomeeka] πλ finances ‖ (ἐπιρ) reasonably, cheaply.
οἰκονομικός [eekonomeekos] economic, financial ‖ (φθηνά) reasonable, cheap.
οἰκονόμος, ὁ, ἡ [eekonomos] steward, stewardess ‖ (μεταφ) thrifty person.
οἰκονομῶ [eekonomo] save, economize ‖ find, get hold of ‖ τά ~ make ends meet, make money.
οἰκόπεδον, τό [eekopeδon] building site, plot.
οἶκον [eekon]: κατ' ~ at home.
οἶκος, ὁ [eekos] house ‖ business house.
οἰκοτροφεῖον, τό [eekotrofeeon] boarding school.
οἰκότροφος, ὁ, ἡ [eekotrofos] boarder.
οἰκουμένη, ἡ [eekoumenee] world, universe.
οἰκουμενική [eekoumeneekee]: ~ κυβέρνησις coalition government.
οἰκουρῶ [eekouro] be confined by illness, keep indoors.
οἰκτείρω [eekteero] feel compassion for, pity ‖ despise, scorn.
οἶκτος, τό [eektos] compassion, pity ‖ contempt, scorn.
οἰκτρός [eektros] deplorable ‖ wretched, miserable.
οἴμοι [eemee] (ἐπιφ) alas!, woe is me!
οἰμωγή, ἡ [eemoyee] lamentation, wailing, moaning.
οἰνόπνευμα, τό [eenopnevma] alcohol ‖ οἰνοπνευματώδης alcoholic.
οἶνος, ὁ [eenos] wine.

οἶον [eeon] such as, for example.
οἱονεί [eeonee] as if, as it were.
οἷος [eeos] such as, who, which, what.
οἱοσδήποτε [eeosdeepote] any(body) ‖ any kind of, whoever, whichever.
οἰσοφάγος, ὁ [eesofayos] oesophagus.
οἶστρος, ὁ [eestros] gadfly ‖ (μεταφ) inspiration, goading.
οἰωνός, ὁ [eeonos] omen, presage, portent.
ὀκνηρός [okneeros] lazy, idle, sluggish.
ὄκνος [oknos] nonchalant, languid, slack.
ὀκρίβας, ὁ [okreevas] easel.
ὀκτάγωνος [oktayonos] octagonal.
ὀκτακόσιοι [oktakosiee] eight hundred.
ὀκταπόδι, τό [oktapodee] octopus.
ὀκτώ [octo] eight.
Ὀκτώβριος, ὁ [oktovreeos] October.
ὅλα, τά [ola] πλ everything ‖ ~ κι' ~ anything else but.
ὁλάκερα [olakera] entirely, completely, wholly.
ὁλάκερος [olakeros] whole, entire, total, complete.
ὄλβιος [olveeos] happy, blissful ‖ wealthy, rich.
ὀλέθριος [olethreeos] ominous, disastrous, destructive.
ὄλεθρος, ὁ [olethros] calamity, destruction, ruin.
ὁλημερίς [oleemerees] all day long.
ὀλιγάκις [oleeyakees] seldom, rarely.
ὀλιγάριθμος [oleeyareethmos] few in number, a few.
ὀλιγαρκής [oleeyarkees] temperate, frugal, moderate.
ὀλιγαρχία, ἡ [oleeyarheea] oligarchy.
ὀλίγιστος [oleeyeestos] very little, tiny.
ὀλιγόλογος [oleeyoloyos] concise, succinct ‖ taciturn.
ὀλίγον [oleeyon] (a) little.
ὀλίγος [oleeyos] short, a little, a few ‖ ὀλίγον κατ' ὀλίγον gradually ‖ παρ' ὀλίγον νά nearly, almost.
ὀλιγοστεύω [oleeyostevo] diminish, decrease, lessen.
ὀλιγοστός [oleeyostos] scarcely enough, scanty, inconsiderable.
ὀλιγοψυχία, ἡ [oleeyopseeheea] timidity.
ὀλιγωρία, ἡ [oleeyoreea] negligence, neglect, indifference.
ὁλικός [oleekos] total, whole, complete.
ὁλικῶς [oleekos] totally, utterly.
ὀλισθαίνω [oleestheno] slip, slide ‖ (μεταφ) lapse into, slip into.
ὀλίσθημα, τό [oleestheema] slip(ping), slide ‖ mistake, fault.
ὀλισθηρός [oleestheeros] slippery, greasy.
ὁλκή, ἡ [olkee] attraction, pull, weight ‖ calibre, bore.
ὅλμος, ὁ [olmos] mortar.
ὅλο [olo] all ‖ ~ καί (περισσότερο) more and more, always.
ὁλογράφως [oloyrafos] written in full.

ὁλόγυρα [oloyeera] all round, in a circle.
ὁλοέν(α) [oloen(a)] incessantly, constantly.
ὁλοήμερος [oloeemeros] lasting a whole day.
ὁλοΐδιος [oloeedeeos] the spitting image.
ὁλοΐσιος [oloeeseeos] direct, straight ‖ upright.
ὁλοκαύτωμα, τό [olokavtoma] holocaust ‖ sacrifice.
ὁλόκληρος [olokleeros] entire, whole, full, complete.
ὁλοκληρῶ [olokleero] complete, finish ‖ (μαθημ) integrate.
ὁλοκληρωτικός [olokleeroteekos] full, entire, complete ‖ totalitarian ‖ (μαθημ) integral.
ὁλολύζω [ololeezo] lament, howl, bewail.
ὁλόμαλλος [olomalos] all wool, pure wool.
ὁλομέλεια, ἡ [olomeleea] total membership, all members present.
ὁλομερής [olomerees] entire, whole, complete.
ὁλομόναχος [olomonahos] quite alone.
ὁλονέν [olonen] always.
ὁλονυχτίς [oloneehtees] the whole night long.
ὁλόρθος [olorthos] straight, upright, standing.
ὅλος [olos] all, whole ‖ ὅλοι everyone, everybody ‖ ὅλοι μας all of us, altogether ‖ ὅλα ὅλα altogether, the total.
ὁλοσχερής [olosherees] utter, complete, full, entire.
ὁλοταχῶς [olotahos] at full speed, at top speed.
ὁλότελα [olotela] entirely, altogether, completely.
ὁλότης, ἡ [olotees] entirety, totality.
ὁλοῦθε [olouthe] from all sides, everywhere, from all directions.
ὁλοφάνερος [olofaneros] obvious, plain, clear.
ὁλοφύρομαι [olofeerome] βλ ὁλολύζω.
ὁλόχαρος [oloharos] joyful, happy.
ὁλοχρονίς [olohronees] throughout the year.
ὁλόχρυσος [olohreesos] all gold, solid gold.
ὁλόψυχος [olopseehos] wholeheartedly.
Ὀλυμπιακός [oleembeeakos] Olympic.
ὅλως [olos] wholly, altogether, totally ‖ ~ διόλου completely, wholly ‖ ~ ὑμέτερος yours truly.
ὁμάδα, ἡ [omada] βλ ὁμάς.
ὁμάδι [omadee] together.
ὁμαδικός [omadeekos] collective, en masse.
ὁμαδικῶς [omadeekos] in a body, collectively.
ὁμαλός [omalos] even ‖ level ‖ smooth, regular ‖ (βίος) uneventful ‖ flat.
ὁμαλότης, ἡ [omalotees] regularity, smoothness, evenness.
ὁμάς, ἡ [omas] group, company, band, gang ‖ (ἀθλητική) team.

ὄμβριος [omvreeos] of rain.
ὀμελέτα, ἡ [omeleta] omelet.
ὀμήγυρις, ἡ [omeeyeerees] party, meeting, assembly, circle.
ὀμῆλιξ, ὁ, ἡ [omeeleeks] person of the same age.
ὄμηρος, ὁ [omeeros] hostage.
ὄμικρον, τό [omeekron] the letter O.
ὀμιλητής, ὁ [omeeleetees] speaker, lecturer.
ὀμιλητικός [omeeleeteekos] sociable, affable.
ὀμιλία, ἡ [omeeleea] talk, conversation ǁ speech, lecture.
ὄμιλος, ὁ [omeelos] company, group, club.
ὀμιλῶ [omeelo] speak, talk.
ὀμίχλη, ἡ [omeehlee] fog, mist.
ὀμιχλώδης [omeehlodees] foggy, misty.
ὄμμα, τό [oma] eye, look.
ὀμματοϋάλια, τά [omatoeealeea] πλ spectacles.
ὀμνύω [omneeo] swear, affirm.
ὀμοβροντία, ἡ [omovronteea] salvo, volley.
ὀμογένεια, ἡ [omoyeneea] homogeneity ǁ fellow Greeks.
ὀμογενής [omoyenees] similar ǁ of the same race ǁ expatriate Greek.
ὀμογνώμων [omoynomon] of the same opinion.
ὀμοεθνής [omoethnees] of the same nation, fellow (countryman).
ὀμοειδής [omoeedees] of the same kind ǁ uniform, similar.
ὀμόθρησκος [omothreeskos] of the same religion.
ὀμόθυμος [omotheemos] unanimous.
ὀμοιάζω [omeeazo] resemble, look like ǁ be like.
ὀμοιογενής [omeeoyenees] homogeneous ǁ uniform.
ὀμοιοκαταληξία, ἡ [omeeokataleekseea] rhyme, rime.
ὀμοιόμορφος [omeeomorfos] uniform, unvarying.
ὀμοιοπαθής [omeeopathees] fellow (sufferer), in the same boat.
ὄμοιος [omeeos] similar, (a)like, same, in conformity with.
ὀμοιότης, ἡ [omeeotees] resemblance, similarity, likeness.
ὀμοιοτρόπως [omeeotropos] likewise, similarly.
ὀμοίωμα, τό [omeeoma] likeness, image ǁ effigy.
ὀμοιωματικά, τά [omeeomateeka] πλ ditto marks.
ὀμόκεντρος [omokentros] concentric.
ὀμολογία, ἡ [omoloyeea] confession, avowal, acknowledgement, admission ǁ (οἴκου) bond, share.
ὀμόλογον, τό [omoloyon] bond, promissory note, obligation.
ὀμολογουμένως [omoloyoumenos] avowedly, admittedly.

ὀμολογῶ [omoloyo] acknowledge, confess, admit.
ὀμόνοια, ἡ [omoneea] concord, agreement, accord, peace.
ὀμόρρυθμος [omoreethmos]: ~ ἑταιρεία partnership (in business).
ὀμορφαίνω [omorfeno] beautify ǁ become beautiful.
ὀμορφιά, ἡ [omorfia] beauty, handsomeness.
ὄμορφος [omorfos] handsome, beautiful, nice.
ὀμοσπονδία, ἡ [omospondeea] federation, confederacy.
ὀμότιμος [omoteemos]: ~ καθηγητής professor emeritus.
ὀμοῦ [omou] together, jointly, in one lot.
ὀμόφρων [omofron] having the same ideas, thinking alike.
ὀμοφυλοφιλία, ἡ [omofeelofeeleea] homosexuality.
ὀμοφωνία, ἡ [omofoneea] unanimity.
ὀμόφωνος [omofonos] unanimous.
ὀμπρέλλα, ἡ [ombrella] umbrella.
ὀμφαλός, ὁ [omfalos] navel ǁ (μεταφ) centre.
ὀμώνυμος [omoneemos] having the same name.
ὄμως [omos] yet, nevertheless, but, however.
ὄν, τό [on] creature, being.
ὄναγρος, ὁ [onayros] wild ass.
ὄναρ, τό [onar] dream, vision.
ὄνειδος, τό [oneedos] disgrace, shame, infamy ǁ blame, reproach.
ὀνειρεύομαι [oneerevome] dream, have visions.
ὀνειροκρίτης, ὁ [oneerokreetees] dream interpreter.
ὄνειρον, τό [oneeron] dream ǁ vision, imagination.
ὀνειροπολῶ [oneeropolo] daydream ǁ dream of, build castles in the air.
ὀνειρώδης [oneerodees] dreamlike, fantastic ǁ grand.
ὀνηλάτης, ὁ [oneelatees] donkey driver.
ὄνομα, τό [onoma] name ǁ (γραμμ) noun ǁ fame, reputation ǁ βγάζω ~ gain renown, become famous ǁ ~ καί πρᾶμα in every sense ǁ ὀνόματι by name of.
ὀνομάζω [onomazo] name, call ǁ appoint.
ὀνομασία, ἡ [onomaseea] name, appellation ǁ designation, appointment.
ὀνομαστί [onomastee] by name, namely.
ὀνομαστική, ἡ [onomasteekee] (γραμμ) nominative (case) ǁ ~ ἑορτή name day.
ὀνομαστικός [onomasteekos] nominal.
ὀνομαστός [onomastos] famous, famed, celebrated.
ὀνοματεπώνυμον, τό [onomateponeemon] name and surname.
ὀνοματολογία, ἡ [onomatoloyeea] nomenclature, terminology.

όνος, ό, ή [onos] ass, donkey.
όντότης, ή [ontotees] entity, being ‖ personality.
όντως [ontos] really, truly, in truth.
όνυξ, ό [oneeks] nail ‖ (ζώου) claw ‖ (όρνέου) talon ‖ (λίθος) onyx.
όξαποδώ, ό [oksapodo] the devil, satan.
όξεῖα, ή [okseea] (γραμμ) acute accent.
όξείδιον, τό [okseedeeon] oxide.
όξείδωσις, ή [okseedosees] oxidation ‖ corrosion, rusting.
όξικός [okseekos] acetic.
όξινος [okseenos] sour, bitter, acid.
όξος, τό [oksos] vinegar.
όξύ, τό [oksee] acid.
όξυά, ή [oksia] beech tree ‖ beech.
όξυγονοκόλλησις, ή [okseeyonokoleesees] oxyacetylene welding.
όξυγόνον, τό [okseeyonon] oxygen.
όξυδέρκεια, ή [okseederkeea] perspicacity, acumen ‖ (μεταφ) discernment.
όξύθυμος [okseetheemos] irritable, touchy.
όξύνους [okseenous] sagacious, acute, keen, clever.
όξύνω [okseeno] sharpen, whet ‖ (τόν νοῦν) sharpen ‖ (αἰσθήματα) stir up, arouse, provoke.
όξύς [oksees] sharp, pointed ‖ piercing, shrill ‖ (γεῦσις) sour, strong.
όξύτης, ή [okseetees] sharpness ‖ keenness, acuteness.
όξύφωνος, ό [okseefonos] (μουσ) tenor.
όξω [okso] βλ ἔξω.
όπαδός, ό, ή [opados] adherent, partisan, supporter.
όπερ [oper] which, what.
όπερα, ή [opera] opera.
όπή, ή [opee] opening, aperture, hole, gap.
όπιον, τό [opeeon] opium.
όπισθεν [opeesthen] behind, in the rear ‖ κάνω ~ go backwards, put in reverse.
όπίσθιος [opeestheeos] hind, posterior, back.
όπισθογραφῶ [opeesthoyrafo] endorse (a cheque).
όπισθοδρομικός [opeesthodromeekos] retrogressive ‖ (στάς ἀπόψεις) reactionary.
όπισθοφυλακή, ή [opeesthofeelakee] rearguard.
όπισθοχώρησις, ή [opeesthohoreesees] retreat, withdrawal.
όπίσω [opeeso] behind, back ‖ again.
όπλα, τά [opla] πλ arms.
όπλή, ή [oplee] hoof.
όπλίζω [opleezo] arm ‖ (μεταφ) reinforce, strengthen.
όπλισμός, ό [opleesmos] armament, equipment ‖ (καλωδίου) sheathing.
όπλιταγωγόν, τό [opleetayoyon] troopship.
όπλίτης, ό [opleetees] soldier.
όπλον, τό [oplon] arm, weapon ‖ rifle ‖ (ἀμύνης) branch of army.

όπλοπολυβόλον, τό [oplopoleevolon] light machine gun.
όπλοστάσιον, τό [oplostaseeon] arsenal, armoury.
όπλοφορία, ή [oploforeea] carrying of arms.
όπόθεν [opothen] whence, from where.
όποιος [opeeos] whoever, whichever ‖ ~ κι' whosoever, anybody.
όποιοσδήποτε [opeeosdeepote] whoever, whatsoever.
όποῖος [opeeos] of what kind ‖ ό ~ who, which.
όπόταν [opotan] whenever, when.
όποτε [opote] whenever, at any time.
όπότε [opote] at which time, when.
όπου [opou] where, wherever.
όποῦ [opou] he who ‖ whom, which.
όπουδήποτε [opoudeepote] wheresoever, wherever.
όπτασία, ή [optaseea] vision, apparition.
όπτική, ή [opteekee] optics.
όπτικός [opteekos] optic(al) ‖ (οὐσ) optician.
όπτός [optos] roast, baked.
όπωρικά, τά [oporeeka] πλ fruit.
όπωροπωλεῖον [oporopoleeon] fruit market.
όπωροφόρος [oporoforos] bearing fruit, fruit-producing.
όπως [opos] as, like ‖ ~ ~ somehow or other, after a fashion ‖ (συνδ) in order that, so as.
όπωσδήποτε [oposdeepote] howsoever, anyway, without fail ‖ definitely.
όπωσοῦν [oposoun] somewhat, rather.
όραμα, τό [orama] vision ‖ ~ τίζομαι have visions, visualize.
όρασις, ή [orasees] sense of sight, vision.
όρατός [oratos] visible, perceptible.
όρατότης, ή [oratotees] visibility.
όργανικός [oryaneekos] organic.
όργανισμός, ό [oryaneesmos] organism ‖ organization.
όργανον, τό [oryanon] organ ‖ (μουσ) instrument ‖ implement, tool ‖ (κατασκοπείας) agent.
όργανώνω [oryanono] organize, constitute, form.
όργάνωσις, ή [oryanosees] organization, arranging.
όργασμός, ό [oryasmos] orgasm, heat ‖ (μεταφ) feverish activity.
όργή, ή [oryee] anger, rage ‖ νά πάρη ή ~ damn it!, damnation!
όργια, τά [oryeea] πλ orgies ‖ (μεταφ) corrupt practices ‖ όργιάζω revel, debauch.
όργίζω [oryeezo] anger, enrage, irritate.
όργίλος [oryeelos] irate, angry ‖ irascible, wrathful.
όργυιά, ή [oryia] fathom.
όργωμα, τό [oryoma] ploughing, tilling, tillage.

όργώνω [oryono] plough, till, furrow.
όρδή, ή [ordee] horde, host, rabble.
όρέγομαι [oreyome] envy, covet, desire.
όρειβασία, ή [oreevaseea] mountain climbing.
όρειβάτης, ό [oreevatees] mountain climber.
όρειβατικός [oreevateekos] of climbing, of mountaineering.
όρεινός [oreenos] mountainous, hilly ‖ of the mountains.
όρείχαλκος, ό [oreehalkos] brass, bronze.
όρεκτικόν, τό [orekteekon] appetizer, titbit ‖ drink.
όρεκτικός [orekteekos] appetizing, savoury ‖ tempting.
όρεξις, ή [oreksees] appetite ‖ desire, liking.
όρθά [ortha] right, rightly ‖ upright ‖ ~ κοφτά flatly, frankly.
όρθάνοιχτος [orthaneehtos] wide open.
όρθιος [ortheeos] on end, upright, erect, standing.
όρθογραφία, ή [orthoyrafeea] spelling, orthography ‖ dictation.
όρθογώνιον, τό [orthoyoneeon] rectangle.
όρθογώνιος [orthoyoneeos] right-angled ‖ rectangular.
όρθοδοξία, ή [orthodokseea] orthodoxy.
όρθόδοξος [orthodoksos] orthodox.
όρθολογισμός, ό [ortholoyeesmos] rationalism.
όρθοπεδική, ή [orthopedeekee] orthopaedics.
όρθοποδῶ [orthopodo] walk straight ‖ stand on sure ground, thrive.
όρθός [orthos] right ‖ correct ‖ proper ‖ upright, erect, standing.
όρθοστασία, ή [orthostaseea] standing.
όρθότης, ή [orthotees] accuracy ‖ soundness ‖ aptness.
όρθρος, ό [orthros] (έκκλ) matins ‖ dawn, daybreak.
όρθώνομαι [orthonome] rise, get up ‖ (άλογο) rear up.
όρθώνω [orthono] raise, pull up, lift up ‖ redress.
όρθῶς [orthos] βλ όρθά.
όριζόντιος [oreezonteeos] horizontal, level.
όρίζω [oreezo] mark, bound, delimit ‖ fix, settle, define ‖ rule, control, govern.
όρίστε [oreeste] I beg your pardon? ‖ come in, take a seat ‖ your pleasure, sir? ‖ καλῶς όρίσατε (έπιφ) welcome!
όρίζων, ό [oreezon] horizon.
όριον, τό [oreeon] boundary, limit, border ‖ (μεταφ) scope, boundary.
όρισμένος [oreesmenos] defined, fixed ‖ certain, special.
όρισμός, ό [oreesmos] designation, fixing ‖ definition ‖ order, instruction.
όριστική, ή [oreesteekee] (γραμμ) indicative (mood).
όριστικός [oreesteekos] definitive, final.

όρκίζομαι [orkeezome] swear, take the oath.
όρκίζω [orkeezo] put on oath, swear in.
όρκος, ό [orkos] oath ‖ vow.
όρκωμοσία, ή [orkomoseea] swearing (in).
όρκωτός [orkotos] sworn ‖ οί όρκωτοί the jury.
όρμαθός, ό [ormathos] string, chain, bunch.
όρμέμφυτον, τό [ormemfeeton] instinct.
όρμή, ή [ormee] vehemence ‖ impulse, impetus ‖ passion.
όρμητήριον, τό [ormeeteereeon] starting place ‖ motive.
όρμητικός [ormeeteekos] impetuous, hot-tempered, fiery.
όρμιά, ή [ormia] fishing line.
όρμόνη, ή [ormonee] hormone.
όρμος, ό [ormos] bay, inlet.
όρμῶ [ormo] dash, rush ‖ ~μαι be urged ‖ come from.
όρνεον, τό [orneon] bird of prey.
όρνιθα, ή [orneetha] hen, chicken, fowl.
όρνιθοσκαλίσματα, τά [orneethoskaleesmata] πλ scrawl, scribble.
όρνιθοτροφεῖον, τό [orneethotrofeeon] poultry farm.
όρνιθών, ό [orneethon] chicken coop, henhouse, hen roost.
όρνιο, τό [orneeo] bird of prey ‖ (μεταφ) dullard, dolt.
όρνις, ή [ornees] βλ όρνιθα.
όροθεσία, ή [orotheseea] fixing of boundaries.
όρολογία, ή [oroloyeea] terminology.
όροπέδιον, τό [oropedeeon] plateau, table-land.
όρος, τό [oros] mountain.
όρος, ό [oros] term, condition, stipulation, proviso ‖ limit, end ‖ (έπιστημονικός) term, definition.
όρ(ρ)ός, ό [oros] serum.
όροσειρά, ή [oroseera] mountain range, mountain chain.
όρόσημον, τό [oroseemon] boundary mark, boundary stone.
όροφή, ή [orofee] ceiling, roof.
όροφος, ό [orofos] floor, storey.
όρτύκι, τό [orteekee] quail.
όρυγμα, τό [oreeyma] pit, trench, ditch, excavation.
όρυζα, ή [oreeza] rice.
όρυκτέλαιον, τό [oreekteleon] petroleum ‖ lubricant.
όρυκτολογία, ή [oreektoloyeea] mineralogy.
όρυκτόν, τό [oreekton] mineral, ore.
όρυκτός [oreektos] mineral, dug-up.
όρύσσω [oreeso] dig, excavate ‖ (φρέαρ) bore, sink.
όρυχεῖον, τό [oreeheeon] mine.
όρφανός [orfanos] orphan.
όρφανοτροφεῖον, τό [orfanotrofeeon] orphanage.
όρχήστρα, ή [orheestra] orchestra.

ὄρχις, ἡ [orhees] testicle ‖ (λουλούδι) orchid.

ὀρχοῦμαι [orhoume] dance.

ὁρῶ [oro] βλ βλέπω.

ὅς [os] who.

ὁσάκις [osakees] whenever, as often as.

ὅσιος [oseeos] holy, blessed ‖ saint.

ὀσμή, ἡ [osmee] odour, smell, scent.

ὅσο(ν) [oso(n)] as, as far as, as long as ‖ ~ γιά as for ‖ ~ ἀφορᾶ as regards, with regard to ‖ ἐφ᾽ ~ as long as, inasmuch as ‖ ~ νἄρθη until he comes ‖ ~ νἄναι nevertheless.

ὁσονούπω [osonoupo] soon, in a while, before long.

ὅσος [osos] as much as, as many as, all.

ὄσπριον, τό [ospreeon] pulse (legume).

ὅστις [ostees] who(ever).

ὀστοῦν, τό [ostoun] bone.

ὀστρακιά, ἡ [ostrakia] scarlet fever.

ὄστρακον, τό [ostrakon] shell ‖ (ἀρχαιολογία) potsherd.

ὀσφραίνομαι [osfrenome] smell, scent ‖ (μεταφ) feel.

ὄσφρησις, ἡ [osfreesees] sense of smell.

ὀσφύς, ἡ [osfees] waist, loins, haunches.

ὅταν [otan] when, at the time when, whenever.

ὀτέ [ote] sometimes.

ὅτι [otee] (συνδ) that ‖ (ἐπίρ) as soon as ‖ just (now).

ὅ τι [otee] what(ever).

ὁτιδήποτε [oteedeepote] whatsoever ‖ anything at all.

ὅτου [otou]: ἕως ~ until ‖ μέχρις ~ until ‖ ἀφ᾽ ~ since.

οὐ [ou] not, no.

οὐγγιά, ἡ [oungia] ounce.

οὐδαμοῦ [oudamou] nowhere, not anywhere.

οὐδαμῶς [oudamos] not at all, not in any way, by no means.

οὐδέ [oude] βλ οὔτε.

οὐδείς [oudees] no(body), no one, none.

οὐδέποτε [oudepote] never.

οὐδέτερος [oudeteros] neither ‖ (ἐπίθ) neutral ‖ (γραμμ) neuter.

οὐδόλως [oudolos] by no means, no wise, by no manner of means.

οὔζο, τό [ouzo] ouzo.

οὐκ [ouk] βλ οὐ.

οὐλή, ἡ [oulee] scar.

οὖλον, τό [oulon] gum (anat).

οὖρα, τά [oura] πλ urine, piss (col).

οὐρά, ἡ [oura] tail ‖ train of dress ‖ queue ‖ (κατσαρόλας) handle ‖ (φάλαγγος) rear ‖ λεφτά μέ ~ loads of money.

οὐραγός, ὁ [ourayos] person bringing up the rear, the last one.

οὐρανής [ouranees] sky-blue.

οὐράνιον, τό [ouraneeon] uranium.

οὐράνιον [ouraneeon]: ~ τόξον rainbow.

οὐράνιος [ouraneeos] heavenly, celestial.

οὐρανίσκος, ὁ [ouraneeskos] palate.

οὐρανισκόφωνος [ouraneeskofonos] palatal.

οὐρανοκατέβατος [ouranokatevatos] heaven-sent ‖ (μεταφ) unexpected.

οὐρανοξύστης, ὁ [ouranokseestees] skyscraper.

οὐρανός, ὁ [ouranos] sky, heaven ‖ canopy.

οὐρητήριον, τό [oureeteereeon] urinal, john (col).

οὐρικός [oureekos] uric, urinary.

οὔριος [oureeos] tail (wind), favourable (wind), fair (wind).

οὐρλιάζω [ourleeazo] howl, roar ‖ (ἀπό πόνο) yell, scream ‖ (ἀπό θυμό) bellow.

οὔρλιασμα, τό [ourleeasma] howl(ing), bellowing, yelling.

οὐροδοχεῖον, τό [ourodoheeon] chamberpot.

οὐρῶ [ouro] urinate.

οὖς, τό [ous] ear.

οὐσία, ἡ [ouseea] matter, substance ‖ essence ‖ (μεταφ) gist, main point.

οὐσιαστικόν, τό [ouseeasteekon] (γραμμ) substantive, noun.

οὐσιαστικός [ouseeasteekos] substantial, essential.

οὐσιώδης [ouseeodees] essential, vital, indispensable, capital.

οὔτε [oute] not even ‖ ~ . . . ~ neither . . . nor.

οὐτιδανός [outeedanos] worthless, useless, vile, base, abject.

οὐτοπία, ἡ [outopeea] Utopia.

οὗτος [outos] he, this one, that, it.

οὕτω(ς) [outo(s)] so, such, thus ‖ ~ ὥστε so that, in order that.

οὐχ [ouh] not ‖ ~ ἧττον nonetheless.

οὐχί [ouhee] βλ ὄχι.

ὀφειλέτης, ὁ [ofeeletees] debtor.

ὀφειλή, ἡ [ofeelee] debt, sum due ‖ (μεταφ) obligation, duty.

ὀφείλομαι [ofeelome] be due.

ὀφείλω [ofeelo] owe ‖ be obliged to ‖ ~ νά πάω I should go.

ὄφελος, τό [ofelos] profit, advantage, benefit.

ὀφθαλμαπάτη, ἡ [ofthalmapatee] optical illusion.

ὀφθαλμίατρος, ὁ, ἡ [ofthalmeeatros] eye specialist, oculist.

ὀφθαλμός, ὁ [ofthalmos] eye ‖ (βιολ) bud.

ὀφθαλμοφανής [ofthalmofanees] obvious, manifest, evident.

ὀφιοειδής [ofeeoeedees] serpentine, meandering, winding.

ὄφις, ὁ [ofees] snake, serpent.

ὀφρύς, ἡ [ofrees] eyebrow ‖ (ὄρους) range ‖ (χάνδακος) edge.

ὀφφίς, τό [ofees] domestic office.

ὄχεντρα, ἡ [ohentra] βλ ὀχιά.

ὀχέτευσις, ἡ [ohetevsees] drainage.

όχετός, ὁ [ohetos] drain, sewer ‖ conduit, pipe.

όχημα, τό [oheema] vehicle, carriage, coach.

όχθη, ἡ [ohthee] (ποταμοῦ) bank ‖ (λίμνης) shore.

όχι [ohee] no ‖ not.

όχιά, ἡ [ohia] viper.

όχλαγωγία, ἡ [ohlaγoγeea] disturbance, riot, tumult.

όχληρός [ohleeros] tiresome, unpleasant, burdensome.

όχλοβοή, ἡ [ohlovoee] uproar, din, hubbub.

όχλοκρατία, ἡ [ohlokrateea] mob rule.

όχλος, ὁ [ohlos] populace, mob, crowd, rabble.

όχυρόν, τό [oheeron] strong point, fort, stronghold.

όχυρώνομαι [oheeronome] (μεταφ) find an excuse, justify.

όχυρώνω [oheerono] fortify, entrench.

όψη [opsee] βλ όψις.

όψιγενής [opseeγenees] posthumous ‖ late, belated.

όψιμος [opseemos] tardy, late, of a late season.

όψις, ἡ [opsees] aspect, appearance, look ‖ view, sight ‖ countenance ‖ face ‖ λαμβάνω ὑπ' όψιν take into account ‖ ἐξ όψεως by sight ‖ ἐν όψει in view of ‖ in view.

όφοφυλάκιον, τό [opsofeelakeeon] larder, pantry.

όψώνια, τά [opsoneea] πλ purchases, supplies, shopping, provisions.

Π, π

παγάνα, ἡ [paγana] trap, snare.

παγανισμός, ὁ [paγaneesmos] paganism.

παγερός [paγeros] icy cold, freezing ‖ (μεταφ) chilly, frigid.

παγετός, ὁ [paγetos] frost.

παγετώδης [paγetodees] icy, icy cold, freezing.

παγετών, ὁ [paγeton] glacier.

παγίδα, ἡ [paγeeda] trap, snare ‖ (τάφρος) pitfall.

παγίδευμα, τό [paγeedevma] ensnaring, trapping.

παγιδεύω [paγeedevo] snare, catch, entice.

πάγιος [paγeeos] fixed, stable, firm ‖ (καθεστώς) secure, durable ‖ (δάνειον) consolidated loan ‖ (πρόσοδος) steady income.

παγίς, ἡ [paγees] βλ παγίδα.

παγιώνω [paγeeono] consolidate, make secure.

παγίως [paγeeos] firmly, securely.

πάγκοινος [pangkeenos] common, universal, public.

πάγκος, ὁ [pangkos] bench, seat.

παγκόσμιος [pangkosmeeos] universal, world-wide.

πάγκρεας, τό [pangkreas] pancreas.

παγόβουνον, τό [paγovounon] iceberg.

παγόδα, ἡ [paγoda] pagoda.

παγοδρομία, ἡ [paγodromeea] skating.

παγοθραύστης, ὁ [paγothravstees] icebreaker.

παγοπέδιλο, τό [paγopedeelo] iceskate.

πάγος, ὁ [paγos] ice, frost.

παγούρι, τό [paγouree] can, tin, flask ‖ (στρατ) canteen.

παγωμένος [paγomenos] frozen, frostbitten.

παγώνι, τό [paγonee] peacock.

παγωνιά, ἡ [paγonia] frost.

παγώνω [paγono] freeze, congeal, frost.

παγωτό, τό [paγoto] ice cream.

παζαρεύω [pazarevo] haggle over, bargain for.

παζάρι, τό [pazaree] market, bazaar ‖ bargaining, haggling.

παθαίνω [patheno] undergo, suffer, be injured.

πάθημα, τό [patheema] mishap, accident.

πάθησις, ἡ [patheesees] complaint, sickness, affliction.

παθητικός [patheeteekos] passive, submissive ‖ (γραμμ) passive (voice) ‖ charged with passion ‖ (οίκ) debit.

παθολογία, ἡ [patholoγeea] pathology.

παθολογικός [patholoγeekos] pathological.

παθολόγος, ὁ [patholoγos] general practitioner.

πάθος, τό [pathos] illness, passion ‖ suffering ‖ (ἔχθρα) animosity.

παιγνίδι, τό [peγneedee] play, game, sport ‖ (γιά παιδιά) toy, plaything.

παιγνιδιάρης [peγneedeearees] playful, gay, mirthful.

παίγνιον, τό [peγneeon] βλ παιγνίδι.

παιγνιόχαρτον, τό [peγneeoharton] playing card.

παιδαγωγεῖον, τό [pedaγoγeeon] children's school.

παιδαγωγία, ἡ [pedaγoγeea] education, pedagogy.

παιδαγωγικός [pedaγoγeekos] educational, pedagogical.

παιδαγωγός, ὁ, ἡ [pedaγoγos] tutor, preceptor, pedagogue.

παιδαγωγῶ [pedaγoγo] educate, instruct, teach.

παιδάκι, τό [pedakee] little child.

παιδαριώδης [pedareeodees] puerile, childish ‖ (εὔκολο) quite simple, trivial.

παιδεία, ἡ [pedeea] education, learning, instruction, culture.

παίδεμα, τό [pedema] torture, trial, ordeal.

παιδεύομαι [pedevome] try hard, struggle.

παιδευτήριον, τό [pedevteereeon] βλ ἐκπαιδευτήριον.

παιδεύω [pedevo] pester, torture, torment.

παιδί, τό [pedee] child, boy ‖ chap.

παιδιά, ή [peδia] game, sport ‖ amusement, distraction.
παιδιαρίζω [peδeeareezo] act like a child.
παιδίατρος, ὁ, ή [peδeeatros] paediatrician, child specialist.
παιδικός [peδeekos] child's, of children ‖ childish ‖ ~ σταθμός day nursery.
παιδίον, τό [peδeeon] βλ παιδί.
παιδίσκη, ἡ [peδeeskee] little girl, lassie.
παίζω [pezo] play ‖ (παιχνίδι) speculate, gamble ‖ (μεταφ) swing, sway.
παίκτης, ὁ [pektees] player ‖ gambler, gamester.
παινεύω [penevo] βλ ἐπαινῶ.
παίξιμο, τό [pekseemo] playing ‖ (μέ κάτι) toying with ‖ (θεάτρου) performance ‖ (παιχνίδι) gaming, gambling.
παίρνω [perno] receive, take hold of, get, contain ‖ (πόλιν κτλ) capture ‖ (διά τῆς βίας) wrench from ‖ (ὑπηρέτην) hire, take on ‖ (καφέ κτλ) take, have ‖ (κρύο κτλ) catch, get ‖ (ὡς παράδειγμα) take, draw ‖ (σημείωσι) take (a note) ‖ (κάτι γιά κάτι) take for, consider (as) ‖ (μέ κάποια ἔννοια) understand, interpret ‖ (χρήματα) be paid, draw, receive ‖ (γιά γυναίκα) marry, wed ‖ τόν ~ fall asleep ‖ ~ ἀπό πίσω follow closely.
παῖς, ὁ, ἡ [pes] βλ παιδί.
πακετάρω [paketaro] pack, box.
πακέτο, τό [paketo] pack, packet, parcel, box, bundle.
παλαβομάρα, ἡ [palavomara] madness, lunacy, foolish act.
παλαβός [palavos] mad, insane, stupid ‖ (παράτολμος) foolhardy.
παλάβρας, ὁ [palavras] braggart, windbag.
πάλαι [pale] of old.
παλαίμαχος [palemahos] veteran.
παλαιογραφία, ή [paleoγrafeea] pal(a)eography.
παλαιόθεν [paleothen] from olden times.
παλαιόκαστρον, τό [paleokastron] old castle, ruined castle.
παλαιοπωλεῖον, τό [paleopoleeon] second-hand shop, antique shop.
παλαιοπώλης, ὁ [paleopolees] secondhand dealer.
παλαιός [paleos] old ‖ (μνημεῖον κτλ) ancient, old ‖ (ἄλλοτε) former.
παλαιστής, ὁ [palestees] wrestler.
παλαίστρα, ἡ [palestra] arena, ring.
παλαίω [paleo] βλ παλεύω.
παλαιώνω [paleono] wear out, become anti-quated.
παλαμάκια, τά [palamakeea] πλ clapping, applause.
παλαμάρι, τό [palamaree] (ναυτ) cable, mooring line.
παλάμη, ἡ [palamee] palm ‖ (μέτρον) span.
παλαμίδα, ή [palameeδa] kind of small tunny.
παλάτι, τό [palatee] palace ‖ mansion.

παλεύω [palevo] wrestle, struggle, fight.
πάλη, ἡ [palee] wrestling ‖ (μεταφ) struggle, strife, contest.
παλιανθρωπιά, ή [palianthropia] villainy, meanness, roguery.
παλιάνθρωπος, ὁ [palianthropos] rogue, rascal, scamp.
παλιάτσος, ὁ [paliatsos] clown, buffoon.
παλιγγενεσία, ή [paleengeneseea] revival, renaissance.
πάλι(ν) [pali(n)] again, once more, over again.
παλινδρομικός [paleenδromeekos] alter-nating, reciprocating, recoiling.
παλιν(ν)οστῶ [paleenosto] repatriate.
παλινόρθωσις, ή [paleenorthosees] restor-ation, re-establishment.
παλινωδῶ [paleenoδo] (μεταφ) retract, recant, take back.
παλιογύναικο, τό [palioγeeneko] street-walker, tart.
παλιοκόριτσο, τό [paliokoreetso] ill-bred girl ‖ prostitute.
παλιόμουτρο, τό [paliomoutro] villain, scoundrel, scamp.
παλιόπαιδο, τό [paliopeδo] bad boy, young scamp.
παλίρροια, ἡ [paleereea] tide, floodtide.
παλλακίς, ἡ [palakees] concubine, mistress.
πάλλευκος [palevkos] pure white, snow-white.
παλληκαράς, ὁ [paleekaras] bully.
παλληκάρι, τό [paleekaree] young man, brave person ‖ (ἐργένης) bachelor.
παλληκαρίσια [paleekareeseea] boldly, bravely.
πάλλω [palo] throb, beat, palpitate ‖ (ἤλεκτ) vibrate.
παλμός, ὁ [palmos] oscillation, vibration ‖ palpitation, throbbing ‖ (ἐνθουσιασμοῦ) feeling, eagerness.
παλούκι, τό [paloukee] stake, pole ‖ (μεταφ) difficulty.
παλτό, τό [palto] overcoat.
παμμακάριστος [pamakareestos] most blessed.
παμπάλαιος [pampaleos] ancient ‖ out-of-date.
πάμπλουτος [pamploutos] extremely wealthy.
παμπόνηρος [pamponeeros] very cunning, very sly.
πάμπτωχος [pamptohos] very poor, very needy.
πάμφθηνος [pamftheenos] very cheap, ex-tremely cheap.
παμψηφεί [pampseefee] unanimously.
πᾶν, τό [pan] the whole world ‖ (τό κεφα-λαιῶδες) essentials, everything.
Πάν, ὁ [pan] Pan.
πανάγαθος [panaγathos] merciful ‖ ex-tremely virtuous.
Παναγία, ἡ [panaγeea] the Virgin Mary.

παναγιότης, ἡ [panaγeeotees] holiness.
πανάδα, ἡ [panaδa] brown patch, freckle.
πανάθλιος [panathleeos] wretched, miserable.
πανάκεια, ἡ [panakeea] panacea.
πανάρχαιος [panarheos] very ancient.
πανδαιμόνιον, τό [panδemoneeon] pandemonium.
πάνδεινος [panδeenos] disastrous, most terrible.
πάνδημος [panδeemos] public, of all the people.
πανδοχεῖον, τό [panδoheeon] inn.
πανδρειά, ἡ [panδria] marriage, matrimony.
πανδρεύω [panδrevo] marry.
πανελλήνιος [paneleeneeos] panhellenic.
πανεπιστημιακός [panepeesteemeeakos] of the university.
πανεπιστήμιον, τό [panepeesteemeeon] university.
πανέρι, τό [paneree] wide basket.
πανευτυχής [panefteehees] very happy.
πανηγυρίζω [paneeγeereezo] celebrate, fête.
πανηγυρικός [paneeγeereekos] festive ‖ (οὐσ) oration, panegyric.
πανήγυρις, ἡ [paneeγeerees] festival, festivity ‖ (ἐμπορική) fair.
πανηγυρισμός, ὁ [paneeγeereesmos] celebration.
πάνθεον, τό [pantheon] pantheon.
πάνθηρ, ὁ [pantheer] panther.
πανί, τό [panee] cloth, linen ‖ (ναυτ) sail.
πανιερότης, ἡ [panierotees] (ὡς τίτλος) His Grace.
πανικόβλητος [paneekovleetos] panic-stricken.
πανικός, ὁ [paneekos] panic.
πανίς, ἡ [panees] fauna.
πανίσχυρος [paneesheeros] all-powerful.
πάν(ν)ινος [paneenos] of cloth, of linen, of cotton.
πανόμοιος [panomeeos] similar, alike.
πανομοιότυπον, τό [panomeeoteepon] facsimile.
πανοπλία, ἡ [panopleea] arms, armour.
πανόραμα, τό [panorama] panorama.
πανοσιότης, ἡ [panoseeotees] reverence.
πανοσιώτατος, ὁ [panoseeotatos] most reverend.
πανούκλα, ἡ [panoukla] plague, pestilence.
πανουργία, ἡ [panourγeea] ruse, trick, cunning.
πανοῦργος [panourγos] malicious, tricky, wily, cunning.
πανσέληνος, ἡ [panseleenos] full moon.
πανσές, ὁ [panses] pansy.
πάντα [panta] forever, always ‖ anyway, in any case.
πανταλόνι, τό [pantalonee] trousers ‖ pants, knickers.
παντάπασι [pantapasee] completely, fully, utterly.

πανταχόθεν [pantahothen] from all parts.
πανταχοῦ [pantahoo] everywhere.
παντελής [pantelees] complete, absolute, entire.
παντελῶς [pantelos] utterly, absolutely, totally.
παντζάρι, τό [pantzaree] beetroot.
παντιέρα, ἡ [pantiera] banner, flag.
παντοδύναμος [pantoδeenamos] omnipotent, all-powerful.
παντοειδῶς [pantoeeδos] in every way.
παντοιοτρόπως [panteeotropos] in every way, by every means.
παντοκράτωρ, ὁ [pantokrator] the Almighty.
παντομίμα, ἡ [pantomeema] pantomime.
παντοπωλεῖον, τό [pantopoleeon] grocer's shop ‖ (US) grocery.
παντοπώλης, ὁ [pantopolees] grocer.
πάντοτε [pantote] always, at all times, forever.
παντοτεινά [pantoteena] perpetually, everlastingly.
παντοῦ [pantou] everywhere.
παντούφλα, ἡ [pantoufla] slipper.
παντρειά, ἡ [pantria] βλ πανδρειά.
παντρεύω [pantrevo] βλ πανδρεύω.
πάντως [pantos] anyhow, in any case, at any rate.
πάνυ [panee] very much, a great deal.
πανωλεθρία, ἡ [panolethreea] heavy loss, total ruin.
πανώλης, ἡ [panolees] plague, pestilence.
πανώριος [panoreeos] very beautiful.
πανωφόρι, τό [panoforee] overcoat.
παξιμάδι, τό [pakseemaδee] rusk ‖ (γιά κοχλία) nut (of screw).
παπαγαλιστί [papaγaleestee] parrot-like.
παπαδιά, ἡ [papaδia] priest's wife.
παπάκι, τό [papakee] duckling.
παπαρούνα, ἡ [paparouna] poppy.
Πάπας, ὁ [papas] Pope.
παπᾶς, ὁ [papas] priest.
παπί, τό [papee] young duck ‖ γίνομαι ~ get wet to the skin.
πάπια, ἡ [papeea] duck ‖ bedpan ‖ κάνω τήν ~ play the fool, keep mum.
παπικός [papeekos] papal.
πάπλωμα, τό [paploma] cotton quilt.
παπουτσάδικο, τό [papoutsaδeeko] shoemaker's shop.
παπουτσῆς, ὁ [papoutsees] shoemaker, bootmaker.
παπούτσι, τό [papoutsee] shoe.
παππούς, ὁ [papoos] grandfather.
παρά [para] than ‖ but ‖ (πρόθ) near, close, by ‖ (προσθήκην) in spite of, against my will ‖ (ἀντίθεσιν) against, contrary to ‖ (ἀφαίρεσιν) by, almost, nearly.
παραβαίνω [paraveno] break, violate, infringe.
παραβάλλω [paravalo] compare.
παραβάν, τό [paravan] (folding) screen.

παραβαρύνω [paravareeno] overload, overburden ‖ become very heavy.

παράβασις, ἡ [paravasees] violation, transgression, breach.

παραβάτης, ὁ [paravatees] violator, transgressor.

παραβιάζω [paraveeazo] (πόρτα κτλ) force entry, break open ‖ (νόμον) violate, infringe.

παραβλέπω [paravlepo] neglect, omit ‖ turn a blind eye (to), ignore.

παραβολή, ἡ [paravolee] comparison, collation ‖ (ἐκκλ) parable ‖ (μαθημ) parabola.

παράβολον, τό [paravolon] fee, deposit.

παραγάδι, ὁ [parayadee] large fishing net.

παραγγελία, ἡ [parangeleea] command, commission, order ‖ (μήνυμα) message ‖ ἐπί ~ made to order.

παραγγέλω [parangelo] order, command ‖ inform.

παραγεμίζω [parayemeezo] fill up ‖ become too full ‖ (μαγειρική) stuff ‖ cram.

παραγίνομαι [parayeenome] grow too much ‖ go too far ‖ get overripe ‖ ~ χοντρός grow too fat.

παράγκα, ἡ [paranga] wooden hut, shack.

παραγκωνίζω [parangoneezo] elbow, thrust aside.

παραγνωρίζω [paraynoreezo] ignore ‖ misinterpret ‖ mistake identity of.

παραγραφή, ἡ [parayrafee] lapse of right, lapse of penalty.

παράγραφος, ὁ [parayrafos] paragraph.

παράγομαι [parayome] be derived from.

παράγω [parayo] produce, bear ‖ derive.

παραγωγή, ἡ [parayoyee] production ‖ output, generation ‖ (γραμμ) derivation.

παραγωγικός [parayoyeekos] productive.

παραγωγός, ὁ [parayoyos] producer, grower.

παράγων, ὁ [parayon] agent, factor ‖ (μαθημ) factor.

παράδειγμα, τό [paradeeyma] example ‖ ~τος χάριν for example, for instance.

παραδειγματίζω [paradeeymateezo] set an example, exemplify.

παράδεισος, ὁ [paradeesos] paradise.

παραδεκτός [paradektos] admitted, accepted ‖ acceptable, admissible.

παραδέχομαι [paradehome] admit, acknowledge, confess, allow.

παραδίδομαι [paradeeodome] surrender, submit, yield.

παραδίδω [paradeeo] hand over ‖ surrender ‖ (μάθημα) teach, give lessons.

παράδοξος [paradoksos] peculiar, odd, singular ‖ unusual.

παραδόπιστος [paradopeestos] greedy, extremely fond of money.

παράδοσις, ἡ [paradosees] delivery, surrender ‖ (τῆς χώρας) tradition ‖ (μαθήματος) teaching.

παραδοτέος [paradoteos] due for delivery.

παραδουλεύτρα, ἡ [paradoulevtra] charwoman.

παραδρομή, ἡ [paradromee] carelessness, oversight.

παραέιμαι [paraeeme] be beyond measure, be too much.

παραζάλη, ἡ [parazalee] confusion, agitation, turmoil.

παραθαλάσσιος [parathalaseeos] by the sea, coastal.

παραθερίζω [parathereezo] spend the summer.

παραθεριστής, ὁ [parathereestees] summer holidaymaker.

παραθετικός [paratheteekos] comparative.

παραθέτω [paratheto] contrast, compare ‖ (ἀναφέρω) cite, quote ‖ (φαγητό) serve, offer.

παράθυρο, τό [paratheero] window.

παραθυρόφυλλο, τό [paratheerofeelo] shutter.

παραίνεσις, ἡ [parenesees] advice, counsel, admonition.

παραίσθησις, ἡ [parestheesees] hallucination, illusion.

παραίτησις, ἡ [pareteesees] resignation, renunciation ‖ abdication.

παραιτοῦμαι [paretoume] resign, give up ‖ (ἀποφεύγω) avoid.

παραιτῶ [pareto] give up, leave, desert.

παρακάθομαι [parakathome] overstay ‖ sit too long.

παράκαιρος [parakeros] unseasonable, inopportune, untimely.

παρακάλια, τά [parakaleea] πλ supplications, pleading.

παρακαλῶ [parakalo] ask, beg, entreat ‖ ~! don't mention it!, please!, a pleasure!

παρακάμ(ν)ω [parakam(n)o] exaggerate, go too far.

παρακάμπτω [parakampto] get round, surpass ‖ (ἔνα θέμα) evade.

παρακαταθήκη, ἡ [parakatatheekee] consignation, deposit ‖ stock ‖ provisions ‖ (παράδοσις) heritage.

παρακάτω [parakato] lower down ‖ at a lower price.

παρακείμενος [parakeemenos] adjoining, adjacent ‖ ὁ ~ (γραμμ) perfect tense.

παρακινῶ [parakeeno] exhort, urge ‖ instigate.

παρακλάδι, τό [parakladee] shoot, bough ‖ (ποταμοῦ) branch.

παράκλησις, ἡ [parakleesees] request, plea ‖ (ἐκκλ) prayer.

παρακμή, ἡ [parakmee] decay, decline.

παρακοή, ἡ [parakoee] disobedience, insubordination.

παρακολουθῶ [parakoloutho] follow, come behind ‖ watch ‖ go after ‖ (τήν ἔννοια) understand.

παρακούω [parakouo] hear wrongly ‖ (ἀπειθαρχῶ) disobey.

παρακρατῶ [parakrato] retain ‖ keep back ‖ (γιά χρόνο) last too long.

παράκτιος [parakteeos] coastal, inshore.

παραλαβή, ἡ [paralavee] receipt, receiving, delivery.

παραλαμβάνω [paralamvano] receive, take delivery of ‖ take possession of.

παραλείπω [paraleepo] leave out, miss, neglect, omit.

παράλειψις, ἡ [paraleepsees] omission, neglect(ing).

παραλέω [paraleo] exaggerate, overcolour.

παραλήπτης, ὁ [paraleeptees] payee, addressee, consignee.

παραλήρημα, τό [paraleereema] delirium, frenzy.

παραλία, ἡ [paraleea] seashore, shore, coast, beach ‖ **παραλιακός** of the seashore, of the coast.

παραλῆς [paralees] rich, wealthy.

παραλλαγή, ἡ [paralayee] change, variation ‖ (ἄστρον) deviation.

παράλληλος [paraleelos] parallel.

παραλογίζομαι [paraloyeezome] talk irrationally, rave.

παράλογος [paraloyos] illogical, absurd, foolish.

παραλυσία, ἡ [paraleeseea] palsy, paralysis ‖ dissoluteness, debauchery.

παράλυσις, ἡ [paraleesees] paralysis ‖ helplessness.

παράλυτος [paraleetos] paralytic, stiff, crippled ‖ (ἰατρ) paralyzed.

παραλύω [paraleo] make loose, make shaky ‖ slacken, relax ‖ (ἰατρ) paralyze.

παραμάννα, ἡ [paramana] nurse, nanny ‖ (καρφίτσα) safety pin.

παραμελῶ [paramelo] neglect, leave undone, disregard.

παραμένω [parameno] stay by ‖ remain, continue to exist ‖ sojourn.

παράμερα [paramera] out of the way, apart.

παραμερίζω [paramereezo] set aside ‖ get out of the way ‖ fend off.

παράμερος [parameros] remote, outlying.

παραμιλῶ [parameelo] speak too much ‖ rave.

παραμονεύω [paramonevo] watch for, waylay.

παραμονή, ἡ [paramonee] stay ‖ eve.

παραμορφώνω [paramorfono] deform, disfigure, twist.

παραμύθι, τό [parameethee] fable, story, fairy tale.

παρανόησις, ἡ [paranoeesees] misunderstanding.

παρανομία, ἡ [paranomeea] illegality ‖ breach of the law.

παράνομος [paranomos] illegal, unlawful.

παρανομῶ [paranomo] transgress a law.

παρανοῶ [paranoo] misunderstand.

παράνυμφος, ὁ, ἡ [paraneemfos] best man ‖ bridesmaid.

παρανυχίδα, ἡ [paraneeheeda] hangnail.

παράξενα [paraksena] oddly, strangely.

παραξενεύομαι [paraksenevome] be astonished, be amazed (at).

παραξενιά, ἡ [paraksenia] caprice, fancy, whim.

παράξενος [paraksenos] peculiar, singular, odd.

παραξηλώνω [parakseelono] unsew, unstitch ‖ τό ~ I go too far, I exaggerate.

παραπανήσιος [parapaneeseeos] superfluous, to spare ‖ (τιμή) excess, overly much.

παραπάνω [parapano] higher up ‖ (ἐπιπρόσθετα) in addition ‖ μέ τό ~ enough and to spare ‖ ~ ἀπό over, more than, greater than.

παραπάτημα, τό [parapateema] false step ‖ (μεταφ) misconduct.

παραπατῶ [parapato] slip, stumble ‖ stagger.

παραπέμπω [parapembo] refer to ‖ send, hand over.

παραπέρα [parapera] further on, over there.

παραπεταμένος [parapetamenos] thrown away ‖ (μεταφ) disdained, scorned.

παραπέτασμα, τό [parapetasma] curtain.

παραπέτο, τό [parapeto] parapet, breastwork.

παραπέφτω [parapefto] βλ **παραπίπτω**.

παράπηγμα, τό [parapeeyma] wooden hut, shack, shanty.

παραπίπτω [parapeepto] be mislaid, get lost, go astray.

παραπλανῶ [paraplano] seduce, mislead, lead astray.

παραπλεύρως [paraplevros] next door ‖ next to, beside.

παραπλήρωμα, τό [parapleeroma] complement, supplement.

παραπλήσιος [parapleeseeos] next to, nearby ‖ (ὅμοιος) very like, similar.

παραποιῶ [parapeeo] counterfeit ‖ forge, tamper with.

παραπομπή, ἡ [parapombee] referring ‖ (σέ βιβλίο) reference, footnote.

παραπονετικός [paraponeteekos] doleful, whining.

παραπονιάρης [paraponeearees] grumbling, grousing.

παραπονιέμαι [paraponieme] complain, grumble.

παράπονον, τό [paraponon] complaint, grievance.

παραπόταμος, ὁ [parapotamos] tributary.

παράπτωμα, τό [paraptoma] fault, mistake ‖ breach.

παράρτημα, τό [pararteema] annexe, supplement ‖ outbuilding ‖ (τραπέζης) branch ‖ (ἐφημερίδος) special edition, extra.

παρᾶς, ὁ [paras] money, cash.

παράσημον, τό [paraseemon] decoration, medal, order, insignia.

παρασημοφορῶ [paraseemoforo] decorate, invest with an order.

παράσιτα, τά [paraseeta] πλ atmospherics || parasites.

παράσιτος, ὁ [paraseetos] sponger, hanger-on, parasite.

παρασιωπῶ [paraseeopo] pass over in silence.

παρασκευάζω [paraskevazo] prepare, get ready, arrange.

παρασκεύασμα, τό [paraskevasma] substance prepared, preparation.

παρασκευή, ἡ [paraskevee] preparation || (ἡμέρα) Friday.

παρασκήνια, τά [paraskeeneea] πλ wings (theat) || παρασκηνιακός behind the scenes.

παρασταίνω [parasteno] βλ παριστάνω.

παράστασις, ἡ [parastasees] representation, portrayal || (παρουσία) presence, demeanour || (θεάτρου) show, performance || (νομ) appearance.

παραστάτης, ὁ [parastatees] assistant, helper || (πόρτας) jamb.

παραστατικός [parastateekos] expressive, descriptive, vivid.

παραστέκω [parasteko] assist, help, support.

παράστημα, τό [parasteema] carriage, bearing, figure.

παραστράτημα, τό [parastrateema] straying, misconduct.

παρασύνθημα, τό [paraseentheema] password.

παρασύρω [paraseero] drag along, sweep away || run over || (σέ σφάλμα) lead astray, carry away.

παράταξις, ἡ [parataksees] array, parade, order || pomp, ceremony || (πολιτική) political party.

παράτασις, ἡ [paratasees] extension, protraction || renewal.

παρατάσσω [parataso] arrange, set in order, line up.

παρατατικός, ὁ [paratateekos] (γραμμ) imperfect tense.

παρατείνω [parateeno] prolong, lengthen || extend, defer.

παρατήρησις, ἡ [parateereesees] observation, remark || (κουβέντα) comment || reproach, reprimand.

παρατηρητής, ὁ [parateereetees] observer, watcher, spotter.

παρατηρητικός [parateereeteekos] observing, keen || reproachful.

παρατηρῶ [parateero] observe, perceive, notice || (ἐπιτιμῶ) reproach, blame.

παράτολμος [paratolmos] reckless, audacious, bold.

παρατραβῶ [paratravo] draw out, prolong || last too long || (μεταφ) go too far.

παρατράγουδο, τό [paratragoudo] untoward incident.

παρατρέχω [paratreho] leave out, omit || run back and forth.

παρατσούκλι, τό [paratsooklee] nickname.

παρατυγχάνω [parateenghano] chance to be present.

παρατυπία, ἡ [parateepeea] breach of formalities || irregularity.

πάραυτα [paravta] immediately, at once, forthwith.

παραφέρνω [paraferno] carry more than necessary || resemble.

παραφέρομαι [paraferome] flare up, lose one's temper.

παραφθορά, ἡ [parafthora] alteration, corruption, change.

παραφορά, ἡ [parafora] frenzy, outburst || rage.

παράφορος [paraforos] hotheaded, hasty, furious.

παραφορτώνομαι [parafortonome] become overburdened || (ἐνοχλῶ) nag, annoy.

παραφορτώνω [parafortono] overload, overburden || (μεταφ) drive too hard.

παράφρασις, ἡ [parafrasees] paraphrase, free translation.

παραφρονῶ [parafrono] become insane, go mad.

παραφροσύνη, ἡ [parafroseenee] madness, insanity, foolish act.

παράφρων [parafron] mad, frenzied.

παραφυάς, ἡ [parafias] sprout, shoot || (οἰκογενείας) scion, offspring.

παραφυλάω [parafeelao] lie in wait for || be on the watch for.

παραφωνία, ἡ [parafoneea] dissonance || (μεταφ) discord, disagreement.

παραχαράκτης, ὁ [paraharaktees] forger, counterfeiter.

παραχειμάζω [paraheemazo] pass the winter, winter.

παραχρήμα [parahreema] immediately, instantly.

παραχώνω [parahono] bury, hide || (γεμίζω) stuff into.

παραχωρῶ [parahoro] grant, yield, concede || (παραδίδω) surrender, resign.

παρδαλός [parðalos] spotted || multicoloured, gaudy.

παρέα, ἡ [parea] company, set, party || κάνω ~ μέ keep company with.

παρειά, ἡ [paria] cheek || (μεταφ) wall.

παρείσακτος [pareesaktos] intrusive, intruding.

παρεκβαίνω [parekveno] digress, deviate.

παρέκβασις, ἡ [parekvasees] digression.

παρέκει [parekee] further on, a little further.

παρεκκλήσι(ον), τό [parekleesee(on)] chapel.

παρεκκλίνω [parekleeno] deviate from, turn aside from || diverge.

παρεκτείνω [parekteeno] prolong, extend.

παρεκτός [parektos] except, save, besides.

παρεκτροπή, ή [parektropee] aberration, deviation ‖ (ἠθική) misconduct, dissoluteness.

παρέλασις, ή [parelasees] parade, march-past, procession.

παρελαύνω [parelavno] march past, parade.

παρέλευσις, ή [parelevsees] passage of time, passing.

παρελθόν [parelthon] past, bygone.

παρελκύω [parelkeeo] drag out, protract, retard, delay.

παρεμβαίνω [paremveno] interfere, intervene, meddle with.

παρεμβάλλω [paremvalo] insert, interpose.

παρέμβασις, ή [paremvasees] intervention, mediation.

παρεμβολή, ή [paremvolee] insertion.

παρεμπιπτόντως [parempeeptontos] by the way.

παρεμφερής [paremferees] similar, of the same nature, resembling.

παρενέργεια, ή [pareneryeea] side effect.

παρένθεσις, ή [parenthesees] insertion ‖ (γραμμ) parenthesis.

παρενθέτω [parentheto] insert, interpose.

παρενοχλῶ [parenohlo] inconvenience, trouble, harass.

παρεξήγησις, ή [parekseeyeesees] misunderstanding.

παρεξηγῶ [parekseeyo] misunderstand, misinterpret, misconstrue.

παρεπιδημῶ [parepeedeemo] live temporarily (abroad).

παρεπόμενα, τά [parepomena] πλ consequences, issues.

πάρεργον, τό [parergon] sideline, hobby.

παρερμηνεία, ή [parermeeneea] misinterpretation.

παρέρχομαι [parerhome] elapse, pass ‖ (τελειώνω) come to an end ‖ (πηδῶ) pass over ‖ omit.

παρεστῶτες, οἱ [parestotes] πλ those present, those attending.

παρευθύς [parevthees] βλ πάραυτα.

παρευρίσκομαι [parevreeskome] be present at, attend.

παρεφθαρμένος [pareftharmenos] defective (linguistically).

παρέχω [pareho] procure ‖ give, supply ‖ (εὐκαιρίαν) occasion, bring about.

παρηγορία, ή [pareeyoreea] consolation, comfort, solace.

παρηγορῶ [pareeyoro] console, comfort.

παρθεναγωγεῖον, τό [parthenaγoγeeon] girls' school.

παρθενία, ή [partheneea] virginity, maidenhood ‖ chastity.

παρθενικός [partheneekos] virginal ‖ (μεταφ) pure ‖ maiden.

παρθένος, ή [parthenos] virgin, maiden.

Παρθενών, ὁ [parthenon] Parthenon.

παρίσταμαι [pareestame] be present at, assist (at) ‖ arise.

παριστάνω [pareestano] represent, portray, depict ‖ (ρόλον) perform ‖ pretend to be.

πάρκο, τό [parko] park.

παρντόν [parnton] pardon me!

παροδικός [paroδeekos] passing, fleeting, momentary.

πάροδος, ή [paroδos] side street ‖ (χρόνον κτλ) passing, course.

παροικία, ή [pareekeea] colony, quarter.

παροιμία, ή [pareemeea] proverb, adage, saying.

παροιμιώδης [pareemeeoδees] proverbial ‖ famous, renowned.

παρομοιάζω [paromeeazo] compare, liken ‖ resemble, be similar.

παρόμοιος [paromeeos] similar, alike.

παρόν, τό [paron] the present.

παρονομασία, ή [paronomaseea] play on words ‖ (παρατσούκλι) nickname.

παρονομαστής, ὁ [paronomastees] (μαθημ) denominator.

παροξυσμός, ὁ [parokseesmos] fit, attack ‖ incitement.

παροξύτονος [parokseetonos] accented on penultimate syllable.

παρόραμα, τό [parorama] mistake, blunder ‖ erratum.

παροργίζω [paroryeezo] irritate, enrage, vex, annoy.

παρόρμησις, ή [parormeesees] prompting, instigation ‖ stimulation, exhortation.

παροτρύνω [parotreeno] βλ παρακινῶ.

παρουσία, ή [parouseea] presence, attendance ‖ δευτέρα ~ second coming, doomsday.

παρουσιάζομαι [parouseeazome] appear ‖ introduce o.s.

παρουσιάζω [parouseeazo] present, show, introduce.

παρουσιαστικόν, τό [parouseeasteekon] presence, demeanour, bearing.

παροχή, ή [parohee] furnishing ‖ contribution, donation ‖ granting.

παρρησία, ή [pareeseea] frankness, candour.

πάρσιμο, τό [parseemo] capture, taking ‖ (ἐλάττωσις) trimming, lessening.

παρτέρι, τό [parteree] flower bed.

παρτίδα, ή [parteeδa] part, portion ‖ (παιγνιδιοῦ) game (of cards).

παρυφή, ή [pareefee] hem ‖ border, edge.

παρωδία, ή [paroδeea] parody, farce, travesty.

παρών [paron] present, actual.

παρωνυμία, ή [paroneemeea] nickname ‖ surname.

παρωνυχίς, ή [paroneehees] hangnail.

παρωπίς, ή [paropees] blinker, blind.

πάρωρα [parora] untimely, too late.

παρωχημένος [paroheemenos] past, gone by.

πᾶς [pas] any, all, every ‖ (οί πάντες) everybody, everyone.

πασαλείβομαι [pasaleevome] be smeared ‖ get a smattering of knowledge.

πασαλείβω [pasaleevo] smear, daub ‖ smudge.

πασᾶς, ὁ [pasas] pasha.

πασίγνωστος [paseeγnostos] well-known, notorious.

πασιέντζα, ἡ [pasientza] patience, solitaire (card game).

πασπαλίζω [paspaleezo] sprinkle, powder (with).

πασπατεύω [paspatevo] pry about, feel, finger.

πάσσαλος, ὁ [passalos] stake, post, pole.

πάσσο, τό [passo] stride, step ‖ πάω ~ (στά χαρτιά) pass (at cards).

πάστα, ἡ [pasta] dough, paste ‖ (γλυκό) pastry, cake ‖ (χαρακτήρ) character, sort.

παστέλι, τό [pastelee] concoction of honey and sesame.

παστίτσιο, τό [pasteetseeo] baked macaroni.

παστός [pastos] salted.

παστουρμᾶς, ὁ [pastourmas] seasoned cured meat.

παστρεύω [pastrevo] clean, cleanse ‖ (μεταφ) destroy, exterminate.

παστρικός [pastreekos] clean, neat ‖ (μεταφ) dishonest, depraved.

Πάσχα, τό [pasha] Easter.

πασχαλιά, ἡ [pashalia] lilac.

πασχίζω [pasheezo] try hard to, strive, endeavour.

πάσχω [pasho] be ill, suffer ‖ ὁ ~ν the patient, the sufferer.

πάταγος, ὁ [pataγos] din, noise, bang ‖ (μεταφ) sensation, stir.

παταγώδης [pataγodees] uproarious, noisy, loud.

πατάρι, τό [pataree] loft, attic.

πατάσσω [patasso] strike, treat severely.

πατάτα, ἡ [patata] potato.

πατατάλευρον, τό [patatalevron] potato flour.

πατέρας, ὁ [pateras] βλ πατήρ.

πατερίτσα, ἡ [patereetsa] crook, crutch ‖ bishop's staff.

πατερό, τό [patero] beam, rafter ‖ floor.

πατηκώνω [pateekono] press down, crush, compress.

πάτημα, τό [pateema] step, footstep ‖ (ἴχνος) footprint ‖ (σταφυλιῶν) treading, pressing ‖ excuse.

πατημασιά, ἡ [pateemasia] footprint, trace, track.

πατήρ, ὁ [pateer] father.

πατινάρω [pateenaro] skate.

πάτος, ὁ [patos] bottom ‖ (ποδός) sole.

πατούσα, ἡ [patousa] sole (anat).

πατριάρχης, ὁ [patreearhees] patriarch.

πατριαρχεῖον, τό [patreearheeon] patriarchate.

πατρίδα, ἡ [patreeda] native country, birthplace.

πατρικός [patreekos] paternal ‖ fatherly.

πάτριος [patreeos] paternal, ancestral ‖ native.

πατρίς, ἡ [patrees] native country, fatherland.

πατριώτης, ὁ [patreeotees] compatriot ‖ patriot.

πατριωτικός [patreeoteekos] patriotic.

πατριωτισμός, ὁ [patreeoteesmos] patriotism.

πατρογονικός [patroγoneekos] paternal, ancestral ‖ hereditary.

πατρόν, τό [patron] pattern (in dressmaking).

πατροπαράδοτος [patroparadotos] usual, customary, traditional ‖ hereditary.

πατρυιός, ὁ [patreeos] stepfather.

πατσαβούρα, ἡ [patsavoura] dish cloth, rag ‖ (μεταφ) rag (newspaper) ‖ prostitute.

πατσᾶς, ὁ [patsas] (soup of) tripe.

πάτσι [patsee] even, quits.

πατῶ [pato] step on ‖ (κουδούνι κτλ) press ‖ press down ‖ ~ τόν πάτο touch bottom ‖ (μεταφ) violate ‖ run over ‖ ~ πόδι I put my foot down.

πάτωμα, τό [patoma] floor, ground ‖ storey.

πατώνω [patono] lay a floor ‖ touch bottom, reach bottom.

παῦλα, ἡ [pavla] dash (punctuation).

παῦσις, ἡ [pavsees] stoppage, cessation, discharge ‖ (μουσ) rest, pause.

παύω [pavo] cease, stop ‖ cause to cease ‖ (ἀπολύω) dismiss ‖ (σταματῶ) stop, finish, give up.

παφλασμός, ὁ [paflasmos] splashing, gushing ‖ bubbling up.

παχαίνω [paheno] βλ παχύνω.

παχιά [pahia] πλ: ~ λόγια empty words, empty promises.

πάχνη, ἡ [pahnee] hoarfrost, rime.

παχνί, τό [pahnee] manger, crib.

πάχος, τό [pahos] plumpness ‖ thickness ‖ (λῖπος) fat, grease ‖ (στρώματος) depth.

παχουλός [pahoulos] plump, chubby.

παχύδερμος [paheedermos] (μεταφ) insensitive.

παχύνω [paheeno] fatten ‖ grow fat.

παχύς [pahees] thick ‖ fleshy, fat ‖ (εἰς λίπος) rich in fat ‖ (λειβάδι) rich.

παχύσαρκος [paheesarkos] fat, stout, obese.

πάω [pao] go ‖ take ‖ carry ‖ τά ~ καλά I get along well with ‖ ~ περίπατο it's a washout ‖ I go for a walk ‖ ~ νά σκάσω I'm ready to burst.

πεδιάδα, ἡ [pedeeada] plain, flat country.

πεδιάς, ἡ [pedias] βλ πεδιάδα.

πεδικλώνομαι [pedeeklonome] trip.

πεδικλώνω [pedeeklono] fetter ‖ hobble ‖ trip up.

πέδιλον, τό [pedeelon] sandal.

πεδινός [pedeenos] flat, level ‖ (ἔδαφος) even, smooth.

πεδίον, τό [pedeeon] plain, flat country, ground ‖ (μάχης) field of battle ‖ (ὀπτικόν) field.

πεζεύω [pezevo] dismount.

πεζῇ [pezee] on foot.

πεζικόν, τό [pezeekon] infantry.

πεζογραφία, ἡ [pezoγrafeea] prose.

πεζογράφος [pezoγrafos] prose writer, novelist.

πεζοδρόμιον, τό [pezoδromeeon] pavement ‖ (US) sidewalk.

πεζοναύτης, ὁ [pezonavtees] marine.

πεζοπορία, ἡ [pezoporeea] walking, walk ‖ (στρατ) march.

πεζός [pezos] pedestrian ‖ (τῆς πρόζας) in prose ‖ (μεταφ) banal, trivial, common.

πεζούλι, τό [pezoulee] parapet ‖ bench ‖ (σέ λόφο) terrace.

πεθαίνω [pethéno] die ‖ (μεταφ) perish ‖ be fond of, be mad about.

πεθαμός, ὁ [pethamos] death ‖ (μεταφ) excessive hardship.

πεθερά, ἡ [pethera] mother-in-law.

πεθερικά, τά [pethereeka] πλ in-laws.

πεθερός, ὁ [petheros] father-in-law.

πειθαναγκάζω [peethanangazo] persuade by force, force, compel.

πειθαρχία, ἡ [peetharheea] discipline.

πειθαρχικός [peetharheekos] disciplinary ‖ (ὑπάκουος) obedient, docile, submissive.

πειθαρχῶ [peetharho] be obedient, obey one's superiors.

πειθήνιος [peetheeneeos] docile, obedient, submissive.

πείθω [peetho] convince, persuade.

πειθώ, ἡ [peetho] persuasion, conviction.

πείνα, ἡ [peena] hunger, famine, starvation ‖ πειναλέος starving, famishing, ravenous ‖ πεινασμένος hungry, famished.

πεινῶ [peeno] be hungry, be starving.

πεῖρα, ἡ [peera] experience, background.

πείραγμα, τό [peeraγma] teasing ‖ annoyance ‖ (ἀσθένεια) malady.

πειραγμένος [peeraγmenos] hurt, offended ‖ (κρέας) tainted, spoilt.

πειράζει [peerazee]: ~; is it all right?, is it important?

πειράζω [peerazo] trouble, anger, annoy ‖ tease ‖ (τήν ὑγεία) upset, be bad for ‖ (ἐνοχλῶ) disturb.

πειρακτικός [peerakteekos] irritating, offensive, cutting.

πείραμα, τό [peerama] experiment ‖ trial, test ‖ πειραματικός experimental.

πειρασμός, ὁ [peerasmos] temptation.

πειρατής, ὁ [peeratees] pirate, corsair ‖ pirate taxi.

πεῖρος, ὁ [peeros] plug, peg.

πεῖσμα, τό [peesma] obstinacy, stubbornness ‖ πεισματάρης obstinate, stubborn ‖ πεισματώδης headstrong, stubborn ‖

πεισματώνομαι be unyielding ‖ πεισματώνω make obstinate, irritate ‖ become obdurate.

πείσμων [peesmon] βλ πεισματάρης.

πειστήριον, τό [peesteereeon] proof.

πειστήριος [peesteereeos] convincing, persuasive.

πειστικός [peesteekos] βλ πειστήριος.

πέλαγος, τό [pelaγos] open sea.

πελαγώνω [pelaγono] (μεταφ) lose one's way, be at a loss, feel at sea.

πελαργός, ὁ [pelarγos] stork.

πελατεία, ἡ [pelateea] clientèle, customers, patronage.

πελάτης, ὁ [pelatees] customer, patron, client ‖ (ξενοδοχείου) guest.

πελεκάνος, ὁ [pelekanos] pelican.

πελεκούδι, τό [pelekouδee] chip, paring, shaving.

πέλεκυς, ὁ [pelekees] axe, hatchet ‖ (μεταφ) punishment.

πελεκῶ [peleko] axe, hew, cut into shape, carve ‖ (μεταφ) thrash.

πελιδνός [peleeδnos] livid.

πέλμα, τό [pelma] sole (anat) ‖ (τεχνική) shoe, flange.

Πελοπόννησος, ἡ [peloponeesos] the Peloponnese.

πελότα, ἡ [pelota] pincushion.

πελτές [peltes] βλ μπελντές.

πελώριος [peloreeos] enormous, mammoth ‖ (σφάλμα) gross.

Πέμπτη, ἡ [pemptee] Thursday.

πέμπτος [pemptos] fifth.

πέμπω [pempo] send, send out ‖ forward.

πενήντα [peneenta] fifty.

πενηνταριά, ἡ [peeneentaria]: καμμιά ~ about fifty.

πένης, ὁ [penees] destitute or needy person.

πενθερά [penthera] βλ πεθερά.

πενθερός [pentheros] βλ πεθερός.

πενθήμερος [pentheemeros] of five days.

πένθιμος [pentheemos] sorrowful, mournful, dismal ‖ in mourning.

πένθος, τό [penthos] bereavement ‖ mourning.

πενθῶ [pentho] lament, mourn ‖ be in mourning.

πενία, ἡ [peneea] poverty, want.

πενιχρός [peneehros] poor, mean ‖ (γεῦμα) poor, scant ‖ paltry.

πέννα, ἡ [pena] pen ‖ (μουσικής) plectrum ‖ (νόμισμα) penny.

πεννάκι, τό [penakee] nib.

πένομαι [penome] be poverty-stricken, be needy.

πένσα, ἡ [pensa] tweezers, forceps ‖ (ραπτικῆς) dart.

πεντάγραμμον, τό [pentaγramon] (μουσ) stave, staff.

πεντακόσιοι [pentakosiee] five hundred.

πεντάμορφος [pentamorfos] extremely beautiful.

πεντάρα, ἡ [pentara] (μεταφ) farthing ‖ (US) nickel.

πεντάρι, τό [pentaree] figure 5 ‖ (στά χαρτιά) five (at cards).

πέντε [pente] five.

πεντήκοντα [penteekonta] βλ πενήντα.

Πεντηκοστή, ἡ [penteekostee] Whit Sunday.

πέος, τό [peos] penis.

πεπαιδευμένος [pepedevmenos] educated, learned, trained.

πεπειραμένος [pepeeramenos] experienced, versed in.

πεπεισμένος [pepeesmenos] convinced, certain, sure.

πέπλος, ὁ [peplos] veil.

πεποίθησις, ἡ [pepeetheesees] conviction, certainty, assurance.

πεπόνι, τό [peponee] melon.

πεπτικός [pepteekos] digestive, peptic.

πέρα [pera] beyond, over, on the other side, over there ‖ ἐκεῖ ~ yonder ‖ ~ γιά ~ through and through ‖ ἐδῶ ~ here ‖ ~ ἀπό beyond, across ‖ τά βγάζω ~ manage, make out.

περαιτέρω [peretero] further ‖ moreover.

πέραμα, τό [perama] passage, ford ‖ ferry.

πέραν [peran] βλ πέρα.

πέρας, τό [peras] end, extremity ‖ completion, close.

πέρασμα, τό [perasma] crossing, passage ‖ (βελόνας) threading ‖ (ἀσθενείας) passing ‖ (τόπος) much-visited spot.

περασμένος [perasmenos] past, gone, last, by.

περαστικά [perasteeka]: ~! get well soon!

περαστικός [perasteekos] passing by ‖ transient, transitory ‖ (δρόμος) frequented, busy.

περατώνω [peratono] finish, bring to an end, complete.

περβάζι, τό [pervazee] doorframe, frame, cornice.

περγαμηνή, ἡ [peryameenee] parchment.

πέρδικα, ἡ [perdeeka] partridge.

περδικλώνομαι [perdeeklonome] βλ πεδικλώνομαι.

περδικλώνω [perdeeklono] βλ πεδικλώνω.

πέρδομαι [perdome] fart (col), break wind.

περηφάνεια, ἡ [pereefaneea] βλ ὑπερηφάνεια.

περηφανεύομαι [pereefanevome] βλ ὑπερηφανεύομαι.

περήφανος [pereefanos] βλ ὑπερήφανος.

περί [peree] about, concerning, regarding, of ‖ (μέ αἰτ) round, near ‖ round about, approximately ‖ ~ τίνος πρόκειται; what's it all about?

περιαυτολογία, ἡ [pereeavtoloyeea] boasting, bragging.

περιαυτολογῶ [pereeavtoloyo] boast.

περιβάλλον, τό [pereevalon] environment, surroundings.

περιβάλλω [pereevalo] encircle, surround ‖ (ροῦχα) clothe, dress.

περίβλημα, τό [pereevleema] wrapper ‖ (καρποῦ) shell, husk ‖ casing.

περιβόητος [pereevoeetos] famous, renowned, infamous.

περιβολάρης, ὁ [pereevolarees] gardener.

περιβολή, ἡ [pereevolee] garment, dress ‖ surrounding.

περιβόλι, τό [pereevolee] garden, orchard.

περίβολος, ὁ [pereevolos] enclosure, yard ‖ (τοῖχος) surrounding wall ‖ park.

περιβρέχω [pereevreho] bathe, wash.

περιγελῶ [pereeyelo] mock, ridicule, deride ‖ dupe, trick.

περίγελως, ὁ [pereeyelos] laughing stock.

περιγιάλι, τό [pereeyialee] seashore, coast.

περιγραφή, ἡ [pereeyrafee] description, account.

περιγράφω [pereeyrafo] describe, portray.

περιδεής [pereedeis] terrified, frightened.

περιδέραιον, τό [pereedereon] necklace.

περίδοξος [pereedoksos] illustrious, famous.

περιεκτικός [periekteekos] capacious ‖ (τροφή) substantial ‖ (λόγος) comprehensive, concise, succinct.

περιεργάζομαι [perieryazome] examine carefully.

περιέργεια, ἡ [perieryeea] curiosity.

περίεργος [perieryos] curious, strange, inquiring.

περιέρχομαι [perierhome] travel through, walk round ‖ come into reach.

περιεχόμενον, τό [periehomenon] contents ‖ (σημασία) meaning.

περιέχω [perieho] contain, hold.

περιζήτητος [pereezeeteetos] in great demand, greatly prized.

περιηγητής, ὁ [perieeyeetees] tourist, traveller.

περιθάλπω [pereethalpo] attend, look after, treat.

περίθαλψις, ἡ [pereethalpsees] attendance, care, relief.

περιθώριον, τό [pereethoreeon] margin, room.

περικάλυμμα, τό [pereekaleema] wrapper, covering, shell.

περικεφαλαία, ἡ [pereekefalea] helmet.

περικλείω [pereekleeo] enclose, include.

περικοκλάδα, ἡ [pereekoklada] climbing plant ‖ convolvulus.

περικοπή, ἡ [pereekopee] cutting off, deduction ‖ (ἀπό βιβλίο) extract, passage.

περικόχλιον, τό [pereekohleeon] nut (for screw).

περικυκλώνω [pereekeeklono] surround.

περιλαίμιον, τό [pereelemeeon] animal's collar ‖ necklace.

περιλάλητος [pereelaleetos] celebrated, famous, renowned.

περιλαμβάνω [pereelamvano] contain, have, hold ‖ (περιέχω) include, comprise.

περιληπτικός [pereeleepteekos] comprehensive ‖ concise, succinct.

περίληψις, ή [pereeleepsees] summary, précis, résumé.

περίλυπος [pereeleepos] sad, sorrowful ‖ (έκφρασις) gloomy, doleful.

περιμαζεύω [pereemazevo] gather up ‖ (άπό τόν δρόμο) rescue, harbour ‖ (περιορίζω) check, control.

περιμένω [pereemeno] wait ‖ wait for, expect.

περίμετρος, ή [pereemetros] circumference, perimeter.

πέριξ [pereeks] about, round ‖ τά ~ the environs, suburb.

περιοδεία, ή [pereeodeea] tour, travelling, trip.

περιοδικόν, τό [pereeodeekon] magazine, periodical.

περιοδικός [pereeodeekos] periodic(al).

περίοδος, ή [pereeodos] period, era, age ‖ season ‖ (γυναικών) monthlies.

περίοπτος [pereeoptos] overlooking, rising, conspicuous ‖ noticeable.

περιορίζω [pereeoreezo] limit, restrict ‖ (έλέγχω) control ‖ (έλαττώνω) reduce, cut down, curtail.

περιορισμός, ό [pereeoreesmos] limitation ‖ detention, restriction ‖ (έλάττωσις) reduction.

περιουσία, ή [pereeouseea] property, estate ‖ (πλούτη) fortune, wealth.

περιοχή, ή [pereeohee] area, region, district ‖ extent, expanse.

περιπαθής [pereepathees] full of feeling, passionate, impetuous.

περιπαίζω [pereepezo] ridicule, mock ‖ dupe, trick, take in.

περίπατο [pereepato]: πάω ~ go for a stroll ‖ (μεταφ) be a failure.

περίπατος, ό [pereepatos] walk, ride, drive, spin.

περιπατώ [pereepato] βλ περπατώ.

περιπέτεια, ή [pereepeteea] misadventure, incident.

περιπέτειες, οί [pereepeties] πλ the ups and downs.

περιπετειώδης [pereepeteeodees] full of adventures ‖ (ίστορία) of adventure.

περιπίπτω [pereepeepto] fall into ‖ be reduced to.

περιπλανώ [pereeplano] send long way round ‖ ~μαι wander, rove, lose one's way.

περιπλέκω [pereepleko] interlace, entangle ‖ complicate, confuse, muddle.

περιπλέον [pereepleon] moreover, besides ‖ τό ~ surplus, excess.

περιπλέω [pereepleo] circumnavigate.

περιπλοκή, ή [pereeplokee] complication, complexity, intricacy.

περίπλοκος [pereeplokos] complex, involved.

περιπόθητος [pereepotheetos] much loved, greatly desired.

περιποίησις, ή [pereepieesees] care, attendance, looking after.

περιποιητικός [pereepieeteekos] considerate, obliging.

περιποιοῦμαι [pereepeeoume] take care of ‖ (άσθενή) nurse.

περίπολος, ή [pereepolos] patrol.

περίπου [pereepou] about, nearly, almost.

περίπτερον, τό [pereepteron] pavilion, kiosk.

περιπτώσει [pereeptosee]: έν πάσει ~ in any case, anyway.

περίπτωσις, ή [pereeptosees] case, condition, circumstance.

περισκελίς, ή [pereeskelees] pair of trousers, pants ‖ (γυναικός) knickers, panties.

περίσκεψις, ή [pereeskepsees] prudence, caution, discretion.

περισπασμός, ό [pereespasmos] diversion, distraction ‖ (μεταφ) embarrassment, perplexity.

περισπῶ [pereespo] distract, divert ‖ (γραμμ) circumflex.

περισπωμένη, ή [pereespomenee] circumflex accent.

περίσσεια, ή [pereeseea] excess, superabundance.

περίσσευμα, τό [pereesevma] surplus, excess.

περισσεύω [pereesevo] be in excess, be left over.

περίσσιος [pereeseeos] (άφθονος) abundant ‖ (περιττός) unnecessary.

περισσοῦ [pereesou]: ὡς ἐκ ~ without absolute necessity, moreover.

περισσότερον [pereesoteron] more.

περισσότερος [pereesoteros] more ‖ ὁ ~ most.

περισταλτικός [pereestalteekos] checking, repressive ‖ (ίατρ) peristaltic.

περίστασις, ή [pereestasees] circumstance, event, fact, occasion, situation.

περιστατικόν, τό [pereestateekon] incident, event.

περιστέλλω [pereestelo] repress, check, restrain, reduce.

περιστερώνας, ό [pereesteronas] dovecote.

περιστέρι, τό [pereesteree] pigeon, dove.

περιστοιχίζω [pereesteeheezo] surround, encircle.

περιστολή, ή [pereestolee] limitation, decrease, restriction, checking.

περιστρέφομαι [pereestrefome] revolve, spin, turn.

περιστρέφω [pereestrefo] (ρόδα κτλ) turn, rotate ‖ (κλειδί) turn, twist.

περιστροφή, ή [pereestrofee] revolution, turn, rotation.

περίστροφον, τό [pereestrofon] revolver.

περισυλλέγω [pereeseelego] collect, gather.

περισφίγγω [pereesfingo] hug, embrace, clasp in one's hand.

περιτειχίζω [pereeteeheezo] build a wall round.

περιτομή, ἡ [pereetomee] circumcision.

περίτρανος [pereetranos] obvious, clear, evident.

περιτριγυρίζω [pereetreeyeereezo] surround, encircle, border.

περίτρομος [pereetromos] terrified, frightened.

περιτροπή, ἡ [pereetropee]: **ἐκ περιτροπῆς** by turns, in turn.

περιττός [pereetos] (προσπάθεια) useless, unavailing || superfluous, unnecessary, needless || ~ ἀριθμός odd number.

περιτύλιγμα, τό [pereeteeleeyma] wrapper, wrapping.

περιτυλίσσω [pereeteeleeso] wrap up || roll up.

περιφανής [pereefanees] manifest, obvious || (ἄνθρωπος) eminent, distinguished.

περιφέρεια, ἡ [pereefereea] (δένδρου) girth || (γεωμ) circumference || (χῶρος) district, region.

περιφέρομαι [pereeferome] stroll, walk up and down, hang about || (ἡ γῆ κτλ) turn round, rotate.

περιφέρω [pereefero] turn, revolve, rotate.

περίφημος [pereefeemos] famous, admirable, celebrated.

περιφορά, ἡ [pereefora] turn, rotation || (ἐκκλ) procession.

περίφραγμα, τό [pereefrayma] enclosure, hedge, fencing.

περίφραξις, ἡ [pereefraksees] enclosing, fencing.

περιφραστικός [pereefrasteekos] periphrastic(al).

περιφρόνησις, ἡ [pereefroneesees] contempt, scorn.

περιφρονητικός [pereefroneeteekos] disdainful, contemptuous, haughty.

περίφροντις [pereefrontees] full of care, concerned.

περιφρονῶ [pereefrono] hold in contempt, despise, spurn.

περιχαρής [pereeharees] cheerful, merry, joyful, gay.

περίχωρα, τά [pereehora] πλ neighbourhood, environs || (πόλεως) suburb, outskirts.

περιώνυμος [pereeoneemos] celebrated, illustrious.

περιωπή, ἡ [pereeopee] eminence || (μεταφ) importance || ἀπό περιωπῆς with detachment.

περνῶ [perno] (ποτάμι, γέφυρα κτλ) pass, cross, go over || (κάτι σέ κάποιον) pass, hand over || (κάτι μέσα σέ κάτι) pass through || (τόν καιρό) spend || (βελόνη) thread (a needle) || (ὑγρό ἀπό φίλτρο) filter, strain || (νόμον) get voted, pass ||

(στό δρόμο) pass, leave behind || ~ γιά mistake for || ~ ἀπό call at, go via.

περονιάζω [peroneeazo] pierce, go through.

περονόσπορος, ὁ [peronosporos] mildew.

περούκα, ἡ [perouka] wig.

περπάτημα, τό [perpateema] walking || gait.

περπατῶ [perpato] walk || go across || (σκύλο κτλ) take for a walk.

πέρ(υ)σι [per(ee)see] last year || **περ(υ)σινός** of last year.

πέσιμο, τό [peseemo] falling, fall.

πεσμένος [pesmenos] fallen || impaired, worsened.

πέστροφα, ἡ [pestrofa] trout.

πέταγμα, τό [petayma] flying, flight || throwing away, casting.

πετάγομαι [petayome] fly up || rush || butt in.

πετάλι, τό [petalee] pedal.

πεταλίδα, ἡ [petaleeda] limpet.

πέταλο, τό [petalo] petal || (ἀλόγου) horseshoe.

πεταλούδα, ἡ [petalouda] butterfly || (λαιμοδέτου) bow, bow tie.

πεταλώνω [petalono] shoe (a horse).

πέταμα [petama] βλ **πέταγμα**.

πεταχτά [petahta]: **στά** ~ hastily, hurriedly, quickly.

πεταχτός [petahtos] nimble || sticking out.

πετεινός, ὁ [peteenos] cock || (ὅπλου) hammer.

πετ(ι)μέζι, τό [pet(ee)mezee] must turned into syrup.

πετονιά, ἡ [petonia] fishing line.

πέτρα, ἡ [petra] stone, rock || precious stone.

πετράδι, τό [petradee] pebble || precious stone.

πετραχήλι, τό [petraheelee] (ἐκκλ) stole.

πετρέλαιον, τό [petreleon] petroleum, oil || (ἀκάθαρτο) crude oil.

πετρελαιοπηγή, ἡ [petreleopeeyee] oil well.

πετρελαιοφόρον, τό [petreleoforon] oil tanker.

πέτρινος [petreenos] made of stone.

πετροβολῶ [petrovolo] pelt with stones.

πέτσα, ἡ [petsa] skin || (ψωμιοῦ) crust || (γάλακτος) cream.

πετσέτα, ἡ [petseta] table napkin || towel.

πετσί, τό [petsee] skin, pelt, hide || leather, dressed skin.

πέτσινος [petseenos] leather.

πετσοκόβω [petsokovo] cut up, carve || cut badly, butcher.

πέττο, τό [peto] lapel.

πετυχαίνω [peteeheno] βλ **ἐπιτυγχάνω**.

πετῶ [peto] fly || (ἀπό χαρά) jump for joy || (στά σκουπίδια) throw away || ~ ἔξω throw out || kick out (col).

πεῦκο, τό [pefko] pine.

πέφτει [peftee]: **δέν σοῦ** ~ **λόγος** you've got no say in the matter.

πέφτω [pefto] tumble, fall || drop, come

down, subside ‖ come off ‖ occur ‖ ~ στό **κρεββάτι** I go to bed ‖ ~ **ἔξω** make a mistake ‖ (ναυτ) run aground ‖ ~ **δίπλα** make up to ‖ ~ **μέ τά μοῦτρα** apply o.s., take up eagerly.

πέψις, ἡ [pepsees] digestion.

πηγάδι, τό [peeyadee] well.

πηγάζω [peeyazo] spring from, originate, emanate.

πηγαινοέλα, τό [peeyenoela] toing and froing.

πηγαινοέρχομαι [peeyenoerhome] go to and fro.

πηγαίνω [peeyeno] go ‖ escort, take ‖ βλ καί **πάω.**

πηγή, ἡ [peeyee] spring, source ‖ (μεταφ) origin, cause.

πηγούνι, τό [peeyounee] chin.

πηδάλιον, τό [peedaleeon] rudder ‖ helm ‖ wheel.

πηδαλιοῦχος, ὁ [peedaleeouhos] helmsman.

πήδημα, τό [peedeema] jump(ing), spring ‖ sudden rise.

πηδῶ [peedo] leap, jump, vault ‖ jump over ‖ (παραλείπω) skip, leave out.

πήζω [peezo] coagulate, thicken, curdle.

πηκτός [peektos] coagulated, thick, curdled.

πηλάλα, ἡ [peelala] quick running ‖ (ἐπίρ) at full speed.

πηλαλῶ [peelalo] run (quickly, at full speed).

πηλήκιον, τό [peeleekeeon] cap.

πηλίκον, τό [peeleekon] quotient.

πήλινος [peeleenos] earthen, of clay.

πηλός, ἡ [peelos] clay ‖ mud, slime, sludge.

πηνίον, τό [peeneeon] bobbin, spool ‖ (ἠλεκ) coil.

πῆξις, ἡ [peeksees] coagulation, congealing ‖ sticking in.

πηρούνι, τό [peerounee] fork.

πῆττα, ἡ [peeta] kind of cake, pie.

πήχη, ἡ [peehee] measure of length (0.46 m).

πηχτή, ἡ [peehtee] galantine.

πηχτός [peehtos] coagulated, jellied ‖ thick.

πῆχυς, ὁ [peehees] cubit ‖ ell.

πῑ, τό [pee] the letter Π ‖ στό ~ **καί φῑ** in two shakes of a lamb's tail.

πιά [pia] not any longer ‖ now, finally, at last, at long last.

πιάνο, τό [peeano] piano.

πιάνομαι [peeanome] be caught at, be paralyzed ‖ (τσακώνομαι) quarrel with ‖ (κατάγομαι) be related to.

πιάνω [peeano] take hold of, catch ‖ occupy ‖ (συζήτησι) engage ‖ (περιέχω) contain, hold ‖ (λιμάνι) land ‖ ~ **σπίτι** rent a house ‖ ~ **τόπο** come in useful ‖ ~ **κουβέντα** get into conversation ‖ ~ **δουλειά** start a job, find a job.

πιάσιμο, τό [peeaseemo] hold, grasp ‖ catching ‖ (ἀφή) feeling, touch ‖ (φυτοῦ κτλ) taking root ‖ (σώματος) stiffness, paralysis.

πιασμένος [peeasmenos] occupied, taken ‖ (στό σῶμα) paralyzed, (feeling) stiff, crippled.

πιατάκι, τό [peeatakee] small plate ‖ saucer.

πιατέλλα, ἡ [peeatela] large dish, flat dish.

πιατικά, τά [peeateeka] πλ crockery, earthenware.

πιάτσα, ἡ [peeatsa] market ‖ (ταξί) taxi rank.

πίδαξ, ὁ [peedaks] jet of water, gush, spirt, fountain.

πιέζω [piezo] press, squeeze, compress ‖ oppress, force.

πίεσις, ἡ [piesees] pressure, oppression ‖ (αἵματος) blood pressure.

πιεστήριον, τό [piesteereeon] press ‖ (ἐλαιῶν) oil-press.

πιεστικός [piesteekos] pressing, oppressive ‖ urgent.

πιέτα, ἡ [pieta] pleat.

πιθαμή, ἡ [peethamee] span of hand.

πιθανός [peethanos] probable, likely.

πιθανότης, ἡ [peethanotees] likelihood, probability.

πιθανῶς [peethanos] probably, likely, in all likelihood.

πίθηκος, ὁ [peetheekos] ape.

πιθάρι, τό [peetharee] jar.

πίθος, ὁ [peethos] βλ **πιθάρι.**

πίκα, ἡ [peeka] umbrage, pique ‖ (στά χαρτιά) spade.

πικάντικος [peekanteekos] piquant, spicy.

πίκρα, ἡ [peekra] grief, bitterness, affliction.

πικράδα, ἡ [peekraδa] bitterness ‖ (μεταφ) sorrow, chagrin.

πικραίνομαι [peekrenome] be grieved, be embittered.

πικραίνω [peekreno] render bitter ‖ grieve, distress.

πικροδάφνη, ἡ [peekroδafnee] oleander.

πικρός [peekros] bitter ‖ biting, harsh.

πικρότης, ἡ [peekrotees] bitterness.

πικρόχολος [peekroholos] (μεταφ) touchy, irritable, snappy.

πιλάφι, τό [peelafee] pilaf, rice dish.

πῖλος, ὁ [peelos] hat.

πιλότος, ὁ [peelotos] pilot.

πινάκιον, τό [peenakeeon] dish, plate ‖ list, roll, register.

πινακίς, ἡ [peenakees] nameplate ‖ (αὐτοκινήτου) licence plate, number plate.

πινακοθήκη, ἡ [peenakotheekee] picture gallery, art gallery.

πίνακας, ὁ [peenakas] βλ **πίναξ.**

πίναξ, ὁ [peenaks] list, table ‖ (τοῦ τείχου) notice board ‖ (σχολείου) blackboard ‖ (περιεχομένων) table of contents.

πινέζα, ἡ [peeneza] drawing pin.

πινέλο, τό [peenelo] artist's paintbrush.

πίνω [peeno] drink, take in ‖ (τσιγάρο) smoke.

πιό [pio] more, greater.

πιοτό, τό [pioto] drinking ‖ drink, liquor.
πίπα, ή [peepa] pipe ‖ cigarette holder.
κιπεράτος [peeperatos] peppery ‖ biting, caustic, piquant.
πιπέρι, τό [peeperee] pepper.
πιπεριά, ή [peeperia] pepper ‖ (δένδρον) pepper tree.
πιπιλίζω [peepeeleezo] suck, sip.
πίπτω [peepto] βλ πέφτω.
πισίνα, ή [peeseena] swimming pool.
πισινός [peeseenos] back, posterior ‖ ὁ ~ backside (col), arse (col), bum (col).
πίσσα, ή [peesa] pitch, tar, asphalt.
πισσόχαρτο, τό [peesoharto] roofing felt.
πισσώνω [peesono] tar, pitch.
πίστα, ή [peesta] ring ‖ racetrack ‖ (χοροῦ) dance floor.
πιστευτός [peestevtos] trustworthy ‖ credible.
πιστεύω [peestevo] believe, have faith in ‖ suppose, fancy, think.
πίστις, ή [peestees] faith, confidence, trust ‖ fidelity ‖ (οἰκον) credit, trustworthiness.
πιστόλι, τό [peestolee] pistol.
πιστοποιητικόν, τό [peestopieeteekon] certificate, testimonial.
πιστοποιῶ [peestopeeo] certify, guarantee, vouch for.
πιστός [peestos] faithful, loyal, devoted ‖ accurate.
πιστώνω [peestono] (οἰκον) credit with, give credit.
πίστωσις, ή [peestosees] credit, trust.
πιστωτής, ὁ [peestotees] creditor.
πίσω [peeso] behind ‖ back ‖ over again ‖ πάει ~ τό ρολόϊ the clock is slow ‖ κάνω ~ move back ‖ ~ μου behind me ‖ ~ ἀπό behind, following.
πίτουρο, τό [peetouro] bran.
πιτσιλάδα, ή [peetseelada] freckle.
πιτσιλίζω [peetseeleezo] splash, sprinkle, dash (with).
πιτσιρίκος, ὁ [peetseereekos] small boy ‖ kid (col).
πιτσούνι, τό [peetsounee] young pigeon, squab.
πίττα [peeta] βλ πήττα.
πιτυρίδα, ή [peeteereeda] scurf, dandruff.
πίτυρον, τό [peeteeron] βλ πίτουρο.
πιωμένος [piomenos] drunk, tipsy.
πλά(γ)ι, τό [pla(γ)ee] side ‖ στό ~ close by, near, beside.
πλαγιά, ή [playia] slope of hill, hillside.
πλαγιάζω [playiazo] go to bed ‖ lie down ‖ put to bed.
πλαγιαστός [playiastos] lying down, reclining.
πλάγιος [playeos] oblique ‖ indirect ‖ crooked, dishonest.
πλαγίως [playeos] indirectly ‖ next door.
πλαδαρός [pladaros] flabby, soft ‖ (προσπάθεια) feeble, ineffective.
πλάζ, ή [plaz] bathing beach.

πλάθω [platho] mould, create, fashion.
πλάϊ [plaee] alongside, next door ‖ ~ ~ side by side ‖ ~ σέ next to, along with.
πλαϊνός [plaeenos] adjoining, next door.
πλαίσιον, τό [pleseeon] frame, framework ‖ chassis ‖ (μεταφ) scope, range.
πλαισιώνω [pleseeono] border, surround, frame, encircle.
πλάκα, ή [plaka] slab, plate, paving stone ‖ plaque ‖ (σχολική) slate ‖ (σαπούνι) cake ‖ (γραμμοφώνου) record ‖ (φωτογραφική) plate ‖ σπάσαμε ~ we had a lot of fun ‖ ἔχει ~ it's funny, it's hilarious.
πλακάκι, τό [plakakee] floor tile, wall tile.
πλακόστρωτος [plakostrotos] paved, laid with tiles.
πλάκωμα, τό [plakoma] pressure, crush ‖ unexpected arrival.
πλακώνω [plakono] crush, press down ‖ happen unexpectedly ‖ come suddenly.
πλακωτός [plakotos] flat(tened), in layers.
πλάνη, ή [planee] mistake, delusion ‖ (ἐργαλεῖον) plane.
πλάνης, ὁ [planees] wanderer, vagrant.
πλανήτης, ὁ [planeetees] planet.
πλανίζω [planeezo] plane, smooth down.
πλανόδιος [planodeeos] travelling ‖ ~ ἔμπορος pedlar, hawker.
πλανταζω [plantazo] be furious, fume, be enraged.
πλανώμαι [planome] ramble, wander ‖ (κάνω λάθος) be mistaken, delude o.s.
πλάξ, ή [plaks] βλ πλάκα.
πλασιέ, ὁ [plasie] commercial traveller, salesman.
πλάσις, ή [plasees] foundation, creation ‖ moulding, formation.
πλάσμα, τό [plasma] creature, being ‖ invention, fiction ‖ beauty.
πλάστιγξ, ή [plasteengks] weighing machine, balance.
πλαστικός [plasteekos] plastic ‖ comely.
πλαστογραφῶ [plastoγrafo] counterfeit ‖ falsify.
πλαστός [plastos] false, forged ‖ artificial, fictitious.
πλατάίνω [plateno] βλ πλατύνω.
πλάτανος, ὁ [platanos] plane tree.
πλατεία, ή [plateea] town square ‖ (θεάτρου) pit.
πλάτη, ή [platee] back ‖ shoulder blade.
πλατιά [platia] widely.
πλάτος, τό [platos] width, broadness, breadth ‖ (γεωγραφικόν) latitude.
πλάττω [plato] βλ πλάθω.
πλατύνω [plateeno] make wider, stretch, let out ‖ become wider, broaden.
πλατύς [platees] wide, broad, large, ample ‖ (μεταφ) far-reaching.
πλέγμα, τό [pleγma] network ‖ (μαλλιῶν) tress, braid.
πλειοδοτῶ [pleeodoto] make highest offer or bid.

πλεῖον [pleeon] more.

πλειονότης, ή [pleeonotees] majority.

πλειο(νο)ψηφία, ή [pleeo(no)pseefeea] majority (of votes).

πλειστάκις [pleestakees] many times, often.

πλειστηριασμός, ὁ [pleesteereeasmos] auction.

πλεῖστος [pleestos] most, very much.

πλεκτός [plektos] knitted, plaited, woven.

πλέκω [pleko] plait, weave || (κάλτσες) knit.

πλεμόνι, τό [plemonee] lung.

πλένω [pleno] βλ πλύνω.

πλέξιμο, τό [plekseemo] knitting || braiding || (σέ ὑπόθεσι) involvement.

πλεξούδα, ή [pleksouda] plait, braid, tress.

πλέον [pleon] more || ἐπί ~ in addition || not any longer || moreover || in now.

πλεονάζω [pleonazo] abound, be plentiful || exceed, be superfluous.

πλεόνασμα, τό [pleonasma] surplus, excess || (βάρους) overweight.

πλεονέκτημα, τό [pleonekteema] advantage, benefit || gift, quality, merit.

πλεονέκτης, ὁ [pleonektees] greedy person, covetous person.

πλεονεκτῶ [pleonekto] have the advantage || be greedy.

πλεονεξία, ή [pleonekseea] cupidity, greed, avidity.

πλέριος [plereeos] full.

πλευρά, ή [plevra] side || rib || (ὄρους) slope, declivity || (μεταφ) point of view.

πλευρίζω [plevreezo] (ναυτ) come alongside.

πλευρῖτις, ή [plevreetees] pleurisy.

πλευρόν, τό [plevron] side || rib || (στρατ) flank.

πλεχτό, τό [plehto] pullover || knitted article.

πλέω [pleo] navigate, sail || float || (μεταφ) wade, wallow.

πληγή, ή [pleeyee] wound, injury, sore || (μεταφ) plague, evil, sore.

πλῆγμα, τό [pleeyma] blow || wound.

πληγώνω [pleeyono] wound, injure || offend, hurt.

πλήθη, τά [pleethee] πλ the masses.

πλῆθος, τό [pleethos] crowd || mass || great number.

πληθυντικός, ὁ [pleetheenteekos] (γραμμ) plural.

πληθύνω [pleetheeno] multiply, increase || augment.

πληθυσμός, ὁ [pleetheesmos] population.

πληθώρα, ή [pleethora] abundance, excess, plenitude.

πληθωρισμός, ὁ [pleethoreesmos] inflation || plenitude.

πληκτικός [pleekteekos] boring, tiresome, irksome, dull, trying.

πλῆκτρον, τό [pleektron] (πιάνο κτλ) key || plectrum || drumstick.

πλημμελειοδικεῖον, τό [pleemeleeodeekeeon] (νομ) magistrate's court.

πλημμέλημα, τό [pleemeleema] misdemeanour, offence.

πλημμελής [pleemelees] faulty, inadequate, defective.

πλημμύρα, ή [pleemeera] flood, inundation || (μεταφ) plenitude.

πλημμυρίζω [pleemeereezo] inundate, overflow || (μεταφ) swarm.

πλήν [pleen] except, save || (ἐπίρ) unless, except that || (σύνδ) but || (μαθημ) minus || ~ τούτου besides, moreover.

πλῆξις, ή [pleeksees] tedium, weariness, boredom.

πληρεξούσιον, τό [pleereksouseeon] power of attorney.

πληρεξούσιος, ὁ, ή [pleereksouseeos] representative, proxy || plenipotentiary, deputy.

πλήρης [pleerees] full, complete, whole || swarming, teeming, packed.

πληροφορία, ή [pleeroforeea] information, report.

πληροφορίες, οἱ [pleerofories] πλ information.

πληροφοροῦμαι [pleeroforoume] learn, discover.

πληροφορῶ [pleeroforo] inform, notify.

πληρῶ [pleero] fill || fulfil, perform.

πλήρωμα, τό [pleeroma] crew || fullness || filling, completion.

πληρωμή, ή [pleeromee] payment, reward || salary, wages.

πληρώνω [pleerono] pay, settle || (μεταφ) pay up, discharge.

πληρωτέος [pleeroteos] payable.

πληρωτής [pleerotees] payer.

πλησιάζω [pleeseeazo] approach, go near, put near, draw near.

πλησιέστερος [pleeseesteros] closer || ὁ ~ the nearest.

πλησίον [pleeseeon] near, close by || ὁ ~ neighbour.

πλησμονή, ή [pleesmonee] abundance, plenitude || satiety.

πλήττω [pleeto] strike, hit, wound, afflict || (παθαίνω πλῆξι) be bored, be weary.

πλιάτσικο, τό [pleeatseeko] booty, pillage, loot.

πλίθ(ρ)α, ή [pleeth(r)a] brick.

πλινθόκτιστος [pleenthokteestos] built of bricks.

πλίνθος, ή [pleenthos] brick, firebrick.

πλοηγός, ὁ [ploeeyos] (ναυτ) pilot.

πλοιάριον, τό [pleeareeon] small boat, launch.

πλοίαρχος, ὁ [pleearhos] (ναυτ) captain || (ἐμπορικοῦ) master, skipper.

πλοῖον, τό [pleeon] ship, vessel, boat.

πλόκαμος, ὁ [plokamos] tress, braid, plait || (κινέζων) pigtail || (ὀκταποδιοῦ) tentacle.

πλοκή, ή [plokee] plot (of play).

πλουμίδι, τό [ploumeedee] embroidery, ornamentation.

πλοῦς, ὁ [plous] sailing, passage ‖ navigating.

πλουσιοπάροχος [plouseeoparohos] copious, generous, abundant.

πλούσιος [plouseeos] rich, wealthy ‖ splendid, magnificent.

πλουταίνω [plouteno] get rich, become wealthy.

πλουτίζω [plouteezo] make rich ‖ get rich.

πλούτη, τά [ploutee] πλ riches, wealth.

πλοῦτος, ὁ [ploutos] opulence, wealth ‖ richness ‖ (ἐδάφους) fertility.

πλυντήριον, τό [pleenteereeon] laundry room ‖ washing machine.

πλύνω [pleeno] wash, clean ‖ brush ‖ scrub.

πλύσιμο, τό [pleeseemo] wash(ing).

πλυσταριό, τό [pleestario] laundry room.

πλύστρα, ή [pleestra] washerwoman ‖ washboard.

πλώρη, ή [ploree] prow ‖ βάζω ~ set sail (for).

πλωτάρχης, ὁ [plotarhees] lieutenant-commander.

πλωτός [plotos] navigable ‖ floating ‖ (γέφυρα) pontoon bridge.

πνεῦμα, τό [pnevma] ghost, soul, breath of life ‖ mind ‖ genius, spirit ‖ (γραμμ) breathing ‖ ῍Αγιον ~ Holy Ghost.

πνευματικός [pnevmateekos] spiritual ‖ intellectual, mental ‖ pneumatic.

πνευμονία, ή [pnevmoneea] pneumonia.

πνεύμων, ὁ [pnevmon] lung.

πνευστός [pnevstos] blown, wind (instrument).

πνέω [pneo] blow ‖ ~ τά λοίσθια I breathe my last.

πνιγηρός [pneeyeros] stifling, suffocating, choking.

πνιγμός, ὁ [pneeymos] suffocation, choking ‖ drowning ‖ throttling.

πνίγω [pneeyo] drown ‖ stifle, suffocate ‖ choke, throttle.

πνικτικός [pneekteekos] suffocating, choking.

πνίξιμο, τό [pneekseemo] drowning ‖ strangulation.

πνοή, ή [pnoee] breath(ing) ‖ (μεταφ) inspiration.

ποδάγρα, ή [podaqra] gout.

ποδάρι, τό [podaree] βλ πόδι.

ποδήλατον, τό [podeelaton] bicycle.

ποδηλατῶ [podeelato] cycle, pedal.

πόδι, τό [podee] foot, leg ‖ (ποτηριοῦ) stem ‖ στό ~ standing ‖ on the go ‖ σηκώνω στό ~ cause a commotion.

ποδιά, ή [podia] apron, overall ‖ (παραθύρου) windowsill.

ποδόγυρος, ὁ [podoyeeros] border, hem ‖ (μεταφ) the fair sex.

ποδοπατῶ [podopato] tread on, trample on, trample underfoot.

ποδόσφαιρα, ή [podosfera] football.

ποδοσφαιριστής, ὁ [podosfereestees] football player.

ποδόσφαιρον, τό [podosferon] game of football.

πόζα, ή [poza] pose, affectation.

ποζάρω [pozaro] pose, sit for ‖ put on.

πόθεν [pothen] whence, from where, from what.

πόθος, ὁ [pothos] desire, wish, yearning.

ποθῶ [potho] desire, long for, wish, be eager for.

ποίημα, τό [pieema] poem.

ποίησις, ή [pieesees] poetry, poesy.

ποιητής, ὁ [pieetees] poet ‖ creator, maker.

ποιητικός [pieeteekos] poetic.

ποικιλία, ή [peekeeleea] variety, diversity, assortment.

ποικίλλω [peekeelo] embellish, adorn ‖ vary, change.

ποικίλος [peekeelos] varied, diverse, different ‖ miscellaneous.

ποιμενικός [peemeneekos] pastoral, bucolic.

ποιμήν, ὁ [peemeen] shepherd, herdsman.

ποίμνιον, τό [peemneeon] flock, herd, drove ‖ (ἐκκλ) flock.

ποινή, ή [peenee] penalty, punishment, pain.

ποινικός [peeneekos] penal, criminal, felonious.

ποιόν, τό [peeon] quality, property, attribute, nature.

ποῖος [peeos] who?, which?, what?

ποιότης, ή [peeotees] quality, property.

ποιῶ [peeo] create, make ‖ do.

πολεμικόν, τό [polemeekon] warship.

πολεμικός [polemeekos] warlike, bellicose ‖ of war, martial.

πολέμιος [polemeeos] unfriendly, hostile ‖ ὁ ~ enemy, adversary.

πολεμιστής, ὁ [polemeestees] fighter, warrior, combatant.

πόλεμος, ὁ [polemos] war, warfare.

πολεμοφόδια, τά [polemofodeea] πλ munitions, ammunition.

πολεμῶ [polemo] fight, make war against ‖ contend, strive (to).

πολεοδομία, ή [poleodomeea] town planning.

πολικός [poleekos] polar.

πολιορκία, ή [poleeorkeea] siege, blockade.

πολιορκῶ [poleeorko] besiege, surround ‖ invest.

πόλις, ή [polees] city, town.

πολιτεία, ή [poleeteea] state, government ‖ country, nation ‖ town.

πολίτευμα, τό [poleetevma] system of government, regime.

πολιτεύομαι [poleetevome] go into politics, meddle in politics.

πολιτευτής, ὁ [poleetevtees] politician, statesman.

πολιτικά, τά [poleeteeka] πλ politics.

πολίτης, ὁ [poleetees] citizen ‖ civilian.

πολιτική, ἡ [poleeteekee] politics ‖ policy ‖ (μεταφ) cunning, shrewdness.

πολιτικός [poleeteekos] civic, civilian ‖ political ‖ (οὐσ) politician.

πολιτισμένος [poleeteesmenos] civilized, cultured.

πολιτισμός, ὁ [poleeteesmos] civilization, culture.

πολιτογραφῶ [poleetoyrafo] naturalize (as citizen).

πολιτοφυλακή, ἡ [poleetofeelakee] militia, civil guard ‖ (US) national guard.

πολίχνη, ἡ [poleehnee] large village, small market town.

πολλάκις [polakees] often, many times, frequently.

πολλαπλασιάζω [polaplaseeazo] multiply ‖ propagate, increase.

πολλαπλασιασμός, ὁ [polaplaseeasmos] multiplication ‖ increase.

πολλαπλάσιον, τό [polaplaseeon] multiple.

πολλοί [polee] πλ many.

πόλο, τό [polo] polo.

πόλος, ὁ [polos] pole.

πολτός, ὁ [poltos] pap ‖ purée ‖ rag pulp.

πολύ [polee] much ‖ numerous, several ‖ great, lot ‖ τό ~ at the most.

πολυάνθρωπος [poleeanthropos] populous, crowded.

πολυάριθμος [poleeareethmos] numerous.

πολυάσχολος [poleeasholos] very busy, very occupied.

πολυβόλον, τό [poleevolon] machine gun.

πολυγαμία, ἡ [poleeyameea] polygamy.

πολύγλωσσος [poleeylosos] polyglot.

πολυγράφος, ὁ [poleeyrafos] duplicator.

πολυέλαιος, ὁ [polieleos] chandelier.

πολυζήτητος [poleezeeteetos] much sought-after.

πολυθρόνα, ἡ [poleethrona] armchair.

πολυκατοικία, ἡ [poleekateekeea] block of flats, apartment building.

πολυκοσμία, ἡ [poleekosmeea] crowds of people.

πολύκροτος [poleekrotos] causing a commotion.

πολυλογάς, ὁ [poleeloyas] chatterbox, babbler, gossip.

πολυλογία, ἡ [poleeloyeea] loquacity, garrulity, babble.

πολυμάθεια, ἡ [poleematheea] erudition, learning.

πολυμελής [poleemelees] having many members, numerous.

πολυμερής [poleemerees] varied, diversified.

πολυμήχανος [poleemeehanos] very ingenious ‖ cunning, crafty.

πολυπαθής [poleepathees] sorely tried, much afflicted.

πολυπληθής [poleepleethees] very numerous, crowded.

πολύπλοκος [poleeplokos] intricate, complicated, very involved.

πολύπους, ὁ [poleepous] polyp ‖ (ἰατρ) polypus.

πολυπράγμων [poleepraymon] meddlesome, inquisitive ‖ fussy.

πολύπτυχος [poleepteehos] with many folds, many-pleated.

πολύς [polees] much, numerous, many, great ‖ (χρόνος) long.

πολυσήμαντος [poleeseemantos] very significant, very important.

πολυσύνθετος [poleeseenthetos] very complex ‖ compound.

πολυτέλεια, ἡ [poleeteleea] luxury.

πολυτελής [poleetelees] sumptuous, splendid, rich.

πολυτεχνεῖον, τό [poleetehneeon] Polytechnic, National Technical School.

πολύτιμος [poleeteemos] valuable, precious, priceless.

πολυφαγία, ἡ [poleefayeea] gluttony, voracity, greediness.

πολύφωτον, τό [poleefoton] chandelier, candelabrum.

πολύχρωμος [poleehromos] multicoloured, variegated.

πολύωρος [poleeoros] lasting many hours, long-drawn-out.

πόμολο, τό [pomolo] door knob, handle.

πομπή, ἡ [pompee] procession, parade ‖ shame, stigma.

πομπός, ὁ [pompos] transmitter.

πομπώδης [pompodees] pompous, bombastic.

πονεμένος [ponemenos] in distress ‖ sad, hurt.

πονηρεύομαι [poneerevome] employ cunning, use wiles ‖ become suspicious.

πονηρεύω [poneerevo] rouse suspicions of ‖ make suspicious ‖ become cunning.

πονηρία, ἡ [poneereea] ruse, trick, guile ‖ suspicion, slyness.

πονηρός [poneeros] cunning, wily, crafty ‖ suspicious, distrustful ‖ diabolical.

πονόδοντος, ὁ [ponodontos] toothache.

πονοκέφαλος, ὁ [ponokefalos] headache.

πονόλαιμος, ὁ [ponolemos] sore throat.

πόνος, ὁ [ponos] suffering, pain ‖ (τοκετοῦ) labour ‖ compassion, pity, sympathy.

ποντάρω [pontaro] punt ‖ back, bet on.

ποντικός, ὁ [ponteekos] mouse, rat ‖ (ἀνατ) muscle.

ποντοπόρος, ὁ [pontoporos] seafarer, navigator.

πόντος, ὁ [pontos] sea ‖ (παιχνιδιοῦ) point ‖ (μέτρον) centimetre ‖ (στή πλεκτική) stitch ‖ Εὔξεινος ~ Black Sea.

πονῶ [pono] feel compassion for, sympathize with ‖ hurt, pain ‖ (ἀμετ) feel pain, suffer.

πορδή, ἡ [pordee] fart (col).

πορεία, ἡ [poreea] march, route ‖ course, run.

πορεύομαι [porevome] proceed, go, walk, march.

πορθμεῖον, τό [porthmeeon] ferry(boat).

πορθμός, ὁ [porthmos] strait, sound, channel.

πορθῶ [portho] sack, pillage ‖ take, capture.

πόρισμα, τό [poreesma] deduction, inference, conclusion ‖ finding ‖ (μαθημ) corollary.

πορνεῖον, τό [porneeon] brothel ‖ (US) whorehouse.

πόρνη, ἡ [pornee] prostitute, whore.

πόρος, ὁ [poros] passage, ford ‖ (τοῦ δέρματος) pore ‖ πλ means, income, resources.

πόρπη, ἡ [porpee] buckle, clasp, brooch.

πόρρω [poro] far off, far away, at a distance.

πορσελάνη, ἡ [porselanee] china, porcelain.

πόρτα, ἡ [porta] door, gate, doorway, gateway.

πορτοκαλάδα, ἡ [portokalaδa] orangeade.

πορτοκάλι, τό [portokalee] orange.

πορτοκαλιά, ἡ [portokalia] orange tree.

πορτοφολᾶς, ὁ [portofolas] pickpocket.

πορτοφόλι, τό [portofolee] wallet.

πορτραῖτο, τό [portreto] portrait.

πορφύρα, ἡ [porfeera] purple.

πορώδης [poroδees] porous.

ποσάκις [posakees] how often?

πόσιμο [poseemo]: ~ νερό drinking water.

πόσιμος [poseemos] drinkable.

ποσόν, τό [poson] quantity, amount ‖ (χρήματος) sum.

πόσο(ν) [poso(n)] how much.

πόσος [posos] how much?, how many?, how large?, how great?

ποσοστόν, τό [pososton] percentage, share, quota.

ποσότης, ἡ [posotees] quantity, amount.

πόστα [posta]: τόν ἔβαλα ~ I berated him.

πόστο, τό [posto] strategic position.

ποσῶς [posos] not at all, in no way, by no means.

ποταμηδόν [potameeδon] in floods, in torrents, in gushes.

ποτάμι, τό [potamee] river.

ποταμός, ὁ [potamos] βλ ποτάμι.

ποταπός [potapos] vile, base, abject.

πότε [pote] when? ‖ ~ ~ sometimes, from time to time ‖ ~ . . . ~ sometimes . . . sometimes.

ποτέ [pote] once, formerly ‖ ever ‖ (μετά ἀπό ἄρνητ) never ‖ ~ πλέον never again.

ποτήρι(ον), τό [poteeree(on)] drinking glass.

πότης, ὁ [potees] heavy drinker, boozer.

ποτίζω [poteezo] water, irrigate ‖ become damp, become saturated.

πότισμα, τό [poteesma] watering, irrigation.

ποτιστήρι, τό [poteesteeree] watering can.

ποτόν, τό [poton] drink, beverage.

ποῦ [pou] where?, whither? ‖ γιά ~ where are you going? ‖ ~ νά ξέρω how should I know? ‖ ~ καί ~ once in a while, now and then.

πού [pou] who, whom, which, that ‖ when ‖ (συνδ) that ‖ (ἐπίρ) somewhere, where.

πουγγί, τό [poungee] purse, bag ‖ money.

πούδρα, ἡ [pouδra] powder.

ποῦθε [pouthe] βλ πόθεν.

πουθενά [pouthena] not anywhere ‖ nowhere.

πουκάμισο, τό [poukameeso] shirt.

πουλάδα, ἡ [poulaδa] young hen, pullet.

πουλάκι, τό [poulakee] little bird ‖ ~ μου my darling, my pet.

πουλάρι, τό [poularee] foal, colt.

πουλερικά, τά [poulereeka] πλ poultry.

πούλημα, τό [pouleema] βλ πώλησις.

πουλί, τό [poulee] bird.

πούλμαν, τό [poulman] (motor) coach.

πουλῶ [poulo] βλ πωλῶ.

πούντα, ἡ [pounda] cold, pleurisy.

πουντιάζω [pounteeazo] cool, chill ‖ feel very cold.

πούπουλο, τό [poupoulo] down, plume, feather.

πουρές, ὁ [poures] purée.

πουρμπουάρ, τό [pourmbouar] gratuity, tip.

πουρνάρι, τό [pournaree] evergreen oak.

πούρο, τό [pouro] cigar.

πούς, ὁ [pous] foot, leg ‖ (μέτρον) foot.

πούσι, τό [pousee] mist, fog.

πούστης, ὁ [poustees] bugger, queen (col), queer (col).

πουτάνα, ἡ [poutana] whore.

πουτίγγα, ἡ [poutinga] pudding.

πωῴδης [pooδees] mossy.

πρᾶγμα, τό [prayma] thing, object ‖ matter, business, affair ‖ (προϊόντα) goods ‖ (ὕφασμα) cloth.

πράγματι [praymatee] in fact, actually.

πραγματεύομαι [praymatevome] deal with, treat, handle ‖ negotiate.

πραγματευτής, ὁ [praymatevtees] tradesman, dealer ‖ pedlar.

πραγματικός [praymateekos] real, actual, substantial, authentic.

πραγματικότης, ἡ [praymateekotees] reality, fact, truth.

πραγματογνώμων, ὁ [praymatoynomon] assessor, valuer ‖ expert.

πραγματοποιῶ [praymatopeeo] carry out, realize, fulfil, work out.

πρακτέον, τό [prakteon] what should be done.

πρακτικά, τά [prakteeka] πλ records, minutes, proceedings.

πρακτικός [prakteekos] useful, practical ‖ vocational.

πρακτορεῖον, τό [praktoreeon] agency, travel agency.

πράκτωρ, ὁ [praktor] agent.

πραμάτεια, ἡ [pramateea] goods, commodities.

πραματευτής, ὁ [pramatevtees] βλ πραγματευτής.

πραξικόπημα, τό [prakseekopeema] coup d'état.

πρᾶξις, ἡ [praksees] action, act ‖ practice, experience ‖ (γεννήσεως κτλ) certificate, registration ‖ (οἴκον) deal, transaction ‖ (μαθημ) operation.

πρᾶος [praos] affable, gentle, kind.

πρασιά, ἡ [prasia] flower bed or lawn round house.

πρασινάδα, ἡ [praseenaδa] verdure, greenery ‖ green colour.

πράσινος [praseenos] green, verdant ‖ unripe.

πράσο, τό [praso] leek.

πρατήριον, τό [prateereeon] specialist shop ‖ ~ βενζίνης petrol station.

πράττω [prato] perform, act ‖ do.

πραΰνω [praeeno] appease, calm, soothe, pacify.

πρέζα, ἡ [preza] pinch.

πρέπει [prepee] it is necessary, it is proper that ‖ ~ νά πάω I must go ‖ καθὼς ~ decent, honourable, a gentleman.

πρεπόντως [prepontos] properly, suitably, fitly ‖ correctly.

πρέπων [prepon] suitable, fitting, proper ‖ decent, correct.

πρεσβεία, ἡ [presveea] embassy, legation ‖ delegation.

πρεσβευτής, ὁ [presvevtees] ambassador, minister ‖ representative.

πρεσβεύω [presvevo] profess, avow, affirm, represent.

πρεσβύτερος [presveeteros] elder, senior, older.

πρεσβυωπία, ἡ [presveeopeea] longsightedness.

πρέφα, ἡ [prefa] card game ‖ τό πῆρε ~ he smelt a rat.

πρήζομαι [preezome] become swollen, swell.

πρήζω [preezo] (μεταφ) infuriate.

πρηνής [preenees] prostrate, prone.

πρήξιμο, τό [preekseemo] swelling, tumour.

πρήσκω [preesko] swell up, become swollen ‖ infuriate.

πρίγκηπας, ὁ [preengkeepas] prince.

πρίζα, ἡ [preeza] plug, socket.

πρίν [preen] before, previously, prior to ‖ ~ ἀπό μένα ahead of me, in front of me ‖ ~ τόν πόλεμο before the war.

πρινάρι, τό [preenaree] evergreen oak, holm oak.

πριόνι, τό [preeonee] saw, handsaw, hacksaw.

πριονίζω [preeoneezo] saw.

πρίσμα, τό [preesma] prism.

πριχοῦ [preehou] before.

πρό [pro] before, in front of, ahead of, in the face of ‖ ~ ἡμερῶν a few days ago ‖ ~ παντός especially, above all.

προαγγέλλω [proangelo] predict, prophesy.

προάγω [proago] put forward, promote, advance ‖ speed up, further ‖ προαγωγή (οὖσ) advancement, promotion ‖ προαγωγός (οὖσ) pimp, pander.

προαίρεσις, ἡ [proeresees] intention, purpose ‖ bent, bias.

προαιρετικός [proereteekos] optional ‖ voluntary.

προαίσθησις, ἡ [proestheesees] presentiment, foreboding.

προάλλες [proales]: τίς ~ just the other day, recently.

προανάκρουσμα, τό [proanakrousma] prelude, preliminary.

προαναφερθείς [proanaferthees] abovementioned.

προασπίζω [proaspeezo] defend, protect, guard.

προάστειον, τό [proasteeon] suburb.

προαύλιον, τό [proavleeon] forecourt, courtyard.

πρόβα, ἡ [prova] fitting of clothes ‖ trial, rehearsal.

προβάδισμα, τό [provaδeesma] precedence, priority.

προβαίνω [proveno] advance, move forward ‖ proceed, make ‖ ~ εἰς carry out, make.

προβάλλω [provalo] project, further ‖ (σκιά) cast ‖ (φίλμ) project, show ‖ (ἀντίστασι) offer resistance ‖ (ἀντίρρησι) raise ‖ (δικαιολογία) put forward an excuse ‖ (ἀμετ) appear suddenly in view.

προβάρω [provaro] try on, go for a fitting.

προβατίνα, ἡ [provateena] ewe, lamb.

πρόβατον, τό [provaton] sheep.

προβιά, ἡ [provia] animal's skin.

προβιβάζω [proveevazo] promote, push forward.

πρόβιος [proveeos] of a sheep.

προβλέπω [provlepo] foresee, forecast ‖ prepare for, provide.

πρόβλεψις, ἡ [provlepsees] forecast, anticipation.

πρόβλημα, τό [provleema] problem ‖ (μεταφ) riddle, puzzle.

προβλής, ἡ [provlees] jetty, mole.

προβολεύς, ὁ [provolevs] searchlight, headlight ‖ (σινεμά) projector.

προβολή, ἡ [provolee] projection ‖ (προϊόντος) promotion.

προβοσκίς, ἡ [provoskees] trunk ‖ (ἐντόμου) proboscis.

προγενέστεροι, οἱ [proyenesteree] πλ predecessors.

προγενέστερος [proyenesteros] anterior, previous, former ‖ (οὖσ) precursor.

πρόγευμα, τό [proyevma] breakfast.

προγεφύρωμα, τό [proyefeeroma] bridge-head.

προγνωστικόν, τό [proynosteekon] prediction, forecast || tip.

πρόγονος, ὁ [proyonos] ancestor, forefather, forbear.

προγονός, ὁ, ἡ [proyonos] stepson, stepdaughter.

πρόγραμμα, τό [proyrama] programme, plan, schedule.

προγραφή, ἡ [proyrafee] proscription.

προγράφω [proyrafo] proscribe, outlaw.

προγυμνάζω [proyeemnazo] exercise, train || tutor.

πρόδηλος [prodeelos] obvious, evident, manifest, plain.

προδιαγράφω [prodeeayrafo] prearrange.

προδιάθεσις, ἡ [prodeeathesees] predisposition, liability (to), prejudice (against).

προδιαθέτω [prodeeatheto] predispose, forewarn, influence, prejudice.

προδίδω [prodeedo] reveal, betray || denounce, inform.

προδοσία, ἡ [prodoseea] betrayal || treachery.

προδότης, ὁ [prodotees] traitor, informer.

πρόδρομος, ὁ [prodromos] forerunner, precursor || herald.

προεδρεία, ἡ [proedreea] presidency, chairmanship.

προεδρεύω [proedrevo] preside, chair.

πρόεδρος, ὁ, ἡ [proedros] president, chairman || presiding judge.

προειδοποίησις, ἡ [proeedopieesees] previous warning, premonition.

προειδοποιῶ [proeedopeeo] let know || warn.

προειρημένος [proeereemenos] aforesaid.

προεισαγωγή, ἡ [proeesayoyee] introduction, preface.

προεκλογικός [proekloyeekos] pre-election.

προέκτασις, ἡ [proektasees] extension, prolongation.

προέλασις, ἡ [proelasees] advance, forward movement.

προελαύνω [proelavno] advance, move forward.

προέλευσις, ἡ [proelevsees] provenance, place of origin.

προεξέχω [proekseho] jut out, project, protrude.

προεξοφλῶ [proeksoflo] (χρέος) pay off in advance || receive in advance || take for granted, rely on.

προεξοχή, ἡ [proeksohee] projection, protrusion, prominence.

προεργασία, ἡ [proeryaseea] preliminary work.

προέρχομαι [proerhome] originate, come from, issue from.

προεστώς [proestos] notable, elder || chief.

προετοιμάζω [proeteemazo] prepare, fit for, train for.

προετοιμασία, ἡ [proeteemaseea] preparation.

προέχω [proeho] jut out || surpass || predominate.

πρόζα, ἡ [proza] prose.

πρόζύμι, τό [prozeemee] leaven, yeast.

προηγοῦμαι [proeeyoume] surpass, be ahead || precede, come before.

προηγούμενα, τά [proeeyoumena]: ἔχουν ~ they have a grudge.

προηγούμενον, τό [proeeyoumenon] precedent.

προηγούμενος [proeeyoumenos] preceding, previous, earlier.

προηγουμένως [proeeyoumenos] previously, beforehand.

προθάλαμος, ὁ [prothalamos] anteroom, antechamber, waiting room.

πρόθεσις, ἡ [prothesees] purpose, design, intention || (γραμμ) preposition, prefix.

προθεσμία, ἡ [prothesmeea] time limit, delay, term, option.

προθήκη, ἡ [protheekee] shop window || showcase.

προθυμία, ἡ [protheemeea] eagerness, readiness, alacrity.

πρόθυμος [protheemos] eager, willing, ready || obliging.

πρόθυρα, τά [protheera] πλ gates, approach || (μεταφ) verge, eve, threshold.

προίκα, ἡ [preeka] dowry, marriage portion.

προικίζω [preekeezo] dower || endow (with), equip (with).

προικοθήρας, ὁ [preekotheeras] fortune hunter, dowry hunter.

προικοσύμφωνον, τό [preekoseemfonon] marriage contract.

προϊόν, τό [proeeon] product, production || proceeds.

προϊόντα, τά [proeeonta] πλ produce, articles, products.

προΐσταμαι [proeestame] direct, manage, supervise.

προϊστάμενος, ὁ [proeestamenos] superior, chief, supervisor.

πρόκα, ἡ [proka] nail, tack.

προκαλύπτω [prokaleepto] hide, screen, cover.

προκαλῶ [prokalo] challenge || provoke, incite.

προκάνω [prokano] catch, overtake || arrive on time || have the time to.

προκαταβολή, ἡ [prokatavolee] prepayment, advance payment || deposit.

προκαταβολικῶς [prokatavoleekos] in advance, beforehand.

προκαταλαμβάνω [prokatalamvano] forestall, occupy beforehand.

προκατάληψις, ἡ [prokataleepsees] bias, prejudice.

προκαταρκτικός [prokatarteekos] preliminary, preparatory.

προκατειλημμένος [prokateeleemenos] biased, prejudiced.

προκάτοχος, ὁ [prokatohos] predecessor ‖ previous holder, previous occupant.

πρόκειται [prokeete] it's a matter of ‖ it's a question of ‖ περί τίνος ~ ; what's it all about? ‖ ~ νά ἔλθω I am due to come.

προκήρυξις, ἡ [prokeereeksees] proclamation, announcement ‖ manifesto.

πρόκλησις, ἡ [prokleesees] affront, challenge ‖ provocation, instigation.

προκλητικός [prokleeteekos] provocative, provoking ‖ seductive.

προκόβω [prokovo] progress, succeed, prosper, make good.

προκομμένος [prokomenos] hard-working, diligent.

προκοπή, ἡ [prokopee] progress ‖ industry ‖ success.

προκρίνω [prokreeno] prefer, choose ‖ predetermine.

πρόκριτος [prokreetos] notable.

προκυμαία, ἡ [prokeemea] quay, pier, jetty.

προκύπτω [prokeepto] arise ‖ result, ensue.

προλαβαίνω [prolaveno] get a start on, forestall ‖ catch, overtake ‖ (σέ χρόνον) be on time, manage ‖ have enough time for.

προλαμβάνω [prolamvano] βλ **προλαβαίνω**.

προλεγόμενα, τά [proleyomena] πλ preface, foreword.

προλέγω [proleyo] forecast, predict ‖ say previously.

προλετάριος [proletareeos] proletarian.

προληπτικός [proleepteekos] precautionary, preventive ‖ superstitious.

πρόληψις, ἡ [proleepsees] avertion, prevention ‖ superstition.

πρόλογος, ὁ [proloyos] prologue, preface, preamble.

προμάμμη, ἡ [promamee] great-grand-mother.

προμαντεύω [promantevo] prophesy, foretell, predict.

πρόμαχος, ὁ [promahos] champion, defender, protector.

προμαχών, ὁ [promahon] bastion, bulwark, rampart.

προμελέτη, ἡ [promeletee] preliminary study ‖ premeditation ‖ ἐκ ~ς deliberately ‖ premeditated.

προμεσημβρία, ἡ [promeseemvreea] forenoon, morning.

προμήθεια, ἡ [promeetheea] supply, provision, supplying, victualling ‖ (ποσοστόν) commission, brokerage.

προμηθευτής, ὁ [promeethevtees] provider, purveyor, supplier.

προμηθεύομαι [promeethevome] get, supply o.s. with.

προμηθεύω [promeethevo] supply, provide, furnish.

προμηνύω [promeeneeo] portend, presage, foretell.

προνοητικός [pronoeeteekos] having foresight, provident, careful.

πρόνοια, ἡ [proneea] care, concern, precaution ‖ providence, welfare.

προνόμιον, τό [pronomeeon] privilege, advantage ‖ gift, talent.

προνομιοῦχος [pronomeeouhos] privileged, favoured.

προνοῶ [pronoo] foresee, forecast ‖ provide for, think of.

προξενεῖον, τό [prokseneeon] consulate.

προξενητής, ὁ [prokseneetees] intermediary, matchmaker.

προξενιά, ἡ [proksenia] matchmaking.

πρόξενος, ὁ [proksenos] author, perpetrator, cause ‖ (διπλωμάτης) consul.

προξενῶ [prokseno] cause, occasion, inflict, bring about.

προοδευτικός [proodevteekos] progressive, forward ‖ (φορολογία) graduated.

προοδεύω [proodevo] progress, make headway ‖ develop.

πρόοδος, ἡ [proodos] advance, progress ‖ development, improvement ‖ (μαθημ) progression.

προοίμιον, τό [proeemeeon] preface, prelude, preamble.

προοπτική, ἡ [proopteekee] perspective ‖ prospect in view.

προορίζω [prooreezo] destine, intend, foreordain.

προορισμός, ὁ [prooreesmos] end, intention ‖ destination.

προπαγάνδα, ἡ [propayanda] propaganda.

πρόπαππος, ὁ [propapos] great-grandfather.

προπαρασκευή, ἡ [proparaskevee] preparation ‖ coaching.

προπέλλα, ἡ [propela] propeller.

προπέμπω [propembo] see off, accompany, go along with.

πρόπερσι [propersee] two years ago.

προπέτασμα [propetasma] screen ‖ ~ καπνοῦ smoke screen.

προπέτεια, ἡ [propeteea] insolence, arrogance.

προπίνω [propeeno] drink to s.o.'s health ‖ toast.

προπληρώνω [propleerono] pay in advance.

πρόποδες, οἱ [propodes] πλ foot of mountain.

προπολεμικός [propolemeekos] prewar.

προπόνησις, ἡ [proponeesees] training, coaching.

πρόποσις, ἡ [proposees] toast (drink).

προπύλαια, τά [propeelea] πλ propylaea.

προπύργιον, τό [propeeryeeon] rampart, bulwark, bastion.

πρός [pros] towards ‖ (γιά) for ‖ at ‖ in ‖ ~ ὀφελός μου to my advantage, to my good ‖ ~ τιμήν του in his honour, for his sake ‖ ~ τό παρόν for the present ‖ ἕνα ~ ἕνα one by one ‖ ὡς ~ ἐμέ as far as I am concerned ‖ ~ Θεοῦ! for God's sake! ‖ ~ τούτοις moreover ‖ ~ δέ in addition, furthermore.

προσαγορεύω [prosaγorevo] address, harangue, greet.

προσάγω [prosaγo] put forward, exhibit, produce.

προσάναμα, τό [prosanama] tinder, firewood ‖ fuel.

προσανατολίζομαι [prosanatoleezome] find one's bearings.

προσανατολίζω [prosanatoleezo] orientate ‖ direct, guide.

προσαράσσω [prosaraso] run aground, be stranded.

προσαρμογή, ἡ [prosarmoγee] adaptation, accommodation ‖ adjustment.

προσαρμόζω [prosarmozo] fit to ‖ adapt, adjust, apply.

προσάρτημα, τό [prosarteema] accessory, annexe, addition.

προσάρτησις, ἡ [prosarteesees] annexation.

προσαρτῶ [prosarto] append, attach ‖ annex.

προσβάλλω [prosvalo] assail, attack ‖ (ὑγείαν) harm, injure ‖ (δυσαρεστῶ) hurt, offend ‖ (διαθήκην) challenge.

προσβλητικός [prosvleeteekos] offensive, abusive, insolent.

προσβολή, ἡ [prosvolee] onset, attack ‖ (ὑγείας) fit, stroke ‖ offence, insult.

προσγειοῦμαι [prosγeeoume] make a landing.

προσγείωσις, ἡ [prosγeeosees] landing, alighting.

προσδένω [prosdeno] tie, attach, fasten.

προσδίδω [prosdeeδo] lend, add to, give.

προσδιορίζω [prosδeeoreezo] determine, define, fix ‖ allocate, assign.

προσδοκῶ [prosδoko] hope, expect, anticipate.

προσεγγίζω [prosengeezo] put near ‖ approach, come near ‖ (κατά προσέγγισιν) approximate ‖ (ναυτ) put in at, land at.

προσεκτικός [prosekteekos] attentive, heedful, mindful ‖ careful.

προσέλευσις, ἡ [proselevsees] arrival, approach.

προσελκύω [proselkeeo] (προσοχήν) attract, win, draw, catch ‖ (ὑποστηρικτές) gain, win over.

προσέρχομαι [proserhome] attend, present o.s. ‖ apply for.

προσέτι [prosetee] also, besides, in addition to, more.

προσευχή, ἡ [prosevhee] prayer.

προσεύχομαι [prosevhome] pray, say one's prayers.

προσεχής [prosehees] next ‖ forthcoming.

προσέχω [proseho] pay attention to, notice ‖ be attentive, be mindful ‖ (κάποιον) take care of.

προσεχῶς [prosehos] shortly, soon, in a short time.

προσηκόντως [proseekontos] becomingly, properly.

προσηλυτίζω [proseeleeteezo] convert, proselytize.

προσηλωμένος [proseelomenos] attached to, devoted to, absorbed in.

προσηλώνω [proseelono] nail, fix ‖ (μεταφ) look fixedly (at).

προσηνής [proseenees] affable, kind, mild, gentle.

πρόσθεσις, ἡ [prosthesees] addition, increase.

πρόσθετος [prosthetos] additional, extra.

προσθέτω [prostheto] add, sum up ‖ mix with.

προσθήκη, ἡ [prostheekee] addition, increase.

πρόσθιος [prostheeos] front, fore.

προσιτός [proseetos] attainable, accessible ‖ (τιμή) reasonable, within one's means.

πρόσκαιρος [proskeros] transitory, passing, momentary.

προσκαλῶ [proskalo] call, send for ‖ (νομ) summon, subpoena ‖ (εἰς γεῦμα κτλ) invite.

προσκεκλημένος [proskekleemenos] invited.

προσκέφαλον, τό [proskefalon] pillow, cushion.

πρόσκλησις, ἡ [proskleesees] call, summons ‖ (τηλεφώνου) telephone call ‖ (εἰς δεξίωσιν κτλ) invitation ‖ (στρατ) calling up ‖ (εἰσιτήριον δωρεάν) complimentary ticket.

προσκλητήριον, τό [proskleeteereeon] invitation (card) ‖ (στρατ) call, roll call ‖ (ναυτ) muster roll.

προσκόλλησις, ἡ [proskoleesees] adherence, attaching ‖ fidelity.

προσκολλῶ [proskolo] stick, attach, paste on ‖ second (attach).

προσκομίζω [proskomeezo] bring forward, bring ‖ offer.

πρόσκομμα, τό [proskoma] obstacle, impediment, hindrance.

πρόσκοπος, ὁ [proskopos] scout ‖ boy scout.

προσκόπτω [proskopto] stumble over ‖ (εἰς ἐμπόδιον) meet with difficulties.

προσκρούω [proskrouo] crash ‖ strike (against) ‖ be opposed to.

προσκύνημα, τό [proskeeneema] adoration ‖ submission ‖ place of pilgrimage.

προσκυνητής, ὁ [proskeeneetees] pilgrim.

προσκυνῶ [proskeeno] adore, worship ‖ pay homage to, yield.

προσλαμβάνω [proslamvano] take on, engage, employ ‖ (ὕφος) put on.

προσμένω [prosmeno] wait for, hope for.

πρόσμειξις, ἡ [prosmeeksees] blending, mixing.

πρόσοδος, ἡ [prosodos] income, revenue || (ἐμπόριον) profit || yield.

προσοδοφόρος [prosodoforos] productive, profitable, lucrative.

προσοικειοῦμαι [proseekeeoume] become familiar with || (συνηθίζω) get accustomed to.

προσόν, τό [proson] aptitude, fitness, qualification || advantage.

προσορμίζομαι [prosormeezome] moor, come to, land.

προσοχή, ἡ [prosohee] attention, notice || caution, precaution, care.

προσόψι(ον), τό [prosopsee(on)] towel.

πρόσοψις, ἡ [prosopsees] façade, front(age).

προσπάθεια, ἡ [prospatheea] endeavour, effort, attempt || labour.

προσπαθῶ [prospatho] try, attempt.

προσπερνῶ [prosperno] overtake || (μεταφ) surpass.

προσποίησις, ἡ [prospieesees] pretence, sham.

προσποιητός [prospieetos] affected, assumed, feigned.

προσποιοῦμαι [prospeeoume] affect, put on || pretend.

προσταγή, ἡ [prostayee] order, ordering, command.

προστάζω [prostazo] order, direct, command.

προστακτική, ἡ [prostakteekee] (γραμμ) imperative (mood).

προστασία, ἡ [prostaseea] protection, defence.

προστατευόμενος, ὁ [prostatevomenos] protégé.

προστατευτικός [prostatevteekos] protecting || condescending.

προστατεύω [prostatevo] defend, protect || extend patronage to.

προστάτης, ὁ [prostatees] protector, patron || (ἀνατ) prostate.

προστίθεμαι [prosteetheme] be added, be mixed (with).

πρόστιμον, τό [prosteemon] fine, penalty.

προστρέχω [prostreho] rush up, run up || resort to, turn to.

προστριβή, ἡ [prostreevee] friction, rubbing || (μεταφ) dispute.

προστυχαίνω [prosteeheno] make vulgar, coarsen || grow vulgar.

προστυχιά, ἡ [prosteehia] vulgarity, rudeness, contemptible act.

πρόστυχος [prosteehos] vile, rude, ill-mannered || of bad quality.

προσύμφωνον, τό [proseemfonon] preliminary agreement, draw-up agreement.

προσφά(γ)ι, τό [prosfa(γ)ee] anything eaten with bread.

πρόσφατος [prosfatos] recent, new || (μόδα) modern.

προσφέρομαι [prosferome] offer || be appropriate, be fitting.

προσφέρω [prosfero] offer, present, give.

προσφεύγω [prosfevγo] have recourse to, turn (to).

προσφιλής [prosfeelees] dear, loved, precious.

προσφορά, ἡ [prosfora] offer, offering, proposal, bid || thing offered || (ἐκκλ) consecrated bread.

πρόσφορος [prosforos] convenient, opportune, suitable.

πρόσφυγας, ὁ [prosfeeγas] refugee.

προσφυγή, ἡ [prosfeeγee] recourse, resort || (νομ) legal redress, appeal.

προσφυής [prosfiees] suitable, well-adapted, fitting.

πρόσφυξ, ὁ, ἡ [prosfeeks] βλ **πρόσφυγας**.

προσφωνῶ [prosfono] address, greet.

πρόσχαρος [prosharos] cheerful, lively, merry, gay.

προσχέδιον, τό [proshedeeon] rough draft, sketch.

πρόσχημα, τό [prosheema] pretext, excuse.

προσχωρῶ [proshoro] join, go over (to) || cleave (to), adhere (to).

πρόσω [proso] forwards, ahead.

προσωδία, ἡ [prosodeea] prosody.

προσωνυμία, ἡ [prosoneemeea] nickname, name.

προσωπάρχης, ὁ [prosoparhees] personnel officer, staff manager.

προσωπεῖον, τό [prosopeeon] mask.

προσωπικόν, τό [prosopeekon] personnel, staff || (σπιτιοῦ) servants.

προσωπικός [prosopeekos] personal.

προσωπικότης, ἡ [prosopeekotees] personality, individuality.

προσωπικῶς [prosopeekos] personally.

προσωπίς, ἡ [prosopees] mask.

προσωπογραφία, ἡ [prosopoγrafeea] portrait painting, portrait.

πρόσωπον, τό [prosopon] face, visage || person || (θεάτρου) role, character, part.

προσωποποίησις, ἡ [prosopopieesees] personification || impersonation.

προσωρινός [prosoreenos] provisional, passing, fleeting.

πρότασις, ἡ [protasees] proposal, suggestion, offer, motion || (γραμμ) sentence || clause.

προτείνω [proteeno] extend, stretch out, put forward || propose, suggest.

προτελευταῖος [protelevteos] last but one.

προτεραία, ἡ [proterea] the preceding day.

προτεραιότης, ἡ [protereotees] priority, primacy.

προτέρημα, τό [protereema] gift, faculty, advantage, talent.

πρότερος [proteros] earlier, previous to, prior (to).

προτέρων [proteron]: ἐκ τῶν ~ beforehand.

προτεσταντισμός, ὁ [protestanteesmos] Protestantism.

προτίθεμαι [proteetheme] intend, propose, mean, think.

προτίμησις, ἡ [proteemeesees] preference, predilection.

προτιμότερος [proteemoteros] preferable to.

προτιμῶ [proteemo] prefer, like better.

προτομή, ἡ [protomee] bust.

προτοῦ [protou] before ‖ previously.

προτρέπω [protrepo] exhort, instigate, incite.

προτρέχω [protreho] run in advance of ‖ (περνῶ) outrun, overtake.

προτροπή, ἡ [protropee] exhortation, prompting.

πρότυπον, τό [proteepon] original, pattern, model, example ‖ mould.

πρότυπος [proteepos] model.

προϋπαντῶ [proeepanto] go to meet s.o.

προϋπάρχω [proeeparho] pre-exist ‖ (εἰς χρόνον) come before.

προϋπόθεσις, ἡ [proeepothesees] assumption, presumption.

προϋποθέτω [proeepotheto] presuppose, presume.

προϋπολογίζω [proeepoloyeezo] estimate, compute beforehand.

προϋπολογισμός, ὁ [proeepoloyeesmos] estimate ‖ budget.

προύχων, ὁ [prouhon] notable.

προφανής [profanees] obvious, evident, plain, clear.

προφανῶς [profanos] obviously, evidently, manifestly.

πρόφασις, ἡ [profasees] pretext, excuse, pretence.

προφέρ(ν)ω [profer(n)o] pronounce, utter, articulate.

προφητεία, ἡ [profeeteea] prophecy, prophetic utterance.

προφητεύω [profeetevo] prophesy, predict.

προφήτης, ὁ [profeetees] prophet.

προφητικός [profeeteekos] prophetic.

προφθάνω [profthano] anticipate, forestall ‖ catch, overtake, overhaul ‖ (εἰς χρόνον) be in time for, have the time to.

προφορά, ἡ [profora] pronunciation, accent.

προφτάνω [proftano] βλ προφθάνω.

προφυλακή, ἡ [profeelakee] vanguard, outpost.

προφυλακίζω [profeelakeezo] hold in custody, detain.

προφυλακτήρ, ὁ [profeelakteer] bumper (aut).

προφυλακτικός [profeelakteekos] wary, careful ‖ precautionary, preventive.

προφύλαξις, ἡ [profeelaksees] precaution, cautiousness.

προφυλάσσομαι [profeelasome] take precautions, protect o.s.

προφυλάσσω [profeelaso] protect, preserve (from), defend.

πρόχειρος [proheeros] ready, handy ‖ impromptu.

προχθές [prohthes] the day before yesterday.

πρόχωμα, τό [prohoma] earthwork ‖ dam, dyke.

προχωρῶ [prohoro] go forward, advance ‖ progress, gain ground.

προωθῶ [prootho] impel ‖ push forward, urge on.

πρόωρος [prooros] premature, untimely, hasty.

πρύμ(ν)η, ἡ [preem(n)ee] stern, poop.

πρυτανεύω [preetanevo] (μεταφ) predominate, prevail, get the better of.

πρύτανις, ὁ [preetanees] head of university, dean.

πρώην [proeen] former, ex-.

πρωθυπουργός, ὁ [protheepouryos] prime minister, premier.

πρωΐ [proee] in the morning ‖ (οὐσ) morning.

πρωΐα, ἡ [proeea] morning, forenoon.

πρώιμος [proeemos] untimely, premature ‖ (γιά φυτά) precocious, early.

πρωινός [proeenos] morning ‖ rising early.

πρωινό, τό [proeeno] morning ‖ (πρόγευμα) breakfast.

πρωκτός, ὁ [proktos] anus.

πρώρα, ἡ [prora] prow, bows.

πρῶτα [prota] first, at first ‖ before, formerly, once.

πρωταγωνιστής, ὁ [protayoneestees] protagonist, hero.

πρωτάθλημα, τό [protathleema] championship.

πρωταίτιος, ὁ [proteteos] ringleader, perpetrator ‖ cause.

πρωτάκουστος [protakoustos] unheard-of, unprecedented.

πρωταρχικός [protarheekos] most important.

πρωτεῖα, τά [proteea] πλ first place, primacy, precedence.

πρωτεργάτης, ὁ [proteryatees] perpetrator, pioneer, cause.

πρωτεύουσα, ἡ [protevousa] capital, metropolis.

πρωτεύω [protevo] be first, lead, surpass, triumph (over).

πρωτεύων [protevon] primary, foremost, first.

πρωτίστως [proteestos] essentially, principally.

πρωτοβάζω [protovazo] wear for the first time.

πρωτοβάθμιος [protovathmeeos] of the first degree.

πρωτόβγαλτος [protovyaltos] inexperienced, unskilful, uninitiated.

πρωτοβουλία, ἡ [protovouleea] initiative.

πρωτοβρόχια, τά [protovroheea] πλ first rains in autumn.

πρωτογέννητος [protoyeneetos] first-born.
πρωτόγονος [protoyonos] primitive ‖ (ἤδη) rough, rude, unpolished.
πρωτοδικεῖον, τό [protoδeekeeon] court of first instance.
πρωτοετής [protoetees] first-year.
πρωτόκολλον, τό [protokolon] register, record ‖ protocol, etiquette.
πρωτοκολλῶ [protokolo] enter in register, record.
Πρωτομαγιά, ἡ [protomayia] May Day.
πρωτομηνιά, ἡ [protomeenia] first day of month.
πρῶτον [proton] first, firstly, in the first place, to start with.
πρωτοπορεία, ἡ [protoporeea] vanguard.
πρωτοπόρος, ὁ [protoporos] pioneer, forerunner, innovator.
πρῶτος [protos] first, foremost ‖ best, top ‖ initial, elementary ‖ (ἀριθμός) prime.
πρωτοστατῶ [protostato] lead.
πρωτότοκος [prototokos] first-born, oldest.
πρωτοτυπία, ἡ [prototeepeea] originality ‖ eccentricity.
πρωτότυπον, τό [prototeepon] original, pattern, model.
πρωτότυπος [prototeepos] original, novel, singular.
πρωτοφανής [protofanees] new, fresh ‖ astonishing.
Πρωτοχρονιά, ἡ [protohronia] New Year's Day.
πρωτύτερα [proteetera] earlier on, at first, before.
πταῖσμα, τό [ptesma] misdemeanour, violation ‖ fault, error.
πταισματοδικεῖον, τό [ptesmatoδeekeeon] police court.
πταίω [pteo] be at fault, be responsible.
πτέρνα, ἡ [pterna] heel.
πτερνιστήρ, ὁ [pterneesteer] spur.
πτερόν, τό [pteron] wing ‖ feather, plume ‖ (προπέλλας) blade, vane.
πτερύγιον, τό [ptereeyeeon] fin ‖ aileron, wing flap.
πτέρυξ, ἡ [ptereeks] wing.
πτέρωμα, τό [pteroma] plumage, feathers.
πτερωτός [pterotos] winged.
πτηνόν, τό [pteenon] bird, fowl.
πτηνοτροφία, ἡ [pteenotrofeea] poultry farming.
πτῆσις, ἡ [pteesees] flight, flying.
πτίλον, τό [pteelon] down, plume.
πτοῶ [ptoo] intimidate, frighten, browbeat.
πτύελον, τό [ptielon] spittle, spit, sputum.
πτυχή, ἡ [pteehee] fold, pleat ‖ wrinkle ‖ (πανταλονιοῦ) crease.
πτυχίον, τό [pteeheeon] diploma, certificate.
πτυχιοῦχος [pteeheeouhos] graduate, holding a diploma.
πτύω [pteeo] spit out ‖ expectorate.
πτῶμα, τό [ptoma] corpse, dead body ‖ (ζώου) carcase.

πτῶσις, ἡ [ptosees] fall, tumble ‖ collapse ‖ drop ‖ (γραμμ) case.
πτώχευσις, ἡ [ptohevsees] bankruptcy, failure, insolvency.
πτωχεύω [ptohevo] go bankrupt ‖ become poor.
πτωχοκομεῖον, τό [ptohokomeeon] poorhouse.
πτωχός [ptohos] poor, needy.
πυγμαῖος, ὁ [peeymeos] pygmy.
πυγμαχία, ἡ [peengmaheea] boxing, pugilism.
πυγμή, ἡ [peeymee] fist ‖ (μεταφ) vigour, determination.
πυγολαμπίς, ἡ [peeyolampees] glow-worm, firefly.
πυθμήν, ὁ [peethmeen] bottom.
πύθων, ὁ [peethon] python.
πυκνά [peekna] closely, densely, thickly.
πυκνός [peeknos] thick, dense, closely-packed, close ‖ (γένεια) bushy.
πυκνότης, ἡ [peeknotees] density, compactness, thickness ‖ (κυμάτων) frequency.
πυκνώνω [peeknono] thicken, condense, grow thick ‖ make more frequent.
πυκνωτής, ὁ [peeknotees] (ἤλεκ) condenser.
πύλη, ἡ [peelee] gate, gateway.
πυλών, ὁ [peelon] gateway, portal, gate, entrance way.
πυνέζα, ἡ [peeneza] drawing pin.
πυξίς, ἡ [peeksees] (mariner's) compass ‖ box.
πύξος, ἡ [peeksos] box tree.
πύον, τό [peeon] pus, matter.
πῦρ, τό [peer] fire, firing.
πυρά, ἡ [peera] fire ‖ (μεταφ) sensation of burning.
πυρακτώνω [peeraktono] make red-hot, glow.
πυραμίς, ἡ [peeramees] pyramid.
πύραυλος, ὁ [peeravlos] rocket.
πύραυνον, τό [peeravnon] brazier.
πυργίσκος, ὁ [peeryeeskos] turret.
πύργος, ὁ [peeryos] tower ‖ castle, palace ‖ (ναυτ) bridge house.
πυρεῖον, τό [peereeon] match (for lighting), lucifer.
πυρετός, ὁ [peeretos] high temperature, fever ‖ (μεταφ) activity, energy.
πυρετώδης [peeretoδees] feverish ‖ (μεταφ) restless, feverish.
πυρήν, ὁ [peereen] stone, pip ‖ centre, core ‖ nucleus.
πυρηνικός [peereeneekos] nuclear.
πυρηνέλαιον, τό [peereeneleon] oil from stones ‖ seed oil.
πύρινος [peereenos] burning, fiery, red-hot ‖ (μεταφ) ardent, fervent.
πυρίτης, ὁ [peereetees] pyrites, flint.
πυριτιδαποθήκη, ἡ [peereeteeδapotheekee] powder magazine.
πυρίτις, ἡ [peereetees] gunpowder, powder.

πυρκαϊά, ἡ [peerkaeea] fire, burning, conflagration.
πυροβολεῖον, τό [peerovoleeon] gun emplacement, gun position.
πυροβολητής, ὁ [peerovoleetees] gunner.
πυροβολικόν, τό [peerovoleekon] artillery.
πυροβολισμός, ὁ [peerovoleesmos] firing, shot.
πυροβολῶ [peerovolo] fire ‖ shoot at ‖ shell.
πυρομαχικά, τά [peeromaheeka] πλ munitions ‖ ammunition.
πυροσβέστης, ὁ [peerosvestees] fireman.
πυροσβεστική [peerosvesteekee]: ~ ὑπηρεσία fire brigade.
πυροτέχνημα, τό [peerotehneema] firework, cracker.
πυρπολικόν, τό [peerpoleekon] fire ship.
πυρπολῶ [peerpolo] set on fire, burn down, consume by fire.
πυρρός [peeros] red-haired ‖ russet, carroty.
πυρσός, ὁ [peersos] torch, brand ‖ beacon.
πυρώνω [peerono] get red-hot, heat.
πιτζάμα, ἡ [peetzama] pyjamas.
πυώδης [peeodees] full of pus.
πώγων, ὁ [poyon] beard ‖ chin.
πωλεῖται [poleete]: '~' 'for sale'.
πώλησις, ἡ [poleesees] sale, selling.
πωλητής, ὁ [poleetees] seller ‖ salesman ‖ shop assistant.
πωλήτρια, ἡ [poleetreea] seller ‖ saleswoman.
πῶλος, ὁ [polos] foal, colt.
πωλῶ [polo] sell ‖ (μεταφ) sell, betray.
πῶμα, τό [poma] stopper, plug ‖ (μποτίλιας) cork ‖ lid, cover.
πωρόλιθος, ὁ [poroleethos] porous stone.
πώρωσις, ἡ [porosees] hardening ‖ (μεταφ) insensibility, callousness.
πῶς [pos] how?, what? ‖ ~ ὄχι; and why not? ‖ ~! yes, certainly.
πώς [pos] that.
πως [pos] somewhat, somehow, in any way.

Ρ, ρ

ραβαϊσι, τό [ravaeesee] banqueting, carousal ‖ uproar.
ραββίνος, ὁ [raveenos] rabbi.
ραβδί, τό [ravdee] cane, stick.
ραβδίζω [ravdeezo] flog, thrash, cane.
ραβδισμός, ὁ [ravdeesmos] flogging.
ράβδος, ἡ [ravdos] stick, staff ‖ (μαγική) wand ‖ (ἐκκλ) pastoral staff ‖ (σιδηροδρομική) rail.
ραβδώσεις, αἱ [ravdosees] πλ fluting, grooves ‖ stripes.
ράβδωσις, ἡ [ravdosees] stripe ‖ (ἀρχιτεκτονική) fluting ‖ groove.
ραβδωτός [ravdotos] striped ‖ fluted ‖ lined, ruled.
ράβω [ravo] sew up, sew on ‖ stitch ‖ (κοστούμι) have a suit made.

ράγα, ἡ [raya] grape, berry ‖ nipple.
ραγάδα, ἡ [rayada] crack, fissure, chink.
ραγδαῖος [raydeos] violent, turbulent ‖ (πτῶσις) rapid, headlong ‖ (πρόοδος) rapid, speedy.
ραγδαίως [raydeos] violently, impetuously, swiftly.
ραγιᾶς, ὁ [rayias] slave, bondsman.
ραγίζω [rayeezo] crack, split.
ράγισμα, τό [rayeesma] crack, fissure, split.
ραγού, τό [rayou] ragout.
ραδιενέργεια, ἡ [radieneryeea] radio-activity.
ραδιενεργός [radieneryos] radioactive.
ραδίκι, τό [radeekee] chicory, dandelion.
ραδιογραφία, ἡ [radeeoyrafeea] X-ray photography.
ραδιοθεραπεία, ἡ [radeeotherapeea] X-ray treatment.
ραδιολογία, ἡ [radeeoloyeea] radiology.
ράδιον, τό [radeeon] radium.
ράδιος [radeeos] easy, not difficult.
ραδιοτηλεγράφημα, τό [radeeoteeleyrafeema] radiotelegram.
ραδιοτηλεγραφία, ἡ [radeeoteeleyrafeea] radiotelegraphy.
ραδιοτηλεφωνία, ἡ [radeeoteelefoneea] radiotelephony.
ραδιουργία, ἡ [radiouryeea] intrigue, machination.
ραδιοῦργος [radiouryos] scheming, intriguing, plotting.
ραδιόφωνον, τό [radeeofonon] radio.
ραδίως [radeeos] easily.
ράθυμος [ratheemos] languid, listless, lazy.
ραιβοποδία, ἡ [revopodeea] bandy-leggedness.
ραίνω [reno] sprinkle, scatter, spread.
ράϊσμα [raeesma] βλ ράγισμα.
ρακένδυτος [rakendeetos] in rags, tattered.
ρακί, τό [rakee] kind of spirit.
ράκος, ὁ [rakos] rag, tatters ‖ (μεταφ) physical wreck.
ράμμα, τό [rama] stitch, thread.
ραμμένος [ramenos] sewn.
ράμνος, ἡ [ramnos] boxthorn.
ραμολῆς, ὁ [ramolees] imbecile, half-wit.
ραμφίζω [ramfeezo] peck at, pick up.
ράμφος, τό [ramfos] (μεγάλων πουλιῶν) bill, beak ‖ (μεταφ) burner, jet.
ρανίς, ἡ [ranees] drop, blob.
ραντεβοῦ, τό [rantevou] meeting, engagement, rendezvous.
ραντίζω [ranteezo] sprinkle, spray, water.
ράντισμα, τό [ranteesma] sprinkling, watering.
ραντιστήρι, τό [ranteesteeree] watering can ‖ (ἐκκλ) sprinkler.
ράντσο, τό [rantso] campbed.
ράξ, ἡ [raks] βλ ράγα.
ραπάνι, τό [rapanee] radish.
ραπίζω [rapeezo] slap or smack s.o. in the face.

P

ράπισμα, τό [rapeesma] clout, slap.

ραπτάδικο, τό [raptadeeko] βλ **ραφτάδικο**.

ράπτης, ὁ [raptees] tailor.

ραπτικά, τά [rapteeka] πλ fees for tailoring, fees for sewing.

ραπτική, ἡ [rapteekee] βλ **ραφτική**.

ραπτομηχανή, ἡ [raptomeehanee] sewing machine.

ράπτρια, ἡ [raptreea] dressmaker ‖ (ἀσπρορρούχων) seamstress.

ράπτω [rapto] βλ **ράβω**.

ράσον, τό [rason] frock, cassock.

ρασοφόρος, ὁ [rasoforos] priest, monk.

ράσπα, ἡ [raspa] rasp.

ράτσα, ἡ [ratsa] race, generation, breed ‖ ἀπό ~ thoroughbred.

ραφεῖον, τό [rafeeon] tailor's shop.

ραφή, ἡ [rafee] dressmaking ‖ stitching, seam.

ράφι, τό [rafee] shelf ‖ (τοίχου) bracket ‖ μένω στὸ ~ be left on the shelf, be an old maid.

ραφινάρισμα, τό [rafeenareesma] refinement.

ραφινάρω [rafeenaro] refine ‖ purify, polish.

ραφίς, ἡ [rafees] sewing needle.

ραφτάδικο, τό [raftadeeko] tailor's shop.

ράφτης [raftees] βλ **ράπτης**.

ραφτικά [rafteeka] βλ **ραπτικά**.

ραφτική, ἡ [rafteekee] dressmaking, sewing, tailoring.

ραχάτι, τό [rahatee] lazing about, idling, leisure.

ράχη, ἡ [rahee] back, backbone ‖ (βιβλίου) spine ‖ (βουνοῦ) crest, ridge.

ράχις [rahees] βλ **ράχη**.

ραχιτικός [raheeteekos] suffering from rickets.

ραχοκοκκαλιά, ἡ [rahokokalia] backbone, spine.

ράψιμο, τό [rapseemo] sewing, stitching ‖ tailoring, dressmaking.

ραψωδία, ἡ [rapsodeea] rhapsody.

ρεαλισμός, ὁ [realeesmos] realism.

ρεαλιστής, ὁ [realeestees] realist.

ρεβεγιόν, τό [reveyion] midnight supper.

ρεβίθι, τό [reveethee] chickpea.

ρεγάλο, τό [reyalo] tip, gratuity, present, gift.

ρέγγα, ἡ [renga] herring.

ρέγουλα, ἡ [reyoula] order, regular arrangement ‖ moderation, measure.

ρεζέρβα, ἡ [rezerva] stock ‖ (λάστιχου κτλ) spare part.

ρεζές, ὁ [rezes] hinge.

ρεζιλεύω [rezeelevo] ridicule, make a fool of ‖ humiliate.

ρεζίλι, τό [rezeelee] shame, derision, object of ridicule ‖ **γίνομαι** ~ become a laughing stock.

ρεζιλίκι [rezeeleekee] βλ **ρεζίλι**.

ρεῖθρον, τό [reethron] watercourse, rivulet ‖ ditch, gutter (of street).

ρεκλάμα, ἡ [reklama] advertisement ‖ show, display.

ρεκλαμάρω [reklamaro] advertise.

ρεκόρ, τό [rekor] record.

ρέκτης, ὁ [rektees] pushing person, enterprising person.

ρεμάλι, τό [remalee] worthless person.

ρεματιά, ἡ [rematia] ravine, torrent, riverbed.

ρεμβάζω [remvazo] muse, daydream, be in a reverie.

ρεμβασμός, ὁ [remvasmos] musing, reverie.

ρεμούλα, ἡ [remoula] plunder, pillage ‖ thieving, graft.

ρέμπελος [rembelos] lazy, sluggish ‖ disorderly.

ρεμπούμπλικα, ἡ [remboumpleeka] trilby, homburg.

ρεπάνι, τό [repanee] radish.

ρεπερτόριον, τό [repertoreeon] repertoire.

ρεπό, τό [repo] time off, break, rest period, rest.

ρέπω [repo] lean, incline, slope ‖ (μεταφ) tend towards.

ρεσιτάλ, τό [reseetal] recital.

ρέστα, τά [resta] πλ change.

ρετάλι, τό [retalee] remnant.

ρετσέτα, ἡ [retseta] prescription.

ρετσίνα, ἡ [retseena] resinated wine.

ρετσινόλαδο, τό [retseenolado] castor oil.

ρεύγομαι [revyome] belch.

ρεῦμα, τό [revma] current, stream, flow ‖ (ἀέρος) draught.

ρευματισμός, ὁ [revmateesmos] rheumatism.

ρεύομαι [revome] βλ **ρεύγομαι**.

ρεῦσις, ἡ [revsees] outflow, flowing ‖ emission.

ρευστοποιῶ [revstopeeo] liquefy.

ρευστός [revstos] fluid, liquid ‖ (μεταφ) fickle, inconstant, changeable.

ρευστότης, ἡ [revstotees] fluidity ‖ (μεταφ) inconstancy.

ρεφενές, ὁ [refenes] share, quota.

ρεφορμιστής, ὁ [reformeestees] reformist.

ρέψιμο, τό [repseemo] belching ‖ decay.

ρέω [reo] flow, stream ‖ (στάγδην) trickle ‖ (δάκρυα) shed.

ρήγας, ὁ [reeyas] king.

ρῆγμα, τό [reeyma] crack, breach, fissure, hole ‖ (μεταφ) rupture.

ρηθείς [reethees] (the) said.

ρῆμα, τό [reema] word, saying ‖ (γραμμ) verb.

ρημάδι, τό [reemadee] ruin ‖ wreckage, derelict ‖ **κλεῖσ'** τό ~ shut the blooming thing!

ρημάζω [reemazo] ruin, destroy ‖ fall into ruins.

ρηξικέλευθος [reekseekelefthos] innovating, modernist.

ρῆξις, ἡ [reeksees] rupture, breach ‖ conflict, quarrel, dispute.

ρῆσις, ἡ [reesees] saying, word.

ρητίνη, ἡ [reeteenee] resin.

ρητόν, τό [reeton] maxim, saying, motto.

ρητορεύω [reetorevo] make speeches, harangue.

ρητορική, ἡ [reetoreekee] oratory.

ρητός [reetos] formal, explicit, flat, positive.

ρήτρα, ἡ [reetra] clause, proviso, provision.

ρήτωρ, ὁ [reetor] orator.

ρητῶς [reetos] explicitly, expressly, flatly.

ρηχά, τά [reeha] πλ shallows.

ρίγα, ἡ [reeya] ruler, measuring rule ‖ line, stripe.

ρίγανη, ἡ [reeyanee] origanum.

ριγέ [reeye] striped.

ρῖγος, τό [reeyos] shiver ‖ thrill.

ριγῶ [reeyo] shiver, tremble, thrill.

ριγώνω [reeyono] draw lines, rule lines (on).

ριγωτός [reeyotos] (χάρτης) lined, ruled ‖ (ὕφασμα) striped.

ρίζα, ἡ [reeza] root ‖ (βουνοῦ) foot, base ‖ (μεταφ) origin, source, cause.

ριζικό, τό [reezeeko] destiny, fortune, lot, fate.

ριζικός [reezeekos] radical, fundamental.

ριζόγαλο, τό [reezoyalo] rice pudding.

ριζόνερο, τό [reezonero] rice water.

ριζοσπάστης, ὁ [reezospastees] radical.

ριζοσπαστικός [reezospasteekos] radical.

ριζώνω [reezono] become established, become fixed, take root, grow.

ρικνός [reeknos] wrinkled, shrivelled, warped.

ρίμα, ἡ [reema] rhyme.

ρίνη, ἡ [reenee] file.

ρινίζω [reeneezo] file.

ρινικός [reeneekos] nasal.

ρινίσματα, τά [reeneesmata] πλ filings.

ρινόκερως, ὁ [reenokeros] rhinoceros.

ριξιά, ἡ [reeksia] throw, cast(ing) ‖ (ὅπλου) charge ‖ shot, firing.

ρίξιμο, τό [reekseemo] casting, throwing ‖ dropping ‖ (ὅπλου) firing, shooting.

ριπή, ἡ [reepee] burst of firing, throwing ‖ (ἀνέμου) gust, blast.

ριπίδιον, τό [reepeeδeeon] fan.

ρίπτω [reepto] βλ **ρίχνω**.

ρίς, ἡ [rees] nose.

ρίχνομαι [reehnome] fling o.s., rush ‖ (στό νερό) plunge.

ρίχνω [reehno] throw, fling, cast ‖ (βόμβα) drop ‖ (ὅπλον) shoot, fire ‖ (ἀνατρέπω) overthrow, defeat ‖ (τοῖχο) pull down, demolish ‖ (δένδρο) hew, fell ‖ **ρίχνει βροχή** it's raining.

ριψοκινδυνεύω [reepsokeenδeenevo] risk, endanger ‖ take risks.

ροβολῶ [rovolo] roll down, rush down.

ρόγχος, ὁ [ronghos] rattle, blowing ‖ death rattle.

ρόδα, ἡ [roδa] wheel.

ροδάκινον, τό [roδakeenon] peach.

ροδαλός [roδalos] rosy, light pink.

ροδάνθη, ἡ [roδanthee] roseola.

ροδάνι, τό [roδanee] spinning wheel.

ροδέλαιον, τό [roδeleon] attar of roses.

ροδέλλα, ἡ [roδela] washer.

ρόδι, τό [roδee] pomegranate.

ρόδινος [roδeenos] rosy ‖ (μεταφ) rose-coloured, bright.

ροδίτης, ὁ [roδeetees] kind of pink grape.

ροδοδάφνη, ἡ [roδoδafnee] oleander.

ροδόδενδρον, τό [roδoδenδron] rhododendron.

ροδοκόκκινος [roδokokeenos] ruddy, rose-red.

ρόδον, τό [roδon] rose.

ροδόστα(γ)μα, τό [roδosta(γ)ma] rose water.

ροδόχρους [roδohrous] rosy, rose-hued.

ρόζ [roz] pink.

ροζιάρικος [rozeeareekos] gnarled.

ρόζος, ὁ [rozos] knot, node ‖ (δακτύλων) knuckle.

ροή, ἡ [roee] flow, flood ‖ (πύου) discharge, running.

ροΐδι, τό [roeeδee] pomegranate.

ρόκα, ἡ [roka] distaff ‖ (χόρτο) rocket.

ροκάνα, ἡ [rokana] (παιχνίδι) rattle.

ροκάνι, τό [rokanee] plane.

ροκανίδι, τό [rokaneeδee] chip, shaving.

ροκανίζω [rokaneezo] plane ‖ (μεταφ) gnaw, crunch.

ροκέτ(τ)α, ἡ [roketa] rocket.

ρολό, τό [rolo] cylindrical roll ‖ shutter.

ρολογᾶς, ὁ [roloyas] watchmaker, clockmaker.

ρολόϊ, τό [roloee] (τοίχου) clock ‖ (χεριοῦ) watch ‖ (μετρητής) meter ‖ **πάει ~** it's going smoothly.

ρόλος, ὁ [rolos] roll ‖ (θεατρικός) part, role ‖ (μεταφ) part ‖ **δέν παίζει ρόλο** it's not important.

ρομάντζο, τό [romantzo] romance.

ρόμβος, ὁ [romvos] rhombus ‖ (ὄργανον παιδιᾶς) spinning top.

ρόμπα, ἡ [romba] dressing gown.

ρομφαία, ἡ [romfea] sword.

ρόπαλον, τό [ropalon] club.

ροπή, ἡ [ropee] inclination, propensity ‖ (μηχανῆς) momentum.

ρούβλιον, τό [rouvleeon] rouble.

ρούζ, τό [rouz] rouge.

ρουθούνι, τό [routhounee] nostril.

ρουθουνίζω [routhouneezo] snort, sniff, snuffle.

ρουκέτ(τ)α, ἡ [rouketa] βλ **ροκέτ(τ)α**.

ρουλεμάν, τό [rouleman] ball bearings, roller bearings.

ρουλέττα, ἡ [rouleta] roulette.

ρουμάνι, τό [roumanee] dense forest, thicket.

Ρουμανία, ἡ [roumaneea] Rumania.

ρούμι, τό [roumee] rum.

ρουμπίνι, τό [roumbeenee] ruby.

ρούπι, τό [roupee] measure of length (.08 m) ‖ **δέν τό κουνάω ~** I refuse to move.

ροῦς, ὁ [rous] βλ ροή.

ρουσφέτι, τό [rousfetee] favour, string pulling, political favour.

ρουτίνα, ἡ [routeena] routine.

ρούφη(γ)μα, τό [roufee(γ)ma] noisy sipping, gulp, sucking in.

ρουφηξιά, ἡ [roufeeksia] mouthful, sip ‖ (πίπας κτλ) puff.

ρουφήχτρα, ἡ [roufeehtra] whirlpool.

ρουφιάνος, ὁ [roufeeanos] pimp ‖ schemer.

ρουφῶ [roufo] draw in, suck up, absorb, sip.

ρουχικά, τά [rouheeka] πλ clothing, garments.

ροῦχο, τό [rouho] cloth, stuff, material ‖ (φόρεμα) dress, attire.

ρόφημα, τό [rofeema] hot drink.

ροφῶ [rofo] βλ ρουφῶ.

ροχαλητό, τό [rohaleeto] snore, snoring.

ροχαλίζω [rohaleezo] snore.

ροχάλισμα, τό [rohaleesma] βλ ροχαλητό.

ρόχαλο, τό [rohalo] phlegm, spit.

ρόχθος, ὁ [rohthos] (κυμάτων) roaring, hissing.

ρύαξ, ὁ [reeaks] stream, brook, rivulet.

ρύγχος, ὁ [reenghos] muzzle, nose, snout ‖ nozzle.

ρύζι, τό [reezee] rice.

ρυζόγαλο, τό [reezoγalo] rice pudding.

ρυθμίζω [reethmeezo] (ὡρολόγι) regulate, set right ‖ (τά τοῦ οἴκου) manage ‖ (ὑποθέσεις) settle ‖ (λογαριασμούς) close, make up.

ρυθμικός [reethmeekos] rhythmical.

ρύθμισις, ἡ [reethmeesees] regulating, adjusting.

ρυθμιστής, ὁ [reethmeestees] regulator.

ρυθμός, ὁ [reethmos] rhythm, rate ‖ (μουσ) cadence ‖ (ἀρχιτεκτονική) order, style.

ρύμη, ἡ [reemee] force, momentum ‖ (φορά) course.

ρυμοτομία, ἡ [reemotomeea] street plan, roadmaking.

ρυμούλκα, ἡ [reemoulka] trailer.

ρυμούλκησις, ἡ [reemoulkeesees] towing, dragging.

ρυμούλκιον, τό [reemoulkeeon] towrope.

ρυμουλκόν, τό [reemoulkon] tugboat, steam tug ‖ (τρακτέρ) tractor.

ρυμουλκῶ [reemoulko] tow, tug, drag, pull ‖ (μεταφ) drag by the nose.

ρυπαίνω [reepeno] make dirty, soil ‖ (μεταφ) defile, tarnish.

ρύπανσις, ἡ [reepansees] dirtying, blemishing, defiling.

ρυπαρός [reeparos] dirty, filthy ‖ (μεταφ) odious, vile.

ρύπος, ὁ [reepos] filth, dirt ‖ ((μεταφ) disgrace, shame.

ρυτίδα, ἡ [reeteeδa] wrinkle, seam, line ‖ (τῆς θάλασσας) ripple.

ρυτιδώνω [reeteeδono] wrinkle, line ‖ get wrinkled.

ρυτίς, ἡ [reetees] βλ ρυτίδα.

ρῶ, τό [ro] the letter P.

ρώγα, ἡ [roγa] nipple.

ρωγμή, ἡ [roγmee] crack, split, cleft, crevice.

ρωγοβύζι, τό [roγoveezee] feeding bottle.

ρόθων, ὁ [rothon] βλ ρουθούνι.

ρωμαίικα, τά [romeïka] modern Greek, demotic Greek ‖ μίλα ~! come to the point!

ρωμαίικο, τό [romeïko] modern Greece.

ρωμαίικος [romeïkos] of modern Greece.

ρωμαϊκός [romaeekos] Roman.

Ρωμαῖος, ὁ [romeos] Roman.

ρωμαλέος [romaleos] robust, strong, vigorous, sturdy.

ρωμάντζα, ἡ [romantza] romantic background, romantic setting.

ρωμαντικός [romanteekos] romantic.

ρωμαντικότης, ἡ [romanteekotees] romanticism.

ρώμη, ἡ [romee] vigour, strength, force, robustness.

Ρώμη, ἡ [romee] Rome.

Ρωμιός, ὁ [romios] modern Greek.

Ρωμιοσύνη, ἡ [romioseenee] the modern Greek people.

Ρωσία, ἡ [roseea] Russia.

Ρῶσος, ὁ [rosos] Russian (person).

ρώτημα, τό [roteema] βλ ἐρώτημα.

ρωτῶ [roto] βλ ἐρωτῶ.

Σ, σ

σά [sa] βλ σάν.

σάβανον, τό [savanon] winding sheet, shroud.

σαββατοκύριακο, τό [savatokeereeako] weekend.

σάββατον, τό [savaton] Saturday.

σαβούρα, ἡ [savoura] rubbish, junk, trash ‖ ballast.

σαγανάκι, τό [saγanakee] frying pan ‖ (φαγητό) dish of fried cheese.

σαγή, ἡ [saγee] harness.

σαγηνεύω [saγeenevo] seduce, charm, attract.

σαγήνη, ἡ [saγeenee] fascination, enchantment.

σάγμα, τό [saγma] packsaddle.

σαγματοποιός, ὁ [saγmatopeeos] packsaddle maker.

σαγόνι, τό [saγonee] chin.

σαδισμός, ὁ [saδeesmos] sadism.

σαδιστής, ὁ [saδeestees] sadist.

σαθρός [sathros] rotted, decayed, rotten ‖ (μεταφ) groundless.

σαθρότης, ἡ [sathrotees] rottenness, decay.

σαιζόν, ἡ [sezon] season.

σαΐτα, ἡ [saeeta] arrow, dart ‖ weaver's shuttle.

σακαράκα, ἡ [sakaraka] (μεταφ) tin

lizzie (col), old motorcar, old bike.

σακατεύω [sakatevo] cripple, mutilate, maim ‖ (μεταφ) wear out, exhaust.

σακάτης, ὁ [sakatees] cripple, maimed person.

σάκκα, ἡ [saka] (μαθητική) satchel ‖ (κυνηγοῦ) game pouch, gamebag ‖ briefcase.

σακκάκι, τό [sakakee] jacket, coat.

σακκί, τό [sakee] sack, bag.

σακκίδιον, τό [sakeedeeon] haversack, satchel, small bag.

σακκοράφα, ἡ [sakorafa] sack needle, packing needle.

σάκκος, ὁ [sakos] sack, bag, sackful ‖ (ταχυδρομικός) mailbag ‖ kitbag.

σακκούλα, ἡ [sakoula] sack, bag ‖ paper bag.

σακκούλι, τό [sakoulee] sack, small bag.

σακκουλιάζω [sakouleeazo] put into a bag, put into a sack, pocket ‖ (ἐπί ἐνδυμασίας) be loose-fitting, not fit well.

σάκχαρις, ἡ [sakharees] sugar.

σακχαροκάλαμον, τό [sakharokalamon] sugar cane.

σάκχαρον, τό [sakharon] sugar.

σαλαμάνδρα, ἡ [salamanδra] salamander ‖ (θερμάστρα) combustion stove.

σαλάμι, τό [salamee] sausage, salami.

σαλαμούρα, ἡ [salamoura] brine.

σαλάτα, ἡ [salata] salad ‖ **τά κάνω ~** make a muddle of it, foul up the works.

σαλατιέρα, ἡ [salatiera] salad bowl.

σάλεμα, τό [salema] moving, stirring, shaking.

σαλέπι, τό [salepee] salep.

σαλεύω [salevo] move, stir, shake ‖ budge.

σάλι, τό [salee] shawl.

σάλιαγκας, ὁ [saleeangas] snail.

σαλιάζω [saleeazo] salivate.

σαλιάρα, ἡ [saleeara] baby's bib.

σαλιάρης, ὁ [saleearees] (μεταφ) babbler, gossip.

σαλιαρίζω [saleeareezo] chatter, prattle.

σαλιγκάρι [saleengaree] βλ **σάλιαγκας.**

σαλιέρα, ἡ [saliera] saltcellar.

σάλιο, τό [saleeo] saliva, spittle.

σαλιώνω [saleeono] lick, moisten, dampen, wet.

σαλόνι, τό [salonee] drawing room ‖ (πλοίου) saloon.

σάλος, ὁ [salos] swell, surge ‖ (πλοίου) rolling ‖ (μεταφ) disturbance ‖ tumult.

σαλπάρω [salparo] weigh anchor.

σάλπιγξ, ἡ [salpeenks] trumpet, bugle ‖ (ἀνατ) tube.

σαλπίζω [salpeezo] sound the trumpet.

σάλπισμα, τό [salpeesma] trumpet call.

σαλτάρω [saltaro] jump, leap.

σαλτιμπάγκος, ὁ [salteembangos] fairground acrobat ‖ (μεταφ) charlatan, buffoon.

σάλτος, ὁ [saltos] jump, leap, bound.

σάλτσα, ἡ [saltsa] gravy, sauce.

σαμάρι, τό [samaree] packsaddle.

σαμαρώνω [samarono] saddle, pack.

σαματᾶς, ὁ [samatas] (φασαρία) noise, din, roar ‖ fight.

σάματι(ς) [samatee(s)] as though.

σαμόλαδο, τό [samolaδo] sesame oil.

σαμούρι, τό [samouree] sable.

σαμπάνια, ἡ [sampaneea] champagne.

σαμποτάζ, τό [sampotaz] sabotage.

σαμποτάρω [sampotaro] sabotage.

σαμπρέλλα, ἡ [sambrela] inner tube.

σάμπως [sambos] as though ‖ it appears that.

σάν [san] when, as soon as, if ‖ like, as if ‖ **~ σήμερα πέρσυ** about a year ago today ‖ **~ τί;** like what? ‖ **~ νά** as though.

σανατόριον, τό [sanatoreeon] sanatorium.

σανδάλιον, τό [sanδaleeon] sandal.

σανδαλοποιός, ὁ [sanδalopeeos] sandal maker.

σανίδα, ἡ [saneeδa] board, beam, plank ‖ (σιδερώματος) ironing board.

σανιδόσκαλα, ἡ [saneeδoskala] gangplank.

σανιδώνω [saneeδono] floor, plank, cover with board.

σανίδωσις, ἡ [saneeδosees] flooring, planking, boarding.

σανίς, ἡ [sanees] βλ **σανίδα.**

σανός, ὁ [sanos] hay, fodder.

σαντιγύ, τό [santeeyee] chantilly.

σάντουιτς, τό [santoueets] sandwich.

σαντούρι, τό [santouree] kind of string instrument.

σαπίζω [sapeezo] rot, spoil, decompose, decay.

σαπίλα, ἡ [sapeela] decay, putridity ‖ (μεταφ) corruption, dishonesty.

σάπιος [sapeeos] decomposed, rotten ‖ corrupt, depraved, wicked.

σαπουνάδα, ἡ [sapounaδa] soapsuds, lather.

σαπούνι, τό [sapounee] soap ‖ (ξυρίσματος) shaving soap.

σαπουνίζω [sapouneezo] soap ‖ lather.

σαπουνόφουσκα, ἡ [sapouηnofouska] soap bubble.

σαπρός [sapros] βλ **σάπιος.**

σάπφειρος, ὁ [sapfeeros] sapphire.

σάπων, ὁ [sapon] βλ **σαπούνι.**

σαπωνοποιός, ὁ [saponopeeos] soap manufacturer.

σάρα, ἡ [sara]: **ἡ ~ καί ἡ μάρα** rabble.

σαράβαλο, τό [saravalo] ruin, wreck ‖ sickly person.

σαράκι, τό [sarakee] woodworm ‖ (μεταφ) remorse, prick of conscience.

σαρακοστή, ἡ [sarakostee] Lent.

σαράντα [saranta] forty.

σαραντάμερο, τό [sarantamero] Advent.

σαρανταποδαρούσα, ἡ [sarantapoδarousa] centipede.

σαρανταριά, ἡ [sarántaria] forty.

Σ

σαραντίζω [saranteezo] become forty ‖ be forty days since.
σαράφης, ὁ [sarafees] moneychanger.
σαρδέλλα, ἡ [sarðela] anchovy ‖ sardine.
σαρδόνιος [sarðoneeos] sardonic, sarcastic.
σαρίδι, τό [sareeðee] sweepings, garbage, refuse.
σαρίκι, τό [sareekee] turban.
σάρκα, ἡ [sarka] flesh.
σαρκασμός, ὁ [sarkasmos] derision, raillery, sarcasm.
σαρκαστικός [sarkasteekos] sarcastic, jeering, mocking.
σαρκικός [sarkeekos] carnal, fleshy, sensual.
σαρκοβόρος [sarkovoros] βλ σαρκοφάγος.
σαρκοφάγος [sarkofayos] carnivorous, flesh-eating ‖ ἡ ~ sarcophagus.
σαρκώδης [sarkoðees] fleshy, ‖ (φροῦτο) pulpy.
σάρκωμα, τό [sarkoma] sarcoma, fleshy growth.
σάρξ, ἡ [sarks] βλ σάρκα.
σάρπα, ἡ [sarpa] scarf.
σάρωθρον, τό [sarothron] broom.
σάρωμα, τό [saroma] sweeping.
σαρώνω [sarono] (δωμάτιο) sweep ‖ (δρόμο) scavenge ‖ (μεταφ) rake.
σᾶς, σας [sas] you ‖ your.
σασ(σ)ί, τό [sasee] chassis.
σαστίζω [sasteezo] disconcert, embarrass, confuse ‖ get disconcerted.
σατανᾶς, ὁ [satanas] Satan ‖ (μεταφ) devilish person.
σατανικός [sataneekos] devilish, satanical, fiendish.
σατέν, τό [saten] satin.
σατίρι, τό [sateeree] meat cleaver.
σατράπης, ὁ [satrapees] satrap ‖ (μεταφ) tyrant.
σάτυρα, ἡ [sateera] satire, skit, lampoon.
σατυρίζω [sateereezo] satirize, ridicule.
σατυρικός [sateereekos] satirical.
σάτυρος, ὁ [sateeros] satyr ‖ (μεταφ) debauchee.
σαύρα, ἡ [savra] lizard.
σαφήνεια, ἡ [safeeneea] clearness, distinctness, lucidity.
σαφηνίζω [safeeneezo] clarify, elucidate, explain.
σαφής [safees] clear, obvious, plain.
σαφῶς [safos] clearly, obviously.
σαχάνι, τό [sahanee] shallow frying pan.
σάχης, ὁ [sahees] Shah.
σάχλα, ἡ [sahla] insipid talk ‖ stupidity.
σαχλαμάρα, ἡ [sahlamara] nonsense, rubbish.
σαχλός [sahlos] flat, flabby ‖ stupid.
σβάρνα, ἡ [svarna] harrow.
σβέλτος [sveltos] nimble ‖ slim, slender.
σβέρκος, ὁ [sverkos] nape of neck, scruff.
σβέσις, ἡ [svesees] (φωτιᾶς κτλ) extinguishing ‖ (κεριοῦ) blowing out ‖ (ἀσβέστου) slaking.

σβήνω [sveeno] extinguish, quench, put out ‖ (γράμματα) erase ‖ (διά τριβῆς) rub out ‖ (μέ πέννα κτλ) strike out ‖ (φωτιά) die out ‖ (χρῶμα) fade ‖ (ἐνθουσιασμός) subside, die down.
σβήσιμο, τό [sveeseemo] extinction ‖ erasure, rubbing out.
σβηστός [sveestos] put out, extinguished, switched off.
σβίγγος, ὁ [sveengos] fritter.
σβουνιά, ἡ [svounia] ox dung.
σβούρα, ἡ [svoura] spinning top.
σβύνω [sveeno] βλ σβήνω.
σβῶλος, ὁ [svolos] lump (of earth) ‖ ball, clod.
σγάρα, ἡ [syara] bird's crop.
σγουραίνω [syoureno] curl ‖ become curly.
σγουρός [syouros] curly, fuzzy, curled ‖ curly-haired.
σέ [se] you ‖ to, at, in.
σέβας, τό [sevas] regard, reverence, deference.
σεβασμός, ὁ [sevasmos] βλ σέβας.
σεβάσμιος [sevasmeeos] venerable, respectable, reverend.
σεβασμιώτης, ἡ [sevasmeeotees]: ἡ ἡμετέρα ~ Your Reverence.
σεβαστός [sevastos] respected ‖ respectable, considerable.
σέβη, τά [sevee] πλ respects.
σεβντάς, ὁ [sevntas] love, yearning.
σέβομαι [sevome] respect, venerate, admire, esteem.
σειρά, ἡ [seera] series, succession ‖ row, line, rank ‖ (στήν τάξη) turn ‖ sequence, order ‖ μέ τήν ~ in turn, in order ‖ μπαίνω σέ ~ settle down.
σειρήν, ἡ [seereen] siren, enchantress ‖ hooter, buzzer, alarm.
σειρήτι, τό [seereetee] stripe, ribbon, braid.
σεισμικός [seesmeekos] seismic.
σεισμογράφος, ὁ [seesmoyrafos] seismograph.
σεισμόπληκτος [seesmopleektos] struck by earthquake.
σεισμός, ὁ [seesmos] earthquake.
σείω [seeo] move, shake, wave.
σεκλέτι, τό [sekletee] nuisance ‖ worry ‖ sorrow, distress.
σελαγίζω [selayeezo] shine, gleam.
σέλας, τό [selas] brightness, brilliance, radiance ‖ βόρειον ~ northern lights, aurora borealis.
σελάχι, τό [selahee] gun belt ‖ (ψάρι) ray.
σελέμης, ὁ [selemees] sponger, parasite.
σελεμίζω [selemeezo] beg, sponge, cadge.
σελήνη, ἡ [seleenee] moon.
σεληνιασμός, ὁ [seleeneeasmos] epilepsy.
σεληνόφως, τό [seleenofos] moonlight.
σελίδα, ἡ [seleeða] page (of book).
σελίνι, τό [seleenee] shilling.
σέλινον, τό [seleenon] celery.
σελίς, ἡ [selees] βλ σελίδα.

σέλλα, ή [sela] saddle.
σελλώνω [selono] saddle.
σεμινάριον, τό [semeenareeon] seminary.
σεμνοπρεπής [semnoprepees] dignified, decent, modest, proper.
σεμνός [semnos] decent, unassuming, modest || (ἐνδυμασία) simple, plain.
σεμνότης, ή [semnotees] dignity, modesty, decency.
σεμνότυφος [semnoteefos] prudish, demure, priggish.
σένα [sena] you.
σεντόνι, τό [sentonee] sheet.
σεντούκι, τό [sentookee] linen closet || box, chest.
σέξ, τό [seks] sex.
σεξουαλισμός, ὁ [seksoualeesmos] sexual instinct, sexuality.
Σεπτέμβρης, ὁ [septemvrees] September.
σεπτός [septos] august, venerable, revered.
σερβίρισμα, τό [serveereesma] waiting on, serving.
σερβίρω [serveero] wait at table, serve.
σερβιτόρα, ή [serveetora] waitress.
σερβιτόρος, ὁ [serveetoros] waiter.
σερβίτσιο, τό [serveetseeo] dinner service || place setting.
σεργιάνι, τό [seryeeanee] walk, promenade.
σεργιανίζω [seryeeaneezo] take for a walk, go for a walk || wander about.
σερμπέτι, τό [sermbetee] sherbet, syrup.
σέρνομαι [sernome] creep, crawl, drag || drag o.s. along.
σέρνω [serno] draw, pull, drag || (βαρύ πρᾶγμα) haul || (χορό) lead || ~ φωνή scream, shriek, cry out.
σέρρα, ή [sera] greenhouse, glasshouse.
σεσημασμένος [seseemasmenos] criminal.
σέσουλα, ή [sesoula] scoop, ladle || (ναυτ) skeet.
σεφτές, ὁ [seftes] first sale (of a day).
σήκαλη, ή [seekalee] rye.
σηκός, ὁ [seekos] shrine || enclosure.
σήκωμα, τό [seekoma] raising, lifting || getting out of bed.
σηκωμός, ὁ [seekomos] rising, rebellion.
σηκώνομαι [seekonome] rise, stand up, get up || (ἐπαναστατῶ) rebel.
σηκώνω [seekono] raise, hoist, pick up, lift up || (μεταφέρω) carry || (ἀφυπνίζω) get up || (ἀνέχομαι) bear, tolerate || ~ τό τραπέζι clear the table || ~ στό πόδι incite, rouse, disturb || ~ κεφάλι become arrogant, rebel.
σηκώτι, τό [seekotee] liver.
σῆμα, τό [seema] signal, sign, mark, badge || ~ κατατεθέν trademark, registration mark.
σημαδεμένος [seemaδemenos] marked || maimed, scarred.
σημαδεύω [seemaδevo] mark || aim at, take aim at.
σημάδι, τό [seemaδee] trace, scar, spot

|| (ἔνδειξις) sign, mark, indication.
σημαδούρα, ή [seemaδoura] buoy.
σημαία, ή [seemea] flag, ensign, colours, standard.
σημαίνω [seemeno] mean, be a sign of, signify || (καμπάνα κτλ) ring, strike, sound, signal || (ἔχων σημασία) matter, be of consequence.
σημαιοφόρος, ὁ [seemeoforos] standard bearer || (ναυτ) ensign, sub-lieutenant || (μεταφ) leader.
σήμανσις, ή [seemansees] marking, stamping || noting of details.
σημαντήρ, ὁ [seemanteer] buoy.
σημαντικός [seemanteekos] important, significant || (πρόσωπον) remarkable, considerable || momentous.
σήμαντρον, τό [seemantron] stamp, seal || (ἐκκλ) special monastery bell.
σημασία, ή [seemaseea] sense, meaning || importance, gravity, significance.
σηματοφόρος, ὁ [seematoforos] semaphore, signal station.
σημεῖον, τό [seemeeon] sign, mark, proof, indication || (θέσις, βαθμοῦ) stage, point || (μαθημ) symbol, sign || ~ τοῦ ὁρίζοντος point of the compass.
σημείωμα, τό [seemeeoma] written note, memorandum, record.
σημειωματάριον, τό [seemeeomatareeon] notebook, agenda, diary.
σημειωμένος [seemeeomenos] noted || scarred.
σημείωσις, ή [seemeeosees] written note || remark, comment.
σημειωτέος [seemeeoteos] to be noted || noticeable, noteworthy.
σήμερα [seemera] today || ~ τό ἀπόγευμα this evening, this afternoon.
σήμερον [seemeron] βλ σήμερα.
σημύδα, ή [seemeeδa] birch tree.
σηπία, ή [seepeea] cuttlefish.
σήπομαι [seepome] rot, decay, decompose.
σηπτικός [seepteekos] septic, putrefactive.
σήπω [seepo] putrefy, rot.
σήραγξ, ή [seeranks] tunnel.
σηροτροφία, ή [seerotrofeea] sericulture.
σησάμι, τό [seesamee] sesame.
σήστρον, τό [seestron] sieve, sifter.
σηψαιμία, ή [seepsemeea] septicaemia, blood poisoning.
σῆψις, ή [seepsees] decay, putrefaction || (ἰατρ) sepsis.
σθεναρός [sthenaros] sturdy, strong, vigorous, powerful, robust.
σθένος, τό [sthenos] vigour, strength, energy || courage, pluck.
σιαγών, ή [seeayon] jaw || (ἀνατ) jawbone.
σιάζω [seeazo] arrange, set in order, straighten, tidy || (ἐπισκευάζω) repair, mend, patch.
σίαλος, ὁ [seealos] saliva, spittle.
σιάξιμον, τό [seeakseemon] tidying,

setting in order, arranging ‖ mending.

σιγά [seeya] softly, lightly, gently, slowly ‖ ~ ~ carefully, by degrees.

σιγαλός [seeyalos] silent, quiet, gentle, still ‖ slowly.

σιγανός [seeyanos] βλ **σιγαλός**.

σιγαρέττον, τό [seeyareton] cigarette.

σιγαροθήκη, ή [seeyarotheekee] cigarette case.

σιγάρον, τό [seeyaron] (πούρο) cigar ‖ (τσιγάρο) cigarette.

σιγαρόχαρτον, τό [seeyaroharton] cigarette paper ‖ tissue paper.

σιγή, ή [seeyee] silence, hush.

σιγηλός [seeyeelos] quiet, silent, noiseless.

σίγμα, τό [seeyma] the letter Σ.

σιγοβράζω [seeyovrazo] simmer.

σίγουρα [seeyoura] for certain, for sure.

σίγουρος [seeyouros] certain, assured, sure ‖ (φάρμακο) infallible.

σιγώ [seeyo] keep quiet, remain silent ‖ die down.

σίδερα, τά [seedera] πλ ironwork ‖ (γραμμές) railway lines ‖ (φυλακή) irons, fetters.

σιδεράς, ό [seederas] blacksmith, ironmonger.

σιδερένιος [seedereneeos] of iron.

σιδερικά, τά [seedereeka] πλ scrap iron ‖ ironware.

σίδερο, τό [seedero] iron ‖ (σιδερώματος) flatiron ‖ (μαλλιών) curling tongs.

σιδέρωμα, τό [seederoma] ironing, pressing.

σιδερώνω [seederono] iron.

σιδηροδρομικός [seedeerodromeekos] of railways.

σιδηροδρομικῶς [seedeerodromeekos] by rail, by train.

σιδηρόδρομος, ό [seedeerodromos] railway, railroad.

σιδηροπυρίτης, ό [seedeeropeereetees] pyrites.

σίδηρος, ό [seedeeros] iron.

σιδηροτροχιά, ή [seedeerotrohia] railway track.

σιδηρουργεῖον, τό [seedeerouryeeon] forge, smithy.

σιδηρουργός, ό [seedeerouryos] blacksmith.

σιδηροῦς [seedeerous] iron, made of iron.

σιδηροῦχος [seedeerouhos] ferruginous.

σιδηρωτής, ό [seedeerotees] one who irons, one who presses.

σιδηρωρυχεῖον, τό [seedeeroreeheeon] iron mine.

σίελος, ό [sielos] βλ **σίαλος**.

σίκ [seek] (οὐσ) chic, stylishness ‖ (ἐπίθ) smart, stylish.

σίκαλις, ή [seekalees] rye.

σιλό, τό [seelo] silo.

σιλουέτ(τ)α, ή [seeloueta] silhouette, figure.

σιμά [seema] near, close by.

σιμιγδάλι, τό [seemeeydalee] semolina.

σιμός [seemos] snub-nosed ‖ (μύτη) snub, flat.

σίμωμα, τό [seemoma] drawing near, approaching.

σιμώνω [seemono] approach, draw near.

σινάπι, τό [seenapee] mustard, mustard seed.

σινδόνη, ή [seendonee] bed sheet.

σινιάλο, τό [seeneealo] βλ **σήμα**.

σινικός [seeneekos]: **σινική μελάνη** India ink.

σιντριβάνι, τό [seentreevanee] fountain.

σιρόκος, ό [seerokos] south-east wind.

σιρόπι, τό [seeropee] syrup.

σιταρένιος [seetareneeos] wheaten, of wheat.

σιτάρι, τό [seetaree] wheat, grain.

σιτεύω [seetevo] fatten ‖ (τό κρέας) hang, make tender.

σιτηρά, τά [seeteera] πλ cereals.

σιτηρέσιον, τό [seeteereseeon] ration, portion, allowance.

σιτίζω [seeteezo] feed, nurture, nourish.

σιτιστής, ό [seeteestees] quartermaster sergeant.

σιτοβολών, ό [seetovolon] granary, barn.

σιτοδεία, ή [seetodeea] scarcity, shortage, famine.

σῖτος, ό [seetos] βλ **σιτάρι**.

σιφόνι, τό [seefonee] siphon.

σιφονιέρα, ή [seefoniera] chest of drawers.

σίφουνας, ό [seefounas] waterspout, whirlwind.

σίφων, ό [seefon] siphon ‖ (σωλήνας) pipe, tube, conduit ‖ (μετεωρολογικός) whirlwind.

σιχαίνομαι [seehenome] loathe, detest, feel disgust for.

σιχαμένος [seehamenos] loathsome, sickening.

σιχαμερός [seehameros] disgusting, repulsive.

σιωπή, ή [seeopee] silence.

σιωπηλός [seeopeelos] silent, quiet, noiseless.

σιωπηρός [seeopeeros] tacit.

σιωπῶ [seeopo] remain silent ‖ hold one's tongue.

σκάβω [skavo] βλ **σκάπτω**.

σκάγι, τό [skayee] small shot, pellet.

σκάζω [skazo] burst, open, split, crack ‖ (ξύλο κτλ) split, splinter ‖ (ὀβίδα) burst, explode ‖ be exasperated, be infuriated (by) ‖ τό ~ make off ‖ **σκάσε!** shut up!

σκαθάρι, τό [skatharee] scarab(ee).

σκαιός [skeos] rough, blunt, abrupt, rude, coarse.

σκαιῶς [skeos] rudely, coarsely, roughly.

σκά(κ)κι, τό [skakee] chess.

σκάλα, ή [skala] stairs, staircase, flight, ladder ‖ (ὑπηρεσίας) backstairs ‖ (ἀποβάθρα) wharf, landing stage ‖ (λιμάνι) port ‖ (πρός ἱππευσιν) stirrup ‖ (μουσ) scale ‖ (μαλλιών) wave.

σκάλεθρον, τό [skalethron] poker.

σκαληνός [skaleenos] oblique ‖ (γεωμ) scalene.

σκαλί, τό [skalee] step, flight, rung ‖ grade.

σκαλίζω [skaleezo] hoe, weed, dig ‖ (μέταλλο) chisel ‖ (πέτρα κτλ) sculpture ‖ (ξύλο) carve ‖ (φωτιά) stir, poke ‖ (βιβλιοθήκη κτλ) rummage, seek, search.

σκάλισμα, τό [skaleesma] weeding, hoeing ‖ searching ‖ carving, sculpting.

σκαλιστήρι, τό [skaleesteeree] hoe, weeding fork.

σκαλιστής, ὁ [skaleestees] carver, engraver, chiseller.

σκαλιστός [skaleestos] engraved, carved, chiselled, sculptured.

σκαλοπάτι, τό [skalopatee] step, rung.

σκάλωμα, τό [skaloma] scaling ‖ (μεταφ) hitch, impediment.

σκαλώνω [skalono] climb, mount ‖ (μεταφ) get held up, meet with an obstacle.

σκαλωσιά, ἡ [skalosia] scaffolding.

σκαμνί, τό [skamnee] stool ‖ chair.

σκαμπίλι, τό [skambeelee] slap, smack.

σκαμπιλίζω [skambeeleezo] slap.

σκανδάλη, ἡ [skanδalee] trigger.

σκανδαλιάρης, ὁ [skanδaliarees] unruly or muddled or mischievous person.

σκανδαλίζομαι [skanδaleezome] be tempted, be shocked.

σκανδαλίζω [skanδaleezo] intrigue, allure ‖ scandalize, shock, offend.

σκάνδαλον, τό [skanδalon] scandal ‖ intrigue.

σκανδαλώδης [skanδaloδees] scandalous, disgraceful.

σκαντζόχοιρος, ὁ [skantzoheeros] hedgehog.

σκαπανεύς, ὁ [skapanevs] sapper ‖ pioneer ‖ digger.

σκαπάνη, ἡ [skapanee] mattock, pickaxe, pick.

σκαπουλάρω [skapoularo] escape from, elude, give the slip.

σκάπτω [skapto] dig up, scoop out ‖ (τάφρον) excavate ‖ (χαράσσω) engrave, carve, chisel.

σκάρα [skara] βλ ἐσχάρα.

σκαρδαμύσσω [skarδameeso] flicker, twinkle.

σκαρί, τό [skaree] slipway ‖ (μεταφ) character, make-up, idiosyncrasy.

σκαρίφημα, τό [skareefeema] sketch, rough outline.

σκαρλατίνα, ἡ [skarlateena] scarlet fever.

σκαρπίνι, τό [skarpeenee] lace-up shoe.

σκάρτος [skartos] defective, useless, unserviceable.

σκαρφάλωμα, τό [skarfaloma] climbing up, scrambling up.

σκαρφαλώνω [skarfalono] climb, clamber up, scramble up.

σκάρωμα, τό [skaroma] (μεταφ) fabrication, invention.

σκαρώνω [skarono] (μεταφ) fabricate, invent, lay on.

σκασίλα, ἡ [skaseela] chagrin, spite, vexation, distress.

σκάσιμο, τό [skaseemo] fissure, cracking ‖ (δέρματος) chap ‖ (διαφυγή) desertion, escape ‖ (μαθήματος) playing truant.

σκασμός, ὁ [skasmos] suffocation ‖ resentment ‖ ~ ! shut up!, hold your tongue!

σκατά, τά [skata] πλ shit (col).

σκαστός [skastos] noisy ‖ loud ‖ (στρατιώτης) AWOL ‖ (μαθητής) playing truant.

σκάφανδρον, τό [skafanδron] diving suit.

σκαφεύς, ὁ [skafevs] digger, labourer.

σκάφη, ἡ [skafee] trough, tub.

σκαφή, ἡ [skafee] digging.

σκάφος, τό [skafos] hull ‖ ship, vessel, boat.

σκάφτω [skafto] βλ σκάπτω.

σκάψιμο, τό [skapseemo] digging, ploughing ‖ carving.

σκάω [skao] βλ σκάζω.

σκεβρός [skevros] crooked, warped, deformed.

σκεβρώνω [skevrono] warp, twist ‖ get warped.

σκέλεθρο, τό [skelethro] βλ σκελετός.

σκελετός, ὁ [skeletos] skeleton ‖ framework, shape ‖ (αὐτοκινήτου) chassis.

σκελετώδης [skeletoδees] bony, emaciated.

σκελίδα, ἡ [skeleeδa] clove of garlic.

σκέλος, τό [skelos] leg ‖ side.

σκεπάζω [skepazo] cover ‖ protect ‖ hide.

σκεπάρνι, τό [skeparnee] adze.

σκέπασμα, τό [skepasma] roofing, covering ‖ blanket ‖ lid.

σκεπαστά [skepasta] secretly, on the quiet.

σκεπαστός [skepastos] covered in, veiled, roofed ‖ (μεταφ) secret.

σκέπαστρον, τό [skepastron] cover, screen, shelter.

σκέπη, ἡ [skepee] shelter, cover ‖ (μεταφ) protection.

σκεπή, ἡ [skepee] roof.

σκεπτικιστής, ὁ [skepteekeestees] sceptic, doubtful person.

σκεπτικός [skepteekos] sceptical ‖ pensive, engrossed.

σκέπτομαι [skeptome] think, reflect ‖ contemplate (doing).

σκέρτσα, τά [skertsa] πλ flirtatious ways.

σκέρτσο, τό [skertso] charm ‖ jesting, playfulness.

σκέτος [sketos] plain, simple ‖ (καφές) without sugar.

σκευασία, ἡ [skevaseea] preparation, composition, disposition.

σκεῦος, τό [skevos] utensil, implement ‖ (ἐκκλ) vessel.

σκευοφόρος, ὁ [skevoforos] luggage van, baggage cart.

σκευωρία, ἡ [skevoreea] scheme, machination, intrigue.

σκέψις, ή [skepsees] thought, consideration ‖ concern.

σκηνή, ή [skeenee] scene, trouble, quarrel ‖ (θεάτρου) action, stage ‖ (τέντα) tent.

σκηνικά, τά [skeeneeka] πλ (stage) scenery.

σκηνικός [skeeneekos] of the stage, theatrical.

σκηνογραφία, ή [skeenoγrafeea] stage designing.

σκηνοθεσία, ή [skeenotheseea] stage production ‖ (μεταφ) fabrication.

σκηνοθέτης, ὁ [skeenothetees] stage manager.

σκήνωμα, τό [skeenoma] (μεταφ) corpse.

σκήπτρα, τά [skeeptra] πλ: κατέχω τά ~ bear the palm.

σκήπτρον, τό [skeeptron] sceptre ‖ (μεταφ) superiority, prevalence.

σκήτη, ή [skeetee] small monastery, cloister.

σκιά, ή [skia] shade, shadow ‖ phantom.

σκιαγραφώ [skeeaγrafo] sketch, line.

σκιάδι, τό [skeeaδee] straw hat ‖ sunshade.

σκιάζομαι [skeeazome] be scared of, take fright (at).

σκιάζω [skeeazo] shade ‖ conceal the sun ‖ veil, hide ‖ (φοβίζω) frighten ‖ (μεταφ) overshadow.

σκιάχτρο, τό [skeeahtro] scarecrow ‖ bogey.

σκιερός [skieros] shady, shadowy.

σκίζα, ή [skeeza] splinter, shaving.

σκίζομαι [skeezome] struggle.

σκίζω [skeezo] split, cleave, tear, rip ‖ ~ τά ρούχα μου I swear I'm innocent.

σκίουρος, ὁ [skeeouros] squirrel.

σκιόφως, τό [skeeofos] partial shadow ‖ twilight, dusk.

σκιρτώ [skeerto] bound, leap, bounce, hop.

σκίσιμο, τό [skeeseemo] tear, rent, laceration ‖ crack.

σκίτσο, τό [skeetso] sketch, cartoon.

σκιώδης [skeeoδees] βλ σκιερός.

σκλαβιά, ή [sklavia] servitude, slavery ‖ (μεταφ) obligation, drudgery.

σκλάβος, ὁ [sklavos] slave ‖ captive.

σκλαβώνω [sklavono] subjugate, enslave ‖ (μεταφ) put under obligation.

σκλήθρος, ὁ [skleethros] alder.

σκληραγωγώ [skleeraγoγo] accustom to hardship, season, toughen.

σκληραίνω [skleereno] harden, make hard ‖ become callous.

σκληρός [skleeros] hard, tough ‖ cruel, heartless.

σκληροτράχηλος [skleerotraheelos] opinionated, headstrong, obstinate.

σκληρύνω [skleereeno] βλ σκληραίνω.

σκνίπα, ή [skneepa] gnat, midge ‖ (μεταφ) drunk as a lord.

σκοινί, τό [skeenee] βλ σχοινί(ον).

σκολειό, τό [skolio] βλ σχολείον.

σκόλη, ή [skolee] holiday, feast day.

σκολιανά, τά [skoleeana] Sunday best.

σκολιός [skolios] tortuous, crooked ‖ (άνθρωπος) difficult, wicked, perverse.

σκολίωσις, ή [skoleeosees] scoliosis.

σκολνώ [skolno] repose ‖ get off (work), leave.

σκολόπενδρα, ή [skolopenδra] centipede.

σκόνη, ή [skonee] dust, powder ‖ (γιά δόντια) tooth powder.

σκονίζω [skoneezo] coat with dust.

σκοντάφτω [skontafto] knock against, stumble ‖ come up against an obstacle.

σκόντο, τό [skonto] discount, deduction.

σκόπελος, ὁ [skopelos] reef, rock, shoal ‖ (μεταφ) stumbling block, danger.

σκοπευτήριον, τό [skopevteereeon] shooting gallery, shooting range.

σκοπεύω [skopevo] take aim at ‖ (μέ όπλον) take aim ‖ (έχω σκοπόν) intend, propose, plan.

σκοπιά, ή [skopia] lookout ‖ sentry box ‖ (σιδηροδρομική) signal box.

σκόπιμος [skopeemos] opportune, convenient, expedient ‖ intentional, deliberate.

σκοπίμως [skopeemos] intentionally, deliberately.

σκοποβολή, ή [skopovolee] target practice, shooting.

σκοπός, ὁ [skopos] purpose, intent, intention ‖ aim, goal ‖ (φρουρός) sentinel ‖ (στόχος) mark, target ‖ (ήχος) tune, air.

σκοπῶ [skopo] βλ **σκοπεύω**.

σκορβούτον, τό [skorvouton] scurvy.

σκορδαλιά, ή [skorδalia] garlic sauce.

σκόρδο, τό [skorδo] garlic.

σκόρος, ὁ [skoros] βλ **σκῶρος**.

σκοροφαγωμένος [skorofaγomenos] motheaten.

σκορπίζω [skorpeezo] scatter, disperse ‖ (περιουσίαν) dissipate, waste ‖ (φῶς) shed, spread ‖ disintegrate, melt away.

σκόρπιος [skorpeeos] dispersed.

σκορπιός, ὁ [skorpios] scorpion.

σκορπώ [skorbo] βλ **σκορπίζω**.

σκοτάδι, τό [skotaδee] darkness, obscurity ‖ gloom.

σκοτεινιάζει [skoteeneeazee] it's getting dark.

σκοτεινιάζω [skoteeneeazo] darken, become overcast ‖ cloud over.

σκοτεινός [skoteenos] dark, dismal, gloomy ‖ (ουρανός) overcast ‖ (νύχτα) murky ‖ (χαρακτήρ) sombre, melancholy ‖ (προθέσεις) underhand, sinister ‖ (λόγια) obscure, abstruse.

σκοτίζομαι [skoteezome] worry, trouble o.s. ‖ care for.

σκοτίζω [skoteezo] darken, obscure ‖ worry, annoy, vex.

σκοτοδίνη, ή [skotoδeenee] dizziness, vertigo.

σκότος, τό [skotos] darkness, obscurity, gloom.

σκοτούρα, ή [skotoura] (μεταφ) care, nuisance ‖ dizziness.

σκοτωμός, ό [skotomos] massacre, killing ‖ (μεταφ) hustle, jostle.

σκοτώνομαι [skotonome] hurt o.s. seriously ‖ (μεταφ) work o.s. to death.

σκοτώνω [skotono] kill ‖ while away (the time), kill time.

σκούζω [skouzo] howl, yell, scream.

σκουλαρίκι, τό [skoulareekee] earring.

σκουλήκι, τό [skouleekee] worm ‖ maggot, mite.

σκουντουφλῶ [skountouflo] stumble, bump against.

σκουντῶ [skounto] push, jostle, shove.

σκούπα, ή [skoupa] broom.

σκουπιδαρειό, τό [skoupeedario] rubbish dump.

σκουπίδι, τό [skoupeedee] rubbish, garbage, refuse.

σκουπιδιάρης, ό [skoupeedeearees] dustman, garbage collector.

σκουπίζω [skoupeezo] sweep, wipe, mop, dust, clean.

σκούρα [skoura]: τά βρῆκα ~ I found things difficult.

σκουραίνω [skoureno] darken ‖ deteriorate.

σκουριά, ή [skouria] rust ‖ ~ζω rust, corrode.

σκοῦρος [skouros] dark-coloured, brown.

σκούφια, ή [skoufeea] cap, baby's bonnet.

σκοῦφος, ό [skoufos] cap, beret, bonnet.

σκύβαλα, τά [skeevala] πλ (μεταφ) sweepings ‖ grain siftings.

σκύβω [skeevo] bend, lean, bow, incline.

σκυθρωπός [skeethropos] sullen, sulky, surly ‖ (ῦφος) morose.

σκύλα, ή [skeela] bitch ‖ (μεταφ) cruel woman.

σκυλεύω [skeelevo] despoil, rob ‖ plunder.

σκυλήσιος [skeeleeseeos] of a dog, like a dog.

σκυλί, τό [skeelee] dog ‖ ἔγινε ~ he got furious.

σκυλιάζω [skeeleeazo] infuriate ‖ become enraged.

σκυλοβρίζω [skeelovreezo] berate rudely.

σκυλολόι, τό [skeeloloee] rabble, mob, riffraff.

σκυλομούρης [skeelomourees] dog-faced ‖ (μεταφ) impudent, without shame.

σκύλος, ό [skeelos] βλ σκυλί.

σκυλόψαρο, τό [skeelopsaro] dogfish ‖ shark.

σκύμνος, ό [skeemnos] lion cub.

σκύρα, τά [skeera] πλ gravel ‖ macadam.

σκυταλοδρομία, ή [skeetalοδromeea] relay race.

σκυφτός [skeeftos] bending, stooping.

σκωληκόβρωτος [skoleekovrotos] worm-eaten.

σκωληκοειδῖτις, ή [skoleekoeeδeetees] appendicitis.

σκώληξ, ό [skoleeks] βλ σκουλήκι.

σκῶμμα, τό [skoma] scoff, gibe ‖ mockery.

σκώπτω [skopto] mock, deride, jeer, taunt.

σκωρία, ή [skoreea] βλ σκουριά.

σκῶρος, ό [skoros] moth.

σκώτι, τό [skotee] βλ σηκώτι.

σλέπι, τό [slepee] lighter.

σμάλτον, τό [smalton] enamel.

σμαράγδι, τό [smaraγδee] emerald.

σμάρι, τό [smaree] βλ σμῆνος.

σμέουρο, τό [smeouro] raspberry.

σμηναγός, ό [smeenaγos] (ἀερο) flight lieutenant.

σμήναρχος, ό [smeenarhos] group captain ‖ (US) colonel.

σμηνίας, ό [smeeneeas] sergeant.

σμηνίτης, ό [smeeneetees] airman.

σμῆνος, τό [smeenos] swarm ‖ (ἀερο) flight, squadron ‖ crowd.

σμίγω [smeeγo] mingle, mix ‖ meet, come face to face with ‖ join.

σμίκρυνσις, ή [smeekreensees] reduction, diminution, decrease.

σμιλάρι, τό [smeelaree] chisel.

σμίλη, ή [smeelee] chisel.

σμίξιμο, τό [smeekseemo] mixing, meeting, mating, joining.

σμιχτοφρύδης [smeehtofreeδees] with eyebrows that meet.

σμόκιν, τό [smokeen] dinner jacket.

σμπαράλια, τά [smbaraleea] πλ tiny pieces.

σμπάρο, τό [smbaro] shot.

σμύρις, ή [smeerees] emery.

σνομπαρία, ή [snombareea] snobbishness.

σοβαρεύομαι [sovarevome] look serious, speak seriously.

σοβαρόν [sovaron]: ~ ποσόν a substantial sum.

σοβαρός [sovaros] serious, grave, solemn.

σοβᾶς, ό [sovas] wall plaster.

σοβατίζω [sovateezo] plaster.

σοβῶ [sovo] be near, be at hand.

σόδα, ή [soδa] soda water ‖ bicarbonate of soda.

σοδειά, ή [soδia] βλ ἐσοδεία.

σόι [soee] lineage, breed ‖ sort, kind ‖ ἀπό ~ from a good family.

σοκάκι, τό [sokakee] narrow street, lane, alley.

σοκάρω [sokaro] shock, upset.

σόκιν [sokeen] shocking, suggestive.

σοκολάτα, ή [sokolata] chocolate.

σόλα, ή [sola] sole (of shoe).

σόλοικος [soleekos] incorrect, ungrammatical ‖ (μεταφ) improper.

σολομός, ό [solomos] salmon.

σόμπα, ή [somba] heater, heating stove.

σόροκος, ό [sorokos] βλ σιρόκος.

σορός, ή [soros] bier, coffin ‖ the dead (person).

σός [sos] your.

σοσιαλιστής, ὁ [soseealeestees] socialist.

σου [sou] your.

σούβλα, ἡ [souvla] skewer.

σουβλάκια, τά [souvlakeea] πλ meat on a skewer.

σουβλερός [souvleros] sharp, pointed.

σουβλί, τό [souvlee] awl || spit.

σουβλιά, ἡ [souvlia] injury from a pointed object || (πόνος) acute pain.

σουβλίζω [souvleezo] run through, pierce || (ψήνω) skewer || (πονῶ) cause pain.

σουγιᾶς, ὁ [souyias] penknife.

σούζα [souza]: στέκομαι ~ obey blindly || (μεταφ) fawn.

σουλατσάρω [soulatsaro] wander about, loaf.

σουλούπι, τό [souloupee] outline, cut, contour.

σουλτανίνα, ἡ [soultaneena] sort of seedless grape.

σουλτάνα, ἡ [soultana] Sultana.

σουλτάνος, ὁ [soultanos] Sultan.

σουμάδα, ἡ [soumada] orgeat (of almonds).

σουμιές, ὁ [soumies] spring mattress.

σούπα, ἡ [soupa] soup.

σουπιά, ἡ [soupia] cuttlefish || (μεταφ) sneaky person.

σούρα, ἡ [soura] fold, wrinkle, crease, pleat.

σουραύλι, τό [souravlee] pipe, reed, flute.

σουρομαδῶ [souromado] tug by the hair.

σούρουπο, τό [souroupo] dusk, nightfall.

σουρούπωμα, τό [souroupoma] nightfall.

σουρτούκης, ὁ [sourtoukees] gadabout.

σουρωμένος [souromenos] intoxicated.

σουρώνω [sourono] strain, filter || fold, pleat, crease || (ἀδυνατίζω) lose weight, grow thin || get drunk.

σουρωτήρι, τό [souroteeree] strainer.

σουσάμι, τό [sousamee] sesame.

σουσουράδα, ἡ [sousourada] wagtail.

σούσουρο, τό [sousouro] noise, din || rustle || (μεταφ) scandal.

σοῦστα, ἡ [sousta] spring (of seat) ||,,(ὄχημα) cart || clasp, clip.

σούτ [sout] (ἐπιφ) hush!, shut up!

σουτζούκι, τό [soutzoukee] type of sausage.

σουτζουκάκια, τά [soutzoukakeea] πλ meatballs.

σουτιέν, τό [soutien] bra(ssière).

σούφρα, ἡ [soufra] pleat, crease, fold || (μεταφ) theft.

σουφρώνω [soufrono] fold, pleat, crease || (μεταφ) pinch, steal.

σοφία, ἡ [sofeea] wisdom, learning || erudition.

σοφίζομαι [sofeezome] devise.

σοφιστεία, ἡ [sofeesteea] sophistry, subtlety.

σοφίτα, ἡ [sofeeta] attic, garret.

σοφός [sofos] wise || learned, lettered.

σπαγγοραμένος [spangoramenos] mean, tight-fisted.

σπάγγος, ὁ [spangos] twine, string || (μεταφ) mean person.

σπάζω [spazo] break, shatter, smash || ~ τό κεφάλι μου think hard || ~ στό ξύλο beat.

σπαθᾶτος [spathatos] sword-bearing || (μεταφ) slim, slender.

σπάθη, ἡ [spathee] sword.

σπαθί, τό [spathee] sabre, sword || (στά χαρτιά) spade.

σπαθιά, ἡ [spathia] sword stroke.

σπανάκι, τό [spanakee] spinach.

σπανίζω [spaneezo] become rare, be exceptional, be scarce.

σπάνιος [spaneeos] few and far between, uncommon.

σπανιότης, ἡ [spaneeotees] rarity, rareness, scarcity.

σπάνις, ἡ [spanees] rarity, shortage.

σπανίως [spaneeos] rarely.

σπανός [spanos] smooth-faced, beardless || raw, very young.

σπάνω [spano] βλ σπάζω.

σπαράγγι, τό [sparangee] asparagus || (US) sparrow grass.

σπαραγμός, ὁ [sparaymos] tearing || heartbreak, anguish.

σπαρακτικός [sparakteekos] heartbreaking, agonizing || (θέαμα) harrowing.

σπαράσσω [sparaso] tear || (μεταφ) cut to the heart.

σπάραχνα, τά [sparahna] πλ gills.

σπάργανα, τά [sparyana] πλ swaddling clothes.

σπαρμένος [sparmenos] spread || strewn, sown.

σπαρτά, τά [sparta] πλ crops.

σπαρταριστός [spartareestos] (ψάρι) fresh || (κορίτσι) beautiful || vivid, very descriptive.

σπαρταρῶ [spartaro] throb, palpitate, jump.

σπαρτός [spartos] βλ σπαρμένος.

σπάσιμο, τό [spaseemo] break, fracture.

σπασμός, ὁ [spasmos] convulsion, twitching.

σπασμωδικός [spasmodeekos] spasmodic || hasty.

σπατάλη, ἡ [spatalee] lavishness, extravagance, waste.

σπάταλος [spatalos] wasteful, extravagant.

σπαταλῶ [spatalo] waste, lavish, squander.

σπάτουλα, ἡ [spatoula] spatula.

σπείρα, ἡ [speera] coil, spiral || (ὁμάδα) band, gang, clique.

σπείρω [speero] sow || propagate.

σπεκουλάρω [spekoularo] speculate.

σπέρμα, τό [sperma] seed, germ || semen, sperm || (μεταφ) offspring || cause, motive.

σπερμολογία, ἡ [spermoloyeea] spreading of rumours.

σπέρνω [sperno] βλ σπείρω.

σπεύδω [spevdo] hurry, make haste.

σπήλαιον, τό [speeleon] cave, cavern, lair.

σπηλιά, ἡ [speelia] βλ σπήλαιον.

σπίθα, ἡ [speetha] spark, flash.

σπιθαμή, ἡ [speethamee] span.

σπιθοβολῶ [speethovolo] sparkle, spark ‖ gleam, glitter.

σπιθούρι, τό [speethouree] pimple.

σπιλῶ [speelo] soil, dirty ‖ (μεταφ) tarnish.

σπινθήρ [speentheer] (αὐτοκινήτου) ignition spark.

σπίνος, ὁ [speenos] finch.

σπιοῦνος, ὁ [speeounos] spy ‖ stool pigeon.

σπιρούνι, τό [speerounee] spur.

σπιρτάδα, ἡ [speertaδa] pungency ‖ (μεταφ) wit, intelligence.

σπίρτο, τό [speerto] alcohol ‖ (πυρεῖον) match.

σπιρτόζος [speertozos] witty, clever, ingenious.

σπιτήσιος [speeteeseeos] home-made, domestic.

σπίτι, τό [speetee] house, home ‖ (μεταφ) family ‖ ἀπό ~ well-born.

σπιτικό, τό [speeteeko] βλ σπίτι.

σπιτικός [speeteekos] βλ σπιτήσιος.

σπιτονοικοκύρης, ὁ [speetoneekokeerees] householder, landlord.

σπιτώνω [speetono] lodge, house ‖ (μεταφ) keep (a woman).

σπλά(γ)χνα, τά [splan(g)hna] πλ entrails, innards ‖ (μεταφ) feelings ‖ offspring.

σπλα(γ)χνικός [splan(g)hneekos] merciful, sympathetic.

σπλά(γ)χνο, τό [splan(g)hno] offspring, child.

σπλήν, ὁ [spleen] spleen.

σπλήνα, ἡ [spleena] βλ σπλήν.

σπληνάντερο, τό [spleenantero] sheep's intestines.

σπληνιάρης [spleeneearees] irritable, hypochondriac.

σπογγαλιεία, ἡ [spongalieea] sponge fishing.

σπογγαλιεύς, ὁ [spongalievs] sponge fisher.

σπογγίζω [spongeezo] sponge up ‖ mop up, wipe away.

σπόγγος, ὁ [spongos] sponge.

σπογγώδης [spongoδees] spongy.

σποδός, ἡ [spoδos] cinders, ashes.

σπονδή, ἡ [sponδee] libation.

σπονδυλική [sponδeeleekee]: ~ στήλη spine, backbone.

σπονδυλικός [sponδeeleekos] vertebral.

σπόνδυλος, ὁ [sponδeelos] vertebra ‖ (κίονος) drum.

σπονδυλωτός [sponδeelotos] vertebrate.

σπόρ, τό [spor] sport, games, pastime.

σπορά, ἡ [spora] sowing ‖ seed time ‖ (μεταφ) generation.

σποράδην [sporaδeen] sporadically.

σποραδικός [sporaδeekos] dispersed, scanty.

σπορέλαιον, τό [sporeleon] seed oil.

σπόρια, τά [sporeea] πλ seeds.

σπόρος, ὁ [sporos] seed, germ ‖ semen.

σπουδάζω [spouδazo] study, attend school.

σπουδαῖος [spouδeos] serious, important ‖ exceptional.

σπουδασμένος [spouδasmenos] learned, educated.

σπουδαστής, ὁ [spouδastees] student.

σπουδή, ἡ [spouδee] haste, keenness ‖ (μελέτη) study.

σπουργίτης, ὁ [spouryeetees] sparrow.

σπρωξιά, ἡ [sproksia] push, hustle, jostle, shoving.

σπρώξιμο, τό [sprokseemo] pushing ‖ encouraging.

σπρώχνω [sprohno] push, thrust, shove ‖ encourage, incite.

σπυρί, τό [speeree] grain ‖ (κολλιέ) bead ‖ (βάρος) grain ‖ (ἐξάνθημα) pimple ‖ boil.

σπυρωτός [speerotos] granular, granulated.

στάβλος, ὁ [stavlos] stable ‖ cowshed.

στάγδην [stayδeen] in drops.

σταγόνα, ἡ [stayona] βλ σταγών.

σταγονόμετρον, τό [stayonometron] dropper ‖ μέ τό ~ in small doses, little by little.

σταγών, ἡ [stayon] drop, dash.

σταδιοδρομία, ἡ [staδeeoδromeea] career, course.

στάδιον, τό [staδeeon] stadium, athletic ground ‖ (μεταφ) career, vocation.

στάζω [stazo] trickle, dribble, drip, leak.

σταθεροποίησις, ἡ [statheropieesees] stabilization, steadying down.

σταθερός [statheros] stable, firm, steadfast, secure.

στάθμα, τά [stathma] πλ weights.

σταθμάρχης, ὁ [stathmarhees] station master.

στάθμευσις, ἡ [stathmevsees] stopping, waiting, parking ‖ stationing.

σταθμεύω [stathmevo] stop, wait, stand, camp, park.

στάθμη, ἡ [stathmee] level, plumbline ‖ (νεροῦ) water level ‖ (τοῦ βίου) standard (of living).

σταθμίζω [stathmeezo] weigh, level ‖ (μεταφ) appreciate, calculate.

σταθμός, ὁ [stathmos] station, halting place ‖ (αὐτοκινήτου) garage ‖ (US) parking lot ‖ (ταξί) taxi rank ‖ stop, stay, wait ‖ (στήν ἱστορία) landmark, stage.

στάκτη, ἡ [staktee] ash, ashes, cinders.

σταλα(γ)ματιά, ἡ [stala(γ)matia] drop, dash.

σταλάζω [stalazo] drip, dribble, trickle.

σταλακτίτης, ὁ [stalakteetees] stalactite.

στάλσιμο, τό [stalseemo] sending.

σταμάτημα, τό [stamateema] stop, halting, checking ‖ pause ‖ block.

σταματῶ [stamato] stop (working), check.

στάμνα, ἡ [stamna] pitcher, jug.

στάμπα, ἡ [stampa] stamp, seal ‖ impression.

στάνη, ή [stanee] sheepfold, pen.

στανιό, τό [stanio]: μέ τό ~ against one's will, involuntarily.

στάξιμο, τό [stakseemo] dripping, trickling.

στασιάζω [staseeazo] mutiny, rebel.

στασίδι, τό [staseedee] pew, stall.

στάσιμος [staseemos] motionless, stationary || (ΰδωρ) stagnant.

στάσις, ή [stasees] halt, stop, bus stop, station || (έργασίας) suspension, stoppage || (τρόπος) posture, position || (ίατρ) retention || (έξέγερσις) revolt, rebellion || (μεταφ) behaviour, attitude.

στατήρ, ό [stateer] hundredweight.

στατική, ή [stateekee] statics.

στατικός [stateekos] static(al).

στατιστική, ή [stateesteekee] statistics.

σταυλάρχης, ό [stavlarhees] stable master.

σταῦλος, ό [stavlos] stable || cowshed || (χοίρων) pigsty.

σταυροδρόμι, τό [stavrodromee] crossroads || crossing.

σταυροειδής [stavroeedees] cruciform, crosslike.

σταυροειδῶς [stavroeedos] crosswise.

σταυροκοπιέμαι [stavrokopieme] cross o.s. over and over again.

σταυρόλεξο, τό [stavrolekso] crossword puzzle.

σταυροπόδι [stavropodee] cross-legged.

σταυρός, ό [stavros] cross, crucifix || stake, pale.

σταυροφορία, ή [stavroforeea] crusade.

σταυρώνω [stavrono] crucify || (τά χέρια) cross || (διασταυρούμαι) cross, meet and pass, cut across.

σταυρωτός [stavrotos] crossways, crosswise || (σακκάκι) double-breasted.

σταφίδα, ή [stafeeda] raisin || κορινθιακή ~ currant || (σμυρναίϊκη) sultana || γίνομαι ~ get intoxicated.

σταφυλή, ή [stafeelee] grapes || (άνατ) uvula.

σταφύλι, τό [stafeelee] grape.

σταφυλόκοκκος, ό [stafeelokokos] staphylococcus.

στάχι, τό [stahee] ear of corn, ear of wheat.

στάχτη, ή [stahtee] βλ στάκτη.

σταχτής [stahtees] ashen, pale.

σταχτόνερο, τό [stahtonero] lye.

Σταχτοπούτα, ή [stahtopouta] Cinderella.

σταχυολόγημα, τό [staheeoloyeema] gleaning || (μεταφ) selection, selecting.

στεατοκήριον, τό [steatokeereeon] tallow candle.

στεγάζω [steyazo] roof || cover, house, shelter.

στεγανόπους [steyanopous] webfooted.

στεγανός [steyanos] airtight, hermetical, waterproof.

στέγασις, ή [steyasees] housing, sheltering.

στέγασμα, τό [steyasma] roof || cover, shelter.

στέγη, ή [steyee] roof || (μεταφ) house, dwelling.

στεγνός [steynos] dry || (μεταφ) skinny, spare.

στεγνώνω [steynono] dry, become dry.

στειλιάρι, τό [steeleearee] helve || cudgel.

στεῖρος [steeros] barren, unproductive || (προσπάθεια) vain.

στέκα, ή [steka] billiard cue || (μεταφ) woman as thin as a rake.

στέκει [stekee]: ~ καλά he is well-off || he is fit and well.

στέκομαι [stekome] stand up || come to a standstill, stop || (μεταφ) prove to be || happen.

στέκω [steko] stand, stand still, come to a stop || it is fit to be.

στελέχη, τά [stelehee] πλ cadres.

στέλεχος, τό [stelehos] stalk, stem || shank, rod || (τσέκ) counterfoil || (χερούλι) handle.

στέλλω [stelo] send, direct, dispatch, forward.

στέλνω [stelno] βλ στέλλω.

στέμμα, τό [stema] crown, diadem.

στεναγμός, ό [stenaymos] sigh, sighing || moan, groan.

στενάζω [stenazo] sigh, heave a sigh || (μεταφ) moan.

στενεύω [stenevo] narrow down, take in, tighten || shrink, get narrow.

στενογραφία, ή [stenoyrafeea] shorthand, stenography.

στενοδακτυλογράφος, ό, ή [stenodakteeloyrafos] shorthand typist.

στενόκαρδος [stenokardos] apt to worry.

στενοκέφαλος [stenokefalos] narrow-minded, strait-laced.

στενόμακρος [stenomakros] long and narrow, oblong.

στενόν, τό [stenon] strait || (όροσειράς) pass, gorge.

στενός [stenos] narrow || tight-fitting || (μεταφ) close, intimate || (φίλος) dear (friend).

στενότης, ή [stenotees] tightness, closeness || narrowness || ~ χρήματος lack of money.

στενοχωρημένος [stenohoreemenos] hard-up || ill at ease.

στενοχωρία, ή [stenohoreea] lack of room || (δυσκολία) difficulty, inconvenience, discomfort.

στενόχωρος [stenohoros] narrow, limited, tight || troublesome.

στενοχωρῶ [stenohoro] worry, embarrass, annoy.

στενωπός, ή [stenopos] narrow street, back street || defile, pass.

στέργω [steryo] content o.s. with, allow, agree to.

στερεά, ή [sterea] mainland || ~ Ἑλλάς central Greece.

στερεοποιῶ [stereopeeo] solidify.

στερεός [stereos] firm, compact, well-built || solid, substantial || (χρῶμα) fast.

στερεότυπος [stereoteepos] stereotyped, invariable.

στερεύω [sterevo] dry up || stop, cease.

στερέωμα, τό [stereoma] consolidation || support, fastening || (οὐρανός) firmament.

στερεώνω [stereono] consolidate || make secure || ~ σέ μιά δουλειά settle down to one job.

στερήσεις, οἱ [stereesees] πλ privation, want, loss.

στέρησις, ἡ [stereesees] deprivation || shortage, absence.

στεριά, ἡ [steria] terra firma.

στεριανός, ὁ [stereeanos] mainlander.

στερλίνα, ἡ [sterleena] pound sterling.

στέρνα, ἡ [sterna] cistern, tank.

στέρνον, τό [sternon] breastbone, chest.

στερνός [sternos] later, last.

στεροῦμαι [steroume] go without, lack || (πένομαι) be needy.

στερῶ [stero] deprive of, take away.

στέφανα, τά [stefana] πλ marriage wreaths.

στεφάνη, ἡ [stefanee] crown || (ἀγγείου) brim || (βαρελιοῦ) hoop || (ἄνθους) corolla || ring, band || (τροχοῦ) tyre.

στεφάνι, τό [stefanee] garland, wreath || (βαρελιοῦ) hoop, band.

στέφανος, ὁ [stefanos] garland, wreath || crown.

στεφανώνομαι [stefanonome] marry, get married.

στεφανώνω [stefanono] crown || be the best man at a wedding.

στέψις, ἡ [stepsees] coronation || wedding ceremony.

στηθαῖον, τό [steetheon] parapet.

στηθικός [steetheekos] of the chest || consumptive.

στηθόδεσμος, ὁ [steethodesmos] βλ σουτιέν.

στῆθος, τό [steethos] chest, breast || (γυναικός) bosom.

στηθοσκοπῶ [steethoskopo] examine with a stethoscope.

στήλη, ἡ [steelee] staff, pillar, column || (μπαταρία) electric battery || (ἐφημερίδος) column.

στηλιτεύω [steeleetevo] defame, slander.

στηλώνω [steelono] prop up, support || bolster up.

στημόνι, τό [steemonee] warp.

στήνω [steeno] raise, hold up, erect, put up || ~ παγίδα lay a trap.

στήριγμα, τό [steereegma] prop, support, stay.

στηρίζομαι [steereezome] lean on, rely on || be based on.

στηρίζω [steereezo]˙ support || prop || base on, reckon on.

στητός [steetos] standing, upright.

στιβάλι, τό [steevalee] ankle boot, laced boot.

στιβαρός [steevaros] strong, robust, steady, firm.

στιβάς, ἡ [steevas] pile, heap, mass.

στίβος, ὁ [steevos] track, ring, racetrack.

στίγμα, τό [steeyma] spot, brand, stain, stigma || disgrace || position, fix.

στιγμή, ἡ [steeymee] instant, moment || (τυπογραφικό) dot, point || τελεία ~ full stop || ἄνω ~ colon.

στιγμιαῖος [steeymieos] instantaneous || momentary, temporary.

στιγμιότυπον, τό [steeymeeoteepon] snapshot, snap.

στικτός [steektos] spotted, dotted, stippled || tattooed.

στίλβω [steelvo] shine, glitter, sparkle.

στιλβώνω [steelvono] polish, varnish, burnish.

στιλβωτήριον, τό [steelvoteereeon] shoe black's.

στιλέττο, τό [steeleto] stiletto, dagger.

στιλπνός [steelpnos] brilliant, polished, bright.

στίξις, ἡ [steeksees] punctuation || dot, spot, speckle.

στιφάδο, τό [steefado] meat stew with onions.

στῖφος, τό [steefos] crowd, horde, throng || rabble, gang.

στιχομυθία, ἡ [steehomeetheea] vivid dialogue.

στίχος, ὁ [steehos] line, row, file || verse.

στιχουργός, ὁ [steehouryos] rhymester, versifier.

στοά, ἡ [stoa] colonnade, portico, arcade || passage || (ὀρυχείου) gallery || (μασωνική) (masonic) lodge.

στοίβα, ἡ [steeva] pile, stack, mass.

στοιβάζω [steevazo] stack, pile up || crowd, squeeze.

στοιχεῖα, τά [steeheea] πλ elements, rudiments || (τυπογραφείου) printing types.

στοιχειό, τό [steehio] ghost, phantom.

στοιχειοθεσία, ἡ [steeheeotheseea] typesetting.

στοιχεῖον, τό [steeheeon] component, element || (νομ) piece of evidence || (ἀλφαβήτου) letter || (ἠλεκτ) cell || (μεταφ) factor.

στοιχειώδης [steeheeodees] elementary, rudimentary || essential, capital.

στοιχειωμένος [steeheeomenos] haunted.

στοιχειώνω [steeheeono] become haunted, haunt.

στοίχημα, τό [steeheema] bet, wager || stake || βάζω ~ lay a bet, wager.

στοιχηματίζω [steeheemateezo] bet, wager.

στοιχίζω [steeheezo] cost || (μεταφ) pain, grieve.

στοῖχος, τό [steehos] row, line, rank.

στόκος, ὁ [stokos] putty, stucco.

στολή, ή [stolee] uniform ‖ costume.
στολίδι, τό [stoleedee] jewellery ‖ (στόλισμα) adornment, decoration.
στολίζω [stoleezo] adorn, decorate, deck, trim, embellish.
στολίσκος, ὁ [stoleeskos] flotilla ‖ flight.
στολισμός, ὁ [stoleesmos] ornamenting, decoration, embellishing.
στόλος, ὁ [stolos] navy, fleet.
στόμα, τό [stoma] mouth ‖ lips.
στομάχι, τό [stomahee] stomach.
στομαχιάζω [stomaheeazo] suffer from indigestion.
στόμαχος, ὁ [stomahos] βλ στομάχι.
στόμιον, τό [stomeeon] mouth, opening, aperture, entrance ‖ muzzle.
στόμφος, ὁ [stomfos] boast, declamation.
στομώνω [stomono] blunt ‖ temper, harden.
στόρ(ι), τό [stor(ee)] blind, roller blind.
στοργή, ή [storyee] affection, tenderness, love.
στουμπίζω [stoumbeezo] pound, grind, crush ‖ beat s.o. mercilessly.
στουμπώνω [stoumbono] stuff, pad, plug ‖ become stuffed.
στουπί, τό [stoupee] oakum, wad, tow ‖ (μεταφ) drunk as a fiddler.
στουπόχαρτο, τό [stoupoharto] blotting paper.
στουπώνω [stoupono] stop, choke up ‖ be choked up.
στουρνάρι, τό [stournaree] flint, gun flint.
στοχάζομαι [stohazome] think, meditate (on) ‖ consider.
στοχασμός, ὁ [stohasmos] thought, meditation.
στοχαστικός [stohasteekos] thoughtful ‖ discreet, wise.
στόχαστρον, τό [stohastron] front sight (of gun).
στόχος, ὁ [stohos] mark, target, objective ‖ aim, end.
στραβά [strava] obliquely, crookedly ‖ wrongly, amiss ‖ τὄβαλε ~ he doesn't give a damn.
στραβισμός, ὁ [straveesmos] squinting.
στραβοβλέπω [stravovlepo] look askance at, leer at.
στραβοκάνης [stravokanees] bandy-legged.
στραβομάρα, ή [stravomara] blindness ‖ (κακοτυχία) bad luck, mischance ‖ (μεταφ) blunder, gross mistake, howler.
στραβόξυλο, τό [stravokseelo] obstinate person, contrary fellow.
στραβοπάτημα, τό [stravopateema] staggering ‖ false step.
στραβός [stravos] crooked, awry, twisted ‖ (λοξός) slanting ‖ (ἐλαττωματικός) faulty ‖ (τυφλός) blind.
στραβώνομαι [stravonome] go blind.
στραβώνω [stravono] bend, distort ‖ make a mess of ‖ spoil ‖ (τυφλώνω) blind ‖ (λυγίζω) become twisted.

στραγάλια, τά [strayaleea] πλ roasted chickpeas.
στραγγαλίζω [strangaleezo] strangle, throttle ‖ stifle.
στραγγαλιστής, ὁ [strangaleestees] strangler.
στραγγίζω [strangeezo] drain, filter, press out, wring out ‖ (κουράζομαι) get exhausted.
στραγγιστήρι, τό [strangeesteeree] strainer, filter, colander.
στραγγουλίζω [strangouleezo] sprain, twist, wrench.
στράκα, ή [straka] crack ‖ (πυροτέχνημα) cracker.
στραμπουλίζω [strambouleezo] sprain, twist.
στραπατσάρω [strapatsaro] harm, damage ‖ ruffle ‖ (ταπεινώνω) humiliate.
στραπάτσο, τό [strapatso] maltreatment ‖ humiliation.
στράτα, ή [strata] way, street, road.
στρατάρχης, ὁ [stratarhees] (field) marshal.
στράτευμα, τό [stratevma] army, troops, forces.
στρατεύματα, τά [stratevmata] πλ troops.
στρατεύομαι [stratevome] serve in the army, take the field.
στρατεύσιμος [stratevseemos] subject to conscription.
στρατηγεῖον, τό [strateeyeeon] headquarters.
στρατήγημα, τό [strateeyeema] stratagem ‖ trick, ruse.
στρατηγία, ή [strateeyeea] generalship.
στρατηγική, ή [strateeyeekee] strategy.
στρατηγικός [strateeyeekos] strategic.
στρατηγός, ὁ [strateeyos] general.
στρατί, τό [stratee] βλ στράτα.
στρατιά, ή [stratia] army, force.
στρατιώτης, ὁ [strateeotees] soldier, private ‖ warrior.
στρατιωτικό, τό [strateeoteeko] military service.
στρατιωτικός [strateeoteekos] military ‖ ~ νόμος martial law.
στρατοδικεῖον, τό [stratodeekeeon] court-martial.
στρατοκρατία, ή [stratokrateea] militarism, military government.
στρατολογία, ή [stratoloyeea] conscription, call-up.
στρατόπεδον, τό [stratopedon] camp, encampment ‖ side, party.
στρατός, ὁ [stratos] army, troops, forces.
στρατόσφαιρα, ή [stratosfera] stratosphere.
στρατώνας, ὁ [stratonas] barracks.
στρεβλός [strevlos] crooked, deformed, twisted ‖ (μεταφ) rough, difficult.
στρείδι, τό [streedee] oyster.
στρέμμα, τό [strema] (approx) quarter of an acre.
στρέφομαι [strefome] turn, rotate ‖ revolve.

στρέφω [strefo] turn, turn about ‖ rotate, revolve.

στρεψοδικία, ή [strepsŏdeekeea] chicanery, quibbling, pettifoggery.

στρίβω [streevo] twist, rotate, turn ‖ τό ~ slip away, slip off.

στρίγ(γ)λα, ή [stree(n)gla] witch, sorceress, shrew.

στριγ(γ)λιά, ή [stree(n)glia] wickedness, shrewishness ‖ (κραυγή) shrill cry, shriek.

στριμμένος [streemenos] twisted ‖ ill-humoured, wicked, malicious.

στρίποδο, τό [streepodo] trestle, tripod.

στριφογυρίζω [streefoγeereezo] move round, turn round ‖ whirl, spin.

στρίφωμα, τό [streefoma] hemming.

στρίψιμο, τό [streepseemo] twisting, turning.

στροβιλίζω [stroveeleezo] whirl, turn round, twirl.

στρόβιλος, ό [stroveelos] spinning top, peg top ‖ (άνεμος) whirlwind ‖ (χιόνος) eddying, swirling (snow) ‖ (μηχανή) turbine ‖ (σκόνης) whirling cloud.

στρογγυλεύω [strongeelevo] make round ‖ grow plump, get stout.

στρογγυλός [strongeelos] round(ed) ‖ (πρόσωπο) full ‖ (άριθμός) round, even.

στρούγγα, ή [strounga] sheepfold, enclosure.

στρουθίον, τό [stroutheeon] sparrow.

στρουθοκάμηλος, ή [strouthokameelos] ostrich.

στρουμπουλός [stroumboulos] dumpy.

στρόφαλος, ό [strofalos] crank, handle ‖ (αύτοκινήτου) starting handle.

στροφείον, τό [strofeeon] winch.

στροφεύς, ό [strofevs] hinge, pivot.

στροφή, ή [strofee] turn, revolution ‖ (όδοΰ) twist, bend ‖ (κατευθύνσεως) detour, change of direction ‖ (ποίηση) stanza ‖ (μουσ) ritornello.

στρόφιγξ, ή [strofeenks] hinge, pivot ‖ tap.

στρυμώ(χ)νω [streemo(h)no] squeeze, crowd, cram ‖ press hard, oppress, annoy.

στρυφνός [streefnos] harsh ‖ peevish ‖ (χαρακτήρ) crabbed ‖ (ϋφος κτλ) obscure, difficult ‖ (είς γεύσιν) sharp, biting.

στρώμα, τό [stroma] couch, bed, mattress ‖ (γεωλογίας) bed, layer, stratum ‖ στό ~ ill in bed.

στρώνομαι [stronome] apply o.s. ‖ install o.s.

στρώνω [strono] spread, lay ‖ (κρεββάτι) make ‖ (δρόμο) pave ‖ (μεταφ) be well under way ‖ ~ τό κρεββάτι make the bed.

στρώση, ή [strosee] layer ‖ strewing ‖ paving, flooring.

στρωσίδι, τό [stroseedee] carpet ‖ bedding.

στρωτός [strotos] strewn ‖ paved ‖ (ζωή) even, normal, regular.

στύβω [steevo] squeeze, wring, press ‖

(μεταφ) rack one's brains ‖ (στειρεύω) dry up, run dry.

στυγερός [steeγeros] abominable, heinous, horrible.

στυγνός [steeγnos] doleful, despondent, gloomy.

στυλό, τό [steelo] fountain pen.

στυλοβάτης, ό [steelovatees] pedestal, base ‖ (μεταφ) pillar, founder.

στυλογράφος, ό [steeloγrafos] βλ στυλό.

στϋλος, ό [steelos] pillar, column, pole ‖ (μεταφ) prop, mainstay, breadwinner.

στυλώνω [steelono] support, prop up ‖ fix.

στυπτηρία, ή [steepteereea] βλ στύψη.

στυπτικός [steepteekos] binding, styptic.

στυφός [steefos] sour, acrid, bitter.

στύψη, ή [steepsee] alum.

στύψιμο, τό [steepseemo] squeezing, pressing, wringing.

στωϊκός [stoeekos] stoic(al).

στωμύλος [stomeelos] eloquent, fluent.

σύ [see] you.

συβαρίτης, ό [seevareetees] sybarite.

σύγγαμβρος, ό [seengamvros] brother-in-law.

συγγένεια, ή [seengeneea] relationship, kinship ‖ affinity, relation, connection.

συγγενής [seengenees] connected, related ‖ (οὐσ) relation, kinsman.

συγγενολό(γ)ι, τό [seengenolo(γ)ee] relations, relatives, kindred.

συγγνώμη, ή [seeγnomee] pardon, excuse ‖ forgiveness.

σύγγραμμα, τό [seengrama] work (of writing), treatise.

συγγραφεύς, ό [seengrafevs] author, writer.

συγγράφω [seengrafo] write a work, compose.

σύγκαιρα [seengkera] in time ‖ simultaneously.

συγκαίομαι [seengkeome] be chafed, be galled.

σύγκαλα, τά [seengkala] πλ: στά ~ μου normal, in good health.

συγκαλύπτω [seengkaleepto] hide, cloak, hush up, cover.

συγκάλυψις, ή [seengkaleepsees] cloaking, masking, suppression.

συγκαλῶ [seengkalo] convene, convoke ‖ (πρόσωπα) assemble, call together.

συγκαταβατικός [seengkatavateekos] accommodating ‖ (τιμή) moderate, reasonable.

συγκατάθεσις, ή [seengkatatheesees] assent, consent, acquiescence.

συγκαταλέγω [seengkataleγo] include, number among ‖ consider, regard.

συγκατανεύω [seengkatanevo] consent, assent, adhere to.

συγκατατίθεμαι [seengkatateetheme] βλ συγκατανεύω.

συγκατοικῶ [seengkateeko] cohabit, live together.

σύγκειμαι [seengkeeme] be composed of, consist of.

συγκεκαλυμμένος [seengkekaleemenos] disguised, indirect.

συγκεκριμένος [seengkekreemenos] concrete, positive, clear, specific.

συγκεκριμένος [seengkekreemenos] plainly, concretely, actually.

συγκεντρώνομαι [seengkentronome] concentrate.

συγκεντρώνω [seengkentrono] collect, bring together, concentrate || centralize.

συγκέντρωσις, ἡ [seengkentrosees] crowd, gathering, . assembly || concentration || centralization.

συγκερασμός, ὁ [seengkerasmos] mixing, mingling || compromise.

συγκεφαλαιώνω [seengkefaleono] summarize, sum up.

συγκεχυμένος [seengkeheemenos] confused, jumbled || (ἦχος) indistinct || (φήμες) vague || (ἰδέες) hazy, dim || (λόγοι) imprecise, obscure.

συγκίνησις, ἡ [seengkeeneesees] emotion, sensation.

συγκινητικός [seengkeeneeteekos] moving, touching, stirring.

συγκινοῦμαι [seengkeenoume] be excited || be touched.

συγκινῶ [seengkeeno] move, affect, touch || excite.

σύγκλησις, ἡ [seengkleesees] convocation, calling together.

σύγκλητος, ἡ [seengkleetos] senate.

συγκλίνω [seengkleeno] converge, concentrate.

συγκλονίζω [seengkloneezo] shake, excite, stir up, shock.

συγκοινωνία, ἡ [seengkeenoneea] communications || means of transport.

συγκοινωνῶ [seengkeenono] communicate, be connected.

συγκολλῶ [seengkolo] glue, join together || (μέταλλα) weld, solder || ~ σαμπρέλα mend a puncture.

συγκομιδή, ἡ [seengkomeedee] harvest, crop.

συγκοπή, ἡ [seengkopee] syncopation || (ἰατρ) heart failure || (γραμμ) contraction.

συγκράτησις, ἡ [seengkrateesees] containing, bridling, restraining.

συγκρατοῦμαι [seengkratoume] control o.s., contain o.s.

συγκρατῶ [seengkrato] check || (πάθη) govern || (θυμόν) contain, control, suppress || (τά πλήθη) restrain.

συγκρίνω [seengkreeno] compare (with), liken (to).

σύγκρισις, ἡ [seengkreesees] comparison, parallel.

συγκριτικός [seengkreeteekos] comparative, compared (to).

συγκρότημα, τό [seengkroteema] group, cluster.

συγκροτῶ [seengkroto] form, compose || convoke, convene.

συγκρούομαι [seengkrouome] bump into, collide || clash, come to blows.

σύγκρουσις, ἡ [seengkrousees] collision, clash, fight, engagement.

σύγκρυο, τό [seengkreeo] shivering, trembling.

συγκυρία, ἡ [seengkeereea]˙ coincidence, occurrence, chance.

συγυρίζω [seeyeereezo] tidy up, arrange || (μεταφ) ill-treat.

συγχαίρω [seenghero] congratulate, compliment.

συγχαρητήρια, τά [seenghareeteereea] πλ congratulations.

συγχέω [seengheo] confound, confuse, perplex.

συγχορδία, ἡ [seenghordeea] harmony of sounds, accord.

συγχρονίζω [seenghroneezo] modernize, bring up to date.

σύγχρονος [seenghronos] contemporary || simultaneous || contemporaneous.

συγχύζω [seengheezo] get mixed up || worry, confound, harass.

σύγχυσις, ἡ [seengheesees] confusion, disorder || chaos, commotion.

συγχωνεύω [seenghonevo] amalgamate, blend, merge.

συγχώρησις, ἡ [seenghoreesees] remission, pardon.

συγχωρητέος [seenghoreeteeos]. pardonable, excusable.

συ(γ)χωρεῖτε [see(ng)horeete]: μέ ~ excuse me, I beg your pardon.

συγχωρῶ [seenghoro] pardon, forgive, excuse || tolerate, permit.

συζήτησις, ἡ [seezeeteesees] discussion, debate || οὔτε ~ it's out of the question.

συζητῶ [seezeeto] discuss, argue, debate.

συζυγία, ἡ [seezeeyeea] conjugation || union.

συζυγικός [seezeeyeekos] conjugal, marital.

σύζυγος, ὁ, ἡ [seezeeyos] consort, spouse, husband, wife.

συζῶ [seezo] live together, cohabit.

συθέμελα [seethemela] to the very roots.

συκιά, ἡ [seekia] fig tree.

σῦκον, τό [seekon] fig.

συκοφάντης, ὁ [seekofantees] slanderer, calumniator.

συκοφαντῶ [seekofanto] slander, calumniate.

συκώτι, τό [seekotee] liver.

σύλησις, ἡ [seeleesees] spoliation, sacking.

συλητής, ὁ [seeleetees] despoiler || looter, pilferer.

συλλαβή, ἡ [seelavee] syllable.

συλλαλητήριον, τό [seelaleeteereeon] mass meeting, demonstration.

συλλαμβάνω [seelamvano] catch, lay hold of, capture, seize, arrest ‖ (ἰδέες) conceive.

συλλέγω [seeleγo] collect, gather.

συλλέκτης, ὁ [seelektees] collector.

συλλήβδην [seeleevδeen] collectively, in one word, as a whole.

σύλληψις, ἡ [seeleepsees] capture, arrest, seizure ‖ (ἰδέας) conception.

συλλογή, ἡ [seeloγee] set, assortment, collection ‖ (σκέψις) thought, concern.

συλλογίζομαι [seeloγeezome] think out, reflect about, consider, reason.

συλλογικός [seeloγeekos] collective.

συλλογισμένος · [seeloγeesmenos] pensive, thoughtful, absorbed (in).

συλλογισμός, ὁ [seeloγeesmos] thought, reflexion ‖ reasoning, syllogism.

σύλλογος, ὁ [seeloγos] society, club, association.

συλλυπητήρια, τά [seeleepeeteereea] πλ condolences, sympathy.

συλλυποῦμαι [seeleepoume] offer condolence ‖ feel sorry for.

συλῶ [seelo] plunder, despoil, loot.

συμβαδίζω [seemvaδeezo] keep up with ‖ go together, coexist.

συμβαίνω [seemveno] happen, take place, come about.

συμβάλλομαι [seemvalome] contract, enter into an agreement.

συμβάλλω [seemvalo] contribute to, pay one's share ‖ (ποτάμι) meet, join, unite.

συμβάν, τό [seemvan] event, accident, occurrence.

σύμβασις, ἡ [seemvasees] agreement, contract, treaty, pact.

συμβεβηκός, τό [seemveveekos] βλ συμβάν.

συμβία, ἡ [seemveea] wife, consort.

συμβιβάζομαι [seemveevazome] compromise, agree with ‖ be compatible with.

συμβιβάζω [seemveevazo] reconcile, arrange, adjust.

συμβιβασμός, ὁ [seemveevasmos] compromise, accommodation, adjustment, settlement.

συμβίωσις, ἡ [seemveeosees] living together, cohabitation.

συμβολαιογράφος, ὁ [seemvoleoγrafos] notary public.

συμβόλαιον, τό [seemvoleon] contract, agreement.

συμβολή, ἡ [seemvolee] contribution ‖ (ποταμῶν) confluence, junction.

συμβολίζω [seemvoleezo] symbolize, represent.

σύμβολον, τό [seemvolon] symbol, mark, sign, emblem, token ‖ ~ τῆς πίστεως Apostles' Creed.

συμβουλεύομαι [seemvoulevome] consult, refer to, take s.o.'s advice.

συμβουλεύω [seemvoulevo] advise, recommend.

συμβουλή, ἡ [seemvoulee] advice, counsel.

συμβούλιον, τό [seemvouleeon] council, board, committee.

σύμβουλος, ὁ [seemvoulos] adviser, counsellor ‖ councillor.

συμμαζεύω [seemazevo] tidy up, collect, assemble, gather together ‖ (ἐλέγχω) restrain, check, hold.

συμμαχία, ἡ [seemaheea] alliance, coalition.

σύμμαχος [seemahos] allied ‖ (οὐσ) ally.

συμμερίζομαι [seemereezome] share, have a part (in).

συμμετέχω [seemeteho] participate in, take part in, be a party to.

συμμετοχή, ἡ [seemetohee] participation ‖ sharing.

συμμετρία, ἡ [seemetreea] symmetry, proportion.

συμμετρικός [seemetreekos] symmetrical ‖ well-proportioned.

συμμιγδην [seemeeγδeen] pell-mell, in confusion.

συμμορία, ἡ [seemoreea] gang, band, body.

συμμορφώνομαι [seemorfonome] comply, conform, agree with, adapt to.

συμμορφώνω [seemorfono] adapt, conform ‖ bring to heel.

συμπαγής [seembaγees] solid, firm, compact, close.

συμπάθεια, ἡ [seempatheea] compassion, sympathy ‖ weakness (for) ‖ favourite.

συμπαθής [seempathees] likeable, lovable.

συμπαθητικός [seempatheeteekos] likeable, lovable ‖ sympathetic.

συμπάθιο, τό [seempatheeo]: μέ τό ~ begging your pardon.

συμπαθῶ [seempatho] feel compassion for ‖ have a liking for.

συμπαιγνία, ἡ [seempeγneea] collusion.

σύμπαν, τό [seempan] universe ‖ everything, all, everybody.

συμπατριώτης, ὁ [seempatreeotees] compatriot, fellow countryman.

συμπεθεριά, ἡ [seempetheria] relationship by marriage.

συμπεθεριό, τό [seempetherio] βλ συμπεθεριά.

συμπέθεροι, οἱ [seempetheree] πλ fathers-in-law ‖ relations by marriage.

συμπεπυκνωμένος [seempepeeknomenos] condensed.

συμπεραίνω [seempereno] conclude, presume, infer, surmise.

συμπέρασμα, τό [seemperasma] conclusion, inference, end.

συμπεριλαμβάνω [seempereelamvano] include, contain, comprise.

συμπεριφέρομαι [seempereeferome] behave, conduct o.s.

συμπεριφορά, ἡ [seempereefora] behaviour, conduct.

σύμπηξις, ἡ [seempeeksees] forming ‖ coagulation, curdling.

συμπίεσις, ή [seempiesees] compression, squeezing.

συμπίπτω [seempeepto] coincide, concur, converge ‖ happen, chance.

σύμπλεγμα, τό [seempleyma] tangle ‖ cluster ‖ network.

συμπλέκομαι [seemplekome] come to blows, quarrel ‖ fight.

συμπλέκω [seempleko] interlace, interweave, entwine.

συμπλήρωμα, τό [seempleeroma] complement ‖ supplement, addition.

συμπληρωματικός [seempleeromateekos] complementary, further ‖ supplementary.

συμπληρώνω [seempleerono] complete, complement, finish ‖ (θέσιν) fill ‖ (φόρμα) fill in.

συμπλήρωσις, ή [seempleerosees] completion, filling, achievement.

συμπλοκή, ή [seemplokee] fight, engagement, clash, brawl.

σύμπνοια, ή [seempneea] harmony, agreement, understanding.

συμπολιτεία, ή [seempoleeteea] confederation, confederacy.

συμπολίτης, ὁ [seempoleetees] fellow citizen, fellow countryman.

συμπονῶ [seempono] feel compassion for, sympathize with.

συμπόσιον, τό [seemposeeon] banquet, feast.

συμποσοῦμαι [seemposoume] come to, run (to).

σύμπραξις, ή [seempraksees] cooperation, contribution.

συμπτύσσομαι [seempteesome] fall back, shorten.

συμπτύσσω [seempteeso] shorten, abridge, abbreviate, cut short.

σύμπτωμα, τό [seemptoma] symptom ‖ sign, indication.

σύμπτωσις, ή [seemptosees] coincidence, accident, chance.

συμπυκνῶ [seempeekno] condense, compress.

συμπυκνωτής, ὁ [seempeeknotees] condenser.

συμφέρει [seemferee] it's worth it, it's to one's advantage.

συμφέρον, τό [seemferon] advantage, interest, profit, benefit.

συμφεροντολογία, ή [seemferontoloyeea] self-interest.

συμφιλιώνω [seemfeeleeono] reconcile, restore friendship, make up.

συμφορά, ή [seemfora] calamity, disaster, misfortune.

συμφόρησις, ή [seemforeesees] traffic jam, congestion ‖ (ἰατρ) stroke.

σύμφορος [seemforos] advantageous, profitable, useful.

συμφυής [seemfiees] innate, inborn, inherent.

συμφυρμός, ὁ [seemfeermos] mixing, blending, jumbling.

συμφύρομαι [seemfeerome] get mixed up with.

συμφύρω [seemfeero] confuse, mingle, mix, jumble.

σύμφωνα [seemfona]: ~ μέ according to, in conformity (with).

συμφωνητικόν, τό [seemfoneeteekon] agreement, deed of contract.

συμφωνία, ή [seemfoneea] agreement, convention ‖ accord, consent ‖ (μουσ) symphony.

σύμφωνον, τό [seemfonon] consonant ‖ compact, agreement, pact.

σύμφωνος [seemfonos] in accord, in conformity with.

συμφωνῶ [seemfono] concur, agree ‖ match, go well together.

συμφώνως [seemfonos] according to ‖ ~ πρός in accordance with.

συμψηφίζω [seempseefeezo] counterbalance, make up for.

σύν [seen] together, with ‖ (μαθημ) plus ‖ ~ τῷ χρόνῳ in time, gradually, eventually ‖ ~ τοῖς ἄλλοις moreover, in addition.

συναγερμός, ὁ [seenayermos] alarm, call to arms, alert ‖ (πολιτικός) rally, mass meeting.

συναγρίδα, ή [seenayreeδa] kind of sea bream.

συνάγω [seenayo] assemble, collect, bring together ‖ (συμπεραίνω) infer, conclude, deduce.

συναγωγή, ή [seenayoyee] collection, gathering, assembly ‖ (ἑβραίων) synagogue.

συναγωνίζομαι [seenayoneezome] rival, compete ‖ fight together.

συναγωνιστής, ὁ [seenayoneestees] rival, competitor ‖ (συμπολεμιστής) brother in arms ‖ (ἀνταγωνιστής) rival.

συνάδελφος, ὁ [seenaδelfos] colleague, fellow member.

συνάζω [seenazo] collect, assemble ‖ gather ‖ heap up.

συναθροίζω [seenathreezo] βλ συνάζω.

συναινῶ [seeneno] consent to, agree to, acquiesce.

συναίρεσις, ή [seeneresees] (γραμμ) contraction.

συναισθάνομαι [seenesthanome] become aware of, be conscious of, feel.

συναίσθημα, τό [seenestheema] sentiment, feeling, sensation.

συναισθήματα, τά [seenestheemata] πλ emotions, feelings.

συναισθηματικός [seenestheemateekos] emotional, sentimental.

συναίσθησις, ή [seenestheesees] feeling, sense, appreciation, consciousness.

συναλλαγή, ή [seenalayee] exchange, dealings, trade ‖ ἐλευθέρα ~ free trade.

συνάλλαγμα, τό [seenalayma] foreign currency ‖ draft, bill ‖ τιμή ~τος rate of exchange.

συναλλαγματική, ή [seenalaymateekee] bill of exchange.

συναλλάσσομαι [seenalasome] deal, trade, traffic ‖ (συναναστρέφομαι) associate with.

συνάμα [seenama] together, in one lot, at the same time, at once.

συναναστρέφομαι [seenanastrefome]· consort with, mix with.

συναναστροφή, ή [seenanastrofee] association, company ‖ party, reception.

συνάντησις, ή [seenanteesees] falling in with, meeting ‖ encounter.

συναντώ [seenanto] meet, happen (upon), run across.

συναντώμαι [seenantome] meet, come together.

σύναξις, ή [seenaksees] concentration, meeting ‖ collecting, receipts.

συναπτός [seenaptos] consecutive, successive ‖ annexed, tied, appended.

συνάπτω [seenapto] annex, attach ‖ (συμμαχίαν) contract, form ‖ (δάνειον) incur ‖ (ειρήνην) conclude ‖ (μάχην) join, give battle ‖ ~ σχέσεις make friends.

συναρμολογώ [seenarmoloyo] fit together ‖ join ‖ make up, piece together.

συναρπάζω [seenarpazo] carry away, enrapture, entrance.

συνάρτησις, ή [seenarteesees] attachment, connection ‖ cohesion.

συνασπισμός, ό [seenaspeesmos] coalition, alliance, league.

συναυλία, ή [seenavleea] concert.

συνάφεια, ή [seenafeea] connection, link, reference.

συναφής [seenafees] adjacent (to) ‖ linked, connected ‖ like.

συνάχι, τό [seenahee] cold (in the head), catarrh.

σύναψις, ή [seenapsees] conclusion, arrangement ‖ contraction ‖ joining.

συνδαιτυμών, ό [seendeteemon] table guest, dinner guest, fellow diner.

συνδαυλίζω [seendavleezo] poke a fire ‖ stir up.

συνδεδεμένος [seendedemenos] closely associated, having ties with.

σύνδεσις, ή [seendesees] joining, binding together.

σύνδεσμος, ό [seendesmos] bond, union ‖ (στρατ) liaison ‖ relationship, affinity ‖ (γραμμ) conjunction.

συνδετήρ, ό [seendeteer] clip, paper clip.

συνδετικός [seendeteekos] joining, connective ‖ (γραμμ) copulative.

συνδέω [seendeo] bind together, unite ‖ (μεταφ) join, link, bind.

συνδιαλέγομαι [seendeealeyome] converse (with), talk to.

συνδιαλλαγή, ή [seendeealayee] reconciliation.

συνδιάσκεψις, ή [seendeeaskepsees] deliberation ‖ conference.

συνδικάτον, τό [seendeekaton] syndicate ‖ (έργατών) trade union.

συνδράμω [seendramo] support, help ‖ contribute to.

συνδρομή, ή [seendromee] coincidence, conjunction ‖ (άρωγή) help, assistance ‖ subscription, contribution ‖ (ιατρ) syndrome.

συνδρομητής, ό [seendromeetees] subscriber.

συνδυάζομαι [seendeeazome] harmonize, go together, match.

συνδυάζω [seendeeazo] unite, combine ‖ match, pair ‖ arrange.

συνδυασμός, ό [seendeeasmos] combination, arrangement ‖ matching.

σύνεγγυς [seenengees]: ἐκ τοῦ ~ very close, from close to.

συνεδριάζω [seenedreeazo] meet, be in session.

συνέδριον, τό [seenedreeon] congress, convention, council.

σύνεδρος, ό [seenedros] delegate ‖ councillor ‖ (δικαστηρίου) judge.

συνείδησις, ή [seeneedeesees] conscience.

συνειδητός [seeneedeetos] conscious, wilful.

συνειρμός, ό [seeneermos] coherence, order, sequence.

συνεισφέρω [seeneesfero] contribute, subscribe.

συνεκτικός [seenekteekos] cohesive, binding, tenacious.

συνέλευσις, ή [seenelevsees] meeting, assembly.

συνεννόησις, ή [seenenoeesees] understanding, concert, concord, agreement ‖ exchange of views.

συνεννοούμαι [seenenooume] agree, come to an agreement ‖ exchange views.

συνενοχή, ή [seenenohee] complicity, abetment, connivance.

συνέντευξις, ή [seenentevksees] interview, appointment, rendezvous.

συνενώ [seeneno] unite, join together.

συνεπάγομαι [seenepayome] lead to, involve, have as consequence, call for.

συνεπαίρνω [seeneperno] transport, carry away.

συνέπεια, ή [seenepeea] result, outcome, consequence ‖ consistency.

συνεπής [seenepees] true, in keeping with, consistent ‖ punctual.

συνεπῶς [seenepos] consequently, accordingly.

συνεπτυγμένος [seenepteeymenos] compact, succinct, brief.

συνεργάζομαι [seeneryazome] cooperate, collaborate ‖ contribute.

συνεργάτης, ὁ [seeneryatees] collaborator ‖ contributor.

συνεργατική, ἡ [seeneryateekee] cooperative.

συνεργεῖον, τό [seeneryeeon] workroom, workshop ‖ gang, shift, team of workers ‖ repair shop.

συνεργία, ἡ [seeneryeea] complicity, abet-ment, confederacy.

σύνεργο, τό [seeneryo] implement, tool, instrument.

συνεργός, ὁ [seeneryos] accessary, accomplice, abettor, party (to).

συνερίζομαι [seenereezome] heed, take into account, keep up rivalry with.

συνέρχομαι [seenerhome] get over, recover ‖ come together, meet, assemble.

σύνεσις, ἡ [seenesees] caution, good sense, prudence, judgment.

συνεσταλμένος [seenestalmenos] shy, modest, timid, circumspect.

συνεταιρισμός, ὁ [seenetereesmos] cooperative, association.

συνέταιρος, ὁ [seeneteros] partner, associate, colleague, copartner.

συνετός [seenetos] wise, discreet, prudent, sensible, cautious.

συνεφέρνω [seeneferno] revive, bring s.o. round ‖ come to.

συνέχεια, ἡ [seeneheea] continuity ‖ continuation, outcome ‖ (ἐπίρ) continuously, successively.

συνεχής [seenehees] continuous, incessant, unceasing, continual ‖ successive ‖ adjacent.

συνεχίζω [seeneheezo] continue, keep on, go on.

συνέχομαι [seenehome] be communicating, be contiguous, adjoin.

συνέχω [seeneho] possess, seize, curb, control, check ‖ adjoin.

συνεχῶς [seenehos] continually, endlessly.

συνήγορος, ὁ [seeneeyoros] advocate, defender, counsel.

συνήθεια, ἡ [seeneetheea] habit, custom, practice, use.

συνήθειο, τό [seeneetheeo] βλ συνήθεια.

συνήθης [seeneethees] habitual, customary, usual, common, ordinary.

συνηθίζεται [seeneetheezete] it is usual, it is the fashion.

συνηθίζω [seeneetheezo] accustom to ‖ get accustomed to ‖ be in the habit of.

συνηθισμένος [seeneetheesmenos] accustomed, familiar with ‖ habitual, customary.

συνημμένος [seeneemenos] attached, connected, annexed, enclosed.

σύνθεσις, ἡ [seenthesees] mixture, composition ‖ collocation ‖ structure, synthesis.

συνθέτης, ὁ [seenthetees] composer ‖ compositor.

συνθετικόν, τό [seentheteekon] component, constituent.

συνθετικός [seentheteekos] constituent, component ‖ artificial, synthetic.

σύνθετον, τό [seentheton] (γραμμ) compound (word).

σύνθετος [seenthetos] compound, composite ‖ intricate.

συνθέτω [seentheto] compose, make up.

συνθῆκες, οἱ [seentheekes] πλ conditions, circumstances, situation.

συνθήκη, ἡ [seentheekee] treaty, agreement, pact ‖ convention.

συνθηκολογῶ [seentheekoloyo] surrender, capitulate ‖ negotiate a treaty.

σύνθημα, τό [seentheema] signal, sign, password, watchword.

συνθηματικός [seentheemateekos] symbolic ‖ in code.

συνθλίβω [seenthleevo] squeeze, compress, crush.

συνίζησις, ἡ [seeneezeesees] synizesis ‖ (χώματος) subsidence.

συνίσταμαι [seeneestame] consist of, be composed of.

συνιστῶ [seeneesto] advise, recommend ‖ (ἐπιτροπήν) establish, set up, form ‖ (γνωρίζω) introduce.

συννεφιά, ἡ [seenefia] cloudy weather ‖ ~ζω become cloudy ‖ (μεταφ) look sullen.

σύννεφο, τό [seenefo] cloud.

συννυφάδα, ἡ [seeneefaδa] wife of one's brother-in-law.

συνοδ(ε)ία, ἡ [seenoδeea] escort, retinue, suite, convoy, procession ‖ (μουσ) accompaniment.

συνοδεύω [seenoδevo] accompany, go with, escort ‖ (ναυτ) convoy.

συνοδοιπόρος, ὁ, ἡ [seenoδeeporos] fellow traveller.

σύνοδος, ἡ [seenoδos] congress, sitting, assembly ‖ (ἐκκλ) synod.

συνοδός, ὁ, ἡ [seenoδos] steward, escort ‖ ἱπταμένη ~ air hostess.

συνοικέσιον, τό [seeneekeseeon] arranged marriage, match.

συνοικία, ἡ [seeneekeea] quarter, neighbourhood, ward.

συνοικιακός [seeneekeeakos] local, suburban.

συνοικισμός, ὁ [seeneekeesmos] settlement ‖ colonization ‖ quarter.

συνολικός [seenoleekos] total, whole.

σύνολον, τό [seenolon] total, entirety.

συνόλω [seenolo] ἐν ~ in all, totally.

συνομήλικος [seenomeeleekos] of the same age.

συνομιλητής, ὁ [seenomeeleetees] interlocutor.

συνομιλία, ἡ [seenomeeleea] conversation, chat, talk ‖ interview.

συνομολογῶ [seenomoloyo] conclude ‖ acknowledge, admit.

συνομοταξία, ἡ [seenomotakseea] branch, group, class.

συνονόματος [seenonomatos] namesake, having the same name.

συνοπτικός [seenopteekos] summary, brief, synoptic, concise.

σύνορα, τά [seenora] πλ frontier, boundaries.

συνορεύω [seenorevo] have a common frontier, border on.

σύνορον, τό [seenoron] boundary, border, frontier.

συνουσία, ἡ [seenouseea] coition, intercourse, copulation.

συνοφρυοῦμαι [seenofreeoume] frown, scowl ‖ look sullen.

συνοχή, ἡ [seenohee] coherence, cohesion ‖ (ἰδεῶν) sequence, chain.

σύνοψις, ἡ [seenopsees] summary, compendium, synopsis ‖ (ἐκκλ) prayer book, breviary.

συνταγή, ἡ [seentayee] formula, prescription ‖ recipe.

σύνταγμα, τό [seentayma] constitution, charter ‖ (στρατ) regiment.

συνταγματάρχης, ὁ [seentaymatarhees] colonel.

συνταγματικός [seentaymateekos] constitutional.

συντάκτης, ὁ [seentaktees] author, writer ‖ (ἐφημερίδος) editor ‖ (συνθήκης) drawer-up, framer.

συντακτικόν, τό [seentakteekon] syntax, book of syntax.

συντακτικός [seentakteekos] component, constituent ‖ (ἐφημερίδος) editorial ‖ (γραμμ) syntactic(al).

συνταξιοῦχος, ὁ, ἡ [seentaksiouhos] pensioner ‖ retired officer.

σύνταξις, ἡ [seentaksees] compilation ‖ wording, writing ‖ organization ‖ (ἐφημερίδος) editing, editorial staff ‖ pension ‖ (γραμμ) construction, syntax.

συνταράσσω [seentaraso] agitate, shake, disturb, trouble ‖ (μεταφ) disconcert.

συντάσσομαι [seentasome] take sides with, fall in with ‖ (γραμμ) govern.

συντάσσω [seentaso] arrange, compile ‖ write, draft, draw up ‖ (γραμμ) construe ‖ constitute, form, organize ‖ (νόμου) frame ‖ (ἐφημερίδα) edit.

συνταυτίζω [seentavteezo] identify, regard as the same.

συντείνω [seenteeno] contribute to, concur.

συντέλεια, ἡ [seenteleea]: ~ τοῦ κόσμου end of the world.

συντελεστής, ὁ [seentelestees] factor, component, contributor ‖ (μαθημ) coefficient.

συντελεστικός [seentelesteekos] contributory, conductive.

συντελῶ [seentelo] finish, complete ‖ contribute to, conduce to.

συντέμνω [seentemno] shorten, curtail, abridge.

συντεταγμένη, ἡ [seentetaymenee] co-ordinate.

συντετριμμένος [seentetreemenos] deeply afflicted, crushed.

συντεχνία, ἡ [seentehneea] guild, fellowship, confraternity ‖ trade union.

συντήρησις, ἡ [seenteereesees] preservation, conservation ‖ (μηχανῆς) maintenance.

συντηρητικός [seenteereeteekos] conservative, preserving.

συντηρῶ [seenteero] preserve, conserve ‖ keep up, maintain ‖ (διατρέφω) maintain, support.

συντίθεμαι [seenteetheme] be composed of, be made up of.

σύντομα [seentoma] in short, briefly ‖ soon, at once, immediately.

συντομεύω [seentomevo] shorten, curtail, abridge.

συντομία, ἡ [seentomeea] shortness, brevity ‖ terseness.

σύντομος [seentomos] short, succinct, brief.

συντόμως [seentomos] in a word, in short ‖ (χρονικῶς) soon.

συντονίζω [seentoneezo] coordinate, harmonize, tune together.

σύντονος [seentonos] unremitting, constant, incessant.

συντρέχω [seentreho] help ‖ meet, converge ‖ contribute.

συντριβή, ἡ [seentreevee] ruin ‖ crushing, smashing.

συντρίβω [seentreevo] shatter, break, crush, smash ‖ ruin, wear out.

σύντριμμα, τό [seentreema] fragment, debris, wreck.

συντρίμματα, τά [seentreemata] πλ debris, fragments, wreckage.

συντριπτικός [seentreepteekos] (μεταφ) crushing, overwhelming.

συντροφιά, ἡ [seentrofia] companionship, company ‖ gathering, society ‖ (ἐπίρ) together.

σύντροφος, ὁ, ἡ [seentrofos] companion, mate, comrade ‖ (ἐμπορ) associate, partner.

συντυχαίνω [seenteeheno] happen, chance ‖ converse with.

συνύπαρξις, ἡ [seeneeparksees] coexistence.

συνυπάρχω [seeneeparho] coexist.

συνυπεύθυνος [seeneepevtheenos] jointly liable.

συνυφαίνω [seeneefeno] entwine ‖ (μεταφ) conspire, intrigue.

συνωθοῦμαι [seenothoume] jostle, push.

συνωμοσία, ἡ [seenomoseea] conspiracy, plot.

συνωμοτῶ [seenomoto] conspire, plot.

συνώνυμον, τό [seenoneemon] synonym.

συνώνυμος [seenoneemos] synonymous.

συνωστισμός, ὁ [seenosteesmos] jostle, crush, scramble.

σύξυλος [seekseelos] with crew and cargo ‖ ἔμεινε ~ he was amazed, he was speechless.

σύριγξ, ἡ [seereenks] Pan's pipe ‖ syringe, tube.

συρίζω [seereezo] hiss, whistle, whizz, whir, wheeze.

σύρμα, τό [seerma] wire.

συρματόπλεγμα, τό [seermatopleyma] barbed wire ‖ wire netting.

συρμός, ὁ [seermos] railway train ‖ (μόδα) fashion, manner, habit.

σύρραξις, ἡ [seeraksees] clash, collision, shock, conflict.

συρρέω [seereo] crowd, throng, flock ‖ flow into.

σύρριζα [seereeza] by the root, root and branch ‖ very closely.

συρροή, ἡ [seeroee] crowd, throng ‖ inflow, influx ‖ abundance, profusion.

συρτάρι, τό [seertaree] drawer.

συρτή, ἡ [seertee] dragnet, trail net.

σύρτης, ὁ [seertees] bolt, bar.

σύρτις, ἡ [seertees] sandbank.

συρτός [seertos] dragged ‖ listless, drawling ‖ (πόρτα) sliding ‖ (οὐ̃ς) kind of circular dance.

συρφετός, ὁ [seerfetos] mob, populace, common people.

σύρω [seero] βλ σέρνω.

συσκέπτομαι [seeskeptome] confer, deliberate, take counsel.

συσκευάζω [seeskevazo] pack, box, wrap, parcel.

συσκευασία, ἡ [seeskevaseea] wrapping up, packing ‖ (φαρμακευτική) preparation.

συσκευή, ἡ [seeskevee] apparatus, contrivance.

σύσκεψις, ἡ [seeskepsees] discussion, deliberation ‖ conference, consultation.

συσκοτίζω [seeskoteezo] obscure, darken, black out ‖ (μεταφ) confuse.

συσκότισις, ἡ [seeskoteesees] blackout ‖ confusion.

σύσπασις, ἡ [seespasees] contraction, writhing, shrinking.

συσπειροῦμαι [seespeeroume] roll into a ball, coil ‖ (μεταφ) snuggle.

συσσίτιον, τό [seeseeteeon] mess, common meal ‖ soup kitchen.

σύσσωμος [seesomos] all together, entire, united, in a body.

συσσωρευτής, ὁ [seesorevtees] accumulator.

συσσωρεύω [seesorevo] accumulate, collect, pile up ‖ amass.

συστάδην [seestaðeen]: ἐκ τοῦ ~ hand-to-hand, at close quarters.

συσταίνω [seesteno] βλ συνιστῶ.

συστάς, ἡ [seestas] clump of trees, cluster, grove.

συστάσεις, οἱ [seestasees] πλ references,

advice ‖ recommendation, introductions.

σύσταση, ἡ [seestasee] address.

σύστασις, ἡ [seestasees] composition, structure ‖ (πάχος) consistency ‖ (σχηματισμός) formation, creation, setting up ‖ (πρότασις) recommendation, recommending ‖ (συμβουλή) advice, counsel.

συστατικά, τά [seestateeka] πλ component parts, ingredients ‖ references, recommendations.

συστατική [seestateekee]: ~ ἐπιστολή letter of introduction, letter of reference.

συστατικός [seestateekos] component, essential, constituent.

συστέλλομαι [seestelome] shrink, contract ‖ feel shy, be timid.

συστέλλω [seestelo] contract, shrink, shrivel.

σύστημα, τό [seesteema] method, system, plan ‖ custom, habitude.

συστηματικός [seesteemateekos] systematic, methodical.

συστημένο [seesteemeno]: ~ γράμμα registered letter.

συστήνω [seesteeno] βλ συνιστῶ.

συστολή, ἡ [seestolee] shrinking, contraction ‖ modesty, shame, bashfulness.

συσφίγγω [seesfeengo] tighten, constrict, draw tighter, grasp.

συσχετίζω [seesheteezo] compare, relate, put together.

σύφιλις, ἡ [seefeelees] syphilis.

συχνά [seehna] often, frequently ‖ ~ κις often, many times.

συχνάζω [seehnazo] frequent, haunt, resort.

συχνός [seehnos] frequent, repeated.

συχνότης, ἡ [seehnotees] frequency.

συχωράω [seehorao] forgive, tolerate.

σφαγεῖον, τό [sfayeeon] slaughterhouse ‖ butchery, slaughter.

σφαγή, ἡ [sfayee] slaughter, carnage, massacre.

σφαγιάζω [sfayeeazo] massacre, slaughter ‖ sacrifice ‖ (μεταφ) violate, transgress.

σφάγιον, τό [sfayeeon] victim, animal for slaughter.

σφαδάζω [sfaðazo] writhe, jerk, squirm.

σφάζω [sfazo] slaughter, kill, massacre, murder.

σφαῖρα, ἡ [sfera] globe, sphere ‖ ball ‖ (ὅπλου) bullet ‖ (μεταφ) sphere, field.

σφαιρίδιον, τό [sfereeðeeon] small shot ‖ (αἵματος) globule.

σφαιριστήριον, τό [sfereesteereeon] billiard table, billiard room ‖ (US) poolroom.

σφαλερός [sfaleros] mistaken, erroneous ‖ (ἐπικίνδυνος) unsafe, unsound, dangerous.

σφαλιάρα, ἡ [sfaleeara] slap in the face ‖ smack.

σφαλίζω [sfaleezo] enclose, shut in ‖ (κλείνω) close, lock, bolt.

σφαλιστός [sfaleestos] shut ‖ sealed, locked.

σφάλλομαι [sfalome] be wrong, make a mistake ‖ misfire.

σφάλλω [sfalo] βλ σφάλλομαι.

σφάλμα, τό [sfalma] wrong act, fault ‖ error, blunder, slip.

σφάξιμο, τό [sfakseemo] butchering.

σφάχτης, ὁ [sfahtees] twinge, sharp pain.

σφένδαμνος, ὁ [sfendamnos] maple tree.

σφενδόνη, ἡ [sfendonee] sling.

σφερδούκλι, τό [sferdooklee] asphodel.

σφετερίζομαι [sfetereezome] purloin, embezzle ‖ appropriate, usurp.

σφή(γ)κα, ἡ [sfee(ng)ka] wasp.

σφήν(α), ἡ [sfeen(a)] wedge.

σφηνώνω [sfeenono] push in, thrust in between ‖ wedge.

σφήξ, ὁ [sfeeks] βλ σφή(γ)κα.

σφίγγομαι [sfeengome] squeeze together ‖ endeavour, try hard.

σφίγγω [sfeengo] squeeze, press ‖ tighten, pull tighter ‖ (σκληρύνω) become tight, stick.

σφίγξ, ἡ [sfeenks] sphinx ‖ (μεταφ) enigmatic.

σφίξη, ἡ [sfeeksee] urgency, necessity.

σφίξιμο, τό [sfeekseemo] pressing, tightening, squeezing ‖ pressure, squeeze.

σφιχτός [sfeehtos] tight, hard, thick ‖ stingy, tight-fisted.

σφόδρα [sfodra] extremely, very, greatly, excessively.

σφοδρός [sfodros] violent, wild, strong, severe, sharp.

σφοδρότης, ἡ [sfodrotees] violence, vehemence, wildness.

σφουγγαράς, ὁ [sfoungaras] sponge fisherman, sponge seller.

σφουγγάρι, τό [sfoungaree] sponge.

σφουγγαρόπανο, τό [sfoungaropano] mop, floorcloth.

σφουγγάτο, τό [sfoungato] omelet.

σφουγγίζω [sfoungeezo] wipe off, sponge ‖ (πιάτα) dry.

σφραγίζω [sfrayeezo] set one's seal to, stamp ‖ (μπουκάλι) cork ‖ (δόντι) fill (tooth).

σφραγίδα, ἡ [sfrayeeda] seal, signet, stamp ‖ (μεταφ) impression.

σφραγίς, ἡ [sfrayees] βλ σφραγίδα.

σφρῖγος, τό [sfreeyos] youthful exuberance, vigour, pep.

σφυγμός, ὁ [sfeeymos] pulse ‖ (μεταφ) caprice, whim.

σφύζω [sfeezo] throb, beat violently, pulsate.

σφύξις, ἡ [sfeeksees] pulsation, throbbing, throb.

σφύρα, ἡ [sfeera] hammer.

σφυρηλατῶ [sfeereelato] hammer, batter, forge, pound away ‖ trump up.

σφυρί, τό [sfeeree] βλ σφύρα.

σφύριγμα, τό [sfeereeyma] whistling, hissing.

σφυρίδα, ἡ [sfeereeda] kind of fish.

σφυρίζω [sfeereezo] whistle, hiss, boo.

σφυρίχτρα, ἡ [sfeereehtra] whistle ‖ (ναυτ) pipe.

σφυροκοπῶ [sfeerokopo] hammer ‖ pound away.

σφυρόν, τό [sfeeron] ankle.

σχεδία, ἡ [shedeea] raft, float.

σχεδιάγραμμα, τό [shedeeayrama] sketch, outline, draft.

σχεδιάζω [shedeeazo] sketch, outline, design, draw ‖ plan, intend, mean.

σχεδιαστής, ὁ [shedeeastees] draughtsman, designer.

σχέδιον, τό [shedeeon] plan, design ‖ sketch, outline ‖ scheme ‖ ~ πόλεως town planning.

σχεδόν [shedon] almost, nearly, all but ‖ not much, scarcely.

σχέσις, ἡ [shesees] relation, connection, reference ‖ intercourse, relations.

σχετίζομαι [sheteezome] be intimate with, get acquainted, make friends with.

σχετίζω [sheteezo] put side by side, connect, compare.

σχετικά [sheteeka] relative to, relatively ‖ ~ μέ with reference to, regarding, referring to.

σχετικός [sheteekos] relative, pertinent.

σχετικότης, ἡ [sheteekotees] relativity.

σχετικῶς [sheteekos] βλ σχετικά.

σχετλιασμός, ὁ [shetleeasmos] complaining, lamenting ‖ grumble, complaint.

σχῆμα, τό [sheema] form, shape ‖ (μέγεθος) format, size ‖ (ἱερατικόν) cloth ‖ gesture ‖ ~ λόγου figure of speech.

σχηματίζω [sheemateezo] form, model, shape ‖ create, produce ‖ constitute.

σχηματισμός, ὁ [sheemateesmos] forming, formation, fashioning, construction.

σχίζα, ἡ [sheeza] split wood, splinter, shaving.

σχίζομαι [sheezome] crack, tear ‖ fork.

σχίζω [sheezo] split, cleave ‖ tear, rend, fissure.

σχῖνος, ἡ [sheenos] lentisk (bush).

σχίσμα, τό [sheesma] crack ‖ schism, dissension, breach.

σχισμάδα, ἡ [sheesmada] crack, split, fissure.

σχισμή, ἡ [sheesmee] crack, fissure, split.

σχιστόλιθος, ὁ [sheestoleethos] schist, slate.

σχιστός [sheestos] split, slit, torn, open.

σχοινάκι, τό [sheenakee] skipping rope.

σχοινί(ον), τό [sheenee(on)] rope, cord ‖ clothes line.

σχοινοβάτης, ὁ [sheenovatees] acrobat, ropedancer.

σχοινοτενής [sheenotenees] long-drawn-out, long-winded, wordy.

σχολάζω [sholazo] stop work ‖ rest, be on vacation ‖ (ἀπό σχολεῖον) let out ‖ (ἀπό ἐργασίαν) dismiss, discharge.

σχολαστικός [sholasteekos] pedantic, scholastic.

σχολεῖον, τό [sholeeon] school.

σχολή, ἡ [sholee] free time, leisure ‖ school, academy.

σχόλη, ἡ [sholee] holiday, feast day.

σχολιάζω [sholeeazo] comment on, pass remarks, criticize ‖ annotate, edit.

σχολιαστής, ὁ [sholeeastees] commentator ‖ editor, annotator, scholiast.

σχολικός [sholeekos] of school, scholastic, educational.

σχόλιον, τό [sholeeon] comment, commentary, annotation.

σώβρακο, τό [sovrako] pants, drawers.

σώζομαι [sozome] escape ‖ remain in existence.

σώζω [sozo] save, rescue ‖ preserve, keep.

σωθικά, τά [sotheeka] πλ entrails, bowels, intestines, innards.

σωλήν, ὁ [soleen] pipe, tube, conduit ‖ hose.

σωληνάριον, τό [soleenareeon] small tube.

σῶμα, τό [soma] body, corpse, corps ‖ ~ στρατοῦ army corps, armed force, army.

σωματάρχης, ὁ [somatarhees] corps commander.

σωματεῖον, τό [somateeon] guild, association.

σωματεμπορία, ἡ [somatemboreea] white slave traffic ‖ slave trade.

σωματέμπορος, ὁ [somatemboros] white slaver ‖ pimp.

σωματικός [somateekos] of the body, physical.

σωματοφυλακή, ἡ [somatofeelakee] bodyguard.

σωματώδης [somatodees] corpulent, stout, portly.

σώνει [sonee]: ~ καί καλά with stubborn insistence.

σώνω [sono] save, rescue, preserve ‖ use up, consume ‖ attain, reach ‖ be enough, be sufficient.

σῶος [soos] safe, entire, whole, unharmed ‖ intact.

σωπαίνω [sopeno] keep silent, say nothing.

σωρεία, ἡ [soreea] heap, pile ‖ abundance of, great number.

σωρηδόν [soreedon] by heaps ‖ in heaps, in piles ‖ in crowds.

σωριάζομαι [soreeazome] collapse, fall in.

σωρός, ὁ [soros] heap, mass, pile ‖ a lot of, stack of.

σωσίας, ὁ [soseeas] living image, double ‖ stand-in.

σωσ(σ)ίβιον, τό [soseeveeon] lifebelt, life jacket.

σώσιμο, τό [soseemo] saving ‖ finishing up, eating.

σωστά [sosta]: μέ τά ~ του in his senses, in earnest.

σωστά [sosta] correctly, precisely, rightly, exactly, absolutely.

σωστός [sostos] correct, just, right ‖ whole, entire ‖ absolute.

σωτήρ, ὁ [soteer] saviour, liberator, rescuer.

σωτηρία, ἡ [soteereea] safety, security ‖ salvation, deliverance, saving.

σωφάρω [sofaro] drive a car.

σωφέρ, ὁ [sofer] chauffeur, driver.

σωφρονίζω [sofroneezo] reform, chastise, correct, bring to reason, render wise.

σωφρονιστήριον, τό [sofroneesteereeon] reformatory, house of correction.

σωφροσύνη, ἡ [sofroseenee] wisdom, prudence, sense, judgment ‖ moderation, composure.

σώφρων [sofron] wise, sensible, prudent ‖ moderate, sober, temperate.

T, τ

τά [ta] πλ the ‖ them.

ταβάνι, τό [tavanee] ceiling.

ταβέρνα, ἡ [taverna] tavern, inn, eating house.

τάβλα, ἡ [tavla] board, plank ‖ table ‖ ~ στό μεθύσι dead drunk.

τάβλι, τό [tavlee] backgammon.

ταγάρι, τό [tayaree] bag, sack, wallet.

ταγγίζω [tangeezo] grow rancid.

ταγγός [tangos] rancid, rank.

ταγή, ἡ [tayee] fodder.

ταγιέρ, τό [tayier] woman's suit.

ταγίζω [tayeezo] feed ‖ (μωρό) nurse.

τάγμα, τό [tayma] order ‖ (στρατ) battalion.

ταγματάρχης, ὁ [taymatarhees] major.

ταγμένος [taymenos] under a vow.

τάδε [tade] as follows, the following, this, that ‖ ὁ ~ Mr so and so ‖ such.

τάζομαι [tazome] make a vow, promise.

τάζω [tazo] promise, dedicate, vow.

ταΐζω [taeezo] βλ ταγίζω.

ταινία, ἡ [teneea] band, stretch, strip, ribbon ‖ (κινηματογράφου) strip, film ‖ (μηχανῆς) tape, ribbon ‖ (ἰατρ) tapeworm ‖ (μετρήσεως) tape measure.

ταίρι, τό [teree] helpmate, partner, mate ‖ one of two ‖ match, equal.

ταιριάζει [tereeazee]: δέν ~ it's not fitting, it's not proper.

ταιριάζω [tereeazo] match, pair, suit, harmonize.

ταιριαστός [tereeastos] well-suited, matched.

τάκος, ὁ [takos] wooden fixing block, stump.

τακούνι, τό [takounee] heel.

τάκτ, τό [takt] tact.

τακτικά [takteeka] regularly, frequently

τακτική, ἡ [takteekee] tactics, strategy ‖ method, regularity.

τακτικός [takteekos] regular ‖ orderly, settled, quiet ‖ fixed ‖ (ἀριϑμός) ordinal.

τακτικῶς [takteekos] regularly, often.

τακτοποίησις, ἡ [taktopieesees] arrangement, accommodation ‖ compromise.

τακτοποιῶ [taktopeeo] arrange, set in order ‖ settle, fix up.

τακτός [taktos] fixed, appointed, settled.

ταλαιπωρία, ἡ [taleporeea] torment, hardship, pain, adversity.

ταλαίπωρος [taleporos] miserable, wretched, unfortunate.

ταλαιπωροῦμαι [taleporoume] suffer, toil, labour.

ταλαιπωρῶ [taleporo] harass, pester, torment.

ταλαντεύομαι [talantevome] swing, sway, rock ‖ waver, hesitate.

τάλαντον, τό [talanton] talent, gift, faculty.

τάλας [talas] βλ **ταλαίπωρος**.

ταλέντο, τό [talento] βλ **τάλαντον**.

τάλ(λ)ηρον, τό [taleeron] coin of five drachmas.

τάμα, τό [tama] βλ **τάξιμο**.

ταμεῖον, τό [tameeon] cashier's office, booking office, cashdesk ‖ treasury, pension fund.

ταμίας, ὁ [tameeas] cashier, teller, treasurer.

ταμιευτήριον, τό [tamievteereeon] savings bank.

ταμπακιέρα, ἡ [tambakiera] cigarette case ‖ snuffbox.

ταμπάκος, ὁ [tambakos] snuff.

ταμπέλα, ἡ [tambela] nameplate, bill ‖ registration plate.

ταμπλό, τό [tamblo] painting, picture ‖ (αὐτοκινήτου) dashboard ‖ switchboard ‖ instrument panel.

ταμπούρι, τό [tambouree] fortification.

ταμπούρλο, τό [tambourlo] drum ‖ (παιδικό) side drum.

τανάλια, τά [tanaleea] πλ pliers, tongs, tweezers.

τανάπαλιν [tanapaleen] inversely, conversely, vice versa.

τάνκ, τό [tank] tank.

τανύζομαι [taneezome] stretch o.s., reach out.

τανύζω [taneezo] stretch, extend.

ταξείδιον, τό [takseedeeon] βλ **ταξίδι(ον)**.

ταξί, τό [taksee] taxi(cab).

ταξιάρχης, ὁ [takseearhees] brigadier ‖ (ἐκκλ) archangel.

ταξιαρχία, ἡ [takseearheea] brigade.

ταξίαρχος, ὁ [takseearhos] brigadier general.

ταξιδεύω [takseedevo] travel, journey.

ταξίδι(ον), τό [takseedee(on)] trip, journey, travel, voyage.

ταξιδιώτης, ὁ [takseedeeotees] traveller.

ταξιθέτις, ἡ [takseethetees] theatre attendant, usher.

ταξικός [takseekos] class.

ταξίμετρον, τό [takseemetron] taximeter.

τάξιμο, τό [takseemo] vow, promise.

ταξινομῶ [takseenomo] classify, class, arrange ‖ grade.

τάξις, ἡ [taksees] order, succession, regularity ‖ class, rank, grade ‖ (σχολείου) form ‖ ἐν τάξει Ο.Κ., all right ‖ τάξεις πλ ranks ‖ πρώτης τάξεως first-rate, first-class.

τάπα, ἡ [tapa] plug, cork, stopper ‖ ~ στό μεθύσι dead drunk.

ταπεινός [tapeenos] modest, humble ‖ abject, vile, base.

ταπεινοφροσύνη, ἡ [tapeenofroseenee] humility, modesty.

ταπεινώνομαι [tapeenonome] be humiliated ‖ lower o.s.

ταπεινώνω [tapeenono] humble, humiliate, mortify, embarrass.

ταπέτο, τό [tapeto] carpet, rug.

ταπετσαρία, ἡ [tapetsareea] tapestry, wall covering ‖ upholstery.

τάπης, ὁ [tapees] βλ **ταπέτο**.

ταπητουργία, ἡ [tapeetouryeea] carpetmaking.

τάραγμα, τό [tarayma] agitation, shaking.

ταράζω [tarazo] shake ‖ disturb, upset.

ταραμᾶς, ὁ [taramas] preserved roe.

ταραξίας, ὁ [tarakseeas] rowdy person, agitator, noisy person.

ταράσσω [tarasso] βλ **ταράζω**.

ταράτσα, ἡ [taratsa] flat roof, terrace.

ταραχή, ἡ [tarahee] agitation, disturbance ‖ upset.

ταραχοποιός, ὁ [tarahopeeos] βλ **ταραξίας**.

ταραχώδης [tarahodees] turbulent, unruly, stormy, disturbed, disorderly.

ταρίφα, ἡ [tareefa] scale of charges, price list, rates.

ταριχεύω [tareehevo] embalm ‖ preserve, cure, smoke.

ταρσανᾶς, ὁ [tarsanas] boatbuilder's yard.

τάρταρα, τά [tartara] πλ bowels of the earth.

τασάκι, τό [tasakee] saucer ‖ ashtray.

τάσι, τό [tasee] shallow bowl, goblet.

τάσις, ἡ [tasees] tension, strain ‖ (ἠλεκτ) voltage ‖ (μεταφ) inclination, proclivity, tendency.

τάσσομαι [tasome] place o.s. ‖ (μεταφ) support.

τάσσω [taso] place, put ‖ post, set ‖ marshal ‖ assign, fix.

ταῦ, τό [tav] the letter T.

ταυρομαχία, ἡ [tavromaheea] bullfight.

ταυρομάχος, ὁ [tavromahos] matador.

ταῦρος, ὁ [tavros] bull.

ταῦτα [tavta] πλ these ‖ μετά ~ afterwards.

ταυτίζω [tavteezo] identify, regard as same.

ταυτόσημος [tavtoseemos] equivalent to, synonymous.

ταυτότης, ἡ [tavtotees] identity, sameness ‖ identity card.

ταυτόχρονος [tavtohronos] simultaneous.

ταφή, ἡ [tafee] burial, interment.

τάφος, ὁ [tafos] grave, tomb, vault.

τάφρος, ὁ [tafros] ditch, trench, drain ‖ (ὀχυροῦ) moat.

ταφτᾶς, ὁ [taftas] taffeta.

τάχα(τες) [taha(tes)] perhaps, apparently, supposedly ‖ as if.

ταχεῖα, ἡ [taheea] express train.

ταχέως [taheos] quickly, rapidly ‖ soon ‖ ὡς τάχιστα as soon as possible.

ταχιά [tahia] tomorrow.

ταχίνι, τό [taheenee] ground sesame.

ταχύ [tahee] tomorrow morning.

ταχυδακτυλουργία, ἡ [taheeðakteelourγeea] conjuring trick, juggling.

ταχυδρομεῖον, τό [taheeðromeeon] post, mail ‖ post office.

ταχυδρομικά, τά [taheeðromeeka] πλ postage.

ταχυδρομικῶς [taheeðromeekos] by post, by mail.

ταχυδρόμος, ὁ [taheeðromos] postman.

ταχυδρομῶ [taheeðromo] mail, post.

ταχύνους [taheenous] quick-thinking, alert, quick-witted.

ταχύνω [taheeno] quicken, speed up, accelerate ‖ hasten, push forward.

ταχυπαλμία, ἡ [taheepalmeea] palpitation.

ταχύς [tahees] quick, brisk, rapid, fleet, swift, fast ‖ prompt ‖ speedy.

ταχύτης, ἡ [taheetees] swiftness, speed, rapidity ‖ promptness ‖ velocity, rate.

ταψί, τό [tapsee] large shallow baking pan.

ταώς, ὁ [taos] peacock.

τέζα [teza] stretched, spread, tight ‖ ἔμεινε ~ he kicked the bucket (col) ‖ ~ στό μεθύσι dead drunk.

τεθλασμένη, ἡ [tethlasmenee] zigzag line, broken line.

τεθλασμένος [tethlasmenos] broken.

τεθλιμμένος [tethleemenos] grief-stricken, heartbroken.

τείνω [teeno] tighten, stretch out ‖ strain ‖ tend (to), lead (to), be inclined (to).

τεϊον, τό [teyon] tea.

τεῖχος, τό [teehos] wall, high wall.

τεκμήριον, τό [tekmeereeon] sign, token, mark, clue, indication.

τέκνον, τό [teknon] child, infant, offspring.

τεκτονισμός, ὁ [tektoneesmos] freemasonry.

τέκτων, ὁ [tekton] bricklayer, mason ‖ freemason.

τελάρο, τό [telaro] embroidery frame ‖ (θύρας) doorframe ‖ (πίνακος) frame.

τελεία, ἡ [teleea] full stop ‖ ἄνω ~ semicolon.

τελειοποιῶ [teleeopeeo] perfect, improve, make better.

τέλειος [teleeos] perfect, faultless ‖ ideal ‖ accomplished.

τελειότης, ἡ [teleeotees] perfection, faultlessness.

τελειόφοιτος [teleeofeetos] final-year (student) ‖ graduate.

τελειωμό [teleeomo]: ~ δέν ἔχει it is interminable, it is inexhaustible.

τελειωμός, ὁ [teleeomos] ending, finishing ‖ exhaustion of supply.

τελειώνω [teleeono] exhaust, finish up ‖ end, conclude, finish ‖ ((μεταφ) die, be exhausted.

τελείως [teleeos] faultlessly, perfectly ‖ completely, fully, entirely, utterly.

τελειωτικός [teleeoteekos] definitive, de-, cisive, final, conclusive.

τελεσίγραφον, τό [teleseeγrafon] ultimatum.

τελεσίδικος [teleseeðeekos] final, irrevocable, decisive.

τέλεσις, ἡ [telesees] ceremony ‖ perpetration ‖ completion.

τελεσφορῶ [telesforo] end in success, meet with success.

τελετάρχης, ὁ [teletarhees] master of ceremonies.

τελετή, ἡ [teletee] celebration, rite ‖ feast, festival.

τελετουργῶ [teletourγo] officiate, celebrate, solemnize.

τελευταῖος [televteos] last ‖ most recent.

τελευταίως [televteos] of late, recently.

τελευτή, ἡ [televtee] end ‖ (μεταφ) death.

τελεύω [televo] βλ τελειώνω.

τέλι, τό [telee] thin wire.

τελικά [teleeka] in the end, finally.

τελικῶς [teleekos] βλ τελικά.

τέλμα, τό [telma] swamp, marsh, bog.

τέλος, τό [telos] end ‖ (φόρος) tax, duty ‖ expiration, close ‖ ~ πάντων at all events, finally ‖ ἐπί τέλους at last, at long last ‖ στό ~ at the end, finally ‖ ἐν τέλει in the end, finally.

τελοῦμαι [teloume] happen, take place.

τελῶ [telo] perform, celebrate ‖ achieve, accomplish.

τελωνεῖον, τό [teloneeon] customs house.

τελώνης, ὁ [telonees] customs officer.

τεμαχίζω [temaheezo] cut in pieces, separate, break up.

τεμάχιον, τό [temaheeon] piece, parcel, bit, fragment, chunk.

τέμενος, τό [temenos] temple, shrine, mosque, house of worship.

τέμνουσα, ἡ [temnousa] secant.

τέμνω [temno] cut, divide, open.

τεμπέλης [tembelees] lazy, indolent, idle.

τεμπελιάζω [tembeleeazo] loaf, get lazy, idle.

τέμπλο, τό [templo] iconostasis, reredos.

τέναγος, τό [tenaγos] shoal ‖ fen ‖ lagoon.

τενεκεδένιος [teneκeðeneeos] made of tin.

τενεκές, ὁ [tenekes] tin ‖ large can ‖ (μεταφ) good-for-nothing.
τενεκετζῆς, ὁ [teneketzees] tinsmith.
τέννις, τό [tenees] tennis.
τενόρος, ὁ [tenoros] tenor.
τέντα, ἡ [tenta] tent ‖ marquee.
τέντζερες, ὁ [tentzeres] cooking pot, kettle, casserole.
τεντώνω [tentono] stretch, tighten, bend ‖ (μεταφ) strain.
τένων, ὁ [tenon] tendon.
τέρας, τό [teras] monster, abortion, freak ‖ (μεταφ) terror.
τεράστιος [terasteeos] prodigious, enormous, huge, vast.
τερατολογία, ἡ [teratoloyeea] extravagant tale, fishy story.
τερατόμορφος [teratomorfos] monstrous, hideous.
τερατούργημα, τό [teratouryeema] monstrosity ‖ atrocious deed.
τερατώδης [teratodees] prodigious, monstrous ‖ ugly, frightful.
τερεβινθέλαιον, τό [terevintheleon] turpentine.
τερετίζω [tereteezo] chirp, warble, twitter.
τέρμα, τό [terma] extremity, terminus, end ‖ (ἀθλητ) goal.
τερματίζω [termateezo] finish, put an end to, terminate, end.
τερματοφύλαξ, ὁ [termatofeelaks] goalkeeper.
τερπνός [terpnos] delightful, agreeable, pleasing.
τέρπω [terpo] delight, please, amuse.
τερτίπι, τό [terteepee] trick.
τέρψις, ἡ [terpsees] delight, pleasure, amusement.
τέσσαρα [tessara] four ‖ μὲ τά ~ on all fours.
τεσσαράκοντα [tessarakonta] forty.
τέσσερις [tesserees] four.
τεταγμένος [tetaymenos] placed, set ‖ determined.
τεταμένος [tetamenos] stretched, extended, strained.
τέτανος, ὁ [tetanos] tetanus.
Τετάρτη, ἡ [tetartee] Wednesday.
τέταρτον, τό [tetarton] quarter of an hour ‖ quarto.
τέταρτος [tetartos] fourth.
τετελεσμένος [tetelesmenos] accomplished, achieved, done ‖ τετελεσμένον γεγονός fait accompli ‖ ~ μέλλων (γραμμ) future perfect tense.
τέτοιος [teteeos] similar, alike, such ‖ ὁ ~ what's-his-name ‖ (US) whatchacallit.
τετραγωνικός [tetrayoneekos] square, quadrangular ‖ (μεταφ) frank, outspoken.
τετράγωνον, τό [tetrayonon] (γεωμ) square, quadrangle ‖ (πόλεως) block.
τετράγωνος [tetrayonos] square ‖ (μεταφ) well-grounded, reasonable.

τετράδιον, τό [tetradeeon] exercise book, copybook.
τετράκις [tetrakees] four times.
τετρακόσιοι [tetrakosiee] four hundred.
τετράπαχος [tetrapahos] very stout, very fat, corpulent.
τετραπέρατος [tetraperatos] very clever, shrewd.
τετραπλάσιος [tetraplaseeos] four times as much.
τετραπλοῦς [tetraplous] βλ τετραπλάσιος.
τετράποδο, τό [tetrapodo] quadruped ‖ (μεταφ) beast, brute.
τετράπους [tetrapous] fourfooted.
τετράς, ἡ [tetras] set of four.
τετράτροχος [tetratrohos] four-wheeled.
τετριμμένος [tetreemenos] worn-out ‖ (μεταφ) hackneyed.
τέττιξ, ὁ [teteeks] cicada ‖ grasshopper.
τεῦτλον, τό [tevtlon] beetroot, beet.
τεῦχος, τό [tevhos] instalment, number, part, issue.
τέφρα, ἡ [tefra] ashes, cinders.
τεφρόχρους [tefrohrous] ashen ‖ grey, grizzled.
τεφτέρι, τό [tefteree] notebook ‖ account book.
τεχνάζομαι [tehnazome] contrive, hatch, think up, invent ‖ imagine.
τέχναι, αἱ [tehne] πλ: καλαί ~ fine arts.
τέχνασμα, τό [tehnasma] ruse, artifice, trick, device.
τέχνη, ἡ [tehnee] art ‖ profession ‖ dexterity ‖ (πολεμική) stratagem.
τεχνηέντως [tehnientos] skilfully, artfully, cleverly.
τεχνητός [tehneetos] sham, false, artificial ‖ simulated, affected.
τεχνική, ἡ [tehneekee] technique, means.
τεχνικός [tehneekos] technical, professional ‖ (οὐσ) technician.
τεχνίτης, ὁ [tehneetees] professional, craftsman ‖ technician, mechanic ‖ (μεταφ) specialist, expert.
τεχνοκρίτης, ὁ [tehnokreetees] art critic.
τεχνολογία, ἡ [tehnoloyeea] technology ‖ (γραμμ) grammatical analysis.
τεχνοτροπία, ἡ [tehnotropeea] artistic style.
τέως [teos] formerly, former, late ‖ ὁ ~ πρόεδρος ex-president.
τζάκι, τό [tzakee] fireplace ‖ heating range.
τζαμαρία, ἡ [tzamareea] glass panelling.
τζάμι, τό [tzamee] window pane, pane of glass.
τζαμί, τό [tzamee] mosque.
τζαμόπορτα, ἡ [tzamoporta] glazed door, glass door.
τζάμπα [tzamba] free, gratis, for nothing ‖ to no purpose, wantonly.
τζαναμπέτης, ὁ [tzanambetees] peevish person ‖ wicked person.
τζάνερο, τό [tzanero] plum ‖ prune.

τζελατίνα, ἡ [tzelateena] gelatine ‖ celluloid holder.

τζίβα, ἡ [tzeeva] vegetable fibre.

τζίγκος, ὁ [tzeengos] βλ τσίγκος.

τζίρος, ὁ [tzeeros] business turnover.

τζίτζικας, ὁ [tzeetzeekas] βλ τέττιξ.

τζιτζιφιά, ἡ [tzeetzeefia] jujube tree.

τζίφρα, ἡ [tzeefra] cipher ‖ initial, monogram.

τζόγος, ὁ [tzoyos] gambling.

τζόκεϋ, ὁ [tzokey] jockey.

τζούτα, ἡ [tzouta] jute.

τήβεννος, ἡ [teevenos] toga ‖ gown, robe.

τηγανητός [teeyaneetos] fried.

τηγάνι, τό [teeyanee] frying pan.

τηγανίζω [teeyaneezo] fry.

τηγανίτα, ἡ [teeyaneeta] fritter, pancake.

τήκομαι [teekome] thaw, melt ‖ wither, pine, languish.

τήκω [teeko] melt, thaw.

τηλεβόας, ὁ [teelevoas] loudhailer, loudspeaker.

τηλεβόλον, τό [teelevolon] cannon.

τηλεγραφεῖον, τό [teeleyrafeeon] telegraph office.

τηλεγράφημα, τό [teeleyrafeema] telegram, cable.

τηλέγραφος, ὁ [teeleyrafos] telegraph.

τηλεγραφῶ [teeleyrafo] telegraph, wire.

τηλεόρασις, ἡ [teeleorasees] television.

τηλεπάθεια, ἡ [teelepatheea] telepathy.

τηλεπικοινωνία, ἡ [teelepeekeenoneea] telecommunications.

τηλεσκόπιον, τό [teeleskopeeon] telescope.

τηλεφώνημα, τό [teelefoneema] telephone call.

τηλεφωνητής, ὁ [teelefoneetees] telephone operator.

τηλέφωνον, τό [teelefonon] telephone, phone.

τηλεφωνῶ [teelefono] telephone, call up.

τῆξις, ἡ [teeksees] melting, thawing ‖ casting.

τήρησις, ἡ [teereesees] observance ‖ maintenance, keeping.

τηρῶ [teero] keep, observe, follow, maintain.

τηρῶ [teero] see, look at ‖ watch.

τί [tee] what? ‖ what, how.

τι [tee] something ‖ a bit.

τίγρις, ἡ [teeyrees] tiger, tigress.

τιθασ(σ)εύω [teethasevo] tame, domesticate.

τίθεμαι [teetheme] be arranged, be placed, be imposed.

τίκτω [teekto] give birth ‖ give rise to.

τίλιο, τό [teeleeo] infusion of lime flowers.

τίλλω [teelo] pluck, pull out ‖ card wool, unweave.

τιμαλφῆ, τά [teemalfee] πλ jewellery, jewels.

τιμαλφής [teemalfees] precious, valuable.

τιμάριθμος, ὁ [teemareethmos] cost of living.

τιμάριον, τό [teemareeon] fief, manor.

τιμή, ἡ [teemee] respect, honour ‖ rate, price ‖ value, worth.

τίμημα, τό [teemeema] cost, price ‖ value.

τιμητικός [teemeeteekos] honorary ‖ honouring.

τίμιος [teemeeos] honest, upright ‖ precious, valuable.

τιμιότης, ἡ [teemeeotees] honesty.

τιμοκατάλογος, ὁ [teemokataloyos] price list, tariff.

τιμολόγιον, τό [teemoloyeeon] invoice, bill.

τιμόνι, τό [teemonee] helm, rudder ‖ tiller, wheel ‖ (αὐτοκινήτου) steering wheel ‖ (ποδηλάτου) handlebars.

τιμονιέρης, ὁ [teemonierees] steersman, helmsman.

τιμῶ [teemo] honour, respect, venerate, do honour to.

τιμῶμαι [teemome] cost, be worth ‖ be honoured.

τιμωρία, ἡ [teemoreea] punishment, chastisement, penalty.

τιμωρῶ [teemoro] punish, chastise ‖ fine.

τίναγμα, τό [teenayma] shake, shaking ‖ jerk, jolt, start.

τινάζομαι [teenazome] leap, spring, start ‖ brush one's clothes.

τινάζω [teenazo] shake off, shake ‖ (πετῶ) hurl, toss ‖ (φτερουγίζω) flap ‖ ~ στόν ἀέρα blow up.

τίποτα [teepota] any, anything ‖ nothing ‖ ~! don't mention it!, forget it!

τιποτένιος [teepoteneeos] mean, trivial, trifling, worthless.

τιράντες, οἱ [teerantes] πλ pair of braces.

τιρμπουσόν, τό [teermbouson] corkscrew.

τίς [tees] who?, what?, which?

τις [tees] someone, somebody ‖ anybody, one ‖ a certain.

τίτλος, ὁ [teetlos] title, right, claim ‖ certificate.

τιτλοφορῶ [teetloforo] entitle, confer a title.

τμῆμα, τό [tmeema] part, segment, section ‖ (ὑπουργείου) branch, department ‖ (ἀστυνομίας) police station.

τμηματάρχης, ὁ [tmeematarhees] chief of a department.

τμηματικῶς [tmeemateekos] partially, bit by bit, by instalments.

τό [to] the ‖ it.

τοιοῦτος [teeoutos] such ‖ (μεταφ) homosexual.

τοιουτοτρόπως [teeoutotropos] thus, in this way, in this manner.

τοιχογραφία, ἡ [teehoyrafeea] fresco, wall painting.

τοιχοκόλλησις, ἡ [teehokoleesees] bill posting, bill sticking.

τοῖχος, ὁ [teehos] wall.

τοίχωμα, τό [teehoma] inner wall, partition wall ‖ inner surface.

τοκετός, ὁ [toketos] childbirth, confinement.

τοκίζω [tokeezo] lend at interest, invest (money).

τοκογλύφος, ὁ [tokoyleefos] usurer.

τοκομερίδιον, τό [tokomereeδeeon] dividend coupon.

τόκος, ὁ [tokos] interest, rate.

τόλμη, ἡ [tolmee] daring || audacity.

τολμηρός [tolmeeros] bold, courageous, daring, venturesome.

τολμῶ [tolmo] dare, risk, hazard.

τολύπη, ἡ [toleepee] ball of raw wool || (μεταφ) flake.

τομάρι, τό [tomaree] hide, skin, leather.

τομάτα, ἡ [tomata] tomato.

τομεύς, ὁ [tomevs] sector || incisor, chisel.

τομή, ἡ [tomee] cut, gash, incision || (διαγράμματος) section.

τόμος, ὁ [tomos] volume, tome.

τονίζω [toneezo] accent || accentuate, stress, lay emphasis on || tone up.

τονισμός, ὁ [toneesmos] accentuation || emphasizing.

τόννος, ὁ [tonos] ton || (ψάρι) tunny.

τόνο [tono]: μιλῶ μέ ~ raise one's voice || δίνω ~ σέ brighten up.

τόνος, ὁ [tonos] tone || (μεταφ) force, energy || (γραμμ) accent || (μους) key.

τονώνω [tonono] fortify, invigorate, brace up.

τονωτικός [tonoteekos] bracing, invigorating, tonic.

τοξεύω [toksevo] shoot with bow, throw a dart.

τοξικομανής, ὁ, ἡ [tokseekomanees] drug addict.

τοξικός [tokseekos] toxic || poisonous.

τοξοειδής [toksoeeδees] bowed, arched, curved, bow-shaped.

τόξον, τό [tokson] bow || (κτιρίου) arch || (γεωμ) arc, curve.

τοξότης, ὁ [toksotees] archer, bowman.

τοπ(ε)ίον, τό [topeeon] landscape || site, locality.

τόπι, τό [topee] ball || (ὑφάσματος) roll of cloth || (κανονιοῦ) cannonball.

τοπικισμός, ὁ [topeekeesmos] localism.

τοπικός [topeekos] local.

τοπιογραφία, ἡ [topeeoyrafeea] landscape painting.

τοπογραφία, ἡ [topoyrafeea] topography.

τοποθεσία, ἡ [topotheseea] locality, situation, site, position, place.

τοποθέτησις, ἡ [topotheteesees] putting, placing || (οἴκον) investment, investing.

τοποθετῶ [topotheto] place, set, put || (οἴκ) invest.

τόπος, ὁ [topos] place, position, site || (χώρα) country || (χῶρο) space, room || (μαθημ) locus || πιάνω τόπο have effect, be of use || ἔμεινε στόν τόπο he died suddenly.

τοπούζι, τό [topouzee] club.

τοπωνυμία, ἡ [toponeemeea] place-name.

τορνευτής, ὁ [tornevtees] turner.

τορνευτός [tornevtos] well-turned, turned.

τορνεύω [tornevo] turn a lathe, work a lathe || (μεταφ) give fine shape to.

τόρνος, ὁ [tornos] lathe.

τορπίλλη, ἡ [torpeelee] torpedo.

τορπιλλίζω [torpeeleezo] torpedo.

τορπιλλοβόλον, τό [torpeelovolon] torpedo boat.

τος [tos]: νά ~ here he is, here he comes.

τοσάκις [tosakees] so many times, so often.

τόσο(ν) [toso(n)] so much || ~ . . . ὅσο(ν) as much . . . as, both . . . and || ὄχι καί ~ not so much.

τόσος [tosos] so big, so large, so great || so much, so many || ~ δά very little, very small, only so small || ἄλλοι τόσοι as many again || κάθε τόσο every now and again || ἑκατόν τόσα a hundred odd.

τοσοῦτος [tosoutos] so large, so much || ἐν τοσούτῳ nevertheless, yet, still || τοσούτῳ μᾶλλον with all the more reason.

τότε [tote] then, at that time || in that case, therefore, thereupon || ~ πού when.

τουαλέττα, ἡ [toualeta] toilet || (γυναικός) dress || (αἴθουσα) dressing room || (τραπέζι) dressing table || (ἀποχωρητήριον) lavatory.

τοῦβλο, τό [touvlo] brick || (μεταφ) simpleton.

τουλάχιστον [toulaheeston] at least, at all events.

τούλι, τό [toulee] tulle.

τουλίπα, ἡ [touleepa] tulip.

τουλούμι, τό [touloumee] goatskin bottle || βρέχει μέ τό ~ it's raining cats and dogs.

τουλούμπα, ἡ [touloumba] pump.

τουλ(ου)πάνι, τό [toul(ou)panee] muslin || veil, small shawl.

τούμπα, ἡ [toumba] somersault, fall || mound || κάνω τοῦμπες kowtow || fall head over heels.

τούμπανο, τό [toumbano] drum.

τουμπάρω [toumbaro] overturn, upset || (μεταφ) persuade || reverse.

τοὐναντίον [tounanteeon] on the contrary.

τουπέ, τό [toupe] cheek, audacity, nerve.

τουρισμός, ὁ [toureesmos] tourism, touring.

τουρίστας, ὁ [toureestas] tourist.

Τουρκάλα, ἡ [tourkala] Turkish woman.

τουρκεύω [tourkevo] (μεταφ) fly into a rage.

Τουρκία, ἡ [tourkeea] Turkey.

τουρκικός [tourkeekos] Turkish.

τουρκοκρατία, ἡ [tourkokrateea] Turkish domination of Greece.

Τοῦρκος, ὁ [tourkos] Turk || γίνομαι ~ get angry.

τούρλα, ἡ [tourla] mound || (ἐπίρ) piled up.

τουρλώνω [tourlono] pile up || swell out, become round.

τουρλωτός [tourlotos] piled up ‖ rounded, bulging.

τουρνέ, ή [tourne] theatrical tour.

τουρσί, τό [toursee] pickle, brine.

τούρτα, ή [tourta] gateau, layer cake, tart.

τουρτουρίζω [tourtoureezo] shiver, tremble, shudder.

τουτέστι [toutestee] that is, in other words, i.e.

τοῦτος [toutos] this one.

τούφα, ή [toufa] tuft, bunch, cluster.

τουφέκι, τό [toufekee] rifle, musket, gun.

τουφεκιά, ή [toufekia] gunshot, rifle shot.

τουφεκίζω [toufekeezo] shoot, fire ‖ execute.

τράβηγμα, τό [traveeyma] pulling, dragging, tug ‖ (ὑγροῦ) drawing off.

τραβηξιά, ή [traveeksia] sip ‖ (πίπας) pull.

τραβῶ [travo] pull, drag, heave, haul ‖ ~ τό δρόμο μου go my own way ‖ (ὅπλο, χρήματα κτλ) draw ‖ τό τραβάει he imbibes ‖ (ἀπορροφάω) absorb ‖ (τυφεκιά) fire, shoot ‖ (ταχύτητα) reach distance of ‖ (προσελκύω) entice, attract ‖ δέν μέ τραβάει it doesn't attract me ‖ (ζητῶ) ask for, want ‖ ὁ καιρός τραβάει πανωφόρι the weather calls for a coat ‖ ἡ καρδιά μου ~ τσιγάρο I need a smoke ‖ (ὑποφέρω) undergo, endure, bear ‖ (ἀμετ) make towards, head for ‖ (move on ‖ (συνεχίζω) last, go on ‖ (τσιμπούκι κτλ) suck, draw ‖ τραβιέμαι (ἀμετ) draw back, leave ‖ (ἐμπόριον) be in demand ‖ (δέν ὑποφέρεται) it's unbearable.

τραγανίζω [trayaneezo] crunch, munch, grind.

τραγανό, τό [trayano] cartilage, grist.

τραγανός [trayanos] crisp, brittle.

τραγέλαφος, ὁ [trayelafos] monstrosity, freak, mix-up.

τραγήσιος [trayeeseeos] of a goat.

τραγί, τό [trayee] kid.

τραγικός [trayeekos] calamitous, tragic ‖ (ποιητής) tragic poet.

τράγος, ὁ [trayos] goat.

τραγούδι, τό [trayoudee] song, air, tune.

τραγουδιστής, ὁ [trayoudeestees] singer, vocalist.

τραγουδιστός [trayoudeestos] sung ‖ (φωνή) tuneful.

τραγουδῶ [trayoudo] sing, chant ‖ (σιγά) hum.

τραγωδία, ή [trayodeea] tragedy.

τραγωδός, ὁ, ή [trayodos] tragic actor, tragedian, tragic actress.

τραῖνο, τό [treno] railway train ‖ (ἐπιβατηγό) passenger train.

τράκ, τό [trak] stage fright.

τρακάρισμα, τό [trakareesma] crash, collision ‖ unexpected meeting.

τρακάρω [trakaro] knock against, collide with ‖ meet by accident ‖ (μεταφ) touch for (a loan), bum (col) (a cigarette).

τρακατρούκα, ή [trakatrouka] firecracker.

τράκο(ς), τό (ὁ) [trako(s)] collision ‖ (μεταφ) attack, assault.

τρακτέρ, τό [trakter] farm tractor.

τράμ, τό [tram] tram, tramcar, tramway.

τραμουντάνα, ή [tramountana] north wind.

τραμπαλίζομαι [trambaleezome] seesaw ‖ go up and down.

τραμποῦκος, ὁ [tramboukos] out-and-out rascal, scoundrel, rotter.

τρανεύω [tranevo] grow, augment.

τρανός [tranos] powerful ‖ large, grand ‖ important, weighty.

τράνταγμα, τό [trantayma] jolting, shake, shaking ‖ jolt, jerk.

τραντάζω [trantazo] jolt, shake up and down.

τρανταχτός [trantahtos] spectacular, dramatic.

τράπεζα, ή [trapeza] table ‖ (ἐμπορ) bank ‖ ἀγία ~ altar.

τραπεζαρία, ή [trapezareea] dining room.

τραπέζι, τό [trapezee] table ‖ dinner ‖ στρώνω ~ set the table ‖ τούς εἴχαμε ~ we invited them to dinner.

τραπέζιον, τό [trapezeeon] small table ‖ (τσίρκου) trapeze ‖ (γεωμ) trapezium, trapezoid.

τραπεζίτης, ὁ [trapezeetees] banker ‖ (δόντι) molar.

τραπεζιτικός [trapezeeteekos] banking ‖ (ὑπάλληλος) bank employee.

τραπεζογραμμάτιον, τό [trapezoyramateeon] banknote.

τραπεζομάντηλο, τό [trapezomanteelo] tablecloth.

τράπουλα, ή [trapoula] pack of cards.

τράτα, ή [trata] seine ‖ fishing boat ‖ (χορός) circular dance.

τρατάρω [trataro] regale ‖ pay for, offer.

τραυλίζω [travleezo] stammer, stutter, lisp.

τραυλός [travlos] stammering, stuttering.

τραῦμα, τό [travma] wound, hurt, injury ‖ (μεταφ) wound, sore.

τραυματίας, ὁ [travmateeas] casualty, wounded person.

τραυματίζω [travmateezo] wound, hurt, injure.

τραχανᾶς, ὁ [trahanas] kind of home-made noodles.

τραχεία, ή [traheea] trachea, windpipe.

τραχέως [traheos] harshly, rudely.

τραχηλιά, ή [traheelia] collar, collaret ‖ bib.

τράχηλος, ὁ [traheelos] neck.

τραχύνω [traheeno] make harsh, make rough ‖ irritate.

τραχύς [trahees] harsh, rough ‖ (τήν γεῦσιν) tart, sharp ‖ (τήν ἀκοήν) harsh, grating ‖ (χαρακτήρ) sour, crabbed.

τρεῖς [trees] three.

τρέλλα, ή [trela] madness, insanity ‖ folly ‖ (ἰατρ) mania ‖ (μεταφ) anything pleasing.

τρελλαίνομαι [trelenome] go insane ‖ be driven mad ‖ be mad about.
τρελλαίνω [treleno] drive mad, bewilder.
τρελλοκομείο, τό [trelokomeeo] madhouse.
τρελλός [trelos] insane, mad ‖ (ούσ) madman ‖ (μωρό) mischievous.
τρεμοσβήνω [tremosveeno] flicker, sparkle.
τρεμούλα, ή [tremoula] shivering, trembling ‖ (φωνῆς) quiver ‖ (ἀπό κρύο) shivering ‖ scare.
τρεμουλιάζω [tremouleeazo] tremble, shiver, shudder.
τρέμω [tremo] tremble ‖ (ἀπό κρύο) shiver ‖ (ἀπό φόβο) shake ‖ (τό φῶς) flicker, waver ‖ (φωνή) quiver.
τρεξίματα, τά [trekseemata] πλ bustle, running around.
τρέξιμο, τό [trekseemo] running ‖ (ὑγροῦ) flowing ‖ (αἵματος) flow, gush.
τρέπομαι [trepome] turn to, turn into.
τρέπω [trepo] change, convert ‖ turn, translate ‖ ~ εἰς φυγήν put to flight.
τρέφω [trefo] nourish, feed, nurture ‖ (ἐλπίδα) cherish, foster ‖ (γένεια) grow ‖ support, keep.
τρεχάλα, ή [trehala] running ‖ (ὡς ἐπίρ) at full speed.
τρεχάματα, τά [trehamata] πλ running about ‖ (μεταφ) cares.
τρεχάμενος [trehamenos] running.
τρεχαντήρι, τό [trehanteeree] small sailing boat.
τρεχάτος [trehatos] running, hasty.
τρέχω [treho] run, race, hurry ‖ (ἐπί ὑγρῶν) flow ‖ leak ‖ τί τρέχει; what's happening?, what's the matter?
τρέχων [trehon] current, present, contemporary.
τρία [treea] three.
τριάδα, ή [treeada] trinity ‖ trio.
τρίαινα, ή [triena] trident.
τριάκοντα [treeakonta] thirty.
τριακόσιοι [treeakosiee] three hundred.
τριακοστός [treeakostos] thirtieth.
τριανδρία, ή [treeanδreea] triumvirate.
τριάντα [treeanta] thirty.
τριαντάφυλλο, τό [treeantafeelo] rose.
τριάρι, τό [treearee] figure 3 ‖ three at cards.
τριάς, ή [treeas] trinity ‖ trio.
τριβέλι, τό [treevelee] drill.
τριβή, ή [treevee] friction, chafing, rubbing ‖ wear and tear ‖ (μεταφ) practice, use, experience.
τρίβολος, ὁ [treevolos] caltrop, thistle.
τρίβομαι [treevome] wear out ‖ disintegrate ‖ (μεταφ) get experienced, get practice in.
τρίβω [treevo] rub ‖ polish up ‖ grate ‖ (τό σῶμα) massage.
τρίγλυφον, τό [treeyleefon] triglyph.
τριγμός, ὁ [treeymos] crackling, creaking ‖ (ὀδόντων) grinding, gnashing.
τριγυρίζω [treeyeereezo] encircle ‖ roam, hang about.

τριγυρίστρα, ή [treeyeereestra] whitlow ‖ (γυναίκα) gadabout.
τριγυρνῶ [treeyeerno] βλ τριγυρίζω.
τριγωνικός [treeyoneekos] triangular.
τριγωνομετρία, ή [treeyonometreea] trigonometry.
τρίγωνον, τό [treeyonon] triangle.
τρίγωνος [treeyonos] three-cornered.
τρίδιπλος [treeδeeplos] triple, three times.
τρίδυμα, τά [treeδeema] πλ triplets.
τριετής [trietees] of three years ‖ (ἡλικία) three years old ‖ (φοιτητής) third-year.
τρίζω [treezo] crackle, crack, creak, squeak ‖ (δόντια) grind, gnash, grit.
τριήρης, ή [trierees] trireme.
τρικαντό, τό [treekanto] three-cornered hat, cocked hat.
τρικλίζω [treekleezo] stagger, totter, wobble, reel.
τρίκλωνος [treeklonos] three-stranded thread.
τρικούβερτος [treekouvertos] (μεταφ) splendid, terrific, wonderful.
τρικυμία, ή [treekeemeea] storm, tempest, hurricane.
τρικυμιώδης [treekeemeeoδees] stormy, tempestuous, rough.
τρίκωχο, τό [treekoho] βλ τρικαντό.
τρίλλια, ή [treeleea] trill.
τριμελής [treemelees] of three members.
τριμερής [treemerees] tripartite.
τριμηνία, ή [treemeeneea] quarter of a year ‖ quarter's rent.
τριμηνιαῖος [treemeenieos] of three months, quarterly.
τρίμηνο, τό [treemeeno] βλ τριμηνία.
τρίμηνος [treemeenos] βλ τριμηνιαῖος.
τρίμμα, τό [treema] fragment, morsel, chip, particle.
τριμμένος [treemenos] showing signs of wear and tear ‖ ground.
τρίξιμο, τό [treekseemo] gnashing, grinding.
τρίπατος [treepatos] three-storeyed.
τριπλασιάζω [treeplaseeazo] treble, triple, triplicate.
τριπλάσιος [treeplaseeos] threefold, triple, treble.
τριπλός [treeplos] βλ τριπλάσιος.
τριποδίζω [treepoδeezo] trot.
τρίποδο, τό [treepoδo] tripod ‖ easel ‖ three-legged support.
τρίπτυχον, τό [treepteehon] triptych.
τρίς [trees] thrice, three times.
τρισάγιον, τό [treesayeeon] canticle ‖ Te Deum.
τρισδιάστατος [treesδeeastatos] three-dimensional.
τρισέγγονο, τό [treesengono] great-great-grandchild.
τρισκατάρατος [treeskataratos] thrice-cursed ‖ abominable.
τριτεύω [treetevo] come third.
Τρίτη, ή [treetee] Tuesday.

τρίτον, τό [treeton] third ‖ (ἐπίρ) thirdly.

τρίτος [treetos] third ‖ third-party.

τρίφτης, ὁ [treeftees] grater, rasp.

τριφύλλι, τό [treefeelee] clover, trefoil.

τρίχα, ἡ [treeha] hair ‖ bristle ‖ fur ‖ στήν ~ spruced up ‖ παρά ~ nearly.

τρίχες, οἱ [treehes] πλ nonsense, rubbish.

τριχιά, ἡ [treehia] rope.

τριχοειδής [treehoeedees] capillary.

τρίχρωμος [treehromos] three-coloured.

τρίχωμα, τό [treehoma] fur ‖ (σώματος) hair.

τριχωτός [treehotos] hairy, shaggy.

τρίψιμο, τό [treepseemo] chafing, massage, rubbing, friction ‖ (στίλβωμα) polishing ‖ grating, grinding, crushing.

τρίωρος [treeoros] of three hours.

τρόλλεϋ, τό [troley] trolley bus.

τρόμαγμα, τό [tromayma] fright, scare.

τρομάζω [tromazo] terrify, frighten ‖ get scared.

τρομακτικός [tromakteekos] fearful, awful, frightening ‖ (μεταφ) terrific.

τρομάρα, ἡ [tromara] dread, fright, fear.

τρομερός [tromeros] terrible, dreadful, frightful ‖ (μεταφ) terrific, astonishing.

τρομοκρατία, ἡ [tromokrateea] terrorism ‖ terror.

τρομοκρατῶ [tromokrato] terrorize.

τρόμος, ὁ [tromos] trembling, shaking ‖ dread, fright.

τρόμπα, ἡ [trompa] pump.

τρομπέτα, ἡ [trompeta] trumpet.

τρομπόνι, τό [tromponee] trombone.

τρόπαιον, τό [tropeon] trophy ‖ triumph.

τροπαιοῦχος [tropeouhos] triumphant, victorious.

τροπάριον, τό [tropareeon] (ἐκκλ) hymn ‖ (μεταφ) same old refrain.

τροπή, ἡ [tropee] change ‖ turn ‖ (μαθημ) conversion.

τροπικός [tropeekos] tropical ‖ (γραμμ) of manner.

τρόπις, ἡ [tropees] keel, bottom.

τροπολογία, ἡ [tropoloyeea] amendment, alteration, change, modification.

τροποποίησις, ἡ [tropopieesees] modification, alteration, change.

τρόποι, οἱ [tropee] πλ manners, behaviour.

τρόπος, ὁ [tropos] way, manner, method ‖ behaviour, conduct ‖ (μουσ) mode ‖ ~ τοῦ λέγειν so to speak.

τροῦλλος, ὁ [troulos] dome, cupola.

τρουλλωτός [troulotos] domed, dome-shaped.

τροφή, ἡ [trofee] food, nutrition ‖ (ζώων) pasture, fodder ‖ sustenance.

τρόφιμα, τά [trofeema] πλ provisions, food, victuals.

τρόφιμος, ὁ, ἡ [trofeemos] lodger, boarder ‖ paying guest ‖ inmate ‖ (μεταφ) nursling.

τροφοδοσία, ἡ [trofodoseea] provisioning, supplying ‖ supply, provisions.

τροφοδότης, ὁ [trofodotees] caterer, purveyor, provider, supplier.

τροφοδοτῶ [trofodoto] feed, provision, keep supplied, supply, serve.

τροφός, ἡ [trofos] wet-nurse.

τροχάδην [trohaðen] hurriedly, hastily, at full speed ‖ (μεταφ) fluently.

τροχαία [trohea]: ~ κίνησις traffic ‖ ἡ ~ traffic police.

τροχαῖον [troheon]: ~ ὑλικόν rolling stock.

τροχαῖος, ὁ [troheos] trochee ‖ (ἐπιθ) wheeled, rolling.

τροχαλία, ἡ [trohaleea] pulley, block.

τροχιά, ἡ [trohia] track, groove, rut ‖ (σιδηροδρόμου) track, rail ‖ (δορυφόρου κτλ) orbit, trajectory.

τροχίζω [troheezo] sharpen, whet, grind (knife) ‖ (μεταφ) train, exercise.

τροχιόδρομος, ὁ [troheeoðromos] tramway.

τρόχισμα, τό [troheesma] sharpening, whetting, grinding ‖ (μεταφ) exercising.

τροχονόμος, ὁ [trohonomos] traffic policeman.

τροχοπέδη, ἡ [trohopeðee] brake, skid, wheel brake.

τροχοπέδιλον, τό [trohopeðeelon] roller skate ‖ scooter.

τροχός, ὁ [trohos] wheel ‖ grindstone, whetstone.

τροχοφόρον, τό [trohoforon] vehicle.

τροχοφόρος [trohoforos] wheeled.

τρυγητής, ὁ [treeyeetees] grape harvester, vintager.

τρυγητός, ὁ [treeyeetos] grape harvest, vintage.

τρυγόνι, τό [treeyonee] turtledove.

τρύγος, ὁ [treeyos] βλ τρυγητός.

τρυγῶ [treeyo] gather grapes ‖ (μεταφ) loot, fleece.

τρῦπα, ἡ [treepa] hole ‖ (βελόνης) eye ‖ (μεταφ) den, lair.

τρυπάνι, τό [treepanee] drill, drilling machine.

τρυπανίζω [treepaneezo] bore, drill, pierce ‖ (ἰατρ) trepan.

τρύπανον, τό [treepanon] βλ τρυπάνι.

τρύπημα, τό [treepeema] perforating, boring, piercing ‖ prick, punch.

τρυπητήρι, τό [treepeeteeree] awl, punch, drill.

τρυπητό, τό [treepeeto] strainer, colander.

τρυπητός [treepeetos] perforated, holed, riddled.

τρύπιος [treepeeos] with holes, perforated, holed, riddled.

τρυπῶ [treepo] bore, make a hole, pierce ‖ prick, punch.

τρυπώνω [treepono] hide, conceal ‖ squeeze in ‖ take refuge.

τρυφερός [treeferos] tender, soft ‖ affectionate, affable, mild.

τρυφερότης, ἡ [treeferotees] tenderness, softness ‖ affection, kindness.

τρωγαλίζω [troyaleezo] gnaw, nibble.

τρώγλη, ή [troylee] hole, lair, den ‖ hovel, shack.

τρωγλοδύτης, ὁ [troylodeetees] troglodyte.

τρώγομαι [troyome] be edible ‖ (μεταφ) be tolerable ‖ **τρώγονται** they are quarrelling.

τρώγω [troyo] eat, bite ‖ **μέ τρώει** it itches ‖ ~ **ξύλο** get a beating ‖ ~ **τόν κόσμο** look everywhere.

τρωκτικόν, τό [trokteekon] rodent.

Τρωϊκός [troeekos] Trojan.

τρωτόν, τό [troton] shortcoming, weak point.

τρωτός [trotos] vulnerable.

τσάγαλο, τό [tsayalo] green almond.

τσαγγός [tsangos] βλ **ταγγός**.

τσαγιέρα, ή [tsayiera] teapot.

τσαγιερό, τό [tsayiero] βγ **τσαγιέρα**.

τσαγκάρης, ὁ [tsangarees] shoemaker.

τσάϊ, τό [tsaee] tea.

τσακάλι, τό [tsakalee] jackal.

τσακίζομαι [tsakeezome] strive, struggle ‖ (διπλώνω) fold.

τσακίζω [tsakeezo] break, shatter, smash ‖ (μεταφ) weaken, wear out, enfeeble.

τσάκιση, ή [tsakeesee] crease, pleat.

τσάκισμα, τό [tsakeesma] breaking, shattering, smashing.

τσακμάκι, τό [tsakmakee] tinderbox ‖ cigarette lighter.

τσάκωμα, τό [tsakoma] seizing, catching ‖ quarrelling, dispute.

τσακώνομαι [tsakonome] quarrel.

τσακώνω [tsakono] catch in the act.

τσαλαβουτῶ [tsalavouto] flounder, wallow, splash about ‖ (μεταφ) do a sloppy job.

τσαλακώνω [tsalakono] crease, crumple, wrinkle.

τσαλαπατῶ [tsalapato] trample underfoot, tread over.

τσάμι, τό [tsamee] Aleppo pine.

τσάμικος, ὁ [tsameekos] kind of circular dance.

τσάμπα [tsamba] βλ **τζάμπα**.

τσαμπί, τό [tsambee] bunch (of grapes), cluster.

τσάμπουρο, τό [tsambouro] grape stalk.

τσανάκι, τό [tsanakee] shallow bowl, earthenware plate.

τσάντα, ή [tsanta] pouch ‖ handbag ‖ briefcase ‖ (ψωνίσματος) shopping bag ‖ (ταχυδρόμου) satchel.

τσαντίρι, τό [tsanteeree] tent.

τσάπα, ή [tsapa] hoe, pickaxe.

τσαπατσούλης [tsapatsoulees] untidy in one's work.

τσαπέλλα, ή [tsapela] string of dried figs.

τσαπί, τό [tsapee] βλ **τσάπα**.

τσάρκα, ή [tsarka] walk, promenade, stroll.

τσάρος, ὁ [tsaros] czar.

τσαρούχι, τό [tsarouhee] rustic shoe with pompom.

τσατσάρα, ή [tsatsara] comb.

τσαχπινιά, ή [tsahpeenia] coquetry, roguery, trickery.

τσέκ, τό [tsek] cheque ‖ (US) check.

τσεκούρι, τό [tsekouree] axe, hatchet.

τσεκουρώνω [tsekourono] cut with an axe.

τσέλιγκας, ὁ [tseleengas] chief shepherd.

τσεμπέρι, τό [tsemberee] kerchief, veil.

τσέπη, ή [tsepee] pocket ‖ pocketful.

τσεπώνω [tsepono] pocket ‖ (μεταφ) filch, swipe.

τσέρι, τό [tseree] cherry brandy.

τσέρκι, τό [tserkee] hoop ‖ stirrup.

τσέτουλα, ή [tsetoula] tally.

τσευδίζω [tsevðeezo] lisp, stammer, falter.

τσευδός [tsevðos] lisping, stammering.

τσιγαρίζω [tseeyareezo] fry lightly, brown, roast brown.

τσιγάρο, τό [tseeyaro] cigarette.

τσιγαροθήκη, ή [tseeyarotheekee] cigarette case.

τσιγαρόχαρτο, τό [tseeyaroharto] tissue paper.

τσιγγάνος, ὁ [tseenganos] gipsy.

τσιγγούνης [tseengounees] miserly, stingy ‖ (οὐσ) miser.

τσιγκέλι, τό [tseengelee] meat hook.

τσιγκλῶ [tseenglo] goad, prick, spur.

τσίγκος, ὁ [tseengos] zinc.

τσίκνα, ή [tseekna] smell of burning meat.

τσικνίζω [tseekneezo] scorch, burn ‖ have burnt smell.

τσικουδιά, ή [tseekouðia] terebinth ‖ (ποτόν) kind of spirit.

τσίμα [tseema]: ~ ~ scarcely ‖ on the brink of.

τσιμέντο, τό [tseemento] cement.

τσιμουδιά, ή [tseemouðia]: δέν ἔβγαλε ~ he remained speechless ‖ ~! not a word!, mum's the word!

τσίμπημα, τό [tseembeema] prick, sting, pinch ‖ bite, peck.

τσιμπιά, ή [tseembia] pinch.

τσιμπίδα, ή [tseembeeða] nippers, tongs, forceps, pincers.

τσιμπιδάκι, τό [tseembeeðakee] tweezers ‖ hairclip.

τσιμπίδι, τό [tseembeeðee] tweezers ‖ clothes peg.

τσίμπλα, ή [tseembla] mucus of eyes.

τσιμπούκι, τό [tseemboukee] tobacco pipe.

τσιμπούρι, τό [tseembouree] (ἔντομον) tick ‖ (μεταφ) troublesome or bothersome person, pest.

τσιμπούσι, τό [tseembousee] spread, repast, regalement, feast.

τσιμπῶ [tseembo] prick, pinch, sting ‖ (ἀγκώνα) bite, peck ‖ (φαγητό) nibble ‖ (μεταφ) cadge ‖ (συλλαμβάνω) seize, collar.

τσίνουρο, τό [tseenouro] eyelash.

τσίπα, ή [tseepa] thin skin, crust ‖ (μεταφ) shame.

τσιπούρα, ή [tseepoura] gilthead.

τσίπουρο, τό [tseepouro] kind of spirit.

τσιράκι, τό [tseerakee] apprentice, boy, novice.

τσιρίζω [tseereezo] screech, shriek, scream.

τσιρίσι, τό [tseereesee] glue.

τσίρκο, τό [tseerko] circus.

τσίρλα, ή [tseerla] diarrhoea.

τσίρος, ό [tseeros] dried mackerel || (μεταφ) skinny person.

τσιρότο, τό [tseeroto] sticking plaster.

τσίτα [tseeta] very tight || ~ ~ scarcely.

τσίτι, τό [tseetee] calico.

τσιτσίδι [tseetseedee] stark naked.

τσιτσιμπύρι, τό [tseetseembeeree] ginger beer.

τσιτσιρίζω [tseetseereezo] sizzle.

τσιτώνω [tseetono] stretch, tighten, strain.

τσιφλίκι, τό [tseefleekee] large country estate, farm, ranch.

τσιφούτης, ό [tseefoutees] miser.

τσίχλα, ή [tseehla] thrush || (άδύνατος) skinny person.

τσόκαρο, τό [tsokaro] wooden shoe.

τσοκολάτα, ή [tsokolata] chocolate.

τσολιάς, ό [tsolias] evzone, kilted soldier.

τσο(μ)πάνης, ό [tso(m)panees] shepherd.

τσοντάρω [tsontaro] join on.

τσότρα, ή [tsotra] gourd, flask.

τσουβάλι, τό [tsouvalee] sackful || sack.

τσουγκράνα, ή [tsoungrana] rake.

τσουγκρανίζω [tsoungraneezo] scratch, rake.

τσουγκρίζω [tsoungreezo] strike against || clink glasses, touch glasses.

τσούζω [tsouzo] smart, sting, hurt.

τσουκάλι, τό [tsoukalee] jug, pot || chamber-pot.

τσουκνίδα, ή [tsoukneeda] nettle.

τσούλα, ή [tsoula] loose-living woman, whore.

τσουλάω [tsoulao] slip along, slide along || (δχημα) push.

τσούλι, τό [tsoulee] doormat.

τσουλίστρα, ή [tsouleestra] slide.

τσουλούφι, τό [tsouloufee] lock of hair.

τσουράπι, τό [tsourapee] woollen sock, stocking.

τσουρέκι, τό [tsourekee] bun, brioche.

τσούρμο, τό [tsourmo] throng || band, troop.

τσουρουφλίζω [tsouroufleezo] grill brown, scorch.

τσουχτερός [tsouhteros] keen, smart, sharp || (κρύο) biting || harsh.

τσούχτρα, ή [tsouhtra] jellyfish.

τσόφλι, τό [tsoflee] shell || rind.

τσόχα, ή [tsoha] felt.

τυγχάνω [teenghano] happen to be || obtain, attain.

τύλιγμα, τό [teeleeyma] winding, rolling, coiling, wrapping.

τυλίγω [teeleeyo] roll up, wind, coil || wrap up, fold round, twist.

τυλίσσω [teeleeso] βλ **τυλίγω**.

τύλος, ό [teelos] callus || corn.

τυλώνω [teelono] fill up.

τύμβος, ό [teemvos] grave, tomb.

τυμβωρύχος, ό [teemvoreehos] grave-robber.

τύμπανον, τό [teembanon] drum, tambour || (αὐτιοῦ) eardrum || tympanum.

τυπικόν, τό [teepeekon] (γραμμ) morphology || formality, ritual.

τυπικός [teepeekos] usual, conventional || typical.

τυπικότης, ή [teepeekotees] formality.

τύπο [teepo]: γιά τόν ~ for the sake of form.

τυπογραφεῖον, τό [teepoyrafeeon] printing press, printer's.

τυπογραφία, ή [teepoyrafeea] printing.

τυπογράφος, ό [teepoyrafos] printer.

τύποι, οἱ [teepee] πλ conventions, form.

τυποποίησις, ή [teepopieesees] standardization.

τύπος, ό [teepos] print, imprint, stamp || (καλούπι) mould, matrix, form || (ὑπόδειγμα) model, type || (συμπεριφορᾶς) formality, rule of procedure || (οἰκίας) type, kind of || (μαθημ) formula || (ἐφημερίδες) the press || (γιά ἄνθρωπο) figure, character.

τύπτω [teepto] beat, strike.

τυπώνω [teepono] print, stamp.

τυραννία, ή [teeraneea] tyranny, oppression || torment, torture.

τύραννος, ό [teeranos] oppressor, tyrant.

τυραννῶ [teerano] oppress || torture, harass.

τυρί, τό [teeree] cheese.

τυροκομία, ή [teerokomeea] cheese-making.

τυρόπηττα, ή [teeropeeta] cheese pie, cheesecake.

τυρός, ό [teeros] βλ **τυρί**.

τύρφη, ή [teerfee] peat.

τύφλα, ή [teefla] blindness || ~ στό μεθύσι dead drunk.

τυφλόμυγα, ή [teeflomeeya] blind man's buff.

τυφλοπόντικας, ό [teefloponteekas] mole.

τυφλός [teeflos] blind.

τυφλώνομαι [teeflonome] grow blind, blind o.s.

τυφλώνω [teeflono] blind || (φῶς) dazzle || (μεταφ) deceive, hoodwink.

τυφοειδής [teefoeedees]: ~ πυρετός typhoid fever.

τῦφος, ό [teefos]: ἐξανθηματικός ~ typhus || κοιλιακός ~ typhoid fever.

τυφών, ό [teefon] typhoon, hurricane, cyclone.

τυχαίνω [teeheno] βλ **τυγχάνω**.

τυχαῖος [teeheos] casual, fortuitous, chance.

τυχαίως [teeheos] by chance, by accident.

τυχερά [teehera] πλ casual profits, tips, perks.

τυχερό, τό [teehero] fortune, destiny.

τυχερός [teeheros] fortunate, lucky.

τύχη, ἡ [teehee] destiny, chance, fortune, lot, fate ‖ (καλή) good luck ‖ στήν ~ haphazard, at random.
τυχηρός [teeheeros] βλ τυχερός.
τυχοδιώκτης, ὁ [teehodeeoktees] adventurer, opportunist.
τυχόν [teehon] by chance ‖ τά ~ ἔξοδα incidental expenses.
τυχών [teehon]: ὁ ~ the first comer, anyone.
τύψις, ἡ [teepsees] remorse, prick of conscience.
τωόντι [toontee] in fact, actually, in effect, indeed.
τώρα [tora] nowadays, at present, now ‖ this minute ‖ at once.
τωρινός [toreenos] present-day, contemporary, of today.

Υ, υ

ὕαινα, ἡ [iena] hyena.
ὑάκινθος, ὁ [eeakeenthos] hyacinth.
ὑαλοπίναξ, ὁ [eealopeenaks] window pane.
ὕαλος, ἡ [eealos] glass.
ὑαλουργία, ἡ [eealouryeea] glassmaking.
ὑαλουργός, ὁ [eealouryos] glassmaker.
ὑαλόφρακτος [eealofraktos] glazed.
ὑαλόχαρτον, τό [eealoharton] emery paper, sandpaper.
ὑαλώδης [eealodees] glassy ‖ vitreous.
ὑάρδα, ἡ [eearda] yard.
ὕβος, ὁ [eevos] hump.
ὑβρεολόγιον, τό [eevreoloyeeon] volley of abuse, tirade.
ὑβρίζω [eevreezo] insult, abuse, swear at.
ὕβρις, ἡ [eevrees] insult, injury ‖ oath.
ὑβριστικός [eevreesteekos] insulting, rude.
ὑγεία, ἡ [eeyeea] health.
ὑγειονομικός [eeyeeonomeekos] sanitary.
ὑγιαίνω [eeyieno] be healthy.
ὑγιεινός [eeyieenos] healthy ‖ wholesome.
ὑγιής [eeyiees] healthy ‖ (μεταφ) sound.
ὑγραίνω [eeyreno] moisten, dampen, wet.
ὑγρασία, ἡ [eeyraseea] moisture, moistness, humidity.
ὑγροποιῶ [eeyropeeo] liquefy.
ὑγρός [eeyros] fluid, liquid ‖ humid, damp ‖ watery.
ὑδαρής [eedarees] watery, aqueous.
ὕδατα, τά [eedata] πλ waters.
ὑδαταγωγός, ὁ [eedatayogos] water pipe.
ὑδατάνθραξ, ὁ [eedatanthraks] carbohydrate.
ὑδατογραφία, ἡ [eedatoyrafeea] watercolour, aquarelle.
ὑδατοπτώσεις, οἱ [eedatoptosees] πλ waterfalls.
ὑδατοστεγής [eedatosteyees] watertight, waterproof.
ὑδατοφράκτης, ὁ [eedatofraktees] dam, weir.

ὑδραγωγεῖον, τό [eedrayogeeon] aqueduct.
ὑδραντλία, ἡ [eedrantleea] water pump.
ὑδράργυρος, ὁ [eedraryeeros] mercury, quicksilver.
ὑδρατμός, ὁ [eedratmos] vapour, steam.
ὑδραυλική, ἡ [eedravleekee] hydraulics.
ὑδραυλικός [eedravleekos] hydraulic ‖ (οὐσ) plumber.
ὑδρεύομαι [eedrevome] draw water.
ὕδρευσις, ἡ [eedrevsees] water supply, drawing of water.
ὑδρία, ἡ [eedreea] pitcher, water jar, jug.
ὑδρόβιος [eedroveeos] aquatic.
ὑδρόγειος, ἡ [eedroyeeos] earth.
ὑδρογόνον, τό [eedroyonon] hydrogen.
ὑδρογραφία, ἡ [eedroyrafeea] hydrography.
ὑδροηλεκτρικός [eedroeelektreekos] hydroelectric.
ὑδροκέφαλος [eedrokefalos] hydrocephalous.
ὑδροκίνητος [eedrokeeneetos] waterpowered.
ὑδροκυάνιον, τό [eedrokeeaneeon] prussic acid.
ὑδρολήπτης, ὁ [eedroleeptees] water consumer, receiver of water.
ὑδρόμυλος, ὁ [eedromeelos] water mill.
ὑδρονομεύς, ὁ [eedronomevs] water distributor ‖ water key.
ὑδροπλάνον, τό [eedroplanon] seaplane.
ὑδρορρόη, ἡ [eedroroee] gutter of roof.
ὑδροσκόπος, ὁ [eedroskopos] water diviner.
ὑδροστάθμη, ἡ [eedrostathmee] water level.
ὑδροστατικός [eedrostateekos] hydrostatic.
ὑδροστρόβιλος, ὁ [eedrostroveelos] water turbine ‖ whirlpool.
ὑδροσωλήν, ὁ [eedrosoleen] water pipe, conduit.
ὑδροφοβία, ἡ [eedrofoveea] rabies, hydrophobia.
ὑδροφόρος [eedroforos] water-carrying ‖ (οὐσ) water carrier.
ὑδροφράκτης, ὁ [eedrofraktees] dam, lock.
ὑδρόφιλος [eedrofeelos] water-loving.
ὑδροχλωρικός [eedrohloreekos] hydrochloric.
ὑδρόχρωμα, τό [eedrohroma] whitewash.
ὑδρόψυκτος [eedropseektos] water-cooled.
ὑδρωπικία, ἡ [eedropeekeea] dropsy.
ὕδωρ, τό [eedor] water.
ὑετός, ὁ [ietos] shower, downpour ‖ rains.
υἱοθεσία, ἡ [eeotheseea] adoption.
υἱοθετῶ [eeotheto] adopt, accept, support.
υἱός, ὁ [eeos] son.
ὑλακή, ἡ [eelakee] barking, baying.
ὑλακτῶ [eelakto] bark, bay.
ὕλη, ἡ [eelee] material, matter, stuff.
ὑλικόν, τό [eeleekon] material, stuff ‖ element, ingredient.
ὑλικός [eeleekos] material, real.
ὑλισμός, ὁ [eeleesmos] materialism.
ὑλιστής, ὁ [eeleestees] materialist.

ὑλιστικός [eeleesteekos] materialistic.
ὑλοτομία, ἡ [eelotomeea] woodcutting, timber-felling.
ὑμεῖς [eemees] you.
ὑμέτερος [eemeteros] your, yours.
ὑμήν, ὁ [eemeen] membrane ‖ tissue, hymen.
ὑμνητής, ὁ [eemneetees] eulogist, praiser, panegyrist.
ὕμνος, ὁ [eemnos] hymn ‖ anthem.
ὑμνῶ [eemno] celebrate, praise, eulogize.
ὑνί, τό [eenee] ploughshare.
ὑπάγομαι [eepayome] belong to, be dependent ‖ be answerable.
ὑπαγόρευσις, ἡ [eepayorevsees] dictation ‖ (μεταφ) suggestion.
ὑπαγορεύω [eepayorevo] dictate ‖ (μεταφ) inspire, suggest.
ὑπάγω [eepayo] go ‖ go under, rank.
ὑπαίθριος [eepethreeos] outdoor, in the open air ‖ field.
ὕπαιθρον, τό [eepethron] open air, open country.
ὕπαιθρος [eepethros]: ἡ ~ χώρα countryside.
ὑπαινιγμός, ὁ [eepeneeymos] hint, allusion, intimation.
ὑπαινίσσομαι [eepeneesome] hint at, allude to.
ὑπαίτιος [eepeteeos] responsible, culpable.
ὑπακοή, ἡ [eepakoee] obedience ‖ submission.
ὑπάκουος [eepakouos] obedient ‖ submissive.
ὑπακούω [eepakouo] obey.
ὑπάλληλος, ὁ, ἡ [eepaleelos] employee, clerk ‖ (ὑπουργείου) official, functionary ‖ δημόσιος ~ civil servant, government employee.
ὑπαναχωρῶ [eepanahoro] withdraw ‖ recant.
ὑπανδρεία, ἡ [eepandreea] marriage.
ὑπανδρεύω [eepandrevo] marry.
ὕπανδρος [eepandros] married.
ὑπαξιωματικός, ὁ [eepakseeomateekos] non-commissioned officer.
Ὑπαπαντή, ἡ [eepapantee] Candlemas.
ὑπαρκτός [eeparktos] existent ‖ subsisting ‖ real.
ὕπαρξις, ἡ [eeparksees] existence ‖ being, life.
ὑπαρχή, ἡ [eeparhee] very beginning ‖ ἐξ ὑπαρχῆς from the very beginning.
ὑπαρχηγός, ὁ [eeparheeyos] deputy commander.
ὑπάρχω [eeparho] exist, be ‖ live ‖ ὑπάρχει there is ‖ τά ὑπάρχοντά μου my possessions, my things.
ὑπασπιστής, ὁ [eepaspeestees] aide-de-camp ‖ (στρατ) adjutant.
ὕπατος, ὁ [eepatos] consul ‖ (ἐπίθ) highest, supreme.
ὑπέδαφος, τό [eepedafos] subsoil.

ὑπείκω [eepeeko] succumb to, obey.
ὑπεισέρχομαι [eepeeserhome] enter secretly ‖ glide into.
ὑπεκμισθώνω [eepekmeesthono] sublet, rent from a tenant.
ὑπεκφεύγω [eepekfevyo] escape, avoid ‖ slip away.
ὑπεκφυγή, ἡ [eepekfeeyee] escape, subterfuge ‖ evasion.
ὑπενθυμίζω [eepenthoemeezo] remind of, call to mind ‖ allude to.
ὑπενοικιάζω [eepeneekeeazo] βλ ὑπεκμισθώνω.
ὑπεξαίρεσις, ἡ [eepekseresees] pilfering, taking away.
ὑπέρ [eeper] over, upwards, above ‖ (γιά) for, on behalf of ‖ τά ~ καί τά κατά pros and cons, for and against.
ὑπεράγαν [eeperayan] too much, exceedingly.
ὑπεραιμία, ἡ [eeperemeea] excess of blood.
ὑπεραμύνομαι [eeperameenome] defend, support.
ὑπεράνθρωπος [eeperanthropos] superhuman ‖ (οὐσ) superman.
ὑπεράνω [eeperano] above, beyond, over.
ὑπεράριθμος [eeperareethmos] supernumerary, redundant.
ὑπερασπίζομαι [eeperaspeezome] defend o.s.
ὑπερασπίζω [eeperaspeezo] defend, protect ‖ maintain.
ὑπεράσπισις, ἡ [eeperaspeesees] defence ‖ protection ‖ the defendants.
ὑπεραστικός [eeperasteekos] long-distance.
ὑπερβαίνω [eeperveno] cross, surmount ‖ exceed, go beyond, overdo.
ὑπερβαλλόντως [eepervalontos] excessively, exceedingly ‖ too, deeply.
ὑπερβάλλω [eepervalo] surpass, outdo, exceed ‖ exaggerate, overdo, magnify.
ὑπέρβασις, ἡ [eepervasees] exceeding ‖ (traffic) violation ‖ trespass.
ὑπερβολή, ἡ [eepervolee] exaggeration ‖ (γεωμ) hyperbola.
ὑπερβολικός [eepervoleekos] excessive ‖ exaggerated, exaggerating.
ὑπέργηρος [eeperyeeros] extremely old, very old.
ὑπερδιέγερσις, ἡ [eeperdieyersees] overexcitement.
ὑπερέντασις, ἡ [eeperentasees] overstrain, overstress.
ὑπερευαίσθητος [eeperevestheetos] oversensitive, hypersensitive.
ὑπερέχω [eepereho] excel, surpass, exceed.
ὑπερήλιξ, ὁ, ἡ [eepereeleeks] elderly person, very old person.
ὑπερηφάνεια, ἡ [eepereefaneea] pride ‖ haughtiness.
ὑπερηφανεύομαι [eepereefanevome] pride o.s. ‖ be proud.

ὑπερήφανος [eepereefanos] proud ‖ haughty.

ὑπερθεματίζω [eeperthemateezo] make higher bid ‖ (μεταφ) outdo.

ὑπερθετικός [eepertheteekos] superlative.

ὑπερίπταμαι [eepereeptame] fly over, fly above.

ὑπερισχύω [eepereesheeo] predominate, prevail over ‖ overcome, triumph.

ὑπεριώδης [eepereeodees] ultraviolet.

ὑπερκέρασις, ἡ [eeperkerasees] outflanking.

ὑπερκόπωσις, ἡ [eeperkoposees] overwork, breakdown.

ὑπέρμαχος, ὁ, ἡ [eepermahos] champion, defender.

ὑπέρμετρος [eepermetros] excessive, huge.

ὑπερνικῶ [eeperneeko] overcome ‖ subdue, master.

ὑπέρογκος [eeperongos] colossal, enormous ‖ outrageous.

ὑπεροπλία, ἡ [eeperopleea] superiority in arms.

ὑπεροπτικός [eeperopteekos] haughty, presumptuous, arrogant.

ὑπεροχή, ἡ [eeperohee] superiority, predominance.

ὑπέροχος [eeperohos] superior, excellent, eminent.

ὑπεροψία, ἡ [eeperopseea] arrogance, disdain, haughtiness.

ὑπερπέραν, τό [eeperperan] the beyond, afterlife.

ὑπερπηδῶ [eeperpeedo] surmount ‖ jump over.

ὑπερπόντιος [eeperponteeos] overseas ‖ transmarine.

ὑπέρποτε [eeperpote] more than ever.

ὑπερσυντέλικος [eeperseenteleekos] (γραμμ) pluperfect (tense).

ὑπέρτασις, ἡ [eepertasees] high blood pressure.

ὑπέρτατος [eepertatos] highest, greatest, supreme.

ὑπέρτερος [eeperteros] superior to.

ὑπερτερῶ [eepertero] excel, exceed, surpass ‖ outnumber.

ὑπερτίμησις, ἡ [eeperteemeesees] overestimation ‖ (οἰκ) rise in price, increase in value.

ὑπερτιμῶ [eeperteemo] overvalue, overestimate ‖ (οἰκ) raise price of.

ὑπερτροφία, ἡ [eepertrofeea] (ἰατρ) hypertrophy.

ὑπέρυθροι [eepereethree] πλ: ~ ἀκτῖνες infrared rays.

ὑπέρυθρος [eepereethros] reddish.

ὑπερύψηλος [eepereepseelos] very high, exceedingly high.

ὑπερυψῶ [eepereepso] raise up ‖ exalt.

ὑπερφαλάγγισις, ἡ [eeperfalangeesees] outflanking.

ὑπερφίαλος [eeperfeealos] overweening, arrogant, insolent.

ὑπερφυσικός [eeperfeeseekos] supernatural ‖ (μεταφ) extraordinary, prodigious.

ὑπερώα, ἡ [eeperoa] palate.

ὑπερωκεάνειον, τό [eeperokeaneeon] liner.

ὑπερῷον, τό [eeperoon] attic, garret ‖ (θεάτρου) gallery.

ὑπερωρία, ἡ [eeperoreea] overtime.

ὑπεύθυνος [eepevtheenos] responsible, answerable.

ὑπέχω [eepeho] bear.

ὑπήκοος [eepeekoos] submissive, obedient ‖ (οὐσ) subject of state.

ὑπηκοότης, ἡ [eepeekootees] nationality, citizenship.

ὑπήνεμος [eepeenemos] (ναυτ) leeward.

ὑπηρεσία, ἡ [eepeereseea] service, attendance ‖ duty, employ ‖ (οἰκίας) domestic servant.

ὑπηρεσιακή [eepeereseeakee]: ~ κυβέρνησις caretaker government.

ὑπηρεσιακός [eepeereseeakos] of service.

ὑπηρέτης, ὁ [eepeeretees] servant.

ὑπηρέτρια, ἡ [eepeeretreea] maid.

ὑπηρετῶ [eepeereto] serve ‖ do one's military service.

ὑπναλέος [eepnaleos] drowsy, sleepy.

ὑπναρᾶς, ὁ [eepnaras] person who enjoys sleeping.

ὑπνοβάτης, ὁ [eepnovatees] sleepwalker.

ὕπνος, ὁ [eepnos] sleep.

ὕπνωσις, ἡ [eepnosees] hypnosis.

ὑπνωτίζω [eepnoteezo] hypnotize.

ὑπνωτικόν, τό [eepnoteekon] soporific drug, sleeping pill.

ὑπνωτισμός, ὁ [eepnoteesmos] hypnotism.

ὑπό [eepo] below, beneath ‖ (μέσον) by, with.

ὑπόβαθρον, τό [eepovathron] base, pedestal, stand.

ὑποβάλλω [eepovalo] submit, hand in ‖ (ὑποτάσσω) subject ‖ suggest, propose.

ὑποβαστάζω [eepovastazo] support, prop up, bear.

ὑποβιβάζω [eepoveevazo] lower ‖ reduce, diminish ‖ demote.

ὑποβλέπω [eepovlepo] suspect ‖ cast glances at, leer.

ὑποβλητικός [eepovleeteekos] evocative.

ὑποβοηθῶ [eepovoeetho] assist, back up, support.

ὑποβολεύς, ὁ [eepovolevs] prompter ‖ instigator.

ὑποβολή, ἡ [eepovolee] submission, presentation ‖ prompting, instigation.

ὑποβολιμαῖος [eepovoleemeos] spurious ‖ interposed, inserted.

ὑποβόσκω [eepovosko] smoulder ‖ lie hidden.

ὑποβρύχιον, τό [eepovreeheeon] submarine ‖ (μεταφ) kind of sweet.

ὑπογεγραμμένη, ἡ [eepoyegramenee] (iota) subscript.

ὑπόγειον, τό [eepoyeeon] basement, cellar.

ὑπόγειος [eepoγeeos] underground.
ὑπόγλυκος [eepoγleekos] sweetish.
ὑπογραμμίζω [eepoγrameezo] underline, emphasize.
ὑπογραφή, ἡ [eepoγrafee] signature.
ὑπογράφω [eepoγrafo] sign ‖ (μεταφ) approve, subscribe.
ὑπογράψας, ὁ [eepoγrapsas] signatory.
ὑποδαυλίζω [eepoδavleezo] fan the flame ‖ (μεταφ) foment, excite.
ὑποδεέστερος [eepoδeesteros] inferior, lower.
ὑπόδειγμα, τό [eepoδeeγma] model, example, specimen ‖ sample.
ὑποδειγματικός [eepoδeeγmateekos] exemplary, representative.
ὑποδεικνύω [eepoδeekneeo] indicate ‖ suggest, propose.
ὑπόδειξις, ἡ [eepoδeeksees] indication ‖ recommendation.
ὑποδέχομαι [eepoδehome] receive, welcome, greet.
ὑποδηλῶ [eepoδeelo] convey, indicate, hint at.
ὑπόδημα, τό [eepoδeema] shoe, boot.
ὑποδηματοποιεῖον, τό [eepoδeematopieeon] shoemaker's shop.
ὑπόδησις, ἡ [eepoδeesees] footgear, footwear.
ὑποδιαίρεσις, ἡ [eepoδieresees] subdivision.
ὑποδιαιρῶ [eepoδiero] subdivide.
ὑποδιαστολή, ἡ [eepoδeeastolee] decimal point ‖ (γραμμ) comma.
ὑποδιευθυντής, ὁ [eepoδieftheentees] assistant director, vice-principal, deputy manager.
ὑπόδικος, ὁ [eepoδeekos] the accused.
ὑπόδουλος [eepoδoulos] enslaved.
ὑποδουλώνω [eepoδoulono] subjugate, enslave, subdue.
ὑποδοχή, ἡ [eepoδohee] reception.
ὑποδύομαι [eepoδeeome] play the part of, assume a role.
ὑποζύγιον, τό [eepozeeγeeon] beast of burden.
ὑποθάλπω [eepothalpo] foment ‖ protect, maintain ‖ entertain, harbour.
ὑπόθεμα, τό [eepothema] suppository.
ὑπόθεσις, ἡ [eepothesees] conjecture, supposition ‖ matter, affair, business ‖ (δικαστηρίου) case, action ‖ (θεατρικοῦ ἔργου κτλ) subject, plot, matter, theme.
ὑποθετικός [eepotheteekos] hypothetical, speculative ‖ imaginary ‖ (γραμμ) conditional.
ὑποθέτω [eepotheto] suppose, assume.
ὑποθηκεύω [eepotheekevo] mortgage.
ὑποθήκη, ἡ [eepotheekee] mortgage.
ὑποθηκοφυλακεῖον, τό [eepotheekofeelakeeon] mortgage office.
ὑποκαθιστῶ [eepokatheesto] replace, substitute.
ὑποκάμισον, τό [eepokameeson] shirt.

ὑποκατάστασις, ἡ [eepokatastasees] replacement, substitution.
ὑποκατάστημα, τό [eepokatasteema] branch office ‖ (US) chain store.
ὑποκάτω [eepokato] below, beneath, under.
ὑπόκειμαι [eepokeeme] be subject to, be liable ‖ lie under.
ὑποκειμενικός [eepokeemeneekos] subjective.
ὑποκείμενον, τό [eepokeemenon] subject ‖ individual ‖ scamp.
ὑποκινῶ [eepokeeno] stir up, excite, incite.
ὑποκλέπτω [eepoklepto] purloin, pilfer.
ὑποκλίνομαι [eepokleenome] bow, bend ‖ yield.
ὑπόκλισις, ἡ [eepokleesees] bow, curtsy.
ὑποκόμης, ὁ [eepokomees] viscount.
ὑποκόπανος, ὁ [eepokopanos] butt of weapon, butt-end.
ὑποκοριστικόν, τό [eepokoreesteekon] diminutive.
ὑπόκοσμος, ὁ [eepokosmos] underworld.
ὑποκρίνομαι [eepokreenome] act, play the part of, impersonate ‖ dissemble.
ὑποκρισία, ἡ [eepokreeseea] hypocrisy.
ὑπόκρισις, ἡ [eepokreesees] pretending, acting ‖ dissembling.
ὑποκριτής, ὁ [eepokreetees] actor ‖ hypocrite.
ὑποκριτικός [eepokreeteekos] feigned, insincere.
ὑπόκρουσις, ἡ [eepokrousees] accompaniment.
ὑποκύπτω [eepokeepto] bend, submit, succumb ‖ yield.
ὑπόκωφος [eepokofos] hollow, deep ‖ smothered.
ὑπόλειμμα, τό [eepoleema] residue, remnant, rest.
ὑπολείπομαι [eepoleepome] be left ‖ be inferior to.
ὑπόληψις, ἡ [eepoleepsees] esteem ‖ credit, reputation.
ὑπολογίζω [eepoloγeezo] estimate, calculate ‖ consider.
ὑπολογισμός, ὁ [eepoloγeesmos] calculation, estimate ‖ account.
ὑπόλογος [eepoloγos] responsible, accountable, liable.
ὑπόλοιπον, τό [eepoleepon] left-over, remainder, balance.
ὑπόλοιπος [eepoleepos] remaining, rest of.
ὑπολοχαγός, ὁ [eepolohaγos] lieutenant.
ὑπομένω [eepomeno] endure, tolerate.
ὑπομιμνήσκω [eepomeemneesko] remind.
ὑπομισθῶνω [eepomeesthono] sublet.
ὑπόμνημα, τό [eepomneema] memorandum.
ὑπομνήματα, τά [eepomneemata] πλ commentary, memorabilia.
ὑπόμνησις, ἡ [eepomneesees] reminder ‖ suggestion.
ὑπομοίραρχος, ὁ [eepomeerarhos] lieutenant of gendarmerie.

ὑπομονεύω [eepomonevo] be patient ‖ endure.

ὑπομονή, ἡ [eepomonee] patience, endurance.

ὑπομονητικός [eepomoneeteekos] patient, enduring.

ὑποναύαρχος, ὁ [eeponavarhos] rear admiral.

ὑπόνοια, ἡ [eeponeea] suspicion ‖ surmise.

ὑπονομεύω [eeponomevo] undermine, sabotage.

ὑπόνομος, ὁ, ἡ [eeponomos] sewer ‖ (στρατ) mine.

ὑπονοώ [eeponoo] infer, mean.

ὑποπίπτω [eepopeepto] commit, fall into ‖ come to s.o.'s notice.

ὑποπλοίαρχος, ὁ [eepopleearhos] lieutenant ‖ first mate.

ὑποπόδιον, τό [eeporodeeon] footstool.

ὑποπροϊόν, τό [eepoproeeon] by-product.

ὑποπρόξενος, ὁ [eepoproksenos] viceconsul.

ὑποπτεύομαι [eepoptevome] suspect, have an idea.

ὕποπτος [eepoptos] suspect, suspicious, suspected.

ὑποσημείωσις, ἡ [eeposeemeeosees] footnote, annotation.

ὑποσιτισμός, ὁ [eeposeeteesmos] undernourishment, malnutrition.

ὑποσκάπτω [eeposkapto] undermine, sabotage.

ὑποσκελίζω [eeposkeleezo] upset . ‖ supplant.

ὑποσμηναγός, ὁ [eeposmeenaγos] flight lieutenant.

ὑποστάθμη, ἡ [eepostathmee] dregs, sediment, residue.

ὑπόστασις, ἡ [eepostasees] existence ‖ foundation, basis ‖ (ιατρ) hypostasis.

ὑποστατικόν, τό [eepostateekon] property, farm.

ὑπόστεγον, τό [eeposteγon] shed, hangar ‖ shelter.

ὑποστέλλω [eepostelo] strike, lower ‖ slow down, reduce.

ὑποστήριγμα, τό [eeposteereeγma] support, prop.

ὑποστηρίζω [eeposteereezo] prop up, support ‖ second, back ‖ maintain.

ὑποστήριξις, ἡ [eeposteereeksees] prop, support ‖ backing.

ὑποστράτηγος, ὁ [eepostrateeγos] majorgeneral.

ὑπόστρωμα, τό [eepostroma] substratum ‖ saddlecloth.

ὑποσυνείδητον, τό [eeposeeneeδeeton] subconscious.

ὑπόσχεσις, ἡ [eeposhesees] promise, pledge, engagement.

ὑπόσχομαι [eeposhome] promise, pledge.

ὑποταγή, ἡ [eepotaγee] obedience, subjection, submission.

ὑποτακτική, ἡ [eepotakteekee] subjective.

ὑποτακτικός [eepotakteekos] obedient, submissive.

ὑπότασις, ἡ [eepotasees] low blood pressure.

ὑποτάσσομαι [eepotasome] submit, give in.

ὑποτάσσω [eepotaso] subjugate, subdue.

ὑποτείνουσα, ἡ [eepoteenousa] hypotenuse.

ὑποτελής [eepotelees] subordinate, tributary, vassal.

ὑποτίθεμαι [eepoteetheme] be supposed ‖ suppose, consider.

ὑποτίμησις, ἡ [eepoteemeesees] reduction in price, depreciation ‖ underestimation.

ὑποτιμῶ [eepoteemo] underestimate ‖ lower the price of, depreciate.

ὑποτονθορύζω [eepotonthoreezo] murmur, mumble, hum.

ὑποτροπή, ἡ [eepotropee] relapse, deterioration.

ὑποτροφία, ἡ [eepotrofeea] scholarship.

ὑποτυπώδης [eepoteepoδees] sketchy, imperfectly formed.

ὕπουλος [eepoulos] shifty, underhand, cunning.

ὑπουργεῖον, τό [eepouryeeon] ministry.

ὑπουργικός [eepouryeekos] ministerial.

ὑπουργός, ὁ [eepouryos] minister ‖ (US) secretary.

ὑποφαινόμενος [eepofenomenos]: ὁ ~ the undersigned.

ὑποφερτός [eepofertos] tolerable ‖ passable.

ὑποφέρω [eepofero] bear, support, endure ‖ feel pain, suffer.

ὑποφώσκω [eepofosko] dawn, glimmer.

ὑποχείριος [eepoheereeos] under the power of, subject.

ὑποχθόνιος [eepohthoneeos] infernal, subterranean.

ὑποχονδρία, ἡ [eepohonδreea] hypochondria ‖ obsession.

ὑπόχρεος [eepohreos] obliged.

ὑποχρεώνω [eepohreono] oblige ‖ compel.

ὑποχρέωσις, ἡ [eepohreosees] obligation, duty.

ὑποχρεωτικός [eepohreoteekos] obligatory ‖ compulsory.

ὑποχώρησις, ἡ [eepohoreesees] withdrawal, yielding ‖ subsidence.

ὑποχωρῶ [eepohoro] withdraw, give way ‖ fall in, cave in.

ὑποψήφιος, ὁ [eepopseefeeos] candidate, applicant.

ὑποψηφιότης, ἡ [eepopseefeeotees] candidature, application.

ὑποψία, ἡ [eepopseea] suspicion, misgiving.

ὑποψιάζομαι [eepopseeazome] suspect, have suspicions.

ὕπτιος [eepteeos] lying on one's back.

ὑπώρεια, ἡ [eeporeea] foot of mountain.

ὕσκα, ἡ [eeska] tinder, touchwood.

ὕστατος [eestatos] last, final.

ὕστερα [eestera] afterwards, then, later ‖

furthermore ‖ ~ ἀπό after, following (this).

ὑστέρημα, τό [eestereema] shortage, deficiency ‖ small savings.

ὑστερία, ἡ [eestereea] hysteria.

ὑστερικός [eestereekos] hysterical.

ὑστερισμός, ὁ [eestereesmos] hysteria, hysterics.

ὑστερ(ι)νός [eester(ee)nos] later, ultimate, last.

ὑστεροβουλία, ἡ [eesterovouleea] afterthought ‖ deceit.

ὑστερόγραφον, τό [eesteroγrafon] postscript.

ὕστερον [eesteron] βλ ὕστερα.

ὕστερος [eesteros] later ‖ inferior ‖ ἐκ τῶν ὑστέρων on second thought, looking back.

ὑστερῶ [eestero] come after ‖ be inferior ‖ deprive.

ὑφάδι, τό [eefaδee] weft, woof.

ὑφαίνω [eefeno] weave, spin ‖ (μεταφ) plot.

ὕφαλα, τά [eefala] πλ beam ‖ part below waterline.

ὕφαλος, ὁ [eefalos] reef, shoal.

ὕφανσις, ἡ [eefansees] weaving ‖ weave.

ὑφαντός [eefantos] woven.

ὑφαντουργία, ἡ [eefantourγeea] textile industry, weaving industry.

ὑφαρπάζω [eefarpazo] obtain by fraud.

ὕφασμα, τό [eefasma] cloth, fabric, stuff, material ‖ ~ τα textiles.

ὕφεσις, ἡ [eefesees] decrease, abatement ‖ (βαρομέτρου) depression ‖ (μουσ) flat (note).

ὑφή, ἡ [eefee] texture, web, weave.

ὑφηγητής, ὁ [eefeeγeetees] lecturer ‖ (US) assistant professor.

ὑφήλιος, ἡ [eefeeleeos] earth, world, globe.

ὑφίσταμαι [eefeestame] bear, undergo, sustain ‖ (εἶμαι) exist, be in force.

ὑφιστάμενος, ὁ [eefeestamenos] subordinate, inferior.

ὕφος, τό [eefos] style ‖ air, look, tone.

ὑφυπουργός, ὁ [eefeepourγos] undersecretary of state.

ὑψηλός [eepseelos] high, towering, tall ‖ (μεταφ) lofty, great.

ὑψηλότης, ἡ [eepseelotees] Highness ‖ ἡ Α.Β. ~ Her Royal Highness.

ὑψηλόφρων [eepseelofron] generous ‖ highminded, haughty.

ὑψικάμινος, ἡ [eepseekameenos] blast furnace.

ὕψιλον, τό [eepseelon] the letter Y.

ὑψίπεδον, τό [eepseepeδon] plateau.

ὕψιστος [eepseestos] highest ‖ (οὐσ) God.

ὑψίφωνος, ὁ, ἡ [eepseefonos] tenor ‖ soprano.

ὑψόμετρον, τό [eepsometron] altitude.

ὕψος, τό [eepsos] height, altitude ‖ (μουσ) pitch.

ὕψωμα, τό [eepsoma] height, elevation ‖ hillock.

ὑψωμός, ὁ [eepsomos] lifting ‖ rise in price.

ὑψώνω [eepsono] raise, elevate ‖ increase ‖ hoist.

ὕψωσις, ἡ [eepsosees] raising, lifting, elevation ‖ rise in price.

Φ, φ

φάβα, ἡ [fava] yellow pea ‖ pea purée.

φαγάνα, ἡ [faγana] dredger.

φαγᾶς, ὁ [faγas] glutton, gourmand.

φαγγρί, τό [fangree] sea bream.

φαγέδαινα, ἡ [faγeδena] canker, cancerous sore.

φαγιάντζα, ἡ [faγeeantza] faïence.

φαγητόν, τό [faγeeton] meal, dish, food ‖ dinner.

φαγί, τό [faγee] food, meal.

φαγκότο, τό [fangoto] bassoon.

φαγοπότι, τό [faγopotee] revel, eating and drinking.

φαγούρα, ἡ [faγoura] itching, irritation.

φάγωμα, τό [faγoma] corrosion, disintegration ‖ (τσακωμός) quarrel, dispute, wrangling.

φαγωμάρα, ἡ [faγomara] itch, irritation ‖ (τσακωμός) discord, arguing, dispute.

φαγωμένος [faγomenos] eaten ‖ eroded ‖ εἶμαι ~ I've eaten.

φαγώσιμα, τά [faγoseema] πλ provisions, victuals.

φαγώσιμος [faγoseemos] eatable, edible.

φαεινή [faeenee]: ~ ἰδέα brainwave, bright idea.

φαΐ, τό [faee] food, meal.

φαιδρός [feδros] merry, cheerful ‖ (μεταφ) ridiculous.

φαιδρύνω [feδreeno] cheer up, gladden, enliven.

φαίνομαι [fenome] appear, come in sight ‖ seem, look ‖ show o.s. to be.

φαινόμενα, τά [fenomena] πλ: κατά τά ~ judging by appearances.

φαινομενικῶς [fenomeneekos] apparently, outwardly.

φαινόμενον, τό [fenomenon] wonder, prodigy ‖ phenomenon.

φαιός [feos] grey ‖ brown, dun.

φάκα, ἡ [faka] mousetrap ‖ snare.

φάκελλος, ὁ [fakelos] envelope ‖ file, cover, dossier, record.

φακή, ἡ [fakee] lentils.

φακίδα, ἡ [fakeeδa] freckle.

φακιόλι, τό [fakeeolee] kerchief, neckerchief.

φακίρης, ὁ [fakeerees] fakir.

φακός, ὁ [fakos] lens ‖ magnifying glass, magnifier.

φάλαγξ, ἡ [falanks] phalanx ‖ (στρατ) column ‖ (στοῖχος) row.

φάλαινα, ἡ [falena] whale.

φαλάκρα, ἡ [falakra] baldness ‖ bald head.

φαλακραίνω [falakreno] go bald.

φαλακρός [falakros] bald(-headed) ‖ bare.

φαλ(λ)ίρω [faleero] go bankrupt, fail, break.

φαλλός, ὁ [falos] phallus.

φαλτσέτα, ἡ [faltseta] shoemaker's knife, paring knife.

φαλτσάρω [faltsaro] be out of tune ‖ make a mistake.

φάλτσο, τό [faltso] wrong note, dissonance ‖ (μεταφ) mistake, fault, error.

φαμελίτης, ὁ [fameleetees] family man, head of the family.

φαμίλια, ἡ [fameeleea] family.

φάμπρικα, ἡ [fambreeka] factory ‖ fabrication, device, artifice.

φαμπρικάρω [fambreekaro] manufacture ‖ (μεταφ) fabricate, concoct, forge, invent.

φανάρι, τό [fanaree] lamp, light, lantern ‖ (αὐτοκινήτου) headlamp ‖ (φάρου) lighthouse.

φαναρτζῆς, ὁ [fanartzees] tinsmith ‖ lampmaker.

φανατίζω [fanateezo] make fanatical, fanaticize.

φανατικός [fanateekos] overzealous, fanatical ‖ (οὐσ) fanatic, zealot.

φανατισμός, ὁ [fanateesmos] fanaticism.

φανέλλα, ἡ [fanela] flannel ‖ vest ‖ woollen cloth.

φανερός [faneros] clear, plain, evident, certain.

φανερώνω [fanerono] reveal, make plain.

φανός, ὁ [fanos] lamp, lantern, street lamp.

φαντάζομαι [fantazome] imagine, fancy, think ‖ (πιστεύω) believe.

φαντάζω [fantazo] make an impression, stand out ‖ look glamorous.

φάνταρος, ὁ [fantaros] infantryman ‖ (US) buck private.

φαντασία, ἡ [fantaseea] imagination ‖ illusion ‖ (ὑπερηφάνεια) vanity, pride ‖ (μουσ) fantasia.

φαντασιοκόπος [fantasiokopos] dreamer, visionary.

φαντασιοπληξία, ἡ [fantaseeopleekseea] extravagant notion ‖ caprice, whim.

φαντασιώδης [fantaseeoðees] illusory, imaginary ‖ fictitious ‖ beyond imagination.

φάντασμα, τό [fantasma] phantom, ghost, spirit.

φαντασμαγορία, ἡ [fantasmaγoreea] phantasmagoria.

φαντασμένος [fantasmenos] presumptuous, vain.

φανταστικός [fantasteekos] illusory, imaginary ‖ fantastic, extravagant.

φανταχτερός [fantahteros] showy, bright ‖ gaudy, glaring.

φάντης, ὁ [fantees] (στά χαρτιά) knave.

φανφαρόνος, ὁ [fanfaronos] braggart, boaster, blusterer.

φάπα, ἡ [fapa] slap, box on the ear, smack.

φάρα, ἡ [fara] race, progeny, breed ‖ crew.

φαράγγι, τό [farangee] βλ **φάραγξ**.

φάραγξ, ἡ [faranks] gorge, gully, precipice, ravine.

φαράσι, τό [farasee] dustpan.

φαρδαίνω [farðeno] widen, broaden, become wider ‖ stretch, extend.

φάρδος, τό [farðos] width, breadth.

φαρδύνω [farðeeno] βλ **φαρδαίνω**.

φαρδύς [farðees] wide, large, broad, ample.

φαρέτρα, ἡ [faretra] quiver.

φαρί, τό [faree] steed.

φαρμακεῖον, τό [farmakeeon] chemist shop.

φαρμακέμπορος, ὁ [farmakemboros] chemist ‖ (US) druggist.

φαρμακερός [farmakeros] venomous ‖ spiteful, bitter.

φαρμάκι, τό [farmakee] poison ‖ (μεταφ) anything bitter.

φαρμακίλα, ἡ [farmakeela] bitter taste.

φάρμακον, τό [farmakon] drug, medicine, remedy.

φαρμακοποιός, ὁ [farmakopeeos] pharmacist, chemist ‖ (US) druggist.

φαρμακώνω [farmakono] poison ‖ (μεταφ) cause grief ‖ mortify.

φάρος, ὁ [faros] lighthouse, beacon.

φάρσα, ἡ [farsa] trick, farce ‖ practical joke.

φάρυγξ, ὁ [fareenks] pharynx, windpipe.

φαρφουρί, τό [farfouree] porcelain, china.

φασαρία, ἡ [fasareea] disturbance ‖ fuss, noise, bustle.

φασιανός, ὁ [faseeanos] pheasant.

φάσις, ἡ [fasees] phase ‖ change, turn ‖ aspect.

φασισμός, ὁ [faseesmos] fascism.

φασιστικός [faseesteekos] fascist.

φασκιά, ἡ [faskia] swaddling band, swaddling clothes.

φασκόμηλο, τό [faskomeelo] three-lobed sage, wild mountain tea.

φάσκω [fasko]: ~ καί ἀντιφάσκω contradict o.s.

φάσμα, τό [fasma] ghost, spirit ‖ (φυσική) spectrum.

φασματοσκόπιον, τό [fasmatoskopeeon] spectroscope.

φασόλι, τό [fasolee] haricot bean, kidney bean.

φασο(υ)λάδα, ἡ [faso(u)laða] bean soup.

φασο(υ)λάκια, τά [faso(u)lakeea] πλ green beans.

φασούλι, τό [fasoulee] βλ **φασόλι**.

φασουλῆς, ὁ [fasoulees] Jack and the Beanstalk ‖ Punch.

φάτνη, ἡ [fatnee] manger, crib, stall.

φατνίον, τό [fatneeon] (ἀνατ) alveolus.

φατρία, ἡ [fatreea] faction, clique, gang.

φατριάζω [fatreeazo] form factions, be factious.

φάτσα, ἡ [fatsa] face ‖ front ‖ (ἐπίρ) opposite.

Φ

φαυλόβιος [favloveeos] licentious, debauched.

φαυλοκρατία, ή [favlokrateea] political corruption.

φαύλος [favlos] wicked, depraved || ~ κύκλος vicious circle.

φαφλατάς, ὁ [faflatas] chatterer, mumbler.

φαφούτης, ὁ [fafoutees] toothless man, very old man.

Φεβρουάριος, ὁ [fevrouareeos] February.

φεγγάρι, τό [fengaree] moon.

φεγγίτης, ὁ [fengeetees] skylight, fanlight, garret window.

φεγγοβολῶ [fengovolo] shine brightly.

φέγγος, τό [fengos] light, gleam, splendour.

φέγγω [fengo] shine, give light.

φείδομαι [feedome] save, spare || be sparing of, be stingy.

φειδώ, ή [feedo] thrift, economy, frugality.

φειδωλός [feedolos] sparing, thrifty || stingy, mean, niggardly.

φελλός, ὁ [felos] cork.

φέλπα, ή [felpa] velveteen, plush.

φενάκη, ή [fenakee] false hair, wig || (μεταφ) deceit, deception.

φεουδαρχικός [feouδarheekos] feudal.

φέουδον, τό [feouδon] fief.

φερέγγυος [ferengeeos] solvent, trustworthy.

φερέλπις [ferelpees] full of promise || hopeful.

φερετζές, ὁ [feretzes] veil (of a Moslem woman).

φέρετρον, τό [feretron] coffin, bier.

φερμένος [fermenos] arrived, brought, imported.

φερμουάρ, τό [fermouar] zip fastener.

φέρνω [ferno] βλ φέρω.

φέρομαι [ferome] conduct, behave || be reputed, be held as.

φέρσιμο, τό [ferseemo] behaviour, conduct.

φέρω [fero] bring, carry, support || (στέλλω) fetch || (ἔχω πάνω μου) carry, have || (προξενῶ) cause || (παράγω) bear, bring forth, bring in, yield || (φορῶ) wear || (κατευθύνω) lead, conduct || ~ ἀντιρρήσεις protest || φερ'εἰπεῖν for example.

φέσι, τό [fesee] fez || γίνομαι ~ get dead drunk.

φέτα, ή [feta] slice || (τυρί) kind of white cheese.

φετινός [feteenos] of this year.

φέτος [fetos] this year.

φεῦ [fev] alas!, ah!, woe!

φευγάλα, ή [fevgala] flight, escape, stampede.

φευγαλέος [fevgaleos] fleeting.

φευγατίζω [fevgateezo] help to escape.

φευγᾶτος [fevgatos] gone, fled, run away, left.

φεύγω [fevgo] leave, depart, get away || escape, flee || run away from, shun.

φευκτέος [fevkteos] avoidable.

φήμη, ή [feemee] report, rumour || reputation || renown, repute || fame.

φημίζομαι [feemeezome] be well-known.

φηρίκι, τό [feereekee] kind of apple.

φθάνω [fthano] catch, overtake, attain || (μεταφ) equal, be equal to || arrive, reach || draw near || ~ σέ reach the point of, be reduced to || φθάνει νά provided that.

φθαρτός [fthartos] perishable, destructible, liable to decay.

φθείρ, ὁ, ή [ftheer] louse.

φθείρομαι [ftheerome] decay, wash away || (μεταφ) lose importance.

φθείρω [ftheero] damage, spoil || corrupt, pervert, taint.

φθινόπωρον, τό [ftheenoporon] autumn.

φθίνω [ftheeno] pine away || decay || decline, fail.

φθισικός [ftheeseekos] consumptive, tubercular.

φθίσις, ή [ftheesees] consumption || decline.

φθόγγος, ὁ [fthongos] voice, sound || (μουσ) note.

φθογγόσημον, τό [fthongoseemon] (musical) note.

φθονερός [fthoneros] envious of, jealous.

φθόνος, ὁ [fthonos] malicious envy, jealousy.

φθονῶ [fthono] be envious of, begrudge.

φθορά, ή [fthora] deterioration, damage, destruction || decay || loss.

φθορεύς, ὁ [fthorevs] seducer, corrupter || destroyer.

φθορισμός, ὁ [fthoreesmos] fluorescence.

φί, τό [fee] the letter Φ.

φιάλη, ή [feealee] bottle, flagon, flask.

φιγούρα, ή [feegoura] figure, image || (μεταφ) expression, air || κάνω ~ cut a fine figure.

φιγουράρω [feegouraro] show off, appear.

φιδές, ὁ [feeδes] vermicelli.

φίδι, τό [feeδee] snake, serpent.

φιδωτός [feeδotos] winding, twisting.

φίλαθλος, ὁ, ή [feelathlos] sports fan.

φιλαλήθης [feelaleethees] truthful.

φιλάνθρωπος, ὁ, ή [feelanthropos] philanthropist, charitable person.

φιλαράκος, ὁ [feelarakos] beau || chum, pal || scoundrel, rascal.

φιλάργυρος [feelaryeeros] niggardly, miserly || (ούσ) miser.

φιλάρεσκος [feelareskos] coquettish, spruce.

φιλαρμονική, ή [feelarmoneekee] (musical) band.

φιλαρχία, ή [feelarheea] love of authority.

φιλάσθενος [feelasthenos] sickly, weakly, puny.

φιλαυτία, ή [feelavteea] egoism, vanity, conceit.

φιλέκδικος [feelekδeekos] vindictive, revengeful.

φιλελευθερισμός, ὁ [feelelevthereesmos] liberalism.
φιλελεύθερος, ὁ [feelelevtheros] liberal.
φιλέλλην, ὁ, ἡ [feeleleen] philhellene.
φιλενάδα, ἡ [feelenaδa] girlfriend || (μεταφ) mistress.
φίλεργος [feeleryos] hard-working, fond of work.
φίλερις [feelerees] quarrelsome, contentious.
φιλές, ὁ [feeles] hairnet.
φιλέτο, τό [feeleto] fillet of meat || (ὕφασμα) piping || (διακόσμηση) strip, border.
φιλεύω [feelevo] make a present || entertain.
φίλη, ἡ [feelee] friend.
φιλήδονος [feeleeδonos] sensual, voluptuous.
φίλημα, τό [feeleema] kiss.
φιλήσυχος [feeleeseehos] peace-loving, calm, quiet, serene.
φιλί, τό [feelee] βλ **φίλημα**.
φιλία, ἡ [feeleea] friendship.
φιλικός [feeleekos] friendly || of a friend.
φίλιππος, ὁ, ἡ [feeleepos] horse lover || racegoer.
φιλιστρίνι, τό [feeleestreenee] porthole.
φιλιώνω [feeleeono] reconcile || be reconciled.
φίλμ, τό [feelm] film.
φίλντισι, τό [feelnteesee] mother-of-pearl || ivory.
φιλόδικος [feeloδeekos] litigious.
φιλόδοξος [feeloδoksos] ambitious || pretentious, showy.
φιλοδοξῶ [feeloδokso] be ambitious || aspire to, desire strongly.
φιλοδώρημα, τό [feeloδoreema] tip || gratuity.
φιλοκερδής [feelokerδees] greedy, covetous, eager for gain.
φιλολογία, ἡ [feeloloyeea] literature || philology.
φιλόλογος, ὁ [feeloloyos] man of letters, philologist || scholar.
φιλομαθής [feelomathees] fond of learning.
φιλόμουσος [feelomousos] lover of music || fond of learning.
φιλον(ε)ικία, ἡ [feeloneekeea] dispute, wrangle.
φιλόν(ε)ικος [feeloneekos] contentious.
φιλον(ε)ικῶ [feeloneeko] quarrel, wrangle.
φιλοξενία, ἡ [feelokseneea] hospitality.
φιλόξενος [feeloksenos] hospitable.
φιλοξενῶ [feelokseno] entertain, give hospitality, receive.
φιλοπαίγμων [feelopeymon] playful, frolicsome.
φιλοπατρία, ἡ [feelopatreea] patriotism.
φιλοπόλεμος [feelopolemos] warlike, martial.
φιλόπονος [feeloponos] assiduous, diligent, industrious.

φιλοπονῶ [feelopono] prepare assiduously.
φιλοπράγμων [feelopraymon] curious, inquiring, inquisitive.
φίλος, ὁ [feelos] friend || (ἐπιϑ) dear, friendly.
φιλοσοφία, ἡ [feelosofeea] philosophy.
φιλοσοφικός [feelosofeekos] philosophical.
φιλόσοφος, ὁ, ἡ [feelosofos] philosopher.
φιλόστοργος [feelostoryos] loving, affectionate.
φιλοτελισμός, ὁ [feeloteleesmos] philately.
φιλοτέχνημα, τό [feelotehneema] work of art.
φιλότεχνος [feelotehnos] art lover || artistic, skilful.
φιλοτιμία, ἡ [feeloteemeea] sense of honour, pride, self-respect, dignity.
φιλότιμο, τό [feeloteemo] βλ **φιλοτιμία**.
φιλότιμος [feeloteemos] eager to excel || obliging || having sense of pride and honour || generous.
φιλοτιμοῦμαι [feeloteemoume] make it a point of honour.
φιλοτιμῶ [feeloteemo] put s.o. on his dignity.
φιλοφρόνησις, ἡ [feelofroneesees] compliment, courtesy.
φιλόφρων [feelofron] courteous, affable, kindly, polite.
φίλτατος [feeltatos] dearest, most beloved.
φίλτρον, τό [feeltron] filter || philtre.
φιλύποπτος [feeleepoptos] distrustful, suspicious.
φιλύρα, ἡ [feeleera] lime tree.
φιλῶ [feelo] kiss, embrace.
φιμώνω [feemono] muzzle, gag || (μεταφ) silence, hush.
φίμωτρον, τό [feemotron] muzzle, gag.
φίνος [feenos] fine.
φιόγκος, ὁ [feeongos] knot, bow.
φιρίκι, τό [feereekee] kind of small apple.
φίρμα, ἡ [feerma] firm || trade name.
φίσα, ἡ [feesa] filing slip || gambling chip.
φίσκα [feeska] brimming over.
φιστίκι, τό [feesteekee] pistachio nut || ~ **ἀράπικο** monkey nut || peanut.
φιτίλι, τό [feeteelee] wick || (δυναμίτιδος) fuse.
φκυάρι, τό [fkeearee] βλ **φτυάρι**.
φλαμούρι, τό [flamouree] lime wood || lime blossom infusion.
φλάμπουρο, τό [flambouro] pennon, standard.
φλάουτο, τό [flaouto] flute.
φλέβα, ἡ [fleva] vein || (μεταλλεύματος) lode || (μεταφ) talent.
Φλεβάρης, ὁ [flevarees] February.
φλέγμα, τό [fleyma] phlegm, mucus || (μεταφ) coolness, unconcern.
φλεγματικός [fleymateekos] phlegmatic || stolid.
φλεγμονή, ἡ [fleymonee] inflammation, soreness.

φλέγομαι [fleyome] burn, ignite ‖ (μεταφ) flare up.

φλέγον [fleyon]: ~ ζήτημα topical problem.

φλερτάρω [flertaro] flirt with.

φλέψ, ἡ [fleps] βλ **φλέβα**.

φληναφῶ [fleenafo] prate, babble, prattle.

φλιτζάνι, τό [fleetzanee] cup(ful).

φλόγα, ἡ [floya] flame, blaze ‖ (μεταφ) passion, ardour.

φλογέρα, ἡ [floyera] shepherd's pipe, reed.

φλογερός [floyeros] burning, flaming ‖ (μεταφ) ardent, fervent.

φλογίζω [floyeezo] inflame, kindle.

φλογοβόλον, τό [floyovolon] flamethrower.

φλόγωσις, ἡ [floyosees] inflammation, soreness.

φλοιός, ὁ [fleeos] peel, rind ‖ (φυστικιοῦ) shell ‖ (δένδρου) bark ‖ (γῆς) crust.

φλοῖσβος, ὁ [fleesvos] rippling of waves ‖ babbling.

φλοκάτη, ἡ [flokatee] thick blanket, peasant's cape.

φλόκος, ὁ [flokos] jib.

φλομώνω [flomono] stun ‖ grow wan.

φλόξ, ἡ [floks] βλ **φλόγα**.

φλούδα, ἡ [flouda] βλ **φλοιός**.

φλουρί, τό [flouree] gold coin.

φλυαρία, ἡ [fleearea] gossiping, chatter, prattle.

φλύαρος [fleearos] talkative.

φλυαρῶ [fleearo] chatter, tattle, prattle.

φλύκταινα, ἡ [fleektena] blister ‖ pustule.

φλυτζάνι, τό [fleetzanee] cup(ful).

φοβᾶμαι [fovame] be afraid (of).

φοβέρα, ἡ [fovera] threat, menace, intimidation.

φοβερίζω [fovereezo] threaten, menace, intimidate.

φοβερός [foveros] terrible, frightful ‖ amazing, formidable.

φόβητρον, τό [foveetron] scarecrow ‖ bogey ‖ fright.

φοβητσιάρης [foveetseearees] fearful, timid, timorous.

φοβία, ἡ [foveea] fear, phobia.

φοβίζω [foveezo] frighten ‖ menace, threaten, intimidate.

φόβος, ὁ [fovos] fear, dread, fright.

φοβοῦμαι [fovoume] βλ **φοβᾶμαι**.

φόδρα, ἡ [fodra] lining.

φοίνιξ, ὁ [feeneeks] palm tree ‖ (καρπός) date ‖ (bird) phoenix.

φοίτησις, ἡ [feeteesees] attendance (at school) ‖ frequenting.

φοιτητής, ὁ [feeteetees] student.

φοιτῶ [feeto] be a student, attend a course of studies ‖ frequent.

φόλα, ἡ [fola] dog poison ‖ (παπουτσιοῦ) patch.

φολίς, ἡ [folees] scale.

φονεύς, ὁ [fonevs] murderer, assassin.

φονεύω [fonevo] murder, kill.

φονιᾶς, ὁ [fonias] murderer.

φονικό, τό [foneeko] murder, homicide, carnage.

φόνος, ὁ [fonos] murder, homicide.

φόντο, τό [fonto] bottom, base, back ‖ (ζωγραφιᾶς) background ‖ (κεφάλαιο) capital.

φόρα, ἡ [fora] impulse, impetus ‖ force ‖ βγάζω στή ~ bring into the open, uncover.

φορά, ἡ [fora] force ‖ course, run, impetus ‖ (κατεύθυνσις) direction ‖ (εὐκαιρία) time ‖ ἄλλη ~ another time ‖ ἄλλη μιά ~ once again ‖ μιά ~ once, only once.

φοράδα, ἡ [forada] mare.

φορατζῆς, ὁ [foratzees] tax collector.

φορβάς, ἡ [forvas] βλ **φοράδα**.

φορβή, ἡ [forvee] fodder, forage.

φορεῖον, τό [foreeon] stretcher, litter.

φόρεμα, τό [forema] dress, garment.

φορεσιά, ἡ [foresia] dress, suit of clothes ‖ attire.

φορεύς, ὁ [forevs] carrier, porter.

φορητός [foreetos] portable, easy to carry.

φόρμα, ἡ [forma] form, shape ‖ mould, matrix ‖ (ἐργάτου) overall ‖ (ντοκουμέντο) form, document ‖ σέ ~ in good form, in tiptop shape.

φοροδιαφυγή, ἡ [forodeeafeeyee] tax evasion.

φορολογία, ἡ [foroloyeea] taxation ‖ tax, rate.

φορολογούμενος, ὁ [foroloyoumenos] taxpayer, ratepayer.

φορολογῶ [foroloyo] tax, put a tax on.

φόρος, ὁ [foros] tax, rate, duty.

φορτηγόν, τό [forteeyon] lorry ‖ (US) truck ‖ (ναυτ) cargo vessel.

φορτηγός [forteeyos] freight-carrying, of transport.

φορτίζω [forteezo] charge with electricity.

φορτικός [forteekos] intrusive, importunate ‖ troublesome.

φορτίον, τό [forteeon] cargo, load ‖ burden, charge, weight.

φορτοεκφορτωτής, ὁ [fortoekfortotees] stevedore.

φόρτος, ὁ [fortos] burden, heavy load.

φορτσάρω [fortsaro] force ‖ intensify ‖ (ἀνέμου) increase, strengthen.

φόρτωμα, τό [fortoma] loading ‖ (μεταφ) burden, care.

φορτώνομαι [fortonome] pester, annoy, bother.

φορτώνω [fortono] load, pile (on) ‖ take on cargo.

φορτωτική, ἡ [fortoteekee] bill of lading.

φορῶ [foro] wear ‖ put on, get into ‖ carry.

φουγάρο, τό [fouyaro] funnel, flue, tall chimney, smokestack.

φουκαράς, ὁ [foukaras] poor devil ‖ unfortunate fellow.

φούμαρα, τά [foumara] πλ boasting ‖ pie in the sky.
φουμάρω [foumaro] smoke.
φοῦμος, ὁ [foumos] soot ‖ lampblack.
φούντα, ἡ [founta] tassel ‖ tuft, crest.
φουντάρω [fountaro] (ναυτ) sink ‖ cast anchor.
φουντούκι, τό [fountoukee] hazelnut.
φουντώνω [fountono] become bushy ‖ stretch out, spread ‖ expand.
φουντωτός [fountotos] bushy, thick.
φούξια, ἡ [foukseea] fuchsia.
φούρια, ἡ [foureea] haste.
φούρκα, ἡ [fourka] rage, anger ‖ (κρεμάλα) gallows, gibbet.
φουρκέτα, ἡ [fourketa] hairpin.
φουρκίζω [fourkeezo] vex, harass ‖ (κρεμῶ) hang.
φούρναρης, ὁ [fournarees] baker.
φουρνάρικο, τό [fournareeko] bakery, baker's shop.
φουρνέλο, τό [fournelo] grid ‖ blasting charge.
φουρνιά, ἡ [fournia] ovenful ‖ (μεταφ) batch.
φοῦρνος, ὁ [fournos] oven ‖ bakery ‖ kiln, furnace.
φουρτούνα, ἡ [fourtouna] tempest, storm ‖ rough sea ‖ (μεταφ) calamity, misfortune.
φούσκα, ἡ [fouska] bladder ‖ (παιχνίδι) balloon ‖ blister ‖ soap bubble.
φουσκάλα, ἡ [fouskala] blister ‖ bubble.
φουσκί, τό [fouskee] manure, dung.
φουσκοθαλασσιά, ἡ [fouskothalasia] surge of sea.
φούσκωμα, τό [fouskoma] inflation, swelling ‖ swaggering.
φουσκωμένος [fouskomenos] swollen, inflated, puffed up.
φουσκώνω [fouskono] swell, inflate, blow up ‖ (λάστιχο) pump ‖ (μεταφ) exaggerate ‖ (ἐνοχλῶ) irritate ‖ (ζύμην) rise ‖ (ἀναπνοή) puff, pant ‖ (μεταφ) puff o.s. up.
φουσκωτός [fouskotos] puffed, inflated ‖ curved.
φούστα, ἡ [fousta] skirt.
φουστανέλλα, ἡ [foustanela] kilt.
φουστάνι, τό [foustanee] gown, dress, frock.
φούχτα, ἡ [fouhta] handful ‖ hollow of hand.
φραγγέλιον, τό [frangeleeon] whip, lash.
Φράγκικος [frangeekos] Frankish ‖ Roman Catholic ‖ West European.
Φράγκος, ὁ [frangos] Frank ‖ Roman Catholic.
φράγκο, τό [frango] franc ‖ drachma.
Φραγκολεβαντίνος, ὁ [frangolevanteenos] Levantine.
φραγκόπαππας, ὁ [frangopapas] Roman Catholic priest.
φραγκοστάφυλο, τό [frangostafeelo] red currant.

φραγκόσυκο, τό [frangoseeko] prickly pear.
φράγμα, τό [frayma] enclosure, fence ‖ barrage, dam ‖ barrier.
φραγμός, ὁ [fraymos] fence, barrier ‖ (στρατ) barrage.
φράζω [frazo] surround, hedge ‖ bar, block up, stop, obstruct.
φράκο, τό [frako] dress coat, tails.
φράκτης, ὁ [fraktees] fence, enclosure, fencing.
φραμπαλᾶς, ὁ [frambalas] furbelow.
φράντζα, ἡ [frantza] fringe.
φραντζόλα, ἡ [frantzola] long loaf.
φράξιμο, τό [frakseemo] enclosing, fencing ‖ stopping up, blockage.
φράουλα, ἡ [fraoula] strawberry.
φράπα, ἡ [frapa] kind of large citrus fruit, grapefruit.
φρασεολογία, ἡ [fraseoloyeea] phraseology.
φράσις, ἡ [frasees] phrase ‖ period.
φράσσω [fraso] βλ φράζω.
φράχτης, ὁ [frahtees] fence, enclosure, fencing, hedge.
φρέαρ, τό [frear] well ‖ (μεταλλεῖον) pit, shaft.
φρεάτιον, τό [freateeon] small well.
φρεγάδα, ἡ [freyada] frigate.
φρένα, τά [frena] πλ reason, senses ‖ brakes.
φρενάρισμα, τό [frenareesma] braking.
φρενάρω [frenaro] brake ‖ (μεταφ) check.
φρένες, οἱ [frenes] πλ mind, reason, wits ‖ ἔξω φρενῶν off one's head, enraged ‖ unbelievable.
φρενιάζω [freneeazo] get furious, fret and fume.
φρενῖτις, ἡ [freneetees] fury, frenzy ‖ insanity.
φρένο, τό [freno] brake.
φρενοβλαβής [frenovlavees] mentally disturbed.
φρενοκομεῖον, τό [frenokomeeon] madhouse, lunatic asylum.
φρενολογία, ἡ [frenoloyeea] phrenology.
φρενοπαθής [frenopathees] βλ φρενοβλαβής.
φρεσκάδα, ἡ [freskada] freshness ‖ coolness, chilliness.
φρεσκάρω [freskaro] freshen, cool ‖ (ὁ καιρός) become worse.
φρέσκο, τό [fresko] fresco ‖ coolness, freshness, chilliness ‖ στό ~ in quod, in prison.
φρέσκος [freskos] fresh, new, recent ‖ cool.
φρικαλέος [freekaleos] horrible, hideous, ghastly.
φρικαλεότης, ἡ [freekaleotees] atrocity, savagery.
φρίκη, ἡ [freekee] terror, horror ‖ (ἐπιφ) frightful!
φρικίασις, ἡ [freekeeasees] shuddering, shivering.
φρικιῶ [freekeeo] shiver, shudder ‖ be disgusted.
φρικτός [freektos] (θέαμα) horrible,

ghastly ‖ (ἐμφάνισις) hideous ‖ (καιρός) horrid, vile ‖ awful.

φρικώδης [freekodees] βλ **φρικτός**.

φρίσσω [freeso] quiver, rustle ‖ shudder ‖ be horrified.

φρόκαλο, τό [frokalo] sweepings, rubbish ‖ broom.

φρόνημα, τό [froneema] opinion, sentiment, morale ‖ ~τα political convictions.

φρονηματίζω [froneemateezo] inspire self-confidence, render self-confident.

φρόνησις, ἡ [froneesees] prudence, wariness, circumspection.

φρόνιμα [froneema] (ἐπιφ) behave yourself!

φρονιμάδα, ἡ [froneemada] wisdom, prudence ‖ moderation ‖ (παιδιοῦ) quietness, good behaviour ‖ (γυναικός) modesty, chastity.

φρονιμεύω [froneemevo] become prudent, grow wise, be well-behaved.

φρονιμίτης, ὁ [froneemeetees] wisdom tooth.

φρόνιμος [froneemos] reasonable, sound, well-behaved ‖ virtuous, wise.

φροντίζω [fronteezo] look after, care for ‖ see to.

φροντίδα, ἡ [fronteeda] concern, care, anxiety.

φροντίδες, οἱ [fronteedes] πλ things to do, cares.

φροντίς, ἡ [frontees] βλ **φροντίδα**.

φροντιστήριον, τό [fronteesteereeon] coaching school ‖ prep school.

φρονῶ [frono] think, suppose, believe, consider.

φροῦδος [froudos] vain, useless, futile.

φρουρά, ἡ [froura] lookout, guard ‖ garrison.

φρούραρχος, ὁ [frourarhos] garrison commander.

φρούριον, τό [froureeon] fortress, stronghold.

φρουρός, ὁ [frouros] guard, sentinel, sentry ‖ (μεταφ) guardian.

φρουρῶ [frouro] guard, keep watch, stand sentry.

φροῦτο, τό [frouto] fruit, dessert.

φρυάττω [freeato] be furious, fume.

φρύγανα, τά [freeyana] πλ dry firewood, twigs.

φρυγανιά, ἡ [freeyania] toast.

φρύδι, τό [freedee] eyebrow.

φταίξιμο, τό [ftekseemo] fault, error, mistake, blame.

φταίχτης, ὁ [ftehtees] person responsible, culprit.

φταίω [fteo] be responsible, be to blame ‖ make a mistake.

φτάνω [ftano] βλ **φθάνω**.

φτελιά, ἡ [ftelia] elm (tree).

φτέρη, ἡ [fteree] fern.

φτέρνα, ἡ [fterna] heel.

φτερνίζομαι [fterneezome] sneeze.

φτέρνισμα, τό [fterneesma] sneeze, sneezing.

φτερό, τό [ftero] feather, plume ‖ wing ‖ (ξεσκονίσματος) feather duster ‖ (αὐτοκινήτου) mudguard ‖ (US) fender.

φτερούγα, ἡ [fterouya] wing.

φτερουγίζω [fterouyeezo] flutter, flap.

φτηναίνω [fteeneno] cheapen, become cheaper, go down.

φτήνεια, ἡ [fteeneea] cheapness, low price.

φτηνός [fteenos] cheap.

φτιά(χ)νομαι [ftea(h)nome] make up one's face ‖ look better.

φτιά(χ)νω [ftea(h)no] arrange, tidy up, correct ‖ (κατασκευάζω) make ‖ have made ‖ do.

φτιασίδι, τό [fteaseedee] rouge, cosmetic ‖ make-up.

φτιαχτός [fteeahtos] fabricated, affected.

φτυάρι, τό [fteearee] shovel, spade, scoop.

φτύνω [fteeno] spit, expectorate ‖ spit out.

φτύσιμο, τό [fteeseemo] spitting.

φτυστός [fteestos]: ~ ὁ πατέρας του the spitting image of his father.

φτωχαίνω [ftoheno] impoverish, make poor ‖ become poor.

φτώχεια, ἡ [ftoheea] poverty, destitution.

φτωχεύω [ftohevo] become poor ‖ go bankrupt.

φτωχικό, τό [ftoheeko] humble abode (of a person).

φτωχικός [ftoheekos] poor, mean, scant ‖ shabby.

φτωχός [ftohos] poor, needy, penniless.

φυγαδεύω [feeyadevo] facilitate s.o.'s escape.

φυγάς, ὁ, ἡ [feeyas] runaway, deserter, fugitive, renegade.

φυγή, ἡ [feeyee] escape, fleeing, flight.

φυγοδικία, ἡ [feeyodeekeea] default.

φυγόδικος, ὁ, ἡ [feeyodeekos] defaulter.

φυγόκεντρος [feeyokentros] centrifugal.

φυγόπονος [feeyoponos] lazy ‖ (οὐσ) slacker, shirker.

φυγόστρατος, ὁ [feeyostratos] defaulting conscript, deserter.

φύκια, τά [feekeea] πλ seaweed.

φυλάγομαι [feelayome] take precautions, take care.

φυλάγω [feelayo] guard, protect ‖ mind, tend ‖ (ἀντικείμενον) keep, lay aside ‖ lie in wait for.

φύλακας, ὁ [feelakas] keeper, guardian, watchman, guard, caretaker.

φυλακεῖον, τό [feelakeeon] guardhouse, post.

φυλακή, ἡ [feelakee] prison, jail.

φυλακίζω [feelakeezo] incarcerate, imprison.

φυλάκισις, ἡ [feelakeesees] imprisonment.

φυλακισμένος, ὁ [feelakeesmenos] prisoner.

φύλαξ, ὁ [feelaks] βλ φύλακας.
φυλά(σσ)ω [feela(s)o] βλ φυλάγω.
φυλάττω [feelato] βλ φυλάγω.
φύλαρχος, ὁ [feelarhos] tribal chief.
φυλαχτό, τό [feelahto] talisman, amulet, charm.
φυλετικός [feeleteekos] tribal, racial.
φυλή, ή [feelee] race, tribe, line.
φυλλάδα, ή [feelada] booklet, pamphlet, brochure.
φυλλάδιον, τό [feeladeeon] pamphlet ‖ instalment, issue, part.
φυλλοκάρδια, τά [feelokarδeea] πλ bottom of one's heart.
φυλλομετρῶ [feelometro] turn pages of, skim over, run through.
φύλλον, τό [feelon] leaf ‖ (λουλουδιοῦ) petal ‖ (χαρτιοῦ κτλ) sheet ‖ (σελίς) page ‖ (πόρτας κτλ) shutter, leaf ‖ (χαρτοπαιξίας) (playing) card ‖ (ἐφημερίς) newspaper ‖ ~ πορείας marching orders.
φυλλοξήρα, ή [feelokseera] phylloxera.
φυλλορροῶ [feeloroo] shed leaves, shed petals ‖ (μεταφ) fade (of hope).
φύλλωμα, τό [feeloma] foliage, leafage.
φῦλον, τό [feelon] sex ‖ race.
φυματικός [feemateekos] consumptive, tubercular.
φυματίωσις, ή [feemateeosees] tuberculosis, consumption.
φύομαι [feeome] grow, bud, sprout.
φύρα, ή [feera] loss of weight, waste.
φυραίνω [feereeno] shorten, shrink ‖ lose weight, lose volume.
φύραμα, τό [feerama] paste, dough ‖ blend ‖ (μεταφ) character, sort.
φύρδην [feerδeen]: ~ μίγδην pell-mell, helter-skelter.
φυρός [feeros] cracked, shrunken ‖ lacking in weight.
φυσαλ(λ)ίς, ή [feesalees] bubble ‖ blister.
φυσαρμόνικα, ή [feesarmoneeka] accordion ‖ mouth organ.
φυσέκι, τό [feesekee] cartridge ‖ roll (of coins).
φυσερό, τό [feesero] bellows.
φύση, ή [feesee] nature.
φύσημα, τό [feeseema] breath ‖ puff ‖ breathing.
φυσίγγιον, τό [feeseengeeon] cartridge.
φῦσιγξ, ή [feeseenks] ampoule for serum.
φυσικά, τά [feeseeka] πλ physics.
φυσικά [feeseeka] naturally, as a matter of fact ‖ φυσικῷ τῷ λόγῳ naturally, of course.
φυσική, ή [feeseekee] physics, natural philosophy.
φυσικό, τό [feeseeko] custom, habit.
φυσικός [feeseekos] natural ‖ physical ‖ (οὐσ) physicist.
φυσικότης, ή [feeseekotees] naturalness, artlessness.
φυσιογνωμία, ή [feeseeoγnomeea] cast of

features ‖ countenance ‖ well-known person.
φυσιοδίφης, ὁ [feeseeoδeefees] naturalist.
φυσιολάτρης, ὁ [feeseeolatrees] lover of nature.
φυσιολογία, ή [feeseeoloγeea] physiology.
φυσιολογικός [feeseeoloγeekos] physiological ‖ (μεταφ) normal.
φύσις, ή [feesees] nature ‖ character, temper ‖ φύσει by nature.
φυσομανῶ [feesomano] rage.
φυσῶ [feeso] blow up ‖ puff, blow out ‖ pant ‖ φυσάει it's windy.
φυτεία, ή [feeteea] plantation ‖ vegetation, bed of vegetables.
φύτε(υ)μα, τό [feete(v)ma] planting.
φυτευτός [feetevtos] planted, cultivated.
φυτεύω [feetevo] plant, lay out ‖ (μεταφ) lodge, stick.
φυτικός [feeteekos] vegetable.
φυτοζωῶ [feetozoo] live in poverty, scrape through.
φυτοκομία, ή [feetokomeea] horticulture.
φυτολογία, ή [feetoloγeea] botany.
φυτόν, τό [feeton] plant, vegetable.
φύτρα, ή [feetra] germ, embryo ‖ (μεταφ) lineage, origin.
φυτρώνω [feetrono] grow, germinate, sprout.
φυτώριον, τό [feetoreeon] nursery, plantation, seedbed.
φώκια, ή [fokeea] seal.
φωλεά, ή [folea] nest, den, lair, hole ‖ (μεταφ) hovel.
φωλιάζω [foleeazo] nestle, nest.
φωνάζω [fonazo] shout, call, summon ‖ cry, scream, shriek.
φωνακλᾶς, ὁ [fonaklas] loud talker, noisy talker.
φωνασκῶ [fonasko] bawl, shout.
φωνή, ή [fonee] sound ‖ voice ‖ cry, shout, scream.
φωνῆεν, τό [fonien] vowel.
φωνητική, ή [foneeteekee] phonetics.
φωνητικός [foneeteekos] vocal ‖ phonetic, phonic.
φωνοληψία, ή [fonoleepseea] recording.
φωνοταινία, ή [fonoteneea] talkie.
φωρῶμαι [forome] be caught red-handed ‖ be shown up.
φῶς, τό [fos] light ‖ (μεταφ) sight ‖ knowledge, illumination.
φωστήρ(ας), ὁ [fosteer(as)] luminary ‖ (μεταφ) learned, erudite person.
φωσφόρος, ὁ [fosforos] phosphorus.
φῶτα, τά [fota] πλ lights ‖ (μεταφ) knowledge, learning ‖ (ἐκκλ) Epiphany.
φωταγωγός, ὁ [fotaγoγos] light well, skylight.
φωταγωγῶ [fotaγoγo] illuminate.
φωταέριον, τό [fotaereeon] gas(lighting).
φωταυγής [fotavγees] bright, brilliant, luminous.

φωταψία, ἡ [fotapseea] illumination.
φωτεινός [foteenos] luminous, light, bright ‖ clear, lucid.
φωτιά, ἡ [fotia] fire ‖ (καπνιστοῦ) light ‖ (μεταφ) great heat ‖ fury ‖ (σέ τιμή) costliness.
φωτίζω [foteezo] illuminate, light up, light ‖ enlighten, inform.
φώτιση, ἡ [foteesee] βλ **φώτισις**.
φώτισις, ἡ [foteesees] enlightenment ‖ inspiration.
φωτισμός, ὁ [foteesmos] lighting, illumination.
φωτοβολία, ἡ [fotovoleea] brightness, luminosity.
φωτοβολίς, ἡ [fotovolees] flare.
φωτογενής [fotoyenees] photogenic.
φωτογραφεῖον, τό [fotoyrafeeon] photographic studio.
φωτογραφία, ἡ [fotoyrafeea] photograph ‖ photography.
φωτογραφική, ἡ [fotoyrafeekee] photography ‖ ~ **μηχανή** camera.
φωτογραφικός [fotoyrafeekos] photographic.
φωτογράφος, ὁ [fotoyrafos] photographer.
φωτόμετρον, τό [fotometron] light meter.
φωτοσκίασις, ἡ [fotoskeeasees] shading, light and shade.
φωτοστέφανος, ὁ [fotostefanos] halo ‖ (μεταφ) glory, prestige.
φωτοτυπία, ἡ [fototeepeea] photostatic copy.
φωτοχυσία, ἡ [fotoheeseea] illumination.

Χ, χ

χαβάνι, τό [havanee] (brass) mortar.
χαβᾶς, ὁ [havas] tune, air, melody.
χαβιάρι, τό [haviaree] caviar.
χαβούζα, ἡ [havouza] cistern, reservoir.
χαγιάτι, τό [hayiatee] upper gallery round courtyard.
χάδια, τά [hadeea] πλ petting, cajolery.
χαζεύω [hazevo] gape ‖ idle about, loiter.
χάζι, τό [hazee] pleasure, delight ‖ τό **κάνω** ~ it entertains me.
χαζός [hazos] stupid, silly, foolish.
χαϊβάνι, τό [haeevanee] beast ‖ (μεταφ) jackass.
χάϊδεμα, τό [haeedema] caressing, pat, stroke ‖ (μεταφ) cajolery.
χαϊδευτικός [haeedevteekos] caressing, affectionate ‖ (ἄνεμος) soft.
χαϊδεμένος [haeedemenos] spoilt.
χαϊδεύομαι [haeedevome] nuzzle, cuddle ‖ seek attention.
χαϊδεύω [haeedevo] caress, fondle, pat ‖ pet, spoil ‖ fawn upon.
χαϊδιάρης [haeedeearees] fond of being caressed.
χαίνω [heno] gape, be wide open.

χαιρέκακος [herekakos] malicious, mischievous.
χαίρετε [herete] (ἐπιφ) hello!, good day! ‖ be seeing you!
χαιρετίζω [hereteezo] hail, greet ‖ salute.
χαιρέτισμα, τό [hereteesma] salute, greeting, salutation, bow.
χαιρετισμός, ὁ [hereteesmos] βλ **χαιρέτισμα**.
χαιρετῶ [hereto] βλ **χαιρετίζω**.
χαίρομαι [herome] be happy ‖ enjoy.
χαίρω [hero] be pleased ‖ ~ **ἄκρας ὑγείας** be in tiptop shape.
χαίτη, ἡ [hetee] mane, shock of hair.
χακί, τό [hakee] khaki.
χάλαζα, ἡ [halaza] βλ **χαλάζι**.
χαλάζι, τό [halazee] hail.
χαλαζίας, ὁ [halazeeas] quartz.
χαλάλι [halalee]: ~ **σου** you merit it, you can have it.
χαλαρός [halaros] relaxed, slack, loose.
χαλαρώνω [halarono] unbend ‖ (σχοινί) loosen, slacken ‖ (μεταφ) relax ‖ (προσπά-θειαν) abate, ease up ‖ (ζῆλον) cool.
χάλασμα, τό [halasma] ruin, demolition ‖ (μηχανῆς) putting out of order ‖ ruin.
χαλασμένος [halasmenos] rotten, turned bad ‖ broken, not working ‖ damaged, demolished.
χαλασμός, ὁ [halasmos] demolition, destruction ‖ (μεταφ) disturbance, storm, excitement ‖ catastrophe.
χαλάστρα, ἡ [halastra]: **μοῦ κάναν** ~ they foiled my plans, they cramped my style.
χαλβᾶς, ὁ [halvas] halva ‖ (μεταφ) indolent person, silly fellow.
χαλεπός [halepos] arduous, difficult, wearisome.
χαλί, τό [halee] carpet, rug.
χάλια, τά [haleea] πλ bad condition, sad plight.
χαλίκι, τό [haleekee] pebble, small stone, gravel.
χαλιμά, ἡ [haleema]: **τά παραμύθια τῆς** ~**ς** Arabian Nights.
χαλιναγωγῶ [haleenayoyo] lead by the bridle ‖ (μεταφ) check, curb ‖ (πάθη) control, curb.
χαλινάρι, τό [haleenaree] bridle, bit, rein ‖ (μεταφ) curbing, holding back.
χαλινός, ὁ [haleenos] βλ **χαλινάρι**.
χαλκᾶς, ὁ [halkas] ring, link.
χαλκεῖον, τό [halkeeon] coppersmith's forge ‖ (μεταφ) fabrication, concoction.
χαλκεύω [halkevo] work copper ‖ (μεταφ) fabricate.
χαλκιᾶς, ὁ [halkeeas] coppersmith ‖ tin-smith.
χάλκινος [halkeenos] of copper.
χαλκογραφία, ἡ [halkoyrafeea] copperplate engraving, art of copperplating.
χαλκομανία, ἡ *[halkomaneea] transfer design.

χαλκός, ὁ [halkos] copper, brass, bronze.
χαλκωματάς, ὁ [halkomatas] βλ χαλκιᾶς.
χαλνῶ [halno] βλ χαλῶ.
χαλύβδινος [haleevðeenos] made of steel.
χάλυψ, ὁ [haleeps] steel.
χαλῶ [halo] demolish, break, ruin, spoil ‖ (φθείρω) wear out ‖ (νεῦρα) fret ‖ (ὑγείαν) break down ‖ (δαπανῶ) spend, consume ‖ (διαφθείρω) corrupt, pervert ‖ (νόμισμα) change ‖ (δόντι) decay ‖ (κρέας) taint, go bad ‖ ~ τόν κόσμον move heaven and earth, make a fuss.
χαμαί [hame] down, on the ground.
χαμαιλέων, ὁ [hameleon] chameleon ‖ (βοτ) ground thistle.
χαμαιπετής [hamepetees] creeping ‖ (μεταφ) grovelling, servile.
χαμαιτυπεῖον, τό [hameteepeeon] brothel, whorehouse.
χαμάλης, ὁ [hamalees] porter ‖ (μεταφ) vulgar fellow, scoundrel.
χαμαλίκι, τό [hamaleekee] hard work, arduous labour.
χαμάμι, τό [hamamee] Turkish bath.
χαμένα [hamena]: τά ἔχω ~ be mixed up, be bewildered.
χαμένος [hamenos] lost, disappeared ‖ (στά χαρτιά) loser ‖ (μεταφ) scoundrel, rascal ‖ scatterbrain.
χαμερπής [hamerpees] vile, mean, crawling, low.
χαμηλός [hameelos] low ‖ (φωνή) gentle, soft, subdued.
χαμηλοφώνως [hameelofonos] in an undertone, softly.
χαμηλώνω [hameelono] lower, reduce, bring down ‖ subside.
χαμίνι, τό [hameenee] street urchin, mischievous youngster.
χαμόγελο, τό [hamoyelo] smile.
χαμογελῶ [hamoyelo] smile.
χαμόκλαδο, τό [hamoklaðo] shrub.
χαμομήλι, τό [hamomeelee] camomile.
χαμός, ὁ [hamos] loss, destruction, ruin ‖ death.
χάμουρα, τά [hamoura] πλ harness, trappings.
χαμπάρι, τό [hambaree] piece of news ‖ παίρνω ~ become aware, perceive.
χαμψί, τό [hampsee] anchovy.
χάμω [hamo] βλ χαμαί.
χάνδαξ, ὁ [hanðaks] ditch, drain, trench ‖ (ὀχυροῦ) moat.
χάνδρα, ἡ [hanðra] bead.
χάνι, τό [hanee] country inn, lodging house.
χανούμισσα, ἡ [hanoumeesa] Turkish lady.
χαντάκι, τό [hantakee] βλ χάνδαξ.
χαντακώνω [hantakono] (μεταφ) destroy, ruin.
χάντρα, ἡ [hantra] βλ χάνδρα.
χάνομαι [hanome] lose o.s., ruin o.s., get lost ‖ νά χαθῆς go to hell! ‖ χάσου get out of my sight!

χάνω [hano] lose, go astray ‖ (εὐκαιρίαν) let slip ‖ (καιρόν) waste time ‖ (τραῖνο) lose, miss ‖ become disconcerted, get confused.
χάος, τό [haos] chaos, wild disorder ‖ bottomless pit.
χάπι, τό [hapee] pill.
χαρά, ἡ [hara] joy ‖ (ὑπερβολική) delight, glee ‖ pleasure, enjoyment ‖ ~ θεοῦ delight ‖ μιά ~ very well, splendidly ‖ γειά ~ so long!, good-bye! ‖ hello! ‖ ~ στό πρᾶμα wonderful!, it's nothing! (ironic).
χαραγή, ἡ [harayee] tracing, engraving ‖ incision, cut.
χάραγμα, τό [harayma] βλ χαραγή.
χαράδρα, ἡ [haraðra] ravine, gorge, gully.
χαράζω [harazo] cut, engrave ‖ rule lines ‖ trace ‖ (δρόμου κτλ) mark out, lay out.
χάρακας, ὁ [harakas] straight edge, ruler.
χαρακιά, ἡ [harakia] scratch, incision, mark ‖ groove ‖ (γραμμή) line, stroke.
χαρακτήρ, ὁ [harakteer] character, letter ‖ temper, nature.
χαρακτηρίζω [harakteereezo] define, qualify ‖ characterize.
χαρακτηριστικά, τά [harakteereesteeka] πλ person's features.
χαρακτηριστικός [harakteereesteekos] typical, distinctive, characteristic.
χαράκτης, ὁ [haraktees] engraver, carver.
χαρακτική, ἡ [harakteekee] art of engraving.
χαράκωμα, τό [harakoma] trench ‖ (γραμμῶν) ruling.
χαρακώνω [harakono] rule lines, line ‖ scratch, incise.
χαραμάδα, ἡ [haramaða] fissure, crack, crevice.
χαράματα, τά [haramata] πλ dawn, daybreak.
χαραματιά, ἡ [haramatia] incision, crack ‖ (ἐπιφανείας) scratch, trace, engraving.
χαραμίζω [harameezo] waste, spend uselessly.
χάραξις, ἡ [haraksees] engraving, tracing, incision ‖ (δρόμου) laying out.
χαράσσω [harasso] engrave, carve ‖ (γραμμές) rule ‖ map out, trace ‖ (δρόμον) lay out.
χαράτσι, τό [haratsee] (μεταφ) oppressive tax.
χαρατσώνω [haratsono] exact money from ‖ tax oppressively.
χαραυγή, ἡ [haravyee] daybreak, dawn.
χάρβαλο, τό [harvalo] ruin, dilapidated building.
χαρέμι, τό [haremee] harem.
χάρη, ἡ [haree] grace, charm ‖ good point ‖ favour ‖ gratitude ‖ ~ σέ σένα thanks to you ‖ λόγου ~ for instance.
χαρίεις [hariees] · graceful, charming, delightful.
χαριεντίζομαι [harienteezome] be in a

teasing mood, jest ‖ become very charming.

χαρίζομαι [hareezome] be indulgent ‖ favour.

χαρίζω [hareezo] give, donate, present ‖ (χρέος κτλ) remit.

χάρις, ἡ [harees] grace, delightfulness ‖ (ποινῆς) remittance, pardon ‖ ~ εἰς thanks to ‖ **χάριν τοῦ** for, on behalf of ‖ **παραδείγματος χάριν** for example, for instance ‖ **πρός χάριν σου** for your sake, on your behalf.

χάρισμα, τό [hareesma] talent, gift ‖ accomplishment ‖ (ἐπίρ) free, gratis, for nothing.

χαριστική [hareesteekee]: ~ **βολή** coup de grâce.

χαριστικός [hareesteekos] prejudiced, partial.

χαριτολογῶ [hareetologo] jest, speak wittily, speak amusingly.

χαριτωμένος [hareetomenos] charming, enchanting.

χάρμα, τό [harma] delight, source of joy.

χαρμάνι, τό [harmanee] mixture, blend.

χαρμόσυνος [harmoseenos] cheerful, glad.

χαροκόπος, ὁ [harokopos] pleasure-loving person, rake.

χάρος, ὁ [haros] death.

χαρούμενος [haroumenos] cheerful, joyful, happy.

χαρούπι, τό [haroupee] carob.

χαρταετός, ὁ [hartaetos] kite.

χαρτένιος [harteneeos] of paper.

χαρτζιλίκι, τό [hartzeeleekee] pocket money.

χάρτης, ὁ [hartees] paper ‖ (γεωγραφικός) map ‖ (συνταγματικός) charter ‖ ~ **ὑγείας** toilet paper.

χαρτί, τό [hartee] paper ‖ (χαρτοπαιξίας) playing card.

χάρτινος [harteenos] βλ **χαρτένιος**.

χαρτόδετος [hartodetos] paper-bound.

χαρτοκοπτήρας, ὁ [hartokopteeras] paper knife.

χαρτόνι, τό [hartonee] cardboard, pasteboard.

χαρτονόμισμα, τό [hartonomeesma] banknote ‖ (US) bill ‖ paper money.

χαρτοπαίκτης, ὁ [hartopektees] gambler, card player.

χαρτοπαιξία, ἡ [hartopekseea] gambling, card playing.

χαρτοπόλεμος, ὁ [hartopolemos] confetti throwing.

χαρτοπώλης, ὁ [hartopolees] stationer, paper merchant.

χαρτόσημον, τό [hartoseemon] stamp tax.

χαρτοφυλάκιον, τό [hartofeelakeeon] letter-case, briefcase ‖ (μεταφ) portfolio.

χαρτοφύλαξ, ὁ [hartofeelaks] briefcase ‖ (ἐκκλ) archivist.

χαρωπός [haropos] cheerful, happy.

χασάπης, ὁ [hasapees] butcher.

χασάπικο, τό [hasapeeko] butcher's shop.

χασάπικος, ὁ [hasapeekos] kind of circular dance.

χασές, ὁ [hases] cotton cloth.

χάση, ἡ [hasee]: **στή ~ καί στή φέξη** once in a blue moon.

χάσιμο, τό [haseemo] loss.

χασίσι, τό [haseesee] hashish.

χάσκω [hasko] yawn, gape ‖ stand ajar.

χάσμα, τό [hasma] abyss, pit ‖ lacuna, gap.

χασμούρημα, τό [hasmoureema] yawning, yawn.

χασμουριέμαι [hasmourieme] yawn.

χασμωδία, ἡ [hasmodeea] hiatus ‖ disorder, confusion.

χασομερῶ [hasomero] be idle ‖ hang around, linger.

χασούρα, ἡ [hasoura] loss.

χαστούκι, τό [hastoukee] slap, smack, clout.

χατζῆς, ὁ [hatzees] pilgrim, hadji.

χατίρι, τό [hateeree] favour, good turn ‖ **γιά τό ~ σου** for your sake.

χαυλιόδους, ὁ [havleeodous] tusk.

χαῦνος [havnos] slack, indolent ‖ faint-hearted.

χαφιές, ὁ [hafies] stool, nark, agent, informer.

χάφτω [hafto] swallow, gobble down ‖ (μεταφ) take in.

χαχανίζω [hahaneezo] burst into laughter, laugh loudly.

χάχας, ὁ [hahas] moron, idiot.

χαψιά, ἡ [hapsia] mouthful.

χαώδης [haodees] chaotic, confused.

χέζομαι [hezome] be in a fright, be scared ‖ **χέστηκα** I don't give a damn.

χέζω [hezo] defecate ‖ send to the devil.

χείλι, τό [heelee] lip ‖ (μεταφ) brink, verge ‖ (ποτηριοῦ) brim, rim.

χειλικός [heeleekos] labial.

χεῖλος, τό [heelos] βλ **χείλι**.

χειμάζομαι [heemazome] undergo hardship.

χείμαρρος, ὁ [heemaros] torrent, torrent bed.

χειμαρρώδης [heemarodees] torrential, impetuous.

χειμερινός [heemereenos] winter, wintry.

χειμών(ας), ὁ [heemon(as)] winter.

χειμωνιάζει [heemoneeazee] winter approaches.

χειμωνιάτικος [heemoneeateekos] βλ **χειμερινός**.

χείρ, ἡ [heer] βλ **χέρι**.

χειραγωγῶ [heeragogo] lead by the hand ‖ (μεταφ) lead, conduct.

χειράμαξα, ἡ [heeramaksa] handbarrow, wheelbarrow.

χειραφετῶ [heerafeto] liberate, emancipate ‖ manumit.

χειραψία, ή [heerapseea] shake of the hand.
χειρίζομαι [heereezome] handle, manipulate, manage ‖ (μηχανήν) drive.
χειρισμός, ό [heereesmos] manipulation, working, driving ‖ (ὑποθέσεως) handling, management.
χειριστήρια, τά [heereesteereea] πλ controls of a machine.
χειριστής, ό [heereestees] operator ‖ pilot.
χείριστος [heereestos] worst.
χειροβομβίς, ή [heerovomvees] grenade.
χειρόγραφον, τό [heeroyrafon] manuscript.
χειροθετῶ [heerotheto] ordain.
χειροκίνητος [heerokeeneetos] hand-operated.
χειροκρότημα, τό [heerokroteema] clapping, applause.
χειροκροτῶ [heerokroto] applaud, cheer, clap.
χειρόκτιον, τό [heerokteeon] glove, gauntlet.
χειρόμακτρον, τό [heeromaktron] towel, napkin.
χειρομαντεία, ή [heeromanteea] palm-reading.
χειρονομία, ή [heeronomeea] flourish, gesture ‖ gesticulation.
χειροπέδη, ή [heeropedee] pair of hand-cuffs.
χειροπιαστός [heeropeeastos] tangible.
χειροπόδαρα [heeropodara] hand and foot.
χειροποίητος [heeropieetos] handmade.
χειρότερα [heerotera] worse.
χειροτερεύω [heeroterevo] worsen, deteriorate.
χειρότερος [heeroteros] worse ‖ ό ~ the worst.
χειροτεχνία, ή [heerotehneea] handicraft.
χειροτονία, ή [heerotoneea] ordination, consecration (of a bishop).
χειρουργεῖον, τό [heerouryeeon] operating theatre.
χειρουργική, ή [heerouryeekee] surgery.
χειρουργικός [heerouryeekos] surgical.
χειρουργός, ό [heerouryos] surgeon.
χειροφίλημα, τό [heerofeeleema] kissing of the hand.
χειρωνακτικός [heeronakteekos] manual.
χέλι, τό [helee] eel.
χελιδόνι, τό [heleedonee] βλ χελιδών.
χελιδών, ή [heleedon] swallow.
χελώνα, ή [helona] tortoise, turtle.
χεράκι, τό [herakee] tiny hand.
χέρι, τό [heree] hand ‖ arm ‖ (χειρολαβή) handle ‖ (μπογιᾶς) coat ‖ (στό πλύσιμο) treatment, going-over ‖ ~ ~ hand-in-hand ‖ ~ μέ ~ quickly, directly ‖ βάζω ἕνα ~ give a hand ‖ βάζω ~ lay hands on, fondle ‖ ἀπό πρῶτο ~ at first hand.
χερούλι, τό [heroulee] handle, haft ‖ (στάμνας) ear.
χερσαῖος [herseos] terrestrial ‖ (κλῖμα) continental.

χερσόνησος, ή [hersoneesos] peninsula.
χέρσος [hersos] uncultivated (land), fallow, waste.
χέσιμο, τό [heseemo] defecation ‖ (μεταφ) fright, terror ‖ volley of abuse.
χηλή, ή [heelee] hoof.
χημεία, ή [heemeea] chemistry.
χημικός [heemeekos] chemical ‖ (οὐσ) chemist.
χήν, ό [heen] gander.
χήνα, ή [heena] goose.
χήρα, ή [heera] widow.
χηρεύω [heerevo] become widowed ‖ (θέσεως) be unoccupied, be vacant.
χῆρος, ό [heeros] widower.
χθές [hthes] yesterday.
χθεσινός [htheseenos] of yesterday ‖ (πρόσφατος) latest, recent.
χθόνιος [hthoneeos] infernal.
χί, τό [hee] the letter X.
χιαστί [heeastee] crossways, crosswise, diagonally.
χίλια [heeleea]: ~ δύο a hundred and one.
χιλιάρικο, τό [heeleeareeko] note of a thousand drachmas.
χιλιάς, ή [heeleeas] thousand.
χιλιετηρίς, ή [heelieteerees] βλ χιλιετία.
χιλιετία, ή [heelieteea] millenium.
χιλιόγραμμον, τό [heelioyramon] kilo-gramme.
χίλιοι [heeliee] thousand.
χιλιόμετρον, τό [heeleeometron] kilometre.
χιλιοστημόριον, τό [heeleeosteemoreeon] thousandth part.
χιλιοστόν, τό [heeleeoston] millimetre ‖ thousandth part.
χιλιοστός [heeleeostos] thousandth.
χίμαιρα, ή [heemera] chimera ‖ (μεταφ) illusion.
χιμαιρικός [heemereekos] fanciful, visionary.
χιμπαντζῆς, ό [heempantzees] chimpanzee.
χιονάνθρωπος, ό [heeonanthropos] snow-man.
χιονᾶτος [heeonatos] snow-white, snowy.
χιόνι, τό [heeonee] snow.
χιονιά, ή [heeonia] snowy weather ‖ snow-ball.
χιονίζει [heeoneezee] it is snowing.
χιονίστρα, ή [heeoneestra] chilblain.
χιονοδρομία, ή [heeonodromeea] skiing.
χιονοθύελλα, ή [heeonothiela] snowstorm, blizzard.
χιονόνερο, τό [heeononero] sleet, melted snow.
χιονοπέδιλον, τό [heeonopedeelon] snow-shoe.
χιονοστιβάς, ή [heeonosteevas] avalanche, snowdrift.
χιοῦμορ, τό [heeoumor] wit, humour ‖ ~ιστικός humorous, humoristic.
χιτών, ό [heeton] robe, tunic ‖ (ματιοῦ) cornea.

χιτώνιον, τό [heetoneeon] tunic ‖ jacket.

χιών, ἡ [heeon] βλ χιόνι.

χλαίνη, ἡ [hlenee] greatcoat ‖ (ναυτ) duffel coat ‖ cloak, capote.

χλαμύς, ἡ [hlamees] mantle.

χλευάζω [hlevazo] mock, scoff at, make fun of.

χλευαστικός [hlevasteekos] mocking, sarcastic, derisive.

χλιαίνω [hlieno] make tepid ‖ become lukewarm.

χλιαρός [hleearos] tepid, lukewarm ‖ (άνεμος) mild ‖ (μεταφ) weak, lax.

χλιδή, ἡ [hleedee] luxury, voluptuousness.

χλιμιντρίζω [hleemeentreezo] neigh, whinny.

χλοερός [hloeros] green, fresh, verdant.

χλόη, ἡ [hloee] grass, turf, lawn ‖ greenness, verdure.

χλωμάδα, ἡ [hlomaδa] paleness.

χλωμιάζω [hlomeeazo] (go) pale ‖ blanch.

χλωμός [hlomos] pale, pallid, wan.

χλώριον, τό [hloreeon] chlorine, chloride.

χλωρίς, ἡ [hlorees] flora.

χλωρός [hloros] green, unseasoned ‖ fresh.

χλωροφόρμιον, τό [hloroformeeon] chloroform.

χλωροφύλλη, ἡ [hlorofeelee] chlorophyll.

χνάρι, τό [hnaree] pattern, model ‖ track.

χνότα, τά [hnota] βλ χνώτο.

χνούδι, τό [hnouδee] down, fuzz, fluff.

χνουδωτός [hnouδotos] downy, fluffy.

χνώτο, τό [hnoto] breath.

χοάνη, ἡ [hoanee] crucible, melting pot ‖ horn.

χόβολη, ἡ [hovolee] embers, burning charcoal.

χοίρειον [heereeon]: ~ λίπος lard.

χοιρίδιον, τό [heereeδeeon] young pig, piglet.

χοιρινό, τό [heereeno] pork.

χοιρομέρι, τό [heeromeree] ham, bacon.

χοίρος, ὁ [heeros] pig, hog, swine.

χολέρα, ἡ [holera] cholera.

χολή, ἡ [holee] bile ‖ (ζώου) gall ‖ (μεταφ) rancour, bitterness.

χολιάζω [holeeazo] get irritated ‖ irritate ‖ lose one's temper.

χολόλιθος, ὁ [hololeethos] gallstone.

χολοσκάνω [holoskano] afflict, grieve, exasperate ‖ get riled.

χολώδης [holoδes] bilious ‖ (μεταφ) irascible.

χονδρεμπόρειος [honδreekos] wholesale.

χονδροειδής [honδroeeδees] rough, clumsy, coarse ‖ (ψεύδος) flagrant ‖ vulgar.

χόνδρος, ὁ [honδros] cartilage ‖ grit.

χονδρός [honδros] big, fat, stout, thick ‖ (εἰς τρόπους) vulgar, unpolished ‖ (ἀστεῖον) coarse.

χονδρύνω [honδreeno] βλ χοντραίνω.

χοντραίνω [hontreno] become fat, make thicker, put on weight.

χοντροκέφαλος [hontrokefalos] stupid, thickheaded ‖ obstinate, headstrong.

χοντροκοπιά, ἡ [hontrokopia] clumsy job of work.

χόντρος, τό [hontros] thickness, stoutness.

χοντρός [hontros] βλ χονδρός.

χορδή, ἡ [horδee] chord, string ‖ (ἀνατ) cord.

χορδίζω [horδeezo] wind up, key, tune.

χορεία, ἡ [horeea] clique, group, body, clan.

χορευτής, ὁ [horevtees] dancer ‖ partner.

χορευτικός [horevteekos] for dancing, of dancing.

χορεύω [horevo] dance ‖ dance with.

χορήγησις, ἡ [horeeyeesees] granting, giving, supplying.

χορηγός, ὁ [horeeyos] purveyor, furnisher, supplier ‖ donor.

χορηγῶ [horeeyo] provide, allocate, supply, grant.

χορογραφία, ἡ [horoyrafeea] choreography.

χοροδιδάσκαλος, ὁ [horoδeeδaskalos] dancing master.

χοροεσπερίς, ἡ [horoesperees] ball, dancing party.

χοροπηδῶ [horopeeδo] leap about, gambol, caper.

χορός, ὁ [horos] dancing, dance ‖ chorus, choir.

χοροστατῶ [horostato] conduct divine service.

χόρτα, τά [horta] πλ green vegetables, wild greens.

χορταίνω [horteno] have enough, satiate ‖ satisfy ‖ (βαρίέμαι) get bored with.

χορτάρι, τό [hortaree] grass.

χορταρικά, τά [hortareeka] πλ vegetables, greens.

χορτασμός, ὁ [hortasmos] satisfaction, satiety.

χορταστικός [hortasteekos] satisfying, substantial, filling ‖ abundant.

χορτᾶτος [hortatos] satisfied, satiated.

χόρτον, τό [horton] grass, herb ‖ (ἄγριον) weed.

χορτόσουπα, ἡ [hortosoupa] vegetable soup.

χορτοφάγος [hortofayos] vegetarian ‖ (ζώον) herbivorous.

χορωδία, ἡ [horoδeea] choir, chorus.

χουζούρι, τό [houzouree] rest, idleness, leisure.

χουλιάρα, ἡ [houleeara] ladle.

χουλιάρι, τό [houleearee] spoon.

χουρμᾶς, ὁ [hourmas] date.

χοῦς, ὁ [hous] dust, earth.

χούφτα, ἡ [houfta] handful ‖ hollow of hand.

χουφτιά, ἡ [houftia] handful.

χοχλακίζω [hohlakeezo] boil, simmer.

χράμι, τό [hramee] handwoven sheet, woollen coverlet.

χρεία, ή [hreea] necessity, lack || indigence, poverty.
χρειάζομαι [hreeazome] lack, want, require || be necessary, be useful.
χρειώδης [hreeodees] necessary, useful.
χρεμετίζω [hremeteezo] neigh, whinny.
χρεόγραφον, τό [hreoγrafon] security, debenture, bond.
χρέος, τό [hreos] debt || obligation.
χρεωκοπία, ή [hreokopeea] bankruptcy, failure.
χρεωκοπῶ [hreokopo] go bankrupt, break.
χρεωλυσία, ή [hreoleeseea] amortization, sinking fund.
χρεώνομαι [hreonome] get into debt.
χρεώνω [hreono] debit, charge.
χρεωστάσιον, τό [hreostaseeon] moratorium.
χρεώστης, ὁ [hreostees] debtor.
χρεωστῶ [hreosto] be in debt, owe, be indebted (to) || be obliged.
χρῆμα(τα) [hreema(ta)] πλ money.
χρηματίζομαι [hreemateezome] take bribes || hoard up money.
χρηματίζω [hreemateezo] serve as, be.
χρηματικός [hreemateekos] of money, monetary.
χρηματιστήριον, τό [hreemateesteereeon] stock exchange.
χρηματιστής, ὁ [hreemateestees] stockbroker.
χρηματοδοτῶ [hreematodoto] finance, invest.
χρηματοκιβώτιον, τό [hreematokeevoteeon] safe, strongbox, cashbox.
χρησιμεύω [hreeseemevo] be useful || be good for, serve.
χρησιμοποίησις, ή [hreeseemopieesees] employment, utilization.
χρησιμοποιῶ [hreeseemopieo] use, utilize, make use of.
χρήσιμος [hreeseemos] useful, handy.
χρησιμότης, ή [hreeseemotees] usefulness, utility, benefit.
χρῆσις, ή [hreesees] use, usage, employment || enjoyment || application || (οἰκ) financial year || πρός χρῆσιν for the use || ἐν χρήσει in use, used.
χρησμός, ὁ [hreesmos] oracle, divination.
χρηστοήθης [hreestoeethees] honest, moral, honourable, upright.
χρηστός [hreestos] honourable, upright, virtuous.
χρίζω [hreezo] βλ χρίω.
χρίσμα, τό [hreesma] chrism, unction || anointing.
χριστιανικός [hreesteeaneekos] Christian.
χριστιανισμός, ὁ [hreesteeaneesmos] Christianity.
χριστιανός, ὁ [hreesteeanos] Christian.
χριστιανοσύνη, ή [hreesteeanoseenee] Christendom.
Χριστός, ὁ [hreestos] Christ.

Χριστούγεννα, τά [hreestouγena] πλ Christmas.
χρίω [hreeo] anoint || plaster.
χροιά, ή [hreea] complexion, colour || shade, tone, nuance.
χρονιά, ή [hroneea] year.
χρονιάτικο, τό [hroneeateeko] year's payment.
χρονίζω [hroneezo] linger on || be persistent || be one year dead.
χρονικά, τά [hroneeka] πλ annals.
χρονικογράφος, ὁ [hroneekoγrafos] chronicler.
χρονικόν, τό [hroneekon] chronicle.
χρονικός [hroneekos] of time, temporal.
χρόνιος [hroneeos] chronic, enduring, lasting.
χρονογράφημα, τό [hronoγrafeema] newspaper column, topical comment.
χρονογράφος, ὁ [hronoγrafos] writer of newspaper articles (special features).
χρονολογία, ή [hronoloγeea] date || chronology.
χρονολογοῦμαι [hronoloγoume] date from, be dated.
χρονόμετρον, τό [hronometron] chronometer.
χρόνος, ὁ [hronos] time, duration || age, period || (γραμμ) tense, quantity || ὁ ~ year || πρό χρόνων some years ago || τοῦ χρόνου next year || χρόνια πολλά! happy name day!, happy birthday!, many happy returns!
χρονοτριβῶ [hronotreevo] linger, loiter.
χρυσαλλίς, ή [hreesalees] chrysalis.
χρυσάνθεμον, τό [hreesanthemon] chrysanthemum.
χρυσάφι, τό [hreesafee] gold.
χρυσαφικά, τά [hreesafeeka] πλ jewellery.
χρυσή, ή [hreesee] jaundice.
χρυσικός, ὁ [hreeseekos] goldsmith || jeweller.
χρυσίον, τό [hreeseeon] wealth, riches.
χρυσόδετος [hreesodetos] mounted in gold.
χρυσοθήρας, ὁ [hreesotheeras] gold digger, prospector.
χρυσοκέντητος [hreesokenteetos] embroidered with gold.
χρυσόμαλλον [hreesomalon]: ~ δέρας golden fleece.
χρυσοπωλεῖον, τό [hreesopoleeon] βλ χρυσοχοεῖον.
χρυσός, ὁ [hreesos] gold || (ἐπίθ) golden || (μεταφ) kind-hearted, adorable.
χρυσοῦς [hreesous] golden, of gold.
χρυσοχοεῖον, τό [hreesohoeeon] jeweller's shop, goldsmith's shop.
χρυσοχόος, ὁ [hreesohoos] goldsmith || jeweller.
χρυσόψαρο, τό [hreesopsaro] goldfish.
χρυσώνω [hreesono] gild, gold-plate.
χρυσωρυχεῖον, τό [hreesoreeheeon] gold mine.

χρῶμα, τό [hroma] colour, tint, hue ‖ (μπογιά) paint, dye ‖ complexion.

χρωματίζω [hromateezo] colour, paint, dye, tint.

χρωματικός [hromateekos] chromatic ‖ of colour.

χρωματισμός, ὁ [hromateesmos] colouring, painting.

χρωματιστός [hromateestos] coloured.

χρώμιον, τό [hromeeon] chromium, chrome.

χρωστήρ, ὁ [hrosteer] paintbrush.

χρωστικός [hrosteekos] colouring.

χρωστῶ [hrosto] βλ χρεωστῶ.

χταπόδι, τό [htapoδee] octopus.

χτένα, ἡ [htena] βλ χτένι.

χτένι, τό [htenee] comb.

χτενίζω [hteneezo] comb ‖ (ὁμιλίαν κτλ) polish up.

χτένισμα, τό [hteneesma] combing ‖ hairstyle.

χτές [htes] βλ χθές.

χτεσινός [hteseenos] βλ χθεσινός.

χτῆμα, τό [hteema] βλ κτῆμα.

χτίζω [hteezo] βλ κτίζω.

χτικιάρης, ὁ [hteekeearees] consumptive person.

χτικιό, τό [hteekio] tuberculosis ‖ (μεταφ) torture, anguish.

χτίριο, τό [hteereeo] βλ κτίριον.

χτίσιμο, τό [hteeseemo] βλ κτίσιμον.

χτίστης, ὁ [hteestees] bricklayer, builder.

χτυπάω [hteepao] βλ χτυπῶ.

χτύπημα, τό [hteepeema] blow, punch, kick, hit, knock ‖ bruise, wound.

χτυπητό, τό [hteepeeto] βλ χτυπητός.

χτυπητός [hteepeetos] beaten ‖ tawdry, garish, loud, striking.

χτυποκάρδι, τό [hteepokarδee] rapid beating of the heart.

χτύπος, ὁ [hteepos] blow, stroke ‖ (καρδιᾶς) throb, beat ‖ (ὡρολογιοῦ) tick(ing).

χτυπῶ [hteepo] knock, thrash, hit, beat, strike ‖ (χέρια) clap ‖ (πόδια) stamp ‖ (χρόνον) beat ‖ (αὐγά κτλ) whisk ‖ (ὡρολογίου κτλ) peal, strike, sound ‖ hurt o.s. ‖ χτυπάει ἄσχημα it jars, it looks bad ‖ μοῦ χτυπάει στὰ νεῦρα it gets on my nerves ‖ χτυπιέμαι come to blows ‖ feel sorry, repent.

χυδαιολογῶ [heeδeologo] speak crudely, swear.

χυδαῖος [heeδeos] vulgar, trivial, crude, rude, coarse.

χυδαιότης, ἡ [heeδeotees] vulgarity, coarseness, foul language.

χυλόπιττα, ἡ [heepoleeta] kind of macaroni ‖ (μεταφ) failure in love.

χυλός, ὁ [heelos] pap, liquid paste.

χύμα [heema] confusedly, pell-mell ‖ loose, unpacked, unbottled.

χυμός, ὁ [heemos] sap, juice.

χυμώδης [heemoδees] juicy, sappy.

χυμῶ [heemo] rush upon, charge.

χύνομαι [heenome] overflow, pour out ‖ flow out ‖ (μεταφ) charge against, rush upon.

χύνω [heeno] spill, tip over, pour out ‖ (δάκρυα) shed ‖ (μέταλλον) cast.

χύσιμο, τό [heeseemo] discharge, pouring out, spilling ‖ casting, moulding.

χυτήριον, τό [heeteereeon] foundry, smelting works.

χυτός [heetos] moulded, cast ‖ (σκορπισμένος) dispersed, scattered ‖ (μαλλιά) flowing, loose ‖ (ροῦχα) perfect (fit).

χυτοσίδηρος, ὁ [heetoseeδeeros] castiron.

χύτρα, ἡ [heetra] cooking pot, pot, porridge pot.

χώλ, τό [hol] hall.

χωλαίνω [holeno] limp, be lame ‖ (μεταφ) halt, hobble, move slowly.

χωλός [holos] lame, limping.

χῶμα, τό [homa] soil, dust, earth ‖ ground.

χωματένιος [homateneeos] earthen.

χώνευσις, ἡ [honevsees] digestion ‖ (μετάλλων) casting, founding.

χωνευτήριον, τό [honevteereeon] crucible, melting pot.

χωνευτικός [honevteekos] digestible, digestive.

χωνευτός [honevtos] cast ‖ fusible ‖ hidden.

χωνεύω [honevo] digest ‖ (μέταλλον) cast, smelt ‖ (μεταφ) tolerate, endure.

χωνί, τό [honee] funnel, horn ‖ (παγωτοῦ) cone.

χώνομαι [honome] squeeze in ‖ hide ‖ (μεταφ) interfere.

χώνω [hono] thrust, force ‖ bury ‖ (κρύβω) hide.

χώρα, ἡ [hora] country, place ‖ chief town ‖ (ἀνατ) region ‖ λαμβάνω ~ν happen.

χωρατό, τό [horato] joke, jest, witticism.

χωρατεύω [horatevo] joke (in a pleasant way).

χωράφι, τό [horafee] field, land.

χωράω [horao] βλ χωρῶ.

χωρητικότης, ἡ [horeeteekotees] volume, capacity ‖ (ναυτ) tonnage.

χώρια [horeea] βλ χωριστά.

χωριανός, ὁ [horeeanos] fellow villager, countryman.

χωριάτης, ὁ [horeeatees] peasant, villager, countryman ‖ (μεταφ) ill-mannered person, unpolished person.

χωριάτικος [horeeateekos] peasant, of the village ‖ rustic.

χωρίζομαι [horeezome] leave, part from.

χωρίζω [horeezo] separate, disconnect, part, split ‖ (δρόμοι) branch off ‖ (ζεῦγος) get a divorce ‖ ~ μέ break up with, part from.

χωρικός [horeekos] village, rural, country ‖ (οὐσ) peasant, villager.

χωριό, τό [horio] village, hamlet ‖ (μεταφ) hometown.

χωρίον, τό [horeeon] village ‖ (βιβλίου) passage.

χωρίς [horees] without, apart from ‖ not including ‖ ~ ἄλλο without fail ‖ μέ ~ without.

χώρισμα, τό [horeesma] sorting, separation ‖ (δωματίου) wall, partition ‖ compartment.

χωρισμένος [horeesmenos] divided ‖ separated, divorced.

χωρισμός, ὁ [horeesmos] separation ‖ partition ‖ separating ‖ divorce.

χωριστά [horeesta] apart, individually ‖ (προθ) not counting, apart from, not including.

χωριστός [horeestos] separate, different, distinct, isolated.

χωρίστρα, ἡ [horeestra] parting of hair.

χῶρος, ὁ [horos] space, area, room ‖ interval, distance.

χωροστάθμησις, ἡ [horostathmeesees] levelling.

χωροφύλαξ, ὁ [horofeelaks] gendarme.

χωροφυλακή, ἡ [horofeelakee] gendarmerie.

χωρῶ [horo] move forward ‖ fit into, get into.

χωρ(ά)ῶ [hor(a)o] fit into, have room ‖ (περιέχω) hold, contain ‖ δέν χωράει ἀμφιβολία there's no doubt, undoubtedly.

χώσιμο, τό [hoseemo] driving in, burying ‖ hiding.

χωστός [hostos] driven in, deep, penetrating.

Ψ, ψ

ψάθα, ἡ [psatha] straw, cane ‖ (χαλί) rush mat ‖ (καπέλλο) straw hat ‖ στήν ~ penniless.

ψαθάκι, τό [psathakee] man's boater, straw hat.

ψάθινος [psatheenos] made of straw.

ψαλίδα, ἡ [psaleeδa] shears ‖ centipede.

ψαλίδι, τό [psaleeδee] scissors, pruning scissors ‖ curling tongs.

ψαλιδίζω [psaleeδeezo] cut, trim ‖ (μεταφ) reduce, cut down.

ψαλιδωτός [psaleeδotos] swallow-tailed.

ψάλλω [psalo] sing, chant ‖ extol, celebrate.

ψαλμός, ὁ [psalmos] psalm, chant.

ψαλμωδία, ἡ [psalmoδeea] chanting of psalms ‖ monotonous delivery.

ψαλτήριον, τό [psalteereeon] psalter, psalm book.

ψάλτης, ὁ [psaltees] chorister, singer, chanter.

ψαμμίασις, ἡ [psameeasees] gravel.

ψαμμίτης, ὁ [psameetees] sandstone.

ψάξιμο, τό [psakseemo] searching, quest, search.

ψαράδικο, τό [psaraδeeko] fishing boat ‖ fishmonger's shop.

ψαράδικος [psaraδeekos] of a fisherman.

ψαράς, ὁ [psaras] fisherman ‖ fishmonger.

ψάρε(υ)μα, τό [psare(v)ma] fishing, angling, netting.

ψαρεύω [psarevo] fish ‖ sound, fish for information.

ψαρής [psarees] grey-haired, grey, grizzled.

ψάρι, τό [psaree] fish.

ψαρόβαρκα, ἡ [psarovarka] fishing boat.

ψαροκόκκαλο, τό [psarokokalo] fish bone ‖ (σχέδιο) herringbone.

ψαρόκολλα, ἡ [psarokola] fish glue.

ψαρομάλλης, ὁ [psaromalees] grey-haired person.

ψαρονέφρι, τό [psaronefree] fillet of meat.

ψαροπούλα, ἡ [psaropoula] fishing boat, smack.

ψαρός [psaros] βλ ψαρής.

ψαῦσις, ἡ [psavsees] touching, feeling, light touch.

ψαύω [psavo] touch, feel, finger.

ψαχνό, τό [psahno] lean meat.

ψάχνομαι [psahnome] look through one's pockets.

ψάχνω [psahno] search for, look for ‖ seek, rummage.

ψαχουλεύω [psahoulevo] search, grope for, fumble around.

ψεγάδι, τό [pseγaδee] fault, failing, shortcoming.

ψέγω [pseγo] blame, reprove, censure.

ψείρα, ἡ [pseera] louse ‖ vermin.

ψειριάζω [pseereeazo] get lousy.

ψειρίζω [pseereezo] delouse ‖ (μεταφ) rob.

ψεκάζω [psekazo] spray.

ψεκαστήρ, ὁ [psekasteer] spray, vapourizer ‖ scent sprayer.

ψελλίζω [pseleezo] stammer, stutter.

ψέλνω [pselno] βλ ψάλλω.

ψέμα, τό [psema] βλ ψεῦδος.

ψές [pses] yesterday.

ψευδαίσθησις, ἡ [psevδestheesees] delusion, hallucination.

ψευδάργυρος, ὁ [psevδarγeeros] zinc.

ψευδής [psevδees] untrue, false ‖ artificial, sham, fictitious ‖ deceptive.

ψευδίζω [psevδeezo] βλ ψελλίζω.

ψευδολογῶ [psevδoloγo] tell lies, tell stories, fib.

ψεύδομαι [psevδome] lie, fib.

ψευδομαρτυρῶ [psevδomarteero] give false witness, commit perjury.

ψευδομάρτυς, ὁ, ἡ [psevδomartees] false witness, perjurer.

ψευδορκία, ἡ [psevδorkeea] perjury.

ψευδορκῶ [psevδorko] commit perjury, perjure.

ψεῦδος, τό [psevδos] lie, falsehood, fib.

ψευδός [psevδos] lisping, stammering, stuttering.

ψευδώνυμον, τό [psevδoneemon] pseudonym, assumed name.

ψεῦμα, τό [psevma] βλ **ψεῦδος**.

ψεύ(σ)της, ὁ [psev(s)tees] liar, fibber || cheat, impostor.

ψευτιά, ἡ [psevtia] untruth, lie.

ψευτίζω [psevteezo] · adulterate || become adulterated.

ψεύτικος [psevteekos] false, untrue || artificial || (σέ ποιότητα) inferior.

ψῆγμα, τό [pseeγma] filings, shavings, chips.

ψῆκτρα, ἡ [pseektra] brush || (μαλλιῶν) hairbrush.

ψηλά [pseela] high up, aloft.

ψηλαφητός [pseelafeetos] tangible, palpable || (μεταφ) obvious, manifest, evident.

ψηλαφῶ [pseelafo] feel, touch, finger || (ψάχνω) feel one's way, grope.

ψηλομύτης [pseelomeetees] haughty, overbearing.

ψηλός [pseelos] high, tall, lofty, great.

ψήλωμα, τό [pseeloma] eminence, elevation || making taller, growing.

ψηλώνω [pseelono] make taller, make higher || grow taller.

ψήνομαι [pseenome] become very hot || (στήν δουλειά) become broken in.

ψήνω [pseeno] bake, roast, cook || (μεταφ) torture, worry, pester.

ψησιά, ἡ [pseesia] potful.

ψήσιμο, τό [pseeseemo] baking, broiling, roasting, cooking, frying.

ψησταριά, ἡ [pseestaria] barbecue apparatus.

ψητό, τό [pseeto] roast meat, grilled meat || (μεταφ) the main point.

ψητός [pseetos] roast, baked, roasted.

ψηφιδωτόν, τό [pseefeeδoton] mosaic.

ψηφίζω [pseefeezo] vote || (νόμον) pass, carry.

ψηφίον, τό [pseefeeon] cipher, figure || (ἀλφαβήτου) letter, character.

ψήφισμα, τό [pseefeesma] decree, enactment, edict.

ψηφοδέλτιον, τό [pseefoδelteeon] ballot paper.

ψηφοδόχος, ἡ [pseefoδohos] ballot box.

ψηφοθηρῶ [pseefotheero] solicit votes, canvass for votes.

ψῆφος, ὁ, ἡ [pseefos] vote, voting, suffrage.

ψηφοφορία, ἡ [pseefoforeea] voting, ballot(ting).

ψηφῶ [pseefo] take into account, consider || appreciate.

ψί, τό [psee] the letter Ψ.

ψίαθος, ὁ [pseeathos] straw, cane.

ψίδι, τό [pseeδee] vamp of shoe, upper part of boot.

ψιθυρίζω [pseetheereezo] mutter, murmur, whisper.

ψιθύρισμα, τό [pseetheereesma] whisper(ing), muttering, murmuring.

ψιθυρισμός, ὁ [pseetheereesmos] βλ **ψιθύρισμα**.

ψίθυρος, ὁ [pseetheeros] murmur, whisper, mutter, growl.

ψιλά, τά [pseela] πλ small change || (μεταφ) cash, money.

ψιλαίνω [pseeleno] thin down || become thinner.

ψιλή, ἡ [pseelee] smooth (soft) breathing.

ψιλικά, τά [pseeleeka] πλ haberdashery || small wares.

ψιλικαντζήδικον, τό [pseeleekantzeeδeekon] haberdashery.

ψιλολογῶ [pseeloloγo] examine carefully, sift.

ψιλός [pseelos] fine, slender, thin || shrill.

ψιλοτραγουδῶ [pseelotraγouδo] hum.

ψιμάρι, τό [pseemaree] late-born lamb || (μεταφ) easily-duped fellow.

ψιμύθιον, τό [pseemeetheeon] rouge, make-up.

ψιττακίζω [pseetakeezo] parrot, jabber.

ψιττακός, ὁ [pseetakos] parrot.

ψίχα, ἡ [pseeha] kernel, crumb || (καρυδιοῦ) edible part of nut || (μεταφ) bit, scrap.

ψιχάλα, ἡ [pseehala] drizzle.

ψιχαλίζει [pseehaleezee] it's drizzling.

ψίχουλο, τό [pseehoulo] crumb.

ψιχίον, τό [pseeheeon] βλ **ψίχουλο**.

ψόγος, ὁ [psoγos] blame, reproach.

ψοφίμι, τό [psofeemee] carcass, carrion.

ψόφιος [psofeeos] (περί ζώων) dead || (μεταφ) worn-out || ~ στήν κούραση dead tired.

ψόφος, ὁ [psofos] noise, tumult || (θάνατος) death || (μεταφ) freezing cold.

ψοφῶ [psofo] die, kick the bucket (col) || (μεταφ) ~ γιά yearn for, be mad on.

ψυγεῖον, τό [pseeγeeon] refrigerator, ice-box || (αὐτοκινήτου) radiator.

ψυκτικός [pseekteekos] cooling.

ψύλλος, ὁ [pseelos] flea || (μεταφ) trifle.

ψῦξις, ἡ [pseeksees] refrigeration || chill, chilling.

ψυχαγωγία, ἡ [pseehaγoγeea] recreation, amusement, diversion, entertainment.

ψυχαγωγικός [pseehaγoγeekos] recreational, entertaining.

ψυχανάλυσις, ἡ [pseehanaleesees] psychoanalysis.

ψυχή, ἡ [pseehee] soul, ghost || heart, core || (θάρρος) energy, spirit.

ψυχιατρεῖον, τό [pseeheeatreeon] mental hospital, asylum.

ψυχιατρική, ἡ [pseeheeatreekee] psychiatry.

ψυχίατρος, ὁ [pseeheeatros] psychiatrist.

ψυχικό, τό [pseeheeko] act of charity || alms, charity.

ψυχικός [pseeheekos] psychical || **ψυχική διάθεσις** humour, mood, disposition || **ψυχική ὀδύνη** mental stress.

ψυχογιός, ὁ [pseehoγios] adopted son.

ψυχοκόρη, ἡ [pseehokoree] adopted daughter.
ψυχολογία, ἡ [pseeholoyeea] psychology.
ψυχολογικός [pseeholoyeekos] psychological.
ψυχολόγος, ὁ [pseeholoyos] psychologist.
ψυχολογῶ [pseeholoyo] read mind of ‖ psychoanalyse.
ψυχομαχῶ [pseehomaho] be at the last gasp.
ψυχοπαθής [pseehopathees] psychopath.
ψυχοπαίδι, τό [pseehopedee] adopted child.
ψυχοπόνια, ἡ [pseehoponeea] commiseration, pity.
ψυχορραγῶ [pseehorayo] βλ **ψυχομαχῶ**.
ψῦχος, τό [pseehos] cold, chilliness.
ψυχοσάββατο, τό [pseehosavato] All Souls' Day.
ψυχοσύνθεσις, ἡ [pseehoseenthesees] person's psychological make-up.
ψύχρα, ἡ [pseehra] chilly weather, cold.
ψυχραιμία, ἡ [pseehremeea] self-control, sangfroid, coolness.
ψύχραιμος [pseehremos] cool, cool-headed.
ψυχραίνομαι [pseehrenome] be on bad terms with.
ψυχραίνω [pseehreno] cool, chill, make cold ‖ (μεταφ) cool off.
ψυχρολουσία, ἡ [pseehrolouseea] (μεταφ) telling off, rebuke.
ψυχρός [pseehros] cold ‖ (μεταφ) indifferent, apathetic.
ψυχρότης, ἡ [pseehrotees] coldness ‖ indifference.
ψυχρούλα, ἡ [pseehroula] freshness of weather, coolness.
ψύχω [pseeho] freeze, chill, make cold.
ψύχωσις, ἡ [pseehosees] psychosis ‖ craze, complex.
ψωμάκι, τό [psomakee] roll, piece of bread.
ψωμᾶς, ὁ [psomas] baker.
ψωμί, τό [psomee] bread ‖ loaf ‖ (μεταφ) living.
ψωμοζῶ [psomozo] eke out one's living, live scantily.
ψωμοτύρι, τό [psomoteeree] bread and cheese.
ψώνια, τά [psoneea] πλ provisions, shopping, purchases.
ψωνίζω [psoneezo] buy, purchase ‖ go shopping ‖ τήν ~ become queer, go mad.
ψώνιο, τό [psoneeo] purchase ‖ (μεταφ) mania.
ψώρα, ἡ [psora] scabies, itch, mange ‖ (μεταφ) pest.
ψωριάζω [psoreeazo] become itchy, be mangy.
ψωριάρης [psoreearees] mangy ‖ (μεταφ) beggar, ragamuffin.
ψωρίασις, ἡ [psoreeasees] psoriasis, itch(ing).
ψωριῶ [psoreeo] be itchy, have scabies.

ψωροκώσταινα, ἡ [psorokostena] poverty-stricken Greece, poor Greece!
ψωροπερηφάνεια, ἡ [psoropereefaneea] pretensions, stupid pride.

Ω, ω

ὤ [o] (ἐπιφ) oh!, ah!, aha!
ὡάριον, τό [oareeon] ovum.
ὧδε [ode] thus, so ‖ here, in this place.
ὠδεῖον, τό [odeeon] conservatory.
ὠδή, ἡ [odee] ode, song.
ὠδική, ἡ [odeekee] singing lesson ‖ art of singing.
ὠδικός [odeekos] singing, melodious.
ὠδῖνες, οἱ [odeenes] πλ childbirth pains ‖ (μεταφ) difficulties.
ὤθησις, ἡ [otheesees] push, pushing, thrust, impulsion.
ὠθῶ [otho] push, thrust, impel ‖ incite, urge.
ὠϊμέ(να) [oeeme(na)] alas!, woe is me!
ὠκεανός, ὁ [okeanos] ocean.
ὠκύπους [okeepous] swift-footed, nimble.
ὠλένη, ἡ [olenee] forearm.
ὠμέγα, τό [omeya] the letter Ω.
ὠμοπλάτη, ἡ [omoplatee] shoulder blade.
ὄμορφος [omorfos] βλ **ὄμορφος**.
ὦμος, ὁ [omos] shoulder.
ὠμός [omos] uncooked, raw ‖ hard, cruel, unrelenting.
ὠμότης, ἡ [omotees] cruelty, ferocity.
ὠμότητες, οἱ [omoteetes] πλ outrages, atrocities.
ὤν [on] being, existing.
ὤνια, τά [oneea] πλ commodities, goods, provisions.
ὠνοῦμαι [onoume] buy, purchase.
ὠοειδής [ooeedees] oval, egg-shaped.
ὠοθήκη, ἡ [ootheekee] ovary ‖ eggcup.
ὠόν, τό [oon] egg.
ὠοτόκος [ootokos] oviparous, egg-laying.
ὥρα, ἡ [ora] hour, time ‖ μέ τήν ~ on the hour ‖ ~ μέ τήν ὥρα any minute ‖ μέ τίς ὧρες for hours ‖ στήν ~ at the right time, on the dot, on time ‖ τῆς ὥρας fresh, cooked to order.
ὡραία [orea] beautiful ‖ very well, perfectly, good.
ὡραῖος [oreos] handsome, comely, lovely ‖ fine, good.
ὡραιότης, ἡ [oreotees] beauty, good looks.
ὡράριον, τό [orareeon] working hours, timetable.
ὡριαῖος [orieos] hourly ‖ lasting an hour.
ὡριμάζω [oreemazo] become ripe, mature, mellow.
ὡρίμανσις, ἡ [oreemansees] ripening, maturity.
ὥριμος [oreemos] ripe, mature, mellow.
ὡριμότης, ἡ [oreemotees] ripeness, maturity, full growth.

ὡρισμένος [oreesmenos] fixed, settled, determined, definite ‖ certain.

ὡρισμένως [oreesmenos] definitely, positively, without fail.

ὡροδείκτης, ὁ [oroδeektees] hourhand.

ὡρολογᾶς, ὁ [oroloγas] watch repairer ‖ clockmaker.

ὡρολόγιον, τό [oroloγeeon] clock, watch ‖ (ἐργασίας) timetable, schedule ‖ (ἐκκλ) breviary.

ὡρολογοποιός, ὁ [oroloγopeeos] watchmaker, clockmaker.

ὡροσκόπιον, τό [oroskopeeon] horoscope.

ὡρυγή, ἡ [oreeγee] howling, roar.

ὡρύομαι [oreeome] howl, roar ‖ yell, scream.

ὡς [os] until, till, down to, up to, as far as ‖ (ἐπίρ) about ‖ ~ ὅτου νά until.

ὡς [os] as, for, like, just as, such as ‖ (συνδ) as, while, as soon as ‖ βλ καί ὡς.

ὡσάν [osan] as if, as, like, when.

ὡσαύτως [osavtos] also, too, likewise, in like manner.

ὡσεί [osee] as though, as if ‖ about, nearly.

ὡσότου [osotou] until, by the time.

ὥσπερ [osper] like, as, such as.

ὥσπου [ospou] until.

ὥστε [oste] thus, and so, so, accordingly, therefore ‖ that ‖ οὕτως ~ thereby.

ὡστόσο [ostoso] nevertheless ‖ meanwhile.

ὠτακουστής, ὁ [otakoustees] eavesdropper.

ὠτίον, τό [oteeon] ear.

ὠτομοτρίς, ἡ [otomotrees] railcar.

ὠτορινολαρυγγολόγος, ὁ [otoreenolareengoloγos] ear, nose and throat doctor.

ὠφέλεια, ἡ [ofeleea] benefit, utility, usefulness, profit, advantage ‖ εἶδα ~ I benefited.

ὠφέλημα, τό [ofeleema] benefit, gain, particular profit, advantage.

ὠφέλιμος [ofeleemos] beneficial, useful, of use, advantageous.

ὠφελοῦμαι [ofeloume] benefit, profit from, turn to good account.

ὠφελῶ [ofelo] do good to, be useful to, benefit, aid.

ὥχρα, ἡ [ohra] ochre.

ὠχραίνω [ohreno] βλ ὠχριῶ.

ὠχριῶ [ohreeo] become pale, make wan.

ὠχρός [ohros] pallid, pale ‖ (μεταφ) indistinct, dim.

ὠχρότης, ἡ [ohrotees] pallor, paleness.

English—Greek

a, an [ei, æn] *indefinite article* ἕνας, μιά, ἕνα.
aback [ə'bæk] *ad*: **to be taken ~** ξαφνιάζομαι, σαστίζω.
abandon [ə'bændən] *vt* ἐγκαταλείπω, ἀφήνω.
abash [ə'bæʃ] *vt* ξεφτελίζω, ντροπιάζω.
abate [ə'beit] *vi* μειώνομαι, κοπάζω, καταργοῦμαι.
abbess ['æbis] *n* ἡγουμένη.
abbey ['æbi] *n* μονή, μοναστήρι.
abbot ['æbət] *n* ἡγούμενος, ἀββᾶς.
abbreviate [ə'bri:vieit] *vt* συντομεύω.
abbreviation [əbri:vi'eiʃən] *n* σύντμησις, συντετμημένη λέξις.
abdicate ['æbdikeit] *vi* παραιτοῦμαι, ἐγκαταλείπω.
abdication [æbdi'keiʃən] *n* παραίτησις.
abdomen ['æbdəmən] *n* κοιλιά.
abdominal [æb'dɔminl] *a* κοιλιακός.
abduction [æb'dʌkʃən] *n* ἀπαγωγή.
aberration [æbə'reiʃən] *n* παρέκκλισις, παρεκτροπή.
abet [ə'bet] *vt* ὑποκινῶ, παρακινῶ.
abeyance [ə'beiəns] *n*: **in ~** ἐκκρεμῶ, ἀχρηστεύομαι.
abhor [əb'hɔ:*] *vt* ἀπεχθάνομαι, σιχαίνομαι ‖ **~rence** *n* ἀπέχθεια ‖ **~rent** *a* ἀπεχθής.
abide [ə'baid] (*irreg v*) *vt* ἀνέχομαι, ἀντέχω ‖ *vi* ἐμμένω, τηρῶ ‖ **to ~ by** τηρῶ, συμμορφοῦμαι.
ability [ə'biliti] *n* ἱκανότης, ἐπιδεξιότης, δύναμη.
abject ['æbʒekt] *a* ἀπαίσιος, ἄθλιος, ἀξιοθρήνητος.
ablaze [ə'bleiz] *a* φλεγόμενος, λάμπων.
able ['eibl] *a* ἱκανός, ἐπιτήδειος.
ably ['eibli] *ad* ἐπιδεξίως, προκομμένα.
abnormal [æb'nɔ:məl] *a* ἀνώμαλος ‖ **~ity** *n* ἀνωμαλία ‖ (*biol*) τερατωδία, δυσμορφία.
aboard [ə'bɔːd] *ad*: **to go ~** ἐπιβιβάζομαι ‖ **to be ~** εὑρίσκομαι ἐπί.
abode [ə'baud] *n* διαμονή, κατοικία.
abolish [ə'bɔliʃ] *vt* καταργῶ.
abolition [æbə'liʃən] *n* κατάργησις.
abominable [ə'bɔminəbl] *a* ἀποτρόπαιος, ἀπεχθής, ἀπαίσιος.
abominably [ə'bɔminəbli] *ad* ἀπαισίως, ἀπεχθῶς.
aborigines [æbə'ridʒini:z] *npl* ἰθαγενεῖς.
abort [ə'bɔːt] *vt* ἀποβάλλω, διακόπτω ‖ *vi* ἀποβάλλομαι, ματαιοῦμαι.
abortion [ə'bɔːʃən] *n* ἔκτρωσι, ἀποβολή ‖ (*col*) ἔκτρωμα, τέρας.
abortive [ə'bɔːtiv] *a* ἀποτυχών, πρόωρος, ἀνεπιτυχής.
abound [ə'baund] *vi* ἀφθονῶ, βρίθω.

about [ə'baut] *prep* περί, γύρω ἀπό, κοντά ‖ *ad* (τρι)γύρω, κοντά ‖ (*estimate*) περίπου ‖ **to be ~ to** μόλις πρόκειται νά.
above [ə'bʌv] *prep* πάνω ἀπό, πέρα ἀπό ‖ (*in rank*) ἀνώτερος ἀπό, μεγαλύτερος ἀπό ‖ *ad* ὑπεράνω, ἐπάνω, στούς οὐρανούς ‖ **the ~** τά προαναφερόμενα, τά ὡς ἄνω ‖ **~board** *a* τίμια καί εἰλικρινή, ἄψογα ‖ **~ ground** ἐπιφανειακός.
abrade [ə'breid] *vt* ξύνω, ἐκτρίβω.
abrasion [ə'breiʒən] *n* ἀπόξεσις, (ἐκ)τριβή.
abrasive [ə'breiziv] *a,n* ἀποξεστικός ‖ **~ material** μέσον λειάνσεως.
abreast [ə'brest] *ad* παραπλεύρως, μαζύ.
abridge [ə'bridʒ] *vt* συντομεύω, συντέμνω.
abroad [ə'brɔ:d] *ad* στό ἐξωτερικό, στά ξένα ‖ (*widely*) εὑρέως, πλατιά.
abrupt [ə'brʌpt] *a* ἀπότομος, ξαφνικός, ἀγενής.
abscess ['æbsis] *n* ἀπόστημα.
abscond [əb'skɔnd] *vi* φυγοδικῶ, δραπετεύω, φεύγω κρυφά.
absence ['æbsəns] *n* ἀπουσία ‖ (*lack of*) ἔλλειψις, ἀνυπαρξία ‖ (*of mind*) ἀφηρημάδα ‖ **leave of ~** ἄδεια.
absent ['æbsənt] *a* ἀπών, ἀπουσιάζων ‖ [æb'sent] *vt*: **he ~ed himself** ἀπουσίαζε ‖ **~ee** *n* ἀπών, ἀπουσιάζων ‖ **~eeism** *n* ἀπουσία ‖ **~-minded** *a* ἀφηρημένος.
absolute ['æbsəlu:t] *a* ἀπόλυτος, τέλειος, ἀπεριόριστος ‖ **~ly** *ad* τελείως.
absolve [əb'zɔlv] *vt* ἀπαλλάσσω, ἀθωώνω.
absorb [əb'zɔ:b] *vt* ἀπορροφῶ.
absorbent [əb'zɔ:bənt] *a,n* ἀπορροφητικός ‖ **~ cotton** (*US*) ἀπορροφητικός βάμβαξ.
absorbing [əb'zɔ:biŋ] *a* ἀπορροφῶν.
abstain [əb'stein] *vi* ἀπέχω, συγκρατοῦμαι ‖ **~er** *n* ὁ μή πίνων ποτά ‖ **to ~ from** ἀποφεύγω.
abstemious [əb'sti:miəs] *a* ἐγκρατής, λιτοδίαιτος.
abstinence ['æbstinəns] *n* ἀποχή, ἐγκράτεια.
abstract ['æbstrækt] *a* ἀφηρημένος, δυσνόητος ‖ *n* τό ἀφηρημένον ‖ (*summary*) περίληψις ‖ (*excerpt*) ἀπόσπασμα ‖ [æb'strækt] *vt* (*remove*) ἀφαιρῶ.
abstruse [æb'stru:s] *a* ἀσαφής, δυσνόητος.
absurd [əb'sə:d] *a* γελοῖος, παράλογος ‖ **~ity** *n* παραλογισμός, μωρία.
abundance [ə'bʌndəns] *n* ἀφθονία, περίσσευμα.
abundant [ə'bʌndənt] *a* ἄφθονος, πλούσιος.
abuse [ə'bju:z] *vt* (*misuse*) κακομεταχειρίζομαι, καταχρῶμαι ‖ (*speak harshly*) βλαστημῶ, ὑβρίζω.
abuse [ə'bju:s] *n* κακομεταχείρησις, κατάχρησις ‖ (*swearing*) βλασφημία.

abusive [ə'bju:siv] *a* καταχρηστικός, ὑβριστικός.

abut [ə'bʌt] *vi* συνορεύω μέ.

abysmal [ə'bizml] *a* φοβερός, ἀπερίγραπτος.

abyss [ə'bis] *n* ἄβυσσος.

acacia [ə'keiʃə] *n* ἀκακία.

academic [ækə'demik] *a* (*unpractical*) σχολαστικόν || *n* ἀκαδημαϊκός.

academy [ə'kædəmi] *n* ἀκαδημία.

accede [æk'si:d] *vi* (*agree*) συμφωνῶ, προσχωρῶ || (*to throne*) ἀνέρχομαι.

accelerate [æk'seləreit] *vt* ἐπιταχύνω, ἐπισπεύδω || *vi* ἐπιταχύνομαι.

acceleration [ækselə'reiʃən] *n* ἐπιτάχυνσις.

accelerator [ək'seləreitə*] *n* (*aut*) ἀξελερατέρ.

accent ['æksent] *n* τόνος, τονισμός || (*of speech*) προφορά.

accent [æk'sent] *vt* τονίζω || ~uate *vt* τονίζω.

accept [ək'sept] *vt* (*gift etc*) δέχομαι, ἀποδέχομαι || (*agree*) παραδέχομαι || ~able *a* (ἀπο)δεκτός, εὐπρόσδεκτος, παραδεκτός || ~ance *n* ἀποδοχή, παραδοχή || ~ation *n* ἀποδοχή.

access ['ækses] *n* (*entrance*) εἴσοδος, μπάσιμο, πλησίασμα || ~ible *a* προσιτός, εὐπρόσιτος || ~ion *n* (*to throne, office*) προσχώρησις, ἄνοδος || (*increase*) προσθήκη, αὔξησις.

accessories [æk'sesəriz] *npl* ἐξαρτήματα, συμπληρώματα || (*toilet*) εἴδη τουαλέτας.

accessory [æk'sesəri] *a* βοηθητικός, συμπληρωματικός || *n* (*to a crime etc*) συνένοχος || (*part*) ἐξάρτημα.

accident ['æksidənt] *n* (*mishap*) δυστύχημα, ἀτύχημα || (*chance*) συμβάν, τύχη || by ~ κατά τύχην || ~ally *ad* τυχαίως, ἐξ ἀπροσεξίας.

acclaim [ə'kleim] *vt* ἐπευφημῶ, ζητωκραυγάζω, ἀναφωνῶ || *n* ζητωκραυγαί.

acclimatize [ə'klaimətaiz] *vt*: to become ~d to ἐγκλιματίζομαι.

accommodate [ə'kɔmədeit] *vt* (*be suitable for*) ἐξοικονομῶ, διευθετῶ, προσαρμόζω || (*lodge*) στεγάζω, παρέχω κατάλυμα || (*supply etc*) ἐξοικονομῶ, ἐφοδιάζω.

accommodating [ə'kɔmədeitiŋ] *a* ἐξυπηρετικός, πρόθυμος.

accommodation [əkɔmə'deiʃən] *n* (*lodging*) κατάλυμα, στέγασις || (*loan*) δάνειον || (*adjustment*) προσαρμογή, διευθέτησις.

accompaniment [ə'kʌmpənimənt] *n* συνοδεία, ἀκκομπανιαμέντο.

accompanist [ə'kʌmpənist] *n* ἀκκομπανιατέρ.

accompany [ə'kʌmpəni] *vt* συνοδεύω, συντροφεύω.

accomplice [ə'kʌmplis] *n* συνένοχος, συνεργός.

accomplish [ə'kʌmpliʃ] *vt* περατώνω, συμπληρώνω, φέρω εἰς πέρας || ~ed *a*

(*skilled*) τέλειος, ὁλοκληρωμένος || ~ment *n* (*ability*) ἱκανότης, προσόντα || (*completion*) ἐκπλήρωσις.

accord [ə'kɔ:d] *n* συμφωνία, ὁμοφωνία || of my own ~ αὐθόρμητα, ἐπειδή θέλω || *vt* (*grant*) παρέχω, χορηγῶ || (*agree with*) συμφωνῶ || ~ance *n* συμφωνία || in ~ance with σύμφωνα μέ || ~ing *ad*, ~ing to *prep* σύμφωνα μέ, κατά τόν || ~ingly *ad* ὅθεν, ἑπομένως.

accordion [ə'kɔ:diən] *n* ἀκκορντεόν.

accost [ə'kɔst] *vt* πλησιάζω, πλευρίζω.

account [ə'kaunt] *n* (*bill*) λογαριασμός, ὑπολογισμός || (*credit*) λογαριασμός || (*story*) ἀφήγησις, περιγραφή || (*financial report*) ἀνάλυσις, ἔκθεσις || on no ~ ἐπ' οὐδενί λόγῳ || on ~ of ἕνεκα, χάριν τοῦ || to ~ for *vt* ἐξηγῶ, λογοδοτῶ διά || to take into ~ λαμβάνω ὑπ'ὄψιν || ~able *a* ὑπόλογος, ὑπεύθυνος || (*explicable*) εὐεξήγητος || ~ant *n* λογιστής.

accredit [ə'kredit] *vt* διαπιστεύομαι, ἀποδίδω.

accredited [ə'kreditid] *a* διαπιστευμένος, παραδεδεγμένος.

accretion [ə'kri:ʃən] *n* ἐπαύξησις, προσαύξησις || (*biol*) προσφυσις.

accrue [ə'kru:] *vi* προκύπτω, ἀπορρέω.

accumulate [ə'kju:mjuleit] *vt* συσσωρεύω, μαζεύω || *vi* συσσωρεύομαι.

accumulation [əkju:mju'leiʃən] *n* συσσώρευσις, μάζεμα, ἄθροισις.

accuracy ['ækjurəsi] *n* ἀκρίβεια.

accurate ['ækjurit] *a* ἀκριβής, ὀρθός || ~ly *ad* μέ ἀκρίβειαν, σωστά.

accusation [ækju:'zeiʃən] *n* κατηγορία.

accusative [ə'kju:zətiv] *n* (*gram*) αἰτιατική.

accuse [ə'kju:z] *vt* κατηγορῶ || ~d *n* κατηγορούμενος || ~r *n* ἐνάγων, μηνυτής, κατήγορος.

accustom [ə'kʌstəm] *vt* συνηθίζω, ἐθίζω || ~ed *a* συνηθισμένος, μαθημένος εἰς.

ace [eis] *n* (*aviat*) ἄσσος || (*cards*) ἄσσος.

ache [eik] *vi* πονῶ.

achieve [ə'tʃi:v] *vt* κατορθώνω, ἐπιτυγχάνω, φθάνω || ~ment *n* κατόρθωμα, ἐπίτευξις.

acid ['æsid] *a* ὀξύς, ξινός || *n* (*chem*) ὀξύ || ~ test *n* ἀποφασιστική δοκιμασία, τελικόν κριτήριον || ~ity *n* (*chem*) ὀξύτης, ξινίλα.

acknowledge [ək'nɔlidʒ] *vt* (*admit*) ἀναγνωρίζω, παραδέχομαι || (*thank*) εἶμαι εὐγνώμων, ἀπαντῶ εἰς || ~ment *n* ἀναγνώρισις, παραδοχή || (*of letter etc*) βεβαίωσις, || ~ments *npl* εὐχαριστίαι.

acme ['ækmi] *n* ἀκμή, ἄκρον ἄωτον.

acne ['ækni] *n* ἀκμή, σπυράκια.

acorn ['eikɔ:n] *n* βαλανίδι.

acoustic [ə'ku:stik] *a* ἀκουστικός || ~s *npl* ἀκουστική.

acquaint [ə'kweint] *vt* γνωρίζω, πληροφορῶ || ~ance *n* (*person*) γνωριμία || (*knowledge*) γνῶσις, ἐξοικείωσις.

acquiesce [ækwi'es] vi συναινῶ, συγκατατίθεμαι, δέχομαι.

acquire [ə'kwaiə*] vt ἀποκτῶ.

acquisition [ækwi'ziʃən] n ἀπόκτημα, ἀπόκτησις.

acquisitive [ə'kwizitiv] a πλεονέκτης, ἁρπακτικός.

acquit [ə'kwit] vt (free from accusation) ἀπαλλάσσω, ἀθωώνω ‖ (conduct o.s.) ἐκπληρῶ, καταφέρνω ‖ ~tal n ἀθώωσις, ἀπαλλαγή.

acre ['eikə*] n ἄκρ (4 στρέμματα) ‖ ~age n στρεμματική ἔκτασις.

acrimonious [ækri'məuniəs] a δηκτικός, πικρός.

acrobat ['ækrəbæt] n ἀκροβάτης.

across [ə'krɔs] prep (through) διά, διά μέσου ‖ ad (crosswise) ἐγκαρσίως, λοξά, σταυροειδῶς ‖ (distance) πλάτος, μῆκος ‖ ~ the road (στό δρόμο) ἀπέναντι.

act [ækt] n (deed) πρᾶξις, ἐνέργεια ‖ (law or decree) νόμος, νομοθέτημα ‖ (of play) πρᾶξις (ἔργου) ‖ vti (take action) ἐνεργῶ, πράττω ‖ (part) παίζω, παριστάνω, κάνω ‖ (pretend) προσποιοῦμαι, ὑποκρίνομαι, ὑποδύομαι ‖ ~ing n (theat) ἠθοποιΐα, παίξιμο ‖ a ἐνεργῶν, ἀναπληρωματικός.

action ['ækʃən] n (deed) πρᾶξις ‖ (motion) λειτουργία, ἐνέργεια ‖ (battle) μάχη ‖ to bring an ~ against κάνω ἀγωγήν κατά ‖ naval ~ n ναυμαχία ‖ to take ~ ἐνεργῶ.

active ['æktiv] a (lively) ἐνεργητικός, ζωηρός ‖ (working) δραστήριος, ἐνεργός ‖ (gram) ἐνεργητικός ‖ on ~ service ἐν ἐνεργεία ‖ ~ly ad ἐνεργῶς.

activity [æk'tiviti] n δραστηριότης, δρᾶσις.

actor ['æktə*] n ἠθοποιός.

actress ['æktris] n (ἡ) ἠθοποιός, θεατρίνα.

actual ['æktjuəl] a πραγματικός, ἀληθινός ‖ ~ly ad πράγματι.

actuate ['æktjueit] vt (παρα)κινῶ, ὠθῶ.

acumen ['ækjumen] n ὀξύνοια, εὐφυΐα.

acute [ə'kju:t] a ὀξύς, διαπεραστικός ‖ ~ly ad ἐντόνως ‖ ~ accent n ὀξεῖα.

Adam ['ædəm] n 'Αδάμ ‖ ~'s apple n καρύδι τοῦ λαιμοῦ.

adamant ['ædəmənt] a ἀμετάπειστος, ἄκαμπτος.

adapt [ə'dæpt] vt προσαρμόζω, ἐναρμόζω ‖ vi: to ~ to προσαρμόζομαι ‖ ~able a προσαρμόσιμος, εὐάρμοστος ‖ ~ation n προσαρμογή ‖ (of play etc) διασκευή ‖ ~er n (elec) προσαρμοστής.

add [æd] vt προσθέτω, ἀθροίζω ‖ to ~ up vt προσθέτω.

addendum [ə'dendəm] n προσθήκη, συμπλήρωμα.

adder ['ædə*] n (snake) ὀχιά, ὄχεντρα.

addict ['ædikt] n -μανής.

addict [ə'dikt] vt ἀφοσιώνω, παραδίδω ‖ ~ed to ἐπιρρεπής εἰς ‖ ~ion n ροπή πρός, ἐθισμός.

adding machine ['ædiŋməʃi:n] n ἀθροιστική μηχανή.

addition [ə'diʃən] n πρόσθεσις, προσθήκη ‖ in ~ ἐπί πλέον, ἐπιπροσθέτως, προσέτι ‖ ~al a πρόσθετος.

address [ə'dres] n διεύθυνσις ‖ (speech) προσφώνησις, λόγος ‖ (manners) συμπεριφορά ‖ vt ἀπευθύνω ‖ (speak) προσφωνῶ ‖ (envelope) γράφω διεύθυνσι.

addressee [ædre'si:] n παραλήπτης.

addressograph [ə'dresəugra:f] n ἀντρεσσογράφος.

adduce [ə'dju:s] vt προσάγω, παραθέτω, παρέχω.

adenoids ['ædinɔidz] npl κρεατάκια.

adept ['ædept] a: ~ at ἔμπειρος εἰς, ἱκανός εἰς.

adequacy ['ædikwəsi] n ἐπάρκεια, ὀρθότης.

adequate ['ædikwit] a ἐπαρκής, ἱκανός ‖ ~ly ad δικαίως, ἐπαρκῶς.

adhere [əd'hiə*] vi (stick to) προσκολλῶμαι ‖ (support) ἐμμένω, προσχωρῶ ‖ to ~ to προσχωρῶ, ἐμμένω.

adhesion [əd'hi:ʒən] n προσκόλλησις, πιάσιμο ‖ (med) σύμφυσις.

adhesive [əd'hi:ziv] a συγκολλητικός, κολλώδης ‖ n κολλητική οὐσία ‖ ~ tape n λευκοπλάστης.

adjacent [ə'dʒeisənt] a παρακείμενος, γειτονικός, συνορεύων.

adjective ['ædʒektiv] n ἐπίθετον.

adjoin [ə'dʒɔin] vi γειτονεύω, συνορεύω μέ, συνάπτω ‖ ~ing a συνεχόμενος, παρακείμενος, γειτνιάζων.

adjourn [ə'dʒə:n] vt (postpone) ἀναβάλλω ‖ vi ἀναβάλλομαι, διακόπτομαι ‖ ~ment n ἀναβολή, διακοπή.

adjudicator [ə'dʒu:dikeitə*] n διαιτητής, δικαστής.

adjunct ['ædʒʌŋkt] n παρεπόμενον, βοηθός ‖ a πρόσθετος.

adjust [ə'dʒʌst] vt (put right) ρυθμίζω, κανονίζω ‖ (to fit) προσαρμόζω, ἐφαρμόζω ‖ ~able a ρυθμιζόμενος, ρυθμιστός ‖ ~ment n ρύθμισις, τακτοποίησις.

adjutant ['ædʒətənt] n ὑπασπιστής.

ad lib [æd'lib] ad κατά βούλησιν ‖ ad-lib vi αὐτοσχεδιάζω.

administer [əd'ministə*] vt (manage) διευθύνω, διαχειρίζομαι, διοικῶ ‖ (dispense) ἀπονέμω ‖ (medicine) παρέχω, δίδω.

administration [ədminis'treiʃən] n διοίκησις, διαχείρισις, διεύθυνσις ‖ ~ of justice n ἀπονομή δικαιοσύνης.

administrative [əd'ministrətiv] a διοικητικός.

administrator [əd'ministreitə*] n διευθυντής, διοικητής ‖ (of will) ἐκτελεστής.

admirable ['ædmərəbl] a θαυμαστός, θαυμάσιος.

admiral ['ædmərəl] n ναύαρχος ‖ ~ty n ναυαρχεῖον.

admiration [ædmə'reiʃən] n θαυμασμός, κατάπληξις.

admire [əd'maiə*] vt θαυμάζω || ~r n θαυμαστής.

admissible [əd'misəbl] a (παρα)δεκτός, ἐπιτρεπτός.

admission [əd'miʃən] n (entrance) εἴσοδος, εἰσαγωγή || (fee) τιμή εἰσητηρίου || (confession) παραδοχή, ἀναγνώρισις.

admit [əd'mit] vt (let in) ἀφήνω νά εἰσέλθη, εἰσέρχομαι || (confess) παραδέχομαι, ἀναγνωρίζω || (receive as true) (ἐπι)δέχομαι || ~tance n εἰσδοχή, εἴσοδος || ~tedly ad ὁμολογουμένως.

admonish [əd'mɔniʃ] vt (warn) προειδοποιῶ || (reprove) ἐπιτιμῶ, ψέγω || (advise) νουθετῶ, παραινῶ.

ado [ə'du:] n: without more ~ χωρίς περισσότερη φασαρία.

adolescence [ædəu'lesns] n ἐφηβική ἡλικία.

adolescent [ædəu'lesnt] a,n ἔφηβος.

adopt [ə'dɔpt] vt υἱοθετῶ || (accept) παραδέχομαι, ἀποδέχομαι || ~ed son n θετός || ~ion n υἱοθεσία || (of idea etc) ἀποχή, ἔγκρισις.

adorable [ə'dɔ:rəbl] a λατρευτός, ἀξιαγάπητος.

adoration [ædə'reiʃən] n λατρεία.

adore [ə'dɔ:*] vt λατρεύω, ὑπεραγαπῶ.

adorn [ə'dɔ:n] vt κοσμῶ, στολίζω, καλλωπίζω.

adrenalin [ə'drenəlin] n ἀδρεναλίνη.

Adriatic [eidri'ætik] n Ἀδριατική.

adrift [ə'drift] ad ἔρμαιον || (col) τά ἔχω χαμένα.

adroit [ə'drɔit] a ἐπιδέξιος, ἐπιτήδειος.

adulation [ædju'leiʃən] n κολακεία, θωπεία.

adult ['ædʌlt] a,n ἐνήλιξ, ἔφηβος || (law) ἐνήλικος.

adulterate [ə'dʌltəreit] vt νοθεύω, ἀλλοιώνω, νερώνω.

adultery [ə'dʌltəri] n μοιχεία.

advance [əd'va:ns] n πρόοδος, προχώρησις || (money) προκαταβολή, πίστωσις || (in prices) αὔξησις, ὕψωσις || vi προχωρῶ || (mil) προελαύνω || (price) ἀνατιμῶμαι, ἀνεβαίνω || ~d a προχωρημένος || (ideas) προοδευτικός || (study etc) ἀνώτερος || ~d ignition n προανάφλεξις, ἀβάνς || in ~ προκαταβολικῶς || in ~ of πρίν ἀπό, ἐνωρίτερα || ~ booking n κλείνω θέσιν.

advantage [əd'va:ntidʒ] n πλεονέκτημα, προτέρημα || to take ~ of (profit by) ἐπωφελοῦμαι ἀπό, ἐκμεταλλεύομαι || (misuse) καταχρῶμαι || ~ over ὑπεροχή.

advantageous [ædvən'teidʒəs] a ἐπωφελής, λυσιτελής.

advent ['ædvənt] n ἔλευσις, ἐμφάνισις || (rel) σαραντάμερο || the Second A~ ἡ Δευτέρα Παρουσία.

adventure [əd'ventʃə*] n περιπέτεια || (bold undertaking) τόλμημα || ~r n τολμηρός || (in bad sense) τυχοδιώκτης.

adventurous [əd'ventʃərəs] a ριψοκίνδυνος, τυχοδιωκτικός.

-adverb ['ædvə:b] n ἐπίρρημα.

adversary ['ædvəsəri] n ἀντίπαλος, ἀνταγωνιστής.

adverse ['ædvə:s] a ἀντίθετος, ἐνάντιος, δυσμενής.

adversity [əd'və:siti] n ἀτυχία, ἀναποδιά.

advertise ['ædvətaiz] vt διαφημίζω, ρεκλαμάρω || ~ment [əd'və:tismənt] n διαφήμησις, ρεκλάμα || (poster) ἀφίσα || ~r n διαφημιστής.

advertising ['ædvətaiziŋ] n διαφήμησις, ρεκλάμα || ~ agency n διαφημιστικόν γραφεῖον.

advice [əd'vais] n συμβουλή || (information) πληροφορία, εἴδησις.

advisability [ədvaizə'biliti] n σκοπιμότης, χρησιμότης.

advisable [əd'vaizəbl] a φρόνιμος, σκόπιμος.

advise [əd'vaiz] vt συμβουλεύω, συνιστῶ || (apprise) εἰδοποιῶ || ~dly ad ἐσκεμμένως || (wisely) κατόπιν σκέψεως || ~r n σύμβουλος.

advisory [əd'vaizəri] a συμβουλευτικός.

advocacy ['ædvəkəsi] n συνηγορία, ὑπεράσπισις.

advocate ['ædvəkit] n (law) δικηγόρος, συνήγορος || (supporter) ὑποστηρικτής || ['ædvəkeit] vt ὑποστηρίζω, συνιστῶ || (law) συνηγορῶ.

aerated ['εəreitid] a ἀεριοῦχος || ~ waters npl ἀεριοῦχα νερά, σόδα.

aerial ['εəriəl] a (ἐν)αέριος || n κεραία || ~ photograph n ἐναέριος φωτογραφία.

aerobatics [εərəu'bætiks] npl ἐναέριοι ἀκροβασίαι.

aeronautics [εərə'nɔ:tiks] n ἀεροναυτική.

aeroplane ['εərəplein] n ἀεροπλάνον.

aerosol ['εərəsɔl] n ἀεροζόλ.

aesthetic [i:s'θetik] a αἰσθητικός || (artistic) καλαίσθητος || ~s npl αἰσθητική.

afar [ə'fa:*] ad: from ~ ἀπό μακράν, μακρόθεν.

affable ['æfəbl] a προσηνής, γλυκομίλητος, καταδεκτικός.

affair [ə'fεə*] n ὑπόθεσις, δουλειά || (matter) πρᾶγμα.

affect [ə'fekt] vt (influence) θίγω, ἐπηρεάζω || (feign) προσποιοῦμαι, κάνω τόν || ~ation n προσποίησις || ~ed a προσποιητός || (moved) συγκινημένος || (med) προσβεβλημένος || n ἀγάπη, στοργή || ~ionate a φιλόστοργος, ἀγαπῶν || ~ionately ad στοργικά, μέ ἀγάπη.

affidavit [æfi'deivit] n ἔνορκος κατάθεσις, γραπτή βεβαίωσις.

affiliate [ə'filieit] vt εἰσάγω, συνεργάζομαι.

affiliation [əfili'eiʃən] n σύνδεσις, δεσμός.

affinity [ə'finiti] *n* συγγένεια.

affirm [ə'fəːm] *vt* ἐπιβεβαιῶ ‖ ~**ation** *n* (δια)βεβαίωσις ‖ (*assent*) κατάφασις ‖ ~**ative** *a* καταφατικός, βεβαιωτικός ‖ *n* κατάφασις ‖ **in the** ~**ative** καταφατικῶς.

affix [ə'fiks] *vt* ἐπισυνάπτω, προσαρτῶ, θέτω.

afflict [ə'flikt] *vt* θλίβω, πικραίνω ‖ (*med*) προσβάλλω ‖ ~**ion** *n* θλίψις, λύπη ‖ (*misfortune*) ἀτύχημα, συμφορά.

affluence ['æfluəns] *n* (*abundance*) ἀφθονία ‖ (*wealth*) πλοῦτος.

affluent ['æfluənt] *a* πλούσιος.

afford [ə'fɔːd] *vt* (*have the means*) δύναμαι, ἔχω τὰ μέσα ‖ (*provide*) παρέχω, προσφέρω.

affront [ə'frʌnt] *vt* προσβάλλω, ντροπιάζω ‖ *n* προσβολή, ὕβρις ‖ ~**ed** *a* προσβεβλημένος.

Afghanistan [æf'gænistæn] *n* Ἀφγανιστάν.

afield [ə'fiːld] *ad*: **far** ~ μακράν.

afloat [ə'fləut] *ad*: **I am** ~ ἐπιπλέω.

afoot [ə'fut] *ad* (*astir*) εἰς κίνησιν, κυκλοφορῶ.

afraid [ə'freid] *a* ἔμφοβος, φοβισμένος ‖ **to be** ~ **of** φοβοῦμαι ‖ **to be** ~ **to** δέν τολμῶ ‖ ~ **that** φοβοῦμαι ὅτι.

afresh [ə'freʃ] *ad* ἐκ νέου, πάλιν.

Africa ['æfrikə] *n* Ἀφρική ‖ ~**n** *n* Ἀφρικανός ‖ *a* ἀφρικανικός.

aft [aːft] *ad* πρός τήν πρύμνην, πρός τά πίσω.

after ['aːftə*] *prep* μετά, κατόπιν, ὕστερα ἀπό ‖ (*according to*) κατά ‖ *ad* ἔπειτα, κατόπιν, ὕστερον ‖ *a* ὕστερος, ἐπόμενος ‖ *cj* ἀφοῦ ‖ **some time** ~ ὀλίγον ἀργότερα ‖ **what is he** ~? τί ζητᾶ; ‖ τί ψάχνει; ‖ ~ **all** τέλος πάντων, ἐπί τέλους ‖ ~ **five** (**o'clock**) περασμένες πέντε ‖ ~ **you, sir**! παρακαλῶ!, περάστε!

after- ['aːftə*] *a* (*in compds*) *a* μετά, μέλλων, ὀπίσθιος.

aftermath ['aːftəmæθ] *n* συνέπεια, ἐπακόλουθον.

afternoon ['aːftə'nuːn] *n* ἀπόγευμα ‖ **good** ~! χαίρετε!, καλό βράδυ!

afterthought ['aːftəθɔːt] *n* μεταγενεστέρα σκέψις.

afterwards ['aːftəwədz] *ad* κατόπιν, ἔκτοτε, ἐν συνεχεία.

again [ə'gen] *ad* πάλιν, ξανά ‖ ~ **and** ~ ἐπανειλημμένως, πάλι καί πάλι.

against [ə'genst] *prep* κατά, ἐναντίον.

agape [ə'geip] *a,ad* μέ ἀνοιχτό στόμα.

age [eidʒ] *n* ἡλικία ‖ (*generation*) γενεά ‖ (*period*) ἐποχή ‖ (*century*) αἰώνας ‖ *vti* γηράσκω, γηράζω ‖ (*wine etc*) ὡριμάζω ‖ ~ **of** ~ ἐνηλικιωμένος, ἐνήλικος ‖ ~**d** *a* ἡλικιωμένος, γέρος ‖ ~**d 20** (**years**) ἡλικίας 20 ἐτῶν ‖ ~**less** *a* ἀγέραστος, αἰώνιος.

agency ['eidʒənsi] *n,a* (ἐπί)δρασις, ἐνέργεια ‖ (*factor*) παράγων, αἴτιον ‖ (*inter-*

vention) ὑπηρεσία, ὀργανισμός ‖ (*office*) πρακτορεῖον, ἀντιπροσωπεία.

agenda [ə'dʒendə] *n* ἡμερησία διάταξις ‖ (*notebook*) ἀτζέντα, σημειωματάριον.

agent ['eidʒənt] *n* πράκτωρ, ἀντιπρόσωπος ‖ (*cause*) παράγων, συντελεστής.

aggravate ['ægrəveit] *vt* ἐπιδεινώνω, χειροτερεύω ‖ (*provoke*) ἐντείνω, ἐρεθίζω.

aggregate ['ægrigit] *n* ἄθροισμα, σύνολον ‖ *a* συνολικός.

aggression [ə'greʃən] *n* ἐπίθεσις, ἐπιδρομή.

aggressive [ə'gresiv] *a* ἐπιθετικός ‖ (*US*) δραστήριος ‖ ~**ly** *ad* ἐπιθετικῶς ‖ ~**ness** *n* ἐπιθετικότης.

aggressor [ə'gresə*] *n* ἐπιτιθέμενος.

aggrieved [ə'griːvd] *a* θλιμμένος, πικραμένος.

aghast [ə'gaːst] *a* κατάπληκτος, ἐμβρόντητος.

agile ['ædʒail] *a* εὐκίνητος, ἐλαφρός.

agility [ə'dʒiliti] *n* εὐκινησία, εὐκαμψία.

agitate ['ædʒiteit] *vt* (*set in motion*) (ἀνα)ταράσσω ‖ (*excite*) ταράσσω, ἀνησυχῶ ‖ (*pol*) κινοῦμαι, κάνω κίνησιν ‖ **to** ~ **for** δημιουργῶ κίνησιν γιά.

agitation [ædʒi'teiʃən] *n* ἀναταραχή.

agitator ['ædʒiteitə*] *n* ὑποκινητής, ταραχοποιός.

agnostic [æg'nɔstik] *a,n* ἀγνωστικός.

agnosticism [æg'nɔstisizəm] *n* ἀγνωστικισμός.

ago [ə'gəu] *ad* περασμένος, παρελθόν, πρό, πρίν ‖ **long** ~ πρό πολλοῦ ‖ **some time** ~ πρό καιροῦ.

agog [ə'gɔg] *a* ἀνυπόμονος.

agonizing ['ægənaiziŋ] *a* σπαρακτικός, φρικτός.

agony ['ægəni] *n* ἀγωνία, βάσανο.

agree [ə'griː] *vti* (*consent*) συγκατατίθεμαι, ἀποδέχομαι ‖ (*have same opinion*) συμφωνῶ, εἶμαι σύμφωνος ‖ (*of climate etc*) ταιριάζω, ὠφελῶ ‖ (*come to an agreement*) συμβιβάζομαι ‖ **it does not** ~ **with me** μέ πειράζει, μ' ἐνοχλεῖ, δέν μοῦ ταιριάζει ‖ ~**able** *a* εὐχάριστος, σύμφωνος ‖ ~**ably** *ad* εὐχαρίστως, συμφώνως πρός ‖ ~**d** *a* (*of persons*) εἶμαι σύμφωνος ‖ (*of things*) ἐγκρίνεται!, σύμφωνοι! ‖ ~**ment** *n* συμφωνία ‖ (*formal*) σύμβασις, συνθήκη.

agricultural [ægri'kʌltʃərəl] *a* γεωργικός.

agriculture ['ægrikʌltʃə*] *n* γεωργία.

aground [ə'graund] *ad* (*naut*) στήν ξέρα, στήν στεριά ‖ **to run** ~ προσαράσσω, καθίζω, ἐξοκέλλω.

ahead [ə'hed] *ad* ἐμπρός, πρό, πρόσω ‖ **to get** ~ προχωρῶ, προηγοῦμαι ‖ ~ **of** μπρός ἀπό.

ahoy [ə'hɔi] *excl*: **boat** ~! αἴ, τῆς λέμβου!, ἔ, ἐσεῖς στῆ βάρκα!

aid [eid] *n* βοήθεια, συνδρομή ‖ (*assistant*) βοηθός ‖ *vt* βοηθῶ, συντρέχω.

ailing ['eiliŋ] *a* πάσχων, ἀσθενής.

ailment ['eilmənt] *n* ἀδιαθεσία, ἀρρώστια.

aim [eim] *n* (*point*) σκόπευσις ‖ (*target*) στόχος ‖ (*purpose*) σκοπός, ἀντικείμενον ‖ *vti* (*throw*) ρίχνω, κτυπῶ ‖ (*point*) σκοπεύω ‖ (*intend*) ἐπιδιώκω ‖ ~**less** *a* ἄσκοπος, ἀσυνάρτητος.

air [εə*] *n* ἀέρας, ἀγέρας ‖ (*tune*) μέλος, σκοπός, ἦχος ‖ (*appearance*) παρουσιαστικό, ἀέρας, ὕφος ‖ *vt* ἀερίζω (*question*) ἐκθέτω, ἀνακινῶ ‖ (*opinions*) ἐπιδεικνύω, ἀποκαλύπτω ‖ ~**borne** *a* ἀεροφερόμενος ‖ ~ **conditioning** *n* κλιματισμός ‖ ~**craft** *n* ἀεροσκάφος, ἀεροπλάνο ‖ ~**craft carrier** *n* ἀεροπλανοφόρο ‖ ~**field** *n* ἀεροδρόμιον ‖ ~**force** *n* (πολεμική) ἀεροπορία ‖ ~ **freight** *n* ἀεροπορικόν φορτίον ‖ ~**gun** *n* σφυρίον πεπιεσμένου ἀέρος ‖ ~ **hostess** *n* ἱπταμένη συνοδός ‖ ~**ily** *ad* εὔθυμα, ἐλαφρά ‖ ~**line** *n* ἀεροπορική γραμμή ‖ ~**liner** *n* ἐπιβατικόν ἀεροπλάνον ‖ ~**mail** *n*: **by** ~**mail** ἀεροπορικῶς ‖ ~**plane** *n* (*US*) ἀεροπλάνον ‖ ~ **pocket** *n* κενόν ἀέρος ‖ ~**port** *n* ἀερολιμήν ‖ ~ **pressure** *n* ἀτμοσφαιρική πίεσις ‖ ~ **pump** *n* ἀεραντλία ‖ ~ **raid** *n* ἀεροπορική ἐπιδρομή ‖ ~-**raid shelter** *n* καταφύγιον ‖ ~**tight** *a* ἀεροστεγές, ἑρμητικός.

aisle [ail] *n* διάδρομος ‖ (*of church*) πτέρυξ.

ajar [ə'dʒɑː*] *ad* μισοανοιγμένος.

akimbo [ə'kimbəu] *ad* ἐπὶ τῶν ἰσχίων.

akin [ə'kin] *a* συγγενεύων.

à la carte [ælæ'kɑːt] *ad* ἀ-λα-κάρτ.

alack [ə'læk] *excl* ἀλλοί!

alarm [ə'lɑːm] *n* (*of danger*) συναγερμός, κραυγή κινδύνου ‖ (*device*) σύστημα εἰδοποιήσεως ‖ (*fright*) φόβος, ἀναταραχή ‖ *vt* τρομάζω, φοβίζω, ταράσσω ‖ ~ **clock** *n* ξυπνητήρι ‖ ~**ing** *a* ἀνησυχητικός ‖ ~**ist** *n* διαδοσίας.

alas [ə'læs] *excl* ἀλλοίμονον!, φεῦ!

Albania [æl'beiniə] *n* 'Αλβανία ‖ ~**n** *a* 'Αλβανός, 'Αρβανίτης.

album ['ælbəm] *n* λεύκωμα, ἄλμπουμ.

alcohol ['ælkəhɔl] *n* ἀλκοόλ, οἰνόπνευμα ‖ ~**ic** *a,n* ἀλκοολικός.

alcove ['ælkəuv] *n* παστάς, ἀλκόβα ‖ (*of wall*) σηκός, ἀψιβάδα.

alder ['ɔːldə*] *n* (σ)κλήθρα, σκλέθρος.

alderman ['ɔːldəmən] *n* δημοτικός σύμβουλος.

ale [eil] *n* μπύρα.

alert [ə'ləːt] *a* ἄγρυπνος, προσεκτικός ‖ (*nimble*) εὐκίνητος, σβέλτος ‖ *n* ἐπιφυλακή, συναγερμός ‖ ~**ness** *n* ἐπαγρύπνησις ‖ (*cleverness*) ἐξυπνάδα, εὐστροφία.

algebra ['ældʒibrə] *n* ἄλγεβρα.

alias ['eiliæs] *ad* ἄλλως, ἤ ‖ *n* ψευδώνυμο, πλαστό ὄνομα.

alibi ['ælibai] *n* ἄλλοθι ‖ (*col*) δικαιολογία.

alien ['eiliən] *n,a* ξένος, ἀλλοδαπός ‖ ~**ate**

vt (*turn away*) ἀποσπῶ, ἀποξενῶ ‖ ~**ation** *n* ἀποξένωσις.

alight [ə'lait] *a* ἀναμμένος, φλεγόμενος ‖ *vi* κατέρχομαι, κατεβαίνω ‖ (*of birds*) κάθομαι.

align [ə'lain] *vt* εὐθυγραμμίζω ‖ ~**ment** *n* εὐθυγράμμισις.

alike [ə'laik] *a* ὅμοιος, παρόμοιος, ἴδιος ‖ *ad* ὁμοίως, ἴδια.

alive [ə'laiv] *a* ζωντανός.‖ (*lively*) ζωηρός ‖ (*teeming*) βρίθων, γεμάτος.

alkali ['ælkəlai] *n* ἄλκαλι.

all [ɔːl] *a,pron* πᾶς, ὅλος, ὅλοι, πάντες ‖ *n* ὅλον, σύνολον, ὁλότης ‖ *ad* ἐντελῶς, τελείως, ὅλο ‖ **after** ~ στό κάτω-κάτω ‖ ~ **in** ἐν συνόλω ‖ **above** ~ πρό παντός.

all- ['ɔːl] (*in compds*) *a* ὁλο-, παν-, παντο-, τελείως.

allay [ə'lei] *vt* καταπραΰνω, γλυκαίνω ‖ (*lessen*) καθησυχάζω, ἀνακουφίζω.

allegation [æle'geiʃən] *n* ἰσχυρισμός, ὑπαινιγμός.

allege [ə'ledʒ] *vt* ἰσχυρίζομαι, ἐπικαλοῦμαι ‖ ~**dly** *ad* δῆθεν.

allegiance [ə'liːdʒəns] *n* πίστις, ὑπακοή.

allegory ['æligəri] *n* ἀλληγορία.

alleluia [æli'luːjə] *n* ἀλληλούϊα.

all-embracing ['ɔːlim'breisiŋ] *a* περιλαμβάνων τά πάντα.

allergic [ə'ləːdʒik] *a* ἀλλεργικός.

allergy ['ælədʒi] *n* ἀλλεργία.

alleviate [ə'liːvieit] *vt* ἐλαφρώνω, ἀνακουφίζω.

alleviation [əliːvi'eiʃən] *n* ἀνακούφισις, ἀλάφρωμα, ξαλάφρωμα.

alley ['æli] *n* δρομίσκος, πάροδος, δρομάκος ‖ ~**way** *n* δρομίσκος, στενόν.

alliance [ə'laiəns] *n* συμμαχία ‖ (*marriage*) ἐπιγαμία, συμπεθεριά.

allied ['ælaid] *a*: ~ **to** συγγενεύω μέ.

alligator ['æligeitə*] *n* ἀλλιγάτωρ.

all-important ['ɔːlim'pɔːtənt] *a* σπουδαιότατος.

all-in ['ɔːlin] *a* (*exhausted*) ἐξηντλημένος.

alliteration [əlitə'reiʃən] *n* παρήχησις.

all-night ['ɔːl'nait] *a* (*cafe etc*) ὁλονύκτιος, διανυκτερεύων.

allocate ['æləukeit] *vt* διαθέτω, παραχωρῶ ‖ (*for special purpose*) κατανέμω, ἀναθέτω.

allocation [æləu'keiʃən] *n* ἐκχώρησις, ἀπονομή.

allot [ə'lɔt] *vt* παραχωρῶ, διαθέτω, κατανέμω ‖ ~**ment** *n* (*share*) μερίδιον, τμῆμα.

all-out ['ɔːl'aut] *ad* μέ ὅλες τίς δυνάμεις.

allow [ə'lau] *vt* ἐπιτρέπω ‖ (*grant*) παρέχω, δίδω ‖ (*acknowledge*) ἀναγνωρίζω, (παρα)δέχομαι ‖ **to** ~ **for** ἀφήνω περιθώριον γιά ‖ ~**able** *a* δεκτός, ἐπιτρεπόμενος ‖ ~**ance** *n* ἐπίδομα, εἰσόδημα.

alloy ['ælɔi] *n* κράμα ‖ *vt* ἀναμιγνύω, συντήκω ‖ (*fig*) νοθεύω.

all-round ['ɔːl'raund] *a* τελειότατος, ἀρτιώτατος.

all-rounder ['ɔːl'raundə*] n ἄνθρωπος γενικῆς μορφώσεως.

all-time ['ɔːl'taim] a παντοτινός.

allude [ə'luːd] vi: to ~ to ἐννοῶ, ὑπονοῶ, ὑπαινίσσομαι.

alluring [ə'ljuəriŋ] a δελεαστικός, γοητευτικός.

allusion [ə'luːʒən] n ὑπαινιγμός, νύξις.

ally ['ælai] n σύμμαχος || [ə'lai] vt συνδέω, ἑνώνω || vi συμμαχῶ, συνδέομαι.

almighty [ɔːl'maiti] a: the A~ ὁ Παντοδύναμος.

almond · ['aːmənd] n ἀμύγδαλο || (tree) ἀμυγδαλιά.

almost ['ɔːlməust] ad σχεδόν, περίπου.

alms [aːmz] npl ἐλεημοσύνη, ψυχικό.

alone [ə'ləun] a μόνος, μονάχος, μοναχός || ad μόνον.

along [ə'lɔŋ] ad: move ~ προχωρῶ, βηματίζω ‖ ἐμπρός!, ἔλα λοιπόν! ‖ prep κατά μήκος ‖ ~side ad,prep πλευρισμένως, πλάϊ-πλάϊ ‖ all ~ ἀπό καιρό, ἀπ' τήν ἀρχή.

aloof [ə'luːf] a,ad μακράν, εἰς ἀπόστασιν.

aloud [ə'laud] ad μεγαλοφώνως, φωναχτά, δυνατά.

alphabet ['ælfəbet] n ἀλφάβητον ‖ ~ical a ἀλφαβητικός ‖ ~ically ad ἀλφαβητικῶς.

alpine ['ælpain] a ἀλπικός.

Alps [ælps] npl: the ~ αἱ Ἄλπεις.

already [ɔːl'redi] ad ἤδη, κιόλας.

alright [ɔːl'rait] = **all right** / see **right**.

also ['ɔːlsəu] ad ἐπίσης, ὡσαύτως, ἀκόμη καί.

altar ['ɔltə*] n βωμός, θυσιαστήριον ‖ (church) Ἁγία Τράπεζα.

alter ['ɔltə*] n vt μεταβάλλω, τροποποιῶ, μεταποιῶ ‖ vi μεταβάλλομαι ‖ ~ation n μεταβολή, ἀλλαγή, ἀλλοίωσις.

alternate [ɔl'təːnit] a ἐναλλάσσων, ἐναλλασσόμενος ‖ ['ɔltəːneit] vt ἐναλλάσσω, χρησιμοποιῶ ἐναλλάξ ‖ vi ἐναλλάσσομαι (with μέ) ‖ ~ly ad ἐναλλάξ, ἀλληλοδιαδόχως.

alternative [ɔl'təːnətiv] n ἐκλογή, λύσις ‖ ~ly ad ἐναλλάξ.

alternator ['ɔltəːneitə*] n (elec) ἐναλλάκτης.

although [ɔːl'ðəu] cj ἄν καί, μόλον ὅτι, καίτοι.

altitude ['æltitjuːd] n ὕψος, ὑψόμετρον.

alto ['æltəu] n (male) ὀξύφωνος ‖ (female) κοντράλτο.

altogether [ɔːltə'geðə*] ad τελείως, ὁλοσχερῶς, ἐντελῶς.

altruistic [æltru'istik] a ἀλτρουϊστικός.

aluminium [ælju'miniəm], (US) **aluminum** [ə'luːminəm] n ἀλουμίνιον, ἀργίλιον.

always ['ɔːlweiz] ad πάντα, πάντοτε, διαρκῶς.

am [æm] see **be**.

amalgam [ə'mælgəm] n ἀμάλγαμα ‖ ~ate vti ἀμαλγαμώνω, συγχωνεύω, ἑνοῦμαι ‖ ~ation n συγχώνευσις.

amass [ə'mæs] vt συσσωρεύω, μαζεύω.

amateur ['æmətə*] n ἐρασιτέχνης ‖ a ἐρασιτεχνική ‖ ~ish a ἐρασιτεχνικός.

amaze [ə'meiz] vt ἐκπλήσσω, καταπλήσσω, θαμπώνω ‖ ~d a ἔκπληκτος, κατάπληκτος ‖ ~ment n κατάπληξις, ἔκπληξις, ξάφνιασμα.

amazing [ə'meiziŋ] a καταπληκτικός, ἀπίστευτος.

ambassador [æm'bæsədə*] n πρεσβευτής, πρέσβυς.

ambiguity [æmbi'gjuiti] n ἀμφιλογία, ἀσάφεια, διφορούμενον.

ambiguous [æm'bigjuəs] a ἀμφίλογος, ἀβέβαιος, ἀσαφής.

ambition [æm'biʃən] n φιλοδοξία.

ambitious [æm'biʃəs] a φιλόδοξος.

amble ['æmbl] vi πηγαίνω ραχβάνι, βαδίζω ἤρεμα.

ambulance ['æmbjuləns] n ἀσθενοφόρον αὐτοκίνητον.

ambush ['æmbuʃ] n ἐνέδρα, καρτέρι ‖ vt παρασύρω εἰς ἐνέδραν.

ameliorate [ə'miːliəreit] vt βελτιώνω, καλυτερεύω.

amelioration [ə'miːliə'reiʃən] n καλυτέρευσις, βελτίωσις.

amen ['aːmen] interj ἀμήν.

amenable [ə'miːnəbl] a ὑπάκουος, πρόθυμος.

amend [ə'mend] vt διορθώνω, τροποποιῶ ‖ vi διορθώνομαι ‖ ~ment n τροποποίησις, διόρθωσις ‖ to make ~s ἐπανορθώνω, ἀποζημιώνω.

amenity [ə'miːniti] n χάρις, ὀμορφιά, ἄνεσις.

America [ə'merikə] n Ἀμερική.

American [ə'merikən] a ἀμερικανικός ‖ n Ἀμερικανός ‖ ~ize vt ἐξαμερικανίζω.

amiable ['eimiəbl] a εὐγενικός, φιλόφρων, γλυκύς.

amicable ['æmikəbl] a φιλικός ‖ ~ settlement n συμβιβασμός.

amid(st) [ə'mid(st)] prep ἀνάμεσα, ἀναμεταξύ.

amiss [ə'mis] a,ad ἐσφαλμένως, κακά, στραβά ‖ to take ~ παίρνω στραβά, παρεξηγῶ.

ammeter ['æmitə*] n ἀμπερόμετρον.

ammunition [æmju'niʃən] n πολεμοφόδια, πυρομαχικά.

amnesia [æm'niːziə] n ἀμνησία.

amnesty ['æmnisti] n ἀμνηστία.

among(st) [ə'mʌŋ(st)] prep μεταξύ, μέσα, ἀνάμεσα.

amoral [æ'mɔrəl] a ἄσχετος μέ τήν ἠθικήν.

amorous ['æmərəs] a ἐρωτόληπτος, ἐρωτιάρης.

amorphous [ə'mɔːfəs] a ἄμορφος.

amount [ə'maunt] n ποσόν, σύνολον, ποσότης ‖ vi ἀνέρχομαι, συμποσοῦμαι, ἰσοδυναμῶ ‖ to ~ to ἀνέρχομαι, συμποσοῦμαι.

ampère ['æmpɛə*] n ἀμπέρ.
amphibious [æm'fibiəs] a ἀμφίβιος.
amphitheatre ['æmfiθiətə*] n ἀμφιθέατρον.
ample ['æmpl] a (enough) ἀρκετός, πλήρης ‖ (big) εὐρύς, πλατύς ‖ (abundant) ἄφθονα, πλούσια.
amplifier ['æmplifaiə*] n ἐνισχυτής.
amputate ['æmpjuteit] vt ἀποκόπτω, ἀκρωτηριάζω.
amputation [æmpju'teiʃən] n ἐκτομή, ἀκρωτηριασμός.
amuck [ə'mʌk] ad: to run ~ παθαίνω ἀμόκ, παραφέρομαι.
amuse [ə'mju:z] vt διασκεδάζω, ξεκουράζω ‖ ~ment n διασκέδασις, θέαμα, ἀναψυχή.
amusing [ə'mju:ziŋ] a διασκεδαστικός, ξεκαρδιστικός.
an [æn] see a.
anachronism [ə'nækrənizəm] n ἀναχρονισμός.
anaemia [ə'ni:miə] n ἀναιμία.
anaemic [ə'ni:mik] a ἀναιμικός.
anaesthetic [ænis'θetik] n ἀναισθητικόν.
anagram ['ænəgræm] n ἀναγραμματισμός.
analgesic [ænæl'dʒi:sik] a,n ἀναλγητικός.
analogous [ə'næləgəs] a ἀνάλογος.
analogy [ə'nælədʒi] n ἀναλογία.
analyse ['ænəlaiz] vt ἀναλύω.
analysis [ə'næləsis] n ἀνάλυσις.
anarchist ['ænəkist] n ἀναρχικός.
anarchy ['ænəki] n ἀναρχία.
anatomical [ænə'tɔmikəl] a ἀνατομικός.
anatomy [ə'nætəmi] n ἀνατομία.
ancestor ['ænsistə*] n πρόγονος, προπάτωρ.
ancestral [æn'sestrəl] a προγονικός, προπατορικός.
ancestry ['ænsistri] n καταγωγή.
anchor ['æŋkə*] n ἄγκυρα ‖ vi ἀγκυροβολῶ, ρίχνω ἄγκυραν, ἀράζω ‖ ~age n ἀγκυροβόλιον, ἀραξοβόλι.
anchovy ['æntʃəvi] n ἀντσούγια, χαμψί.
ancient ['einʃənt] a ἀρχαῖος, παλαιός.
and [ænd, ənd] cj καί.
anecdote ['ænikdəut] n ἀνέκδοτον.
anemone [ə'neməni] n ἀνεμώνη.
anew [ə'nju:] ad ἐκ νέου, πάλιν, ξανά.
angel ['eindʒəl] n ἄγγελος, ἀγγελούδι ‖ ~ic a ἀγγελικός.
anger ['æŋgə*] n ὀργή, θυμός, παραφορά ‖ vt ἐξοργίζω, θυμώνω.
angle ['æŋgl] n γωνία ‖ (viewpoint) ἄποψις ‖ vi ψαρεύω ‖ ~r n ψαρᾶς (μέ καλάμι).
Anglican ['æŋglikən] n Ἀγγλικανός.
anglicize ['æŋglisaiz] vt χρησιμοποιῶ ἀγγλισμούς.
angling ['æŋgliŋ] n ψάρεμα.
Anglo- ['æŋgləu] prefix ἀγγλο-.
angrily ['æŋgrili] ad ὠργισμένα, θυμωμένα.
angry ['æŋgri] a ὠργισμένος, θυμωμένος.
anguish ['æŋgwiʃ] n ἀγωνία, ἀδημονία, πόνος.
angular ['æŋgjulə*] a γωνιακός, γωνιώδης.
animal ['æniməl] n ζῷον, a ζωϊκός.

animate ['ænimit] a ἔμψυχος, ζωντανός ‖ ['ænimeit] vt ζωογονῶ, δίδω κίνησιν ‖ ~d a ζωντανός, ζωηρός.
animation [æni'meiʃən] n ζωηρότης, θέρμη, σφρῖγος.
animosity [æni'mɔsiti] n ἐχθρότης, ἔχθρα.
aniseed ['ænisi:d] n γλυκάνισον.
ankle ['æŋkl] n ἀστράγαλος, σφυρόν.
annex(e) ['æneks] n παράρτημα ‖ annex [ə'neks] vt προσαρτῶ.
annihilate [ə'naiəleit] vt ἐκμηδενίζω, ἐξαφανίζω.
anniversary [æni'və:səri] n ἐπέτειος.
annotate ['ænəuteit] vt σχολιάζω.
announce [ə'nauns] vt (ἀν)αγγέλλω, ἀνακοινῶ ‖ ~ment n ἀναγγελία, ἀνακοίνωσις ‖ ~r n ἐκφωνητής.
annoy [ə'nɔi] vt ἐνοχλῶ, πειράζω ‖ ~ance n ἐνόχλησις, μπελᾶς, στενοχωρία ‖ ~ing a ἐνοχλητικός, ὀχληρός.
annual ['ænjuəl] a ἐτήσιος, χρονιάρικος ‖ n (book) ἐπετηρίς, ἡμερολόγιον ‖ ~ly ad ἐτησίως.
annuity [ə'nju:iti] n πρόσοδος, ἐπίδομα.
annul [ə'nʌl] vt ἀκυρώνω, διαλύω, καταργέλλω ‖ ~ment n ἀκύρωσις, κατάργησις.
anoint [ə'nɔint] vt χρίω, ἀλείφω.
anomalous [ə'nɔmələs] a ἀνώμαλος.
anomaly [ə'nɔməli] n ἀνωμαλία.
anonymity [ænə'nimiti] n ἀνωνυμία.
anonymous [ə'nɔniməs] a ἀνώνυμος.
another [ə'nʌðə*] a,pron ἄλλος (ἕνας), ἀκόμη (ἕνας) ‖ one ~ ὁ ἕνας τόν ἄλλον.
answer [ɑ:nsə*] n ἀπάντησις ‖ (solution) λύσις ‖ vt ἀπαντῶ ‖ (suit) ἀνταποκρίνομαι ‖ to ~ for vt ἐγγυῶμαι διά ‖ ~able a ὑπεύθυνος, ὑπόλογος.
ant [ænt] n μυρμήγκι.
antagonism [æn'tægənizəm] n ἀνταγωνισμός, ἀντιζηλία, ἐχθρότης.
antagonist [æn'tægənist] n ἀνταγωνιστής, ἀντίπαλος ‖ ~ic a ἐχθρικός, ἀνταγωνιστικός.
antagonize [æn'tægənaiz] vt προκαλῶ ἀνταγωνισμόν, προκαλῶ ἐχθρότητα.
Antarctic [ænt'ɑ:ktik] a ἀνταρκτικός.
antecedent [ænti'si:dənt] n ἡγούμενον ‖ a προηγούμενος.
antelope ['æntiləup] n ἀντιλόπη.
antenatal [ænti'neitl] a πρό τῆς γεννήσεως.
antenna [æn'tenə] n κεραία.
anthem ['ænθəm] n ὕμνος.
anthology [æn'θɔlədʒi] n ἀνθολογία.
anthropologist [ænθrə'pɔlədʒist] n ἀνθρωπολόγος.
anthropology [ænθrə'pɔlədʒi] n ἀνθρωπολογία.
anti-aircraft ['ænti'eəkrɑ:ft] a ἀντιαεροπορικός.
antibiotic ['æntibai'ɔtik] n ἀντιβιοτικόν.
anticipate [æn'tisipeit] vt προλαμβάνω ‖ (foresee) προβλέπω, προσδοκῶ.

anticipation [æntisi'peiʃən] *n* πρόληψις, πρόβλεψις ‖ (*expectation*) προσδοκία.

anticlimax ['ænti'klaimæks] *n* ἀντικλῖμαξ, κατάπτωσις, παρακμή.

anticlockwise ['ænti'klɔkwaiz] *ad* = **counterclockwise** ‖ *see* **counter**.

antics ['æntiks] *npl* κόλπα, ἀστεῖα, φάρσες.

anticyclone ['ænti'saikləun] *n* ἀντικυκλών.

antidote ['æntidəut] *n* ἀντίδοτον.

antifreeze ['ænti'friːz] *n* ἀντιψυκτικός, ἀντιπηκτικός.

antipathy [æn'tipəθi] *n* ἀντιπάθεια.

antiquarian [ænti'kwɛəriən] *n* ἀρχαιοδίφης, ἀρχαιόφιλος.

antiquated ['æntikweitid] *a* ἀρχαϊκός, ἀπηρχαιωμένος, πεπαλαιωμένος.

antique [æn'tiːk] *n* ἀρχαῖον, παλαιόν, ἀντίκα ‖ ~s *npl* ἀρχαιότητες, ἀντίκες.

antiquity [æn'tikwiti] *n* ἀρχαιότης.

antiseptic [ænti'septik] *a,n* ἀντισηπτικόν.

antisocial ['ænti'səuʃəl] *a* ἀντικοινωνικός.

antithesis [æn'tiθisis] *n* ἀντίθεσις.

antlers ['æntləz] *npl* κέρατα (ἐλάφου).

anus ['einəs] *n* δακτύλιος, ἕδρα.

anvil ['ænvil] *n* ἄκμων, ἀμόνι.

anxiety [æŋ'zaiəti] *n* ἀνησυχία, φόβος.

anxious ['æŋkʃəs] *a* ἀνήσυχος, στενοχωρημένος ‖ (*impatient*) ἀνυπόμονος ‖ ~**ly** *ad* ἀνήσυχα, ἀνυπόμονα.

any ['eni] *pron,a* κανείς, καμμιά, κανένα ‖ (*whosoever*) ὁποιοσδήποτε, κάθε ‖ *ad* καθόλου, πιά ‖ ~**body** *pron* κανείς, καμμιά, οἱοσδήποτε, καθένας ‖ ~**how** *ad* ὁπωσδήποτε, ὅπως κιάν εἶναι ‖ ~**one** *pron* ὁποιοσδήποτε, καθένας, ὅλοι ‖ ~**thing** *pron* τίποτε, κάτι, ὁτιδήποτε ‖ ~**way** *ad* ὁπωσδήποτε, κουτσά-στραβά ‖ *cj* ὁπωσδήποτε, ἐν πάσῃ περιπτώσει ‖ ~**where** *ad* ὁπουδήποτε, πουθενά.

apace [ə'peis] *ad* γρήγορα, ταχέως.

apart [ə'paːt] *ad* κεχωρισμένως, χωριστά, κατά μέρος ‖ ~ **from** ἐκτός τοῦ ὅτι.

apartheid [ə'paːteit] *n* διαχωρισμός, φυλετική διάκρισις.

apartment [ə'paːtmənt] *n* δωμάτιον ‖ (*flat*) διαμέρισμα.

apathetic [æpə'θetik] *a* ἀπαθής, ἀδιάφορος.

apathy ['æpəθi] *n* ἀπάθεια, ἀδιαφορία.

ape [eip] *n* πίθηκος, μαϊμοῦ ‖ *vt* μιμοῦμαι.

apéritif [ə'peritiv] *n* ὀρεκτικόν.

aperture ['æpətʃjuə*] *n* ἄνοιγμα, ὀπή, σχισμή.

apex ['eipeks] *n* κορυφή.

apiece [ə'piːs] *ad* ἕκαστος, καθένας.

Apollo [ə'pɔləu] *n* ᾿Απόλλων.

apologetic [əpɔlə'dʒetik] *a* ἀπολογητικός, τῆς συγγνώμης.

apologize [ə'pɔlədʒaiz] *vi* ζητῶ συγγνώμην.

apology [ə'pɔlədʒi] *n* ἀπολογία, συγγνώμη.

apoplexy ['æpəpleksi] *n* ἀποπληξία, συμφόρικός.

apostle [ə'pɔsl] *n* ἀπόστολος.

apostrophe [ə'pɔstrəfi] *n* ἀπόστροφος.

appal [ə'pɔːl] *vt* τρομάζω, προκαλῶ φρίκην ‖ ~**ling** *a* τρομερός, φρικτός.

apparatus [æpə'reitəs] *n* συσκευή, μηχάνημα.

apparel [ə'pærəl] *n* ἔνδυμα, ντύσιμο.

apparent [ə'pærənt] *a* φαινόμενος, ἐμφανής, φανερός ‖ ~**ly** *ad* προφανῶς, ὅπως φαίνεται.

apparition [æpə'riʃən] *n* φάντασμα.

appeal [ə'piːl] *n* (ἔκ)κλησις, προσφυγή ‖ (*law*) κλῆσις, ἔφεσις ‖ (*charm*) γοητευτική, ἑλκυστική ‖ *vi* προσφεύγω, ἀπευθύνομαι ‖ ~**ing** *a* συγκινητικός, συμπαθητικός.

appear [ə'piə*] *vi* φαίνομαι, ἐμφανίζομαι ‖ ~**ance** *n* ἐμφάνισις, παρουσία, παρουσιαστικό ‖ **to put in** *or* **make an** ~**ance** ἐμφανίζομαι, παρουσιάζομαι.

appease [ə'piːz] *vt* κατευνάζω, ἱκανοποιῶ.

appendage [ə'pendidʒ] *n* προσάρτημα, παράρτημα ‖ (*anat*) ἀπόφυσις, ἐξάρτημα.

appendicitis [əpendi'saitis] *n* σκωληκοειδῖτις.

appendix [ə'pendiks] *n* παράρτημα, ἐξάρτημα ‖ (*anat*) σκωληκοειδής ἀπόφυσις.

appetite ['æpitait] *n* ὄρεξη ‖ **loss of** ~ *n* ἀνορεξία.

appetizer ['æpitaizə*] *n* ὀρεκτικόν, μεζές.

appetizing ['æpitaiziŋ] *a* ὀρεκτικός, ἑλκυστικός.

applaud [ə'plɔːd] *vt* χειροκροτῶ, ἐπευφημῶ.

applause [ə'plɔːz] *n* χειροκροτήματα, ἐπιδοκιμασία.

apple ['æpl] *n* μῆλον ‖ ~ **pie** *n* μηλόπητα ‖ ~ **tree** *n* μηλιά.

appliance [ə'plaiəns] *n* ὄργανον, μηχάνημα, ἐργαλεῖον.

applicable [ə'plikəbl] *a* ἐφαρμόσιμος, κατάλληλος.

applicant ['æplikənt] *n* αἰτῶν, ὑποψήφιος, αἰτητής.

application [æpli'keiʃən] *n* (*request*) αἴτησις, παράκλησις ‖ (*hard work*) ἐπιμέλεια, προσοχή, προσήλωσις ‖ (*putting into practice*) ἐφαρμογή, χρῆσις.

applied [ə'plaid] *a* προσηρμοσμένος, ἐφηρμοσμένος.

apply [ə'plai] *vi* ἐφαρμόζω ‖ (*place on*) ἐπιθέτω, βάζω ‖ (*for job etc*) ἀπευθύνομαι, ὑποβάλλω αἴτησιν ‖ **to ~ the brake** πατῶ φρένο, φρενάρω ‖ **to ~ o.s.** προσηλοῦμαι, ἀφοσιώνομαι.

appoint [ə'point] *vt* (δι)ορίζω, ὀνομάζω ‖ ~**ment** *n* συνάντησις, ραντεβού, συνέντευξις.

apportion [ə'pɔːʃən] *vt* κατανέμω, διανέμω, μοιράζω.

appreciable [ə'priːʃəbl] *a* ὑπολογίσιμος, αἰσθητός.

appreciate [ə'priːʃieit] *vt* ἐκτιμῶ, ὑπολογίζω, ἀποδίδω σημασίαν ‖ *vi* (*econ*) ἀνατιμοῦμαι, ὑπερτιμοῦμαι.

appreciation [əpriːʃiˈeiʃən] *n* ἐκτίμησις ‖ (*econ*) ὑπερτίμησις, ἀνατίμησις, ὑπεραξία.

apprehend [æpriˈhend] *vt* συλλαμβάνω, ἀντιλαμβάνομαι.

apprehension [æpriˈhenʃən] *n* (*fear*) φόβος, ἀνησυχία ‖ (*understanding*) ἀντίληψις, νόησις ‖ (*arrest*) σύλληψις, τσάκισμα.

apprehensive [æpriˈhensiv] *a* (*worried*) ἀνήσυχος, ἔμφοβος, φοβισμένος.

apprentice [əˈprentis] *n* μαθητευόμενος ‖ *vt* τοποθετῶ ὡς μαθητευόμενον ‖ ~ship *n* μαθητεία, μαθήτευσις.

approach [əˈprəutʃ] *n* προσέγγισις, πλησίασμα ‖ (*path*) εἴσοδος, ὁδός ‖ (*golf*) κτύπημα ‖ *vti* πλησιάζω, προσεγγίζω ‖ ~able *a* εὐπρόσιτος, προσηνής, προσιτός.

approbation [æprəˈbeiʃən] *n* ἔγκρισις, ἐπιδοκιμασία.

appropriate [əˈprəupriit] *a* κατάλληλος, ἁρμόδιος, ταιριαστός ‖ [əˈprəuprieit] *vt* οἰκειοποιοῦμαι, ἰδιοποιοῦμαι, παίρνω.

appropriation [əprəupriˈeiʃən] *n* (*pol*) πίστωσις, κονδύλιον ‖ (*setting apart*) διάθεσις, πρόβλεψις.

approval [əˈpruːvəl] *n* ἔγκρισις.

approve [əˈpruːv] *vti* ἐγκρίνω, ἐπιδοκιμάζω, ἐπικυρώνω ‖ ~d *a* ἐγκριθείς, ἐγκεκριμένος.

approximate [əˈprɔksimit] *a* κατά προσέγγισιν ‖ [əˈprɔksimeit] *vt* προσεγγίζω, πλησιάζω.

approximation [əprɔksiˈmeiʃən] *n* προσέγγισις, ἐγγύτης.

apricot [ˈeiprikɔt] *n* βερύκκοκο.

April [ˈeiprəl] *n* Ἀπρίλιος.

apron [ˈeiprən] *n* ποδιά, μπροστέλλα.

apse [æps] *n* κόγχη, ἀψίς.

apt [æpt] *a* (*suitable*) κατάλληλος, ἁρμόζων ‖ (*ready*) ὑποκείμενος εἰς.

aptitude [ˈæptitjuːd] *n* ἱκανότης.

aqualung [ˈækwəlʌŋ] *n* συσκευή καταδύσεως, ἀκουαλάγκ.

aquarium [əˈkweəriəm] *n* ἐνυδρεῖον, ἀκουάριον.

aquatic [əˈkwætik] *a* ὑδρόβιος ‖ ~ sports *npl* θαλάσσια σπόρ.

aqueduct [ˈækwidʌkt] *n* ὑδραγωγεῖον.

Arab [ˈærəb] *a* ἀραβικός ‖ ~ia [əˈreibiə] *n* Ἀραβία ‖ ~ian [əˈreibiən] *a* Ἄραψ, ἀραβικός ‖ *n* Ἄραψ, Ἀράπης ‖ ~ic *a* ἀραβικός ‖ *n* ἀραβική γλῶσσα.

arable [ˈærəbl] *a* καλλιεργήσιμος.

arbiter [ˈɑːbitə*] *n* διαιτητής, κριτής.

arbitrary [ˈɑːbitrəri] *a* αὐθαίρετος.

arbitration [ɑːbiˈtreiʃən] *n* διαιτησία ‖ ~ court *n* διαιτητικόν δικαστήριον.

arbitrator [ˈɑːbitreitə*] *n* διαιτητής.

arc [ɑːk] *n* τόξον.

arcade [ɑːˈkeid] *n* στοά, καμάρα.

arch [ɑːtʃ] *n* ἀψίς, καμάρα ‖ *a* (*chief*) ἀρχι- ‖ *vt* (*bend*) λυγίζω, καμπουριάζω.

archaeologist [ɑːkiˈɔlədʒist] *n* ἀρχαιολόγος.

archaeology [ɑːkiˈɔlədʒi] *n* ἀρχαιολογία.

archaic [ɑːˈkeiik] *a* ἀρχαϊκός.

archbishop [ˈɑːtʃˈbiʃəp] *n* ἀρχιεπίσκοπος.

arch-enemy [ˈɑːtʃˈenimi] *n* μέγας ἐχθρός.

archer [ˈɑːtʃə*] *n* τοξότης ‖ ~y *n* τοξοβολία.

archetype [ˈɑːkitaip] *n* ἀρχέτυπον.

archimandrite [ˈɑːkiˈmændrait] *n* ἀρχιμανδρίτης.

archipelago [ɑːkiˈpeligəu] *n* ἀρχιπέλαγος, πολύνησον.

architect [ˈɑːkitekt] *n* ἀρχιτέκτων ‖ ~ure *n* ἀρχιτεκτονική ‖ ~ural *a* ἀρχιτεκτονικός.

archives [ˈɑːkaivz] *npl* ἀρχεῖα, ἔγγραφα.

archway [ˈɑːtʃwei] *n* στοά, ἁψιδωτή εἴσοδος.

arc lamp [ˈɑːklæmp] *n* λυχνία βολταϊκοῦ τόξου.

Arctic [ˈɑːktik] *a* Ἀρκτικός.

ardent [ˈɑːdənt] *a* φλογερός, διακαής, ζωηρός.

ardour [ˈɑːdə*] *n* ζέσις, μανία, πόθος.

arduous [ˈɑːdjuəs] *a* τραχύς, δύσκολος, κοπιώδης.

are [ɑː*] *see* be.

area [ˈɛəriə] *n* περιοχή, ἔκτασις, χῶρος ‖ (*math*) ἐμβαδόν.

arena [əˈriːnə] *n* παλαίστρα, κονίστρα, ἀρένα.

aren't [ɑːnt] = are not ‖ *see* be.

argue [ˈɑːgjuː] *vti* (*discuss*) συζητῶ, πραγματεύομαι ‖ (*prove*) (ἀπο)δεικνύω ‖ (*reason*) φέρω ἐπιχειρήματα, παρατάσσω.

argument [ˈɑːgjumənt] *n* ἐπιχείρημα, συζήτησις ‖ (*dispute*) φιλονεικία, λογομαχία ‖ (*of play*) σύνοψις, περίληψις ‖ ~ative *a* συζητητικός.

aria [ˈɑːriə] *n* ἦχος, σκοπός, ἄρια.

arid [ˈærid] *a* ξηρός, ἄνυδρος.

arise [əˈraiz] (*irreg* v) *vi* ἐγείρομαι, σηκώνομαι ‖ (*appear*) ἐμφανίζομαι, ἀπορρέω.

aristocracy [ærisˈtɔkrəsi] *n* ἀριστοκρατία.

aristocrat [ˈæristəkræt] *n* ἀριστοκράτης ‖ ~ic *a* ἀριστοκρατικός, ἀρχοντικός.

arithmetic [əˈriθmətik] *n* ἀριθμητική.

arm [ɑːm] *n* βραχίων, μπράτσο ‖ (*hand*) χέρι ‖ (*weapon*) ὅπλον ‖ *vt* (ἐξ)ὁπλίζω, ἁρματώνω ‖ ~s *npl* ὅπλα ‖ ~ed forces *npl* ἔνοπλοι δυνάμεις.

armchair [ˈɑːmtʃɛə*] *n* πολυθρόνα.

armful [ˈɑːmful] *n* ἀγκαλιά.

armistice [ˈɑːmistis] *n* ἀνακωχή.

armour, (*US*) **armor** [ˈɑːmə*] *n* θωράκισις ‖ (*panoply*) ἁρματωσιά ‖ ~ed car *n* τεθωρακισμένο ἅρμα μάχης.

armoury [ˈɑːməri] *n* ὁπλοστάσιον, ὁπλαποθήκη.

armpit [ˈɑːmpit] *n* μασχάλη.

army [ˈɑːmi] *n* στρατός ‖ (*of people etc*) πλῆθος.

aroma [ə'rəumə] *n* άρωμα, μυρωδιά ‖ **~tic** *a* αρωματικός.

around [ə'raund] *ad* πέριξ, (τρι)γύρω, ολόγυρα ‖ (*about*) (*US*) περίπου ‖ *prep* περί, γύρω.

arouse [ə'rauz] *vt* διεγείρω, αφυπνίζω, ξυπνώ.

arrange [ə'reindʒ] *vt* τακτοποιῶ, διαρρυθμίζω, διευθετῶ, κανονίζω ‖ **~ment** *n* τακτοποίησις, ρύθμισις, διευθέτησις.

array [ə'rei] *n* (*in lines*) σειρά, παράταξις ‖ (*dress*) στολή.

arrears [ə'riəz] *npl* καθηστερούμενα, εκπρόθεσμος ‖ **in ~** καθυστερούμενα ‖ **~ of pay** *n* καθυστερούμενοι μισθοί.

arrest [ə'rest] *n* (*making prisoner*) σύλληψις, κράτησις ‖ (*halt*) αναχαίτησις, σταμάτημα ‖ *vt* σταματῶ, αναχαιτίζω ‖ (*law*) συλλαμβάνω.

arrival [ə'raivəl] *n* άφιξις, ερχομός ‖ **new ~** *n* νεοαφιχθείς ‖ (*baby*) νεογέννητον.

arrive [ə'raiv] *vi* αφικνούμαι, φθάνω (*at* εἰς) ‖ (*at a conclusion*) καταλήγω.

arrogance ['ærəgəns] *n* αλαζονεία, έπαρσις, αυθάδεια.

arrogant ['ærəgənt] *a* αλαζών, υπερόπτης, αυθάδης.

arrow ['ærəu] *n* βέλος, σαΐτα.

arsenal ['a:sinl] *n* οπλοστάσιον.

arsenic ['a:snik] *n* αρσενικόν.

arson ['a:sn] *n* εμπρησμός.

art [a:t] *n* τέχνη ‖ **~ gallery** *n* πινακοθήκη.

artery ['a:təri] *n* αρτηρία.

artesian well [a:'ti:ziən'wel] *n* αρτεσιανόν φρέαρ.

artful ['a:tful] *a* (*person*) επιδέξιος, εφευρετικός ‖ (*crafty*) πονηρός, δόλιος.

arthritis [a:'θraitis] *n* αρθρῖτις.

artichoke ['a:titʃəuk] *n* αγκινάρα.

article ['a:tikl] *n* (*of agreement etc*) άρθρον, όρος ‖ (*gram*) άρθρον ‖ (*newspaper etc*) άρθρον ‖ (*items*) είδος, αντικείμενον.

articulate [a:'tikjulit] *a* αρθρωτός, έναρθρος ‖ (*in expression*) σαφής, ευκρινής ‖ **~d** *a* έναρθρος.

artifice ['a:tifis] *n* τέχνασμα, κόλπο ‖ (*skill*) τέχνη, επιδεξιότης.

artificial [a:ti'fiʃəl] *a* τεχνητός, ψεύτικος ‖ **~ respiration** *n* τεχνητή αναπνοή.

artillery [a:'tiləri] *n* πυροβολικόν.

artisan ['a:tizæn] *n* τεχνίτης, βιοτέχνης, εργάτης.

artist ['a:tist] *n* καλλιτέχνης ‖ (*painter*) ζωγράφος ‖ **~ic** *a* καλλιτεχνικός.

artless ['a:tlis] *a* άτεχνος ‖ (*natural*) απέριττος, φυσικός ‖ (*naive*) αφελής, απονήρευτος.

as [æz, əz] *ad* (*in main clause*) επίσης, εξ ίσου, τόσον . . . όσον ‖ **~ regards** όσο γιά ‖ *cj* (*in subject clause*) όσον, τόσον . . . όσον, σάν ‖ (*time*) ενῶ, καθώς ‖ (*because*) επειδή ‖ (*manner*) **do ~ you**

G.P.D.-H

like κάμετε όπως σᾶς αρέσει ‖ **~ is** όπως είναι.

asbestos [æz'bestəs] *n* αμίαντος, άσβεστος.

ascend [ə'send] *vi* ανέρχομαι, ανεβαίνω ‖ **~ant** *a* ανερχόμενος ‖ *n* άνοδος ‖ **~ancy** *n* (*influence*) επιρροή, επιβολή ‖ (*rule*) ηγεμονία, υπεροχή.

ascension [ə'senʃən] *n* ανάβασις, άνοδος, ανάληψις ‖ **A~ Day** *n* τῆς Αναλήψεως.

ascent [ə'sent] *n* άνοδος, ανάβασις ‖ (*incline*) ανήφορος, ανωφέρεια, κλίσις.

ascertain [æsə'tein] *vt* διαπιστώνω, εξακριβώνω.

ascetic [ə'setik] *a* ασκητικός. ·

ash [æʃ] *n* τέφρα, στάχτη ‖ (*tree*) μελία, φλαμούρι.

ashamed [ə'ʃeimd] *a*: **to be ~** είμαι ντροπιασμένος, ντρέπομαι.

ashen ['æʃən] *a* σταχτής ‖ (*person*) ωχρός, κίτρινος.

ashore [ə'ʃɔ:*] *ad* στήν ξηρά, προσηραγμένος.

ashtray ['æʃtrei] *n* στακτοδοχείο.

Asia ['eiʒə] *n* Ασία ‖ **~n** *a* ασιατικός ‖ **~tic** *a* ασιατικός ‖ **~ Minor** *n* Μικρά Ασία.

aside [ə'said] *ad* κατά μέρος, πλάϊ, παράμερα ‖ **~ from** εκτός, πέραν.

ask [a:sk] *vt* (ε)ρωτῶ, ζητῶ, προσκαλῶ ‖ **to ~ a question** υποβάλλω ερώτησιν.

askance [ə'ska:ns] *ad*: **to look at s.o. ~** κοιτάζω μέ δυσπιστίαν.

askew [ə'skju:] *ad* λοξά, στραβά.

asleep [ə'sli:p] *a*,*ad* κοιμισμένος ‖ (*foot*) μουδιασμένος ‖ **to fall ~** αποκοιμιέμαι.

asparagus [əs'pærəgəs] *n* σπαράγγι.

aspect ['æspekt] *n* θέα, όψις, προσανατολισμός.

asphalt ['æsfælt] *n* άσφαλτος ‖ **~ road** *n* ασφαλτοστρωμένος (δρόμος).

asphyxiate [æs'fiksieit] *vt* πνίγω.

asphyxiation [æsfiksi'eiʃən] *n* ασφυξία.

aspirate ['æspəreit] *vt* δασύνω.

aspiration [æspə'reiʃən] *n* φιλοδοξία, βλέψις ‖ (*gram*) δασεία προφορά.

aspire [əs'paiə*] *vt*: **to ~ to** φιλοδοξῶ, εποφθαλμιῶ.

aspirin ['æsprin] *n* ασπιρίνη.

ass [æs] *n* γάϊδαρος.

assail [ə'seil] *vt* επιτίθεμαι, προσβάλλω ‖ **~ant** *n* επιτιθέμενος.

assassin [ə'sæsin] *n* δολοφόνος ‖ **~ate** *vt* δολοφονῶ ‖ **~ation** *n* δολοφονία.

assault [ə'sɔ:lt] *n* έφοδος, επίθεσις ‖ *vt* επιτίθεμαι, εξορμῶ ‖ (*person*) βιάζω.

assemblage [ə'semblidʒ] *n* σύνδεσις, συναρμολόγησις.

assemble [ə'sembl] *vt* συγκεντρώνω, συναθροίζω ‖ (*machine etc*) ενώνω, συναρμολογῶ ‖ *vi* συγκεντρούμαι, συγκεντρώνομαι.

assembly [ə'sembli] *n* συνέλευσις, συγκέντρωσις ‖ (*machines*) συναρμολόγησις, συγκρότημα ‖ ~ **line** *n* τράπεζα συναρμολογήσεως, ἀλυσίδα.

assent [ə'sent] *n* συγκατάθεσις, ἔγκρισις ‖ *vi* συγκατατίθεμαι, συναινῶ, ἐπικυρῶ.

assert [ə'sə:t] *vt* ἐπιβάλλω, διεκδικῶ ‖ (*ascertain*) βεβαιῶ, ὑποστηρίζω ‖ ~**ion** *n* ἰσχυρισμός, ὑποστήριξις ‖ ~**ive** *a* κατηγορηματικός, θετικός.

assess [ə'ses] *vt* καταλογίζω, ὑπολογίζω, ἐπιβάλλω (φόρον) ‖ (*property*) ἐκτιμῶ, φορολογῶ ‖ ~**ment** *n* καταλογισμός, ἐκτίμησις ‖ (*tax*) φόρος ‖ ~**or** *n* ἐλεγκτής (ἐφοριακός).

asset ['æset] *n* περιουσιακόν στοιχεῖον ‖ (*qualities*) προσόν, ἀξία, ἀτού ‖ ~**s** *npl* περιουσία ‖ (*econ*) ἐνεργητικόν, λαβεῖν.

assiduity [æsi'djuəti] *n* ἐπιμονή, προσήλωσις, ἐπιμέλεια.

assiduous [ə'sidjuəs] *a* ἐπιμελής, προσεκτικός.

assign [ə'sain] *vt* προορίζω, παρέχω, παραχωρῶ, δίδω ‖ ~**ment** *n* ἀνατιθεμένη ἐργασία.

assimilate [ə'simileit] *vt* ἐξομοιώνω ‖ (*food*) ἀφομοιώνω.

assimilation [əsimi'leiʃən] *n* ἀφομοίωσις.

assist [ə'sist] *vt* συνδρῶ, ὑποστηρίζω, μετέχω ‖ ~**ance** *n* βοήθεια, ἀρωγή ‖ ~**ant** *n* βοηθός ‖ *a* βοηθητικός, ἀναπληρωματικός.

assizes [ə'saiziz] *npl*: **court of** ~ ὁρκωτόν δικαστήριον.

associate [ə'səuʃiit] *n* ἑταῖρος, συνέταιρος, συνεργάτης ‖ [ə'səuʃieit] *vti*: **to** ~ **with** συνδέω, συνεταιρίζω, συνεργάζομαι, συναναστρέφομαι.

association [əsəusi'eiʃən] *n* (*club*) ἑταιρεία, ὀργανισμός, σωματεῖον ‖ (*keeping company*) συναναστροφή, σχέσις ‖ ~ **football** *n* ποδόσφαιρον.

assort [ə'sɔːt] *vt* (*arrange*) ταξινομῶ, τακτοποιῶ ‖ (*match*) ταιριάζω, προσαρμόζω ‖ ~**ed** *a* ταιριασμένος, ἀσορτί ‖ ~**ment** *n* συλλογή, ἀσορτιμέντο ‖ (*arrangement*) τακτοποίησις, ταξινόμησις.

assuage [ə'sweidʒ] *vt* κατευνάζω, ἀνακουφίζω, καλμάρω.

assume [ə'sjuːm] *vt* (*take for granted*) ὑποθέτω, θεωρῶ ‖ (*duty*) ἀναλαμβάνω, ἀναδέχομαι ‖ ~**d name** *n* ψευδώνυμον.

assumption [ə'sʌmpʃən] *n* (*supposition*) ὑπόθεσις, εἰκασία ‖ (*eccl*) Κοίμησις τῆς Θεοτόκου.

assurance [ə'ʃuərəns] *n* (*certainty*) βεβαιότης ‖ (*confidence*) διαβεβαίωσις, ὑπόσχεσις ‖ (*insurance*) ἀσφάλεια (ζωῆς).

assure [ə'ʃuə*] *vt* (δια)βεβαιῶ, ἐξασφαλίζω ‖ ~**d** *a* βέβαιος.

aster ['æstə*] *n* ἀστήρ, ἀστράκι.

asterisk ['æstərisk] *n* ἀστερίσκος.

astern [ə'stə:n] *ad* ὀπίσω, πρός τά ὀπίσω.

asthma ['æsmə] *n* ἄσθμα ‖ ~**tic** *a* ἀσθματικός.

astonish [ə'stɔniʃ] *vt* ἐκπλήσσω, καταπλήσσω ‖ ~**ing** *a* ἐκπληκτικός, καταπληκτικός ‖ ~**ment** *n* ἔκπληξις, κατάπληξις.

astound [ə'staund] *vt* καταπλήσσω, ξαφνίζω ‖ ~**ing** *a* καταπληκτικός, πρωτοφανής.

astray [ə'strei] *ad*: **to go** ~ περιπλανῶμαι, παραστρατίζω, ξεστρατίζω.

astride [ə'straid] *a,prep* καβάλλα, ἀσεβάλ.

astringent [əs'trindʒənt] *n* στυπτικόν ‖ *a* στυπτικός.

astrologer [əs'trɔlədʒə*] *n* ἀστρολόγος.

astrology [əs'trɔlədʒi] *n* ἀστρολογία.

astronaut ['æstrənɔːt] *n* ἀστροναύτης.

astronomer [əs'trɔnəmə*] *n* ἀστρονόμος.

astronomy [əs'trɔnəmi] *n* ἀστρονομία.

astute [əs'tjuːt] *a* ἔξυπνος, τετραπέρατος ‖ (*crafty*) πανοῦργος, πονηρός.

asunder [ə'sʌndə*] *ad* κεχωρισμένως, κομματιαστά.

asylum [ə'sailəm] *n* (*refuge*) ἄσυλον, καταφύγιον ‖ (*for insane*) ψυχιατρεῖον.

at [æt] *prep* (*of place*) εἰς ‖ (*of time*) εἰς, κατά, περί ‖ ~ **six o'clock** στίς ἕξι ‖ ~ **first** στήν ἀρχή ‖ ~ **home** στό σπίτι ‖ ~ **least** τουλάχιστο ‖ ~ **last** ἐπί τέλους ‖ (*of cause*) γιά ‖ ~ **all** καθόλου ‖ **not** ~ **all** οὐδόλως ‖ ~ **sea** (*col*) τά ἔχω χαμένα.

ate [eit] *pt of* eat.

atheism ['eiθiizəm] *n* ἀθεϊσμός.

atheist ['eiθiist] *n* ἄθεος, ἀθεϊστής.

athlete ['æθliːt] *n* ἀθλητής.

athletic [æθ'letik] *a* ἀθλητικός ‖ ~**s** *n* ἀθλητισμός, σπόρ.

atlas ['ætləs] *n* ἄτλας.

atmosphere ['ætməsfiə*] *n* ἀτμόσφαιρα.

atmospheric [ætməs'ferik] *a* ἀτμοσφαιρικός ‖ ~**s** *npl* παράσιτα (ἀτμοσφαιρικά).

atoll ['ætɔl] *n* ἀτόλλη.

atom ['ætəm] *n* ἄτομον ‖ ~**ic bomb** *n* ἀτομική βόμβα ‖ ~**ic energy** *n* ἀτομική ἐνέργεια.

atonement [ə'təunmənt] *n* ἔκτισις, ἐπανόρθωσις.

atrocious [ə'trəuʃəs] *a* φρικτός, φρικώδης, φρικαλέος.

atrocity [ə'trɔsiti] *n* ἀγριότης, φρίκη (ἐγκλήματος).

attach [ə'tætʃ] *vt* συνδέω, προσαρτῶ, (ἐπι)συνάπτω ‖ **to** ~ **importance to** δίνω σημασίαν ‖ ~**ed** *a* ἀπεσπασμένος, προσηρτημένος ‖ ~**ment** *n* προσάρτησις, προσκόλλησις ‖ (*devotion to*) ἀφοσίωσις, στοργή.

attaché [ə'tæʃei] *n* ἀκόλουθος ‖ ~ **case** *n* χαρτοφύλαξ.

attack [ə'tæk] *n* ἐπίθεσις, προσβολή ‖ *vt* ἐπιτίθεμαι, προσβάλλω ‖ ~**er** *n* ἐπιτιθέμενος.

attain [ə'tein] *vt* φθάνω, ἀφικνοῦμαι,

κατορθώνω ‖ ~**able** *a* ἐφικτός, κατορθωτός ‖ ~**ment** *n* ἐπίτευξις, πραγματοποίησις ‖ (*learning*) γνῶσις, προσόν.

attempt [ə'tempt] *n* ἀπόπειρα, προσπάθεια, δοκιμή ‖ *vt* ἀποπειρῶμαι, προσπαθῶ.

attend [ə'tend] *vt* (*be present*) παρευρίσκομαι ‖ (*visit*) ἐπισκέπτομαι, συχνάζω ‖ (*wait on*) ὑπηρετῶ ‖ *vi* (*listen*) εἰσακούω ‖ (*look after*) ἀσχολοῦμαι ‖ **to ~ to** προσέχω, φροντίζω ‖ ~**ance** *n* (*presence*) συμμετοχή, παρουσία ‖ ~**ant** *n* ἀκόλουθος, ὑπηρέτης ‖ *a* συνοδεύων.

attention [ə'tenʃən] *n* προσοχή ‖ (*care*) περιποίησις, φροντίδα.

attentive [ə'tentiv] *a* προσεκτικός, περιποιητικός ‖ ~**ly** *ad* προσεκτικά.

attenuate [ə'tenjueit] *vt* μετριάζω, ἀμβλύνω, ἀραιώνω.

attest [ə'test] *vt* ἐπικυρῶ, (ἐπι)βεβαιῶ, καταθέτω ὡς μάρτυς.

attic ['ætik] *n* σοφίτα.

attire [ə'taiə*] *n* ἐνδυμασία, ἔνδυμα, ντύσιμο, φορεσιά ‖ *vt* ἐνδύομαι, στολίζομαι, ντύνομαι.

attitude ['ætitju:d] *n* στάσις.

attorney [ə'tə:ni] *n* δικηγόρος, πληρεξούσιος ‖ **district ~** *n* εἰσαγγελεύς ‖ **A~ general** *n* γενικός εἰσαγγελεύς ‖ **power of ~** *n* πληρεξούσιον.

attract [ə'trækt] *vt* ἑλκύω, ἕλκω, τραβῶ, γοητεύω ‖ ~**ion** *n* (*phys*) ἕλξις ‖ (*of person*) γοητεία, χάρες ‖ (*theat*) ἀτραξιόν ‖ ~**ive** *a* ἑλκυστικός, γοητευτικός.

attribute ['ætribju:t] *n* χαρακτηριστικόν γνώρισμα ‖ (*gram*) ἐπίθετον ‖ [ə'tribju:t] *vt*: **to ~ to** ἀποδίδω (εἰς).

attrition [ə'triʃən] *n* τριβή, φθορά, ξύσιμο.

auburn ['ɔ:bən] *a* πυρόξανθα.

auction ['ɔ:kʃən] *n* πλειστηριασμός, δημοπρασία ‖ *vt* πλειστηριάζω, βγάζω στό σφυρί ‖ ~ **room** *n* αἴθουσα δημοπρασιῶν ‖ ~**eer** *n* προΐστάμενος δημοπρασιῶν.

audacious [ɔ:'deiʃəs] *a* τολμηρός, παράτολμος ‖ (*insolent*) θρασύς, ἀναιδής.

audacity [ɔ:'dæsiti] *n* τόλμη, θάρρος ‖ (*insolence*) ἀναίδεια, ἰταμότης.

audible ['ɔ:dibl] *a* ἀκουστός, ἀκουόμενος.

audience ['ɔ:diəns] *n* (*formal interview*) ἀκρόασις ‖ (*gathering*) ἀκροατήριον ‖ (*theat*) θεαταί.

audit ['ɔ:dit] *n* ἔλεγχος, ἐπαλήθευσις ‖ *vt* ἐλέγχω ‖ ~**or** *n* ἐλεγκτής ‖ (*student*) ἀκροατής.

audition [ɔ:'diʃən] *n* ἀκρόασις (τραγουδιστοῦ κτλ).

auditorium [ɔ:di'tɔ:riəm] *n* αἴθουσα, θέατρον.

augment [ɔ:g'ment] *vt* (ἐπ)αυξάνω, μεγαλώνω.

augur [ɔ:gə*] *vi* προοιωνίζομαι, προβλέπω.

augury ['ɔ:gjuri] *n* οἰωνός, προφητεία, προμήνυμα.

August ['ɔ:gəst] *n* Αὔγουστος.

august [ɔ:'gʌst] *a* σεβάσμιος, μεγαλοπρεπής.

aunt [ɑ:nt] *n* θεία ‖ ~**y**, ~**ie** *n* θείτσα.

aura ['ɔ:rə] *n* αὔρα, φωτοστέφανος.

auspices ['ɔ:spisiz] *npl* αἰγίς ‖ (*omens*) οἰωνοί ‖ **under the ~ of** ὑπό τήν αἰγίδα τοῦ.

auspicious [ɔ:s'piʃəs] *a* εὐνοϊκός, εὐοίωνος.

austere [ɔs'tiə*] *a* αὐστηρός.

austerity [ɔs'teriti] *n* αὐστηρότης ‖ (*of habits etc*) λιτότης.

Australia [ɔs'treiliə] *n* Αὐστραλία ‖ ~**n** *a,n* Αὐστραλός, αὐστραλιακός.

Austria ['ɔstriə] *n* Αὐστρία ‖ ~**n** *a,n* Αὐστριακός.

authentic [ɔ:'θentik] *a* αὐθεντικός, γνήσιος ‖ ~**ity** *n* αὐθεντικότης.

authenticate [ɔ:'θentikeit] *vt* ἐπισημοποιῶ, βεβαιῶ.

author ['ɔ:θə*] *n* συγγραφεύς ‖ (*cause*) δημιουργός, πρωταίτιος.

authoritarian [ɔ:θɔri'teəriən] *a* ἀπολυταρχικός.

authority [ɔ:'θɔriti] *n* ἐξουσία, ἄδεια, ἐντολή ‖ (*specialist*) αὐθεντία ‖ (*pol*) ὑπηρεσία.

authorize ['ɔ:θəraiz] *vt* ἐξουσιοδοτῶ, ἐπιτρέπω.

auto ['ɔ:təu] *n* (*US*) = **automobile**.

autobiographical ['ɔ:təubaiəu'græfikəl] *a* αὐτοβιογραφικός.

autobiography [ɔ:təubai'ɔgrəfi] *n* αὐτοβιογραφία.

autocracy [ɔ:'tɔkrəsi] *n* μονοκρατορία, ἀπολυταρχία.

autocratic [ɔ:təu'krætik] *a* αὐτοκρατορικός, αὐταρχικός.

autograph ['ɔ:təgrɑ:f] *n* αὐτόγραφον.

automatic [ɔ:tə'mætik] *a* αὐτόματος ‖ ~**ally** *ad* αὐτομάτως.

automation [ɔ:tə'meiʃən] *n* αὐτοματοποίησις.

automaton [ɔ:'tɔmətən] *n* αὐτόματον.

automobile ['ɔ:təməbi:l] *n* (*US*) αὐτοκίνητο, ἁμάξι.

autonomous [ɔ:'tɔnəməs] *a* αὐτόνομος.

autonomy [ɔ:'tɔnəmi] *n* αὐτονομία.

autopsy ['ɔ:tɔpsi] *n* αὐτοψία, νεκροψία.

autumn ['ɔ:təm] *n* φθινόπωρο.

auxiliary [ɔ:g'ziliəri] *a* βοηθητικός, ἐπικουρικός.

avail [ə'veil] *n* χρησιμότης, ὠφέλεια, ὄφελος ‖ *vti* ὠφελῶ, βοηθῶ, ἐξυπηρετῶ ‖ ~**able** *a* διαθέσιμος, προσιτός ‖ ~**ability** *n* διαθεσιμότης.

avalanche ['ævəlɑ:nʃ] *n* χιονοστιβάδα ‖ (*fig*) συρροή, πλημμύρα.

avant-garde ['ævɑ:ŋ'gɑ:d] *n* προφυλακή.

avarice ['ævəris] *n* τσιγγουνιά.

avaricious [ævə'riʃəs] *a* τσιγγούνης.

avenge [ə'vendʒ] *vt* ἐκδικοῦμαι.

avenue ['ævənju:] *n* λεωφόρος.

average ['ævəridʒ] n μέσον, μέσος ὅρος ‖ (naut) ἀβαρία ‖ a μέσος, μέτριος ‖ vti ἐξάγω τόν μέσον ὅρον.

averse [ə'vɔ:s] a ἀντίθετος, ἐνάντιος ‖ to be ~ to ἐναντιοῦμαι εἰς.

aversion [ə'vɔ:ʃən] n ἀποστροφή, ἀπέχθεια ‖ (col) ἀντιπάθεια.

avert [ə'vɔ:t] vt ἀποστρέφω ‖ (prevent) ἀποτρέπω, ἀπομακρύνω.

aviary ['eiviəri] n πτηνοτροφεῖον.

aviation [eivi'eiʃən] n ἀεροπορία.

avid ['ævid] a: ~ for ἄπληστος, ἀχόρταγος γιά ‖ ~ly ad ἀπλήστως.

avocado [ævə'ka:dəu] n ἀβοκάντο.

avoid [ə'vɔid] vt ἀποφεύγω ‖ ~able a φευκτέος ‖ ~ance n ἀποφυγή.

avow [ə'vau] vt ὁμολογῶ ‖ ~al n ὁμολογία.

await [ə'weit] vt ἀναμένω, περιμένω.

awake [ə'weik] (irreg v) vti ξυπνῶ, ἀφυπνίζω, ἐφυπνίζομαι ‖ a ξύπνιος, ἄγρυπνος.

awakening [ə'weikniŋ] n ἀφύπνισις, ξύπνημα.

award [ə'wɔ:d] n βραβεῖον ‖ (law) διαιτησία ‖ vt ἐπιδικάζω ‖ (reward) ἀπονέμω.

aware [ə'wεə*] a: ~ (of) πληροφορημένος, γνώστης ‖ ~ness n συνείδησις.

away [ə'wei] ad μακράν, μακρυά ‖ (absent) ἀπουσιάζω, λείπω ‖ ~ with! πάρτο ἀπ' ἐδῶ!

awe [ɔ:] n φόβος, τρόμος ‖ (deep respect) σεβασμός ‖ vt τρομάζω ‖ ~-inspiring a ἐπιβλητικός.

awful ['ɔ:fəl] a (very bad) τρομερός, φοβερός ‖ ~ly ad τρομερά, τρομακτικά.

awhile [ə'wail] ad ὀλίγον, ἐπ' ὀλίγον, μιά στιγμή.

awkward ['ɔ:kwəd] a ἀδέξιος, ἀνεπιτήδειος ‖ ~ness n (embarrassment) στενοχώρια, ἀμηχανία.

awning ['ɔ:niŋ] n σκηνή, τέντα.

awoke [ə'wəuk] pt, pp of awake.

awry [ə'rai] ad λοξός, στραβός ‖ to go ~ πηγαίνω στραβά.

ax [æks] (US) = axe.

axe [æks] n τσεκούρι ‖ vt περιορίζω ‖ (dismiss) ἀπολύω.

axiom ['æksiəm] n ἀξίωμα ‖ ~atic a ἀξιωματικός, προφανής.

axis ['æksis] n ἄξων.

axle ['æksl] n ἄξων.

ay(e) [ai] interj (yes) the ~es npl τά ναί, τά ὑπέρ.

azure ['eiʒə*] a κυανοῦς, γαλανός.

B, b

babble ['bæbl] n μωρολογία, τραύλισμα ‖ vi τραυλίζω, φλυαρῶ.

babe [beib] n μωρό, μπέμπης.

baboon [bə'bu:n] n μπαμπουίνος.

baby ['beibi] n βρέφος, νήπιον, μωρό ‖ ~ carriage n (US) καροτσάκι μωροῦ ‖ ~ish a μωρουδίστικος ‖ ~-sit vi μπέϊμπισιτ, φυλάω νήπιον, προσέχω μωρό ‖ ~-sitter n φύλακας νηπίων, μπέϊμπισιτερ.

bachelor ['bætʃələ*] n ἄγαμος, ἐργένης ‖ B~ of Arts n πτυχιοῦχος (φιλολογίας) ‖ B~ of Science n πτυχιοῦχος ἐπιστημῶν.

back [bæk] n (person, horse) ράχη, πλάτη, νῶτα ‖ (house etc) ὀπίσθιος, πισινός ‖ (sport) μπάκ ‖ vt (support) ὑποστηρίζω ‖ (movement) κάνω πίσω ‖ (sport) ποντάρω ‖ vi (go backwards) ὀπισθοχωρῶ, κάνω πίσω ‖ a ὀπίσθιος, πισινός ‖ ad (ὀ)πίσω, πρός τά πίσω ‖ (again) πάλι ‖ (in time) ἐδῶ καί λίγα χρόνια ‖ to ~ out vi ἀνακαλῶ, ξελέω ‖ (col) τό σκάω ‖ ~biting n κουτσομπολιό ‖ ~bone n ραχοκοκκαλιά ‖ (firmness) θάρρος, κουράγιο ‖ ~-cloth n φόντο ‖ ~er n (sport) παίκτης ‖ (comm) χρηματοδότης ‖ ~fire n πρόωρος ἔκρηξις ‖ ~ground n (scene) βάθος, φόντο ‖ (information) προϊστορία, τό ἱστορικό ‖ (education etc) προσόντα ‖ ~hand n (blow) ἀνάποδη καρπαζιά ‖ ~handed a ὕπουλον ‖ (compliment) διφορούμενον κομπλιμέντο, διφορούμενη φιλοφρόνησις ‖ ~ing n ὑποστήριξις ‖ (movement) ὀπισθοδρόμησις ‖ ~ number n (newspaper etc) παλαιόν φύλλον ‖ ~ pay n καθυστερούμενος μισθός ‖ ~side n (col) πισινός ‖ ~ward a ὀπίσθιος, πρός τά πίσω ‖ (child etc) καθυστερημένο ‖ ~wardness n καθυστέρησις ‖ (hesitation) δειλία, δισταγμός ‖ ~wards ad πρός τά πίσω ‖ (flow) ἀντίθετα ‖ ~yard n ὀπισθία αὐλή.

bacon ['beikən] n καπνιστό χοιρινό, μπέϊκον.

bacteria [bæk'tiəriə] npl μικρόβια.

bad [bæd] a κακός, ἄσχημος.

badge [bædʒ] n διακριτικό, σῆμα, ἔμβλημα.

badger ['bædʒə*] n ἀσβός ‖ vt παρενοχλῶ, βασανίζω.

badly ['bædli] ad κακῶς, ἄσχημα ‖ ~ off σέ δύσκολη θέση, φτωχός.

bad-tempered ['bæd'tempəd] a δύστροπος, γκρινιάρης.

baffle ['bæfl] vt (puzzle) ματαιώνω, τά χάνω.

bag [bæg] n σάκκος, σακκούλα ‖ (handbag) τσάντα ‖ vt σακκουλιάζω ‖ (capture etc) σκοτώνω, πιάνω ‖ ~ful n σακκουλιά ‖ ~gage n ἀποσκευές, βαλίτσες ‖ ~pipes npl γκάϊντα.

bail [beil] n ἐγγύησις ‖ vt (prisoner) ἐλευθερώνω μέ ἐγγύησι ‖ to ~ out (boat) βγάζω τά νερά, ἀδειάζω ‖ see also bale.

bailiff ['beilif] n δικαστικός κλητήρας.

bait [beit] n δόλωμα ‖ vt δελεάζω, δολώνω ‖ (harass) βασανίζω.

bake [beik] vt ψήνω σέ φοῦρνο ‖ vi ψήνομαι ‖ ~r n φούρναρης ‖ ~ry n φουρνάρικο.

baking ['beikiŋ] n ψήσιμο.

balance ['bæləns] n ζυγός, ζυγαριά ‖ (equilibrium) ισορροπία ‖ (of account) υπόλοιπον ‖ (econ) ισολογισμός ‖ vt ζυγίζω, σταθμίζω ‖ (counterbalance) ισορροπῶ, ισοζυγίζω ‖ ~d a ισορροπημένος ‖ (equal) ίσος, ισοδύναμος ‖ ~ sheet n ισολογισμός.

balcony ['bælkəni] n εξώστης, μπαλκόνι.

bald [bɔ:ld] a φαλακρός, καραφλός ‖ (plain) γυμνός, ξηρός.

bale [beil] n δέμα, μπάλλα, κόλος ‖ to ~ or bail out (aviat) πηδῶ μέ ἀλεξίπτωτο.

balk [bɔ:k] vt ματαιώνω, ἀνατρέπω.

Balkan ['bɔ:lkən] a Βαλκανικός.

ball [bɔ:l] n σφαίρα, μπάλλα, τόπι ‖ (dance) χοροεσπερίς, χορός.

ballad ['bæləd] n μπαλάντα.

ballast ['bæləst] n ἕρμα, σαβούρα.

ball bearing ['bɔ:l'bɛəriŋ] n σφαιροτριβεύς, ρουλεμάν.

ballerina [bælə'ri:nə] n μπαλλαρίνα.

ballet ['bælei] n μπαλλέτο.

balloon [bə'lu:n] n ἀερόστατο, μπαλόνι.

ballot ['bælət] n ψηφοδέλτιον.

ballpoint (pen) ['bɔ:lpɔint (pen)] n μπίκ, στυλό, πέννα διαρκείας.

ballroom ['bɔ:lrum] n αἴθουσα χορού.

balmy ['ba:mi] a γλυκύς, κατευναστικός ‖ (col) παλαβός.

balustrade [bæləs'treid] n κιγκλίδωμα, κάγκελλα.

bamboo [bæm'bu:] n μπαμπού, καλάμι.

bamboozle [bæm'bu:zl] vt ἐξαπατῶ, κοροϊδεύω.

ban [bæn] n προγραφή ‖ (church) ἀφορισμός ‖ vt ἀπαγορεύω.

banal [bə'na:l] a κοινός, χυδαῖος.

banana [bə'na:nə] n μπανάνα.

band [bænd] n δεσμός, δέσιμο, στεφάνι ‖ (group) ὁμάδα, συντροφία ‖ (mus) ὀρχήστρα, μπάντα ‖ vi (+together) συνασπίζομαι ‖ vt (tie) δένω ‖ ~age n ἐπίδεσμος, φάσκιά.

bandit ['bændit] n ληστής.

bandy ['bændi] vt ἀνταλλάσσω.

bandy-legged ['bændi'legd] a στραβοπόδης, στραβοκάνης.

bang [bæŋ] n (blow) κτύπημα ‖ (noise) θόρυβος ‖ vti κτυπάω, κρούω.

banish ['bæniʃ] vt ἐξορίζω, ἐκτοπίζω.

banister(s) ['bænistə*(z)] n(pl) κιγκλίδωμα, κάγκελλα.

banjo ['bændʒəu] n μπάντζο.

bank [bæŋk] n τράπεζα ‖ (ground) ἀνάχωμα, ὕψωμα ‖ (of river) ὄχθη ‖ vt (tilt) κλίνω, στρέφω ‖ (pile up) σωριάζω ‖ (money) καταθέτω, βάζω ‖ ~ account n τραπεζιτικός λογαριασμός ‖ ~er n τραπεζίτης ‖ ~ holiday n ἀργία τραπεζῶν ‖ ~note n τραπεζογραμμάτιον, μπανκανότα ‖ ~rupt n πτωχεύσας, χρεωκοπημένος ‖ vt πτωχεύω ‖ ~ruptcy n πτώχευσις, χρεωκοπία.

banner ['bænə*] n σημαία, μπαντιέρα.

banns [bænz] npl ἀγγελία γάμου.

banquet ['bæŋkwit] n συμπόσιο, γλέντι, τσιμπούσι.

banter ['bæntə*] n χαριτολόγημα, σκέρτσο.

baptism ['bæptizəm] n βάφτισμα.

Baptist ['bæptist] n βαπτιστής.

baptize [bæp'taiz] vt βαφτίζω.

bar [ba:*] n (rod) ράβδος, κοντάρι ‖ (of soap etc) κομμάτι, πλάκα ‖ (pub) μπάρ, ποτοπωλείον ‖ (obstacle) φραγμός, ἐμπόδιον ‖ (in court) ἐδώλιον ‖ (mus) μπάρα ‖ vt (fasten) κλείνω, ἀμπαρώνω, κιγκλιδώνω ‖ (hinder) φράσσω, ἐμποδίζω ‖ (exclude) ἀπαγορεύω, ἀποκλείω ‖ the B~ δικηγορικόν ἐπάγγελμα.

barbarian [ba:'bɛəriən] n βάρβαρος.

barbaric [ba:'bærik] a βάρβαρος, ἀγροῖκος.

barbarity [ba:'bæriti] n βαρβαρότης, ἀγριότης.

barbarous ['ba:bərəs] a βάρβαρος.

barbecue ['ba:bikju:] n ψησταριά.

barbed wire ['ba:bd'waiə*] n συρματόπλεγμα.

barber ['ba:bə*] n κουρέας, μπαρμπέρης.

barbiturate [ba:'bitjurit] n βαρβιτουρικόν.

bare [bɛə*] a γυμνός ‖ (living etc) λιγοστός, μόλις ‖ vt γυμνώνω ‖ (reveal) ἀποκαλύπτω ‖ ~back ad χωρίς σέλλα ‖ ~faced a ξεδιάντροπος, ἀναιδής ‖ ~foot a ξυπόλητος ‖ ~headed a ξεσκούφωτος, ἀσκεπής ‖ ~ly ad μόλις ‖ ~ness n γύμνια.

bargain ['ba:gin] n συναλλαγή, ἀγορά ‖ (bought cheaply) εὐκαιρία ‖ into the ~ ἐπί πλέον, ἀπό πάνω.

barge [ba:dʒ] n φορτηγίς, μαούνα ‖ to ~ in vi ἐπεμβαίνω.

baritone ['bæritəun] n βαρύτονος.

bark [ba:k] n (tree) φλοιός, φλούδα ‖ (dog) γαύγισμα ‖ vi (dog) γαυγίζω.

barley ['ba:li] n κριθάρι.

barmaid ['ba:meid] n σερβιτόρα τοῦ μπάρ.

barman ['ba:mən] n μπάρμαν.

barn [ba:n] n (σιτ)ἀποθήκη ‖ (US) στάβλος.

barnacle ['ba:nəkl] n ἀνατίφη, στρειδόνι.

barometer [bə'rɔmitə*] n βαρόμετρον.

baron ['bærən] n βαρῶνος ‖ ~ess n βαρώνη.

baroque [bə'rɔk] a μπαρόκ.

barracks ['bærəks] npl στρατώνας, μπαράκα.

barrage ['bæra:ʒ] n (dam) φράγμα ‖ (mil) πῦρ φραγμοῦ, μπαράζ.

barrel ['bærəl] n βυτίον, βαρέλι ‖ (measure) βαρέλιον ‖ (gun) κάννη ‖ ~ organ n λατέρνα.

barren ['bærən] a στεῖρος, ἄγονος.

barricade [bæri'keid] n προπέτασμα, φράγμα ‖ vt φράσσω.

barrier ['bæriə*] n φραγμός ‖ (obstruction) ἐμπόδιον.

barrister ['bæristə*] n δικηγόρος.

barrow ['bærəu] *n* (*cart*) μονότροχον, χειραμάξιον.
bartender ['bɑːtendə*] *n* (*US*) = **barman**.
base [beis] *n* βάσις ‖ *vt* βασίζω, στηρίζω ‖ *a* ταπεινός, πρόστυχος ‖ (*inferior*) φθηνός ‖ ~ **ball** *n* μπέϊζ-μπώλ ‖ ~ **less** *a* ἀβάσιμος, ἀστήρικτος ‖ ~ **ment** *n* ὑπόγειον.
bash [bæʃ] *vt* (*col*) κτυπῶ, τσακίζω.
bashful ['bæʃful] *a* ντροπαλός.
basic ['beisik] *a* βασικός, θεμελιώδης ‖ ~ **ally** *ad* βασικά.
basilica [bə'zilikə] *n* βασιλική.
basin ['beisn] *n* λεκάνη ‖ (*naut*) νεωδόχος, δεξαμενή.
basis ['beisis] *n* βάσις.
bask [bɑːsk] *vi* λιάζομαι.
basket ['bɑːskit] *n* καλάθι, πανέρι ‖ ~ **ball** *n* καλαθόσφαιρα, μπάσκετ.
bass [bæs] *n* (*fish*) πέρκα ‖ [beis] (*mus*) βαθύφωνος, μπάσος.
bassoon [bə'suːn] *n* φαγκότο.
bastard ['bɑːstəd] *n* νόθος, μπάσταρδος.
baste [beist] *vt* (*sewing*) παρραράβω, ξυλίζω, ραβδίζω ‖ (*cooking*) βουτυρώνω.
bastion ['bæstiən] *n* (*stronghold*) προμαχώνας.
bat [bæt] *n* (*sport*) ρόπαλον, μαγγούρα ‖ (*zool*) νυκτερίδα ‖ *vt* κτυπῶ μέ τό ρόπαλο ‖ **off one's own** ~ ἐξ ἰδίας πρωτοβουλίας.
batch [bætʃ] *n* φουρνιά (ψωμί) ‖ (*set*) σωρός, ὁμάδα.
bath [bɑːθ] *n* λουτρό, μπάνιο ‖ (*tub*) λουτήρας, μπανιέρα ‖ *vt* λούω, μπανιαρίζω ‖ ~ **s** *npl* δημόσια λουτρά, μπάνια, χαμάμ ‖ ~ **chair** *n* καρροτσάκι (ἀναπήρων), ἀναπηρική καρέκλα.
bathe [beið] *vi* λούομαι, κάνω μπάνιο ‖ *vt* λούω, πλένω ‖ ~ **r** *n* κολυμβητής, λουόμενος.
bathing ['beiðiŋ] *n* κολύμπι ‖ ~ **cap** *n* σκοῦφος τοῦ μπάνιου ‖ ~ **costume** *n* μπανιερό, μαγιό.
bathmat ['bɑːθmæt] *n* ψάθα τοῦ μπάνιου.
bathroom ['bɑːθrum] *n* λουτρόν.
bath towel ['bɑːθtauəl] *n* πετσέτα τοῦ μπάνιου.
batman ['bætmən] *n* ὑπηρέτης, ὀρντινάντσα.
baton ['bætən] *n* ράβδος ‖ (*conductor's*) μπαγκέτα ‖ (*truncheon*) γκλώμπ.
battalion [bə'tæliən] *n* τάγμα.
batter ['bætə*] *n* κουρκούτι ‖ *vt* κτυπῶ, κοπανίζω.
battery ['bætəri] *n* (*mil*) πυροβολαρχία ‖ (*cell*) συστοιχία.
battle ['bætl] *n* μάχη ‖ *vi* μάχομαι, πολεμῶ ‖ ~ **field** *n* πεδίον μάχης ‖ ~ **ments** *npl* ἐπάλξεις, παραπέτο, πολεμίστρες ‖ ~ **ship** *n* θωρηκτόν.
bawdy ['bɔːdi] *a* ἀσελγής, αἰσχρός.
bawl [bɔːl] *vi* κραυγάζω, σκούζω.
bay [bei] *n* (*of sea*) κόλπος, κόρφος ‖ (*tree*)

δάφνη ‖ **at** ~ σέ δύσκολη θέσι, στά στενά.
bayonet ['beiənit] *n* ξιφολόγχη, μπαγιονέττα.
bay window ['bei'windəu] *n* σαχνισί, θολωτό παράθυρο.
bazaar [bə'zaː*] *n* παζάρι ‖ (*for charity*) φιλανθρωπική ἀγορά.
bazooka [bə'zuːkə] *n* μπαζούκα.
be [biː] (*irreg v*) *vi* (*exist*) εἶμαι, ὑπάρχω ‖ (*live*) εἶμαι, ζῶ, κατοικῶ ‖ (*stay*) εἶμαι, κάνω ‖ (*cost*) εἶμαι, κοστίζω ‖ (*location*) εἶμαι, εὑρίσκομαι ‖ (*visit*) εἶμαι, ἐπισκέπτομαι ‖ (*take place*) εἶμαι, γίγνομαι.
beach [biːtʃ] *n* παραλία, ἀκρογιαλιά ‖ *vt* προσγιαλῶ, ἀράζω ‖ (*run aground*) προσαράσσω.
beacon ['biːkən] *n* φάρος, φανάρι.
bead [biːd] *n* χάντρα, πέρλα ‖ (*perspiration*) σταγονίδι.
beak [biːk] *n* ράμφος, μύτη.
beaker ['biːkə*] *n* ὑάλινο ποτήρι ζέσεως.
beam [biːm] *n* δοκός, δοκάρι ‖ (*of balance*) ζυγοστάτης, μπράτσο ‖ (*of light*) ἀχτίδα, δέσμη ‖ (*smile*) λάμψη, ἀκτινοβολία ‖ *vi* ἀκτινοβολῶ, λάμπω.
bean [biːn] *n* (*broad*) κουκί ‖ (*kidney*) φασόλι ‖ (*string*) φασολάκι.
bear [bɛə*] (*irreg v*) *n* ἀρκούδα ‖ *vt* (*carry*) φέρω, βαστῶ, σηκώνω ‖ (*support*) ὑποβαστάζω, στηρίζω ‖ (*put up with*) ὑποφέρω, ἀντέχω, ἀνέχομαι ‖ (*produce*) γεννῶ, παράγω ‖ ~ **able** *a* ὑποφερτός, ἀνεκτός.
beard [biəd] *n* γένι, μοῦσι ‖ ~ **ed** *a* μέ γένεια.
bearer ['bɛərə*] *n* (*person*) κομιστής, φορέας.
bearing ['bɛəriŋ] *n* (*behaviour*) συμπεριφορά, ὕφος ‖ (*relation*) σχέσις, ἔννοια ‖ ~ **s** *npl*: **I lose my** ~ **s** χάνω τό μπούσουλα.
beast [biːst] *n* ζῶον, κτῆνος, θηρίον ‖ (*person*) ζῶον, παλιάνθρωπος ‖ ~ **ly** *ad* κτηνώδης, βρώμικος.
beat [biːt] (*irreg v*) *n* (*stroke*) κτύπημα ‖ (*pulsation*) σφυγμός, παλμός ‖ (*of policeman*) περιπολία ‖ (*mus*) χρόνος, μέτρον ‖ *vt* κτυπῶ, δέρνω, ματσουκώνω ‖ (*defeat*) ὑπερτερῶ, νικῶ ‖ **to** ~ **about the bush** χρονοτριβῶ, ταλαντεύομαι ‖ **to** ~ **time** κρατῶ τόν χρόνον ‖ **to** ~ **off** *vt* διώχνω, ἀπωθῶ ‖ **to** ~ **up** *vt* σπάζω στό ξύλο ‖ ~ **en track** *n* πεπατημένη ‖ ~ **er** *n* (*for eggs, cream*) κτυπητήρι.
beautiful ['bjuːtiful] *a* ὡραῖος, ἐξαίσιος, ὑπέροχος ‖ ~ **ly** *ad* θαυμάσια, ὑπέροχα.
beautify ['bjuːtifai] *vt* ἐξωραΐζω, ὀμορφαίνω.
beauty ['bjuːti] *n* ὀμορφιά ‖ (*woman*) καλλονή.
beaver ['biːvə*] *n* καστόρι, κάστορας.
becalm [bi'kɑːm] *vt* ἀπαγκιάζω.

because [bi'kɔz] *ad,cj* διότι, γιατί, ἐπειδή.

beckon ['bekən] *vt* γνέφω, κάνω νόημα.

become [bi'kʌm] *vt* (*befit*) ἁρμόζω, ταιριάζω ‖ *vi* γίνομαι, καταντῶ.

becoming [bi'kʌmiŋ] *a* ἁρμόζων ‖ (*dress etc*) ταιριαστός, πού πηγαίνει.

bed [bed] *n* κρεββάτι ‖ (*of river*) κοίτη ‖ (*foundation*) στρῶμα, στρῶσις ‖ (*garden*) πρασιά ‖ ~ **and breakfast** *n* δωμάτιο μέ πρωϊνό ‖ ~**clothes** *npl* σεντόνια καί κουβέρτες ‖ ~**ding** *n* στρώματα.

bedlam ['bedləm] *n* (*uproar*) φασαρία, θόρυβος.

bedraggled [bi'drægld] *a* κουρελιασμένος.

bedridden ['bedridn] *a* κρεββατωμένος, κατάκοιτος.

bedroom ['bedrum] *n* ὑπνοδωμάτιο, κρεββατοκάμαρα.

bed-sitter ['bed'sitə*] *n* ὑπνοδωμάτιο.

bedtime ['bedtaim] *n* ὥρα γιά ὕπνο.

bee [bi:] *n* μέλισσα.

beech [bi:tʃ] *n* ὀξυά.

beef [bi:f] *n* βωδινό.

beehive ['bi:haiv] *n* κυψέλη.

beeline ['bi:lain] *n*: **to make a ~ for** πηγαίνω κατ' εὐθεῖαν.

been [bi:n] *pp of* be.

beer [biə*] *n* μπύρα.

beetle ['bi:tl] *n* σκαθάρι.

beetroot ['bi:tru:t] *n* πατζάρι, κοκκινογούλι.

befall [bi'fɔ:l] *vti* συμβαίνω, τυχαίνω.

before [bi'fɔ:*] *prep* (*in place*) πρό, ἐμπρός, ἐνώπιον ‖ (*of time*) πρίν, πρό ‖ *cj* πρό, πρίν, πρίν νά ‖ *ad* (*of place*) ἐμπρός, πρό, μπροστά ‖ (*of time*) πρίν, πρωτύτερα, προτοῦ.

befriend [bi'frend] *vt* βοηθῶ, προστατεύω.

beg [beg] *vti* ζητῶ, παρακαλῶ ‖ (*for alms*) ζητιανεύω ‖ ~**gar** *n* ζητιάνος, ἐπαίτης.

began [bi'gæn] *pt of* begin.

begin [bi'gin] (*irreg v*) *vti* ἀρχίζω, ἀρχινῶ, ἄρχομαι ‖ **to ~ with** *vt* πρῶτα-πρῶτα, πρίν ν'ἀρχίσουμε ‖ ~**ner** *n* ἀρχάριος, πρωτάρης ‖ ~**ning** *n* ἀρχή.

begrudge [bi'grʌdʒ] *vt* δίνω μέ τό ζόρι, λυποῦμαι.

begun [bi'gʌn] *pp of* begin.

behalf [bi'ha:f] *n* ἐκ μέρους, ὑπέρ ‖ **on ~ of** γιά λογαριασμό του, ἐκ μέρους.

behave [bi'heiv] *vi* (συμπερι)φέρομαι.

behaviour, (*US*) **behavior** [bi'heivjə*] *n* συμπεριφορά, φέρσιμο.

behead [bi'hed] *vt* ἀποκεφαλίζω.

behind [bi'haind] *prep* πίσω ἀπό ‖ (*time*) καθυστερημένος ‖ *ad* ὄπισθεν, ὀπίσω, πίσω ἀπό ‖ *n* πισινός.

behold [bi'həuld] *vt* βλέπω, ἀντικρύζω.

beige [beiʒ] *a* μπέζ.

being ['bi:iŋ] *n* ὕπαρξις, γέννησις ‖ (*person*) ὄν, εἶναι.

belch [beltʃ] *vti* ρεύομαι.

belfry ['belfri] *n* καμπαναριό.

Belgium ['beldʒəm] *n* Βέλγιον.

belie [bi'lai] *vt* διαψεύδω, ξεγελῶ.

belief [bi'li:f] *n* (*trust*) πίστη ‖ (*idea*) γνώμη, δοξασία.

believable [bi'li:vəbl] *a* πιστευτός.

believe [bi'li:v] *vt* πιστεύω, δέχομαι ‖ *vi* πιστεύω, ἔχω ἐμπιστοσύνη ‖ ~**r** *n* πιστός ὀπαδός.

belittle [bi'litl] *vt* ὑποτιμῶ, περιφρονῶ.

bell [bel] *n* καμπάνα ‖ (*in house*) κουδούνι.

belligerent [bi'lidʒərənt] *a* (*fig*) καυγατζῆς.

bellow ['beləu] *vti* μουγγρίζω, γκαρίζω ‖ *n* μουγκρητό.

bellows ['beləuz] *npl* φυσερό.

belly ['beli] *n* κοιλιά.

belong [bi'lɔŋ] *vi* ἀνήκω ‖ **it does not ~ here** δέν ἀνήκει ἐδῶ ‖ **to ~ to** *vt* ἀνήκω, μετέχω εἰς ‖ (*a place*) κατάγομαι ἀπό ‖ ~**ings** *npl* περιουσία, ὑπάρχοντα.

beloved [bi'lʌvid] *a* πολυαγαπημένος ‖ *n* ἀγαπητός.

below [bi'ləu] *prep* ὑπό, κάτω, κάτωθεν ‖ *ad* κάτω ἀπό, ἀπό κάτω.

belt [belt] *n* ζώνη, ταινία ‖ (*round waist*) ζωνάρι, λουρί ‖ *vt* ζώνω ‖ (*beat*) δέρνω μέ λουρί.

bench [bentʃ] *n* κάθισμα, μπάγκος ‖ (*workshop*) τεζάκι, μπάγκος ‖ (*of judge*) ἕδρα.

bend [bend] (*irreg v*) *n* καμπή, στροφή, γωνία ‖ *vt* κάμπτω, λυγίζω ‖ (*naut*) δένω ‖ *vi* (*stoop*) σκύβω.

beneath [bi'ni:θ] *prep* κάτωθεν, χαμηλότερα, ὑπό ‖ *ad* (ὑπο)κάτω.

benefactor ['benifæktə*] *n* εὐεργέτης, δωρητής.

beneficial [beni'fiʃəl] *a* ὠφέλιμος, χρήσιμος.

beneficiary [beni'fiʃəri] *n* δικαιοῦχος.

benefit ['benifit] *n* ὄφελος, ὠφέλεια ‖ *vt* ὠφελῶ ‖ *vi* ἐπωφελοῦμαι.

benevolent [bi'nevələnt] *a* ἀγαθοεργός, καλοπροαίρετος.

benign [bi'nain] *a* (*tumour etc*) καλοήθης.

bent [bent] *n* (*inclination*) κλίσις, ροπή ‖ *a*: **to be ~ on** ἀποφασισμένος νά ‖ *pt,pp of* bend.

bequeath [bi'kwi:ð] *vt* κληροδοτῶ, ἀφήνω.

bequest [bi'kwest] *n* κληροδότημα.

bereaved [bi'ri:vd] *n* (*person*) τεθλιμμένος.

bereavement [bi'ri:vmənt] *n* ἀπώλεια, πένθος.

beret ['berei] *n* μπερέ, σκοῦφος.

berry ['beri] *n* ρόγα, μοῦρο.

berserk [bə'sə:k] *a*: **to go ~** γίνομαι ἔξω φρενῶν.

berth [bə:θ] *n* (*anchoring*) ὅρμος ‖ (*ship, train*) κλίνη, καμπίνα ‖ *vt* προσορμίζω, πλευρίζω ‖ *vi* ἀγκυροβολῶ, πλευρίζω.

beseech [bi'si:tʃ] (*irreg v*) *vt* ἱκετεύω, ἐκλιπαρῶ.

beset [bi'set] *vt* κυκλώνω, περισφίγγω.

beside [bi'said] *prep* πλάϊ, πλησίον, δίπλα ‖ **to be ~ o.s.** εἶμαι ἐκτός ἑαυτοῦ.

besides [bi'saidz] *prep* ἐκτός ἀπό ‖ *ad* ἐκτός αὐτοῦ, ἀκόμη, ἄλλωστε.
besiege [bi'si:dʒ] *vt* πολιορκῶ.
bespectacled [bi'spektikld] *a* μέ γυαλιά.
best [best] *a* καλύτερος ‖ *ad* καλύτερα ‖ **at ~** τό καλύτερον, ἀκόμα καί ‖ **to make the ~ of it** ὅσον μπορῶ καλύτερα ‖ **~ man** *n* παράνυμφος, κουμπάρος.
bestow [bi'stəu] *vt* παρέχω, ἀπονέμω.
bestseller ['best'selə*] *n* βιβλίον μεγάλης κυκλοφορίας.
bet [bet] (*irreg v*) *n* στοίχημα ‖ *vt* στοιχηματίζω, βάζω στοίχημα ‖ **you ~**! ἀσφαλῶς!, ἔχεις δίκαιο!, σίγουρα!
betray [bi'trei] *vt* προδίδω, ἀποκαλύπτω ‖ (*be false*) ἐξαπατῶ ‖ **~al** *n* προδοσία.
better ['betə*] *a* καλύτερος ‖ *ad* καλύτερα ‖ *vt* καλυτερεύω, βελτιώνω ‖ *n*: **to get the ~ of** νικῶ κάποιον, ὑπερέχω ‖ **he thought ~ of it** ἄλλαξε γνώμην ‖ **~ off** *a* (*richer*) πιό εὔπορος, πλουσιώτερος.
betting ['betiŋ] *n* στοίχημα(τα).
between [bi'twi:n] *prep* μεταξύ, ἀνάμεσα ‖ *ad* ἀνάμεσα.
bevel ['bevəl] *n* λοξά, φάλτσο.
beverage ['bevəridʒ] *n* ποτό.
beware [bi'weə*] *vt* προσέχω, φοβοῦμαι ‖ **'~ of the dog'** 'προσοχή, σκύλος'.
bewildered [bi'wildəd] *a* ζαλισμένος, χαμένος.
bewildering [bi'wildəriŋ] *a* ἐκπληκτικός, κάτι πού ζαλίζει.
bewitching [bi'witʃiŋ] *a* γοητευτικός, μαγευτικός.
beyond [bi'jɔnd] *prep* (*of place*) πέρα ἀπό ‖ (*of time*) πέραν τοῦ ‖ (*in addition*) ἐκτός, πέραν ‖ *ad* πέραν, ἐκεῖθεν.
bias ['baiəs]. *n* (*slant*) λοξότης, λοξά ‖ (*prejudice*) προκατάληψις, συμπάθεια ‖ **~(s)ed** *a* προκατειλημμένος, ἐπηρεασμένος.
bib [bib] *n* σαλιάρα, μπούστος.
Bible ['baibl] *n* Βίβλος, Εὐαγγέλιον.
bibliography [bibli'ɔgrəfi] *n* βιβλιογραφία.
bicentenary [baisen'ti:nəri] *n* δισεκατονταετηρίδα.
biceps ['baiseps] *npl* δικέφαλος (μῦς).
bicker ['bikə*] *vi* καυγαδίζω ‖ **~ing** *n* καυγάς.
bicycle ['baisikl] *n* ποδήλατο.
bid [bid] (*irreg v*) *n* προσφορά ‖ (*cards*) δήλωσις ‖ *vt* (*command*) διατάσσω, προστάζω ‖ (*offer*) προσφέρω, πλειοδοτῶ ‖ (*greeting*) καλημερίζω ‖ (*goodbye*) ἀποχαιρετῶ ‖ **~der** *n* (*person*) πλειοδότης ‖ **~ding** *n* (*order*) ἐντολή, παραγγελία ‖ (*offer*) πλειοδοσία.
bidet ['bi:dei] *n* μπιντέ.
big [big] *a* μεγάλος, σπουδαῖος.
bigamy ['bigəmi] *n* διγαμία.
big-hearted ['big'ha:tid] *a* μεγαλόψυχος, μέ χρυσή καρδιά.
bigot ['bigət] *n* στενοκέφαλος, φανατικός

‖ **~ed** *a* στενοκέφαλος ‖ **~ry** *n* μισαλλοδοξία.
bigwig ['bigwig] *n* σπουδαῖο πρόσωπο, μεγιστάνος, προσωπικότης.
bike [baik] *n* ποδήλατο.
bikini [bi'ki:ni] *n* μπικίνι.
bile [bail] *n* χολή.
bilingual [bai'liŋgwəl] *a* δίγλωσσος.
bilious ['biliəs] *a* χολερικός ‖ (*peevish*) πικρόχολος.
bill [bil] *n* (*notice*) ἀγγελία, ἀφίσα ‖ (*account*) λογαριασμός ‖ (*law*) νομοσχέδιον ‖ (*note*) γραμμάτιον ‖ (*beak*) ράμφος, μύτη ‖ (*US*) χαρτονόμισμα.
billet ['bilit] *n* (*mil*) κατάλυμα ‖ (*job*) θέσι.
billfold ['bilfəuld] *n* (*US*) πορτοφόλι.
billiards ['biliədz] *n* μπιλιάρδος.
billion ['biliən] *n* (*Brit*) τρισεκατομμύριο ‖ (*US*) δισεκατομμύριο.
billy goat ['biligəut] *n* τράγος.
bin [bin] *n* κασέλα, κασόνι, κιβώτιον.
bind [baind] (*irreg v*) *vt* (*tie*) δένω ‖ (*together*) προσδένω ‖ (*a book*) δένω ‖ (*oblige*) δεσμεύω, δένω ‖ **~ing** *n* (σύν)δεσις, δέσιμο ‖ (*book*) βιβλιοδεσία.
binoculars [bi'nɔkjuləz] *npl* κιάλια.
biochemistry ['baiəu'kemistri] *n* βιοχημεία.
biographer [bai'ɔgrəfə*] *n* βιογράφος.
biographic(al) [baiəu'græfik(əl)] *a* βιογραφικός.
biography [bai'ɔgrəfi] *n* βιογραφία.
biological [baiə'lɔdʒikəl] *a* βιολογικός.
biologist [bai'ɔlədʒist] *n* βιολόγος.
biology [bai'ɔlədʒi] *n* βιολογία.
birch [bə:tʃ] *n* (*tree*) σημύδα ‖ (*for whipping*) βέργα.
bird [bə:d] *n* πουλί ‖ **~'s-eye view** *n* κάτοψη.
birth [bə:θ] *n* γέννα, τοκετός ‖ (*beginning*) γέννησις ‖ **of good ~** καλῆς καταγωγῆς ‖ **~ certificate** *n* πιστοποιητικόν γεννήσεως ‖ **~ control** *n* ἔλεγχος γεννήσεων ‖ **~day** *n* γενέθλια ‖ **~place** *n* τόπος γεννήσεως ‖ **~ rate** *n* γεννήσεις.
biscuit ['biskit] *n* παξιμάδι, μπισκότα.
bisect [bai'sekt] *vt* διχοτομῶ.
bishop ['biʃəp] *n* ἐπίσκοπος, δεσπότης.
bit [bit] *n* (*piece*) κομμάτι ‖ (*of tool*) τρυπάνι ‖ (*of horse*) στομίς, χαβιά, χαλινάρι.
bitch [bitʃ] *n* (*dog*) σκύλα ‖ (*unpleasant woman*) παλιοθήλυκο.
bite [bait] (*irreg v*) *n* δάγκωμα ‖ (*mouthful*) μπουκιά ‖ *vti* δαγκώνω ‖ (*insect*) τσιμπῶ ‖ **a ~ to eat** μπουκιά, λίγο φαγητό.
biting ['baitiŋ] *a* δηκτικός.
bitter ['bitə*] *a* πικρός ‖ (*feeling*) φαρμακερός, δηκτικός, πικρά ‖ *n* (*beer*) πικρή μπύρα ‖ **to the ~ end** μέχρι τέλους, μέχρις-ἐσχάτων ‖ **~ness** *n* πικρία, πίκρα ‖ **~sweet** *a* γλυκόπικρος.
bivouac ['bivuæk] *n* καταυλισμός.
bizarre [bi'za:*] *a* παράξενος, ἀλλόκοτος.
blab [blæb] *vti* τά λέω ὅλα, προδίδω.
black [blæk] *a* μαῦρος ‖ (*without light*)

σκοτάδι ‖ *vt* (*shoes*) βάφω, λουστράρω ‖ (*eye*) μαυρίζω τό μάτι ‖ ~ **and blue** γεμάτος σημάδια, καταμαυρισμένος ‖ ~ **berry** *n* βατόμουρον ‖ ~ **bird** *n* κότσυφας ‖ ~ **board** *n* πίνακας, μαυροπίνακας ‖ ~ **currant** *n* μαύρο φραγκοστάφυλλο ‖ ~ **en** *vt* μαυρίζω, λερώνω ‖ ~ **guard** *n* παλιάνθρωπος, μασκαράς ‖ ~ **leg** *n* ἀπεργοσπάστης ‖ ~ **list** *n* μαύρος πίνακας ‖ ~ **mail** *vt* ἐκβιάζω ‖ ~ **mailer** *n* ἐκβιαστής ‖ ~ **market** *n* μαύρη ἀγορά ‖ ~ **ness** *n* μαυράδα, μαυρίλα ‖ ~ **out** *n* (*mil*) συσκότισις ‖ (*elec*) διακοπή ρεύματος ‖ (*faint*) σκοτοδίνη, λιποθυμία ‖ ~ **sheep** *n* (*fig*) ζιζάνιον, ἄσωτος ‖ ~ **smith** *n* σιδεράς.
bladder ['blædə*] *n* κύστις ‖ (*of football etc*) σαμπρέλλα.
blade [bleid] *n* (*leaf etc*) φύλλον ‖ (*of tool etc*) λεπίδα, λάμα ‖ (*of oar etc*) πτερύγιον, φτερό.
blame [bleim] *n* μομφή, ψόγος, φταίξιμο ‖ *vt* κατηγορῶ, ψέγω ‖ ~ **less** *a* ἄψογος, ἀνεύθυνος.
bland [blænd] *a* ἤπιος, μειλίχιος.
blank [blæŋk] *a* (*page*) λευκός, ἄγραφος ‖ (*vacant*) ἀνέκφραστος, χαμένα, συγχισμένα ‖ *n* κενό ‖ (*cartridge*) ἄσφαιρο φυσίγγι.
blanket ['blæŋkit] *n* κλινοσκέπασμα, κουβέρτα.
blankly ['blæŋkli] *ad* μέ ἀνέκφραστον βλέμμα.
blare [blεə*] *n* ἰσχυρός ἦχος, οὔρλιασμα ‖ *vi* ἀντηχῶ, διασαλπίζω.
blarney ['blɑ:ni] *n* κολακεία, γαλιφιά.
blasé ['blɑ:zei] *a* μπλαζέ.
blaspheme [blæs'fi:m] *vi* βλαστημῶ.
blasphemous ['blæsfiməs] *a* ἀσεβής, ἀπρεπής.
blasphemy ['blæsfimi] *n* βλαστήμια.
blast [blɑ:st] *n* (*gust*) φύσημα, ριπή ‖ (*naut*) σφύριγμα ‖ (*mining*) φουρνέλο ‖ *vt* βάζω φουρνέλο ‖ ~ **off** *n* (*space*) ἐκτόξευσις.
blatant ['bleitənt] *a* κραυγαλέος, φωνακλάδικος.
blaze [bleiz] *n* (*fire*) φλόγα, ἀνάφλεξις, φωτιά ‖ *vi* παίρνω φωτιά ‖ (*person*) ἐξάπτομαι ‖ *vt*: **to** ~ **a trail** χαράσσω δρόμον.
blazer ['bleizə*] *n* ἀθλητικό σακάκι.
bleach [bli:tʃ] *n* ἄσπρισμα, μπουγάδα ‖ *vt* ἀσπρίζω, ξεβάφω ‖ (*hair*) ἀποχρωματίζω.
bleak [bli:k] *a* ψυχρός, μελαγχολικός.
bleary-eyed ['bliəriaid] *a* μέ θολωμένα μάτια.
bleat [bli:t] *n* βέλασμα ‖ *vi* βελάζω.
bled [bled] *pt,pp of* **bleed**.
bleed [bli:d] (*irreg v*) *vi* χύνω αἷμα, χάνω αἷμα ‖ *vt* φλεβοτομῶ, παίρνω αἷμα.
bleeding ['bli:diŋ] *a* ματωμένος.
blemish ['blemiʃ] *n* ἐλάττωμα, κηλίδα ‖ *vt* κηλιδώνω ‖ (*reputation*) καταστρέφω.

blench [blentʃ] *vi* κιτρινίζω (ἀπό φόβο).
blend [blend] *n* χαρμάνι ‖ *vt* ἀνακατεύω, συγχωνεύω ‖ *vi* (*colours etc*) ταιριάζω.
bless [bles] *vt* εὐλογῶ, δοξάζω ‖ ~ **ing** *n* εὐλογία, εὐτύχημα.
blew [blu:] *pt of* **blow**.
blight [blait] *n* (*disease*) ἐρυσίβη, συρίκι, συναπίδι ‖ (*fig*) πληγή ‖ *vt* καταστρέφω.
blimey ['blaimi] *excl* (*col*) νά μέ πάρη ὁ διάβολος!
blind [blaind] *a* τυφλός, στραβός ‖ (*alley etc*) ἀδιέξοδος ‖ *n* τέντα, περσίς ‖ (*excuse*) πρόσχημα, ὑποκρισία ‖ *vt* τυφλώνω, στραβώνω ‖ ~ **fold** *a* μέ δεμένα μάτια ‖ *vt* δένω τά μάτια ‖ ~ **ly** *ad* στά τυφλά, στά στραβά ‖ ~ **ness** *n* τυφλότης, στραβομάρα.
blink [bliŋk] *vti* ἀνοιγοκλείνω τά μάτια, μισοκλείνω τά μάτια ‖ ~ **ers** *npl* παρωπίδες.
blinking ['bliŋkiŋ] *a* (*col*) = **bloody**.
bliss [blis] *n* μακαριότητα, εὐδαιμονία ‖ ~ **fully** *ad* εὐτυχισμένα.
blister ['blistə*] *n* (*on skin*) φυσαλίδα, φουσκάλα ‖ (*on surfaces etc*) φουσκάλα ‖ *vti* φουσκαλιάζω, φλυκταινοῦμαι.
blithe [blaið] *a* χαρούμενος, εὔθυμος ‖ ~ **ly** *ad* φαιδρά, χαρούμενα.
blithering ['bliðəriŋ] *a*: ~ **idiot** τελείως βλάκας.
blitz [blits] *n* μπλίτς, βίαιη ἐπίθεσις.
blizzard ['blizəd] *n* χιονοθύελλα.
bloated ['bləutid] *a* φουσκωμένος, πρησμένος.
bloc [blɔk] *n* (*pol*) συνασπισμός, μπλόκ.
block [blɔk] *n* (*piece*) τεμάχι, μεγάλο κομμάτι ‖ (*for chopping*) ἐπικόπανον, πικόπι ‖ (*traffic*) συνωστισμός, διακοπή ‖ (*obstacle*) ἐμπόδιον ‖ (*city*) τετράγωνον ‖ *vt* φράσσω, ἐμποδίζω ‖ ~ **ade** *n* ἀποκλεισμός, μπλόκο ‖ *vt* ἀποκλείω, μπλοκάρω ‖ ~ **age** *n* ἐμπλοκή, μπλοκάρισμα.
bloke [bləuk] *n* (*col*) ἄνθρωπος.
blond(e) [blɔnd] *a* ξανθός, ξανθή ‖ *n* ξανθός, ξανθιά.
blood [blʌd] *n* αἷμα ‖ (*kinship*) συγγένεια ‖ (*descent*) καταγωγή ‖ ~ **donor** *n* αἱμοδότης ‖ ~ **group** *n* ὁμάδα αἵματος ‖ ~ **less** *a* (*victory etc*) ἀναίμακτος ‖ ~ **poisoning** *n* δηλητηρίασις αἵματος ‖ ~ **pressure** *n* πίεσις αἵματος ‖ ~ **shed** *n* αἱματοχυσία ‖ ~ **shot** *a* κόκκινο (μάτι) ‖ ~ **stained** *a* αἱματοσταγής, ματωμένος ‖ ~ **stream** *n* κυκλοφοριακό σύστημα ‖ ~ **thirsty** *a* αἱμοβόρος ‖ ~ **transfusion** *n* μετάγγισις αἵματος ‖ ~ **y** *a* (*col*) παλιο-, βρωμο- ‖ (*lit*) αἱματηρός ‖ ~ **y-minded** *a* τζαναμπέτης.
bloom [blu:m] *n* (*flower*) λουλούδι ‖ (*perfection*) ἄνθησις, ἀκμή ‖ *vi* ἀνθίζω ‖ **in** ~ στήν ἄνθησί του.
blossom ['blɔsəm] *n* ἄνθος ‖ *vi* ἀνθίζω.
blot [blɔt] *n* λεκές ‖ (*disgrace*) κηλίδα ‖ *vt*

(stain) λεκιάζω ‖ *(dry ink)* στυπώνω, τραβῶ ‖ to ~ out *vt* ἐξαφανίζω, σβήνω.
blotchy ['blɔtʃi] *a* γεμᾶτος κοκκινίλες.
blotting paper ['blɔtiŋpeipə*] *n* στυπόχαρτο.
blouse [blauz] *n* μπλούζα.
blow [bləu] *(irreg v) n (with fist)* κτύπημα, γρονθιά ‖ *(with stick)* ραβδισμός ‖ *(of air)* φύσημα ‖ *(of fate)* πλῆγμα ‖ *vt* φυσάω ‖ *(a fuse)* καίομαι ‖ *(col: squander)* σπαταλάω ‖ **at a single ~** μ'ἕνα κτύπημα ‖ to ~ **one's top** ξεσπάω ‖ to ~ **over** *vi* περνῶ, ξεθυμαίνω ‖ to ~ **up** *vi* σκάω, ἀνατινάσσω ‖ *vt (tyre)* φουσκώνω ‖ ~**lamp** *n* καμινευτήρ ‖ ~-**out** *n (aut)* κλατάρισμα ‖ ~**y** *a* ἀνεμώδης.
blubber ['blʌbə*] *n* λίπος φάλαινας.
blue [blu:] *a* γαλάζιος, γαλανός ‖ *(paint)* μπλέ ‖ *(with cold etc)* μελανισμένος ‖ *n:* **to have the ~s** μελαγχολῶ ‖ ~**bell** *n* ζιμπούλι ‖ ~-**blooded** *a* γαλαζοαίματος ‖ ~**bottle** *n* κρεατόμυγα ‖ ~**print** *n* κυανοτυπία, σχέδιον.
bluff [blʌf] *n (deception)* μπλόφα, ἀπάτη ‖ *vt* μπλοφάρω, ἐξαπατῶ ‖ *a* ντόμπρος.
bluish ['blu:iʃ] *a* γαλαζωπός.
blunder ['blʌndə*] *n* μεγάλο λάθος, χοντροκοπιά ‖ *vi* κάνω γκάφα.
blunt [blʌnt] *a* ἀμβλύς, στομωμένος ‖ *(person)* μονοκόμματος ‖ *vt* ἀμβλύνω, στομώνω ‖ ~**ly** *ad* ἀπότομα, ντόμπρα.
blur [blə:*] *n* θολούρα, θαμπάδα ‖ *(stain)* μουτζούρα ‖ *vti* θολώνω, θαμπώνω.
blurt [blə:t] to ~ **out** *vti* προδίδω, ἀποκαλύπτω.
blush [blʌʃ] *vi* κοκκινίζω ‖ *n* κοκκίνισμα ‖ ~**ing** *a* ντροπαλός.
bluster ['blʌstə*] *vi (of wind)* φυσῶ δυνατά ‖ *(of person)* κάνω φασαρία, κομπάζω.
boa ['bəuə] *n* βόας.
boar [bɔ:*] *n* γουρούνι ἀρσενικό, καπρί.
board [bɔ:d] *n (of wood)* σανίδα, τάβλα ‖ *(notice)* πινακίδα, ταμπλώ ‖ *(of paper)* χαρτόνι ‖ *(meal)* φαΐ ‖ *(of men)* συμβούλιον, ἐπιτροπή ‖ *vt (feed)* δίδω τροφήν ‖ *(ship, train)* ἐπιβαίνω, μπαρκάρω ‖ *(with planks)* σανιδώνω ‖ ~ **and lodging** φαΐ καί ὕπνος ‖ to ~ **up** *vt (περι)* φράσσω μέ σανίδες ‖ ~**er** *n* οἰκότροφος ‖ *(lodger)* ἔνοικος ‖ ~**ing house** *n* πανσιόν ‖ ~**ing school** *n* σχολή μέ οἰκοτροφεῖον ‖ ~**ing school pupil** *n* ἐσωτερικός.
boast [bəust] *vi* καυχῶμαι, κομπορρημονῶ ‖ *n* κομπασμός, καυχησιολογία ‖ ~**ful** *a* καυχησιάρης, φανφαρόνος ‖ ~**fulness** *n* κομπασμός.
boat [bəut] *n* βάρκα, καΐκι ‖ *(ship)* καράβι ‖ ~**er** *n (hat)* ναυτικὴ ψάθα ‖ ~**ing** *n* λεμβοδρομία μέ βάρκα ‖ ~**swain** ['bəusən] *n* λοστρόμος.
bob [bɔb] *vi* ἀποδοκατεβαίνω.
bobbin ['bɔbin] *n* πηνίον, κουβαρίστρα ‖ *(elec)* μπομπίνα.

bobsleigh ['bɔbslei] *n* μπόπ-σλέϊ, ἕλκηθρο.
bodice ['bɔdis] *n* στῆθος φορέματος, μπούστος.
bodily ['bɔdili] *ad* σωματικῶς ‖ *(together)* συλλογικῶς, ὅλοι μαζί.
body ['bɔdi] *n* σῶμα, κορμί ‖ *(legislative etc)* σῶμα, σωματεῖον ‖ *(collection)* μέγα πλῆθος, μάζα ‖ *(of car etc)* σῶμα, κύριον μέρος ‖ ~**guard** *n* σωματοφύλακας ‖ ~**work** *n* καρρότσα.
bog [bɔg] *n* ἕλος ‖ *vi:* **to get ~ged down** βουλιάζω.
boggle ['bɔgl] *vi* διστάζω.
bogie ['bəugi] *n* τροχοφορεύς.
bogus ['bəugəs] *a* ψευδής, ψεύτικος.
boil [bɔil] *vt (potatoes etc)* βράζω ‖ *vi* βράζω, κοχλάζω ‖ *n (med)* καλόγερος ‖ **to come to the ~** παίρνω βράση ‖ ~**er** *n* λέβης, καζάνι ‖ ~**ing point** *n* σημεῖον βρασμοῦ.
boisterous ['bɔistərəs] *a* θορυβώδης, ταραχώδης.
bold [bəuld] *a* τολμηρός, θαρραλέος ‖ ~**ly** *ad* θαρραλέα, μέ τόλμην ‖ ~**ness** *n* τολμηρότης, θάρρος.
bollard ['bɔləd] *n* δέστρα.
bolster ['bəulstə*] *n* μαξιλάρα ‖ to ~ **up** *vt* (ὑπο)στηρίζω.
bolt [bəult] *n (of door etc)* σύρτης, μάνταλον ‖ *(rush away)* ἐξόρμησις, φυγή ‖ *vt (a door etc)* μανταλώνω, κλειδώνω ‖ *(food)* καταβροχθίζω ‖ *vi (rush away)* φεύγω, ἐξορμῶ ‖ *(escape)* δραπετεύω.
bomb [bɔm] *n* βόμβα ‖ *vt* βομβαρδίζω ‖ ~**ard** *vt* βομβαρδίζω, σφυροκοπῶ ‖ ~**ardment** *n* βομβαρδισμός ‖ ~**er** *n (person)* βομβαρδιστής ‖ *(aviat)* βομβαρδιστικό ‖ ~**ing** *n* βομβαρδισμός ‖ ~**shell** *n (fig)* κατάπληξις, σάν βόμβα.
bona fide ['bəunə'faidi] *a* καλῆς πίστεως.
bond [bɔnd] *n (link)* δεσμός, συνάφεια ‖ *(promise)* ὑπόσχεσις, σύμβασις ‖ *(econ)* ὁμολογία.
bone [bəun] *n* κόκκαλο ‖ *vt* ξεκοκκαλίζω ‖ ~-**dry** *a* ἐντελῶς ξηρός, κατάξερος ‖ ~**r** *n (US)* γκάφα.
bonfire ['bɔnfaiə*] *n* φωτιά.
bonnet ['bɔnit] *n* γυναικεῖο καπέλλο ‖ *(child's)* σκουφίτσα ‖ *(cap)* σκοῦφος, μπερές ‖ *(Brit: of car)* καπό.
bonus ['bəunəs] *n* ἐπιμίσθιον, ἐπίδομα.
bony ['bəuni] *a* κοκκαλιάρης.
boo [bu:] *vt* ἀποδοκιμάζω, γιουχαΐζω.
book [buk] *n* βιβλίον, κιτάπι ‖ *vt (ticket etc)* βγάζω εἰσιτήριο ‖ *(a room)* κλείνω δωμάτιο ‖ *(person)* πληρώνω, τιμωροῦμαι ‖ ~-**case** *n* βιβλιοθήκη ‖ ~**ing office** *n* πρακτορεῖον εἰσιτηρίων ‖ ~-**keeping** *n* λογιστική ‖ ~-**let** *n* φυλλάδιον, βιβλιαράκι ‖ ~**maker** *n (racing)* μπουκμέκερ ‖ ~**seller** *n* βιβλιοπώλης ‖ ~**shop** *n* βιβλιοπωλεῖον ‖ ~**stall** *n* πάγκος βιβλιοπώλου ‖ ~**store** *n* = ~**shop**.

boom [bu:m] n (noise) κρότος, βόμβος ‖ (naut) ἀπώστης ‖ (port) φράγμα ‖ (busy period) μπούμ, κῦμα εὐημερίας, αἰχμή εὐημερίας ‖ vi ἀνέρχομαι, ἀνεβαίνω.

boon [bu:n] n (blessing) ὄφελος.

boorish ['buərɪʃ] a ἄξεστος, ἀγροῖκος.

boost [bu:st] n προώθησις ‖ vt προωθῶ, διαφημίζω.

boot [bu:t] n μπόττα ‖ (Brit: of car) πόρτ-μπαγκάζ ‖ vt (kick) λακτίζω, κλωτσάω ‖ to ~ (in addition) ἐπί πλέον.

booze [bu:z] n ποτόν ‖ vi ξεφαντώνω, μεθοκοπῶ.

border ['bɔ:də*] n (frontier) σύνορον, μεθόριος ‖ (edge) γῦρος, σειρίτι, μπορ-ντούρα ‖ (page etc) πλαίσιον, βινιέτα ‖ to ~ on vt συνορεύω μέ ‖ ~line n (fig) ἐγγίζω τά ὅρια.

bore [bɔ:*] pt of bear ‖ n (person or thing) πληκτικός, ἐνοχλητικός, ἀφόρητος ‖ (of gun etc) διαμέτρημα ‖ vt τρυπῶ, ἀνοίγω ὀπήν ‖ (weary) πλήττω, λιμάρω ‖ ~dom n πλῆξις, ἀνία.

boring ['bɔ:rɪŋ] a ἀνιαρός, βαρετός.

born [bɔ:n] pp: to be ~ γεννιέμαι.

borough ['bʌrə] n (διοικητική) περιφέρεια.

borrow ['bɔrəu] vt δανείζομαι.

bosom ['buzəm] n στῆθος, κόρφος.

boss [bɔs] n κύφωμα, καμπούρα ‖ (master) τό ἀφεντικό ‖ vt διευθύνω, κάνω τόν διευθυντή ‖ ~y a κάνω τό δερβέναγα.

bosun ['bəusn] n = boatswain ‖ see boat.

botanical [bə'tænɪkəl] a βοτανικός.

botanist ['bɔtənɪst] n βοτανολόγος.

botany ['bɔtənɪ] n βοτανική.

botch [bɔtʃ] vt φτιάνω τσαπατσούλικα, κουτσοφτιάχνω ‖ (patch) κουτσομπα-λώνω.

both [bəuθ] a,pron ἀμφότεροι, καί οἱ δύο ‖ ad καί . . . καί ‖ cj ὄχι μόνον . . . ἀλλά καί . . . .

bother ['bɔðə*] n ἐνόχλησις, μπελᾶς ‖ vt ἐνοχλῶ, πειράζω, σκοτίζω ‖ vi στενα-χωριέμαι, νοιάζομαι.

bottle ['bɔtl] n φιάλη, μπουκάλι, μποτίλια ‖ vt ἐμφιαλώνω, μπουκαλάρω, μποτιλ-λιάρω ‖ ~neck n (production) δυσχέρεια ‖ (traffic) συνωστισμός.

bottom ['bɔtəm] n κάτω μέρος, βάθος ‖ (of sea etc) πυθμήν, βυθός ‖ (seat) πισινός, ποπός ‖ (ship) πλοῖον ‖ a κάτω μέρος, κάτω-κάτω ‖ (lowest) κατώτατος ‖ ~less a ἀπύθμενος.

bough [bau] n κλάδος, κλαδί.

bought [bɔ:t] pt,pp of buy.

boulder ['bəuldə*] n λίθος, λιθάρι, ὀγκό-λιθος.

bounce [bauns] n (rebound) ἀναπήδησις, γκέλ ‖ vi κάνω γκέλ, ἀναπηδῶ ‖ (col: person) μπαίνω—βγαίνω ξαφνικά ‖ vt κάνω μπάλλα νά κάνει γκέλ.

bound [baund] pt,pp of bind ‖ n ὅριον, σύνορον ‖ (restriction) ὅρια ‖ (leap)

πήδημα ‖ vi (spring, leap) πηδῶ, σκιρτῶ ‖ (limit) περιορίζω ‖ a προοριζόμενον γιά, κατευθυνόμενον εἰς ‖ ~ary n ὅριον, σύνορον ‖ ~less a ἀπεριόριστος.

bouquet ['bukeɪ] n μπουκέτο.

bourgeois ['buəʒwa:] a μπουρζουάζ, ἀστός.

bout [baut] n (contest) γῦρος, ἀγών, συνάντησις ‖ (of illness) προσβολή.

bow [bəu] n (curve) καμπή ‖ (ribbon) φιόγκος ‖ (weapon) τόξο, δοξάρι ‖ (mus) δοξάρι βιολιοῦ.

bow [bau] vi ὑποκλίνομαι, σκύβω τό κεφάλι ‖ vt κλίνω, κάμπτω ‖ (submit) ὑποκύπτω, ὑποτάσσομαι ‖ n ὑπόκλισις, κλίσις (τῆς κεφαλῆς) ‖ (of ship) πλώρη.

bowels [bauəlz] npl ἔντερα, σπλάχνα ‖ (fig) σπλάχνα.

bowl [bəul] n (basin) λεκάνη, γαβάθα ‖ (of pipe) λουλᾶς (τσιμπουκιοῦ) ‖ (wooden ball) σφαίρα ‖ vti παίζω μπάλλα, ρίχνω μπάλλα ‖ ~s npl παιχνίδι τῆς μπάλλας.

bow-legged ['bəulegid] a στραβοπόδης, στραβοκάνης.

bowler ['bəulə*] n παίκτης τῆς μπάλλας ‖ (hat) μελόν.

bowling ['bəulɪŋ] n (game) παιχνίδι τῆς μπάλλας, μπόλιγκ.

bow tie ['bəu'taɪ] n παπιγιόν, πεταλούδα.

box [bɔks] n κιβώτιον ‖ (small) κουτί ‖ (theat) θεωρεῖον ‖ vt (s.o.'s ears) καρπα-ζώνω ‖ (package) πακετάρω ‖ vi πυγμαχῶ, παίζω μπόξ ‖ ~er n (person) πυγμάχος, μποξέρ ‖ (dog) μπόξερ ‖ ~ing n (sport) πυγμαχία, μπόξ ‖ ~ office n ταμεῖον (θεάτρου) ‖ ~ room n ἀποθήκη οἰκίας.

boy [bɔɪ] n ἀγόρι, παιδί.

boycott ['bɔɪkɔt] n μποϋκοττάρισμα ‖ vt ἀποκλείω, μποϋκοττάρω.

boyfriend ['bɔɪfrend] n φίλος, ἀγαπημένος.

boyish ['bɔɪɪʃ] a παιδιάστικος, ἀγορίστικος.

bra [bra:] n σουτιέν, στηθόδεσμος.

brace [breis] n (clamp) δεσμός ‖ (pair) ζευγάρι ‖ (support) στύλωμα ‖ (tool) ματικάπι ‖ vt συνδέω, στερεώνω ‖ (o.s.) τονώνω, δυναμώνω ‖ ~s npl τιράντες.

bracelet ['breislit] n βραχιόλι.

bracing ['breisiŋ] a τονωτικός.

bracken ['brækən] n φτέρη.

bracket ['brækit] n (support) ὑποστήριγμα, ὠτίς, κρεμάθρα ‖ (round) παρένθεσις ‖ (square) ἀγκύλη ‖ (group) ὁμάδα, ἰσάξιοι ‖ vt θέτω ἐν παρενθέσει ‖ (associate) συνδέω.

brag [bræg] vi καυχῶμαι.

braid [breid] n (of hair) πλεξίδα, πλεξούδα ‖ (officer's etc) σειρήτι, κορδόνι.

Braille [breil] n Μπράϊλ.

brain [brein] n ἐγκέφαλος, μυαλό ‖ (person) διάνοια ‖ ~s npl μυαλά ‖ ~less a ἀμυ-αλος, βλάκας ‖ ~washing n πλύσις ἐγκεφάλου ‖ ~wave n ἔμπνευσις, ἐπίνόησις ‖ ~y a εὐφυής.

braise [breiz] vt ψήνω στήν κατσαρόλα.

brake ['breik] n (on vehicle) τροχοπέδη, φρένο ‖ vti φρενάρω, πατῶ φρένο.
bramble ['bræmbl] n βάτος.
branch [bra:ntʃ] n (of tree) κλάδος, κλαδί ‖ (division) κλάδος ‖ (office) ὑποκατάστημα ‖ vi διακλαδοῦμαι, χωρίζομαι.
brand [brænd] n (trademark) μάρκα ‖ (on cattle) σφράγισις μέ ἀναμμένο σίδηρο.
brand-new ['brænd'nju:] a κατακαίνουργος, ὁλοκαίνουργος, τοῦ κουτιοῦ.
brandy ['brændi] n κονιάκ.
brash [bræʃ] a ἀναιδής, ἀδιάντροπος.
brass [bra:s] n μπροῦτζος ‖ ~ **band** n μπάντα, φανφάρα.
brassière ['bræsiəз*] n σουτιέν, στηθόδεσμος.
brat [bræt] n κουτσούβελο, διαβολάκι.
bravado [brə'va:dəu] n παλληκαρισμός.
brave [breiv] a γενναῖος ‖ (show) περίφημος ‖ n ἐρυθρόδερμος πολεμιστής ‖ vt ἀψηφῶ ‖ ~ **ly** ad γενναία, παλληκαρίσια ‖ ~ **ry** n θάρρος, ἀνδρεία.
bravo [bra:'vəu] excl εὖγε!, μπράβο!
brawl [brɔ:l] n καυγάς ‖ vi καυγαδίζω.
brawn [brɔ:n] n μυϊκή δύναμις, δύναμι ‖ (cooking) πηχτή ‖ ~ **y** a γεροδεμένος.
bray [brei] n γκάρισμα ‖ vi γκαρίζω.
brazen ['breizn] a (metal) μπρούτζινος ‖ (shameless) ἀναιδής, ξετσίπωτος ‖ vt: **to ~ it out** καυχῶμαι ξετσίπωτα.
brazier ['breiziə*] n μαγκάλι, φουρφού.
Brazil [brə'zil] n Βραζιλία ‖ ~ **ian** a βραζιλιανός ‖ n Βραζιλιάνος ‖ ~ **nut** n Βραζιλιανόν καρύδι.
breach [bri:tʃ] n (gap) ῥῆγμα, τρύπα ‖ (of trust, duty) παραβίασις, παράβασις ‖ (quarrel) ῥῆξις, τσάκωμα ‖ vt γκρεμίζω.
bread [bred] n ψωμί ‖ (living) καθημερινό ψωμί ‖ ~ **and butter** n μέσα συντηρήσεως ‖ ~ **crumbs** npl ψύχουλα ‖ ~ **winner** n στήριγμα τῆς οἰκογενείας.
break [breik] (irreg v) vt (crush) συντρίβω, τσακίζω ‖ (apart) σπάω ‖ (promise) ἀθετῶ ‖ (silence etc) διακόπτω ‖ (habit) κόβω ‖ (the law) παραβιάζω ‖ vi θραύομαι, τσακίζομαι ‖ (friendship etc) τά χαλῶ ‖ (dissolve) διαλύομαι ‖ n (gap) ῥῆξις, ἄνοιγμα, χάσμα ‖ (rest) διακοπή, διάλειμμα ‖ (chance) εὐκαιρία, τύχη ‖ (fracture) ῥωγμή ‖ **to ~ free** or **loose** vi δραπετεύω, ἀπελευθερώνομαι ‖ **to ~ in** vt (a horse etc) δαμάζω ‖ (conversation) διακόπτω ‖ vi (burglar) κάνω διάρρηξι ‖ **to ~ out** vi (escape) δραπετεύω ‖ (of prison) δραπετεύω ‖ **to ~ up** vi διαλύομαι ‖ vt χωρίζω, συντρίβω, τεμαχίζω ‖ ~ **able** a εὔθραστος ‖ ~ **age** n σπάσιμο, ῥάγισμα ‖ ~ **down** n (in discussions) διακοπή ‖ (of health) κατάρρευσις ‖ (mental) χάσιμο τοῦ μυαλοῦ ‖ ~ **er** n (naut) κῦμα ‖ ~ **fast** n πρωϊνό, κολατσό ‖ ~ **through** n δίοδος, ῥῆγμα ‖ ~ **water** n κυματοθραύστης.
breast [brest] n (of woman) μαστός, βυζί ‖

(of man, animal) στῆθος ‖ ~ -**stroke** n ἁπλωτή.
breath [breθ] n πνοή, ἀναπνοή ‖ **out of ~** λαχανιασμένος.
breathe [bri:ð] vti ἀναπνέω ‖ ~ **r** n ἀνάσα.
breathing ['bri:ðiŋ] n ἀναπνοή.
breathless ['breθlis] a λαχανιασμένος.
breathtaking ['breθteikiŋ] a καταπληκτικός, τρομακτικός.
bred [bred] pt,pp of **breed**.
breed [bri:d] (irreg v) n γενεά, ῥάτσα ‖ vt γεννῶ, φέρνω ‖ (animals) τρέφω ‖ vi ἀναπαράγομαι ‖ ~ **er** n (person) ἀναπαραγωγός, τροφεύς ‖ ~ **ing** n ἀνατροφή.
breeze [bri:z] n αὖρα, ἀεράκι.
breezy ['bri:zi] a εὔαερος ‖ (person) γεμάτος ζωή.
brevity ['breviti] n βραχύτης, συντομία.
brew [bru:] vt (drinks) παρασκευάζω, μπύρα, ἀποστάζω ‖ (tea) βράζω ‖ (plot) μηχανορραφῶ ‖ vi βράζομαι ‖ (storm etc) ἔρχεται ‖ ~ **ery** n ζυθοποιία, ποτοποιία.
bribe [braib] n δωροδοκία ‖ vt δωροδοκῶ, λαδώνω ‖ ~ **ry** n δωροδοκία, μπούκωμα.
brick [brik] n πλίνθος, τοῦβλο ‖ ~ **layer** n τουβλᾶς ‖ ~ **work** n πλινθοδομή.
bridal ['braidl] a νυφικός, γαμήλιος.
bride [braid] n νύφη ‖ ~ **groom** n γαμπρός ‖ ~ **smaid** n παράνυφη.
bridge [bridʒ] n γεφύρι, γιοφύρι ‖ (naut) γέφυρα ‖ (cards) μπρίτζ ‖ (of nose) ῥάχη τῆς μύτης ‖ vt γεφυρώνω.
bridle ['braidl] n χαλινάρι, γκέμι ‖ vt (a horse) χαλινώνω ‖ (control) χαλιναγωγῶ.
brief [bri:f] a σύντομος, βραχύς ‖ n (law) δικογραφία, φάκελλος ‖ vt δίδω ὁδηγίες, ἐνημερώνω ‖ ~ **s** npl κοντή κυλόττα ‖ ~ **case** n χαρτοφύλακας ‖ ~ **ing** n καταρτισμός, ὁδηγίες ‖ ~ **ly** ad σύντομα, μέ λίγα λόγια ‖ ~ -**ness** n βραχύτης, συντομία.
brigade [bri'geid] n (mil) ταξιαρχία ‖ see **fire**.
brigadier [brigə'diə*] n ταξίαρχος.
bright [brait] a (as light) φωτεινός, λαμπερός, γυαλιστερός ‖ (weather) φωτεινός, καθαρός ‖ (clever) ἔξυπνος, εὐφυής ‖ (colour) ζωηρός, λαμπρός ‖ ~ **en** vti ζωηρεύω, φωτίζομαι, ἀστράφτω ‖ ~ **ly** ad λαμπρά, λαμπερά.
brilliance ['briljəns] n λαμπρότης, ἐξυπνάδα ‖ (of surface etc) φωτεινότης ‖ (of style) ζωηρότης.
brilliant ['briljənt] a φωτεινός, λαμπρός ‖ (person) σπουδαῖος, λαμπρός ‖ (splendid) ἔξοχος ‖ ~ **ly** ad λαμπρά.
brim [brim] n (of cup) χεῖλος ‖ (of hat) γῦρος, μπόρ ‖ vi ξεχειλίζω ‖ ~ **ful** a ξέχειλος.
brine [brain] n σαλαμούρα, ἅρμη.
bring [briŋ] (irreg v) vt φέρω, φέρνω ‖ **to ~ about** vt ἐπιτυγχάνω, καταφέρνω ‖ **to ~ off** vt φέρω εἰς πέρας ‖ **to ~ round** or

to vt ἐπαναφέρω, συνεφέρω ‖ **to ~ up** vt (raise) ἀνατρέφω, μεγαλώνω ‖ (introduce) προβάλλω, θέτω.

brisk [brisk] a ζωηρός.

bristle ['brisl] n γουρουνότριχα ‖ vi ἀνατριχιάζω ‖ **bristling with** γεμάτος μέ.

Britain ['britən] n Βρεττανία.

British ['britiʃ] a Βρεττανικός, Ἀγγλικός ‖ **the ~** npl οἱ Ἄγγλοι ‖ **~ Isles** npl Βρεττανικαί Νῆσοι.

Briton ['britən] n Βρεττανός, Ἄγγλος.

brittle ['britl] a εὔθραυστος.

broach [brəutʃ] vt (subject) θίγω (ζήτημα).

broad [brɔːd] a εὐρύς, φαρδύς, πλατύς ‖ (daylight) στό φῶς τῆς ἡμέρας ‖ (general) ἁπλό, γενικό ‖ (accent) χωριάτικη προφορά ‖ **~cast** n ἐκπομπή ‖ vti μεταδίδω διά ραδιοφώνου ‖ **~casting** n ἐκπομπή, μετάδοσις ‖ **~en** vt εὐρύνω, πλαταίνω ‖ vi εὐρύνομαι, ἀνοίγω ‖ **~ly** ad εὐρέως, πλατειά ‖ **~-minded** a μέ ἀνοικτό μυαλό, ἀνεκτικός, εὐρείας ἀντιλήψεως.

brocade [brəu'keid] n μπροκάρ.

broccoli ['brɔkəli] n μπρόκολο.

brochure ['brəuʒjuə*] n φυλλάδιον, μπροσούρα.

broiler ['brɔilə*] n ψησταριά.

broke [brəuk] pt of **break** ‖ a ἀπένταρος ‖ **~n** pp of **break** ‖ **~n-hearted** a μέ ραγισμένη καρδιά.

broker ['brəukə*] n μεσίτης, χρηματιστής.

bronchitis [brɔŋ'kaitis] n βρογχίτιδα.

bronze [brɔnz] n μπροῦντζος ‖ **~d** a ἡλιοψημένος, μαυρισμένος.

brooch [brəutʃ] n καρφίτσα.

brood [bruːd] n κλώσσισμα, γενιά ‖ vi κλωσσῶ ‖ (meditate) μελαγχολῶ ‖ **~y** a ἀφηρημένος.

brook [bruk] n (stream) ρυάκι, ρέμα.

broom [brum] n σκούπα ‖ **~ stick** n σκουπόξυλο.

broth [brɔθ] n ζουμί κρέατος, σούπα.

brothel ['brɔθl] n μπορντέλο, οἴκος ἀνοχῆς.

brother ['brʌðə*] n ἀδελφός ‖ **~hood** n ἀδελφοσύνη, ἀδελφότης ‖ **~-in-law** n γαμπρός, κουνιάδος ‖ **~ly** a ἀδελφικός.

brought [brɔːt] pt,pp of **bring**.

brow [brau] n (forehead) κούτελο, μέτωπο ‖ (eyebrow) φρύδι ‖ (of hill etc) χεῖλος, φρύδι ‖ **~beat** vt φοβίζω, τρομάζω.

brown [braun] a καστανό, καφετής ‖ n καφετής ‖ vti σκουραίνω, μαυρίζω ‖ (cooking) καβουρδίζω ‖ **~ie** n (girl guide) προσκοπίνα.

browse [brauz] vi (examine casually) ξεφυλλίζω, βόσκω, τριγυρίζω.

bruise [bruːz] n μώλωψ, κτύπημα ‖ vti κτυπῶ, κτυπιέμαι.

brunette [bruː'net] n μελαχροινή.

brunt [brʌnt] n ὁρμή, φόρα.

brush [brʌʃ] n βούρτσα ‖ (paint) πινέλο ‖ (fight) σύγκρουσις ‖ vt βουρτσίζω ‖

(lightly) ξεσκονίζω ‖ **to ~ aside** vt παραμερίζω ‖ **~wood** n θάμνοι, χαμόκλαδα.

brusque [bruːsk] a ἀπότομος, τραχύς.

Brussels sprout ['brʌslz'spraut] n (Βελγικό) λαχανάκι, πετί-σού.

brutal ['bruːtl] a κτηνώδης ‖ **~ity** n κτηνωδία.

brute [bruːt] n κτῆνος, θηρίον.

brutish ['bruːtiʃ] a ἀποκτηνωμένος, κτηνώδης.

bubble ['bʌbl] n μπουρμπουλήθρα, φουσκάλα ‖ vi κοχλάζω ‖ (river, wine) ἀφρίζω ‖ **to ~ over** (fig) ξεχειλίζω.

buck [bʌk] n ἐλάφι ἀρσενικό ‖ (rabbit) κούνελος ‖ vi ἐνθαρρύνω, δίνω κουράγιο ‖ **to ~ up** vi ἐνθαρρύνομαι, (ξανα)παίρνω κουράγιο.

bucket ['bʌkit] n κουβάς, κάδος.

buckle ['bʌkl] n πόρπη, φιούμπα ‖ vt κουμπώνω, θηλυκώνω ‖ (bend) λυγίζω, στραβώνω.

bud [bʌd] n μπουμπούκι.

Buddha ['budə] n Βούδδας.

Buddhism ['budizəm] n Βουδδισμός.

Buddhist ['budist] n βουδδιστής ‖ a βουδδικός.

budding ['bʌdiŋ] a πού μπουμπουκιάζει.

buddy ['bʌdi] n φιλαράκος.

budge [bʌdʒ] vti κινοῦμαι, ὑποχωρῶ.

budgerigar ['bʌdʒəriga:*] n παπαγαλάκι.

budget ['bʌdʒit] n προϋπολογισμός.

buff [bʌf] a (colour) σαμουά, κρεατί.

buffalo ['bʌfələu] n βουβάλι.

buffer ['bʌfə*] n ἀποσβεστήρ, ἀμορτισέρ.

buffet ['bʌfit] n πλῆγμα, κτύπημα ‖ ['bufei] (bar) ἀναψυκτήριον ‖ (food) μπουφές ‖ vt πλήττω, κτυπῶ.

buffoon [bə'fuːn] n παλιάτσος, καραγκιόζης.

bug [bʌg] n (insect) κοριός ‖ (US) ζωΰφιον ‖ (spy device) κρυφό μικρόφωνο ‖ **~bear** n ἀντιπάθεια, φόβητρον.

buggy ['bʌgi] n ἁμαξάκι.

bugle ['bjuːgl] n σάλπιγγα.

build [bild] (irreg v) vt οἰκοδομῶ, χτίζω ‖ **~er** n οἰκοδόμος, κατασκευαστής ‖ **~ing** n χτίριο, οἰκοδομή ‖ **~ing society** n οἰκοδομικός συνεταιρισμός ‖ **~-up** n διαφήμισις.

built [bilt] pt,pp of **build** ‖ **well-~** a (person) γεροδεμένος ‖ **~-in** a (cupboard) ἐντοιχισμένος.

bulb [bʌlb] n (bot) βολβός ‖ (elec) λάμπα, γλόμπος ‖ **~ous** a βολβώδης.

Bulgaria [bʌl'geəriə] n Βουλγαρία.

bulge [bʌldʒ] n διόγκωσις, φούσκωμα ‖ vti προεξέχω, ἐξογκοῦμαι, φουσκώνω.

bulk [bʌlk] n μέγεθος, ὄγκος ‖ (greater part) μέγιστον μέρος ‖ **~head** n διάφραγμα ‖ **~y** a ὀγκώδης, χονδρός.

bull [bul] n ταῦρος ‖ (rubbish) ψέμματα, ἀρλούμπες ‖ **~dog** n μπουλντόγκ.

bulldozer ['buldəuzə*] n μπουλντόζα.

bullet ['bulit] *n* σφαῖρα, βόλι.
bulletin ['bulitin] *n* δελτίον, ἀνακοινωθέν.
bullfight ['bulfait] *n* ταυρομαχία.
bullion ['buljən] *n* χρυσός (ἄργυρος) εἰς ράβδους.
bullock ['bulək] *n* βόδι, μοσχάρι.
bull's-eye ['bulzai] *n* κέντρον (στόχου).
bully ['buli] *n* τύραννος ‖ *vt* ἀπειλῶ, τρομοκρατῶ.
bum [bʌm] *n* (*col*) πισινός ‖ (*tramp*) ἀλήτης, ἀκαμάτης ‖ **to ~ around** *vi* κοπροσκυλιάζω.
bump [bʌmp] *n* (*blow*) κτύπημα, τίναγμα ‖ (*bruise*) πρήξιμο, καρούλα, καρούμπαλο ‖ *vti* κτυπῶ, σκοντάφτω ‖ **~er** *n* (*car*) προφυλακτήρας ‖ *a* πλουσία (ἐσοδεία).
bumptious ['bʌmpʃəs] *a* ψηλομύτης.
bumpy ['bʌmpi] *a* ἀνώμαλος (δρόμος).
bun [bʌn] *n* σταφιδόψωμο, κουλουράκι.
bunch [bʌntʃ] *n* μάτσο, φούχτα, χούφτα, δέμα.
bundle ['bʌndl] *n* δέμα, μπόγος ‖ *vt* πακετάρω, δένω ‖ (*also ~* **off**) ξεφορτώνομαι.
bung [bʌŋ] *n* πῶμα, τάπα ‖ *vt* (*throw*) ρίχνω, χώνω.
bungalow ['bʌŋgələu] *n* μπάγκαλο, ἐξοχικό σπίτι.
bungle ['bʌŋgl] *vt* τά κάνω θάλασσα, εἶμαι ἀδέξιος.
bunion ['bʌnjən] *n* κάλος.
bunk [bʌŋk] *n* κλίνη, κουκέτα.
bunker ['bʌŋkə*] *n* ἀποθήκη καυσίμων, καρβουνιέρα.
bunny ['bʌni] *n* κουνελάκι.
Bunsen burner ['bʌnsn'bə:nə*] *n* λυχνία Μποῦνσεν.
bunting ['bʌntiŋ] *n* σακκελίς, σημαιοστολισμός.
buoy [bɔi] *n* (*naut*) σημαδούρα ‖ (*lifebuoy*) σωσσίβιο ‖ **~ancy** *n* πλευστότης ‖ **~ant** *a* (*of person*) εὔθυμος, κεφάτος ‖ **to ~ up** *vt* ἐνισχύω, ἀναθαρρύνω, ἐνθαρρύνω.
burden ['bə:dn] *n* φόρτωμα, βάρος, δυσβάστακτον βάρος ‖ *vt* (ἐπι)βαρύνω, φορτώνω.
bureau [bjuə'rəu] *n* γραφεῖον πού κλείνει ‖ (*for information etc*) ὑπηρεσία πληροφοριῶν.
bureaucracy [bjuə'rɔkrəsi] *n* γραφειοκρατία.
bureaucrat ['bjuərəukræt] *n* γραφειοκράτης ‖ **~ic** *a* γραφειοκρατικός.
burglar ['bə:glə*] *n* διαρρήκτης ‖ **~ alarm** *n* κουδούνι ἀσφαλείας ‖ **~ize** *vt* (*US*) διαρρηγνύω ‖ **~y** *n* διάρρηξις.
burgle ['bə:gl] *vt* διαρρηγνύω.
burial ['beriəl] *n* ταφή ‖ **~ ground** *n* νεκροταφεῖον.
burlesque [bə:'lesk] *n* ἐπιθεώρησις, μπυρλέσκ.
burly ['bə:li] *a* γεροδεμένος.
burn [bə:n] (*irreg v*) *n* ἔγκαυμα ‖ *vt* καίω ‖ *vi* φλέγομαι ‖ **to ~ one's fingers** (*fig*)

βρίσκω τό μπελά μου ‖ **~ing question** *n* φλέγον ζήτημα.
burnish ['bə:niʃ] *vt* στιλβώνω, γυαλίζω.
burnt [bə:nt] *pt,pp of* **burn** ‖ *a* καμένος, ψημένος.
burrow ['bʌrəu] *n* φωλιά, τρύπα, λαγούμι ‖ *vti* σκάβω λαγούμι, ἀνοίγω τρύπα.
burst [bə:st] (*irreg v*) *n* ἔκρηξις, ριπή ‖ *vt* (*explode*) προκαλῶ ἔκρηξιν ‖ (*break*) σπάζω ‖ (*break out*) διαρρηγνύω, σπάω ‖ *vi* (*tank etc*) διαρρηγνύομαι, σπάζω ‖ (*flower*) σκάζω, ἀνοίγω ‖ (*into pieces*) γίνομαι κομμάτια.
bury ['beri] *vt* (*inter*) θάβω ‖ (*hide*) κρύβομαι, χώνω, βυθίζομαι.
bus [bʌs] *n* λεωφορεῖον, μπούσι.
bush [buʃ] *n* θάμνος, χαμόκλαδο.
bushel ['buʃl] *n* μπούσελ (36 λίτρα).
bushy ['buʃi] *a* δασύς, πυκνός.
busily ['bizili] *ad* δραστηρίως.
business ['biznis] *n* ἐπιχείρησις, δουλειά ‖ (*concern*) ἐνδιαφέρον, δουλειά ‖ **~man** *n* ἐπιχειρηματίας.
bus stop ['bʌsstɔp] *n* στάσις λεωφορείου.
bust [bʌst] *n* (*statue*) προτομή, μποῦστος ‖ (*of woman*) στῆθος.
bustle ['bʌsl] *n* (θορυβώδης) κίνησις, πάταγος ‖ *vi* πηγαινοέρχομαι, βιάζομαι.
bustling ['bʌsliŋ] *a* δραστήριος, πολυάσχολος.
bust-up ['bʌstʌp] *n* (*col*) χρεωκόπησις, ἀποτυχία.
busy ['bizi] *a* ἀπησχολημένος, πολυάσχολος ‖ *vt* ἀσχολοῦμαι, φροντίζω ‖ **~body** *n* πολυπράγμων, παπατρέχας.
but [bʌt] *cj* (*still, yet, besides*) ἀλλά, μά ‖ *ad* (*only, except, as*) μόνον, μόλις, δέν . . . παρά ‖ *prep* (*except*) ἐκτός, πλήν, παρά.
butane ['bju:tein] *n* βουτάνιον.
butcher ['butʃə*] *n* χασάπης ‖ (*savage*) σφαγεύς ‖ *vt* σφάζω.
butler ['bʌtlə*] *n* κελλάρης, μπάτλερ, ἀρχιϋπηρέτης.
butt [bʌt] *n* (*cask*) βαρέλι, βουτσί ‖ (*target*) στόχος ‖ (*of cigarette*) ἀποτσίγαρο, γόπα ‖ (*thick end*) χονδρόν ἄκρον ‖ *vt* κτυπῶ μέ τό κεφάλι.
butter ['bʌtə*] *n* βούτυρο ‖ *vt* βουτυρώνω ‖ (*fig*) **to ~ s.o. up** κολακεύω, ξεσκονίζω ‖ **~fly** *n* πεταλούδα.
buttocks ['bʌtəks] *npl* γλουτοί, τά ὀπίσθια.
button ['bʌtn] *n* κουμπί ‖ *vti* κουμπώνω ‖ **~hole** *n* κουμπότρυπα.
buttress ['bʌtris] *n* ἀντέρεισμα.
buy [bai] (*irreg v*) *vt* ἀγοράζω ‖ **to ~ up** *vt* ἀγοράζω χονδρικῶς ‖ **~er** *n* ἀγοραστής.
buzz [bʌz] *n* βούϊσμα ‖ *vi* βουΐζω.
buzzard ['bʌzəd] *n* ἰκτίνος.
buzzer ['bʌzə*] *n* βομβητής, ψιθυριστής.
by [bai] *prep* (*near, beside*) παρά, πλησίον, πλάϊ, δίπλα, κοντά ‖ (*through*) διά, ἀπό ‖

(*with*) ἀπό, μέ ‖ ~ **and large** κατά κανόνα ‖ ~-**election** n ἀναπληρωματικές ἐκλογές ‖ ~**gone** a περασμένος, παλιός ‖ n: **let** ~**gones be** ~**gones** περασμένα, ξεχασμένα ‖ ~ **far** κατά πολύ ‖ ~-**name** κατ' ὄνομα ‖ ~**pass** n βοηθητική δίοδος ‖ ~-**product** n ὑποπροϊόν ‖ ~**stander** n παριστάμενος ‖ ~**word** n παροιμία ‖ (*person*) περίγελως, τό κορόϊδο.
Byzantine [bai'zæntain] a Βυζαντινός.

C, c

cab [kæb] n ἁμάξι, ταξί ‖ (*of train, truck*) θέσις ὁδηγοῦ.
cabaret ['kæbərei] n καμπαρέ.
cabbage ['kæbidʒ] n λάχανο.
cabin ['kæbin] n καλύβα ‖ (*naut*) καμπίνα ‖ ~ **cruiser** n θαλαμηγός χωρίς κατάρτια.
cabinet ['kæbinit] n κομό ‖ (*pol*) ὑπουργικόν συμβούλιον ‖ ~**maker** n ἐπιπλοποιός.
cable ['keibl] n καλώδιον ‖ (*message*) τηλεγράφημα ‖ vti τηλεγραφῶ ‖ ~**gram** n τηλεγράφημα ‖ ~ **railway** n κρεμαστός σιδηρόδρομος.
cache [kæʃ] n (*place*) κρύπτη ‖ (*material*) ἀποκρυπτόμενα εἴδη.
cackle ['kækl] n κακάρισμα ‖ vi κακαρίζω.
cactus ['kæktəs] n κάκτος.
caddie, caddy ['kædi] n κάντι.
cadet [kə'det] n (*naut*) δόκιμος ‖ (*mil*) εὔελπις ‖ (*aviat*) ἴκαρος.
cadge [kædʒ] vt ζητιανεύω, σελεμίζω.
Caesarean [si:'zɛəriən] a: ~ (**section**) καισαρική (τομή).
cafe ['kæfei] n καφενεῖον ‖ (*with food*) καφεστιατόριον ‖ (*bar*) καφεμπάρ ‖ ~**teria** n καφετέρια.
cage [keidʒ] n κλουβί ‖ vt ἐγκλουβίζω.
cagey ['keidʒi] a (*col*) πονηρός.
cajole [kə'dʒəul] vt καλοπιάνω.
cake [keik] n κέῖκ, γλύκισμα ‖ (*pie*) πήττα ‖ (*of soap etc*) πλάκα.
calamitous [kə'læmitəs] a καταστρεπτικός.
calamity [kə'læmiti] n συμφορά, καταστροφή.
calcium ['kælsiəm] n ἀσβέστιον.
calculate ['kælkjuleit] vti ὑπολογίζω, λογαριάζω.
calculating ['kælkjuleitiŋ] a ὑπολογιστικός, ἐσκεμμένη.
calculation [kælkju'leiʃən] n ὑπολογισμός.
calculus ['kælkjuləs] n λογισμός.
calendar ['kæləndə*] n ἡμερολόγιον.
calf [ka:f] n (*cow*) μοσχάρι ‖ (*skin*) βιδέλο ‖ (*anat*) κνήμη, γάμπα.
calibre, (US) caliber ['kælibə*] n διαμέτρημα ‖ (*fig*) ἀξία, ἱκανότης.
call [kɔ:l] vt καλῶ, φωνάζω ‖ (*meeting*) συγκαλῶ ‖ (*tel*) κλῆσις, πρόσκλησις ‖ vi (*visit*) ἐπισκέπτομαι, ἔρχομαι ‖ n

(*shout*) φωνή, κραυγή ‖ (*visit*) ἐπίσκεψις ‖ ~**box** n τηλεφωνικός θάλαμος ‖ ~**er** n (*visitor*) ἐπισκέπτης ‖ ~ **girl** n κοκότα ‖ ~**ing** n (*profession*) ἐπάγγελμα ‖ **to** ~ **for** vt καλῶ, ζητῶ, ἔρχομαι ‖ **to** ~ **off** vt ἀκυρώνω, σταματῶ, διακόπτω ‖ **to** ~ **on** vt (*visit*) ἐπισκέπτομαι ‖ '**to** ~ **up** vt (*mil*) (ἐπι)στρατεύω ‖ (*tel*) (πρόσ)καλῶ, τηλεφωνῶ.
callous ['kæləs] a σκληρός, ἄκαρδος ‖ ~**ly** ad σκληρά ‖ ~**ness** n ἀναισθησία.
calm [ka:m] n ἀταραξία ‖ vti καθησυχάζω ‖ a ἤρεμος, ἀτάραχος ‖ ~**ly** ad ἠρέμως ‖ ~**ness** n ἡσυχία, κάλμα ‖ **to** ~ **down** vi καταπραΰνω, καλμάρω ‖ vi ἠρεμῶ, καθησυχάζω.
calorie ['kæləri] n θερμίδα.
calve [ka:v] vi γεννῶ ἀγελάδα.
cam [kæm] n ἔκκεντρον, κάμα.
camber ['kæmbə*] n καμπυλότης, κυρτότης.
came [keim] pt of **come**.
camel ['kæməl] n καμήλα.
camellia [kə'mi:liə] n καμέλια.
cameo ['kæmiəu] n καμέα.
camera ['kæmərə] n φωτογραφική μηχανή ‖ ~**man** n ὀπερατέρ.
camouflage ['kæməfla:ʒ] n καμουφλάρισμα ‖ vt καμουφλάρω.
camp [kæmp] n κατασκήνωσις ‖ (*mil*) στρατόπεδον ‖ vi κατασκηνώνω ‖ (*mil*) στρατοπεδεύω.
campaign [kæm'pein] n ἐκστρατεία ‖ vi (*also fig*) ἐκστρατεύω, κάνω καμπάνια.
campbed ['kæmp'bed] n κρεββάτι ἐκστρατείας, ράντσο.
camper ['kæmpə*] n σκηνίτης, ἐκδρομεύς.
camping ['kæmpiŋ] n: **to go** ~ πηγαίνω εἰς κατασκήνωσιν.
campsite ['kæmpsait] n τόπος κατασκηνώσεως.
can [kæn] auxiliary v (*be able*) δύναμαι, μπορῶ ‖ (*be allowed*) ἐπιτρέπεται, μπορῶ ‖ (*know how*) γνωρίζω, ξέρω ‖ n τενεκές, κουτί ‖ vt κονσερβοποιῶ.
Canada ['kænədə] n Καναδᾶς.
Canadian [kə'neidiən] a καναδικός ‖ n Καναδός.
canal [kə'næl] n (*waterway*) διώρυγα, κανάλι ‖ (*anat*) σωλήν, πόρος.
canary [kə'neəri] n καναρίνι ‖ a καναρινί (χρῶμα).
cancel ['kænsəl] vt (*check etc*) ἀκυρώνω ‖ (*strike out*) διαγράφω ‖ (*math*) ἐξαλείφω ‖ ~**lation** n ἀκύρωσις, ματαίωσις.
cancer ['kænsə*] n καρκίνος.
candid ['kændid] a εἰλικρινής, ντρίτα ‖ ~**ly** ad εἰλικρινά.
candidate ['kændideit] n ὑποψήφιος.
candle ['kændl] n κερί ‖ ~**light** n φῶς κεριοῦ ‖ ~**stick** n κηροπήγιον.
candour ['kændə*] n εὐθύτης, ντομπροσύνη.

candy ['kændi] n καραμέλα.
cane [kein] n (bamboo etc) καλάμι ‖ (stick) μπαστούνι ‖ vt (beat) ραβδίζω.
canine ['kænain] a σκυλήσιος.
canister ['kænistə*] n τενεκεδάκι, κουτί.
cannabis ['kænəbis] n κάνναβις.
canned ['kænd] a (food) κονσερβοποιημένο.
cannibal ['kænibəl] n καννίβαλος, ἀνθρωποφάγος ‖ ~ism n ἀνθρωποφαγία.
cannon ['kænən] n (gun) πυροβόλον, κανόνι.
cannot ['kænɔt] = can not ‖ see can.
canoe [kə'nu:] n μονόξυλο, κανό ‖ ~ing n κανό ‖ ~ist n φίλος τοῦ κανό.
canon ['kænən] n κανών ‖ (criterion) κριτήριον ‖ (clergyman) κανονικός.
canonize ['kænənaiz] vt ἁγιοποιῶ.
can opener ['kænəupnə*] n ἀνοιχτήρι.
canopy ['kænəpi] n σκιάς, προστέγασμα.
can't [kænt] = can not ‖ see can.
cantankerous [kæn'tæŋkərəs] a διεστραμμένος, καυγατζῆς.
canteen [kæn'ti:n] n (shop) καντίνα ‖ (mil) παγούρι.
canter ['kæntə*] n τριποδισμός ‖ vi καλπάζω ἐλαφρῶς.
canvas ['kænvəs] n κανναβάτσο ‖ (naut) πανιά ‖ (art) μουσαμάς ‖ under ~ εἰς σκηνάς.
canvass ['kænvəs] vt (election) ψηφοθηρῶ ‖ (discuss) συζητῶ, ἐρευνῶ.
canyon ['kænjən] n φαράγγι, χαράδρα.
cap [kæp] n (hat) σκοῦφος, τραγιάσκα ‖ (top) κάλυμμα ‖ vt στέφω, στεφανώνω ‖ (bottle etc) πωματίζω, σφραγίζω ‖ (outdo) ὑπερβάλλω.
capability [keipə'biləti] n ἱκανότης.
capable ['keipəbl] a ἱκανός ‖ to be ~ of ἱκανός νά.
capacity [kə'pæsiti] n (space) χωρητικότης ‖ (ability) ἱκανότης ‖ (position) ἰδιότης.
cape [keip] n (garment) κάπα, μπελερίνα ‖ (geog) ἀκρωτήρι.
capital ['kæpitl] n (city) πρωτεύουσα ‖ (econ) κεφάλαιον ‖ (letter) κεφαλαῖον γράμμα ‖ ~ism n καπιταλισμός, κεφαλαιοκρατία ‖ ~ist n καπιταλιστής ‖ ~ punishment n θανατική ποινή.
capitulate [kə'pitjuleit] vi συνθηκολογῶ.
capitulation [kəpitju'leiʃən] n συνθηκολόγησις.
capricious [kə'priʃəs] a ἰδιότροπος, ἀσταθής.
capsize [kæp'saiz] vti ἀνατρέπω, μπατάρω.
capstan ['kæpstən] n ἐργάτης.
capsule ['kæpsju:l] n (anat) κάψα ‖ (med) καψούλα.
captain ['kæptin] n (leader) ἀρχηγός ‖ (mil) λοχαγός ‖ (naut) πλοίαρχος ‖ vt ὁδηγῶ, διευθύνω.
caption ['kæpʃən] n ἐπικεφαλίς ‖ (of picture) λεζάντα.

captivate ['kæptiveit] vt γοητεύω, σαγηνεύω, δελεάζω.
captive ['kæptiv] n,a αἰχμάλωτος.
captivity [kæp'tiviti] n αἰχμαλωσία.
capture ['kæptʃə*] vt συλλαμβάνω, αἰχμαλωτίζω ‖ (fort etc) κυριεύω ‖ n σύλληψις ‖ (objective) κατάληψις.
car [ka:*] n (motor) αὐτοκίνητον, ἁμάξι ‖ (railway) βαγόνι.
carafe [kə'ræf] n καράφα.
caramel ['kærəməl] n καραμέλα.
carat ['kærət] n καράτι.
caravan ['kærəvæn] n καραβάνι ‖ (house on wheels) τροχοφόρον οἴκημα.
caraway ['kærəwei] ~ seed n κύμινο.
carbon ['ka:bən] n ἄνθραξ ‖ (paper) καρμπόν ‖ ~ copy n ἀκριβές ἀντίγραφον.
carburettor [ka:bju'retə*] n καρμπυρατέρ.
carcass ['ka:kəs] n πτῶμα, κουφάρι, ψοφίμι.
card [ka:d] n (playing) τραπουλόχαρτο ‖ (visiting) ἐπισκεπτήριον ‖ (general) δελτάριον n χαρτόνι ‖ ~ board n χαρτόνι ‖ ~ game n χαρτοπαιξία.
cardiac ['ka:diæk] a καρδιακός.
cardigan ['ka:digən] n πλεκτό γιλέκο.
cardinal ['ka:dinl] a: ~ number ἀπόλυτος ἀριθμός.
care [keə*] n (worry, attention) φροντίδα, μέριμνα, προσοχή ‖ vi φροντίζω, μέ νοιάζει ‖ ~ of (abbr c/o) τῇ φροντίδι τοῦ ‖ to ~ about vt μέ ἐνδιαφέρει, μέ νοιάζει ‖ to take ~ προσέχω ‖ to take ~ of vt ἐνδιαφέρομαι γιά, φροντίζω γιά ‖ to ~ for vt ἐνδιαφέρομαι ‖ (love) ἀγαπῶ, ἀρέσω.
career [kə'riə*] n σταδιοδρομία, καρριέρα ‖ vi τρέχω, ὁρμῶ.
carefree ['keəfri:] a ἀμέριμνος, ξένοιαστος.
careful ['keəful] a προσεκτικός, ἐπιμελής ‖ ~ly ad προσεχτικά.
careless ['keəlis] a ἀπρόσεκτος, ἀπερίσκεπτος ‖ ~ly ad ἀδιάφορα, ἀπρόσεκτα ‖ ~ness n ἀπροσεξία, ἀμέλεια.
caress [kə'res] n θωπεία, χάδι ‖ vt θωπεύω, χαϊδεύω.
caretaker ['keəteikə*] n ἐπιστάτης ‖ ~ government n ὑπηρεσιακή κυβέρνησις.
car-ferry ['ka:feri] n πορθμεῖον ὀχημάτων, φέρρυ-μποτ.
cargo ['ka:gəu] n φορτίον.
caricature ['kærikətjuə*] n γελοιογραφία, καρικατούρα.
carnal ['ka:nl] a σαρκικός.
carnation [ka:'neiʃən] n γαρύφαλλο.
carnival ['ka:nivəl] n (public celebration) ἀποκρηές, καρναβάλι.
carob ['kærəb] n χαρούπι, ξυλοκέρατον.
carol ['kærəl] n (Christmas) κάλαντα.
carp [ka:p] n (fish) κυπρῖνος, σαζάνι ‖ to ~ at vt ἐπικρίνω, κατσαδιάζω, ἀντιλέγω.
car park ['ka:pa:k] n χῶρος παρκαρίσματος.

carpenter ['ka:pintǝ*] n μαραγκός.

carpentry ['ka:pintri] n ξυλουργική.

carpet ['ka:pit] n τάπης, χαλί ‖ vt στρώνω μέ χαλί.

carping ['ka:piŋ] a (critical) ἐπικριτικός.

carriage ['kærid3] n (vehicle) ἅμαξα, ὄχημα ‖ (carrying) μεταφορά ‖ (fees) μεταφορικά ‖ (bearing) συμπεριφορά, ὕφος ‖ ~way n (part of road) ἁμαξιτή ὁδός.

carrier ['kæriǝ*] n (μετα)φορεύς, κομιστής ‖ ~-bag n μεγάλη χαρτοσακκούλα ‖ ~ pigeon n ταχυδρομική περιστερά.

carrot ['kærǝt] n καρότο.

carry ['kæri] vt (transport, hold) (μετα)-φέρω, βαστάζω, κουβαλῶ ‖ (responsibility) ἔχω εὐθύνες ‖ to be carried away (fig) παρασύρομαι ‖ to ~ on vti συνεχίζω, ἐπιμένω ‖ to ~ out vt (orders) ἐκτελῶ.

cart [ka:t] n κάρρο ‖ vt μεταφέρω μέ κάρρο.

cartilage ['ka:tilid3] n χόνδρος, τραγανό.

carton ['ka:tǝn] n κουτί ἀπό χαρτόνι.

cartoon [ka:'tu:n] n (press) γελοιογραφία, σκίτσο ‖ (cine) κινούμεναι εἰκόνες, μίκυ-μάους.

cartridge ['ka:trid3] n (for gun) φυσίγγι, φυσέκι.

carve [ka:v] vti σκαλίζω, χαράσσω, κόβω.

carving ['ka:viŋ] n (in wood etc) γλυπτική, σκάλισμα ‖ ~ knife n μαχαίρι γιά κόψιμο.

car wash ['ka:woʃ] n πλύσιμο αὐτοκινήτου.

cascade [kæs'keid] n καταρράκτης.

case [keis] n (box) θήκη, κιβώτιο, κασόνι ‖ (instance) περίπτωσις ‖ (state) κατάστασις, ζήτημα ‖ (gram) πτῶσις ‖ (law) ὑπόθεσις ‖ in ~ εἰς περίπτωσιν πού ‖ in any ~ ἐν πάσει περιπτώσει.

cash [kæʃ] n μετρητά (χρήματα) ‖ vt ξαργυρώνω ‖ ~desk n ταμεῖον ‖ ~ier n ταμίας, κασιέρης ‖ ~ register n μηχανή ταμείου, ταμειακή μηχανή.

cashmere [kæʃ'miǝ*] n κασμίρι.

casing ['keisiŋ] n περίβλημα, πλαίσιον, θήκη.

casino [kǝ'si:nǝu] n καζίνο.

cask [ka:sk] n βαρέλι.

casket ['ka:skit] n (box) κουτί, κασετίνα ‖ (US) φέρετρον.

casserole ['kæsǝrǝul] n (pot) τσουκάλι, νταβᾶς ‖ (meal) γκιουβέτσι.

cassock ['kæsǝk] n ράσον.

cast [ka:st] (irreg v) vt (throw) ρίπτω, ρίφνω, πετῶ ‖ (shed) βγάζω, ἀπορρίπτω ‖ (theat) διανέμω ρόλους, ἀναθέτω ρόλον ‖ (metal) χύνω, καλουπώνω ‖ n (theat) θίασος ‖ to ~ off vti βγάζω ‖ (naut) ἀποπλέω.

castanets [kæstǝ'nets] npl καστανιέτες.

caste [ka:st] n κοινωνική τάξις, κάστα.

casting ['ka:stiŋ] a: ~ vote ἀποφασιστική ψῆφος.

castiron ['ka:st'aiǝn] n χυτοσίδηρος.

castle ['ka:sl] n (fortress) φρούριον ‖ (mansion) πύργος.

castor ['ka:stǝ*] n (wheel) καρούλι, ρόδα ‖ ~ oil n ρετσινόλαδο ‖ ~ sugar n ψιλή ζάχαρι.

castrate [kæs'treit] vt μουνουχίζω.

casual ['kæʒjul] a (occasional) τυχαία ‖ (work, attitude) τυχαῖος, ἀπερίσκεπτος ‖ (meeting) τυχαῖος ‖ ~ly ad παρεπιπτόντως.

casualty ['kæʒjulti] n τραυματίας.

cat [kæt] n γάτα.

catalogue, (US) catalog ['kætǝlɔg] n κατάλογος ‖ vt ἐγγράφω εἰς κατάλογον.

catalyst ['kætǝlist] n καταλύτης.

catapult ['kætǝpʌlt] n καταπέλτης.

cataract ['kætǝrækt] n (waterfall) καταρράκτης ‖ (med) καταρράκτης.

catarrh [kǝ'ta:*] n καταρρους.

catastrophe [kǝ'tæstrǝfi] n καταστροφή, συμφορά.

catastrophic [kætǝ'strɔfik] a καταστροφικός.

catch [kætʃ] (irreg v) n (for window etc) δόντι, μπετούγια, ἀσφάλεια ‖ (sport, breath) πιάσιμο ‖ (fish) πιάνω (πολλά ψάρια) ‖ (hunt) θήραμα ‖ vt (seize) πιάνω, ἁρπάζω ‖ (surprise) συλλαμβάνω ‖ (in time) (προ)φθάνω, πιάνω στά πράσα ‖ to ~ a cold ἁρπάζω κρύο.

catching ['kætʃiŋ] a (med) μεταδοτικό, κολλητικό.

catch phrase ['kætʃfreiz] n σύνθημα.

catchy ['kætʃi] a (tune) ἑλκυστικός.

catechism ['kætikizǝm] n (rel) κατήχησις.

categorical [kæti'gɔrikǝl] a κατηγορηματικός ‖ ~ly ad κατηγορηματικῶς.

categorize ['kætigǝraiz] vt κατατάσσω εἰς κατηγορίες.

category ['kætigǝri] n κατηγορία, τάξις.

cater ['keitǝ*] vi (food) τροφοδοτῶ, σερβίρω ‖ ~ing n προμήθεια, τροφοδοσία ‖ to ~ for (fig) φροντίζω, ἱκανοποιῶ.

caterpillar ['kætǝpilǝ*] n κάμπια ‖ ~ tread n ἑρπύστρια.

cathedral [kǝ'θi:drǝl] n καθεδρικός ναός, μητρόπολις.

catholic ['kæθǝlik] a καθολικός, παγκόσμιος, εὐρύς ‖ C~ n Καθολικός ‖ a καθολικός.

cattle ['kætl] npl κτήνη, ζῶα.

catty ['kæti] a δηκτικός, πονηρός.

cauliflower ['kɔliflauǝ*] n κουνουπίδι.

cause [kɔ:z] n (reason) αἰτία, ἀφορμή, λόγος ‖ (object) ὑπόθεσις, χάρις ‖ vt προξενῶ, κάνω νά.

causeway ['kɔ:zwei] n ὑψωμένος δρόμος.

caustic ['kɔ:stik] a (burning) καυστικός ‖ (sarcastic) σαρκαστικός.

cauterize ['kɔ:tǝraiz] vt καυτηριάζω.

caution ['kɔ:ʃǝn] n (care) προσοχή ‖ (warning) προειδοποίησις ‖ vt προειδοποιῶ.

cautious ['kɔ:ʃəs] a προσεκτικός ‖ ~ly ad προσεκτικά.

cavalcade [kævəl'keid] n ἔφιππος παρέλασις.

cavalier [kævə'liə*] a εὔθυμος, ξένοιαστος.

cavalry ['kævəlri] npl ἱππικόν.

cave [keiv] n σπηλιά ‖ ~man n τρωγλοδύτης ‖ to ~ in vi καταρρέω, σωριάζομαι.

cavern ['kævən] n σπηλιά ‖ ~ous a σπηλαιώδης.

caviar(e) ['kævia:*] n χαβιάρι.

cavity ['kæviti] n κοίλωμα, τρύπα.

cease [si:s] vti παύω, σταματῶ, τελειώνω ‖ ~fire n ἀνακωχή ‖ ~less a ἀκατάπαυστος, ἀδιάκοπος.

cedar ['si:də*] n κέδρος.

cede [si:d] vt παραχωρῶ, ἐκχωρῶ.

ceiling ['si:liŋ] n ταβάνι ‖ (fig) ἀνώτατον ὕψος.

celebrate ['selibreit] vt γιορτάζω ‖ (wedding etc) τελῶ ‖ ~d a διάσημος.

celebration [seli'breiʃən] n γιορτασμός, τέλεσις.

celebrity [si'lebriti] n (person) διασημότης.

celery ['seləri] n σέλινο.

celestial [si'lestiəl] a οὐράνιος.

celibacy ['selibəsi] n ἀγαμία.

cell [sel] n (in monastery) κελλί ‖ (in jail) φυλακή ‖ (elec) στοιχεῖον ‖ (biol) κύτταρον.

cellar ['selə*] n ὑπόγειον, κελλάρι ‖ (wine) κάβα.

'cellist ['tʃelist] n βιολοντσελλίστας.

'cello ['tʃeləu] n βιολοντσέλλο.

cellophane ['seləfein] n ® σελλοφάν.

cellular ['seljulə*] a κυτταρικός, κυψελοειδής.

cellulose ['seljuləus] n κελλουλόζη, κυτταρίνη.

Celtic ['keltik, 'seltik] a Κελτικός.

cement [sə'ment] n τσιμέντο ‖ vt (lit) συγκολλῶ μέ τσιμέντο ‖ (fig) στερεώνω, κατοχυρώνω.

cemetery ['semitri] n νεκροταφεῖον.

cenotaph ['senəta:f] n κενοτάφιον.

censer ['sensə*] n θυμιατήρι, λιβανιστήρι.

censor ['sensə*] n λογοκριτής, ἐλεγκτής ‖ ~ship n λογοκρισία.

censure ['senʃə*] vt ἐπικρίνω, ψέγω.

census ['sensəs] n ἀπογραφή.

cent [sent] n σέντ ‖ (col) πεντάρα.

centenary [sen'ti:nəri] n ἑκατονταετηρίς.

center ['sentə*] n (US) = centre.

centigrade ['sentigreid] a ἑκατονταβάθμιος.

centilitre, (US) ~liter ['sentili:tə*] n ἑκατοστόλιτρον.

centimetre, (US) ~meter ['sentimi:tə*] n ἑκατοστόμετρον.

centipede ['sentipi:d] n σαρανταποδαρούσα.

central ['sentrəl] a κεντρικός ‖ ~ heating n κεντρική θέρμανσις ‖ ~ize vt συγκεντρώνω.

centre ['sentə*] n κέντρον.

centrifugal [sen'trifjugəl] a φυγόκεντρος.

century ['sentjuri] n αἰῶνας.

ceramic [si'ræmik] a κεραμικός.

cereal ['siəriəl] n (any grain) δημητριακά, σιτηρά.

ceremonial [seri'məuniəl] a ἐθιμοτυπικός.

ceremony ['seriməni] n ἐθιμοτυπία ‖ (religious) τελετή.

certain ['sɜ:tən] a (sure) βέβαιος, σίγουρος, ἀσφαλής ‖ (some, one) ὡρισμένος, κάποιος ‖ for ~ σίγουρα ‖ ~ly ad ἀσφαλῶς, σίγουρα ‖ ~ty n βεβαιότης, σιγουριά.

certificate [sə'tifikit] n πιστοποιητικόν, βεβαίωσις.

certify ['sɜ:tifai] vti πιστοποιῶ, βεβαιῶ, κυρώνω.

cessation [se'seiʃən] n κατάπαυσις, λῆξις.

chafe [tʃeif] vti τρίβω, ἐρεθίζομαι, φθείρομαι.

chaffinch ['tʃæfintʃ] n σπίνος.

chagrin ['ʃægrin] n λύπη, πικρία.

chain [tʃein] n ἀλυσίδα, καδένα ‖ (mountains) σειρά ‖ vt (also ~ up) δένω μέ ἀλυσίδες, δεσμεύω ‖ ~ reaction n ἀλυσωτὴ ἀντίδρασις ‖ ~ smoker n μεγάλος καπνιστής ‖ ~ store n ὑποκατάστημα.

chair [tʃeə*] n καρέκλα ‖ (univ etc) ἕδρα ‖ vt (preside) προεδρεύω ‖ ~man n πρόεδρος ‖ (director) διευθυντής.

chalet ['ʃælei] n σαλέ.

chalice ['tʃælis] n δισκοπότηρο.

chalk [tʃɔ:k] n (geol) ἀσβεστόλιθος ‖ (crayon) κιμωλία.

challenge ['tʃælindʒ] n πρόκλησις ‖ vt προκαλῶ ‖ (dispute) ἀμφισβητῶ ‖ ~r n διεκδικητής.

challenging ['tʃælindʒiŋ] a προκλητικό.

chamber ['tʃeimbə*] n (compartment) δωμάτιον ‖ (of gun etc) θαλάμη (ὅπλου) ‖ ~ of commerce n Ἐμπορικόν Ἐπιμελητήριον ‖ ~maid n καμαριέρα ‖ ~ music n μουσικὴ δωματίου ‖ ~pot n καθίκι.

chamois ['ʃæmwa:] n: ~ leather n σαμουά.

champagne [ʃæm'pein] n σαμπάνια.

champion ['tʃæmpiən] n (sport) πρωταθλητής ‖ (of cause) πρόμαχος ‖ ~ship n πρωτάθλημα.

chance [tʃa:ns] n (opportunity) εὐκαιρία ‖ (possibility) ἐλπίδα, πιθανότης ‖ a τυχαῖος ‖ vt: to ~ it διακινδυνεύω, παίζω στήν τύχη ‖ to take a ~ δοκιμάζω.

chancel ['tʃa:nsəl] n ἱερόν (ναοῦ).

chancellor ['tʃa:nsələ*] n (univ) πρύτανις ‖ C~ of the Exchequer n Ὑπουργός Οἰκονομικῶν.

chandelier [ʃændə'liə*] n πολύφωτο, πολυέλαιο.

change [tʃeindʒ] vt ἀλλάζω, τροποποιῶ ‖ (exchange) ἀνταλλάσσω ‖ (trains) ἀλλάζω

‖ *vi* ἀλλάζω, μεταβάλλομαι ‖ *n (alteration)* ἀλλαγή, μεταβολή ‖ *(coins)* ψιλά ‖ *(balance)* ρέστα ‖ ~**able** *a (weather)* ἄστατος ‖ ~ **over** *n (to new system)* ἀλλαγή συστήματος.

changing ['tʃeindʒiŋ] *a* εὐμετάβλητος, ἀλλάζων ‖ ~-**room** *n (in shop)* βεστιάριον.

channel ['tʃænl] *n (of stream)* κοίτη ‖ *(of bay etc)* δίαυλος, μπούκα ‖ *(strait)* πορθμός, στενόν ‖ *(of communication)* ὁδός, δρόμος ‖ *(rad etc)* ζώνη συχνοτήτων ‖ *(TV)* κανάλι ‖ *vt* αὐλακώνω ‖ **the (English) C~** ἡ Μάγχη ‖ **C~ Islands** *npl* νησιά τῆς Μάγχης.

chant [tʃɑ:nt] *n* τραγούδι ‖ *(church)* ψαλμός ‖ *vt* τραγουδῶ ‖ *(church)* ψάλλω.

chaos ['keiɔs] *n* χάος.

chaotic [kei'ɔtik] *a* χαῶδης.

chap [tʃæp] *n* ρωγμή, σκάσιμο ‖ *vt (skin)* σκάζω ἀπό τό κρύο.

chapel ['tʃæpəl] *n* παρεκκλήσι.

chaperon ['ʃæpərəun] *n* συνοδός κοριτσιοῦ ‖ *vt* συνοδεύω.

chaplain ['tʃæplin] *n* ἐφημέριος.

chapter ['tʃæptə*] *n (of book)* κεφάλαιον.

char [tʃɑ:*] *vt (burn)* μαυρίζω μέ κάψιμο ‖ *n (cleaner)* παραδουλεύτρα.

character ['kæriktə*] *n (qualities)* χαρακτήρ ‖ *(liter, theat etc)* πρόσωπον, χαρακτήρ ‖ *(peculiar person)* τύπος, χαρακτήρας ‖ *(letter, sign)* χαρακτήρ, στοιχεῖον, γράμμα ‖ ~**istic** *a* χαρακτηριστικός ‖ *n* χαρακτηριστικόν γνώρισμα ‖ ~**ize** *vt* χαρακτηρίζω.

charade [ʃə'rɑ:d] *n* συλλαβόγριφος.

charcoal ['tʃɑ:kəul] *n* ξυλοκάρβουνο.

charge [tʃɑ:dʒ] *n (price)* τίμημα, τιμή ‖ *(accusation)* κατηγορία ‖ *(load for gun)* γόμωσις ‖ *(attack)* ἔφοδος, προσβολή ‖ *vt (fill, load)* γεμίζω, φορτίζω ‖ *(a price)* ζητῶ (τιμήν), χρεώνω ‖ *(a battery)* ἐπιφορτίζω ‖ *(attack)* ἐφορμῶ ‖ *(accuse)* κατηγορῶ ‖ *vi* ἐπιπίπτω, προσβάλλω ‖ **in ~ of** φροντίζω, πού φροντίζει ‖ **to take ~** ἀναλαμβάνω, εἰμαι ὑπεύθυνος.

chariot ['tʃæriət] *n* ἄρμα.

charitable ['tʃæritəbl] *a* φιλάνθρωπος, ἐλεήμων.

charity ['tʃæriti] *n (institution)* φιλανθρωπικόν ἵδρυμα ‖ ἀγαθοεργία.

charlady ['tʃɑ:leidi] *n* παραδουλεύτρα.

charlatan ['ʃɑ:lətən] *n* ἀγύρτης, τσαρλατάνος.

charm [tʃɑ:m] *n (attractiveness)* γοητεία ‖ *(for luck)* φυλαχτό ‖ *vt* μαγεύω, γοητεύω ‖ ~**ing** *a* γοητευτικός.

chart [tʃɑ:t] *n (of information)* γραφική παράστασις, διάγραμμα ‖ *(naut)* χάρτης.

charter ['tʃɑ:tə*] *vt* ναυλώνω ‖ *n* καταστατικός χάρτης ‖ ~ **flight** *n* ναυλωμένη πτῆσις ‖ ~**ed accountant** *n* λογιστής.

charwoman ['tʃɑ:wumən] *n* = **charlady.**

chase [tʃeis] *vt (run after)* κυνηγῶ, (κατα)-

διώκω ‖ *n (act of chasing)* κυνήγι, καταδίωξις.

chasm ['kæzəm] *n* χάσμα, κενόν.

chassis ['ʃæsi] *n* σασσί.

chaste [tʃeist] *a* ἁγνός.

chastity ['tʃæstiti] *n* ἁγνότης, παρθενία.

chat [tʃæt] *vi* κουβεντιάζω ‖ *n (friendly, casual talk)* φιλική κουβεντούλα.

chatter ['tʃætə*] *vi* φλυαρῶ ‖ *(of teeth)* τρέμω, κτυπῶ ‖ *n* φλυαρία, τερετισμός ‖ ~**box** *n (esp child)* φλύαρος.

chatty ['tʃæti] *a (style)* ὁμιλιτικός, πολυλογᾶς.

chauffeur ['ʃəufə*] *n* ὁδηγός, σωφέρ.

cheap [tʃi:p] *a (joke)* ἄνοστο (ἀστεῖο) ‖ *(poor quality)* φτηνός, πρόστυχος, μικρᾶς ἀξίας ‖ ~**en** *vt (person)* ὑποτιμῶ, ξευτελίζω ‖ ~**ly** *ad* φτηνά.

cheat [tʃi:t] *vti (ἐξ)ἀπατῶ*, κοροϊδεύω ‖ *n* ἀγύρτης, κατεργάρης ‖ ~**ing** *n (at cards)* κλέψιμο ‖ *(general)* παγανοντιά.

check [tʃek] *vt (examine)* ἐλέγχω ‖ *(halt)* σταματῶ, ἀναχαιτίζω ‖ *n (examination)* ἔλεγχος, ἐπαλήθευσις ‖ *(restraint)* περιορισμός ‖ *(restaurant bill)* λογαριασμός ‖ *(pattern)* καρρώ ‖ *(US)* = **cheque** ‖ ~**ers** *npl (US)* ντάμα ‖ ~**list** *n* κατάλογος ἐλέγχου ‖ ~**mate** *n* μάτ ‖ ~**point** *n* σημεῖον ἐλέγχου ‖ ~**up** *n (med)* γενική ἐξέτασις.

cheek [tʃi:k] *n* παρειά, μάγουλο ‖ *(impudence)* ἀναίδεια ‖ ~**bone** *n* μῆλον (παρειᾶς) ‖ ~*y* *a* ἀναιδής.

cheer [tʃiə*] *n (joy)* εὐθυμία ‖ *(shout)* ζητωκραυγή ‖ *vt (shout)* ἐπευφημίζω, ζητωκραυγάζω ‖ *(comfort)* χαροποιῶ ‖ *(encourage)* ἐνθαρρύνω ‖ *vi*: **to ~ up** κάνω κέφι ‖ **good ~** *n* φαγητά ‖ ~**ful** *a* χαρωπός, καλόκεφος ‖ ~**fulness** *n* εὐθυμία ‖ *(of fireplace etc)* ζεστασιά ‖ ~**ing** *n* ζητοκραυγαί, χειροκροτήματα ‖ *a* ἐνθαρρυντικός, προκαλῶν τό κέφι ‖ ~**io** *interj (in departure)* γειά χαρά! ‖ *(greeting)* γειά σου ‖ ~**less** *a* μελαγχολικός, κακόκεφος.

cheese [tʃi:z] *n* τυρί.

chef [ʃef] *n* ἀρχιμάγειρας.

chemical ['kemikəl] *a* χημικός.

chemist ['kemist] *n (med)* φαρμακοποιός ‖ *(scientist)* χημικός ‖ ~**ry** *n* χημεία ‖ ~**'s (shop)** *n* φαρμακεῖον.

cheque [tʃek] *n* ἐπιταγή ‖ ~ **book** *n* βιβλιάριον ἐπιταγῶν.

chequered ['tʃekəd] *a (fig)* περιπετειώδης.

cherish ['tʃeriʃ] *vt (a hope)* τρέφω ‖ *(love)* λατρεύω ‖ *(look after)* περιποιοῦμαι.

cheroot [ʃə'ru:t] *n* εἶδος φτηνοῦ πούρου.

cherry ['tʃeri] *n (tree)* κερασιά ‖ *(fruit)* κεράσι.

chess [tʃes] *n* σκάκι ‖ ~**board** *n* σκακιέρα ‖ ~**man** *n* πιόνι, πεσσός ‖ ~**player** *n* σκακιστής.

chest [tʃest] *n (anat)* στῆθος ‖ *(box)*

κιβώτιον, μπαούλο ‖ **to get sth off one's ~** ξελαφρώνω ‖ ~ **of drawers** n σιφονιέρα, κομό.

chestnut ['tʃesnʌt] n κάστανο ‖ ~ **(tree)** n καστανιά.

chew [tʃu:] vti μασῶ ‖ ~ **ing gum** n τσίχλα.

chic [ʃi:k] a κομψός, σίκ.

chicanery [ʃi'keinəri] n στρεψοδικία, κατεργαριά.

chick [tʃik] n πουλάκι ‖ ~ **en** n (bird, food) κοτόπουλο ‖ ~ **enpox** n ἀνεμοβλογιά.

chicory ['tʃikəri] n κιχώρι, ἀντίδι, ραδίκι.

chief [tʃi:f] n ἀρχηγός, διευθυντής ‖ a κύριος, πρωτεύων, πρῶτος ‖ ~ **ly** ad κυρίως, προπάντων.

chiffon ['ʃifon] n σιφφόν.

chilblain ['tʃilblein] n χιονίστρα.

child [tʃaild] n παιδί ‖ ~ **birth** n τοκετός, γέννα ‖ ~ **hood** n παιδικά χρόνια ‖ ~ **ish** a παιδαριώδης, παιδιάστικος ‖ ~ **like** a ἀφελής, παιδιάστικος ‖ ~ **ren** ['tʃildrən] npl of **child** παιδιά, παιδάκια.

chill [tʃil] n (coldness) ψυχρότης, κρυάδα ‖ (cold) κρυολόγημα ‖ a ψυχρός, κρύος ‖ ~ **y** a ψυχρός, κρύος.

chime [tʃaim] n κωδωνοκρουσία ‖ vi ἠχῶ ἁρμονικῶς.

chimney ['tʃimni] n καπνοδόχος, καμινάδα.

chimpanzee [tʃimpæn'zi:] n χιμπαντζῆς.

chin [tʃin] n πηγούνι.

china ['tʃainə] n πορσελάνη ‖ (dishes, cups) πιάτα.

China ['tʃainə] n Κίνα.

Chinese ['tʃai'ni:z] a Κινέζικος ‖ n (person) Κινέζος ‖ (language) κινεζική.

chink [tʃiŋk] n (opening) ρωγμή, σκάσιμο ‖ (noise) ἦχος (μετάλλου κτλ).

chintz [tʃints] n τσίτι.

chip [tʃip] n ἀπόκομμα, θρύμμα ‖ vt θραύω, θρυμματίζω, ἀποκόπτω ‖ **to ~ in** vi (cards) ποντάρω ‖ (interrupt) παρεμβαίνω ‖ συνεισφέρω.

chiropodist [ki'rɔpədist] n πεντικιουρίστας.

chirp [tʃə:p] n τερετισμός, τιτίβισμα, κελάδημα ‖ vi τερετίζω, τιτιβίζω, κελαϊδῶ.

chisel ['tʃizl] n σμίλη.

chit [tʃit] n σημείωμα, γραπτή ἄδεια ‖ ~ **chat** n κουβέντα.

chivalrous ['ʃivəlrəs] a ἱπποτικός, εὐγενικός.

chivalry ['ʃivəlri] n (knighthood) ἱπποτισμός ‖ (courtesy) εὐγένεια.

chloride ['klɔ:raid] n χλωρίδιον.

chlorine ['klɔ:ri:n] n χλώριον.

chloroform ['klɔrəfɔ:m] n χλωροφόρμιον.

chock [tʃɔk] n μόρσος, τάκος ‖ ~ **-a-block** a παραγεμισμένος.

chocolate ['tʃɔklit] n σοκολάτα.

choice [tʃɔis] n ἐκλογή, προτίμησις ‖ (variety) ποικιλία ‖ a ἐκλεκτός.

choir ['kwaiə*] n χορός ‖ ~ **boy** n παιδί χορωδίας.

choke [tʃəuk] vi (be unable to breathe) πνίγομαι ‖ vt (stop breathing of) ἀσφυκτιῶ, στραγγαλίζω ‖ (block) ἐμφράσσω ‖ n (aut) διαχύτης, ἐμφράκτης.

cholera ['kɔlərə] n χολέρα.

choose [tʃu:z] (irreg v) vt διαλέγω, προτιμῶ ‖ (decide) ἀρέσω, προτιμῶ.

chop [tʃɔp] vt (cut with a blow) κόπτω, ἀποκόπτω ‖ (into pieces) κατακόπτω, διαμελίζω, λιανίζω ‖ vi: **to ~ and change** πωλῶ καί ἀγοράζω ‖ n (blow) κτύπημα ‖ (meat) μπριζολάκι ‖ ~ **py** a ταραγμένος, κυματώδης ‖ ~ **sticks** npl ξυλαράκια (γιά τό πιλάφι), κινέζικο πηρούνι.

choral ['kɔ:rəl] a χορικός.

chord [kɔ:d] n χορδή.

chore [tʃɔə*] n βαρετή δουλειά.

choreographer [kɔri'ɔgrəfə*] n χορογράφος.

chorister ['kɔristə*] n ψάλτης.

chortle ['tʃɔ:tl] vi καγχάζω, κακαρίζω.

chorus ['kɔ:rəs] n (choir etc) χορός, χορωδία ‖ (many voices) τραγούδι ἐν χορῷ ‖ ~ **of praise** n (fig) συναυλία ἐπαίνων.

chose [tʃəuz] pt of **choose** ‖ ~ **n** pp of **choose**.

chow [tʃau] n (dog) τσάου (εἶδος πεκινουά).

Christ [kraist] n Χριστός ‖ **c ~ en** ['krisn] vt βαπτίζω ‖ **c ~ ening** n βάπτισμα ‖ ~ **ian** ['kristiən] n Χριστιανός ‖ a χριστιανικός ‖ ~ **ian name** n μικρόν ὄνομα ‖ ~ **ianity** n χριστιανισμός ‖ ~ **mas** ['krisməs] n Χριστούγεννα ‖ ~ **mas card** n χριστουγεννιάτικη κάρτα ‖ ~ **mas tree** n χριστουγεννιάτικο δένδρο.

chrome [krəum] n = **chromium plating** ‖ see **chromium**.

chromium ['krəumiəm] n χρώμιον ‖ ~ **-plating** n ἐπιχρωμίωσις.

chronic ['krɔnik] a (med) χρόνιος.

chronicle ['krɔnikl] n χρονικόν, χρονογράφημα.

chronological [krɔnə'lɔdʒikəl] a χρονολογικός.

chrysalis ['krisəlis] n χρυσαλλίς, νύμφη.

chrysanthemum [kri'sænθəməm] n χρυσάνθεμον.

chubby ['tʃʌbi] a παχουλός, στρουμπουλός.

chuck [tʃʌk] vt πετῶ, ρίπτω ‖ n σφιγκτήρ, τσόκ.

chuckle ['tʃʌkl] vi γελῶ χαμηλοφώνως.

chum [tʃʌm] n στενός φίλος.

chunk [tʃʌŋk] n χονδρό κομμάτι.

church [tʃə:tʃ] n (building) ἐκκλησία, ναός ‖ ~ **service** n λειτουργία ‖ ~ **yard** n αὐλόγυρος ἐκκλησίας, νεκροταφεῖον.

churlish ['tʃə:liʃ] a ἄξεστος, δύστροπος.

churn [tʃə:n] n (for butter) βουτίνα, καρδάρα, ντουρβάνι.

chute [ʃu:t] n τσουλήθρα.

chutney ['tʃʌtni] n τσάτνυ (ἀρωματικόν).

cicada [si'ka:də] n τζίτζικας.

cider ['saidə*] n μηλίτης (οἶνος).

cigar [si'ga:*] n ποῦρο ‖ ~ **ette** n τσιγάρο, σιγαρέττο ‖ ~ **ette case** n τσιγαροθήκη.

ταμπακιέρα ‖ ~ette end n γόπα, ἀποτσίγαρο ‖ ~ette holder n πίπα.
cinch [sintʃ] n (sl) σιγουριά.
cinder ['sində*] n ἀνθρακιά, θράκα, στάκτη.
Cinderella [sində'relə] n Σταχτοπούτα.
cine ['sini] ~-camera n κινηματογραφική
μηχανή ‖ ~-film n κινηματογραφική
ταινία.
cinema ['sinəmə] n (theat) σινεμά ‖ (motion
pictures) κινηματογράφος.
cine-projector [siniprə'dʒektə*] n κινημα-
τογραφικός προβολεύς.
cinnamon ['sinəmən] n κανέλλα.
cipher ['saifə*] n (zero) μηδενικόν ‖ (code)
κρυπτογράφησις ‖ (person) μηδενικός.
circle ['sɜ:kl] n (ring, figure) κύκλος, γύρος
‖ (of friends) κύκλος, συντροφιά ‖ vi
περιστρέφομαι, στριφογυρίζω ‖ vt
(surround) περικυκλώνω ‖ vi (move in a
circle) κάνω τόν κύκλον, κάνω κύκλους.
circuit ['sɜ:kit] n (moving around) κυκλικός
δρόμος, περιστροφή ‖ (tour by judges)
περιοδεία (δικαστοῦ) ‖ (elec) κύκλωμα ‖
~ous a κυκλικός, ἔμμεσος.
circular ['sɜ:kjulə*] a κυκλικός ‖ (in a circle)
κυκλοτερής ‖ n ἐγκύκλιος, διαφημιστι-
κόν γράμμα.
circulate ['sɜ:kjuleit] vi κυκλοφορῶ ‖ vt
θέτω εἰς κυκλοφορίαν.
circulation [sɜ:kju'leiʃən] n κυκλοφορία.
circumcise ['sɜ:kəmsaiz] vt περιτέμνω.
circumference [sə'kʌmfərəns] n περιφέρεια.
circumflex ['sɜ:kəmfleks] n περισπωμένη.
circumspect ['sɜ:kəmspekt] a προσεκτικός,
μετρημένος.
circumstances ['sɜ:kəmstənsiz] npl (facts
connected with sth) περιστάσεις, συνθῆκες, συμβάντα ‖ (financial condition)
οἰκονομική κατάστασις.
circus ['sɜ:kəs] n τσίρκος.
cistern ['sistən] n δεξαμενή, ντεπόσιτο.
cite [sait] vt (mention, quote) ἀναφέρω,
παραπέμπω.
citizen ['sitizn] n (city dweller) ἀστός ‖
πολίτης ‖ ~ship n πολιτικά δικαιώματα.
citrus ['sitrəs] ~ fruit n ἐσπεριδοειδῆ.
city ['siti] n πόλις ‖ the C~ τό Ἐμπορικόν
κέντρον Λονδίνου.
civic ['sivik] a ἀστικός, πολιτικός.
civil ['sivl] a πολιτικός ‖ (polite) εὐγενικός
‖ ~ engineer n πολιτικός μηχανικός ‖
~ engineering n πολιτική μηχανική ‖
~ian n πολίτης, ἰδιώτης ‖ a πολιτικός
‖ ~ization n πολιτισμός ‖ ~ized a πολιτισμένος ‖ ~ law n ἀστικόν δίκαιον ‖
~ servant n δημόσιος ὑπάλληλος ‖ C~
Service n Δημόσιαι Ὑπηρεσίαι ‖ ~ war
n ἐμφύλιος πόλεμος.
claim [kleim] vt ἀπαιτῶ, ζητῶ, διεκδικῶ ‖
n αἴτησις, ἀπαίτησις, ἀξίωσις ‖ ~ant n
ἀπαιτητής ‖ (law) ἐνάγων, δικαιοῦχος.
clam [klæm] n ἀχιβάδα.
clamber ['klæmbə*] vi σκαρφαλώνω.

clammy ['klæmi] a ἱδρωμένος, κολλώδης.
clamp [klæmp] n σφιγκτήρ, σύνδεσμος ‖ vt
(συσ)σφίγγω.
clan [klæn] n φυλή, πατριά.
clang [klæŋ] n κλαγγή, κρότος ‖ vti ἀντηχῶ,
κροτῶ.
clap [klæp] vti κτυπῶ, χειροκροτῶ ‖ ~ping
n χειροκρότημα.
claret ['klærət] n μαῦρο κρασί, μπορντῶ.
clarification [klærifi'keiʃən] n (fig) διευκρί-
νισις.
clarify ['klærifai] vt διευκρινίζω.
clarinet [klæri'net] n κλαρίνο.
clarity ['klæriti] n διαύγεια.
clash [klæʃ] n σύγκρουσις, ἀντίθεσις ‖
(sound) ἰσχυρόν καί ἠχηρόν κτύπημα ‖
vi συγκρούομαι.
clasp [kla:sp] n πόρπη, κόπιτσα ‖ vt ἐναγκα-
λιάζω, σφίγγω.
class [kla:s] n (rank) τάξις ‖ (sort) τάξις,
εἶδος, κατηγορία ‖ (sch) τάξις ‖ vt ταξινομῶ, βαθμολογῶ.
classic ['klæsik] n κλασσικός ‖ a (traditional) κλασσικός, ἀκαδημαϊκός ‖ ~al a
κλασσικός ‖ (mus) κλασσική (μουσική).
classification [klæsifi'keiʃən] n ταξινόμησις, κατάταξις.
classify ['klæsifai] vt ταξινομῶ, κατατάσσω.
classroom ['kla:srum] n αἴθουσα παραδό-
σεων, τάξις.
classy ['kla:si] a (posh) καλῆς τάξεως.
clatter ['klætə*] n θόρυβος, γδοῦπος ‖ vi
κροτῶ, θορυβῶ.
clause [klɔ:z] n (of contract etc) ὅρος,
ἄρθρον, διάταξις ‖ (gram) πρότασις.
claustrophobia [klɔ:strə'fəubiə] n κλειστο-
φοβία.
claw [klɔ:] n νύχι ‖ (of quadrupeds) χηλή,
ὁπλή ‖ vt νυχιάζω, γρατσουνίζω.
clay [klei] n ἄργιλος, πηλός.
clean [kli:n] a (free from dirt) καθαρός,
παστρικός ‖ (guiltless) καθαρός, τίμιος ‖
(lines) καθαρός (γραμμές), σαφές περίγραμμα ‖ vt καθαρίζω, παστρεύω ‖ ~er
n (person) καθαριστής ‖ ~ing n καθαρ-
σις, καθάρισμα ‖ ~liness n καθαριότης,
πάστρα ‖ ~ly ad καθαρά, παστρικά ‖
~se [klenz] vt ἀποκαθαίρω, καθαρίζω,
πλένω ‖ ~-shaven a φρεσκοξυρισμένος
‖ ~up n καθαρισμός ‖ to ~ out vt καθαρίζω ‖ (col) ξεπεντιαρίζω ‖ to ~ up vt
κάνω καθαρισμόν, σιάζω ‖ (col) κερδίζω.
clear [kliə*] a (water etc) καθαρό, διαυγές ‖
(sound) καθαρό (ἦχο) ‖ (meaning) σαφής,
καθαρή ‖ (certain) σαφής ‖ (road) ἀνοικτός ‖ vt καθαρίζω, ξεκαθαρίζω ‖ vi
(become clear) διευκρινίζεται ‖ ~ance n
(sale) ἐκποίησις, ξεπούλημα ‖ (free
space) ἀπελευθέρωσις, ἐκκένωσις ‖ (permission) ἄδεια ‖ ~-cut a σαφής, συγκεκριμένος ‖ ~ing n καθάρισμα ‖ ~ly ad
σαφῶς, προφανῶς, ἀσφαλῶς ‖ ~way n
(Brit) ἐθνική ὁδός ἄνευ σταθμεύσεως ‖

to ~ up *vi* διαλύω, ξεκαθαρίζω ‖ *vt* τακτοποιῶ, στάζω ‖ ξεκαθαρίζω.

clef [klef] *n* κλειδί.

clematis ['klemətis] *n* κληματίς, ἀμπελίνα.

clench [klentʃ] *vt (teeth etc)* σφίγγω.

clergy ['klə:dʒi] *n* κλῆρος, ἱερατεῖον ‖ ~**man** *n* κληρικός, ἱερωμένος, παπᾶς.

clerical ['klerikəl] *a* κληρικός, ἱερατικός ‖ τοῦ γραφείου ‖ ~ **error** *n* λάθος ἀντιγραφῆς.

clerk [kla:k, (US) klə:rk] *n* (US) (*salesman, woman*) ὑπάλληλος ‖ (*in office*) γραφεύς.

clever ['klevə*] *a* (*with hands*) ἐπιδέξιος, καπάτσος ‖ (*in mind*) εὐφυής, σπιρτόζος ‖ ~**ly** *ad* εὐφυῶς, ἔξυπνα.

cliché ['kli:ʃei] *n* στερεότυπον, κλισέ.

click [klik] *vi* κτυπῶ, κάνω τίκ-τάκ ‖ *n* κλίκ, ξηρός κρότος.

client ['klaiənt] *n* πελάτης ‖ ~**ele** [kli:ã:n'tel] *n* πελατεία.

cliff [klif] *n* γκρεμός.

climate ['klaimit] *n* κλῖμα.

climax ['klaimæks] *n* ἀποκορύφωμα.

climb [klaim] *vti* ἀνέρχομαι, ἀνεβαίνω, σκαρφαλώνω ‖ *n* ἀνέβασμα, ἀνηφοριά ‖ ~ **er** *n* (*of mountains*) ὀρειβάτης ‖ ~**ing**: to go ~**ing** κάνω ὀρειβασία.

clinch [klintʃ] *vt (fig: decide)* συνάπτω, κλείνω.

cling [kliŋ] *vi* προσκολλῶμαι, πιάνομαι.

clinic ['klinik] *n* κλινική ‖ ~**al** *a* κλινικός.

clink [kliŋk] *n* κτύπημα (ποτηριῶν) ‖ *vti* κτυπῶ, ἠχῶ.

clip [klip] *n* συνδετήρ, τσιμπιδάκι ‖ *vt* (*papers*) συνδέω ‖ (*hair*) κουρέβω, ψαλιδίζω ‖ (*hedge*) κόβω ‖ ~**pers** *npl* (*instrument*) κουρευτική μηχανή.

clique [kli:k] *n* κλίκα, φάρα.

cloak [kləuk] *n* πανωφόρι ‖ (*fig*) κάλυμμα, πέπλον ‖ ~**room** *n* (*for coats etc*) γκαρνταρόπα ‖ (*W.C.*) ἀποχωρητήριον, μέρος, καμπινέτο.

clock [klɔk] *n* ὡρολόγι, ρολόϊ ‖ ~**wise** *ad* δεξιόστροφος ‖ ~**work** *n* μηχανισμός ὡρολογιοῦ.

clog [klɔg] *n* (*shoe*) τσόκαρο ‖ *vti* ἐμποδίζω, κωλύω, φράσσω.

close [kləus] *a* (*near*) πλησίον, ἐγγύς, διπλανός ‖ (*atmosphere etc*) ἀσφυκτικός, πνιγηρός, στενός ‖ (*mean*) σφιχτός ‖ (*weather*) κλειστός, βαρύς ‖ *ad* (*near*) κοντά, ἀπό κοντά, σφιχτά ‖ ~**ly** *ad* προσεκτικά, στενά, κατά πόδας ‖ ~ **shave** *n* (*fig*) γλυτωμός παρά τρίχα ‖ ~ **-up** *n* λεπτομέρεια.

close [kləuz] *vt* (*shut*) κλείνω ‖ (*end*) τελειώνω, τερματίζω ‖ *vi* κλείομαι ‖ (*end*) τερματίζομαι ‖ *n* (*end*) τέλος ‖ to ~ **down** *vti* κλείνω, διακόπτω ‖ ~**d** *a* (*road*) 'ἀπαγορεύεται ἡ διάβασις' ‖ ~**d shop** *n* κλειστόν κατάστημα.

closet ['klɔzit] *n* μικρό δωμάτιο ‖ (*storeroom*) ἀποθήκη.

closure ['kləuzə*] *n* κλείσιμο, τερματισμός.

clot [klɔt] *n* (*esp blood*) θρόμβος, σβῶλος ‖ *vi* θρομβοῦμαι, πήζω.

cloth [klɔθ] *n* (*material*) ὕφασμα, πανί ‖ (*for cleaning*) πατσαβούρα.

clothe [kləuð] *vt* ντύνω, καλύπτω ‖ ~**s** *npl* ροῦχα ‖ ~**sbrush** *n* βούρτσα ‖ ~**s line** *n* σχοινί ἀπλώματος ρούχων ‖ ~**s peg** *n* μανταλάκι.

clothing ['kləuðiŋ] *n* = **clothes** ‖ *see* **clothe**.

cloud [klaud] *n* σύννεφο ‖ (*of dust etc*) νέφος, σύννεφο ‖ ~**burst** *n* μπόρα ‖ ~**y** *a* συνεφιασμένος ‖ (*wine etc*) θολωμένο.

clout [klaut] *n* κτύπημα ‖ *vt* κτυπῶ, καρπαζώνω.

clove [kləuv] *n* γαρύφαλο.

clover ['kləuvə*] *n* τριφύλλι ‖ ~**leaf** *n* τριφύλλι.

clown [klaun] *n* παλιάτσος, κλάουν ‖ *vi* κάνω τόν παλιάτσο.

club [klʌb] *n* (*stick*) ρόπαλο, ματσούκα ‖ (*society*) λέσχη ‖ (*golf*) κλόμπ ‖ (*cards*) σπαθί ‖ *vt* κτυπῶ μέ ρόπαλο, μέ κλόμπ ‖ *vi*: to ~ **together** συνεισφέρω, βάζω ρεφενέ ‖ ~**house** *n* λέσχη.

cluck [klʌk] *vi* κακαρίζω.

clue [klu:] *n* νύξις, ἔνδειξις ‖ he hasn't a ~ δέν ἔχει ἰδέα.

clump [klʌmp] *n* συστάς (δένδρων), μεγάλο κομμάτι.

clumsy ['klʌmzi] *a* (*person*) ἀδέξιος, ἀτζαμῆς ‖ (*object*) βαρύς, ἄκομψος.

clung [klʌŋ] *pt,pp* of **cling**.

cluster ['klʌstə*] *n* συστάς, ὁμάς ‖ (*of grapes*) τσαμπί ‖ (*of stars*) ἀστέρισμα ‖ *vi* φύομαι βοτρηδόν, μαζευόμαστε.

clutch [klʌtʃ] *n* (*grip, grasp*) ἅρπαγμα, σφικτό πιάσιμο ‖ (*aut*) ἀμπραγιάζ, συμπλέκτης ‖ *vt* ἀρπάζω, πιάνω σφικτά.

clutter ['klʌtə*] *vt* παραγεμίζω, κάνω ἄνωκάτω.

coach [kəutʃ] *n* (*bus*) λεωφορεῖον, πούλμαν ‖ (*teacher*) φροντιστής ‖ (*rail*) ἅμαξα, βαγόνι ‖ (*trainer*) προγυμναστής ‖ *vt* προγυμνάζω.

coagulate [kəu'ægjuleit] *vti* πηγνύω, πήζω.

coal [kəul] *n* ἄνθραξ, κάρβουνο, γαιάνθραξ.

coalfield ['kəulfi:ld] *n* ἀνθρακοφόρος περιοχή.

coalition [kəuə'liʃən] *n* συνασπισμός.

coalmine ['kəulmain] *n* ἀνθρακωρυχεῖον.

coarse [kɔ:s] *a* (*lit*) τραχύς, ἀκατέργαστος ‖ (*fig*) ἄξεστος, χυδαῖος.

coast [kəust] *n* παραλία, ἀκτή ‖ ~**al** *a* παράκτιος, παραλιακός ‖ ~**er** *n* ἀκτοπλοϊκόν ‖ ~**guard** *n* ἀκτοφυλακή ‖ ~**line** *n* ἀκτή, παραλία.

coat [kəut] *n* (*garment*) σακάκι ‖ (*of animal*) προβειά ‖ (*layer etc*) στρῶμα, χέρι ‖ *vt* (*with paint etc*) ἐπιχρίω ‖ ~ **of arms** *n* οἰκόσημον ‖ ~ **hanger** *n* κρεμαστάρι ‖ ~**ing** *n* ἐπίστρωμα, χέρι.

coax [kəuks] *vt* καλοπιάνω, καταφέρνω.

cobbler ['kɔblə*] n μπαλωματής.

cobble(stone)s ['kɔbl(stəun)z] npl βότσαλα, καλντερίμι.

cobra ['kəubrə] n κόμπρα.

cobweb ['kɔbweb] n ἱστός ἀράχνης, ἀράχνη.

cocaine [kə'kein] n (med) κοκαΐνη.

cock [kɔk] n (poultry) κόκκορας, πετεινός || (bird etc) ἀρσενικό πουλί || (tap, faucet etc) κρουνός, κάνουλα || vt σηκώνω, βάζω στραβά (τό καπέλλο) || (a gun) σηκώνω τόν λύκο || ~erel n κοκκοράκι || ~eyed a (fig) στραβός, λοξός.

cockle ['kɔkl] n κοχύλι.

cockney ['kɔkni] n Λονδρέζος κατωτέρας τάξεως, κόκνυ.

cockpit ['kɔkpit] n (aviat) θέσις χειριστοῦ.

cockroach ['kɔkrəutʃ] n κατσαρίδα.

cocktail ['kɔkteil] n (drink) κοκτέϊλ || ~ cabinet n μπάρ || ~ party n πάρτυ κοκτέϊλ || ~ shaker n κτυπητήρι τοῦ κοκτέϊλ, σαῖκερ.

cocoa ['kəukəu] n κακάο.

coconut ['kəukənʌt] n καρύδα.

cocoon [kə'ku:n] n κουκούλι.

cod [kɔd] n μουρούνα.

code [kəud] n (of laws) κώδιξ || (signals) σύστημα κρυπτογραφίας.

codify ['kəudifai] vt κωδικοποιῶ.

coeducational ['kəuedju'keiʃənl] a (school) μικτόν σχολεῖον.

coerce [kəu'ə:s] vt πιέζω, ἀναγκάζω.

coercion [kəu'ə:ʃən] n καταπίεσις.

coexistence ['kəuig'zistəns] n συνύπαρξις.

coffee ['kɔfi] n καφές || ~ bar n καφέ-μπάρ.

coffin ['kɔfin] n φέρετρον, κάσα.

cog [kɔg] n (of wheel etc) δόντι.

cogent ['kəudʒənt] a πειστικός.

cognac ['kɔnjæk] n κονιάκ.

coherent [kəu'hiərənt] a (consistent) συναφής, συνεπής.

coil [kɔil] n κουλούρα, σπείρωμα || (elec) μπομπίνα || vt συσπειρώνω, τυλίγω, κουλουριάζω.

coin [kɔin] n νόμισμα, κέρμα || ~age n (system) νομισματικόν σύστημα || νόμισμα.

coincide [kəuin'said] vt συμπίπτω, συμφωνῶ || ~nce [kəu'insidəns] n σύμπτωσις || ~ntal [kəuinsi'dentl] a συμπτωματικός.

coke [kəuk] n κώκ.

colander ['kʌləndə*] n τρυπητό, σουρωτήρι.

cold [kəuld] a ψυχρός, κρύος || n ψύχος, κρύο || (illness) κρυολόγημα || to have ~ feet (γ)κιοτέβω || to give s.o. the ~ shoulder φέρομαι ψυχρά || ~ly a ψυχρά, κρύα.

coleslaw ['kəulslɔ:] n λαχανοσαλάτα.

colic ['kɔlik] n κωλικόπονος.

collaborate [kə'læbəreit] vi (+ with) συνεργάζομαι μέ.

collaboration [kəlæbə'reiʃən] n συνεργασία.

collaborator [kə'læbəreitə*] n συνεργάτης.

collapse [kə'læps] vi καταρρέω || n κατάρρευσις.

collapsible [kə'læpsəbl] a πτυσσόμενος, διπλωτός.

collar ['kɔlə*] n (of coat, shirt) κολλάρο, γιακάς || ~bone n κλειδί τοῦ ὤμου.

collate [kɔ'leit] vt (ἀντι)παραβάλλω.

colleague ['kɔliːg] n συνάδελφος, συνεργάτης.

collect [kə'lekt] vt συλλέγω, μαζεύω || vi συναθροίζομαι || ~ed a συγκεντρωμένος || (fig) ἀτάραχος || ~ion n συλλογή || (money) εἴσπραξις || ~ive a συλλογικός || (pol) κολλεκτίβο || ~or n (of art etc) συλλέκτης || (of money) εἰσπράκτωρ.

college ['kɔlidʒ] n (non-specialized) κολλέγιον || (esp Oxford and Cambridge) πανεπιστήμιον.

collide [kə'laid] vi συγκρούομαι, τρακάρω.

collie ['kɔli] n κόλι.

colliery ['kɔliəri] n ἀνθρακωρυχεῖον.

collision [kə'liʒən] n σύγκρουσις.

colloquial [kə'ləukwiəl] a τῆς καθομιλουμένης.

collusion [kə'lu:ʒən] n συμπαιγνία.

colon ['kəulən] n (gram) διπλῆ στιγμή.

colonel ['kə:nl] n συνταγματάρχης.

colonial [kə'ləuniəl] a ἀποικιακός.

colonize ['kɔlənaiz] vt ἀποικίζω.

colonnade [kɔlə'neid] n περιστύλιον, κιονοστοιχία.

colony ['kɔləni] n ἀποικία || (of immigrants etc) παροικία.

color ['kʌlə*] n (US) = colour.

colossal [kə'lɔsl] a κολοσσιαῖος.

colour ['kʌlə*] n χρῶμα || (paints etc) βαφή, μπογιά || (of skin) χρῶμα || vt χρωματίζω, βάφω || (news) χρωματίζω, γαρνίρω || ~s npl χρώματα || (naut) σημαία || ~ bar n φυλετική διάκρισις || ~-blind a δαλτωνικός || ~ed a χρωματιστός, ἔγχρωμος || (fig) ἐξωγκωμένος || ~ed man n νέγρος || ~ film n (for camera) ἔγχρωμο φίλμ || ~ful a ζωντανός || ~ television n ἔγχρωμη τηλεόρασι.

colt [kəult] n πῶλος, πουλάρι.

column ['kɔləm] n (pillar) κίων, στύλος, κολώνα || (of troops) φάλαγγα || (of page) στήλη || ~ist n ἀρθρογράφος.

coma ['kəumə] n κῶμα, λήθαργος.

comb [kəum] n (for hair) κτένι, χτένα || (of cock) λειρί || (honey) κηρήθρα || vt (hair) κτενίζω || (search) ἐρευνῶ, ψάχνω.

combat ['kɔmbæt] n πάλη, διαμάχη || vt (κατα)πολεμῶ.

combination [kɔmbi'neiʃən] n συνδυασμός, ἕνωσις.

combine [kəm'bain] vti συνδυάζω, συνεργάζομαι, ἑνοῦμαι || ['kɔmbain] n συνδυασμός, ἑταιρεία, συνδικᾶτον || ~ harvester n θεριστική καί ἁλωνιστική μηχανή.

combustible [kəm'bʌstibl] *a* καύσιμος, εὔφλεκτος.

combustion [kəm'bʌstʃən] *n* καῦσις, ἀνάφλεξις.

come [kʌm] (*irreg v*) *vi* (*approach*) ἔρχομαι, φθάνω || (*reach*) τελειώνω, φθάνω, βρίσκομαι || (*become*) γίνομαι, συμβαίνω || (*result*) καταλήγω || **to ~ about** *vi* συμβαίνω, γίνομαι || **to ~ across** *vt* συναντῶ || **to ~ by** *vt* (*visit*) περνῶ || (*find*) βρίσκω, ἀποκτῶ || **to ~ in for** *vt* ἔχω μερίδιο, μετέχω || **to ~ into** *vt* (*enter*) μπαίνω μέσα, ἐμφανίζομαι || (*inherit*) κληρονομῶ || (*fashion*) γίνομαι τῆς μόδας || **to ~ out with** *vt* βγαίνω, βγάζω || **to ~ to** *vt* (*bill*) φθάνω || (*grief*) μοῦ συμβαίνει δυστύχημα || (*nothing*) ἀποτυγχάνω || (*notice*) ἀντιλαμβάνομαι || **to ~ up to** *vt* ἀνεβαίνω || (*amount*) φθάνω || **to ~ up with** *vt* προφθάνω || **~back** *n* ἐπάνοδος.

comedian [kə'mi:diən] *n* κωμικός.

comedown ['kʌmdaun] *n* ξεπεσμός.

comedy ['kɔmidi] *n* κωμωδία.

comet ['kɔmit] *n* κομήτης.

comfort ['kʌmfət] *n* (*of body*) ἄνεσις || (*of mind*) παρηγοριά || *vt* παρηγορῶ || **~s** *npl* ἀνέσεις, ἀπολαύσεις || **~able** *a* ἀναπαυτικός, ἄνετος || **~ station** *n* (*US*) ἀποχωρητήριο.

comic ['kɔmik] *n* (*actor*) κωμικός || (*magazine*) κόμικς || *a* (*also* **~al**) κωμικός, ἀστεῖος.

comma ['kɔmə] *n* (*gram*) κόμμα.

command [kə'ma:nd] *n* (*order*) διαταγή || (*control*) ἐξουσία, κυριαρχία, διοίκησις || *vt* (*order*) διατάσσω || (*be in charge*) διοικῶ, ἐξουσιάζω, ἐλέγχω || (*be able to get*) κατέχω, διαθέτω || *vi* προστάζω || **~eer** [kɔmən'diə*] *vt* ἐπιτάσσω || **~er** *n* (*mil*) διοικητής || (*naut*) πλωτάρχης || **~ing officer** *n* διοικητής || **~ment** *n* ἐντολή || **~o** *n* κομμάντο, καταδρομεύς.

commemorate [kə'meməreit] *vt* ἑορτάζω.

commemoration [kəmemə'reiʃən] *n*: **in ~ of** εἰς μνήμην τοῦ.

commemorative [kə'memərətiv] *a* ἀναμνηστικός.

commence [kə'mens] *vti* ἀρχίζω.

commend [kə'mend] *vt* συνιστῶ, ἐπαινῶ || **~able** *a* ἀξιέπαινος || **~ation** [kɔmən'deiʃən] *n* ἔπαινος.

commensurate [kə'menʃərit] *a* (+ *with*) ἀνάλογος.

comment ['kɔment] *n* σχόλιον, ἐξήγησις || *vi* (+ *on*) σχολιάζω, ἐπεξηγῶ || **~ary** *n* (*sport*) ρεπορτάζ || σχόλιον || **~ator** *n* σχολιαστής.

commerce ['kɔmə:s] *n* ἐμπόριον.

commercial [kə'mə:ʃəl] *a* ἐμπορικός || (*TV*) διαφήμισις || **~ize** *vt* ἐμπορεύομαι || **~ vehicle** *n* δημοσίας χρήσεως.

commiserate [kə'mizəreit] *vi* (+ *with*) συμπονῶ, συλλυποῦμαι.

commission [kə'miʃən] *n* (*duty*) ἐντολή, παραγγελία || (*fee*) προμήθεια || (*mil*) βαθμός ἀξιωματικοῦ || (*reporting body*) ἐπιτροπή || *vt* ἐντέλλομαι, ἐπιφορτίζω || **out of ~** ἐκτός ἐνεργείας, χαλασμένο || **~aire** *n* θυρωρός || **~er** *n* μέλος ἐπιτροπῆς, ἁρμοστής.

commit [kə'mit] *vt* (*a crime*) διαπράττω (ἔγκλημα) || (*to paper*) καταγράφω || (*to memory*) ἀπομνημονεύω || (*entrust*) ἐμπιστεύομαι, ἀναθέτω || **~ment** *n* δέσμευσις, ὑποχρέωσις.

committee [kə'miti] *n* ἐπιτροπή.

commodious [kə'məudiəs] *a* εὐρύχωρος.

commodity [kə'mɔditi] *n* ἐμπόρευμα.

common ['kɔmən] *a* (*shared*) κοινός || (*knowledge etc*) κοινός, συνήθης || (*ordinary, usual*) συνήθης, συνηθισμένος || (*mean, low*) χυδαῖος, πρόστυχος || (*frequent*) συνήθης || *n*: **in ~** ἀπό κοινοῦ || **~ly** *ad* συνήθως || **C~ Market** *n* Κοινή Ἀγορά || **~ place** *a* κοινοτοπία, πεζός || **~room** *n* αἴθουσα καθηγητῶν || **~sense** *n* κοινός νοῦς || **the C~wealth** *n* Κοινοπολιτεία.

commotion [kə'məuʃən] *n* ταραχή.

communal ['kɔmju:nl] *a* κοινοτικός.

commune ['kɔmju:n] *n* (*group of people living communally*) κοινότης || [kə'mju:n] *vi* (+ *with*) συναναστρέφομαι.

communicate [kə'mju:nikeit] *vt* (*transmit*) ἀνακοινώνω, μεταδίδω || *vi* (*connect*) συγκοινωνῶ || (*be in touch*) (+ *with*) ἐπικοινωνῶ.

communication [kəmju:ni'keiʃən] *n* ἀνακοίνωσις, μετάδοσις || συγκοινωνία, ἐπικοινωνία || **~s** *npl* (*transport etc*) συγκοινωνία || **~ cord** *n* κώδων κινδύνου.

communion [kə'mju:niən] *n* κοινότης || (*rel*) θρησκευτική ὁμάς || (Holy) **C~** *n* (Ἁγία) Μετάληψις.

communiqué [kə'mju:nikei] *n* ἀνακοινωθέν.

communism ['kɔmjunizəm] *n* κομμουνισμός.

communist ['kɔmjunist] *n* κομμουνιστής || *a* κομμουνιστικός.

community [kə'mju:niti] *n* κοινότης || (*the public*) κοινωνία, τό κοινόν || **~ centre** *n* αἴθουσα ἀναψυχῆς || **~ chest** *n* (*US*) φιλανθρωπικόν ταμεῖον.

commutation ticket [kɔmju'teiʃəntikit] *n* (*US*) εἰσιτήριον διαρκείας.

compact [kəm'pækt] *a* συμπαγής, σφικτός || ['kɔmpækt] *n* (*agreement*) σύμβασις, συμφωνία || (*powder*) πουδριέρα.

companion [kəm'pæniən] *n* σύντροφος, συνάδελφος, ταῖρι || **~ship** *n* συντροφιά.

company ['kʌmpəni] *n* (*business*) ἑταιρεία || (*of people*) παρέα, συντροφιά || (*mil*) λόχος || (*guests*) κόσμο || **to keep s.o. ~** κάνω παρέα.

comparable ['kɔmpərəbl] *a* συγκρίσιμος, ἀνάλογος, παραβλητός.

comparative [kəm'pærətiv] *a* συγκριτικός, σχετικός ‖ ~ **ly** *ad* συγκριτικῶς.

compare [kəm'pɛə*] *vt* συγκρίνω, παραβάλλω ‖ (+*with*) παρομοιάζω ‖ *vi* συγκρίνομαι.

comparison [kəm'pærisn] *n* σύγκρισις ‖ παρομοίωσις ‖ **in** ~ (**with**) συγκρινόμενος (μέ).

compartment [kəm'pɑ:tmənt] *n* (*naut*) διαμέρισμα ‖ (*rail*) βαγκόν-λί.

compass ['kʌmpəs] *n* (*instrument*) πυξίς ‖ ~ **es** *npl* διαβήτης.

compassion [kəm'pæʃən] *n* εὐσπλαχνία, οἶκτος ‖ ~ **ate** *a* φιλεύσπλαχνος.

compatible [kəm'pætibl] *a* συμβιβάσιμος, σύμφωνος.

compel [kəm'pel] *vt* ἀναγκάζω, ὑποχρεώνω.

compendium [kəm'pendiəm] *n* σύνοψις, ἐπιτομή.

compensate ['kɔmpenseit] *vt* ἀμείβω, ἀποζημιώνω ‖ *vi*: **to** ~ **for** ἀντισταθμίζω.

compensation [kɔmpen'seiʃən] *n* ἀμοιβή ‖ (*money*) ἀποζημίωσις ‖ (*satisfaction*) ἱκανοποίησις.

compere ['kɔmpɛə*] *n* κομπέρ.

compete [kəm'pi:t] *vi* συναγωνίζομαι, ἀνταγωνίζομαι ‖ (*for prize*) διαγωνίζομαι.

competence ['kɔmpitəns] *n* ἱκανότης, ἐπιδεξιότης.

competent ['kɔmpitənt] *a* ἱκανός, ἐπιδέξιος ‖ (*office etc*) ἁρμόδιος.

competition [kɔmpi'tiʃən] *n* ἅμιλλα ‖ (*rivalry*) ἀνταγωνισμός, συναγωνισμός.

competitive [kəm'petitiv] *a* ἀνταγωνιστικός, συναγωνιστικός.

competitor [kəm'petitə*] *n* ἀνταγωνιστής, ἀντίπαλος.

compile [kəm'pail] *vt* συλλέγω, συναθροίζω.

complacency [kəm'pleisnsi] *n* αὐταρέσκεια.

complacent [kəm'pleisənt] *a* αὐτάρεσκος, ἐπηρμένος.

complain [kəm'plein] *vi* παραπονιέμαι, γκρινιάζω ‖ ~ **t** *n* παράπονο, γκρίνια ‖ (*illness*) ἀρρώστια.

complement ['kɔmplimənt] *n* πληρότης ‖ (*math*) συμπλήρωμα ‖ (*esp ship's crew etc*) πλῆρες ‖ ~ **ary** *a* συμπληρωματικός.

complete [kəm'pli:t] *a* πλήρης, συμπληρωμένος, τέλειος ‖ *vt* συμπληρώνω, ἀποτελειώνω ‖ ~ **ly** *ad* πλήρως, ἐντελῶς.

completion [kəm'pli:ʃən] *n* συμπλήρωσις, ἀποπεράτωσις.

complex ['kɔmpleks] *a* πολύπλοκος, πολυσύνθετος ‖ *n* (*mental*) σύμπλεγμα, κόμπλεξ ‖ (*of buildings*) σύμπλεγμα.

complexion [kəm'plekʃən] *n* χρῶμα, χροιά.

complexity [kəm'pleksiti] *n* περιπλοκή.

complicate ['kɔmplikeit] *vt* περιπλέκω ‖ ~ **d** *a* μπλεγμένος.

complication [kɔmpli'keiʃən] *n* περιπλοκή.

compliment ['kɔmplimənt] *n* φιλοφρόνησις, κομπλιμέντο ‖ ['kɔmpliment] *vt* κομπλι-

μεντάρω, συγχαίρω ‖ ~ **s** *npl* εὐχές, χαιρετισμοί ‖ ~ **ary** *a* φιλοφρονητικός, κομπλιμεντόζος.

comply [kəm'plai] *vi*: **to** ~ **with** συμφωνοῦμαι, ἐνδίδω, ἐκπληρῶ.

component [kəm'pəunənt] *a* συνθετικός, συστατικός ‖ *n* συστατικόν ‖ (*phys*) συνιστῶσα δύναμις.

compose [kəm'pəuz] *vt* συντάσσω, γράφω ‖ (*mus*) μελοποιῶ, συνθέτω ‖ (*calm*) ἠρεμῶ ‖ ~ **d** *a* ἀτάραχος, ἤρεμος ‖ ~ **r** *n* (*mus*) μουσουργός, συνθέτης.

composite ['kɔmpəzit] *a* σύνθετος, μικτός.

composition [kɔmpə'ziʃən] *n* σύνθεσις ‖ (*structure*) σύστασις.

compost ['kɔmpɔst] *n* (*fertilizer*) φουσκί.

composure [kəm'pəuʒə*] *n* ἠρεμία, ἀταραξία.

compound ['kɔmpaund] *n* (*gram*) σύνθετος λέξις ‖ (*enclosure*) κλειστός χῶρος ‖ *a* σύνθετος ‖ (*chem*) ἕνωσις ‖ ~ **fracture** *n* τέλειο κάταγμα ‖ ~ **interest** *n* ἀνατοκισμός.

comprehend [kɔmpri'hend] *vt* (*understand*) καταλαβαίνω ‖ (*include*) συμπεριλαμβάνω.

comprehension [kɔmpri'henʃən] *n* κατανόησις, ἀντίληψις.

comprehensive [kɔmpri'hensiv] *a* περιεκτικός, νοήμων.

compress [kəm'pres] *vt* συμπιέζω ‖ ['kɔmpres] *n* (*med*) ἐπίθεμα, κομπρέσσα ‖ ~ **ion** *n* (συμ)πίεσις, σύμπτυξις.

comprise [kəm'praiz] *vi* ἀποτελοῦμαι ἀπό.

compromise ['kɔmprəmaiz] *n* συμβιβασμός ‖ *vt* (*expose*) ἐκθέτω ‖ *vi* (*agree*) συμβιβάζομαι.

compulsion [kəm'pʌlʃən] *n* βία, καταναγκασμός.

compulsory [kəm'pʌlsəri] *a* (*obligatory*) ὑποχρεωτικός.

computer [kəm'pju:tə*] *n* ὑπολογιστής.

comrade ['kɔmrid] *n* σύντροφος, συνάδελφος ‖ ~ **ship** *n* καμαραντερί.

concave ['kɔn'keiv] *a* κοῖλος, βαθουλός.

conceal [kən'si:l] *vt* (ἀπο)κρύπτω.

concede [kən'si:d] *vt* (*admit*) παραδέχομαι ‖ *vi* (*yield*) παραχωρῶ.

conceit [kən'si:t] *n* ματαιοδοξία, ξηπασιά ‖ ~ **ed** *a* φαντασμένος, ξηπασμένος.

conceivable [kən'si:vəbl] *a* διανοητός, δυνατός.

conceive [kən'si:v] *vt* (*imagine*) φαντάζομαι ‖ (*child*) συλλαμβάνω.

concentrate ['kɔnsəntreit] *vi* (+*on*) συγκεντρώνομαι ‖ *vt* συγκεντρώνω.

concentration [kɔnsən'treiʃən] *n* συγκέντρωσις ‖ ~ **camp** *n* στρατόπεδον συγκεντρώσεως.

concentric [kən'sentrik] *a* ὁμόκεντρος.

concept ['kɔnsept] *n* ἰδέα, ἔννοια ‖ ~ **ion** *n* σύλληψις, ἀντίληψις.

concern [kən'sə:n] *n* (*affair*) ἐνδιαφέρον,

συμφέρον ‖ (business) ἐπιχείρησις ‖ (anxiety) ἀνησυχία ‖ vt ἐνδιαφέρομαι, ἐνδιαφέρω ‖ ~ed a (anxious) ἀνήσυχος ‖ ~ing prep ὅσον ἀφορᾶ.

concert ['kɔnsət] n συνεννόησις, συμφωνία ‖ (mus) συναυλία ‖ in ~ ἐκ συμφώνου, μαζί ‖ ~ed [kən'sɔ:tid] a συμπεφωνημένος ‖ ~ hall n αἴθουσα συναυλιῶν.

concertina [kɔnsə'ti:nə] n ἀκορντεόν.

concerto [kən'tʃeətəu] n κονσέρτο.

concession [kən'seʃən] n παραχώρησις, ἐκχώρησις.

conciliation [kənsili'eiʃən] n συμφιλίωσις.

conciliatory [kən'siliətəri] a διαλλακτικός.

concise [kən'sais] a σύντομος, βραχυλόγος.

conclave ['kɔnkleiv] n κογκλάβιον, συμβούλιον.

conclude [kən'klu:d] vt (end) τελειώνω, περαίνω ‖ (settle) συνάπτω, κλείνω ‖ (decide) συμπεραίνω, καταλήγω ‖ vi τερματίζω.

conclusion [kən'klu:ʒən] n συμπέρασμα, τέλος ‖ in ~ ἐν τέλει.

conclusive [kən'klu:siv] a ἀποφασιστικός, πειστικός ‖ ~ly ad ἀποφασιστικῶς, ἀναμφισβητήτως.

concoct [kən'kɔkt] vt (drink etc) κατασκευάζω ‖ (plan etc) ἐφευρίσκω, καταστρώνω.

concrete ['kɔnkri:t] n σκυροκονίαμα, μπετόν ‖ a συγκεκριμένος.

concur [kən'kə:*] vi συμπίπτω, συμφωνῶ.

concurrently [kən'kʌrəntli] ad ἀπό κοινοῦ.

concussion [kən'kʌʃən] n τράνταγμα ‖ (med) διάσεισις.

condemn [kən'dem] vt καταδικάζω ‖ ~ation n καταδίκη, μομφή.

condensation [kɔndən'seiʃən] n συμπύκνωσις.

condense [kən'dens] vi συμπυκνοῦμαι ‖ vt συμπυκνώνω ‖ ~d milk n συμπεπυκνωμένο γάλα.

condescend [kɔndi'send] vi καταδέχομαι ‖ ~ing a καταδεκτικός, εὐπροσήγορος.

condition [kən'diʃən] n (state) κατάστασις, συνθήκη ‖ (term) ὅρος ‖ vt ρυθμίζω, καθορίζω ‖ on ~ that ὑπό τόν ὅρον νά ‖ ~s npl (circumstances, weather) συνθῆκες ‖ ~al a ὑπό ὅρους, προϋποθετικός.

condolences [kən'dəulənsiz] npl συλλυπητήρια.

condone [kən'dəun] vt συγχωρῶ, παραβλέπω. .

conducive [kən'dju:siv] a (+to) συντελεστικός.

conduct ['kɔndʌkt] n (behaviour) διαγωγή ‖ (management) διεξαγωγή ‖ [kən'dʌkt] vt (people) ὁδηγῶ, φέρω ‖ (affairs) διευθύνω, ἐκτελῶ ‖ (mus) διευθύνω ‖ ~ed tour n ξενάγησις ‖ ~or n (orchestra) μαέστρος ‖ (bus) εἰσπράκτωρ ‖ ~ress n (bus) εἰσπράκτόρισσα.

cone [kəun] n (math) κῶνος ‖ (ice cream)

παγωτό χωνάκι ‖ (pine) κουκουνάρι.

confectioner [kən'fekʃənə*] n ζαχαροπλάστης ‖ ~'s (shop) n ζαχαροπλαστεῖον ‖ ~y n ζαχαροπλαστεῖον.

confederation [kɔnfedə'reiʃən] n συνομοσπονδία.

confer [kən'fə:*] vt (grant) ἀπονέμω, παρέχω ‖ vi (consult) συζητῶ, διασκέπτομαι ‖ ~ence ['kɔnfərəns] n (συν)διάσκεψις, συμβούλιον.

confess [kən'fes] vti (admit) (ἐξ)ὁμολογῶ ‖ (rel) ἐξομολογοῦμαι ‖ ~ion n ὁμολογία ‖ (rel) ἐξομολόγησις ‖ ~ional n ἐξομολογητήριον ‖ ~or n ὁμολογητής ‖ (priest) πνευματικός.

confetti [kən'feti] n χαρτοπόλεμος, κονφετί.

confide [kən'faid] vi: to ~ in ἐμπιστεύομαι ‖ ~nce ['kɔnfidəns] n (trust) ἐμπιστοσύνη ‖ (secret) μυστικόν ‖ ~nce trick n κόλπο, ἀπάτη.

confident ['kɔnfidənt] a βέβαιος, μέ θάρρος ‖ ~ial a (secret) ἐμπιστευτικός ‖ (trusted) τῆς ἐμπιστοσύνης.

confine [kən'fain] vt περιορίζω ‖ (shut up) ἐγκλείω ‖ ~s ['kɔnfainz] npl ὅρια ‖ ~d a (space) περιορισμένος ‖ ~ment n (limiting) περιορισμός ‖ (birth) λοχεία, τοκετός.

confirm [kən'fə:m] vt (report) ἐπιβεβαιώνω ‖ (appointment) ἐπικυρώνω ‖ ~ation n (general) ἐπιβεβαίωσις ‖ (rel) χρίσμα, μύρωσις ‖ ~ed a ἔμμονος, πείσμων.

confiscate ['kɔnfiskeit] vt δημεύω.

confiscation [kɔnfis'keiʃən] n δήμευσις.

conflagration [kɔnflə'greiʃən] n πυρκαϊά.

conflict ['kɔnflikt] n σύγκρουσις, διαμάχη, ἀντίθεσις ‖ [kən'flikt] vi συγκρούομαι, διαφέρω, ἀντιμάχομαι ‖ ~ing a ἀντιφατικός, συγκρουόμενος.

conform [kən'fɔ:m] vi (+to) συμμορφώνομαι, προσαρμόζομαι.

confront [kən'frʌnt] vt ἀντιμετωπίζω ‖ ~ation n ἀντιμετώπισις.

confuse [kən'fju:z] vt συγχύζω, ταράσσω.

confusing [kən'fju:ziŋ] a συγκεχυμένος.

confusion [kən'fju:ʒən] n (disorder) σύγχυσις ‖ (tumult) ἀνακτάσωσις, ἀναμπουμπούλα ‖ (embarrassment) σάστισμα.

congeal [kən'dʒi:l] vi πήζω.

congenial [kən'dʒi:niəl] a ταιριαστός, εὐχάριστος.

congested [kən'dʒestid] a (overcrowded) συνωστισμένος.

congestion [kən'dʒestʃən] n (of traffic etc) συμφόρησις, συνωστισμός.

conglomeration [kɔnglɔmə'reiʃən] n σύμφυρμα, σύμπηγμα.

congratulate [kən'grætjuleit] vt (+on) συγχαίρω.

congratulations [kəngrætju'leiʃənz] npl συγχαρητήρια.

congregate ['kɔŋgrigeit] vi συναθροίζομαι.

congregation [kɔŋgri'geiʃən] *n* συνάθροισις, πλήρωμα ἐκκλησίας.

congress ['kɔŋgres] *n* συνέλευσις, συνέδριον ‖ (*US*) Κογκρέσσον ‖ ~**ional** *a* κοινοβουλευτικός ‖ ~**man** *n* (*US*) μέλος τοῦ Κογκρέσσου.

conical ['kɔnikəl] *a* κωνικός, κωνοειδής.

conifer ['kɔnifə*] *n* κωνοφόρον (δένδρον) ‖ ~**ous** [kə'nifərəs] *a* κωνοφόρος.

conjecture [kən'dʒektʃə*] *n* εἰκασία, συμπερασμός ‖ *vti* εἰκάζω, συμπεραίνω.

conjugal ['kɔndʒugəl] *a* συζυγικός.

conjunction [kən'dʒʌŋkʃən] *n* σύνδεσμος ‖ **in ~ with** ἀπό κοινοῦ μέ.

conjure ['kʌndʒə*] *vti* πλέκω, μηχανεύω ‖ **to ~ up** *vt* ἐπινοῶ, ἐπικαλοῦμαι ‖ ~**r** *n* ταχυδακτυλουργός.

conjuring ['kʌndʒəriŋ] *n*: ~ **trick** *n* ταχυδακτυλουργία.

conk [kɔŋk]: **to ~ out** *vi* (*col*) σβήνω.

connect [kə'nekt] *vti* (*train*) συνδέω, συνδέομαι, συνδυάζω ‖ ~**ion** *n* (*joining*) σύνδεσις, συνάφεια ‖ (*relation*) σχέσις, συσχετισμός ‖ **in ~ion with** σχετικῶς μέ.

connexion [kə'nekʃən] *n* = **connection** ‖ *see* **connect**.

connoisseur [kɔnə'sə:*] *n* εἰδήμων, τεχνοκρίτης.

conquer ['kɔŋkə*] *vt* (*overcome*) ὑπερνικῶ, ὑποτάσσω ‖ (*by war*) κατακτῶ, κυριεύω ‖ ~**or** *n* κατακτητής, νικητής.

conquest ['kɔŋkwest] *n* κατάκτησις.

conscience ['kɔnʃəns] *n* συνείδησις.

conscientious [kɔnʃi'enʃəs] *a* εὐσυνείδητος ‖ ~ **objector** *n* ἀντιρρησίας συνειδήσεως.

conscious ['kɔnʃəs] *a* συνειδός, συναισθανόμενος ‖ ~**ness** *n* συναίσθησις.

conscript ['kɔnskript] *n* στρατεύσιμος, κληρωτός ‖ ~**ion** [kən'skripʃən] *n* στρατολογία.

consecrate ['kɔnsikreit] *vt* ἐγκαινιάζω, χειροτονῶ ‖ (*devote*) ἀφιερώνω.

consecutive [kən'sekjutiv] *a* διαδοχικός.

consensus [kən'sensəs] *n* κοινή συναίνεσις, ἐπικρατοῦσα γνώμη.

consent [kən'sent] *n* συγκατάθεσις, συναίνεσις ‖ *vi* (+*to*) συγκατατίθεμαι.

consequence ['kɔnsikwəns] *n* (*importance*) σπουδαιότης ‖ (*result, effect*) συνέπεια, ἐπακόλουθον.

consequently ['kɔnsikwəntli] *ad* ἑπομένως, συνεπῶς.

conservation [kɔnsə'veiʃən] *n* συντήρησις, διατήρησις.

conservative [kən'sə:vətiv] *a* συντηρητικός, μετριοπαθής ‖ **C~** *a* (*party*) συντηρητικός ‖ *npl* οἱ Συντηρητικοί.

conservatory [kən'sə:vətri] *n* (*greenhouse*) θερμοκήπιον, σέρρα ‖ (*mus*) ὠδεῖον.

conserve [kən'sə:v] *vt* συντηρῶ, διατηρῶ.

consider [kən'sidə*] *vt* (*think over*) μελετῶ ‖ (*take into account*) λαμβάνω ὑπ'ὄψιν ‖ (*deem*) θεωρῶ ‖ ~**able** *a* σημαντικός,

ἀξιόλογος ‖ ~**ate** *a* διακριτικός, ἁβρόφρων ‖ ~**ation** *n* (*thoughtfulness*) ἁβροφροσύνη, διακριτικότης ‖ (*serious thought*) μελέτη, σκέψις ‖ (*reason*) λόγος ‖ (*reward*) ἀμοιβή ‖ ~**ing** *prep* λαμβανομένου ὑπ'ὄψιν.

consign [kən'sain] *vt* ἀποστέλλω, παραδίδω ‖ ~**ment** *n* ἀποστολή.

consist [kən'sist] *vi* (+*of*) συνίσταμαι, ἀποτελοῦμαι.

consistency [kən'sistənsi] *n* (*firmness*) συνοχή, συνέπεια, σταθερότης ‖ (*density*) πυκνότης, στερεότης.

consistent [kən'sistənt] *a* σταθερός, συνεπής, σύμφωνος.

consolation [kɔnsə'leiʃən] *n* παρηγοριά ‖ ~ **prize** *n* βραβεῖον παρηγορίας.

console [kən'səul] *vt* παρηγορῶ.

consolidate [kən'sɔlideit] *vt* συγχωνεύω, παγιώνω.

consommé [kən'sɔmei] *n* ζωμός κρέατος, κονσομέ.

consonant ['kɔnsənənt] *n* (*gram*) σύμφωνον.

consortium [kən'sɔ:tiəm] *n* κοινοπραξία, κονσόρτιουμ.

conspicuous [kən'spikjuəs] *a* καταφανής, περίβλεπτος ‖ (*prominent*) ἀξιοσημείωτος, σημαντικός.

conspiracy [kən'spirəsi] *n* συνωμοσία.

conspire [kən'spaiə*] *vi* συνωμοτῶ, συνεργῶ.

constable ['kʌnstəbl] *n* ἀστυφύλαξ, χωροφύλαξ.

constabulary [kən'stæbjuləri] *n* ἀστυνομία.

constancy ['kɔnstənsi] *n* σταθερότης, εὐστάθεια.

constant ['kɔnstənt] *a* σταθερός, συνεχής ‖ (*math*) σταθερόν ‖ ~**ly** *ad* σταθερῶς, συνεχῶς.

constellation [kɔnstə'leiʃən] *n* ἀστερισμός.

consternation [kɔnstə'neiʃən] *n* κατάπληξις.

constipated ['kɔnstipeitid] *a* δυσκοίλιος.

constipation [kɔnsti'peiʃən] *n* δυσκοιλιότης.

constituency [kən'stitjuənsi] *n* ἐκλογική περιφέρεια.

constituent [kən'stitjuənt] *n* (*elector*) ψηφοφόρος ‖ (*essential part*) συστατικόν.

constitute ['kɔnstitju:t] *vt* (*amount to*) συνιστῶ, ἀποτελῶ.

constitution [kɔnsti'tju:ʃən] *n* (*laws*) σύνταγμα ‖ (*health*) κρᾶσις ‖ ~**al** *a* συνταγματικός.

constrain [kən'strein] *vt* ἐξαναγκάζω ‖ ~**t** *n* ἐξαναγκασμός ‖ (*feelings*) ταραχή, τράκ.

constrict [kən'strikt] *vt* συσφίγγω ‖ ~**ion** *n* σύσφιγξις, σφίξιμο.

construct [kən'strʌkt] *vt* κατασκευάζω, οἰκοδομῶ ‖ ~**ion** *n* κατασκευή, οἰκοδόμησις ‖ (*gram*) σύνταξις, ἑρμηνεία ‖ **under** ~**ion** ὑπό κατασκευήν ‖ ~**ive** *a* ἐποικοδομητικός, δημιουργικός.

construe [kən'stru:] *vt* ἑρμηνεύω.

consul ['kɔnsəl] *n* πρόξενος ‖ ~**ate** ['kɔnsjulit] *n* προξενεῖον.

consult [kən'sʌlt] *vt* συμβουλεύομαι ‖ ~**ant** *n* (*med*) συμβουλεύων ἰατρός ‖ (*other specialist*) σύμβουλος ‖ ~**ation** *n* συμβούλιον, συνδιάσκεψις ‖ ~**ing room** *n* ἰατρεῖον.

consume [kən'sju:m] *vt* καταναλίσκω ‖ ~**r** *n* καταναλωτής.

consumption [kən'sʌmpʃən] *n* κατανάλωσις ‖ (*med*) φθίσις, φυματίωσις.

contact ['kɔntækt] *n* ἐπαφή ‖ *vt* ἔρχομαι εἰς ἐπαφήν μέ ‖ ~ **lenses** *npl* φακοί ἐπαφῆς.

contagious [kən'teidʒəs] *a* μεταδοτικός, κολλητικός.

contain [kən'tein] *vt* περιέχω ‖ **to ~ o.s.** συγκρατοῦμαι ‖ ~**er** *n* (*small*) δοχεῖον ‖ (*transport*) (ἐμπορευματικό) κιβώτιον.

contaminate [kən'tæmineit] *vt* μολύνω, μιαίνω.

contamination [kəntæmi'neiʃən] *n* μόλυνσις, μίανσις.

contemplate ['kɔntempleit] *vt* (*look at*) κυττάζω, παρατηρῶ ‖ (*meditate*) μελετῶ, ἀναπολῶ ‖ (*intend*) σχεδιάζω.

contemplation [kɔntem'pleiʃən] *n* σκέψις, συλλογή.

contemporary [kən'tempərəri] *a* σύγχρονος ‖ *n* σύγχρονος, συνομίληκος.

contempt [kən'tempt] *n* περιφρόνησις ‖ ~**ible** *a* ἀξιοκαταφρόνητος ‖ ~**uous** *a* περιφρονητικός.

contend [kən'tend] *vt* (*strive*) (συν)αγωνίζομαι ‖ (*argue*) ἰσχυρίζομαι ‖ ~**er** *n* (*competitor*) ἀνταγωνιστής.

content [kən'tent] *a* ἱκανοποιημένος, εὐχαριστημένος ‖ *vt* ἱκανοποιῶ ‖ ['kɔntent] *n* (*of article etc*) περιεχόμενον ‖ ~**s** *npl* (*of room*) περιεχόμενα ‖ (*of book*) (πίναξ) περιεχομένων ‖ (*of barrel*) περιεκτικότης ‖ ~**ed** *a* ἱκανοποιημένος.

contention [kən'tenʃən] *n* (*dispute*) ἀγών, διαμάχη ‖ (*opinion*) ἰσχυρισμός.

contentment [kən'tentmənt] *n* ἱκανοποίησις.

contest ['kɔntest] *n* ἀγών, πάλη ‖ [kən'test] *vt* διαμφισβητῶ, διεκδικῶ, ἀγωνίζομαι ‖ ~**ant** *n* ἀγωνιζόμενος, διεκδικητής.

context ['kɔntekst] *n* συμφραζόμενα.

continent ['kɔntinənt] *n* ἤπειρος ‖ **the C~** Εὐρώπη ‖ ~**al** *a* ἠπειρωτικός.

contingency [kən'tindʒənsi] *n* ἐνδεχόμενον, σύμπτωσις.

contingent [kən'tindʒənt] *n* ἐνδεχόμενος ‖ (*mil*) τμῆμα στρατοῦ ἤ ναυτικοῦ ‖ *a* (+(*up*)*on*) ἐξηρτημένος ἀπό.

continual [kən'tinjuəl] *a* (*endless*) συνεχής, ἀδιάκοπος ‖ (*often repeated*) συχνά ‖ ~**ly** *ad* συνεχῶς.

continuation [kəntinju'eiʃən] *n* συνέχεια, συνέχισις.

continue [kən'tinju:] *vi* συνεχίζομαι ‖ (*remain*) (παρα)μένω ‖ *vt* συνεχίζω ‖ (*resume*) ἐξακολουθῶ.

continuity [kɔnti'nju:iti] *n* συνέχεια.

continuous [kən'tinjuəs] *a* συνεχής, ἀδιάκοπος.

contort [kən'tɔ:t] *vt* συστρίβω, παραμορφώνω ‖ ~**ion** *n* στρίψιμο ‖ (*of face*) μορφασμός ‖ ~**ionist** *n* ἀκροβάτης.

contour ['kɔntuə*] *n* (*shape*) περίγραμμα ‖ (*of map*) ἰσοΰψεῖς καμπύλαι.

contraband ['kɔntrəbænd] *n* λαθρεμπόριον, κοντραμπάντο.

contraception [kɔntrə'sepʃən] *n* πρόληψις συλλήψεως.

contraceptive [kɔntrə'septiv] *n* ἀντισυλληπτικός.

contract ['kɔntrækt] *n* συμβόλαιον, συμφωνία ‖ [kən'trækt] *vi* (*to do sth*) συμφωνῶ, συμβάλλομαι ‖ (*become smaller*) συστέλλομαι, στενεύω ‖ ~**ion** *n* συστολή, μάζεμα ‖ ~**or** *n* ἐργολάβος, προμηθευτής.

contradict [kɔntrə'dikt] *vt* (*say the opposite*) ἀντιλέγω ‖ (*deny*) διαψεύδω ‖ ~**ion** *n* (*in terms*) ἀντίφασις ‖ (*denial*) διάψευσις.

contralto [kən'træltəu] *n* μεσόφωνος, κοντράλτο.

contraption [kən'træpʃən] *n* μηχανή, μαραφέτι.

contrary ['kɔntrəri] *a* (*opposite*) ἐνάντιος, ἀντίθετος ‖ (*unfavourable*) ἀντίθετος, δυσμενής ‖ [kən'treəri] (*perverse*) διεστραμμένος ‖ *n* ἀντίθετον ‖ **on the ~** τουναντίον ‖ **to the ~** ἀντιθέτως.

contrast ['kɔntra:st] *n* σύγκρισις, ἀντίθεσις ‖ [kən'tra:st] *vt* συγκρίνω, ἀντιπαραβάλλω.

contravene [kɔntrə'vi:n] *vt* (*a rule etc*) παραβαίνω, καταπατῶ ‖ (*conflict with*) διαψεύδω, προσκρούω.

contribute [kən'tribju:t] *vi* (*help*) συμβάλλω, βοηθῶ ‖ (*subscribe*) συνεισφέρω ‖ *vt* καταβάλλω.

contribution [kɔntri'bju:ʃən] *n* συνεισφορά, συνεργασία.

contributor [kən'tribjutə*] *n* συνεισφέρων, συνεργάτης.

contrite ['kɔntrait] *a* συντετριμμένος, μετανοῶν.

contrivance [kən'traivəns] *n* τέχνασμα, ἐπινόησις.

contrive [kən'traiv] *vt* (*bring about*) καταφέρνω.

control [kən'trəul] *vt* (*check*) συγκρατῶ, χαλιναγωγῶ ‖ (*direct*) διευθύνω, ἐξουσιάζω ‖ *n* (*check*) ἔλεγχος, ἐπίβλεψις ‖ (*restraint*) χαλινός ‖ ~**s** *npl* χειριστήριον, ἔλεγχος, ἔλεγχος ‖ ~ **point** *n* σημεῖον ἐλέγχου ‖ **out of ~** ἀκυβέρνητος ‖ **under ~** ὑπό ἔλεγχον.

controversial [kɔntrə'və:ʃəl] *a* συζητήσιμος.

controversy [kən'trɔvəsi] *n* συζήτησις, λογομαχία.

convalesce [kɔnvə'les] vi ἀναρρωνύω ‖ ~nce n ἀνάρρωσις ‖ ~nt a,n ἀναρρωνύων.

convene [kən'vi:n] vti συγκαλῶ, συνέρχομαι.

convenience [kən'vi:niəns] n (being convenient) καταλληλότης, συμφωνία ‖ (thing) εὐκολία, ἄνεσις.

convenient [kən'vi:niənt] a κατάλληλος, βολικός, χρήσιμος.

convent ['kɔnvənt] n μονὴ γυναικῶν.

convention [kən'venʃən] n (assembly) συνέδριον, συνέλευσις ‖ (custom) ἔθιμον, συνήθεια ‖ ~al a (traditional) ἐθιμοτυπικός, συνήθης.

converge [kən'və:dʒ] vi συγκλίνω.

conversant [kən'və:sənt] a (+with) οἰκεῖος, γνωστός.

conversation [kɔnvə'seiʃən] n συνδιάλεξις, συνομιλία, κουβέντα ‖ ~al a ὁμιλητικός, καθομιλούμενος.

converse [kən'və:s] vi συνομιλῶ, συνδιαλέγομαι ‖ ['kɔnvə:s] a ἀντίθετος ‖ ~ly ad ἀντιστρόφως, ἀντιθέτως.

conversion [kən'və:ʃən] n μετατροπὴ ‖ (esp rel) προσηλύτισις ‖ ~ table n πίναξ μετατροπῶν.

convert [kən'və:t] vt (change) μετατρέπω ‖ (esp rel) προσηλυτίζω ‖ ['kɔnvə:t] n προσήλυτος ‖ ~ible n (aut) καμπριολέ.

convex ['kɔn'veks] a κυρτός.

convey [kən'vei] vt (carry) μεταφέρω ‖ (communicate) μεταβιβάζω, μεταδίδω ‖ ~or belt n μεταφορεύς.

convict [kən'vikt] vt καταδικάζω ‖ ['kɔnvikt] n κατάδικος ‖ ~ion n (verdict) καταδίκη ‖ (belief) πεποίθησις.

convince [kən'vins] vt πείθω.

convincing [kən'vinsiŋ] a πειστικός.

convivial [kən'viviəl] a εὔθυμος, κεφάτος.

convoy ['kɔnvɔi] n συνοδεία, νηοπομπή.

convulse [kən'vʌls] vt (esp with laughter) ξεραίνομαι στὰ γέλια.

convulsion [kən'vʌlʃən] n σπασμός.

coo [ku:] vi (dove) τερετίζω σὰν περιστέρι.

cook [kuk] vt μαγειρεύω ‖ vi ψήνεται ‖ n μάγειρας ‖ ~book n βιβλίον μαγειρικῆς ‖ ~er n συσκευὴ μαγειρέματος ‖ ~ery n μαγειρικὴ ‖ ~ery book n = cookbook ‖ ~ie n μπισκότο ‖ ~ing n μαγειρική.

cool [ku:l] a (fairly cold) δροσερὸς ‖ (calm) ψύχραιμος ‖ (unfriendly) ψυχρός, ἀδιάφορος ‖ (impudent) ἀναιδής, θρασὺς ‖ vti δροσίζω, κρυώνω ‖ ~ness n ψύχρα, ψυχρότης.

coop [ku:p] n κοττέτσι, κλούβα ‖ vt: to ~ up (fig) περιορίζω, κλείνω.

co-op ['kəu'ɔp] n = cooperative.

cooperate [kəu'ɔpəreit] vi συνεργάζομαι.

cooperation [kəuɔpə'reiʃən] n συνεργασία.

cooperative [kəu'ɔpərətiv] a συνεργατικὸς ‖ n (farmers) συνεταιρισμὸς ‖ ~ store n (retail) πρατήριον συνεταιρισμοῦ.

coordinate [kəu'ɔ:dineit] vt συνδυάζω, συντονίζω.

coordination [kəuɔ:di'neiʃən] n συντονισμός.

coot [ku:t] n φαλαρίδα, λούφα.

cope [kəup] vi (+with) ἀντιμετωπίζω, ἀνταπεξέρχομαι.

co-pilot ['kəu'pailət] n δεύτερος χειριστής.

copper ['kɔpə*] n χαλκός, μπακίρι ‖ (coin) δεκάρα ‖ (sl: policeman) ἀστυφύλακας.

coppice ['kɔpis] n, copse [kɔps] n δασύλλιον, λόγγος.

copulate ['kɔpjuleit] vi συνουσιάζομαι, γαμῶ.

copy ['kɔpi] n (imitation) ἀντίγραφον, ἀντιγραφὴ ‖ (of book) ἀντίτυπον ‖ vt ἀντιγράφω, ἀπομιμοῦμαι ‖ ~book n τετράδιο ‖ ~cat n μιμήτρια ‖ ~right n πνευματικὴ ἰδιοκτησία ‖ ~right reserved ἀπαγορεύεται ἢ ἀναδημοσίευσις.

coral ['kɔrəl] n κοράλλιον ‖ ~ reef n κοραλλιογενὲς νησί.

cord [kɔ:d] n σχοινί, χορδὴ ‖ see vocal.

cordial ['kɔ:diəl] a ἐγκάρδιος ‖ ~ly ad (invite) ἐγκαρδίως, θερμῶς.

cordon ['kɔ:dn] n (ornamental) κορδόνι ‖ (of police etc) ζώνη.

corduroy ['kɔ:dərɔi] n κοτλέ.

core [kɔ:*] n πυρήν, καρδία ‖ vt ἀφαιρῶ τὸν πυρήνα.

cork [kɔ:k] n φελλός ‖ (of bottle) πῶμα ‖ ~screw n τιρ-μπουσόν.

cormorant ['kɔ:mərənt] n φαλακροκόραξ, καλικατζοῦ.

corn [kɔ:n] n σιτηρά, δημητριακὰ ‖ (US: maize) καλαμπόκι ‖ (on foot) κάλος.

cornea ['kɔ:niə] n κερατοειδής.

corned ['kɔ:nd] ~ beef n εἶδος ἀλιπάστου κρέατος.

corner ['kɔ:nə*] n (of street) γωνία ‖ (of room) γωνία, κώχη ‖ (fig) δύσκολη θέσι ‖ vt φέρω εἰς δύσκολον θέσιν, στριμώχνω ‖ (econ) μονοπωλῶ ‖ vi (turn) παίρνω στροφὴν ‖ ~ kick n κόρνερ ‖ ~stone n ἀκρογωνιαῖος λίθος, βάσις.

cornet ['kɔ:nit] n (mus) κορνέττα ‖ (ice cream) χωνάκι.

cornflour ['kɔ:nflauə*] n καλαμποκάλευρο, κορνφλάουερ.

cornice ['kɔ:nis] n κορνίζα.

cornstarch ['kɔ:nsta:tʃ] n (US) = cornflour.

corny ['kɔ:ni] a (joke) σαχλό.

coronary ['kɔrənəri] a στεφανιαῖος ‖ n στεφανιαία ‖ ~ thrombosis n θρόμβωσι τῆς στεφανιαίας.

coronation [kɔrə'neiʃən] n στέψις.

coroner ['kɔrənə*] n ἰατροδικαστής.

corporal ['kɔ:pərəl] n (mil) δεκανέας ‖ (aviat) ὑποσμηνίας ‖ a σωματικός.

corporation [kɔ:pə'reiʃən] n σωματεῖον ‖ (esp business) ἑταιρεία.

corps [kɔ:*] n (στρατιωτικόν) σῶμα.

corpse [kɔ:ps] n πτῶμα, κουφάρι.

corpulent ['kɔ:pjulənt] *a* παχύσαρκος.
corpuscle ['kɔ:pʌsl] *n* σωματίδιον ‖ *(blood corpuscle)* αἱμοσφαίριον.
corral [kə'rɑ:l] *n* μάνδρα.
correct [kə'rekt] *a (accurate)* ἀκριβής, ὀρθός, διορθωμένος ‖ *(proper)* ἄψογος, ὅπως πρέπει ‖ *vt (papers etc)* διορθώνω ‖ *(make right)* ἐπανορθώνω ‖ ~**ion** *n* διόρθωσις ‖ ~**ly** *ad* ὀρθῶς, σωστά.
correlate ['kɔrileit] *vt* σχετίζομαι, φέρω εἰς σχέσιν.
correlation [kɔri'leiʃən] *n* συσχετισμός, συσχέτισις.
correspond [kɔris'pɔnd] *vi (agree with)* ἀνταποκρίνομαι, ταιριάζω ‖ *(write)* ἀλληλογραφῶ ‖ ~**ence** *n (letters)* ἀλληλογραφία ‖ *(similarity)* ἀντιστοιχία, ἀνταπόκρισις ‖ ~**ence course** *n* μάθημα ἀλληλογραφίας ‖ ~**ent** *n (reporter)* ἀνταποκριτής ‖ ~**ing** *a* ἀντίστοιχος.
corridor ['kɔridɔ:*] *n* διάδρομος.
corroborate [kə'rɔbəreit] *vt* ἐπιβεβαιώνω, ἐνισχύω.
corroboration [kərɔbə'reiʃən] *n* ἐπιβεβαίωσις, ἐπίρρωσις.
corrode [kə'rəud] *vti* διαβιβρώσκω, σκουριάζω.
corrosion [kə'rəuʒən] *n* διάβρωσις, σκωρίασις.
corrugated ['kɔrəgeitid] *a* κυματοειδής ‖ ~ **cardboard** *n* κυματοειδὲς χαρτόνι ‖ ~ **iron** *n* αὐλακωτὸν ἔλασμα.
corrupt [kə'rʌpt] *a* διεφθαρμένος ‖ *vt* διεφθείρω ‖ ~**ion** *n* διαφθορά, δεκασμός.
corset ['kɔ:sit] *n* κορσές.
cortège [kɔ:'teiʒ] *n* νεκρώσιμος πομπή.
cortisone ['kɔ:tizəun] *n* κορτιζόνη.
cosh [kɔʃ] *n* μαγκούρα, βούρδουλας ‖ *vt* κτυπῶ μὲ βούρδουλα.
cosine ['kəusain] *n* συνημίτονον.
cosiness ['kəuzinis] *n* ἄνεσις.
cosmetic [kɔz'metik] *n* καλλυντικόν.
cosmic ['kɔzmik] *a* κοσμικός.
cosmonaut ['kɔzmənɔ:t] *n* ἀστροναύτης, κοσμοναύτης.
cosmopolitan [kɔzmə'pɔlitən] *a* κοσμοπολιτικός.
cosmos ['kɔzmɔs] *n* κόσμος, τὸ σύμπαν.
cost [kɔst] *(irreg v) n* κόστος, τιμή, δαπάνη ‖ *vt* κοστίζω, στοιχίζω ‖ **it** ~**s £5** στοιχίζει πέντε λίρες ‖ **it** ~**s too much** στοιχίζει πολλά ‖ **it** ~ **him his life** τοῦ κόστιζε τὴν ζωή ‖ **at all** ~**s** πάση θυσία.
costing ['kɔstiŋ] *n* κοστολόγησις.
costly ['kɔstli] *a (expensive)* δαπανηρός ‖ *(jewellery etc)* πολύτιμος.
cost price ['kɔstprais] *n* τιμή κόστους.
costume ['kɔstju:m] *n (style of dress)* ἔνδυμα, φορεσιά, μόδα ‖ *(woman's outer clothes)* ἐνδυμασία, κοστούμι ‖ *(for bathing)* μπανιερό, μαγιώ ‖ ~ **jewellery** *n* κοσμήματα.
cosy ['kəuzi] *a* ἀναπαυτικός, ζεστός.

cot [kɔt] *n (child's bed)* κρεββατάκι.
cottage ['kɔtidʒ] *n* ἐξοχικὸ σπιτάκι ‖ ~ **cheese** *n* ἄσπρο τυρί, φέτα.
cotton ['kɔtn] *n* βαμβάκι, μπαμπάκι ‖ *a*: ~ **dress** *etc* μπαμπακερό ‖ ~ **wool** *n* ἀκατέργαστος βάμβαξ.
couch [kautʃ] *n* ντιβάνι, καναπές ‖ *vt* ἐκφράζω, συγκαλύπτω.
cough [kɔf] *vi* βήχω ‖ *n* βήχας ‖ ~ **drop** *n* παστίλια.
could [kud] *pt of* **can** ‖ ~**n't** = **could not** ‖ *see* **can**.
council ['kaunsl] *n* συμβούλιον ‖ ~**lor** *n* σύμβουλος.
counsel ['kaunsəl] *n (law)* δικηγόρος ‖ *(opinion)* συμβουλή ‖ ~**lor** *n* σύμβουλος.
count [kaunt] *vt (add up)* μετρῶ, ἀριθμῶ ‖ *(include)* ὑπολογίζω, συμπεριλαμβάνω ‖ *vi (be of importance)* ὑπολογίζομαι, στηρίζομαι ‖ *n (reckoning)* ἀρίθμησις, μέτρησις, λογαριασμός ‖ *(nobleman)* κόμης ‖ **to** ~ **on** *vt* ὑπολογίζω, στηρίζομαι εἰς ‖ **to** ~ **up** *vt* μετρῶ ἕως, προσθέτω.
counter ['kauntə*] *n* θυρίς, γκισέ ‖ *(machine that counts)* μετρητής ‖ *vt* ἀντιτίθεμαι, ἀνταπαντῶ ‖ *ad* ἐναντίον, ἀντιθέτως ‖ ~**act** *vt* ἀντιδρῶ, ἐξουδετερώνω ‖ ~**-attack** *n* ἀντεπίθεσις ‖ ~**balance** *vt* ἀντισταθμίζω ‖ ~**-clockwise** *ad* ἀριστερόστροφα ‖ ~**-espionage** *n* ἀντικατασκοπεία ‖ ~**feit** *a* πλαστός, κίβδηλος ‖ *n* παραποίησις, ἀπάτη ‖ *vt* πλαστογραφῶ ‖ ~**foil** *n* στέλεχος ‖ ~**part** *n* ἀντίστοιχον, ταίρι.
countess ['kauntis] *n* κόμισσα, κοντέσσα.
countless ['kauntlis] *a* ἀναρίθμητος, ἀμέτρητος.
country ['kʌntri] *n (land)* χώρα ‖ *(of birth)* πατρίδα ‖ *(rural district)* ὕπαιθρος, ἐξοχή, ἐπαρχία ‖ *(region)* περιοχή ‖ ~ **dancing** *n* ἐθνικός χορός, λαϊκός χορός ‖ ~ **house** *n* ἐξοχικό σπίτι ‖ ~**man** *n (national)* (συμ)πατριώτης ‖ *(rural)* ἐπαρχιώτης, χωριάτης ‖ ~**side** *n* ὕπαιθρος.
county ['kaunti] *n* κομητεία ‖ ~ **town** *n* πρωτεύουσα κομητείας.
coup [ku:] *n (also* ~ **d'état)** πραξικόπημα.
coupé ['ku:pei] *n* κουπέ.
couple ['kʌpl] *n* ζευγάρι, δύο ‖ *vt* ἑνώνω, ζευγαρώνω.
couplet ['kʌplit] *n* δίστοιχον.
coupling ['kʌpliŋ] *n* σύζευξις.
coupon ['ku:pɔn] *n* κουπόνι, ἀπόκομμα.
courage ['kʌridʒ] *n* θάρρος, γενναιότητα ‖ ~**ous** *a* θαρραλέος.
courier ['kuriə*] *n* ἀγγελιαφόρος.
course [kɔ:s] *n (path, track)* διαδρομή ‖ *(line of action)* πορεία, δρόμος ‖ *(series, procedure)* μάθημα, κούρ ‖ *(career, journey)* πορεία ‖ *(part of meal)* φαγητό, πιάτο ‖ **of** ~ φυσικά, καὶ βέβαια ‖ **in the** ~ **of** κατὰ τὴν διάρκειαν τοῦ ‖ **in due** ~ ἐν καιρῷ τῷ δέοντι ‖ *see* **golf**.

court [kɔːt] *n* (*attendants of sovereign*) αὐλή ‖ (*residence of sovereign*) (βασιλική) αὐλή ‖ (*of justice*) δικαστήριον ‖ *vt* κορτάρω, προσκαλῶ, ἐπιδιώκω ‖ *see* tennis.

courteous ['kɔːtiəs] *a* εὐγενής.

courtesy ['kɔːtisi] *n* εὐγένεια.

courthouse ['kɔːthaus] *n* (*US*) δικαστικόν μέγαρον.

courtier ['kɔːtiə*] *n* αὐλικός.

court-martial ['kɔːt'mɑːʃəl] *n* στρατοδικεῖον.

court room ['kɔːtrum] *n* αἴθουσα δικαστηρίου.

courtyard ['kɔːtjɑːd] *n* αὐλή.

cousin ['kʌzn] *n* ξάδελφος, ξαδέλφη.

cove [kəuv] *n* ὅρμος.

cover ['kʌvə*] *vt* (*place over*) καλύπτω, σκεπάζω ‖ (*shield, screen*) καλύπτω, προστατεύω, κρύβω ‖ (*deal with*) καλύπτω, περιλαμβάνω ‖ (*protect*) προστατεύω ‖ *n* κάλυμμα, σκέπασμα ‖ ~age *n* (*of news*) ρεπορτάζ ‖ ~ charge *n* κουβέρ ‖ ~ing *n* κάλυψις, σκέπασμα, ἐπένδυσις ‖ ~ing letter *n* ἐπιβεβαιωτική ἐπιστολή.

covet ['kʌvit] *vt* ἐποφθαλμιῶ.

covetous ['kʌvitəs] *a* ἄπληστος.

cow [kau] *n* ἀγελάδα.

coward ['kauəd] *n* ἄνανδρος, δειλός ‖ ~ice *n* δειλία ‖ ~ly *a* ἄνανδρος, δειλός.

cowboy ['kaubɔi] *n* κάου-μπόϊ.

cower ['kauə*] *vi* μαζεύομαι, τρέμω.

co-worker ['kəu'wəːkə*] *n* συνεργάτης.

cowshed ['kauʃed] *n* βουστάσιον.

coxswain ['kɔksn] *n* (*abbr* cox) πηδαλιοῦχος.

coy [kɔi] *a* ντροπαλός, σεμνός.

crab [kræb] *n* κάβουρας ‖ ~apple *n* ἀγριόμηλον.

crack [kræk] *n* (*sharp noise*) κρότος, τριγμός ‖ (*of whip*) στράκα ‖ (*split*) ρωγμή, σκάσιμο ‖ *vt* (*noise*) κροτῶ ‖ (*split*) θραύω, ραγίζω ‖ *a* λαμπρός, ἐκλεκτός ‖ ~er *n* (*firework*) βαρελότο, στράκα ‖ (*biscuit*) παξιμαδάκι, μπισκότο ‖ to ~ up *vi* κομματιάζω ‖ (*fig*) καταρρέω.

crackling ['kræklŋ] *n* κροταλισμός, τρίξιμο ‖ (*of pig*) πέτσα ψημένου γουρουνιοῦ.

cradle ['kreidl] *n* κοιτίς, λίκνον, κούνια.

craft [krɑːft] *n* (*skill*) τέχνη, χειροτεχνία, ἐπάγγελμα ‖ (*cunning*) πανουργία, δόλος ‖ (*boat*) σκάφος, βάρκα ‖ ~sman *n* τεχνίτης ‖ ~smanship *n* τέχνη ‖ ~y *a* πανοῦργος, πονηρός, πολυμήχανος.

crag [kræg] *n* κατσάβραχο, γκρεμός ‖ ~gy *a* ἀπόκρημνος, βραχώδης.

cram [kræm] *vt* μπάζω, χώνω.

cramp [kræmp] *n* σπασμός, κράμπα ‖ *vt* ἐμποδίζω, περιορίζω.

crane [krein] *n* γερανός, κρένι.

cranium ['kreiniəm] *n* κρανίον.

crank [kræŋk] *n* (*lever*) (χειρο)στρόφαλος, μανιβέλλα ‖ (*person*) ἰδιότυπος,

ἐκκεντρικός ‖ *vt* βάζω μπρός μέ μανιβέλλα ‖ ~shaft *n* στροφαλοφόρος (ἄξων).

cranny ['kræni] *n* σχισμή, ρωγμή.

crap [kræp] *n* (*nonsense*) τρίχες.

craps [kræps] *n* ζάρι.

crash [kræʃ] *n* κρότος, βρόντος ‖ (*aviat*) συντριβή, πτῶσις ‖ (*aut*) σύγκρουσις ‖ (*econ*) κράχ ‖ *vti* πέφτω, συντρίβομαι ‖ ~ helmet *n* προστατευτικόν κράνος ‖ ~ landing *n* ἀναγκαστική προσγείωσις.

crate [kreit] *n* κασόνι, κοφίνι, καφάσι.

crater ['kreitə*] *n* κρατήρ.

cravat(e) [krə'væt] *n* γραβάτα.

crave [kreiv] *vi* (+*for*) ἐκλιπαρῶ, ποθῶ.

craving ['kreiviŋ] *n* πόθος, λαχτάρα.

crawl [krɔːl] *vi* ἕρπω, σέρνομαι ‖ *n* σύρσιμο, βραδυπορία ‖ (*swimming*) κρώουλ.

crayon ['kreiən] *n* κραγιόνι, παστέλ.

craze [kreiz] *n* μανία, λόξα.

crazy ['kreizi] *a* (*foolish*) ἀνόητος ‖ (*insane*) παράφρων, τρελλός, μουρλός ‖ (*madly eager for*) ἔχω μανία γιά ‖ ~ paving *n* ἀκανόνιστο πλακόστρωμα.

creak [kriːk] *n* τριγμός ‖ *vi* τρίζω.

cream [kriːm] *n* καϊμάκι, κρέμα, σαντιγί ‖ (*polish*) ἀλοιφή ‖ (*cosmetic*) κρέμα ‖ (*colour*) ἰβουάρ, μπέζ ‖ ~ cake *n* πάστα, τούρτα ‖ ~ery *n* γαλατάδικο ‖ ~y *a* καϊμακλίδικος, βουτιράτος.

crease [kriːs] *n* πτυχή, τσάκισμα, τσαλάκωμα ‖ *vti* διπλώνω, ζαρώνω, τσαλακώνω.

create [kriː'eit] *vt* (*bring into being*) δημιουργῶ ‖ (*cause*) προξενῶ.

creation [kriː'eiʃən] *n* δημιούργημα.

creative [kriː'eitiv] *a* δημιουργικός.

creator [kriː'eitə*] *n* δημιουργός.

creature ['kriːtʃə*] *n* πλάσμα, ὄν.

credentials [kri'denʃəlz] *npl* (*papers*) διαπιστευτήρια, πιστοποιητικά.

credibility [kredə'biləti] *n* ἀξιοπιστία, (τό) πιστευτόν.

credible ['kredibl] *a* πιστευτός, ἀξιόπιστος.

credit ['kredit] *n* πίστις, πίστωσις ‖ (*recognition*) ἀναγνώρισις ‖ *vt* πιστεύω ‖ to one's ~ πρός τιμήν τοῦ ‖ ~able *a* ἔντιμος, ἀξιέπαινος ‖ ~ card *n* κάρτα πιστώσεως ‖ ~or *n* πιστωτής.

creed [kriːd] *n* πίστις, θρήσκευμα.

creek [kriːk] *n* κολπίσκος ‖ (*US*) ρέμα.

creep [kriːp] (*irreg v*) *vi* ἕρπω, σύρομαι ‖ ~er *n* (*animal*) ἑρπετόν ‖ (*plant*) ἀναρριχητικόν ‖ ~y *a* (*frightening*) ἀνατριχιαστικόν.

cremate [kri'meit] *vt* ἀποτεφρώνω (νεκρόν).

cremation [kri'meiʃən] *n* καῦσις (νεκροῦ).

crematorium [kremə'tɔːriəm] *n* κρεματόριον.

crêpe [kreip] *n* κρέπ(ι).

crept [krept] *pt,pp* of creep.

crescent ['kresnt] *n* ἡμισέληνος ‖ (*esp street*) ἡμικυκλικός δρόμος.

cress [kres] *n* κάρδαμο.
crest [krest] *n* (*tuft*) λοφίον, λειρί ‖ (*of wave*) κορυφή ‖ (*badge*) κορωνίς, οἰκόσημον ‖ ~**fallen** *a* κατηφής, ἀποθαρρημένος.
Crete [kri:t] *n* Κρήτη.
cretin ['kretin] *n* ἠλίθιος ‖ (*med*) κρετῖνος.
crevasse [kri'væs] *n* σχισμή.
crevice ['krevis] *n* ρωγμή, χαραμάδα.
crew [kru:] *n* πλήρωμα ‖ ~-**cut** *n* πολύ κοντό μαλλί.
crib [krib] *n* (*child's bed*) παιδικό κρεββάτι ‖ (*copy*) ἀντιγραφή.
cribbage ['kribidʒ] *n* κρίμπιτζ.
crick [krik] *n* πιάσιμο.
cricket ['krikit] *n* (*insect*) γρύλλος, τριζόνι ‖ (*game*) κρίκετ ‖ ~**er** *n* παίκτης τοῦ κρίκετ.
crime [kraim] *n* (*wicked act*) κακούργημα ‖ (*lawbreaking*) ἔγκλημα.
criminal ['kriminl] *n* ἐγκληματίας, κακοῦργος ‖ *a* ἐγκληματικός, ἐνοχικός.
crimson ['krimzn] *n* βαθύ ἐρυθρόν, βυσσινί ‖ *a* κατακόκκινος.
cringe [krindʒ] *vi* φέρομαι δουλοπρεπῶς, σκύβω.
crinkle ['kriŋkl] *vt* ζαρώνω, τσαλακώνω ‖ (*rustle*) τρίβω.
cripple ['kripl] *n* ἀνάπηρος, χωλός ‖ *vt* τραυματίζω, σακατεύω, παραλύω.
crisis ['kraisis] *n* (*time of danger etc*) κρίσις.
crisp [krisp] *a* εὔθριπτος, ἀφράτος, φρέσκος ‖ *n* ξεροτηγανισμένη πατάτα.
criss-cross ['kriskrɔs] *a* σταυρωτός, καφασιτός.
criterion [krai'tiəriən] *n* κριτήριον.
critic ['kritik] *n* (*theat etc*) τεχνοκρίτης, κριτικός ‖ ἐπικριτής ‖ ~**al** *a* (*like a critic*) κριτικός ‖ (*danger*) κρίσιμος ‖ (*severe*) αὐστηρός ‖ ~**ally** *ad* μέ κριτική διάθεσι, κρίσιμος ‖ ~**ism** ['kritisizəm] *n* (*judgment*) κριτική ‖ (*finding fault*) ἐπίκρισις ‖ ~**ize** ['kritisaiz] *vt* (ἐπι)κρίνω, κατακρίνω.
croak [krəuk] *vi* (*crow*) κρώζω ‖ (*frog*) κοάζω ‖ *n* (*of crow*) κρωγμός ‖ (*of frog*) κοασμός.
crochet ['krəuʃei] *n* κροσέ.
crockery ['krɔkəri] *n* πήλινα σκεύη.
crocodile ['krɔkədail] *n* κροκόδειλος.
crocus ['krəukəs] *n* κρόκος.
crony ['krəuni] *n* γέρος, παλιόφιλος.
crook [kruk] *n* (*criminal*) λωποδύτης, ἀπατεών ‖ (*of shepherd*) γκλίτσα ‖ ~**ed** *a* ἀγκυλωτός.
crop [krɔp] *n* συγκομιδή, σοδιά ‖ **to ~ up** *vi* (*fig*) παρουσιάζομαι, προκύπτω.
croquet ['krəukei] *n* κροκέ.
croquette [krəu'ket] *n* κροκέτα, κεφτές.
cross [krɔs] *n* (*of Christ*) σταυρός ‖ (*mark*) σταυρό ‖ (*breed*) διασταύρωσις ‖ (*misfortune*) ἐμπόδιον, δυσκολία, ‖ *vt* (*pass*

over) διασχίζω, περνῶ ‖ (*make sign*) σταυροκοπιέμαι ‖ (*place across*) σταυρώνω ‖ (*mix breeds*) διασταυρώνω ‖ (*cheque*) διαγραμμίζω ‖ *a* θυμωμένος, κακόκεφος ‖ ~**breed** *n* μιγάς ‖ ~-**country** (*race*) *n* ἀνώμαλος δρόμος ‖ ~-**examination** *n* ἐξέτασις κατ'ἀντιπαράστασιν ‖ ~-**examine** *vt* ἐξετάζω κατ'ἀντιπαράστασιν ‖ ~-**eyed** *a* ἀλλοίθωρος ‖ ~**ing** *n* (*road etc*) διάβασις, πέρασμα ‖ (*sea passage*) διάπλους ‖ (*place for crossing*) διάβασις ‖ **at** ~-**purposes** παρεξηγημένοι, σέ ἀντίθεσι ‖ ~-**reference** *n* παραπομπή ‖ ~**roads** *n* σταυροδρόμι ‖ ~ **section** *n* ἐγκαρσία τομή ‖ ~**wind** *n* πλάγιος ἄνεμος ‖ ~**word** (**puzzle**) *n* σταυρόλεξον.
crotch [krɔtʃ] *n* διακλάδωσις δένδρου, καβάλος τοῦ πανταλονιοῦ.
crotchet ['krɔtʃit] *n* ἰδιοτροπία, βίδα.
crotchety ['krɔtʃiti] *a* (*person*) ἰδιότροπος.
crouch [krautʃ] *vi* σκύβω, μαζεύομαι, ὀκλάζω.
crow [krəu] *n* κορώνη, κουρούνα ‖ *vi* κράζω, λαλῶ ‖ (*fig*) κομπάζω.
crowbar ['krəuba:*] *n* λοστός.
crowd [kraud] *n* πλῆθος, ὄχλος, συρροή ‖ *vt* (*fill*) γεμίζω ‖ *vi* (*flock together*) συνωθοῦμαι, συνωστίζομαι ‖ ~**ed** *a* γιομάτος.
crown [kraun] *n* (*royal headdress*) στέμμα, κορώνα ‖ (*of tooth*) κορώνα, μύλη ‖ (*top of head etc*) κορυφή, κορφή ‖ (*of flowers*) στεφάνι ‖ *vt* (*put crown on*) στεφανώνω ‖ (*be at top of*) πάνω ἀπ'ὅλα, ἀποκορυφώνω ‖ ~ **jewels** *npl* κοσμήματα τοῦ Στέμματος ‖ ~ **prince** *n* διάδοχος τοῦ θρόνου.
crucial ['kru:ʃəl] *a* ἀποφασιστικός, κρίσιμος.
crucifix ['kru:sifiks] *n* ἐσταυρομένος ‖ ~**ion** *n* σταύρωσις.
crucify ['kru:sifai] *vt* σταυρώνω, βασανίζω.
crude [kru:d] *a* (*unfinished*) ἀκατέργαστος ‖ (*petroleum*) ἀργόν πετρέλαιον ‖ (*harsh*) ὠμός, ἄξεστος ‖ (*humour*) χονδρό χιοῦμορ ‖ ~**ly** *ad* ὠμῶς, χονδρά, πρόστυχα ‖ ~**ness** *n* τραχύτης, σκληρότης ‖ (*of thought*) χοντροκοπιά.
crudity ['kru:diti] *n* = **crudeness** // *see* **crude**.
cruel ['kruəl] *a* (*vicious*) αἱμοβόρος, ἀμείλικτος ‖ (*severe, distressing*) σκληρός, ὠμός ‖ (*hard-hearted*) σκληρόκαρδος ‖ ~**ty** *n* σκληρότης, ἀσπλαγχνία ‖ (*to wife*) κακοποίησις.
cruise [kru:z] *n* περίπλους, κρουαζιέρα ‖ *vi* κάνω κρουαζιέρα, περιπλέω ‖ ~**r** *n* καταδρομικόν.
crumb [krʌm] *n* ψιχίον, ψίχουλο ‖ (*fig*) ἀπομεινάρι.
crumble ['krʌmbl] *vti* καταρρέω, θρυμματίζομαι.
crumbly ['krʌmbli] *a* εὔθρυπτος.
crumpet ['krʌmpit] *n* εἶδος κέϊκ.

crumple ['krʌmpl] vt τσαλακώνω, ζαρώνω.

crunch [krʌntʃ] n δαγκωνιά || (sound) τρίξιμο || vt μασῶ, τραγανίζω || ~y a τραγανιστός.

crusade [kruːˈseid] n σταυροφορία || ~r n σταυροφόρος.

crush [krʌʃ] n σύνθλιψις, συνωστισμός || vt συνθλίβω || (a rebellion) συντρίβω, καταβάλλω || vi (material) τσαλακώνω || ~ing a συντριπτικός.

crust [krʌst] n (of bread) κόρα || (of cake etc) κρούστα || (of earth etc) φλοιός, κρούστα.

crutch [krʌtʃ] n δεκανίκι, πατερίτσα.

crux [krʌks] n οὐσία, κεντρικόν σημεῖον.

cry [krai] vi (sell etc) διαλαλῶ || (shout) φωνάζω, βάζω τίς φωνές || (weep) κλαίω, θρηνῶ || n φωνή, κλάμα || ~ing a ἐπείγων, κραυγαλέα.

crypt [kript] n κρύπτη.

cryptic ['kriptik] a μυστικός, δυσνόητος.

crystal ['kristl] n (natural form) κρύσταλλος || (clear glass) κρύσταλλον || ~-clear a κρυστάλλινος || ~lize vti (lit) (ἀπο)κρυσταλλώνω || (fig) (ἀπο)κρυσταλλοῦμαι.

cub [kʌb] n νεογνόν ζῶον.

cube [kjuːb] n (figure) κύβος.

cubic ['kjuːbik] a κυβικός.

cubicle ['kjuːbikəl] n θαλαμίσκος.

cubism ['kjuːbizəm] n κυβισμός.

cuckoo ['kuːkuː] n κοῦκος || (fig) χαζός || ~ clock n ρολόϊ κούκου.

cucumber ['kjuːkʌmbə*] n ἀγγούρι.

cuddle ['kʌdl] vti ἀγκαλιάζω, κουκουλώνομαι || n ἀγκάλιασμα.

cue [kjuː] n (hint) νύξι, ὑπαινιγμός || (in billiards) στέκα.

cuff [kʌf] n (of shirt, coat etc) μανικέτι || (US) ~ turnup || ~link n μανικετόκουμπα.

cuisine [kwiˈziːn] n μαγειρική.

cul-de-sac ['kʌldəˈsæk] n ἀδιέξοδον.

culinary ['kʌlinəri] a μαγειρικός.

culminate ['kʌlmineit] vi ἀποκορυφώνομαι, μεσουρανῶ.

culmination [kʌlmiˈneiʃən] n μεσουράνημα, κολοφών.

culprit ['kʌlprit] n ἔνοχος.

cult [kʌlt] n (religious) λατρεία || (mode) μόδα, λόξα.

cultivate ['kʌltiveit] vt καλλιεργῶ || ~d a καλλιεργημένος.

cultivation [kʌltiˈveiʃən] n καλλιέργεια.

cultural ['kʌltʃərəl] a πνευματικός, μορφωτικός.

culture ['kʌltʃə*] n (refinement) καλλιέργεια || (intellectual development) ἀνάπτυξις, κουλτούρα || ~d a μορφωμένος, καλλιεργημένος.

cumbersome ['kʌmbəsəm] a ἐνοχλητικός, βαρύς, δυσκίνητος.

cumulative ['kjuːmjulətiv] a ἐπισωρευτικός, ἀθροιστικός.

cunning ['kʌniŋ] n πανουργία, καπατσοσύνη || a πονηρός, τετραπέρατος.

cup [kʌp] n κούπα, φλυτζάνι || (prize) κύπελλον || ~board ['kʌbəd] n ντουλάπι, ἀρμάρι || ~ful n τελικός (πρωταθλήματος) || ~ful n φλυτζανιά.

Cupid ['kjuːpid] n ῏Ερως.

cupola ['kjuːpələ] n θόλος, τροῦλλος.

cup-tie ['kʌptai] n ἡμιτελικός (ἀγών).

curable ['kjuərəbl] a ἰάσιμος, πού γιατρεύεται.

curator [kjuəˈreitə*] n ἔφορος (μουσείου).

curb [kəːb] vt χαλιναγωγῶ, ἐλέγχω || n χαλινός, φραγμός || βλ καί kerb(stone).

curfew ['kəːfjuː] n σβέσις φώτων.

curiosity [kjuəriˈɔsiti] n περιέργεια || (strange object) περίεργον ἀντικείμενον.

curious ['kjuəriəs] a (φιλο)περίεργος || (strange) περίεργος, παράξενος || ~ly ad περιέργως.

curl [kəːl] n βόστρυχος, μπούκλα || (of lips etc) στρίψιμο || vti (hair etc) σγουραίνω || (lips) στρίβω, στραβώνω || (wrap) τυλίγω || ~er n ρολό, μπικουτί.

curlew ['kəːluː] n νουμήνιος.

curling ['kəːliŋ] n κατσάρωμα.

curly ['kəːli] a κατσαρός, σγουρός.

currant ['kʌrənt] n Κορινθιακή σταφίς.

currency ['kʌrənsi] n νόμισμα, κυκλοφοροῦν νόμισμα || (of ideas) κυκλοφορία, πέραση.

current ['kʌrənt] n ρεῦμα, ροή, ρέμα || a κυκλοφορῶν, ἐν χρήσει || ~ account n τρέχων λογαριασμός || ~ affairs npl ἐπίκαιρα || ~ly ad γενικῶς, κοινῶς.

curriculum [kəˈrikjuləm] n κύκλος μαθημάτων || ~ vitae n περίληψις προσόντων.

curry ['kʌri] n κάρρι || ~ powder n σκόνη κάρρι.

curse [kəːs] vi βλαστημῶ, ὑβρίζω || vt καταριέμαι, ἀναθεματίζω || n κατάρα, ἀνάθεμα || (bad language) βλαστημιά.

cursory ['kəːsəri] a γρήγορος, βιαστικός.

curt [kəːt] a ἀπότομος, κοφτός.

curtail [kəːˈteil] vt περικόπτω, περιορίζω.

curtain ['kəːtn] n (esp at window) κουρτίνα || (theat) αὐλαία, παραπέτασμα.

curtsy ['kəːtsi] n ὑπόκλισις || vi κάνω ὑπόκλισιν.

curve [kəːv] n καμπή.

cushion ['kuʃən] n μαξιλαράκι.

custard ['kʌstəd] n ψημένη κρέμα.

custodian [kʌsˈtəudiən] n φύλακας, ἐπιστάτης.

custody ['kʌstədi] n ἐπιτήρησις, κηδεμονία || (under arrest) κράτησις.

custom ['kʌstəm] n (fashion) ἔθιμον, συνήθεια || (business) πελατεία || ~s n (taxes) δασμοί || C~s n (place) τελωνεῖον || ~ary a ἐθιμικόν, συνήθης || ~er n πελάτης || ~-made n συνώνυμο ἐπί παραγγελία || ~s officer n τελωνειακός ὑπάλληλος.

cut [kʌt] vt (irreg v) (divide) κόβω, χαράζω

‖ *(wound)* πληγώνω, πονῶ ‖ *(reduce)* κατεβάζω (τιμές) ‖ *n (sharp stroke)* κόψις, κόψιμο ‖ *(wound)* τομή, κόψιμο, πληγή ‖ *(reduction)* περικοπή, μείωσις ‖ *(share)* μερίδιον.

cute [kju:t] *a* χαριτωμένος.

cuticle ['kju:tikl] *n (on nail)* ἐπιδερμίς.

cutlery ['kʌtləri] *n* μαχαιροπήρουνα.

cutlet ['kʌtlit] *n* κοτολέττα.

cutout ['kʌtaut] *n (elec)* διακόπτης.

cut-price ['kʌtprais] *a* τιμή ἠλαττωμένη.

cutting ['kʌtiŋ] *n* αἰχμή, κόψη.

cyanide ['saiənaid] *n* κυανίδη.

cybernetics [saibə'netiks] *n* κυβερνητική.

cyclamen ['sikləmən] *n* κυκλάμινον.

cycle ['saikl] *n (bicycle)* ποδήλατον ‖ *(series)* κύκλος, περίοδος ‖ *(of poems etc)* κύκλος ‖ *vi* πηγαίνω μέ ποδήλατο.

cycling ['saikliŋ] *n* ποδηλατοδρομία, ποδήλατο.

cyclist ['saiklist] *n* ποδηλατιστής.

cyclone ['saikləun] *n* κυκλών.

cygnet ['signit] *n* μικρός κύκνος.

cylinder ['silində*] *n* κύλινδρος ‖ *(of gas etc)* φιάλη, μπουκάλα ‖ ~ **block** *n* συγκρότημα κυλίνδρου ‖ ~ **capacity** *n* ὄγκος κυλίνδρου ‖ ~ **head** *n* κεφαλή κυλίνδρου.

cymbals ['simbəlz] *npl* κύμβαλα.

cynic ['sinik] *n* κυνικός ‖ ~ **al** *a* κυνικός, δύσπιστος ‖ ~ **ism** ['sinisizəm] *n* κυνισμός, χονδροκουβέντα.

cypress ['saipris] *n* κυπαρίσσι.

Cyprus ['saiprəs] *n* Κύπρος.

cyst [sist] *n* κύστις.

czar [za:*] *n* τσάρος ‖ ~ **ina** *n* τσαρίνα.

Czech [tʃek] *a* Τσεχικός ‖ *n* Τσέχος ‖ ~ **oslovakia** *n* Τσεχοσλοβακία.

D, d

dab [dæb] *vt* ἐπιψαύω, ἐπαλείφω ‖ *n (tap)* ἐλαφρό κτύπημα, φάπα ‖ *(smear)* μικρή ποσότης, λίγο.

dad(dy) ['dæd(i)] *n* μπαμπάς, μπαμπάκας ‖ **daddy-long-legs** *n* τιπούλη, ἀλογατάκι.

daffodil ['dæfədil] *n* ἀσφόδελος.

daft [da:ft] *a* ἀνόητος, τρελλός.

dagger ['dægə*] *n* ἐγχειρίδιον, στιλέττο.

dahlia ['deiliə] *n* ντάλια.

daily ['deili] *a* ἡμερήσιος ‖ *n* καθημερινή (ἐφημερίς).

dainty ['deinti] *a* κομψός, νόστιμος.

dairy ['deəri] *n (shop)* γαλακτοπωλεῖον, γαλατάδικο ‖ *(on farm)* γαλακτοκομεῖον ‖ *a* γαλακτοκομικός.

daisy ['deizi] *n* μαργαρίτα.

dally ['dæli] *vi* χασομερῶ.

dam [dæm] *n (for water)* φράγμα, ἀνάχωμα ‖ *vt* φράσσω.

damage ['dæmidʒ] *n* βλάβη, ζημιά ‖ *vt*

βλάπτω, ζημιώνω ‖ ~ **s** *npl (law)* ἀποζημιώσις.

dame [deim] *n* κυρία, κυρά.

damn [dæm] *vt* καταδικάζω ‖ *a (col)* διαβολο- ‖ ~ it! νά πάρη ὁ διάβολος!, νά πάρη ἡ εὐχή! ‖ ~ **ing** *a* καταδικαστικός, ἐπιβαρυντικός.

damp [dæmp] *a* ὑγρός, νοτερός ‖ *n* ὑγρασία, ὑγρότης ‖ *vt (also* ~ **en)** ὑγραίνω, μουσκεύω ‖ *(discourage)* μειώνω, ἐλαττώνω, κόβω ‖ ~ **ness** *n* ὑγρασία, ὑγρότης.

damson ['dæmzən] *n* δαμάσκηνον.

dance [da:ns] *n* χορός ‖ *(party)* χορευτική συγκέντρωσις, πάρτυ ‖ *vi* χορεύω ‖ ~ **hall** *n* χορευτικόν κέντρον ‖ ~ **r** *n* χορευτής, χορεύτρια.

dancing ['da:nsiŋ] *n* χορός.

dandelion ['dændilaiən] *n* ἀγριοραδίκι.

dandruff ['dændrəf] *n* πιτυρίδα.

dandy ['dændi] *n* κομψευόμενος, δανδής.

Dane [dein] *n* Δανός.

danger ['deindʒə*] *n* κίνδυνος ‖ ~ ! *(sign)* προσοχή! ‖ **in** ~ διατρέχω κίνδυνον ‖ ~ **ous** *a* ἐπικίνδυνος ‖ ~ **ously** *ad* ἐπικινδύνως.

dangle ['dæŋgl] *vti* αἰωροῦμαι, ταλαντεύομαι, κρέμομαι.

Danish ['deiniʃ] *a* Δανικός ‖ *n* Δανική γλώσσα.

dare [dɛə*] *vt* τολμῶ, ἀψηφῶ ‖ *vi*: **to** ~ **(to) do sth** τολμῶ, κοτῶ ‖ **I** ~ **say** ἀσφαλῶς, πιθανῶς.

daring ['dɛəriŋ] *a* τολμηρός, ἄφοβος.

dark [da:k] *a (dim)* σκοτεινός, μαῦρος ‖ *(gloomy)* σκοτεινός, μελαγχολικός ‖ *(colour)* μελαχροινός, μελαψός ‖ *n* σκοτάδι ‖ *(ignorance)* ἐν πλήρει ἀγνοία ‖ **after** ~ ἀφοῦ νυχτώσει ‖ **D** ~ **Ages** *npl* Μεσαίων ‖ ~ **en** *vti* σκοτεινιάζω ‖ ~ **ness** *n* σκότος, σκοτάδι ‖ ~ **room** *n* σκοτεινός θάλαμος.

darling ['da:liŋ] *n* πολυαγαπημένος.

darn [da:n] *n* μαντάρισμα ‖ *vt* μπαλώνω, καρικώνω.

dart [da:t] *n (quick move)* ὁρμή ‖ *(weapon)* βέλος, σαΐτα ‖ *vi* ἐξακοντίζω, ὁρμῶ ‖ ~ **s** *n* σαΐτα ‖ ~ **board** *n* στόχος σαΐτας.

dash [dæʃ] *n (rush)* ἐξόρμησις ‖ *(waves)* χτύπημα, πλάτς ‖ *(mark)* παῦλα ‖ *vt (lit)* ρίχνω, χτυπῶ, καταστρέφω ‖ *vi* ἐφορμῶ, πέφτω ‖ ~ **board** *n* ταμπλώ ‖ ~ **ing** *a (person)* ὁρμητικός, ζωηρός.

data ['deitə] *npl* δεδομένα, στοιχεῖα ‖ ~ **processing** *n* κατεργασία στοιχείων.

date [deit] *n (point in time)* χρονολογία, ἡμερομηνία ‖ *(with person)* ραντεβοῦ ‖ *(fruit)* χουρμᾶς ‖ *vt (letter etc)* βάζω ἡμερομηνία ‖ *(person)* δίνω ραντεβοῦ ‖ ~ **d** *a* μέ χρονολογίαν . . . ‖ ~ **-line** *n* γραμμή ἀλλαγῆς ἡμερομηνίας.

dative ['deitiv] *a* δοτική.

daub [dɔ:b] *vt (smear)* πασαλείβω, ἀλείφω ‖ *(paint badly)* μουντζουρώνω.

daughter ['dɔ:tə*] *n* θυγατέρα, κόρη ‖ ~ **-in-law** *n* νύφη.

dawdle ['dɔ:dl] *vi* χασομερῶ, κοπροσκυλιάζω.

dawn [dɔ:n] *n* αὐγή ‖ *vi* ὑποφώσκω, χαράζω ‖ (*become apparent*) ἀποκαλύπτω.

day [dei] *n* ἡμέρα, μέρα ‖ (*24 hours*) εἰκοσιτετράωρον ‖ (*date, time*) ἡμερομηνία ‖ (*daylight*) φῶς τῆς ἡμέρας ‖ ~ **by** ~ ἡμέρα μέ τήν ἡμέρα ‖ ~ **break** *n* αὐγή, χάραμα ‖ ~ **dream** *n* ὀνειροπόλημα, ρεμβασμός ‖ *vi* ὀνειροπολῶ, ρεμβάζω ‖ ~ **light** *n* φῶς τῆς ἡμέρας ‖ ~ **time** *n* ἡμέρα.

daze [deiz] *vt* θαμπώνω, γυαλίζω ‖ *n* θάμβος, ζάλη.

dazzle ['dæzl] *vt* θαμπώνω, τυφλώνω ‖ *n* θάμβωμα, θάμβος.

deacon ['di:kən] *n* διάκονος.

dead [ded] *a* νεκρός, πεθαμένος ‖ (*without feeling*) ἀναίσθητος ‖ (*exact*) πλήρης, ἀκριβής ‖ *ad* τελείως, ἀκριβῶς, ἀπολύτως ‖ **the** ~ *npl* οἱ νεκροί, οἱ πεθαμένοι ‖ ~ **en** *vt* νεκρώνω, κατασιγάζω ‖ ~ **end** *n* ἀδιέξοδον ‖ ~ **heat** *n* ἰσοπαλία ‖ ~ **line** *n* (χρονικόν) ὅριον ‖ ~ **lock** *n* ἀδιέξοδον ‖ ~ **ly** *a* θανατηφόρος, θανάσιμος ‖ ἀδυσώπητος, ἀφόρητος ‖ ~ **pan** *a* (ἠθοποιός) χωρίς ἔκφρασιν ‖ ~ **wood** *n* (*fig*) ἄχρηστος, χαραμοφάης.

deaf [def] *a* κουφός ‖ ~ **-aid** *n* ἀκουστικόν κωφῶν ‖ ~ **en** *vt* (ξε)κουφαίνω ‖ ~ **ening** *a* ἐκκωφαντικός ‖ ~ **ness** *n* κωφότης, κουφαμάρα ‖ ~ **-mute** *n* κωφάλαλος.

deal [di:l] (*irreg v*) *n* συμφωνία, δουλειά ‖ *vti* (*cards*) μοιράζω, δίνω ‖ **a great** ~ **of** ποσότης, πολύ ‖ **to** ~ **with** *vt* ἀντιμετωπίζω, λαμβάνω μέτρα ‖ ~ **er** *n* ἔμπορος, ἀντιπρόσωπος ‖ (*cards*) μοιραστής.

dear [diə*] *a* (*beloved*) ἀγαπητός, προσφιλής ‖ (*expensive*) ἀκριβός, δαπανηρός ‖ *n* προσφιλής, ἀγαπημένος ‖ ~ **me**! Θεέ μου! ‖ **D** ~ **Sir** ἀξιότιμε, ἀγαπητέ κύριε ‖ **D** ~ **John** ἀγαπητέ Γιάννη ‖ ~ **ly** *ad* (*love*) πολυαγαπημένος ‖ (*pay*) ἀκριβά.

death [deθ] *n* θάνατος ‖ ~ **bed** *n* νεκροκρέββατο ‖ ~ **certificate** *n* πιστοποιητικόν θανάτου ‖ ~ **duties** *npl* (*Brit*) φόρος κληρονομίας ‖ ~ **ly** *a* νεκρικός, ὠχρός ‖ ~ **penalty** *n* ποινή θανάτου ‖ ~ **rate** *n* θνησιμότης.

debase [di'beis] *vt* ξεφτελίζω, ὑποβιβάζω.

debatable [di'beitəbl] *a* συζητήσιμος.

debate [di'beit] *n* συζήτησις ‖ *vt* συζητῶ ‖ (*consider*) σκέπτομαι.

debauched [di'bɔ:tʃt] *a* διεφθαρμένος, ἀκόλαστος.

debauchery [di'bɔ:tʃəri] *n* ἀκολασία.

debit ['debit] *n* δοῦναι, παθητικόν ‖ *vt* χρεώνω.

debris ['debri:] *n* συντρίμματα, μπάζα.

debt [det] *n* χρέος, ὀφειλή ‖ **to be in** ~ χρεωστῶ ‖ ~ **or** *n* ὀφειλέτης, χρεώστης.

début ['deibu:] *n* πρώτη ἐμφάνισις, ντεμποῦτο.

decade ['dekeid] *n* δεκαετία.

decadence ['dekədəns] *n* παρακμή.

decanter [di'kæntə*] *n* καράφα.

decay [di'kei] *n* παρακμή, φθορά, κατάπτωσις ‖ *vi* παρακμάζω, μαραίνομαι.

decease [di'si:s] *n* θάνατος ‖ ~ **d** *n* μακαρίτης.

deceit [di'si:t] *n* ἀπάτη, δόλος ‖ ~ **ful** *a* δόλιος, ἀπατηλός.

deceive [di'si:v] *vt* ἐξαπατῶ, ἀπατῶ.

decelerate [di:'seləreit] *vti* ἐπιβραδύνω, κόβω ταχύτητα.

December [di'sembə*] *n* Δεκέμβρης.

decency ['di:sənsi] *n* (*fit behaviour*) εὐπρέπεια, σεμνότης ‖ (*respectability*) κοσμιότης.

decent ['di:sənt] *a* (*respectable*) εὐπρεπής, συμμαζεμένος ‖ (*pleasant*) ἀρκετό καλό.

decentralization [di:sentrəlai'zeiʃən] *n* ἀποκέντρωσις.

deception [di'sepʃən] *n* ἐξαπάτησις, τέχνασμα.

deceptive [di'septiv] *a* ἀπατηλός.

decibel ['desibel] *n* ντεσιμπέλ.

decide [di'said] *vt* (*settle*) κρίνω, ἀποφασίζω ‖ *vi* (*determine*) ἀποφασίζω, καταλήγω ‖ **to** ~ **to do** ἀποφασίζω ‖ ~ **d** *a* ἀποφασισμένος, ὁριστικός ‖ ~ **dly** *ad* ἀποφασιστικά, βεβαίως.

deciduous [di'sidjuəs] *a* φυλλοβόλος.

decimal ['desiməl] *a* δεκαδικός ‖ *n* δεκαδικόν ‖ ~ **point** *n* ὑποδιαστολή ‖ ~ **system** *n* δεκαδικόν σύστημα.

decimate ['desimeit] *vt* ἀποδεκατίζω.

decipher [di'saifə*] *vt* ξεδιαλύνω, βγάζω.

decision [di'siʒən] *n* ἀπόφασις.

decisive [di'saisiv] *a* ἀποφασιστικός.

deck [dek] *n* (*naut*) κατάστρωμα, κουβέρτα ‖ (*of bus*) ὄροφος ‖ (*of cards*) τράπουλα ‖ ~ **chair** *n* σαίζ-λόγκ ‖ ~ **hand** *n* ναύτης καταστρώματος.

declaration [deklə'reiʃən] *n* δήλωσις, διακήρυξις.

declare [di'kleə*] *vt* (*state*) δηλώνω ‖ (*war*) κηρύσσω ‖ (*in customs*) δηλώνω.

decline [di'klain] *n* (*decay*) παρακμή, πτῶσις, πέσιμο ‖ (*lessening*) πέσιμο, κατάπτωση ‖ *vt* (*refuse*) ἀρνοῦμαι ‖ (*gram*) κλίνω ‖ *vi* φθίνω, ἐξασθενίζω, ἀδυνατίζω.

declutch ['di:'klʌtʃ] *vi* ντεμπραγιάρω.

decode ['di:'kəud] *vt* ἀποκρυπτογραφῶ.

decompose [di:kəm'pəuz] *vi* (*rot*) ἀποσυντίθεμαι, σαπίζω.

decomposition [di:kɔmpə'ziʃən] *n* ἀποσύνθεσις.

decontaminate [di:kən'tæmineit] *vt* ἀπολυμαίνω.

décor ['deikɔ:*] *n* διακόσμησις, ντεκόρ.

decorate ['dekəreit] *vt* (*renew paint etc*) χρωματίζω, βάφω ‖ (*adorn*) (δια)κοσμῶ,

στολίζω ‖ (*give medal etc*) παρασημο-
φορώ.
decoration [dekə'reiʃən] *n* (*of house*) διακόσμησις ‖ παράσημον.
decorative ['dekərətiv] *a* διακοσμητικός.
decorator ['dekəreitə*] *n* διακοσμητής.
decorum [di'kɔːrəm] *n* εὐπρέπεια.
decoy ['diːkɔi] *n* δέλεαρ, δόλωμα.
decrease [diː'kriːs] *n* μείωσις, ἐλάττωσις ‖
vti μειώνω, ἐλαττοῦμαι.
decree [di'kriː] *n* διάταγμα, βούλευμα.
decrepit [di'krepit] *a* παραγηρασμένος ‖
(*furniture etc*) ἐξαρβαλωμένος.
dedicate ['dedikeit] *vt* ἀφιερώνω.
dedication [dedi'keiʃən] *n* ἀφιέρωσις.
deduce [di'djuːs] *vt* συμπεραίνω.
deduct [di'dʌkt] *vt* ἀφαιρῶ ‖ ~**ion** *n* ἀφαίρεσις, συμπέρασμα ‖ (*in price etc*)
ἔκπτωσις.
deed [diːd] *n* πρᾶξις, ἔργον ‖ (*law*) ἔγγραφον.
deep [diːp] *a* (*water*) βαθύς ‖ (*breath*) βαθειά
‖ (*voice*) βαθειά, βαρειά ‖ **in** ~ **water** εἰς
μεγάλην δυσκολίαν ‖ ~**en** *vt* ἐκβαθύνω,
βαθαίνω ‖ ~**-freeze** *n* κατάψυξις ‖
~**-seated** *a* βαθειά ριζωμένος.
deer [diə*] *n* ἐλάφι.
deface [di'feis] *vt* παραμορφώνω.
defamation [defə'meiʃən] *n* δυσφήμησις.
default [di'fɔːlt] *n* παράλειψις, ἀθέτησις ‖
(*law*) ἀπουσία ‖ *vi* παραλείπω καθῆκον,
φυγοδικῶ ‖ **by** ~ ἐρήμην ‖ ~**er** *n* φυγόδικος.
defeat [di'fiːt] *n* (*overthrow*) ἀνατροπή,
ματαίωσις ‖ ἦττα, συντριβή ‖ *vt* νικῶ,
ἀνατρέπω ‖ ~**ist** *a* ἡττοπαθής.
defect ['diːfekt] *n* ἀτέλεια, ἐλάττωμα ‖
[di'fekt] *vi* λιποτακτῶ ‖ ~**ive** a ἐλλιπής,
ἐλαττωματικός.
defence [di'fens] *n* (*mil*, *sport*) ἄμυνα,
ὑπεράσπισις ‖ δικαιολογία ‖ ~**less** *a*
ἀνυπεράσπιστος.
defend [di'fend] *vt* ὑπερασπίζω ‖ ~**ant** *n*
ἐναγόμενος ‖ ~**er** *n* ὑπερασπιστής,
ὑπέρμαχος.
defensive [di'fensiv] *a* ἀμυντικός ‖ *n* ἄμυνα.
defer [di'fəː*] *vt* ἀναβάλλω ‖ ~**ence**
['defərəns] *n* σεβασμός ‖ ~**ential**
[defə'renʃəl] *a* εὐλαβής, πλήρης σεβα-
σμοῦ.
defiance [di'faiəns] *n* ἀψηφισιά, περιφρόνησις.
defiant [di'faiənt] *a* προκλητικός, ἀψηφῶν.
deficiency [di'fiʃənsi] *n* ἔλλειψις, ἀτέλεια.
deficient [di'fiʃənt] *a* ἀτελής, ἐλλιπής.
deficit ['defisit] *n* ἔλλειψμα.
define [di'fain] *vt* (καθ)ορίζω ‖ (*explain*)
ἐξηγῶ, καθορίζω.
definite ['definit] *a* (*fixed*) (καθ)ωρισμένος
‖ (*clear*) σαφής ‖ (*gram*) ὁριστικόν ‖ ~**ly**
ad σαφῶς, ὁριστικῶς.
definition [defi'niʃən] *n* (καθ)ορισμός.
definitive [di'finitiv] *a* ὁριστικός, τελικός.

deflate [diː'fleit] *vt* ξεφουσκώνω ‖ (*currency*) ὑποτιμῶ.
deflation [diː'fleiʃən] *n* (*fin*) ὑποτίμησις.
deflect [di'flekt] *vt* ἐκτρέπω, παρεκκλίνω.
deform [di'fɔːm] *vt* παραμορφώνω, ἀσχημίζω ‖ ~**ed** *a* δύσμορφος, παραμορφωμένος ‖ ~**ity** *n* δυσμορφία, ἀσκατηλίκι.
defraud [di'frɔːd] *vt* ἐξαπατῶ, κλέβω.
defray [di'frei] *vt* πληρώνω, καταβάλλω.
defrost [di'frɔst] *vt* (*fridge*) ξεπαγώνω.
deft [deft] *a* ἐπιτήδειος, ἐπιδέξιος.
defunct [di'fʌŋkt] *a* μακαρίτης.
defy [di'fai] *vt* (*challenge*) προκαλῶ ‖
(*ignore*) ἀψηφῶ.
degenerate [di'dʒenəreit] *vi* ἐκφυλίζομαι ‖
[di'dʒenərit] *a* ἐκφυλισμένος.
degradation [degrə'deiʃən] *n* ξεφτελισμός,
ὑποβιβασμός.
degrading [di'greidiŋ] *a* ξεφτελιστικός,
ταπεινωτικός.
degree [di'griː] *n* (*step*, *stage*) βαθμός ‖
(*univ*) πτυχίον ‖ (*measurement*) μοῖρα ‖
by ~**s** βαθμηδόν.
dehydrated [diːhai'dreitid] *a* ἀφυδατω-
μένος.
de-ice [diː'ais] *vt* (*windscreen*) ξεπαγώνω.
deign [dein] *vi* καταδέχομαι, εὐαρεστοῦμαι.
deity ['diːiti] *n* θεότης.
dejected [di'dʒektid] *a* κατηφής, ἄκεφος.
dejection [di'dʒekʃən] *n* κατήφεια, ἀκεφιά.
delay [di'lei] *vt* ἀναβάλλω, καθυστερῶ ‖
vi βραδύνω, ἀργῶ ‖ *n* ἀργοπορία, ἀναβολή, ἐπιβράδυνσις ‖ **without** ~ ἄνευ
ἀναβολῆς ‖ ~**ed action** *n* ἐπιβραδυνο-
μένη, καθυστερημένη.
delegate ['deligit] *n* ἀντιπρόσωπος, ἀπεσταλμένος ‖ ['deligeit] *vt* ἐντέλλομαι,
ἐξουσιοδοτῶ.
delegation [deli'geiʃən] *n* ἀντιπροσωπεία.
delete [di'liːt] *vt* ἀφαιρῶ, σβήνω.
deliberate [di'libərit] *a* (*intentional*) ἐσκεμμένος ‖ (*slow*) ἀργός, ἐπιφυλακτικός ‖
[di'libəreit] *vi* διαλογίζομαι, συνδι-
ασκέπτομαι ‖ ~**ly** *ad* ἐσκεμμένως.
delicacy ['delikəsi] *n* (*daintiness*) εὐαισθησία, λεπτότης ‖ (*refinement*) λεπτότης ‖
(*choice food*) λιχουδιές.
delicate ['delikit] *a* (*fine*) λεπτός, ἁπαλός ‖
(*fragile*) λεπτός ‖ (*situation*) λεπτός,
δύσκολος ‖ (*med*) λεπτή, εὐπαθής ‖ ~**ly**
ad μέ λεπτότητα.
delicious [di'liʃəs] *a* νόστιμος, εὐχάριστος.
delight [di'lait] *n* εὐχαρίστησις, τέρψις ‖
vt χαιροποιῶ, τέρπω ‖ ~**ful** *a* γοητευτικός, πολύ εὐχάριστος.
delinquency [di'liŋkwənsi] *n* πλημμέλημα,
ἀδίκημα.
delinquent [di'liŋkwənt] *n* ἐγκληματίας,
παραπτωματίας ‖ *a* παραπτωματικός ‖
(*econ*) ἐκπρόθεσμος.
delirium [di'liriəm] *n* παραλήρημα.
deliver [di'livə*] *vt* (*distribute*) (παρα)δίδω,
διανέμω ‖ (*pronounce*) ἐκφωνῶ, μεταδίδω

‖ (*free*) ἀπαλλάσσω, ἐλευθερώνω, σῴζω ‖ ~**y** *n* παράδοσις, διανομή ‖ (*of speech*) παράδοσις, ἐκφώνησις.

delouse ['di:'laus] *vt* ξεψειριάζω.

delta ['deltə] *n* δέλτα.

delude [di'lu:d] *vt* ἐξαπατῶ.

deluge ['delju:dʒ] *n* κακακλυσμός.

delusion [di'lu:ʒən] *n* (αὐτ)ἀπάτη.

de luxe [di'lʌks] *a* ντέ λούξ.

demand [di'ma:nd] *vt* ἀπαιτῶ, ἀξιώνω ‖ *n* ἀξίωσις, ἀπαίτησις ‖ (*call for a commodity*) ζήτησις ‖ **in** ~ ζητοῦμαι ‖ **on** ~ ἐπί τῇ ἐμφανίσει ‖ ~**ing** *a* ἀπαιτητικός, διεκδικητικός.

demarcation [di:ma:'keiʃən] *n* ὁροθεσία.

demented [di'mentid] *a* παράφρων, τρελλός.

demi- ['demi] *prefix* ἡμι-.

demise [di'maiz] *n* ἀποβίωσις.

demobilization ['di:məubilai'zeiʃən] *n* ἀποστράτευσις.

democracy [di'mɔkrəsi] *n* δημοκρατία.

democrat ['deməkræt] *n* δημοκράτης ‖ ~**ic** *a* δημοκρατικός ‖ ~**ically** *ad* δημοκρατικῶς.

demolish [di'mɔliʃ] *vt* (*lit*) κατεδαφίζω, κατακρημνίζω ‖ (*fig*) συντρίβω.

demolition [demə'liʃən] *n* κατεδάφισις.

demon ['di:mən] *n* δαίμων.

demonstrate ['demənstreit] *vt* ἀποδεικνύω ‖ (*protest*) διαδηλώνω.

demonstration [demən'streiʃən] *n* ἀπόδειξις, ἐπίδειξις ‖ (*pol*) διαδήλωσις.

demonstrative [di'mɔnstrətiv] *a* ἐκδηλωτικός ‖ (*gram*) δεικτικός.

demonstrator ['demənstreitə*] *n* (*pol*) διαδηλωτής.

demoralize [di'mɔrəlaiz] *vt* ἐξαχρειώνω, ἀποθαρρύνω.

demote [di'məut] *vt* ὑποβιβάζω.

demure [di'mjuə*] *a* σοβαρός, μετριόφρων.

den [den] *n* τρώγλη, φωλιά ‖ (*room*) καμαρούλα.

denationalize [di:'næʃnəlaiz] *vt* ἀπεθνικοποιῶ.

denial [di'naiəl] *n* ἄρνησις.

denigrate ['denigreit] *vt* δυσφημῶ.

Denmark ['denma:k] *n* Δανία.

denomination [dinɔmi'neiʃən] *n* (*name*) ὀνομασία ‖ (*rel*) δόγμα, θρήσκευμα.

denote [di'nəut] *vt* δείχνω, ἐμφαίνω.

denounce [di'nauns] *vt* καταγγέλω.

dense [dens] *a* πυκνός ‖ (*stupid*) βλάκας, ἀμαθής ‖ ~**ly** *ad* πυκνῶς.

density ['densiti] *n* πυκνότης.

dent [dent] *n* κοίλωμα, βαθούλωμα ‖ *vt* κοιλαίνω, ζουλίζω.

dental ['dentl] *a* (*gram*) ὀδοντόφωνος ‖ ~ **surgeon** *n* = **dentist**.

dentist ['dentist] *n* ὀδοντίατρος ‖ ~**ry** *n* ὀδοντιατρική.

denture ['dentʃə*] *n* ὀδοντοστοιχία, μασέλα.

denude [di'nju:d] *vt* ἀπογυμνώνω.

deny [di'nai] *vt* (*declare untrue*) διαψεύδω, ἀρνοῦμαι ‖ (*disown*) ἀπαρνιέμαι, ἀνακαλῶ ‖ (*refuse*) ἀρνοῦμαι.

deodorant [di:'əudərənt] *n* ἀποσμητικόν.

depart [di'pa:t] *vi* ἀναχωρῶ.

department [di'pa:tmənt] *n* τμῆμα, ὑπηρεσία, κλάδος ‖ (*univ, sch*) τμῆμα ‖ (*pol*) διεύθυνσις, γραφεῖον ‖ (*US*) ὑπουργεῖον ‖ ~**al** [di:pa:t'mentl] *a* ὑπηρεσιακός ‖ ~ **store** *n* μεγάλο ἐμπορικό κατάστημα.

departure [di'pa:tʃə*] *n* ἀναχώρησις ‖ **new** ~ *n* νέα τάσις.

depend [di'pend] *vi*: **it** ~**s** ἐξαρτᾶται ‖ **to** ~ **on** *vti* ἐξαρτῶμαι ἀπό ‖ ~**able** *a* ἀξιόπιστος ‖ (*car, machine etc*) ἀξιόπιστου ἀσφαλείας ‖ ~**ent** *n* (*person*) προστατευόμενος ‖ *a* (+*on*) ἐξαρτώμενος ἀπό ‖ ~**ence** *n* ἐξάρτησις ‖ (*trust*) ἐμπιστοσύνη.

depict [di'pikt] *vt* περιγράφω, ἀπεικονίζω.

depleted [di'pli:tid] *a* ἐξηντλημένος.

deplorable [di'plɔ:rəbl] *a* θλιβερός, ἀξιοθρήνητος.

deplore [di'plɔ:*] *vt* θρηνῶ, λυποῦμαι πολύ.

deploy [di'plɔi] *vt* ἀναπτύσσω.

depopulation ['di:pɔpju'leiʃən] *n* ἐλάττωσις πληθυσμοῦ.

deport [di'pɔ:t] *vt* ἐκτοπίζω, ἀπελαύνω ‖ ~**ation** *n* ἀπέλασις, ἐκτοπισμός ‖ ~**ment** *n* συμπεριφορά.

depose [di'pəuz] *vt* ἐκθρονίζω.

deposit [di'pɔzit] *n* κατάθεσις ‖ (*down payment*) προκαταβολή, καπάρο ‖ (*chem*) ἵζημα, κατακάθι ‖ *vt* (*bank*) (παρα)καταθέτω, ἀποταμιεύω ‖ (*place*) τοποθετῶ, βάζω ‖ ~ **account** *n* λογαριασμός καταθέσεως ‖ ~**or** *n* καταθέτης.

depot ['depəu] *n* ἀποθήκη ‖ (*mil*) βάσις ἀνεφοδιασμοῦ ‖ (*US: for buses etc*) σταθμός.

deprave [di'preiv] *vt* διαφθείρω, ἐξαχρειώνω ‖ ~**d** *a* διεφθαρμένος.

depravity [di'præviti] *n* ἀχρειότης, διαφθορά.

depreciate [di'pri:ʃieit] *vt* ὑποτιμῶ ‖ *vi* ὑποτιμοῦμαι, πέρτω.

depreciation [dipri:ʃi'eiʃən] *n* ὑποτίμησις, πέσιμο.

depress [di'pres] *vt* (*make sad*) συντρίβω, ἀποθαρρύνω ‖ (*press down*) καταπιέζω, κατεβάζω ‖ ~**ed** *a* (*person*) μελαγχολικός, ἀποκαρδιωμένος ‖ (*area*) φτωχή (συνοικία), ὑποανάπτυκτος ‖ ~**ing** *a* καταθλιπτικός, ἀποθαρρυντικό ‖ ~**ion** *n* (*econ*) ὕφεσις, κρίσις ‖ (*hollow*) κοίλωμα, λακούβα ‖ (*meteorology*) βαρομετρική ὕφεσις.

deprivation [depri'veiʃən] *n* στέρησις.

deprive [di'praiv] *vt* (+ *of*) στερῶ τοῦ ‖ ~**d** *a* ἐστερημένος.

depth [depθ] *n* βάθος, πυθμήν, βαθύτης ‖ **in the** ~**s of** στήν καρδιά τοῦ.

deputation [depju'teiʃən] *n* ἀποστολή, ἐπιτροπή.

deputize ['depjutaiz] *vi* (+*for*) ἀναπληρῶ, ἀντιπροσωπεύω.

deputy ['depjuti] *a* ἀναπληρωτικός, βοηθητικός ‖ *n* ἀναπληρωτής, ἀντικαταστάτης.

derail [di'reil] *vt* ἐκτροχιάζω ‖ ~ment *n* ἐκτροχίασις.

deranged [di'reindʒd] *a* παράφρων, στριμμένος.

derby ['da:bi] *n* (*US: bowler hat*) ἡμίψηλον, μελόν.

derelict ['derilikt] *a* ἐγκαταλελειμμένος.

deride [di'raid] *vt* χλευάζω, ἐμπαίζω.

derision [di'riʒən] *n* ἐμπαιγμός, χλευασμός.

derisory [di'raisəri] *a* σκωπτικός, εἰρωνικός.

derivation [deri'veiʃən] *n* καταγωγή ‖ (*math etc*) παραγωγή.

derivative [di'rivətiv] *a* παράγωγος.

derive [di'raiv] *vt* παράγω, ἀποκομίζω ‖ *vi* κατάγομαι, παράγομαι.

dermatitis [də:mə'taitis] *n* δερματῖτις.

derogatory [di'rɔgətəri] *a* ξεφτελιστικός, δυσφημιστικός, μειωτικός.

derrick ['derik] *n* γερανός ‖ (*of oil well*) ἰκρίωμα γεωτρήσεως.

desalination [di:sæli'neiʃən] *n* ἀφαλάτωσις.

descend [di'send] *vti* κατεβαίνω ‖ (*rain etc*) πέφτω ‖ *vi*: **to ~ from** κατάγομαι ‖ ~ant *n* ἀπόγονος.

descent [di'sent] *n* (*coming down*) κάθοδος, κατέβασμα ‖ (*origin*) καταγωγή.

describe [dis'kraib] *vt* περιγράφω.

description [dis'kripʃən] *n* περιγραφή ‖ (*kind, sort*) εἶδος, τύπος.

descriptive [dis'kriptiv] *a* περιγραφικός.

desecrate ['desikreit] *vt* βεβηλώνω.

desert ['dezət] *n* ἔρημος ‖ [di'zə:t] *vt* ἐγκαταλείπω ‖ *vi* (*mil*) λιποτακτῶ ‖ ~er *n* λιποτάκτης ‖ ~ion *n* λιποταξία.

deserve [di'zə:v] *vt* ἀξίζω.

deserving [di'zə:viŋ] *a* ἄξιος, ἀξιόλογος.

design [di'zain] *n* (*plan*) σχέδιον, σκοπός, ἐπιδίωξις ‖ (*drawing*) σχέδιον, τύπος ‖ (*the art*) σχέδιον ‖ *vt* (*plan*) σχεδιάζω ‖ (*purpose*) προορίζω ‖ **to have ~s on** ἔχω βλέψεις σέ.

designate ['dezigneit] *vt* (προ)ὁρίζω, διορίζω ‖ ['dezignit] *a* ἐκλεγείς.

designation [dezig'neiʃən] *n* ὁρισμός, τίτλος.

designer [di'zainə*] *n* (*tech*) μελετητής ‖ (*art*) σχεδιαστής.

desirability [dizaiərə'biliti] *n* τό ἐπιθυμητόν.

desirable [di'zaiərəbl] *a* ἐπιθυμητός.

desire [di'zaiə*] *n* ἐπιθυμία, πόθος ‖ *vt* ἐπιθυμῶ, ποθῶ ‖ (*ask for*) ζητῶ.

desk [desk] *n* γραφεῖον ‖ (*of student*) θρανίον.

desolate ['desəlit] *a* (*barren, dismal*) ἔρημος.

desolation [desə'leiʃən] *n* ἐρήμωσις, καταστροφή.

despair [dis'pεə*] *n* ἀπόγνωσις, ἀπελπισία ‖ *vi* (+ *of*) ἀπελπίζομαι διά.

despatch [dis'pætʃ] = **dispatch**.

desperate ['despərit] *a* (*hopeless*) ἀπελπιστικός ‖ (*reckless*) ἀπεγνωσμένος, σκληρός ‖ ~ly *ad* ἀπεγνωσμένως.

desperation [despə'reiʃən] *n* ἀπόγνωσις.

despicable [dis'pikəbl] *a* ἀηδής, σιχαμερός, εὐτελής.

despise [dis'paiz] *vt* περιφρονῶ.

despite [dis'pait] *prep* παρά, εἰς πεῖσμα.

despondent [dis'pɔndənt] *a* ἀπελπισμένος, συντετριμμένος.

dessert [di'zə:t] *n* ἐπιδόρπιον ‖ ~spoon *n* κουταλάκι τοῦ γλυκοῦ.

destination [desti'neiʃən] *n* προορισμός.

destine ['destin] *vt* προορίζω.

destiny ['destini] *n* προορισμός ‖ (*fate*) μοῖρα.

destitute ['destitju:t] *a* ἄπορος.

destroy [dis'trɔi] *vt* καταστρέφω ‖ ~er *n* (*naut*) ἀντιτορπιλλικόν.

destruction [dis'trʌkʃən] *n* καταστροφή.

destructive [dis'trʌktiv] *a* καταστρεπτικός.

detach [di'tætʃ] *vt* ἀποσπῶ, ἀφαιρῶ ‖ ~able *a* ἀφαιρούμενον, κινητός ‖ ~ed *a* (*attitude*) ἀνεμπρέαστος ‖ ~ment *n* (*mil*) ἀπόσπασμα ‖ ἀπόπασις, ἀμεροληψία.

detail ['di:teil] *n* λεπτομέρεια, ἀπόσπασμα ‖ *vt* ἐκθέτω λεπτομερῶς ‖ (*mil*) ὁρίζω, ἀποσπῶ ‖ **in ~** λεπτομερῶς.

detain [di'tein] *vt* κρατῶ, ἐμποδίζω ‖ (*imprison*) φυλακίζω, κρατῶ.

detect [di'tekt] *vt* ἀνακαλύπτω, διακρίνω ‖ ~ion *n* ἀνακάλυψις ‖ ~ive *n* μυστικός ἀστυνομικός, ντετέκτιβ ‖ ~ive story *n* ἀστυνομικόν μυθιστόρημα ‖ ~or *n* ἀνιχνευτής.

detention [di'tenʃən] *n* κράτησις.

deter [di'tə:*] *vt* ἀποτρέπω.

detergent [di'tə:dʒənt] *n* ἀπολυμαντικόν, καθαρτικόν.

deteriorate [di'tiəriəreit] *vi* ἐπιδεινοῦμαι, χειροτερεύω.

deterioration [ditiəriə'reiʃən] *n* ἐπιδείνωσις.

determination [ditə:mi'neiʃən] *n* ἀπόφασις, ἀποφασιστικότης.

determine [di'tə:min] *vt* (κα9)ὁρίζω, ἀποφασίζω ‖ ~d *a* ἀποφασιστικός, ἀποφασισμένος.

deterrent [di'terənt] *n* προληπτικόν ‖ *a* ἀποτρεπτικός.

detest [di'test] *vt* ἀπεχθάνομαι, ἀποστρέφομαι, σιχαίνομαι ‖ ~able *a* ἀπεχθής, σιχαμένος.

detonate ['detəneit] *vti* ἐκρηγνύω, ἐκπυρσοκροτῶ.

detonator ['detəneitə*] *n* ἐπικρουστήρ, πυροκροτητής.

detour ['di:tuə*] *n* ἀπόκλισις, στροφή, λοξοδρόμησις.

detract [di'trækt] *vi* (+*from*) δυσφημῶ, μειώνω.

detriment ['detrimənt] *n*: to the ~ of πρός ζημίαν τοῦ ‖ ~al *a* ἐπιβλαβής, ἐπιζήμιος.
devaluation [divælju'eiʃən] *n* ὑποτίμησις.
devalue ['di:'vælju:] *vt* ὑποτιμῶ.
devastate ['devəsteit] *vt* ἐρημώνω, καταστρέφω.
devastating ['devəsteitiŋ] *a* ἐξολοθρευτικός.
develop [di'veləp] *vt* (*make grow*) ἀναπτύσσω ‖ (*film*) ἐμφανίζω ‖ *vi* (*unfold*) ἀναπτύσσομαι, ἐκδηλοῦμαι ‖ (*grow*) ἀναπτύσσομαι ‖ ~er *n* (*phot*) ἐμφανιστής ‖ ~ing *a* (*country*) ἀναπτυσσομένη ‖ ~ment *n* ἀνάπτυξις.
deviate ['di:vieit] *vi* ἐκτρέπομαι, παρεκκλίνω.
deviation [di:vi'eiʃən] *n* παρέκκλισις.
device [di'vais] *n* ἐπινόημα, τέχνασμα.
devil ['devl] *n* διά(β)ολος, δαίμονας ‖ ~ish *a* διαβολικός.
devious ['diviəs] *a* (*means*) ἔμμεσος, παρεκκλίνων ‖ (*person*) ἀνέντιμος.
devise [di'vaiz] *vt* ἐπινοῶ, μηχανεύομαι.
devoid [di'vɔid] *a*: ~ of ἐστερημένος, ξένοιαστος.
devote [di'vəut] *vt* ἀφιερώνω ‖ ~d *a* ἀφοσιωμένος ‖ ~e *n* λάτρης, ὀπαδός.
devotion [di'vəuʃən] *n* ἀφοσίωσις, λατρεία.
devour [di'vauə*] *vt* καταβροχθίζω.
devout [di'vaut] *a* εὐσεβής, ἔνθερμος.
dew [dju:] *n* δρόσος, δροσιά.
dexterity [deks'teriti] *n* ἐπιδεξιότης.
diabetes [daiə'bi:ti:z] *n* διαβήτης.
diabetic [daiə'betik] *a,n* διαβητικός.
diagnose ['daiəgnəuz] *vt* κάνω διάγνωσιν.
diagnosis [daiəg'nəusis] *n* διάγνωσις.
diagonal [dai'ægənl] *a,n* διαγώνιος.
diagram ['daiəgræm] *n* διάγραμμα, σχέδιον.
dial ['daiəl] *n* (*esp tel*) δίσκος ἐπιλογῆς, καντράν ‖ *vt* καλῶ, παίρνω ἕνα νούμερο ‖ ~ling tone *n* ἔνδειξις ἐλευθέρας γραμμῆς.
dialect ['daiəlekt] *n* διάλεκτος.
dialogue ['daiəlɔg] *n* διάλογος.
diameter [dai'æmitə*] *n* διάμετρος.
diamond ['daiəmənd] *n* διαμάντι ‖ (*cards*) καρρό.
diapers ['daiəpəz] *npl* (*US*) πάνες.
diaphragm ['daiəfræm] *n* διάφραγμα.
diarrhoea [daiə'ri:ə] *n* διάρροια.
diary ['daiəri] *n* ἡμερολόγιον.
dice [dais] *npl* ζάρια ‖ *vt* (*vegetables*) κόβω σέ κύβους.
dictate [dik'teit] *vt* ὑπαγορεύω ‖ (*impose*) ἐπιβάλλω ‖ ['dikteit] *n* πρόσταγμα, διαταγή.
dictation [dik'teiʃən] *n* ὑπαγόρευσις.
dictator [dik'teitə*] *n* δικτάτωρ.
dictatorship [dik'teitəʃip] *n* δικτατορία.
diction ['dikʃən] *n* ὕφος λόγου, λεκτικόν.
dictionary ['dikʃənri] *n* λεξικόν.
did [did] *pt of* do ‖ ~n't = did not ‖ *see* do.

die [dai] *vi* πεθαίνω, τά τινάζω ‖ (*end*) σβήνω ‖ to ~ away *vi* ἐξασθενίζω, σβήνω ‖ to ~ down *vi* ἐξασθενίζω, πέφτω ‖ to ~ out *vi* ἀποθνήσκω, σβήνω.
Diesel ['di:zəl] ~ engine *n* ντῆζελ.
diet ['daiət] *n* (*food*) (δια)τροφή ‖ (*special course*) δίαιτα ‖ *vi* κάνω δίαιτα.
differ ['difə*] *vi* διαφέρω, ξεχωρίζω ‖ (*disagree*) διαφωνῶ ‖ ~ence *n* διαφορά ‖ (*disagreement*) διαφωνία, διαφορά ‖ ~ent *a* διάφορος, διαφορετικός ‖ ~ently *ad* διαφορετικά ‖ ~ential [difə'renʃəl] *n* (*aut*) διαφορικόν ‖ (*wages*) διαφορική ‖ ~entiate *vti* διαφοροποιῶ, ξεχωρίζω.
difficult ['difikəlt] *a* δύσκολος ‖ ~y *n* δυσκολία, δυσχέρεια.
diffidence ['difidəns] *n* ἐπιφυλακτικότης, ντροπαλότης.
diffident ['difidənt] *a* διστακτικός, ντροπαλός.
diffuse [di'fju:s] *a* διάχυτος ‖ [di'fju:z] *vt* διαχέω, σκορπῶ.
dig [dig] (*irreg v*) *vt* (*hole*) σκάβω ‖ (*garden*) σκάβω ‖ (*nails*) μπήζω ‖ (*delve into*) ψάχνω, τρυπῶ ‖ *n* (*prod*) κάρφωμα, πείραγμα ‖ (*arch*) ἐκσκαφή ‖ to ~ up *vt* ἐκσκάπτω, ξερριζώνω, ξεθάβω.
digest [dai'dʒest] *vt* χωνεύω ‖ (*work over*) ἐπεξεργάζομαι ‖ ['daidʒest] *n* περίληψις, σύνοψις ‖ ~ible [di'dʒestəbl] *a* εὐκολοχώνευτος ‖ ~ion *n* χώνευσις.
digit ['didʒit] *n* (*number*) ψηφίον, ἀριθμός ‖ (*toe, finger*) δάκτυλος.
dignified ['dignifaid] *a* ἀξιοπρεπής.
dignify ['dignifai] *vt* τιμῶ, ἐξυψώνω.
dignitary ['dignitəri] *n* ἀξιωματοῦχος.
dignity ['digniti] *n* ἀξιοπρέπεια.
digress [dai'gres] *vi* ἐκτρέπομαι, ξεφεύγω ‖ ~ion *n* ἐκτροπή, παρέκβασις.
digs [digz] *npl* (*Brit col*) δωμάτιο.
dilapidated [di'læpideitid] *a* σαραβαλιασμένος.
dilate [dai'leit] *vti* διαστέλλω, πλαταίνω, διαστέλλομαι.
dilemma [dai'lemə] *n* δίλημμα.
diligence ['dilidʒəns] *n* ἐπιμέλεια.
diligent ['dilidʒənt] *a* ἐπιμελής.
dilute [dai'lu:t] *vt* ἀραιώνω, νερώνω ‖ *a* ἀραιός.
dim [dim] *a* ἀμυδρός, μουντός, σκοτεινός ‖ (*stupid*) κουτός ‖ *vt* χαμηλώνω, θολώνω.
dime [daim] *n* (*US*) δέκατον τοῦ δολλαρίου.
dimension [di'menʃən] *n* διάστασις, ἔκτασις ‖ ~s *npl* διαστάσεις.
diminish [di'miniʃ] *vti* ἐλαττώνω, ἐλαττώνομαι.
diminutive [di'minjutiv] *a* ὑποκοριστικός ‖ *n* ὑποκοριστικόν.
dimly ['dimli] *ad* ἀμυδρῶς, θαμπά.
dimple ['dimpl] *n* λακκάκι, λακκίτσα.
dim-witted ['dim'witid] *a* (*col*) βλάκας.
din [din] *n* θόρυβος, πάταγος.

dine [dain] *vi* γευματίζω, τρώγω ‖ **~r** *n* τραπεζαρία τραίνου ‖ (*person*) γευματίζων.

dinghy ['diŋgi] *n* μικρά λέμβος.

dingo ['diŋgəu] *n* ντίγκο.

dingy ['dindʒi] *a* μαυρισμένος, σκοτεινός.

dining car ['daininŋka:*] *n* βαγκόν-ρεστωράν.

dining room ['daininŋrum] *n* τραπεζαρία.

dinner ['dinə*] *n* γεῦμα, φαΐ ‖ (*public*) ἐπίσημον γεῦμα ‖ **~ jacket** *n* σμόκιν ‖ **~ party** *n* τραπέζι ‖ **~ time** *n* ὥρα φαγητοῦ.

dinosaur ['dainɔ:*] *n* δεινόσαυρος.

diocese ['daiəsis] *n* ἐπισκοπή.

dip [dip] *n* (*slope*) κλίσις, πλαγιά ‖ (*bath*) βουτιά ‖ *vt* ἐμβαπτίζω, βουτῶ ‖ (*aut*) χαμηλώνω ‖ (*flag*) κατεβάζω ‖ *vi* (*slope*) γέρνω, κατηφορίζω, χαμηλώνω.

diphtheria [dif'θiəriə] *n* διφθερῖτις.

diphthong ['difθɒŋ] *n* δίφθογγος.

diploma [di'pləumə] *n* δίπλωμα.

diplomacy [di'pləuməsi] *n* διπλωματία.

diplomat ['dipləmæt] *n* διπλωμάτης ‖ **~ic** *a* διπλωματικός ‖ **~ic corps** *n* διπλωματικόν σῶμα.

dipstick ['dipstik] *n* βυθομετρική ράβδος.

dire [daiə*] *a* καταστρεπτικός, τρομερός, ἔσχατος.

direct [dai'rekt] *a* (*straight*) εὐθύς, ἴσιος ‖ (*immediate*) ἄμεσος ‖ *vt* (*manage*) διευθύνω, διοικῶ ‖ (*aim*) κατευθύνω, δείχνω ‖ ~ **current** *n* συνεχές ρεῦμα ‖ ~ **hit** *n* εὐστοχία ‖ **~ion** [di'rekʃən] *n* (*control*) διεύθυνσις, διαχείρησις ‖ (*of traffic*) ρύθμισις ‖ (*of movement*) κατεύθυνσις, φορά ‖ **~ions** *npl* (*for use*) ὁδηγίες ‖ **~ional** *a* κατά διεύθυνσιν ‖ ~ **ly** *ad* (*in straight line*) εὐθέως, ἴσια ‖ (*at once*) ἀμέσως ‖ **~or** *n* διευθυντής, ὁ γενικός ‖ ~ **ory** *n* (*esp tel*) (τηλεφωνικός) κατάλογος.

dirt [də:t] *n* ἀκαθαρσία, βρωμιά, ρύπος ‖ ~ **road** *n* (*US*) χωματόδρομος ‖ ~ **y** *a* ρυπαρός, λερωμένος, ἀκάθαρτος ‖ (*mean*) βρώμικο, πρόστυχο ‖ *vt* λερώνω, μουντζουρώνω.

dis- [dis] *prefix* ἀπο-, ξε-, ἐξ-, δυσ-, ἀ-, ἀν-.

disability [disə'biliti] *n* ἀνικανότης ‖ (*physical*) ἀναπηρία.

disabled [dis'eibld] *a* ἀνίκανος, σακατεμένος, ἀνάπηρος.

disadvantage [disəd'va:ntidʒ] *n* μειονέκτημα, ἐλάττωμα ‖ (*sell at*) ζημία ‖ **~ous** [disædvə:n'teidʒəs] *a* ἀσύμφορος, δυσμενής.

disagree [disə'gri:] *vi* διαφωνῶ ‖ **to ~ with** *vt* δέν ταιριάζω, δέν πηγαίνω ‖ (*food*) πειράζω ‖ ~ **able** *a* δυσάρεστος, ἀντιπαθής ‖ **~ment** *n* διαφωνία, διάστασις, ἀσυμφωνία.

disallow ['disə'lau] *vt* ἀρνοῦμαι, ἀπορρίπτω, ἀπαγορεύω.

disappear [disə'piə*] *vi* ἐξαφανίζομαι ‖ **~ance** *n* ἐξαφάνισις.

disappoint [disə'pɔint] *vt* ἀπογοητεύω, χαλῶ, στενοχωροῦμαι ‖ **~ing** *a* ἀπογοητευτικός ‖ **~ment** *n* ἀπογοήτευσις, λύπη.

disapproval [disə'pru:vəl] *n* ἀποδοκιμασία.

disapprove [disə'pru:v] *vi* (+*of*) ἀποδοκιμάζω, ἐπικρίνω.

disarm [dis'a:m] *vt* ἀφοπλίζω ‖ **~ament** *n* ἀφοπλισμός.

disaster [di'za:stə*] *n* συμφορά, δυστύχημα.

disastrous [di'za:strəs] *a* ὀλέθριος, καταστρεπτικός.

disband [dis'bænd] *vt* ἀπολύω, διαλύω.

disbelief ['disbə'li:f] *n* δυσπιστία.

disc [disk] *n* δίσκος.

discard [dis'ka:d] *vt* ἀπορρίπτω, ἀφήνω.

disc brake ['diskbreik] *n* δισκόφρενο.

discern [di'sə:n] *vt* διακρίνω, ξεχωρίζω ‖ **~ing** *a* ὀξυδερκής, ἀνοιχτομάτης.

discharge [dis'tʃa:dʒ] *vt* (*unload ship etc*) ξεφορτώνω ‖ (*fire a gun*) πυροβολῶ ‖ (*dismiss*) ἀπολύω ‖ (*mil*) ἀποστρατεύω ‖ (*perform duties*) ἐκτελῶ, ἐκπληρῶ ‖ *n* (*med*) ἀπέκκριμα ‖ (*mil*) ἀποστράτευσις ‖ (*flow*) ἐκκένωσις.

disciple [di'saipl] *n* μαθητής, ὀπαδός.

disciplinary ['disiplinəri] *a* πειθαρχικός.

discipline [disiplin] *n* πειθαρχία ‖ *vt* πειθαρχῶ, τιμωρῶ.

disclaim [dis'kleim] *vt* ἀπαρνοῦμαι.

disclose [dis'kləuz] *vt* ἀποκαλύπτω.

disclosure [dis'kləuʒə*] *n* ἀποκάλυψις, ἐκδήλωσις.

disco ['diskəu] *n abbr of* **discothèque**.

discoloured [dis'kʌləd] *a* ξεβαμμένος, μουντζουρωμένος.

discomfort [dis'kʌmfət] *n* (*uneasiness*) δυσφορία, στενοχωριά ‖ (*lack of comfort*) ἔλλειψις ἀνέσεως, κακουχία.

disconcert [diskən'sə:t] *vt* ταράσσω, συγχύζω.

disconnect ['diskə'nekt] *vt* διασπῶ, διαχωρίζω.

discontent ['diskən'tent] *n* δυσαρέσκεια ‖ **~ed** *a* δυσαρεστημένος.

discontinue ['diskən'tinju:] *vti* διακόπτω, καταργῶ.

discord ['diskɔ:d] *n* (*quarrelling*) διαφωνία, διχόνοια ‖ (*mus*) παραφωνία ‖ **~ant** *a* ἀσύμφωνος, παράφωνος.

discothèque ['diskəutek] *n* ντισκοτέκ.

discount ['diskaunt] *n* ἔκπτωσις, σκόντο ‖ (*bank*) προεξόφλησις, ὑφαίρεσις ‖ [dis'kaunt] *vt* (*disbelieve*) περιφρονῶ, δέν πιστεύω.

discourage [dis'kʌridʒ] *vt* (*take away confidence*) ἀποθαρρύνω ‖ (*disapprove*) ἀποδοκιμάζω, ἀποτρέπω.

discouraging [dis'kʌridʒiŋ] *a* ἀποθαρρυντικός.

discourteous [dis'kə:tiəs] *a* ἀγενής.

discover [dis'kʌvə*] *vt* ἀνακαλύπτω ‖ ~**y** *n* ἀνακάλυψις.

discredit [dis'kredit] *vt* δυσπιστῶ, ὑποτιμῶ.

discreet [dis'kri:t] *a* νουνεχής, διακριτικός ‖ ~**ly** *ad* συνετῶς, ἐπιφυλακτικά.

discrepancy [dis'krepənsi] *n* διαφορά, ἀσυμφωνία.

discretion [dis'kreʃən] *n* (*prudence*) διακριτικότης, σύνεσις ‖ (*right to decide*) βούλησις, φρόνησις.

discriminate [dis'krimineit] *vi* κάνω διάκρισιν, ξεχωρίζω.

discriminating [dis'krimineitiŋ] *a* διακριτικός, μεροληπτικός.

discrimination [diskrimi'neiʃən] *n* διάκρισις, ὀρθοφροσύνη.

discus ['diskəs] *n* δίσκος.

discuss [dis'kʌs] *vt* συζητῶ ‖ ~**ion** *n* συζήτησις.

disdain [dis'dein] *vt* περιφρονῶ ‖ *n* περιφρόνησις ‖ ~**ful** *a* ὑπεροπτικός, περιφρονητικός.

disease [di'zi:z] *n* νόσημα, ἀσθένεια ‖ ~**d** *a* νοσῶν, ἄρρωστος.

disembark [disim'ba:k] *vti* ἀποβιβάζω, ἀποβιβάζομαι.

disenchanted ['disin'tʃa:ntid] *a* ἀπογοητευμένος, ξεμαγεμένος.

disengage [disin'geidʒ] *vt* (*aut*) ἀποσυμπλέκω.

disentangle ['disin'tæŋgl] *vt* διαχωρίζω, ξεμπλέκω.

disfigure [dis'figə*] *vt* παραμορφώνω.

disgrace [dis'greis] *n* (*general*) δυσμένεια ‖ (*thing*) ὄνειδος, ἐντροπή ‖ *vt* ντροπιάζω, ξεφτελίζω ‖ ~**ful** *a* ἐπονείδιστος.

disgruntled [dis'grʌntld] *a* δυσαρεστημένος, κατσουφιασμένος.

disguise [dis'gaiz] *vt* (*change appearance*) μεταμφιέζω ‖ (*hide*) ἀποκρύπτω ‖ *n* μεταμφίεσις, ἀπόκρυψις.

disgust [dis'gʌst] *n* ἀηδία ‖ *vt* ἀηδιάζω ‖ ~**ing** *a* ἀηδιαστικός, σιχαμερός.

dish [diʃ] *n* πιάτο ‖ (*meal*) φαγητό ‖ ~ **up** *vt* παρουσιάζω, σερβίρω ‖ ~**cloth** *n* πιατόπανο.

dishearten [dis'ha:tn] *vt* ἀποθαρρύνω, ἀπελπίζω.

dishevelled [di'ʃevəld] *a* ξεμαλλιασμένος, ἀνακατωμένος.

dishonest [dis'ɔnist] *a* ἀνέντιμος, κακοήθης, πρόστυχος ‖ ~**y** *n* κακοήθεια, ἀτιμία.

dishonour [dis'ɔnə*] *n* αἶσχος, ἀτιμία.

dishwasher ['diʃwɔʃə*] *n* πλυντήριο πιάτων.

disillusion [disi'lu:ʒən] *vt* ἀπογοητεύω.

disinfect [disin'fekt] *vt* ἀπολυμαίνω ‖ ~**ant** *n* ἀπολυμαντικός.

disintegrate [dis'intigreit] *vi* ἀποσυντίθεμαι, θρυμματίζομαι.

disinterested [dis'intristid] *a* ἀμερόληπτος, ἀδιάφορος.

disjointed [dis'dʒɔintid] *a* ἀσυνάρτητος, ἐξηρθρωμένος.

disk [disk] *n* = **disc**.

dislike [dis'laik] *n* ἀντιπάθεια, ἀποστροφή ‖ *vt* ἀντιπαθῶ, ἀπεχθάνομαι.

dislocate ['disləukeit] *vt* (*bone*) ἐξαρθρώνω, στραμπουλίζω ‖ ξεχαρβαλώνω, χαλνῶ.

dislodge [dis'lɔdʒ] *vt* ἐκτοπίζω, ἐκδιώκω.

disloyal ['dis'lɔiəl] *a* ἄπιστος.

dismal ['dizməl] *a* ζοφερός, μελαγχολικός.

dismantle [dis'mæntl] *vt* παροπλίζω, λύω.

dismay [dis'mei] *n* κατάπληξις, φόβος ‖ *vt* (*dishearten*) πτοῶ, φοβίζω, ἀπογοητεύω.

dismiss [dis'mis] *vt* (*discharge*) ἀπολύω, παύω ‖ (*out of mind*) διώχνω, βγάζω ‖ (*send away*) ἀπομακρύνω, διώχνω ‖ (*law*) ἀπορρίπτω, ἀπαλλάσσω ‖ ~**al** *n* ἀπόλυσις, παῦσις.

disobedience [disə'bi:diəns] *n* ἀνυπακοή, παρακοή.

disobedient [disə'bi:diənt] *a* ἀνυπάκουος, πεισματάρης.

disobey ['disə'bei] *vt* παρακούω, παραβαίνω.

disorder [dis'ɔ:də*] *n* (*confusion*) ἀκαταστασία, ἀταξία ‖ (*commotion*) ταραχή, φασαρία ‖ (*med*) διαταραχή.

disorderly [dis'ɔ:dəli] *a* (*untidy*) ἀκατάστατος ‖ (*unruly*) ἄτακτος, ἀπείθαρχος.

disown [dis'əun] *vt* ἀπαρνοῦμαι, ἀποκηρύττω.

disparaging [dis'pæridʒiŋ] *a* δυσφημιστικό.

disparity [dis'pæriti] *n* ἀνισότης, διαφορά.

dispassionate [dis'pæʃnit] *a* ψύχραιμος, ἀμερόληπτος.

dispatch [dis'pætʃ] *vt* (*goods*) στέλνω, διεκπεραιώνω ‖ *n* ἀποστολή, διεκπεραίωσις ‖ (*esp mil*) ἀναφορά, μήνυμα.

dispel [dis'pel] *vt* διασκορπίζω.

dispensary [dis'pensəri] *n* θεραπευτήριον.

dispense [dis'pens] *vt* διανέμω, χορηγῶ ‖ **to ~ with** *vt* κάνω χωρίς.

dispersal [dis'pə:səl] *n* διασκορπισμός.

disperse [dis'pə:s] *vt* διασκορπίζω ‖ *vi* διασκορπίζομαι.

dispirited [dis'piritid] *a* ἀπελπισμένος.

displace [dis'pleis] *vt* ἐκτοπίζω, μετατοπίζω ‖ ~**d person** *n* πρόσφυγας.

display [dis'plei] *n* (*of goods*) ἔκθεσις, ἐπίδειξις ‖ (*of feeling*) ἐκδήλωσις ‖ (*mil*) ἐπίδειξις ‖ *vt* ἐπιδεικνύω, ἐκθέτω.

displease [dis'pli:z] *vt* δυσαρεστῶ.

displeasure [dis'pleʒə*] *n* δυσαρέσκεια.

disposal [dis'pəuzəl] *n* (*of property*) ἐκχώρησις, διάθεσις ‖ **at one's ~** στήν διάθεσι.

dispose [dis'pəuz] **to ~ of** *vt* ἀπαλλάσσομαι, ξεφορτώνομαι.

disposed [dis'pəuzd] *a* διατεθειμένος.

disposition [dispə'ziʃən] *n* (*character*) προδιάθεσι, χαρακτήρ.

disproportionate [disprə'pɔ:ʃnit] *a* δυσανάλογος.

disprove [dis'pru:v] *vt* ἀναιρῶ, ἀνασκευάζω.

dispute [dis'pju:t] *n* ἀμφισβήτησις, φιλονεικία ‖ *vt* ἀμφισβητῶ, διεκδικῶ.

disqualify [dis'kwɔlifai] *vt* (*sport*) ἀποκλείω ǁ καθιστῶ ἀνίκανον.

disregard ['disri'gɑːd] *vt* παραβλέπω, ἀγνοῶ, περιφρονῶ.

disreputable [dis'repjutəbl] *a* ἀνυπόληπτος, κακόφημος.

disrespectful [disris'pektful] *a* ἀσεβής.

disrupt [dis'rʌpt] *vt* διασπῶ, διαλύω ǁ ~ **ion** *n* διάσπασις.

dissatisfaction ['dissætis'fækʃən] *n* δυσαρέσκεια.

dissatisfied ['dis'sætisfaid] *a* δυσαρεστημένος.

dissect [di'sekt] *vt* κατατέμνω, διαμελίζω.

disseminate [di'semineit] *vt* διασπείρω.

dissent [di'sent] *n* διχογνωμία, διαφωνία ǁ *vi* διαφωνῶ.

dissident ['disidənt] *a* διϊστάμενος, διαφωνῶν.

dissimilar ['di'similə*] *a* ἀνόμοιος, διαφορετικός.

dissipate ['disipeit] *vt* (*waste*) σπαταλῶ, ἀσωτεύω ǁ (δια)σκορπίζω ǁ ~ **d** *a* ἔκλυτος, ἀκόλαστος.

dissipation [disi'peiʃən] *n* διασκόρπησις, ἀσωτεία.

dissociate [di'səuʃieit] *vt* ἀποσπῶ, διαχωρίζω, ἀπομακρύνω.

dissolute ['disəluːt] *a* ἄσωτος, ἔκλυτος.

dissolve [di'zɔlv] *vt* διαλύω ǁ *vi* διαλύομαι, λυώνω.

dissuade [di'sweid] *vt* ἀποτρέπω, μεταπείθω.

distance ['distəns] *n* ἀπόστασις, διάστημα ǁ **in the ~** μακρυά.

distant ['distənt] *a* (*far away*) μακρυά, μακρυνός ǁ ἀπομεμακρυσμένος, ἐπιφυλακτικός.

distaste [dis'teist] *n* ἀποστροφή, ἀπέχθεια ǁ ~ **ful** *a* δυσάρεστος, ἀπεχθής.

distemper [dis'tempə*] *n* (*paint*) ἀσβεστόχρωμα ǁ (*disease*) ἀρρώστεια τῶν σκύλων.

distend [dis'tend] *vti* ἐκτείνω, τεντώνω.

distil [dis'til] *vt* ἀποστάζω, διϋλίζω ǁ ~ **lery** *n* ποτοποιεῖον.

distinct [dis'tiŋkt] *a* (*different*) διαφορετικός ǁ (*clear*) εὐδιάκριτος, σαφής ǁ ~ **ion** *n* (*difference*) διαφορά ǁ (*honour etc*) διάκρισις, τιμή ǁ (*medal etc*) παράσημον ǁ ~ **ive** *a* διακριτικός, χαρακτηριστικός ǁ ~ **ly** *ad* εὐδιακρίτως, καθαρά.

distinguish [dis'tiŋgwiʃ] *vt* διακρίνω, ξεχωρίζω, διαφοροποιῶ ǁ ~ **ed** *a* (*eminent*) διακεκριμένος ǁ ~ **ing** *a* χαρακτηριστικός, διακριτικός.

distort [dis'tɔːt] *vt* (*out of shape*) διαστρέφω, στραβώνω ǁ διαστρεβλώνω, παραποιῶ ǁ ~ **ion** *n* παραμόρφωσις, διαστρέβλωσις.

distract [dis'trækt] *vt* ἀποσπῶ, περισπῶ ǁ (*drive mad*) περιπλέκω, τρελλαίνω ǁ ~ **ing** *a* τρομακτικός, ἐνοχλητικός ǁ ~ **ion** *n* (*inattention*) περίσπασις, ἀφηρη-

μάδα ǁ (*distress*) διατάραξις, ἀναστάτωσις ǁ (*diversion*) διασκέδασις.

distraught [dis'trɔːt] *a* ταραγμένος, συγχυσμένος.

distress [dis'tres] *n* (*grief*) ἀπελπισία, ἀγωνία, πίκρα ǁ (*suffering*) ἀθλιότης, δυστυχία ǁ (*difficulty*) κίνδυνος, σέ δύσκολη θέσι ǁ *vt* θλίβω, στενοχωρῶ ǁ ~ **ing** *a* δυσάρεστος, ὀδυνηρός ǁ ~ **signal** *n* σῆμα κινδύνου.

distribute [dis'tribjuːt] *vt* (*give out*) διανέμω, μοιράζω ǁ (*spread*) ἐξαπλώνω.

distribution [distri'bjuːʃən] *n* διανομή, κατανομή.

distributor [dis'tribjutə*] *n* (*one who distributes*) διανομεύς, ἀντιπρόσωπος ǁ (*aut etc*) διανομεύς.

district ['distrikt] *n* (*of country*) περιοχή, περιφέρεια ǁ (*of town*) συνοικία ǁ ~ **attorney** *n* (*US*) εἰσαγγελεύς ǁ ~ **nurse** *n* (*Brit*) ἐπισκέπτρια νοσοκόμος.

distrust [dis'trʌst] *n* δυσπιστία, ὑποψία ǁ *vt* δυσπιστῶ πρός, ὑποπτεύομαι.

disturb [dis'təːb] *vt* (*upset*) ταράσσω, ἐνοχλῶ ǁ (*agitate*) ταράσσω, κλονίζω ǁ ~ **ance** *n* διατάραξις, φασαρία ǁ ~ **ing** *a* ἐνοχλητικός, ἀνησυχητικός.

disused ['dis'juːzd] *a* ἀχρηστευμένος, ἀπηρχαιωμένος.

ditch [ditʃ] *n* τάφρος, χανδάκι.

ditto ['ditəu] *n* ὁμοίως.

divan [di'væn] *n* (*bed*) ντιβάνι.

dive [daiv] *n* (*into water*) βουτιά ǁ (*aviat*) βύθισις ǁ *vi* βυθίζομαι, βουτῶ ǁ ~ **r** *n* (*professional*) δύτης.

diverge [dai'vəːdʒ] *vi* διΐσταμαι, ἀποκλίνω.

diverse [dai'vəːs] *a* διάφορος, ποικίλος.

diversification [daivəsifi'keiʃən] *n* διαφοροποίησις.

diversify [dai'vəːsifai] *vt* διαφοροποιῶ, ποικίλλω.

diversion [dai'vəːʃən] *n* ἀπόκλισις, λοξοδρομία ǁ (*of traffic*) διοχέτευσις ǁ (*pastime*) διασκέδασις.

diversity [dai'vəːsiti] *n* ἀνομοιότης, ποικιλία.

divert [dai'vəːt] *vt* ἀποσπῶ, ἐκτρέπω ǁ (*entertain*) διασκεδάζω.

divide [di'vaid] *vt* διανέμω, (δια)μοιράζω, χωρίζω ǁ *vi* διαιρῶ, χωρίζω.

dividend ['dividend] *n* μέρισμα, τοκομερίδιον ǁ (*math*) διαιρετέος.

divine [di'vain] *a* θεῖος, θεϊκός.

diving board ['daiviŋbɔːd] *n* ἐξέδρα γιά βουτιές.

divinity [di'viniti] *n* θεότης ǁ (*study*) θεολογία.

divisible [di'vizəbl] *a* διαιρετός.

division [di'viʒən] *n* (*dividing*) διανομή, μοιρασιά ǁ (*math*) διαίρεσις ǁ (*mil*) μεραρχία ǁ (*part*) τμῆμα ǁ (*of opinion*) διχόνοια, διαίρεσις.

divorce [di'vɔːs] *n* διαζύγιον, διάζευξις

‖ *vt* διαζευγνύω ‖ ~**d** *a* χωρισμένος.
divulge [dai'vʌldʒ] *vt* ἀποκαλύπτω, φανερώνω.
dizziness ['dizinis] *n* ἴλιγγος, ζάλη.
dizzy ['dizi] *a* ζαλισμένος.
do [du:] (*irreg v*) *vt* κάνω, ἐκτελῶ, ἐκπληρῶ, τελειώνω, ταιριάζω, ἀρκῶ ‖ *vi* (*act, proceed*) κάνω ‖ (*be suitable*) ταιριάζω, κάνω ‖ *n* (*party*) πάρτυ.
docile ['dousail] *a* εὐάγωγος, ὑπάκοος.
dock [dɔk] *n* (*naut*) νηοδόχη, ντόκος, δεξαμενή ‖ (*court*) ἐδώλιον ‖ *vi* (*naut*) δεξαμενίζομαι ‖ ~**er** *n* φορτοεκφορτωτής, λιμενεργάτης.
docket ['dɔkit] *n* περιληπτική ἐπιγραφή.
dockyard ['dɔkja:d] *n* ναύσταθμος.
doctor ['dɔktə*] *n* (*med*) ἰατρός, γιατρός ‖ (*univ*) διδάκτωρ.
doctrinaire [dɔktri'nɛə*] *a* θεωρητικός.
doctrine ['dɔktrin] *n* δόγμα, θεωρία.
document ['dɔkjumənt] *n* ἔγγραφον ‖ ~**ary** [dɔkju'mentəri] *n* (*film*) ντοκυμαντέρ.
dodge [dɔdʒ] *n* ὑπεκφυγή, τέχνασμα ‖ *vt* ξεφεύγω, ἀποφεύγω ‖ *vi* ἐκφεύγω, παραμερίζω, κάνω πλάι.
dog [dɔg] *n* σκυλί ‖ (*human*) παλιάνθρωπος ‖ ~ **biscuit** *n* μπισκότο γιά σκύλους ‖ ~ **collar** *n* λαιμοδέτης (σκύλου) ‖ (*col*) κολλάρο κληρικοῦ ‖ ~-**eared** *a* τσάκκισμα γωνίας τῆς σελίδος ‖ ~**fish** *n* σκυλόψαρο ‖ ~ **food** *n* φαγητό γιά σκύλους.
dogged ['dɔgid] *a* ἰσχυρογνώμων, πεισματάρης.
dogma ['dɔgmə] *n* δόγμα ‖ ~ **tic** [dɔg'mætik] *a* (*stubborn*) κατηγορηματικός, δογματικός.
doings ['du:iŋz] *npl* (*activities*) πράξεις, ἔργα.
doldrums ['dɔldrəmz] *npl*: **in the** ~ ἄκεφος.
dole [doul] *n* (*Brit: for unemployed*) ἐπίδομα ἀνεργίας ‖ **on the** ~ παίρνω ἐπίδομα ὡς ἄνεργος ‖ **to** ~ **out** *vt* διανέμω, μοιράζω.
doleful ['doulful] *a* λυπητερός, πένθιμος.
doll [dɔl] *n* κούκλα ‖ *vt*: **to** ~ **o.s. up** στολίζομαι.
dollar ['dɔlə*] *n* δολλάριο, τάληρο.
dolphin ['dɔlfin] *n* δελφίνι.
dome [doum] *n* θόλος, τροῦλλος.
domestic [də'mestik] *a* (*of the house*) οἰκιακός, τοῦ σπιτιοῦ ‖ (*of the country*) ἐσωτερικος, ἐγχώριος ‖ (*tame: of animal*) οἰκιακό ζῶον ‖ ~**ated** *a* ἐξημερωμένος.
domicile ['dɔmisail] *n* διαμονή.
dominant ['dɔminənt] *a* ἐπικρατῶν, ὑπερισχύων.
dominate ['dɔmineit] *vt* δεσπόζω, κυριαρχῶ.
domination [dɔmi'neiʃən] *n* κυριαρχία.
domineering [dɔmi'niəriŋ] *a* δεσποτικός, αὐταρχικός.
dominion [də'miniən] *n* (*rule*) κυριαρχία, ἐξουσία ‖ (*land*) κτῆσις (ἀποικία).
dominoes ['dɔminəuz] *npl* ντόμινο.

don [dɔn] *n* καθηγητής πανεπιστημίου.
donate [dəu'neit] *vt* δωρίζω.
donation [dəu'neiʃən] *n* δωρεά.
done [dʌn] *pp of* **did**.
donkey ['dɔŋki] *n* γάιδαρος, γαϊδούρι.
donor ['dəunə*] *n* δωρητής.
don't [dəunt] = **do not** ‖ *see* **do**.
doom [du:m] *n* (*fate*) μοῖρα ‖ (*death*) θάνατος, καταστροφή ‖ *vt*: **to be** ~**ed** εἶμαι καταδικασμένος.
door [dɔ:*] *n* πόρτα, θύρα ‖ ~**bell** *n* κουδούνι (τῆς πόρτας) ‖ ~**handle** *n* πόμολο, (χειρο)λαβή ‖ ~**man** *n* θυρωρός, πορτιέρης ‖ ~**mat** *n* ψάθα ἐξώπορτας ‖ ~**step** *n* σκαλοπάτι ‖ ~**way** *n* εἴσοδος.
dope [dəup] *n* (*drug*) ναρκωτικόν.
dopey ['dəupi] *a* (*col*) βλάκας ‖ (*doped*) χασικλωμένος.
dormant ['dɔ:mənt] *a* λανθάνων, κοιμώμενος.
dormitory ['dɔ:mitri] *n* ὑπνοθάλαμος.
dormouse ['dɔ:maus] *n* μυωξός.
dosage ['dəusidʒ] *n* δόσις.
dose [dəus] *n* δόσις ‖ *vt* δίδω φάρμακον.
dossier ['dɔsiei] *n* φάκελλος.
dot [dɔt] *n* στιγμή ‖ **on the** ~ στήν στιγμήν, στήν ὥρα.
dote [dəut] **to** ~ **on** *vt* ἀγαπῶ τρελλά.
double ['dʌbl] *a* διπλός, διπλάσιος ‖ *ad* διπλά, διπλάσια, δύο-δύο ‖ *n* (*match*) σωσίας, ταῖρι ‖ *vt* διπλασιάζω ‖ (*fold in two*) διπλώνω ‖ *vi* διπλασιάζομαι, διπλώνομαι ‖ **at the** ~ τροχάδην ‖ ~**s** *npl* (*tennis*) διπλοῦς (ἀγών) ‖ ~ **bass** *n* κοντραμπάσσο ‖ ~ **bed** *n* διπλό κρεββάτι ‖ ~-**breasted** *a* σταυρωτός ‖ ~-**cross** *n* προδοσία ‖ *vt* προδίδω, ἐξαπατῶ ‖ ~-**decker** *n* διόροφον (λεωφορεῖον) ‖ ~ **room** *n* δίκλινο.
doubly ['dʌbli] *ad* διπλασίως.
doubt [daut] *n* ἀμφιβολία ‖ *vt* ἀμφιβάλλω, διαμφισβητῶ ‖ **without** ~ χωρίς καμμιά ἀμφιβολίαν ‖ ~**ful** *a* ἀμφίβολος ‖ ~**less** *ad* ἀναμφιβόλως.
dough [dəu] *n* ζυμάρι ‖ ~**nut** *n* τηγανίτα, λουκουμάς.
dove [dʌv] *n* περιστέρι ‖ ~**tail** *n* ψαλιδωτή ἕνωσις ‖ *vt* ταιριάζω.
dowdy ['daudi] *a* ἄκομψος, κακοντυμένος.
down [daun] *n* (*fluff*) πούπουλο, χνούδι ‖ *ad* κάτω, χάμω ‖ *prep* πιό κάτω, πρός τά κάτω, χαμηλότερα ‖ *vi* καταβιβάζω, καταρρίπτω, νικῶ ‖ ~ **with X!** κάτω ὁ Χ! ‖ ~-**and-out** *a* κατεστραμμένος, στήν ψάθα ‖ ~-**at-heel** *a* μπατίρης ‖ ~**cast** *a* κατηφής ‖ ~**fall** *n* πτῶσις, παρακμή ‖ ~**hearted** *a* ἀποθαρρυμένος, κακόκεφος ‖ ~**hill** *ad* κατηφορικῶς, πρός τά κάτω ‖ ~**pour** *n* μπόρα ‖ ~**right** *a* εὐθύς, εἰλικρινής, ἀπόλυτος ‖ ~**stairs** *ad* κάτω ‖ ~**stream** *a* κάτω, εἰς τό κάτω πάτωμα ‖ ~**stream** *ad* μέ τό ρεῦμα ‖ ~**town** *ad* στήν πόλι ‖

~**ward** *a* κατηφορικός, κατερχόμενος ‖ ~**wards** *ad* πρός τά κάτω, καί κάτω.

dowry ['dauri] *n* προίκα.

doze [dəuz] *vi* λαγοκοιμᾶμαι ‖ *n* ὑπνάκος.

dozen ['dʌzn] *n* δωδεκάδα.

drab [dræb] *a* (*dull*) μονότονος, ἀνιαρός.

drachma ['drækmə] *n* δραχμή.

draft [dra:ft] *n* (*rough copy*) (προ)σχέδιον ‖ (*econ*) γραμμάτιον, συναλλαγματική ‖ (*US mil*) στρατολογία ‖ *vt* συντάσσω, ἑτοιμάζω προσχέδιον ‖ *see* **draught**.

drag [dræg] *vt* (*pull*) σέρνω ‖ (*naut*) βυθοκορῶ ‖ *vi* βραδυπορῶ, σέρνομαι ‖ *n* (*bore*) φορτικός ἄνθρωπος ‖ **to ~ on** *vi* συνεχίζω ἀνιαρά.

dragon ['drægən] *n* δράκος.

drain [drein] *n* (*lit*) ὀχετός, ἀγωγός, αὐλάκι ‖ (*fig*) φυγή, διαρροή, ἐξάντλησις ‖ *vt* (*water*) ἀποχετεύω ‖ ἀδειάζω, ἀπομυζῶ, μαδῶ ‖ *vi* (*of water*) στάζω, στραγγίζω ‖ ~**age** *n* ἀποχέτευσις, ἀποστράγγισις ‖ ~**pipe** *n* σωλήν ἀποχετεύσεως, ὑδρορρόη.

dram [dræm] *n* δράμι ‖ (*col*) σταγόνα.

drama ['dra:mə] *n* δρᾶμα ‖ ~**tic** [drə'mætik] *a* δραματικός ‖ ~**tist** *n* δραματογράφος, δραματουργός.

drank [dræŋk] *pt of* **drink**.

drape [dreip] *vt* κοσμῶ μέ ὕφασμα, ντύνω ‖ ~**s** *npl* (*US*) κουρτίνες ‖ ~**r** *n* ὑφασματέμπορος.

drastic ['dræstik] *a* δραστικός, ἀποφασιστικός.

draught [dra:ft] *n* (*air*) ρεῦμα (ἀέρος) ‖ (*naut*) βύθισμα ‖ ~**s** *n* (*game*) ντάμα, νταμιέρα ‖ (*beer*) **on ~** μπύρα τοῦ βαρελιοῦ ‖ ~**board** *n* ἀβάκιον ‖ ~**sman** *n* σχεδιαστής ‖ ~**y** *a* μέ πολλά ρεύματα.

draw [drɔ:] (*irreg v*) *vt* (*pull*) σέρνω, τραβῶ, σηκώνω ‖ (*attract*) ἑλκύω, τραβῶ ‖ (*a picture*) χαράσσω, σχεδιάζω, ζωγραφίζω ‖ (*take out*) ἐξάγω, βγάζω, τραβάω ‖ *vi* (*sport*) ἔρχομαι ἰσόπαλος ‖ *n* (*sport*) ἰσοφάρισις ‖ (*lottery*) κλήρωσις ‖ **to ~ to a close** πλησιάζω στό τέλος ‖ **to ~ out** *vi* (*train*) ξεκινῶ ‖ (*lengthen*) παρατείνω, τραβῶ σέ μάκρος ‖ *vt* (*take out*) ἀποσύρω, τραβῶ ‖ **to ~ up** *vi* (*stop*) φθάνω ‖ *vt* (*document*) συντάσσω, καταστρώνω ‖ ~**back** *n* μειονέκτημα, ἐλάττωμα ‖ ~**bridge** *n* κρεμαστή γέφυρα ‖ ~**er** *n* συρτάρι ‖ ~**ing** *n* σχέδιον, σκίτσο ‖ (*art of drawing*) σχέδιον ‖ ~**ing pin** *n* πινέζα ‖ ~**ing room** *n* σαλόνι, σάλα.

drawl [drɔ:l] *n* συρτή φωνή ‖ *vi* σέρνω τή φωνή.

dread [dred] *n* τρόμος, φόβος, ἀνησυχία ‖ *vt* φοβοῦμαι, τρέμω ‖ ~**ful** *a* φοβερός, τρομερός.

dream [dri:m] (*irreg v*) *n* ὄνειρο ‖ (*fancy*) ὀνειροπόλησις ‖ *vi* ὀνειρεύομαι ‖ *a* ὀνειρώδης ‖ ~**er** *n* ὀνειροπόλος ‖ ~**y** *a* ὀνειροπόλος, φαντασιόπληκτος, θολός.

dreary ['driəri] *a* μονότονος, πληκτικός.

dredge [dredʒ] *vt* βυθοκορῶ, ἐκβαθύνω ‖ ~**r** *n* βυθοκόρος.

dregs [dregz] *npl* κατακάθι, μούργα.

drench [drentʃ] *vt* καταβρέχω, μουσκεύω.

dress [dres] *n* ἐνδυμασία, ροῦχα, ντύσιμο ‖ (*esp woman's*) φόρεμα, φουστάνι ‖ *vt* ντύνω, στολίζω ‖ (*a wound*) ἐπενδύω ‖ (*food*) ἑτοιμάζω γιά μαγείρευμα ‖ **to ~ up** *vi* ντύνομαι ‖ ~ **circle** *n* πρῶτος ἐξώστης ‖ ~**er** *n* (*person*) πού ντύνεται καλά ‖ (*US*) κομψός ‖ ~**ing** *n* (*med*) ἐπίδεσις ‖ (*of food*) ἑτοιμασία, σάλτσα ‖ ~**ing gown** *n* ρόμπα ‖ ~**ing room** *n* (*theat*) καμαρίνι ‖ ~**ing table** *n* τουαλέττα (ἔπιπλον) ‖ δωμάτιον καλλωπισμοῦ ‖ ~**maker** *n* ράφτρα, μοδίστρα ‖ ~**making** *n* ραπτική ‖ ~ **rehearsal** *n* τελευταία πρόβα, γενική δοκιμή.

drew [dru:] *pt of* **draw**.

dribble ['dribl] *vi* (*trickle*) στάζω ‖ *vt* (*sport*) κάνω τρίπλες.

dried [draid] *a* ξηρός, ἀπεξηραμένος, στεγνός.

drift [drift] *n* (*driven by tide etc*) κατεύθυνσις, διεύθυνσις, ταχύτης ‖ (*mass of snow etc*) χιονοστιβάς, συσσώρευσις ‖ (*meaning*) ἔννοια, νόημα ‖ *vi* (*of course*) παρασύρομαι, ξεπέφτω ‖ (*aimlessly*) περιφέρομαι ἀσκόπως ‖ ~**wood** *n* ἐπιπλέον ξύλον.

drill [dril] *n* (*tool*) τρυπάνι, δράπανο ‖ (*mil*) γυμνάσια, ἄσκησις ‖ *vt* (*bore*) τρυπῶ, ἀνοίγω ‖ (*exercise*) ἐκπαιδεύω, γυμνάζω ‖ *vi* (+*for*) κάνω γεώτρησι ‖ ~**ing** *n* (*of well etc*) διάτρησις, γεώτρησις.

drink [driŋk] (*irreg v*) *n* (*liquid*) ποτόν, ἀναψυκτικόν ‖ (*alcoholic*) ποτό ‖ *vti* (*swallow liquid*) πίνω ‖ ~**able** *a* πόσιμος ‖ ~**er** *n* πότης ‖ ~**ing water** *n* πόσιμο νερό.

drip [drip] *n* στάξιμο, σταλαγματιά ‖ *vi* στάζω, σταλάζω ‖ ~**ping** *n* στάξιμο ‖ (*fat*) λίπος ψητοῦ ‖ ~**ping wet** *a* μουσκεμένος.

drive [draiv] (*irreg v*) *n* (*trip in car*) κούρσα, διαδρομή ‖ (*road*) δρόμος πάρκου ‖ (*campaign*) καμπάνια, ἔρανος ‖ (*energy*) ἐνεργητικότητα, δραστηριότητα ‖ (*sport*) κτήπυμα ‖ *vt* (*car etc*) ὁδηγῶ, σοφάρω ‖ (*urge*) διώχνω, σπρώχνω ‖ (*nail etc*) καρφώνω, μπάζω ‖ (*operate*) κινῶ, βάζω μπρός ‖ (*force*) ἀναγκάζω, παρακινῶ ‖ *vi* (*at controls*) ὁδηγῶ, χειρίζομαι ‖ (*travel*) πηγαίνω, τρέχω.

driver ['draivə*] *n* ὁδηγός ‖ ~'s **license** *n* (*US*) ἄδεια ὁδηγοῦ.

driving ['draiviŋ] *a* (*rain*) νεροποντή ‖ ~ **instructor** *n* δάσκαλος ὁδηγήσεως ‖ ~ **lesson** *n* μάθημα ὁδηγήσεως ‖ ~ **licence** *n* (*Brit*) ἄδεια ὁδηγοῦ ‖ ~ **school** *n* σχολή ὁδηγῶν ‖ ~ **test** *n* ἐξέτασις δι'ἄδειαν ὁδηγοῦ.

drizzle ['drizl] *n* ψιχάλισμα ‖ *vi* ψιχαλίζω.

droll [drəul] *a* ἀστεῖος, κωμικός.

dromedary ['drɔmidəri] *n* κάμηλος ἡ δρομάς.

drone [drəun] *n* (*bee*) κηφήν ‖ (*sound*) βόμβος, βουητό ‖ *vi* σαλιαρίζω, μωρολογῶ.

droop [dru:p] *vi* πέφτω, γέρνω, σκύβω.

drop [drɔp] *n* (*of liquid*) σταγόνα, στάλλα ‖ (*fall*) πτῶσις, πέσιμο ‖ (*med*) σταγών ‖ *vt* (*let fall*) ρίχνω, ἀφήνω νά πέση ‖ (*lower*) κατεβάζω, χαμηλώνω ‖ (*cease*) ἐγκαταλείπω, παρατῶ, ἀφήνω ‖ *vi* (*fall*) πέφτω ‖ **to ~ off** *vi* (*sleep*) ἀποκοιμιέμαι ‖ **to ~ out** *vi* (*withdraw*) ἀποσύρομαι ‖ **~ kick** *n* κλωτσιά ἀπό γκέλι.

dross [drɔs] *n* ἀκαθαρσίες, ἀπορρίμματα.

drought [draut] *n* ξηρασία.

drove [drəuv] *pt of* **drive** ‖ *n* (*crowd*) πλῆθος ἀνθρώπων, κοπάδι.

drown [draun] *vt* πνίγω ‖ (*flood*) πλημμυρίζω ‖ *vi* πνίγομαι.

drowsy ['drauzi] *a* νυσταλέος, νυσταγμένος.

drudgery ['drʌdʒəri] *n* μόχθος, ἀγγαρεία.

drug [drʌg] *n* (*med*) φάρμακον ‖ (*narcotic*) ναρκωτικόν ‖ *vt* δίδω ναρκωτικόν εἰς, ντοπάρω ‖ **~ addict** *n* τοξικομανής, πρεζάκιας ‖ **~gist** *n* (*US*) φαρμακοποιός ‖ **~ store** *n* (*US*) φαρμακεῖον.

drum [drʌm] *n* (*mus*) τύμπανον, τούμπανο ‖ βαρέλι ‖ **~mer** *n* τυμπανιστής.

drunk [drʌŋk] *pp of* **drink** ‖ *n* μέθυσος, μπεκρής ‖ **~ard** *n* μεθύστακας ‖ **~en** *a* μεθυσμένος ‖ **~enness** *n* μέθη, μεθύσι.

dry [drai] *a* (*not wet*) ξηρός, ξερός ‖ (*of well*) στερεμένος ‖ (*rainless*) ἄνυδρος ‖ (*uninteresting*) ξερό, κρύο ‖ (*wine*) μπρούσκο ‖ *vt* ξηραίνω, στεγνώνω, στίβω ‖ *vi* ξεραίνομαι, στεγνώνω ‖ **to ~ up** *vi* ξεραίνομαι ‖ (*of well*) στερεύω ‖ **~ cleaner** *n* καθαριστήριον ‖ **~er** *n* στεγνωτής, στεγνωτήριον ‖ **~ goods** *npl* νεωτερισμοί ‖ **~ness** *n* ξηρασία, ξηρότης ‖ **~ rot** *n* σαράκι.

dual ['djuəl] *a* διπλός, διττός, δυϊκός ‖ **~ nationality** *n* διπλή ὑπηκοότης ‖ **~-purpose** *a* διπλῆς χρήσεως.

dubbed [dʌbd] *a* (*cine*) ντουμπλαρισμένο.

dubious ['dʌ:biəs] *a* ἀμφίβολος, ἀμφιβάλλων, ἀβέβαιος.

duchess ['dʌtʃis] *n* δούκισσα.

duck [dʌk] *n* πάπια ‖ *vt* βουτῶ, σκύβω ‖ *vi* βουτῶ ‖ **~ling** *n* παπάκι.

duct [dʌkt] *n* ἀγωγός, σωλήν.

dud [dʌd] *n* μή ἐκραγεῖσα ὀβίς ‖ *a* ἄχρηστος, τενεκές, ἀποτυχημένος.

due [dju:] *a* (*owing*) ὀφειλόμενος, λήγων ‖ (*deserved*) ἀνήκων, δίκαιος, σωστός ‖ (*expected*) ἀναμενόμενος ‖ *ad* κατ'εὐθείαν, ἴσια πρός ‖ **~s** *npl* (*debt*) τέλη, δασμός ‖ ὀφειλόμενον, ἀνῆκον ‖ **~ to** ὀφειλόμενος εἰς, λόγω.

duel ['djuəl] *n* μονομαχία.

duet [dju:'et] *n* δυωδία, ντουέτο.

dug [dʌg] *pt,pp of* **dig**.

duke [dju:k] *n* δούξ, δούκας.

dull [dʌl] *a* (*person*) βραδύνους, μπουνταλᾶς ‖ (*boring*) πληκτικός, ἀνιαρός ‖ (*weather*) βαρύς, σκοτεινός ‖ *vt* (*soften, weaken*) ἐξασθενίζω, ξεθωριάζω.

duly ['dju:li] *ad* δεόντως, ἐγκαίρως.

dumb [dʌm] *a* (*lit*) βουβός, μουγγός ‖ (*stupid*) ἀνόητος, κουτός, ἠλίθιος.

dummy ['dʌmi] *n* (*model*) κούκλα, ἀνδρείκελον ‖ (*substitute*) ὁμοίωμα ‖ (*for baby*) πιπιλίστρα ‖ *a* πλαστός, ψεύτικος, εἰκονικός.

dump [dʌmp] *n* σκουπιδότοπος ‖ (*storing place*) ἀποθήκη ‖ *vt* ξεφορτώνω, ἀπορρίπτω ‖ **~ing** *n* (*comm*) ντάμπιγκ ‖ (*rubbish*) ἀνατροπή, ἐκφόρτισις.

dumpling ['dʌmpliŋ] *n* βρασμένη μπουλέττα ‖ (*pie*) πίττα.

dunce [dʌns] *n* ἀμαθής, ντουβάρι.

dune [dju:n] *n* ἀμμόλοφος.

dung [dʌŋ] *n* κοπριά.

dungarees [dʌŋgə'ri:z] *npl* φόρμα ἐργάτου.

dungeon ['dʌndʒən] *n* μπουντρούμι, φυλακή.

duodenal [dju:əu'di:nl] *a* δωδεκαδακτυλικός.

dupe [dju:p] *n* θῦμα, ἀπάτη, κορόϊδο ‖ *vt* ἐξαπατῶ, κοροϊδεύω.

duplicate ['dju:plikit] *a* διπλοῦς, διπλάσιος ‖ *n* διπλότυπον ‖ ['dju:plikeit] *vt* ἀντιγράφω ‖ **in ~** εἰς διπλοῦν.

duplicator ['dju:plikeitə*] *n* πολύγραφος.

durability [djuərə'biliti] *n* ἀνθεκτικότης, στερεότης.

durable ['djuərəbl] *a* ἀνθεκτικός, διαρκής.

duration [djuə'reiʃən] *n* διάρκεια.

during ['djuəriŋ] *prep* ἐπί, κατά τήν διάρκειαν.

dusk [dʌsk] *n* σούρουπο.

dust [dʌst] *n* σκόνη, κονιορτός, στάκτη ‖ *vt* ξεσκονίζω, πασπαλίζω ‖ **~bin** *n* (*Brit*) τενεκές σκουπιδιῶν ‖ **~er** *n* ξεσκονόπανο ‖ (*feather*) φτερό ‖ **~man** *n* (*Brit*) ὁδοκαθαριστής, σκουπιδιάρης ‖ **~storm** *n* κονιορτοθύελλα ‖ **~y** *a* σκονισμένος.

Dutch [dʌtʃ] *a* 'Ολλανδικός ‖ *n* (*ling*) ὁλλανδικά ‖ **the ~** *npl* 'Ολλανδοί ‖ **~man** *n* 'Ολλανδέζος ‖ **~woman** *n* 'Ολλανδέζα.

dutiable ['dju:tiəbl] *a* φορολογήσιμος.

duty ['dju:ti] *n* καθῆκον ‖ (*job*) καθῆκον(τα), ὑποχρέωσις ‖ (*mil*) ὑπηρεσία ‖ (*tax*) δασμός, φόρος ‖ **on ~** ἐν ὑπηρεσία ‖ **~-free** *a* ἀφορολόγητος ‖ *n* ἀφορολόγητον.

dwarf [dwɔ:f] *n* νάνος.

dwell [dwel] (*irreg v*) *vi* διαμένω, κατοικῶ ‖ **to ~ on** *vi* ἐμμένω εἰς, ἐπιμένω ‖ **~ing** *n* κατοικία.

dwindle ['dwindl] *vi* ἐλαττώνομαι, μικραίνω.
dye [dai] *n* βαφή, χρωματισμός ‖ *vt* βάφω.
dying ['daiiŋ] *a (man)* ἑτοιμοθάνατος.
dynamic [dai'næmik] *a* δυναμικός ‖ ~s *n* δυναμική.
dynamite ['dainəmait] *n* δυναμῖτις.
dynamo ['dainəməu] *n* γεννήτρια, δυναμό.
dynasty ['dinəsti] *n* δυναστεία.
dysentery ['disntri] *n* δυσεντερία.
dyspepsia [dis'pepsiə] *n* δυσπεψία.

E, e

each [i:tʃ] *a* ἕκαστος, πᾶς, καθένας, κάθε ‖ *pron* ἕκαστος, κάθε ‖ ~ other ὁ ἕνας τόν ἄλλον, ἀλλήλους.
eager ['i:gə*] *a* ἔνθερμος, ἀνυπόμονος, παθιασμένος ‖ ~ly *ad* ἐντόνως, ζωηρῶς ‖ ~ness *n* ζῆλος, ζέσις, ἀνυπομονησία.
eagle ['i:gl] *n* ἀετός.
ear [iə*] *n* αὐτί ‖ *(for music)* λεπτή ἀκοή ‖ *(of corn)* στάχυς ‖ ~ache *n* ὠταλγία, αὐτόπονος ‖ ~drum *n* τύμπανον.
earl [ə:l] *n* κόμης, κόντες.
early ['ə:li] *a (before the season)* πρώϊμος, πρόωρος ‖ *(in the morning)* πρωϊνός ‖ *ad (in the morning)* πρωΐ ‖ *(in time)* ἐνωρίς.
earn [ə:n] *vt* κερδίζω, βγάζω ‖ *(acquire)* ἀποκτῶ, κατακτῶ.
earnest ['ə:nist] *a* σοβαρός ‖ *(ardent)* διάπυρος, ἔνθερμος ‖ in ~ *ad* στά σοβαρά.
earnings ['ə:niŋz] *npl* ἀπολαβαί, ἀποδοχαί ‖ *(of a firm)* κέρδη.
earphones ['iəfəunz] *npl* ἀκουστικά.
earring ['iəriŋ] *n* σκουλαρίκι.
earth [ə:θ] *n (planet)* γῆ, κόσμος ‖ *(soil)* γῆ, ἔδαφος, χῶμα ‖ *(elec)* γῆ, προσγείωσις ‖ *vt (elec)* προσγειώνω ‖ ~enware *n* πήλινα ‖ ~quake *n* σεισμός.
earwig ['iəwig] *n (insect)* φορφικούλη, ψαλλίδα.
ease [i:z] *n (facility)* εὐχέρεια, εὐκολία, ἄνεσις ‖ *(comfort)* ἀνάπαυσις, ἄνεσις, ξεκούρασμα ‖ *vt (reduce pain etc)* ἀνακουφίζω, καταπραΰνω ‖ *(remove pressure)* καθησυχάζω, ξεφορτώνω ‖ at ~! ἀνάπαυσις! ‖ to ~ off *or* up *vi* ἐλαττώνω, ἐργάζομαι ἀργότερα.
easily ['i:zili] *ad* ἠρέμως, ἤρεμα, εὔκολα.
east [i:st] *n (direction)* ἀνατολή ‖ *(in direction)* ἀνατολικά ‖ *a* ἀνατολικός ‖ *ad* πρός ἀνατολάς, ἀνατολικά ‖ the E~ Ἀνατολή.
Easter ['i:stə*] *n* Πάσχα, Λαμπρή.
eastern ['i:stən] *a (from, of the east)* ἀνατολικός.
eastward(s) ['i:stwəd(z)] *ad* πρός ἀνατολάς.
easy ['i:zi] *a (not difficult)* εὐχερής, εὔκολος ‖ *(life)* ξεκούραστη, ἄνετη ‖ *(manner)* ἄνετος, ἀβίαστος ‖ *(yielding)* καλόβολος ‖ *ad* εὔκολα, ἤρεμα, ἥσυχα.

eat [i:t] *(irreg v)* *vt (swallow)* τρώγω ‖ *(one's words)* καταπίνω ‖ *(consume)* (κατα)-τρώγω, ὑπονομεύω ‖ to ~ away *vt* κατατρώγω, προσβάλλω ‖ ~able *a* φαγώσιμος.
eau de Cologne ['əudəkə'ləun] *n* κολώνια.
eavesdrop ['i:vzdrɔp] *vi (+ on)* κρυφακούω.
ebb [eb] *n* ἄμπωτις ‖ *(fig)* παρακμή, πέσιμο ‖ *vi* κατεβαίνω, πέφτω.
ebony ['ebəni] *n* ἔβενος, ἀμπανός.
ebullient [i'buliənt] *a (enthusiastic)* ἐκχειλίζων, ἐνθουσιώδης.
eccentric [ik'sentrik] *a (odd)* ἐκκεντρικός, παράξενος ‖ *n (person)* ἰδιότροπος.
ecclesiastical [ikli:zi'æstikl] *a* ἐκκλησιαστικός.
echo ['ekəu] *n* ἠχώ, ἀντήχησις, ἀντίλαλος ‖ *vt* ἀντηχῶ ‖ *vi* ἀντηχῶ, ἀπηχῶ, ἀντιλαλῶ.
eclipse [i'klips] *n* ἔκλειψις ‖ *vt* προκαλῶ ἔκλειψιν ‖ *(fig)* ἐπισκιάζω.
economic [i:kə'nɔmik] *a* οἰκονομικός ‖ ~al *a* οἰκονομικός ‖ *(of person)* φειδωλός ‖ ~s *npl* οἰκονομικά.
economist [i'kɔnəmist] *n* οἰκονομολόγος.
economize [i'kɔnəmaiz] *vi (+ on)* οἰκονομῶ, κάνω οἰκονομία σέ.
economy [i'kɔnəmi] *n (thrift)* οἰκονομία ‖ *(of country)* οἰκονομία.
ecstasy ['ekstəsi] *n* ἔκστασις, μάγευμα.
ecstatic [ek'stætik] *a* ἐκστατικός.
ecumenical [i:kju'menikl] *a* οἰκουμενικός.
eczema ['eksimə] *n* ἔκζεμα.
Eden ['i:dn] *n* Ἐδέμ.
edge [edʒ] *n (boundary)* ὄχθη, παρυφή, ἄκρη ‖ *(of garment)* οὔγια ‖ *(brink)* ἀκμή, χεῖλος, ἄκρη ‖ *(of knife)* κόψη, ἀκμή ‖ on ~ = edgy.
edging ['edʒiŋ] *n*: ~ strip *n* πλαίσιον, μπορντούρα.
edgy ['edʒi] *a* ἐκνευρισμένος.
edible ['edibl] *a* φαγώσιμος.
edict ['i:dikt] *n* ἔδικτον, διάταγμα.
edifice ['edifis] *n* οἰκοδόμημα, κτίριον.
edit ['edit] *vt* ἐκδίδω, διευθύνω ‖ ~ion [i'diʃən] *n* ἔκδοσις ‖ ~or *n (of newspaper)* (ἀρχι)συντάκτης ‖ *(of book)* ἐκδότης, ἐπιμελητής ἐκδόσεως ‖ ~orial *a* ἐκδοτικός, συντακτικός ‖ *n* (κύριον) ἄρθρον.
educate ['edjukeit] *vt* ἐκπαιδεύω, σπουδάζω, μαθαίνω.
education [edju'keiʃən] *n (system)* ἐκπαίδευσις ‖ *(schooling)* σπουδαί, ἐκπαίδευσις, μόρφωσις ‖ ~al *a* ἐκπαιδευτικός, μορφωτικός.
eel [i:l] *n* χέλι.
eerie ['iəri] *a* μυστηριώδης, παράξενος, τρομακτικός.
efface [i'feis] *vt* ἐξαλείφω, ἀπαλείφω, σβήνω.
effect [i'fekt] *n (result)* ἐνέργεια, ἐπίδρασις, ἐπιρροή, ἀποτέλεσμα ‖ *(impression)* ἐντύπωσις, αἴσθησις ‖ *vt* πραγματοποιῶ,

ἐπιτυγχάνω ‖ **~s** npl (sound, visual) σκηνικά ἐφφέ ‖ **in** ~ πράγματι, πραγματικά ‖ **~ive** a ἀποτελεσματικός, οὐσιαστικός.

effeminate [i'feminit] a θηλυπρεπής, γυναικωτός.

effervescent [efə'vesnt] a (ἀνα)βράζων, ἀεριοῦχος ‖ (person) ζωηρός.

efficiency [i'fiʃənsi] n ἀποτελεσματικότης, δραστικότης ‖ (of machine) ἀπόδοσις.

efficient [i'fiʃənt] a ἀποτελεσματικός ‖ (person) ἱκανός, ἐπιδέξιος ‖ **~ly** ad ἀποτελεσματικῶς, μέ ἐπιδεξιότητα.

effigy ['efidʒi] n ὁμοίωμα, εἰκών.

effort ['efət] n προσπάθεια ‖ **~less** a ἄνευ προσπαθείας, εὔκολος.

effrontery [i'frʌntəri] n αὐθάδεια, ἀδιαντροπία.

egalitarian [igæli'teəriən] a ἰσοπεδωτικός.

egg [eg] n αὐγό ‖ **boiled.~** n βραστό αὐγό ‖ **to ~ on** vt ἐξωθῶ, παρακινῶ, σπρώχνω ‖ **~cup** n αὐγουλήθρα ‖ **~plant** n μελιτζανιά ‖ **~shell** n τσόφλι αὐγοῦ.

ego ['i:gəu] n τό ἐγώ.

egotism ['egətizəm] n ἐγωπάθεια, περιαυτολογία.

egotist ['egətist] n περιαυτολόγος.

Egypt ['i:dʒipt] n Αἴγυπτος ‖ **~ian** n Αἰγύπτιος ‖ a αἰγυπτιακός.

eiderdown [aidədaun] n (quilt) πουπουλένιο πάπλωμα.

eight [eit] num ὀκτώ, ὀχτώ ‖ **~een** num δέκα ὀκτώ ‖ **~h** a ὄγδοος ‖ **~y** num ὀγδόντα.

Eire ['eərə] n Ἰρλανδία.

either ['aiðə*] a ἑκάτερος, ἕκαστος, καθένας ‖ pron ὁ εἷς ἤ ὁ ἄλλος, ἕκαστος ‖ cj ἤ . . . ἤ, εἴτε . . . εἴτε ‖ ad οὔτε . . . οὔτε.

eject [i'dʒekt] vt ἐκβάλλω, βγάζω ‖ (throw out) διώχνω, βγάζω ἔξω ‖ **~or seat** n ἐκτοξευόμενον κάθισμα.

elaborate [i'læbərit] a ἐπιμελημένος, ἐξονυχιστικός, περίπλοκος ‖ [i'læbəreit] vt ἐπεξεργάζομαι, δουλεύω, ἐπιμελοῦμαι ‖ **~ly** ad ἐπιμελῶς, μετά προσοχῆς.

elapse [i'læps] vi παρέρχομαι, περνῶ.

elastic [i'læstik] n ἐλαστικόν, λάστιχο ‖ a ἐλαστικός, εὔκαμπτος ‖ **~ band** n λαστιχάκι.

elated [i'leitid] a συνεπαρμένος, ἔξαλλος.

elation [i'leiʃən] n ἔπαρσις, χαρά, κέφι.

elbow ['elbəu] n ἀγκώνας, ἄγκωνας.

elder ['eldə*] a πρεσβύτερος, μεγαλύτερος ‖ n μεγαλύτερος ‖ (tree) ἀκτή, σαμπποῦκος ‖ **~ly** a ἡλικιωμένος.

elect [i'lekt] vt ἐκλέγω ‖ a ἐκλεκτός ‖ **~ion** n ἐκλογή ‖ **~ioneering** n ψηφοθηρία ‖ **~or** n ψηφοφόρος ‖ **~oral** a ἐκλογικός ‖ **~orate** n οἱ ψηφοφόροι.

electric [i'lektrik] a (appliance) ἠλεκτρικός ‖ **~al** a ἠλεκτρικός ‖ **~ blanket** n θερμοφόρα κουβέρτα ‖ **~ chair** n (US) ἠλεκτρική καρέκλα ‖ **~ cooker** n ἡ κουζίνα,

μάτι ‖ **~ current** n ἡ. ρεῦμα ‖ **~ fire** n ἠλεκτρική σόμπα ‖ **~ian** [ilek'triʃən] n ἠλεκτρολόγος ‖ **~ity** [ilek'trisiti] n ἠλεκτρισμός.

electrification [i'lektrifi'keiʃən] n ἐξηλεκτρισμός.

electrify [i'lektrifai] vt (ἐξ)ηλεκτρίζω.

electro- [i'lektrəu] prefix ἠλεκτρο-.

electrocute [i'lektrəkju:t] vt θανατώνω δι'ἠλεκτρισμοῦ, δι'ἠλεκτροπληξίας.

electrocution [ilektrə'kju:ʃən] n ἠλεκτροπληξία.

electron [i'lektrən] n ἠλεκτρόνιον.

electronic [elək'trɔnik] a ἠλεκτρονικός ‖ **~s** n ἠλεκτρονική.

elegance [eligəns] n κομψότης.

elegant ['eləgənt] a κομψός.

element ['eləmənt] n (chem) στοιχεῖον ‖ (fig) στοιχεῖον ‖ (elec) στοιχεῖον ‖ **~ary** [eli'mentəri] a στοιχειώδης.

elephant ['elifənt] n ἐλέφας.

elevate ['eliveit] vt (ἀν)ὑψώνω.

elevation [eli'veiʃən] n (height) ὕψος, ὕψωμα.

elevator ['eliveitə*] n ἀνελκυστήρ, ἀσανσέρ.

eleven [i'levən] a ἕντεκα ‖ n (team) ὁμάς ἕνδεκα παικτῶν ‖ **~ses** npl κολατσό.

elf [elf] n ἔλφα, ἀγερικό, ξωτικό.

elicit [i'lisit] vt ἐξάγω, ἀποσπῶ, βγάζω.

eligible ['elidʒibl] a ἐκλέξιμος, κατάλληλος.

eliminate [i'limineit] vt ἀποβάλλω, διαγράφω ‖ (math) ἐξαλείφω.

elimination [ilimi'neiʃən] n ἀποκλεισμός, διαγραφή.

élite [i'li:t] n ἐκλεκτόν μέρος.

elm [elm] n φτελιά.

elocution [elə'kju:ʃən] n εὐγλωττία, ἀπαγγελία.

elongated ['i:lɔŋgeitid] a ἐπιμήκης, μακρύς.

elope [i'ləup] vi ἀπάγομαι, φεύγω (ἑκουσίως), κλέβομαι ‖ **~ment** n ἑκουσία ἀπαγωγή.

eloquence ['eləkwəns] n εὐφράδεια.

eloquent ['eləkwənt] a εὐφραδής, εὔγλωττος ‖ **~ly** ad εὐγλώττως.

else [els] ad ὁποιοσδήποτε ἄλλος, ἐπί πλέον, ἀλλοῦ ‖ (otherwise) ἄλλως, εἰδεμή, ἀλλοιῶς ‖ **~where** ad ἀλλαχοῦ, ἀλλοῦ.

elucidate [i'lu:sideit] vt διευκρινίζω, διασαφίζω.

elude [i'lu:d] vt ξεφεύγω, διαφεύγω.

elusive [i'lu:siv] a ἄπιαστος, ἀπατηλός.

emaciated [i'meisieitid] a ἀδυνατισμένος, πετσί καί κόκκαλο.

emanate ['eməneit] vi ἀπορρέω, προέρχομαι, πηγάζω.

emancipate [i'mænsipeit] vt ἀπελευθερώνω ‖ **~d** a χειραφετός, ἐλευθερωθείς.

emancipation [imænsi'peiʃən] n χειραφέτησις, ἀπελευθέρωσις.

embalm [im'ba:m] vt ταριχεύω, βαλσαμώνω.

embankment [im'bæŋkmənt] n ἀνάχωμα.

embargo [im'ba:gəu] n ἀπαγόρευσις, περιορισμός.

embark [im'ba:k] vt ἐπιβιβάζω ‖ vi ἐπιβιβάζομαι ‖ to ~ on vt ἀρχίζω ‖ ~ation [emba:'keiʃən] n μπαρκάρισμα.

embarrass [im'bærəs] vt φέρω εἰς ἀμηχανίαν, στενοχωρῶ ‖ ~ing a (humiliating) ἐνοχλητικός, ξεφτελιστικός ‖ ~ment n στεναχώρια, ἀμηχανία, μπλέξιμο.

embassy ['embəsi] n πρεσβεία.

embed [im'bed] vt ἐνθέτω, χώνω, θάβω.

embellish [im'beliʃ] vt καλλωπίζω, γαρνίρω.

embers ['embəz] npl θράκα.

embezzle [im'bezl] vt καταχρῶμαι ‖ ~ment n κατάχρησις, σφετερισμός.

embitter [im'bitə*] vt πικραίνω.

emblem ['embləm] n (symbol) σύμβολον ‖ (badge etc) ἔμβλημα.

embodiment [im'bɔdimənt] n ἐνσάρκωσις, προσωποποίησις.

embody [im'bɔdi] vt (ideas) ἐνσαρκώνω, πραγματοποιῶ ‖ (new features) ἐνσωματώνω, περιλαμβάνω.

emboss [im'bɔs] vt ἀναγλύφω, χαράσσω ἀναγλύφως.

embrace [im'breis] vt (clasp) ἐναγκαλίζομαι, ἀγκαλιάζω ‖ (include) περιλαμβάνω, περικλείω ‖ n ἐναγκαλισμός, ἀσπασμός.

embroider [im'brɔidə*] vt κεντῶ, κάνω κέντημα ‖ ~y n κέντημα.

embryo ['embriəu] n (fig) ἔμβρυον.

emerald ['emərld] n σμαράγδι.

emerge [i'mə:dʒ] vi ἀναδύομαι, (ξε)προβαίνω, ξεπροβάλλω ‖ ~nce n ἐμφάνισις ‖ ~ncy n ἐπείγουσα ἀνάγκη ‖ a (action) βοηθητικός, ἔκτακτος ‖ ~ncy exit n ἔξοδος κινδύνου.

emery ['eməri] n: ~ board n γυαλόχαρτο ‖ ~ paper n σμυριδόχαρτον.

emetic [i'metik] n ἐμετικόν.

emigrant ['emigrənt] n μετανάστης ‖ a μεταναστευτικός.

emigrate ['emigreit] vi μεταναστεύω.

emigration [emi'greiʃən] n μετανάστευσις.

eminence ['eminəns] n (distinction) ἀνωτερότης, διασημότης ‖ (eccl) ἐξοχότης.

eminent ['eminənt] a διακεκριμένος, ἔξοχος, διάσημος.

emission [i'miʃən] n (of gases) ἐκπομπή, ἀποβολή.

emit [i'mit] vt ἐκπέμπω, ἀναδίδω.

emotion [i'məuʃən] n συγκίνησις, (ψυχική) ἀναταραχή ‖ ~al a (person) εὐσυγκίνητος, εὐαίσθητος ‖ (scene) συγκινητικός ‖ ~ally ad συγκινητικῶς, εὐαίσθητως.

emotive [i'məutiv] a συγκινητικός.

emperor ['empərə*] n αὐτοκράτορας.

emphasis ['emfəsis] n ἔμφασις.

emphasize ['emfəsaiz] vt τονίζω, ὑπογραμμίζω.

emphatic [im'fætik] a ἐμφατικός ‖ ~ally ad ἐντόνως, ἐμφατικῶς.

empire ['empaiə*] n αὐτοκρατορία.

empirical [em'pirikl] a ἐμπειρικός.

employ [em'plɔi] vt (use) χρησιμοποιῶ, ἐφαρμόζω ‖ (hire) ἀπασχολῶ, ἔχω ‖ ~ee n ὑπάλληλος ‖ ~er n ἐργοδότης ‖ ~ment n (job) ἀπασχόλησις, δουλειά, ἐργασία ‖ (jobs collect) χρῆσις, χρησιμοποίησις.

empress ['empris] n αὐτοκράτειρα.

emptiness ['emptinis] n κενότης.

empty ['empti] a κενός, ἄδειος ‖ vt (contents) κενώνω, ἀδειάζω ‖ (container) ἀδειάζω ‖ ~-handed a μέ ἄδεια χέρια.

emulate ['emjuleit] vt ἁμιλλῶμαι, μιμοῦμαι, ἀκολουθῶ.

emulsion [e'mʌlʃən] n γαλάκτωμα.

enable [i'neibl] vt καθιστῶ ἱκανόν, διευκολύνω, ἐπιτρέπω.

enamel [i'næml] n βερνίκι, σμάλτο, λάκα ‖ (of teeth) σμάλτο.

enamoured [i'næməd] a (+of) ἐρωτευμένος.

encase [in'keis] vt ἐγκιβωτίζω, καλύπτω.

enchant [in'tʃa:nt] vt (bewitch) μαγεύω ‖ (delight) γοητεύω ‖ ~ing a (delightful) γοητευτικός.

encircle [in'sə:kl] vt (περι)κυκλώνω, (περι)σφίγγω.

enclose [in'kləuz] vt (shut in) περικλείω, (περι)μαντρώνω ‖ (in a letter etc) ἐγκλείω, ἐσωκλείω.

enclosure [in'kləuʒə*] n (space) φράκτης, μανδρότοιχος ‖ (in a letter) συνημμένον, ἐσώκλειστον.

encore ['ɔnkɔ:*] n πάλιν, μπίς.

encounter [in'kauntə*] n συνάντησις ‖ (battle) σύγκρουσις ‖ vt (meet) συναντῶ.

encourage [in'kʌridʒ] vt ἐνθαρρύνω, δίνω κουράγιο ‖ ~ment n ἐμψύχωσις, ἐνθάρρυνσις.

encouraging [in'kʌridʒiŋ] a ἐνθαρρυντικός.

encroach [in'krəutʃ] vi (+(up)on) καταπατῶ.

encyclop(a)edia [ensaikləu'pi:diə] n ἐγκυκλοπαίδεια.

end [end] n (finish) τέρμα, τέλος ‖ (book, day, rope, street, queue) ἄκρη, τέλος, οὐρά ‖ (purpose) σκοπός, ἐπιδίωξις ‖ a τελικός, ἀκραῖος ‖ vt τερματίζω, τελειώνω ‖ vi τερματίζομαι, καταλήγω.

endanger [in'deindʒə*] vt διακινδυνεύω, (ἐκ)θέτω εἰς κίνδυνον.

endeavour [en'devə*] n προσπάθεια ‖ vi προσπαθῶ, πασχίζω.

ending ['endiŋ] n τέλος, κατάληξις.

endive ['endaiv] n ἀντίδι, ραδίκι.

endless ['endlis] a ἀτελείωτος, ἀπέραντος.

endorse [in'dɔ:s] vt (cheque etc) ὀπισθογραφῶ, θεωρῶ ‖ (approve) ὑποστηρίζω, ἐγκρίνω ‖ ~ment *n* ὀπισθογράφησις ‖ (*of action*) ἔγκρισις.

endow [en'dau] *vt* προικίζω ‖ (*equip*) διωρίζω.

end product ['endprodʌkt] *n* τελικόν προϊόν.

endurable [en'djuərəbl] *a* ἀνεκτός, ὑποφερτός.

endurance [en'djuərəns] *n* ἀντοχή.

endure [en'djuə*] *vt* ὑπομένω, ἀνέχομαι ‖ *vi* διαρκῶ, ἀντέχω.

enemy ['enəmi] *n* ἐχθρός ‖ *a* ἐχθρικός.

energetic [enə'dʒetik] *a* ἐνεργητικός, δραστήριος.

energy ['enədʒi] *n* (*of person*) ἐνέργεια, δύναμις ‖ (*phys*) ἐνέργεια.

enforce [en'fo:s] *vt* ἐπιβάλλω, ἐκτελῶ, ἐφαρμόζω.

engage [en'geidʒ] *vt* (*hire*) προσλαμβάνω, παίρνω ‖ (*take part in*) ἀπασχολῶ, ἐπισύρω, τραβῶ ‖ (*begin fight*) ἐπιτίθεμαι ‖ (*tech*) συνδέω, βάζω ‖ ~d *a* (*to marry*) ἀρραβωνιασμένος ‖ (*tel*) κατειλημμένη, μιλάει ‖ (*in use*) ἀπησχολημένος, πιασμένος ‖ (*person*) εἶμαι προσκεκλημένος, ἔχω κλείσει ‖ ~ment *n* (*appointment*) δέσμευσις, ραντεβοῦ ‖ (*to marry*) μνηστεία, ἀρραβώνιασμα ‖ (*mil*) συμπλοκή, σύγκρουσις ‖ ~ment ring *n* βέρα.

engaging [en'geidʒiŋ] *a* θελκτικός, πού τραβάει.

engender [en'dʒendə*] *vt* γεννῶ, προκαλῶ.

engine ['endʒin] *n* (*aut*) μηχανή, κινητήρ, μοτέρ ‖ (*rail*) ἀτμομηχανή, ἀτμοατρίς ‖ ~er *n* μηχανικός ‖ (*US rail*) μηχανοδηγός ‖ ~ering *n* μηχανολογία ‖ ~ failure *or* trouble *n* βλάβη μηχανῆς ἤ κινητήρος.

England ['iŋglənd] *n* Ἀγγλία.

English ['iŋgliʃ] *a* ἀγγλικός ‖ *n* (*ling*) (τά) ἀγγλικά ‖ the ~ *npl* οἱ Ἀγγλοι ‖ ~ Channel *n* ἡ Μάγχη ‖ ~man *n* Ἀγγλος, Ἐγγλέζος ‖ ~woman *n* Ἀγγλίδα.

engrave [en'greiv] *vt* χαράσσω.

engraving [en'greiviŋ] *n* χαρακτική.

engrossed [en'grəust] *a* ἀπορροφημένος.

engulf [en'gʌlf] *vt* καταβροχθίζω, καταποντίζω.

enhance [en'ha:ns] *vt* ἐξαίρω, ἀνυψῶ, ἀνεβάζω.

enigma [e'nigmə] *n* αἴνιγμα ‖ ~tic [enig'mætik] *a* αἰνιγματικός, μυστηριώδης.

enjoy [en'dʒoi] *vt* μοῦ ἀρέσει, χαίρομαι (κάτι) ‖ (*privileges etc*) ἀπολαμβάνω, κατέχω ‖ ~able *a* ἀπολαυστικός, εὐχάριστος ‖ ~ment *n* ἀπόλαυσις.

enlarge [en'la:dʒ] *vt* μεγεθύνω, ἐπεκτείνω ‖ (*phot*) μεγεθύνω, μεγαλώνω ‖ ~ment *n* μεγέθυνσις.

enlighten [en'laitn] *vt* διαφωτίζω ‖ ~ed *a* φωτισμένος ‖ ~ment *n* διαφώτισις.

enlist [en'list] *vt* στρατολογῶ, προσλαμ-

βάνω ‖ *vi* στρατολογοῦμαι, κατατάσσομαι.

enmity ['enmiti] *n* ἔχθρα, ἐχθρότης.

enormity [i'no:miti] *n* φρικαλεότης, τερατωδία.

enormous [i'no:məs] *a* τεράστιος, πελώριος, κολοσσιαῖος ‖ ~ly *ad* κολοσσιαίως, καταπληκτικῶς.

enough [e'nʌf] *n* ἀρκετός, ἐπαρκής, ἱκανός ‖ *a* ἀρκετό ‖ *ad* ἐπαρκῶς, ἀρκετά ‖ ~! ἀρκετά!, φθάνει!, φθάνει πιά!

enquire [en'kwaiə*] = inquire.

enrich [en'ritʃ] *vt* (ἐμ)πλουτίζω.

enrol [en'rəul] *vt* (*mil*) στρατολογῶ ‖ *vi* ἐγγράφω, προσλαμβάνω, παίρνω ‖ ~ment *n* στρατολογία ‖ (*sch*) ἀριθμός μαθητῶν.

en route [ã'ru:t] *ad* καθ'ὁδόν.

ensign ['ensain] *n* (*flag*) σημαία ‖ (*naut*) σημαιοφόρος.

enslave [en'sleiv] *vt* ὑποδουλώνω, σκλαβώνω.

ensue [en'sju:] *vi* ἕπομαι, ἐπακολουθῶ.

ensuing [en'sju:iŋ] *a* ἑπόμενος, κατοπινός.

ensure [in'ʃuə*] *vt* (*make certain*) (ἐξ)ἀσφαλίζω.

entail [en'tail] *vt* συνεπάγομαι, ἐπιφέρω.

enter ['entə*] *vt* (*go into*) εἰσέρχομαι, μπαίνω ‖ (*join*) εἰσέρχομαι, κατατάσσομαι, γίνομαι ‖ (*write in*) ἐγγράφω, γράφω ‖ *vi* εἰσέρχομαι, μπαίνω ‖ to ~ for *vt* ἐγγράφω ‖ to ~ into *vt* (*agreement*) μπαίνω, συνάπτω, μετέχω ‖ (*argument*) μπαίνω ‖ to ~ upon *vt* ἀναλαμβάνω, ἀρχίζω.

enterprise ['entəpraiz] *n* τόλμη, θάρρος ‖ (*comm*) ἐπιχείρησις.

enterprising ['entəpraiziŋ] *a* τολμηρός.

entertain [entə'tein] *vt* (*as guest*) φιλοξενῶ, περιποιοῦμαι ‖ (*amuse*) διασκεδάζω ‖ ~er *n* ντιζέρ ‖ ~ing *a* διασκεδαστικός ‖ ~ment *n* (*amusement*) διασκέδασις ‖ (*show*) θέαμα.

enthralled [in'θro:ld] *a* γοητευμένος, κατακτημένος.

enthusiasm [in'θu:ziæzəm] *n* ἐνθουσιασμός.

enthusiast [in'θu:ziæst] *n* θαυμαστής, λάτρης ‖ ~ic [inθu:zi'æstik] *a* ἐνθουσιώδης, μανιώδης.

entice [in'tais] *vt* (*tempt*) δελεάζω, ξεμυαλίζω.

entire [en'taiə*] *a* ὁλόκληρος, ὁλάκαιρος, πλήρης ‖ ~ly *ad* ἀκέραια, πλήρως ‖ ~ty *n*: in its ~ty συνολικά.

entitle [en'taitl] *vt* (*allow*) ἐξουσιοδοτῶ, δίδω τό δικαίωμα, ἐπιτρέπω ‖ (*name*) τιτλοφορῶ.

entrance ['entrəns] *n* εἴσοδος, μπάσιμο ‖ [en'tra:ns] *vt* γοητεύω, μαγεύω ‖ ~ examination *n* εἰσαγωγικές ἐξετάσεις ‖ ~ fee *n* τιμή εἰσητηρίου, τιμή ἐγγραφῆς.

entrancing [in'trɑːnsiŋ] a γοητευτικός, μαγευτικός.

entrant ['entrənt] n ἀρχάριος, μαθητευόμενος.

entrée ['ɔntrei] n πρῶτο πιάτο, ἐντράδα.

entrenched [in'trentʃd] a ὀχυρωμένος.

entrust [in'trʌst] vt (confide) ἐμπιστεύομαι || (put in charge) ἐπιφορτίζω, ἀναθέτω.

entry ['entri] n (place) εἴσοδος || (act) εἴσοδος, ἐμφάνισις || (in dictionary) ἐγγραφή, καταχώρισις || 'no ~' ἀπαγορεύεται ἡ εἴσοδος' || ~ form n αἴτησις ἐγγραφῆς, δελτίον ἐγγραφῆς.

enunciate [i'nʌnsieit] vt προφέρω.

envelop [in'veləp] vt (περι)καλύπτω, τυλίγω, σκεπάζω || ~e ['envələup] n φάκελλος.

enviable ['enviəbl] a ἐπίζηλος, ἀξιοζήλευτος.

envious ['enviəs] a ζηλόφθονος, φθονερός, ζηλιάρης.

environment [in'vaiərənmənt] n περιβάλλον || ~al a τοῦ περιβάλλοντος.

envoy ['envɔi] n ἀπεσταλμένος.

envy ['envi] n φθόνος, ζήλεια || (object of envy) ἀντικείμενον ζήλειας || vt φθονῶ, ζηλεύω.

enzyme ['enzaim] n ἔνζυμον.

ephemeral [i'femərəl] a ἐφήμερος.

epic ['epik] n ἔπος, ἐπικόν ποίημα || a ἐπικός.

epidemic [epi'demik] n ἐπιδημία.

epigram ['epigræm] n ἐπίγραμμα.

epilepsy ['epilepsi] n ἐπιληψία.

epileptic [epi'leptik] a,n ἐπιληπτικός.

epilogue ['epilɔg] n ἐπίλογος.

episode ['episəud] n ἐπισόδειον.

epistle [i'pisl] n ἐπιστολή, γράμμα.

epitaph ['epitɑːf] n ἐπιτάφιον.

epitome [i'pitəmi] n ἐπιτομή, περίληψις, σύνοψις.

epitomize [i'pitəmaiz] vt συνοψίζω, κάνω περίληψιν.

epoch ['iːpɔk] n ἐποχή.

equable ['ekwəbl] a ὁμοιόμορφος, ἴσος.

equal ['iːkwl] a (same) ἴσος || (qualified) ἀντάξιος, ἀνταποκρίνομαι πρός || n ἴσος, ὁμότιμος, ὅμοιος || vt ἰσοῦμαι, εἰμαι ἴσος || ~ to ὁμοιῶ του, ἀνταποκρινόμενος || without ~ ἀσυναγώνιστος || ~ity n ἰσότης || ~ize vt ἐξισώνω, ἀντισταθμίζω || ~izer n ἐξισωτής, ἀντισταθμιστής || ~ly ad ἐξ ἴσου, ὁμοίως || ~(s) sign n σημεῖον ἰσότητος.

equanimity [ekwə'nimiti] n γαλήνη, ἠρεμία.

equate [i'kweit] vt ἐξισώνω.

equation [i'kweiʒən] n ἐξίσωσις.

equator [i'kweitə*] n ἰσημερινός || ~ial [ekwə'tɔːriəl] a ἰσημερινός.

equilibrium [iːkwi'libriəm] n ἰσορροπία.

equinox ['iːkwinɔks] n ἰσημερία.

equip [i'kwip] vt ἐφοδιάζω, ἐξοπλίζω || ~ment n ἐφόδια, ἐφοδιασμός, ὑλικά.

equitable ['ekwitəbl] a δίκαιος.

equity ['ekwiti] n δίκαιον, τιμιότης.

equivalent [i'kwivələnt] a ἰσότιμος || (tech) ἰσοδύναμος || n ἰσόποσον.

equivocal [i'kwivəkl] a (doubtful) διφορούμενος, ἀμφίβολος || (suspicious) ὕποπτος.

era ['iərə] n ἐποχή.

eradicate [i'rædikeit] vt ξερριζώνω.

erase [i'reiz] vt ἐξαλείφω, σβήνω || ~r n γομολάστιχα, γόμα.

erect [i'rekt] a ὀρθός, ὄρθιος, στητός, σηκωμένος || vt ὑψώνω, ἀναγείρω, κτίζω || ~ion n ὀρθωσις, σήκωμα, ἀνέργεσις.

ermine ['əːmin] n ἐρμίνα.

erode [i'rəud] vt διαβιβρώσκω, τρώγω.

erosion [e'rəuʒən] n διάβρωσις.

erotic [i'rɔtik] a ἐρωτικός || ~ism [i'rɔtisizəm] n ἐρωτισμός.

err [əː*] vi (make mistakes) σφάλλω, σφάλλομαι || (sin) πλανῶμαι, ἁμαρτάνω.

errand ['erənd] n παραγγελία, ἀποστολή || ~ boy n ὁ μικρός.

erratic [i'rætik] a ἄτακτος, ἀκανόνιστος, ἐκκεντρικός.

erroneous [e'rəuniəs] a ἐσφαλμένος, λαθεμένος.

error ['erə*] n σφάλμα, λάθος.

erudite ['erjudait] a πολυμαθής, διαβασμένος.

erupt [i'rʌpt] vi ἐκρήγνυμι || ~ion n ἔκρηξις, ξέσπασμα.

escalate ['eskəleit] vt ἀνεβάζω || vi ἀνεβαίνω.

escalator ['eskəleitə*] n κυλιωμένη κλίμαξ.

escapade [eskə'peid] n ξέσκασμα, κασκαρίκα.

escape [is'keip] n (getting away) (δια)φυγή, δραπέτευσις, σκάσιμο || (leakage) ἐκφυγή, διαρροή || vi (get free) δραπετεύω, (δια)σώζομαι || (unpunished) ξεφεύγω, γλυτώνω || (leak) διαφεύγω, διαρρέω, τρέχω || vt (be forgotten) διαφεύγω, εἰμαι ἀπαρατήρητος.

escapist [is'keipist] a τῆς φυγῆς.

escort ['eskɔːt] n (mil) συνοδεία, φρουρά || (of lady) συνοδός, καβαλιέρος || [is'kɔːt] vt (lady) συνοδεύω || (mil) συνοδεύω.

Eskimo ['eskiməu] n Ἐσκιμῶος.

especially [is'peʃəli] ad εἰδικῶς, ἰδιαιτέρως, κυρίως.

espionage ['espiənɑːʒ] n κατασκοπεία.

esplanade ['espləneid] n τόπος περιπάτου.

esquire [es'kwaiə*] n: J. Brown E~ (Κύριον).

essay ['esei] n (sch) ἔκθεσις || (liter) δοκίμιον, διατριβή.

essence ['esns] n (quality) οὐσία || (perfume) ἄρωμα, μυρουδιά.

essential [i'senʃl] a (necessary) οὐσιώδης, οὐσιαστικός || (basic) βασικός, ἀπαραίτητος || n οὐσία, τό ἀπαραίτητον || ~ly ad οὐσιαστικά, κυρίως.

establish [es'tæbliʃ] vt (set up) ἰδρύω,

θεμελιώνω, ἐγκαθιστῶ ‖ (prove) στηρίζω, στερεώνω, ἀποδεικνύω ‖ ~ment n (setting up) ἵδρυσις, δημιουργία, ἐπιβολή ‖ (house of business) ἵδρυμα, κατάστημα, οἴκος ‖ (mil) σύνθεσις (μονάδος) ‖ the E~ment τό Κατεστημένον.

estate [es'teit] n (landed property) κτῆμα, ἀκίνητον ‖ (property left) κληρονομία ‖ ~ agent n κτηματομεσίτης ‖ ~ car n (Brit) στέϊσον-βάγκον.

esteem [es'ti:m] n ἐκτιμῶ, θεωρῶ.

estimate ['estimit] n (opinion) ἐκτίμησις ‖ (price quoted) (προϋπολογισμός, τιμολόγιον ‖ ['estimeit] vt ἐκτιμῶ, ὑπολογίζω, λογαριάζω.

estimation [esti'meiʃən] n (judgment) κρίσις, γνώμη ‖ (esteem) ἐκτίμησις, ὑπόληψις.

estuary ['estjuəri] n ἐκβολή.

etching ['etʃiŋ] n γκραβούρα.

eternal [i'tə:nl] a αἰώνιος, ἀτελείωτος ‖ ~ly ad αἰωνίως.

eternity [i'tə:niti] n αἰωνιότης.

ether ['i:θə*] n αἰθέρας.

ethical ['eθikl] a ἠθικός.

ethics ['eθiks] npl ἠθική.

ethnic ['eθnik] a ἐθνικός.

etiquette ['etiket] n ἐθιμοτυπία, ἐτικέττα.

Eucharist ['ju:kərist] n Εὐχαριστία, Ἁγία Μετάληψις.

eulogy ['ju:lədʒi] n ἐγκώμιον.

eunuch ['ju:nək] n εὐνοῦχος, μουνοῦχος.

euphemism ['ju:fəmizəm] n εὐφημισμός.

euphoria [ju:'foriə] n εὐφορία.

Europe ['juərəp] n Εὐρώπη ‖ ~an a εὐρωπαῖκός.

euthanasia [ju:θə'neiziə] n εὐθανασία.

evacuate [i'vækjueit] vt ἐκκενώνω, διακομίζω.

evacuation [ivækju'eiʃən] n ἐκκένωσις, διακομιδή.

evade [i'veid] vt ἀποφεύγω, ξεφεύγω, διαφεύγω.

evaluate [i'væljueit] vt ἐκτιμῶ, ὑπολογίζω.

evangelical [ivæn'dʒelikl] a εὐαγγελικός.

evangelist [i'vændʒəlist] n Εὐαγγελιστής.

evaporate [i'væpəreit] vi ἐξατμίζομαι, ξεθυμαίνω ‖ vt ἐξατμίζω ‖ ~d milk n γάλα ἐβαπορέ.

evaporation [ivæpə'reiʃən] n ἐξάτμισις.

evasion [i'veiʒən] n (avoiding question) ὑπεκφυγή, πρόφασις.

evasive [i'veisiv] a πού ξεφεύγει, πού διαφεύγει.

even ['i:vən] a ὁμαλός, ἐπίπεδος, ἴσιος ‖ (score etc) ἰσόπαλος, πάτσι ‖ (number) ἄρτιος, ζυγός ‖ vt σιάζω, ἰσώνω, ἐξισώνω ‖ ad ἀκόμη, καί ἄν, ἤ ἀκόμη ‖ (emphasis) καί ἄν ἀκόμη ‖ ~ if κἄν ‖ to ~ out or up vi πατσίζω, ἀνταποδίδω τά ἴσα.

evening ['i:vniŋ] n (time) ἑσπέρα, βράδυ ‖ (event) ἑσπερίς, βραδυνή συγκέντρωσις ‖ in the ~ τό βράδυ ‖ ~ class n βραδυνό

μάθημα ‖ ~ dress n (man's) φράκο ‖ (woman's) βραδυνή τουαλέττα.

evenly ['i:vənli] ad ὁμοιομόρφως, ὁμαλῶς, κανονικά.

evensong ['i:vənsɔŋ] n (eccl) ἑσπερινός.

event [i'vent] n (happening) γεγονός, περίπτωσις, ἔκβασις ‖ (sport) ἄθλημα, ἀγών, μάτς ‖ in the ~ of εἰς περίπτωσιν ‖ ~ful a πλήρης γεγονότων, ἀλησμόνητος.

eventual [i'ventʃuəl] a (final) ὁριστικός, ἀναπόφευκτος, τελικός ‖ ~ity n πιθανότης ‖ ~ly ad (at last) τελικά ‖ (given time) πιθανῶς.

ever ['evə*] ad ποτέ, καμμιά φορά ‖ (always) πάντα, πάντοτε ‖ ~ so big τόσος δά ‖ ~ so many τόσοι καί τόσοι ‖ ~green a ἀειθαλής ‖ ~lasting a αἰώνιος, διαρκής, ἄφθαρτος.

every ['evri] a ἕκαστος, κάθε ‖ ~ other day μέρα παρά μέρα ‖ ~body pron ὅλοι, ὅλος ὁ κόσμος, καθένας ‖ ~day a (daily) κάθε μέρα, καθημερινός ‖ (commonplace) συνηθισμένος, κοινός ‖ ~one = ~body ‖ ~thing pron τά πάντα, ὅλα, κάθε τι ‖ ~where ad παντάχοῦ, παντοῦ.

evict [i'vikt] vt ἐκδιώκω, ἐξώνω, διώχνω ‖ ~ion n ἔξωσις, ἐκβολή.

evidence ['evidəns] n (sign) σημάδι, σημεῖον, ἔνδειξις ‖ (proof) ἀπόδειξις, μαρτυρία ‖ in ~ (obvious) διακρίνομαι, ξεχωρίζω.

evident ['evidənt] a προφανής, κατάδηλος, φανερός ‖ ~ly ad προφανῶς, ὁλοφάνερα.

evil ['i:vil] a κακός ‖ n τό κακόν ‖ (sin) κακία, ἁμαρτία.

evocative [i'vɔkətiv] a ἐπικλητικός.

evoke [i'vəuk] vt ἐπικαλοῦμαι, ἀναπολῶ.

evolution [i:və'lu:ʃən] n ἐξέλιξις, ἀνέλιξις.

evolve [i'vɔlv] vt ἀναπτύσσω, συνάγω ‖ vi ἐξελίσσομαι, ἀπορρέω.

ewe [ju:] n προβατίνα.

ex- [eks] a (former) πρώην, τέως.

exact [eg'zækt] a ἀκριβής, σωστός ‖ vt (obedience etc) ἀπαιτῶ, ζητῶ ‖ (payment) ἀποσπῶ, παίρνω ‖ ~ing a ἀπαιτητικός, κουραστικός ‖ ~itude n ἀκρίβεια ‖ ~ly ad ἀκριβῶς, σωστά ‖ ~ness n ἀκρίβεια.

exaggerate [eg'zædʒəreit] vti ὑπερβάλλω, μεγαλοποιῶ, (παρα)φουσκώνω ‖ ~d a ὑπερβολικός, ὑπερβάλλων.

exaggeration [egzædʒə'reiʃən] n ὑπερβολή, μεγαλοποίησις.

exalt [eg'zɔ:lt] vt ἐξυμνῶ, ἐκθειάζω, ἐπαινῶ.

exam [eg'zæm] n (col, sch, univ) see examination.

examination [egzæmi'neiʃən] n (sch, univ) ἐξετάσεις, διαγωνισμός ‖ (med) (ἰατρική) ἐξέτασις ‖ (inquiry) ἀνάκρισις, ἐξέτασις ‖ (customs) ἔλεγχος, ἔρευνα.

examine [eg'zæmin] vt (sch) ἐξετάζω ‖ (med) ἐξετάζω ‖ (consider) ἐξετάζω, ἐρευνῶ ‖ (baggage) ἐρευνῶ, ἐλέγχω ‖ ~r n ἐξεταστής, ἐπιθεωρητής.

example 262 expand

example [ig'za:mpl] *n* (παρά)δειγμα, ὑπόδειγμα || **for ~** παραδείγματος χάριν, λόγου χάριν.

exasperate [eg'za:spəreit] *vt* ἐξάπτω, ἐξαγριώνω.

exasperating [eg'za:spəreitiŋ] *a* ἐρεθιστικός, ἐξοργιστικός.

exasperation [egza:spə'reiʃən] *n* ἐκνευρισμός, ἔξαψις, ἀπόγνωσις.

excavate ['ekskəveit] *vt* (*hollow out*) σκάπτω, ἀνοίγω, βαθαίνω || (*unearth*) ἀνασκάπτω, κάνω ἀνασκαφές.

excavation [ekskə'veiʃən] *n* ἀνασκαφή.

excavator ['ekskəveitə*] *n* ἐκσκαφεύς.

exceed [ek'si:d] *vt* (*number*) ὑπερβαίνω, (ξε)περνῶ || (*limit*) ὑπερβαίνω || (*powers*) ὑπερβαίνω, ἐξέρχομαι || (*hopes*) ὑπερβάλλω || **~ingly** *ad* ὑπερβολικά, πολύ.

excel [ek'sel] *vi* διακρίνομαι, διαπρέπω, ξεχωρίζω || *vt* ὑπερέχω, ὑπερτερῶ, ξεπερνῶ || **~lence** ['eksələns] *n* ἀξία, ὑπεροχή, ἀρετή || **His E~lency** *n* ἡ Αὐτοῦ Ἐξοχότης || **~lent** *a* ἐξαίρετος, θαυμάσιος, ἐξαίσιος.

except [ek'sept] *prep* (*also ~* **for**) ἐκτός, ἔξω ἀπό, ἐξαιρουμένου τοῦ || *vt* ἐξαιρῶ, ἀποκλείω || **~ing** *prep* = **except** || **~ion** *n* ἐξαίρεσις || **to take ~ion** *to* προσβάλλομαι, ἀντιλέγω || **~ional** *a* ἐξαιρετικός, ἔξοχος, ἀσύγκριτος || **~ionally** *ad* ἐξαιρετικά, ὑπερβολικά.

excerpt ['eksə:pt] *n* ἀπόσπασμα.

excess [ek'ses] *n* ὑπερβολή, πληθώρα || *a* (*fare, baggage*) ὑπερβάλλων || **~ive** *a* ὑπερβολικός || **~ively** *ad* ὑπερβολικά.

exchange [eks'tʃeindʒ] *n* ἀνταλλαγή || (*foreign money*) συνάλλαγμα || (*tel*) κέντρον || *vt* (*goods*) ἀνταλλάσσω, ἀλλάζω || (*greetings*) ἀνταλλάσσω χαιρετισμούς || (*blows*) ἀνταλλάσσω γροθιές || *see* **rate.**

exchequer [eks'tʃekə*] *n* δημόσιον ταμεῖον, θησαυροφυλάκιον.

excisable [ek'saizəbl] *a* φορολογήσιμος.

excise ['eksaiz] *n* φόρος || [ek'saiz] *vt* φορολογῶ.

excitable [ek'saitəbl] *a* εὐερέθιστος, εὐέξαπτος.

excite [ek'sait] *vt* (ἐξ)ερεθίζω, ἐξεγείρω, κεντρίζω || **~d** *a* συγκεκινημένος, ἐκνευρισμένος || **to get ~d** ἐξάπτομαι || **~ment** *n* ἔξαψις, ἀναστάτωσις.

exciting [ek'saitiŋ] *a* συναρπαστικός, συγκινητικός.

exclaim [eks'kleim] *vi* φωνάζω, ἀναφωνῶ.

exclamation [eksklə'meiʃən] *n* ἀναφώνησις, κραυγή || **~ mark** *n* θαυμαστικόν.

exclude [iks'klu:d] *vt* ἀποκλείω.

exclusion [iks'klu:ʒən] *n* ἀποκλεισμός.

exclusive [iks'klu:siv] *a* (*select*) κλειστή, περιορισμένη || (*sole*) ἀποκλειστικότης || μοναδικός || (*news etc*) ἀποκλειστικότητε || **~ly** *ad* ἀποκλειστικῶς, μόνον.

excommunicate [ekskə'mju:nikeit] *vt* ἀφορίζω, ἀναθεματίζω.

excrement ['ekskrimənt] *n* ἀποπάτημα, σκατά.

excruciating [eks'kru:ʃieitiŋ] *a* φρικτός, ἀνυπόφορος.

excursion [eks'kə:ʃən] *n* ἐκδρομή.

excusable [eks'kju:zəbl] *a* συγχωρητός.

excuse [eks'kju:s] *n* δικαιολογία, πρόφασις || [eks'kju:z] *vt* (*let off*) ἀπαλλάσσω, συγχωρῶ || (*overlook*) δικαιολογῶ || **~ me!** συγγνώμη, μέ συγχωρεῖτε.

execute ['eksikju:t] *vt* (*perform*) ἐκτελῶ, ἐκπληρῶ, ἐνεργῶ || (*put to death*) ἐκτελῶ, θανατώνω.

execution [eksi'kju:ʃən] *n* ἐκτέλεσις || **~er** *n* δήμιος, μπόγιας.

executive [eg'zekjutiv] *n* (*comm*) διευθυντής || (*pol*) ἐκτελεστική ἐξουσία || *a* ἐκτελεστικός.

executor [eg'zekjutə*] *n* ἐκτελεστής.

exemplary [ig'zempləri] *a* ὑποδειγματικός.

exemplify [ig'zemplifai] *vt* παραδειγματίζω.

exempt [ig'zempt] *a* ἀπηλλαγμένος, ἐξηρημένος || *vt* ἐξαιρῶ, ἀπαλλάσσω || **~ion** *n* ἀπαλλαγή.

exercise ['eksəsaiz] *n* (*of duties*) ἄσκησις || (*physical*) γυμναστική || (*sch*) σχολική ἄσκησις, γυμναστική || (*mil*) ἄσκησις, γυμνάσια || *vt* (*muscle*) ἐξασκῶ, γυμνάζω || (*power*) ἐξασκῶ || (*patience*) ἐξαντλῶ ὑπομονήν, κάνω ὑπομονή || **~ book** *n* τετράδιον (μαθητοῦ).

exhaust [ig'zɔ:st] *n* (*fumes*) ἐξάτμισις, καυσαέρια || (*pipe*) σωλήν ἐξαγωγῆς || *vt* (*weary*) ἐξαντλῶ, κατακουράζω || (*use up*) ἐξαντλῶ, στειρεύω || **~ed** *a* ἐξηντλημένος || **~ing** *a* ἐξαντλητικός, κουραστικός || **~ion** *n* ἐξάντλησις, ἀποκάμωμα, τσάκισμα || **~ive** *a* ἐξαντλητικός, πλήρης.

exhibit [ig'zibit] *n* (*art*) ἔκθεμα, ἔκθεσις || (*law*) τεκμήριον || *vt* ἐκθέτω, παρουσιάζω, ἐπιδεικνύω || **~ion** [eksi'biʃən] *n* (*art*) ἔκθεσις || (*of temper etc*) ἐπίδειξις, γελοιοποίησις || **~ionist** *n* ἐπιδειξίας || **~or** *n* ἐκθέτης.

exhilarating [ig'ziləreitiŋ] *a* φαιδρυντικός, εὐχάριστος.

exhilaration [igzilə'reiʃən] *n* χαρά, εὐθυμία, κέφι.

exhort [eg'zɔ:t] *vt* προτρέπω, ἐνθαρρύνω.

exile ['eksail] *n* ἐξορία || (*person*) ἐξόριστος.

exist [eg'zist] *vi* ὑπάρχω, ὑφίσταμαι, εἶμαι, ζῶ || **~ence** *n* (*state of being*) ὕπαρξις || (*way of life*) ζωή || **~ing** *a* ὑπάρχων, παρών, σημερινός.

exit ['eksit] *n* ἔξοδος.

exorbitant [eg'zɔ:bitənt] *a* ὑπερβολικός, ὑπέρμετρος.

exotic [ig'zɔtik] *a* ἐξωτικός.

expand [iks'pænd] *vt* (*spread*) διαστέλλω,

εὐρύνω, ἀπλώνω ‖ (*operations*) ἐπεκτείνω, ἀναπτύσσω ‖ *vi* διαστέλλομαι, φουσκώνω.

expanse [eks'pæns] *n* ἔκτασις.

expansion [iks'pænʃən] *n* ἐπέκτασις, ἀνάπτυξις ‖ (*phys*) διαστολή, ἐκτόνωσις.

expatriate [eks'pætrieit] *vt* ἐκπατρίζω, ἐκπατρίζομαι.

expect [iks'pekt] *vt* (*anticipate*) ἀναμένω, προσδοκῶ, περιμένω ‖ (*require*) ἀπαιτῶ, ἀναμένω ‖ (*suppose*) σκέπτομαι, φρονῶ, πιστεύω ‖ (*baby*) περιμένω ‖ *vi*: **to be ~ing** περιμένω παιδί ‖ **~ant** *a* (*hopeful*) περιμένων, ἀναμένων ‖ (*mother*) ἐπίτοκος ‖ **~ation** [ekspek'teiʃən] *n* (*hope*) προσδοκία, ἐλπίδα ‖ **~ations** *npl* ἐλπίδες.

expedience [eks'pi:diəns] *n*, **expediency** [eks'pi:diənsi] *n* σκοπιμότης, ὠφελιμότης.

expedient [eks'pi:diənt] *a* σκόπιμος, πρόσφορος, κατάλληλος ‖ *n* μέσον, τρόπος, τέχνασμα.

expedite ['ekspidait] *vt* ἐπισπεύδω, ἐπιταχύνω.

expedition [ekspi'diʃən] *n* (*journey*) ἀποστολή, ἐκστρατεία.

expel [eks'pel] *vt* διώχνω, βγάζω ‖ (*alien*) ἀπελαύνω.

expend [eks'pend] *vt* (*time*) ἀφιερώνω, διαθέτω ‖ (*money*) δαπανῶ, ξοδεύω ‖ (*effort*) δαπανῶ, ἐξαντλῶ ‖ **~able** *a* ἀναλώσιμος ‖ **~iture** *n* δαπάνη, κατανάλωσις, ἔξοδα.

expense [eks'pens] *n* (*cost*) δαπάνη, ἔξοδα ‖ (*high cost*) βάρος, ἀκρίβεια ‖ **~s** *npl* ἀποζημίωσις, δαπάναι ‖ **at the ~ of** μέ τήν θυσία τοῦ, εἰς βάρος τοῦ ‖ **~ account** *n* ἔξοδα παραστάσεως.

expensive [eks'pensiv] *a* πολυδάπανος, δαπανηρός, ἀκριβός.

experience [eks'piəriəns] *n* (*happening*) δοκιμασία, περιπέτεια ‖ (*knowledge*) πεῖρα, ἐμπειρία ‖ *vt* δοκιμάζω, ὑφίσταμαι, αἰσθάνομαι ‖ **~d** *a* πεπειραμένος, ἔμπειρος.

expert ['ekspə:t] *n* εἰδικός, ἐμπειρογνώμων, πραγματογνώμων ‖ *a* πεπειραμένος, εἰδικός ‖ **~ise** *n* πραγματογνωμοσύνη.

expiration [ekspi'reiʃən] *n* ἐκπνοή.

expire [eks'paiə*] *vi* (*end*) ἐκπνέω, λήγω, τελειώνω ‖ (*die*) ἀποθνήσκω, πεθαίνω ‖ (*ticket*) λήγω.

expiry [eks'paiəri] *n* ἐκπνοή, λῆξις.

explain [eks'plein] *vt* (*make clear*) ἐξηγῶ, λύω, ἑρμηνεύω ‖ (*account for*) ἐξηγοῦμαι, δικαιολογοῦμαι ‖ **to ~ away** *vt* ἐξηγῶ, δικαιολογῶ.

explanation [eksplə'neiʃən] *n* ἐξήγησις.

explanatory [eks'plænətəri] *a* ἑρμηνευτικός, ἐξηγητικός.

explicable [eks'plikəbl] *a* ἐξηγήσιμος.

explicit [eks'plisit] *a* ρητός, σαφής, καθα-

ρός, κατηγορηματικός ‖ **~ly** *ad* κατηγορηματικῶς, ρητῶς.

explode [eks'pləud] *vi* σκάω, ἀνατινάζομαι.

exploit ['eksplɔit] *n* κατόρθωμα, ἀνδραγάθημα ‖ [iks'plɔit] *vt* ἐκμεταλλεύομαι ‖ **~ation** *n* ἐκμετάλλευσις.

exploration [eksplə'reiʃən] *n* ἐξερεύνησις, ἔρευνα.

exploratory [eks'plɔrətəri] *a* (*fig*) δοκιμαστικός.

explore [eks'plɔ:*] *vt* (*for discovery*) ἐξερευνῶ ‖ (*examine*) ἐξετάζω, (ἐξ)ἐρευνῶ ‖ **~r** *n* ἐξερευνητής.

explosion [eks'pləuʒən] *n* (*lit*) ἔκρηξις, ἐκτόνωσις ‖ (*fig*) ξεχείλισμα, ξέσπασμα.

explosive [eks'pləuziv] *a* ἐκρηκτικός ‖ *n* ἐκρηκτικόν, ἐκρηκτική ὕλη.

exponent [eks'pəunənt] *n* ἑρμηνευτής, ὑπέρμαχος ‖ (*math*) ἐκθέτης.

export [eks'pɔ:t] *vt* ἐξάγω ‖ ['ekspɔ:t] *n* ἐξαγωγή ‖ *a* (*trade*) ἐξαγωγικός ‖ **~ation** *n* ἐξαγωγή ‖ **~er** *n* ἐξαγωγεύς.

expose [eks'pəuz] *vt* (*uncover*) ἐκθέτω, ἀποκαλύπτω, ξεσκεπάζω ‖ (*leave unprotected*) ἀφήνω ἀπροστάτευτον, ἐκθέτω ‖ (*plot*) ἀποκαλύπτω.

exposé [eks'pəuzei] *n* (*of scandal*) ἀποκάλυψις σκανδάλων.

exposed [eks'pəuzd] *a* (*position*) ἐκτεθειμένος.

exposure [eks'pəuʒə*] *n* τράβηγμα, πόζα, φωτογραφία ‖ (*med*) ἔκθεσις ‖ **~ meter** *n* φωτόμετρον.

expound [eks'paund] *vt* ἀναπτύσσω, ἐκθέτω, ἐξηγῶ.

express [eks'pres] *a* (*clearly stated*) σαφής, ρητός ‖ (*speedy*) ταχύς ‖ *n* (*fast train*) ταχεῖα, ἐξπρές ‖ *ad* (*speedily*) γρήγορα, ἄνευ σταθμοῦ ‖ *vt* (*idea*) ἐκφράζω, διατυπώνω ‖ (*feeling*) ἐκφράζω, ἐκδηλώνω ‖ **to ~ o.s.** ἐκφράζομαι ‖ **~ion** *n* (*phrase*) (ἐκ)φρασις, τρόπος ἐκφράσεως ‖ (*look on face*) ἔκφρασις ‖ (*showing*) ἐκδήλωσις ‖ **~ive** *a* ἐκφραστικός ‖ **~ly** *ad* ρητῶς, ἐπίτηδες.

expropriate [eks'prəuprieit] *vt* ἀπαλλοτριῶ.

expulsion [eks'pʌlʃən] *n* ἀπέλασις, ἀποβολή.

exquisite [eks'kwizit] *a* ἄριστος, εὐχάριστος, λεπτός ‖ **~ly** *ad* μέ λεπτότητα, ἐξαιρετικά.

extend [eks'tend] *vt* (*visit*) παρατείνω ‖ (*building*) ἐπεκτείνω, μεγαλώνω ‖ (*hand*) τείνω, δίνω (τό χέρι) ‖ (*welcome*) εὔχομαι, καλωσορίζω.

extension [eks'tenʃən] *n* (*general*) ἔκτασις, ἐπέκτασις, ἅπλωμα ‖ (*building*) ἐπέκτασις, εὔρυνσις ‖ (*tel*) ἐσωτερική γραμμή.

extensive [eks'tensiv] *a* ἐκτεταμένος, ἐκτενής, μεγάλος ‖ **~ly** *ad* (*travel*) εὐρέως ‖ (*use*) ἐκτεταμένα.

extent [eks'tent] *n* ἔκτασις, σημασία, μέγεθος.

extenuating [eks'tenjuːeitiŋ] *a* ἐλαφρυντικόν.

exterior [eks'tiəriə*] *a* ἐξωτερικός ‖ *n* ἐξωτερικόν, ἔξω.

exterminate [eks'tə:mineit] *vt* ἐξοντώνω, ἐξολοθρεύω.

extermination [ekstə:mi'neiʃən] *n* ἐξολόθρευσις, ἐκρίζωσις.

external [eks'tə:nl] *a* ἐξωτερικός ‖ ~**ly** *ad* ἐξωτερικῶς, ἀπέξω.

extinct [eks'tiŋkt] *a* (*animal etc*) ἐκλειπών, ἐξαφανισθείς ‖ ~**ion** *n* ἐξαφάνισις, σβήσιμο.

extinguish [eks'tiŋgwiʃ] *vt* σβήνω ‖ ~**er** *n* πυροσβεστήρ.

extort [iks'tɔ:t] *vt* (+*from*) ἀποσπῶ ‖ ~**ion** [iks'tɔ:ʃən] *n* ἀναγκαστική εἴσπραξις, ἀπόσπασις ‖ ~**ionate** *a* ὑπερβολικός.

extra ['ekstrə] *a* πρόσθετος, ἔκτακτος, ἔξτρα ‖ *ad* ἄνω τοῦ συνήθους, ἐξαιρετικῶς, πολύ ‖ *n* συμπλήρωμα ‖ (*newspaper*) ἔκτακτος ἔκδοσις ‖ (*theat*) κομπάρσος.

extract [eks'trækt] *vt* (*distil*) ἀποστάζω ‖ (*select*) ἐξάγω, βγάζω, παίρνω ‖ ['ekstrækt] *n* (*liter*) ἀπόσπασμα, ἐκλογή ‖ (*cooking*) ἐκχύλισμα ‖ ~**ion** *n* ἐξαγωγή, βγάλσιμο ‖ (*origin*) καταγωγή, προέλευσις.

extradite ['ekstrədait] *vt* ἐκδίδω (ἐγκληματίαν).

extradition [ekstrə'diʃən] *n* ἔκδοσις (ἐγκληματίου).

extraneous [eks'treiniəs] *a* ξένος, ἄσχετος.

extraordinary [eks'trɔːdnri] *a* ἔκτακτος, ἐξαιρετικός ‖ (*strange*) παράξενος, ἀλλόκοτος.

extravagance [eks'trævəgəns] *n* (*wasteful spending*) σπατάλη ‖ (*no restraint*) ὑπερβολή, παραλογισμός.

extravagant [eks'trævəgənt] *a* (*lavish*) ὑπερβολικός, παράλογος ‖ (*wasteful*) σπάταλος, ἄσωτος.

extreme [eks'tri:m] *a* (*last*) ἀκραῖος, ἔσχατος, μακρυνός ‖ (*very great*) ὑπερβολικός, μέγιστος ‖ (*not moderate*) τῶν ἄκρων, ἐξαιρετικός ‖ *n* ἄκρον, ἐσχατιά, ἄκρη ‖ ~**s** *npl* ἄκρα ‖ ~**ly** *ad* ἄκρως, εἰς τὸ ἔπακρον.

extremist [eks'tri:mist] *a* ἀδιάλλακτος, τῶν ἄκρων ‖ *n* ἐξτρεμιστής.

extremity [eks'tremiti] *n* (*farthest end*) ἄκρον, ἐσχατιά, ἄκρη ‖ (*necessity*) ἐσχάτη ἀνάγκη ‖ (*anat*) τά ἄκρα.

extricate ['ekstrikeit] *vt* ἐξάγω, βγάζω, ξεμπλέκω.

extrovert ['ekstrəuvə:t] *a,n* ἐξώστροφος.

exuberance [ig'zju:bərəns] *n* ὑπερεκχείλισις, διάχυσις.

exuberant [ig'zju:bərənt] *a* διαχυτικός, ὑπερεκχειλίζων.

exude [ig'zju:d] *vt* ἐξιδρῶ, ἐκχύνω.

exult [ig'zʌlt] *vi* χαίρομαι, ἀγάλλομαι,

θριαμβεύω ‖ ~**ation** [egzʌl'teiʃən] *n* ἀγαλλίασις.

eye [ai] *n* (*anat*) ὀφθαλμός, μάτι ‖ (*of needle*) μάτι, τρύπα ‖ (*for perception*) καλό μάτι, μάτι ζωγράφου κτλ ‖ (*in the public eye*) διάσημος ‖ *vt* ὑποβλέπω, ἐποφθαλμιῶ, κοιτάζω ‖ to keep an ~ on προσέχω, ἐπιβλέπω, παρακολουθῶ ‖ in the ~**s** of ἐνώπιον, στά μάτια ‖ up to the ~**s** in πνιγμένος στό, φορτωμένος μέ ‖ ~**ball** *n* βολβός ὀφθαλμοῦ ‖ ~**brow** *n* φρύδι ‖ ~**lash** *n* βλεφαρίδα, ματοτσίνουρο ‖ ~**lid** *n* βλέφαρον ‖ ~**-opener** *n* ἔκπληξις, ἀποκάλυψις ‖ ~**shadow** *n* σκιά ματιῶν ‖ ~**sight** *n* ὅρασις ‖ ~**sore** *n* ἀσχημιά ‖ ~**wash** *n* (*lit*) κολλύριον ὑγρόν ‖ (*fig*) ἀπάτη, φούμαρα ‖ ~**witness** *n* αὐτόπτης μάρτυς.

F, f

fable ['feibl] *n* μύθος, παραμύθι.

fabric ['fæbrik] *n* (*cloth*) ὕφασμα, πανί.

fabulous ['fæbjuləs] *a* (*imaginary*) μυθικός, μυθώδης ‖ (*wonderful*) μυθικός ‖ (*unbelievable*) ὑπερβολικής.

façade [fə'sɑ:d] *n* πρόσοψις.

face [feis] *n* (*anat*) πρόσωπον, φάτσα, μούρη ‖ (*appearance*) φυσιογνωμία ‖ (*grimace*) μορφασμός ‖ (*front*) ὄψις, ἐμφάνισις ‖ (*of clock*) καντράν ‖ *vt* (*look towards*) ἀντικρύζω, γυρίζω ‖ (*bravely*) ἀντιμετωπίζω ‖ in the ~ of ἐνώπιον, μπρός ἀπό, εἰς ‖ to ~ up to *vt* ἀντιμετωπίζω ‖ ~ **cream** *n* κρέμα (τοῦ προσώπου) ‖ ~ **powder** *n* πούδρα (τοῦ προσώπου).

facet ['fæsit] *n* (*single part*) μέρος, πλευρά ‖ (*of gem*) ἕδρα διαμαντιοῦ.

facetious [fə'si:ʃəs] *a* εὐτράπελος, ἀστεῖος, περιπαικτικός ‖ ~**ly** *ad* εὐτράπελα, πειραχτά.

face to face ['feistu:'feis] *ad* πρόσωπο μέ πρόσωπο, φάτσα μέ φάτσα.

face value ['feis'vælju:] *n* ὀνομαστική ἀξία.

facial ['feiʃəl] *a* τοῦ προσώπου, καθάρσις, μάσκα.

facile ['fæsail] *a* (*US: easy*) εὔκολος.

facilitate [fə'siliteit] *vt* (δι)ευκολύνω.

facility [fə'siliti] *n* (*ease*) εὐκολία, εὐχέρεια, εὐκολία ‖ **facilities** *npl* ἀνέσεις, εὐκολίες.

facing ['feisiŋ] *a,prep* ἀπέναντι ἀπό, ἀντίκρυ.

facsimile [fæk'simili] *n* πανομοιότυπον.

fact [fækt] *n* γεγονός, πραγματικότης ‖ *see* **matter**.

faction ['fækʃən] *n* φατρία, κόμμα.

factor ['fæktə*] *n* παράγων, συντελεστής.

factory ['fæktəri] *n* ἐργοστάσιον.

factual ['fæktjuəl] *a* πραγματικός.

faculty ['fækəlti] *n* (*ability*) ἱκανότης, προσόν ‖ (*univ*) σχολή ‖ (*US: teaching staff*) διδακτικόν προσωπικόν.

fade [feid] *vt* (*cause to fade*) ξεθωριάζω, ξεβάφω ‖ *vi* (*grow dim*) ἐξασθενίζω, ἀδυνατίζω, πέφτω ‖ (*lose colour*) ξασπρίζω, ξεθωριάζω, ξεβάφω ‖ (*wither*) μαραίνομαι ‖ ~**d** *a* ξεβαμμένος, ξεθωριασμένος, ‖ (*of flower*) μαραμένος.

fag [fæg] *n* ἀγγαρεία, μόχθος ‖ (*col: cigarette*) τσιγάρο ‖ ~**ged** *a* (*exhausted*) ἐξηντλημένος.

Fahrenheit ['færənhait] *n* Φαρενάϊτ.

fail [feil] *vt* (*exam*) ἀπορρίπτω, ἀποτυγχάνω ‖ *vi* (*run short*) ἐλείπω, λείπω, δέν ὑπάρχω ‖ (*lose power*) ἐγκαταλείπω, χάνω, ἐξασθενίζω ‖ (*light*) ἐξασθενίζω, πέφτω, σβήνω ‖ (*remedy*) ἀποτυγχάνω ‖ **to ~ to do sth** (*neglect*) παραλείπω, ἐγκαταλείπω ‖ (*be unable*) ἀποτυγχάνω ‖ **without ~** χωρίς ἄλλο ‖ ~**ing** *n* (*shortcoming*) ἐλάττωμα, ἀδυναμία ‖ *prep* ἐλλείψει ‖ ~**ure** *n* (*person*) ἀποτυχημένος ‖ (*mech*) διακοπή, βλάβη.

faint [feint] *a* ἀδύνατος, ἀσθενής, ἀμυδρός, δειλός ‖ *n* λιποθυμία, ἀναισθησία ‖ *vi* λιποθυμῶ ‖ ~**hearted** *a* δειλός, μικρόψυχος, φοβιτσιάρης ‖ ~**ly** *ad* ντροπαλά, ἀδύνατα, ἄτονα, μόλις ‖ ~**ness** *n* (*of voice*) ἀδυναμία ‖ (*of light*) ἀμυδρότης.

fair [fεə*] *a* (*beautiful*) ὡραῖος, ὅμορφος ‖ (*light*) ξανθός, ἄσπρος ‖ (*weather*) καλός καιρός, καλοκαιριά ‖ (*just, honest*) δίκαιος, ἔντιμος, τίμιος ‖ (*tolerable*) ὑποφερτός ‖ (*conditions*) ἔτσι καί ἔτσι ‖ (*sizeable*) ἀρκετός, μεγάλος ‖ *ad* (*play*) τίμια, δίκαια, ἐντίμως ‖ *n* (*comm*) πανήγυρις, Ἔκθεσις ‖ (*fun fair*) λούνα-πάρκ, πανηγύρι ‖ ~**ly** *ad* ἔντιμα, δίκαια ‖ (*rather*) ἀρκετά καλό, σχεδόν, καλούτσικα ‖ ~**ness** *n* τιμιότης, ἐντιμότης ‖ ~**way** *n* (*golf*) κανονική διαδρομή.

fairy ['fεəri] *n* νεράϊδα ‖ ~**land** *n* χώρα τῶν παραμυθιῶν ‖ ~ **tale** *n* παραμύθι.

faith [feiθ] *n* (*trust*) ἐμπιστοσύνη, πίστις ‖ (*rel*) πίστις, θρήσκευμα, θρησκεία ‖ **on good** ~ μέ καλή πίστι ‖ ~**ful** *a* πιστός ‖ ~**fully** *ad* πιστῶς, ἐντίμως ‖ (*in letter*) ὑμέτερος.

fake [feik] *n* (*thing*) ψεύτικο εἶδος, ἀπομίμησις ‖ (*person*) ἀπατεών ‖ *a* ψεύτικο, πλαστό ‖ *vt* παραποιῶ, πλαστογραφῶ.

falcon ['fɔːlkən] *n* γεράκι.

fall [fɔːl] (*irreg v*) *n* πτῶσις, κατέβασμα ‖ (*drop*) πτῶσις, πέσιμο ‖ (*of snow*) πτῶσις ‖ (*US: autumn*) φθινόπωρον ‖ *vi* πέφτω, πίπτω ‖ ~**s** *npl* (*waterfall*) καταρράκτης ‖ **to ~ down** *vi* (*person*) πέφτω χάμω ‖ (*building*) καταρρέω, γκρεμίζομαι ‖ (*fail*) ἀποτυγχάνω, πέφτω ‖ **to ~ flat** *vi* πάω χαμένο, πέφτω στά κούφια, πέφτω ‖ **to ~ for** *vt* (*trick*) πιάνομαι κορόϊδο, πέφτω στήν παγίδα ‖ **to ~ off** *vi* (*drop off*) πέφτω ‖ (*diminish*) πέφτω, φθίνω, μειοῦμαι, ὀλιγοστεύω ‖ **to ~ out** *vi* τσακώνομαι, τά χαλῶ ‖ **to ~ through** *vi* ἀποτυγχάνω,

γκρεμίζομαι ‖ **to ~ under** *vi* ὑπάγομαι εἰς.

fallacy ['fæləsi] *n* σόφισμα, πλάνη.

fallen ['fɔːlən] *pp* *of* **fall**.

fallible ['fæləbl] *a* σφαλερός.

fallout ['fɔːlaut] *n* ραδιενεργός κόνις.

fallow ['fæləu] *a* χέρσος, ἀκαλλιέργητος.

false [fɔːls] *a* (*untrue*) ψευδής, ψεύτικος, λαθεμένος ‖ (*sham*) πλαστός, τεχνητός, κίβδηλος ‖ **under ~ pretences** δι'ἀπάτης ‖ ~ **alarm** *n* ἀδικαιολόγητος φόβος ‖ ~**ly** *ad* ψεύτικα, ἀπατηλά ‖ ~ **teeth** *npl* μασέλλες.

falter ['fɔːltə*] *vi* διστάζω, κοντοστέκω, κομπιάζω ‖ (*in speech*) τραυλίζω, ψευδίζω ‖ ~**ing** *a* διστακτικός, ἀσταθής.

fame [feim] *n* φήμη.

familiar [fə'miliə*] *a* (*well-known*) γνωστός, γνώριμος ‖ (*intimate*) οἰκεῖος, στενός, φιλικός ‖ **to be ~ with** ξαίρω, γνωρίζω ‖ ~**ity** *n* οἰκειότης, ἐξοικείωσις ‖ ~**ize** *vt* ἐξοικειοῦμαι μέ, συνηθίζω.

family ['fæmili] *n* οἰκογένεια, φαμίλια ‖ ~ **allowance** *n* ἐπίδομα οἰκογενείας ‖ ~ **business** *n* οἰκογενειακή ἐπιχείρησις ‖ ~ **doctor** *n* οἰκογενειακός ἰατρός ‖ ~ **life** *n* οἰκογενειακή ζωή.

famine ['fæmin] *n* λιμός, πεῖνα.

famished ['fæmiʃt] *a* πειναμένος.

famous ['feiməs] *a* διάσημος, περίφημος, φημισμένος ‖ ~**ly** *ad* περίφημα, σπουδαῖα.

fan [fæn] *n* (*folding*) βεντάλια ‖ (*elec*) ἀνεμιστήρας ‖ (*sport etc*) φανατικός θαυμαστής, φάν ‖ *vt* ἀεριζω, ἀνεμίζω ‖ **to ~ out** *vi* ἀναπτύσσω, ἁπλώνω.

fanatic [fə'nætik] *n* φανατικός ‖ ~**al** *a* φανατικός.

fan belt ['fænbelt] *n* ἱμάς, ταινία, λουρί.

fancied ['fænsid] *a* φανταστικός, φαντασιώδης.

fanciful ['fænsiful] *a* (*odd*) παράξενος, ἰδιότροπος ‖ (*imaginative*) φανταστικός.

fancy ['fænsi] *n* (*liking*) συμπάθεια, ἀγάπη, τσίμπημα ‖ (*imagination*) φαντασία, φανταστικόν πρᾶγμα ‖ *a* φαντασιώδης, φανταχτερός, φανταιζί ‖ *vt* (*like*) συμπαθῶ, μοῦ ἀρέσει ‖ (*imagine*) φαντάζομαι, ὑποθέτω ‖ (*just*) ~ (**that**)! γιά φαντάσου! ‖ ~ **dress** *n* μεταμφίεσις ‖ ~**-dress ball** *n* χορός μεταμφιεσμένων, μπάλ μασκέ.

fanfare ['fænfεə*] *n* σάλπισμα.

fang [fæŋ] *n* δόντι ‖ (*of snake*) φαρμακερό δόντι.

fantastic [fæn'tæstik] *a* παράξενος, φαντασιώδης, ἀλλόκοτος.

fantasy ['fæntəzi] *n* φαντασία, καπρίτσιο.

far [fɑː*] *a* μακρυνός, ἀπώτερος ‖ *ad* μακρυά, μακράν ‖ (*very much*) πολύ, τόσο πολύ ‖ ~ **away**, ~ **off** πολύ μακρυά ‖ **by** ~ ἀσυγκρίτως, κατά πολύ ‖ **so** ~

ἕως ἐδῶ, μέχρι τοῦδε ‖ ~**away** a μακρυνός ‖ the F~ East ˝Απω ᾿Ανατολή.

farce [fɑːs] n κωμωδία, φάρσα.

farcical [ˈfɑːsikəl] a γελοῖος, κωμικός, σάν φάρσα.

fare [fɛə*] n εἰσιτήριον, ναῦλα ‖ (food) φαΐ ‖ vi τά πάω, πηγαίνω ‖ ~**well** n ἀποχαιρετισμός ‖ excl ἀντίο!, χαίρετε!, γειά σου! ‖ a ἀποχαιρετιστήριος.

far-fetched [ˈfɑːˈfetʃt] a ἐξεζητημένος, παρατραβηγμένος.

farm [fɑːm] n ἀγρόκτημα, φάρμα ‖ vt καλλιεργῶ ‖ ~**er** n γεωργός, ἀγρότης, φαρμαδόρος ‖ ~**hand** n ἀγροτικός ἐργάτης ‖ ~**house** n ἀγροικία ‖ ~**ing** n γεωργία, καλλιέργεια ‖ ~**land** n ἀγροτική ἔκτασις ‖ ~**yard** n περίβολος ἀγροικίας.

far-reaching [ˈfɑːˈriːtʃiŋ] a μεγάλης ἐκτάσεως, μεγάλης σημασίας.

far-sighted [ˈfɑːˈsaitid] a προνοητικός, διορατικός.

fart [fɑːt] (col) n πορδή ‖ vi πέρδομαι, κλάνω.

farther [ˈfɑːðə*] a μακρυνότερος, ἀπώτερος ‖ ad μακρύτερα, περαιτέρω.

farthest [ˈfɑːðist] a ἀπώτατος, μακρυνότερος ‖ ad μακρύτατα, πιό μακρά.

fascinate [ˈfæsineit] vt γοητεύω, μαγεύω.

fascinating [ˈfæsineitiŋ] a γοητευτικός, μαγευτικός.

fascination [fæsiˈneiʃən] n γοητεία, μάγεμα.

fascism [ˈfæʃizəm] n φασισμός.

fascist [ˈfæʃist] n φασιστής, φασίστας ‖ a φασιστικός.

fashion [ˈfæʃən] n (custom) ράψιμο, μόδα ‖ (manner) τρόπος, συνήθεια, μορφή ‖ vt σχηματίζω, διαμορφώνω, πλάθω ‖ **in** ~ τῆς μόδας ‖ **out of** ~ ντεμοντέ ‖ **after a** ~ ὅπως-ὅπως, ἔτσι κι ἔτσι ‖ ~**able** a (clothes) τῆς μόδας, μοντέρνος ‖ (place) κοσμικός ‖ ~ **show** n ἐπίδειξις μόδας.

fast [fɑːst] a (swift) ταχύς, γρήγορος ‖ (ahead of time) πού τρέχει, πού πάει ἐμπρός ‖ (steady, firm) σταθερός, στερεός, σφικτός ‖ (firmly fixed) στερεός, γερός ‖ ad (rapidly) ταχέως, γρήγορα ‖ (firmly) στερεά, γερά ‖ n νηστεία ‖ vi νηστεύω.

fasten [ˈfɑːsn] vt (attach) στερεώνω, σφίγγω ‖ (with rope) δένω ‖ (coat) κουμπώνω ‖ vi δένομαι, κουμπώνομαι ‖ ~**er** n, ~**ing** n (on box) συνδετήρας, ἐνδέτης ‖ (on clothes) ἀγκράφα, φερμουάρ.

fastidious [fæsˈtidiəs] a δύσκολος, δύστροπος, στριφνός.

fat [fæt] a παχύς, χονδρός, εὔσωμος ‖ n (of person) ξύγγι, πάχος ‖ (on meat) λίπος, ξύγγι ‖ (for cooking) λίπος.

fatal [ˈfeitl] a (ending in death) θανάσιμος ‖ (disastrous) μοιραῖος, καταστρεπτικός, ὀλέθριος ‖ ~**ism** n μοιρολατρεία, φαταλισμός ‖ ~**ity** n (road death etc) θάνατος,

θύμα ‖ ~**ly** ad μοιραία, ἀναπόφευκτα, θανάσιμα.

fate [feit] n (destiny) μοῖρα, πεπρωμένον, τό γραφτό ‖ (death) μοῖρα, θάνατος ‖ ~**ful** a (prophetic) προφητικός ‖ (important) ὑψίστης σημασίας, ἀποφασιστικός.

father [ˈfɑːðə*] n (parent) πατέρας ‖ (priest) πάτερ, πατήρ ‖ (early leader) πατήρ, δημιουργός ‖ ~**-in-law** n πεθερός ‖ ~**ly** a πατρικός, σάν πατέρας.

fathom [ˈfæðəm] n ὀργυιά ‖ vt (sound) βυθομετρῶ ‖ (understand) βολιδοσκοπῶ, καταλαβαίνω.

fatigue [fəˈtiːg] n (weariness) κούρασις, κόπωσις, κάματος ‖ vt κουράζω, καταπονῶ.

fatness [ˈfætnis] n πάχος, πολυσαρκία, χόντρος.

fatten [ˈfætn] vt παχαίνω, σιτεύω ‖ vi παχαίνω, χοντραίνω.

fatty [ˈfæti] a (food) παχύς, λιπαρός.

fatuous [ˈfætjuəs] a ἀνόητος, ἠλίθιος, χαζός.

faucet [ˈfɔːsit] n (US) κάνουλα, βρύση.

fault [fɔːlt] n (offence) σφάλμα, λάθος ‖ (defect) ἐλάττωμα ‖ (blame) λάθος, φταίξιμο ‖ (geol) ρῆγμα, ρωγμή ‖ **at** ~ σφάλλω, λαθεύω, εἶμαι πταίστης ‖ ~**less** a ἄψογος, τέλειος ‖ ~**y** a ἐλαττωματικός, λανθασμένος.

fauna [ˈfɔːnə] n πανίς.

favour, (US) **favor** [ˈfeivə*] n (approval) εὔνοια, συμπάθεια ‖ (kindness) χάρις, χατήρι ‖ vt (plan) προτιμῶ, ὑποστηρίζω, μεροληπτῶ ‖ (in race) παίζω τό φαβορί ‖ **in** ~ **of** ὑπέρ ‖ ~**able** a εὐνοϊκός ‖ ~**ably** ad εὐνοϊκά, συμπαθητικά ‖ ~**ite** a εὐνοούμενος, ἀγαπητός ‖ n εὐνοούμενος ‖ ~**itism** n εὐνοιοκρατία, ρουσφετολογία.

fawn [fɔːn] a,n (colour) πυρόξανθο.

fear [fiə*] n φόβος, τρόμος ‖ vt φοβοῦμαι, τρέμω, ἀνησυχῶ ‖ **no** ~! μή φοβᾶσαι!, δέν εἶναι πιθανόν! ‖ ~**ful** a (timid) δειλός, φοβιτσιάρης ‖ (terrible) φοβερός, τρομερός ‖ ~**less** a ἀτρόμητος, ἄφοβος ‖ ~**lessly** ad ἄφοβα, ἀτρόμητα ‖ ~**lessness** n ἀφοβία, θάρρος, τόλμη.

feasibility [fiːzəˈbiliti] n (τό) πραγματοποιήσιμον.

feasible [ˈfiːzəbl] a δυνατός, κατορθωτός.

feast [fiːst] n τραπέζι, φαγοπότι, γλέντι ‖ vi (+ on) ἀπολαμβάνω, χορταίνω ‖ ~ **day** n (rel) γιορτή.

feat [fiːt] n κατόρθωμα.

feather [ˈfeðə*] n φτερό.

feature [ˈfiːtʃə*] n χαρακτηριστικόν ‖ (article) κύριον ἄρθρον ‖ (film) κυρία ταινία ‖ vti χαρακτηρίζω, τονίζω, ἐμφανίζω ‖ ~**less** a πλαδαρός, ἀσήμαντος.

February [ˈfebruəri] n Φλεβάρης.

fed [fed] pt,pp of **feed** ‖ **to be** ~ **up** vi βαριέμαι, μπουχτώνω, ἀηδιάζω.

federal ['fedərəl] a ὁμόσπονδος, ὁμοσπονδιακός.

federation [fedə'reiʃən] n ὁμοσπονδία, συνασπισμός.

fee [fiː] n (payment) ἀμοιβή || (for entrance) δίδακτρα, τέλος.

feeble ['fiːbl] a (person) φιλασθενής, ἀρρωστιάρης || (excuse) ἀδύνατος, ἀμφίβολος || ~-minded a διανοητικῶς ἀνεπαρκής.

feed [fiːd] (irreg v) n τροφή, τάϊσμα, τροφοδότησις || vt τρέφω, θρέφω || (machine etc) τροφοδοτῶ || to ~ back n ἀνάδρασις.

feel [fiːl] (irreg v) n (touch) ἀφή, πιάσιμο || (feeling) αἴσθησις, αἴσθημα || vt (touch) ἀγγίζω, ἅπτομαι || (examine) ψηλαφῶ, ψαύω, πιάνω || (be mentally aware of) αἰσθάνομαι, νοιώθω || (think, believe) νοιώθω || vi (give impression) αἰσθάνομαι, νοιώθω || ~er n βολιδοσκόπησις || ~ing n (sensation) ἀφή, αἴσθημα || (emotion) εὐαισθησία, συγκίνησις || (opinion) ἐντύπωσις, γνώμη, αἴσθημα.

feet [fiːt] npl of foot.

feign [fein] vt προσποιοῦμαι, ὑποκρίνομαι || ~ed a προσποιητός, ψεύτικος.

feint [feint] n προσποίησις || (mil) ψευδεπίθεσις.

fell [fel] pt of fall || vt (tree) κόβω, ρίπτω κάτω || n (hill) βραχώδης λόφος.

fellow ['felou] n (companion) σύντροφος, συνάδελφος || (member of society) ἑταῖρος, μέλος || (man or boy) ἄνθρωπος, βλάμης, παιδί τζιμάνι || ~ citizen n συμπολίτης || ~ countryman n συμπατριώτης || ~ feeling n συναδελφοσύνη || ~ men npl συνάνθρωποι || ~ship n (group) (συν)αδελφότης, ἑταιρεία || (friendliness) συντροφιά, συντροφικότης || ~ worker n συνεργάτης, συνάδελφος.

felony ['feləni] n κακούργημα.

felt [felt] pt,pp of feel || n πίλημα, κετσές.

female ['fiːmeil] n θῆλυ, γυναίκα || a θηλυκός, γυναικεῖος.

feminine ['feminin] a (gram) θηλυκόν || (qualities) θηλυκός, γυναικείος.

feminist ['feminist] n φεμινιστής, φεμινίστρια.

fence [fens] n φράγμα, φράχτης || vt (also ~ in, ~ off) περιφράσσω, (περι)μαντρώνω || vi ξιφομαχῶ.

fencing ['fensiŋ] n (swordplay) ξιφασκία, ξιφομαχία || (fences) περίφραξις, φράκτης.

fend [fend] vi: to ~ for o.s. φροντίζω, συντηροῦμαι, καταφέρνω.

fender ['fendə*] n κυγκλίδωμα, πυρομάχος || (US: wing, mudguard) προφυλακτήρας.

fennel ['fenl] n μάραθο.

ferment [fə'ment] vi ζημούμαι, βράζω || ['fəːment] n ζύμωσις, ἀναβρασμός || ~ation n ζύμωσις, βράσιμο.

fern [fəːn] n φτέρη.

ferocious [fə'rouʃəs] a ἄγριος, θηριώδης || ~ly ad θηριωδῶς, ἄγρια.

ferry ['feri] n (small) πέραμα, πορθμεῖον || (large: also ~boat) φέρρυ-μπότ || vt διεκπεραιῶ, διαπορθμεύω, περνῶ.

fertile ['fəːtail] a (agr) εὔφορος, γόνιμος || (biol) γονιμοποιός.

fertility [fə'tiliti] n εὐφορία, γονιμότης.

fertilization [fəːtilai'zeiʃən] n γονιμοποίησις.

fertilize ['fəːtilaiz] vt γονιμοποιῶ || ~r n λίπασμα.

fervent ['fəːvənt] a θερμός, φλογερός.

festival [festivəl] n (rel etc) ἑορτή, πανηγύρι || (art, mus) φεστιβάλ.

festive ['festiv] a γιορταστικός, γιορτάσιμος || (person) εὔθυμος, κεφάτος || the ~ season (Christmas) ἐποχή γιορτῶν.

festivity [fes'tiviti] n γιορτή, γλέντι || festivities npl γιορτή.

fetch [fetʃ] vt πηγαίνω νά φέρω || (a price) ἀποφέρω, πιάνω.

fetching ['fetʃiŋ] a γοητευτικός, ἑλκυστικός.

fête [feit] n γιορτή, πανηγύρι.

fetters ['fetəz] npl δεσμά, ἁλυσίδες.

fetus ['fiːtəs] n (US) = foetus.

feud [fjuːd] n ἔχθρα, ἔρις, βεντέτα || vi εἶμαι στά χέρια μέ || ~al a φεουδαλικός, τιμαριωτικός || ~alism n φεουδαλισμός.

fever ['fiːvə*] n πυρετός, θέρμη || ~ish a (med) ἐμπύρετος || (fig) πυρετώδης || ~ishly ad (fig) πυρετωδῶς, μέ τά μοῦτρα.

few [fjuː] a ὀλίγοι, λίγοι, μερικοί || a ~ μερικοί, ὀλίγοι || ~er ὀλιγώτεροι, σπανιώτεροι || ~est ἐλάχιστοι, λιγοστά.

fiancé [fi'ɑ̃:nsei] n μνηστήρ, ἀρραβωνιαστικός || ~e n ἀρραβωνιαστικιά.

fiasco [fi'æskou] n φιάσκο, ἀποτυχία.

fib [fib] n ψεμματάκι, μπούρδα || vi ψεύδομαι.

fibre, (US) **fiber** ['faibə*] n ἴνα, ἴνες || ~glass n ὑαλοβάμβαξ.

fickle ['fikl] a ἀλλοπρόσαλος, ἀλαφρόμυαλος || ~ness n ἀστάθεια, ἄστατος χαρακτήρ.

fiction ['fikʃən] n (invention) φαντασία || (novels) μυθιστορήματα || ~al a τῶν μυθιστορημάτων.

fictitious [fik'tiʃəs] a φανταστικός.

fiddle ['fidl] n (violin) βιολί, βιολιστής || (swindle) κομπίνα || vt (cheat) ξεγελῶ || vi παίζω, μαστορεύω, χάνω (τόν χρόνον) || to ~ with vt παίζω, μαστορεύω || ~r n βιολιστής.

fidelity [fi'deliti] n πίστις, ἀφοσίωσις, πιστότης.

fidget ['fidʒit] vi κάνω νευρικές κινήσεις || ~y a ἀεικίνητος, νευρικός, ἀνήσυχος.

field [fiːld] n (land) χωράφι, κάμπο, περιοχή || (sport: ground) γήπεδον || (sport: in race) τά ἄλογα || (range) ἔκτασις, πεδίον

‖ (battleground) πεδίον ‖ ~ **day** n (gala)
μεγάλη ἡμέρα ‖ ~ **marshal** n στρατάρχης
‖ ~ **work** n (mil) ἔργον ἐκστρατείας.

fiend [fi:nd] n δαίμονας, τέρας ‖ ~**ish** a
διαβολικός.

fierce [fiəs] a θηριώδης, μανιασμένος ‖
~**ly** ad βιαίως, ἀπότομα, λυσσασμένα ‖
~**ness** n ἀγριότης, θηριωδία, σκληρότης.

fiery ['faiəri] a (of fire) φλογερός, καφτερός, φλεγόμενος ‖ (person) ζωηρός,
ὁρμητικός, ζωντανός.

fifteen [fif'ti:n] num δέκα πέντε.

fifth [fifθ] a πέμπτος.

fiftieth ['fiftiiθ] a πεντηκοστός.

fifty ['fifti] num πενήντα.

fig [fig] n σῦκο ‖ (tree) συκιά.

fight [fait] (irreg v) n (between people)
καυγᾶς, πιάσιμο ‖ (campaign) μάχη,
ἀγών, πάλη ‖ vt πολεμῶ, μάχομαι ‖ vi
(struggle against) μάχομαι, ἀγωνίζομαι,
παλεύω ‖ ~**er** n πολεμιστής, μαχητής ‖
(aviat) καταδιωκτικόν ‖ ~**ing** n μάχη,
καυγᾶς ‖ (sport) πυγμαχία.

figurative ['figərətiv] a μεταφορικός, παραστατικός.

figure ['figə*] n (shape) μορφή, σχῆμα ‖
(of person) παράστημα, κορμοστασιά,
σιλουέττα ‖ (picture) εἰκών, ἀπεικόνισις
‖ (person) πρόσωπον, ἄνθρωπος ‖ προσωπικότης ‖ (math) σχῆμα ‖ (cipher)
ἀριθμός, ψηφίον, νούμερο ‖ vt (US:
imagine) ὑπολογίζω, λογαριάζω ‖ vi
(appear) ἐμφανίζομαι, φαντάζομαι ‖ **to**
~ **out** vt ὑπολογίζω, λογαριάζω ‖ ~**head**
n (naut) ξόανον, γοργόνα ‖ (fig) διακο-
σμητικόν πρόσωπον ‖ ~-**skating** n
φιγούρες (τῆς παγοδρομίας).

filament ['filəmənt] n νῆμα.

file [fail] n (tool) ρίνη, λίμα ‖ (dossier)
φάκελλος, ἀρχεῖον ‖ (folder) φάκελλος,
σεμίζ ‖ (row) στοῖχος, γραμμή, ἀράδα ‖
vt (wood) λιμάρω ‖ (nails) λιμάρω ‖
(papers) ταξινομῶ, ἀρχειοθετῶ ‖ (claim)
καταθέτω, ὑποβάλλω ‖ vi: **to** ~ **in, out**
μπαίνω (βγαίνω) ἔνας-ἔνας ‖ **in single** ~
κατ'ἄνδρα.

filing ['failiŋ] n (of papers) ταξινόμησις,
ἀρχειοθέτησις ‖ ~**s** npl ρινίσματα, λιμα-
δούρα ‖ ~ **cabinet** n δελτιοθήκη, ἀρχειο-
θήκη.

fill [fil] vt (make full) πληρῶ, γεμίζω ‖
(occupy completely) συμπληρώνω, γεμίζω
‖ (satisfy) ἱκανοποιῶ, χορταίνω ‖ (position etc) κατέχω, γεμίζω ‖ n πλησμονή,
κορεσμός, γέμισμα ‖ **to** ~ **the bill** (fig)
ἀνταποκρίνομαι ‖ **to** ~ **in** vt (hole)
γεμίζω, βουλώνω ‖ (form) συμπληρώνω
‖ **to** ~ **up** vt (container) γεμίζω τελείως ‖
(form) συμπληρώνω.

fillet ['filit] n (food) φιλέτο ‖ vt χωρίζω τά
φιλέτα.

filling ['filiŋ] n (for cakes, pies etc) γέμιση ‖

(for tooth) σφράγισμα, βούλωμα ‖ ~
station n πρατήριον βενζίνης, βενζινάδικο.

fillip ['filip] n (reviver) ἀναζωογόνησις,
τόνωσις.

film [film] n (thin layer) ἐλαφρόν στρῶμα,
μεμβράνη ‖ (phot) (φωτο)ταινία, φίλμ,
πλάκα ‖ (moving picture) ταινία, φίλμ ‖
vt (scene) γυρίζω ταινίαν, φιλμάρω ‖ ~
script n σενάριο, σκρίπτ ‖ ~ **star** n
ἀστήρ τοῦ κινηματογράφου.

filter ['filtə*] n φίλτρον ‖ (phot) φίλτρον ‖
vt διυλίζω, φιλτράρω, λαμπικάρω ‖ vi
(fig) διεισδύω, εἰσχωρῶ ‖ ~ **tip** n ἐπιστόμιον φίλτρου ‖ ~-**tipped cigarette** n
τσιγάρο φίλτρο.

filth [filθ] n (lit) ἀκαθαρσίες, σκουπίδια,
βρῶμα ‖ (fig) ἠθική φθορά, βρωμιά,
αἰσχρολογία ‖ ~**y** a ἀκάθαρτος, ρυπαρός, βρώμικος.

fin [fin] n (fish) πτερύγιον, φτερό.

final ['fainl] a τελικός, τελευταῖος, ὁριστικός ‖ n (sport) τελικός (ἀγώνας) ‖ ~**s**
npl (univ) ἀπολυτήριοι ἐξετάσεις ‖ ~**e**
[fi'na:li] n (theat) φινάλε ‖ (mus) φινάλε
‖ ~**ist** n (sport) φιναλιστής ‖ ~**ize** vt
ὁριστικοποιῶ ‖ ~**ly** ad (lastly) τελικῶς ‖
(eventually) εἰς τό τέλος ‖ (irrevocably)
ὁριστικῶς, τελεσιδίκως.

finance [fai'næns] n οἰκονομία ‖ vt χρηματοδοτῶ ‖ ~**s** npl οἰκονομικά.

financial [fai'nænʃəl] a (policy) οἰκονομική
(πολιτική) ‖ (year) οἰκονομικόν (ἔτος) ‖
~**ly** ad οἰκονομικῶς.

financier [fai'nænsiə*] n κεφαλαιοῦχος,
χρηματοδότης.

find [faind] (irreg v) vt (come across)
εὑρίσκω, βρίσκω ‖ (discover, get) ἀνακαλύπτω, (ἀνε)βρίσκω ‖ (learn) ἀνακαλύπτω, διαπιστώνω ‖ (declare) ἀποφαίνομαι, κηρύσσω ‖ n ἀνακάλυψις,
εὕρημα ‖ **to** ~ **out** (about) ἀνακαλύπτω,
ἀναζητῶ, πληροφοροῦμαι ‖ ~**ings** npl
(law) ἀπόφασις, ἐτυμηγορία ‖ (of report)
διαπίστωσις, συμπέρασμα.

fine [fain] a (thin, slender) λεπτός, ψιλός,
ψιλόλιγνος ‖ (delicate) λεπτός, φίνος ‖
(handsome) ὡραῖος, ὄμορφος ‖ (pure)
καθαρός ‖ (rainless) ὡραῖος, καλός ‖ ad
(well) θαυμάσια, περίφημα ‖ (small)
λεπτός, λεπτομερῶς, ψιλά ‖ n (law)
ποινική ρήτρα, πρόστιμον ‖ vt (law) ἐπιβάλλω πρόστιμον ‖ ~ **arts** n καλαί
τέχναι ‖ ~**ness** n λεπτότης, κομψότης ‖
~**ry** n στολίδια, στόλισμα ‖ ~**sse** [fi'nes]
n τέχνασμα, πανουργία, φινέτσα.

finger ['fiŋgə*] n δάκτυλος, δάχτυλο ‖ vt
ψαύω, ψηλαφῶ, πιάνω ‖ ~**nail** n νύχι ‖
~**print** n δακτυλικόν ἀποτύπωμα ‖ ~**stall**
n δακτυλήθρα ‖ ~**tip** n ἄκρα τοῦ δακτύ-
λου.

finicky ['finiki] a μικρολόγος, λεπτολόγος.

finish ['finiʃ] n (end) τέλος ‖ -(sport) τερματισμός, τέλος, τέρμα ‖ (completion) τελείωμα, αποπεράτωσις, συμπλήρωμα ‖ vt (also ~ off, ~ up) τερματίζω, τελειώνω, αποτελειώνω ‖ vi (general) τελειώνω, τερματίζομαι, λήγω ‖ (sport) τερματίζω ‖ ~ing line n τέρμα ‖ ~ing school n σχολείον γενικής μορφώσεως.

finite ['fainait] a πεπερασμένος, περιωρισμένος.

Finland ['finlənd] n Φινλανδία.

Finn [fin] n Φινλανδός ‖ ~ish a φινλανδικός ‖ n (ling) φιννική.

fiord [fjɔ:d] n φιόρδ.

fir [fə:*] n έλατο.

fire [faiə*] n (element) πυρ ‖ (in grate) φωτιά ‖ (damaging) πυρκαϊά ‖ (mil) πυρ, βολή ‖ vt (cause to burn) ανάβω, βάζω φωτιά ‖ (gun etc) πυροδοτώ, βάλλω, ρίχνω ‖ (fig: imagination) ενθουσιάζω, εξάπτω ‖ (col: dismiss) απολύω, παύω, διώχνω ‖ vi (gun) πυροβολώ ‖ on ~ καίομαι, παίρνω φωτιά ‖ ~ alarm n κώδων πυρκαϊάς ‖ ~ arm n (πυροβόλον) όπλον ‖ ~ brigade n πυροσβεστική (υπηρεσία) ‖ ~ engine n αντλία πυρκαϊάς ‖ ~ escape n κλίμαξ πυρκαϊάς ‖ ~ extinguisher n πυροσβεστήρ ‖ ~man n πυροσβέστης ‖ (rail) θερμαστής ‖ ~place n τζάκι ‖ ~proof a πυρίμαχος, αλεξίπυρος ‖ ~side n παραστιά, τζάκι ‖ ~ station n πυροσβεστικός σταθμός ‖ ~wood n καυσόξυλα ‖ ~works npl (lit) πυροτεχνήματα.

firing ['faiəriŋ] n (mil) βολή, πυροβολισμός, πυρ ‖ ~ squad n εκτελεστικόν απόσπασμα.

firm [fə:m] a (solid) στεριός, σφιχτός ‖ (determined) αμετακίνητος, σταθερός ‖ n οίκος, εταιρεία, φίρμα ‖ ~ly ad σταθερώς, στερεά, γερά ‖ ~ness n σταθερότης, στερεότης.

first [fə:st] a (time) πρώτος ‖ (place) πρώτος ‖ ad (before others) πρώτος ‖ (firstly = in the first place) πρωτίστως, πρώτα-πρώτα ‖ (sooner = before then) στην αρχή, μάλλον, καλύτερα ‖ n (person: in race) πρώτος ‖ (univ) λίαν καλώς, άριστα ‖ (aut) πρώτη (ταχύτητα) ‖ at ~ κατά πρώτον, στην αρχή ‖ ~ of all πρίν απ'όλα, κατ'αρχήν ‖ ~ aid n πρώται βοήθειαι ‖ ~-aid kit n σακκίδιον πρώτων βοηθειών ‖ ~-class a πρώτης τάξεως ‖ ~-hand a από πρώτο χέρι ‖ ~ lady n (US) πρώτη κυρία ‖ ~ly ad πρωτίστως, πρώτα-πρώτα ‖ ~ name n μικρόν όνομα ‖ ~ night n πρώτη, πρεμιέρα ‖ ~-rate a πρώτης τάξεως.

fiscal ['fiskəl] a οικονομικός.

fish [fiʃ] n ψάρι ‖ vt αλιεύω, ψαρεύω ‖ vi ψαρεύω ‖ to go ~ing πάω γιά ψάρεμα ‖ ~erman n ψαράς ‖ ~ery n αλιεία, ψαρική ‖ ~ hook n αγκίστρι ‖ ~ing boat n ψαρόβαρκα ‖ ~ing line n αρμίδι,

αρμιθιά ‖ ~ing rod n καλάμι ‖ ~ing tackle n σύνεργα ψαρικής ‖ ~ market n ιχθυαγορά ‖ ~monger n ιχθυοπώλης ‖ ~y a (suspicious) ύποπτος, βρώμικος.

fission ['fiʃən] n διάσπασις.

fissure ['fiʃə*] n σχισμή, ρωγμή.

fist [fist] n πυγμή, γροθιά.

fit [fit] a (med, sport) σέ φόρμα, υγιής ‖ (suitable) κατάλληλος, αρμόζων, καλός ‖ (qualified, worthy) ικανός ‖ vt (suit) συμφωνώ, ταιριάζω ‖ (insert, attach) πηγαίνω, μπαίνω ‖ vi (correspond) εφαρμόζω, πιάνω ‖ (of clothes) πηγαίνω, έρχεται ‖ n (of clothes) εφαρμογή, ταίριασμα ‖ (med: mild, of coughing) παροξυσμός ‖ (med: serious, epilepsy) προσβολή ‖ (of anger) ξέσπασμα, έκρηξις ‖ (of laughter) ξέσπασμα ‖ to ~ in vi συμφωνώ, ταιριάζω ‖ vt ενώνω, συνδέω ‖ to ~ out vt εξαρτίζω, εφοδιάζω, ντύνω ‖ to ~ up vt εφαρμόζω, ταιριάζω, μοντάρω ‖ ~fully, by ~s and starts ακανόνιστα, άστατα ‖ ~ness n (suitability) ικανότης, καταλληλότης ‖ (med) υγεία ‖ ~ter n εφαρμοστής ‖ (of clothes) δοκιμαστής α κατάλληλος, πρέπων, ταιριαστός ‖ n (of dress) πρόβα, προβάρισμα ‖ (piece of equipment) εφαρμογή, μοντάρισμα ‖ ~tings npl επιπλώσεις, εξαρτήματα, σύνεργα.

five [faiv] num πέντε ‖ ~r n (Brit) πεντάρι (λίρες).

fix [fiks] vt (fasten) τοποθετώ, στερεώνω, καρφώνω ‖ (determine) καθορίζω, (προσδι)ορίζω, ρυθμίζω ‖ (repair) επισκευάζω, επιδιορθώνω ‖ (drink) ετοιμάζω, φτιάχνω ‖ n: in a ~ μπελάδες, μπλέξιμο, σκοτούρες ‖ ~ed a σταθερός, αμετάβλητος, στερεωμένος ‖ ~ture n ακινητοποιημένο έπιπλον, εξάρτημα.

fizz [fiz] n σπίθισμα, τσιτσίρισμα ‖ vi σπιθίζω.

fizzle ['fizl] vi αφρίζω, τσιρίζω ‖ to ~ out vi βγαίνω τζίφος, αποτυγχάνω.

fizzy ['fizi] a αεριούχος, αφρώδης.

fjord [fjɔ:d] n = **fiord**.

flabbergasted ['flæbəgɑ:stid] a κατάπληκτος, ξερός.

flabby ['flæbi] a πλαδαρός, άτονος.

flag [flæg] n (banner) σημαία ‖ (also ~stone) πλάκα, πλακόλιθος ‖ vi (strength) εξασθενίζω, χαλαρούμαι ‖ (spirit) κάμπτομαι, πέφτω, σπάω ‖ to ~ down vt σταματώ.

flagon ['flægən] n καράφα.

flagpole ['flægpəul] n κοντάρι.

flagrant ['fleigrənt] a κατάφωρος, καταφανής.

flair [fleə*] n οξυδέρκεια, ικανότης.

flake [fleik] n (of rust) λέπι, τρίμα, φύλλο ‖ (of snow) νιφάς, στούπα ‖ vi (also ~ off) ξελεπίζω, ξεφλουδίζομαι.

flame [fleim] n φλόγα.

flaming ['fleimiŋ] *a* (*col*) φλογερός, ἀστρα-φτερός.

flamingo [flə'miŋgəu] *n* φλαμίγκος.

flange [flændʒ] *n* φλάντζα.

flank [flæŋk] *n* (*side*) λαγόνα, πλαγιά ǁ (*mil*) πλευρά ǁ *vt* εὑρίσκομαι πλάϊ.

flannel ['flænl] *n* φανέλλα ǁ ~s *npl* (*trousers*) φανελλένιο παντελόνι.

flap [flæp] *n* καπάκι ǁ (*of pocket*) καπάκι (τσέπης) ǁ (*of envelope*) κλείσιμο (φακέλλου) ǁ *vt* (*of birds*) φτερουγίζω ǁ *vi* (*sail, flag*) ἀνεμίζομαι, κυματίζω.

flare [flɛə*] *n* φωτοβολίς ǁ (*in skirt etc*) φάρδεμα ǁ **to ~ up** *vi* (*into flame*) ἀστράφτω, ἀνάβω ǁ (*in anger*) ἀνάβω, ἐξάπτομαι.

flash [flæʃ] *n* ἀναλαμπή, λάμψις ǁ (*news flash*) τελευταία εἴδησις ǁ (*phot*) φλάς ǁ *vt* (*light*) κάνω νά λάμψη, ρίχνω ǁ (*torch*) ρίπτω, ἀνάβω ǁ (*message*) μεταδίδω ǁ *vi* ἀστράφτω, γυαλίζω ǁ **in a ~** στή στιγμή ǁ **to ~ by** *or* **past** *vt* περνῶ σάν ἀστραπή ǁ **~back** *n* ἀναδρομή ǁ **~ bulb** *n* λάμπα φλάς ǁ **~ er** *n* (*aut*) φανάρι τοῦ στόπ.

flashy ['flæʃi] *a* (*pej*) φανταχτερός, χτυπητός.

flask [flɑːsk] *n* τσότρα, φλασκί ǁ (*chem*) φιάλη ǁ (*vacuum flask*) θερμό.

flat [flæt] *a* (*level*) ἐπίπεδος, ἴσιος ǁ (*dull*) ἄνευ προοπτικῆς, θαμπό ǁ (*below pitch*) σέ ὕφεσι, μπεμόλ ǁ (*beer*) ξεθυμασμένο ǁ (*tyre*) ξεφουσκωμένο, πεσμένο ǁ *n* (*rooms*) διαμέρισμα ǁ (*mus*) ὕφεσις ǁ (*aut*) ξεφουσκωμένο λάστιχο ǁ **~ broke** *a* ἀπένταρος, πατήρης ǁ **~footed** *a* μέ πλατειά πόδια ǁ **~ly** *ad* σαφῶς, κατηγορηματικῶς ǁ **~ness** *n* ἐπιπεδότης ǁ (*of beer*) ξεθύμασμα ǁ **~ten** *vt* (*also* **~ten out**) ἐπιπεδώνω, ἰσώνω.

flatter ['flætə*] *vt* κολακεύω ǁ **~er** *n* κόλακας ǁ **~ing** *a* κολακευτικός ǁ **~y** *n* κολακεία.

flaunt [flɔːnt] *vt* ἐπιδεικνύω, δείχνω.

flavour, (*US*) **flavor** ['fleivə*] *n* γεῦσις ǁ *vt* καρικεύω, ἀρωματίζω ǁ **~ing** *n* καρίκευμα, ἄρωμα.

flaw [flɔː] *n* ἐλάττωμα ǁ **~less** *a* ἄψογος, τέλειος.

flax [flæks] *n* λινάρι ǁ **~en** *a* κατάξανθος.

flea [fliː] *n* ψύλλος.

fled [fled] *pt,pp* of **flee**.

flee [fliː] (*irreg v*) *vi* (κατα)φεύγω ǁ *vt* φεύγω.

fleece [fliːs] *n* δορά, δέρμα, τομάρι ǁ *vt* (*rob*) ληστεύω, γδέρνω, γδύνω.

fleet [fliːt] *n* (*naut*) στόλος ǁ (*of cars*) συνοδεία, πομπή.

fleeting ['fliːtiŋ] *a* φευγαλέος, περαστικός.

Flemish ['flemiʃ] *a* φλαμανδικός ǁ *n* (*ling*) φλαμανδική.

flesh [fleʃ] *n* σάρξ, σάρκα ǁ (*meat*) κρέας ǁ (*of fruit*) σάρξ ǁ **~ wound** *n* ἐλαφρόν τραῦμα.

flew [fluː] *pt* of **fly**.

flex [fleks] *n* εὔκαμπτον καλώδιον ǁ *vt* κάμπτομαι ǁ **~ibility** *n* εὐκαμψία ǁ **~ible** *a* εὔκαμπτος ǁ (*plans*) ἐλαστικός.

flick [flik] *vt* κτυπῶ ἐλαφρά.

flicker ['flikə*] *n* (*of light*) τρεμούλιασμα, παίξιμο ǁ *vi* τρέμω, τρεμοσβύνω.

flier ['flaiə*] *n* ἱπτάμενος, ἀεροπόρος.

flight [flait] *n* (*flying*) πτῆσις, πέταμα ǁ (*of squadron*) σμῆνος ǁ (*journey*) διαδρομή ǁ (*also* **~ of steps**) σκαλοπάτια, κλίμαξ ǁ **to take ~** τρέπομαι εἰς φυγήν ǁ **to put to ~** τρέπω εἰς φυγήν ǁ **~ deck** *n* κατάστρωμα ἀπογειώσεως ǁ **~y** *a* ἄστατος, κουφιοκέφαλος.

flimsy ['flimzi] *a* σαθρός, λεπτός, μικρᾶς ἀντοχῆς ǁ (*weak*) ἀδύνατος, ἀσθενής, πρόχειρος.

flinch [flintʃ] *vi* ὑποχωρῶ, δειλιάζω.

fling [fliŋ] (*irreg v*) *vt* ρίχνω, πετῶ.

flint [flint] *n* (*in lighter*) τσακμακόπετρα.

flip [flip] *vt* δίνω ἐλαφρόν κτύπημα.

flippancy ['flipənsi] *n* ἀπεριακεψία, ἀφέλεια.

flippant ['flipənt] *a* ἐλαφρός, ἀφελής.

flirt [fləːt] *vi* φλερτάρω ǁ *n* φιλάρεσκη, κοκέττα ǁ **~ation** *n* φλέρτ, φλερτάρισμα.

flit [flit] *vi* πηγαινοέρχομαι.

float [fləut] *n* πλωτήρ, φλοτέρ ǁ (*esp in procession*) ἀποκριάτικο ἅρμα ǁ *vi* (*επι*)πλέω ǁ (*swimming*) κολυμπῶ ἀνάσκελα ǁ (*in air*) πλέω ǁ *vt* (*company*) ἱδρύω ǁ (*loan*) ἐκδίδω δάνειον ǁ (*rumour*) διαδίδω, κυκλοφορῶ ǁ **~ing** *a* (*lit*) ἐπιπλέων ǁ (*fig: population*) κινητός πληθυσμός.

flock [flɔk] *n* ποίμνιον, κοπάδι ǁ (*of people*) πλῆθος, κοπάδι.

flog [flɔg] *vt* μαστιγώνω, ραβδίζω.

flood [flʌd] *n* πλημμύρα, κατακλυσμός ǁ *vt* πλημμυρίζω, κατακλύζω ǁ **~ing** *n* πλημμύρισμα, ὑπερεκχείλισις ǁ **~light** *n* προβολεύς ǁ *vt* φωτίζω διά προβολέως ǁ **~lighting** *n* φωτισμός διά προβολέως.

floor [flɔː*] *n* (*of room*) δάπεδον, πάτωμα ǁ (*storey*) ὄροφος, πάτωμα ǁ *vt* (*person*) ρίχνω κάτω ǁ **ground ~** (*Brit*), **first ~** (*US*) ἰσόγειον ǁ **first ~** (*Brit*), **second ~** (*US*) πρῶτο πάτωμα ǁ **~board** *n* σανίδα ǁ **~ show** *n* νούμερα.

flop [flɔp] *vi* (*fail*) ἀποτυγχάνω, καταρρέω ǁ (*fall*) κάνω πλάφ, σωριάζομαι.

floppy ['flɔpi] *a* πλαδαρός.

flora ['flɔːrə] *npl* χλωρίς ǁ **~l** *a* ἀνθικός, λουλουδένιος.

florid ['flɔrid] *a* ἀνθηρός, γεμᾶτος φιοριτούρες.

florist ['flɔrist] *n* ἀνθοπώλης ǁ **~'s (shop)** *n* ἀνθοπωλεῖον.

flounce [flauns] *n* βολλάν ǁ *vi:* **to ~ in, out** μπαίνω, βγαίνω ἀπότομα.

flounder ['flaundə*] *vi* παραπατῶ, σπαρταρῶ, τσαλαβουτῶ.

flour ['flauə*] *n* ἀλεύρι.

flourish ['flʌriʃ] vi (thrive, prosper) προοδεύω, ἀνθῶ, προκόβω ‖ vt κραδαίνω, κουνῶ ‖ n (ornament) ποίκιλμα, κόσμημα, τζίφρα ‖ ἐπίδειξις, φανφάρα ‖ ~ing a (thriving) ἀκμάζων, ἀνθοῦν.

flout [flaut] vt ἐμπαίζω, περιφρονῶ.

flow [fləu] n (movement) ῥοή, ῥεῦμα ‖ (stream: lit, fig) ῥοῦς, χύσις, χείμαρρος ‖ (of dress) χυτές γραμμές, ντραπέ ‖ vi ῥέω, χύνομαι ‖ κυλῶ ‖ (traffic, supply) κυκλοφορῶ, 'κινοῦμαι ‖ (robes, hair) χύνομαι, πέφτω.

flower ['flauə*] n ἄνθος, λουλούδι ‖ vi ἀνθίζω ‖ ~ bed n παρτέρι, βραγιά ‖ ~pot n βάζο ‖ ~y a πολυγαρνισμένος.

flowing ['fləuiŋ] a (movement) ῥέων ‖ (hair) χυτός, μακρυά ‖ (style) ῥέων, ἄνετος.

flown [fləun] pp of fly.

flu [flu:] n γρίπ̄πη.

fluctuate ['flʌktjueit] vi κυμαίνομαι.

fluctuation [flʌktju'eiʃən] n διακύμανσις.

fluency ['flu:ənsi] n εὐλωττία, εὐφράδεια.

fluent ['flu:ənt] a εὐφράδης, στρωτός ‖ ~ly ad εὐχερῶς,.ἄνετα.

fluff [flʌf] n χνούδι ‖ ~y a χνουδάτος.

fluid ['flu:id] n ῥευστόν, ὑγρόν ‖ a (lit) ῥευστός, ῥέων ‖ (fig: plans) ῥευστός, εὐμετάβλητος.

fluke [flu:k] n (col: lucky stroke) κατά τύχην.

flung [flʌŋ] pt, pp of.fling.

fluorescent [fluə'resnt] a φθορίζων.

fluoride ['fluəraid] n φθοριοῦχον.

flurry ['flʌri] n (of activity) ἀναστάτωσις, πανικός.

flush [flʌʃ] n (blush) κοκκίνισμα, ἐρύθημα ‖ (of excitement) ξέσπασμα ‖ (cards) χρῶμα, φλός ‖ vt ποτίζω, καθαρίζω, τραβῶ (τό καζανάκι) ‖ vi (blush) κοκκινίζω ‖ a ἐπίπεδος, λεῖος, στό ντουζένι ‖ ~ed a (blushing) κόκκινο, ξαναμμένο ‖ (with anger) κόκκινος.

fluster ['flʌstə*] n ἀναστάτωσις ‖ ~ed a ταραγμένος.

flute [flu:t] n φλογέρα, φλάουτο.

fluted ['flu:tid] a αὐλακωτός.

flutter ['flʌtə*] n (of wings) φτερούγισμα ‖ (of excitement) ἀναστάτωσις, συγκίνησις ‖ vi (of birds) φτερουγίζω ‖ τρέμω, ταράσσομαι.

flux [flʌks] n: in a state of ~ σέ ῥευστή κατάστασι.

fly [flai] (irreg v) n (insect) μύγα ‖ (on trousers: also flies) μπροστινό ἄνοιγμα ‖ vt (plane) πετῶ, ὁδηγῶ ‖ (passengers) μεταφέρω ἀεροπορικῶς ‖ vi (travel by air) ἵπταμαι, πετῶ ‖ (flee) φεύγω, τρέχω ‖ (of flag) κυματίζω ‖ ~er n = flier ‖ ~ing n (activity) πτῆσις, ἀεροπορία ‖ a (rapid visit) ταχύς, γρήγορος, πεταχτός, σύντομος, βιαστικός ‖ ~ing saucer n ἱπτάμενος δίσκος ‖ ~ing start n καλή ἀρχή, ταχύ ξεκίνημα ‖ ~over n (Brit)

ἐναέριος διάβασις ‖ ~paper n μυγοπαγίδα ‖ ~past n παρέλασις ἀεροπλάνων ‖ ~swatter n μυγοδιώχτης ‖ ~wheel n σφόνδυλος, βολάν.

foal [fəul] n πουλάρι.

foam [fəum] n ἀφρός ‖ (plastic etc) ἀφρολέξ ‖ vi ἀφρίζω.

fob [fɔb] to ~ off vt πασσάρω, κοροϊδεύω.

focal ['fəukəl] a ἑστιακός.

focus ['fəukəs] n ἑστία ‖ vt συγκεντρώνω, ρυθμίζω ‖ in ~ ρυθμισμένος, εὐκρινής ‖ out of ~ μή ρυθμισμένος, θαμπός.

fodder ['fɔdə*] n φορβή, χόρτο.

foe [fəu] n ἐχθρός, ἀντίπαλος.

foetus ['fi:təs] n ἔμβρυον.

fog [fɔg] n ὁμίχλη ‖ vt (issue) θολώνω, περιπλέκω ‖ ~gy a ὁμιχλώδης.

foible ['fɔibl] n ἀδυναμία.

foil [fɔil] vt ἀνατρέπω, προλαμβάνω ‖ n (of metal) ἔλασμα, φύλλον ‖ (person) κοντράστο ‖ (fencing) ξίφος.

fold [fəuld] n (bend, crease) πτυχή, ζάρα, δίπλα ‖ vt διπλώνω, πτυχώνω ‖ to ~ up vi (map etc) τυλίγω, διπλώνω ‖ (business) κλείνω τό μαγαζί, χρεωκοπῶ ‖ ~er n (pamphlet) (πτυσσομένη) διαφήμισις ‖ (portfolio) φάκελλος, σεμίζ ‖ ~ing a (chair, bed etc) πτυσσόμενος, τσακιστός.

foliage ['fəuliidʒ] n φυλλωσιά.

folio ['fəuliəu] n φύλλον, ἴν φόλιο.

folk [fəuk] n ἄνθρωποι ‖ a λαϊκός ‖ ~s npl ἄνθρωποι, συγγενεῖς, δικοί μου ‖ ~lore n λαογραφία ‖ ~song n δημοτικό τραγούδι.

follow ['fɔləu] vt (come after) (παρ)ἀκολουθῶ ‖ (obey) ἀκολουθῶ ‖ (go along path) ἀκολουθῶ, παίρνω ‖ (profession) ἀκολουθῶ, ἀσκῶ ‖ (understand) καταλαβαίνω, παρακολουθῶ ‖ vi (after) ἀκολουθῶ, συνοδεύω ‖ (result) ἕπομαι, προκύπτω ‖ to ~ up vt συνεχίζω, ἐκμεταλλεύομαι ‖ ~er n ὀπαδός ‖ ~ing n ἀκολουθῶν, ἑπόμενος ‖ n ὀπαδοί, ἀκολουθία.

folly ['fɔli] n ἀνοησία, τρέλλα.

fond [fɔnd] a: to be ~ of (person) εἶμαι ἀφοσιωμένος, συμπαθῶ, ἀγαπῶ ‖ (thing) μοῦ ἀρέσει, τρελλαίνομαι γιά ‖ ~ly ad ἀφελῶς ‖ (with affection) στοργικά ‖ ~ness n (+for) ἀφοσίωσις, συμπάθεια .σέ ‖ ἀγάπη γιά, τάσι στό.

font [fɔnt] n κολυμβήθρα.

food [fu:d] n τροφή, τρόφιμα, φαΐ, φαγητόν ‖ ~ mixer n μίξερ, ἀνάμικτρον ‖ ~ poisoning n δηλητηρίασι ‖ ~stuffs npl εἴδη διατροφῆς.

fool [fu:l] n (silly person) ἠλίθιος, βλάκας, κουτός, χαζός ‖ (clown) παλιάτσος ‖ vt (deceive) ἐξαπατῶ, γελῶ ‖ vi (act like a fool) κάνω τόν βλάκα ‖ ~hardy a παράτολμος, ἀπερίσκεπτος ‖ ~ish a παράλογος, γελοῖος ‖ ~ishly ad παράλογα, ἀνόητα ‖ ~ishness n ἀπερισκεψία, ἀνοησία ‖ ~**proof** a (plan etc) ἀλάνθαστος.

foot [fut] n (of person) πόδι, ποδάρι ‖ (of animal) πόδι ‖ (base) πέλμα, πόδι, κάτω ἄκρον ‖ (measure) ἀγγλικός πούς, πόδι (0.3μ) ‖ vt (bill) πληρώνω, κάνω τά ἔξοδα ‖ **on** ~ πεζῆ, μέ τά πόδια ‖ ~**ball** n (ball) μπάλλα ‖ (game) ποδόσφαιρον ‖ ~**baller** n ποδοσφαιριστής ‖ ~**brake** n ποδόφρενο ‖ ~**bridge** n γέφυρα πεζῶν ‖ ~**hills** npl χαμηλοί λόφοι ‖ ~**hold** n πάτημα, στήριγμα ‖ ~**ing** n (lit) ἀσφαλής θέσις, πάτημα ‖ (fig) θέσις, κατάστασις ‖ ~**lights** npl ράμπα, προσκήνιον ‖ ~**man** n (servant) ὑπηρέτης, λακές ‖ ~-**and-mouth** (disease) n ἀφθώδης πυρετός ‖ ~**note** n ὑποσημείωσις ‖ ~**path** n μονοπάτι ‖ ~**sore** a μέ πονεμένα πόδια ‖ ~**step** n βῆμα, πάτημα ‖ (trace) ἴχνος, πατησιά ‖ ~**wear** n παπούτσι.

for [fɔː*] prep διά, γιά ‖ (in spite of) μόλον ‖ cj διότι, γιατί ‖ **what** ~? γιατί;, γιά ποιό λόγο;.

forage [ˈfɔrɪdʒ] n βοσκή, χορτονομή, χόρτο ‖ vi (col) ψάχνω γιά.

foray [ˈfɔreɪ] n ἐπιδρομή, διαρπαγή.

forbearing [fɔːˈbɛərɪŋ] a ὑπομονητικός, ἀνεκτικός.

forbid [fəˈbid] (irreg v) vt ἀπαγορεύω ‖ ~**den** a ἀπηγορευμένον ‖ ~**ding** a ἀποκρουστικός, δυσάρεστος.

force [fɔːs] n (strength) δύναμις, ἰσχύς ‖ (compulsion) ἐξαναγκασμός, ζόρι ‖ (body of men) δύναμις ‖ vt (compel) ἐξαναγκάζω, ἐκβιάζω ‖ (break open) παραβιάζω ‖ **to** ~ **into** vt πιέζω, σπρώχνω, μπάζω ‖ **in** ~ ἰσχύον ‖ **the F**~**s** npl αἱ δυνάμεις ‖ ~**d** a (smile) προσποιητό, ψεύτικο ‖ (landing) ἀναγκαστική ‖ ~**ful** a ἀποφασιστικός, δραστήριος.

forcible [ˈfɔːsəbl] a ρωμαλέος, βίαιος.

forcibly [ˈfɔːsəbli] ad μέ τό ζόρι, ἀποφασιστικά.

ford [fɔːd] n πέραμα ‖ vt περνῶ.

fore [fɔː*] a πρόσθιος, μπροστινός ‖ n: **to the** ~ στό προσκήνιον, διαπρέπων.

forearm [ˈfɔːrɑːm] n ἀντιβράχιον.

foreboding [fɔːˈbəʊdɪŋ] n κακόν προαίσθημα, κακός οἰωνός.

forecast [ˈfɔːkɑːst] n πρόβλεψις, πρόγνωσις ‖ vt προβλέπω.

forecourt [ˈfɔːkɔːt] n προαύλιον.

forefathers [ˈfɔːfɑːðəz] npl πρόγονοι.

forefinger [ˈfɔːfɪŋgə*] n δείκτης.

forefront [ˈfɔːfrʌnt] n πρόσοψις ‖ (fig) πρώτη σειρά.

forego [fɔːˈgəʊ] vt προηγοῦμαι ‖ ~**ing** a προειρημένος ‖ ~**ne** [ˈfɔːgɔn] a (conclusion) προκαθορισμένο.

foreground [ˈfɔːgraund] n πρῶτο πλάνο.

forehead [ˈfɔrid] n μέτωπον, κούτελο.

foreign [ˈfɔrin] a (country) ξένος, ἄσχετος ‖ (trade) ἐξωτερικόν ‖ (accent) ξενική ‖ (body) ξένος ‖ ~**er** n ξένος, ἀλλοδαπός ‖ ~ **exchange** n συνάλλαγμα ‖ **F**~ **Minister** n ὑπουργός ἐξωτερικῶν.

foreman [ˈfɔːmən] n προϊστάμενος, ἐργοδηγός.

foremost [ˈfɔːməust] a πρῶτος, πρώτιστος, ἐπί κεφαλῆς.

forensic [fəˈrensik] a: ~ **medicine** n ἰατροδικαστική.

forerunner [ˈfɔːrʌnə*] n πρόδρομος.

foresee [fɔːˈsiː] vt προβλέπω ‖ ~**able** a δυνάμενος νά προβλεφθῆ.

foresight [ˈfɔːsait] n πρόβλεψις, πρόνοια.

forest [ˈfɔrist] n δάσος, ρουμάνι.

forestall [fɔːˈstɔːl] vt προλαμβάνω.

forestry [ˈfɔristri] n δασοκομία.

foretaste [ˈfɔːteist] n προαίσθησις.

foretell [fɔːˈtel] vt προλέγω, προμηνύω.

forever [fəˈrevə*] ad παντοτεινά, γιά πάντα.

foreword [ˈfɔːwəːd] n πρόλογος.

forfeit [ˈfɔːfit] n ποινική ρήτρα ‖ vt χάνω (διά κατασχέσεως), χάνω.

forge [fɔːdʒ] n καμίνι, σιδεράδικο ‖ vt (falsely) πλάθω, πλαστογραφῶ ‖ (shape) σφυρηλατῶ ‖ **to** ~ **ahead** vi προηγοῦμαι, προχωρῶ ‖ ~**r** n (criminal) πλαστογράφος, παραχαράκτης ‖ ~**ry** n (activity) πλαστογράφησις ‖ (article) πλαστόν, κίβδηλον (ἀντικείμενον).

forget [fəˈget] vti λησμονῶ, ξεχνῶ, παραλείπω ‖ ~**ful** a ξεχασιάρης, ἀπρόσεκτος ‖ ~**fulness** n ἀπερισκεψία, ἔλλειψι μνήμης.

forgive [fəˈgiv] vt συγχωρῶ ‖ ~**ness** n συγχώρησις.

forgo [fɔːˈgəu] vt παραιτοῦμαι, ἀποφεύγω, κάνω χωρίς.

fork [fɔːk] n (for food) πηρούνι ‖ (farm tool) δικράνα, διχάλα ‖ (branch) διακλάδωσις ‖ vi (road) διχάζομαι, χωρίζομαι ‖ **to** ~ **out** vti (col: pay) πληρώνω ‖ ~**ed** a (lightning) ζίγκ-ζάγκ.

forlorn [fəˈlɔːn] a (person) ἀπελπισμένος, ἐγκαταλελειμμένος ‖ (hope) ἀπελπισμένος, ἄπελπις.

form [fɔːm] n (structure) μορφή, σχῆμα, φόρμα ‖ (class) τάξις ‖ (bench) μπάγκος ‖ (document) ἔντυπον, τύπος ‖ (also mental, physical condition) κατάστασις, φόρμα ‖ vt (shape) διαμορφώνω, σχηματίζω, φτιάνω ‖ (make part of) συγκροτῶ, σχηματίζω.

formal [ˈfɔːməl] a (according to rule) ἐπίσημος, ἐθιμοτυπικός ‖ (stiff) τυπικός ‖ (dress) ἐπίσημος ‖ ~**ity** n (of occasion) τύπος, τυπικότης ‖ ~**ities** npl διατυπώσεις, ἐθιμοτυπία ‖ ~**ly** ad (ceremoniously) τυπικῶς, μέ διατυπώσεις ‖ (officially) ἐπισήμως, τυπικῶς.

format [ˈfɔːmæt] n σχῆμα.

formation [fɔːˈmeiʃən] n διαμόρφωσις, σχηματισμός ‖ (forming) σχηματισμός, διάπλασις ‖ (group) σχηματισμός, διάταξις, τάξις.

formative ['fɔ:mətiv] a (years) διαπλαστικός, μορφωτικός.

former ['fɔ:mə*] a παλαιότερος, προγενέστερος, πρώην, τέως ‖ (opposite of latter) πρῶτος ‖ ~ly ad ἄλλοτε, παλαιότερα.

formica [fɔ:'maikə] n φορμάικα.

formidable ['fɔ:midəbl] a φοβερός, τρομερός.

formula ['fɔ:mjulə] n τύπος ‖ (fig) τύπος, στερεοτυπία, κλισέ ‖ (math) τύπος ‖ ·~te ['fɔ:mjuleit] vt διατυπώνω.

forsake [fə'seik] (irreg v) vt ἐγκαταλείπω, ἀφήνω, ἀρνοῦμαι.

fort [fɔ:t] n φρούριον.

forte [fɔ:t] n δύναμις, φόρτε.

forth [fɔ:θ] ad πρός τά ἐμπρός, πρός τά ἔξω ‖ (in space) πρόσω, ἐμπρός, μπροστά ‖ (in time) ἀπό τοδὲ, ἀπό τώρα καί ἐμπρός ‖ ~coming a (ἐπ)ερχόμενος, προσεχής.

fortieth ['fɔ:tiiθ] a τεσσαρακοστός.

fortification [fɔ:tifi'keiʃən] n (walls etc) ὀχύρωμα, ὀχύρωσις.

fortify ['fɔ:tifai] vt (strengthen) ἐνισχύω, δυναμώνω, τονώνω ‖ (protect) ὀχυρώνω.

fortnight ['fɔ:tnait] n δεκαπενθήμερον ‖ ~ly a δεκαπενθήμερος ‖ ad ἀνά δεκαπενθήμερον.

fortress ['fɔ:tris] n φρούριον, κάστρο.

fortunate ['fɔ:tʃənit] a εὐτυχής, τυχερός, εὐμενής ‖ ~ly ad εὐτυχῶς.

fortune ['fɔ:tʃən] n (chance) τύχη, σύμπτωσις, καλοτυχία ‖ (wealth) πλοῦτος, περιουσία ‖ ~teller n μάντις, χαρτορίχτρα.

forty ['fɔ:ti] num σαράντα.

forward ['fɔ:wəd] a (lying ahead) πρόσθιος, μπροστινός ‖ (movement) κίνησις πρός τά πρόσω, προοδευτικός ‖ (advanced) μέ πρόωρον ἀνάπτυξιν ‖ ad (πρός τά) ἐμπρός, μπρός ‖ n (sport) κυνηγός ‖ vt (mail etc) ἀποστέλλω, διεκπεραιώνω ‖ (help) προωθῶ, εὐνοῶ, προάγω ‖ ~s ad ἀπό τώρα καί στό ἑξῆς.

fossil ['fɔsl] n ἀπολίθωμα.

foster ['fɔstə*] vt καλλιεργῶ, τρέφω ‖ ~ child n 3ετόν τέκνον ‖ ~ mother n μητρυιά, ψυχομάννα.

fought [fɔ:t] pt,pp of fight.

foul [faul] a ἀκάθαρτος, ρυπαρός, βρωμερός, μολυσμένος ‖ (language) βωμολόγος, πρόστυχος, αἰσχρός ‖ (weather) κακοκαιρίας ‖ n (sport) φάουλ ‖ vt (mechanism) φράσσω, μπλέκω, πιάνω ‖ (sport) κάνω φάουλ.

found [faund] pt,pp of find ‖ vt (establish) ἱδρύω, 3εμελιώνω, κτίζω ‖ ~ation n (act) ἵδρυσις, 3εμελίωσις, 3εμέλιον ‖ (fig) ἵδρυμα, κληροδότημα ‖ ~ations npl (building) 3εμέλια.

founder ['faundə*] n ἱδρυτής ‖ vi (naut) βυθίζομαι, βουλιάζω.

foundry ['faundri] n χυτήριον.

fount [faunt] n (source) πηγή ‖ ~ain n πηγή ‖ (jet of water) συντριβάνι ‖ ~ain pen n στυλογράφος, στυλό.

four [fɔ:*] num τέσσερα ‖ on all ~s μέ τά τέσσερα ‖ ~some n διπλή παρτίδα ‖ ~teen num δέκα τέσσερα ‖ ~teenth a δέκατος τέταρτος ‖ ~th a τέταρτος.

fowl [faul] n πουλί, πουλερικός.

fox [fɔks] n ἀλεποῦ ‖ ~hunting n κυνήγι τῆς ἀλεπούς ‖ ~trot n φόξ-τρότ.

foyer ['fɔiei] n φουαγιέ.

fraction ['frækʃən] n (part) τεμάχιον, κομμάτι ‖ (math) κλάσμα.

fracture ['fræktʃə*] n (of bone) κάταγμα ‖ vt 3ραύω, τσακίζω, προκαλῶ κάταγμα.

fragile ['frædʒail] a εὔθραυστος.

fragment ['frægmənt] n 3ραύσμα, 3ρύμμα, σύντριμμα ‖ (part) τεμάχιον, ἀπόκομμα, ἀπόσπασμα ‖ ~ary a ἀποσπασματικός, κλαστικός.

fragrance ['freigrəns] n ἄρωμα, μυρωδιά.

fragrant ['freigrənt] a εὔοσμος, μυρωδάτος.

frail [freil] a εὐπαθής, ἀσθενικός.

frame [freim] n σκελετός, πλαίσιον ‖ (border) πλαίσιον, κορνίζα ‖ vt (put into frame) πλαισιώνω, κορνιζάρω ‖ (put together) κατασιτρώνω, διαμορφώνω, κατασκευάζω ‖ (col: incriminate) μηχανορραφῶ, σκηνοθετῶ ‖ ~ of mind n πνευματική κατάσταση, διάθεση ‖ ~work n σκελετός, πλαίσιον.

France [fra:ns] n Γαλλία.

franchise ['fræntʃaiz] n προνόμιον.

frank [fræŋk] a εἰλικρινής ‖ ~ly ad εἰλικρινά, ντόμπρα ‖ ~ness n εἰλικρίνεια, παρρησία.

frankincense ['fræŋkinsens] n λιβάνι.

frantic ['fræntik] a φρενητιώδης, μανιώδης ‖ ~ally ad μανιασμένα, τρομερά.

fraternal [frə'tə:nl] a ἀδελφικός.

fraternity [frə'tə:niti] n (club) ὀργάνωσις ‖ (spirit) ἀδελφότης ‖ (US sch) φοιτητική ὀργάνωσις.

fraternization [frætənai'zeiʃən] n συναδέλφωσις.

fraternize ['frætənaiz] vi (+ with) συναδελφώνομαι μέ.

fraud [frɔ:d] n (trickery) δόλος, ἀπάτη ‖ (trick) κόλπο, ἀπάτη, παγίδα ‖ (person) ἀπατεών, κατεργάρης.

fraudulent ['frɔ:djulənt] a δόλιος, ἀπατηλός.

fray [frei] n σύρραξις, καυγᾶς, σύγκρουσι ‖ vt τρίβω, ταράζω, ξεφτίζω ‖ vi ξεφτίζομαι, τρίβομαι ‖ ~ed a τριμμένος, φαγωμένος.

freak [fri:k] n ἰδιοτροπία, καπρίτσιο ‖ (col) τέρας ‖ a περίεργον φαινόμενον.

freckle ['frekl] n πανάδα ‖ ~d a μέ πανάδες.

free [fri:] a (at liberty) ἀνεξάρτητος, ἐλεύθερος ‖ (loose) ἐλεύθερος ‖ (not *occupied*) ἐλεύθερος ‖ (*gratis*) δωρεάν, τζάμπα ‖ (*liberal*) φιλελεύθερος, γενναιόφρων, ἀνοιχτός ‖ *vt* (*set free*) (ἀπ)ελευθερώνω ‖ (*unblock*) ἀποφράσσω, καθαρίζω ‖ ~**dom** *n* ἐλευθερία, ἀνεξαρτησία ‖ ~**lance** *a* ἀνεξάρτητος ‖ ~**ly** *ad* ἐλευθέρως, ἀβίαστα ‖ ~**mason** *n* μασῶνος ‖ ~**masonry** *n* τεκτωνισμός, μασωνία ‖ ~ **trade** *n* ἐλεύθερον ἐμπόριον ‖ ~**way** *n* (US) αὐτοκινητόδρομος ‖ ~**wheel** *vi* πηγαίνω μέ ἐλεύθερον τροχόν ‖ ~ **will** *n* ἐλευθέρα θέλησις.

freesia ['fri:ziə] *n* φρισία.

freeze [fri:z] (*irreg v*) *vi* (*become ice*) ψύχω, καταψύχω, παγώνω ‖ (*feel cold*) κρυώνω ‖ *vt* (*lit*) (κατα)ψύχω, παγώνω ‖ (*fig*) δεσμεύω, ἀκινητοποιῶ ‖ *n* (*lit*) (κατά)ψυξις, παγωνιά ‖ (*fig, econ*) δέσμευσις ‖ ~**r** *n* παγωτιέρα, ψυγεῖον καταψύξεως.

freezing ['fri:zɪŋ] *a*: ~ **cold** *a* παγερό κρύο ‖ ~ **point** *n* σημεῖον ψύξεως, πήξεως.

freight [freit] *n* (*goods*) φορτίον, ἐμπορεύματα ‖ (*money charged*) ναῦλος ‖ ~ **car** *n* (US) φορτηγόν βαγόνι ‖ ~**er** *n* (*naut*) φορτηγόν.

French [frentʃ] *a* γαλλικός ‖ *n* (*ling*) (τά) γαλλικά ‖ **the** ~ *npl* οἱ Γάλλοι ‖ ~ **fried potatoes** *npl* πατάτες τηγανιτές ‖ ~**man** *n* Γάλλος ‖ ~ **window** *n* τζαμόπορτα ‖ ~**woman** *n* Γαλλίδα.

frenzy ['frenzi] *n* φρενῖτις, τρέλλα, παραλήρημα.

frequency ['fri:kwənsi] *n* συχνότης, πυκνότης ‖ (*phys*) συχνότης.

frequent ['fri:kwənt] *a* (*happening often*) συχνός, διαδεδομένος, συνήθης ‖ (*numerous*) ἄφθονος, πολυάριθμος ‖ [fri:'kwent] *vt* συχνάζω ‖ ~**ly** *ad* συχνά.

fresco ['freskəu] *n* νωπογραφία, φρέσκο.

fresh [freʃ] *a* (*new, additional*) νέος, καινούριος, φρέσκος ‖ (*recent*) νέος, πρωτότυπος ‖ (*not stale*) νωπός, φρέσκος ‖ (*not tired*) ρωμαλαῖος, ξεκούραστος, φρέσκος ‖ (*cool*) καθαρός, δροσερός ‖ (*cheeky*) ἀναιδής, ζωηρός ‖ ~**en** (*also* ~ **up**) *vi* φρεσκάρω, συνέρχομαι ‖ *vt* ἀναζωογονῶ, φρεσκάρω ‖ ~**ly** *ad* προσφάτως, νεο-, φρεσκο- ‖ ~**ness** *n* φρεσκάδα, δροσερότης ‖ ~**water** *a* τοῦ γλυκοῦ νεροῦ.

fret [fret] *vi* ταράσσομαι, ἀνησυχῶ, στεναχωριέμαι.

friar ['fraɪə*] *n* μοναχός, καλόγηρος.

friction ['frikʃən] *n* (*resistance*) τριβή, τρίψιμο ‖ (*disagreement*) προστριβή, τσάκωμα.

Friday ['fraidi] *n* Παρασκευή ‖ *see* **good**.

fridge [fridʒ] *n* ψυγεῖον.

fried [fraid] *a* τηγανισμένο.

friend [frend] *n* φίλος, γνωστός, γνώριμος ‖ ~**liness** *n* φιλία, καλωσύνη ‖ ~**ly** *a* (*person*) εὐμενής, φιλικός ‖ (*attitude*) φιλικός ‖ ~**ship** *n* φιλία.

frieze [fri:z] *n* (*archit*) διάζωμα, ζωφόρος.

frigate ['frigit] *n* φρεγάτα.

fright [frait] *n* τρόμος, φόβος ‖ (*ugly*) ἄσχημος, σχιάχτρο ‖ ~**en** *vt* (κατα)τρομάζω, φοβίζω ‖ ~**ening** *a* τρομακτικός, τρομερός ‖ ~**ful** *a* (*col*) τρομερός, φρικτός ‖ ~**fully** *ad* τρομερά, τρομακτικά.

frigid ['fridʒid] *a* ψυχρός, παγερός, κρύος ‖ ~**ity** *n* ψυχρότης ‖ (*sexual*) ἀναφροδισία.

frill [fril] *n* βολάκι.

fringe [frindʒ] *n* (*border*) κροσσός, κρόσι ‖ (*fig*) περιθώριον, παρυφή.

frisky ['friski] *a* παιχνιδιάρης, κεφάτος.

fritter ['fritə*] *n* τηγανίτα, σβίγγος ‖ **to** ~ **away** *vt* σπαταλῶ.

frivolity [fri'voliti] *n* ἐπιπολαιότης.

frivolous ['frivələs] *a* ἐπιπόλαιος.

frizzy ['frizi] *a* σγουρός.

fro [frəu] *see* **to**.

frock [frɔk] *n* (*of monk*) ράσο ‖ (*of woman*) φουστάνι.

frog [frɔg] *n* βάτραχος ‖ ~**man** *n* βατραχάνθρωπος.

frolic ['frɔlik] *n* παιχνίδι, γλέντι ‖ *vi* διασκεδάζω, παιχνιδίζω.

from [frɔm] *prep* ἀπό, ἐκ, ἐξ.

front [frʌnt] *n* (*of house*) πρόσοψις, μπροστινό, φάτσα ‖ (*mil*) μέτωπον ‖ (*pol*) μέτωπον ‖ (*meteorology*) μέτωπον ‖ (*fig: appearances*) ὄψις, μούτρα, ἀναίδεια ‖ *a* (*forward*) πρόσθιος, μπροστινός ‖ (*first*) μπροστινός, πρῶτος ‖ (*door*) κυρία εἴσοδος, μπροστινή πόρτα ‖ ~**age** *n* πρόσοψις ‖ ~**al** *a* μετωπικός ‖ ~**ier** *n* σύνορον, μεθόριος ‖ ~**-page** *a* τῆς πρώτης σελίδος ‖ ~**-wheel drive** *n* κίνησις στούς προσθίους τροχούς.

frost [frɔst] *n* παγετός, παγωνιά ‖ ~**bite** *n* κρυοπάγημα ‖ ~**ed** *a* (*glass*) μάτ, ἀδιαφανής ‖ ~**y** *a* παγερός, παγωμένος.

froth [frɔθ] *n* ἀφρός ‖ (*on beer*) κολλάρο ‖ ~**y** *a* ἀφρισμένος, ἀφρώδης.

frown [fraun] *n* συνοφρύωσις, κατσούφιασμα ‖ *vi* συνοφρυοῦμαι, σκυθρωπάζω ‖ **to** ~ **upon** *vt* κάνω μούτρα σέ.

froze [frəuz] *pt of* **freeze** ‖ ~**n** *pp of* **freeze** ‖ (*comm*) παγωμένος ‖ ~**n food** *n* κατεψυγμένα.

frugal ['fru:gəl] *a* λιτός, οἰκονομικός.

fruit [fru:t] *n* φροῦτον, καρπόν ‖ ~**s** *npl* καρποί, κέρδη ‖ ~**erer** *n* ὀπωροπώλης ‖ ~**ful** *a* καρποφόρος, γόνιμος ‖ ~**ion** [fru:'iʃən] *n* ἐκπλήρωσις, ἀπόλαυσις.

frustrate [frʌs'treit] *vt* ματαιώνω, ἐξουδετερώνω, ἐμποδίζω ‖ ~**d** *a* ἀπογοητευμένος.

frustration [frʌs'treiʃən]· *n* ματαίωσις, ἀπογοήτευσις.

fry [frai] *vt* τηγανίζω ‖ **small** ~ *npl* οἱ ἀνθρωπάκοι, τά κατακάθια ‖ ~**ing pan** *n* τηγάνι.

fuchsia ['fju:ʃə] *n* φούξια.

fudge [fʌdʒ] *n* ζαχαρωτόν, καραμέλα.

fuel [fjuəl] *n* (*oil*) καύσιμος ύλη, πετρέλαιον ‖ (*petrol*) καύσιμον, βενζίνη ‖ (*wood*) καυσόξυλα ‖ (*coal*) κάρβουνο ‖ (*gas*) καύσιμον ἀέριον ‖ ~ **oil** *n* (*diesel fuel*) ἀκάθαρτον πετρέλαιον ‖ ~ **tank** *n* ντεπόζιτο βενζίνης.

fugitive [ˈfjuːdʒitiv] *n* φυγάς, δραπέτης.

fulfil [fulˈfil] *vt* (*accomplish*) ἐκπληρώνω ‖ (*obey*) ἐκτελῶ, εἰσακούω ‖ ~**ment** *n* ἐκπλήρωσις, ἐκτέλεσις.

full [ful] *a* (*box, bottle*) πλήρης, γεμᾶτος ‖ (*vehicle*) πλήρης, γεμᾶτος ‖ (*person: satisfied*) χορτάτος, μπουκωμένος ‖ (*session*) ὁλομέλεια ‖ (*complete*) ὁλόκληρος ‖ (*moon*) πανσέληνος ‖ (*price*) ὁλόκληρο ‖ (*speed*) ὁλοταχῶς ‖ (*skirt*) φαρδύς, μπουφφάν ‖ **in** ~ χωρίς ἐκπτώσιν, ὁλογράφως, ἀκέραιον ‖ ~**back** *n* ὀπισθοφύλαξ ‖ ~**ness** *n* πληρότης, τελειότης ‖ ~ **stop** *n* τελεία ‖ ~**time** *a* (*work*) μέ πλήρες ὡράριον ‖ *ad* ἀκριβῶς, τελείως ‖ ~**y** *ad* πλήρως, τελείως, ἀπολύτως ‖ ~**y-fledged** *a* ὥριμος.

fumble [ˈfʌmbl] *vti* ψαχουλεύω, χειρίζομαι ἀτζαμίστικα.

fume [fjuːm] *vi* (*smoke*) ἀναδίδομαι, καπνίζω ‖ (*be furious*) ἐξάπτομαι, λυσσάζω ‖ ~**s** *npl* ἀτμοί, ἀναθυμιάσεις, καπνιές.

fumigate [ˈfjuːmigeit] *vt* ἀπολυμαίνω.

fun [fʌn] *n* διασκέδασις, κέφι, ἀστεῖο, χωρατό ‖ **to make** ~ **of** κοροϊδεύω, περιπαίζω.

function [ˈfʌŋkʃən] *n* (*use*) λειτουργία, ἔργον, λειτούργημα ‖ (*public occasion*) τελετή, δεξίωσις ‖ *vi* λειτουργῶ ‖ ~**al** *a* λειτουργικός.

fund [fʌnd] *n* (*capital*) ταμεῖον, κεφάλαιον, παρακαταθήκη ‖ (*store*) ἀπόθεμα, πηγή.

fundamental [fʌndəˈmentl] *a* θεμελιώδης ‖ ~**s** *npl* στοιχεῖα, βασικές ἀρχές ‖ ~**ly** *ad* οὐσιαστικῶς, βασικῶς.

funeral [ˈfjuːnərəl] *n* κηδεία ‖ *a* νεκρώσιμος, πένθιμος.

fun fair [ˈfʌnfɛə*] *n* λούνα-πάρκ.

fungus [ˈfʌŋgəs] *n* μύκης, μανιτάρι.

funnel [ˈfʌnl] *n* χωνί ‖ (*of ship*) φουγάρο.

funnily [ˈfʌnili] *ad* κωμικά, περίεργα ‖ ~ **enough** περίεργως.

funny [ˈfʌni] *a* (*comical*) ἀστεῖος, κωμικός ‖ (*strange*) παράξενος, περίεργος.

fur [fəː*] *n* γοῦνα, γουναρικό ‖ ~ **coat** *n* γούνινο παλτό.

furious [ˈfjuəriəs] *a* μαινόμενος, λυσσαλέος, ἀγριεμένος ‖ ~**ly** *ad* ἄγρια, λυσσωδῶς.

furlong [ˈfəːlɒŋ] *n* = 220 ὑάρδες (201 μέτρα).

furlough [ˈfəːləu] *n* (*US*) ἄδεια.

furnace [ˈfəːnis] *n* κλίβανος, κάμινος, φοῦρνος.

furnish [ˈfəːniʃ] *vt* (*with furniture*) ἐπιπλώνω

‖ (*supply*) παρέχω, προμηθεύω, προσφέρω ‖ ~**ings** *npl* ἔπιπλα, ἐπίπλωσις.

furniture [ˈfəːnitʃə*] *n* ἔπιπλα.

furrow [ˈfʌrəu] *n* αὐλακώνω.

furry [ˈfəːri] *a* γούνινος.

further [ˈfəːðə*] *comp of* **far** ‖ *a* (*additional*) νέος, πρόσθετος, μεταγενέστερος ‖ (*more distant*) πιό πέρα ‖ *ad* (*more*) περαιτέρω, περισσότερον ‖ (*moreover*) ἄλλωστε, ἐπί πλέον ‖ *vt* προάγω, ὑποστηρίζω ‖ ~**more** *ad* ἐκτός ἀπ'αὐτό, ἐξ ἄλλου.

furthest [ˈfəːðist] *superl of* **far**.

furtive [ˈfəːtiv] *a* λαθραῖος, κρυμμένος, ὕπουλος ‖ ~**ly** *ad* κρυφά, λαθραία.

fury [ˈfjuəri] *n* ὀργή, θυμός, μάνιτα.

fuse [fjuːz] *n* (*elec*) ἀσφάλεια ‖ (*cord*) φυτίλι ‖ *vt* τήκω, λειώνω ‖ *vi* (*elec*) τήκομαι, λυώνω ‖ ~ **box** *n* κιβώτιον ἀσφαλειῶν.

fuselage [ˈfjuːzəlɑːʒ] *n* ἄτρακτος, σκελετός.

fusion [ˈfjuːʒən] *n* (*union*) συγχώνευσις, σύμπραξις.

fuss [fʌs] *n* (*dispute*) φασαρία, θόρυβος, ταραχή ‖ (*bustle*) φασαρία, ἀναστάτωσις, μπερδέματα ‖ ~**y** *a* πολυπράγμων, λεπτολόγος, ἰδιότροπος.

futile [ˈfjuːtail] *a* (*useless*) φροῦδος, μάταιος ‖ (*unimportant*) ἀσήμαντος, κούφιος.

futility [fjuːˈtiliti] *n* ματαιότης.

future [ˈfjuːtʃə*] *a* μέλλων, μελλοντικός ‖ *n* μέλλον ‖ **in (the)** ~ στό μέλλον.

futuristic [fjuːtʃəˈristik] *a* φουτουριστικός.

fuze [fjuːz] (*US*) = **fuse**.

fuzzy [ˈfʌzi] *a* (*indistinct*) θαμπός ‖ (*from drink*) σουρωμένος.

G, g

gabble [ˈgæbl] *vi* φλυαρῶ.

gable [ˈgeibl] *n* ἀέτωμα.

gadget [ˈgædʒit] *n* μαραφέτι.

gag [gæg] *n* φίμωτρον ‖ (*funny phrase*) ἀστεῖο, κασκαρίκα ‖ *vt* φιμώνω, ἀποστομώνω.

gaiety [ˈgeiiti] *n* εὐθυμία.

gaily [ˈgeili] *ad* εὔθυμα, χαρούμενα.

gain [gein] *vt* (*obtain*) ἀποκτῶ, κερδίζω ‖ (*win over*) κερδίζω, παίρνω ‖ (*make progress*) προχωρῶ, προηγοῦμαι ‖ *vi* (*improve*) κερδίζω, κατακτῶ ‖ (*clock etc*) τρέχω μπρός ‖ *n* κέρδος, αὔξησις ‖ ~**ful** *a* ἐπικερδής.

gala [ˈgɑːlə] *n* γιορτή.

galaxy [ˈgæləksi] *n* (*stars*) γαλαξίας.

gale [geil] *n* θύελλα, φουρτούνα ‖ ~ **warning** *n* ἀναγγελία θυέλλης.

gallant [ˈgælənt] *a* (*fine, brave*) γενναῖος, ἡρωϊκός ‖ (*to women*) γαλάντης, περιποιητικός ‖ ~**ry** *n* γενναιότης, λεβεντιά ‖ (*to women*) περιποιητικότης.

gall-bladder ['gɔːlblædə*] *n* χοληδόχος κύστις.

gallery ['gæləri] *n* (*art*) πινακοθήκη ‖ (*theat*) γαλαρία, ἐξώστης.

galley ['gæli] *n* (*of ship*) μαγειρεῖον ‖ (*vessel*) γαλέρα.

gallon ['gælən] *n* γαλλόνι (04.54 χλγρ.).

gallop ['gæləp] *n* καλπασμός, γκάλοπ ‖ *vi* καλπάζω.

gallows ['gæləuz] *npl* ἀγχόνη, κρεμάλα.

gallstone ['gɔːlstəun] *n* χολόλιθος.

gamble ['gæmbl] *vi* παίζω ‖ *vt* (*risk*) ριψοκινδυνεύω ‖ *n* (τυχηρόν) παιχνίδι ‖ ~**r** *n* (χαρτο)παίκτης.

gambling ['gæmblin] *n* παιχνίδι, παίξιμο.

game [geim] *n* (*play*) παιχνίδι, διασκέδασις ‖ (*animals*) θήραμα, κυνήγι ‖ *a* θαρραλέος, τολμηρός ‖ ~**keeper** *n* φύλαξ κυνηγιοῦ.

gammon ['gæmən] *n* ὀπίσθια μποῦτια, χοιρομέρι.

gang [gæn] *n* συμμορία, σπεῖρα.

gangrene ['gængriːn] *n* γάγγραινα.

gangster ['gænstə*] *n* γκάγκστερ.

gangway ['gænwei] *n* (*of ship*) διαβάθρα, μαδέρι ‖ (*aisle*) διάδρομος.

gaol [dʒeil] *n* = **jail.**

gap [gæp] *n* (*opening*) τρύπα, ῥῆγμα ‖ (*empty space*) διάκενον.

gape [geip] *vi* χάσκω, χασμουριέμαι.

gaping ['geipin] *a* χαίνων.

garage ['gærɑːʒ] *n* γκαράζ.

garbage ['gɑːbidʒ] *n* σκουπίδια ‖ ~ **can** *n* (*US*) σκουπιδοτενεκές.

garbled ['gɑːbld] *a* (*story*) παραμορφωμένος, ἀλλοιωμένος.

garden ['gɑːdn] *n* κῆπος, μπαξές ‖ *vi* ἀσχολοῦμαι μέ κηπουρικήν ‖ ~**er** *n* κηπουρός, περιβολάρης ‖ ~**ing** *n* κηπουρική ‖ ~ **party** *n* γκάρντεν-πάρτυ.

gargle ['gɑːgl] *vi* γαργαρίζω ‖ *n* γαργάρα.

gargoyle ['gɑːgɔil] *n* ὑδρορρόη.

garish ['gɛəriʃ] *a* φανταχτερός, κακόγουστος.

garland ['gɑːlənd] *n* στέφανος, γιρλάντα.

garlic ['gɑːlik] *n* σκόρδο.

garment ['gɑːmənt] *n* φόρεμα.

garnish ['gɑːniʃ] *vt* (*food*) γαρνίρω ‖ *n* γαρνιτούρα.

garret ['gærit] *n* σοφίτα.

garrison ['gærisən] *n* φρουρά ‖ *vt* ἐγκαθιστῶ φρουράν.

garrulous ['gærələs] *a* φλύαρος, πολυλογᾶς.

garter ['gɑːtə*] *n* καλτσοδέτα.

gas [gæs] *n* ἀέριον ‖ (*coalgas*) φωταέριον, γκάζ ‖ (*med*) ἀναισθητικόν ‖ (*US: gasoline*) βενζίνη ‖ *vt* δηλητηριάζω (δι'ἀερίου) ‖ ~ **cooker** *n* κουζίνα ‖ ~ **cylinder** *n* φιάλη ἀερίου ‖ ~ **fire** *n* σόμπα τοῦ γκαζιοῦ.

gash [gæʃ] *n* ἐγκοπή, μαχαιριά ‖ *vt* κόβω, πληγώνω.

gasket ['gæskit] *n* (*tech*) παρένθεμα.

gasmask ['gæsmɑːsk] *n* προσωπίς ἀερίων, μάσκα.

gas meter ['gæsmiːtə*] *n* μετρητής τοῦ γκαζιοῦ.

gasoline ['gæsəliːn] *n* (*US*) βενζίνη.

gasp [gɑːsp] *vi* ἀσθμαίνω, λαχανιάζω ‖ *n* κομμένη ἀναπνοή, ρόγχος.

gas ring ['gæsrin] *n* μάτι τοῦ γκαζιοῦ.

gas station ['gæssteiʃən] *n* (*US*) βενζινάδικο.

gas stove ['gæs'stəuv] *n* κουζίνα τοῦ γκαζιοῦ.

gassy ['gæsi] *a* (*drink*) ἀεριοῦχος.

gastric ['gæstrik] *a* γαστρικός ‖ ~ **ulcer** *n* ἕλκος τοῦ στομάχου.

gastronomy [gæs'trɔnəmi] *n* γαστρονομία.

gate [geit] *n* πύλη, πόρτα ‖ (*of estate etc*) καγκελόπορτα, αὐλόπορτα ‖ ~**crasher** *n* (*party*) σελέμης, τζαμπατζῆς ‖ ~**way** *n* πύλη, εἴσοδος.

gather ['gæðə*] *vt* συλλέγω, μαζεύω ‖ (*gain*) συμπεραίνω, συνάγω ‖ *vi* (*assemble*) συγκεντρώομαι, μαζεύομαι ‖ ~**ing** *n* συγκέντρωσις, μάζεμα.

gauche [gəuʃ] *a* χωρίς τάκτ.

gaudy ['gɔːdi] *a* ἐπιδεικτικός, φανταχτερός.

gauge [geidʒ] *n* (*of metal*) διάμετρος, διαμέτρημα ‖ (*rail*) πλάτος, μετατρόχιον ‖ (*measure*) μετρητής, (ἐν)δείκτης ‖ *vt* (δια)μετρῶ, ἐκτιμῶ.

gaunt [gɔːnt] *a* (*lean*) ἰσχνός, κοκκαλιάρης ‖ (*grim*) ἄγριος, συντετριμμένος.

gauze [gɔːz] *n* γάζα.

gave [geiv] *pt of* give.

gay [gei] *a* (*merry*) εὔθυμος ‖ (*brightly coloured*) λαμπρός, ζωηρός ‖ (*col*) τοιοῦτος.

gaze [geiz] *n* ἀτενές βλέμμα ‖ to ~ at *vt* ἀτενίζω, καρφώνω.

gazelle [gə'zel] *n* γαζέλλα.

gazetteer [gæzi'tiə*] *n* γεωγραφικόν λεξικόν.

gear [giə*] *n* (*equipment*) εἴδη ‖ (*mech*) μηχανισμός, ὀδοντωτός τροχός ‖ (*aut*) γρανάζι ‖ in ~ κινούμενος, στήν ταχύτητα ‖ out of ~ νεκρό σημεῖον, ἐκτός λειτουργίας ‖ ~**box** *n* κιβώτιον ταχυτήτων ‖ ~-**lever**, (*US*) ~**shift** *n* μοχλός ταχυτήτων.

geese [giːs] *npl of* goose.

gelatin(e) ['dʒelətiːn] *n* ζελατίνη, πηκτή.

gelignite ['dʒelignait] *n* ζελινίτης.

gem [dʒem] *n* πολύτιμος λίθος, πέτρα.

gender ['dʒendə*] *n* γένος.

general ['dʒenərəl] *n* στρατηγός ‖ *a* γενικός ‖ ~ **election** *n* γενικαί ἐκλογαί ‖ ~**ization** *n* γενίκευσις ‖ ~**ize** *vi* γενικεύω, ἐκλαϊκεύω ‖ ~**ly** *ad* γενικά, κατά κανόνα.

generate ['dʒenəreit] *vt* παράγω, (ἐπι)φέρω, προκαλῶ ‖ (*elec*) παράγω.

generation [dʒenə'reiʃən] *n* (*into being*) γέννησις, γένεσις ‖ (*descent in family*) γενεά, γενιά || (of same period) (σημερινή) γενεά ||· (about 30 years) (μιά) γενεά.

generator ['dʒenəreitə*] n γεννήτρια.

generosity [dʒenə'rɔsiti] n γενναιοδωρία, γενναιοψυχία.

generous ['dʒenərəs] a γενναιόδωρος, μεγαλόψυχος || (col) γενναίο, πλούσιο || ~ly ad γενναιόδωρα, μεγαλόψυχα.

genetics [dʒi'netiks] npl γενετική.

genial ['dʒi:niəl] a εὔκρατος, ἤπιος, προσηνής.

genitals ['dʒenitlz] npl γεννητικά ὄργανα.

genitive ['dʒenitiv] n γενική (πτῶσις).

genius ['dʒi:niəs] n (person) ἰδιοφυΐα, μεγαλοφυΐα || (ability) πνεῦμα.

genteel [dʒen'ti:l] a εὐγενής, κομψός.

gentile ['dʒentail] n ἐθνικός, μὴ Ἰουδαῖος.

gentle ['dʒentl] a ἤπιος, μαλακός, εὐγενής || ~man n (of manners) κύριος, τζέντλεμαν || ~ness n λεπτότης.

gently ['dʒentli] ad ἤρεμα, μαλακά.

gentry ['dʒentri] n ἀρχοντολόϊ.

gents [dʒents] n ἄνδρες, κύριοι.

genuine ['dʒenjuin] a γνήσιος, αὐθεντικός, ἀληθινός || ~ly ad εἰλικρινά, γνησίως.

geographical [dʒiə'græfikəl] a γεωγραφικός.

geography [dʒi'ɔgrəfi] n γεωγραφία.

geological [dʒiəu'lɔdʒikəl] a γεωλογικός.

geologist [dʒi'ɔlədʒist] n γεωλόγος.

geology [dʒi'ɔlədʒi] n γεωλογία.

geometric(al) [dʒiə'metrik(əl)] a γεωμετρικός.

geometry [dʒi'ɔmitri] n γεωμετρία.

geranium [dʒə'reiniəm] n γεράνι.

germ [dʒə:m] n (of disease) μικρόβιον || (bud or seed) σπέρμα || (beginning) σπέρμα.

German ['dʒə:mən] a γερμανικός || n (person) Γερμανός || (ling) γερμανικά || ~y n Γερμανία.

germination [dʒə:mi'neiʃən] n βλάστησις, κύησις.

gesticulate [dʒes'tikjuleit] vi χειρονομῶ.

gesticulation [dʒestikju'leiʃən] n χειρονομία.

gesture ['dʒestʃə*] n χειρονομία, νεῦμα.

get [get] (irreg v) vt (fetch) (πηγαίνω νά) φέρω || (become) γίνομαι || (persuade) πείθω, καταφέρνω || (catch) (συλ)λαμβάνω, πιάνω || vi (reach) πηγαίνω, φθάνω, γίνομαι || to ~ along vi (of people) πηγαίνω καλά || (depart) προχωρῶ, (ὥρα) νά φύγω || to ~ at vi (facts) φθάνω, βρίσκω, πλησιάζω || to ~ away vi (leave) ἀναχωρῶ, ἀπομακρύνω || (escape) φεύγω, τό σκάω || to ~ down vt κατεβάζω, γράφω || to ~ in vi (train) μπαίνω, πιάνω φιλίες || to ~ on vi (well, badly etc) εὐδοκιμῶ, συμφωνῶ, τά πάω καλά || to ~ out vi βγάζω, ἀφαιρῶ, βγαίνω || to ~ over vt (illness) συνέρχομαι, τελειώνω || to ~ up

vi (in morning) σηκώνομαι || ~away n φυγή, δραπέτευσις.

geyser ['gi:zə*] n θερμοπίδαξ, γκάϊζερ || (heater) θερμοσίφων.

ghastly ['ga:stli] a φρικτός, τρομερός || (pale) ὠχρός.

gherkin ['gə:kin] n ἀγγουράκι.

ghetto ['getəu] n γκέττο, ὀβριακή.

ghost [gəust] n φάντασμα || ~ly a φαντασμακικός.

giant ['dʒaiənt] n γίγας || a γιγαντιαῖος.

gibberish ['dʒibəriʃ] n ἀλαμπουρνέζικα.

gibe [dʒaib] n σκῶμμα, πείραγμα.

giblets ['dʒiblits] npl ἐντόσθια (πουλερικῶν).

giddiness ['gidinis] n ἴλιγγος, ζάλη.

giddy ['gidi] a (dizzy) ζαλισμένος || (frivolous) ἐπιπόλαιος.

gift [gift] n δῶρον || (talent) προσόν, τάλαντον || ~ed a προικισμένος, μέ ταλέντο.

gigantic [dʒai'gæntik] a γιγαντιαῖος.

giggle ['gigl] vi χασκογελῶ || n κακάρισμα.

gild [gild] (irreg v) vt (ἐπι)χρυσώνω.

gill [dʒil] n (measure = ¼ pint) ⅛ τοῦ λίτρου || [gil] n (fish) βράγχιον, σπάραχνο.

gilt [gilt] pp of gild || n ἐπιχρύσωσις, χρύσωμα || a (ἐπι)χρυσωμένος.

gin [dʒin] n (liquor) τζίν.

ginger ['dʒindʒə*] n πιπερόρριζα || ~ beer n τζιτζιμπύρα || ~bread n μελόψωμο || ~-haired a κοκκινοτρίχης.

gingerly ['dʒindʒəli] ad προσεκτικά, μαλακά.

gipsy ['dʒipsi] n τσιγγάνος, γύφτος.

giraffe [dʒi'ra:f] n καμηλοπάρδαλις.

girder ['gə:də*] n δοκός.

girdle ['gə:dl] n ζωνάρι || vt (περι)ζώνω.

girl [gə:l] n (child) κοριτσάκι, κορίτσι || (young woman) νέα, κοπέλα || ~friend n (of girl) φιλινάδα || (of boy) φιλινάδα, φίλη || ~ish a κοριτσίστικος.

girth [gə:θ] n (measurement) περιφέρεια, περίμετρος || (strap) ἔποχον, ἴγγλα.

gist [dʒist] n οὐσία, ἔννοια.

give [giv] (irreg v) vt (hand over) δίνω, χαρίζω || (supply) παρέχω, ἀπονέμω || vi (break) ὑποχωρῶ, λυγίζω || to ~ away vt (give free) χαρίζω || (betray) καταδίδω, προδίδω || to ~ back vt ἀποδίδω, ξαναδίδω, γυρίζω || to ~ in vi (yield, agree) ὑποχωρῶ, ὑποκύπτω || vt (hand in) παραδίδω || to ~ up vi (surrender) παραδίδομαι || vt (post, office) παραιτοῦμαι, ἐγκαταλείπω || to ~ way vi θραύομαι, ὑποχωρῶ, ἀντικαθίσταμαι || ~r n δωρητής, δότης.

glacier ['glæsiə*] n παγετών.

glad [glæd] a εὐχαριστημένος, εὐχάριστος || ~den vt χαροποιῶ.

gladiator ['glædieitə*] n μονομάχος.

gladioli [glædi'əulai] npl γλαδιόλες.

gladly ['glædli] ad εὐχαρίστως, μέ χαρά.

glamorous ['glæmərəs] *a* γοητευτικός, μαγευτικός.

glamour ['glæmə*] *n* γοητεία, μαγεία.

glance [glɑ:ns] *n* βλέμμα, ματιά ‖ *vi* (+ *at*) (*look*) ρίχνω ματιά ‖ γλιστρώ πλαγίως.

glancing ['glɑ:nsiŋ] *a* (*blow*) πλάγιος.

gland [glænd] *n* αδήν ‖ ~**ular** *a* αδενικός.

glare [glɛə*] *n* (*light*) εκτυφλωτική λάμψη ‖ (*fierce stare*) άγριο βλέμμα ‖ *vi* απαστράπτω, λάμπω ‖ (*angrily*) αγριοκοιτάζω.

glaring ['glɛəriŋ] *a* (*mistake*) έκδηλος, ολοφάνερος.

glass [glɑ:s] *n* (*substance*) ύαλος, γυαλί ‖ (*vessel*) ποτήρι ‖ (*mirror*) καθρέπτης ‖ ~**es** *npl* γυαλιά ‖ ~**house** *n* (*agr*) θερμοκήπιον, σέρρα ‖ ~**ware** *n* γυαλικά ‖ ~**y** *a* (*eye*) σαν γυαλί, ανέκφραστος.

glaze [gleiz] *vt* (*furnish with glass*) βάζω τζάμια ‖ (*finish*) βερνικώνω, γυαλίζω ‖ *n* βερνίκι.

glazier ['gleiziə*] *n* τζαμιτζής.

gleam [gli:m] *n* ακτίδα, λάμψις ‖ *vi* ακτινοβολώ, λάμπω ‖ ~**ing** *a* απαστράπτων, λάμπον.

glee [gli:] *n* ευθυμία, χαρά ‖ ~**ful** *a* εύθυμος, χαρούμενος.

glen [glen] *n* χαράδρα, δερβένι.

glib [glib] *a* εύγλωττος, επιπόλαιος ‖ ~**ly** *ad* εύκολα, πονηρά.

glide [glaid] *vi* ολισθαίνω, γλυστρώ, κυλώ ‖ *n* ολίσθησις, βολπλανέ ‖ ~**r** *n* (*aviat*) ανεμόπτερον.

gliding ['glaidiŋ] *n* ολίσθησις, ανεμοπορία.

glimmer ['glimə*] *n* αμυδρόν φώς.

glimpse [glimps] *n* γρήγορη ματιά ‖ *vt* βλέπω φευγαλέα.

glint [glint] *n* λάμψις ‖ *vi* λάμπω, αστράφτω.

glisten ['glisn] *vi* απαστράπτω, σπιθίζω.

glitter ['glitə*] *vi* λάμπω, σπινθηροβολώ ‖ *n* λαμποκόπημα, γυάλισμα ‖ ~**ing** *a* αστράπτων, λαμπερός.

gloat [gləut] **to** ~ **over** *vt* κοιτάζω με χαιρεκακίαν.

global ['gləubl] *a* παγκόσμιος.

globe [gləub] *n* (*light*) γλόμπος, λάμπα ‖ (*earth*) σφαίρα, υδρόγειος σφαίρα.

gloom [glu:m] *n* (*also* ~**iness**) (*darkness*) σκότος, σκοτάδι ‖ (*depression*) μελαγχολία, ακεφιά ‖ ~**ily** *ad* μελαγχολικά, σκυθρωπά ‖ ~**y** *a* σκοτεινός, βαρύς, μελαγχολικός.

glorification [glɔ:rifi'keiʃən] *n* εξύμνησις.

glorify ['glɔ:rifai] *vt* εκθειάζω, εξυμνώ, δοξάζω.

glorious ['glɔ:riəs] *a* ένδοξος, δοξασμένος, λαμπρός.

glory ['glɔ:ri] *n* (*splendour*) δόξα, μεγαλείον ‖ (*fame*) τιμή, φήμη, δόξα.

gloss [glɔs] *n* (*shine*) στιλπνότης, λούστρο, γυαλάδα.

glossary ['glɔsəri] *n* λεξιλόγιον, γλωσσάριον.

glossy ['glɔsi] *a* (*surface*) στιλπνός, γυαλιστερός.

glove [glʌv] *n* γάντι.

glow [gləu] *vi* πυρακτούμαι, κοκκινίζω ‖ (*look hot*) ζεσταίνομαι, ανάβω ‖ (*with emotion*) αστράφτω, λάμπω ‖ *n* (*heat*) πυράκτωσις ‖ (*colour*) ροδαλότης, κοκκινάδα ‖ (*feeling*) σφρίγος, φλόγα.

glower ['glauə*] *vi* στραβοκοιτάζω.

glucose ['glu:kəus] *n* γλυκόζη.

glue [glu:] *n* κόλλα ‖ *vt* κολλώ.

glum [glʌm] *a* σκυθρωπός, κατσούφης.

glut [glʌt] *n* υπεραφθονία ‖ *vt* (*econ*) πλημμυρίζω.

glutton ['glʌtn] *n* λαίμαργος, φαγάς ‖ ~**ous** *a* αδηφάγος ‖ ~**y** *n* λαιμαργία.

glycerin(e) ['glisərin] *n* γλυκερίνη.

gnarled [nɑ:ld] *a* ροζιάρικος.

gnat [næt] *n* σκνίπα.

gnaw [nɔ:] *vt* ροκανίζω, τραγανίζω.

gnome [nəum] *n* (*goblin*) καλικάντζαρος.

go [gəu] (*irreg v*) *vi* (*travel*) πηγαίνω, πάω ‖ (*progress*) κινούμαι, πάω ‖ (*function*) πάω, τρέχω, λειτουργώ ‖ (*depart*) αναχωρώ, φεύγω ‖ (*disappear*) χάνομαι ‖ (*be sold*) (+ *for*) πουλιέται γιά ‖ (*fit, suit*) πηγαίνω, ταιριάζω ‖ (*become*) γίνομαι ‖ (*break etc*) σπάζω, κόβομαι, πωλούμαι ‖ *n* (*energy*) δραστηριότης, διάθεσις ‖ (*attempt*) δοκιμή, προσπάθεια, απόπειρα ‖ **to** ~ **ahead** *vi* (*proceed*) προχωρώ, προοδεύω ‖ **to** ~ **along with** *vt* (*agree to support*) συμφωνώ, ταιριάζω ‖ **to** ~ **away** *vi* (*depart*) φεύγω ‖ **to** ~ **back** *vi* (*return*) επιστρέφω ‖ **to** ~ **back on** *vt* (*promise*) παραβαίνω, προδίδω ‖ **to** ~ **by** *vi* (*years, time*) περνώ ‖ **to** ~ **down** *vi* (*sun*) κατεβαίνω, γέρνω, πέφτω ‖ **to** ~ **for** *vt* (*fetch*) πάω γιά ‖ (*like*) συμπαθώ ‖ **to** ~ **in** *vi* (*enter*) εισέρχομαι, μπαίνω ‖ (*fit*) μπαίνω ‖ **to** ~ **into** *vt* (*enter*) μπαίνω ‖ (*study*) εξετάζω, μελετώ ‖ **to** ~ **off** *vi* (*depart*) εξέρχομαι, φεύγω ‖ (*milk*) ξυνίζω ‖ (*explode*) εκπυρσοκροτώ ‖ *vt* (*dislike*) ξεθυμαίνω, αντιπαθώ ‖ **to** ~ **on** *vi* (*continue*) συνεχίζω, εξακολουθώ ‖ ~ **out** *vi* (*fire, light*) σβήνω ‖ (*of house*) βγαίνω ‖ **to** ~ **over** *vt* (*examine, check*) εξετάζω, επαναλαμβάνω ‖ **to** ~ **up** *vi* (*price*) ανεβαίνω ‖ (*explode*) ανατινάσσομαι ‖ **to** ~ **without** *vt* περνώ χωρίς.

goad [gəud] *vt* κεντρίζω, προκαλώ ‖ *n* βούκεντρον, κίνητρον.

go-ahead ['gəuəhed] *a* δραστήριος.

goal [gəul] *n* (*purpose*) σκοπός ‖ (*sports field*) τέρμα ‖ (*score*) γκώλ ‖ ~**keeper** *n* τερματοφύλαξ ‖ ~**-post** *n* δοκός.

goat [gəut] *n* κατσίκα, γίδα.

gobble ['gɔbl] *vt* καταβροχθίζω.

go-between ['gəubitwi:n] *n* μεσάζων, μεσολαβητής.

god [gɔd] *n* θεός ‖ **G**~ *n* Θεός ‖ ~**child** *n* βαπτησιμιός ‖ ~**dess** *n* θεά ‖ ~**father**

n νουνός ‖ ~**forsaken** *a* ἐγκαταλελειμμένος, καταραμένος ‖ ~**mother** *n* νουνά ‖ ~**send** *n* θεῖον δῶρον, κελεποὺρι.

goggle ['gɔgl] *vi* γουρλώνω ‖ ~s *npl* προστατευτικά γυαλιά.

going ['gəuiŋ] *n* (*condition of ground*) κατάστασις ἐδάφους ‖ *a* (*rate*) τρέχουσα (τιμή) ‖ (*concern*) δραστήριος ‖ ~s-on *npl* συμβάντα, συμπεριφορά.

gold [gəuld] *n* χρυσός, χρυσάφι ‖ ~en *a* χρυσοῦς, χρυσαφένια ‖ ~fish *n* χρυσόψαρο ‖ ~ mine *n* χρυσορυχεῖον.

golf [gɔlf] *n* γκόλφ ‖ ~ club *n* (*society*) λέσχη τοῦ γκόλφ ‖ (*stick*) κλώμπ ‖ ~ course *n* γήπεδον τοῦ γκόλφ ‖ ~er *n* παίκτης τοῦ γκόλφ.

gondola ['gɔndələ] *n* γόνδολα.

gone [gɔn] *pp* of **go**.

gong [gɔŋ] *n* γκόγκ, κώδων.

good [gud] *n* (*well-being*) καλόν, ὄφελος ‖ (*goodness*) ἀρετή, καλόν ‖ *a* (*well-behaved*) καλός, ἔντιμος ‖ (*virtuous*) τίμιος, ἀγαθός, καλός ‖ (*well-done*) ἐξαιρετικός, καλός ‖ (*suitable*) ταιριαστός, ποὺ πάει ‖ (*sound*) σέ καλή κατάστασι ‖ ~s *npl* κινητά, ἀγαθά, εἴδη ‖ **a ~ deal, a ~ many** ἀρκετός, πολὺς ‖ ~**bye!** ἀντίο! ‖ γειά σου! ‖ στό καλό ‖ **G~ Friday** *n* Μεγάλη Παρασκευή ‖ ~-**looking** *a* εὔμορφος ‖ ~ **morning!** καλημέρα! ‖ ~**ness** *n* καλωσύνη, ἀρετή ‖ ~**will** *n* καλή θέλησι, κέφι.

goose [gu:s] *n* χήνα ‖ ~**berry** *n* φραγκοστάφυλο ‖ ~**flesh** *n* ἀνατριχίλα.

gore [gɔ:*] *vi* κερατίζω ‖ *n* πηκτόν αἷμα.

gorge [gɔ:dʒ] *n* στενόν, φαράγγι ‖ *vti* παρατρώγω.

gorgeous ['gɔ:dʒəs] *a* πολύχρωμος, ἐξαίσιος.

gorilla [gə'rilə] *n* γορίλλας.

gorse [gɔ:s] *n* σπάρτο.

gory ['gɔ:ri] *a* (*details*) αἱματοβαφής.

go-slow ['gəu'sləu] *n* ἀπεργία κωλυσιεργίας.

gospel ['gɔspəl] *n* εὐαγγέλιον.

gossip ['gɔsip] *n* (*idle talk*) κουβεντολόϊ ‖ (*person*) κουτσομπόλης ‖ *vi* κουτσομπολεύω, φλυαρῶ.

got [gɔt] *pt,pp* of **get** ‖ ~**ten** (*US*) *pp* of **get**.

gout [gaut] *n* ἀρθρῖτις, ποδάγρα.

govern ['gʌvən] *vt* (*general*) κυβερνῶ, διοικῶ, διευθύνω ‖ (*gram*) συντάσσομαι μέ ‖ ~**ess** *n* γκουβερνάντα, νταντά ‖ ~**ing** *a* διευθύνων, διοικῶν, κατευθυντήριος ‖ ~**ment** *n* κυβέρνησις, (*management*) διοίκησις ‖ ~**mental** *a* κυβερνητικός ‖ ~**or** *n* κυβερνήτης, διοικητής.

gown [gaun] *n* φόρεμα, φουστάνι ‖ (*of judge etc*) τήβεννος.

grab [græb] *vt* ἀρπάζω, πιάνω ‖ *n* ἁρπαγή ‖ (*excavator*) ἀρπάγη.

grace [greis] *n* (*charm*) χάρις, χάρη ‖ (*favour, kindness*) εὔνοια, χάτηρι ‖ (*God's blessing*) θεία χάριτι ‖ (*short prayer*) προσευχή ‖ *vt* (*honour*) τιμῶ ‖ (*adorn*) στολίζω, ὀμορφαίνω ‖ **5 days' ~ful** *a* πενθήμερος χάρις ‖ ~**ful** *a* χαριτωμένος, κομψός ‖ ~**fully** *ad* χαριτωμένα.

gracious ['greiʃəs] *a* (*kind, courteous*) καλός, ἀγαθός, καλόβολος.

gradation [grə'deiʃən] *n* διαβάθμισις.

grade [greid] *n* (*degree, rank*) βαθμός, τάξις, βαθμίδα ‖ (*slope*) κλίσις ‖ *vt* (*classify*) διαβαθμίζω, ταξινομῶ ‖ ~ **crossing** *n* (*US*) ἰσόπεδος διάβασις.

gradient ['greidiənt] *n* κλίσις.

gradual ['grædjuəl] *a* βαθμιαῖος ‖ ~**ly** *ad* βαθμηδόν.

graduate ['grædjuit] *n* πτυχιοῦχος ‖ ['grædjueit] *vi* ἀποφοιτῶ.

graduation [grædju'eiʃən] *n* ἀποφοίτησις ‖ (*grade*) διαβάθμισις.

graft [gra:ft] *n* (*shoot*) μπόλι, κεντρί ‖ (*on humans*) μόσχευμα ‖ (*unfair means*) δωροδοκία, ρεμούλα ‖ *vt* μπολιάζω ‖ ~**ing** *n* μεταμόσχευσις.

grain [grein] *n* (*seed*) κόκκος, σπυρί ‖ (*crop*) δημητριακά ‖ (*small particle*) ψῆγμα, κόκκος ‖ (*fibre*) κόκκος, ὑφή, ἷς.

grammar ['græmə*] *n* γραμματική.

grammatical [grə'mætikəl] *a* γραμματικός.

gram(me) [græm] *n* γραμμάριον.

gramophone ['græməfəun] *n* γραμμόφωνον.

granary ['grænəri] *n* σιταποθήκη.

grand [grænd] *a* (*fine, splendid*) μέγας, μεγαλοπρεπής ‖ (*final*) πλήρης, ὁλόκληρος ‖ ~**daughter** *n* ἐγγονή ‖ ~**eur** *n* μεγαλεῖον, μεγαλοπρέπεια ‖ ~**father** *n* πάππος, παπποὺς ‖ ~**iose** *a* (*imposing*) μεγαλοπρεπής ‖ (*pompous*) πομπώδης, φαντασμένος ‖ ~**mother** *n* μάμη, γιαγιά ‖ ~ **piano** *n* πιάνο μέ οὐρά ‖ ~**son** *n* ἔγγονος ‖ ~**stand** *n* ἐξέδρα.

granite ['grænit] *n* γρανίτης.

granny ['græni] *n* (*col*) γιαγιά, γρηούλα.

grant [gra:nt] *vt* (*bestow*) ἀπονέμω, δίδω ‖ (*allow*) (ἀπο)δέχομαι ‖ *n* δωρεά, ἐπιχορήγησις.

granule ['grænju:l] *n* κοκκίδιον, κοκκίον.

grape [greip] *n* σταφύλι, ρώγα ‖ ~**fruit** *n* φράπα, γκρέϊπ-φρούτ ‖ ~ **juice** *n* χυμός σταφυλιοῦ.

graph [gra:f] *n* διάγραμμα, γραφική παράστασις ‖ ~**ic** *a* (*vivid*) ζωηρός, ἐκφραστικός ‖ (*drawing, writing*) γραφικός.

grapple ['græpl] *vi* (+ *with*) πιάνομαι, ἔρχομαι στά χέρια.

grasp [gra:sp] *vt* πιάνω, σφίγγω, ἁρπάζω ‖ (*understand*) συλλαμβάνω, κατανοῶ ‖ *n* (*handgrip*) λαβή, πιάσιμο, σφίξιμο ‖ (*possession*) ἔλεγχος, ἐξουσία ‖ (*understanding*) ἀντίληψις, γνῶσις ‖ ~**ing** *a* ἄπληστος, πλεονέκτης.

grass [grɑːs] n χορτάρι, γρασίδι ‖ ~-**hopper** n ἀκρίδα ‖ ~**land** n λιβάδι ‖ ~ **snake** n νερόφιδο ‖ ~**y** a χορταρια-σμένος, πράσινος.

grate [greit] n ἐσχάρα, κάγκελο ‖ vi (scrape) ξύω ‖ (make harsh sound) τρίζω ‖ (irritate) ἐνοχλῶ ‖ vt (into small pieces) τρίβω.

grateful ['greitful] a εὐγνώμων, εὐχάριστος ‖ ~**ly** ad εὐγνωμόνως.

grater ['greitə*] n ξύστρα, τρίφτης.

gratification [grætifi'keiʃən] n ἱκανοποί-ησις.

gratify ['grætifai] vt εὐχαριστῶ, ἱκα-νοποιῶ.

gratifying ['grætifaiiŋ] a εὐχάριστος.

grating ['greitiŋ] n (iron bars) κιγκλίδωμα, κάγκελα ‖ a (noise) κακόηχος, στρίγ-γλικος.

gratitude ['grætitjuːd] n εὐγνωμοσύνη.

gratuitous [grə'tjuːitəs] a (uncalled for) ἀδικαιολόγητος ‖ (given free) δωρεάν, χαριστικός.

gratuity [grə'tjuːiti] n φιλοδώρημα, πουρ-μπουάρ.

grave [greiv] n τάφος ‖ a βαρύς, σοβαρός, δυσάρεστος ‖ ~**digger** n νεκροθάπτης.

gravel ['grævəl] n χαλίκι, ἄμμο.

gravely ['greivli] ad σοβαρά, βαρειά.

gravestone ['greivstəun] n ἐπιτάφιος πλάκα.

graveyard ['greivjɑːd] n νεκροταφεῖον.

gravitate ['græviteit] vi ἕλκομαι, ρέπω πρός.

gravity ['græviti] n βαρύτης, βάρος ‖ (seriousness) σοβαρότης.

gravy ['greivi] n σάλτσα.

gray [grei] a = **grey**.

graze [greiz] vi (feed) βόσκω ‖ vt (touch) ψαύω, ἐγγίζω ‖ (scrape) ξύνω ‖ n (med) ξέγδαρμα.

grease [griːs] n (fat) λίπος, ξύγγι ‖ (lubricant) γράσο, λάδι ‖ vt λαδώνω, γρασάρω ‖ ~ **gun** n γρασαδόρος ‖ ~**proof** a μή διαπερατός ἀπό λάδι.

greasy ['griːsi] a λιπαρός, λαδωμένος.

great [greit] a (large) μεγάλος ‖ (important) σπουδαῖος ‖ (distinguished) μεγάλος ‖ G~ **Britain** n Μεγάλη Βρεττανία ‖ ~-**grandfather** n πρόπαππος ‖ ~-**grand-mother** n προμάμη ‖ ~**ly** ad μεγάλως, πολύ ‖ ~**ness** n μεγαλεῖον, μέγεθος.

Greece [griːs] n Ἑλλάς.

greed [griːd] n (also ~**iness**) ἀπληστία, πλεονεξία ‖ ~**ily** ad ἀπλήστως ‖ ~**y** a ἄπληστος, πλεονέκτης ‖ (gluttonous) λαίμαργος, ἀδηφάγος.

Greek [griːk] n (person) Ἕλλην, Ρωμαιός ‖ (ling) ἑλληνικά ‖ a ἑλληνικός.

green [griːn] a πράσινος, ἄγουρος ‖ (inexperienced) ἄπειρος ‖ ~**gage** n πράσινο δαμάσκηνο ‖ ~**grocer** n μανάβης ‖ ~**house** n θερμοκήπιον ‖ ~**ish** a πρασινωπός.

greet [griːt] vt χαιρετίζω ‖ ~**ing** n χαιρετι-σμός ‖ ~**ings**! χαιρετισμούς!

gregarious [gri'gɛəriəs] a κοινωνικός.

grenade [gri'neid] n (χειρο)βομβίδα.

grew [gruː] pt of **grow**.

grey [grei] a σταχτής, γκρίζος, ψαρός ‖ (dismal) σκοτεινός ‖ ~-**haired** a γκρι-ζομάλλης, ψαρομάλλης ‖ ~**hound** n λαγωνικό ‖ ~**ish** a γκριζωπός.

grid [grid] n (of bars) ἐσχάρα, σχάρα, πλέγμα ‖ (network) πλέγμα, δίκτυον ‖ (of map) δικτυωτόν, τετραγωνισμός ‖ ~**iron** n σχάρα.

grief [griːf] n θλίψις, λύπη, ἀτύχημα.

grievance ['griːvəns] n παράπονο.

grieve [griːv] vi λυποῦμαι, θλίβομαι ‖ vt λυπῶ, πικραίνω.

grill [gril] n (on cooker) σχάρα, τῆς σχάρας ‖ vt ψήνω στή σχάρα ‖ (interrogate) ἀνακρίνω.

grille [gril] n (on car etc) γρίλλιες.

grilled [grild] a (food) τῆς σχάρας, τῆς ὥρας.

grim [grim] a φρικαλέος, ἀπειλητικός, σκληρός.

grimace [gri'meis] n γκριμάτσα ‖ vi μορφάζω.

grime [graim] n ἀκαθαρσία, λέρα, φοῦμο.

grimly ['grimli] ad ἀπαίσια, σκληρά, αὐστηρά.

grimy ['graimi] a ἀκάθαρτος, βρώμικος.

grin [grin] n χαμόγελο, μειδίαμα ‖ vi χαμογελῶ, μορφάζω.

grind [graind] (irreg v) vt (crush) τρίβω, ἀλέθω, κοπανίζω ‖ (sharpen) τροχίζω, τορνάρω, λειαίνω ‖ (teeth) τρίζω ‖ n (bore) ἀγγαρεία, μαγγανοψηνάδο.

grip [grip] n (firm hold) σφίξιμο, πιάσιμο, χειραψιά ‖ (handle) λαβή ‖ (mastery) πυγμή, γνώσις, ἐπιβάλλω ‖ (suitcase) βαλιτσάκι ‖ vt πιάνω, σφίγγω.

gripes [graips] npl (bowel pains) κωλικό-πονοι.

gripping ['gripiŋ] a (exciting) συγκινητικό, συναρπαστικό.

grisly ['grizli] a φρικιαστικός, τρομακτι-κός.

gristle ['grisl] n χόνδρος, τραγανό.

grit [grit] n (sand) ἀμμόλιθος, ἀκαθαρσίες ‖ (courage) τόλμη, θάρρος ‖ vt τρίζω τά δόντια.

groan [grəun] n ἀναστεναγμός ‖ vi (ἀνα)στενάζω.

grocer ['grəusə*] n μπακάλης ‖ ~**ies** npl εἴδη μπακαλικῆς.

groggy ['grɔgi] a (dazed, staggering) κλονιζόμενος, σουρωμένος, ἀσταθής.

groin [grɔin] n βουβών.

groom [gruːm] n ἱπποκόμος ‖ (bridegroom) γαμπρός ‖ vt (o.s.) προετοιμάζω, ντύ-νομαι.

groove [gruːv] n αὐλάκι, διάξυσμα ‖ (rut) ρουτίνα.

grope [grəup] *vi* ψηλαφῶ, ψάχνω.

gross [grəus] *a* (*coarse*) χονδροειδής, σωματώδης ‖ (*very bad*) χοντρός, καταφανής ‖ (*total*) ὁλικός, χονδρικός ‖ *n* γρόσσα, δώδεκα δωδεκάδες ‖ ~**ly** *ad* χονδροειδῶς, χονδρά.

grotesque [grəu'tesk] *a* μασκαρένιος, παράλογος.

grotto ['grɔtəu] *n* σπηλαιά, κρύπτη.

ground [graund] *pt,pp of* **grind** ‖ *n* (*surface*) ἔδαφος, γῆ, ἄργος ‖ (*land*) οἰκόπεδο, γῆ ‖ ,(*generally pl: reason*) λόγος, αἰτία, βάσις ‖ ~**s** *npl* (*dregs*) κατακάθι, ἵζημα ‖ (*land*) περιοχή, κῆποι, πάρκο ‖ *vt* (*run ashore*) προσαράσσω, ἐξοκέλλω ‖ (*compel to stay*) καθηλώνω ‖ (*instruct*) διδάσκω ἐντατικά ‖ *vi* ἐξοκέλλω ‖ ~**ing** *n* (*instruction*) οἱ βάσεις ‖ ~**sheet** *n* μουσαμᾶς ἐδάφους ‖ ~**work** *n* θεμέλια, βάσις.

group [gru:p] *n* ὁμάδα, παρέα ‖ *vt* συνδυάζω, συνδέω, συγκεντρώνω.

grouse [graus] *n* (*bird*) χαμωτίδα, ἀγριόγαλλος ‖ (*complaint*) γκρίνια ‖ *vi* (*complain*) γκρινιάζω.

grove [grəuv] *n* ἄλσος, ἀσύλιον.

grovel ['grɔvl] *vi* (*in fear*) σέρνομαι, κυλιόμαι ‖ (*abase o.s.*) ταπεινοῦμαι, πέφτω στά πόδια.

grow [grəu] (*irreg v*) *vi* (*in size*) μεγαλώνω, ἀναπτύσσομαι ‖ (*be produced*) φύομαι ‖ (*become*) καθίσταμαι, γίνομαι ‖ *vt* (*raise crops etc*) καλλιεργῶ ‖ **to ~ up** *vi* μεγαλώνω ‖ ~**er** *n* καλλιεργητής ‖ ~**ing** *a* αὐξανόμενος, πού μεγαλώνει.

growl [graul] *vi* μουγγρίζω ‖ *n* μούγγρισμα, βρυχηθμός.

grown-up ['grəun'ʌp] *a* ὥριμος ‖ *n* ἐνήλιξ.

growth [grəuθ] *n* (*development*) ἀνάπτυξις ‖ (*increase*) αὔξησις, μεγάλωμα ‖ (*what has grown*) καλλιέργεια ‖ (*med*) σάρκωμα.

grub [grʌb] *n* (*larva*) σκουλίκι ‖ (*col: food*) φαγητό ‖ ~**by** *a* ἀκάθαρτος, βρώμικος.

grudge [grʌdʒ] *n* (*μνησι*)κακία, ἔχθρα ‖ *vt* ζηλεύω γιά, δεικνύω ἀπροθυμίαν ‖ **to bear a ~** κρατάω κακία γιά.

grudging ['grʌdʒiŋ] *a* ἀπρόθυμος, φειδωλός.

gruelling ['gruəliŋ] *a* ἐξαντλητικός.

gruesome ['gru:səm] *a* φρικτός, ἀπαίσιος.

gruff [grʌf] *a* τραχύς, ἀπότομος.

grumble ['grʌmbl] *vi* γκρινιάζω, μουγγρίζω ‖ *n* μουγγρητό, γκρίνια.

grumpy ['grʌmpi] *a* κατσούφης, γκρινιάρης.

grunt [grʌnt] *n* γρύλλισμα ‖ *vi* γρυλλίζω.

guarantee [gærən'ti:] *n* (*of goods*) ἐγγύησις ‖ (*promise to pay*) ἐγγύησις, ἐνέχυρον ‖ *vt* ἐγγυῶμαι.

guard [ga:d] *n* (*defence*) φρουρά, προφύλαξίς ‖ (*sentry*) σκοπός ‖ (*official*) φύλαξ ‖ *vt* φυλάσσω, προστατεύω, φρουρῶ ‖ ~**ed** *a* ὑπό φρούρησιν ‖ (*words etc*)

ἐπιφυλακτικός ‖ ~**ian** *n* (*keeper*) φύλαξ, προστάτης ‖ (*of child*) κηδεμών.

guerilla [gə'rilə] *n* ἀντάρτης ‖ ~ **warfare** *n* ἀνταρτοπόλεμος.

guess [ges] *vti* μαντεύω ‖ (*US*) νομίζω ‖ *n* εἰκασία, γνώμη ‖ ~**work** *n* εἰκασία.

guest [gest] *n* καλεσμένος, ξένος ‖ (*of hotel*) πελάτης ‖ ~-**house** *n* πανσιόν ‖ ~ **room** *n* (*in private house, for friends*) δωμάτιον τῶν ξένων.

guffaw [gʌ'fɔ:] *n* καγχασμός ‖ *vi* ξεσπῶ στά γέλια.

guidance ['gaidəns] *n* (*control*) καθοδήγησις ‖ (*advice*) συμβουλές, ὁδηγίες.

guide [gaid] *n* (*person*) ὁδηγός, συνοδός, ξεναγός ‖ (*book etc*) ὁδηγός ‖ *vt* (καθ)ὁδηγῶ ‖ **girl ~** *n* προσκοπίνα ‖ ~**book** *n* ὁδηγός ‖ ~**d missile** *n* κατευθυνόμενον βλῆμα ‖ ~ **lines** *npl* ὁδηγός.

guild [gild] *n* (*old: company*) συντεχνία ‖ (*society*) ἕνωσις, σωματεῖον ‖ ~**hall** *n* (*Brit: town hall*) δημαρχεῖον.

guile [gail] *n* τέχνασμα, δόλος ‖ ~**less** *a* ἄδολος.

guillotine ['giləti:n] *n* λαιμητόμος, γκιλοτίνα.

guilt [gilt] *n* ἐνοχή ‖ ~**y** *a* ἔνοχος.

guise [gaiz] *n* (*appearance*) μορφή, ἐμφάνισις.

guitar [gi'ta:*] *n* κιθάρα ‖ ~**ist** *n* κιθαριστής.

gulf [gʌlf] *n* κόλπο, κόρφος ‖ (*abyss*) χάσμα.

gull [gʌl] *n* γλάρος.

gullet ['gʌlit] *n* οἰσοφάγος.

gullible ['gʌlibl] *a* εὔπιστος, κορόϊδο.

gully ['gʌli] *n* ρεματιά, στενό, ὑπόνομος.

gulp [gʌlp] *vi* (*hastily*) καταπίνω, καταβροχθίζω ‖ (*choke*) κομπιάζομαι, πνίγομαι ‖ *n* ρουφηξιά, γουλιά.

gum [gʌm] *n* (*of teeth*) οὖλον ‖ (*for sticking*) γόμα, γόμμι ‖ (*for chewing*) τσίκλα, μαστίχα ‖ *vt* κολλῶ, ἀλείφω μέ γόμα ‖ ~**boil** *n* ἀπόστημα, φουσκάλα ‖ ~**boots** *npl* μπότες ἀπό καουτσούκ.

gum tree ['gʌmtri:] *n* εὐκάλυπτος.

gun [gʌn] *n* (*cannon*) πυροβόλον, κανόνι ‖ (*rifle*) τουφέκι ‖ (*revolver*) πιστόλι ‖ ~**fire** *n* βολή, πῦρ, κανονιοβολισμός ‖ ~**man** *n* ληστής, κακοποιός ‖ ~**ner** *n* πυροβολητής ‖ ~**powder** *n* πυρῖτις, μπαρούτι ‖ ~**shot** *n* τουφεκιά, κανονιά.

gurgle ['gə:gl] *n* παφλασμός, κελάρισμα.

gush [gʌʃ] *n* ἐκροή, διάχυσις, ξέσπασμα ‖ *vi* (*out*) ἐκχύνομαι, ἀναπηδῶ ‖ (*be moved*) συγκινοῦμαι, ἀναλύομαι εἰς.

gusset ['gʌsit] *n* ἐπένθεμα.

gust [gʌst] *n* ἀνεμοριπή, μπουρίνι.

gut [gʌt] *n* (*intestine*) ἔντερον, σπλάχνον ‖ (*string*) χορδή ‖ ~**s** *npl* θάρρος.

gutter ['gʌtə*] *n* (*channel*) λούκι, σούγελο ‖ (*of street*) ρεῖθρον, χαντάκι.

guttural ['gʌtərəl] *a* λαρυγγικός.

guy [gai] *n* (*naut*) πρόδρομος, γκάγια ‖ (*effigy*) ἀνδρείκελον, σκιάχτρο ‖ (*man, fellow*) τύπος, παιδί.
guzzle ['gʌzl] *vi* καταβροχθίζω, ρουφῶ.
gym(nasium) [dʒim('neiziəm)] *n* γυμναστήριον.
gymnast ['dʒimnæst] *n* γυμναστής ‖ ~ics *n* γυμναστική.
gyn(a)ecologist [gaini'kɔlədʒist] *n* γυναικολόγος.
gypsy ['dʒipsi] *n* = **gipsy**.
gyrate [dʒai'reit] *vi* περιστρέφομαι.

H, h

habit ['hæbit] *n* συνήθεια, ἔθιμον ‖ (*dress*) φόρεμα.
habitable ['hæbitəbl] *a* κατοικήσιμος.
habitation [hæbi'teiʃən] *n* κατοικία, διαμονή.
habitual [hə'bitjuəl] *a* συνήθης, συνηθισμένος ‖ ~ly *ad* συνήθως.
hack [hæk] *vt* κατακόβω, πετσοκόβω ‖ *n* ἀγοραῖον ἄλογον.
hackneyed ['hæknid] *a* ξεφτελισμένος, φθαρμένος.
had [hæd] *pt,pp* of **have**.
haddock ['hædək] *n* βακαλάος.
hadn't ['hædnt] = **had not** ‖ *see* **have**.
haemorrhage, (*US*) **hemo**~ ['heməridʒ] *n* αἱμορραγία.
haemorroids, (*US*) **hemo**~ ['hemərɔidz] *npl* ζοχάδες.
haggard ['hægəd] *a* κάτωχρος, χαμένος.
haggle ['hægl] *vi* κάνω παζάρι.
hail [heil] *n* (*meteorology*) χαλάζι ‖ *vt* (*greet*) χαιρετῶ ‖ *vi* (*meteorology*) ρίχνει χαλάζι ‖ **to ~ from** vt προέρχομαι ἀπό ‖ ~**stone** *n* κόκκος χαλάζης.
hair [hɛə*] *n* (*general*) τρίχα, μαλλιά ‖ (*one hair*) τρίχα ‖ ~**'s breadth** *n* παρά τρίχα ‖ ~**brush** *n* βούρτσα μαλλιῶν ‖ ~**cut** *n* κούρεμα ‖ ~**do** *n* κτένισμα ‖ ~**dresser** *n* κομμωτής, κουρέας ‖ ~-**drier** *n* σεσουάρ ‖ ~**net** *n* δίχτυ γιά τά μαλλιά ‖ ~ **oil** *n* λάδι γιά τά μαλλιά ‖ ~**pin** *n* (*lit*) φουρκέτα ‖ (*bend*) ἀπότομος στροφή ‖ ~-**raising** *a* τρομακτικός ‖ ~ **style** *n* κόμμωσις, χτενισιά ‖ ~**y** *a* τριχωτός, μαλλιαρός.
half [hɑːf] *n* ἥμισυ, μισό ‖ *a* μισός ‖ *ad* κατά τό ἥμισυ, μισό ‖ ~-**breed**, ~-**caste** *n* μιγάς ‖ ~-**hearted** *a* χλιαρός, μέ μισή καρδιά ‖ ~-**hour** *n* ἡμίωρον, μισή (ὥρα) ‖ ~**penny** *n* μισή πέννα ‖ ~-**price** μισή τιμή, μισό εἰσιτήριο ‖ ~-**way** *ad* στό ἥμισυ τῆς ἀποστάσεως, μισοστρατής.
halibut ['hælibət] *n* ἱππόγλωσσος, εἶδος γλώσσας.
hall [hɔːl] *n* μεγάλη αἴθουσα ‖ (*building, house*) δημόσιον κτίριον ‖ (*dining*) τραπεζαρία ‖ (*entrance*) εἴσοδος, χώλ.

hallo [hʌ'ləu] *excl* = **hello**.
hallucination [həluːsi'neiʃən] *n* παραίσθησις, αὐταπάτη.
halo ['heiləu] *n* (*of saint*) φωτοστέφανος ‖ (*of sun, moon*) ἅλως, ἀλώνι.
halt [hɔːlt] *n* στάσις, σταμάτημα ‖ *vt* σταματῶ ‖ *vi* σταθμεύω, σταματῶ.
halve [hɑːv] *vt* χωρίζω στά δύο, μοιράζω.
ham [hæm] *n* χοιρομέρι, ζαμπόν ‖ ~**burger** *n* μπιφτέκι ἀπό κιμά.
hamlet ['hæmlət] *n* χωριουδάκι.
hammer ['hæmə*] *n* σφυρί ‖ *vt* κτυπῶ δυνατά, σφυρηλατῶ.
hammock ['hæmək] *n* ἁμάκ, κούνια ‖ (*naut*) αἰώρα, μπράντα.
hamper ['hæmpə*] *n* καλάθι ‖ *vt* ἐμποδίζω, παρακωλύω.
hand [hænd] *n* χέρι ‖ (*of clock*) δείκτης ‖ (*factory*) ἐργάτης ‖ (*help*) βοήθεια ‖ *vt* δίδω ‖ βοηθῶ ‖ *n* (*naut*) πλήρωμα ‖ **to ~ down** *vt* μεταβιβάζω ‖ **to ~ over** *vt* παραδίδω ‖ **at ~** κοντά ‖ **in ~** στήν διάθεσί μου ‖ ὑπό τόν ἕλεγχό μου ‖ ~**s up!** ψηλά τά χέρια! ‖ ~ **bag** *n* τσάντα ‖ ~**book** *n* ἐγχειρίδιον ‖ (*guide*) ὁδηγός ‖ ~**brake** *n* χειρόφρενο ‖ ~**cuffs** *npl* χειροπέδες ‖ ~**ful** *n* φούχτα, φουχτιά.
handicap ['hændikæp] *n* ἐμπόδιον, μειονέκτημα ‖ (*sport*) χάντικαπ ‖ *vt* παρεμποδίζω, δυσχεραίνω ‖ (*sport*) βάζω χάντικαπ.
handicraft ['hændikrɑːft] *n* χειροτεχνία, τέχνη.
handkerchief ['hæŋkətʃif] *n* μαντήλι.
handle ['hændl] *n* (*of door etc*) πόμολο, (χειρο)λαβή ‖ (*of cup etc*) χερούλι ‖ (*for winding*) χειρολαβή, χερούλι ‖ *vt* (*use, treat*) μεταχειρίζομαι ‖ (*manipulate*) χειρίζομαι ‖ (*touch*) πιάνω, πασπατεύω ‖ (*comm*) διεκπεραιώνω, διαχειρίζομαι.
hand-luggage ['hændlʌgidʒ] *n* ἀποσκευαί τοῦ χεριοῦ.
handmade ['hændmeid] *a* χειροποίητος.
handshake ['hændʃeik] *n* χειραψία, σφίξιμο τοῦ χεριοῦ.
handsome ['hænsəm] *a* ὡραῖος, ὅμορφος ‖ (*generous*) σημαντικός, γενναιόδωρος.
handwriting ['hændraitiŋ] *n* γραφή, γράψιμο.
handy ['hændi] *a* ἐπιδέξιος ‖ (*useful*) βολικός, χρήσιμος.
handyman ['hændimən] *n* πολυτεχνίτης.
hang [hæŋ] (*irreg v*) *vt* ἀναρτῶ, κρεμῶ ‖ (*one's head*) σκύβω ‖ (*wallpaper*) κολλῶ ‖ *vi* κρέμομαι ‖ **to ~ about** *vi* περιφέρομαι, τριγυρίζω, τεμπελιάζω.
hangar ['hæŋə*] *n* ὑπόστεγον.
hanger ['hæŋə*] *n* κρεμάστρα.
hanger-on ['hæŋər'ɔn] *n* κολλιτσίδα.
hangover ['hæŋəuvə*] *n* (*med*) πονοκέφαλο (ἀπό μεθύσι).
hanker ['hæŋkə*] *vi*: **to ~ after** ποθῶ διακαῶς, λαχταρῶ.

haphazard [hæp'hæzəd] *a* στήν τύχη, τυχαίως.

happen ['hæpən] *vi* συμβαίνω, τυγχάνω ‖ ~**ing** *n* συμβάν, γεγονός.

happily ['hæpili] *ad* εὐτυχῶς.

happiness ['hæpinis] *n* εὐτυχία.

happy ['hæpi] *a* εὐτυχής, τυχερός, ἐπιτυχημένος ‖ ~**-go-lucky** *a* ξένοιαστος.

harass ['hærəs] *vt* παρενοχλῶ, βασανίζω.

harbour, (*US*) **harbor** ['ha:bə*] *n* λιμάνι, καταφύγιο ‖ *vt* στεγάζω, παρέχω ἄσυλον.

hard [ha:d] *a* σκληρός, στερεός ‖ (*task*) δύσκολος, δυσχερής ‖ (*person etc*) αὐστηρός, ἀλύπητος ‖ (*work*) ἐπίπονος, σκληρός ‖ *ad* δυνατά, σκληρά, δύσκολα ‖ ~ **by** κοντά ‖ ~**-boiled** *a* (*egg*) σφιχτό ‖ (*person*) σκληρός ‖ ~**en** *vi* σκληραίνω ‖ ~**-hearted** *a* σκληρόκαρδος, ἀλύπητος ‖ ~**ly** *ad* μόλις ‖ ~**ship** *n* κακουχία, δοκιμασία, ταλαιπωρία ‖ ~ **up** *a* ἀπένταρος ‖ ~**ware** *n* σιδηρικά, εἴδη καγκελαρίας.

hardy ['ha:di] *a* σκληραγωγημένος ‖ (*brave*) τολμηρός, θαρραλέος.

hare [hεə*] *n* λαγός.

harem [ha:'ri:m] *n* χαρέμι.

harm [ha:m] *n* κακόν, βλάβη, ζημία ‖ *vt* βλάπτω, θίγω ‖ ~**ful** *a* ἐπιβλαβής, βλαβερός ‖ ~**less** *a* ἄκακος, ἀβλαβής, ἀκίνδυνος.

harmonica [ha:'mɔnikə] *n* φυσαρμόνικα.

harmonious [ha:'məuniəs] *a* ἁρμονικός ‖ (*mus*) μελωδικός.

harmonize ['ha:mənaiz] *vt* ἐναρμονίζω ‖ (*agree*) συμφωνῶ ‖ *vi* ἐναρμονίζομαι, ταιριάζω.

harmony ['ha:məni] *n* (*mus*) ἁρμονία ‖ (*agreement*) συμφωνία.

harness ['ha:nis] *n* σαγή, χάμουρα, χαμούρωμα ‖ *vt* (*horse*) χαμουρώνω.

harp [ha:p] *n* ἅρπα ‖ ~**ist** *n* ἁρπιστής.

harpoon [ha:'pu:n] *n* καμάκι.

harrow ['hærəu] *n* βωλοκόπος, σβάρνα ‖ *vt* βωλοκοπῶ.

harrowing ['hærəuiŋ] *a* θλιβερός, σπαρακτικός.

harsh [ha:ʃ] *a* σκληρός, τραχύς ‖ ~**ly** *ad* σκληρά, ἀπότομα ‖ ~**ness** *n* τραχύτης, σκληρότης ‖ (*of taste*) ξυνίλα.

hart [ha:t] *n* ἐλάφι.

harvest ['ha:vist] *n* συγκομιδή, ἐσοδεία ‖ (*season*) θέρος, ἐποχή θερισμοῦ ‖ *vt* θερίζω, μαζεύω.

harvester ['ha:vistə*] *n* θεριστική μηχανή.

has [hæz] *see* **have**.

hash [hæʃ] *n* κιμάς ‖ *vt* κατακόπτω, κάνω κιμά.

hashish ['hæʃi:ʃ] *n* χασίς.

haste [heist] *n* βία, βιασύνη, γρηγοράδα ‖ ~**n** *vt* σπεύδω, ἐπιταχύνω ‖ *vi* βιάζομαι, κάνω γρήγορα.

hastily ['heistili] *ad* βιαστικά.

hasty ['heisti] *a* βιαστικά, ὀξύθυμος.

hat [hæt] *n* καπέλλο.

hatch [hætʃ] *n* καταπακτή, μπουκαπόρτα ‖ *vi* ἐκκολάπτομαι, βγαίνω, σκάω ‖ *vt* κλωσσῶ.

hatchet ['hætʃit] *n* τσεκούρι.

hate [heit] *vt* μισῶ ‖ *n* μῖσος ‖ ~**ful** *a* μισητός.

hatred ['heitrid] *n* ἔχθρα, μῖσος.

haughty ['hɔ:ti] *a* ὑπεροπτικός, αὐθάδης.

haul [hɔ:l] *n* τράβηγμα ‖ (*fish*) διχτυά ‖ *vt* ἕλκω, τραβῶ, σύρω ‖ ~**age** *n* μεταφορά ἐμπορευμάτων.

haunch [hɔ:ntʃ] *n* ἰσχίον, γοφός.

haunt [hɔ:nt] *n* λημέρι, στέκι ‖ *vt* συχνάζω εἰς ‖ (*of ghosts*) στοιχειώνω.

have [hæv] (*irreg v*) *vt* ἔχω, κατέχω ‖ (*be obliged*) ἀναγκάζω, ἔχω νά, πρέπει νά ‖ (*meal*) λαμβάνω, παίρνω ‖ (*obtain*) παίρνω ‖ (*children etc*) γεννῶ, κάνω ‖ **to** ~ **on** *vt* φορῶ.

haven ['heivən] *n* λιμάνι ‖ (*refuge*) καταφύγιον, ἄσυλον.

haversack ['hævəsæk] *n* σακκίδιον ‖ (*mil*) γυλιός.

havoc ['hævək] *n* πανωλεθρία, καταστροφή.

hawk [hɔ:k] *n* γεράκι.

hawser ['hɔ:zə*] *n* (*naut*) λαντσάνα ‖ παλαμάρι.

hay [hei] *n* σανός, ἄχυρο ‖ ~ **fever** *n* φθινοπωρινός κατάρρους ‖ ~**stack** *n* θημωνιά.

haywire ['haiwaiə*] *a* (*col*) **it's gone** ~ δέν πάει καλά.

hazard ['hæzəd] *n* (*chance*) τύχη ‖ (*danger*) κίνδυνος ‖ *vt* διακινδυνεύω, ριψοκινδυνεύω ‖ ~**ous** *a* ριψοκίνδυνος.

haze [heiz] *n* καταχνιά.

hazelnut ['heizlnʌt] *n* φουντούκι.

hazy ['heizi] *a* (*weather*) καταχνιασμένος ‖ (*vague*) ἀμυδρός, ἀόριστος.

he [hi:] *pron* αὐτός, ἐκεῖνος ‖ ἀρσενικός.

head [hed] *n* (*anat*) κεφάλι ‖ (*leader*) ἀρχηγός, προϊστάμενος, διευθυντής ‖ (*top*) ἄκρον ‖ *a* πρωτεύων, κύριος ‖ *vt* ἡγοῦμαι, διευθύνω, διοικῶ ‖ **to** ~ **for** *vt* κινοῦμαι πρός, κατευθύνομαι ‖ ~**ache** *n* κεφαλόπονος, πονοκέφαλος ‖ ~**ing** *n* ἐπικεφαλίς, τίτλος ‖ ~**lamp** *n* πρόσθιον φῶς, φανάρι ‖ ~**land** *n* ἀκρωτήρι ‖ ~**light** = ~**lamp** ‖ ~**line** *n* ἐπικεφαλίς, τίτλος ‖ ~**long** *ad* μέ τό κεφάλι, ἀπερίσκεπτος ‖ ~**master** *n* διευθυντής σχολείου ‖ ~**mistress** *n* διευθύντρια (σχολείου) ‖ ~ *a* κατά μέτωπον ‖ ~**quarters** *npl* ἀρχηγεῖον, στρατηγεῖον ‖ ~**rest** *n* κουμπιστήρι ‖ ~**strong** *a* ἰσχυρογνώμων, ξεροκέφαλος ‖ ~ **waiter** *n* ἀρχισερβιτόρος, μαίτρ ‖ ~**way** *n* πρόοδος ‖ ~**wind** *n* ἀντίθετος ἄνεμος, ἀέρας κόντρα ‖ ~**y** *a* ὁρμητικός, φουριόζος ‖ (*drink etc*) πού ζαλίζει, βαράει στό κεφάλι.

heal [hi:l] *vt* θεραπεύω, γιατρεύω ‖ *vi* ἐπουλώνομαι, γιατρεύομαι.

health [helθ] *n* ὑγεία ‖ (*toast*) πρόποσις ‖ ~y *a* ὑγιής, εὔρωστος, γερός.

heap [hi:p] *n* σωρός ‖ πλῆθος ‖ *vt* γεμίζω, συσσωρεύω.

hear [hiə*] (*irreg v*) *vt* ἀκούω ‖ ἀκροῶμαι ‖ (*learn*) ἀκούω, μαθαίνω ‖ ~ing *n* (*sense*) ἀκοή ‖ ἀκρόασις ‖ (*law*) (ἀκροαματική) ἐξέτασις μαρτύρων ‖ ~ing aid *n* ἀκουστικά βαρυκοΐας ‖ ~say *n* ' φήμη, διάδοσις.

hearse [hə:s] *n* νεκροφόρος.

heart [ha:t] *n* (*anat*) καρδία ‖ (*centre*) καρδιά ‖ (*courage*) θάρρος ‖ (*emotion*) ψυχή ‖ (*tenderness*) καρδιά, ψυχή ‖ (*cards*) κούπα ‖ ~ attack *n* καρδιακή προσβολή ‖ ~beat *n* παλμός καρδίας ‖ ~breaking *a* θλιβερός, λυπητερός ‖ ~broken *a* περίλυπος, θλιμμένος ‖ ~burn *n* καρδιαλγία, καύσα (στομάχου) ‖ ~ failure *n* συγκοπή ‖ ~felt *a* ἐγκάρδιος, γκαρδιακός.

hearth [ha:θ] *n* τζάκι ‖ πυροστιά.

heartily [ˈha:tili] *ad* εἰλικρινά, μέ ὄρεξι, τελείως.

heartless [ˈha:tlis] *a* ἄκαρδος.

hearty [ˈha:ti] *a* ἐγκάρδιος ‖ (*healthy*) εὔρωστος ‖ (*meal*) πλούσια, θρεπτικός.

heat [hi:t] *n* θερμότης ‖ (*weather*) ζέστη, κάψα ‖ (*anger*) ἔξαψις, ὀργή ‖ (*sport*) ἀγών δρόμου, κούρσα ‖ *vt* θερμαίνω, ζεσταίνω ‖ to ~ up *vi* ἀνάβω, (ὑπερ)θερμαίνομαι ‖ ~ed *a* ζεστός, θερμασμένος ‖ ~er *n* θερμαστής ‖ θερμάστρα, σόμπα.

heath [hi:θ] *n* (*Brit*) χέρσος γῆ, ρεικιά ‖ ρείκη.

heathen [ˈhi:ðən] *n* εἰδωλολάτρης, ἐθνικός ‖ *a* εἰδωλολατρικός.

heather [ˈheðə*] *n* (δ)ρείκι.

heating [ˈhi:tiŋ] *n* θέρμανσις.

heatstroke [ˈhi:tstrəuk] *n* θερμοπληξία.

heatwave [ˈhi:tweiv] *n* κῦμα ζέστης, καύσων.

heave [hi:v] (*irreg v*) *vt* σηκώνω, ἀνυψώνω ‖ (*throw*) ρίπτω ‖ *vi* ἀνυψοῦμαι ‖ (*naut*) βιράρω ‖ *n* ἀνύψωσις, σήκωμα ‖ φούσκωμα.

heaven [ˈhevən] *n* οὐρανός ‖ for ~'s sake! γιά ὄνομα τοῦ Θεοῦ! ‖ good ~s! Θεέ μου! ‖ ~ly *a* οὐράνιος ‖ (*col*) περίφημα.

heavily [ˈhevili] *ad* βαρειά, δυνατά.

heavy [ˈhevi] *a* βαρύς ‖ (*difficult*) δύσκολος, δύσβατος ‖ (*abundant*) ἄφθονος ‖ ~ eater *n* μεγάλος φαγᾶς.

Hebrew [ˈhi:bru:] *n* (*person*) Ἑβραῖος ‖ (*ling*) ἑβραϊκά ‖ *a* ἑβραϊκός.

heckle [ˈhekl] *vt* βομβαρδίζω μέ ἐνοχλητικές ἐρωτήσεις.

hectare [ˈhekta:*] *n* ἑκτάριον.

hectic [ˈhektik] *a* πυρετώδης ‖ ταραχώδης.

hedge [hedʒ] *n* φράχτης, φραγμός ‖ *vt*

(*surround*) περιφράσσω, φράττω ‖ *vi* ὑπεκφεύγω, μασῶ τά λόγια μου.

hedgehog [ˈhedʒhɔg] *n* σκαντζόχοιρος.

heed [hi:d] *vt* προσέχω ‖ *n* προσοχή ‖ ~ful *a* προσεκτικός ‖ ~less *a* ἀπρόσεκτος, ἀμέριμνος.

heel [hi:l] *n* φτέρνα ‖ (*of shoe*) τακούνι ‖ *vt* (*shoe*) βάζω τακούνι εἰς.

hefty [ˈhefti] *a* δυνατός, ρωμαλέος.

heifer [ˈhefə*] *n* δάμαλι.

height [hait] *n* (*of person*) ἀνάστημα, μπόϊ ‖ (*of object*) ὕψος, ὕψωμα ‖ ἀκμή ‖ (*of mountain*) κορυφή ‖ ~en *vt* ὑψώνω, αὐξάνω.

heir [eə*] *n* κληρονόμος ‖ ~ess *n* ἡ κληρονόμος ‖ ~loom *n* οἰκογενειακόν κειμήλιον.

held [held] *pt,pp* of hold.

helicopter [ˈhelikɔptə*] *n* ἑλικόπτερο.

hell [hel] *n* κόλασις.

he'll [hi:l] = he will, he shall ‖ see will, shall.

hellish [ˈheliʃ] *a* ἀπαίσιος, καταχθόνιος.

hello [hʌˈləu] *excl* (*greeting*) γιάσου! ‖ (*tel*) ἀλλό! ‖ (*surprise*) μπά, μπά!

helm [helm] *n* τιμόνι, δοιάκι.

helmet [ˈhelmit] *n* κράνος, κάσκα ‖ περικεφαλαία.

helmsman [ˈhelmzmən] *n* πηδαλιοῦχος.

help [help] *n* βοήθεια ‖ *vt* βοηθῶ, ἐνισχύω ‖ (*prevent*) ἀποφεύγω, ἐμποδίζω ‖ (*serve food*) σερβίρω ‖ ~er *n* βοηθός ‖ ~ful *a* χρήσιμος ‖ ~ing *n* μερίδα ‖ ~less *a* ἀβοήθητος, εἰς ἀμηχανίαν.

hem [hem] *n* στρίφωμα ‖ to ~ in *vt* περικυκλώνω, στρυμώνω.

hemisphere [ˈhemisfiə*] *n* ἡμισφαίριον.

hemp [hemp] *n* κάνναβις, καννάβι.

hen [hen] *n* κότα, θηλυκό πτηνό ‖ ~coop *n* κοτέτσι.

hence [hens] *ad* ἀπ'ἐδῶ, ἀπό τώρα ‖ (*therefore*) ἀπ'αὐτό.

henchman [ˈhentʃmən] *n* πιστός ὀπαδός, μπράβος.

her [hə:*] *pron* αὐτήν ‖ *a* δικός της.

herald [ˈherəld] *n* κήρυκας, πρόδρομος ‖ *vt* ἀναγγέλω, προμηνύω, προαγγέλω.

heraldry [ˈherəldri] *n* οἰκοσημολογία.

herb [hə:b] *n* βότανο, χόρτο.

herd [hə:d] *n* (*general*) κοπάδι.

here [hiə*] *ad* ἐδῶ ‖ *n* ἐδῶ ‖ ~! ἰδού νά! ‖ come ~! ἔλα (δῶ)! ‖ ~after *ad* στό ἑξῆς ‖ *n* μέλλουσα ζωή ‖ ~by *ad* μ'αὐτό, διά τοῦ παρόντος.

hereditary [hiˈreditri] *a* κληρονομικός.

heredity [hiˈrediti] *n* κληρονομικότης.

heresy [ˈherisi] *n* αἵρεσις.

heretic [ˈherətik] *n* αἱρετικός ‖ ~al [hiˈretikəl] *a* αἱρετικός.

herewith [ˈhiəˈwið] *ad* μετ'αὐτοῦ, μ'αὐτό.

heritage [ˈheritidʒ] *n* κληρονομία.

hermit [ˈhə:mit] *n* ἐρημίτης.

hernia [ˈhə:niə] *n* κήλη.

hero ['hiərəu] n ἥρωας, παληκάρι ‖ (of a story) πρωταγωνιστής ‖ ~ic a ἡρωϊκός.
heroin ['herəuin] n ἡρωΐνη.
heroine ['herəuin] n ἡρωΐδα, πρωταγωνίστρια.
heroism ['herəuizm] n ἡρωϊσμός.
heron ['hern] n ἐρωδιός, τσικνιάς.
herring ['heriŋ] n ρέγγα.
hers [hə:z] pron αὐτῆς, δικός της.
herself [hə:'self] pron ἡ ἴδια, τόν ἑαυτόν της.
he's [hi:z] = he is, he has ‖ see be, have.
hesitant ['hezitnt] a διστακτικός.
hesitate ['heziteit] vi διστάζω.
hesitation [hezi'teiʃən] n δισταγμός, ἐνδοιασμός.
het up ['het'ʌp] a θυμωμένος, στενοχωρημένος.
hew [hju:] (irreg v) vt κατακόπτω, πελεκῶ.
hexagon ['heksəgən] n ἑξάγωνον.
heyday ['heidei] n ἀκμή, ἄνθος, καλές μέρες.
hi [hai] excl ἔ!, σύ! ‖ (US) καλημέρα!, γιάσου!
hibernate ['haibəneit] vi διαχειμάζω.
hibernation [haibə'neiʃən] n χειμερία νάρκη.
hiccough, hiccup ['hikʌp] vi ἔχω λόξυγγα ‖ ~s npl λόξυγγας.
hid [hid] pt of hide.
hidden ['hidn] pp of hide.
hide [haid] (irreg v) n δέρμα, πετσί, τομάρι ‖ vt (ἀπό) κρύβω ‖ vi κρύβομαι ‖ ~-and-seek n κρυφτό.
hideous ['hidiəs] a φρικτός, ἀποκρουστικά ἄσχημος ‖ ~ly ad ἀπαίσια, φρικτά.
hiding ['haidiŋ] n (beating) σπάσιμο στό ξύλο ‖ in ~ a (concealed) κρυμμένος ‖ ~ place n κρυψώνας.
hierarchy ['haiəra:ki] n ἱεραρχία.
high [hai] a (far up) ψηλά ‖ (tall) ψηλός ‖ (rank) ἀνώτερος, σπουδαῖος ‖ (class) ἀνώτερος ‖ (price) ἀκρίβεια, ψηλή (τιμή) ‖ (pressure etc) ὑψηλός, μεγάλος ‖ (opinion) μεγάλη ἐκτίμηση σέ ‖ ad ψηλά, πλούσια ‖ ~-chair n ψηλό καρεκλάκι γιά μωρά ‖ ~-handed a αὐθαίρετα ‖ ~-heeled a μέ ψηλά τακούνια ‖ ~-level a στό ἀνώτερο ἐπίπεδο, σέ μεγάλο ὕψος ‖ ~light n (fig) ἀποκορύφωμα, τό μεγάλο νούμερο ‖ ~ly ad ἐξαιρετικά, πάρα πολύ ‖ ~ly strung a εὐερέθιστος, νευρικός ‖ H~ Mass n μεγάλη λειτουργία (τῶν Καθολικῶν) ‖ ~ness n (title) ὑψηλότης ‖ ~-pitched a (voice) διαπεραστικά, ὀξύς ‖ ~ school n γυμνάσιον ‖ ~-speed a μεγάλης ταχύτητος ‖ ~ tide n φουσκονεριά, πλημμυρίδα ‖ ~way n ἐθνική ὁδός.
hijack ['haidʒæk] vt κάνω ἀεροπειρατία ‖ ~er n (aviat) ἀεροπειρατής.
hike [haik] vi πεζοπορῶ ‖ n πεζοπορία ‖ ~r n πεζοπόρος.

hiking ['haikiŋ] n πεζοπορία.
hilarious [hi'leəriəs] a ἱλαρός, εὔθυμος.
hilarity [hi'læriti] n ἱλαρότης, εὐθυμία.
hill [hil] n λόφος ‖ ~y a λοφώδης.
hilt [hilt] n λαβή (ξίφους) ‖ up to the ~ τελείως.
him [him] pron αὐτόν, σ'αὐτόν.
himself [him'self] pron τόν ἑαυτόν του, (αὐτός) ὁ ἴδιος.
hind [haind] a ὀπίσθιος ‖ n ἔλαφος.
hinder ['hində*] vt ἐμποδίζω, κωλύω.
hindrance ['hindrəns] n ἐμπόδιον.
Hindu ['hin'du:] n Ἰνδός.
hinge [hindʒ] n ἄρθρωσις, μεντεσές ‖ vt κρεμῶ σέ μεντεσέδες ‖ vi (fig) ἐξαρτῶμαι.
hint [hint] n νύξις, ὑπαινιγμός ‖ vi ὑπαινίσσομαι.
hip [hip] n ἰσχίον, γοφός.
hippopotamus [hipə'potəməs] n ἱπποπόταμος.
hire ['haiə*] n μίσθωσις, ἐνοικίασις ‖ vt (worker) μισθώνω, πληρώνω, προσλαμβάνω ‖ (rent) ἐνοικιάζω ‖ (car) νοικιάζω ‖ 'for ~' 'ἐλεύθερον', ἐνοικιάζεται ‖ ~ purchase n μέ δόσεις.
his [hiz] pron δικός του ‖ a αὐτοῦ, (δικός) του.
hiss [his] n σφύριγμα ‖ vi ἀποδοκιμάζω, σφυρίζω.
historian [his'tɔ:riən] n ἱστορικός.
historic(al) [his'tɔrik(əl)] a ἱστορικός.
history ['histəri] n ἱστορία.
hit [hit] (irreg v) n κτύπημα ‖ (success) ἐπιτυχία ‖ vt κτυπάω, πλήττω ‖ (target) εὐστοχῶ.
hitch [hitʃ] n τίναγμα, τράβηγμα ‖ (bend) θηλειά ‖ (fig) ἐμπόδιο ‖ vt δένω, προσδένω ‖ (jerk) τραντάζω.
hitch-hike ['hitʃhaik] vi κάνω ὠτοστόπ ‖ ~r n ὁ κάνων ὠτοστόπ.
hive [haiv] n κυψέλη.
hoard [hɔ:d] n θησαυρός, σωρός ‖ vt συσσωρεύω, θησαυρίζω, ἀποκρύπτω.
hoarding ['hɔ:diŋ] n ἀποθησαυρισμός, ἀπόκρυψις.
hoarfrost ['hɔ:'frɔst] n πάχνη.
hoarse [hɔ:s] a βραχνιασμένος.
hoax [həuks] n ἀστεῖο, τέχνασμα, φάρσα.
hobble ['hɔbl] vi χωλαίνω, κουτσαίνω.
hobby ['hɔbi] n μεράκι, χόμπυ.
hobo ['həubəu] n (US) ἀλήτης.
hock [hɔk] n (wine) ἄσπρο κρασί τοῦ Ρήνου.
hockey ['hɔki] n χόκεϋ.
hoe [həu] n τσάπα ‖ vt τσαπίζω.
hog [hɔg] n γουρούνι.
hoist [hɔist] n ἀνελκυστήρας ‖ τράβηγμα, σπρώξιμο ‖ vt ἀνυψώνω.
hold [həuld] (irreg v) n λαβή, πιάσιμο ‖ (influence) ἔχω ἐπιρροήν πάνω σέ ‖ (naut) ἀμπάρι ‖ vt (grasp) κρατῶ ‖ (keep) κρατῶ, φέρω ‖ (contain) περιέχω ‖ (keep

back) συγκρατῶ, σταματῶ ‖ (meeting etc) συγκαλῶ, κάνω ‖ (title) κατέχω, ἔχω ‖ to ~ back vt συγκρατῶ ‖ (secret) ἀποκρύβω ‖ (control) ἀναχαιτίζω ‖ to ~ down vt κρατῶ ‖ to ~ out vt ἐκτείνω ‖ (resist) ἀντέχω ‖ to ~ up vt (support) ὑποστηρίζω ‖ (display) ἐπιδεικνύω ‖ (stop) σταματῶ, καθυστερῶ ‖ (rob) ληστεύω ‖ vi (withstand pressure) ἀντέχω ‖ ~er n κάτοχος ‖ (handle) λαβή, σφυγκτήρας ‖ ~ing n (share) μετοχή ‖ ~ings npl ἀποθεματικόν ‖ ~up n παρακώλησις ‖ (robbery) ληστεία.

hole [həul] n τρύπα ‖ vt τρυπῶ, ἀνοίγω.

holiday [ˈhɔlidei] n γιορτή, ἀργία ‖ (annual) διακοπές ‖ ~-maker n γιορταστής ‖ παραθεριστής.

holiness [ˈhəulinis] n ἁγιότης.

Holland [ˈhɔlənd] n Ὀλλανδία.

hollow [ˈhɔləu] a βαθουλός, κοῖλος ‖ (empty) κούφιος ‖ (false) ψεύτικος ‖ n κοίλωμα, βαθούλωμα, γούβα ‖ to ~ out vt βαθουλώνω, σκάβω.

holly [ˈhɔli] n (tree) πουρνάρι.

holster [ˈhəulstə*] n πιστολιοθήκη.

holy [ˈhəuli] a ἅγιος, ἱερός ‖ (divine) θεῖος.

homage [ˈhɔmidʒ] n ὑποταγή.

home [həum] n σπίτι, κατοικία ‖ (native country) πατρίδα ‖ (institution) ἄσυλον ‖ a (country) σπιτικό ‖ ἐγχώριος, ἐντόπιος ‖ ad στό σπίτι, στήν πατρίδα ‖ at ~ στό σπίτι ‖ (at ease) ἄνετα ‖ ~coming n ἐπάνοδος, ἐπαναπατρισμός ‖ ~less a ἄστεγος ‖ ~-made a σπιτήσιος, ντόπιος ‖ ~sick a νοσταλγός ‖ ~ward(s) ad πρός τό σπίτι ‖ ~work n κατ᾽οἴκον ἐργασία.

homicide [ˈhɔmisaid] n (US) ἀνθρωποκτονία.

homogeneous [hɔməˈdʒiːniəs] a ὁμοιογενής.

homosexual [ˈhɔmɔuˈseksjuəl] a ὁμοφυλόφιλος ‖ n ὁμοφυλόφιλος, ἀνώμαλος.

hone [həun] n ἀκόνι ‖ vt ἀκονίζω.

honest [ˈɔnist] a τίμιος, ἔντιμος, εὐθύς ‖ ~ly ad τίμια ‖ ~y n ἐντιμότης.

honey [ˈhʌni] n μέλι ‖ ~comb n κερήθρα ‖ ~moon n μήνας τοῦ μέλιτος.

honk [hɔŋk] n (aut) κορνάρισμα ‖ vi κορνάρω.

honor [ˈɔnə*] (US) = honour.

honorary [ˈɔnərəri] a τιμητικός ‖ (degree etc) ἐπίτιμος.

honour [ˈɔnə*] n τιμή, ὑπόληψις ‖ vt τιμῶ ‖ (bill) ἐξοφλῶ, πληρώνω ‖ ~s npl (univ) τίτλος, τιμητική διάκρισις ‖ ~able a ἔντιμος ‖ (title) ἐντιμώτατος.

hood [hud] n κουκούλα, σκοῦφος ‖ (cover) κάλυμμα ‖ (US aut) καπό ‖ ~wink vt ἐξαπατῶ, κοροϊδεύω.

hoof [huːf] n ὁπλή, πέλμα, νύχι.

hook [huk] n ἀγκίστρι, γάντζος ‖ vt ἀγκιστρώνω, γαντζώνω.

hooligan [ˈhuːligən] n ταραξίας, ἀλήτης.

hoop [huːp] n στεφάνι, τσέρκι.

hoot [huːt] n (of owl) γρούξιμο ‖ (aut) κορνάρισμα ‖ vi γιουχάρω, σφυρίζω ‖ ~er n (naut) σειρήνα, σφυρίχτρα ‖ (aut) κλάξον, κόρνα.

hop [hɔp] n χοροπήδημα, πήδημα ‖ vi σκιρτῶ, πηδῶ, χοροπηδῶ.

hope [həup] n ἐλπίδα ‖ vi ἐλπίζω ‖ ~ful a γεμᾶτος ἐλπίδες, ἐλπιδοφόρος ‖ ~less a (without hope) ἀπελπισμένος ‖ (useless) μάταιον.

hops [hɔps] npl λυκίσκος.

horde [hɔːd] n ὀρδή, στῖφος.

horizon [həˈraizn] n ὁρίζων ‖ ~tal [hɔriˈzɔntl] a ὁριζόντιος.

hormone [ˈhɔːməun] n ὁρμόνη.

horn [hɔːn] n κέρατο ‖ (insect) κεραία ‖ (mus) κέρας, κόρνα ‖ (aut) κλάξον ‖ ~ed a μέ κέρατα.

hornet [ˈhɔːnit] n σφήκα.

horny [ˈhɔːni] a κεράτινος, σκληρός.

horoscope [ˈhɔrəskəup] n ὡροσκόπιον.

horrible [ˈhɔribl] a φρικτός, φρικώδης, ἀπαίσιος.

horrid [ˈhɔrid] a φρικτός, ἀποτρόπαιος ‖ (col) κακός.

horrify [ˈhɔrifai] vt τρομάζω ‖ (shock) σκανδαλίζω.

horror [ˈhɔrə*] n φρίκη, τρόμος.

hors d'oeuvres [ɔːˈdəːvr] npl ὀρεκτικά, μεζεδάκια, ὀρντέβρ.

horse [hɔːs] n ἄλογο ‖ on ~back καβάλλα ‖ ~ chestnut n ἀγριοκάστανο ‖ ~-drawn a ἱπποκίνητο ‖ ~power n ἱπποδύναμις ‖ ~-racing n ἱπποδρομίες ‖ ~shoe n πέταλο.

horticulture [ˈhɔːtikʌltʃə*] n κηπουρική.

hose [həuz] n (water) σωλήνας ποτίσματος ‖ ~pipe n μάνικα, σωλήνας.

hosiery [ˈhəuʒəri] n πλεκτά εἴδη.

hospitable [hɔsˈpitəbl] a φιλόξενος.

hospital [ˈhɔspitl] n νοσοκομεῖο.

hospitality [hɔspiˈtæliti] n φιλοξενία.

host [həust] n οἰκοδεσπότης ‖ (hotel) ξενοδόχος, χανιτζῆς ‖ (large number) πλῆθος, στρατιά.

hostage [ˈhɔstidʒ] n ὅμηρος.

hostel [ˈhɔstəl] n οἰκοτροφεῖον, χάνι.

hostess [ˈhəustes] n οἰκοδέσποινα.

hostile [ˈhɔstail] a ἐχθρικός.

hostility [hɔsˈtiliti] n ἐχθρότης ‖ hostilities npl ἐχθροπραξίες.

hot [hɔt] a θερμός, ζεστός ‖ (fiery) ὀξύθυμος, ἀναμμένος ‖ ~ dog n λουκάνικο ‖ ~-water bottle n θερμοφόρα.

hotel [həuˈtel] n ξενοδοχεῖον ‖ (residential) πανσιόν.

hound [haund] n σκυλί, λαγωνικό ‖ vt καταδιώκω, παροτρύνω.

hour [ˈauə*] n ὥρα ‖ ~ly a,ad κάθε ὥρα.

house [haus] n σπίτι, κατοικία ‖ (parl) βουλή ‖ (theat) ἀκροατήριον ‖ [hauz] vt στεγάζω ‖ (store) ἀποθηκεύω ‖ ~boat n πλωτό σπίτι ‖ ~**breaking** *n* διάρρηξι σπιτιοῦ ‖ ~**hold** *n* σπίτι ‖ οἰκογένεια, σπιτικό ‖ ~**keeper** *n* νοικοκυρά ‖ ~**keeping** *n* νοικοκυριό, σπιτικό ‖ ~**maid** *n* ὑπηρέτρια, ὑπηρεσία ‖ ~**wife** *n* νοικοκυρά ‖ ~**work** *n* νοικοκυριό.

housing ['hauziŋ] *n* στέγασις.

hovel ['hɔvl] *n* καλύβα.

hover ['hɔvə*] *vi* μετεωρίζομαι, πλανῶμαι ‖ (*between*) διστάζω, ταλαντεύομαι ‖ ~**craft** *n* χόβερκραφτ.

how [hau] *ad* πῶς, μέ ποιό τρόπο ‖ (*extent*) πόσο ‖ **and** ~! (*US*) καί βέβαια!, ἀσφαλῶς! ‖ ~**ever** *ad* ὁπωσδήποτε, ὅπως κι ἄν ‖ (*much*) ὁσονδήποτε, ὅσο κι ἄν ‖ (*yet*) παρά ταῦτα, κι ὅμως.

howl [haul] *n* οὑρλιασμα, οὑρλιαχτό ‖ *vi* οὑρλιάζω, σκούζω.

howler ['haulə*] *n* ὠρυόμενος ‖ (*mistake*) γκάφα, χοντροκοπιά.

hub [hʌb] *n* (*of wheel*) ἀφαλός ‖ (*of activity*) κέντρον.

hubbub ['hʌbʌb] *n* φασαρία, θόρυβος, ὀχλοβοή.

hub cap ['hʌbkæp] *n* καπάκι τῆς ρόδας.

huddle ['hʌdl] *n* σωρός, σωρό κουβάρι ‖ *vi* συσσωρεύω, συνωθοῦμαι, κουλουριάζω.

hue [hju:] *n* χροιά, χρῶμα, ἀπόχρωσις.

huff [hʌf] *n* παραφορά, θυμός.

hug [hʌg] *n* ἀγκάλιασμα ‖ *vt* ἀγκαλιάζω, σφίγγω ‖ (*naut*) παραπλέω, πηγαίνω κόστα-κόστα.

huge [hju:dʒ] *a* πελώριος, θεόρατος, τεράστιος.

hulk [hʌlk] *n* (*naut*) ξαρματωμένο πλοῖο, σαπιοκάραβο ‖ (*person*) μπατάλης, χοντράνθρωπος ‖ ~**ing** *a* δυσκίνητος, χοντρός, βαρύς.

hull [hʌl] *n* σκάφος, γάστρα.

hullo [hʌ'ləu] *excl* = **hello**.

hum [hʌm] *n* βόμβος, βουητό, ψίθυρος ‖ *vi* βουΐζω, ψιθυρίζω ‖ *vt* μουρμουρίζω.

human ['hju:mən] *a* ἀνθρώπινος ‖ *n* ἄνθρωπος.

humane [hju'mein] *a* ἀνθρωπιστικός, φιλάνθρωπος.

humanity [hju'mæniti] *n* ἀνθρωπότης ‖ (*kindness*) φιλανθρωπία.

humble ['hʌmbl] *a* ταπεινός, ἁπλός ‖ (*unimportant*) ἀσήμαντος ‖ *vt* ταπεινώνω, ξευτελίζω.

humbly ['hʌmbli] *ad* ταπεινά, ἁπλά.

humdrum ['hʌmdrəm] *a* μονότονος, ἀνιαρός, πληκτικός.

humid ['hju:mid] *a* ὑγρός, νοτερός ‖ ~**ity** *n* ὑγρασία, νότισμα.

humiliate [hju'milieit] *vt* ταπεινώνω, ξευτελίζω, κουρελιάζω.

humiliation [hju:mili'eiʃən] *n* ταπείνωσις, κουρέλιασμα.

humility [hju'militi] *n* ταπεινότης, μετριοφροσύνη.

humor ['hju:mə*] (*US*) = **humour**.

humorist ['hju:mərist] *n* χιουμορίστας.

humorous ['hju:mərəs] *a* γεμάτος χιοῦμορ, εὔθυμος.

humour ['hju:mə*] *n* χιοῦμορ, κέφι, διάθεσις ‖ *vt* κάνω τά χατήρια, κάνω τά κέφια.

hump [hʌmp] *n* καμπούρα.

hunch [hʌntʃ] *n* ὕβος, καμπούρα ‖ (*suspicion*) ὑποψία ‖ *vi* κυρτώνω, καμπουριάζω ‖ ~**back** *n* καμπούρης.

hundred ['hʌndrid] *num,n* ἑκατόν ‖ ~**weight** *n* στατήρ (112 λίτρες).

hung [hʌŋ] *pt,pp of* **hang**.

Hungarian [hʌŋ'gɛəriən] *a* οὐγγρικός ‖ *n* (*person*) Οὔγγρος ‖ (*ling*) οὐγγρική.

Hungary ['hʌŋgəri] *n* Οὐγγαρία.

hunger ['hʌŋgə*] *n* πεῖνα ‖ (*desire*) σφοδρά ἐπιθυμία ‖ *vi* πεινῶ, ποθῶ ἐντόνως ‖ ~ **strike** *n* ἀπεργία πείνης.

hungrily ['hʌŋgrili] *ad* ἄπληστα, ἀχόρταγα, πεινασμένα.

hungry ['hʌŋgri] *a* πεινασμένος.

hunt [hʌnt] *n* κυνήγι ‖ (*seeking*) ἀναζήτησις ‖ *vt* κυνηγῶ ‖ (*search*) διώχνω ‖ *vi* κυνηγῶ ‖ (*seek*) ψάχνω ‖ ~**er** *n* κυνηγός ‖ ~**ing** *n* κυνήγι.

hurdle ['hə:dl] *n* (*lit*) φράκτης ‖ (*fig*) ἐμπόδιον.

hurl [hə:l] *vt* ἐκσφενδονίζω, ρίχνω.

hurrah [hu'ra:] *n*, **hurray** [hu'rei] *n* ζητοκραυγή.

hurricane ['hʌrikən] *n* καταιγίδα, λαίλαπας.

hurried ['hʌrid] *a* βιαστικός ‖ ~**ly** *ad* βιαστικά.

hurry ['hʌri] *n* βία, βιασύνη ‖ *vi* βιάζομαι, εἶμαι βιαστικός ‖ *vt* ἐπισπεύδω, βιάζω.

hurt [hə:t] (*irreg v*) *n* κακόν ‖ (*wound*) τραῦμα, πληγή ‖ (*damage*) βλάβη, ζημία ‖ *vt* κτυπῶ, τραυματίζω, πληγώνω ‖ (*insult*) προσβάλλω, πειράζω ‖ *vi* πονῶ, θίγομαι ‖ ~**ful** *a* βλαβερός.

hurtle ['hə:tl] *vt* ἐκσφενδονίζω ‖ *vi* (*rush*) ἐφορμῶ, ρίχνομαι.

husband ['hʌzbənd] *n* ἄνδρας.

hush [hʌʃ] *n* σιωπή, σιγή ‖ *vt* (καθ)ἠσυχάζω, καλμάρω ‖ *vi* σωπαίνω ‖ ~! σιωπή!, σούτ!

husk [hʌsk] *n* φλοιός, φλούδα, τσόφλι.

husky ['hʌski] *a* (*voice*) βραχνός ‖ γεροδεμένος ‖ *n* σκύλος ἑλκύθρου.

hustle ['hʌsl] *n* σπουδή, βιασύνη ‖ (*push*) σπρωξίδι ‖ *vt* (*push*) σπρώχνω ‖ σκουντῶ, βιάζω.

hut [hʌt] *n* καλύβα ‖ (*mil*) παράπηγμα.

hutch [hʌtʃ] *n* κονικλοτροφεῖον.

hyacinth ['haiəsinθ] *n* ὑάκινθος.

hybrid ['haibrid] *n* μιγάς, μικτογενής, νόθος ‖ *a* νόθος, μπασταρδεμένος.

hydrant ['haidrənt] *n* σωλήν πυρκαϊᾶς, στόμιον ὑδρολήψιας.

hydraulic [hai'drɔ:lik] *a* ὑδραυλικός.

hydroelectric ['haidrəui'lektrik] a ὑδροηλεκτρικός.
hydrogen ['haidrədʒen] n ὑδρογόνον.
hyena [hai'i:nə] n ὕαινα.
hygiene ['haidʒi:n] n ὑγιεινή.
hygienic [hai'dʒi:nik] a ὑγιεινός.
hymn [him] n ὕμνος, ὑμνῳδία.
hyphen ['hǎifən] n ἑνωτικόν.
hypnosis [hip'nəusis] n ὕπνωσις.
hypnotism ['hipnətizəm] n ὑπνωτισμός.
hypnotist ['hipnətist] n ὑπνωτιστής.
hypnotize ['hipnətaiz] vt ὑπνωτίζω.
hypochondriac [haipə'kɔndriæk] n ὑπόχόν-
δριος.
hypocrisy [hi'pɔkrisi] n ὑποκρισία.
hypocrite ['hipəkrit] n ὑποκριτής.
hypocritical [hipə'kritikl] a ὑποκριτικός.
hypothesis [hai'pɔθisis] n ὑπόθεσις.
hypothetic(al) [haipə'θetik(əl)] a ὑποθετικός.
hysteria [his'tiəriə] n ὑστερία.
hysterical [his'terikl] a ὑστερικός.
hysterics [his'teriks] npl ὑστερία.

I, i

I [ai] pron ἐγώ.
ice [ais] n πάγος ‖ (refreshment) παγωτό ‖
vt (cake) γκλασάρω ‖ vi (also ~ up)
παγώνω ‖ ~ axe n πέλεκυς πάγου ‖
~berg n παγόβουνο ‖ ~box n (US)
ψυγεῖον ‖ ~ cream n παγωτό ‖ ~cold
a παγερός, παγωμένος ‖ ~ cube n παγάκι
‖ ~ hockey n χόκεϋ ἐπί πάγου.
icicle ['aisikl] n σταλακτίτης πάγου.
icing ['aisiŋ] n κρούστα γιά κέϊκ, γκλασά-
ρισμα.
icon ['aikɔn] n εἰκόνα.
icy ['aisi] a (slippery) γλιστερός ‖ (frozen)
παγετώδης, παγωμένος.
I'd [aid] = I would, I had ‖ see would, have.
idea [ai'diə] n ἰδέα ‖ (plan) σκοπός, ἰδέα.
ideal [ai'diəl] n ἰδανικόν, ἰδεῶδες ‖ a
ἰδανικός, ἰδεώδης ‖ ~ism n ἰδεαλισμός ‖
~ist n ἰδεαλιστής ‖ ~ly ad ἰδανικῶς,
ἰδεωδῶς.
identical [ai'dentikəl] a ὅμοιος, ἴδιος,
ἀπαράλλακτος.
identification [aidentifi'keiʃən] n ἐξακρί-
βωσις ταυτότητος, συναύτισις.
identify [ai'dentifai] vt (person) διαπιστώνω, ἐξακριβώνω ‖ (regard as same)
ταυτίζω.
identity [ai'dentiti] n ταυτότης.
ideology [aidi'ɔlədʒi] n ἰδεολογία.
idiocy ['idiəsi] n ἠλιθιότης.
idiom ['idiəm] n ἰδίωμα ‖ (dialect) διάλεκτος.
idiosyncrasy [idiə'siŋkrəsi] n ἰδιοσυγκρασία.
idiot ['idiət] n ἠλίθιος, ἀνόητος ‖ ~ic
[idi'ɔtik] a ἠλίθιος.

idle ['aidl] a ἀργός ‖ (lazy) ὀκνηρός,
τεμπέλης ‖ (useless) μάταιος, ἀνωφελής ‖
~ness n ἀργία, τεμπελιά ‖ ~r n
ἀργόσχολος.
idol ['aidl] n εἴδωλον ‖ ~ize vt λατρεύω,
θαυμάζω.
idyllic [i'dilik] a εἰδυλλιακός.
if [if] cj (condition) ἐάν, ἄν, ὅταν ‖ (whether)
ἄν.
ignite [ig'nait] vt ἀναφλέγω, ἀνάβω.
ignition [ig'niʃən] n ἀνάφλεξις ‖ ~ key n
(aut) κλειδί (ξεκινήσεως).
ignorance ['ignərəns] n ἄγνοια.
ignorant ['ignərənt] a ἀμαθής, ἀγνοῶν.
ignore [ig'nɔ:*] vt ἀγνοῶ, ἀψηφῶ.
ikon ['aikɔn] n = icon.
I'll [ail] = I will, I shall ‖ see will, shall.
ill [il] a ἄρρωστος ‖ (evil) κακός ‖ n κακόν,
ἀτυχία ‖ ~advised a ἀσύνετος, ἀπερίσκεπτος ‖ ~-at-ease a στενοχωρημένος,
ἀνήσυχος.
illegal [i'li:gəl] a παράνομος ‖ ~ly ad
παράνομα.
illegible [i'ledʒəbl] a δυσανάγνωστος.
illegitimate [ili'dʒitimit] a νόθος.
ill-fated ['il'feitid] a κακότυχος.
ill-feeling ['il'fi:liŋ] n κακία, ἔχθρα.
illicit [i'lisit] a παράνομος, ἀθέμιτος.
illiterate [i'litərit] a ἀγράμματος.
ill-mannered ['il'mænəd] a κακότροπος,
κακομαθημένος.
illness ['ilnis] n ἀσθένεια, ἀρρώστεια.
illogical [i'lɔdʒikəl] a παράλογος.
ill-treat ['il'tri:t] vt κακομεταχειρίζομαι.
illuminate [i'lu:mineit] vt φωτίζω, φωταγωγῶ.
illumination [ilu:mi'neiʃən] n φωτισμός,
φωταγώγησις.
illusion [i'lu:ʒən] n αὐταπάτη, πλάνη.
illusive [i'lu:siv] a, illusory [i'lu:səri] a
ἀπατηλός.
illustrate ['iləstreit] vt εἰκονογραφῶ.
illustration [iləs'treiʃən] n εἰκονογράφη-
σις, εἰκόνα.
illustrious [i'lʌstriəs] a ἔνδοξος, ἐπιφανής.
ill will ['il'wil] n κακοβουλία, κακία.
I'm [aim] = I am ‖ see be.
image ['imidʒ] n (statue) εἰκών, εἴδωλον ‖
(likeness) ὁμοίωμα, ἀναπαράστασις ‖
(reflection) εἴδωλον ‖ ~ry n ῥητορικά
σχήματα.
imaginable [i'mædʒinəbl] a διανοητός.
imaginary [i'mædʒinəri] a φανταστικός.
imagination [imædʒi'neiʃən] n φαντασία.
imaginative [i'mædʒinətiv] a εὐφάνταστος,
ἐπινοητικός.
imagine [i'mædʒin] vt φαντάζομαι, διανο-
οῦμαι.
imbalance [im'bæləns] n ἀνισότης, ἀνισορ-
ροπία.
imbecile ['imbəsi:l] n βλάκας, ἠλίθιος.
imbue [im'bju:] vt (ἐμ)ποτίζω, διαποτίζω.
imitate ['imiteit] vt μιμοῦμαι, ἀντιγράφω.

imitation [imi'teiʃən] *n* (άπο)μίμησις.
imitator ['imiteitə*] *n* μιμητής.
immaculate [i'mækjulit] *a* άσπιλος, άμόλυντος.
immaterial [imə'tiəriəl] *a* · άσήμαντος, άϋλος.
immature [imə'tjuə*] *a* άνώριμος, άγουρος.
immediate [i'mi:diət] *a* (*near*) άμεσος, προσεχές ‖ (*present*) έπείγων, άμεσος ‖ (*not separated*) πλησιέστερος ‖ (*instant*) άμεσος, στιγμιαίος ‖ ~ly *ad* (*at once*) άμέσως, στή στιγμή.
immense [i'mens] *a* άπέραντος, άπειρος ‖ ~ly *ad* άπέραντα.
immerse [i'mə:s] *vt* έμβαπτίζω, βυθίζω, βουτῶ.
immigrant ['imigrənt] *n* μετανάστης.
immigration [imi'greiʃən] *n* μετανάστευσις.
imminent ['iminənt] *a* έπικείμενος, άμεσος.
immobilize [i'məubilaiz] *vt* άκινητοποιῶ.
immoderate [i'mɔdərit] *a* ύπερβολικός, ύπέρμετρος.
immoral [i'mɔrəl] *a* άνήθικος, κακοήθης ‖ ~ity [imə'ræliti] *n* άνηθικότης.
immortal [i'mɔ:tl] *a* άθάνατος, άφθαρτος ‖ *n* άθάνατος ‖ ~ity *n* άθανασία ‖ ~ize *vt* άποθανατίζω.
immune [i'mju:n] *a* άπρόσβλητος.
immunity [i'mju:niti] *n* άπαλλαγή ‖ (*med*) άνοσία.
immunization [imjunai'zeiʃən] *n* άνοσοποίησις.
immunize ['imjunaiz] *vt* άνοσοποιῶ.
impact ['impækt] *n* (*lit*) σύγκρουσις, κτύπημα ‖ (*fig*) έπίδρασις.
impair [im'pɛə*] *vt* βλάπτω, έξασθενίζω.
impale [im'peil] *vt* άνασκολοπίζω, παλουκώνω.
impartial [im'pa:ʃəl] *a* άμερόληπτος ‖ ~ity *n* άμεροληψία.
impassable [im'pa:səbl] *a* άδιάβατος.
impassioned [im'pæʃnd] *a* έμπαθής, παθιασμένος.
impatience [im'peiʃəns] *n* άνυπομονησία.
impatient [im'peiʃənt] *a* άνυπόμονος ‖ ~ly *ad* άνυπόμονα, βιαστικά.
impeccable [im'pekəbl] *a* άψογος, τέλειος.
impede [im'pi:d] *vt* έμποδίζω, παρακωλύω.
impediment [im'pedimənt] *n* κώλυμα, έμπόδιον.
impending [im'pendiŋ] *a* έπικείμενος.
impenetrable [im'penitrəbl] *a* άδιαπέραστος, άνεξιχνίαστος.
imperative [im'perətiv] *a* έπιτακτικός ‖ *n* (*gram*) προστακτική.
imperceptible [impə'septəbl] *a* άνεπαίσθητος, άδιόρατος.
imperfect [im'pa:fikt] *a* έλαττωματικός ‖ (*incomplete*) έλλειπής ‖ ~ion *n* άτέλεια, έλάττωμα.
imperial [im'piəriəl] *a* αὐτοκρατορικός ‖

(*majestic*) μεγαλοπρεπής ‖ ~ism *n* ίμπεριαλισμός.
imperil [im'peril] *vt* διακινδυνεύω, έκθέτω εἰς κίνδυνον.
impersonal [im'pə:snl] *a* άπρόσωπος.
impersonate [im'pə:səneit] *vt* προσωποποιῶ, ὑποδύομαι, παριστάνω.
impersonation [impə:sə'neiʃən] *n* προσωποποίησις, ένσάρκωσις, μίμησις.
impertinence [im'pə:tinəns] *n* αὐθάδεια.
impertinent [im'pə:tinənt] *a* αὐθάδης, άσχετος.
imperturbable [impə'tə:bəbl] *a* άτάραχος.
impervious [im'pə:viəs] *a* άδιαπέραστος, στεγανός, άνεπηρέαστος.
impetuous [im'petjuəs] *a* όρμητικός, βίαιος.
impetus ['impitəs] *n* ὤθησις, όρμή.
impinge [im'pindʒ] **to ~ on** *vt* συγκρούομαι, καταπατῶ.
implausible [im'plɔ:zəbl] *a* άπίθανος.
implement ['implimənt] *n* όργανον, έργαλεῖον, σύνεργο ‖ ['impliment] *vt* έφαρμόζω.
implicate ['implikeit] *vt* έμπλέκω, άναμιγνύω.
implication [impli'keiʃən] *n* ένοχοποίησις, ὑπαινιγμός.
implicit [im'plisit] *a* ὑπονοούμενος, σιωπηρός ‖ (*complete*) άπόλυτος, άμέριστος.
implore [im'plɔ:*] *vt* ίκετεύω, έκλιπαρῶ.
imply [im'plai] *vt* ὑπονοῶ, ὑπαινίσσομαι, προϋποθέτω.
impolite [impə'lait] *a* άγενής, βάναυσος.
imponderable [im'pondərəbl] *a* άστάθμητος, άνεξιχνίαστος.
import [im'pɔ:t] *vt* εἰσάγω ‖ ['impɔ:t] *n* εἰσαγωγή ‖ (*meaning*) σημασία ‖ ~ **duty** *n* (εἰσαγωγικός) δασμός ‖ ~ **licence** *n* άδεια εἰσαγωγής.
importance [im'pɔ:təns] *n* σπουδαιότης, σοβαρότης ‖ (*value*) σημασία, άξία.
important [im'pɔ:tənt] *a* σημαντικός, σπουδαῖος.
importation [impɔ:'teiʃən] *n* εἰσαγωγή.
importer [im'pɔ:tə*] *n* εἰσαγωγεύς.
impose [im'pəuz] *vt* έπιβάλλω, έπιτάσσω ‖ (*on s.o.*) έπωφελοῦμαι.
imposing [im'pəuziŋ] *a* έπιβλητικός.
imposition [impə'ziʃən] *n* (*burden*) φόρος, φορολογία ‖ (*punishment*) ποινή.
impossibility [impɔsə'biliti] *n* (τό) άδύνατον.
impossible [im'pɔsəbl] *a* άδύνατος, άκατόρθωτος, άνυπόφορος.
impostor [im'pɔstə*] *n* άγύρτης, λαοπλάνος.
impotence ['impətəns] *n* (*esp sexual*) άνικανότης.
impotent ['impətənt] *a* άνίκανος, άνίσχυρος.
impound [im'paund] *vt* κατάσχω.
impoverished [im'pɔvəriʃt] *a* πάμπτωχος, έξηντλημένος.

impracticable [im'præktikəbl] *a* ἀκατόρθωτος, ἀπραγματοποίητος.

impractical [im'præktikəl] *a* οὐχί πρακτικόν.

impregnable [im'pregnəbl] *a* ἀπόρθητος.

impregnate ['impregneit] *vt* γονιμοποιῶ, ἐμποτίζω.

impress [im'pres] *vt* (*influence*) κάνω ἐντύπωσιν ‖ (*imprint*) ἐντυπώνω, ἐγχαράσσω ‖ ~**ion** *n* (*mark*) ἀποτύπωσις, ἀποτύπωμα ‖ (*printed copy*) ἔκδοσις ‖ (*effect*) ἐντύπωσις, αἴσθησις ‖ (*belief*) ἰδέα, ἐντύπωσις, γνώμη ‖ ~**ionable** *a* εὐαίσθητος, εὐσυγκίνητος ‖ ~**ionist** *n* ἰμπρεσσιονιστής ‖ ~**ive** *a* ἐντυπωσιακός, συγκινητικός.

imprison [im'prizn] *vt* φυλακίζω ‖ ~**ment** *n* φυλάκισις.

improbable [im'prɔbəbl] *a* ἀπίθανος.

impromptu [im'prɔmptju:] *a* αὐτοσχέδιος, ἐκ τοῦ προχείρου ‖ *ad* ἐκ τοῦ προχείρου.

improper [im'prɔpə*] *a* (*wrong*) ἐσφαλμένος ‖ (*unsuitable*) ἀνάρμοστος ‖ (*indecent*) ἀπρεπής.

impropriety [imprə'praiəti] *n* ἀπρέπεια, ἀκαταλληλότης.

improve [im'pru:v] *vt* βελτιώνω, κάνω καλύτερον ‖ *vi* (*become better*) βελτιοῦμαι, καλυτερεύω ‖ ~**ment** *n* βελτίωσις, πρόοδος.

improvisation [imprəvai'zeiʃən] *n* αὐτοσχεδιασμός.

improvise ['imprəvaiz] *vi* αὐτοσχεδιάζω ‖ *vt* κάνω ἐκ τοῦ προχείρου.

imprudence [im'pru:dəns] *n* ἀφροσύνη, ἀπερισκεψία.

imprudent [im'pru:dənt] *a* ἀσύνετος, ἀστόχαστος.

impudence ['impjudəns] *n* ἀναίδεια, θράσος.

impudent ['impjudənt] *a* ἀναιδής, ἀναίσχυντος.

impulse ['impʌls] *n* (*sudden desire*) ὁρμή, ὁρμέμφυτον ‖ ὤθησις, πρόωσις.

impulsive [im'pʌlsiv] *a* αὐθόρμητος, ὁρμέμφυτος.

impunity [im'pju:niti] *n* ἀτιμωρησία.

impure [im'pjuə*] *a* ἀκάθαρτος ‖ (*bad*) μιαρός, αἰσχρός.

impurity [im'pjuəriti] *n* ἀκαθαρσία, ξένο σῶμα.

in [in] *prep* εἰς, ἐν, ἐντός, σέ ‖ (*made of*) σέ ‖ (*expressed in*) εἰς, μέ ‖ (*dressed in*) μέ ‖ *ad* ἐντός, μέσα ‖ ~**s and outs** *npl* τά μέσα καί τά ἔξω.

inability [inə'biliti] *n* ἀνικανότης, ἀδυναμία.

inaccessible [inæk'sesəbl] *a* ἀπρόσιτος, ἀπλησίαστος.

inaccuracy [in'ækjurəsi] *n* ἀνακρίβεια.

inaccurate [in'ækjurit] *a* ἀνακριβής, ἐσφαλμένος.

inaction [in'ækʃən] *n* ἀδράνεια, ἀπραξία.

inactivity [inæk'tiviti] *n* ἀδράνεια, ἀργία.

inadequacy [in'ædikwəsi] *n* ἀνεπάρκεια, ἀτέλεια.

inadequate [in'ædikwit] *a* ἀνεπαρκής, ἀτελής.

inadvertently [inəd'və:təntli] *ad* ἀπρόσεκτα, ἐξ ἀμελείας.

inadvisable [inəd'vaizəbl] *a* ἀσύμφορος.

inane [i'nein] *a* κενός, ἀνόητος.

inanimate [in'ænimit] *a* ἄψυχος.

inapplicable [in'æplikəbl] *a* ἀνεφάρμοστος.

inappropriate [inə'prəupriit] *a* ἀκατάλληλος, ἀνάρμοστος.

inapt [in'æpt] *a* ἀνεπιτήδειος, ἀδέξιος ‖ ~**itude** *n* ἀνικανότης, ἀδεξιότης.

inarticulate [ina:'tikjulit] *a* ἄναρθρος, βουβός, ἀσύνδετος.

inartistic [ina:'tistik] *a* ἀφιλόκαλος.

inasmuch [inəz'mʌtʃ] ~ **as** ἐπειδή, ἐφ' ὅσον.

inattention [inə'tenʃən] *n* ἀπροσεξία, ἀφηρημάδα.

inattentive [inə'tentiv] *a* ἀπρόσεκτος, ἀμελής.

inaudible [in'ɔ:dəbl] *a* ἀνεπαίσθητος, ἀσθενής.

inaugural [i'nɔ:gjurəl] *a* ἐναρκτήριος.

inaugurate [i'nɔ:gjureit] *vt* ἐγκαινιάζω.

inauguration [inɔ:gju'reiʃən] *n* ἐγκαινιασμός, ἐγκαίνια.

inborn ['in'bɔ:n] *a* ἔμφυτος.

inbred ['in'bred] *a* ἔμφυτος, φυσικός. ,

incalculable [in'kælkjuləbl] *a* ἀνυπολόγιστος.

incapability [inkeipə'biliti] *n* ἀνικανότης.

incapable [in'keipəbl] *a* ἀνίκανος.

incapacitate [inkə'pæsiteit] *vt* καθιστῶ ἀνίκανον.

incapacity [inkə'pæsiti] *n* ἀνικανότης, ἀναρμοδιότης.

incarcerate [in'ka:səreit] *vt* φυλακίζω.

incarnate [in'ka:nit] *a* ἐνσαρκωμένος.

incarnation [inka:'neiʃən] *n* ἐνσάρκωσις.

incendiary [in'sendiəri] *a* ἐμπρηστικός ‖ *n* ἐμπρηστής.

incense ['insens] *n* θυμίαμα, λιβάνι ‖ [in'sens] *vt* ἐξοργίζω, ἐξαγριώνω.

incentive [in'sentiv] *n* κίνητρον, ἐλατήριον, τονωτικόν.

incessant [in'sesnt] *a* ἀδιάκοπος ‖ ~**ly** *ad* ἀδιάκοπα.

incest ['insest] *n* αἱμομιξία.

inch [intʃ] *n* ἴντσα (.0254 μ.).

incidence ['insidəns] *n* πρόσπτωσις, περίπτωσις.

incident ['insidənt] *n* ἐπεισόδιον, περιπέτεια ‖ ~**al** *a* τυχαῖος, συμπτωματικός ‖ ~**ally** *ad* παρεμπιπτόντως.

incinerator [in'sinəreitə*] *n* ἀποτεφρωτήρ.

incision [in'siʒən] *n* ἐντομή, χαραματιά.

incisive [in'saisiv] *a* κοφτερός ‖ (*cutting*) δηκτικός.

incite [in'sait] *vt* ὑποκινῶ, παροτρύνω.

inclement [in'klemənt] a δριμύς, κακός.

inclination [inkli'neiʃən] n κλίσις, τάσις, διάθεσις.

incline ['inklain] n κλίσις ‖ [in'klain] vi κλίνω, γέρνω ‖ (be disposed) ρέπω, τείνω.

include [in'klu:d] vt (συμ)περιλαμβάνω, περιέχω.

inclusion [in'klu:ʒən] n συμπερίληψις.

inclusive [in'klu:siv] a συμπεριλαμβάνων, περιέχων.

incognito [in'kɔgnitəu] ad ινκόγνιτο.

incoherent [inkəu'hiərənt] a ασυνάρτητος.

income ['inkʌm] n εισόδημα ‖ ~ tax n φόρος εισοδήματος.

incoming [in'kʌmiŋ] a (tide) ανερχόμενος, εισερχόμενος.

incomparable [in'kɔmpərəbl] a ασύγκριτος, απαράμιλλος.

incompatible [inkəm'pætəbl] a ασυμβίβαστος. .

incompetence [in'kɔmpitəns] n αναρμοδιότης, ανικανότης.

incompetent [in'kɔmpitənt] a ανίκανος, αναρμόδιος.

incomplete [inkəm'pli:t] a ατελής.

incomprehensible [inkɔmpri'hensəbl] a ακατανόητος, ακατάληπτος.

inconceivable [inkən'si:vəbl] a ασύλληπτος, απίστευτος.

inconclusive [inkən'klu:siv] a μή πειστικός.

incongruity [inkɔŋ'gru:iti] n ασυνέπεια, ασυναρτησία.

incongruous [in'kɔŋgruəs] a ασύμφωνος, ανάρμοστος.

inconsequential [inkɔnsi'kwenʃəl] a ανακόλουθος, ασήμαντος.

inconsiderable [inkən'sidərəbl] a ασήμαντος.

inconsiderate [inkən'sidərit] a απερίσκεπτος, αδιάκριτος.

inconsistency [inkən'sistənsi] n ασυνέπεια, αντίφασις.

inconsistent [inkən'sistənt] a ασυνεπής, αντιφατικός.

inconspicuous [inkən'spikjuəs] a αφανής, όχι κτυπητός.

inconstancy [in'kɔnstənsi] n αστάθεια.

inconstant [in'kɔnstənt] a ευμετάβολος, ασταθής.

incontinence [in'kɔntinəns] n ακολασία, ακράτεια.

incontinent [in'kɔntinənt] a ακόλαστος, ακρατής.

inconvenience [inkən'vi:niəns] n δυσχέρεια, ενόχλησις, μπελάς.

inconvenient [inkən'vi:niənt] a στενόχωρος, ενοχλητικός, ακατάλληλος.

incorporate [in'kɔ:pəreit] vt ενσωματώνω, συγχωνεύω.

incorporated [in'kɔ:pəreitid] a ενσωματωμένος, συγχωνευμένος ‖ (US) ανώνυμος (εταιρεία).

incorrect [inkə'rekt] a εσφαλμένος, ανακριβής.

incorrigible [in'kɔridʒəbl] a αδιόρθωτος.

incorruptible [inkə'rʌptəbl] a αδιάφθορος, ακέραιος, αδέκαστος.

increase ['inkri:s] n αύξησις ‖ [in'kri:s] vt αυξάνω, μεγαλώνω ‖ vi αυξάνομαι.

increasingly [in'kri:siŋli] ad διαρκώς περισσότερον.

incredible [in'kredəbl] a απίστευτος.

incredibly [in'kredəbli] ad απίστευτα.

incredulity [inkri'dju:liti] n δυσπιστία, ολιγοπιστία.

incredulous [in'kredjuləs] a δύσπιστος.

increment ['inkrimənt] n αύξησις.

incriminate [in'krimineit] vt ενοχοποιώ.

incubation [inkju'beiʃən] n επώασις, κλώσημα.

incubator ['inkjubeitə*] n κλωσσομηχανή.

incur [in'kə:*] vt υφίσταμαι, διατρέχω, προκαλώ.

incurable [ink'juərəbl] a ανίατος, αγιάτρευτος.

incursion [in'kɔ:ʃən] n επιδρομή.

indebted [in'detid] a υποχρεωμένος, υπόχρεως.

indecency [in'di:snsi] n απρέπεια.

indecent [in'di:snt] a απρεπής, άσεμνος.

indecision [indi'siʒən] n αναποφασιστικότης, αοριστία.

indecisive [indi'saisiv] a μή αποφασιστικός.

indeed [in'di:d] ad πράγματι, πραγματικά, αληθινά.

indefinable [indi'fainəbl] a απροσδιόριστος.

indefinite [in'definit] a αόριστος ‖ ~ly ad αορίστως.

indelible [in'deləbl] a ανεξίτηλος.

indemnify [in'demnifai] vt αποζημιώνω, εξασφαλίζω.

indentation [inden'teiʃən] n (typing) οδόντωσις, δόντιασμα.

independence [indi'pendəns] n ανεξαρτησία.

independent [indi'pendənt] a ανεξάρτητος.

indescribable [indis'kraibəbl] a απερίγραπτος.

index ['indeks] n ευρετήριον ‖ ~ finger n δείκτης.

India ['indiə] n 'Ινδία ‖ ~n n 'Ινδός ‖ (of America) ερυθρόδερμος ‖ a ινδικός, ινδιάνικος.

indicate ['indikeit] vt δεικνύω, εμφαίνω, δηλώ.

indication [indi'keiʃən] n ένδειξις, σημείον.

indicative [in'dikətiv] a (gram) οριστική (έγκλισις).

indicator ['indikeitə*] n (sign) δείκτης.

indict [in'dait] vt μηνύω, ενάγω, καταγγέλλω ‖ ~able a ενακτέος ‖ ~ment n μήνυσις, κατηγορία.

indifference [in'difrəns] n αδιαφορία.

indifferent [in'difrənt] *a* (*not caring*) ἀδιάφορος ‖ (*unimportant*) ἀδιάφορος ‖ (*neither good nor bad*) συνηθισμένος, ἔτσι καί ἔτσι ‖ (*moderate*) μέτριος, οὐδέτερος ‖ (*impartial*) ἀμερόληπτος.

indigenous [in'didʒinəs] *a* γηγενής, ἰθαγενής, ντόπιος.

indigestible [indi'dʒestəbl] *a* δυσκολοχώνευτος.

indigestion [indi'dʒestʃən] *n* δυσπεψία.

indignant [in'dignənt] *a* ἀγανακτισμένος.

indignation [indig'neiʃən] *n* ἀγανάκτησις.

indignity [in'digniti] *n* προσβολή, ταπείνωσις, ὕβρις.

indigo ['indigəu] *n* λουλάκι ‖ *a* ἰνδικόν.

indirect [indi'rekt] *a* πλάγιος, ἔμμεσος ‖ ~ly *ad* ἐμμέσως.

indiscernible [indi'sə:nəbl] *a* δυσδιάκριτος.

indiscreet [indis'kri:t] *a* ἀδιάκριτος, ἀπρόσεκτος.

indiscretion [indis'kreʃən] *n* ἀδιακρισία, ἀκριτομύθια.

indiscriminate [indis'kriminit] *a* χωρίς διακρίσεις, τυφλός.

indispensable [indis'pensəbl] *a* ἀπαραίτητος.

indisposed [indis'pəuzd] *a* ἀδιάθετος, ἀπρόθυμος.

indisposition [indispə'ziʃən] *n* ἀδιαθεσία, ἀπροθυμία.

indisputable [indis'pju:təbl] *a* ἀναμφισβήτητος, ἀναμφίβολος.

indistinct [indis'tiŋkt] *a* ἀδιόρατος, συγκεχυμένος, ἀμυδρός.

indistinguishable [indis'tiŋgwiʃəbl] *a* δυσδιάκριτος, ἀνεπαίσθητος.

individual [indi'vidjuəl] *n* ἄτομον, πρόσωπο ‖ *a* ἰδιαίτερος, ἰδιωτικός, ἀτομικός ‖ ~ist *n* ἀτομικιστής ‖ ~ity *n* ἀτομικότης, προσωπικότης ‖ ~ly *ad* προσωπικῶς, ἀτομικῶς.

indoctrinate [in'dɔktrineit] *vt* διδάσκω, κατηχῶ, ἐμποτίζω.

indoctrination [indɔktri'neiʃən] *n* ἐμποτισμός, διδασκαλία.

indolence ['indələns] *n* νωθρότης, τεμπελιά, βαρεμάρα.

indolent ['indələnt] *a* νωθρός, τεμπέλης.

indoor ['indɔ:*] *a* τοῦ σπιτιοῦ, κατ'οἶκον ‖ ~s *ad* στό σπίτι.

indubitable [in'dju:bitəbl] *a* ἀναμφίβολος, βέβαιος.

induce [in'dju:s] *vt* πείθω, προτρέπω, προκαλῶ ‖ ~ment *n* προτροπή, κίνητρον.

induct [in'dʌkt] *vt* ἐγκαθιστῶ, εἰσάγω, μυῶ.

indulge [in'dʌldʒ] *vt* ἰκανοποιῶ ‖ (*allow pleasure*) ἐντρυφῶ, παραδίδομαι ‖ ~nce *n* ἐπιείκεια, διασκέδασις, ἐντρύφησις ‖ ~nt *a* ἐπιεικής, συγκαταβατικός.

industrial [in'dʌstriəl] *a* βιομηχανικός ‖ ~ist *n* βιομήχανος ‖ ~ize *vt* ἐκβιομηχανίζω.

industrious [in'dʌstriəs] *a* φιλόπονος, ἐπιμελής.

industry ['indəstri] *n* βιομηχανία ‖ (*diligence*) φιλοπονία.

inebriated [i'ni:brieitid] *a* μεθυσμένος.

inedible [in'edibl] *a* ἀκατάλληλος πρός βρῶσιν.

ineffective [ini'fektiv] *a*, **ineffectual** [ini'fektjuəl] *a* ἀτελέσφορος, μάταιος.

inefficiency [ini'fiʃənsi] *n* ἀνικανότης, ἀνεπάρκεια.

inefficient [ini'fiʃənt] *a* ἀνίκανος, ἀτελέσφορος.

inelegant [in'eligənt] *a* ἄκομψος, ἄγαρμπος.

ineligible [in'elidʒəbl] *a* μή ἐκλέξιμος, ἀκατάλληλος.

inept [i'nept] *a* ἄτοπος, ἀνόητος.

inequality [ini'kwɔliti] *n* ἀνισότης.

ineradicable [ini'rædikəbl] *a* ἀξερρίζωτος.

inert [i'nə:t] *a* ἀδρανής.

inertia [i'nə:ʃə] *n* ἀδράνεια.

inescapable [inis'keipəbl] *a* ἀναπόφευκτος.

inessential ['ini'senʃəl] *a* μή ἀπαραίτητος.

inestimable [in'estimabl] *a* ἀνεκτίμητος.

inevitability [inevitə'biliti] *n* (τό) ἀναπόφευκτον.

inevitable [in'evitəbl] *a* ἀναπόφευκτος.

inexact [inig'zækt] *a* ἀνακριβής.

inexcusable [iniks'kju:zəbl] *a* ἀσυγχώρητος.

inexhaustible [inig'zɔ:stəbl] *a* ἀνεξάντλητος.

inexorable [in'eksərəbl] *a* ἀδυσώπητος, ἀμείλικτος.

inexpensive [iniks'pensiv] *a* φθηνός, ἀνέξοδος.

inexperience [iniks'piəriəns] *n* ἀπειρία ‖ ~d *a* ἄπειρος.

inexplicable [iniks'plikəbl] *a* ἀνεξήγητος.

inexpressible [iniks'presəbl] *a* ἀνέκφραστος.

inextricable [iniks'trikəbl] *a* ἀδιέξοδος, ἄλυτος.

infallibility [infælə'biliti] *n* (τό) ἀλάνθαστον.

infallible [in'fæləbl] *a* ἀλάνθαστος, σίγουρος.

infamous ['infəməs] *a* ἐπονείδιστος, κακοήθης.

infamy ['infəmi] *n* ἀτιμία, κακοήθεια.

infancy ['infənsi] *n* νηπιότης ‖ (*early stages*) ἀπαρχαί, πρώτη περίοδος.

infant ['infənt] *n* νήπιον, βρέφος ‖ ~ile *a* παιδικός, παιδιάστικος ‖ ~ school *n* νηπιαγωγεῖον.

infantry ['infəntri] *n* πεζικόν ‖ ~man *n* στρατιώτης, φαντάρος.

infatuated [in'fætjueitid] *a* ξεμυαλισμένος, συνεπαρμένος.

infatuation [infætju'eiʃən] *n* ξεμυάλισμα, τρέλλα.

infect [in'fekt] *vt* μολύνω, μιαίνω, βρωμίζω ‖ (*influence*) ἐπηρεάζω ‖ ~ion *n* μόλυνσις, ἐπίδρασις ‖ ~ious *a* μολυσματικός, μεταδοτικός.

infer [in'fə:*] vt συνάγω, συμπεραίνω, ὑπονοῶ ‖ ~ence ['infərəns] n συμπέρασμα, πόρισμα.

inferior [in'fiəriə*] a κατώτερος, ὑποδεέστερος ‖ n κατώτερος, ὑφιστάμενος ‖ ~ity n κατωτερότης, μειονεκτικότης ‖ ~ity complex n (σύμ)πλέγμα κατωτερότητος.

infernal [in'fə:nl] a καταχθόνιος, διαβολικός, ἀπαίσιος.

inferno [in'fə:nəu] n κόλασις.

infertile [in'fə:tail] a ἄγονος, ἄκαρπος.

infertility [infə:'tiliti] n (τό) ἄγονον, στειρότης.

infest [in'fest] vt λυμαίνομαι, κατακλύζω.

infidel [infidəl] n ἄπιστος.

infidelity [infi'deliti] n ἀπιστία.

infiltrate ['infiltreit] vti (δι)εἰσδύω, εἰσχωρῶ.

infinite ['infinit] a ἄπειρος, ἀπέραντος.

infinitive [in'finitiv] n ἀπαρέμφατον.

infinity [in'finiti] n ἄπειρον, ἀπεραντοσύνη.

infirm [in'fə:m] a ἀσθενής, ἀδύνατος ‖ (irresolute) ἀσταθής, ταλαντευόμενος.

infirmary [in'fə:məri] n νοσοκομεῖον, θεραπευτήριον.

infirmity [in'fə:miti] n ἀδυναμία, ἀναπηρία.

inflame [in'fleim] vt (excite) ἐξάπτω, ἐρεθίζω.

inflammable [in'flæməbl] a εὔφλεκτος.

inflammation [inflə'meiʃən] n φλόγωσις, ἐρεθισμός.

inflate [in'fleit] vt φουσκώνω ‖ (econ) προκαλῶ πληθωρισμόν.

inflation [in'fleiʃən] n πληθωρισμός.

inflexible [in'fleksəbl] a ἄκαμπτος, ἀλύγιστος.

inflict [in'flikt] vt καταφέρω, δίνω, ἐπιβάλλω ‖ ~ion n ἐπιβολή, βάρος, τιμωρία.

inflow [infləu] n εἰσροή.

influence ['influəns] n ἐπίδρασις, ἐπιρροή ‖ vt ἐπηρεάζω, ἐπιδρῶ.

influential [influ'enʃəl] a σημαίνων, μέ ἐπιρροήν.

influenza [influ'enzə] n γρίππη.

influx ['inflaks] n εἰσροή, διείσδυσις.

inform [in'fə:m] vt πληροφορῶ, εἰδοποιῶ.

informal [in'fə:məl] a ἀνεπίσημος, παράτυπος ‖ ~ity n ἀνεπισημότης.

information [infə'meiʃən] n πληροφορίες, εἴδησις.

informative [in'fə:mətiv] a κατατοπιστικός, πληροφοριακός.

informer [in'fə:mə*] n καταδότης, χαφιές.

infrared [infrə'red] a ὑπέρυθρος.

infrequent [in'fri:kwənt] a σπάνιος.

infringe [in'frindʒ] vt παραβαίνω, παραβιάζω ‖ vi καταπατῶ ‖ ~ment n παράβασις.

infuriate [in'fjuərieit] vt ἐξαγριώνω.

infuriating [in'fjuərieitiŋ] a ἐξοργιστικό.

ingenious [in'dʒi:niəs] a ὀξύνους, πολυμήχανος.

ingenuity [indʒi'nju:iti] n εὐφυΐα, ὀξύνοια.

ingot ['iŋgət] n ράβδος, χελώνα.

ingratiate [in'greiʃieit] vt ἀποκτῶ εὔνοιαν.

ingratitude [in'grætitju:d] n ἀγνωμοσύνη.

ingredient [in'gri:diənt] n συστατικόν.

inhabit [in'hæbit] vt κατοικῶ, μένω ‖ ~ant n κάτοικος.

inhale [in'heil] vt εἰσπνέω, ρουφῶ.

inherent [in'hiərənt] a (+ in) συμφυής, ἔμφυτος.

inherit [in'herit] vt κληρονομῶ ‖ ~ance n κληρονομία.

inhibit [in'hibit] vt ἐμποδίζω, ἀναχαιτίζω, ἀπαγορεύω ‖ ~ion n ἀπαγόρευσις, ἀναχαίτισις.

inhospitable [inhɔs'pitəbl] a ἀφιλόξενος.

inhuman [in'hju:mən] a ἀπάνθρωπος.

inimitable [i'nimitəbl] a ἀμίμητος.

iniquity [i'nikwiti] n ἀδικία, κακοήθεια.

initial [i'niʃəl] a ἀρχικός, πρῶτος ‖ n ἀρχικόν ‖ vt μονογράφω ‖ ~ly ad ἀρχικῶς, κατ' ἀρχήν.

initiate [i'niʃieit] vt ἀρχίζω, εἰσάγω ‖ (in a society) μυῶ.

initiation [iniʃi'eiʃən] n μύησις.

initiative [i'niʃətiv] n πρωτοβουλία.

inject [in'dʒekt] vt ἐγχέω, εἰσάγω, κάνω ἔνεσιν ‖ ~ion n ἔγχυσις, ἔνεσις.

injure ['indʒə*] vt βλάπτω, ζημιώνω, πληγώνω.

injury ['indʒəri] n βλάβη, τραῦμα, ζημία.

injustice [in'dʒʌstis] n ἀδικία.

ink [iŋk] n μελάνι.

inkling ['iŋkliŋ] n ὑποψία, ὑπόνοια.

inky ['iŋki] a μελανωμένος, μαῦρος.

inlaid [in'leid] a ἐμπαιστός.

inland ['inlænd] a ἐσωτερικός, μεσόγειος ‖ ad στό ἐσωτερικό, στά ἐνδότερα ‖ ~ revenue n (Brit) φορολογία.

in-laws ['inlɔ:z] npl πεθερικά.

inlet [inlet] n ὁρμίσκος, εἴσοδος.

inmate ['inmeit] n ἔνοικος.

inn [in] n πανδοχεῖον, ξενοδοχεῖον.

innate [i'neit] a ἔμφυτος.

inner ['inə*] a ἐσωτερικός.

innocence ['inəsns] n ἀθωότης, ἀφέλεια.

innocent ['inəsnt] a ἄθωος, ἀγνός, ἀφελής.

innocuous [i'nɔkjuəs] a ἀβλαβής.

innovation [inəu'veiʃən] n καινοτομία, νεωτερισμός.

innuendo [inju'endəu] n ὑπαινιγμός.

innumerable [i'nju:mərəbl] a ἀναρίθμητος.

inoculation [inɔkju'leiʃən] n μπόλιασμα.

inopportune [in'ɔpətju:n] a ἄκαιρος, ἄτοπος.

inordinately [i'nɔ:dinitli] ad ὑπερβολικά.

inorganic [inɔ:'gænik] a ἀνόργανος.

in-patient ['inpeiʃənt] n ἐσωτερικός (ἀσθενής).

input ['input] n εἰσαγωγή.

inquest ['inkwest] n ἀνάκρισις, ἔρευνα.

inquire [in'kwaiə*] vi ρωτῶ, ζητῶ ‖ vt (price) ρωτῶ τήν τιμήν ‖ to ~ into vt ἐρευνῶ, ἐξετάζω.

inquiring [in'kwaiəriŋ] a (*mind*) ἐρευνητικός.

inquiry [in'kwaiəri] n ἐρώτησις ‖ (*search*) ἔρευνα, ἀνάκρισις ‖ ~ **office** n ὑπηρεσία πληροφοριῶν.

inquisitive [in'kwizitiv] a περίεργος, ἀδιάκριτος.

inroad ['inrəud] n εἰσβολή, ἐπιδρομή.

insane [in'sein] a παράφρων, τρελλός.

insanitary [in'sænitəri] a ἀνθυγιεινός.

insanity [in'sæniti] n παραφροσύνη, τρέλλα.

insatiable [in'seiʃəbl] a ἀκόρεστος, ἄπληστος.

inscription [in'skripʃən] n ἐπιγραφή, ἀφιέρωσις.

inscrutable [in'skru:təbl] a ἀνεξιχνίαστος, μυστηριώδης.

insect ['insekt] n ἔντομον, ζουζούνι ‖ ~**icide** n ἐντομοκτόνον.

insecure [insi'kjuə*] a ἐπισφαλής.

insecurity [insi'kjuəriti] n ἀνασφάλεια, (τό) ἐπισφαλές.

insensible [in'sensəbl] a ἀνεπαίσθητος, ἀναίσθητος.

insensitive [in'sensitiv] a ἀναίσθητος, χωρίς ντροπή.

inseparable [in'sepərəbl] a ἀχώριστος, ἀναπόσπαστος.

insert [in'sə:t] vt παρεμβάλλω, καταχωρῶ, εἰσάγω ‖ ['insə:t] n παρεμβολή, ἔνθεμα ‖ ~**ion** n παρεμβολή, καταχώρησις, βάλσιμο.

inshore ['in'ʃɔ:*] a,ad κοντά στὴν ἀκτή.

inside [in'said] n (τό) μέσα, ἐσωτερικόν (μέρος) ‖ a ἐσωτερικός ‖ ad ἐσωτερικά, μέσα ‖ prep ἐντός, μέσα ‖ ~-**forward** n (*sport*) μέσος κυνηγός ‖ ~ **out** ad ἀνάποδα, τό μέσα ἔξω ‖ ~**r** n μεμυημένος, γνώστης.

insidious [in'sidiəs] a ὕπουλος, δόλιος.

insight ['insait] n διορατικότης, ὀξύνοια.

insignificant [insig'nifikənt] a ἀσήμαντος, τιποτένιος.

insincere [insin'siə*] a ἀνειλικρινής.

insincerity [insin'seriti] n ἀνειλικρίνεια.

insinuate [in'sinjueit] vt παρεισάγω, ὑπαινίσσομαι.

insinuation [insinju'eiʃən] n ὑπαινιγμός, παρεισαγωγή.

insipid [in'sipid] a ἀνούσιος, σαχλός.

insist [in'sist] vi (+ *on*) ἐπιμένω, ἐμμένω ‖ ~**ence** n ἐπιμονή ‖ ~**ent** a ἐπίμονος, ἐπείγων.

insolence ['insələns] n ἀναίδεια, θρασύτης.

insolent ['insələnt] a ἀναιδής, θρασύς.

insoluble [in'soljubl] a ἄλυτος, ἀδιάλυτος.

insolvent [in'sɔlvənt] a ἀφερέγγυος, ἀναξιόχρεος.

insomnia [in'sɔmniə] n ἀϋπνία.

inspect [in'spekt] vt ἐπιθεωρῶ, ἐπιτηρῶ, ἐπιβλέπω ‖ ~**ion** n ἐπιθεώρησις,

ἐπιτήρησις ‖ ~**or** n ἐπιθεωρητής ‖ (*rail*) ἐπιστάτης, ἐπόπτης.

inspiration [inspə'reiʃən] n ἔμπνευσις.

inspire [in'spaiə*] vt ἐμπνέω.

inspiring [in'spaiəriŋ] a ἐμπνέων.

instability [instə'biliti] n ἀστάθεια.

install [in'stɔ:l] vt ἐγκαθιστῶ, μοντάρω ‖ (*in office*) ἐγκαθιστῶ ‖ ~**ation** n ἐγκατάστασις, τοποθέτησις.

instalment, (*US*) **installment** [in'stɔ:lmənt] n δόσις, παρτίδα.

instance ['instəns] n περίπτωσις, παράδειγμα ‖ **for** ~ παραδείγματος χάριν.

instant [instənt] n στιγμή ‖ a ἄμεσος, ἐπείγων ‖ ~ **coffee** n καφέ τῆς στιγμῆς ‖ ~**ly** ad ἀμέσως, στή στιγμή.

instead [in'sted] ad ἀντ'αὐτοῦ ‖ ~ **of** ἀντί.

instigation [insti'geiʃən] n παρακίνησις, ὑποκίνησις.

instil [in'stil] vt ἐμποτίζω, βάζω.

instinct ['instiŋkt] n ἔνστικτον, ὁρμέμφυτον ‖ ~**ive** a ἐνστικτώδης ‖ ~**ively** ad ἐνστικτωδῶς.

institute [in'stitju:t] n ἵδρυμα, ἰνστιτοῦτον ‖ vt θεσπίζω, ἱδρύω, ἐγκαθιστῶ.

institution [insti'tju:ʃən] n (*custom*) θεσμός, θέσμιον ‖ (*organization*) ἵδρυμα, ὀργάνωσις ‖ (*beginning*) ἵδρυσις, σύστασις.

instruct [in'strʌkt] vt (*order*) παραγγέλλω, διατάσσω ‖ (*teach*) διδάσκω, μαθαίνω ‖ ~**ion** n διδασκαλία ‖ (*direction*) ὁδηγία ‖ ~**ions** npl ἐντολές, ὁδηγίες ‖ ~**ive** a διδακτικός, ἐνημερωτικός ‖ ~**or** ,n διδάσκαλος, ἐκπαιδευτής ‖ (*US*) ἐπιμελητής.

instrument ['instrumənt] n (*implement*) ἐργαλεῖον, ὄργανον ‖ (*mus*) ὄργανον ‖ ~**al** a ἐνόργανος ‖ (*helpful*) συντελεστικός, συμβάλλων ‖ ~**alist** n ὀργανοπαίκτης ‖ ~ **panel** n ταμπλώ.

insubordinate [insə'bɔ:dənit] a ἀνυπότακτος, ἀνυπάκουος.

insubordination ['insəbɔ:di'neiʃən] n ἀνυπακοή, ἀνυποταξία.

insufferable [in'sʌfərəbl] a ἀνυπόφορος, ἀφόρητος.

insufficient [insə'fiʃənt] a ἀνεπαρκής, λειψός ‖ ~**ly** ad ἀνεπαρκῶς.

insular ['insjələ*] a (*narrow-minded*) μέ στενές ἀντιλήψεις ‖ ~**ity** n στενές ἀντιλήψεις.

insulate ['insjuleit] vt μονώνω ‖ (*set apart*) ἀπομονώνω.

insulating ['insjuleitiŋ] ~ **tape** n μονωτική ταινία.

insulation [insju'leiʃən] n (*elec*) μόνωσις.

insulin ['insjulin] n (*for diabetic*) ἰνσουλίνη.

insult ['insʌlt] n προσβολή, ὕβρις ‖ [in'sʌlt] vt ὑβρίζω, προσβάλλω ‖ ~**ing** a προσβλητικός.

insuperable [in'su:pərəbl] a ἀνυπέρβλητος.

insurance [in'ʃurəns] n ἀσφάλεια ‖ ~

agent n πράκτωρ ἀσφαλειῶν ‖ **~ policy** n ἀσφαλιστήριον.

insure [in'ʃuə*] vt (ἐξ)ἀσφαλίζω.

insurmountable [insə'mauntəbl] a ἀνυπέρβλητος.

insurrection [insə'rekʃən] n ἐπανάστασις, ἐξέγερσις.

intact [in'tækt] a ἄθικτος, ἀπείραχτος.

intake ['inteik] n (mech) εἰσαγωγή.

intangible [in'tændʒəbl] a (difficult) δυσνόητος.

integral ['intigrəl] a (essential) ἀναπόσπαστος ‖ (complete) ὁλοκληρωτικός.

integrate ['intigreit] vti ὁλοκληρώνω.

integration [inti'greiʃən] n ὁλοκλήρωσις.

integrity [in'tegriti] n ἀκεραιότης, ἐντιμότης.

intellect ['intilekt] n διάνοια, νόησις, μυαλό ‖ **~ual** a διανοητικός, πνευματικός ‖ n διανοούμενος.

intelligence [in'telidʒəns] n νοημοσύνη ‖ (information) πληροφορία.

intelligent [in'telidʒənt] a εὐφυής, νοήμων, μυαλωμένος ‖ **~ly** ad εὐφυῶς, ἔξυπνα.

intelligible [in'telidʒəbl] a (κατα)νοητός, καταληπτός.

intemperate [in'tempərit] a ἀκρατής, μέθυσος.

intend [in'tend] vt (mean) προτίθεμαι ‖ **to ~ to do sth** σκοπεύω.

intense [in'tens] a ἔντονος, ἰσχυρός ‖ **~ly** ad ὑπερβολικά, ἐντόνως.

intensify [in'tensifai] vt ἐντείνω, ἐπιτείνω.

intensity [in'tensiti] n ἔντασις, σφοδρότης, ὁρμή.

intensive [in'tensiv] a ἐντατικός ‖ **~ly** ad ἐντόνως, ἐντατικά.

intent [in'tent] n = **intention** ‖ see below ‖ **to all ~s and purposes** οὐσιαστικά, πραγματικά ‖ **~ion** n πρόθεσις ‖ (plan) τελικός σκοπός ‖ **~ional** a σκόπιμος, ἐσκεμμένος ‖ **~ionally** ad ἠθελημένως, σκοπίμως ‖ **~ly** ad προσεκτικά, ἔντονα.

inter [in'tə:*] vt ἐνταφιάζω, θάβω.

inter- ['intə*] prefix διά-, μεσ(ο)-, μεταξύ.

interact [intər'ækt] vi ἀλληλεπιδρῶ ‖ **~ion** n ἀλληλεπίδρασις.

intercede [intə'si:d] vi ἐπεμβαίνω, μεσολαβῶ, μεσιτεύω.

intercept [intə'sept] vt ἀνακόπτω, συλλαμβάνω, πιάνω ‖ **~ion** n σύλληψις, ὑποκλοπή.

interchange ['intə'tʃeindʒ] n (exchange) ἀνταλλαγή ‖ (roads) μεταλλαγή ‖ [intə'tʃeindʒ] vt ἀνταλλάσσω ‖ **~able** a ἀνταλλάξιμος, ἐναλλάξιμος.

intercom ['intəkɔm] n ἐνδοσυνεννόησις.

interconnect [intəkə'nekt] vi ἀλληλοσυνδέω.

intercontinental ['intəkɔnti'nentl] a διηπειρωτικός.

intercourse ['intəkɔ:s] n συναλλαγή, σχέσεις ‖ (sexual) συνουσία, γαμήσι.

interdependence [intədi'pendəns] n ἀλληλεξάρτησις.

interest ['intrist] n (curiosity) ἐνδιαφέρον ‖ (advantage) συμφέρον ‖ (money paid) τόκος ‖ (comm: stake) συμμετοχή, συμμετοχή ‖ vt ἐνδιαφέρω, προσελκύω ‖ **~ed** a ἐνδιαφερόμενος ‖ (attentive) μέ ἐνδιαφέρον ‖ **to be ~ed in** ἐνδιαφέρομαι γιά ‖ **~ing** a ἐνδιαφέρων.

interfere [intə'fiə*] vi ἐπεμβαίνω ‖ (+ with) συγκρούομαι μέ, ἀνακατεύομαι ‖ **~nce** n (general) ἐπέμβασις, ἀνάμιξις ‖ (TV) παράσιτα.

interim ['intərim] a προσωρινός ‖ n: **in the ~** στό μεταξύ.

interior [in'tiəriə*] n ἐσωτερικόν ‖ (inland) ἐνδοχώρα ‖ a ἐσωτερικός.

interjection [intə'dʒekʃən] n (gram) ἐπιφώνημα.

interlock [intə'lɔk] vi συνδέομαι, διασταυρούμαι ‖ vt συνδέω, συμπλέκω.

interloper ['intələupə*] n παρείσακτος.

interlude ['intəlu:d] n διάλειμμα ‖ (theat) ἰντερμέτζο.

intermarriage [intə'mæridʒ] n ἐπιγαμία, ἐπιμιξία.

intermarry ['intə'mæri] vi ἐπιμιγνύομαι.

intermediary [intə'mi:diəri] n μεσάζων, μεσίτης.

intermediate [intə'mi:diət] a μεσολαβῶν, ἐνδιάμεσος.

interminable [in'tə:minəbl] a ἀτελείωτος.

intermission [intə'miʃən] n διάλειμμα, διακοπή.

intermittent [intə'mitənt] a διαλείπων ‖ **~ly** ad διακεκομμένα.

intern [in'tə:n] vt θέτω ὑπό περιορισμόν ‖ ['intə:n] n (US) ἐσωτερικός ἰατρός.

internal [in'tə:nl] a ἐσωτερικός ‖ **~ly** ad (med) ἐσωτερικῶς ‖ **~ revenue** n (US) φορολογία.

international [intə'næʃnəl] a διεθνής ‖ n (sport) διεθνής (παίκτης).

internment [in'tə:nmənt] n ἐγκάθειρξις, περιορισμός.

interplanetary [intə'plænitəri] a διαπλανητικός.

interplay ['intəplei] n ἀλληλεπίδρασις.

Interpol ['intəpɔl] n Ἰντερπόλ.

interpret [in'tə:prit] vt ἐξηγῶ ‖ (translate) μεταφράζω ‖ (theat) ἑρμηνεύω ‖ **~ation** n ἑρμηνεία, ἐξήγησις ‖ **~er** n διερμηνεύς.

interrelated [intəri'leitid] a ἀλληλένδετος.

interrogate [in'terəgeit] vt ἐρωτῶ, ἀνακρίνω.

interrogation [interə'geiʃən] n ἀνάκρισις, ἐξέτασις.

interrogative [intə'rɔgətiv] a ἐρωτηματικός.

interrogator [in'terəgeitə*] n ἀνακριτής.

interrupt [intə'rʌpt] vt διακόπτω, ἐμποδίζω ‖ **~ion** n διακοπή.

intersect [intə'sekt] vt τέμνω, διακόπτω,

κόβω ‖ *vi* (*roads*) διασταυρούμαι ‖ **~ion** *n* (*roads*) διασταύρωσις, σταυροδρόμι.

intersperse [intə'spəːs] *vt* διασπείρω, αναμιγνύω.

interval ['intəvəl] *n* διάλειμμα, διάστημα ‖ (*mus*) διάστημα ‖ **at ~s** κατά διαστήματα.

intervene [intə'viːn] *vi* μεσολαβώ, παρεμβαίνω, επεμβαίνω.

intervening [intə'viːniŋ] *a* παρεμβαίνων, μεσολαβών.

intervention [intə'venʃən] *n* μεσολάβησις, παρέμβασις.

interview ['intəvjuː] *n* (*press etc*) συνέντευξις ‖ (*for job*) συνάντησις, ραντεβού ‖ *vt* παίρνω συνέντευξιν ‖ **~er** *n* ο λαμβάνων συνέντευξιν.

intestate [in'testit] *a* χωρίς διαθήκην.

intestinal [intes'tainl] *a* εντερικός.

intestine [in'testin] *n* έντερον.

intimacy ['intiməsi] *n* οικειότης ‖ (*sexual*) συνουσία.

intimate ['intimit] *a* ενδόμυχος, ιδιαίτερος ‖ (*familiar*) οικείος, στενός ‖ ['intimeit] *vt* υποδηλώ, εκδηλώνω, υπαινίσσομαι ‖ **~ly** *ad* στενά, κατά βάθος.

intimidate [in'timideit] *vt* (εκ)φοβίζω, φοβερίζω.

intimidation [intimi'deiʃən] *n* εκφοβισμός.

into ['intu] *prep* (*movement*) εις, εντός, μέσα ‖ (*change*) εις.

intolerable [in'tɔlərəbl] *a* ανυπόφορος, αφόρητος.

intolerance [in'tɔlərəns] *n* μισαλλοδοξία.

intolerant [in'tɔlərənt] *a* μισαλλόδοξος, αδιάλλακτος.

intonation [intəu'neiʃən] *n* διακύμανσις της φωνής.

intoxicate [in'tɔksikeit] *vt* μεθώ, ζαλίζω ‖ **~d** *a* μεθυσμένος.

intoxication [intɔksi'keiʃən] *n* μεθύσι, παραζάλη.

intractable [in'træktəbl] *a* ανυπάκουος, ατίθασος.

intransigent [in'trænsidʒənt] *a* αδιάλλακτος.

intransitive [in'trænsitiv] *a* αμετάβατος.

intravenous [intrə'viːnəs] *a* ενδοφλέβιος.

intrepid [in'trepid] *a* ατρόμητος, άφοβος.

intricacy ['intrikəsi] *n* περιπλοκή, (τό) περίπλοκον.

intricate ['intrikit] *a* περίπλοκος ‖ (*of thoughts*) συγκεχυμένος.

intrigue [in'triːg] *n* μηχανορραφία ‖ *vt* (*make curious*) προσελκύω, μαγεύω.

intriguing [in'triːgiŋ] *a* (*fascinating*) περίεργος, μυστηριώδης.

intrinsic [in'trinsik] *a* ουσιαστικός, πραγματικός.

introduce [intrə'djuːs] *vt* (*person*) συνιστώ, συστήνω ‖ (*sth new*) παρουσιάζω, μπάζω ‖ (*subject*) εισάγω.

introduction [intrə'dʌkʃən] *n* παρουσίασις, σύστασις ‖ (*book*) εισαγωγή, πρόλογος.

introductory [intrə'dʌktəri] *a* εισαγωγικός.

introspective [intrəu'spektiv] *a* ενδοσκοπικός.

introvert ['intrəuvəːt] *a,n* ενδόστροφος.

intrude [in'truːd] *vi* (+ *on*) επιβάλλω, επεμβαίνω ‖ **~r** *n* παρείσακτος.

intrusion [in'truːʒən] *n* επέμβασις, διείσδυσις.

intrusive [in'truːsiv] *a* παρείσακτος, ενοχλητικός.

intuition [intjuː'iʃən] *n* διαίσθησις, ενόρασις.

intuitive [in'tjuːitiv] *a* διαισθητικός, ενστικτώδης ‖ **~ly** *ad* ενστικτωδώς.

inundate ['inʌndeit] *vt* (*fig*) κατακλύζω, πλημμυρίζω.

invade [in'veid] *vt* εισβάλλω, καταπατώ ‖ **~r** *n* επιδρομεύς, εισβολεύς.

invalid ['invəlid] *n* ασθενής, ανάπηρος ‖ [in'vælid] *a* (*not valid*) άκυρος ‖ **~ate** *vt* ακυρώνω, αναιρώ.

invaluable [in'væljuəbl] *a* ανεκτίμητος.

invariable [in'veəriəbl] *a* αμετάβλητος.

invariably [in'veəriəbli] *ad* αμεταβλήτως.

invasion [in'veiʒən] *n* εισβολή, επιδρομή.

invective [in'vektiv] *n* βρισιά, λοιδωρία.

invent [in'vent] *vt* εφευρίσκω ‖ (*make up*) πλάθω ‖ **~ion** *n* εφεύρεσις ‖ **~ive** *a* εφευρετικός, δημιουργικός ‖ **~iveness** *n* εφευρετικότης ‖ **~or** *n* εφευρέτης.

inventory ['invəntri] *n* απογραφή, κατάλογος.

inverse ['invəːs] *n* αντίστροφος, ανάστροφος ‖ **~ly** *ad* αντιστρόφως.

invert [in'vəːt] *vt* αντιστρέφω ‖ **~ed commas** *npl* εισαγωγικά.

invertebrate [in'vəːtibrit] *n* ασπόνδυλον.

invest [in'vest] *vt* (*econ*) επενδύω ‖ (*control*) παρέχω, αναθέτω.

investigate [in'vestigeit] *vt* ερευνώ, εξετάζω.

investigation [investi'geiʃən] *n* έρευνα, εξέτασις.

investigator [in'vestigeitə*] *n* ερευνητής, αναζητητής.

investiture [in'vestitʃə*] *n* εγκαθίδρυσις.

investment [in'vestmənt] *n* επένδυσις.

investor [in'vestə*] *n* κεφαλαιούχος, επενδύτης.

inveterate [in'vetərit] *a* (*habitual*) φανατικός, αδιόρθωτος.

invigorating [in'vigəreitiŋ] *a* αναζωογονητικός, τονωτικός.

invincible [in'vinsəbl] *a* αήττητος.

inviolate [in'vaiəlit] *a* απαραβίαστος, απαράβατος.

invisible [in'vizəbl] *a* (*general*) αόρατος, άδηλος ‖ (*ink*) συμπαθητική μελάνι.

invitation [invi'teiʃən] *n* πρόσκλησις.

invite [in'vait] *vt* (προσ)καλώ ‖ (*attract*) ελκύω, προκαλώ.

inviting [in'vaitiŋ] *a* δελεαστικός, ελκυστικός.

invoice ['invɔis] *n* τιμολόγιον ‖ *vt* τιμολογῶ.

invoke [in'vəuk] *vt* ἐπικαλοῦμαι, ἀπαιτῶ.

involuntarily [in'vɔləntərili] *ad* ἀκουσίως, ἀθέλητα.

involuntary [in'vɔləntəri] *a* ἀκούσιος, ἀθέλητα.

involve [in'vɔlv] *vt (include)* συνεπάγομαι ‖ *(entangle)* (περι)πλέκω, ἀνακατώνω ‖ ~d *a* περιπεπλεγμένος ‖ ~ment *n* ἀνάμιξις, μπλέξιμο.

invulnerable [in'vʌlnərəbl] *a* ἄτρωτος.

inward ['inwəd] *a* ἐσωτερικός, πρός τά μέσα ‖ ~(s) *ad* πρός τά ἔσω ‖ ~ly *ad* ἐσωτερικῶς, μέσα.

iodine ['aiədi:n] *n* ἰώδιον.

iota [ai'əutə] *n (fig)* γιώτα, τίποτε, ἐλάχιστη ποσότης.

Iran [i'ra:n] *n* Ἰράν, Περσία.

Iraq [i'ra:k] *n* Ἰράκ.

irascible [i'ræsibl] *a* εὐέξαπτος, ὀξύθυμος.

irate [ai'reit] *a* θυμωμένος, ἐξηγριωμένος.

Ireland ['aiələnd] *n* Ἰρλανδία.

iris ['aiəris] *n (anat)* ἴρις ‖ *(bot)* ἴρις, ρίδι.

Irish ['aiəriʃ] *a* Ἰρλανδικός ‖ **the** ~ *npl* οἱ Ἰρλανδοί ‖ ~ **man** *n* Ἰρλανδός ‖ ~ **woman** *n* Ἰρλανδή.

irk [ə:k] *vt* ἐνοχλῶ, στενοχωρῶ.

iron ['aiən] *n* σίδηρος ‖ *(flat iron)* σίδερο ‖ *(golf club)* ρόπαλον τοῦ γκόλφ ‖ *a* σιδερένιος ‖ *vt* σιδερώνω ‖ ~**s** *npl (chains)* ἁλυσίδες, δεσμά ‖ **to** ~ **out** *vt (crease)* σιδερώνω ‖ *(difficulties)* ἐξομαλύνω ‖ ~ **curtain** *n* σιδηροῦν παραπέτασμα.

ironic(al) [ai'rɔnik(əl)] *a* εἰρωνικός ‖ ~ **ally** *ad* εἰρωνικά.

ironing ['aiəniŋ] *n* σιδέρωμα ‖ ~ **board** *n* σιδερώστρα, τάβλα.

ironmonger ['aiənmʌŋgə*] *n* σιδηροπώλης ‖ ~'s **(shop)** *n* σιδηροπωλείο.

iron ore ['aiənɔ:*] *n* σιδηρομετάλλευμα.

ironworks ['aiənwə:ks] *n* σιδηρουργεῖον.

irony ['aiərəni] *n* εἰρωνεία.

irrational [i'ræʃənl] *a* παράλογος.

irreconcilable [irekən'sailəbl] *a* ἀδιάλλακτος, ἀσυμβίβαστος.

irredeemable [iri'di:məbl] *a (comm)* ἀνεξαγόραστος.

irrefutable [iri'fju:təbl] *a* ἀκαταμάχητος, ἀδιάψευστος.

irregular [i'regjulə*] *a (not regular)* ἀκανόνιστος, ἄτακτος ‖ *(not smooth)* ἀνώμαλος ‖ *(against rule)* ἀντικανονικός, ἀντίθετος ‖ ~ **ity** *n* ἀνωμαλία.

irrelevance [i'reləvəns] *n* (τό) ἄσχετον.

irrelevant [i'reləvənt] *a* ἄσχετος, ξεκάρφωτος.

irreligious [iri'lidʒəs] *a* ἄθρησκος, ἀσεβής.

irreparable [i'repərəbl] *a* ἀνεπανόρθωτος, ἀγιάτρευτος.

irreplaceable [iri'pleisəbl] *a* ἀναντικατάστατος.

irrepressible [iri'presəbl] *a* ἀκατάσχετος, ἀκάθεκτος.

irreproachable [iri'prəutʃəbl] *a* ἄμεμπτος, ἄψογος.

irresistible [iri'zistəbl] *a* ἀσυγκράτητος, ἀκαταμάχητος.

irresolute [i'rezəlu:t] *a* ἀναποφάσιστος, διστακτικός.

irrespective [iri'spektiv] ~ **of** *prep* ἀνεξάρτητα ἀπό.

irresponsibility ['irispɔnsə'biliti] *n* (τό) ἀνεύθυνον, ἀμυαλιά.

irresponsible [iris'pɔnsəbl] *a* ἀπερίσκεπτος, ἐλαφρόμυαλος.

irretrievably [iri'tri:vəbli] *ad* ἀνεπανορθώτως, ὁριστικά.

irreverence [i'revərəns] *n* ἀνευλάβεια, ἀσέβεια.

irreverent [i'revərənt] *a* ἀσεβής, ἀναιδής.

irrevocable [i'revəkəbl] *a* ἀμετάκλητος, ἀνέκκλητος.

irrigate [i'rigeit] *vt* ἀρδεύω, ποτίζω.

irrigation [iri'geiʃən] *n* ἄρδευσις, πότισμα.

irritability [iritə'biliti] *n* ὀξυθυμία, (τό) εὐέξαπτον.

irritable ['iritəbl] *a* ὀξύθυμος, εὐέξαπτος.

irritant ['iritənt] *n* ἐρεθιστικόν.

irritate ['iriteit] *vt (annoy)* (ἐξ)ἐρεθίζω, ἐκνευρίζω ‖ *(skin etc)* ἐρεθίζω.

irritating ['iriteitiŋ] *a* ἐρεθιστικός, ἐκνευριστικός.

irritation [iri'teiʃən] *n* ἐρεθισμός, θυμός.

is [iz] *see* be.

Islam ['izla:m] *n* Ἰσλάμ.

island ['ailənd] *n* νησί ‖ ~**er** *n* νησιώτης.

isle [ail] *n* νησίς, νησάκι.

isn't ['iznt] = **is not** ‖ *see* be.

isobar ['aisəuba:*] *n* ἰσοβαρής.

isolate ['aisəuleit] *vt* (ἀπο)μονώνω ‖ ~**d** *a* ἀπομονωμένος, ἀπόμερος.

isolation [aisəu'leiʃən] *n* ἀπομόνωσις.

isotope ['aisəutəup] *n* ἰσότοπον.

Israel ['izreil] *n* Ἰσραήλ ‖ ~**i** *n* Ἰσραηλινός.

issue ['iʃu:] *n (question)* ὑπόθεσις, ζήτημα ‖ *(giving out)* ἔκδοσις, διανομή, χορήγησις ‖ *(copy)* τεῦχος, φύλλον ‖ *(offspring)* ἀπόγονοι ‖ *vt (rations)* διανέμω ‖ *(orders)* ἐκδίδω, δημοσιεύω ‖ *(equipment)* διανέμω, ἐκδίδω ‖ *a* ὑπό συζήτησιν.

isthmus ['isməs] *n* ἰσθμός.

it [it] *pron* τόν, τήν, τό, αὐτό.

Italian [i'tæliən] *a* ἰταλικός ‖ *n (person)* Ἰταλός ‖ *(ling)* ἰταλικά.

italic [i'tælik] *a* κυρτός, πλάγιος ‖ ~**s** *npl* πλαγία γραφή.

Italy ['itəli] *n* Ἰταλία.

itch [itʃ] *n (fig)* πόθος, ὄρεξι ‖ *(med)* φαγούρα, ψώρα ‖ *vi* ἔχω φαγούρα ‖ ~**ing** *n* φαγούρα.

it'd ['itd] = **it would, it had** ‖ *see* would, have.

item ['aitəm] *n (on list)* εἶδος, κονδύλιον,

ἐγγραφή ‖ (in programme) νούμερο ‖ (in agenda) θέμα ‖ (in newspaper) εἴδησις ‖ ~ize vt ἀναλύω.
itinerant [i'tinərənt] a περιοδεύων.
itinerary [ai'tinərəri] n δρομολόγιον.
it'll ['itl] = it will, it shall ‖ see will, shall.
its [its] poss a του ‖ poss pron ἰδικός του.
it's [its] = it is, it has ‖ see be, have.
itself [it'self] pron τόν ἑαυτόν του.
I've [aiv] = I have ‖ see have.
ivory ['aivəri] n ἐλεφαντοστοῦν ‖ ~ tower n (fig) τόπος μονώσεως.
ivy ['aivi] n κισσός.

J, j

jab [dʒæb] vti κτυπῶ, κεντῶ, μπήζω.
jabber ['dʒæbə*] vi φλυαρῶ, τραυλίζω.
jack [dʒæk] n (mech) γρύλλος ‖ (cards) βαλές, φάντης ‖ to ~ up vt σηκώνω μέ γρύλλο.
jackdaw ['dʒækdɔː] n κολοιός, καλιακούδα.
jacket ['dʒækit] n ζακέττα, σακκάκι ‖ (mech) χιτώνιον, πουκάμισο.
jack-knife ['dʒæknaif] n μεγάλος σουγιᾶς, κολοκοτρώνης.
jade [dʒeid] n (stone) νεφρίτης.
jaded ['dʒeidid] a κουρασμένος, τσακισμένος.
jagged ['dʒægid] a ἀνώμαλος, ὀδοντωτός, μυτερός.
jail [dʒeil] n φυλακή ‖ ~ break n δραπέτευσις ‖ ~er n δεσμοφύλαξ.
jam [dʒæm] n (fruit) μαρμελάδα ‖ (stoppage) ἐμπλοκή, φρακάρισμα, στρίμωγμα ‖ vt ἐνσφηνώνω, σφίγγω, στριμώχνω ‖ vi σφίγγομαι, φρακάρω, κολλῶ.
jangle ['dʒæŋgl] vti ἠχῶ κακόηχα, κουδουνίζω.
janitor ['dʒænitə*] n (caretaker) θυρωρός, ἐπιστάτης.
January ['dʒænjuəri] n Γενάρης.
Japan [dʒə'pæn] n Ἰαπωνία ‖ ~ese a Ἰαπωνικός ‖ n (ling) ἰαπωνική.
jar [dʒɑː*] n (glass) βάζο, λαγήνι, στάμνα ‖ vi τραντάζω, συγκρούομαι.
jargon ['dʒɑːgən] n ἀλαμπουρνέζικα.
jarring ['dʒɑːriŋ] a (sound) κακόηχος, σοκάρων, ἐνοχλητικός.
jasmin(e) ['dʒæzmin] n γιασεμί.
jaundice ['dʒɔːndis] n ἴκτερος, χρυσή ‖ ~d a (attitude) κακόβουλος, φθονερός.
jaunt [dʒɔːnt] n βόλτα, περίπατος ‖ ~y a ζωηρός, ξένοιαστος.
javelin ['dʒævlin] n ἀκόντιον, κοντάρι.
jaw [dʒɔː] n σαγόνι, μασέλα ‖ ~s npl (fig) στόμα.
jazz [dʒæz] n τζάζ ‖ to ~ up vt ζωηρεύω, ἐπιταχύνω ‖ ~ band n τζάζ-μπάντ.
jealous ['dʒeləs] a (envious) ζηλιάρης ‖ (watchful) ζηλότυπος, προσεκτικός ‖

~ly ad ζηλοτύπως, ἐπιμελῶς ‖ ~y n ζήλεια.
jeans [dʒiːnz] npl ντρίλινο παντελόνι.
jeep [dʒiːp] n τζίπ.
jeer [dʒiə*] vi (+ at) κοροϊδεύω, χλευάζω, γιουχαΐζω ‖ n ἐμπαιγμός, γιούχα ‖ ~ing a σκωπτικός.
jelly ['dʒeli] n ζελέ(ς) ‖ ~fish n μέδουσα, τσούχτρα.
jeopardize ['dʒepədaiz] vt διακινδυνεύω.
jeopardy ['dʒepədi] n: in ~ ἐν κινδύνω.
jerk [dʒəːk] n τίναγμα,· τράνταγμα ‖ (US: idiot) χαζός ‖ vti τινάζω, τραντάζω.
jerkin ['dʒəːkin] n πέτσινο σακκάκι.
jerky ['dʒəːki] a ἀπότομος, κοφτός.
jersey ['dʒəːzi] n φανέλλα.
jest [dʒest] n ἀστεϊσμός, χωρατό, ἀστεῖο ‖ vi κάνω ἀστεῖα, ἀστειεύομαι.
jet [dʒet] n (stream) ἐκροή, ἀναπήδησις ‖ (spout) στόμιον, μπέκ ‖ (aviat) τζέτ ‖ ~-black a κατάμαυρος ‖ ~ engine n κινητήρ τζέτ.
jettison ['dʒetisn] vt ἀπορρίπτω.
jetty ['dʒeti] n μῶλος, λιμενοβραχίων.
Jew [dʒuː] n Ἑβραῖος.
jewel ['dʒuːəl] n κόσμημα ‖ (fig) διαμάντι, χρυσός ‖ ~ler, (US) ~er n κοσμηματοπώλης ‖ ~(l)er's (shop) n κοσμηματοπωλεῖον ‖ ~(le)ry n κοσμήματα, διαμαντικά.
Jewess ['dʒuːis] n Ἑβραία.
Jewish ['dʒuːiʃ] a ἑβραϊκός.
jib [dʒib] n (naut) ἀρτέμων, φλόκος ‖ vi ἀρνοῦμαι, κωλώνω, κλωτσῶ.
jibe [dʒaib] n πείραγμα, ἀστεῖο.
jiffy ['dʒifi] n (col) in a ~ στή στιγμή, ἀμέσως.
jigsaw ['dʒigsɔː] n (also ~ puzzle) (παιχνίδι) συναρμολογήσεως.
jilt [dʒilt] vt διώχνω, στρίβω.
jingle ['dʒiŋgl] n κουδούνισμα, γκλίνγκλίν ‖ vi κουδουνίζω.
jinx [dʒiŋks] n (col) γρουσούζης.
jitters ['dʒitəz] npl (col) to get the ~ τρέμω, φοβᾶμε.
jittery ['dʒitəri] a (col) φοβιτσιάρικος, ἐκνευριστικός.
jiujitsu [dʒuː'dʒitsuː] n ζίου-ζίτσου.
job [dʒɔb] n ἔργον, ἐργασία ‖ (position) θέσις, δουλειά ‖ (difficult task) ἀγγαρεία, χαμαλήκι ‖ ~bing a μέ τό κομμάτι, κατ' ἀποκοπήν ‖ ~less a ἄνεργος.
jockey ['dʒɔki] n τζόκεϋ ‖ vi ἑλίσσομαι, μανουβράρω.
jocular ['dʒɔkjulə*] a ἀστεῖος, εὔθυμος.
jog [dʒɔg] vt σπρώχνω, σκουντῶ ‖ vi (move jerkily) κλυδωνίζω, τραντάζω.
john [dʒɔn] n (US col: loo) ἀποχωρητήριον.
join [dʒɔin] vt (fasten) ἑνώνω, συνδέω, ματίζω ‖ (club) ἐγγράφομαι, γίνομαι μέλος ‖ vi (the army) κατατάσσομαι ‖ n ἕνωσις, ραφή ‖ ~er n μαραγκός ‖ ~ery n ξυλουργική ‖ ~t n (tech) ἁρμός,

ἄρθρωσις ‖ (*of meat*) τεμάχιον κρέατος ‖ (*col: place*) καταγώγιον, τρώγλη ‖ ~**tly** *ad* ὁμοῦ, μαζί.
joist [dʒɔist] *n* δοκάρι, πατερό.
joke [dʒəuk] *n* ἀστεῖο, χωρατό, καλαμπούρι ‖ *vi* ἀστείζομαι ‖ ~**r** *n* ἀστειολόγος ‖ (*cards*) μπαλλαντέρ.
joking [ˈdʒəukiŋ] *a* ἀστεῖος, ἀστιευόμενος ‖ ~**ly** *ad* ἀστεῖα.
jollity [ˈdʒɔliti] *n* εὐθυμία, χαρά, γιορτή.
jolly [ˈdʒɔli] *a* εὔθυμος, χαρούμενος, κεφάτος ‖ *ad* (*col*) ἐξαιρετικά, πολύ ‖ **to** ~ **s.o. along** διασκεδάζω κάποιον.
jolt [dʒəult] *n* τίναγμα, τράνταγμα ‖ (*col*) ξάφνιασμα ‖ *vt* τινάζω, κουνῶ.
jostle [ˈdʒɔsl] *vi* σπρώχνω.
jot [dʒɔt] *n*: **not one** ~ οὔτε ἴχνος, οὐδέ κατά κεραίαν ‖ **to** ~ **down** *vt* σημειώνω, γράφω ‖ ~**ter** *n* σημειωματάριον.
journal [ˈdʒəːnl] *n* ἐφημερίδα, περιοδικόν ‖ ~**ese** *n* δημοσιογραφικόν ὕφος ‖ ~**ism** *n* δημοσιογραφία ‖ ~**ist** *n* δημοσιογράφος.
journey [ˈdʒəːni] *n* ταξίδι, διαδρομή.
jovial [ˈdʒəuviəl] *a* εὔθυμος, κεφάτος, φαιδρός.
joy [dʒɔi] *n* χαρά, εὐθυμία ‖ ~**ful** *a* περιχαρής, χαρμόσυνος ‖ ~**fully** *ad* χαρούμενα ‖ ~**ous** *a* εὔθυμος ‖ ~ **ride** *n* περίπατος μέ αὐτοκίνητο.
jubilant [ˈdʒuːbilənt] *a* χαρούμενος, πανηγυρίζων.
jubilation [dʒuːbiˈleiʃən] *n* ἀγαλλίασις, χαρά.
jubilee [ˈdʒuːbiliː] *n* γιορτή.
judge [dʒʌdʒ] *n* (*in court*) δικαστής ‖ (*race-track*) κριτής ‖ (*in dispute*) πραγματογνώμων, κριτής ‖ *vt* δικάζω, κρίνω ‖ *vi* (*estimate*) ὑπολογίζω, θεωρῶ ‖ ~**ment**, **judgment** *n* (*sentence*) δικαστική ἀπόφασις ‖ (*opinion*) κρίσις, γνώμη.
judicial [dʒuːˈdiʃəl] *a* (*law*) δικαστικός ‖ (*discerning*) κριτικός, δίκαιος.
judicious [dʒuːˈdiʃəs] *a* συνετός, σώφρων, φρόνιμος.
judo [ˈdʒuːdəu] *n* τζούντο.
jug [dʒʌg] *n* κανάτι, στάμνα.
juggle [ˈdʒʌgl] *vi* ταχυδακτυλουργῶ, ἐξαπατῶ ‖ ~**r** *n* ταχυδακτυλουργός.
Jugoslav [ˈjuːgəuˈslaːv] = **Yugoslav**.
jugular [ˈdʒʌgjulə*] *a* (*vein*) σφαγῖτις.
juice [dʒuːs] *n* χυμός, ζουμί.
juiciness [ˈdʒuːsinis] *n* ζουμεράδα.
juicy [ˈdʒuːsi] *a* χυμώδης, ζουμερός.
jukebox [ˈdʒuːkbɔks] *n* τζούκ μπόξ.
July [dʒuːˈlai] *n* Ἰούλιος.
jumble [ˈdʒʌmbl] *n* ἀνακάτεμα, κυκεών, μπέρδεμα ‖ *vt* (*also* ~ **up**) ἀνακατεύω, μπερδεύω.
jumbo [ˈdʒʌmbəu] *attr*: ~ **jet** *n* τζάμπο τζέτ.
jump [dʒʌmp] *vi* πηδῶ ‖ *vt* πηδῶ πάνω ἀπό, ὑπερπηδῶ ‖ *n* πήδημα, ἅλμα ‖ ~**ed-up** *a* (*col*) νεόπλουτος ‖ ~**er** *n* μπλούζα,

ριχτή ζακέττα ‖ ~**y** *a* νευρικός.
junction [ˈdʒʌŋkʃən] *n* (*road*) διασταύρωσις ‖ (*rail*) διακλάδωσις.
juncture [ˈdʒʌŋktʃə*] *n*: **at this** ~ στό σημείο αὐτό.
June [dʒuːn] *n* Ἰούνιος.
jungle [ˈdʒʌŋgl] *n* (*tropical*) ζούγκλα.
junior [ˈdʒuːniə*] *a* (*in age*) νεώτερος ‖ (*in rank*) κατώτερος, ὑφιστάμενος ‖ *n* (*US: school*) προτελειόφοιτος.
junk [dʒʌŋk] *n* (*rubbish*) σκουπίδια, παλιοπράγματα ‖ (*ship*) τζόγκα ‖ ~**shop** *n* παλιατζίδικο.
junta [ˈdʒʌntə] *n* χούντα.
jurisdiction [dʒuərisˈdikʃən] *n* δικαιοδοσία.
jurisprudence [dʒuərisˈpruːdəns] *n* νομολογία, νομομάθεια.
juror [ˈdʒuərə*] *n* ἔνορκος.
jury [ˈdʒuəri] *n* ἔνορκοι ‖ (*of contest*) κριτική ἐπιτροπή ‖ ~**man** *n* = **juror**.
just [dʒʌst] *a* (*fair, right*) δίκαιος, σωστός ‖ (*exact*) ἀκριβής ‖ *ad* (*exactly*) ἀκριβῶς ‖ (*barely*) μόλις ‖ ~ **as I arrived** μόλις ἔφθασα ‖ **I have** ~ **arrived** μόλις ἦλθα ‖ ~ **a little** τόσο δά, ὀλίγο ‖ ~ **now** πρό ὀλίγου, μόλις τώρα ‖ ~ **you and me** ἐμεῖς μόνον, σύ κι᾽ἐγώ.
justice [ˈdʒʌstis] *n* (*fairness*) δικαιοσύνη ‖ (*magistrate*) δικαστικός, δικαστής.
justifiable [ˈdʒʌstifaiəbl] *a* δικαιολογήσιμος, εὔλογος.
justifiably [ˈdʒʌstifaiəbli] *ad* δικαιολογημένα.
justification [dʒʌstifiˈkeiʃən] *n* δικαίωσις, δικαιολογία.
justify [ˈdʒʌstifai] *vt* (*prove right*) αἰτιολογῶ ‖ (*defend etc*) δικαιώνω, δικαιολογῶ.
justly [ˈdʒʌstli] *ad* δίκαια, ὀρθῶς.
justness [ˈdʒʌstnis] *n* ὀρθότης, τό δίκαιον.
jut [dʒʌt] *vi* (*also* ~ **out**) προεξέχω.
juvenile [ˈdʒuːvənail] *a* νεανικός, παιδικός ‖ *n* νέος, νεανίας.
juxtapose [ˈdʒʌkstəpəuz] *vt* (ἀντι)παραθέτω.
juxtaposition [dʒʌkstəpəˈziʃən] *n* (ἀντι)παράθεσις.

K, k

kaleidoscope [kəˈlaidəskəup] *n* καλειδοσκόπιον.
kangaroo [kæŋgəˈruː] *n* καγκουρώ.
keel [kiːl] *n* τρόπις, καρίνα.
keen [kiːn] *a* ζωηρός, ἐπιμελής, θερμός ‖ ~**ly** *ad* ἔντονα, βαθειά, σφόδρα ‖ ~**ness** *n* ζῆλος, ἐνθουσιασμός.
keep [kiːp] (*irreg v*) *vt* (*have*) ἔχω, κρατῶ, συντηρῶ ‖ (*take care of*) φυλάω, συντηρῶ, τρέφω ‖ (*detain*) (κατα)κρατῶ, καθυστερῶ ‖ (*be faithful*) τηρῶ, σέβομαι, μένω πιστός εἰς ‖ *vi* (*continue*) συνεχίζω, ἐξακολουθῶ ‖ (*of food*) διατηροῦμαι,

J

K

κρατῶ ‖ (*remain: quiet etc*) μένω, στέκομαι ‖ *n* τροφή, συντήρησις, ἔξοδα συντηρήσεως ‖ (*tower*) (ἀκρό)πύργος ‖ **to ~ back** *vti* κρατῶ πίσω, ἀπομακρύνομαι, κρύπτω ‖ **to ~ on** *vi* συνεχίζω, ἐξακολουθῶ νά φορῶ ‖ **to ~ out** *vt* μένω ἔξω, ἀπέχω ‖ ' ~ out!' 'ἀπαγορεύεται ἡ εἴσοδος!' ‖ **to ~ up** *vi* (+ *with*) διατηρῶ, καλλιεργῶ ‖ ~ing *n* (*care*) φύλαξις, συντήρησις ‖ **in** ~ing **with** σύμφωνος μέ, ἀνάλογα μέ.

keg [keg] *n* βαρελάκι.

kennel ['kenl] *n* σπιτάκι σκύλου.

kept [kept] *pt,pp of* **keep.**

kerb(stone) ['kɜːb(stəun)] *n* κράσπεδον πεζοδρομίου.

kernel ['kɜːnl] *n* πυρήν, κόκκος, ψύχα.

kerosene ['kerəsiːn] *n* φωτιστικόν πετρέλαιον, παραφίνη.

kestrel ['kestrəl] *n* γεράκι, κιρκινέζι.

ketchup ['ketʃəp] *n* κετσάπ, σάλτσα τομάτας.

kettle ['ketl] *n* χύτρα, τσαγιέρα ‖ ~drum *n* εἶδος τυμπάνου.

key [kiː] *n* κλειδί ‖ (*of problem*) κλείς ‖ (*set of answers*) κλείς, λύσις ‖ (*lever*) πλῆκτρον ‖ (*mus*) τόνος ‖ *a* (*position etc*) βασικός, καίριος ‖ ~board *n* πλῆκτρον, κλαβιέ ‖ ~hole *n* κλειδαρότρυπα ‖ ~note *n* κυρία ἰδέα, γνώμων ‖ ~ring *n* κρίκος κλειδιῶν.

khaki ['kɑːki] *n,a* χακί.

kibbutz [ki'buts] *n* κιμπούτς.

kick [kik] *vt* λακτίζω, κλωτσῶ ‖ *vi* (*col*) παραπονιέμαι, ἀντιδρῶ ‖ *n* λάκτισμα, κλωτσιά ‖ (*thrill*) συγκίνησις ‖ **to ~ around** *vi* (*col*) σέρνομαι, χαζεύω ‖ **to ~ off** *vi* (*sport*) δίνω τή πρώτη κλωτσιά ‖ **to ~ up** *vt* (*col*) κάνω φασαρία ‖ ~-off *n* (*sport*) ἐναρκτήριον λάκτισμα.

kid [kid] *n* (*child*) πιτσιρίκος, παιδάκι ‖ (*goat*) κατσικάκι, ρίφι ‖ (*leather*) σεβρό.

kidnap ['kidnæp] *vt* ἀπάγω, κλέβω ‖ ~per *n* ἀπαγωγεύς ‖ ~ping *n* ἀπαγωγή.

kidney ['kidni] *n* νεφρό.

kill [kil] *vt* (*murder*) φονεύω, σκοτώνω ‖ (*destroy*) ξερριζώνω, ἀφανίζω ‖ *n* κυνήγι ‖ ~er *n* φονέας, φονιάς.

kiln [kiln] *n* καμίνι, κλίβανος.

kilo ['kiːləu] *n* κιλό ‖ ~gramme, (*US*) ~gram *n* χιλιόγραμμον ‖ ~metre, (*US*) ~meter *n* χιλιόμετρον ‖ ~watt *n* κιλοβάτ.

kilt [kilt] *n* φουστανέλλα.

kimono [ki'məunəu] *n* κιμονό.

kin [kin] *n* συγγενεῖς, συγγενολόϊ.

kind [kaind] *a* καλός, καλοκάγαθος, καλόβολος ‖ *n* εἶδος ‖ **a ~ of** ἅς τόν ποῦμε, κάποιος ‖ (**two**) **of a ~** τοῦ ἰδίου φυράματος ‖ **in ~** (*merchandise*) εἰς εἶδος ‖ (*same way*) μέ τό ἴδιο νόμισμα.

kindergarten ['kindəgɑːtn] *n* νηπιαγωγεῖον.

kind-hearted ['kaind'hɑːtid] *a* καλόκαρδος.

kindle ['kindl] *vt* ἀνάβω ‖ (*rouse*) ἐξάπτω, προκαλῶ.

kindliness ['kaindlinis] *n* καλωσύνη.

kindly ['kaindli] *a* καλός, εὐγενικός ‖ *ad* εὐγενικά, μαλακά, φιλικά.

kindness ['kaindnis] *n* ἀγαθότης, καλωσύνη.

kindred ['kindrid] *a* συγγενής, συγγενικός.

kinetic [ki'netik] *a* (*energy*) κινητικός.

king [kiŋ] *n* βασιλιᾶς ‖ (*cards*) ρήγας ‖ ~dom *n* βασίλειον ‖ ~fisher *n* ψαροφάγος, μπιρμπίλι ‖ ~pin *n* (*of game*) κεντρικός πασσαλίσκος ‖ (*indispensable person*) κινητήριος μοχλός.

kink [kiŋk] *n* ζάρα, στράβωμα ‖ ~y *a* (*fig*) ἰδιότροπος ‖ (*hair*) σγουρός.

kiosk ['kiːɔsk] *n* (*tel*) θάλαμος ‖ (*shop*) κιόσκι, περίπτερον.

kipper ['kipə*] *n* καπνιστή ρέγγα.

kiss [kis] *n* φιλί, φίλημα ‖ *vt* φιλῶ ‖ *vi*: **they ~ed** φιλήθηκαν.

kit [kit] *n* σύνεργα, ἀτομικά εἴδη ‖ ~bag *n* σάκκος.

kitchen ['kitʃin] *n* κουζίνα ‖ **~ garden** *n* λαχανόκηπος ‖ **~ sink** *n* νεροχύτης.

kite [kait] *n* (χαρτ)ἀετός ‖ (*bird*) τσίφτης.

kith [kiθ] *n*: **~ and kin** φίλοι καί συγγενεῖς.

kitten ['kitn] *n* γατάκι.

kitty ['kiti] *n* (*pool of money*) γκανιότα, βιδάνιο.

kleptomaniac [kleptəu'meiniæk] *n* κλεπτομανής.

knack [næk] *n* ἐπιδεξιότης, κόλπο.

knapsack ['næpsæk] *n* δισάκκι, γυλιός.

knave [neiv] *n* (*cards*) βαλές, φάντης.

knead [niːd] *vt* ζυμώνω.

knee [niː] *n* γόνατο ‖ ~cap *n* ἐπιγονατίς ‖ ~-deep *a* ὡς τό γόνατο.

kneel [niːl] (*irreg v*) *vi* γονατίζω.

knell [nel] *n* καμπάνισμα, κωδωνοκρουσία.

knelt [nelt] *pt,pp of* **kneel.**

knew [njuː] *pt of* **know.**

knickers ['nikəz] *npl* κυλόττα.

knife [naif] *n* μαχαίρι ‖ *vt* μαχαιρώνω.

knight [nait] *n* ἱππότης ‖ (*chess*) ἄλογο ‖ ~hood *n* ἱπποτισμός, ἱπποσύνη.

knit [nit] *vt* πλέκω ‖ *vi* συγκολλῶ ‖ ~ting *n* πλέξιμο, πλεκτική ‖ **~ting machine** *n* πλεκτομηχανή ‖ **~ting needle** *n* βελόνα (τοῦ πλεξίματος) ‖ ~wear *n* πλεκτό, τρικό.

knives [naivz] *npl of* **knife.**

knob [nɔb] *n* (*of door*) πόμολο ‖ (*butter etc*) κομμάτι.

knock [nɔk] *vt* (*criticize*) βρίζω, κακολογῶ ‖ *vi* προσκρούω, κτυπῶ ‖ *n* κτύπημα ‖ **to ~ off** *vi* (*finish*) σταματῶ ‖ **to ~ out** *vt* βγάζω, τινάζω ‖ (*sport*) βγάζω νόκ-ἄουτ ‖ ~er *n* (*on door*) κτυπητήρι ‖ ~-kneed *a* στραβοπόδης, στραβοκάνης ‖ ~out *n* (*lit*) νόκ-ἄουτ ‖ (*fig*) σπουδαῖο πρᾶγμα.

knot [nɔt] *n* (*of rope etc*) κόμπος, δεσμός ‖

(of ribbon) κόμπος ‖ (lump) ρόζος ‖ (measure) κόμβος ‖ vt δένω κόμπο ‖ ~ted a κομπιασμένος.

know [nəu] (irreg v) vti (be aware of) ξέρω ‖ (recognize) γνωρίζω, διακρίνω, ξέρω ‖ **to ~ how to do** ξέρω πώς ‖ **~-how** n μέθοδος, τέχνη ‖ ~ing a νοήμων, έξυπνος, πονηρός ‖ ~ingly ad σκοπίμως, πονηρά ‖ ~-(it-)all n παντογνώστης.

knowledge ['nɔlidʒ] n (what one knows) γνῶσις, μάθησις ‖ (information) εἴδησις, πληροφορίες ‖ ~able a καλῶς πληροφορημένος, μορφωμένος.

known [nəun] pp of know.

knuckle ['nʌkl] n φάλαγξ, κλείδωσις ‖ (of meat) κότσι.

Koran [kɔ'raːn] n Κοράνιον.

L, l

lab [læb] n (col) ἐργαστήριον.

label ['leibl] n ἐτικέττα ‖ vt ἐπιγράφω, κολλῶ ἐτικέττα.

labor ['leibə*] n (US) = labour.

laboratory [lə'bɔrətəri] n ἐργαστήριον.

laborious [lə'bɔːriəs] a κοπιώδης, ἐπίπονος.

labour ['leibə*] n ἐργασία, μόχθος ‖ (workmen) ἐργάτες ‖ ~er n ἐργάτης ‖ **L~ Party** n Ἐργατικόν Κόμμα.

laburnum [lə'bɔːnəm] n κύτισος, λαβοῦρνον, λιβάρνο.

labyrinth ['læbərinθ] n λαβύρινθος.

lace [leis] n δαντέλλα ‖ (braid) σειρήτι ‖ (cord) κορδόνι ‖ vt δένω, πλέκω, βάζω δαντέλλες.

lacerate ['læsəreit] vt ξεσχίζω.

lack [læk] vt στεροῦμαι ‖ n ἔλλειψις ‖ **for ~ of** λόγω ἐλλείψεως.

lackadaisical [lækə'deizikəl] a ἄτονος, νωθρός.

laconic [lə'kɔnik] a λακωνικός.

lacquer ['lækə*] n βερνίκι, λάκα.

lad [læd] n (boy) ἀγόρι ‖ (young man) παλληκάρι.

ladder ['lædə*] n (lit) σκάλα, ἀνεμόσκαλα ‖ (fig) (κοινωνική) κλίμαξ.

laden ['leidn] a φορτωμένος.

ladle ['leidl] n κουτάλα.

lady ['leidi] n κυρία ‖ (title) λαίδη ‖ **'Ladies'** (lavatory) 'Κυριῶν', 'Γυναικῶν' ‖ ~-bird, (US) ~bug n λαμπρίτσα, πασχαλίτσα ‖ ~-in-waiting n Κυρία τῶν Τιμῶν ‖ ~like a ἀρχοντική, εὐγενική ‖ ~ship n κυρία, ἡ εὐγένεια της.

lag [læg] n (delay) ὑστέρησις, ἐπιβράδυνσις ‖ vi (also ~ behind) βραδυπορῶ ‖ vt (pipes) ἐπενδύω, φασκιώνω.

lager ['laːgə*] n ἐλαφρά μπύρα, λάγκερ.

lagging ['lægiŋ] n μονωτική ἐπένδυσις.

lagoon [lə'guːn] n λιμνοθάλασσα.

laid [leid] pt,pp of lay ‖ **to be ~ up** εἶμαι κρεβατωμένος.

lair [lεə*] n φωλιά, ἄντρον.

laity ['leiiti] n οἱ λαϊκοί, οἱ κοσμικοί.

lake [leik] n λίμνη.

lamb [læm] n ἀρνάκι ‖ (meat) ἀρνί ‖ ~ **chop** n παϊδάκι.

lame [leim] a κουτσός ‖ (excuse) μή πειστικός.

lament [lə'ment] n θρῆνος ‖ vt θρηνῶ, ὀδύρομαι ‖ ~able a ἀξιοθρήνητος ‖ ~ation n θρῆνος.

laminated ['læmineitid] a φυλλωτός.

lamp [læmp] n λύχνος, λυχνάρι ‖ (globe) λάμπα ‖ (in street) φανάρι ‖ ~post n φανοστάτης ‖ ~shade n ἀμπαζούρ.

lance [laːns] n λόγχη ‖ vt ἐγχειρίζω, ἀνοίγω ‖ ~ **corporal** n ὑποδεκανεύς.

lancet ['laːnsit] n νυστέρι.

land [lænd] n γῆ, στερεά ‖ (ground) γῆ, ἔδαφος ‖ (country) γῆ, χώρα ‖ (estate) κτῆμα ‖ vi (from ship) ἀποβιβάζομαι ‖ (aviat) προσγειοῦμαι ‖ (fig: arrive, fall) πέφτω ‖ vt (obtain) πιάνω, λαμβάνω ‖ (passengers, goods) ἀποβιβάζω, ξεφορτώνω ‖ ~ed a κτηματικός ‖ ~ing n ἀπο(βί)βασις ‖ (aviat) προσγείωσις ‖ (platform) πλατύσκαλον ‖ ~ing craft n ἀποβατικόν σκάφος ‖ ~ing stage n ἀποβάθρα ‖ ~ing strip n λωρίδα προσγειώσεως ‖ ~lady n σπιτονοικοκυρά ‖ ~locked a μεσόγειος ‖ ~lord n σπιτονοικοκύρης ‖ (innkeeper) ξενοδόχος ‖ ~lubber n στεριανός ‖ ~mark n δρόσημον ‖ ~owner n γαιοκτήμων ‖ ~scape n -τοπίον ‖ (painting) ζωγραφική τοπίων ‖ ~slide n (geog) (κατ)ὀλίσθησις ‖ (pol) ἐντυπωσιακή στροφή.

lane [lein] n δρομίσκος, μονοπάτι ‖ (of road) λωρίδα, διάδρομος ‖ (sport) ἀτομική πίστα, λωρίδα.

language ['læŋgwidʒ] n γλώσσα ‖ (national) γλῶσσα, διάλεκτος ‖ (style) γλῶσσα, ὁμιλία.

languid ['læŋgwid] a νωθρός, ἀδρανής.

languish ['læŋgwiʃ] vi κυττάζω τρυφερά, λιγώνω.

lank [læŋk] a μακρυά καί ἴσια ‖ ~y a μακρυός καί λεπτός.

lanolin ['lænəulin] n λανολίνη.

lantern ['læntən] n φανάρι.

lanyard ['lænjəd] n κορδόνι.

lap [læp] n ἀγκαλιά ‖ (sport) γύρος, βόλτα ‖ vt γλείφω ‖ vi (of waves) παφλάζω ‖ ~dog n χαϊδεμένο σκυλάκι.

lapel [lə'pel] n πέτο.

lapse [læps] n σφάλμα ‖ (fall from virtue) παράβασις ‖ (of time) παρέλευσις, ἐκπνοή.

larceny ['laːsəni] n κλοπή.

lard [laːd] n λαρδί.

larder ['laːdə*] n ἀποθήκη τροφίμων, κελλάρι.

large [laːdʒ] a (broad) εὐρύχωρος, ἐκτενής ‖ (big, numerous) μεγάλος ‖ **at ~** (free) ἐλεύθερος ‖ (*extensively*) γενικά ‖ **by and** ~ γενικά ‖ ~**ly** *ad* μεγάλως, σέ μεγάλο βαθμό ‖ ~**-scale** *a* εἰς μεγάλη κλίμακα, μεγάλος ‖ ~**sse** *n* (*generosity*) γενναιοδωρία.

lark [la:k] *n* (*bird*) κορυδαλλός ‖ (*joke*) ἀστεῖο, φάρσα ‖ **to** ~ **about** *vi* (*col*) ἀστειεύομαι, κάνω φάρσες.

larva ['la:və] *n* νύμφη.

laryngitis [lærin'dʒaitis] *n* λαρυγγῖτις.

larynx ['læriŋks] *n* λάρυγγι.

lash [læʃ] *n* (*stroke*) καμτσικιά ‖ *vt* (*beat against*) δέρνω, ξεσπῶ, κτυπῶ ‖ (*whip*) μαστιγώνω ‖ (*bind*) (προσ)δένω ‖ **to** ~ **out** *vi* (*with fists*) ἐπιτίθεμαι, ἐφορμῶ ‖ (*spend money*) κάνω σπατάλες ‖ ~**ing** *n* (*beating*) μαστίγωσις ‖ (*tie*) πρόσδεσις, δέσιμο ‖ ~**ings of** (*col*) ἀφθονία.

lass [læs] *n* κορίτσι, κοπέλλα.

lasso [læ'su:] *n* λάσσο ‖ *vt* πιάνω μέ λάσσο.

last [la:st] *a* τελευταῖος, τελικός ‖ *ad* τελευταῖον ‖ *n* (*person or thing*) τελευταῖος, ὕστατον ‖ (*for shoe*) καλαπόδι ‖ *vi* (*continue, hold out*) διαρκῶ, παραμένω ‖ (*remain*) συντηροῦμαι, διατηροῦμαι ‖ **at** ~ ἐπί τέλους ‖ ~ **night** χθές τό βράδυ ‖ ~ **week** τήν περασμένη βδομάδα ‖ ~**ing** *a* διαρκείας, πού κρατά ‖ ~**-minute** *a* τῆς τελευταίας στιγμῆς ‖ **the** ~ **straw** *n* (*fig*) τό τελειωτικόν κτύπημα.

latch [lætʃ] *n* μάνταλο, σύρτης ‖ (*yale lock*) λουκέτο ‖ ~**key** *n* ἀπλό κλειδί, ἀντικλείδι.

late [leit] *a* καθυστερημένος, ἀργοπορημένος ‖ (*not early*) ἀργά ‖ (*recent*) παλαιός, πρώην, τέως ‖ (*recently dead*) μακαρίτης ‖ *ad* ἐν καθυστερήσει, ἀργά ‖ (*late hour*) ἀργά ‖ **of** ~ προσφάτως ‖ ~ **in the day** ἀργά τό βραδάκι ‖ ~**comer** *n* ἀργοπορημένος ‖ ~**ly** *ad* ἐσχάτως, τελευταῖα.

lateness ['leitnis] *n* (*of person*) ἀργοπορία ‖ (*of hour*) ἡ προχωρημένη ὥρα.

latent ['leitənt] *a* ἀφανής, κρυφός ‖ (*existing*) λανθάνων.

later ['leitə*] *comp a, comp ad of* late.

lateral ['lætərəl] *a* πλάγιος, πλευρικός.

latest ['leitist] *sup a, sup ad of* late ‖ *n* (*news*) τό νεώτερον ‖ **at the** ~ τό ἀργότερον.

lathe [leið] *n* τόρνος.

lather ['lɑːðə*] *n* σαπουνάδα ‖ *vt* σαπουνίζω ‖ *vi* κάνω ἀφρό.

Latin ['lætin] *n* λατινική (γλῶσσα) ‖ *a* λατινικός ‖ ~ **America** *n* Λατινοαμερική ‖ ~**-American** *a* λατινοαμερικανικός ‖ *n* Λατινοαμερικανός.

latitude ['lætitju:d] *n* γεωγραφικόν πλάτος ‖ (*freedom*) εὐρυχωρία, περιθώριο.

latrine [lə'tri:n] *n* ἀποχωρητήριον, μέρος.

latter ['lætə*] *a* (*more recent*) ὁ δεύτερος, ἕτερος ‖ (*later*) τελευταῖος, πρόσφατος ‖ *n* (*opposite of* former) ὁ δεύτερος, ἕτερος ‖ ~**ly** *ad* τώρα τελευταῖα, ἀργότερα.

lattice work ['lætiswə:k] *n* δικτυωτόν, καφάσι.

laudible ['lɔ:dəbl] *a* ἀξιέπαινος.

laugh [la:f] *n* γέλιο ‖ *vi* γελῶ ‖ **to** ~ **at** *vt* διασκεδάζω, περιγελῶ, γελῶ γιά ‖ **to** ~ **off** *vt* γελοιοποιῶ ‖ ~**able** *a* γελοῖος, ἀστεῖος, διασκεδαστικός ‖ ~**ing** *a* γελαστός ‖ ~**ing stock** *n* περίγελως, κορόϊδο ‖ ~**ter** *n* γέλιο.

launch [lɔ:ntʃ] *n* (*of ship*) καθέλκυσις ‖ (*of rocket*) ἐκτόξευσις ‖ (*ship*) σκαμπαβία ‖ (*motor*) βενζινάκατος ‖ *vt* (*ship*) καθελκύω ‖ προβάλλω, βάζω ἐμπρός ‖ ~**ing** *n* καθέλκυσις, ἐκτόξευσις ‖ ~(**ing**) **pad** *n* πλατφόρμα ἐκτοξεύσεως.

launder ['lɔ:ndə*] *vt* πλένω καί σιδερώνω ‖ ~**ette** *n* πλυντήριον αὐτοεξυπηρετήσεως.

laundry ['lɔ:ndri] *n* (*place*) πλυντήριον ‖ (*clothes*) ῥούχα γιά πλύσιμο.

laureate ['lɔ:riit] *a see* poet.

laurel ['lɔrəl] *n* δάφνη.

lava ['la:və] *n* λάβα.

lavatory ['lævətri] *n* ἀποχωρητήριον, τουαλέτα.

lavender ['lævində*] *n* λεβάντα.

lavish ['læviʃ] *a* γενναιόδωρος, σπάταλος ‖ (*abundant*) ἄφθονος, πλούσιος ‖ *vt* κατασπαταλῶ, διασπαθίζω ‖ ~**ly** *ad* ἄφθονα, σπάταλα.

law [lɔ:] *n* νόμος, νομικά ‖ (*system of laws*) δίκαιον ‖ (*of game etc*) κανόνες ‖ ~**-abiding** *a* νομοταγής ‖ ~**breaker** *n* παραβάτης τοῦ νόμου ‖ ~ **court** *n* δικαστήριον ‖ ~**ful** *a* νόμιμος ‖ ~**fully** *ad* νομίμως ‖ ~**less** *a* ἄνομος, παράνομος.

lawn [lɔ:n] *n* πρασιά, γρασίδι ‖ ~**mower** *n* χορτοκόπτης ‖ ~ **tennis** *n* τέννις.

law school ['lɔ:sku:l] *n* σχολή νομικῆς.

law student ['lɔ:stju:dənt] *n* φοιτητής νομικῆς.

lawsuit ['lɔ:su:t] *n* δίκη.

lawyer ['lɔ:jə*] *n* νομικός, δικηγόρος.

lax [læks] *a* χαλαρός ‖ (*morals etc*) ἔκλυτος, ἄτακτος.

laxative ['læksətiv] *n* καθάρσιον.

laxity ['læksiti] *n* χαλαρότης.

lay [lei] (*irreg v*) *pt of* lie ‖ *a* λαϊκός, μή εἰδικός ‖ *vt* (*put down*) τοποθετῶ, θέτω, βάζω ‖ (*lay low*) ξαπλώνω, σωριάζω ‖ (*prepare*) βάζω, στρώνω ‖ (*eggs*) γεννῶ, κάνω ‖ **to** ~ **aside** *vt* θέτω κατά μέρος, βάζω ‖ **to** ~ **by** *vt* ἀποταμιεύω, οἰκονομῶ ‖ **to** ~ **down** *vt* παραδίδω ‖ (*plan*) σχεδιάζω ‖ **to** ~ **off** *vt* (*workers*) ἀπολύω ‖ **to** ~ **on** *vt* ἐπιβάλλω, ἐπιθέτω ‖ **to** ~ **out** *vt* ἀπλώνω ‖ (*spend*) ξοδεύω ‖ (*plan*) σχεδιάζω ‖ **to** ~ **up** *vt* (*store*) ἀποθηκεύω ‖ (*ship*) παροπλίζω ‖ ~**-by** *n* πλάτυσμα σταθμεύσεως ‖ ~**er** *n* στρῶμα ‖ ~**ette** *n* τά μωρουδιακά ‖ ~**man** *n* λαϊκός ‖ ~**out** *n* σχέδιον.

laze [leiz] *vi* τεμπελιάζω, χασομερῶ.

lazily ['leizili] ad τεμπέλικα.

laziness ['leizinis] n τεμπελιά, χάζεμα.

lazy ['leizi] a όκνηρός, τεμπέλης.

lead [led] n μόλυβδος || (of pencil) μολυβδίς, γραφίτης || a μολύβδινος.

lead [li:d] (irreg v) n (front position) πρώτη θέσις, άρχηγία || (distance, time ahead) προπορεία || (example) καθοδήγησις, παράδειγμα || (clue) ύπαινιγμός || (theat) πρωταγωνιστής || vi όδηγῶ, καθοδηγῶ || (group etc) ήγοῦμαι, διευθύνω || vi ἄγω, καταλήγω, πηγαίνω || **to ~ astray** vt παραπλανῶ || **to ~ away** vt (παρα)σύρω || **to ~ back** vi ἐπαναφέρω || **to ~ on** vt προτρέπω, κεντρίζω || **to ~ to** vt (street) όδηγῶ εἰς, πηγαίνω εἰς || (result in) καταλήγω || **to ~ up to** vt όδηγῶ εἰς || **~er** n άρχηγός, ήγέτης || (newspaper) κύριον ἄρθρον || **~ership** n ήγεσία, άρχηγία || **~ing** a κύριος, ήγετικός, σημαίνων || **~ing lady** n (theat) πρωταγωνίστρια || **~ing light** n (person) ήγετική φυσιογνωμία || **~ing man** n (theat) πρωταγωνιστής.

leaf [li:f] n φύλλον || (thin sheet) φύλλον || (table) φύλλο (τραπεζιοῦ) || **to ~** vt φυλλάδιον || **~y** a φυλλατός, φυλλώδης.

league [li:g] n σύνδεσμος, ἕνωσις, συμμαχία || (measure) λεύγα.

leak [li:k] n διαφυγή, διαρροή || (hole) τρύπα || vt (liquid etc) διαρρέω, (δια)φεύγω || (naut) κάνω νερά || vi (of pipe etc) διαρρέω, τρέχω || **to ~ out** vi (liquid etc) διαρρέω || (information) διαδίδομαι.

lean [li:n] (irreg v) a (thin) λιγνός || (meat) άπαχος || (poor) ἰσχνός, φτωχός || n άπαχο κρέας || vi κλίνω, γέρνω || vt άκουμπῶ, στηρίζομαι || **to ~ back** vi γέρνω πρός τά πίσω || **to ~ forward** vi γέρνω πρός τά ἐμπρός || **to ~ on** vt στηρίζομαι, άκουμπῶ || **to ~ over** vi κύπτω || **~ing** n κλίσις, τάσις || **~t** [lent] pt,pp of **lean** || **~-to** n ὑπόστεγον.

leap [li:p] (irreg v) n πήδημα || vi πηδῶ || **by ~s and bounds** άλματωδῶς, καλπάζων || **~frog** n καβάλες, τά βαρελάκια || **~t** [lept] pt,pp of **leap** || **~ year** n δίσεκτον ἔτος.

learn [lə:n] (irreg v) vti μαθαίνω || **~ed** a μορφωμένος, πολυμαθής || **~er** n (also aut) μαθητευόμενος, άρχάριος || **~ing** n (έκ)μάθησις, μόρφωσις.

lease [li:s] n ἐκμίσθωσις, ἐνοικίασις, συμβόλαιον || vt ἐκμισθώνω, ἐνοικιάζω.

leash [li:ʃ] n λουρί, άλυσίδα.

least [li:st] a ἐλάχιστος, μικρότατος, όλίγιστος || n (τό) λιγώτερον, (τό) μικρότερον || **at ~** τουλάχιστον || **not in the ~** καθόλου, ποτέ.

leather ['leðə*] n δέρμα, πετσί || a δερμάτινο, πέτσινο || **~y** a σάν πετσί, σάν δέρμα.

leave [li:v] (irreg v) vt (go away from) φεύγω,

ἐγκαταλείπω || (go without taking) άφήνω || (let stay) άφήνω || (give by will) άφήνω || vi (depart) φεύγω || n ἄδεια || (mil) ἄδεια || **on ~** σέ ἄδεια || **to take one's ~ of** άποχαιρετῶ, φεύγω || **to ~ off** vi ἐγκαταλείπω, σταματῶ, κόβω || **to ~ out** vt παραλείπω.

leaves [li:vz] npl of **leaf**.

Lebanon ['lebənən] **the ~** τό Λίβανον.

lecherous ['letʃərəs] a λάγνος, άσελγής.

lectern ['lektə(:)n] n άναγνωστήριον, άναλόγιον.

lecture ['lektʃə*] n διάλεξις, μάθημα || vi κάνω διάλεξιν, κάνω μάθημα || **~r** n όμιλητής, ὑφηγητής.

led [led] pt,pp of **lead**.

ledge [ledʒ] n ἄκρον, χεῖλος, ράφι || (of rock) ὕφαλος, ξέρα.

ledger ['ledʒə*] n καθολικόν (κατάστιχον).

lee [li:] n (from wind) προκάλυμμα.

leech [li:tʃ] n βδέλλα.

leek [li:k] n πράσο.

leer [liə*] n λοξό βλέμμα, στραβοκοίταγμα || vi στραβοκοιτάζω.

leeway ['li:wei] n (fig) χαμός χρόνου, κενόν.

left [left] pt,pp of **leave** || a άριστερός || n (τό) άριστερόν, ή άριστερά || **the L~** (pol) ή άριστερά || **~-hand drive** n άριστερό τιμόνι || **~-handed** a ζερβός, άριστερός || **~-luggage (office)** n γραφεῖον κατατεθέσεως άποσκευῶν || **~-overs** npl πλεονάσματα, ὑπολείμματα || **~-wing** n (pol) άριστερός.

leg [leg] n πόδι, γάμπα || (of table etc) πόδι || (on trouser etc) γάμπα.

legacy ['legəsi] n κληροδότημα || (from ancestors) κληρονομία.

legal ['li:gəl] a νομικός || (allowed) νόμιμος || **~ize** vt νομιμοποιῶ || **~ly** ad νομίμως, νομικῶς || **~ tender** n νόμισμα (ὑποχρεωτικῶς δεκτόν).

legation [li'geiʃən] n πρεσβεία.

legend ['ledʒənd] n θρύλος, μύθος || **~ary** a θρυλικός, μυθικός.

-legged ['legid] a μέ πόδια.

leggings ['leginz] npl γκέτες.

legibility [ledʒi'biliti] n τό εὐανάγνωστον.

legible ['ledʒəbl] a εὐανάγνωστος.

legibly ['ledʒəbli] ad εὐανάγνωστα.

legion ['li:dʒən] n λεγεών || a (countless) άναρίθμητος.

legislate ['ledʒisleit] vi νομοθετῶ.

legislation [ledʒis'leiʃən] n νομοθεσία.

legislative ['ledʒislətiv] a νομοθετικός.

legislator ['ledʒisleitə*] n νομοθέτης.

legislature ['ledʒislətʃə*] n νομοθετικόν σῶμα.

legitimacy [li'dʒitiməsi] n νομιμότης, γνησιότης.

legitimate [li'dʒitimit] a νόμιμος, λογικός.

leisure ['leʒə*] n σχόλη, άργία, ἄνεσις, ἐλεύθερες ὥρες || a τῆς σχόλης, τῆς άργίας ‖ at ~ ἐλεύθερος, ἔχων καιρό ‖ ~ly a ἀβίαστα, ἀργά, ἄνετα.

lemon ['lemən] n λεμόνι ‖ (colour) λεμονής ‖ ~ade n λεμονάδα.

lend [lend] (irreg v) vt δανείζω ‖ (dignity etc) (προσ)δίδω ‖ it ~s itself to προσφέρεται, κάνει γιά ‖ ~er n δανειστής ‖ ~ing library n δανειστική βιβλιοθήκη.

length [leŋθ] n μῆκος, μάκρος ‖ (of road, pipe etc) μῆκος ‖ (of material) τεμάχιον ‖ at ~ (finally) ἐπὶ τέλους ‖ (time) γιά πολλήν ὥραν ‖ (extent) ἐν ἐκτάσει ‖ ~en vt μακραίνω, ἐπιμηκύνω ‖ vi ἐπεκτείνομαι, παρατείνομαι ‖ ~ways ad κατά μῆκος, στό μάκρος ‖ ~y a μακροσκελής, ἐκτενής.

leniency ['li:niənsi] n ἠπιότης, ἐπιείκεια.

lenient ['li:niənt] a ἤπιος, ἐπιεικής ‖ ~ly ad ἐπιεικῶς.

lens [lenz] n φακός.

lent [lent] pt,pp of **lend** ‖ L~ n Σαρακοστή.

lentil ['lentl] n φακή.

leopard ['lepəd] n λεοπάρδαλις.

leper ['lepə*] n λεπρός.

leprosy ['leprəsi] n λέπρα.

lesbian ['lezbiən] a λεσβιακός ‖ n λεσβία.

less [les] a comp of **little** ‖ (ὀ)λιγώτερος ‖ ad (ὀ)λιγώτερον ‖ n ὀλιγώτερον.

lessen ['lesn] vi μειοῦμαι, μικραίνω, λιγοστεύω ‖ vt μειώνω, ἐλαττώνω, μικραίνω.

lesson ['lesn] n μάθημα.

lest [lest] cj μήπως, μὴ τυχόν.

let [let] (irreg v) vt (allow) ἀφήνω, ἐπιτρέπω ‖ (lease) ἐνοικιάζω, ἐκμισθώνω ‖ n: without ~ or hindrance ἄνευ κωλύματος, ἐλεύθερα ‖ ~ us pray ἄς προσευχηθοῦμε ‖ ~'s go ἄς πᾶμε ‖ 'to ~' 'ἐνοικιάζεται' ‖ to ~ down vt καταθλίβω ‖ (disappoint) ἀπογοητεύω, ἐγκαταλείπω ‖ to ~ go vti ἐλευθερώνω, χαλαρώνω ‖ to ~ off vt ἀπαλλάσσω, ἀφήνω, συγχωρῶ, ἀπολύω ‖ to ~ out vt ἀφήνω ‖ (garment) ἀνοίγω ‖ (scream) ἀφήνω (κραυγήν) ‖ to ~ up vi μειοῦμαι, ἐλαττοῦμαι ‖ ~-down n ἀπογοήτευσις.

lethal ['li:θəl] a θανατηφόρος.

lethargic [le'θa:dʒik] a ληθαργικός, νυσταλέος.

lethargy ['leθədʒi] n λήθαργος, ἀτονία.

letter ['letə*] n (sign) γράμμα, στοιχεῖον ‖ ἐπιστολή, γράμμα ‖ ~s npl (literature) γράμματα, φιλολογία ‖ ~box n γραμματοκιβώτιον ‖ ~ing n γράμματα, μαρκάρισμα.

lettuce ['letis] n μαρούλι.

let-up ['letʌp] n (col) μείωσις, χαλάρωσις.

leukaemia, (US) **leukemia** [lu:'ki:miə] n λευχαιμία.

Levant [li'vænt] the ~ ἡ Ἀνατολή.

level ['levl] a ἐπίπεδος, ὁριζόντιος ‖ ad ὁριζοντίως ‖ n ἐπίπεδον, ἐπίπεδος ἐπιφάνεια ‖ (height) στάθμη ‖ vt ἰσοπε-

δώνω, ὁριζοντιώνω ‖ on the ~ (lit) ἐπίπεδος, στό ἀλφάδι ‖ (fig: honest) τίμια, ἐν τάξει ‖ to ~ off or out vi ἐξισώνω ‖ ~ crossing n ἐπίπεδος διάβασις ‖ ~-headed a ἰσορροπημένος, ψύχραιμος.

lever ['li:və*] n μοχλός ‖ vt κινῶ μοχλόν ‖ ~age n ἐνέργεια μοχλοῦ, μόχλευσις.

levity ['leviti] n ἐλαφρότης, ἔλλειψις σοβαρότητος.

levy ['levi] n (taxes) εἴσπραξις ‖ (mil) στρατολογία ‖ vt εἰσπράττω, ἐπιβάλλω ‖ (mil) στρατολογῶ.

lewd [lu:d] a λάγνος, ἀσελγής.

liability [laiə'biliti] n (being liable) εὐθύνη, ὑποχρέωσις ‖ (debt) ὑποχρέωσις, ὀφειλή ‖ (disadvantage) προδιάθεσις, τάσις.

liable ['laiəbl] a (responsible) ὑπεύθυνος ‖ (likely) ὑποκείμενος.

liaison [li:'eizɔn] n (coordination) σύνδεσμος.

liar ['laiə*] n ψεύτης.

libel ['laibəl] n λίβελλος, δυσφήμισις ‖ vt διασύρω, δυσφημῶ ‖ ~lous, (US) ~ous a δυσφημιστικός.

liberal ['libərəl] a (generous) γενναιόδωρος ‖ (open-minded) φιλελεύθερος ‖ n φιλελεύθερος ‖ L ~ Party Φιλελεύθερον Κόμμα ‖ ~ly ad (abundantly) γενναιόδωρα, πλούσια.

liberate ['libəreit] vt ἀπελευθερώνω.

liberation [libə'reiʃən] n ἀπελευθέρωσις.

liberty ['libəti] n ἐλευθερία ‖ at ~ ἐλεύθερος, εὔκαιρος ‖ to take liberties with παίρνω θάρρος, γίνομαι ἀναιδής.

librarian [lai'brɛəriən] n βιβλιοθηκάριος.

library ['laibrəri] n βιβλιοθήκη.

libretto [li'bretəu] n λιμπρέττο.

Libya ['libiə] n Λιβύη ‖ ~n a λιβυκός ‖ n (person) ἐκ Λιβύης.

lice [lais] npl of **louse**.

licence, (US) **license** ['laisəns] n (permit) ἄδεια, ἔγκρισις, προνόμιον ‖ (lack of control) κατάχρησις ‖ ~ plate n (US aut) πινακίδα.

license ['laisəns] vt δίνω ἄδειαν, παρέχω ἄδειαν ‖ ~d a (for alcohol: premises) μέ ἄδεια πωλήσεως ποτοῦ ‖ ~e n προνομιοῦχος.

licentious [lai'senʃəs] a ἀκόλαστος.

lichen ['laikən] n λειχήνα.

lick [lik] vt γλείφω ‖ (of flames etc) παίζω μέ, ἐγγίζω, καταβροχθίζω ‖ n γλείψιμο ‖ (small amount) μικρή ποσότης.

licorice ['likəris] n γλυκόρριζα.

lid [lid] n κάλυμμα, καπάκι.

lido ['li:dəu] n (for swimming) δημοσία πισίνα.

lie [lai] (irreg v) n ψέμμα ‖ vi (speak) ψεύδομαι ‖ (rest) εἶμαι ξαπλωμένος, μένω ‖ (of object: be situated) κεῖμαι, εὑρίσκομαι ‖ to ~ idle μένω ἀκίνητος ‖ ~ detector n ἀνιχνευτής ψεύδους.

lieu [lu:] *n*: **in ~ of** ἀντί του, εἰς θέσιν τοῦ.

lieutenant [lef'tenənt] *n* (*army*) ὑπολοχαγός ‖ [lu:'tenənt] (*US*) ὑποσμηναγός.

life [laif] *n* (*being alive*) ζωή ‖ (*way of living*) τρόπος ζωῆς, ζωή ‖ (*time of life*) ζωή, διάρκεια ζωῆς, βίος ‖ (*story*) βίος, βιογραφία ‖ (*energy, vigour*) ζωηρότης, ζωή, κίνησις ‖ **~ assurance** *n* ἀσφάλεια ζωῆς ‖ **~belt** *n* σωσίβιος ‖ **~boat** *n* ναυαγοσωστική λέμβος ‖ **~guard** *n* ναυαγοσώστης ‖ **~ jacket** *n* σωσίβιος χιτών ‖ **~less** *a* (*dead*) νεκρός ‖ χωρίς ζωή, χωρίς κέφι ‖ **~like** *a* ρεαλιστικός, ζωντανός ‖ **~line** *n* (*lit*) σωσίβιον σχοινί ‖ **~long** *a* ἰσόβιος, ὁλοκλήρου ζωῆς ‖ **~ preserver** *n* σωσίβιον ‖ **~ raft** *n* σωσίβιος σχεδία ‖ **~-sized** *a* φυσικού μεγέθους ‖ **~ span** *n* διάρκεια ζωῆς, μέσος ὅρος ζωῆς ‖ **~time** *n* ζωή.

lift [lift] *vt* (ἀν)ὑψώνω, σηκώνω ‖ (*col: steal*) κλέβω ‖ *vi* ὑψοῦμαι, σηκώνομαι ‖ *n* ἀνύψωσις, σήκωμα ‖ (*aviat*) ἄνωσις ‖ (*machine, elevator*) ἀνελκυστήρ, ἀσανσέρ ‖ (*free ride*) παίρνω στό αὐτοκίνητο.

ligament ['ligəmənt] *n* σύνδεσμος.

light [lait] (*irreg v*) *n* φῶς ‖ (*giving light*) φῶς, φωτισμός ‖ (*for cigarette*) φωτιά ‖ (*lamp*) φῶς, λάμπα ‖ (*brightness*) λάμψις ‖ (*of dawn*) λάμψις ‖ (*information*) διαφώτισις ‖ (*aspect*) φῶς, ὄψις, ἄποψις ‖ *vt* ἀνάβω ‖ (*set burning*) ἀνάβω ‖ (*brighten*) φωτίζω, φέγγω ‖ *a* (*bright*) φωτεινός ‖ (*colour*) ἀνοιχτόχρωμος, ξανθός ‖ (*not heavy*) ἐλαφρός ‖ (*easy to do*) εὔκολος ‖ (*delicate*) ἐλαφρός, ἀπαλός ‖ (*cheerful*) εὔθυμος ‖ **to ~ up** *vi* (*lamps*) ἀνάβω, φωτίζω ‖ (*face*) ἀστράφτω, λάμπω ‖ *vt* (*illuminate*) (δια)φωτίζω ‖ **~ bulb** *n* λάμπα, λαμπτήρ ‖ **~en** *vi* (*brighten*) φωτίζομαι ‖ (*flash lightning*) ἀστράπτω ‖ *vt* (*give light to*) φωτίζω ‖ (*make less heavy*) ἐλαφρώνω ‖ **~er** *n* (*cigarette lighter*) ἀναπτήρας ‖ (*boat*) φορτηγίδα ‖ **~-headed** *a* ζαλισμένος ‖ (*thoughtless*) ἐπιπόλαιος, ἀπερίσκεπτος ‖ **~-hearted** *a* εὔθυμος, χαρούμενος ‖ **~house** *n* φάρος ‖ **~ing** *n* (*on road*) φωτισμός ‖ (*in theatre*) φωτισμός ‖ **~ing-up time** *n* ὥρα ἀφῆς φώτων ‖ **~ly** *ad* ἐλαφρῶς, ἐλαφρά ‖ **~ meter** *n* (*phot*) μετρητής φωτός ‖ **~ness** *n* ἐλαφρότης ‖ **~ning** *n* ἀστραπή, κεραυνός ‖ **~ning conductor** *n* ἀλεξικέραυνον ‖ **~ship** *n* φαρόπλοιον ‖ **~-year** *n* ἔτος φωτός.

lignite ['lignait] *n* λιγνίτης.

like [laik] *vt* μοῦ ἀρέσει, συμπαθῶ, προτιμῶ ‖ *prep* σάν, ὅπως, ὡς ‖ *a* (*similar*) ὅμοιος, ὁμοίαζω ‖ (*equal*) τά ἴσα, παρόμοια ‖ *ad* ὅπως, σάν ‖ *n* ὅμοιος ‖ **~able** *a* εὐχάριστος, συμπαθής ‖ **~lihood** *n* πιθανότης ‖ **~ly** *a* πιθανός, πού μπορεῖ νά ‖ *ad* πιθανόν, ἴσως ‖ **~-minded** *a* μέ τήν αὐτήν γνώμην ‖ **~n**

vt συγκρίνω, παρομοιάζω ‖ **~wise** *ad* ὁμοίως, ἐπίσης, ἐπί πλέον.

liking ['laikiŋ] *n* κλίσις, τάσις, συμπάθεια, γοῦστο.

lilac ['lailək] *n* πασχαλιά.

lilting ['liltiŋ] *a* ρυθμικός, μουσικός.

lily ['lili] *n* κρίνον.

limb [lim] *n* μέλος, ἄκρον ‖ (*of tree*) κλάδος.

limber ['limbə*] **to ~ up** *vi* γίνομαι εὐλύγιστος.

limbo ['limbəu] *n*: **to be in ~** (*fig*) εἶμαι στή φυλακή, στό φρέσκο.

lime [laim] *n* (*tree*) γλυκολεμονιά, κίτριον ‖ φιλύρα ‖ (*fruit*) γλυκολέμονο, κίτρο ‖ (*geol*) ἀσβέστης ‖ **~ juice** *n* χυμός γλυκολεμονιοῦ ‖ **~light** *n* (*fig*) τό προσκήνιον, δημοσιότης.

limestone ['laimstəun] *n* ἀσβεστόλιθος.

limit ['limit] *n* ὅριον, σύνορον, πέρας ‖ *vt* περιορίζω ‖ **~ation** *n* περιορισμός, ἀνικανότης ‖ **~ed** *a* περιωρισμένος, στενός ‖ **~ed company** *n* ἑταιρεία περιωρισμένης εὐθύνης.

limousine ['liməzi:n] *n* λιμουζίνα.

limp [limp] *n* χωλότης ‖ *vi* χωλαίνω, κουτσαίνω ‖ *a* ἀπαλός, πλαδαρός, μαλακός ‖ (*without energy*) λυωμένος, τσακισμένος.

limpet ['limpit] *n* πεταλίδα.

line [lain] *n* (*cord, wire, string*) σχοινί, γραμμή, σύρμα ‖ (*narrow mark*) γραμμή ‖ (*row, series*) σειρά, γραμμή ‖ (*course, direction*) κατεύθυνσις, τρόπος, πορεία ‖ (*class of goods*) σειρά, συλλογή, εἶδος ‖ (*poetry etc*) στίχος, γραμμή ‖ *vt* (*coat etc*) φοδράρω ‖ (*border*) χαράσσω ‖ **in ~ with** σύμφωνα μέ ‖ **to ~ up** *vi* μπαίνω στή γραμμή ‖ σχηματίζω οὐράν ‖ *vt* παρατάσσω, βάζω στή γραμμή.

linear ['liniə*] *a* (*of length*) τοῦ μήκους, γραμμική.

linen ['linin] *n* λινόν ὕφασμα ‖ (*articles*) ἀσπρόρουχα.

liner ['lainə*] *n* πλοῖον γραμμῆς.

linesman ['lainzmən] *n* (*sport*) λάϊνσμαν.

line-up ['lainʌp] *n* παράταξις.

linger ['liŋgə*] *vi* (*remain long*) χρονοτριβῶ, παρατείνομαι ‖ (*delay*) ἀργοπορῶ, βραδύνω.

lingerie ['lænʒəri:] *n* γυναικεῖα ἐσώρουχα.

lingering ['liŋgəriŋ] *a* παρατεταμένος, βραδύς, ἀνιαρός.

lingo ['liŋgəu] *n* (*col*) γλῶσσα, διάλεκτος.

linguist ['liŋgwist] *n* γλωσσολόγος, γλωσσομαθής.

linguistic [liŋ'gwistik] *a* γλωσσολογικός ‖ **~s** *n* γλωσσολογία.

liniment ['linimənt] *n* ὑγρόν ἐντριβῆς, ἐπάλειψις.

lining ['lainiŋ] *n* φόδρα.

link [liŋk] *n* (*of chain*) κρίκος ‖ δεσμός, σύνδεσμος ‖ *vt* συνδέω, ἑνώνω ‖ **~s** *npl* γήπεδον γκόλφ ‖ ~-**up** n (communication) σύνδεσις.

linoleum [li'nəuliəm] n λινοτάπης, λινόλεουμ.

linseed oil ['linsi:d'ɔil] n λινέλαιον.

lint [lint] n ξαντόν.

lion ['laiən] n λιοντάρι ‖ ~**ess** n λέαινα.

lip [lip] n χείλι, χεῖλος ‖ (**to pay**) ~ **service** (+ to) κάνω ψεύτικες ὑποσχέσεις ‖ ~**stick** n κραγιόν.

liquefy ['likwifai] vt ὑγροποιῶ.

liqueur [li'kjuə*] n λικέρ.

liquid ['likwid] n ὑγρόν ‖ a (substance) ὑγρός, ρευστός ‖ (asset) ρευστός, διαθέσιμος ‖ ~**ate** vt διαλύω, ξεκαθαρίζω, χρεωκοπῶ ‖ ~**ation** n διάλυσις, ἐξόφλησις, χρεωκόπησις.

liquor ['likə*] n (strong drink) οἰνοπνευματῶδες ποτόν.

lisp [lisp] n τραυλισμός, ψεύδισμα.

list [list] n (of names etc) κατάλογος ‖ (on ship) κλίσις, γέρσιμο ‖ vt (write down) ἐγγράφω, καταγράφω ‖ vi (of ship) κλίνω, γέρνω.

listen ['lisn] vi ἀκούω, προσέχω ‖ **to** ~ **to** vt ἀκούω ‖ ~**er** n ἀκροατής.

listless ['listlis] a ἄτονος, νωθρός, ἀδιάφορος ‖ ~**ly** ad ἀδιάφορα, ἀπαθῶς ‖ ~**ness** n ἀδιαφορία, ἀπάθεια.

lit [lit] pt,pp of **light**.

litany ['litəni] n λιτανεία.

liter ['li:tə*] n (US) = **litre**.

literacy ['litərəsi] n βαθμός μορφώσεως.

literal ['litərəl] a (word for word) κατά λέξιν ‖ (usual meaning) κατά κυριολεξίαν ‖ ~**ly** ad κυριολεκτικά.

literary ['litərəri] a λογοτεχνικός, φιλολογικός.

literate ['litərit] a ἐγγράμματος.

literature ['litəritʃə*] n φιλολογία, λογοτεχνία.

lithograph ['liθəugra:f] n λιθόγραφον, λιθογραφία.

litigate ['litigeit] vi βρίσκομαι εἰς δίκην, δικάζομαι.

litmus ['litməs] n: ~ **paper** χάρτης ἡλιοτροπίου.

litre ['li:tə*] n λίτρον.

litter ['litə*] n (untidy bits) σκουπίδια ‖ (young animals) γέννα, νεογνά ‖ vt κάνω ἄνω-κάτω, βρωμίζω μέ σκουπίδια.

little ['litl] a (small) μικρός, ὀλίγος, κοντός ‖ (unimportant) ἀσήμαντος ‖ ad ἐλάχιστα, λίγο ‖ n ὀλίγον, λίγο.

liturgy ['litədʒi] n λειτουργία.

live [liv] vi ζῶ ‖ (pass one's life) ζῶ ‖ (last) ζῶ, διαρκῶ ‖ (dwell) κατοικῶ, διαμένω, ζῶ ‖ **to** ~ **down** vt κάνω νά ξεχασθῆ, ὑπερνικῶ ‖ **to** ~ **on** vt τρέφομαι μέ, συντηροῦμαι μέ ‖ **to** ~ **up to** vt ἐφαρμόζω, τιμῶ, ἐκπληρώνω.

live [laiv] a (living) ζωντανός ‖ (burning) ἀναμμένος ‖ (wire) ἡλεκτρισμένον, μέ

ρεῦμα ‖ (broadcast) ζωντανόν πρόγραμμα.

livelihood ['laivlihud] n τά πρός τό ζῆν.

liveliness ['laivlinis] n ζωηρότης, ζωτικότης.

lively ['laivli] a ζωηρός.

liver ['livə*] n (anat) σηκότι ‖ ~**ish** a ἡπατικός, εὐερέθιστος.

livery ['livəri] n στολή ὑπηρέτου.

lives [laivz] npl of **life**.

livestock ['laivstɔk] n ζῶα, κτήνη.

livid ['livid] a (lit) πελιδνός, ὠχρός ‖ (furious) φουριόζος.

living ['liviŋ] n τά πρός τό ζῆν, βίος ‖ a ζωντανός, ζῶν ‖ (wage) βασικός μισθός ‖ ~ **room** n καθημερινόν δωμάτιον.

lizard ['lizəd] n σαύρα.

load [ləud] n φορτίον, φόρτωμα ‖ vt φορτώνω, γεμίζω.

loaf [ləuf] n καρβέλι ‖ vi χαζεύω, τεμπελιάζω.

loan [ləun] n δάνειον, δανεισμός ‖ vt δανείζω ‖ **on** ~ ἀπεσπασμένος.

loathe [ləuð] vt σιχαίνομαι.

loathing ['ləuðiŋ] n σιχαμός, ἀηδία.

loaves [ləuvz] npl of **loaf**.

lobby ['lɔbi] n προθάλαμος, εἴσοδος ‖ vt ἐπηρεάζω βουλευτάς.

lobe [ləub] n λοβός.

lobster ['lɔbstə*] n ἀστακός.

local ['ləukəl] a τοπικός, ἐπιτόπιος ‖ n (pub) ταβέρνα ‖ **the** ~**s** npl ντόπιοι ‖ ~ **colour** n τοπικόν χρῶμα ‖ ~**ity** n θέσις, μέρος, τοποθεσία ‖ ~**ly** ad τοπικῶς, ἐπιτοπίως.

locate [ləu'keit] vt ἐντοπίζω ‖ (establish) τοποθετῶ.

location [ləu'keiʃən] n τοποθεσία.

loch [lɔx] n λίμνη.

lock [lɔk] n (of door) κλειδαριά ‖ (of canal etc) ὑδροφράκτης, φράγμα ‖ (of hair) βόστρυχος, μπούκλα ‖ vt κλειδώνω σφίγγω, στερεώνω ‖ vi (door etc) ἀσφαλίζομαι ‖ (wheels) σφηνώνω, μπλοκάρομαι.

locker ['lɔkə*] n ἀρμάρι, ντουλάπι, ἀποθήκη.

locket ['lɔkit] n μενταγιόν.

locomotive [ləukə'məutiv] n ἀτμάμαξα, ἀτμομηχανή.

locust ['ləukəst] n ἀκρίδα.

lodge [lɔdʒ] n ἐξοχική οἰκία ‖ (at gate) οἰκίσκος τοῦ φύλακος ‖ (meeting place) στοά ‖ vi φιλοξενοῦμαι, διαμένω ‖ (rent a room) εἰμαι νοικάρης ‖ (stick) ἐνσφηνοῦμαι, πιάνομαι ‖ vt καταθέτω, ὑποβάλλω ‖ ~**r** n ἔνοικος.

lodgings ['lɔdʒiŋz] npl δωμάτια.

loft [lɔft] n ὑπερῶον, σοφίτα.

lofty ['lɔfti] a ὑψηλός ‖ (proud) ὑπεροπτικός, ἀγέρωχος.

log [lɔg] n (of wood) κούτσουρο ‖ (of ship etc) ἡμερολόγιον.

logarithm ['lɔgəriθəm] *n* λογάριθμος.
logbook ['lɔgbuk] *n* ἡμερολόγιον (πλοίου).
loggerheads ['lɔgəhədz] *n*: at ~ τσακωμένος, στά μαχαίρια.
logic ['lɔdʒik] *n* λογική ‖ ~al *a* λογικός ‖ ~ally *ad* λογικά.
loin [lɔin] *n* ὀσφύς, λαγών.
loiter ['lɔitə*] *vi* χρονοτριβῶ, χαζεύω.
loll [lɔl] *vi* ξαπλώνω, χουζουρεύω.
lollipop ['lɔlipɔp] *n* γλειφιτζούρι.
London ['lʌndən] *n* Λονδῖνον ‖ ~er *n* (*person*) Λονδρέζος.
lone [ləun] *a* (*solitary*) μόνος, μοναχικός ‖ ~liness *n* μοναξιά, ἐρημιά ‖ ~ly *a* (*sad*) μελαγχολικός, ἔρημος, ἀκατοίκητος.
long [lɔŋ] *a* μακρύς, μακρά, ἐκτενής ‖ (*length*) μάκρος ‖ *ad* (*time*) ἐπὶ μακρόν, πολλή ὥρα ‖ (*during*) ὅλη, σ' ὅλη ‖ *vi* (+ *for*) ποθῶ, λαχταρῶ ‖ ~ ago πρό πολλοῦ, τοῦ παλαιοῦ καιροῦ ‖ before ~ ἐντός ὀλίγου, σύντομα ‖ as ~ as ἐφ' ὅσον ‖ in the ~ run στό τέλος, τελικά ‖ ~-distance *a* (*tel*) ὑπεραστικόν ‖ (*sport*) μεγάλων δρόμων ‖ ~-haired *a* μακρυμάλλης ‖ ~hand *n* συνήθης γραφή ‖ ~ing *n* πόθος, λαχτάρα ‖ *a* λαχταρῶν, ποθῶν ‖ ~ish *a* μακρούτσικος ‖ ~itude *n* μῆκος ‖ ~ jump *n* ἅλμα εἰς μῆκος ‖ ~-lost *a* χαμένος πρό πολλοῦ ‖ ~-playing record *n* δίσκος μακρᾶς διαρκείας ‖ ~-range *a* μεγάλης διαρκείας, μεγάλης ἀκτῖνος ‖ ~-sighted *a* πρεσβύωψ, ὀξύδερκής ‖ ~-standing *a* παλαιός, μακροχρόνιος ‖ ~-suffering *a* ὑπομονητικός, μακρόθυμος ‖ ~-term *a* μακροπρόθεσμος, μακροχρόνιος ‖ ~ wave *n* μακρόν κῦμα ‖ ~-winded *a* ἀτελείωτος, φλύαρος.
loo [lu:] *n* μέρος.
loofah ['lu:fə] *n* (ἐλ)λύφι.
look [luk] *vi* (*see*) κοιτάζω, βλέπω ‖ (*seem*) φαίνομαι ‖ (*face*) βλέπω, ἀντικρύζω ‖ *n* βλέμμα, ματιά ‖ ~s *npl* ὄψις, ἐμφάνισις ‖ to ~ after *vt* φροντίζω γιά ‖ to ~ down on *vt* (*fig*) περιφρονῶ ‖ to ~ for *vt* ψάχνω, ζητῶ ‖ (*expect*) προσδοκῶ ‖ to ~ forward to *vt* προσδοκῶ ‖ to ~ out for *vt* ἀναζητῶ, ψάχνω, προσέχω ‖ to ~ to *vt* φροντίζω γιά, βασίζομαι εἰς ‖ to ~ up *vi* βελτιοῦμαι ‖ *vt* ἐπισκέπτομαι, ψάχνω (εἰς βιβλίον) ‖ to ~ up to *vt* σέβομαι ‖ ~out *n* (*watch*) προσοχή ‖ (*view*) θέα ‖ (*mil*) φρούρησις, φρουρός.
loom [lu:m] *n* ἀργαλειός ‖ *vi* διαφαίνομαι, διακρίνομαι ἀσαφῶς.
loop [lu:p] *n* βρόχος, θηλιά ‖ *vt* κάνω θηλιά, πλέκω σὲ θηλιά ‖ ~hole *n* (*for escape*) ὑπεκφυγή, διέξοδος.
loose [lu:s] *a* χαλαρός ‖ (*free*) ἐλεύθερος, λυμένος ‖ (*slack*) ἀπρόσεκτος, ἀπαλός ‖ *vt* λύνω, λασκάρω, χαλαρῶνω ‖ at a ~ end χωρίς ἀπασχόλησιν ‖ ~ly *ad*

χαλαρά, ἀσαφῶς ‖ ~n *vt* λύνω, λασκάρω ‖ ~ness *n* χαλαρότης.
loot [lu:t] *n* λάφυρον, λεία, πλιάτσικο ‖ *vt* λαφυραγωγῶ, λεηλατῶ ‖ ~ing *n* λεηλασία.
lop [lɔp] to ~ off *vt* (ἀπο)κόπτω, κλαδεύω.
lop-sided ['lɔp'saidid] *a* ἑτεροβαρής, πού γέρνει.
lord [lɔːd] *n* ἄρχων, ἀφέντης ‖ (*Brit*) λόρδος ‖ the L~ ὁ Κύριος ‖ ~ly *a* μεγαλοπρεπής, ἀγέρωχος ‖ ~ship *n* (*title*) ἐξοχότης.
lore [lɔː*] *n* εἰδική γνῶσις, παραδόσεις.
lorry ['lɔri] *n* φορτηγόν (αὐτοκίνητον), καμιόνι ‖ ~ driver *n* ὀδηγός φορτηγοῦ.
lose [lu:z] (*irreg v*) *vt* χάνω ‖ (*be robbed of*) χάνω ‖ (*waste*) σπαταλῶ, χάνω ‖ (*miss*) χάνω ‖ (*be defeated*) χάνω ‖ *vi* χάνω ‖ ~r *n* ἡττημένος, χαμένος.
losing ['lu:ziŋ] *a* χάνων.
loss [lɔs] *n* ἀπώλεια, χάσιμο ‖ (*what is lost*) ἀπώλεια ‖ (*harm*) ζημία ‖ at a ~ ἔχω χαμένα, βρίσκομαι εἰς ἀμηχανίαν.
lost [lɔst] *pt,pp* of **lose** ‖ *a* ἀπωλεσθείς, χαμένος ‖ ~ cause *n* χαμένη ὑπόθεσις ‖ ~ property *n* (γραφεῖον) ἀπολεσθέντων ἀντικειμένων.
lot [lɔt] *n* (*large quantity*) πολύ ‖ (*for prize*) κλῆρος ‖ (*group of objects*) σύνολον, σὲ μεγάλη ποσότητα ‖ a ~ of ἕνα σωρό, πολύ ‖ ~s of πλῆθος, ἕνα σωρό.
lotion ['ləuʃən] *n* λοσιόν.
lottery ['lɔtəri] *n* λαχεῖον.
loud [laud] *a* βροντερός, θορυβώδης, μεγαλόφωνος ‖ (*showy*) κτυπητός ‖ *ad* δυνατά, μεγαλοφώνως ‖ ~ly *ad* δυνατά, θορυβωδῶς ‖ ~ness *n* ἠχηρότης, δύναμις θορύβου ‖ ~speaker *n* μεγάφωνον.
lounge [laundʒ] *n* μικρό σαλόνι, χώλ ξενοδοχείου ‖ *vi* περιφεραμαι ἀσκόπως, χαζεύω ‖ ~ suit *n* καθημερινό κοστούμι.
louse [laus] *n* ψείρα.
lousy ['lauzi] *a* (*lit*) ψειριάρης ‖ (*fig*) βρωμερός, ἄθλιος.
lout [laut] *n* ἄξεστος, ντουβάρι.
lovable ['lʌvəbl] *a* ἀξιαγάπητος.
love [lʌv] *n* ἀγάπη, ἔρως, στοργή ‖ (*person loved*) ἀγαπημένος, ἐρωμένη ‖ (*sport*) μηδέν ‖ *vt* (*person*) ἀγαπῶ ‖ (*activity*) λατρεύω, ἀγαπῶ ‖ to ~ to do μοῦ ἀρέσει νά κάνω ‖ to make ~ κάνω ἔρωτα, φλερτάρω ‖ ~ affair *n* ἐρωτική ὑπόθεσι ‖ ~ letter *n* ἐρωτικό γράμμα ‖ ~ life *n* ἐρωτική ζωή ‖ ~ly *a* ὡραῖος, χαριτωμένος, εὐχάριστος ‖ ~-making *n* ἐρωτοτροπία, κόρτε ‖ ~r *n* (*general*) φιλο- ‖ (*man*) ἐραστής, φίλος ‖ ~song *n* ἐρωτικό τραγούδι.
loving ['lʌviŋ] *a* τρυφερός, στοργικός ‖ ~ly *ad* στοργικά, μέ ἀγάπη.
low [ləu] *a* (*not tall*) χαμηλός ‖ (*rank*) ταπεινός, κατώτερος ‖ (*common*) χυδαῖος, ἄξεστος ‖ (*not loud*) ἀδύνατος,

χαμηλός ‖ (*weak*) κακόκεφος ‖ (*tide*) ἄμπωτις ‖ *ad* χαμηλά ‖ (*not loudly*) χαμηλόφωνα, χαμηλά ‖ *n* (*low point*) ναδίρ ‖ (*meteorology*) βαρομετρικόν χαμηλόν ‖ ~-cut *a* (*dress*) ντεκολτέ.
lower ['ləuə*] *vt* κατεβάζω, χαμηλώνω ‖ (*make less*) ἐλαττώνω.
lowly ['ləuli] *a* ταπεινός, μετριόφρων.
loyal ['lɔiəl] *a* πιστός, ἀφοσιωμένος ‖ ~ly *ad* πιστῶς, πιστά ‖ ~ty *n* πίστις, ἀφοσίωσις.
lozenge ['lozindʒ] *n* παστίλια.
lubricant ['lu:brikənt] *n* λιπαντικόν, γράσο.
lubricate ['lu:brikeit] *vt* λιπαίνω, λαδώνω, γρασάρω.
lubrication [lu:bri'keiʃən] *n* λίπανσις, γρασάρισμα.
lucid ['lu:sid] *a* σαφής, διαυγής ‖ ~ity *n* σαφήνεια, διαύγεια ‖ ~ly *ad* σαφῶς, καθαρά.
luck [lʌk] *n* τύχη ‖ ~ily *ad* εὐτυχῶς ‖ ~y *a* τυχερός.
lucrative ['lu:krətiv] *a* ἐπικερδής.
ludicrous ['lu:dikrəs] *a* ἀλλόκοτος, γελοῖος, ἀστεῖος.
lug [lʌg] *vt* σέρνω μέ δυσκολία.
luggage ['lʌgidʒ] *n* ἀποσκευές ‖ ~ rack *n* (*in train etc*) σκευοθέσιον, δίχτυ γιά βαλίτσες.
lugubrious [lu:'gu:briəs] *a* πένθιμος, λυπητερός.
lukewarm ['lu:kwɔ:m] *a* χλιαρός ‖ (*indifferent*) ἀδιάφορος.
lull [lʌl] *n* ἀνάπαυλα, κόπασις ‖ *vt* νανουρίζω ‖ (*calm*) καθησυχάζω, καταπραΰνω ‖ ~aby *n* νανούρισμα.
lumbago [lʌm'beigəu] *n* ὀσφυαλγία.
lumber ['lʌmbə*] *n* (*old articles*) παλιατσοῦρες ‖ (*wood*) ξυλεία ‖ ~jack *n* ξυλοκόπος.
luminous ['lu:minəs] *a* φωτεινός, λάμπων.
lump [lʌmp] *n* (σ)βῶλος, μεγάλο τεμάχιον ‖ (*swelling*) ἐξόγκωμα, καρούμπαλο ‖ (*of sugar*) κομμάτι ζάχαρι ‖ *vt* σβωλιάζω, συσσωρεύω ‖ **a ~ sum** στρογγυλόν ποσόν, ὁλική τιμή ‖ ~y *a* σβωλιασμένος.
lunacy ['lu:nəsi] *n* παραφροσύνη.
lunar ['lu:nə*] *a* σεληνιακός.
lunatic ['lu:nətik] *n* παράφρων ‖ *a* παράφρων, τρελλός.
lunch [lʌntʃ] *n* (*also* ~eon) γεῦμα ‖ ~ hour *n* μεσημβρινή διακοπή ‖ ~time *n* = ~ **hour.**
lung [lʌŋ] *n* πνευμόνι ‖ ~ cancer *n* καρκῖνος πνευμονιοῦ.
lunge [lʌndʒ] *vi* μπήζω, κτυπῶ ξαφνικά, ἐφορμῶ.
lupin ['lu:pin] *n* λούπινον.
lurch [lə:tʃ] *vi* τρικλίζω, μποτζάρω ‖ *n* κλυδώνισμα, μπότζι.
lure [ljuə*] *n* δέλεαρ, δόλωμα, ἕλξις ‖ *vt* δελεάζω, θέλγω.
lurid ['ljuərid] *a* (*shocking*) τρομερός.

lurk [lə:k] *vi* παραμονεύω, κρύβομαι.
luscious ['lʌʃəs] *a* γευστικός, χυμώδης, γλυκύτατος.
lush [lʌʃ] *a* γεμάτος χυμούς ‖ (*countryside*) πλούσιον εἰς βλάστησι.
lust [lʌst] *n* σαρκική ἐπιθυμία ‖ *vi* (+ *after*) ἐποφθαλμιῶ, ὀρέγομαι ‖ ~ful *a* λάγνος.
lustre, (*US*) **luster** ['lʌstə*] *n* λάμψις, στιλπνότης.
lusty ['lʌsti] *a* εὔρωστος, σφριγηλός.
lute [lu:t] *n* λαοῦτο.
luxuriant [lʌg'zjuəriənt] *a* ἄφθονος, πλούσιος.
luxurious [lʌg'zjuəriəs] *a* πολυτελής, πλούσιος.
luxury ['lʌkʃəri] *n* πολυτέλεια, λοῦσο.
lying ['laiiŋ] *n* κείμενος ‖ (*not truthful*) ψευδόμενος ‖ *a* ψεύτικος.
lynch [lintʃ] *vt* λυντσάρω.
lyre ['laiə*] *n* λύρα.
lyric ['lirik] *n* λόγια τραγουδιοῦ ‖ *a* λυρικός ‖ ~al *a* (*fig*) ἐνθουσιάδης, πομπώδης.

M, m

mac [mæk] *n* (*raincoat*) ἀδιάβροχο.
macaroni [mækə'rəuni] *n* μακαρόνια.
macaroon [mækə'ru:n] *n* ἐργολάβος.
mace [meis] *n* κηρύκειον ‖ (*spice*) μοσχοκάρυδο.
machine [mə'ʃi:n] *n* (*general*) μηχανή, μηχάνημα ‖ *vt* (*dress etc*) ἐπεξεργάζομαι, κατεργάζομαι ‖ ~ gun *n* πολυβόλον ‖ ~ry *n* μηχανές ‖ (*parts*) μηχανήματα ‖ (*of government*) μηχανισμός ‖ ~ tool *n* ἐργαλειομηχανή.
machinist [mə'ʃi:nist] *n* μηχανουργός.
mackerel ['mækrəl] *n* σκουμπρί.
mackintosh ['mækintɔʃ] *n* ἀδιάβροχο.
macro- ['mækrəu] *prefix* μακρο-.
mad [mæd] *a* παράφρων, τρελλός ‖ (*foolish*) παράλογος ‖ ~ about ξετρελαμένος ‖ (*very angry*) ἐξαγριωμένος.
madam ['mædəm] *n* κυρία.
madden ['mædn] *vt* τρελλαίνω ‖ ~ing *a* ἐκνευριστικός, τρομερός.
made [meid] *pt,pp of* **make** ‖ ~-to-measure *a* κατασκευασθέν ἐπί παραγγελία ‖ ~-up *a* τεχνητός, φτιαστός.
madly ['mædli] *ad* τρελλά, ἀγρίως.
madman ['mædmən] *n* (*maniac*) φρενοβλαβής, τρελλός.
madness ['mædnis] *n* παραφροσύνη, τρέλλα.
Madonna [mə'dɔnə] *n* Παναγία.
magazine [mægə'zi:n] *n* περιοδικόν.
maggot ['mægət] *n* σκουλίκι.
magic ['mædʒik] *n* μαγεία ‖ *a* μαγικός, μαγεμένος ‖ ~al *a* μαγικός ‖ ~ian *n* μάγος.

magistrate ['mædʒistreit] n δικαστικός ὑπάλληλος ‖ (*judge*) δικαστής.
magnanimity [mægnə'nimiti] n μεγαλοψυχία, γενναιοφροσύνη.
magnanimous [mæg'næniməs] a μεγαλόψυχος.
magnate ['mægneit] n μεγιστάν.
magnet ['mægnit] n μαγνήτης ‖ ~ic a μαγνητικός ‖ ~ism n μαγνητισμός.
magnification [mægnifi'keiʃən] n μεγέθυνσις.
magnificence [mæg'nifisəns] n μεγαλοπρέπεια.
magnificent [mæg'nifisənt] a μεγαλοπρεπής ‖ ~ly ad μεγαλοπρεπῶς.
magnify ['mægnifai] νt μεγεθύνω, ὑπερβάλλω ‖ ~ing glass n μεγεθυντικός φακός.
magnitude ['mægnitju:d] n μέγεθος, σπουδαιότης.
magnolia [mæg'nəuliə] n μανόλια.
magpie ['mægpai] n καρακάξα.
maharajah [mɑ:hə'rɑ:dʒə] n μαχαραγιᾶς.
mahogany [mə'hɔgəni] n μαόνι.
maid [meid] n (*servant*) ὑπηρέτρια ‖ ~en n κορίτσι, παρθένος ‖ a (*lady*) ἄγαμος ‖ ~en name n οἰκογενειακὸν ὄνομα ‖ ~en speech n παρθενικὸς λόγος ‖ ~en voyage n παρθενικὸν ταξίδι.
mail [meil] n ἐπιστολές, ταχυδρομεῖον ‖ (*system*) ταχυδρομεῖον ‖ νt (*US*) ταχυδρομῶ ‖ ~box n (*US*) γραμματοκιβώτιον ‖ ~order n ταχυδρομικὴ ἐντολή.
maim [meim] νt ἀκρωτηριάζω, σακατεύω.
main [mein] a κύριος, πρωτεύων ‖ n (*pipe*) κεντρικὸς ἀγωγός ‖ in the ~ γενικά, ὡς ἐπὶ τό πλεῖστον ‖ ~land n στερεά, ἠπειρωτικὴ χώρα ‖ ~ road n κεντρικὴ ὁδὸς ‖ ~stay n (*fig*) κύριον ἔρεισμα, στήριγμα.
maintain [mein'tein] νt (*machine*) διατηρῶ, συντηρῶ ‖ (*support*) συντηρῶ, τρέφω ‖ (*traditions*) συντηρῶ, συνεχίζω ‖ (*an opinion*) ὑποστηρίζω.
maintenance ['meintinəns] n (*tech*) συντήρησις.
maisonette [meizə'net] n διαμέρισμα, μονοκατοικία.
maize [meiz] n ἀραποσίτι, καλαμπόκι.
majestic [mə'dʒestik] a μεγαλοπρεπής.
majesty ['mædʒisti] n μεγαλεῖον ‖ His, Her M~ ἡ Αὐτοῦ Μεγαλειότης, ἡ Αὐτὴ Μεγαλειότης ‖ Your M~ ἡ Μεγαλειότης σας.
major ['meidʒə*] n (*mil*) ταγματάρχης ‖ a (*mus*) μείζων.
majority [mə'dʒɔriti] n πλειοψηφία ‖ (*number*) πλειονότης.
make [meik] (*irreg v*) νt (*build, shape, produce*) κάνω, φτιάνω, δημιουργῶ ‖ (*appoint*) κάνω, ὁρίζω ‖ (*cause to do*) ἀναγκάζω, κάνω, ὑποχρεώνω ‖ (*reach*) φθάνω ‖ (*earn*) κάνω, ἀποκτῶ, κερδίζω,

βγάζω ‖ (*do, perform*) κάνω ‖ (*amount to*) κάνω ‖ (*prepare*) φτιάνω ‖ n (*style*) κατασκευή, τύπος ‖ (*kind*) μάρκα ‖ to ~ for νt (*place*) κατευθύνομαι, πηγαίνω ‖ to ~ out νi ἐπιτυγχάνω, καταφέρνω ‖ νt (*write out*) συντάσσω, βγάζω, ἑτοιμάζω ‖ (*understand*) καταλήγω, καταλαμβάνω ‖ (*pretend*) προσποιοῦμαι, παριστάνω ‖ to ~ up νt (*make*) συντάσσω, φτιάνω, πλάθω ‖ (*face*) βάφομαι, μακιγιάρομαι, φτιάνομαι ‖ (*settle*) ρυθμίζω, συμφιλιώνω, διευθετῶ ‖ to ~ up for νt ἀνακτῶ, καλύπτω ‖ ~-believe n προσποίησις, ὑπόκρισις ‖ a προσποιητός, ψεύτικος ‖ ~r n κατασκευαστής, δημιουργός ‖ ~shift a προσωρινή λύσις ‖ ~-up n (*cosmetics*) μακιγιάζ, ψιμύθιον ‖ (*theat*) μακιγιάζ, βάψιμο.
making ['meikiŋ] n: in the ~ ἐν ἐξελίξει.
maladjusted ['mælə'dʒʌstid] a ἀπροσάρμοστος.
malaise [mæ'leiz] n ἀδιαθεσία.
malaria [mə'lɛəriə] n ἑλονοσία.
Malaysia [mə'leiziə] n Μαλαισία.
male [meil] n ἄρρην, ἄνδρας ‖ a ἀρσενικός.
malevolence [mə'levələns] n κακοβουλία, μοχθηρία.
malevolent [mə'levələnt] a κακόβουλος.
malfunction [mæl'fuŋkʃən] νi λειτουργῶ ἐλαττωματικῶς.
malice ['mælis] n κακεντρέχεια, ἔχθρα.
malicious [mə'liʃəs] a κακόβουλος, μοχθηρός ‖ ~ly ad μοχθηρά, μέ κακίαν.
malign [mə'lain] νt δυσφημίζω, κακολογῶ.
malignant [mə'lignənt] a (*tumour*) κακοήθης.
malleable ['mæliəbl] a ἐλάσιμος, μαλακός.
mallet ['mælit] n ξύλινο σφυρί, κόπανος.
malnutrition ['mælnju'triʃən] n ὑποσιτισμός.
malpractice ['mæl'præktis] πl ἀδίκημα, κατάχρησις.
malt [mɔ:lt] n βύνη.
Malta ['mɔ:ltə] n Μάλτα.
maltreat [mæl'tri:t] νt κακομεταχειρίζομαι.
mammal ['mæməl] n θηλαστικόν, μαστοφόρον.
mammoth ['mæməθ] a γιγαντιαῖος, πελώριος.
man [mæn] n ἄνθρωπος ‖ (*male*) ἀνήρ, ἄνδρας ‖ (*race*) ἀνθρωπότης ‖ νt ἐπανδρώνω.
manage ['mænidʒ] νi (*succeed*) καταφέρνω ‖ νt χειρίζομαι, διευθύνω, διοικῶ ‖ ~able a εὐχείριστος ‖ (*person*) εὔκολος ‖ ~ment n χειρισμός, διαχείρισις ‖ (*directors*) διεύθυνσις, διοίκησις ‖ ~r n διευθυντής ‖ ~ress n διευθύντρια ‖ ~rial a διευθυντικός, τεχνοκρατικός.
managing ['mænidʒiŋ] a: ~ director n γενικός διευθυντής.
mandarin ['mændərin] n (*orange*) μανταρίνι ‖ μανδαρῖνος.

M

mandate ['mændeit] n (*instruction*) ἐντολή ‖ (*commission*) ἐντολή.
mandatory ['mændətəri] a ἐπιτακτικός.
mandolin(e) ['mændəlin] n μαντολίνο.
mane [mein] n χαίτη.
maneuver [mə'nu:və*] (*US*) = **manoeuvre**.
manful ['mænful] a ρωμαλέος, θαρραλέος ‖ ~ly ad παλληκαρίσια.
mangle ['mæŋgl] vt καταξεσκίζω, κατακόπτω.
mango ['mæŋgəu] n μάγγο.
manhandle ['mænhændl] vt ξυλοφορτώνω, κακομεταχειρίζομαι.
manhole ['mænhəul] n ἀνθρωποθυρίς, εἴσοδος ὑπονόμου.
manhood ['mænhud] n ἀνδρικότης, ἀνδρική ἡλικία.
man-hour ['mæn'auə*] n ὡριαία ἐργασία.
manhunt ['mænhʌnt] n ἀνθρωποκυνήγι.
mania ['meiniə] n (*craze*) μανία, πάθος ‖ τρέλλα ‖ ~c n μανιακός.
manicure ['mænikjuə*] n μανικιούρ ‖ vt φτιάχνω τά νύχια ‖ ~ set n κασετίνα τοῦ μανικιούρ.
manifest ['mænifest] vt ἐπιδεικνύω, ἐκδηλώνω ‖ a ἔκδηλος, προφανής ‖ ~ation n ἐκδήλωσις ‖ ~ly ad προφανῶς ‖ ~o n διακήρυξις, μανιφέστο.
manipulate [mə'nipjuleit] vt χειρίζομαι, μανουβράρω.
manipulation [mənipju'leiʃən] n χειρισμός, τέχνασμα.
mankind [mæn'kaind] n ἀνθρωπότης, οἱ ἄνδρες.
manliness ['mænlinis] n ἀνδρικότης, ἀνδρισμός.
manly ['mænli] a ἀνδρικός, ἀνδροπρεπής, ἀντρίκιος.
manner ['mænə*] n τρόπος ‖ (*custom*) συμπεριφορά, εἴδος ‖ ~s npl συμπεριφορά, τρόποι ‖ ~ism n (*of person*) ἰδιορρυθμία, ἰδιοτροπία.
manoeuvrable [mə'nu:vrəbl] a εὐέλικτος, εὐχείριστος.
manoeuvre [mə'nu:və*] vti ἑλίσσομαι, μανουβράρω ‖ n (*mil*) ἑλιγμός, ἄσκησις ‖ ἑλιγμός, μηχανορραφίες, μανοῦβρες ‖ ~s npl γυμνάσια.
manor ['mænə*] n τιμάριον, κτῆμα ‖ ~ house n ἀρχοντικό σπίτι.
manpower ['mænpauə*] n δύναμις εἰς ἄνδρας.
manservant ['mænsə:vənt] n ὑπηρέτης, καμαριέρης.
mansion ['mænʃən] n μέγαρον.
manslaughter ['mænslɔ:tə*] n ἀνθρωποκτονία.
mantelpiece ['mæntlpi:s] n γείσωμα τζακιοῦ.
mantle ['mæntl] n μανδύας.
manual ['mænjuəl] a χειρωνακτικός ‖ n ἐγχειρίδιον.
manufacture [mænju'fæktʃə*] vt κατασκευ-

άζω, βιομηχανοποιῶ ‖ n κατασκευή, βιομηχανία ‖ ~r n βιομήχανος.
manure [mə'njuə*] n κοπριά, λίπασμα.
manuscript ['mænjuskript] n χειρόγραφον.
many ['meni] a πολλοί, ἀρκετοί ‖ n ἀρκετοί, πολλοί, ὅσοι.
map [mæp] n χάρτης ‖ vt χαρτογραφῶ ‖ to ~ out vt χαράσσω, καθορίζω, κανονίζω.
maple ['meipl] n σφενδάμι.
mar [ma:*] vt βλάπτω, χαλῶ, παραμορφώνω.
marathon ['mærəθən] n μαραθώνιος.
marauder [mə'rɔ:də*] n λεηλάτης, ληστής.
marble ['ma:bl] n μάρμαρον ‖ pl (*game*) βῶλος, μπίλλι.
March [ma:tʃ] n Μάρτης.
march [ma:tʃ] vi βαδίζω, βηματίζω, ὁδηγῶ ‖ n (*time*) ἐμβατήριον ‖ πορεία, βάδισμα ‖ ~-past n παρέλασις.
mare [mɛə*] n φοράδα.
margarine [ma:dʒə'ri:n] n μαργαρίνη.
margin ['ma:dʒin] n (*page*) περιθώριον ‖ (*extra amount*) περιθώριον ‖ ~al a περιθωριακός.
marigold ['mærigəuld] n χρυσάνθεμο.
marijuana [mæri'hwa:nə] n μαριχουάνα.
marina [mə'ri:nə] n (*for boats*) μαρίνα.
marine [mə'ri:n] a θαλάσσιος, ναυτικός, πεζοναυτικός ‖ n πεζοναύτης ‖ ~r ['mærinə*] n ναύτης, ναυτιλόμενος.
marionette [mæriə'net] n μαριονέττα.
marital ['mæritl] a συζυγικός.
maritime ['mæritaim] a θαλασσινός, ναυτικός ‖ (*power*) ναυτική (δύναμις).
marjoram ['ma:dʒərəm] n μαντζουράνα.
mark [ma:k] n (*coin*) μάρκα ‖ (*scar etc*) σημάδι, ἴχνος, στίγμα ‖ (*sign*) σημεῖον, ἔνδειξις ‖ (*target*) στόχος, σημάδι ‖ (*grade*) βαθμός ‖ vt (*make a mark*) μαρκάρω, σημαδεύω ‖ (*indicate*) δεικνύω, ἐκδηλώνω, δείχνω ‖ (*watch etc*) προσέχω, κοιτάζω ‖ (*exam*) διορθώνω, βαθμολογῶ ‖ to ~ time κάνω βῆμα σημειωτόν ‖ (*make no progress*) δέν προχωρῶ ‖ to ~ out vt σημαδεύω ‖ ~ed a ἔντονος, σαφής, φανερός, ἐμφανής ‖ ~edly ad ἐντόνως, σαφῶς, καταφανῶς ‖ ~er n (*sign*) δείκτης.
market ['ma:kit] n ἀγορά ‖ (*overseas*) ἀγορά ‖ (*demand*) ζήτησις ‖ vt (*comm: new product*) πωλῶ ‖ (*project*) προβάλλω ‖ ~ day n ἡμέρα ἀγορᾶς ‖ ~ garden n (*Brit*) περιβόλι (κηπουρικῶν) ‖ ~ing n ἀγορά, πώλησις ‖ ~ place n ἀγορά, παζάρι.
marksman ['ma:ksmən] n σκοπευτής ‖ ~ship n σκοπευτική ἱκανότης.
marmalade ['ma:məleid] n μαρμελάδα.
maroon [mə'ru:n] vt (*usually passive*) ἐγκαταλείπω εἰς ἔρημον ἀκτήν ‖ a (*colour*) ἐρυθρόφαιος.
marquee [ma:'ki:] n μεγάλη τέντα.

marquess, marquis ['ma:kwis] n μαρκήσιος.
marriage ['mærɪdʒ] n (institution) παντρειά ‖ (wedding) γάμος.
married ['mærɪd] a (person) έγγαμος ‖ (life) έγγαμος βίος, παντρειά.
marrow ['mærəu] n μυελός, μεδούλι ‖ (vegetable) κολοκύθι.
marry ['mæri] vt νυμφεύω, παντρεύω ‖ vi (also get married) νυμφεύομαι, παντρεύομαι.
Mars [ma:z] n ˮΑρης.
marsh [ma:ʃ] n έλος, βάλτος.
marshal ['ma:ʃəl] n (US) σερίφης ‖ vt παρατάσσω, συγκεντρώνω ‖ see field.
marshy ['ma:ʃi] a ελώδης.
martial ['ma:ʃəl] a πολεμικός, στρατιωτικός ‖ ~ law n στρατιωτικός νόμος.
martyr ['ma:tə*] n μάρτυρας ‖ (fig) βασανιζόμενος, πάσχων άπό ‖ ~dom n μαρτύριον.
marvel ['ma:vəl] n θαύμα ‖ vi (+ at) έκπλήσσομαι, ξαφνίζομαι ‖ ~lous, (US) ~ous a θαυμάσιος, καταπληκτικός ‖ ~lously, (US) ~ously ad θαυμάσια, υπέροχα.
Marxism ['ma:ksizəm] n μαρξισμός.
Marxist ['ma:ksist] n μαρξιστής.
mascara [mæs'ka:rə] n μάσκαρα.
mascot ['mæskət] n μασκώτ.
masculine ['mæskjulin] a άρρην, άρσενικός ‖ (manly) άνδροπρεπής, ρωμαλέος ‖ (gram) άρσενικός ‖ n τό άρσενικόν.
masculinity [mæskju'liniti] n άρρενότης, άνδρικόν ύφος.
mashed [mæʃt] a: ~ potatoes npl πατάτες πουρέ.
mask [ma:sk] n προσωπίς, μάσκα ‖ (pretence) προσωπεῖον ‖ vt καλύπτω, άποκρύπτω.
masochist ['mæzəukist] n μαζοχιστής.
mason ['meisn] n (stonemason) κτίστης ‖ (freemason) τέκτων ‖ ~ic [mə'sɔnik] a τεκτονικός, μασονικός ‖ ~ry ['meisnri] n λιθοδομή, χτίσιμο.
masquerade [mæskə'reid] n μεταμφίεσις ‖ vi μεταμφιέζομαι.
mass [mæs] n (phys) μάζα ‖ (information, people) όγκος, μάζα, πλήθος ‖ τό μεγαλύτερον μέρος, ή πλειονηφία ‖ (rel) λειτουργία ‖ vi συγκεντρώνω, άθροίζω, μαζεύω ‖ vi συγκεντρούμαι, μαζεύομαι.
massacre ['mæsəkə*] n σφαγή, μακελειό ‖ vt σφάζω.
massage ['mæsa:ʒ] n μάλαξις, μασσάζ ‖ vt μαλάσσω, κάνω μασσάζ.
masseur [mæ'sə:*] n μασσέρ.
masseuse [mæ'sə:z] n μασσέζ.
massive ['mæsiv] a ὀγκώδης, δυνατός.
mass media ['mæs'mi:diə] npl μέσα μαζικής έπικοινωνίας.
mass-produce ['mæsprə'dju:s] vt παράγω μαζικῶς.

mass production ['mæsprə'dʌkʃən] n μαζική παραγωγή.
mast [ma:st] n ἱστός, κατάρτι ‖ (pole) στήλη, στύλος.
master ['ma:stə*] n κύριος, άφεντικό ‖ (teacher) δάσκαλος, καθηγητής ‖ (head) άρχηγός ‖ (of ship) καπετάνιος ‖ (artist) μεγάλος καλλιτέχνης ‖ vt έξουσιάζω, έλέγχω ‖ (learn) μαθαίνω τέλεια ‖ ~ly a έντεχνος, άριστοτεχνικός ‖ ~mind n ἰθύνων νοῦς ‖ vt συλλαμβάνω, πραγματοποιῶ ‖ M~ of Arts n πτυχιοῦχος φιλολογίας ‖ ~piece n άριστούργημα ‖ ~ stroke n άριστοτεχνικόν κτύπημα ‖ ~y n έξουσία, ὑπεροχή, μαεστρία.
masturbate ['mæstəbeit] vi μαλακίζομαι.
masturbation [mæstə'beiʃən] n μαλακία.
mat [mæt] n ψάθα, χαλάκι ‖ (material for table) στρωσίδι τραπεζιοῦ ‖ (tangled mass) μπλεγμένα νήματα κτλ ‖ vti μπλέκω, μπερδεύω.
matador ['mætədɔ*] n ταυρομάχος.
match [mætʃ] n (matchstick) σπίρτο ‖ (game) άγών ‖ (equal) ταίρι ‖ (marriage) συνοικέσιον ‖ vt (be like) έναρμονίζω, ταιριάζω ‖ (equal strength etc) έξισοῦμαι μέ, φθάνω ‖ vi συμβιβάζομαι, συμφωνῶ, ταιριάζω ‖ ~box n κουτί σπίρτα ‖ ~ing a προσαρμογή, ταίριασμα ‖ ~less a άπαράμιλλος.
mate [meit] n σύντροφος, συνάδελφος ‖ (husband, wife) σύζυγος, ταίρι ‖ (naut) ὑποπλοίαρχος ‖ vi (chess) κάνω μάτ ‖ (of animal) ζευγαρώνομαι.
material [mə'tiəriəl] n ὕλη, ὑλικόν ‖ a σημαντικός, οὐσιώδης ‖ (of matter) ὑλικός ‖ (opposite of spirit) ὑλικός ‖ ~s npl ὑλικά, έφόδια ‖ ~istic a ὑλιστικός ‖ ~ize vi πραγματοποιοῦμαι, γίνομαι ‖ ~ly ad ὑλικῶς, οὐσιαστικά.
maternal [mə'tə:nl] a μητρικός ‖ (relatives) άπό τήν μητέρα.
maternity [mə'tə:niti] n (dress) φόρεμα έγγύου ‖ μητρότης ‖ (hospital) μαιευτήριον.
matey ['meiti] a (col) φιλικός.
mathematical [mæθə'mætikəl] a μαθηματικός ‖ (exact) μαθηματική (άκρίβεια) ‖ ~ly ad μαθηματικῶς.
mathematician [mæθəmə'tiʃən] n μαθηματικός.
mathematics [mæθə'mætiks] n (also maths) μαθηματικά.
matinée ['mætinei] n παράστασις (άπογευματινή).
mating ['meitiŋ] n ζευγάρωμα, βάτεμα.
matins ['mætinz] npl ὄρθρος.
matriarchal [meitri'a:kl] a μητριαρχικός.
matrimonial [mætri'məuniəl] a γαμήλιος, συζυγικός.
matrimony ['mætriməni] n γάμος, έγγαμος βίος.
matron ['meitrən] n (med) προϊσταμένη ‖

matt (sch) ἐπιμελήτρια, οἰκονόμος ‖ ~ly a σεβάσμιος, ἀτάραχος.

matt [mæt] a (paint) μουντός, μάτ.

matter ['mætə*] n οὐσία, ὕλη ‖ (affair) ὑπόθεσις, θέμα, πρᾶγμα ‖ (question, issue etc) ζήτημα ‖ (discharge) πύον, ἔμπυον ‖ vi ἔχω σημασίαν, ἐνδιαφέρω ‖ what is the ~ ? τί συμβαίνει; ‖ as a ~ of fact τῷ ὄντι ‖ ~-of-fact a πεζός, πρακτικός.

matting ['mætiŋ] n ψάθα, πλέγμα.

mattress ['mætris] n στρῶμα.

mature [mə'tjuə*] a ὥριμος ‖ vi ὡριμάζω.

maturity [mə'tjuəriti] n (fin) λῆξις.

maul [mɔːl] vt κακοποιῶ, κοπανίζω.

mausoleum [mɔːsə'liːəm] n μαυσωλεῖον.

mauve [məuv] a (colour) μώβ.

mawkish ['mɔːkiʃ] a ἀνούσιος, ἀηδής.

maxim ['mæksim] n ἀπόφθεγμα, γνωμικόν.

maximize ['mæksimaiz] vt φέρω εἰς μέγιστον.

maximum ['mæksiməm] a ἀνώτατος, μέγιστος ‖ n μέγιστον, μάξιμουμ.

May [mei] n Μάης.

may [mei] (irreg v) vi (be possible) ἐνδέχεται νά, ἴσως νά ‖ (have permission) ἔχω τήν ἄδειαν νά, μπορῶ νά ‖ ~be ad ἴσως, δυνατόν.

May Day ['meidei] n Πρωτομαγιά.

mayonnaise [meiə'neiz] n μαγιονέζα.

mayor [mɛə*] n δήμαρχος ‖ ~ess n (wife) κυρία δημάρχου ‖ (lady mayor) ἡ δήμαρχος.

maze [meiz] n (network) λαβύρινθος ‖ (confused state) κυκεών.

me [miː] pron (after prep) (ἐ)μέ, σ᾽ ἐμένα.

meadow ['medəu] n λειβάδι.

meagre, (US) meager ['miːgə*] a ἰσχνός, πενιχρός.

meal [miːl] n φαγητό ‖ (grain) χονδράλευρον ‖ ~time n ὥρα φαγητοῦ ‖ ~y-mouthed a γλυκομίλητος, μέ παχειά λόγια.

mean [miːn] (irreg v) a ἄθλιος, φτωχός, ταπεινός ‖ (stingy) φιλάργυρος, τσιγκούνης ‖ (average) μέσος, μεσαῖος ‖ vt (signify) ἐννοῶ, σημαίνω, θέλω νά πῶ ‖ (intend) προτίθεμαι, σκοπεύω ‖ (be resolved) προορίζω ‖ n (average) μέσος ὅρος, μέσον ‖ ~s npl μέσα, τρόποι ‖ (wealth) πόροι, μέσα, περιουσία ‖ by ~s of διά, μέ τήν βοήθειαν τοῦ ‖ by all ~s ὁπωσδήποτε.

meander [mi'ændə*] vi ἐλίσσομαι, σχηματίζω μαιάνδρους.

meaning ['miːniŋ] n (intention) λόγος, σκοπός ‖ (sense of word) ἔννοια, σημασία, νόημα ‖ ~less a χωρίς νόημα.

meanness ['miːnnis] n μικρότης, μικροπρέπεια.

meant [ment] pt,pp of mean.

meantime ['miːn'taim] ad, meanwhile

['miːn'wail] ad ἐν τῷ μεταξύ, στό μεταξύ.

measles ['miːzlz] n ἱλαρά ‖ German ~ n ἐρυθρά.

measly ['miːzli] a (col) ἀσήμαντος, ἀνάξιος, τιποτένιος.

measurable ['meʒərəbl] a καταμετρητός, μετρήσιμος.

measure ['meʒə*] vt (find size) μετρῶ ‖ (test) δοκιμάζω, ἀναμετρῶμαι ‖ vi (be certain size) εἶναι, ἔχει διαστάσεις . . . ‖ n (unit) μέτρον ‖ (tape measure) μεζούρα, μέτρον ‖ (plan) μέτρον, ἐνέργεια, πρᾶξις ‖ (a law) μέτρον ‖ ~d a μετρημένος ‖ ~ment n (way of measuring) μέτρησις, μέτρημα ‖ (amount measured) μέτρα, διαστάσεις.

meat [miːt] n (flesh) κρέας ‖ ~ pie n κρεατόπιττα ‖ ~y a (lit) σαρκώδης ‖ (fig) οὐσιαστικός, δεμένος, ζουμερός.

Mecca ['mekə] n Μέκκα ‖ (fig) Μέκκα.

mechanic [mi'kænik] n τεχνίτης, μηχανικός ‖ ~s n μηχανική ‖ ~al a μηχανικός ‖ (automatically) μηχανικός, αὐτόματος.

mechanism ['mekənizəm] n μηχανισμός.

mechanization [mekənai'zeiʃən] n μηχανοποίησις.

mechanize ['mekənaiz] vt μηχανοποιῶ, κάνω μηχανοκίνητο.

medal ['medl] n μετάλλιον ‖ ~lion [mi'dæliən] n μενταγιόν ‖ ~list, (US) ~ist n κάτοχος μεταλλίου.

meddle ['medl] vi (+ with) ἀνακατεύομαι, ἐπεμβαίνω ‖ ~some a πολυπράγμων, ἀνακατωσούρης.

media ['miːdiə] npl (of communication) μέσα.

mediate ['miːdieit] vi μεσολαβῶ.

mediation [miːdi'eiʃən] n μεσολάβησις.

mediator ['miːdieitə*] n μεσολαβητής.

medical ['medikəl] a (science) ἰατρικός ‖ (student) (φοιτητής) ἰατρικῆς ‖ ~ly ad ἰατρικῶς.

medicated ['medikeitid] a ἐμποτισμένος μέ φάρμακον.

medicinal [me'disinl] a φαρμακευτικός, ἰατρικός, θεραπευτικός.

medicine ['medsin] n ἰατρική ‖ (drugs) φάρμακα, ἰατρικά ‖ ~ chest n φαρμακεῖον.

medieval [medi'iːvəl] a μεσαιωνικός.

mediocre [miːdi'əukə*] a μέτριος, τῆς ἀράδας.

mediocrity [miːdi'ɔkriti] n μετριότης.

meditate ['mediteit] vi (+ on) μελετῶ, σκέπτομαι, συλλογίζομαι.

meditation [medi'teiʃən] n συλλογισμός, διαλογισμός.

Mediterranean (Sea) [meditə'reiniən(siː)] n Μεσόγειος (θάλασσα).

medium ['miːdiəm] a μεσαῖος, μέτριος ‖ n μέσον, μέσος ὅρος ‖ (means) μέσον, διά τοῦ.

medley ['medli] n σύμφυρμα, κυκεών, μίγμα.

meek [mi:k] *a* πρᾶος, ἤρεμος, πειθήνιος ‖ ~**ly** *ad* ἤρεμα, μαλακά.

meet [mi:t] (*irreg v*) *a* (*old*) πρέπων, σωστός, πού ταιριάζει ‖ *vt* συναντῶ, ἀπαντῶ, ἀνταμώνω ‖ (*come across*) βρίσκω, ἀπαντῶ, διασταυροῦμαι ‖ (*go towards*) προχωρῶ πρός συνάντησιν, πηγαίνω ‖ (*pay, satisfy*) ἐκπληρώνω, ἀνταποκρίνομαι, τιμῶ ‖ *vi* (*by arrangement*) συναντῶμαι, βλέπομαι ‖ (*fight*) ἀντιμετωπίζω ‖ (*join*) συναντῶμαι, συναθροίζομαι, συνέρχομαι ‖ **to ~ with** *vt* (*problems*) συναντῶ, ἀντιμετωπίζω ‖ (*US: people*) συναντῶ, γνωρίζω ‖ ~**ing** *n* συνάντησις, συνάθροισις, συνέλευσις ‖ ~ **ing place** *n* τόπος συναντήσεως.

megaphone ['megəfəun] *n* μεγάφωνον.

melancholy ['melənkəli] *n* μελαγχολία, κατήφεια ‖ *a* μελαγχολικός.

mellow ['meləu] *a* ὥριμος ‖ (*delicate*) ἁπαλός, γλυκός ‖ (*aged*) ἁπαλός ‖ *vi* ὡριμάζω, ἁπαλύνομαι.

melodious [mi'ləudiəs] *a* μελωδικός.

melodrama ['meləudra:mə] *n* μελόδραμα ‖ ~**tic** *a* μελοδραματικός.

melody ['melədi] *n* μελωδία.

melon ['melən] *n* πεπόνι.

melt [melt] *vi* τήκομαι, λυώνω ‖ (*disappear*) χάνομαι, διαλύομαι ‖ *vt* τήκω, λυώνω ‖ **to ~ away** *vi* λυώνω, διαλύομαι ‖ **to ~ down** *vt* λυώνω, τήκω ‖ ~**ing point** *n* σημεῖον τήξεως ‖ ~**ing pot** *n* (*fig*) χωνευτήριον, ρευστή κατάστασις.

member ['membə*] *n* μέλος ‖ (*parl*) βουλευτής ‖ ~**ship** *n* ἰδιότης μέλους ‖ τά μέλη, ἀριθμός μελῶν.

membrane ['membrein] *n* μεμβράνη.

memento [mə'mentəu] *n* ἐνθύμιον, ἐνθύμησις.

memo ['meməu] *n* (*comm*) ὑπόμνημα, σημείωμα.

memoir ['memwa:*] *n* ὑπόμνημα ‖ ~**s** *npl* ἀπομνημονεύματα.

memorable ['memərəbl] *a* ἀξιομνημόνευτος, ἀξέχαστος.

memorandum [memə'rændəm] *n* (*comm*) ὑπόμνημα, σημείωμα.

memorial [mi'mɔːriəl] *n* μνημεῖον ‖ *a* ἀναμνηστικός, ἐπιμνημόσυνος.

memorize ['meməraiz] *vt* ἀποστηθίζω, μαθαίνω ἀπ' ἔξω.

memory ['meməri] *n* μνήμη, μνημονικό, θυμητικό ‖ (*thing recalled*) ἀνάμνησις, θύμηση ‖ **in ~ of** εἰς μνήμην τοῦ, εἰς ἀνάμνησιν τοῦ.

men [men] *npl of* **man**.

menace ['menis] *n* ἀπειλή, φοβέρα ‖ *vt* ἀπειλῶ, φοβερίζω.

menacing ['menisiŋ] *a* ἀπειλητικός ‖ ~**ly** *ad* ἀπειλητικά.

ménage [me'na:ʒ] *n* νοικοκυριό.

menagerie [mi'nædʒəri] *n* θηριοτροφεῖον.

mend [mend] *vt* (ἐπι)διορθώνω, βελτιώνω ‖ *vi* ἀναρρωνύω ‖ *n* ἐπιδιόρθωσις, ἐπισκευή ‖ **on the ~** συνέρχομαι, πάω καλύτερα.

menial ['mi:niəl] *a* ταπεινός, δουλοπρεπής.

meningitis [menin'dʒaitis] *n* μηνιγγῖτις.

menopause ['menəupɔːz] *n* ἐμμηνόπαυσις.

menstrual ['menstruəl] *a* καταμήνιος, ἔμμηνος.

menstruation [menstru'eiʃən] *n* ἔμμηνα, περίοδος.

mental ['mentl] *a* διανοητικός, νοερός, πνευματικός ‖ (*col: abnormal*) τρελλός ‖ ~**ity** *n* νοοτροπία ‖ ~**ly** *ad* πνευματικῶς.

mentholated ['menθəleitid] *a* περιέχον μινθόλην.

mention ['menʃən] *n* μνεία ‖ *vt* ἀναφέρω ‖ **don't ~ it!** παρακαλῶ!

menu ['menju:] *n* μενοῦ.

mercantile ['mə:kəntail] *a* ἐμπορικός.

mercenary ['mə:sinəri] *a* φιλοχρήματος, πλεονέκτης ‖ *n* μισθοφόρος.

merchandise ['mə:tʃəndaiz] *n* ἐμπορεύματα.

merchant ['mə:tʃənt] *n* ἔμπορος ‖ *a* ἐμπορικός ‖ ~ **navy** *n* ἐμπορικόν ναυτικόν.

merciful ['mə:siful] *a* εὐσπλαχνος ‖ ~**ly** *ad* σπλαχνικά.

merciless ['mə:silis] *a* ἀνηλεής, ἄσπλαχνος ‖ ~**ly** *ad* ἀνηλεῶς, ἀλύπητα.

mercurial [mə:'kjuəriəl] *a* ὑδραργυρικός, ζωηρός.

mercury ['mə:kjuri] *n* ὑδράργυρος.

mercy ['mə:si] *n* εὐσπλαχνία, ἔλεος ‖ (*blessing*) εὐλογία ‖ **at the ~ of** στό ἔλεος τοῦ.

mere [miə*] *a* ἁπλός, τίποτε ἄλλο ἀπό ‖ ~**ly** *ad* ἁπλῶς, μόνον.

merge [mə:dʒ] *vt* ἀπορροφῶ, συγχωνεύω ‖ *vi* (*become absorbed*) ἀπορροφοῦμαι, συγχωνεύομαι ‖ ~**r** *n* (*comm*) συγχώνευσις.

meridian [mə'ridiən] *n* μεσημβρινός.

meringue [mə'ræŋ] *n* μαρέγγα.

merit ['merit] *n* ἀξία, προσόν ‖ *vt* ἀξίζω.

mermaid ['mə:meid] *n* γοργόνα.

merrily ['merili] *ad* εὔθυμα, χαρούμενα.

merriment ['merimənt] *n* εὐθυμία, διασκέδασις.

merry ['meri] *a* εὔθυμος, φαιδρός, χαρωπός ‖ (*col: after drink*) στό κέφι, πιωμένος.

mesh [meʃ] *n* θηλειά (δικτύου) ‖ *vti* (*gears*) ἐμπλέκω, ἐμπλέκομαι.

mesmerize ['mezməraiz] *vt* μαγνητίζω, ὑπνωτίζω.

mess [mes] *n* σαλάτα, θάλασσα ‖ (*untidy state*) ἀκαθαρσία, ἄνω-κάτω ‖ (*mil*) συσσίτιον, τραπέζι ‖ (*officers' mess*) λέσχη ἀξιωματικῶν ‖ **to ~ about** *vi* χασομερῶ ‖ **to ~ about with** *vt* πασπατεύω, σαχλαμαρίζω ‖ **to ~ up** *vt* χαλῶ, μπλέκω, περιπλέκω.

message ['mesidʒ] *n* μήνυμα, διάγγελμα, εἴδησις.

messenger ['mesindʒə*] *n* ἀγγελιαφόρος.

messy ['mesi] *a* ἀκάθαρτος, φύρδην-μύγδην.

met [met] *pt,pp of* meet.

metabolism [me'tæbəlizəm] *n* μεταβολισμός.

metal ['metl] *n* μέταλλον ‖ ~**lic** *a* μεταλλικός ‖ ~**lurgy** *n* μεταλλουργία.

metamorphosis [metə'mɔːfəsis] *n* μεταμόρφωσις.

metaphor ['metəfɔː*] *n* μεταφορά ‖ ~**ical** *a* μεταφορικός.

metaphysics [metə'fiziks] *n* μεταφυσική.

meteor ['miːtiə*] *n* μετέωρον ‖ ~**ic** *a* μετεωρικός, λαμπρός ‖ ~**ite** *n* μετεωρίτης ‖ ~**ological** *a* μετεωρολογικός ‖ ~**ology** *n* μετεωρολογία.

meter ['miːtə*] *n* (*instrument*) μετρητής (*US*) = **metre**.

method ['meθəd] *n* μέθοδος ‖ ~**ical** *a* μεθοδικός.

Methodist ['meθədist] *a,n* μεθοδιστής.

methodology [meθə'dɔlədʒi] *n* μεθοδολογία.

methylated spirit ['meθileitid'spirit] *n* (*also* **meths**) μεθυλικόν οἰνόπνευμα.

meticulous [mi'tikjuləs] *a* λεπτολόγος, λεπτομερειακός.

metre ['miːtə*] *n* μέτρον.

metric(al) ['metrik(əl)] *a* μετρικός ‖ ~ **system** *n* μετρικόν σύστημα.

metronome ['metrənəum] *n* μετρονόμος.

metropolis [mi'trɔpəlis] *n* μητρόπολις.

mews [mjuːz] *n* ἀδιέξοδος.

Mexican ['meksikən] *a* μεξικανικός ‖ *n* Μεξικανός.

Mexico ['meksikəu] *n* Μεξικόν.

mezzanine ['mezəniːn] *n* μετζοπάτωμα, μέτζο.

miaow [miːˈau] *vi* νιαουρίζω.

mice [mais] *npl of* mouse.

mickey ['miki] *n* (*col*) **to take the** ~ **out of s.o.** κοροϊδεύω, τή σκάω.

microbe ['maikrəub] *n* μικρόβιον.

microfilm ['maikrəufilm] *n* μικροφίλμ.

microphone ['maikrəfəun] *n* μικρόφωνον.

microscope ['maikrəskəup] *n* μικροσκόπιον.

microscopic [maikrə'skɔpik] *a* μικροσκοπικός.

mid [mid] *a* μέσος, μεσαῖος ‖ **in** ~ **course** στό μέσον, στήν ἀκμήν.

midday ['mid'dei] *n* μεσημέρι.

middle ['midl] *n* μέσον ‖ *a* μέσος, μεσαῖος ‖ ~-**aged** *a* μεσῆλιξ ‖ **the M** ~ **Ages** *npl* ὁ Μεσαίων ‖ ~ **class** *n* μεσαία τάξις, ἀστική τάξις ‖ ~-**class** *a* ἀστικός ‖ **M** ~ **East** *n* Μέση 'Ανατολή ‖ ~**man** *n* μεταπωλητής, μεσίτης ‖ ~ **name** *n* ὄνομα πατρός.

middling ['midliŋ] *ad* μέτρια, καλούτσικα.

midge [midʒ] *n* σκνίπα.

midget ['midʒit] *n* νάνος, ἀνθρωπάκι ‖ *a* μικρός, μικροσκοπικός.

Midlands ['midləndz] *n* (*of England*) κεντρικές κομητεῖες (τῆς 'Αγγλίας).

midnight ['midnait] *n* μεσάνυκτα.

midst [midst] *n*: **in the** ~ **of** στό μέσον.

midsummer ['mid'sʌmə*] *n* μεσοκαλόκαιρο.

midway ['mid'wei] *ad* (+ *between*) στό μέσον ‖ *a* μέσος.

midweek ['mid'wiːk] *ad* στά μέσα τῆς ἑβδομάδος.

midwife ['midwaif] *n* μαία, μαμμή ‖ ~**ry** ['midwifəri] *n* μαιευτική.

midwinter ['mid'wintə*] *n* στό μέσον τοῦ χειμῶνος, μεσοχείμωνο.

might [mait] *pt of* may ‖ *n* ἰσχύς, δύναμις ‖ ~**ily** *ad* (*very*) πάρα πολύ, περίφημα ‖ ἰσχυρῶς, μέ δύναμιν ‖ ~**n't** = **might not**, *see* **may** ‖ ~**y** *a* ἰσχυρός, δυνατός ‖ *ad* (*col*) πολύ, τρομερά.

migraine ['miːgrein] *n* ἡμικρανία.

migrant ['maigrənt] *n* μεταναστευτικός, περαστικός ‖ *a* ἀποδημητικός, μεταναστευτικός.

migrate [mai'greit] *vi* (*birds*) ἀποδημῶ.

migration [mai'greiʃən] *n* μετανάστευσις.

mike [maik] *n* (*microphone*) μικρόφωνον.

mild [maild] *a* (*rebuke*) ἐπιεικής, μαλακός ‖ (*warm*) ἤπιος, εὔκρατος ‖ (*not sour*) ἐλαφρό ‖ (*slight*) ἐλαφρό ‖ *n* (*beer*) ἐλαφριά μπύρα.

mildew ['mildjuː] *n* μούχλα, σείρηκας.

mildly ['maildli] *ad* ἤρεμα, μαλακά.

mildness ['maildnis] *n* ἠπιότης, γλύκα, ἐπιείκεια.

mile [mail] *n* μίλι (1609 μ) ‖ ~**age** *n* ἀπόστασις εἰς μίλια ‖ ~**stone** *n* μιλιοδείκτης ‖ (*fig*) ἰστορικός σταθμός.

militant ['militənt] *n* ὀπαδός τῆς ἀμέσου δράσεως ‖ *a* μαχητικός.

militarism ['militərizəm] *n* μιλιταρισμός.

military ['militəri] *a* στρατιωτικός ‖ *n* οἱ στρατιωτικοί, στρατός.

militate ['militeit] *vi* (+ *against*) ἀντιστρατεύομαι, ἀντιμάχομαι.

militia [mi'liʃə] *n* ἐθνοφυλακή.

milk [milk] *n* γάλα ‖ *vt* (*cow*) ἀρμέγω ‖ (*fig*) ἐκμεταλλεύομαι, μαδῶ ‖ ~ **chocolate** *n* σοκολάτα γάλακτος ‖ ~**ing** *n* ἄρμεγμα ‖ ~**man** *n* γαλατάς ‖ **M** ~ **y Way** *n* Γαλαξίας.

mill [mil] *n* μύλος ‖ (*building*) μύλος ‖ (*factory*) ἐργοστάσιον ‖ *vt* (*grind*) ἀλέθω ‖ *vi* (*move around*) στριφογυρίζω ‖ ~**ed** *a* ὀδοντωτός, μέ ραβδώσεις.

millenium [mi'leniəm] *n* χιλιετηρίς.

miller ['milə*] *n* μυλωνάς.

millet ['milit] *n* κεχρί, σόργον.

milligram(me) ['miligræm] *n* χιλιοστόγραμμον.

millilitre, (*US*) ~**liter** ['mililiːtə*] *n* χιλιοστόλιτρον.

millimetre, (*US*) ~**meter** [milimiːtə*] *n* χιλιοστόμετρον.

milliner ['milinə*] *n* καπελλοῦ ‖ ~**y** *n* γυναικεῖα καπέλλα ‖ ἐμπόριον γυναικείων καπέλλων.

million ['miljən] *n* ἐκατομμύριον ‖ ~**aire** *n* ἐκατομμυριοῦχος ‖ ~**th** *a* ἐκατομμυριοστός.

mime [maim] *n* μῖμος, μιμόδραμα ‖ *vti* μιμοῦμαι, παίζω μέ μιμικήν.

mimic ['mimik] *n* μῖμος, μιμητής ‖ *vti* μιμοῦμαι, κοροϊδεύω, ἀντιγράφω ‖ ~**ry** *n* μίμησις, μιμική.

mince [mins] *vt* ψιλοκόβω, κάνω κιμᾶ ‖ (*words*) μασῶ ‖ *vi* βαδίζω μέ προσποιητήν χάριν ‖ *n* (*meat*) κιμᾶς ‖ ~**meat** *n* κομπόστα ‖ ~ **pie** *n* σκαλτσούνι, κρεατόπιττα ‖ ~**r** *n* κρεατομηχανή.

mincing ['minsiŋ] *a* (*manner*) προσποιητός, φτιαστός, ψεύτικος.

mind [maind] *n* νοῦς, μυαλό ‖ (*intelligence*) σκέψις, γνώμη, ἰδέα ‖ (*memory*) μνήμη, ἀνάμνησις, θύμησις ‖ *vti* φροντίζω, προσέχω ‖ (*be careful*) προσέχω ‖ (*object to*) ἀντιτίθεμαι πρός, ἐνοχλοῦμαι, πειράζομαι ‖ **on my** ~ στή σκέψι μου, ἀνησυχῶ ‖ **to my** ~ κατά τήν γνώμην μου ‖ **out of one's** ~ τρελλός ‖ **never** ~ ! δέν πειράζει, ἄστο, μήν ἀνησυχεῖς ‖ **to bear** *or* **keep in** ~ δέν ξεχνῶ, λαμβάνω ὑπ' ὄψιν ‖ **to make up one's** ~ ἀποφασίζω ‖ '~ **the step**' 'πρόσεχε τήν σκάλα' ‖ ~**ed** *a* διατεθειμένος, μέ πνεῦμα ‖ ~**ful** *a* προσεκτικός ‖ ~**less** *a* ἀπερίσκεπτος, ἀδιάφορος, ἐπιλήσμων.

mine [main] *poss pron* δικός μου, δική μου, δικό μου ‖ *n* ὀρυχεῖον, μεταλλεῖον ‖ (*naut*) νάρκη ‖ (*source*) πηγή ‖ *vi* ἐξορύσσω ‖ (*naut*) ναρκοθετῶ ‖ *vi* ἐκμεταλλεύομαι ‖ ~**field** *n* ναρκοπέδιον ‖ ~**r** *n* μεταλλορύχος, ἀνθρακορύχος.

mineral ['minərəl] *a* ὀρυκτός, μεταλλευτικός ‖ *n* ὀρυκτόν, μετάλλευμα ‖ ~**ogy** *n* ὀρυκτολογία ‖ ~ **water** *n* ἀεριοῦχο ποτό, μεταλλικόν ὕδωρ.

minesweeper ['mainswi:pə*] *n* ναρκαλιευτικόν.

mingle ['miŋgl] *vt* ἀναμιγνύω ‖ *vi* (+ *with*) ἀναμιγνύομαι.

mingy ['mindʒi] *a* (*col*) στριμμένος, γύφτος, μίζερος.

mini- ['mini] *prefix* μικρο-.

miniature ['minitʃə*] *a* μικρογραφικός ‖ *n* μικρογραφία, μινιατούρα ‖ (*model*) μακέτα ‖ **in** ~ μικρού σχήματος.

minibus ['minibʌs] *n* μικρό λεωφορεῖο.

minicab ['minikæb] *n* μικρό ταξί.

minimal ['miniml] *a* ἐλάχιστος.

minimize ['minimaiz] *vt* ἐλαττώνω, μικραίνω, περιορίζω.

minimum ['miniməm] *n* ἐλάχιστον, κατώτατον ὅριον, μίνιμουμ ‖ *a* κατώτατος, ἐλάχιστος.

mining ['mainiŋ] *n* ἐξόρυξις ‖ (*naut*) ναρκοθέτησις ‖ *a* μεταλλευτική, ὀρυκτική.

minion ['minjən] *n* (*pej*) εὐνοούμενος, δοῦλος.

miniskirt ['miniskə:t] *n* κοντή φοῦστα, μίνι.

minister ['ministə*] *n* ὑπουργός ‖ (*eccl*) ἱερεύς ‖ ~**ial** [minis'tiəriəl] *a* ὑπουργικός, κυβερνητικός.

ministry ['ministri] *n* (*government*) ὑπουργεῖον, κυβέρνησις ‖ (*eccl*) τό ἱερατεῖον, κλῆρος.

mink [miŋk] *n* εἶδος νιφίτσας ‖ *a*: ~ **coat** *n* παλτό ἀπό μίνκ.

minor ['mainə*] *a* μικρότερος, μικρός ‖ (*mus*) ἐλάσσων ‖ *n* (*under 18: Brit*) ἀνήλικος ‖ ~**ity** [mai'nɔriti] *n* μειοψηφία, μειονότης.

minster ['minstə*] *n* καθεδρικός ναός ‖ (*of monastery*) ἐκκλησία μονῆς.

minstrel ['minstrəl] *n* ραψωδός, τραγουδιστής.

mint [mint] *n* (*plant*) δυόσμος ‖ (*sweet*) μέντα ‖ (*for coins*) νομισματοκοπεῖον ¶ (*large amount*) μέ τό τσουβάλι ‖ *a* (*condition*) καινούργιος, κατακαίνουργος ‖ ~ **sauce** *n* σάλτσα μέ δυόσμο.

minuet [minju'et] *n* μενουέτο.

minus ['mainəs] *n* σημεῖον τοῦ πλήν ‖ *prep* πλήν, μεῖον.

minute [mai'nju:t] *a* μικροσκοπικός, ἐλάχιστος ‖ (*detailed*) λεπτομερής ‖ ['minit] *n* λεπτόν (τῆς ὥρας) ‖ (*moment*) στιγμή ‖ ~**s** *npl* πρακτικά ‖ ~**ly** *ad* ἐπιμελῶς, λεπτομερειακῶς.

miracle ['mirəkl] *n* (*esp rel*) θαῦμα ‖ ~ **play** *n* θρησκευτικόν δρᾶμα.

miraculous [mi'rækjuləs] *a* θαυματουργός, ὑπερφυσικός, θαυμαστός ‖ ~**ly** *ad* ὡς ἐκ θαύματος.

mirage ['mira:ʒ] *n* ἀντικατοπτρισμός, ὀπτική ἀπάτη.

mirror ['mirə*] *n* καθρέπτης, κάτοπτρον ‖ *vt* ἀντικατοπτρίζω, ἀντανακλῶ.

mirth [mə:θ] *n* εὐθυμία, χαρά, κέφι.

misadventure [misəd'ventʃə*] *n* κακοτυχία, ἀτύχημα.

misanthropist [mi'zænθrəpist] *n* μισάνθρωπος.

misapply ['misə'plai] *vt* ἐφαρμόζω κακῶς.

misapprehension ['misæpri'henʃən] *n* (*misunderstanding*) παρεξήγησις.

misappropriate ['misə'prəuprieit] *vt* (*take dishonestly*) καταχρῶμαι.

misappropriation ['misəprəupri'eiʃən] *n* κατάχρησις, διασπάθισις.

misbehave ['misbi'heiv] *vi* φέρομαι ἄσχημα.

miscalculate ['mis'kælkjuleit] *vt* ὑπολογίζω ἐσφαλμένα.

miscalculation ['miskælkju'leiʃən] *n* ἐσφαλμένος ὑπολογισμός.

miscarriage ['miskæridʒ] *n* ἀποτυχία ‖ (*of justice*) δικαστικόν λάθος ‖ (*med*) ἀποβολή.

miscellaneous [misi'leiniəs] *a* ποικίλος, ἀνάμικτος.

mischance [mis'tʃa:ns] *n* ἀποτυχία, ἀτύχημα.

mischief ['mistʃif] n σκανταλιά, κατεργαριά.
mischievous ['mistʃivəs] a κατεργάρης, σκανταλιάρης ‖ **~ly** ad βλαβερά, κατεργάρικα.
misconception ['miskən'sepʃən] n έσφαλμένη άντίληψις.
misconduct [mis'kɔndʌkt] n παράπτωμα, κακή διαγωγή.
misconstrue ['miskən'stru:] vt (misunderstand) παρερμηνεύω.
miscount ['mis'kaunt] vt μετρώ έσφαλμένα.
misdemeanour, (US) **misdemeanor** [misdi'mi:nə*] n (less important offence) πταῖσμα, πλημμέλημα.
misdirect [misdi'rekt] vt (person, letter) κατευθύνω έσφαλμένα, διευθύνω κακῶς.
miser ['maizə*] n φιλάργυρος, τσιγκούνης.
miserable ['mizərəbl] a δυστυχής, θλιβερός ‖ (poor) ἄθλιος, ἐλεεινός, φτωχός.
miserably ['mizərəbli] ad θλιβερά, ἄθλια.
miserly ['maizəli] a τσιγκούνικος.
misery ['mizəri] n δυστυχία, βάσανον ‖ (poverty) ἀθλιότης, φτώχια.
misfire ['mis'faiə*] vi ρετάρω, παθαίνω ἀφλογιστίαν ‖ (plan) πέφτω στό κενό.
misfit [misfit] n (person) ἀπροσάρμοστος.
misfortune [mis'fɔ:tʃən] n άτυχία, ἀτύχημα.
misgiving [mis'givin] n (often pl) άνησυχία, ἀμφιβολία, φόβος.
misguided ['mis'gaidid] a πλανόμενος, παρασυρόμενος.
mishandle ['mis'hændl] vt (manage badly) κακομεταχειρίζομαι.
mishap ['mishæp] n ἀτυχία, ἀναποδιά.
mishear ['mis'hiə*] vt (hear wrongly) παρακούω.
misinform ['misin'fɔ:m] vt πληροφορῶ κακῶς.
misinterpret ['misin'tə:prit] vt παρερμηνεύω ‖ **~ation** n παρερμηνεία.
misjudge ['mis'dʒʌdʒ] vt κρίνω έσφαλμένα.
mislay [mis'lei] vt (misplace, lose) παραπετῶ, χάνω.
mislead [mis'li:d] vt (deceive) παραπλανῶ, ἐξαπατῶ ‖ **~ing** a παραπλανητικός.
misnomer ['mis'nəumə*] n έσφαλμένη ὀνομασία.
misogynist ['mi'sɔdʒinist] n μισογύνης.
misplace ['mis'pleis] vt (mislay) τοποθετῶ κατά λάθος, χάνω.
misprint ['misprint] n τυπογραφικόν λάθος.
mispronounce ['misprə'nauns] vt προφέρω έσφαλμένα.
misread ['mis'ri:d] vt κακοδιαβάζω, παρερμηνεύω.
misrepresent ['misrepri'zent] vt διαστρέφω, παριστάνω κακῶς.
miss [mis] vt άστοχῶ, ἀποτυγχάνω ‖ (not notice) δέν βλέπω, χάνω ‖ (train etc) χάνω ‖ (omit) παραλείπω ‖ (regret absence) μοῦ λείπει, ἀποζητῶ ‖ vi ἀντιλαμβάνομαι ‖ n (shot) άστοχία ‖ (failure) ἀποτυχία ‖

(title) δεσποινίδα ‖ **to ~ the bus** or **boat** (fig) χάνω εὐκαιρίαν ‖ **M~ Smith** Δεσποινίδα Σμίθ, Δις Σμίθ.
misshapen ['mis'ʃeipən] a παραμορφωμένος.
missile ['misail] n (esp nuclear) βλῆμα.
missing ['misin] a (person) ἀπών, ἀγνοούμενος ‖ (thing) χαμένος.
mission ['miʃən] n ἀποστολή ‖ (church) ἱεραποστολή ‖ **~ary** n ἱεραπόστολος.
misspent ['mis'spent] a (youth) χαμένα (νειάτα).
mist [mist] n ὀμίχλη, καταχνιά ‖ vi (also **~ over, ~ up**) σκεπάζω μέ ὀμίχλην, θαμπώνω.
mistake [mis'teik] n σφάλμα, λάθος ‖ vt παρανοῶ, παρερμηνεύω ‖ (for another) παίρνω γιά ἄλλον, παραγνωρίζω ‖ **~n** a (person) σφάλλω, κάνω λάθος ‖ (identity) σφάλλω περί τό πρόσωπον.
mister ['mistə*] n (abbr Mr) κύριος (Κος) ‖ **Mr Smith** Κος Σμίθ.
mistletoe ['misltəu] n ἰξός, γκί.
mistranslation ['mistræns'leiʃən] n άνακριβής μετάφρασις.
mistreat [mis'tri:t] vt κακομεταχειρίζομαι.
mistress ['mistris] n (teacher) δασκάλα ‖ (of house) κυρία, οἰκοδέσποινα ‖ (lover) ἐρωμένη, μαιτρέσσα ‖ (abbr Mrs) κυρία (Κα) ‖ **Mrs Smith** Κα Σμίθ.
mistrust ['mis'trʌst] vt δυσπιστῶ πρός, ὑποπτεύομαι.
misty ['misti] a ὀμιχλώδης, θαμπός, σκοτεινιασμένος.
misunderstand ['misʌndə'stænd] vti παρανοῶ, παρεξηγῶ ‖ **~ing** n παρανόησις, παρεξήγησις.
misunderstood ['misʌndə'stud] a (person) παρεξηγημένος.
misuse ['mis'ju:s] n κακή χρῆσις ‖ ['mis'ju:z] vt κάνω κατάχρησιν, χρησιμοποιῶ έσφαλμένως.
mite [mait] n (insect) σκουλήκι.
miter ['maitə*] n (US) = **mitre**.
mitigate ['mitigeit] vt μετριάζω, καταπραΰνω.
mitre ['maitə*] n λοξή ἔνωσις, ὀνυχωτή ἔνωσις ‖ (eccl) μίτρα.
mitt(en) ['mit(n)] n εἶδος γαντιοῦ.
mix [miks] vt ἀναμιγνύω, άνακατώνω ‖ vi ἀναμιγνύομαι, ταιριάζω ‖ n (mixture) μῖξις, μῖγμα ‖ **to ~ up** vt ἀνακατεύω ‖ (confuse) μπερδεύω ‖ **~ed** a (assorted) ἀνάμικτος ‖ (school etc) μικτός ‖ **~ed grill** n μίξτ γκρίλλ ‖ **~ed-up** a (confused) ζαλισμένος, ἄνω-κάτω ‖ **~r** n (for food) μίξερ ‖ (person) κοινωνικός ‖ **~ture** n (assortment) ἀμάλγαμα, ἀνακάτεμα ‖ (med) μῖγμα ‖ **~-up** n (confusion) σύγχυσις, άνακατωσούρα.
moan [məun] n (groan) γογγυσμός, βογγητό ‖ (complaint) γκρίνια, μουρμουρητό

‖ *vi* στενάζω, βογγῶ, γογγύζω ‖ ~**ing** *n* βογγητό, κλάμα.

moat [məut] *n* τάφρος.

mob [mɔb] *n* ὄχλος, τό πλῆθος ‖ *vt* (*star etc*) πολιορκῶ, κυκλώνω.

mobile ['məubail] *a* εὐκίνητος, κινητός, εὐμετάβολος.

mobility [məu'biliti] *n* εὐκινησία, κινητικότης.

mock [mɔk] *vt* ἐμπαίζω, κοροϊδεύω, περιπαίζω ‖ *a* ψεύτικος, φτιαστός ‖ ~**ery** *n* (*derision*) ἐμπαιγμός, κοροϊδία ‖ (*object*) περίγελως, κοροῖδο ‖ ~**ing** *a* (*tone*) εἰρωνικός, σαρκαστικός ‖ ~**up** *n* ὑπόδειγμα, μακέττα.

model ['mɔdl] *n* ὁμοίωμα, μοντέλλο ‖ (*example*) πρότυπον, ὑπόδειγμα ‖ (*person*) μοντέλλο ‖ (*of clothes*) μανεκέν ‖ *vt* (δια)πλάθω, διαμορφώνω, σχεδιάζω ‖ (*display clothes*) κάνω ἐπίδειξι (ρούχων) ‖ *a* (*railway: toy*) τραινάκι ‖ (*child*) πρότυπον, ἰδεώδης ‖ ~**ling**, (*US*) ~**ing** *n* σχεδίασμα, πλάσιμο ‖ (*of styles*) ἐπίδειξις μόδας.

moderate ['mɔdərit] *a* μέτριος, μέσος ‖ (*fairly good*) μέτριος, τῆς σειρᾶς ‖ *n* (*pol*) μετριοπαθής ‖ ['mɔdəreit] *vi* προΐσταμαι, προεδρεύω ‖ *vt* μετριάζω, περιορίζω ‖ ~**ly** *ad* μετρημένα, συγκρατημένα, μέτρια.

moderation [mɔdə'reiʃən] *n* μετριασμός, μετριοπάθεια.

modern ['mɔdən] *a* σύγχρονος, μοντέρνος ‖ ~**ization** *n* (ἐκ)συγχρονισμός ‖ ~**ize** *vt* συγχρονίζω, ἀνανεώνω.

modest ['mɔdist] *a* (*attitude*) μετριόφρων, σεμνός ‖ (*meal, home*) ταπεινός, μέτριος ‖ ~**ly** *ad* μετριοπαθῶς, σεμνά, ντροπαλά ‖ ~**y** *n* μετριοφροσύνη, σεμνότης, ταπεινότης.

modicum ['mɔdikəm] *n*: with a ~ of μέ ἐλάχιστο, μέ λίγο.

modification [mɔdifi'keiʃən] *n* τροποποίησις, μετριασμός.

modify ['mɔdifai] *vt* τροποποιῶ, μετριάζω.

module ['mɔdju:l] *n* (*space*) σεληνάκατος.

mohair ['məuheə*] *n* μαλλί μοχαίρ.

moist [mɔist] *a* ὑγρός, νοτισμένος ‖ ~**en** *vt* ὑγραίνω, μουσκεύω ‖ ~**ure** *n* ὑγρασία.

molar ['məulə*] *n* γομφίος, μυλίτης, τραπεζίτης.

mold [məuld] (*US*) = **mould**.

mole [məul] *n* (*spot*) κρεατοελιά ‖ (*animal*) τυφλοπόντικας ‖ (*pier*) κυματοθραύστης, μῶλος.

molecular [mə'lekjulə*] *a* μοριακός.

molecule ['mɔlikju:l] *n* μόριον.

molest [məu'lest] *vt* (παρ)ενοχλῶ, πειράζω.

molt [məult] (*US*) = **moult**.

molten ['məultən] *a* τετηγμένος, λυωμένος.

moment ['məumənt] *n* στιγμή ‖ (*importance*) βαρύτης, σπουδαιότης ‖ ~**arily** *ad* σέ μιά στιγμή ‖ ~**ary** *a* στιγμιαῖος, προσω-

ρινός ‖ ~**ous** *a* βαρυσήμαντος, σημαντικός ‖ ~**um** *n* ὁρμή, φορά.

monarch ['mɔnək] *n* μονάρχης ‖ ~**ist** *n* μοναρχικός ‖ ~**y** *n* μοναρχία.

monastery ['mɔnəstri] *n* μοναστήρι.

monastic [mə'næstik] *a* μοναχικός, μοναστικός.

Monday ['mʌndi] *n* Δευτέρα.

monetary ['mʌnitəri] *a* νομισματικός, χρηματικός.

money ['mʌni] *n* χρῆμα, νόμισμα, παράς ‖ (*wealth*) χρήματα, πλούτη ‖ ~**ed** *a* πλούσιος ‖ ~**lender** *n* τοκιστής, τοκογλύφος ‖ ~**making** *a* ἐπικερδής, κερδοφόρος ‖ *n* ἀπόκτησις χρημάτων ‖ ~ **order** *n* ταχυδρομική ἐπιταγή.

mongol ['mɔŋgəl] *n* (*child*) πάσχων ἐκ μογγολισμοῦ ‖ *a* μογγολικός.

mongrel ['mʌŋgrəl] *n* μιγάς ‖ *a* μιγαδικός, μιξιγενής.

monitor ['mɔnitə*] *n* παρεναίτης, ἐπιμελητής ‖ (*television monitor*) ἐλεγκτής ‖ *vt* (*broadcasts*) ἐλέγχω.

monk [mʌŋk] *n* καλόγηρος, μοναχός.

monkey ['mʌŋki] *n* πίθηκος, μαϊμοῦ ‖ ~ **nut** *n* ἀραποφύστικο ‖ ~ **wrench** *n* γαλλικό κλειδί.

mono- ['mɔnəu] *prefix* μον(ο)-.

monochrome ['mɔnəkrəum] *a* (*TV*) μονόχρωμος.

monocle ['mɔnəkl] *n* μονύαλος, μονόκλ.

monogram ['mɔnəgræm] *n* μονόγραμμα, μονογραφή.

monolithic [mɔnəu'liθik] *a* μονολιθικός.

monologue ['mɔnəlɔg] *n* μονόλογος.

monopolize [mə'nɔpəlaiz] *vt* μονοπωλῶ.

monopoly [mə'nɔpəli] *n* μονοπώλιον.

monorail ['mɔnəureil] *n* μονόραβδος.

monosyllabic ['mɔnəusi'læbik] *a* (*person*) μονοσυλλαβικός.

monotone ['mɔnətəun] *n* μονοτονία ἤχου, μονότονος ὁμιλία.

monotonous [mə'nɔtənəs] *a* μονότονος.

monotony [mə'nɔtəni] *n* μονοτονία.

monsoon [mɔn'su:n] *n* (*with rains*) θερινός μουσῶν.

monster ['mɔnstə*] *n* (*huge animal*) τέρας, τερατούργημα ‖ (*wicked person*) τέρας ‖ *a* (*col*) κολοσσιαῖος, πελώριος.

monstrosity [mɔns'trɔsiti] *n* τερατωδία, κτηνωδία.

monstrous ['mɔnstrəs] *a* τερατώδης, ἐκτρωματικός.

montage [mɔn'ta:ʒ] *n* (*picture*) μοντάζ, μοντάρισμα.

month [mʌnθ] *n* μήν, μήνας ‖ ~**ly** *a* μηνιαῖος, μηνιάτικος ‖ *ad* μηνιαίως, κάθε μήνα ‖ *n* (*magazine*) μηνιαῖον περιοδικόν ‖ **monthlies** *npl* ἔμμηνα.

monument ['mɔnjumənt] *n* μνημεῖον ‖ ~**al** *a* μνημειακός ‖ (*work etc*) μνημειώδης.

moo [mu:] *vi* (*cow*) μηκῶμαι, μουγκρίζω.

mood [mu:d] *n* διάθεσις, κέφι ‖ (*gram*)

ἔγκλισις ‖ in the ~ καλόκεφος, ἔχω ὄρεξι γιά ‖ ~ily ad κακόκεφα, σκυθρωπά ‖ ~iness n σκυθρωπότης, κακοκεφιά ‖ ~y a κακόκεφος, κατσούφης, σκυθρωπός, ἰδιότροπος.

moon [mu:n] n σελήνη, φεγγάρι ‖ ~less a χωρίς φεγγάρι ‖ ~light n σεληνόφως, φεγγάρι ‖ ~lit a φεγγαρόλουστος.

moor [muə*] n (Brit: heath) ἕλος, βάλτος, ρεικότοπος ‖ vt (ship) πρυμνοδετῶ, δένω (πλοῖον) ‖ vi πλευρίζω, πέφτω δίπλα ‖ M~ n (person) Μαυριτανός, Ἀράπης ‖ ~ings npl πρυμνήσια, πρυμάτσες, ναύδετα ‖ M~ish a μαυριτανικός ‖ ~land n ἕλος, βάλτος, ρεικότοπος.

moose [mu:s] n ἄλκη ἡ Ἀμερικανική.

moot [mu:t] vt ἀνακοινῶ, φέρω πρός συζήτησιν ‖ a: ~ point n συζητήσιμον ζήτημα.

mop [mɔp] n πατσαβούρα ‖ (duster) ξεσκονιστήρι ‖ vt σφουγγαρίζω ‖ ~ of hair n ξεχτένιστα μαλλιά.

mope [məup] vi μελαγχολῶ, πλήττω.

moping ['məupiŋ] n κατήφεια, ἀθυμία.

moral ['mɔrəl] a ἠθικός, ψυχικός ‖ n ἐπιμύθιον, ἠθικόν δίδαγμα ‖ ~s npl ἤθη ‖ ~e n ἠθικόν ‖ ~ity n ἠθικότης, ἠθικόν αἴσθημα ‖ ~ly ad ἠθικῶς.

morass [mə'ræs] n ἕλος ‖ (fig) βόρβορος.

morbid ['mɔ:bid] a νοσηρός, ἀρρωστιάρικος.

more [mɔ:*] a περισσότερος ‖ ad περισσότερον, πλέον, πιό ‖ ~ or less σχεδόν, πάνω κάτω ‖ ~ than ever περισσότερον παρά ποτέ ‖ ~over ad ἐπί πλέον, ἐκτός τούτου.

morgue [mɔ:g] n νεκροτομεῖον.

moribund ['mɔribʌnd] a ἑτοιμοθάνατος.

morning ['mɔ:niŋ] n πρωΐ ‖ a πρωϊνός ‖ in the ~ τό πρωΐ ‖ ~ sickness n πρωϊνή ἀδιαθεσία.

Moroccan [mə'rɔkən] a,n Μαροκινός.

Morocco [mə'rɔkəu] n Μαρόκον.

moron ['mɔ:rɔn] n καθυστερημένος ‖ (col) ἠλίθιος, βλάκας ‖ ~ic [mə'rɔnik] a ἠλίθιος, βλακώδης.

morose [mə'rəus] a κακότροπος, σκυθρωπός.

morphine ['mɔ:fi:n] n μορφίνη.

Morse [mɔ:s] ~ code n μορσικός κώδιξ.

morsel ['mɔ:sl] n (of food) μπουκιά, κομματάκι.

mortal ['mɔ:tl] a θνητός ‖ (deadly) θανάσιμος, θανατηφόρος ‖ (very great) τρομερός ‖ n (human being) θνητός (ἄνθρωπος) ‖ ~ity n θνητότης ‖ (death rate) θνησιμότης ‖ ~ly ad (wounded) θανάσιμα ‖ (offended) θανάσιμα.

mortar ['mɔ:tə*] n ἀσβεστοκονίαμα, πηλός, λάσπη ‖ (bowl) γουδί ‖ (weapon) ὅλμος.

mortgage ['mɔ:gidʒ] n ὑποθήκη.

mortified ['mɔ:tifaid] a ντροπιασμένος, ταπεινωμένος.

mortuary ['mɔ:tjuəri] n νεκροθάλαμος.

mosaic [məu'zeiik] n μωσαϊκόν, ψηφιδωτόν.

Moscow ['mɔskəu] n Μόσχα.

Moslem ['mɔzlem] n Μουσουλμάνος ‖ a μουσουλμανικός.

mosque [mɔsk] n τέμενος, τζαμί.

mosquito [mɔs'ki:təu] n κουνούπι ‖ ~ net n κουνουπιέρα.

moss [mɔs] n βρύον ‖ ~y a βρυώδης, βρυόφυτος.

most [məust] a πλεῖστος, περισσότερος ‖ πιό πολύς ‖ ad πλέον, πιό, πιό πολύ, πάρα πολύ ‖ n οἱ περισσότεροι ‖ at the (very) ~ τό πιό πολύ ‖ to make the ~ of ἐπωφελοῦμαι ‖ ~ly ad ὡς ἐπί τό πλεῖστον, κυρίως, συνήθως.

motel [məu'tel] n μοτέλ.

moth [mɔθ] n βότριδα, σκῶρος ‖ ~ball n ναφθαλίνη (σέ μπάλλες) ‖ ~-eaten a σκωροφαγωμένος.

mother ['mʌðə*] n μητέρα, μάννα ‖ vt (spoil) χαϊδεύω, κανακεύω ‖ a (tongue, country) μητρική (γλῶσσα) ‖ ~hood n μητρότης ‖ ~-in-law n πεθερά ‖ ~ly a μητρικά, σάν μάννα ‖ ~-to-be n σέ ἐνδιαφέρουσα.

motif [məu'ti:f] n μοτίφ, θέμα, μοτίβο.

motion ['məuʃən] n κίνησις ‖ (proposal) πρότασις ‖ vi κάνω νόημα, νεύω ‖ ~less a ἀκίνητος ‖ ~ picture n ταινία, φίλμ.

motivated ['məutiveitid] a αἰτιολογούμενος, κινητήριος.

motivation [məuti'veiʃən] n κίνητρον, ἐλατήριον.

motive ['məutiv] n κίνητρον, αἴτιον, ἐλατήριον ‖ a κινητήριος.

motley ['mɔtli] a (heterogeneous) πολύχρωμος, ἑτερογενής.

motor ['məutə*] n κινητήρ, μηχανή ‖ (automobile) αὐτοκίνητο ‖ vi ταξιδεύω μέ αὐτοκίνητον ‖ ~bike n μοτοσυκλέτα ‖ ~boat n βενζινάκατος ‖ ~car n αὐτοκίνητον ‖ ~cycle n = ~bike ‖ ~cyclist n μοτοσυκλετιστής ‖ ~ing n χρῆσις τοῦ αὐτοκινήτου, ὁδήγησις ‖ a τοῦ αὐτοκινήτου, τῆς ὁδηγήσεως ‖ ~ist n αὐτοκινητιστής ‖ ~ oil n ἔλαιον κινητήρων ‖ ~ racing n αὐτοκινητοδρομία ‖ ~ scooter n σκούτερ, βέσπα ‖ ~ vehicle n αὐτοκίνητον ‖ ~way n (Brit) αὐτοκινητόδρομος.

mottled ['mɔtld] a διάστικτος, μέ νερά.

motto ['mɔtəu] n ρητόν, μόττο, ἀρχή.

mould [məuld] n τύπος, μήτρα, καλούπι ‖ (shape) τύπωμα, πρότυπον ‖ (mildew) εὐρώς, μούχλα ‖ vt χύνω σέ τύπους ‖ (fig) διαπλάθω, διαμορφώνω ‖ ~er vi (decay) σαπίζω, φθείρομαι ‖ ~ing n (in plaster) τυποποιία, χυτόν ἀντικείμενον ‖ (in wood) κορνίζα ‖ ~y a (food etc) μουχλιασμένος.

moult [məult] vi μαδῶ.

mound [maund] *n* ἀνάχωμα, λοφίσκος, πρόχωμα.

mount [maunt] *n* (*high hill*) ὄρος, βουνό ‖ (*horse*) ἄλογο ‖ (*for jewel etc*) κορνίζα, ὑποστήριγμα, σκελετός ‖ *vt* (*get on horse*) ἀνεβάζω, ἀνεβαίνω στό ‖ (*put in setting*) μοντάρω, δένω, κορνιζάρω ‖ (*exhibition*) ἀνεβάζω ‖ (*attack*) ὀργανώνω ἐπίθεσιν ‖ *vi* (*also* ~ up) ἀνέρχομαι, ἀνεβαίνω ‖ ~**ain** *n* ὄρος, βουνό ‖ (*pile*) σωρός, πλῆθος ‖ ~**aineer** *n* (*climber*) ὀρειβάτης ‖ ~**aineering** *n* ὀρειβασία ‖ **to go** ~**aineering** κάνω ὀρειβασίαν ‖ ~**ainous** *a* ὀρεινός ‖ ~**ainside** *n* πλευρά βουνοῦ.

mourn [mɔːn] *vt* πενθῶ, θρηνῶ ‖ *vi* (+ *for*) θρηνῶ, κλαίω ‖ ~**er** *n* πενθῶν, πενθοφορῶν ‖ ~**ing** *n* πένθος ‖ **in** ~**ing** (*period etc*) ἔχω πένθος ‖ (*dress*) πένθιμα ροῦχα, μαῦρα.

mouse [maus] *n* ποντικός ‖ ~**trap** *n* ποντικοπαγίδα, φάκα.

moustache [məsˈtaːʃ] *n* μουστάκι.

mouth [mauθ] *n* (*anat*) στόμα ‖ (*opening*) στόμιον ‖ (*entrance*) ἐκβολή, στόμιον ‖ [mauð] *vt* (*words*) λέγω πομπωδῶς, ὁμιλῶ μέ στόμφον ‖ ~**ful** *a* πένθιμος ‖ ~ **down in the** ~ τσακισμένος, χαμένα ‖ ~**ful** *n* μπουκιά ‖ ~ **organ** *n* φυσαρμόνικα ‖ ~**piece** *n* ἐπιστόμιον ‖ (*speaker*) ὄργανον, φερέφωνον, ἐκπρόσωπος ‖ ~**wash** *n* γαργάρα ‖ ~**-watering** *a* γαργαλιστικός.

movable [ˈmuːvəbl] *a* κινητός.

move [muːv] *n* (*movement*) κίνησις ‖ (*in game*) κίνησις ‖ (*step*) ἐνέργεια, βῆμα ‖ (*from house*) μετακόμισις ‖ *vt* (μετα)κινῶ, μετατοπίζω ‖ (*stir, rouse*) συγκινῶ, γίνομαι (ἐξωφρενῶν κλ) ‖ *vi* (*general*) κινοῦμαι, κουνιέμαι ‖ (*travel*) μετακινοῦμαι, φεύγομαι ‖ (*take action*) ἐνεργῶ ‖ (*go elsewhere*) μετακομίζω ‖ **to get a** ~ **on** σπεύδω, κάνω γρήγορα ‖ **to** ~ **house** μετοικῶ, μετακομίζω ‖ **to** ~ **about** *vi* περιφέρομαι, τριγυρίζω ‖ **to** ~ **away** *vi* ἀπομακρύνομαι, φεύγω ‖ **to** ~ **back** *vi* ὑποχωρῶ, ξαναγυρίζω πίσω ‖ **to** ~ **forward** *vi* προχωρῶ ‖ *vt* κινῶ πρός τά ἐμπρός ‖ **to** ~ **in** *vi* (*house*) μετακομίζω (στό νέο σπίτι), ἐγκαθίσταμαι ‖ **to** ~ **on** *vi* προχωρῶ, τραβῶ τόν δρόμο μου ‖ *vt* κάνω νά κυκλοφορῇ ‖ **to** ~ **out** *vi* (*house*) μετακομίζω (ἀλλοῦ), ἀδειάζω ‖ ~**ment** *n* κίνησις, μετακίνησις ‖ (*social etc*) κίνημα, κίνησις ‖ (*mus*) μέρος.

movie [ˈmuːvi] *n* (*film*) φίλμ ‖ **the** ~**s** (*cinema*) σινεμά ‖ ~ **camera** *n* (*amateur*) κινηματογραφική μηχανή.

moving [ˈmuːviŋ] *a* (*lit*) κινούμενος, κινητός ‖ (*stirring*) συνταρακτικός, συγκινητικός ‖ (*touching*) συγκινητικός.

mow [məu] (*irreg v*) *vt* θερίζω ‖ **to** ~ **down** *vt* θερίζω ‖ ~**er** *n* (*machine*) θεριστική μηχανή.

Mr [ˈmistə*] *see* **mister**.

Mrs [ˈmisiz] *see* **mistress**.

much [mʌtʃ] *a* πολύς ‖ *ad* πολύ, μεγάλως, καλή, συχνά, σχεδόν ‖ *n* πολλά, πολύ ‖ **how** ~ **is it?** πόσον κάνει; ‖ **too** ~ πάραπολυ.

muck [mʌk] *n* (*lit*) κοπριά, βρωμιά ‖ (*fig*) σύγχυσις, καταστροφή ‖ **to** ~ **about** *vi* (*col*) περιφέρομαι ἀσκόπως, χαζεύω ‖ *vt* (*col*) λασπώνω, βρωμίζω ‖ **to** ~ **up** *vt* (*col*) (*ruin*) χαλάω μιά δουλειά ‖ ~**y** *a* (*dirty*) βρώμικος, βρωμερός.

mud [mʌd] *n* λάσπη.

muddle [ˈmʌdl] *n* ἀκαταστασία, σαλάτα, μπέρδεμα ‖ *vt* (*also* ~ up) μπερδεύω, κάνω ἄνω-κάτω ‖ **to** ~ **through** *vi* καταφέρνω κουτσά-στραβά.

muddy [ˈmʌdi] *a* λασπώδης, λασπωμένος.

mud flats [ˈmʌdflæts] *npl* παραλία μέ λάσπη.

mudguard [ˈmʌdgɑːd] *n* φτερό (αὐτοκινήτου).

mudpack [ˈmʌdpæk] *n* μάσκα (ἀπό πηλό).

mud-slinging [ˈmʌdsliŋiŋ] *n* συκοφαντία, κακογλωσσιά.

muff [mʌf] *n* (*for hands*) μανσόν.

muffle [ˈmʌfl] *vt* πνίγω (ἤχον) ‖ (*wrap up*) κουκουλώνω, σκεπάζω ‖ ~**d** *a* ὑπόκουφος, πνιγμένος.

mug [mʌg] *n* (*cup*) μεγάλο φλυτζάνι, φλυτζάνα ‖ (*col: face*) μοῦτρο, φάτσα ‖ (*col: dupe*) χαζός, κορόιδο ‖ *vt* (*assault*) κτυπῶ ἀπό πίσω ‖ ~**ging** *n* (*assault*) ἐπίθεσι ἀπό πίσω.

muggy [ˈmʌgi] *a* (*weather*) βαρύς (καιρός), ὑγρός.

mulatto [mjuːˈlætəu] *n* μιγᾶς, μουλάτος.

mule [mjuːl] *n* ἡμίονος, μουλάρι.

mull [mʌl] **to** ~ **over** *vt* γυροφέρνω στό μυαλό.

mulled [mʌld] *a* (*wine*) ζεστό κρασί μέ κανέλλα.

multi- [ˈmʌlti] *prefix* πολύ-.

multicoloured, (*US*) **multicolored** [ˈmʌltiˈkʌləd] *a* πολύχρωμος.

multilateral [ˈmʌltiˈlætərəl] *a* πολύπλευρος.

multiple [ˈmʌltipl] *n* πολλαπλάσιον ‖ *a* πολλαπλός ‖ ~ **store** *n* κατάστημα μέ πολλά ὑποκαταστήματα.

multiplication [mʌltipliˈkeiʃən] *n* πολλαπλασιασμός.

multiply [ˈmʌltiplai] *vt* πολλαπλασιάζω ‖ *vi* πολλαπλασιάζομαι.

multiracial [ˈmʌltiˈreiʃəl] *a* πολλῶν φυλῶν.

multitude [ˈmʌltitjuːd] *n* πλῆθος.

mum [mʌm] *n* (*col*) μαμά.

mumble [ˈmʌmbl] *vt* μουρμουρίζω, μασῶ ‖ *n* μπερδεμένα λόγια, μουρμούρα.

mummy [ˈmʌmi] *n* μούμια ‖ (*col*) μαμά.

mumps [mʌmps] *n* παρωτίτις.

munch [mʌntʃ] *vti* μασουλίζω, τραγανίζω.

mundane [ˈmʌnˈdein] *a* ἐγκόσμιος, γήϊνος.

municipal [mjuːˈnisipəl] *a* δημοτικός.

munificence [mju:'nifisns] *n* γενναιοδωρία.
munitions [mju:'niʃənz] *npl* πολεμοφόδια.
mural ['mjuərəl] *n* τοιχογραφία.
murder ['mɔːdə*] *n* φόνος, δολοφονία ‖ (*fig: col*) φονικό ‖ *vt* φονεύω, σκοτώνω, δολοφονῶ ‖ ~**er** *n* φονιάς, δολοφόνος ‖ ~**ess** *n* φόνισσα ‖ ~**erous** *a* (δολο)-φονικός.
murky ['mɔːki] *a* σκοτεινός, ζοφερός.
murmur ['mɔːmə*] *n* ψίθυρος, μουρμουρητό ‖ *vi* ψιθυρίζω, μουρμουρίζω, παραπονοῦμαι.
muscle ['mʌsl] *n* μῦς.
muscular ['mʌskjulə*] *a* μυϊκός, γεροδεμένος.
Muse [mju:z] *n* Μοῦσα.
muse [mju:z] *vi* ρεμβάζω, ὀνειροπολῶ.
museum [mju:'ziəm] *n* μουσεῖον.
mush [mʌʃ] *n* πολτός ‖ ~**room** *n* μανιτάρι ‖ *a* ἐφήμερος.
mushy ['mʌʃi] *a* πολτώδης, μαλακός.
music ['mju:zik] *n* μουσική ‖ **to face the** ~ ἀκούω ἐξάψαλμον ‖ ~ **stand** *n* ἀναλόγιον μουσικοῦ ‖ ~**al** *n* μουσική παράστασις ‖ *a* μουσικός, φιλόμουσος ‖ ~**ian** *n* μουσικός.
musk [mʌsk] *n* μόσχος.
musket ['mʌskit] *n* τουφέκι ‖ ~**eer** *n* σωματοφύλαξ.
musky ['mʌski] *a* μοσχοβολῶν.
muslin ['mʌzlin] *n* μουσελίνα.
mussel ['mʌsl] *n* μύδι.
must [mʌst] *auxiliary v* (*obligation*) **I** ~ **do it** πρέπει νά τό κάνω ‖ **I** ~ **not do it** δέν πρέπει νά τό κάνω ‖ (*probability*) **he** ~ **be there by now** πρέπει νά εἶναι ἐκεῖ τώρα ‖ *n* γλῦκος, μοῦστος ‖ **it is a** ~ εἶναι ἀναγκαῖον.
mustache ['mʌstæʃ] *n* (*US*) = moustache.
mustard ['mʌstəd] *n* (*condiment*) μουστάρδα.
mustiness ['mʌstinis] *n* μοῦχλα, ὑγρασία.
mustn't ['mʌsnt] = **must not** ‖ *see* **must.**
musty ['mʌsti] *a* τῆς μούχλας ‖ (*col*) παλιατσούρα, μπαγιάτικος.
mute [mju:t] *a* βουβός, μουγγός ‖ (*gram*) ἄφωνος ‖ *n* βουβός, μουγγός ‖ (*on instrument*) σουρντίνα.
mutilate ['mju:tileit] *vt* ἀκρωτηριάζω, σακατεύω.
mutilation [mju:ti'leiʃən] *n* ἀκρωτηριασμός, σακάτεμα.
mutinous ['mju:tinəs] *a* στασιαστικός, ἀντάρτικος.
mutiny ['mju:tini] *n* στάσις, ἀντάρσια ‖ *vi* στασιάζω.
mutter ['mʌtə*] *vti* μουρμουρίζω.
mutton ['mʌtn] *n* ἀρνήσιο κρέας.
mutual ['mju:tjuəl] *a* ἀμοιβαῖος, κοινός ‖ ~**ly** *ad* ἀμοιβαίως.
muzzle ['mʌzl] *n* (*mouth and nose*) ρύγχος, μουσούδα ‖ (*straps*) φίμωτρον ‖ (*of gun*) στόμιον, στόμα ‖ *vt* φιμώνω.

my [mai] *poss a* ἰδικός μου, μου.
myopic [mai'ɔpik] *a* μυωπικός.
myrrh [mɔː*] *n* σμύρνα, μύρρα.
myself [mai'self] *pron* ἐγώ ὁ ἴδιος, τόν ἑαυτόν μου.
mysterious [mis'tiəriəs] *a* μυστηριώδης ‖ ~**ly** *ad* μυστηριωδῶς.
mystery ['mistəri] *n* μυστήριον ‖ ~ **play** *n* μυστήριον.
mystic ['mistik] *n* μυστικός, ἐσωτερικός ‖ ~**al** *a* μυστικιστικός, μυστηριώδης ‖ ~**ism** *n* μυστικισμός, μυστικοπάθεια.
mystification [mistifi'keiʃən] *n* παραζάλη, συσκότισις, ἀπάτη.
mystify ['mistifai] *vt* ἐξαπατῶ, ζαλίζω.
myth [miθ] *n* μῦθος ‖ ~**ical** *a* μυθικός ‖ ~**ological** *a* μυθολογικός ‖ ~**ology** *n* μυθολογία.

N, n

nab [næb] *vt* ἁρπάζω, συλλαμβάνω.
nadir ['neidiə*] *n* ναδίρ.
nag [næg] *n* (*horse*) μικρό ἄλογο (ἱππασίας) ‖ (*person*) γρινιάρης, καυγατζῆς ‖ *vti* γρινιάζω, καυγαδίζω ‖ ~**ging** *a* (*doubt*) σαράκι (ἀμφιβολίας) ‖ *n* καυγάς, φασαρία.
nail [neil] *n* νύχι ‖ (*spike*) καρφί, πρόκα ‖ *vt* καρφώνω ‖ **to** ~ **down** *vt* (*fig*) δεσμεύω ‖ ~**brush** *n* βούρτσα τῶν νυχιῶν ‖ ~**file** *n* λίμα (γιά νύχια) ‖ ~ **polish** *n* βερνίκι τῶν νυχιῶν, μανόν ‖ ~ **scissors** *npl* ψαλιδάκι (γιά νύχια) ‖ ~ **varnish** *n* βερνίκι γιά τά νύχια.
naive [nai'i:v] *a* ἀφελής ‖ ~**ly** *ad* ἀφελῶς.
naked ['neikid] *a* γυμνός ‖ (*uncovered*) ἐκτεθειμένος, καθαρός ‖ ~**ness** *n* γυμνότης.
name [neim] *n* ὄνομα ‖ (*reputation*) φήμη, ὑπόληψις ‖ *vt* ὀνομάζω ‖ (*call by name*) ἀναφέρω, κατονομάζω ‖ (*appoint*) ὁρίζω, διορίζω ‖ **in the** ~ **of** ἐξ ὀνόματος του ‖ (*authority of*) ἐν ὀνόματι ‖ ~**less** *a* ἄγνωστος, ἀνώνυμος ‖ ~**ly** *ad* δηλαδή ‖ ~**sake** *n* ὁμώνυμος, συνωνόματος.
nanny ['næni] *n* (*for child*) νταντά.
nap [næp] *n* (*sleep*) ὑπνάκος ‖ **to have a** ~ τόν παίρνω λιγάκι.
nape [neip] *n* αὐχήν, σβέρκος.
napkin ['næpkin] *n* πετσέτα φαγητοῦ ‖ (*Brit*) χαρτοπετσέτα, πάνα (βρέφους).
nappy ['næpi] *n* (*for baby*) πάνα.
narcissus [na:'sisəs] *n* νάρκισσος, ζαμπάκι.
narcotic [na:'kɔtik] *n* ναρκωτικόν.
nark [na:k] *vt* (*col: annoy*) ἐξερεθίζω, ἐξαργιώνω.
narrate [nə'reit] *vt* διηγοῦμαι.
narration [nə'reiʃən] *n* διήγησις.
narrative ['nærətiv] *n* διήγημα, ἀφήγησις ‖ *a* ἀφηγηματικός.
narrator [nə'reitə*] *n* ἀφηγητής.

narrow ['nærəu] *a* στενός, στενόχωρος ‖ *vi* στενεύω ‖ **to ~ sth down to** περιορίζω ‖ **~ly** *ad* (*miss*) μόλις, ὀλίγον νά ‖ **~-minded** *a* στενοκέφαλος ‖ **~-mindedness** *n* στενοκεφαλιά.

nasal ['neizəl] *a* ἔνρινος, ρινικός, τῆς μύτης.

nastily ['nɑːstili] *ad* δυσάρεστα, πρόστυχα, χυδαῖα.

nastiness ['nɑːstinis] *n* κακία, ἀχρειότης, προστυχιά.

nasty ['nɑːsti] *a* (*mess*) δυσάρεστος, βρώμικος ‖ (*business*) δύσκολος, ἐπικίνδυνος, φοβερός ‖ (*person*) πρόστυχος, ρεμάλι, κακός.

nation ['neiʃən] *n* ἔθνος ‖ **~al** ['næʃənl] *a* ἐθνικός ‖ *n* ὑπήκοος, πολίτης ‖ **~al anthem** *n* ἐθνικός ὕμνος ‖ **~alism** *n* ἐθνικισμός ‖ **~alist** *a,n* ἐθνικιστής, ἐθνικόφρων ‖ **~ality** *n* ἐθνικότης ‖ **~alization** *n* ἐθνικοποίησις ‖ **~alize** *vt* ἐθνικοποιῶ ‖ **~ally** *ad* ἀπό ἐθνικῆς ἀπόψεως ‖ **~wide** *a* πανεθνικόν ‖ *ad* καθ' ὁλόκληρον τήν χώραν.

native ['neitiv] *n* ἐντόπιος ‖ (*non-European*) ἰθαγενής ‖ *a* ἐγχώριος ‖ (*country etc*) γενέθλιος, μητρικός ‖ (*inborn*) ἔμφυτος, φυσικός.

natter ['nætə*] *vi* (*col: chat*) κουβεντιάζω.

natural ['nætʃrəl] *a* φυσικός ‖ (*inborn*) ἔμφυτος, φυσικός ‖ **~ist** *n* φυσιοδίφης ‖ **~ize** *vt* πολιτογραφῶ ‖ (*plant etc*) ἐγκλιματίζω ‖ **~ly** *ad* φυσικά, βέβαια ‖ **~ness** *n* φυσικότης.

nature ['neitʃə*] *n* φύσις ‖ (*sort, kind*) εἶδος, χαρακτήρ ‖ **by ~** ἐκ φύσεως.

naught [nɔːt] *n* τίποτε, μηδενικόν.

naughtily ['nɔːtili] *ad* ἄτακτα, κακά.

naughtiness ['nɔːtinis] *n* κακή συμπεριφορά, ἀνυπακοή.

naughty ['nɔːti] *a* (*child*) ἄτακτος, κακός.

nausea ['nɔːsiə] *n* ναυτία, ἀναγούλα ‖ (*disgust*) ἀηδία, ἀποστροφή ‖ **~te** *vt* ἀηδιάζω (κάτι), προξενῶ ναυτίαν.

nauseating ['nɔːsieitiŋ] *a* ἀηδιαστικός, σιχαμερός.

nautical ['nɔːtikəl] *a* ναυτικός.

naval ['neivəl] *a* ναυτικός.

nave [neiv] *n* κλῖτος, νάρθηξ.

navel ['neivəl] *n* ὀμφαλός, ἀφαλός.

navigable ['nævigəbl] *a* πλωτός.

navigate ['nævigeit] *vt* (*ship etc*) κυβερνῶ, διευθύνω ‖ *vi* ναυσιπλοῶ, πλέω, ταξιδεύω.

navigation [nævi'geiʃən] *n* ναυτιλία, πλοῦς, διάπλους.

navigator ['nævigeitə*] *n* ναυτίλος, πλοηγός ‖ (*explorer*) θαλασσοπόρος ‖ (*aviat*) ἀεροναυτίλος.

navvy ['nævi] *n* ἀνειδίκευτος ἐργάτης, σκαφτιᾶς.

navy ['neivi] *n* ναυτικόν ‖ **~ blue** *n* (*colour*) σκοῦρος μπλέ, μπλέ μαρίν.

nay [nei] *ad* (*no*) ὄχι ‖ (*also*) τί λέω, ἤ καλύτερα.

Nazi ['nɑːtsi] *n* Ναζιστής.

neap [niːp] *a* (*tide*) ἄμπωτις.

near [niə*] *a* (*close*) ἐγγύς, πλησίον ‖ κοντά ‖ (*related*) πλησίον, στενός ‖ *ad* (*space*) κοντά, πλησίον ‖ (*time*) περί, ἐγγύς, κοντά ‖ *prep* (*also ~ to*) κοντά σέ, παρά, πλησίον ‖ (*space*) παρά, πλησίον ‖ (*time*) περί, κοντά ‖ *vt* πλησιάζω ‖ **~by** *a* κοντινός, πλαϊνός ‖ *ad* πολύ κοντά, ἐγγύτατα ‖ **N ~ East** *n* Μέση Ἀνατολή, Ἐγγύς Ἀνατολή ‖ **~ly** *ad* σχεδόν, περίπου ‖ **~ miss** *n* λίγο ἔλειψε (νά), παρ' ὀλίγον (νά) ‖ **~ness** *n* ἐγγύτης, στενότης ‖ **~side** *n* (*aut*) ἀριστερά πλευρά.

neat [niːt] *a* (*tidy*) καθαρός, καλοβαλμένος, κομψός ‖ (*clever*) καλοβαλμένος, ἐπιτυχής, κομψός ‖ (*pure*) καθαρός, ἄγνός, χωρίς νερό ‖ **~ly** *ad* μέ τάξιν, περιποιημένα ‖ **~ness** *n* ἁπλότης, κομψότης, τάξις, καθαρότης.

nebulous ['nebjuləs] *a* νεφελώδης.

necessarily ['nesisərili] *ad* ἀπαραιτήτως, κατ' ἀνάγκην.

necessary ['nesisəri] *a* ἀναγκαῖος, ἀπαραίτητος.

necessitate [ni'sesiteit] *vt* κάνω ἀναγκαῖον, ὑποχρεώνω.

necessity [ni'sesiti] *n* ἀνάγκη.

neck [nek] *n* λαιμός, αὐχήν, τράχηλος, σβέρκος ‖ (*narrow part*) λαιμός, στένωμα ‖ **~ and ~** στά ἴσια, ἰσόπαλος, πλάι-πλάι ‖ **~lace** *n* περιδέραιον, κολλιέ ‖ **~line** *n* λαιμός, ντεκολτέ ‖ **~tie** *n* γραβάτα.

née [nei] *a* τό γένος.

need [niːd] *n* ἀνάγκη, χρειά ‖ (*poverty*) ἔνδεια, φτώχια ‖ *vt* (*of person*) χρειάζομαι ‖ (*of thing*) ἀπαιτῶ, ζητῶ (κάτι), ἀπαιτεῖται ‖ **to ~ to do** ἔχω ἀνάγκην νά κάνω (κάτι).

needle ['niːdl] *n* βελόνι ‖ (*knitting*) βελόνα ‖ (*compass etc*) βελόνη.

needless ['niːdlis] *a* ἄχρηστος, περιττός ‖ **~ly** *ad* ἀνωφελῶς, χωρίς ἀνάγκην.

needlework ['niːdlwəːk] *n* ἐργόχειρον.

needy ['niːdi] *a* ἐνδεής, ἄπορος.

negation [ni'geiʃən] *n* ἄρνησις.

negative ['negətiv] *n* (*phot*) ἀρνητικόν ‖ *a* ἀρνητικός.

neglect [ni'glekt] *vt* παραμελῶ ‖ *n* ἀμέλεια, παραμέλησις.

negligee ['negliʒei] *n* νυχτικό.

negligence ['neglidʒəns] *n* ἀμέλεια.

negligent ['neglidʒənt] *a* ἀμελής, ἀπρόσεκτος ‖ **~ly** *ad* ἀπρόσεκτα, ἀμελῶς.

negligible ['neglidʒəbl] *a* ἀμελητέος.

negotiable [ni'gəuʃiəbl] *a* (*cheque*) ἐμπορεύσιμος, μετατρεπτός, μεταβιβάσιμος.

negotiate [ni'gəuʃieit] *vi* διαπραγματεύομαι ‖ *vt* (*treaty*) διαπραγματεύομαι ‖

(difficulty) διαβαίνω, ξεπερνῶ.

negotiation [nigəuʃiˈeiʃən] n διαπραγμά-τευσις.

negotiator [niˈgəuʃieitə*] n διαπραγματευ-τής.

Negress [ˈniːgres] n νέγρα, μαύρη.

Negro [ˈniːgrəu] n νέγρος, μαῦρος.

neighbour, (US) **neighbor** [ˈneibə*] n γείτων, γείτονας || ~**hood** n γειτονιά, περιοχή || ~**ing** a γειτονικός || ~**ly** a καλός γείτονας, γειτονικός.

neither [ˈnaiðə*] a οὔτε ὁ ἕνας οὔτε ὁ ἄλλος, κανένας || cj οὔτε ... οὔτε, οὔτε (καί) || pron κανένας.

neo– [ˈniːəu] prefix νεο–.

neon [ˈniːɔn] n νέον || ~ **light** n φῶς μέ νέον.

nephew [ˈnevjuː] n ἀνεψιός.

nerve [nɜːv] n νεῦρον || (courage) σθένος, θάρρος || (impudence) θράσος || ~-racking a ἐκνευριστικός.

nervous [ˈnɜːvəs] a νευρικός || (timid) ντροπαλός, νευρικός, δειλός || ~ **breakdown** n νευρικός κλονισμός || ~**ly** ad δειλά, φοβισμένα || ~**ness** n νευρικό-της, δειλία.

nest [nest] n φωλιά.

nestle [ˈnesl] vi φωλιάζω, κουλουριάζομαι.

net [net] n δίκτυον, δίχτυ || (hair) φιλές, δίχτυ || a καθαρός, νέτος.

Netherlands [ˈneðələndz] npl Ὁλλανδία.

netting [ˈnetiŋ] n δικτύωμα, πλέγμα.

network [ˈnetwɜːk] n δίκτυον.

neurosis [njuəˈrəusis] n νεύρωσις.

neurotic [njuəˈrɔtik] a νευρωτικός || n νευροπαθής.

neuter [ˈnjuːtə*] a οὐδέτερος || n οὐδέ-τερον.

neutral [ˈnjuːtrəl] a οὐδέτερος || ~**ity** n οὐδετερότης.

never [ˈnevə*] ad ποτέ || ~-**ending** a ἀτελείωτος || ~**theless** ad οὐχ ἧττον, μόλον τοῦτο, κι᾽ ὅμως.

new [njuː] a νέος, καινούργιος || (clothes etc) καινουργής, καινούργιος || (modern) σύγχρονος, μοντέρνος || (at work etc) ἀρχάριος, ἄπειρος || ~**born** a νεογέν-νητος || ~**comer** n φρεσκοφερμένος, ἄρτι ἀφιχθείς || ~**ly** ad νεωστί, προσφά-τως || ~ **moon** n καινούργιο φεγγάρι || ~**ness** n νεότης, φρεσκάδα.

news [njuːz] n νέα, εἰδήσεις || ~ **agent** n πράκτωρ ἐφημερίδων || ~ **flash** n ἔκτα-κτος εἴδησις || ~**letter** n δελτίον εἰδήσεων || ~**paper** n ἐφημερίδα || ~**reel** n ταινία ἐπικαίρων.

New Year [njuːˈjiə*] n νέον ἔτος || ~᾽s **Day** n Πρωτοχρονιά || ~᾽s **Eve** n παρα-μονή τῆς Πρωτοχρονιᾶς.

New Zealand [njuːˈziːlənd] n Νέα Ζηλανδία.

next [nekst] a πλησιέστερος, γειτονικός, πλαϊνός || (in time) προσεχής, ἑπόμενος || ad ἔπειτα, κατόπιν, μετά || prep: ~ **to** κοντά εἰς, σχεδόν || **the** ~ **day** τήν ἄλλην ἡμέραν, ἡ ἑπομένη || ~ **year** ἑπόμενον ἔτος, ἄλλος χρόνος, τοῦ χρόνου || ~ **of kin** n πλησιέστερος συγγενής.

nibble [ˈnibl] vt δαγκώνω, μασουλίζω, τρώγω σιγά-σιγά.

nice [nais] a εὐχάριστος, καλός, ὡραῖος || (exact) λεπτός, εὐαίσθητος || ~-**looking** a ὡραῖος, ὄμορφος || ~**ly** ad ὡραία, εὐχάριστα.

nick [nik] n χαραγή, ἐγκοπή || κατάλληλος στιγμή.

nickel [ˈnikl] n νικέλιον || (US) πεντάρα (5 σέντς).

nickname [ˈnikneim] n παρατσούκλι.

nicotine [ˈnikətiːn] n νικοτίνη.

niece [niːs] n ἀνεψιά.

niggardly [ˈnigədli] a φιλάργυρος, τσιγ-γούνης.

niggling [ˈnigliŋ] a ἀσημαντολόγος.

night [nait] n νύχτα, βράδυ, σκότος || **good** ~ ! καλή νύχτα! || **at** or **by** ~ τήν νύχτα || ~**cap** n (drink) νυκτερινό ρόφημα || ~ **club** n νυκτερινόν κέντρον || ~**dress** n νυχτικό || ~**fall** n σούρουπο || ~-**ingale** n ἀηδόνι || ~ **life** n νυχτερινή ζωή || ~**ly** a νυκτερινός, βραδυνός || ad κάθε νύχτα, κάθε βράδυ || ~**mare** n ἐφιάλτης || ~ **school** n βραδυνή σχολή || ~-**time** n νύχτα || ~ **watchman** n νυκτοφύλαξ.

nil [nil] n μηδέν, τίποτε.

nimble [ˈnimbl] a εὔστροφος, εὐκίνητος.

nine [nain] num ἐννέα, ἐνιά || ~**teen** num δεκαεννιά || ~**ty** num ἐνενήντα.

ninth [nainθ] a ἔνατος.

nip [nip] vt (pinch etc) τσιμπῶ, δαγκώνω || n τσίμπημα, δάγκωμα.

nipple [ˈnipl] n (anat) θηλή, ρώγα.

nippy [ˈnipi] a (person) ζωηρός, ξύπνιος, σβέλτος.

nitrogen [ˈnaitrədʒən] n ἄζωτον.

no [nəu] a κανείς, καθόλου || ad ὄχι, καθόλου, μή || n ἄρνησις, ἀρνητική ψῆφος.

nobility [nəuˈbiliti] n (social class) εὐγε-νεῖς.

noble [ˈnəubl] a εὐγενής, μεγαλοπρεπής || (splendid) θαυμαστός || n εὐγενής, εὐπατρίδης.

nobly [ˈnəubli] ad εὐγενικά, μεγαλοπρε-πῶς.

nobody [ˈnəubədi] pron κανείς, κανένας, οὐδείς || n (unimportant person) μηδα-μινότης, τιποτένιος.

nod [nɔd] vi νεύω, νέφω, κάνω νόημα || (droop with sleep) νυστάζω, κουτουλῶ || n νεῦμα, νόημα, κουτούλισμα.

noise [nɔiz] n κρότος, βοή || (unpleasant) θόρυβος.

noisily [ˈnɔizili] ad θορυβωδῶς, μέ φα-σαρία.

noisy [ˈnɔizi] a θορυβώδης.

nomad ['nəʊmæd] *n* νομάς ‖ ~**ic** *a* νομαδικός.

nominal ['nɔminl] *a* ὀνομαστικός, μή πραγματικός.

nominate ['nɔmineit] *vt* προτείνω, ὀνομάζω ‖ (*appoint*) διορίζω.

nomination [nɔmi'neiʃən] *n* πρότασις, ὑποψηφιότης, διορισμός.

nominee [nɔmi'ni:] *n* ὑποψήφιος.

non- [nɔn] *prefix* μή-, ἀντι-, ἀν-, ἀ- ‖ ~-**alcoholic** *a* ἄνευ οἰνοπνεύματος.

nonchalant ['nɔnʃələnt] *a* ψύχραιμος, ἀδιάφορος.

nondescript ['nɔndiskript] *a* ἀκαθόριστος, ἀχαρακτήριστος.

none [nʌn] *a* κανείς ‖ *pron* κανείς, καμμία, κανέν ‖ *ad* καθόλου.

nonentity [nɔ'nentiti] *n* μηδαμινότης, ἀσήμαντος ἄνθρωπος.

nonplussed ['nɔn'plʌst] *a* (τά ἔχω) χαμένα, (εἶμαι) ζαλισμένος.

nonsense ['nɔnsəns] *n* ἀνοησία, παραλογισμός.

non-stop ['nɔn'stɔp] *a* ἄνευ σταθμοῦ.

noodles ['nu:dlz] *npl* χυλοπῆτες.

noon [nu:n] *n* μεσημέρι.

no one ['nəʊwʌn] *pron* = **nobody**.

noose [nu:s] *n* βρόχος, θηλειά.

nor [nɔ:*] *cj* οὔτε, μήτε.

norm [nɔ:m] *n* κανών, τύπος, μέτρον.

normal ['nɔ:məl] *a* κανονικός, συνήθης, ὁμαλός ‖ ~**ly** *ad* κανονικῶς.

north [nɔ:θ] *n* βορράς, βοριάς ‖ (*of country etc*) τά βόρεια ‖ *a* βόρειος ‖ *ad* βορείως, πρός βορᾶν ‖ ~-**east** *n* βορειοανατολικόν ‖ ~**ern** *a* βόρειος, βορεινός ‖ N~ **Pole** *n* Βόρειος Πόλος ‖ N~ **Sea** *n* Βόρειος Θάλασσα ‖ ~**ward(s)** *ad* πρός βορράν ‖ ~-**west** *n* βορειοδυτικόν.

Norway ['nɔ:wei] *n* Νορβηγία.

Norwegian [nɔ:'wi:dʒən] *a* νορβηγικός ‖ *n* Νορβηγός.

nose [nəʊz] *n* μύτη ‖ (*smell*) ὄσφρησις, μύτη ‖ ~**bleed** *n* ρινορραγία, μάτωμα τῆς μύτης ‖ ~-**dive** *n* κάθετος ἐφόρμησις ‖ ~**y** *a* περίεργος, ἀδιάκριτος.

nostalgia [nɔs'tældʒiə] *n* νοσταλγία.

nostalgic [nɔs'tældʒik] *a* νοσταλγικός.

nostril ['nɔstril] *n* ρουθούνι.

not [nɔt] *ad* δέν, μή, ὄχι.

notable ['nəʊtəbl] *a* ἀξιοσημείωτος, σημαντικός.

notably ['nəʊtəbli] *ad* ἰδιαιτέρως, εἰδικῶς.

notch [nɔtʃ] *n* ἐγκοπή, χαραγή, ὀδόντωσις.

note [nəʊt] *n* νότα, τόνος, πλῆκτρον ‖ (*short letter*) γραμματάκι, σημείωμα ‖ (*remark*) σημείωσις, ὑπόμνημα ‖ (*reputation*) φήμη, διάκρισις ‖ *vt* σημειώνω, παρατηρῶ ‖ (*write down*) σημειώνω, (κατα)γράφω ‖ ~**book** *n* σημειωματάριον, καρνέ ‖ ~-**case** *n* πορτοφόλι ‖ ~**d** *a* σημαίνων, διακεκριμένος, διάσημος ‖ ~**paper** *n* χαρτί ἀλληλογραφίας.

nothing ['nʌθiŋ] *n* μηδέν, τίποτε ‖ **for** ~ (*free*) δωρεάν, τζάμπα.

notice ['nəʊtis] *n* (*announcement*) ἀγγελία, ἀναγγελία ‖ (*attention*) προσοχή, παρατήρησις ‖ (*warning*) εἰδοποίησις, προειδοποίησις ‖ *vt* (*observe*) παρατηρῶ, ἀντιλαμβάνομαι, προσέχω ‖ ~**able** *a* ἀξιοσημείωτος, ἀξιοπρόσεκτος ‖ ~ **board** *n* (*Brit*) ἐνοικιαστήριον, πίναξ ἀνακοινώσεων.

notification [nəʊtifi'keiʃən] *n* (ἀν)ἀγγελία, ἀνακοίνωσις, δήλωσις, γνωστοποίησις.

notify ['nəʊtifai] *vt* πληροφορῶ, εἰδοποιῶ, γνωστοποιῶ.

notion ['nəʊʃən] *n* ἀντίληψις, ἰδέα ‖ (*fancy*) γνώμη, ἰδέα, σκέψις.

notorious [nəʊ'tɔ:riəs] *a* περιβόητος, πασίγνωστος.

notwithstanding [nɔtwið'stændiŋ] *ad* παρ' ὅλα ταῦτα, ἐν τούτοις, παρ' ὅλον.

nougat ['nu:gɑ:] *n* χαλβαδόπητα.

nought [nɔ:t] *n* (*zero*) μηδέν ‖ τίποτε, μηδέν.

noun [naʊn] *n* ὄνομα, οὐσιαστικόν.

nourish ['nʌriʃ] *vt* (δια)τρέφω ‖ ~**ing** *a* θρεπτικός ‖ ~**ment** *n* (δια)τροφή, θρέψις.

novel ['nɔvəl] *n* μυθιστόρημα ‖ *a* νέος, πρωτότυπος ‖ ~**ist** *n* μυθιστοριογράφος ‖ ~**ty** *n* νεωτερισμός.

November [nəʊ'vembə*] *n* Νοέμβρης.

novice ['nɔvis] *n* ἀρχάριος, μαθητευόμενος.

now [naʊ] *ad* τώρα, λοιπόν ‖ **right** ~ ἀμέσως, στή στιγμή ‖ ~ **and then**, ~ **and again** κάπου-κάπου, κάθε τόσο, καμμιά φορά, μερικές φορές, πού καί πού ‖ ~**adays** *ad* σήμερα.

nowhere ['nəʊwɛə*] *ad* πουθενά.

nozzle ['nɔzl] *n* στόμιον (σωλῆνος), προφύσιον, ἀκροφύσιον.

nuance ['nju:ɑ:ns] *n* ἀπόχρωσις.

nuclear ['nju:kliə*] *a* (*energy etc*) πυρηνικός.

nucleus ['nju:kliəs] *n* πυρήν ‖ (*of atom*) πυρήν.

nude [nju:d] *a* γυμνός, γδυτός ‖ *n* (*art*) γυμνόν.

nudge [nʌdʒ] *vt* ἀγκωνίζω, σκουντῶ.

nudist ['nju:dist] *n* γυμνιστής.

nudity ['nju:diti] *n* γυμνότης.

nuisance ['nju:sns] *n* ἐνόχλησις, μπελάς.

null [nʌl] *a* ἄκυρος ‖ ~**ify** *vt* ἀκυρώνω.

numb [nʌm] *a* ναρκωμένος, μουδιασμένος ‖ *vt* ναρκώνω, μουδιάζω.

number ['nʌmbə*] *n* ἀριθμός, ψηφίον, νούμερο ‖ (*sum*) ἀριθμός, σύνολον, ἄθροισμα ‖ (*quantity*) πολλοί, πλῆθος ‖ (*gram*) ἀριθμός ‖ (*issue*) ἀριθμός (τεύχους) ‖ *vt* (ἀ)ριθμῶ, μετρῶ ‖ (*amount to*) ἀνέρχομαι, φθάνω, ἀριθμῶ ‖ ~ **plate** *n* (*Brit aut*) πίναξ (αὐτοκινήτου).

numbness ['nʌmnis] *n* νάρκωσις, μούδιασμα,

numeral ['nju:mərəl] *n* ἀριθμός.
numerical [nju:'merikəl] *a* (*order*) ἀριθμητικός.
numerous ['nju:mərəs] *a* πολυάριθμος.
nun [nʌn] *n* μοναχή, καλόγρηα.
nurse [nə:s] *n* νοσοκόμος ‖ (*for children*) παραμάννα, τροφός ‖ *vt* (*patient, invalid*) περιποιοῦμαι, νοσηλεύω ‖ (*fig*) φροντίζω, ἐπιμελοῦμαι, συγκρατῶ ‖ ~**ry** *n* παιδικός σταθμός, βρεφοκομεῖον ‖ (*plants*) φυτώριον ‖ ~**ry rhyme** *n* παιδικό τραγουδάκι ‖ ~**ry school** *n* νηπιαγωγεῖον.
nursing ['nə:siŋ] *n* (*profession*) ἐπάγγελμα νοσοκόμου ‖ ~ **home** *n* (ἰδιωτική) κλινική.
nut [nʌt] *n* περικόχλιον, παξιμάδι ‖ (*fruit*) καρύδι, ξηρός καρπός ‖ ~**s** *a* (*col: crazy*) τρελλός.
nutcrackers ['nʌtkrækəz] *npl* καρυοθραύστης.
nutmeg ['nʌtmeg] *n* μοσχοκάρυδο.
nutrient ['nju:triənt] *n* θρεπτικόν, τρόφιμον.
nutrition [nju:'triʃən] *n* θρέψις, διατροφή.
nutritious [nju:'triʃəs] *a* θρεπτικός.
nutshell ['nʌtʃel] *n*: **in a ~** σύντομος, μέ λίγα λόγια.
nylon ['nailɔn] *a,n* νάϋλον.

O, o

O, o [əu] *exel* = **oh.**
oaf [əuf] *n* ἀδέξιος, ἄξεστος.
oak [əuk] *n* δρῦς, βαλανιδιά ‖ *a* δρύινος.
oar [ɔ:*] *n* κώπη, κουπί.
oasis [əu'eisis] *n* ὄασις.
oath [əuθ] *n* ὄρκος ‖ (*swearword*) βλαστήμια.
oats [əuts] *npl* βρώμη.
obedience [ə'bi:diəns] *n* ὑπακοή, εὐπείθεια.
obedient [ə'bi:diənt] *a* ὑπάκουος.
obelisk ['ɔbilisk] *n* ὀβελίσκος.
obesity [əu'bi:siti] *n* παχυσαρκία.
obey [ə'bei] *vti* ὑπακούω.
obituary [ə'bitjuəri] *n* νεκρολογία.
object ['ɔbdʒikt] *n* ἀντικείμενον ‖ (*target*) στόχος, σκοπός, ἀντικείμενον ‖ (*gram*) ἀντικείμενον ‖ [əb'dʒekt] *vi* (+ *to*) (*proposal*) ἀντιτίθεμαι, ἀποδοκιμάζω ‖ (*a noise etc*) ἀποκρούω, ἐπικρίνω ‖ ~**ion** *n* ἀντίρρησις, ἀντιλογία ‖ (*obstacle*) ἐμπόδιον, δυσκολία ‖ ~**ionable** *a* ἀπαράδεκτος, ἀνεπιθύμητος ‖ ~**ive** *n* ἀντικειμενικός σκοπός ‖ *a* (*impartial*) ἀντικειμενικός ‖ ~**ively** *ad* ἀντικειμενικά ‖ ~**ivity** *n* ἀντικειμενικότης ‖ ~**or** *n* ἀντιρρησίας, ἀντιλέγων.
obligation [ɔbli'geiʃən] *n* ὑποχρέωσις.
obligatory [ə'bligətəri] *a* ὑποχρεωτικός.
oblige [ə'blaidʒ] *vt* ὑποχρεώνω, ἐπιβάλλω ‖ (*do a favour*) ἐξυπηρετῶ, ὑποχρεώνω.

obliging [ə'blaidʒiŋ] *a* ὑποχρεωτικός, ἐξυπηρετικός.
oblique [ə'bli:k] *a* λοξός, πλάγιος.
obliterate [ə'blitəreit] *vt* ἐξαλείφω, σβήνω, καταστρέφω.
oblivion [ə'bliviən] *n* λήθη.
oblivious [ə'bliviəs] *a* (+ *of*) ἐπιλήσμων, ξεχασιάρης.
oblong ['ɔblɔŋ] *n* ἐπίμηκες σχῆμα, ὀρθογώνιον ‖ *a* ἐπιμήκης, μακρουλός.
obnoxious [əb'nɔkʃəs] *a* ἀπεχθής, δυσάρεστος.
oboe ['əubəu] *n* ὄμπος.
obscene [əb'si:n] *a* αἰσχρός, πρόστυχος.
obscenity [əb'seniti] *n* αἰσχρότης, ἀχρειότης.
obscure [əb'skjuə*] *a* σκοτεινός, σκοῦρος ‖ (*unnoticed*) ἄσημος, ταπεινός ‖ *vt* συσκοτίζω, σκεπάζω.
obscurity [əb'skjuəriti] *n* σκοτάδι, ἀφάνεια.
obsequious [əb'si:kwiəs] *a* δουλοπρεπής.
observable [əb'zə:vəbl] *a* ὁρατός, εὐδιάκριτος.
observance [əb'zə:vəns] *n* τήρησις, ἑορτασμός.
observant [əb'zə:vənt] *a* παρατηρητικός, προσεκτικός.
observation [ɔbzə'veiʃən] *n* παρατήρησις, παρακολούθησις.
observatory [əb'zə:vətri] *n* ἀστεροσκοπεῖον.
observe [əb'zə:v] *vt* (*the law etc*) τηρῶ, κρατῶ ‖ (*study*) παρατηρῶ, κοιτάζω ‖ (*understand*) διακρίνω, ἀντιλαμβάνομαι ‖ ~**r** *n* παρατηρητής, τηρητής.
obsess [əb'ses] *vt* κατέχω, βασανίζω ‖ ~**ion** *n* ἔμμονος ἰδέα ‖ ~**ive** *a* καταθλιπτικός, βασανιστικός.
obsolescence [ɔbsə'lesns] *n* τάσις πρός ἀχρηστίαν, παλαίωμα.
obsolete ['ɔbsəli:t] *a* ἀπηρχαιωμένος.
obstacle ['ɔbstəkl] *n* ἐμπόδιον, πρόσκομμα ‖ ~ **race** *n* δρόμος μετ' ἐμποδίων.
obstetrics [ɔb'stetriks] *n* μαιευτική.
obstinacy ['ɔbstinəsi] *n* ἰσχυρογνωμοσύνη, ἐπιμονή.
obstinate ['ɔbstinit] *a* ἐπίμονος, πείσμων ‖ ~**ly** *ad* ἐπίμονα.
obstreperous [əb'strepərəs] *a* φασαρίας, ταραχοποιός.
obstruct [əb'strʌkt] *vt* φράσσω, ἐμποδίζω ‖ ~**ion** *n* κωλυσιεργία, ἐμπόδιον ‖ ~**ive** *a* κωλυσιεργός.
obtain [əb'tein] *vt* παίρνω, ἀποκτῶ, ἐπιτυγχάνω ‖ ~**able** *a* ἐπιτευκτός, εὐαπόκτητος.
obtrusive [əb'tru:siv] *a* ἐνοχλητικός, φορτικός.
obtuse [əb'tju:s] *a* (*person*) ἀμβλύνους.
obvious ['ɔbviəs] *a* προφανής, εὐνόητος ‖ ~**ly** *ad* προφανώς, φανερά.
occasion [ə'keiʒən] *n* (*time*) εὐκαιρία, φορά ‖ (*event*) ἀφορμή, περίστασις ‖ (*reason*)

λόγος, αἰτία ‖ vt προξενῶ ‖ ~ **al** a σποραδικός, τυχαῖος ‖ (drink) πού καί πού ‖ ~ **ally** ad κάπου-κάπου.

occult [ɔ'kʌlt] n: **the** ~ οἱ ἀπόκρυφοι ἐπιστῆμες.

occupant ['ɔkjupənt] n κάτοχος ‖ (of house) ἔνοικος.

occupation [ɔkju'peiʃən] n ἀπασχόλησις, ἀσχολία, ἐπάγγελμα ‖ (of country) κατάληψις, κτῆσις ‖ ~ **al** a (hazard) ἐπαγγελματικός.

occupier ['ɔkjupaiə*] n (of house) ἔνοικος.

occupy ['ɔkjupai] vt (take possession) κατέχω, κατακτῶ ‖ (live in) κατοικῶ ‖ (hold) κατέχω ‖ (employ) ἀπασχολῶ. συμβάν.

occur [ə'kə:*] vi συμβαίνω, γίνομαι, λαμβάνω χώραν ‖ (be found) συναντῶμαι, ἐμφανίζομαι ‖ (+ to) παρουσιάζομαι στήν σκέψιν, μοῦ ἔρχεται ‖ ~ **rence** n γεγονός, συμβάν.

ocean ['əuʃən] n ὠκεανός ‖ ~ **-going** a ὑπερωκεάνειος.

ochre ['əukə*] n ὤχρα.

o'clock [ə'klɔk] ad: **it is 5** ~ εἶναι πέντε (ὥρα).

octagonal [ɔk'tægənl] a ὀκταγώνιος.

octane ['ɔktein] n ὀκτάνιον.

octave ['ɔktiv] n ὀχτάβα.

October [ɔk'təubə*] n 'Οκτώβρης.

octopus ['ɔktəpəs] n χταπόδι.

odd [ɔd] a (number) περιττός, μονός ‖ (not part of set) μονό, παράταιρος ‖ (with some left over) περισσεύων, τόσα, καί κάτι ‖ (strange) περίεργος, παράξενος ‖ (casual) τυχαῖος ‖ ~ **ity** n παραδοξότης ‖ παράξενος ἄνθρωπος ‖ ~ **ly** ad περίεργως, περίεργα ‖ ~ **ly enough** τό περίεργον εἶναι ‖ ~ **ments** npl ὑπολείμματα ‖ ~ **s** npl ἀνισότης, διαφορά ‖ (balance of advantage) πλεονέκτημα, πιθανότητες ‖ (chances) πιθανότητες ‖ (at racetrack) στοίχημα, ποντάρισμα ‖ **at** ~ **s** διαφωνῶ, εἶμαι τσακωμένος ‖ ~ **s and ends** npl ρετάλια, μικροπράγματα.

ode [əud] n ᾠδή.

odious ['əudiəs] a ἀπεχθής, μισητός.

odour, (US) **odor** ['əudə*] n ὀσμή, μυρουδιά ‖ ~ **less** a ἄοσμος.

of [ɔv, əv] prep ἀπό, περί, ὡς πρός.

off [ɔf] ad (absent) μακρυά ‖ (of switch) 'κλειστόν' ‖ (milk) ὄχι φρέσκο, χαλασμένη ‖ prep ἀπό, μακρυά ἀπό, ὀλιγώτερον ἀπό.

offal ['ɔfəl] n ἐντόσθια.

off-colour, (US) **off-color** ['ɔf'kʌlə*] a (ill) χλωμός.

offence [ə'fens] n (crime) παράπτωμα, πταῖσμα ‖ (insult) προσβολή.

offend [ə'fend] vt προσβάλλω ‖ ~ **er** n παραβάτης ‖ ~ **ing** a προσβλητικός, πειρακτικός.

offense [ə'fens] n (US) = **offence**.

offensive [ə'fensiv] a προσβλητικός, δυσάρεστος ‖ (weapon) ἐπιθετικός.

offer ['ɔfə*] n προσφορά ‖ vt προσφέρω, προτείνω ‖ ~ **ing** n (esp rel) θυσία, προσφορά.

offhand ['ɔf'hænd] a αὐθόρμητος, ἀπότομος ‖ ad στή στιγμή, ἀπότομα.

office ['ɔfis] n (position) γραφεῖον ‖ ~ **r** n (mil) ἀξιωματικός ‖ δημόσιος ὑπάλληλος, ἀξιωματοῦχος ‖ ~ **work** n ἐργασία γραφείου.

official [ə'fiʃəl] a (authorized) ἐπίσημος, ὑπηρεσιακός ‖ n ὑπάλληλος (δημόσιος) ‖ ~ **ly** ad ἐπισήμως.

officious [ə'fiʃəs] a ἐπεμβαίνων, ἐνοχλητικός.

offing ['ɔfiŋ] n: **in the** ~ ἐν ὄψει, στά ἀνοιχτά.

off-season ['ɔfsi:zn] a μή ἐποχιακός, ἐκτός ἐποχῆς, νεκρά ἐποχή.

offset ['ɔfset] vt ἀντισταθμίζω, ἀποζημιώνω.

offshore ['ɔf'ʃɔ:*] ad στά ἀνοιχτά ‖ a χερσαῖος, στεριανός ‖ ἀπόγειος.

offside ['ɔf'said] a (aut) ἔξω πλευρά, δεξιά πλευρά ‖ n (sport) ὄφ-σάϊντ.

offspring ['ɔfspriŋ] n ἀπόγονος, βλαστός ‖ ἀποτέλεσμα.

often ['ɔfən] ad συχνά, πολλές φορές.

ogle ['əugl] vt γλυκοκοιτάζω.

oh [əu] excl ὤ!, ἄχ!

oil [ɔil] n ἔλαιον ‖ πετρέλαιον, λάδι ‖ vt λαδώνω ‖ ~ **can** n λαδωτήρι ‖ ~ **field** n πετρελαιοφόρος περιοχή ‖ ~ **-fired** a καίων πετρέλαιον ‖ ~ **level** n στάθμη ἐλαίου ‖ ~ **painting** n ἐλαιογραφία ‖ ~ **refinery** n διυλιστήριον ‖ ~ **skins** npl μουσαμᾶς ‖ ~ **tanker** n δεξαμενόπλοιον ‖ ~ **well** n πετρελαιοπηγή ‖ ~ **y** a ἐλαιώδης, λαδερός.

ointment ['ɔintmənt] n ἀλοιφή.

O.K., okay ['əu'kei] excl πολύ καλά!, ἐν τάξει! ‖ n ἔγκρισις ‖ vt ἐγκρίνω.

old [əuld] a (γέρων, γέρος, ἡλικιωμένος ‖ (of age) τῆς ἡλικίας, χρονῶν ‖ (worn) παλαιός, σαραβαλωμένος ‖ (former) παλαιός, πρώην, τέως ‖ (friend) παλαιός (σύντροφος) ‖ ~ **age** n (βαθειά) γηράματα ‖ ~ **en** a (old) παλιό, τοῦ παλιοῦ ‖ ~ **-fashioned** a ὀπαδός τοῦ παλιοῦ καιροῦ ‖ (out of date) ἀπηρχαιωμένος, παλαιᾶς μόδας ‖ ~ **maid** n γεροντοκόρη.

olive ['ɔliv] n (fruit) ἐλαία, ἐλιά ‖ a (colour) λαδής, ἐλαιόχρους ‖ ~ **oil** n ἐλαιόλαδον, λάδι.

Olympic [əu'limpik] a 'Ολυμπιακός ‖ ~ **Games** npl (also ~ **s**) 'Ολυμπιακοί 'Αγῶνες.

omelet(te) ['ɔmlit] n ὀμελέττα.

omen ['əumen] n οἰωνός, σημάδι.

ominous ['ɔminəs] a δυσοίωνος, δυσμενής.

omission [əu'miʃən] n παράλειψις, παραδρομή.

omit [əu'mit] vt παραλείπω.

on [ɔn] prep ἐπί, πάνω σέ, εἰς, κατά, περί ‖ ad ἐμπρός, πρός τά ἐμπρός, ἐν λειτουργία ‖ ~ **and off** ἐνίοτε, κάπου-κάπου ‖ ~ **the left** ἀριστερά, στ' ἀριστερά ‖ ~ **Friday** τήν Παρασκευή.

once [wʌns] ad μιά φορά, ἅπαξ, ἄλλοτε, κάποτε ‖ cj μόλις, ἀπό τή στιγμή που, μιά καί ‖ **at** ~ ἀμέσως, στή στιγμή ‖ (same time) ταυτοχρόνως, συγχρόνως ‖ **all at** ~ ὅλως αἰφνιδίως ‖ ὅλοι μαζί ‖ ~ **more** ἀκόμη μιά φορά ‖ **more than** ~ πολλές φορές ‖ ~ **and for all** μιά καί καλή ‖ ~ **upon a time** μιά φορά (καί ἕναν καιρό).

oncoming ['ɔnkʌmiŋ] a (traffic) ἐπερχόμενος, προσεγγίζων.

one [wʌn] a ἕνα, μία, ἕνα ‖ (united) ἕνας, μιά, ἕνα ‖ (only) μόνος, μοναδικός ‖ n ἕνα, ἕνας, μιά ‖ pron ἕνα, αὐτός, κανείς, τέτοιος ‖ **this** ~ αὐτός ἐδῶ ‖ **that** ~ αὐτός ἐκεῖ ‖ ~ **by** ~ ἕνας-ἕνας ‖ ~ **never knows** ποτέ δέν ξέρει κανείς ‖ ~ **another** ἀλλήλους ‖ ~**man** a (business) (δουλειά) γιά ἕνα ἄνθρωπο ‖ ~**self** pron ἑαυτόν ‖ ~**way** a (street, traffic) μονῆς κατευθύνσεως.

onion ['ʌnjən] n κρομμύδι.

onlooker ['ɔnlukə*] n θεατής.

only ['əunli] ad μόνον ‖ a μόνος.

onset ['ɔnset] n (beginning) ἀπαρχή.

onshore ['ɔnʃɔ:*] a,ad πρός τήν ἀκτήν.

onslaught ['ɔnslɔ:t] n ἐφόρμησις, ἐπίθεσις.

onto ['ɔntu] prep = **on to**.

onus ['əunəs] n βάρος, εὐθύνη, καθῆκον.

onwards ['ɔnwədz] ad (place) πρός τά ἐμπρός, καί πέραν ‖ (time) καί εἰς τό ἑξῆς.

ooze [u:z] vi (liquid) στάζω, ἐκρέω, διεισδύω.

opacity [əu'pæsiti] n ἀδιαφάνεια, θολότης.

opaque [əu'peik] a ἀδιαφανής, θαμπός.

open ['əupən] a ἀνοιχτός ‖ (unlimited) ἀνοικτός, ἀπεριόριστος ‖ (without cover) ἀκάλυπτος, ξέσκεπος ‖ (clear) φανερός, ἔκδηλος ‖ (question) φανερός, ἔκδηλος ‖ (free) ἐλεύθερος, ἀνοιχτός ‖ (sincere) εἰλικρινής, ἀπροκάλυπτος ‖ vt (mouth) ἀνοίγω ‖ (letter) ἀποσφραγίζω, ἀνοίγω ‖ (box) λύνω, ἀνοίγω ‖ (door) ἀνοίγω ‖ (account) ἀνοίγω ‖ vi ἀρχίζω, ἀνοίγω ‖ (shop) ἀνοίγω ‖ (play) ἀρχίζω ‖ **to** ~ **out** vt ἀνοίγω, ξεδιπλώνω ‖ **to** ~ **up** vt (route) ἀνοίγω, χαράσσω, διανοίγω ‖ ~**air** a ὑπαίθριος ‖ ~**er** n (for cans) ἀνοικτήρι ‖ ~**ing** n ἄνοιγμα, ρωγμή ‖ (beginning) ἔναρξις ‖ (good chance) εὐκαιρία ‖ ~**ly** ad φανερά, εἰλικρινή, δημοσία ‖ ~**-minded** a εὐρύνους, μέ ἀνοιχτό μυαλό ‖ ~**-necked** a ἀνοιχτό ‖ (φόρεμα) ντεκολτέ.

opera ['ɔpərə] n μελόδραμα, ὄπερα ‖ ~ **house** n λυρική σκηνή, ὄπερα.

operate ['ɔpəreit] vt (machine) ἐνεργῶ, κινῶ, διευθύνω ‖ vi λειτουργῶ, δρῶ, ἐνεργῶ ‖ (med) (+ on) χειρουργῶ, ἐγχειρίζω.

operatic [ɔpə'rætik] a μελοδραματικός.

operation [ɔpə'reiʃən] n λειτουργία, δρᾶσις ‖ (med) ἐγχείρησις ‖ (mil) ἐπιχείρησις ‖ ~**al** a τῆς ἐπιχειρήσεως.

operative ['ɔpərətiv] a ἐνεργός, ἰσχύων ‖ χειρουργικός ‖ n ἐργάτης, τεχνίτης.

operator ['ɔpəreitə*] n (of machine) χειριστής, ὀπερατέρ ‖ (tel) τηλεφωνήτρια.

operetta [ɔpə'retə] n ὀπερέττα.

opinion [ə'pinjən] n γνώμη, ἰδέα, δοξασία.

opium ['əupiəm] n ὄπιον.

opponent [ə'pəunənt] n ἀντίπαλος.

opportune ['ɔpətju:n] a ἐπίκαιρος, εὔθετος, κατάλληλος.

opportunist [ɔpə'tju:nist] n καιροσκόπος.

opportunity [ɔpə'tju:niti] n εὐκαιρία.

oppose [ə'pəuz] vt ἀντιτάσσω, ἀντικρούω, καταπολεμῶ ‖ ~**d** a (+ to) ἀντίθετος (πρός), ἀντιτιθέμενος.

opposing [ə'pəuziŋ] a (side) ἀντίθετος, ἀντίπαλος.

opposite ['ɔpəzit] a ἀντίθετος, ἀντικρυνός ‖ (direction) ἀντίθετος ‖ ad ἔναντι, ἀπέναντι, ἀντίκρυ ‖ prep ἔναντι, ἀπέναντι ‖ n ἀντίστοιχον, ἀντίθετον ‖ ~ **number** n (person) ἀντίστοιχος.

opposition [ɔpə'ziʃən] n ἀντίστασις, ἀντίθεσις ‖ (party) ἀντιπολίτευσις.

oppress [ə'pres] vt καταπιέζω, καταδυναστεύω ‖ (heat etc) καταθλίβω, βασανίζω ‖ ~**ion** n καταπίεσις, στενοχωρία ‖ ~**ive** a καταθλιπτικός, πνιγηρός.

opt [ɔpt] vi: **to** ~ **for sth** διαλέγω, ἐπιλέγω.

optical ['ɔptikəl] a ὀπτικός.

optician [ɔp'tiʃən] n ὀπτικός.

optimism ['ɔptimizəm] n αἰσιοδοξία.

optimist ['ɔptimist] n αἰσιόδοξος ‖ ~**ic** a αἰσιόδοξος.

optimum ['ɔptiməm] a εὐνοϊκός, ἄριστος.

option ['ɔpʃən] n ἐκλογή ‖ δικαίωμα ἐκλογῆς ‖ ~**al** a προαιρετικός.

opulence ['ɔpjuləns] n πλοῦτος, ἀφθονία.

opulent ['ɔpjulənt] a πλούσιος, ἄφθονος.

opus ['əupəs] n μουσική σύνθεσις, ἔργον.

or [ɔ:*] cj ἤ.

oracle ['ɔrəkl] n χρησμός, μαντεῖον.

oral ['ɔ:rəl] a ~ροφορικός ‖ n (exam) προφορικαί (ἐξετάσεις).

orange ['ɔrindʒ] n πορτοκάλι ‖ (colour) πορτοκαλλί.

oration [ɔ:'reiʃən] n λόγος.

orator ['ɔrətə*] n ρήτωρ.

oratorio [ɔrə'tɔ:riəu] n ὀρατόριον.

orbit ['ɔ:bit] n τροχιά ‖ vt (earth) περιστρέφομαι.

orchard ['ɔ:tʃəd] n ὀπωρόκηπος, περιβόλι.

orchestra ['ɔ:kistrə] n ὀρχήστρα ‖ ~**l** [ɔ:'kestrəl] a ὀρχηστρικός.

orchid ['ɔ:kid] n ὀρχεοειδές φυτόν.

ordain [ɔː'dein] *vt* (προ)ορίζω, θεσπίζω, διορίζω ‖ (*eccl*) χειροτονῶ.

ordeal [ɔː'diːl] *n* βασανιστήριον.

order ['ɔːdə*] *n* (*arrangement*) τάξις, σειρά, διαδοχή ‖ (*instruction*) διαταγή, ἐντολή, διάταγμα ‖ (*rank, class*) τάξις ‖ (*eccl*) βαθμός ἱερωσύνης ‖ τάγμα ‖ (*decoration*) παράσημον ‖ (*comm*) ἐπιταγή, παραγγελία ‖ *vt* διατάσσω ‖ διευθετῶ, ταξινομῶ ‖ (*comm*) παραγγέλλω ‖ ~ **form** *n* ἔντυπον ἐντολῆς ‖ ~**ly** *n* ἀγγελιαφόρος, ὀρτινάντσα ‖ *a* φρόνιμος, τακτικός, ἥσυχος ‖ (*tidy*) συγυρισμένος, τακτικός.

ordinal ['ɔːdinl] *a* (*number*) τακτικός.

ordinarily ['ɔːdnrili] *ad* συνήθως, κανονικά.

ordinary ['ɔːdnri] *a* συνήθης, συνηθισμένος ‖ (*commonplace*) τῆς ἀράδας, κοινός.

ordination [ɔːdi'neiʃən] *n* χειροτονία.

ordnance ['ɔːdnəns] *n* ὑλικόυ πολέμου, τηλεβόλα, πυροβόλα.

ore [ɔː*] *n* ὀρυκτόν, μετάλλευμα.

organ ['ɔːgən] *n* (*mus*) ὄργανον ‖ (*of sight etc*) ὄργανον·‖ (*means of action*) ὄργανον ‖ ~**ic** [ɔː'gænik] *a* ὀργανικός, ἐνόργανος ‖ ~**ism** *n* ὀργανισμός ‖ ~**ist** *n* ὀργανοπαίκτης.

organization [ɔːgənai'zeiʃən] *n* ὀργάνωσις, ὀργανισμός.

organize ['ɔːgənaiz] *vt* ὀργανώνω ‖ ~**r** *n* (δι)ὀργανωτής.

orgasm ['ɔːgæzəm] *n* ὀργασμός, παροξυσμός.

orgy ['ɔːdʒi] *n* ὄργιον.

Orient ['ɔːriənt] *n*: the ~ Ἀνατολή, Ἄπω Ἀνατολή.

oriental [ɔːri'entəl] *a* ἀνατολικός, ἀσιατικός ‖ *n* Ἀσιάτης.

orientate ['ɔːrienteit] *vt* προσανατολίζω.

origin ['ɔridʒin] *n* ἀρχή, γένεσις, καταγωγή.

original [ə'ridʒinl] *a* (*first*) ἀρχικός ‖ (*new*) πρωτότυπος ‖ (*individual*) ἰδιότυπος, πρωτότυπος ‖ *n* πρωτότυπον ‖ ~**ity** [əridʒi'næliti] *n* πρωτοτυπία ‖ ~**ly** *ad* ἀρχικῶς ‖ ἐξ ἀρχῆς.

originate [ə'ridʒineit] *vi* κατάγομαι, προέρχομαι ‖ *vt* γεννῶ, δημιουργῶ.

originator [ə'ridʒineitə*] *n* δημιουργός, ἐγκαινιαστής.

Orlon ['ɔːlɒn] *n* ® ὀρλόν.

ornament ['ɔːnəmənt] *n* κόσμημα, στολίδι ‖ ~**al** *a* (δια)κοσμητικός ‖ ~**ation** *n* διακόσμησις.

ornate [ɔː'neit] *a* κεκοσμημένος, φανταχτερός.

ornithologist [ɔːni'θɒlədʒist] *n* ὀρνιθολόγος.

ornithology [ɔːni'θɒlədʒi] *n* ὀρνιθολογία.

orphan ['ɔːfən] *n* ὀρφανός ‖ *vt* ἀπορφανίζω ‖ ~**age** *n* ὀρφανοτροφεῖον.

orthodox ['ɔːθədɒks] *a* ὀρθόδοξος ‖ (*conventional*) καθιερωμένος.

orthopaedic, (*US*) ~**pedic** [ɔːθəu'piːdik] *a* ὀρθοπεδικός.

oscillation [ɒsi'leiʃən] *n* αἰώρησις, ταλάντευσις.

ostensible [ɒs'tensəbl] *a* προφανής, φαινομενικός, δῆθεν.

ostensibly [ɒs'tensəbli] *ad* κατά τά φαινόμενα, δῆθεν.

ostentation [ɒsten'teiʃən] *n* ἐπίδειξις, φιγούρα.

ostentatious [ɒsten'teiʃəs] *a* ἐπιδεικτικός, φιγουρατζῆς, φανταχτερός.

ostracize ['ɒstrəsaiz] *vt* ἐξοστρακίζω.

ostrich ['ɒstritʃ] *n* στρουθοκάμηλος.

other ['ʌðə*] *a* ἄλλος ‖ (*additional*) ἄλλος, ἐπιπρόσθετος ‖ (*opposite*) ἄλλος, ἀπέναντι ‖ *pron* ἄλλος ‖ *ad*: ~ **than** διαφορετικός ἀπό, ἐκτός ἀπό ‖ ~**wise** *ad* ἄλλως, ἀλλοιώτικα ‖ (*in other ways*) κατά τά ἄλλα ‖ (*or else*) διαφορετικά, ἀλλοιῶς, εἰδεμή.

otter ['ɒtə*] *n* ἐνιδρύς, βύδρα.

ought [ɔːt] *auxiliary v* πρέπει, θέ ἔπρεπε ‖ I ~ **to do it** πρέπει νά τό κάνω ‖ **you** ~ **to go** πρέπει νά φύγης ‖ **he** ~ **to win** πρέπει νά κερδίση.

ounce [auns] *n* οὐγγιά.

our [auə*] *poss a* ἰδικός μας ‖ ~**s** *poss pron* ἰδικός μας ‖ ~**selves** *pron* ἐμεῖς οἱ ἴδιοι.

oust [aust] *vt* ἐκβάλλω, ἐκτοπίζω.

out [aut] *ad* ἔξω ‖ (*not indoors*) ἐκτός ‖ (*not alight*) σβησμένος ‖ (*open*) πού βγῆκαν, βγαλμένα ‖ (*made known*) γνωστόν, πού ἀπεκαλύφθη ‖ (*in reckoning*) εἰς λάθος, ἔξω ‖ ~ **of** *prep* ἔξω ἀπό ‖ (*from among*) ἀπό ‖ (*without*) χωρίς ‖ **made** ~ **of wood** καμωμένο ἀπό ξύλο ‖ ~-**of-bounds** *a* ἀπαγορευμένος ‖ ~-**of-date** *a* ξεπερασμένος ‖ ~ **of doors** *ad* ἔξω, στό ὕπαιθρον ‖ ~ **of order** *a* βεβλαμένος, χαλασμένος ‖ ~-**of-the-way** *a* παράμερος, ἀπόμερος ‖ (*unusual*) ἀσυνήθης, ἀσυνήθιστος.

outback ['autbæk] *n* τό ἐσωτερικόν.

outboard (**motor**) ['autbɔːd('məutə*)] *n* ἐξωλέμβιος (κινητήρ).

outbreak ['autbreik] *n* ἔκρηξις, ξέσπασμα, ἔναρξις.

outbuilding ['autbildiŋ] *n* παράρτημα οἰκοδομῆς.

outburst ['autbəːst] *n* ἔκρηξις, ξέσπασμα.

outcast ['autkɑːst] *n* ἀπόβλητος.

outclass [aut'klɑːs] *vt* ὑπερτερῶ, ὑπερβαίνω.

outcome ['autkʌm] *n* ἔκβασις, πέρας.

outcry ['autkrai] *n* (κατα)κραυγή.

outdated ['aut'deitid] *a* παλιωμένος, ξεπερασμένος.

outdo [aut'duː] *vt* ὑπερβαίνω, ὑπερέχω.

outdoor ['autdɔː*] *a* ὑπαίθριος, ἐξωτερικός.

outdoors [aut'dɔːz] *ad* στό ὕπαιθρον.

outer ['autə*] *a* ἐξωτερικός ‖ ~ **space** *n* διάστημα.

outfit ['autfit] n ἐξοπλισμός, ἐργαλεῖα, ἀπαιτούμενα ‖ ~ **ters** npl (of clothes) ἔμπορος ἀνδρικῶν ἐνδυμάτων.

outgoings ['autgəuiŋz] npl (expenses) ἔξοδα, πληρωμές.

outgrow [aut'grəu] vt γίνομαι ὑψηλότερος ἀπό, ξεπερνῶ ‖ ἀπαλλάσσομαι.

outing ['autiŋ] n ἐκδρομή.

outlandish [aut'lændiʃ] a παράξενος, ἀσυνήθιστος.

outlaw ['autlɔ:] n ληστής, παράνομος ‖ vt προγράφω.

outlay ['autlei] n δαπάνη, ἔξοδα.

outlet ['autlet] n διέξοδος, ἄνοιγμα.

outline ['autlain] n περίμετρος, περίγραμμα ‖ περίληψις.

outlive [aut'liv] vt ἐπιζῶ.

outlook ['autluk] n (prospect) πρόβλεψις.

outlying ['autlaiiŋ] a ἀπόκεντρος, ἀπόμερος.

outmoded [aut'məudid] a ντεμοντέ.

outnumber [aut'nʌmbə*] vt ὑπερτερῶ ἀριθμητικῶς.

outpatient ['autpeiʃənt] n ἐξωτερικός ἀσθενής.

outpost ['autpəust] n (people, also place) προφυλακή, φυλάκιον.

output ['autput] n παραγωγή, ἀπόδοσις, προϊόν.

outrage ['autreidʒ] n προσβολή, κατάφωρον ἀδίκημα ‖ vt προσβάλλω, πληγώνω, ταράζω ‖ ~**ous** a σκανδαλώδης, τερατώδης, ἀχρεῖος.

outright ['autrait] ad ἀπεριφράστως, ὠμά, ξάστερα ‖ (once for all) τελείως, ἐντελῶς ‖ a τέλειος, ὁριστικός.

outset ['autset] n ἀρχή, ξεκίνημα.

outside ['aut'said] n ἐξωτερικόν ‖ a ἐξωτερικός, πιθανός ‖ ad ἀπ' ἔξω, ἔξω ‖ prep ἔξω ἀπό, ἐκτός ἀπό, πέραν τοῦ ‖ ~-**forward** n ἔξω κυνηγός ‖ ~**r** n (in race etc) χωρίς πιθανότητες ‖ (independent) ξένος, θεατής.

outsize ['autsaiz] a μεγάλων διαστάσεων.

outskirts ['autskə:ts] npl προάστια, περίχωρα.

outspoken [aut'spəukən] a εἰλικρινής, ντόμπρος.

outstanding [aut'stændiŋ] a προέχων, κύριος, σημαντικός ‖ (person) διακεκριμένος, σπουδαῖος, διαπρεπής ‖ (unsettled) ἐκκρεμής, ἀπλήρωτος.

outstay [aut'stei] vt (welcome) μένω περισσότερον ἀπό.

outstretched ['autstretʃt] a (hand) ἀπλωμένος, μέ ἀνοιχτάς ἀγκάλας.

outward ['autwəd] a (sign) ἐξωτερικός ‖ (journey) πρός τά ἔξω, ἔξω ‖ ~**ly** ad ἐξωτερικῶς, φαινομενικῶς.

outweigh [aut'wei] vt (in importance) βαρύνω περισσότερον, ὑπερτερῶ.

outwit [aut'wit] vt ξεγελῶ.

outworn [aut'wɔ:n] a (dated) παλιωμένος.

oval ['əuvəl] a ὠοειδής, ἐλλειψοειδής ‖ n ὠοειδές σχῆμα.

ovary ['əuvəri] n ὠοθήκη.

ovation [əu'veiʃən] n ἐπευφημία.

oven ['ʌvn] n κλίβανος, φοῦρνος.

over ['əuvə*] ad (above) ἄνωθεν, πάνω ἀπό ‖ (across) ἀπέναντι, πέραν ‖ (finished) περασμένος, τελειωμένος ‖ (too much) πέραν τοῦ δέοντος, ἐπί πλέον ‖ (again) φορές (συνέχεια), πάλι ‖ prep (above) ἄνωθεν, ἀπό πάνω, πάνω ‖ (across) ἀπέναντι ‖ (in rank) ὑπεράνω, ὑψηλότερος, ἀνώτερος ‖ (about) περί, γιά ‖ **all** ~ (everywhere) παντοῦ, σ' ὅλο ‖ (finished) τελειωμένο, τετέλεσται, περασμένα ‖ ~ **and** ~ πολλές φορές, ἐπανειλημμένος ‖ ~ **and above** πέραν ἀπό.

over- ['əuvə*] prefix ὑπέρ-, παρά-.

overact ['əuvər'ækt] vi ὑπερβάλλω, παρακάνω.

overall ['əuvərɔ:l] n (Brit) (coat for woman etc) μπλούζα, ποδιά ‖ ~**s** npl (including trousers, for man) φόρμα.

overawe [əuvər'ɔ:] vt ἐκφοβίζω, τρομοκρατῶ, ἐπιβάλλομαι (εἰς).

overbalance [əuvə'bæləns] vi ἀνατρέπω, ὑπερέχω.

overbearing [əuvə'bɛəriŋ] a αὐταρχικός, δεσποτικός, ὑπεροπτικός.

overboard ['əuvəbɔ:d] ad στή θάλασσα (ἀπό πλοῖον).

overcast ['əuvəka:st] a συννεφιασμένος, σκοτεινιασμένος.

overcharge ['əuvə'tʃa:dʒ] vt (price) παίρνω πολλά, γδύνω, ἐπιβαρύνω.

overcoat ['əuvəkaut] n ἐπανωφόρι, παλτό.

overcome [əuvə'kʌm] vt νικῶ, καταβάλλω.

overcrowded [əuvə'kraudid] a ὑπερπλήρες, παραγεμισμένος.

overcrowding [əuvə'kraudiŋ] n ὑπερπλήρωσις, ὑπερπληθυσμός.

overdo [əuvə'du:] vt (cook) παραψήνω ‖ (exaggerate) ὑπερβάλλω, μεγαλοποιῶ, παρακάνω.

overdose ['əuvədəus] n ὑπερβολική δόσις.

overdraft ['əuvədra:ft] n ἀκάλυπτος λογαριασμός.

overdrawn ['əuvə'drɔ:n] a (account) see **overdraft.**

overdrive ['əuvədraiv] n (aut) πολλαπλασιασμένη ταχύτης.

overdue ['əuvə'dju:] a καθυστερημένος, ἐκπρόθεσμος.

overestimate ['əuvər'estimeit] vt ὑπερεκτιμῶ, ὑπερτιμῶ.

overexcited ['əuvərik'saitid] a ὑπερδιεγειρόμενος.

overexertion ['əuvərig'zə:ʃən] n ὑπερκόπωσις, ξεθέωμα.

overexpose ['əuvəriks'pəuz] vt (phot) ὑπερεκθέτω, ὑπερφωτίζω.

overflow [əuvə'fləu] vi ξεχειλίζω ‖ ['əuvəfləu] n ὑπερχείλησις, ξεχείλισμα.

overgrown ['əuvə'grəun] a (garden) κατάφυτος, γεμάτο ἀπό, σκεπασμένο μέ.

overhaul [əuvə'hɔːl] vt (repair) ἐξετάζω, ἐπιθεωρῶ, ἐλέγχω ‖ ['əuvəhɔːl] n προσεκτική ἐξέτασις, ἐπιθεώρησις, ἐπισκευή.

overhead ['əuvəhed] a ἐναέριος, γενικός ‖ ['əuvə'hed] ad ἐπάνω, ὑπεράνω, ψηλά ‖ ~s npl γενικά ἔξοδα.

overhear [əuvə'hiə*] vt ἀκούω τυχαία, κρυφακούω.

overjoyed [əuvə'dʒɔid] a περιχαρής, γεμάτος χαρά.

overland ['əuvəlænd] a χερσαῖος, στεριανός ‖ [əuvə'lænd] ad (journey) διά ξηρᾶς.

overlap [əuvə'læp] vi καβαλικεύω, σκεπάζω μερικῶς ‖ ['əuvəlæp] n ἐπικάλυψις, καβαλίκεμα.

overleaf [əuvə'liːf] ad ὄπισθεν (τῆς σελίδος).

overload ['əuvə'ləud] vt παραφορτώνω, ὑπερφορτίζω.

overlook [əuvə'luk] vt κοιτάζω ἐπάνω ἀπό, δεσπόζω ‖ (not notice) παραβλέπω, παραμελῶ ‖ (pardon) παραβλέπω, συγχωρῶ.

overlord ['əuvəlɔːd] n ἀνώτατος ἄρχων, ἐπικυρίαρχος.

overnight ['əuvə'nait] a ὁλονύκτιος, ξενυχτισμένος ‖ ad ὅλην τήν νύκτα, ξενύχτι.

overpass ['əuvəpaːs] n (road) ἀνυψωμένη διάβασις.

overpower [əuvə'pauə*] vt καταβάλλω, συντρίβω, καταπνίγω ‖ ~ing a συντριπτικός, ἀποπνικτικός.

overrate [əuvə'reit] vt ὑπερτιμῶ.

override [əuvə'raid] vt (invalidate) ὑπερβαίνω, ἀνατρέπω.

overriding [əuvə'raidiŋ] a πρωταρχικός, δεσπόζων.

overrule [əuvə'ruːl] vt ἀνατρέπω, ἀγνοῶ, ἀναιρῶ.

overseas [əuvə'siːz] ad στό ἐξωτερικόν ‖ a (trade) ἐξωτερικός.

overseer ['əuvəsiə*] n ἐπιτηρητής, ἐπιστάτης.

overshadow [əuvə'ʃædəu] vt ἐπισκιάζω.

overshoot ['əuvə'ʃuːt] vt (runway) προσγειώνομαι μακρυά.

oversight ['əuvəsait] n παράβλεψις, παραδρομή.

oversimplify ['əuvə'simplifai] vt ὑπεραπλοποιῶ.

oversleep ['əuvə'sliːp] vi παρακοιμᾶμαι.

overstate ['əuvə'steit] vt (case) μεγαλοποιῶ, ὑπερβάλλω ‖ ~ment n ὑπερβολή, μεγαλοποίησις.

overt ['əu'vɔːt] a ἔκδηλος, κατάφανής, ἐμφανής.

overtake [əuvə'teik] vt (κατα)φθάνω, ξεπερνῶ ‖ vi συμβαίνω εἰς, τυχαίνω εἰς.

overtaking [əuvə'teikiŋ] n ξεπέρασμα.

overthrow [əuvə'θrəu] vt (vanquish) συντρίβω, ἀνατρέπω, τσακίζω.

overtime ['əuvətaim] n ὑπερωρίες.

overtone ['əuvətəun] n (mus) ἁρμονική.

overture ['əuvətjuə*] n (mus) εἰσαγωγή, 'οὐβερτούρα.

overturn [əuvə'təːn] vt ἀνατρέπω, ἀναποδογυρίζω ‖ vi ἀνατρέπομαι.

overweight ['əuvə'weit] a μέ βάρος ἀνώτερον τοῦ κανονικοῦ.

overwhelm [əuvə'welm] vt συντρίβω, κατακλύζω, καταβάλλω ‖ ~ing a συντριπτικός, ἀκαταμάχητος.

overwork ['əuvə'wəːk] n καταπόνησις, ὑπερκόπωσις ‖ vt παραφορτώνω, παρακουράζω ‖ vi ἐργάζομαι ὑπερβολικά, παρακουράζομαι.

overwrought ['əuvə'rɔːt] a πολυδουλεμένος, πολυκουρασμένος.

owe [əu] vt ὀφείλω, χρεωστῶ, χρωστῶ.

owing ['əuiŋ] ~ to prep λόγω, ἔνεκα, συνεπεία, ἐξ αἰτίας.

owl [aul] n κουκουβάγια.

own [əun] vt (κατ)ἔχω, κέκτημαι ‖ ὁμολογῶ ‖ a ἴδιος, δικός (μου) ‖ n δικός (μου), ἰδιαίτερος ‖ all my ~ μοῦ ἀνήκει, ὅλο δικό μου ‖ on one's ~ ἀνεξάρτητα, μόνος (μου) ‖ to ~ up vi (confess) ὁμολογῶ ‖ ~er n' ἰδιοκτήτης, κύριος ‖ ~ership n κυριότης, ἰδιοκτησία.

ox [ɔks] n βόδι, βοῦς.

oxide ['ɔksaid] n ὀξείδιον.

oxyacetylene ['ɔksiə'setiliːn] a ὀξυακετυλενικός.

oxygen ['ɔksidʒən] n ὀξυγόνον ‖ ~ mask n μάσκα ὀξυγόνου ‖ ~ tent n ἀσκός ὀξυγόνου.

oyster ['ɔistə*] n στρείδι.

ozone ['əuzəun] n ὄζον.

P, p

pa [paː] n (col: father) πατέρας, μπαμπᾶς.

pace [peis] n βῆμα, βάδισμα ‖ (speed) ταχύτης ‖ vi βαδίζω, βηματίζω, περπατῶ ‖ to keep ~ with συμβαδίζω ‖ ~maker n προπονητής ‖ (med) βηματοδότης.

pacification [pæsifi'keiʃən] n εἰρήνευσις.

Pacific (Ocean) [pə'sifik('əuʃən)] n Εἰρηνικός ('Ωκεανός).

pacifism ['pæsifizəm] n εἰρηνοφιλία, πα(τ)σιφισμός.

pacifist ['pæsifist] n εἰρηνόφιλος.

pacify ['pæsifai] vt εἰρηνεύω, καθησυχάζω.

pack [pæk] n (bundle) δέμα, πακέτο ‖ (wolves) ἀγέλη, κοπάδι ‖ (cards) δεσμίς, τράπουλα ‖ (gang) συμμορία ‖ vt (case) συσκευάζω, πακετάρω, κάνω δέμα ‖ (clothes) μαζεύω (τά ροῦχα μου) ‖ ~age n δέμα ‖ ~et n δεματάκι, πακέτο ‖ ~ ice n σωρός πάγων, ὀγκόπαγοι ‖ ~ing n (action) πακετάρισμα ‖ (material)

P

συσκευασία ‖ ~ing case n κιβώτιον συσκευασίας, κασόνι.

pact [pækt] n συμφωνία, συνθήκη.

pad [pæd] n μαξιλαράκι ‖ μπλόκ ‖ (for inking) ταμπόν ‖ vt (παρα)γεμίζω.

paddle ['pædl] n (oar) κουπί, ἀναδευτήρ ‖ vt (boat) κωπηλατῶ, τραβῶ κουπί ‖ vi (in sea) κωπηλατῶ ἤρεμα, τσαλαβουτῶ.

paddling pool ['pædliŋpu:l] n λιμνούλα (γιά παιδιά).

paddock ['pædək] n περίβολος, μάνδρα (γιά ἄλογα).

paddy ['pædi] ~ field n ὀρυζοφυτεία.

padlock ['pædlɔk] n λουκέτο.

padre ['pa:dri] n παπᾶς.

paediatrics [pi:di'ætriks] n παιδιατρική.

pagan ['peigən] a εἰδωλολατρικός.

page [peidʒ] n (of book) σελίδα ‖ (boy servant) νεαρός ὑπηρέτης, γκρούμ ‖ (wedding) ἀκόλουθος, παράνυμφος ‖ vt (in hotel etc) στέλνω μικρόν νά φωνάξη (κάποιον).

pageant ['pædʒənt] n φαντασμαγορικόν θέαμα, ἐπιβλητική πομπή ‖ ~ry n ἐπίδειξις, θεαματικότης, πομπή.

pagoda [pə'gəudə] n παγόδα.

paid [peid] pt,pp of pay.

pail [peil] n κάδος, κουβάς.

pain [pein] n πόνος ‖ ~s npl (efforts) κόπος ‖ ~ed a (expression) θλιμμένος, πικραμένος, πονεμένος ‖ ~ful a (physically) πού πονεῖ ‖ (difficult) ἐπίπονος ‖ ὀδυνηρός ‖ ~killing drug n παυσίπονον ‖ ~less a ἀνώδυνος ‖ ~staking a φιλόπονος, προσεκτικός.

paint [peint] n χρῶμα, μπογιά ‖ vt ζωγραφίζω, ἀπεικονίζω ‖ (house etc) μπογιατίζω, χρωματίζω ‖ ~brush n χρωστήρ, πινέλλο ‖ ~er n (art) ζωγράφος ‖ (decorator) χρωματιστής, μπογιατζῆς ‖ ~ing n (action) ζωγραφική ‖ (picture) πίναξ, ζωγραφιά.

pair [pɛə*] n (of shoes) ζεῦγος, ζευγάρι ‖ ~ of scissors n ψαλίδι ‖ ~ of trousers n πανταλόνι.

pajamas [pə'dʒa:məz] npl (US) πυτζάμες.

pal [pæl] n (col) βλάμης, μακαντάσης, φίλος.

palace ['pælis] n ἀνάκτορον, παλάτι.

palatable ['pælətəbl] a εὔγευστος, νόστιμος.

palate ['pælit] n ὑπερῴα, οὐρανίσκος ‖ (taste) γεῦσις.

pale [peil] a (face) ὠχρός, χλωμός ‖ (colour) ἀνοιχτό ‖ ~ness n ὠχρότης, χλωμάδα.

palette ['pælit] n παλέττα.

palisade [pæli'seid] n φράκτης ἀπό πασσάλους.

pall [pɔ:l] n (of smoke) σύννεφο ‖ vi ξεθυμαίνω, μπουχτίζω.

pally ['pæli] a (col) πού πιάνει εὔκολα φιλίες.

palm [pa:m] n (tree) φοῖνιξ, βάϊον ‖ (of hand) παλάμη ‖ ~ist n χειρομάντης ‖

P~ Sunday n Κυριακή τῶν Βαΐων ‖ ~ tree n φοῖνιξ, χουρμαδιά.

palpable ['pælpəbl] a (obvious) φανερός, καταφανής.

palpitation [pælpi'teiʃən] n παλμός, σπαρτάρισμα.

paltry ['pɔ:ltri] a μηδαμινός, τιποτένιος, ἄθλιος.

pamper ['pæmpə*] vt (παρα)χαϊδεύω.

pamphlet ['pæmflit] n φυλλάδιον.

pan [pæn] n τηγάνι, κατσαρόλα ‖ vi (+ out) ἐπιτυγχάνω, ἀποδίδω.

pan- [pæn] prefix παν-.

panacea [pænə'siə] n (fig) πανάκεια.

pancake ['pænkeik] n τηγανίτα.

panda ['pændə] n πάνδα.

pandemonium [pændi'məuniəm] n πανδαιμόνιον.

pander ['pændə*] vi (+ to) κάνω τόν ρουφιάνο, κολακεύω πρόστυχα.

pane [pein] n τζάμι.

panel ['pænl] n (of wood) φάτνωμα, φύλλο ‖ (of people) ἐπιτροπή ‖ ~ling, (US) ~ing n ξυλεπένδυσις.

pang [pæŋ] n δυνατός πόνος ‖ ἀγωνία.

panic ['pænik] n πανικός ‖ a (reaction) πανικόβλητος ‖ vi πανικοβάλλομαι ‖ ~ky a (person) πανικόβλητος, ἔντρομος, φοβισμένος.

pannier ['pæniə*] n κοφίνι, πανέρι.

panorama [pænə'ra:mə] n πανόραμα.

panoramic [pænə'ræmik] a πανοραματικός.

pansy ['pænzi] n (flower) πανσές.

pant [pænt] vi λαχανιάζω.

panther ['pænθə*] n πάνθηρ.

panties ['pæntiz] npl (woman's) κυλότα.

pantomime ['pæntəmaim] n παντομίμα.

pantry ['pæntri] n κελλάρι ‖ (butler's) κάβα.

pants [pænts] npl (woman's) κυλότα ‖ (man's) σώβρακο ‖ (US: trousers) πανταλόνι.

papal ['peipəl] a παπικός.

paper ['peipə*] n (material) χαρτί ‖ (newspaper) ἐφημερίδα ‖ (essay) μελέτη, διατριβή, ὑπόμνημα ‖ a χάρτινος ‖ vt σκεπάζω μέ χαρτί, στολίζω μέ χαρτί ‖ ~s npl (identity) πιστοποιητικά ‖ ἔγγραφα ‖ ~back n χαρτόδετον (βιβλίον) ‖ ~ bag n χαρτοσακούλα ‖ ~ clip n συνδετήρας ‖ ~weight n πρές-παπιέ ‖ ~ work n γραφική ἐργασία.

papier-mâché ['pæpiei'mæʃei] n πεπιεσμένος χάρτης.

par [pa:*] n (comm) ἰσοτιμία, ἄρτιον, ἰσότης ‖ on a ~ with ἴσον μέ, ἴση ἀξία μέ.

parable ['pærəbl] n παραβολή.

parachute ['pærəʃu:t] n ἀλεξίπτωτον ‖ vi κατέρχομαι δι' ἀλεξιπτώτου ‖ ~ jump n πτῶσις μέ ἀλεξίπτωτον.

parade [pə'reid] n (procession) παρέλασις ‖ (review) παράταξις, παρέλασις ‖ vt ἐπιδεικνύω, κάνω παρέλασιν ‖ vi παρελαύνω.

paradise ['pærədais] n παράδεισος.
paradox ['pærədɔks] n παράδοξον, παραδοξολογία ǁ ~ical a παράδοξος ǁ ~ically ad παραδόξως.
paraffin ['pærəfin] n παραφίνη.
paragraph ['pærəgraːf] n παράγραφος.
parallel ['pærəlel] a παράλληλος ǁ (similar) δμοιος, παράλληλος, ἀνάλογος ǁ n παράλληλος.
paralysis [pə'ræləsis] n παράλυσις.
paralyze ['pærəlaiz] vt παραλύω.
paramount ['pærəmaunt] a ὕψιστος, ὑπέρτατος, ἐξαίρετος.
paranoia [pærə'nɔiə] n παράνοια.
parapet ['pærəpit] n στηθαῖον, παραπέτο, πρόχωμα.
paraphernalia [pærəfə'neiliə] n διάφορα, καλαμπαλίκια.
paraphrase ['pærəfreiz] vt παραφράζω.
paraplegic [pærə'pliːdʒik] a παραπληγικός.
parasite ['pærəsait] n παράσιτον.
parasol ['pærə'sɔl] n ὀμπρέλλα ἡλίου.
paratrooper ['pærətruːpə*] n ἀλεξιπτωτιστής.
parcel ['paːsl] n δέμα, πακέτο ǁ vt (also ~ up) πακετάρω.
parch [paːtʃ] vt ξηραίνω, καψαλίζω, ψήνω ǁ ~ed a ξηρός, στεγνός, ἄνυδρος.
parchment ['paːtʃmənt] n περγαμηνή.
pardon ['paːdn] n συγγνώμη, συγχώρησις ǁ vt (free from punishment) δίδω χάριν εἰς ǁ ~! συγγνώμη! ǁ ~ me! μέ συγχωρεῖτε! **I beg your** ~! συγγνώμη! ǁ **I beg your** ~? παρακαλῶ;.
parent ['peərənt] n γονεύς ǁ ~al a πατρικός, μητρικός.
parenthesis [pə'renθisis] n παρένθεσις.
parish ['pæriʃ] n ἐνορία, κοινότης ǁ ~ioner n ἐνορίτης.
parity ['pæriti] n (fin) ἰσότης, ἰσοτιμία, παρίτέ.
park [paːk] n πάρκο ǁ (cars) χῶρος σταθμεύσεως ǁ vti σταθμεύω, παρκάρω ǁ ~ing n στάθμευσις, παρκάρισμα, πάρκιν ǁ 'no ~ing' 'ἀπαγορεύεται ἡ στάθμευσις' ǁ ~ing lot n (US) χῶρος σταθμεύσεως ǁ ~ing meter n παρκόμετρον ǁ ~ing place n θέσις σταθμεύσεως.
parliament ['paːləmənt] n κοινοβούλιον ǁ (in Britain) κοινοβούλιον, Βουλή ǁ ~ary a κοινοβουλευτικός.
parochial [pə'rəukiəl] a ἐνοριακός, κοινοτικός ǁ (narrow-minded) περιωρισμένος, τοπιστικός.
parody ['pærədi] n παρωδία.
parole [pə'rəul] n: **on** ~ ἐλεύθερος (προσωρινῶς) ἐπί λόγου.
parquet ['paːkei] n παρκέτο.
parrot ['pærət] n παπαγάλος ǁ ~ **fashion** ad (learn) παπαγαλίστικα.
parry ['pæri] vt ἀποκρούω, ἀποφεύγω, ξεφεύγω.
parsimonious [paːsi'məuniəs] a φειδωλός,

σφιχτός, τσιγγούνης ǁ ~ly ad μετά φειδοῦς, μετρημένα.
parsley ['paːsli] n μαϊντανός.
parsnip ['paːsnip] n δαυκί.
parson ['paːsn] n ἐφημέριος, παπᾶς.
part [paːt] n μέρος, κομμάτι ǁ (in play) ρόλος ǁ (of machine) τμῆμα, μέρος, ἐξάρτημα, τεμάχιον ǁ a μερικό, ἡμι-, μισο- ǁ ad = **partly** ǁ vt χωρίζω, διαιρῶ, κόβω ǁ vi (people) χωρίζουμε, χωρίζομαι ǁ (roads) παρεκκλίνω, χωρίζομαι ǁ **for my** ~ ὅσο γιά μένα ǁ **for the most** ~ ὡς ἐπί τό πλεῖστον ǁ **to** ~ **with** vt ἐγκαταλείπω, παραδίδω ǁ ~ial ['paːʃəl] a μερικός ǁ (favouring) μεροληπτικός ǁ (+ to) ἔχω συμπάθειαν πρός, ἔχω κλῆσιν ǁ ~ially ad μερικῶς, ἐν μέρει.
participate [paː'tisipeit] vi (+ in) συμμετέχω, παίρνω μέρος.
participation [paːtisi'peiʃən] n συμμετοχή.
participle ['paːtisipl] n μετοχή.
particular [pə'tikjulə*] a συγκεκριμένος ǁ (single) ἰδιαίτερος ǁ (hard to please) ἰδιότροπος, ἀκριβολόγος ǁ n λεπτομέρεια, ἰδιομορφία ǁ ~s npl (details) χαρακτηριστικά, περιγραφή ǁ ~ly ad ἰδιαιτέρως, εἰδικῶς, συγκεκριμένως.
parting ['paːtiŋ] n (separation) ἀναχώρησις, χωρισμός ǁ (of hair) χωρίστρα ǁ a ἀποχαιρετιστήριος ǁ διαχωριστικός.
partisan [paːti'zæn] n ὀπαδός, παρτιζάνος ǁ a μεροληπτικός.
partition [paː'tiʃən] n διαχωρισμός, διαίρεσις ǁ (wall) χώρισμα, μεσότοιχος.
partly ['paːtli] ad ἐν μέρει.
partner ['paːtnə*] n ἑταῖρος, συνέταιρος ǁ (in dance etc) καβαλιέρος, ντάμα ǁ vt συνεταιρίζομαι, συμπράττω ǁ ~ship n συνεταιρισμός, συνεργασία ǁ ἑταιρεία.
partridge ['paːtridʒ] n πέρδικα.
part-time ['paːt'taim] ad γιά λίγες ῶρες, μερικῶς ἄνεργος.
party ['paːti] n (pol) κόμμα ǁ (group) ὁμάς, συντροφιά ǁ (lawsuit, agreement) διάδικος ǁ μέτοχος, πρόσωπον ǁ (celebration) πάρτυ ǁ a (dress) τοῦ πάρτυ, τῆς διασκεδάσεως ǁ (pol) τοῦ κόμματος, κομματικός.
pass [paːs] vt περνῶ, διέρχομαι, παρέρχομαι ǁ διαβαίνω ǁ (surpass) ὑπερβαίνω, ξεπερνῶ, προσπερνῶ ǁ (move one to another) μεταβιβάζω, διαβιβάζω, δίνω ǁ (spend time) περνῶ ǁ (be successful) ἐπιτυγχάνω, περνῶ ǁ (approve) ἐγκρίνω ǁ vi μεταβαίνω, διαβαίνω, διέρχομαι ǁ n (passage) στενόν, πέρασμα, δερβένι ǁ (permission) ἄδεια ǁ (success) περνῶ (ἴσα-ἴσα) ǁ (sport) πάσσα ǁ **to** ~ **away** vi (die) πεθαίνω ǁ ἐξαφανίζομαι ǁ **to** ~ **by** vi (ἀντιπαρέρχομαι ǁ παραμελῶ ǁ **to** ~ **for** vt θεωροῦμαι ὡς, περνῶ γιά ǁ **to** ~ **out** vi (faint) λιποθυμῶ ǁ ~able a

διαβατός ‖ (*fairly good*) ὑποφερτός, καλούτσικος ‖ **~age** *n* (*corridor*) διάδρομος ‖ (*part of book etc*) χωρίον, ἀπόσπασμα, κομμάτι ‖ (*crossing*) διάβασις, δίοδος, διάβα ‖ **~ageway** *n* δίοδος, πέρασμα, πάροδος.

passenger ['pæsindʒə*] *n* ἐπιβάτης.

passer-by ['pɑ:sə'bai] *n* διαβάτης, περαστικός.

passing ['pɑ:siŋ] *n* (*death*) θάνατος ‖ *a* (*car*) διερχόμενος, διαβατικός ‖ **in ~** παρεμπιπτόντως.

passion ['pæʃən] *n* πάθος, θέρμη, μανία ‖ (*love*) ἔρως, πάθος ‖ **~ate** *a* σφοδρός, φλογερός, βίαιος ‖ **~ately** *ad* περιπαθῶς, θερμά.

passive ['pæsiv] *a* (*gram*) παθητικός.

Passover ['pɑ:səuvə*] *n* Λαμπρή, Πάσχα.

passport ['pɑ:spɔ:t] *n* διαβατήριον.

password ['pɑ:swɔ:d] *n* σύνθημα, παρασύνθημα.

past [pɑ:st] *ad,prep* (*beyond*) πέραν, πέρα ἀπό, ἐκεῖθεν ‖ (*with numbers*) περασμένος ‖ (*with time*) παρωχημένος, περασμένα ‖ *a* (*years*) περασμένος, τόν παλιό καιρό ‖ (*president etc*) τέως, πρώην.

paste [peist] *n* (*for paper*) κόλλα ‖ (*for cooking*) πάστα, ζυμάρι.

pastel ['pæstəl] *a* (*colour*) παστέλ.

pasteurized ['pæstəraizd] *a* παστεριωμένον.

pastille ['pæstil] *n* παστίλλια.

pastime ['pɑ:staim] *n* διασκέδασις, παιχνίδι.

pastor ['pɑ:stə*] *n* πάστωρ, παπᾶς.

pastoral ['pɑ:stərəl] *a* ποιμενικός, βουκολικός.

pastry ['peistri] *n* ζύμη, πάστα ‖ (*pies, tarts etc*) γλυκό.

pasture ['pɑ:stʃə*] *n* (*ground*) βοσκοτόπι.

pasty ['pæsti] *n* κρεατόπιττα ‖ ['peisti] *a* ζυμώδης, ὠχρός.

pat [pæt] *n* ἐλαφρόν κτύπημα, χάδι ‖ *vt* κτυπῶ ἐλαφρά, χαϊδεύω.

patch [pætʃ] *n* ἐπίρραμα, μπάλωμα ‖ τσιρότο ‖ (*stain*) λεκές ‖ *vt* μπαλώνω ‖ **~work** *n* σύρραμα, συνονθύλευμα ‖ **~y** *a* (*irregular*) ἀνομοιόμορφος.

pate [peit] *n* κεφάλι, κούτρα.

patent ['peitənt] *n* προνόμιον, δίπλωμα εὐρεσιτεχνίας, πατέντα ‖ *vt* πατεντάρω ‖ *a* προφανής, ἁπλός, προνομιακός, πρωτότυπος ‖ **~ leather** *n* λουστρίνι ‖ **~ly** *ad* φανερά, ὁλοφάνερα ‖ **~ medicine** *n* εἰδικόν φάρμακον, ἰδιοσκεύασμα.

paternal [pə'tɜ:nl] *a* πατρικός.

paternity [pə'tɜ:niti] *n* πατρότης.

path [pɑ:θ] *n* μονοπάτι, μονοπάτι ‖ (*of sun etc*) διαδρομή, πορεία, γραμμή, ἴχνος.

pathetic [pə'θetik] *a* συγκινητικός, περιπαθής ‖ **~ally** *ad* παθητικά, συγκινητικά.

pathological [pæθə'lɔdʒikəl] *a* παθολογικός.

pathologist [pə'θɔlədʒist] *n* παθολόγος.

pathology [pə'θɔlədʒi] *n* παθολογία.

pathos ['peiθɔs] *n* πάθος, συγκινητικότης.

pathway ['pɑ:θwei] *n* μονοπάτι, ἀτραπός.

patience ['peiʃəns] *n* ὑπομονή.

patient ['peiʃənt] *n* νοσηλευόμενος, ἄρρωστος ‖ *a* ὑπομονητικός ‖ **~ly** *ad* ὑπομονετικά.

patio ['pætiəu] *n* πλακόστρωτος αὐλή.

patriarch ['peitriɑ:k] *n* πατριάρχης.

patriotic [pætri'ɔtik] *a* πατριωτικός.

patriotism ['pætriətizəm] *n* πατριωτισμός.

patrol [pə'trəul] *n* περίπολος, περιπολία ‖ *vti* περιπολῶ ‖ **on ~** εἰς περιπολίαν ‖ **~ car** *n* περιπολικόν ‖ **~man** *n* (*US*) ἀστυφύλαξ.

patron ['peitrən] *n* πάτρων, προστάτης, ὑποστηρικτής ‖ (*comm*) τακτικός πελάτης ‖ **~age** ['pætrənidʒ] *n* προστασία, πατρονάρισμα ‖ **~ize** ['pætrənaiz] *vt* πατρωνάρω ‖ (*manner*) μεταχειρίζομαι συγκαταβατικά ‖ **~izing** *a* (*attitude*) συγκαταβατικός ‖ **~ saint** *n* προστάτης ἅγιος.

patter ['pætə*] *n* (*sound*) ἐλαφρά συνεχή χτυπήματα ‖ (*sales talk*) φλυαρία, κοράκίστικα ‖ *vi* χτυπῶ ἐλαφρά καί συνεχῶς.

pattern ['pætən] *n* ὑπόδειγμα, πρότυπον, μοντέλο ‖ (*design*) σχέδιον, τύπος, μοντέλο.

paunch [pɔ:ntʃ] *n* κοιλιά.

pauper ['pɔ:pə*] *n* ἄπορος, πτωχός.

pause [pɔ:z] *n* παῦσις, διακοπή, ἀνάπαυλα, διάλειμμα ‖ *vi* σταματῶ, διστάζω, κοντοστέκομαι.

pave [peiv] *vt* ἐπιστρώνω ‖ **to ~ the way for** ἀνοίγω τόν δρόμον, προετοιμάζω τό ἔδαφος ‖ **~ment** *n* (*Brit*) πεζοδρόμιον.

pavilion [pə'viliən] *n* (*building*) περίπτερον, ὑπόστεγον.

paving ['peiviŋ] *n* στρώσιμο.

paw [pɔ:] *n* πέλμα ζώου, πόδι ‖ *vt* χτυπῶ μέ τό πόδι ‖ (*person*) πασπατεύω.

pawn [pɔ:n] *n* ἐνέχυρον ‖ *vt* ἐνεχυριάζω, βάζω ἐνέχυρον ‖ **~broker** *n* ἐνεχυροδανειστής ‖ **~shop** *n* ἐνεχυροδανειστήριον.

pay [pei] (*irreg v*) *n* πληρωμή, μισθός ‖ *vt* πληρώνω, καταβάλλω, ξοδεύω ‖ (*be profitable to*) συμφέρω, ἀποδίδω ‖ *vi* πληρώνομαι, εἶναι συμφέρον ‖ **to ~ attention (to)** προσέχω ‖ **to ~ for** *vt* πληρώνω, κερνῶ ‖ **to ~ up** *vi* ἐξοφλῶ ‖ **~able** *a* πληρωτέος ‖ **~day** *n* ἡμέρα πληρωμῆς ‖ **~ee** *n* πληρωνόμενος ‖ **~ing** *a* ἐπικερδής, ἀποδοτικός ‖ **~ment** *n* πληρωμή ‖ (*compensation*) ἀποζημίωσις, ἀνταπόδοσις ‖ **~roll** *n* μισθοδοτική κατάστασις.

pea [pi:] *n* (*seed*) μπιζέλι.

peace [pi:s] *n* εἰρήνη, ἡσυχία ‖ **~ably** *ad* εἰρηνικά, ἥσυχα, ἤρεμα ‖ **~ful** *a* γαλή-

νιος, ἥσυχος, εἰρηνόφιλος ‖ ~ **offering** *n* δῶρον συμφιλιώσεως.
peach [pi:tʃ] *n* ῥοδάκινον.
peacock ['pi:kɔk] *n* παγώνι.
peak [pi:k] *n* κορυφή ‖ *(of cap)* γεῖσος.
peal [pi:l] *n* κωδωνοκρουσία, κτύπημα.
peanut ['pi:nʌt] *n* ἀράπικο φυστίκι.
pear [pɛə*] *n* ἀπίδι, ἀχλάδι.
pearl [pə:l] *n* μαργαριτάρι.
peasant ['pezənt] *n* χωρικός, χωριάτης, ἀγρότης.
peat [pi:t] *n* τύρφη, πόανθραξ.
pebble ['pebl] *n* χαλίκι.
peck [pek] *vti* ῥαμφίζω, τσιμπῶ ‖ *n (with beak)* ῥαμφισμός, τσίμπημα ‖ *(kiss)* φιλάκι.
peckish ['pekiʃ] *a (col)* to feel ~ νοιώθω τό στομάχι ἄδειο.
peculiar [pi'kju:liə*] *a (interest)* εἰδικός, ἰδιαίτερος ‖ *(+ to)* τελείως δικό (του), χαρακτηριστικόν, ἰδιάζων ‖ ~**ity** *n* ἰδιάζων χαρακτήρ, ἰδιορρυθμία ‖ *(oddness)* παραξενιά ‖ ~**ly** *ad* ἰδιαίτερα, περίεργα.
pedal ['pedl] *n* ποδωστήριον, πετάλι ‖ *vti* κάνω πετάλι ‖ ποδηλατῶ.
pedantic [pi'dæntik] *a* σχολαστικός.
peddle ['pedl] *vt* κάνω τόν μικροπωλητήν, πωλῶ στούς δρόμους.
pedestal ['pedistl] *n* βάθρον, βάσις ἀγάλματος.
pedestrian [pi'destriən] *n* πεζός, διαβάτης ‖ *a* μέ τά πόδια, πεζός ‖ *(humdrum)* μονότονος, πεζός ‖ ~ **crossing** *n* διάβασις πεζῶν.
pediatrics [pi:di'ætriks] *n (US)* = **paediatrics**.
pedigree ['pedigri:] *n* γενεαλογικόν δένδρον, καταγωγή ‖ *a (animal)* καθαρόαιμος.
pee [pi:] *(col) n* οὖρα ‖ *vi* κατουρῶ, κάνω πιπί.
peek [pi:k] *n* ματιά ‖ *vi* κρυφοκοιτάζω, ξεπροβάλλω.
peel [pi:l] *n* φλούδα ‖ *vi (paint etc)* ξεφλουδίζομαι, φεύγω ‖ ~**ings** *npl* φλοῦδες, φλούδια.
peep [pi:p] *n (look)* φευγαλέον βλέμμα, ματιά ‖ *(sound)* τιτίβισμα, σκούξιμο, τσίριγμα ‖ *vi (look)* κρυφοκοιτῶ.
peer [piə*] *vi* κοιτάζω ἐπισταμένως ‖ *(+ at)* κοιτάζω προσεκτικά ‖ *(peep)* κρυφοκοιτάζω ‖ *n (nobleman)* λόρδος, εὐγενής ‖ *(equal)* ἰσάξιος, ἴσος, ταίρι ‖ ~ **age** *n* τάξις εὐγενῶν ‖ ~**less** *a* ἀπαράμιλλος, ἀσύγκριτος.
peeve [pi:v] *vt (col)* ἐκνευρίζω ‖ ~**d** *a* ἐκνευρισμένος.
peevish ['pi:viʃ] *a* εὐερέθιστος, δύστροπος ‖ ~**ness** *n* ὀξυθυμία, γκρίνια.
peg [peg] *n* γόμφος, πάσσαλος, κρεμάστρα ‖ **off the** ~ στά στραβά, μέ κλειστά μάτια.
pekinese [pi:ki'ni:z] *n* πεκινουά.

pelican ['pelikən] *n* πελεκάνος.
pellet ['pelit] *n (of paper, bread etc)* σφαιρίδιον, σκάγιον ‖ δισκίον.
pelt [pelt] *vt* πετροβολῶ, πετῶ, κτυπῶ ‖ *vi (fall heavily)* πίπτω καταρρακτωδῶς ‖ *n* δορά, δέρμα, προβειά.
pelvis ['pelvis] *n* λεκάνη.
pen [pen] *n (for writing)* γραφίς, πέννα, στυλό ‖ *(for sheep)* μάντρα.
penal ['pi:nl] *a* ποινικός ‖ ~**ize** *vt* ἐπιβάλλω ποινήν εἰς, τιμωρῶ ‖ ~**ty** ['penlti] *n* ποινή, τιμωρία ‖ ~**ty kick** *n* πέναλτυ.
penance ['penəns] *n* αὐτοτιμωρία, μετάνοια.
pence [pens] *npl* πέννες.
penchant ['pã:ŋʃã:ŋ] *n (+ for)* κλίσις (γιά).
pencil ['pensl] *n* μολύβι ‖ *(of light)* δέσμη ‖ ~ **sharpener** *n* ξύστρα.
pendant ['pendənt] *n* κρεμαστόν κόσμημα.
pending ['pendiŋ] *prep* κατά τήν διάρκειαν τοῦ, μέχρι ‖ *a* ἐκκρεμής.
pendulum ['pendjuləm] *n* ἐκκρεμές.
penetrate ['penitreit] *vt* εἰσχωρῶ εἰς, διεισδύω ‖ *(pierce)* διαπερνῶ, τρυπῶ ‖ **penetrating** *a* διαπεραστικός, ὀξύς.
penetration [peni'treiʃən] *n (lit)* διείσδυσις.
penfriend ['penfrend] *n* φίλος ἐξ ἀλληλογραφίας.
penguin ['peŋgwin] *n* πιγκουῖνος.
penicillin [peni'silin] *n* πενικιλλίνη.
peninsula [pi'ninsjulə] *n* χερσόνησος.
penis ['pi:nis] *n* πέος.
penitence ['penitəns] *n* μετάνοια.
penitent ['penitənt] *a* μετανοημένος ‖ ~**iary** *n (US)* σωφρονιστήριον.
penknife ['pennaif] *n* σουγιάς.
pen name ['penneim] *n* ψευδώνυμον (φιλολογικόν).
pennant ['penənt] *n* ἐπισείων, φλάμπουλα.
penniless ['penilis] *a* ἀπένταρος.
penny ['peni] *n* πέννα.
pension ['penʃən] *n (from job)* σύνταξις ‖ ~**able** *a* δικαιούμενος σύνταξιν ‖ ~**er** *n* συνταξιοῦχος.
pensive ['pensiv] *a* ἔμφροντις, σκεπτικός, συλλογισμένος.
pentagon ['pentəgən] *n* πεντάγωνον.
Pentecost ['pentikɔst] *n* Πεντηκοστή.
penthouse ['penthaus] *n* πρόστεγον, ὑπόστεγον.
pent-up ['pentʌp] *a (feelings)* συγκρατουμένη συγκίνησις.
penultimate [pi'nʌltimit] *a* προτελευταῖος.
people ['pi:pl] *n* ἄνθρωποι, κόσμος ‖ *(nation)* λαός, ἔθνος ‖ *vt* κατοικῶ, οἰκίζω.
pep [pep] *n (col)* κέφη, ζωή ‖ **to ~ up** *vt* ἐνθαρρύνω, δίνω κέφι εἰς.
pepper ['pepə*] *n* πιπέρι ‖ *(green)* πιπεριά ‖ *vt (pelt)* πιπερώνω, βομβαρδίζω ‖ ~**mint** *n (plant)* ἡδύοσμος, μέντα ‖ *(sweet)* μέντα (καραμέλα).
per [pə:*] *prep* κατά, ἀνά, διά ‖ ~ **cent** τοῖς ἑκατόν.
perceive [pə'si:v] *vt* διακρίνω, βλέπω ‖

(*understand*) ἀντιλαμβάνομαι, καταλαβαίνω.

percentage [pə'sentidʒ] *n* ποσοστόν, τοῖς ἑκατόν.

perceptible [pə'septəbl] *a* αἰσθητός.

perception [pə'sepʃən] *n* ἀντίληψις, αἴσθησις.

perceptive [pə'septiv] *a* ἀντιληπτικός.

perch [pɜːtʃ] *n* κούρνια, ξύλο ‖ (*fish*) πέρκα ‖ *vi* κουρνιάζω, τοποθετῶ ψηλά.

percolator ['pɜːkəleitə*] *n* σουρωτήρι, φίλτρο.

percussion [pə:'kʌʃən] *n* (*mus*) κρουστά ὄργανα.

peremptory [pə'remptəri] *a* τελικός, ἀμετάκλητος, ἀποφασιστικός.

perennial [pə'reniəl] *a* αἰώνιος, χρόνιος, ἀέναος ‖ *n* πολυετές φυτόν.

perfect [pɜː'fikt] *a* τέλειος, πλήρης, τελειωμένος ‖ (*gram*) τετελεσμένος ‖ *n* (*gram*) παρακείμενος ‖ [pə'fekt] *vt* τελειοποιῶ, συμπληρώνω ‖ ~**ion** [pə'fekʃən] *n* τελειότης, ἐντέλεια, τελειοποίησις ‖ ~**ly** *ad* ἐντελῶς, τέλεια.

perforate ['pɜːfəreit] *vt* διατρυπῶ, διεισδύω ‖ ~**d** *a* διάτρητος.

perforation [pɜːfə'reiʃən] *n* διάτρησις, τρυπούλα.

perform [pə'fɔːm] *vt* ἐκτελῶ, ἐκπληρῶ, ἐπιτελῶ ‖ (*theat*) παριστάνω, παίζω ‖ *vi* (*theat*) παίζεται, παίζω ‖ ~**ance** *n* ἐκτέλεσις, κατόρθωμα ‖ (*theat*) παράστασις ‖ ~**er** *n* ἐκτελεστής, ἠθοποιός ‖ ~**ing** *a* (*animal*) γυμνασμένο (ζῶο).

perfume ['pɜːfjuːm] *n* ὀσμή, μυρωδιά ‖ (*scent*) ἄρωμα, μυρωδικό.

perhaps [pə'hæps] *ad* ἴσως.

peril ['peril] *n* κίνδυνος ‖ ~**ous** *a* ἐπικίνδυνος ‖ ~**ously** *ad* ἐπικινδύνως.

perimeter [pə'rimitə*] *n* περίμετρος.

period ['piəriəd] *n* ἐποχή, περίοδος ‖ (*stop*) τελεία ‖ (*med*) στάδιον, φάσις, περίοδος ‖ *a* (*costume*) τῆς ἐποχῆς ‖ ~**ic** *a* περιοδικός ‖ ~**ical** *n* περιοδικός ‖ *n* περιοδικόν ‖ ~**ically** *ad* κατὰ περιόδους.

peripheral [pə'rifərəl] *a* περιφερειακός, περιμετρικός.

periphery [pə'rifəri] *n* περιφέρεια, περίμετρος.

periscope ['periskəup] *n* περισκόπιον.

perish ['periʃ] *vi* χάνομαι, ἀφανίζομαι, πεθαίνω ‖ ~ **the thought!** μακρὰν ἐμοῦ ἡ σκέψις ‖ ~**able** *a* φθαρτός ‖ ~**ing** *a* (*col: cold*) τρομερό, ψῶφο.

perjury ['pɜːdʒəri] *n* ἐπιορκία, ψευδομαρτυρία.

perk [pɜːk] **to** ~ **up** *vi* ξανακάνω κέφι, ξαναζωντανεύω ‖ ~**y** *a* (*cheerful*) ζωηρός, εὔθυμος.

perm [pɜːm] *n* περμανάντ.

permanence ['pɜːmənəns] *n* μονιμότης.

permanent ['pɜːmənənt] *a* μόνιμος, διαρκής ‖ ~**ly** *ad* μονίμως.

permissible [pə'misəbl] *a* ἐπιτρεπόμενος, ἀνεκτός.

permission [pə'miʃən] *n* ἄδεια, ἔγκρισις.

permissive [pə'misiv] *a* ἐπιτρέπων.

permit ['pɜːmit] *n* (ἔγγραφος) ἄδεια ‖ [pə'mit] *vt* ἐπιτρέπω.

permutation [pɜːmju'teiʃən] *n* (ἀντι)μετάθεσις, ἀντιμετάταξις.

pernicious [pɜː'niʃəs] *a* ὀλέθριος, καταστρεπτικός.

perpendicular [pɜːpən'dikjulə*] *a* κάθετος, κατακόρυφος.

perpetrate ['pɜːpitreit] *vt* διαπράττω.

perpetual [pə'petjuəl] *a* διηνεκής, συνεχής, παντοτεινός ‖ ~**ly** *ad* παντοτεινά, ἀδιάκοπα.

perpetuate [pə'petjueit] *vt* διαιωνίζω, ἀποθανατίζω.

perplex [pə'pleks] *vt* περιπλέκω, φέρω εἰς ἀμηχανίαν, μπερδεύω ‖ ~**ed** *a* εἰς ἀμηχανίαν ‖ ~**ing** *a* στενόχωρος, σκοτεινός ‖ ~**ity** *n* ἀμηχανία, παραζάλη, δίλημμα.

persecute ['pɜːsikjuːt] *vt* (*oppress*) καταδιώκω, διώκω.

persecution [pɜːsi'kjuːʃən] *n* διωγμός, καταδίωξις.

perseverance [pɜːsi'viərəns] *n* καρτερία, ἐμμονή, ἐπιμονή.

persevere [pɜːsi'viə*] *vi* ἐμμένω, ἐπιμένω.

Persia ['pɜːʃə] *n* Περσία ‖ ~**n** *a* περσικός ‖ *n* (*person*) Πέρσης ‖ (*ling*) περσικά ‖ ~**n Gulf** *n* Περσικός Κόλπος.

persist [pə'sist] *vi* ἐξακολουθῶ, διαρκῶ, συνεχίζομαι ‖ (*keep saying*) ἐπιμένω, ἐμμένω ‖ ~**ence** *n* ἐπιμονή, ἐμμονή ‖ ~**ent** *a* ἐπίμονος, διαρκής ‖ ~**ently** *ad* ἐπιμόνως.

person ['pɜːsn] *n* πρόσωπον, ἄνθρωπος, ἄτομον ‖ ~**able** *a* εὐπαρουσίαστος, ὡραῖος ‖ ~**al** *a* προσωπικός, ἀτομικός ‖ (*of body*) σωματικός ‖ ~**ality** *n* προσωπικότης ‖ ~**ally** *ad* προσωπικῶς ‖ ~**ify** *vt* προσωποποιῶ.

personnel [pɜːsə'nel] *n* προσωπικόν ‖ ~ **manager** *n* διευθυντής προσωπικοῦ.

perspective [pə'spektiv] *n* προοπτική ‖ (*view*) ἄποψις, θέα.

Perspex ['pɜːspeks] *n* ® ἄθραυστος ὕαλος, περσπέξ.

perspiration [pɜːspə'reiʃən] *n* ἐφίδρωσις, ἱδρώτας.

perspire [pəs'paiə*] *vi* ἱδρώνω.

persuade [pə'sweid] *vt* πείθω, καταφέρνω.

persuasion [pə'sweiʒən] *n* πειθώ, πειστικότης ‖ (*belief*) πεποίθησις, θρήσκευμα.

persuasive [pə'sweisiv] *a* πειστικός ‖ ~**ly** *ad* πειστικά.

pert [pɜːt] *a* ἀναιδής, αὐθάδης, τσαχπίνης.

pertaining [pɜː'teiniŋ] ~ **to** σχετικά μέ.

pertinent ['pɜːtinənt] *a* σχετικός, κατάλληλος, σωστό.

perturb [pə'tə:b] vt διαταράσσω, ἀναστατώνω.

perusal [pə'ru:zəl] n ἀνάγνωσις, διάβασμα.

pervade [pə:'veid] vt ἐμποτίζω, διαπερῶ, ἐπικρατῶ.

perverse [pə'və:s] a διεστραμμένος, κακότροπος ‖ ~ly ad διεστραμμένα ‖ ~ness n διαστροφή, κακία.

perversion [pə'və:ʃən] n διαστροφή, ἀνωμαλία.

perversity [pə'və:siti] n διαστροφή, δυστροπία.

pervert ['pə:və:t] n διεστραμμένος, ἀνώμαλος τύπος, ἐκφυλισμένος ‖ [pə'və:t] vt διαστρέφω, στρεβλώνω, διαφθείρω.

pessimism ['pesimizəm] n ἀπαισιοδοξία.

pessimist ['pesimist] n ἀπαισιόδοξος ‖ ~ic a ἀπαισιόδοξος.

pest [pest] n ἐπιβλαβές φυτόν (ἢ ἔντομον) ‖ (fig: person, thing) ἐνοχλητικός, πληγή.

pester ['pestə*] vt ἐνοχλῶ, πειράζω.

pestle ['pesl] n κόπανος, γουδοχέρι.

pet [pet] n ἀγαπημένος, εὐνοούμενος, χαϊδεμένος ‖ vt χαϊδεύω.

petal ['petl] n πέταλον.

peter ['pi:tə*] to ~ out vi ἐξαφανίζομαι, σβήνω.

petite [pə'ti:t] a μικροκαμωμένη.

petition [pə'tiʃən] n αἴτησις, ἀναφορά.

petrified ['petrifaid] a ἀπολιθωμένος.

petrol ['petrəl] n (Brit) βενζίνη ‖ ~ engine n βενζινομηχανή ‖ ~eum [pi'trəuliəm] n πετρέλαιον ‖ ~ pump n (in car) ἀντλία βενζίνης ‖ (at garage) πρατήριον βενζίνης ‖ ~ station n πρατήριον βενζίνης ‖ ~ tank n δεξαμενή, ντεπόζιτο βενζίνης.

petticoat ['petikəut] n μισοφόρι.

pettifogging ['petifɔgiŋ] a στρεψόδικος, τιποτένιος.

pettiness ['petinis] n σμικρότης.

petty ['peti] a μικρός, ἀσήμαντος, κατώτερος ‖ (mean) μικρόνους, στενοκέφαλος ‖ ~ cash n μικροέξοδα, πρόχειρον ταμεῖον ‖ ~ officer n ὑπαξιωματικός, ὑποκελευστής.

petulant ['petjulənt] a ὀξύθυμος, εὐερέθιστος.

pew [pju:] n στασίδι.

pewter ['pju:tə*] n κράμα κασσιτέρου καί μολύβδου.

phantom ['fæntəm] n φάντασμα.

Pharaoh ['fεərəu] n Φαραώ.

pharmacist ['fɑ:məsist] n φαρμακοποιός.

pharmacy ['fɑ:məsi] n (shop) φαρμακεῖον ‖ φαρμακευτική.

phase [feiz] n φάσις.

pheasant ['feznt] n φασιανός.

phenomenal [fi'nɔminl] a φαινομενικός, ἐξαιρετικός ‖ ~ly ad ἐξαιρετικά, θαυμάσια.

phenomenon [fi'nɔminən] n φαινόμενον.

phew [fju:] excl οὐφ! ‖ Πφ!

phial ['faiəl] n φιαλίδιον.

philanthropic [filən'θrɔpik] a φιλάνθρωπος, φιλανθρωπικός.

philanthropist [fi'lænθrəpist] n φιλάνθρωπος.

philatelist [fi'lætəlist] n φιλοτελιστής.

philately [fi'lætəli] n φιλοτελισμός.

philosopher [fi'lɔsəfə*] n φιλόσοφος.

philosophical [filə'sɔfikəl] a φιλοσοφικός.

philosophy [fi'lɔsəfi] n φιλοσοφία.

phlegm [flem] n φλέγμα ‖ (calmness) ἠρεμία, ἀδιαφορία ‖ ~atic [fleg'mætik] a φλεγματικός, ἤρεμος.

phobia ['fəubiə] n φοβία, φοβοπάθεια.

phoenix ['fi:niks] n φοῖνιξ.

phone [fəun] (abbr of telephone) n τηλέφωνον ‖ vt τηλεφωνῶ.

phonetics [fəu'netiks] n φωνολογία, φωνητική γραφή.

phon(e)y ['fəuni] (col) a ψευδής, ψεύτικος ‖ n ἀπατεώνας.

phonograph ['fəunəgra:f] n (US) φωνογράφος.

phonology [fəu'nɔlədʒi] n φωνολογία.

phosphate ['fɔsfeit] n φωσφορικόν ἅλας.

phosphorus ['fɔsfərəs] n φωσφόρος.

photo ['fəutəu] n abbr of photograph.

photocopier ['fəutəu'kɔpiə*] n φωτοτυπική μηχανή.

photocopy ['fəutəukɔpi] n φωτοαντίτυπον, φωτοτυπία ‖ vt κάνω φωτοτυπία.

photoelectric ['fəutəui'lektrik] a φωτοηλεκτρικόν.

photogenic [fəutəu'dʒenik] a φωτογενής.

photograph ['fəutəugræf] n φωτογραφία ‖ vt φωτογραφίζω, βγάζω φωτογραφίες ‖ ~er [fə'tɔgrəfə*] n φωτογράφος ‖ ~ic a φωτογραφικός ‖ ~y n φωτογραφική τέχνη, φωτογράφισις.

photostat ['fəutəustæt] n φωτοστατικόν ἀντίτυπον.

phrase [freiz] n φράσις ‖ vt διατυπώνω ‖ ~book n συλλογή ἐκφράσεων.

physical ['fizikəl] a φυσικός ‖ (of the body) σωματικός ‖ ~ly ad φυσικῶς, σωματικῶς.

physician [fi'ziʃən] n ἰατρός.

physicist ['fizisist] n φυσικός.

physics ['fiziks] n φυσική.

physiology [fizi'ɔlədʒi] n φυσιολογία.

physiotherapist [fiziə'θerəpist] n φυσιοθεραπευτής.

physiotherapy [fiziə'θerəpi] n φυσιοθεραπεία.

physique [fi'zi:k] n σωματική διάπλασις.

pianist ['piənist] n πιανίστας.

piano ['pjɑ:nəu] n πιάνο.

pick [pik] n (tool) ἀξίνα, κασμᾶς, σκαπάνη ‖ (choice) ἐκλογή ‖ (best) δ, τι ἐκλεκτόν, ἀφρόκρεμα ‖ vti μαζεύω, κόβω, συλλέγω ‖ (choose) ἐκλέγω, διαλέγω ‖ to ~ s.o.'s pocket βουτῶ ἀπό τήν τσέπη, κλέβω τό πορτοφόλι ‖ to ~ out vt διαλέγω ‖ to ~ up vi (improve) ἀποκτῶ πάλιν, ἀνακτῶ ‖

vt (*arrest*) συλλαμβάνω, πιάνω ‖ (*from ground*) σηκώνω, μαζεύω ‖ (*in car etc*) παίρνω ‖ ~ **axe** *n* σκαπάνη, κασμᾶς.

picket ['pikit] *n* (*stake*) πάσσαλος, παλούκι ‖ (*strikers*) σκοπός ἀπεργῶν, ἀπεργός φρουρῶν ‖ *vt* βάζω σκοπούς.

pickle ['pikl] *n* (*also* ~**s**: *as condiment*) τουρσί, ἄλμη ‖ *vt* διατηρῶ εἰς ἄλμην, παστώνω.

pick-me-up ['pikmiːʌp] *n* στυλωτικό, πού δυναμώνει.

pickpocket ['pikpɔkit] *n* πορτοφολᾶς.

pickup ['pikʌp] *n* (*on record player*) φωνολήπτης, πικάπ ‖ (*small truck*) μικρό φορτηγό ‖ (*casual acquaintance*) ψάρεμα, τσίμπημα πελάτου.

picnic ['piknik] *n* ἐκδρομή, πικνίκ ‖ *vi* τρώγω στήν ἐξοχή ‖ ~**ker** *n* ἐκδρομεύς.

pictorial [pik'tɔːriəl] *a* εἰκονογραφικός ‖ γραφικός ‖ (*illustrated*) εἰκονογραφημένον.

picture ['piktʃə*] *n* εἰκών, ζωγραφιά, προσωποποίησις ‖ *vt* ζωγραφίζω, ἀπεικονίζω, φαντάζομαι ‖ **the** ~**s** *npl* κινηματογράφος ‖ ~ **book** *n* βιβλίον μέ εἰκόνες ‖ ~**sque** *a* γραφικός.

pidgin ['pidʒin] *a*: ~ **English** *n* παρεφθαρμένα Ἀγγλικά.

pie [pai] *n* πίττα.

piece [piːs] *n* τεμάχιον, κομμάτι ‖ **in** ~**s** (*broken*) (σέ) κομματάκια ‖ (*taken apart*) σέ τεμάχια ‖ ~**meal** *ad* λίγο-λίγο, κατά τεμάχια ‖ ~**work** *n* ἐργασία μέ τό κομμάτι.

pier [piə*] *n* (*landing place*) προβλής, ἀποβάθρα.

pierce [piəs] *vt* τρυπῶ, διεισδύω, εἰσχωρῶ.

piercing ['piəsiŋ] *a* (*cry*) διαπεραστικός.

piety ['paiəti] *n* εὐσέβεια, θρησκοληψία.

piffling ['pifliŋ] *a* ἀσήμαντος, τιποτένιος.

pig [pig] *n* γουρούνι ‖ (*person*) παλιάνθρωπος, γουρούνι.

pigeon ['pidʒən] *n* περιστέρι ‖ ~**hole** *n* (*compartment*) θυρίδα, γραμματοθήκη ‖ *vt* βάζω στό χρονοντούλαπο.

piggy bank ['pigibæŋk] *n* κουμπαρᾶς.

pigheaded ['pig'hedid] *a* πείσμων, ξεροκέφαλος.

piglet ['piglit] *n* γουρουνόπουλο.

pigment ['pigmənt] *n* χρῶμα, βαφή ‖ ~**ation** *n* σχηματισμός τοῦ χρωμοφόρου.

pigmy ['pigmi] *n* = **pygmy**.

pigskin ['pigskin] *n* γουρουνόδερμα.

pigsty ['pigstai] *n* χοιροστάσιον.

pigtail ['pigteil] *n* κοτσίδα.

pilchard ['piltʃəd] *n* μεγάλη σαρδέλλα.

pile [pail] *n* (*of books*) σωρός, στοίβα ‖ (*in ground*) πάσσαλος, παλούκι, κολώνα ‖ (*on carpet*) τρίχα, χνούδι, μαλλί ‖ *vti* (*also* ~ **up**) συσσωρεύω, στοιβάζομαι.

piles [pailz] *npl* αἱμορροΐδες, ζοχάδες.

pilfer ['pilfə*] *vt* ὑπεξαιρῶ, βουτῶ, σουφρώνω ‖ ~**ing** *n* μικροκλοπή, σούφρωμα.

pilgrim ['pilgrim] *n* προσκυνητής ‖ ~**age** *n* προσκύνημα.

pill [pil] *n* χάπι ‖ **the P**~ *n* χάπι ἀντισυλληπτικό.

pillage ['pilidʒ] *vt* λεηλατῶ.

pillar ['pilə*] *n* κίων, κολώνα, στύλος ‖ (*fig*) στύλος ‖ ~ **box** *n* (*Brit*) γραμματοκιβώτιον.

pillion ['piljən] *n* ὀπίσθιον κάθισμα ‖ ~ **passenger** *n* ἐπιβάτης (ἀπό πίσω).

pillory ['piləri] *n* κυφών, γεβεντιστήρι ‖ *vt* διαπομπεύω, στηλιτεύω.

pillow ['piləu] *n* προσκέφαλο, μαξιλάρι ‖ ~**case** *n* μαξιλαροθήκη.

pilot ['pailət] *n* πλοηγός, πιλότος ‖ (*aviat*) χειριστής, πιλότος ‖ *vt* (*aviat*) ὁδηγῶ, πιλοτάρω ‖ ~ **light** *n* καυστήρ (θερμάστρας φωταερίου).

pimp [pimp] *n* μαστρωπός, ρουφιάνος.

pimple ['pimpl] *n* ἐξάνθημα, σπυρί.

pimply ['pimpli] *a* σπυριάρης.

pin [pin] *n* καρφίτσα ‖ (*peg*) περόνη ‖ *vt* καρφιτσώνω ‖ (*hold fast*) καρφώνω, πλακώνομαι ‖ (**on**) ~**s and needles** 'στά κάρβουνα' ‖ **to** ~ **down** *vt* (*fig: person*) καθηλώνω.

pinafore ['pinəfɔː*] *n* ποδιά.

pincers ['pinsəz] *npl* τανάλια.

pinch [pintʃ] *n* μικρά ποσότης, πρέζα ‖ (*nip*) τσίμπημα, τσιμπιά ‖ *vt* (*with fingers*) τσιμπῶ ‖ (*col: steal*) ἀποσπῶ, σουφρώνω, βουτῶ ‖ *vi* (*shoe*) στενεύω, κτυπῶ, σφίγγω ‖ **at a** ~ στήν ἀνάγκη, εἰς ὥραν ἀνάγκης.

pincushion ['pinkuʃən] *n* μαξιλαράκι γιά καρφίτσες.

pine [pain] *n* (*also* ~ **tree**) πεῦκο ‖ *vi*: **to** ~ **for** ποθῶ, φθίνω, μαραζώνω.

pineapple ['painæpl] *n* ἀνανᾶς.

ping [piŋ] *n* (*noise*) σφύριγμα, κουδούνισμα ‖ ~**-pong** *n* (*US*) πίγκ-πόγκ.

pink [piŋk] *n* (*plant*) γαρουφαλιά ‖ (*pale red*) ροδόχρουν χρῶμα, ρόζ ‖ *a* ροδόχρους, ρόζ, ρόδινος.

pin money ['pinmʌni] *n* χαρτζιλίκι.

pinnacle ['pinəkl] *n* (*highest point*) κορυφή, κολοφών.

pinpoint ['pinpoint] *vi* ὑποδεικνύω ἐπακριβῶς.

pint [paint] *n* πίντα (.567 λ.), μπουκάλι.

pioneer [paiə'niə*] *n* πρωτοπόρος.

pious ['paiəs] *a* εὐσεβής, θρῆσκος.

pip [pip] *n* (*seed*) κουκούτσι ‖ (*on uniform*) ἄστρον (ἐπωμίδος).

pipe [paip] *n* σωλήνας, ὀχετός ‖ (*smoking*) πίπα, τσιμπούκι ‖ (*instrument*) αὐλός ‖ (*of bird*) κελάδημα ‖ **to** ~ **down** *vi* (*be quiet*) τό βουλώνω ‖ ~ **dream** *n* ματαία ἐλπίς ‖ ~**line** *n* ἀγωγός ‖ ~**r** *n* αὐλητής, παίκτης γκάϊντας ‖ ~ **tobacco** *n* καπνό πίπας.

piping ['paipiŋ] *ad*: ~ **hot** καυτερός, ζεματιστός, ἀχνιστό.

piquant ['pi:kənt] *a* πικάντικος.
pique [pi:k] *n* μνησικακία, φούρκα.
piracy ['paiərəsi] *n* πειρατεία.
pirate ['paiərit] *n* πειρατής ‖ ~ **radio** *n* πειρατικός σταθμός.
pirouette [piru'et] *n* πιρουέτα ‖ *vi* κάνω πιρουέτες, περιστρέφομαι.
pissed [pist] *a* (*col*) μεθυσμένος.
pistol ['pistil] *n* πιστόλι.
piston ['pistən] *n* έμβολον, πιστόνι.
pit [pit] *n* λάκκος, ἀνθρακωρυχεῖον ‖ *vt* σημαδεύω, κόβω ‖ (*put to test*) ἔχω κάποιον ὡς ἀντίπαλον.
pitch [pitʃ] *n* (*way of throwing*) βολή, ριξιά ‖ (*ground*) γήπεδον ‖ (*degree*) βαθμός, κλίσις ‖ (*of note*) ὕψος τόνου, διαπασσῶν ‖ (*tar*) πίσσα, κατράμι ‖ *vt* (*throw*) πετῶ ‖ (*tent*) στήνω (σκηνήν) ‖ *vi* (*fall head-long*) πέφτω ‖ (*of ship*) σκαμπανεβάζω ‖ ~-**black** *a* μαῦρος σάν κατράμι ‖ ~**ed battle** *n* μάχη ἐκ τοῦ συστάδην.
pitcher ['pitʃə*] *n* στάμνα, κανάτα.
pitchfork ['pitʃfɔ:k] *n* δίκρανον, τσουγκράνα, φούρκα ‖ *vt* φορτώνω μέ δικράνι.
pitfall ['pitfɔ:l] *n* (*trap*) παγίδα.
pith [piθ] *n* (*essence*) οὐσία, σθένος.
pithead ['pithed] *n* στόμιον φρέατος.
pithy ['piθi] *a* (*concise*) μέ οὐσίαν, οὐσιαστικός.
pitiable ['pitiəbl] *a* ἀξιολύπητος, ἀξιοθρήνητος, οἰκτρός.
pitiful ['pitiful] *a* ἀξιολύπητος ‖ (*mean*) ἐλεεινός ‖ ~**ly** *ad* θλιβερά, ἐλεεινά.
pitiless ['pitilis] *a* ἀνηλεής, ἄσπλαγχνος, ἄκαρδος ‖ ~**ly** *ad* σκληρά, ἀνηλεῶς.
pittance ['pitəns] *n* γλίσχρος μισθός, ἐξευτελιστικός μισθός.
pity ['piti] *n* ἔλεος, οἶκτος, λύπησι ‖ (*of regret*) κρῖμα ‖ **what a** ~! τί κρῖμα! ‖ ~**ing** *a* συμπονετικός.
pivot ['pivət] *n* ἄξων, κέντρον περιστροφῆς, κεντρικόν σημεῖον ‖ *vi* (*turn*) περιστρέφομαι.
pixie ['piksi] *n* ξωτικό, νεράιδα.
placard ['plækɑ:d] *n* τοιχοκόλλησις, ταμπέλλα, πλακάρ.
placate [plə'keit] *vt* κατευνάζω.
place [pleis] *n* τόπος, μέρος, τοποθεσία ‖ (*position*) σημεῖον, μέρος ‖ θέσις ‖ τοποθεσία ‖ (*town etc*) τόπος ‖ (*employment, rank*) θέσις, ὑπηρεσία, βαθμός ‖ (*seat*) θέσις, κάθισμα ‖ *vt* (*object*) τοποθετῶ, θέτω, βάζω ‖ (*order*) τοποθετῶ, πωλῶ ‖ (*in race*) ἔρχομαι πλασέ ‖ **in** ~ ἁρμόζων, ταιριαστός ‖ **out of** ~ ἄτοπος ‖ **in the first** ~ ἐν πρώτοις.
placid ['plæsid] *a* γαλήνιος, ἥρεμος, ἀτάραχος ‖ ~**ity** *n* πραότης, γαλήνη, ἀταραξία.
plagiarism ['pleidʒiərizəm] *n* λογοκλοπή, λογοκλοπία.
plague [pleig] *n* πληγή, μάστιξ, λοιμός, πανούκλα.

plaice [pleis] *n* γλῶσσα (ψάρι).
plaid [plæd] *n* καρώ.
plain [plein] *a* (*clear*) σαφής, φανερός ‖ (*simple*) ἁπλός, λιτός ‖ (*not beautiful*) κοινός, ὄχι ὡραῖος ‖ *ad* σαφῶς, καθαρά, εὐδιακρίτως, εἰλικρινῶς ‖ *n* πεδιάς, κάμπος ‖ **in** ~ **clothes** (*police*) μέ πολιτικά ‖ ~**ly** *ad* προφανῶς, ὁλοφάνερα ‖ ἁπλά ‖ ~**ness** *n* ἁπλότης, σαφήνεια.
plaintiff ['pleintif] *n* ἐνάγων, μηνυτής.
plait [plæt] *n* πλόκαμος, πλεξούδα ‖ *vt* πλέκω.
plan [plæn] *n* σχέδιον, προσχέδιον, πρόγραμμα ‖ (*of house etc*) σχέδιο, πλάνο, σχεδιάγραμμα ‖ (*pol, econ*) σχέδιον ‖ *vt* (*holiday etc*) σχεδιάζω ‖ *vi* (*make a plan*) καταστρώνω, σχεδιαγραφῶ.
plane [plein] *n* (*tree*) πλάτανος ‖ (*tool*) πλάνη, ροκάνι, πλάνια ‖ (*level*) ἐπίπεδον, ἐπίπεδος (ἐπιφάνεια) ‖ (*aviat*) ἀεροπλάνον ‖ *a* ἐπίπεδος ‖ *vt* (*with tool*) ροκανίζω, πλανιάρω, ἰσιάζω.
planet ['plænit] *n* πλανήτης.
plank [plæŋk] *n* σανίδα, μαδέρι.
plankton ['plæŋktən] *n* πλαγκτόν.
planner ['plænə*] *n* προγραμματιστής, σχεδιαστής.
planning ['plæniŋ] *n* χάραξις (σχεδίου), κατάστρωσις, προγραμματισμός.
plant [plɑ:nt] *n* φυτόν ‖ (*factory*) ἐγκατάστασις, ἐργοστάσιον, μηχανήματα ‖ *vt* φυτεύω ‖ (*set firmly*) ἐμπηγνύω, καρφώνω, ἐγκαθιστῶ.
plantain ['plæntin] *n* ἀρνόγλωσσον.
plantation [plæn'teiʃən] *n* φυτεία.
plaque [plæk] *n* (*on wall*) πλάκα (ἀναμνηστική).
plasma ['plæzmə] *n* πλάσμα, πρωτόπλασμα.
plaster ['plɑ:stə*] *n* σουβάς, κονία, γύψος ‖ (*for wounds*) ἔμπλαστρον, τσιρότο ‖ *vt* σοβατίζω ‖ φορτώνω, γεμίζω, σκεπάζω ‖ **in** ~ (*leg etc*) σέ γύψο ‖ ~**ed** *a* (*col*) μεθυσμένος ‖ ~**er** *n* σουβατζῆς.
plastic ['plæstik] *n* πλαστική ὕλη ‖ *a* πλαστικός ‖ (*easily shaped*) εὔπλαστος ‖ **P**~**ine** ® *n* πλαστιλίνη ‖ ~ **surgery** *n* πλαστική ἐγχείρησις.
plate [pleit] *n* πιάτο, δίσκος, σκεύη ‖ (*table utensils*) χρυσά ἤ ἀργυρά ἐπιτραπέζια σκεύη, ἀσημικά ‖ (*flat sheet*) πλάκα, λάμα, φύλλον.
plateau ['plætəu] *n* ὑψίπεδον, ὀροπέδιον.
plateful ['pleitful] *n* πιάτο γεμάτο.
plate glass ['pleit'glɑ:s] *n* κρύσταλλον, ὑαλοπίναξ.
platform ['plætfɔ:m] *n* (*at meeting*) ἐξέδρα, βῆμα ‖ (*rail*) ἀποβάθρα, ἐξέδρα.
platinum ['plætinəm] *n* λευκόχρυσος, πλατίνη.
platitude ['plætitju:d] *n* κοινοτοπία, πλαδαρότης.
platoon [plə'tu:n] *n* διμοιρία, οὐλαμός.
platter ['plætə*] *n* καραβάνα, πινάκιον.

plausibility [plɔːzə'biliti] *n* εὐλογοφάνεια.
plausible ['plɔːzəbl] *a* εὔλογος, εὐλογοφανής.
plausibly ['plɔːzəbli] *ad* ἀληθοφανῶς, εὐλογοφανῶς.
play [plei] *n* παιχνίδι, διασκέδασις ‖ *(stage)* ἔργον ‖ *(of shadows etc)* παίξιμο, λαμποκόπημα ‖ *(mech)* ἀνοχή, παίξιμο, τζόγος ‖ *vi* παίζω, διασκεδάζω ‖ *(trick)* παιχνιδιάζω, κάνω ἀστεῖο ‖ *(part)* παίζω, ὑποδύομαι ρόλον, ἑρμηνεύω ‖ *(instrument)* παίζω ‖ *vi (amuse o.s.)* διασκεδάζω, παίζω ‖ *(of light etc)* σπιθοβολῶ, παίζω, χοροπηδῶ ‖ ~**boy** *n* γλεντζές, ἔκλυτος νέος ‖ ~**ed-out** *a* ἐξηντλημένος, ἀποκαμωμένος ‖ ~**er** *n* παίκτης, ἠθοποιός ‖ ~**ful** *a* παιχνιδιάρικος, παιχνιδιάρης ‖ ~**goer** *n* θεατρόφιλος ‖ ~**ground** *n* προαύλιον, τόπος διασκεδάσεως ‖ ~**ing card** *n* τραπουλόχαρτο ‖ ~**ing field** *n* γήπεδον ‖ ~**mate** *n* συμπαίκτης, σύντροφος στὸ παιχνίδι ‖ ~**thing** *n* παιχνίδι, παιχνιδάκι ‖ ~**wright** *n* θεατρικὸς συγγραφεύς.
plea [pliː] *n* (law) ἔκκλησις, ἀγωγή, ἔνστασις.
plead [pliːd] *vt* ἐπικαλοῦμαι, προβάλλω ‖ *vi* παρακαλῶ, ἱκετεύω ‖ *(law)* ὑποστηρίζω, ὑπερασπίζω, ἀπολογοῦμαι.
pleasant ['plɛznt] *a* εὐχάριστος ‖ ~**ly** *ad* εὐχάριστα ‖ ~**ness** *n* χάρις, θέλγητρον, καλωσύνη ‖ ~**ry** *n* εὐθυμία, κέφι, χιούμορ.
please [pliːz] *vt* ἀρέσκω εἰς, ἀρέσω, εὐχαριστῶ ‖ ~! παρακαλῶ! ‖ **my bill,** ~ τόν λογαριασμόν, παρακαλῶ ‖ ~ **yourself!** κάνε τό κέφι σου! ‖ ~**d** *a (happy, glad)* εὐχαριστημένος, ἱκανοποιημένος.
pleasing ['pliːzɪŋ] *a* εὐχάριστος.
pleasurable ['plɛʒərəbl] *a* εὐχάριστος, τερπνός.
pleasurably ['plɛʒərəbli] *ad* εὐχάριστα, τερπνά.
pleasure ['plɛʒə*] *n* τέρψις, εὐχαρίστησις, χαρά ‖ *(amusement)* ἀπολαύσεις, ἡδοναί, χαρές ‖ **it's a** ~! χαίρομαι!, παρακαλῶ!
pleat [pliːt] *n* πτυχή, πιέτα.
plebiscite ['plebisit] *n* δημοψήφισμα.
plebs [plebz] *npl* λαουτζίκος.
plectrum ['plektrəm] *n* πλῆκτρον.
pledge [pledʒ] *n* ἐνέχυρον, δεσμευτική ὑπόσχεσις, ἐχέγγυον ‖ *vi* ἐγγυῶμαι, ὑπόσχομαι.
plentiful ['plentiful] *a* ἄφθονος, πλουσιοπάροχος.
plenty ['plenti] *n* ἀφθονία, πλῆθος ‖ *(enough)* ἀρκετόν ‖ *ad (col)* πάραπολυ ‖ ~ **of** ἄφθονα, μέ τό τσουβάλι.
plethora ['pleθərə] *n* πληθώρα.
pleurisy ['pluərisi] *n* πλευρῖτις.
pliability [plaiə'biliti] *n* εὐκαμψία, εὐστροφία.
pliable ['plaiəbl] *a* εὔκαμπτος, εὐλύγιστος.

pliers ['plaiəz] *npl* τανάλια, λαβίς.
plight [plait] *n* κατάστασις, θέσις.
plinth [plinθ] *n* πλίνθος, πλινθίον.
plod [plɔd] *vi* περπατῶ βαρειά, σέρνομαι ‖ ~**der** *n* φιλόπονος, εὐσυνείδητος ‖ ~**ding** *a* (βῆμα) συρτό ‖ πού μοχθεῖ, ἀργός καί ἐπίπονος.
plot [plɔt] *n (conspiracy)* συνωμοσία ‖ *(of story)* πλοκή, ὑπόθεσις ‖ *(land)* οἰκόπεδον, χωράφι ‖ *vt* χαράσσω, σχεδιάζω ‖ *vt (plan secretly)* συνωμοτῶ, μηχανορραφῶ ‖ ~**ter** *n* συνωμότης ‖ ~**ting** *n* γραφική παράστασις.
plough, *(US)* **plow** [plau] *n* ἄροτρον, ἀλέτρι ‖ *vt (earth)* ἀροτριῶ, ἀλετρίζω ‖ *(col: exam candidate)* ἀπορρίπτω (μαθητήν) ‖ **to** ~ **back** *n (comm)* ἐπενδύω (τά κέρδη) ἐκ νέου ‖ **to** ~ **through** *vt (book)* διαβάζω μέ κόπο ‖ ~**ing** *n* ἄροσις, ἀλέτρισμα.
pluck [plʌk] *vt (fruit)* κόβω ‖ *(feathers)* μαδῶ ‖ *n (col)* κουράγιο, θάρρος ‖ **to** ~ **up courage** παίρνω κουράγιο ‖ ~**y** *a* θαρραλέος, παληκάρι.
plug [plʌg] *n (for hole)* πῶμα, βούλωμα, τάπα ‖ *(wall socket)* πρίζα ‖ *(col: publicity)* διαφήμισις, προβολή ‖ *(aut)* μπουζί ‖ *vt (hole)* βουλώνω, ταπώνω ‖ *(col: advertise)* διαφημίζω, προβάλλω.
plum [plʌm] *n (fruit)* δαμάσκηνο ‖ *a* ἐκλεκτό πρᾶμα ‖ καλύτερη θέσις.
plumage ['pluːmidʒ] *n* πτέρωμα, φτερά.
plumb [plʌm] *a* κατακόρυφος ‖ πλήρης, ἀληθής ‖ *ad (exactly)* ἀκριβῶς ‖ τελείως ‖ *vt* βυθομετρῶ, βολίζω.
plumber ['plʌmə*] *n* ὑδραυλικός.
plumbing ['plʌmɪŋ] *n (craft)* ὑδραυλική τέχνη ‖ *(piping)* σωληνώσεις, ὑδραυλικά.
plume [pluːm] *n* λοφίον, φτερόν.
plump [plʌmp] *a* στρογγυλός, παχουλός, ἀφράτος ‖ *vi* σωριάζομαι, κάνω πλάφ ‖ *vt* πετῶ ἀπότομα ‖ **to** ~ **for** *vt (col: choose)* ὑποστηρίζω, ψηφίζω ὑπέρ ‖ ~**ness** *n* πολυσαρκία, πάχος.
plunder ['plʌndə*] *n* λεία, λεηλασία, πλιάτσικο ‖ *vt* λεηλατῶ, λαφυραγωγῶ.
plunge [plʌndʒ] *n* κατάδυσις, βουτιά ‖ *vt* (κατα)βυθίζω, βουτῶ, χώνω ‖ *vi* καταδύομαι, βουτῶ, πέφτω.
plunging ['plʌndʒiŋ] *a (neckline)* μεγάλο (ντεκολτέ).
pluperfect ['pluː'pəːfikt] *n* ὑπερσυντέλικον.
plural ['pluərəl] *a* πληθυντικός, πολλαπλός ‖ *n* πληθυντικός.
plus [plʌs] *prep* πλέον, σύν, μαζί μέ ‖ *a* θετικός.
plush [plʌʃ] *a (col: luxurious)* πολυτελής, πλούσιος ‖ *n* βελοῦδο.
ply [plai] *n as in* three-~ *(wood)* φύλλον, φλοίωμα ‖ *(wool)* πτυχή, δίπλα ‖ *vt (a trade)* ἀσκῶ ἐπάγγελμα ‖ *(with questions)* ταλαιπωρῶ (μέ ἐρωτήσεις) ‖ *vi* ταξιδεύω,

ἐκτελῶ γραμμήν ‖ ~**wood** *n* κόντρα-πλακέ.

pneumatic [nju:'mætik] *a* πνευματικός, τοῦ πεπιεσμένου ἀέρος.

pneumonia [nju:'məuniə] *n* πνευμονία.

poach [pəutʃ] *vt* (*cook*) βράζω ξεφλουδισμένο αὐγό, ποσάρω ‖ (*steal*) κλέβω ‖ *vi* λαθροθηρῶ ‖ ~**ed** *a* (*egg*) αὐγό ποσέ ‖ ~**er** *n* λαθροθήρας ‖ ~**ing** *n* λαθροθηρία, κλοπή.

pocket ['pɔkit] *n* τσέπη ‖ (*hollow*) θύλαξ, λάκκος ‖ (*of resistance*) νησίς ἀντιστά-.σεως ‖ *vt* τσεπώνω, βάζω στήν τσέπη ‖ **out of** ~ ζημιωμένος, βγαίνω χαμένος ‖ ~**book** *n* πορτοφόλι ‖ σημειωματάριον (τῆς τσέπης) ‖ βιβλίον τσέπης ‖ ~**ful** *n* (ὅσο χωρεῖ μιά) τσέπη ‖ ~ **knife** *n* σουγιᾶς (τῆς τσέπης) ‖ ~ **money** *n* χαρτζιλίκι.

pockmarked ['pɔkmɑːkt] *a* (*face*) βλογιοκομμένος.

pod [pɔd] *n* περικάρπιον.

podgy ['pɔdʒi] *a* κοντόχονδρος, χοντρός.

poem ['pəuim] *n* ποίημα.

poet ['pəuit] *n* ποιητής ‖ ~**ic** [pəu'etik] *a* ποιητικός ‖ ~ **laureate** *n* ἐπίσημος ποιητής ‖ ~**ry** *n* ποίησις.

poignant ['pɔinjənt] *a* ὀξύς, δριμύς, τσουχτερός, δυνατός ‖ ~**ly** *ad* πικάντικα, σπαρακτικά.

point [pɔint] *n* (*sharp end*) ἀκίς, ἄκρα, αἰχμή, μύτη ‖ (*dot*) στίξις, σημεῖον ‖ (*moment*) στιγμή, σημεῖον ‖ (*detail*) λεπτομέρεια, στοιχεῖον, σημεῖον ‖ (*headland*) ἀκρωτήριον ‖ (*rail*) κλειδί, διασταύρωσις ‖ (*of compass*) ρόμβος πυξίδος, κάρτα ‖ (*degree*) βαθμός, σημεῖον ‖ (*decimal point*) κόμμα ‖ *vt* στρέφω, κατευθύνω, δείχνω ‖ (*gun etc*) σκοπεύω μέ, σημαδεύω ‖ *vi* δείχνω, δακτυλοδεικτῶ ‖ ~**s** *npl* κλειδί ‖ ~ **of view** *n* ἄποψις, ἔποψις ‖ **what's the** ~? τί τό ὄφελος; ‖ **to** ~ **out** *vt* δείχνω, ἐπισύρω τήν προσοχήν, ὑπογραμμίζω ‖ **to** ~ **to** *vt* δείχνω, δακτυλοδεικτῶ, ἐμφαίνω ‖ ~-**blank** *ad* κατ' εὐθείαν, ἀπερίστροφος ‖ ~ **duty** *n* ὑπηρεσία τροχαίας ‖ ~**ed** *a* (*shape*) αἰχμηρός, μυτερός ‖ (*remark*) δηκτικός, καυστικός, τσουχτερός ‖ ~**edly** *ad* ἀπροκάλυπτα, θμά ‖ σαρκαστικά ‖ ~**er** *n* δείκτης ‖ ~**less** *a* ἄσκοπος, ξεκάρφωτος ‖ ~**lessly** *ad* ἄσκοπα, ἄσχετα ‖ ~**lessness** *n* ἀσημαντότης ‖ ἀστοχία.

poise [pɔiz] *n* παρουσιαστικό, κορμοστασιά ‖ *vti* ἰσορροπῶ, σταθμίζω ‖ περιΐπταμαι.

poison ['pɔizn] *n* δηλητήριον ‖ *vt* δηλητηριάζω, μολύνω ‖ ~**ing** *n* δηλητηρίασις ‖ ~**ous** *a* δηλητηριώδης, φαρμακερός.

poke [pəuk] *vt* (*stick into sth*) κτυπῶ, χώνω ‖ (*fire*) ἀναζωπυρῶ, σκαλίζω ‖ *n* (*jab*) κτύπημα, σπρωξιά ‖ **to** ~ **one's nose into** ἀνακατεύομαι ‖ **to** ~ **about** *vi* ψηλαφῶ,

ψάχνω ‖ ~**r** *n* σκαλιστήρι ‖ (*cards*) πόκερ ‖ ~**r-faced** *a* μέ ἀνέκφραστο πρόσωπο, ἀπαθές πρόσωπο.

poky ['pəuki] *a* μικρός, στενάχωρος.

Poland ['pəuland] *n* Πολωνία.

polar ['pəulə*] *a* πολικός ‖ ~ **bear** *n* πολική ἄρκτος ‖ ~**ize** *vt* πολώνω ‖ *vi* πολοῦμαι.

pole [pəul] *n* (*of wood*) στῦλος, ἱστός, κοντάρι ‖ (*elec*) στῦλος ‖ (*geog*) πόλος ‖ ~**cat** *n* (*US*) εἶδος νυφίτσας ‖ ~ **star** *n* πολικός ἀστήρ ‖ ~ **vault** *n* ἅλμα ἐπί κοντῶ.

police [pə'li:s] *n* ἀστυνομία ‖ *vt* ἀστυνομεύω, ἐλέγχω, τηρῶ (τήν τάξιν) ‖ ~ **car** *n* ἀστυνομικόν (αὐτοκίνητον) ‖ ~**man** *n* ἀστυφύλαξ, ἀστυνόμος, πολισμάνος ‖ ~ **state** *n* ἀστυνομικόν κράτος ‖ ~ **station** *n* ἀστυνομικόν τμῆμα ‖ ~**woman** *n* ἡ ἀστυνόμος.

policy ['pɔlisi] *n* πολιτική ‖ (*prudence*) φρόνησις ‖ (*insurance*) ἀσφαλιστήριον.

polio ['pəuliəu] *n* πολυομυελῖτις.

Polish ['pəuliʃ] *a* πολωνικός ‖ *n* (*ling*) πολωνικά.

polish ['pɔliʃ] *n* βερνίκι ‖ (*surface*) γυαλάδα, στιλπνότης, λοῦστρο ‖ (*fig: refinement*) εὐγένεια, καλοί τρόποι ‖ *vt* στιλβώνω, γυαλίζω, λουστράρω ‖ (*refine*) ἐξευγενίζω ‖ **to** ~ **off** *vt* (*work*) τελειώνω βιαστικά ‖ (*food*) ἀδειάζω, κατεβάζω, καθαρίζω ‖ ~**ed** *a* (*fig*) εὐγενικός, λεπτός ‖ ἐκλεπτισμένος.

polite [pə'lait] *a* εὐγενής, φιλόφρων ‖ ~**ly** *ad* εὐγενικά ‖ ~**ness** *n* εὐγένεια, λεπτότης.

politic ['pɔlitik] *a* (*wise*) συνετός, προνοητικός ‖ ~**al** [pə'litikəl] *a* πολιτικός ‖ ~**ally** *ad* πολιτικῶς ‖ ~**ian** [pɔli'tiʃən] *n* πολιτικός, πολιτικάντης ‖ ~**s** *npl* (ἡ) πολιτική ‖ (*US*) πολιτικολογία.

polka ['pɔlkə] *n* πόλκα ‖ ~ **dot** (φόρεμα) μέ πίκες, μέ βούλες, πουαντιγιέ.

poll [pəul] *n* ψηφοφορία, ἀριθμός ψήφων ‖ *vt* λαμβάνω ψήφους, δίνω ψήφος.

pollen ['pɔlən] *n* γῦρις (λουλουδιοῦ).

pollination [pɔli'neiʃən] *n* ἐπικονίασις, γονιμοποίησις.

polling booth ['pəulinbuːð] *n* ἀπομονωτήριον ἐκλογικοῦ τμήματος.

polling day ['pəulindei] *n* ἡμέρα ἐκλογῶν.

polling station ['pəulinsteiʃən] *n* ἐκλογικόν τμῆμα.

pollute [pə'luːt] *vt* μολύνω, βρωμίζω.

pollution [pə'luːʃən] *n* μίανσις, μόλυνσις.

polo ['pəuləu] *n* πόλο.

poly- ['pɔli] *prefix* πολυ-.

polygamy [pɔ'ligəmi] *n* πολυγαμία.

polytechnic [pɔli'teknik] *n* (*college*) τεχνική σχολή, πολυτεχνεῖον.

polythene ['pɔliθiːn] *n* πολυθένιον.

pomegranate ['pɔməgrænit] *n* ρόδι.

pommel ['pʌml] *vt* γρονθοκοπῶ, κοπανίζω.

pomp [pɔmp] *n* λαμπρότης, πομπή, ἐπίδειξις.

pompous ['pɔmpəs] *a* πομπώδης, φανφαρόνος ‖ ~**ly** *ad* πομπωδῶς, μέ στόμφον.

ponce [pɔns] *n* (*col*) σωματέμπορος.

pond [pɔnd] *n* λιμνοστάσιον, νερόλακκος, λιμνούλα.

ponder ['pɔndə*] *vti* σταθμίζω, ξανασκέπτομαι, μελετῶ, ζυγίζω ‖ ~**ous** *a* βαρύς, στιβαρός, βραδύς, ἀνιαρός.

pontiff ['pɔntif] *n* ποντίφηξ, πάπας.

pontificate [pɔn'tifikeit] *vi* (*fig*) τά λέω μέ ὕφος ποντίφηκος.

pontoon [pɔn'tu:n] *n* ἐπιπλέων στήριγμα γέφυρας ‖ (*cards*) εἴκοσι-ἕνα (περίπου 31).

pony ['pəuni] *n* ἀλογάκι ‖ ~**tail** *n* ἀλογοουρά.

poodle ['pu:dl] *n* μαλλιαρό σκυλάκι.

pooh-pooh [pu:'pu:] *vt* γελοιοποιῶ, κοροϊδεύω, ἀδιαφορῶ.

pool [pu:l] *n* (*of liquid*) λιμνούλα, νερόλακκος, δεξαμενή ‖ (*at cards*) πόστα, πότ ‖ (*football*) προ-πό ‖ (*billiards*) μπάτσικα ‖ *vt* (*money etc*) ἐνώνω, συγκεντρώνω ‖ σχηματίζω κοινοπραξίαν.

poor [puə*] *a* πτωχός, δυστυχής ‖ (*feeble*) ἀδύνατος, ἄθλιος ‖ (*pitied*) κακόμοιρος, ἀξιολύπητος ‖ *n*: **the** ~ οἱ φτωχοί ‖ ~**ly** *ad* φτωχικά, ἄθλια ‖ *a* ἀδιάθετος.

pop [pɔp] *n* (*noise*) ξηρός κρότος ‖ (*mus*) μουσική πόπ ‖ (*col US: father*) μπαμπάς ‖ *vt* (*put suddenly*) θέτω ἀπότομα ‖ *vi* (*explode*) κάνω πόπ, κροτῶ ‖ (*come suddenly*) μπαίνω ξαφνικά, βγαίνω ‖ ~ **concert** *n* λαϊκή συναυλία (πόπ) ‖ ~**corn** *n* ψημένο καλαμπόκι, πόπ-κόρν.

Pope [pəup] *n* Πάπας.

poplar ['pɔplə*] *n* λεύκη.

poplin ['pɔplin] *n* ποπλίνα.

poppy ['pɔpi] *n* παπαρούνα ‖ ~**cock** *n* (*col*) κουταμάρα, μπούρδα.

populace ['pɔpjuləs] *n* λαός, τό πλῆθος.

popular ['pɔpjulə*] *a* δημοφιλής, κοσμοαγάπητος ‖ (*of the people*) λαϊκός ‖ ~**ity** *n* δημοτικότης, δημοφιλία ‖ ~**ize** *vt* ἐκλαϊκεύω ‖ ἐπιβάλλω μόδαν, καθιστῶ δημοφιλῆ ‖ ~**ly** *ad* λαϊκῶς ‖ κοινῶς.

populate ['pɔpjuleit] *vt* (συν)οἰκίζω, κατοικῶ.

population [pɔpju'leiʃən] *n* πληθυσμός.

populous ['pɔpjuləs] *a* πολυάνθρωπος, πυκνοκατοικημένος.

porcelain ['pɔ:slin] *n* πορσελάνη.

porch [pɔ:tʃ] *n* πρόστεγον ‖ (*US*) βεράνδα.

porcupine ['pɔ:kjupain] *n* σκαντζόχοιρος.

pore [pɔ:*] *n* ὁ πόρος ‖ **to** ~ **over** *vt* ἀπορροφῶμαι ἀπό.

pork [pɔ:k] *n* χοιρινό.

pornographic [pɔ:nə'græfik] *a* πορνογραφικός.

pornography [pɔ:'nɔgrəfi] *n* πορνογραφία.

porous ['pɔ:rəs] *a* πορώδης.

porpoise ['pɔ:pəs] *n* φώκαινα.

porridge ['pɔridʒ] *n* χυλός (βρώμης).

port [pɔ:t] *n* λιμήν, λιμάνι ‖ (*town*) πόρτο ‖ (*naut: left side*) ἀριστερά πλευρά ‖ (*wine*) πορτό, οἶνος Πορτογαλίας.

portable ['pɔ:təbl] *a* φορητός.

portal ['pɔ:tl] *n* πυλών, πύλη.

portcullis [pɔ:t'kʌlis] *n* καταρρακτή θύρα, καταρραχτή.

portend [pɔ:'tend] *vt* προοιωνίζομαι, προμηνύω.

portent ['pɔ:tent] *n* κακός οἰωνός ‖ (*good*) θαυμάσιον πρᾶγμα, οἰωνός.

porter ['pɔ:tə*] *n* ἀχθοφόρος, χαμάλης ‖ μικρός ὑπηρέτης (ξενοδοχείου) ‖ (*doorkeeper*) θυρωρός, πορτιέρης.

porthole ['pɔ:thəul] *n* (*naut*) φινιστρίνι.

portico ['pɔ:tikəu] *n* πρόστωον, στοά.

portion ['pɔ:ʃən] *n* μερίς, μερίδιον.

portly ['pɔ:tli] *a* παχύς, θεωρητικός.

portrait ['pɔ:trit] *n* προσωπογραφία, πορτραῖτο, πορτρέτο ‖ ~**ure** *n* προσωπογραφία.

portray [pɔ:'trei] *vt* (*describe*) περιγράφω ‖ ~**al** *n* ἀπεικόνισις, περιγραφή.

Portugal ['pɔ:tjugəl] *n* Πορτογαλία.

Portuguese [pɔ:tju'gi:z] *a* πορτογαλικός ‖ *n* (*person*) Πορτογάλος ‖ (*ling*) πορτογαλικά.

pose [pəuz] *n* (*position*) στάσις ‖ (*affectation*) προσποίησις, πόζα ‖ *vi* (*take up attitude*) ποζάρω ‖ (*assume false pose*) ἐμφανίζομαι, παριστάνω ‖ *vt* (*put question*) θέτω ‖ ~ **r** *n* (*problem*) δύσκολον πρόβλημα ‖ ~**ur** [pəu'zə:*] *n* (*person*) ἄνθρωπος πού κάνει καμώματα.

posh [pɔʃ] *a* (*col*) ὡραῖος, κομψός, φίνος, μοντέρνος.

position [pə'ziʃən] *n* θέσις, στάσις ‖ (*place*) θέσις, σειρά ‖ (*attitude*) θέσις, πρότασις ‖ (*rank*) θέσις, βαθμός ‖ (*job*) θέσις, ἐργασία.

positive ['pɔzitiv] *a* θετικός, καταφατικός ‖ (*confident*) πεπεισμένος, βέβαιος, σίγουρος ‖ (*real*) πραγματικός, ἀληθινός ‖ (*character*) θετικός, κατηγορηματικός ‖ ~**ly** *ad* κατηγορηματικά, θετικά.

posse ['pɔsi] *n* (*US*) ἀπόσπασμα (ἀστυνομικῶν).

possess [pə'zes] *vt* (κατ)έχω, διατηρῶ ‖ ~**ion** *n* κατοχή, κτῆσις, κτῆμα ‖ (*owning*) κατοχή ‖ ~**ive** *a* κτητικός, παθολογικά στοργικός ‖ (*gram*) κτητικόν ‖ ~**or** *n* κάτοχος, κύριος, κτήτωρ.

possibility [pɔsə'biliti] *n* (*chance*) πιθανότης ‖ (*event*) δυνατότης.

possible ['pɔsəbl] *a* δυνατός, ἐνδεχόμενος, λογικός ‖ **if** ~ ἄν μπορῶ, εἰ δυνατόν.

possibly ['pɔsəbli] *ad* κατά τό δυνατόν, πιθανόν, ἴσως, πιθανώς.

post [pəust] *n* (*pole*) στύλος, πάσσαλος, κολώνα ‖ (*mail*) ταχυδρομεῖον ‖ (*delivery*) ταχυδρόμος, ταχυδρομεῖον ‖ (*station*) θέσις, φυλακή, πόστο ‖ (*job*) θέσις, πόστο ‖ *vt* (*notice*) τοιχοκολλῶ ‖ (*letters*) ταχυδρομῶ, ρίχνω (στὸ κουτί) ‖ (*station*) ἐγκαθιστῶ, τοποθετῶ ‖ ~age *n* ταχυδρομικά, γραμματόσημα ‖ ~al *a* ταχυδρομικός ‖ ~al order *n* ταχυδρομικὴ ἐπιταγή ‖ ~box *n* γραμματοκιβώτιον ‖ ~card *n* κάρτ-ποστάλ, κάρτα ‖ ~date *vt* (*cheque*) μεταχρονολογῶ, ἐπιχρονολογῶ ‖ ~er *n* διαφήμισις, ἀφίσα ‖ ~e restante *n* πόστ-ρεστάντ.

posterior [pɔs'tiəriə*] *n* (*col*) ὁ πισινός, κῶλος.

posterity [pɔs'teriti] *n* (οἱ) μεταγενέστεροι.

postgraduate ['pəust'grædjuit] *n* πτυχιοῦχος συνεχίζων σπουδάς.

posthumous ['pɔstjuməs] *a* (*works*) κατάλοιπα ‖ ~ly *ad* μετά τόν θάνατον (τοῦ συγγραφέως).

postman ['pəustmən] *n* ταχυδρόμος.

postmark ['pəustma:k] *n* ταχυδρομικὴ σφραγίς.

postmaster ['pəustma:stə*] *n* διευθυντὴς ταχυδρομείου.

post-mortem ['pəust'mɔ:tem] *n* (*examination*) νεκροψία.

post office ['pəustɔfis] *n* ταχυδρομεῖον.

postpone [pəust'pəun] *vt* ἀναβάλλω ‖ ~ment *n* ἀναβολή.

postscript ['pəusskript] *n* ὑστερόγραφον.

postulate ['pɔstjuleit] *vt* ἀπαιτῶ, ἀξιώνω ‖ ὑποθέτω.

posture ['pɔstʃə*] *n* στάσις, θέσις, κατάστασις ‖ *vi* τοποθετῶ, στήνω, ποζάρω.

postwar ['pəust'wɔ:*] *a* μεταπολεμικός.

posy ['pəuzi] *n* μπουκέτο (ἀπό λουλούδια), ἀνθοδέσμη.

pot [pɔt] *n* (*for cooking*) χύτρα, δοχεῖον, γλάστρα ‖ (*sl: marijuana*) ναρκωτικά ‖ *vt* (*plant*) βάζω σέ γλάστρα, φυτεύω εἰς γλάστρα.

potash ['pɔtæʃ] *n* ποτάσσα, κάλιον.

potato [pə'teitəu] *n* πατάτα.

potency ['pəutənsi] *n* δύναμις, ἰσχύς, ἱκανότης.

potent ['pəutənt] *a* ἰσχυρός, πειστικός, ἱκανός.

potentate ['pəutənteit] *n* ἡγεμών, δυνάστης.

potential [pəu'tenʃəl] *a* δυνητικός, λανθάνων, δυναμικός ‖ *n* δυναμικόν, πιθανός, δυνατός ‖ ~ly *ad* δυνάμει.

pothole ['pɔthəul] *n* φρέαρ, σπήλαιον ‖ (*in road*) λακκούβα, λάκκος ‖ ~r *n* σπηλαιολόγος.

potholing ['pɔthəuliŋ] *n* σπηλαιολογία.

potion ['pəuʃən] *n* δόσις (φαρμάκου).

potshot ['pɔtʃɔt] *n* πυροβολισμὸ στὴν τύχη.

potted ['pɔtid] *a* (*food*) διατηρημένον ‖ (*plant*) στὴν γλάστρα, τῆς γλάστρας.

potter ['pɔtə*] *n* κεραμοποιός, τσουκαλᾶς ‖ *vi* χασομερῶ, ψευδοδουλεύω ‖ ~y *n* ἀγγειοπλαστική, κεραμεική ‖ (*place*) κεραμοποιεῖον.

potty ['pɔti] *a* (*mad*) λοξός, παράφρων ‖ *n* (*child's potty*) δοχεῖον (μωροῦ).

pouch [pautʃ] *n* (*zool*) θύλακος ‖ (*tobacco*) ταμπακιέρα.

poultice ['pəultis] *n* κατάπλασμα.

poultry ['pəultri] *n* πουλερικά ‖ ~ farm *n* ὀρνιθοτροφεῖον.

pounce [pauns] *vi* (+ *on*) ἐφορμῶ, ἐπιπίπτω, χυμῶ ‖ *n* πήδημα, ἐφόρμησις.

pound [paund] *n* (*weight*) λίμπρα (435 γρ), λίβρα, λίτρα ‖ (*sterling*) λίρα ('Αγγλίας) ‖ (*area*) περίβολος, μάντρα ‖ *vt* κτυπῶ, κοπανίζω ‖ (*crush to powder*) λειοτριβῶ, κονιοποιῶ, κοπανίζω ‖ ~ing *n* σφυροκόπημα ‖ γδοῦπος.

pour [pɔ:*] *vt* (*cause*) χύνω ‖ *vi* μπαίνω σάν ποτάμι, τρέχω, χύνομαι ‖ to ~ away *or* off *vt* χύνω (ἔξω), ἐκχέω ‖ to ~ in *vi* (*people*) μπαίνω κατά κύματα ‖ ~ing rain *n* βροχὴ μέ τό τουλούμι, καταρρακτώδης βροχή.

pout [paut] *n* κατσούφιασμα ‖ *vi* κατσουφιάζω, στραβομουριάζω.

poverty ['pɔvəti] *n* φτώχεια, ἔνδεια ‖ ~-stricken *a* ἐξαθλιωμένος, ἄπορος.

powder ['paudə*] *n* κόνις, σκόνη ‖ (*medicine*) κόνις ‖ (*cosmetic*) πούδρα ‖ *vt* (*make into powder*) κονιοποιῶ, τρίβω ‖ (*put on powder*) πουδράρω μέ ‖ to ~ one's nose πουδράρομαι ‖ πάω στό μέρος ‖ ~ room *n* τουαλέττα ‖ ~y *a* κονιώδης, σάν σκόνη.

power [pauə*] *n* (*ability to act*) ἐξουσία, δύναμις, μπόρεση ‖ (*strength*) δύναμις, μέσα ‖ (*mighty nation*) (μεγάλη) δύναμις ‖ (*mental*) ἱκανότης, ἰδιοφυΐα, ταλέντο ‖ (*elec*) ἐνέργεια, δύναμις ‖ (*pol: of party or leader*) ἐξουσία, ἐπιρροή, ἰσχύς ‖ *vt* παρέχω ἐνέργειαν εἰς, κινῶ ‖ ~ cut *n* κοπὴ ρεύματος ‖ ~ful *a* (*person*) ρωμαλέος, μεγάλος, δυνατός ‖ (*government*) ἰσχυρός ‖ (*engine*) ἰσχυρός, ἀποδοτικός, μέ δύναμιν ‖ ~less *a* ἀνίσχυρος, ἀδύναμος ‖ ~ line *n* γραμμὴ μεταφορᾶς ‖ ~ station *n* ἐργοστάσιον παραγωγῆς ρεύματος.

powwow ['pauwau] *n* συνέδριον, συγκέντρωσις ‖ *vi* ὀργανώνω συνέδριον, συζητῶ.

practicability [præktikə'biliti] *n* (τό) δυνατόν (γενέσθαι), ἐπιτευκτόν.

practicable ['præktikəbl] *a* δυνατός, κατορθωτός, ἐφαρμόσιμος.

practical ['præktikəl] *a* πρακτικός, ἔμπειρος, ἐφαρμόσιμος ‖ ~ joke *n* βαρύ ἀστεῖο, φάρσα ‖ ~ly *ad* (*almost*) σχεδόν, οὐσιαστικῶς.

practice ['præktis] *n* ἄσκησις, ἐξάσκησις, γυμναστική ‖ (*habit*) συνήθεια, ἔθιμον, ἕξις ‖ (*business*) ἄσκησις, ἐξάσκησις, πελατεία ‖ in ~ (*in reality*) στὴν πραγματικότητα ‖ out of ~ (*sport*) ξεσυνηθίζω, δέν εἶμαι σέ φόρμα.

practicing ['præktisiŋ] *a (US)* = **practising**.
practise, *(US)* **practice** ['præktis] *vt* ἀσκῶ, ἐφαρμόζω, ἀκολουθῶ, συνηθίζω ‖ *(sport)* ἐκγυμνάζω ‖ *(piano)* μελετῶ, κάνω ἀσκήσεις ‖ *(profession)* ἐπαγγέλομαι, (ἐξ)ασκῶ.
practising ['præktisiŋ] *a (Christian etc)* ἄσκησις.
practitioner [præk'tiʃənə*] *n* ἀσκῶν, ἐπαγγελματίας.
pragmatic [præg'mætik] *a* πρακτικός, πραγματικός.
pragmatism ['prægmətizəm] *n* πραγματισμός, σχολαστικότης.
prairie ['prɛəri] *n* λιβάδι, κάμπος, στέππα.
praise [preiz] *n* ἔπαινος, ἐγκώμιον ‖ *vt* ἐπαινῶ, ἐξυμνῶ ‖ *(worship)* λατρεύω, δοξάζω ‖ ~**worthy** *a* ἀξιέπαινος.
pram [præm] *n* καροτσάκι μωροῦ.
prance [pra:ns] *vi* ἀνασκιρτῶ, ἀναπηδῶ ‖ *(strut)* κορδώνομαι, κοκορεύομαι.
prank [præŋk] *n* τρέλλα, κατεργαριά, κόλπο.
prattle ['prætl] *vi* φλυαρῶ, λογοκοπανῶ.
prawn [prɔ:n] *n* εἶδος γαρίδας.
pray [prei] *vi* προσεύχομαι, παρακαλῶ ‖ ~**er** *n* προσευχή ‖ *(praying)* παράκλησις ‖ ~**er book** *n* εὐχολόγιον, προσευχητήριον.
pre- [pri:] *prefix* προ-.
preach [pri:tʃ] *vi* κηρύττω ‖ προτρέπω, νουθετῶ ‖ ~**er** *n* ἱεροκῆρυξ, παπᾶς.
preamble [pri:'æmbl] *n* προοίμιον, εἰσαγωγή.
prearranged ['pri:ə'reindʒd] *a* προκαθωρισμένος, προσυμπεφωνημένος.
precarious [pri'kɛəriəs] *a* ἐπισφαλής, ἐπικίνδυνος, ἀβέβαιος ‖ ~**ly** *ad* ἐπισφαλῶς, ἀβέβαια.
precaution [pri'kɔ:ʃən] *n* προφύλαξις ‖ ~**ary** *a (measure)* προφυλακτικός, προληπτικός.
precede [pri'si:d] *vti* προηγοῦμαι, προπορεύομαι ‖ ~**nce** ['presidəns] *n (of position)* πρωτεῖα ‖ ~**nt** *n* προηγούμενον.
preceding [pri'si:diŋ] *a* προηγούμενος.
precept ['pri:sept] *n* κανών, δίδαγμα, διαταγή.
precinct ['pri:siŋkt] *n* περίβολος, περιοχή.
precious ['preʃəs] *a* πολύτιμος ‖ *(affected)* μέ ἐπιτήδευσιν, προσποιητός.
precipice ['presipis] *n* κρημνός.
precipitate [pri'sipitit] *a (hasty)* βιαστικός, ἐσπευσμένος ‖ ~**ly** *ad* βιαστικά.
precipitation [prisipi'teiʃən] *n (rainfall)* ὄμβρος, βροχόπτωσις.
precipitous [pri'sipitəs] *a (steep)* κρημνώδης ‖ ~**ly** *ad* ἀπότομα.
précis ['preisi:] *n* περίληψις, ἐπιτομή, σύνοψις.
precise [pri'sais] *a* ἀκριβός, ὡρισμένος, συγκεκριμένος ‖ *(careful)* ἀκριβολόγος, τυπικός ‖ ~**ly** *ad* ἀκριβῶς, σωστά.

preclude [pri'klu:d] *vt* ἀποκλείω, προλαμβάνω, ἐμποδίζω.
precocious [pri'kəuʃəs] *a* πρόωρος.
preconceived ['pri:kən'si:vd] *a (idea)* προκαταληπτικός.
precondition [pri:kən'diʃən] *n* προϋπόθεσις.
precursor [pri:'kə:sə*] *n* πρόδρομος.
predator ['predətə*] *n* ληστής, διαγουμιστής ‖ ~**y** *a (of animals)* ἁρπακτικός.
predecessor ['pri:disesə*] *n* προκάτοχος.
predestination [pri:desti'neiʃən] *n* προκαθορισμός, μοιρολατρεία.
predetermine ['pri:di'tə:min] *vt* προκαθορίζω, προαποφασίζω.
predicament [pri'dikəmənt] *n* δύσκολη θέσις, δυσχέρεια, ἀμηχανία.
predicate ['predikit] *n* βεβαιώνω, ὑποδηλῶ, βεβαιῶ.
predict [pri'dikt] *vt* προλέγω, προφητεύω ‖ ~**ion** *n* πρόρρησις, προφητεία.
predominance [pri'dominəns] *n* ἐπικράτησις, ὑπεροχή.
predominant [pri'dominənt] *a* ὑπερισχύων, ἐπικρατῶν ‖ ~**ly** *ad* κυρίως, ἐπί τό πλεῖστον, κατά τό ἐπικρατέστερον.
predominate [pri'domineit] *vi* ἐπικρατῶ, ὑπερισχύω.
pre-eminent [pri:'eminənt] *a* ἐξέχων, ὑπερέχων, ἀνώτερος.
pre-empt [pri:'empt] *vt* ἀποκτῶ πρῶτος.
preen [pri:n] *vt*: **to ~ o.s.** σιάζομαι, κορδώνομαι.
prefabricated ['pri:'fæbrikeitid] *a* προκατασκευασμένος.
preface ['prefis] *n* πρόλογος, εἰσαγωγή, προοίμιον.
prefect ['pri:fekt] *n (of school)* ἐπιμελητής.
prefer [pri'fə:*] *vt* προτιμῶ, ὑποβάλλω, προάγω ‖ ~**able** ['prefərəbl] *a (+ to)* προτιμώτερος, καλύτερος (ἀπό) ‖ ~**ably** *ad* προτιμώτερα, καλύτερα ‖ ~**ence** *n* προτίμησις ‖ ~**ential** *a* προνομιακός, προνομιούχος.
prefix ['pri:fiks] *n* πρόθεμα.
pregnancy ['pregnənsi] *n* ἐγκυμοσύνη, γκαστρώματα.
pregnant ['pregnənt] *a* ἔγκυος, γκαστρωμένη ‖ *(of ideas)* γόνιμος (εἰς), γεμᾶτος συνέπειας.
prehistoric ['pri:his'tɔrik] *a* προϊστορικός.
prehistory [pri:'histəri] *n* προϊστορία.
prejudice ['predʒudis] *n* προκατάληψις, πρόληψις ‖ *(harm)* ζημία, βλάβη ‖ *vt* ζημιώνω, ἐπηρεάζω ‖ ~**d** *a* προκατειλημμένος, προδιατεθειμένος.
prelate ['prelit] *n* ἱεράρχης.
preliminary [pri'liminəri] *a* προκαταρκτικός ‖ **the preliminaries** *npl* προεισαγωγικά, προκαταρκτικά.
prelude ['prelju:d] *n* πρόλογος, προοίμιον ‖ *(mus)* προανάκρουσμα, πρελούντιο.
premarital ['pri:'mæritl] *a* προγαμιαῖος.

premature ['prematʃuə*] *a* πρόωρος ‖ ~**ly** *ad* πρόωρα.

premeditated [pri:'mediteitid] *a* προεσκεμμένος, ἐκ προμελέτης.

premeditation [pri:medi'teiʃən] *n* προμελέτη.

premier ['premiə*] *a* πρῶτος, κύριος ‖ *n* πρωθυπουργός ‖ ~**e** [premi'εə*] *n* πρεμιέρα.

premise ['premis] *n* πρότασις ‖ ~**s** *npl* οἴκημα, κτίριον, κατάστημα.

premium ['pri:miəm] *n* (*insurance*) ἀσφάλιστρον.

premonition [pri:mə'niʃən] *n* προειδοποίησις, προαίσθημα.

preoccupation [pri:ɔkju'peiʃən] *n* προκατάληψις, ἀφηρημάδα, ἀπορρόφησις.

preoccupied [pri:'ɔkjupaid] *a* ἀπορροφημένος, ἀφηρημένος.

prep [prep] *n* (*sch: study*) ὥρα μελέτης ‖ φροντιστήριον.

preparation [prepə'reiʃən] *n* προπαρασκευή, προετοιμασία.

preparatory [pri'pærətəri] *a* (*sch*) προπαρασκευαστικός, προεισαγωγικός.

prepare [pri'pεə*] *vt* προετοιμάζω, προπαρασκευάζω ‖ *vi* προετοιμάζομαι, προπαρασκευάζομαι, ‖ ~**d** **for** εἶμαι ἕτοιμος γιά ‖ ~**d** **to** εἶμαι διατεθειμένος νά.

preponderance [pri'pondərəns] *n* ὑπεροχή, ἐπικράτησις.

preposition [prepə'ziʃən] *n* πρόθεσις.

preposterous [pri'postərəs] *a* παράλογος, γελοῖος.

prerequisite ['pri:'rekwizit] *n* προϋπόθεσις, ἀναγκαῖος ὅρος.

prerogative [pri'rɔgətiv] *n* προνόμιον.

Presbyterian [prezbi'tiəriən] *a,n* πρεσβυτεριανός.

presbytery ['prezbitəri] *n* (*house*) κατοικία ἱερέως.

preschool ['pri:'sku:l] *a* προσχολικός.

prescribe [pris'kraib] *vt* ὁρίζω, παραγγέλλω ‖ (*medicine*) δίνω συνταγήν.

prescription [pris'kripʃən] *n* (*for medicine*) συνταγή.

prescriptive [pris'kriptiv] *a* ὁριζόμενος ὑπό τοῦ νόμου, διατακτικός.

presence ['prezns] *n* παρουσία ‖ (*bearing*) ὕφος, παρουσιαστικό, ἐμφάνισις ‖ ~ **of mind** *n* ψυχραιμία, ἑτοιμότης πνεύματος.

present ['preznt] *a* παρών ‖ (*time*) σημερινός ‖ *n* (*time*) παρόν, τά τωρινά, τό σήμερα ‖ (*gift*) δῶρον ‖ (*gram*) ἐνεστώς ‖ [pri'zent] *vt* παρουσιάζω, παρουσιάζομαι ‖ (*introduce*) συστήνω, παρουσιάζω ‖ (*offer, give*) καταθέτω, προσφέρω, δίνω ‖ **at** ~ τώρα, πρός τό παρόν ‖ ~**able** *a* παρουσιάσιμος ‖ ~**ation** *n* παρουσίασις, παράστασις ‖ ~**-day** *a* σημερινός ‖ ~**ly** *ad* (*soon*) σέ λίγο, ἀμέσως, εὐθύς ‖ (*at present*) τώρα ‖ ~ **participle** *n* μετοχή ἐνεστῶτος ‖ ~ **tense** *n* ἐνεστώς.

preservation [prezə'veiʃən] *n* διατήρησις, διαφύλαξις.

preservative [pri'zə:nətiv] *n* προφυλακτικόν, ἀντισηπτικόν.

preserve [pri'zə:v] *vt* διαφυλάσσω ‖ (*keep up*) συντηρῶ, διατηρῶ ‖ *n* μέρος διατηρήσεως ζώων ‖ (*jam*) γλυκό κουταλιοῦ, μαρμελάδα.

preside [pri'zaid] *vi* προεδρεύω.

presidency ['prezidənsi] *n* προεδρεία.

president ['prezidənt] *n* διευθυντής, πρύτανις, πρόεδρος ‖ (*of a country*) πρόεδρος ‖ ~**ial** *a* προεδρικός.

press [pres] *n* (*machine*) πιεστήριον, πρέσσα ‖ (*printing house*) (τυπογραφικόν) πιεστήριον, τυπογραφεῖον ‖ (*newspapers*) τύπος, ἐφημερίδες ‖ (*journalists*) τύπος, δημοσιογράφοι ‖ *vt* πιέζω, ὠθῶ, συνθλίβω ‖ (*urge*) πιέζω, ἐπιμένω ‖ (*clothes*) σιδερώνω ‖ *vi* πιέζομαι, σφίγγομαι ‖ **to be** ~**ed for** χρειάζομαι, εἶμαι στενοχωρημένος, πιέζομαι ἀπό ‖ **to** ~ **for sth** κινηγῶ, ἐπιμένω εἰς, ἀσκῶ πίεσιν γιά ‖ **to** ~ **on** *vi* σπεύδω, ἐπισπεύδω, συνεχίζω ‖ ~ **agency** *n* πρακτορεῖον εἰδήσεων ‖ ~ **conference** *n* συνέντευξις δημοσιογραφική ‖ ~ **cutting** *n* ἀπόκομμα ἐφημερίδος ‖ ~**ing** *a* ἐπείγων, ἐπίμονος, πιεστικός ‖ ~ **stud** *n* κουμπί μέ πίεσιν.

pressure ['preʃə*] *n* πίεσις ‖ ~ **cooker** *n* χύτρα ταχύτητος, κατσαρόλα ταχύτητος ‖ ~ **gauge** *n* θλιβόμετρον, πιεζόμετρον, μανόμετρον ‖ ~ **group** *n* ὁμάς μέ ἰσχυράν ἐπιρροήν.

pressurized ['preʃəraizd] *a* πιεζόμενος, ὑπό πίεσιν.

prestige [pres'ti:ʒ] *n* γόητρον.

presumably [pri'zju:məbli] *ad* κατά τό φαινόμενον, πιθανῶς.

presume [pri'zju:m] *vti* ὑποθέτω, προϋποθέτω ‖ (*venture*) τολμῶ, λαμβάνω τό θάρρος.

presumption [pri'zʌmpʃən] *n* ὑπόθεσις, παραδοχή ‖ (*impudence*) ἀλαζονεία, ἀναίδεια.

presumptuous [pri'zʌmptjuəs] *a* ἀναιδής.

presuppose [pri:sə'pəuz] *vt* προϋποθέτω.

pretence [pri'tens] *n* προσποίησις ‖ (*false excuse*) πρόσχημα, πρόφασις.

pretend [pri'tend] *vt* (*feign*) προσποιοῦμαι, ὑποκρίνομαι ‖ *vi* προσποιοῦμαι.

pretense [pri'tens] *n* (*US*) = **pretence**.

pretension [pri'tenʃən] *n* (*claim to merit*) ἀξίωσις, ἀπαίτησις.

pretentious [pri'tenʃəs] *a* ἀπαιτητικός, ἐπιδεικτικός.

pretext ['pri:tekst] *n* πρόφασις, πρόσχημα.

prettily ['pritili] *ad* ὄμορφα, μέ χάριν.

pretty ['priti] *a* χαριτωμένος, ἑλκυστικός.

prevail [pri'veil] *vi* ἐπικρατῶ, ὑπερισχύω ‖ (*succeed*) ἐπιβάλλω, πείθω ‖ ~**ing** *a* (*current*) ἐπικρατῶν, ἰσχύων.

prevalent ['prevələnt] *a* διαδεδομένος, ἐπικρατῶν.

prevarication [priværi'keiʃən] *n* ὑπεκφυγή, στρίψιμο, ψεῦδος.

prevent [pri'vent] *vt* ἀποτρέπω, προλαμβάνω, προφυλάσσω ἀπό ‖ (*hinder*) ἐμποδίζω, (παρα)κωλύω ‖ ~**able** *a* ἀποφεύξιμος ‖ ~**ative** *n* προληπτικόν (φάρμακον) ‖ ~**ion** *n* πρόληψις, ἐμπόδισις ‖ ~**ive** *a* προληπτικός, προφυλακτικός.

preview ['pri:vju:] *n* προκαταρκτική προβολή, δοκιμαστική προβολή.

previous ['pri:viəs] *a* προηγούμενος ‖ ~**ly** *ad* προηγουμένως, προτύτερα.

prewar ['pri:'wɔ:*] *a* προπολεμικός.

prey [prei] *n* λεία, βορά, θῦμα ‖ **to ~ on** *vt* καταδιώκω, κινηγῶ, τρώγω ‖ (*mind*) βασανίζω.

price [prais] *n* τιμή, τίμημα ‖ (*value*) ἀξία ‖ *vt* διατιμῶ, καθορίζω τιμή ‖ ~**less** *a* ἀνεκτίμητος ‖ ~ **list** *n* τιμοκατάλογος, τιμολόγιον.

prick [prik] *n* τσίμπημα ‖ *vt* τσιμπῶ, κεντρῶ, τρυπῶ.

prickle ['prikl] *n* ἀγκάδι.

prickly ['prikli] *a* (*lit*) ἀκανθῶδες, τσουχτερός ‖ (*fig: person*) δύσκολος.

pride [praid] *n* (*self-respect*) φιλότιμο ‖ (*something to be proud of*) ὑπερηφάνεια, καμάρι ‖ (*conceit*) ἀλαζονεία, ὑπεροφία ‖ **to ~ o.s. on sth** ὑπερηφανεύομαι, καυχῶμαι.

priest [pri:st] *n* ἱερεύς, παπᾶς ‖ ~**ess** *n* ἱέρεια ‖ ~**hood** *n* ἱερωσύνη, (οἱ) ἱερεῖς.

prig [prig] *n* φαντασμένος, ξιππασμένος.

prim [prim] *a* ἀκριβής, τυπικός, μαζεμένος.

primarily ['praimərili] *ad* πρωτίστως, κυρίως ‖ (*at first*) ἀρχικά, πρῶτα-πρῶτα.

primary ['praiməri] *a* πρῶτος, ἀρχικός, ἀρχέτυπος ‖ (*first in importance*) πρωτεύων, κύριος, οὐσιώδης ‖ (*education*) στοιχειώδης ‖ (*election*) προκριματική ἐκλογή ‖ ~ **colours** *npl* πρωτεύοντα χρώματα ‖ ~ **school** *n* δημοτικόν σχολεῖον.

primate ['praimit] *n* ἀρχιεπίσκοπος, πριμᾶτος ‖ ['praimeit] (*zool*) πρωτεύων.

prime [praim] *a* πρῶτος, πρώτιστος, κύριος ‖ (*excellent*) ἐξαίρετος, πρώτης ποιότητος ‖ *vt* κατηχῶ, δασκαλεύω ‖ (*gun, pump*) γεμίζω, γομῶ ‖ ~ **minister** *n* πρωθυπουργός ‖ ~**r** *n* ἀλφαβητάριον, πρῶτον βιβλίον ‖ ~**val** [prai'mi:vəl] *a* πρωτόγονος, ἀρχέγονος, προϊστορικός.

primitive ['primitiv] *a* πρωτόγονος, ἀρχικός, ἁπλός.

primrose ['primrəuz] *n* ἡράνθεμο, δακράκι, πασχαλούδα.

primula ['primjulə] *n* πριμούλη.

primus (*stove*) ['praiməs(stəuv)] *n* ® γκαζιέρα.

prince [prins] *n* ἡγεμών, μεγιστάν ‖ (*of royal family*) πρίγκηψ, βασιλόπαις ‖ ~**ss** *n* πριγκήπισσα.

principal ['prinsipəl] *a* κύριος, κυριώτερος ‖ (*capital*) κεφάλαιον ‖ (*of school*) προϊστάμενος, διευθυντής ‖ ~**ity** *n* πριγκηπᾶτον ‖ ~**ly** *ad* κυρίως, πρό παντός, κατά τό πλεῖστον.

principle ['prinsəpl] *n* ἀρχή, τιμιότης.

print [print] *n* σφραγίς, τύπος, ἀποτύπωμα ‖ (*phot*) ἀντίτυπον, κόπια ‖ (*picture*) εἰκών, γραβούρα ‖ (*pattern*) ἐμπριμέ ‖ *vt* τυπώνω, ἐκτυπώνω ‖ ~**ed matter** *n* ἔντυπα ‖ ~**er** *n* τυπογράφος ‖ ~**ing** *n* (ἐκ)τύπωσις, τυπογραφία ‖ ~**ing press** *n* πιεστήριον (τυπογραφείου).

prior ['praiə*] *a* προγενέστερος, προηγούμενος ‖ *n* ἡγούμενος ‖ ~**ity** *n* προτεραιότης ‖ ~**y** *n* μοναστήρι, κοινόβιον.

prise [praiz] *vt*: **to ~ open** ἀνοίγω μέ μοχλό.

prism ['prizəm] *n* πρίσμα.

prison ['prizn] *n* φυλακή ‖ ~**er** *n* φυλακισμένος, ὑπόδικος, κατάδικος ‖ (*of war*) αἰχμάλωτος.

prissy ['prisi] *a* (*col*) λεπτολόγος, μικρολόγος.

pristine ['pristain] *a* πρωτόγονος, ἀρχικός.

privacy ['privəsi] *n* μοναξιά ‖ μυστικότης.

private ['praivit] *a* ἰδιωτικός, ἰδιαίτερος, μυστικός ‖ *n* φαντάρος ‖ '~' (*sign*) 'ἰδιωτικόν', 'ἰδιαίτερον' ‖ **in ~** ἰδιαιτέρως, μυστικά ‖ ~ **eye** *n* ἰδιωτικός ἀστυνομικός ‖ ~**ly** *ad* ἰδιωτικῶς, ἀτομικῶς.

privet ['privit] *n* λιγούστρον, ἀγριομυρτιά.

privilege ['privilidʒ] *n* προνόμιον ‖ ~**d** *a* προνομιοῦχος.

privy ['privi] *a*: ~ **council** ἀνακτοβούλιον.

prize [praiz] *n* βραβεῖον, ἔπαθλον ‖ *a* (*example*) λαμπροῦ (ὑπο)δείγματος ‖ (*idiot*) ὑποδείγματος ἠλιθίου ‖ *vt* ἐκτιμῶ, τιμῶ ‖ ~ **fight** *n* πυγμαχικός ἀγών ‖ ~ **giving** *n* βράβευσις ‖ ~**winner** *n* βραβευθείς.

pro- [prəu] *prefix* (*in favour*) ὑπέρ-, ἀντί- ‖ **the pros and cons** τά ὑπέρ καί τά κατά.

pro [prəu] *n* (*professional*) ἐπαγγελματίας.

probability [prɔbə'biliti] *n* πιθανότης.

probable ['prɔbəbl] *a* ἐνδεχόμενος, πιθανός.

probably ['prɔbəbli] *ad* πιθανῶς, πιθανόν.

probation [prə'beiʃən] *n* δοκιμασία ‖ (*in court etc*) ἀστυνομική ἐπιτήρησις ‖ **on ~** ὑπό δοκιμασίαν ‖ ~**ary** *a* (περίοδος) δοκιμασίας ‖ ~**er** *n* δόκιμος.

probe [prəub] *n* (*med*) καθετήρ, μήλη ‖ (*enquiry*) ἐξερεύνησις, διερεύνησις ‖ *vti* (ἐξ)ἐρευνῶ, διερευνῶ.

probity ['prəubiti] *n* χρηστότης, τιμιότης, ἀκεραιότης.

problem ['prɔbləm] *n* πρόβλημα ‖ ~**atic** *a* προβληματικός.

procedure [prə'si:dʒə*] *n* διαδικασία, μέθοδος, πορεία.

proceed [prə'si:d] *vi* προχωρῶ, συνεχίζω, τραβῶ ‖ (*begin*) προβαίνω, ἀρχίζω ‖ ~**ings** *npl* συζητήσεις, πρακτικά ‖ (*law*) δικαστική ἐνέργεια, δίκη ‖ ~**s** ['prəusi:dz] *npl* εἰσπραχθέν ποσόν, εἰσπράξεις.

process ['prəuses] *n* πορεία, ἐξέλιξις ‖ (*method*) μέθοδος, τρόπος ‖ *vt* ἐπεξεργάζω, κατεργάζω.

procession [prə'seʃən] *n* πομπή, παρέλασις ‖ (*orderly progress*) παράταξις, σειρά, συνοδεία.

proclaim [prə'kleim] *vt* κηρύττω, ἀνακηρύσσω, ἀναγορεύω ‖ (*show*) φανερώνω, δείχνω.

proclamation [prɔklə'meiʃən] *n* (προ)κήρυξις, ἀνακήρυξις.

procrastination [prəukræsti'neiʃən] *n* ἀναβολή, χρονοτριβή, χασομέρι.

procreation [prəukri'eiʃən] *n* γέννησις, τεκνοποιία.

procure [prə'kjuə*] *vt* προμηθεύω, προμηθεύομαι, ἐξευρίσκω.

prod [prɔd] *vt* σκαλίζω, κεντρίζω, ἐξάπτω ‖ *n* (*push, jab*) μπήξιμο, κέντρισμα.

prodigal ['prɔdigəl] *a* ἄσωτος, σπάταλος.

prodigious [prə'didʒəs] *a* τεράστιος, καταπληκτικός, θαυμάσιος.

prodigy ['prɔdidʒi] *n* φαινόμενον, θαῦμα.

produce ['prɔdju:s] *n* (*agr*) προϊόν, καρπός ‖ [prə'dju:s] *vt* (*show*) παρουσιάζω, ἐπιδεικνύω ‖ (*make*) παράγω, γεννῶ, προξενῶ ‖ (*play*) ἀνεβάζω, παρουσιάζω ‖ ~**r** *n* παραγωγός ‖ (*theat*) σκηνοθέτης, παραγωγός.

product ['prɔdʌkt] *n* προϊόν, ἀποτέλεσμα ‖ ~**ion** *n* παραγωγή, κατασκευή, γένεσις ‖ προϊόντα, παραγωγή ‖ (*theat*) σκηνοθέτησις, παράστασις, ἀνέβασμα ‖ ~**ion line** *n* γραμμή παραγωγής ‖ ~**ive** *a* παραγωγικός ‖ (*fertile*) γόνιμος.

productivity [prɔdʌk'tiviti] *n* παραγωγικότης, γονιμότης.

profane [prə'fein] *a* βέβηλος ‖ (*language*) βλάσφημος.

profess [prə'fes] *vt* διακηρύττω, ὁμολογῶ ‖ (*claim*) προσποιοῦμαι ‖ ~**ion** *n* ἐπάγγελμα ‖ (*declaration*) ὁμολογία, διακήρυξις ‖ ~**ional** *n* ἐπαγγελματίας ‖ *a* ἐπαγγελματικός ‖ ~**ionalism** *n* ἐπαγγελματισμός ‖ ~**or** *n* καθηγητής.

proficiency [prə'fiʃənsi] *n* εἰδικότης, ἐπιδεξιότης, ἱκανότης.

proficient [prə'fiʃənt] *a* ἱκανός, εἰδικός, ἐγκρατής.

profile ['prəufail] *n* (*of face*) κατατομή, προφίλ ‖ (*fig: report*) σύντομος βιογραφία.

profit ['prɔfit] *n* κέρδος, ὄφελος, ὠφέλεια ‖ *vi* (+ *by, from*) ὠφελοῦμαι (ἀπό), ἐπωφελοῦμαι ‖ ~**able** *a* ἐπικερδής, ἐπωφελής ‖ ~**ably** *ad* ἐπωφελῶς, ἐπικερδῶς, ὠφέλιμα ‖ ~**eering** *n* κερδοσκοπία.

profound [prə'faund] *a* βαθύς, μυστηριώδης ‖ ~**ly** *ad* βαθέως, βαθύτατα.

profuse [prə'fju:s] *a* ἄφθονος, γενναιόδωρος ‖ ~**ly** *ad* ἀφθόνως, ἄφθονα.

profusion [prə'fju:ʒən] *n* ἀφθονία.

progeny ['prɔdʒini] *n* ἀπόγονοι, νεογνά, παιδιά.

programing ['prəugræmiŋ] *n* (*US*) = **programming**.

programme, (*US*) **program** ['prəugræm] *n* πρόγραμμα.

programming ['prəugræmiŋ] *n* προγραμματισμός.

progress ['prəugres] *n* πρόοδος, ἐξέλιξις ‖ [prə'gres] *vi* προοδεύω, προχωρῶ, ἐξελίσσομαι ‖ *to* **make** ~ σημειώνω πρόοδον, προκόβω ‖ ~**ion** *n* πρόοδος ‖ ~**ive** *a* προοδευτικός ‖ ~**ively** *ad* προοδευτικῶς, βαθμηδόν.

prohibit [prə'hibit] *vt* ἀπαγορεύω ‖ ~**ion** *n* (*US*) ἀπαγόρευσις, ποταπαγόρευσις ‖ ~**ive** *a* (*price etc*) ἀπαγορευτικός, ἀπλησίαστος.

project ['prɔdʒekt] *n* (*plan*) σχέδιον ‖ (*final project*) μελέτη ‖ [prə'dʒekt] *vt* (*throw*) ρίπτω, ἐξακοντίζω ‖ (*extend*) προεκτείνω ‖ (*film etc*) προβάλλω ‖ *vi* (προ)ἐξέχω, προβάλλω ‖ ~**ile** *n* βλῆμα ‖ ~**ion** *n* προεξοχή, προβολή ‖ ~**or** *n* (*film*) προβολεύς, μηχάνημα προβολῆς.

proletarian [prəulə'tɛəriən] *a* προλεταριακός ‖ *n* προλετάριος.

proletariat [prəulə'tɛəriət] *n* προλεταριάτον.

proliferate [prə'lifəreit] *vi* πολλαπλασιάζομαι.

proliferation [prəlifə'reiʃən] *n* πολλαπλασιασμός.

prolific [prə'lifik] *a* γόνιμος, ἄφθονος.

prologue ['prəulɔg] *n* πρόλογος.

prolong [prə'lɔŋ] *vt* παρατείνω, προεκτείνω.

prom [prɔm] *n abbr of* **promenade** ‖ *abbr of* **promenade concert** ‖ (*US: college ball*) φοιτητικός χορός.

promenade [prɔmi'na:d] *n* περίπατος, τόπος περιπάτου ‖ ~ **concert** *n* συναυλία ‖ ~ **deck** *n* (*naut*) κατάστρωμα περιπάτου.

prominence ['prɔminəns] *n* ὑπεροχή, προεξοχή.

prominent ['prɔminənt] *a* προεξέχων, περίβλεπτος, διακεκριμμένος.

promiscuity [prɔmis'kju:iti] *n* συγχρονισμός, σμίξιμο, ἀνακάτεμα.

promise ['prɔmis] *n* ὑπόσχεσις, τάξιμο ‖ (*hope*) ὑπόσχεσις ‖ *vti* ὑπόσχομαι, παρέχω ὑποσχέσεις, φαίνομαι καλά.

promising ['prɔmisiŋ] *a* γεμάτος ὑποσχέσεις, παρέχων ἐλπίδας.

promontory ['prɔməntri] *n* ἀκρωτήριον.

promote [prə'məut] *vt* προάγω, προβιβάζω ‖ (*help on*) ὑποστηρίζω, ὑποκινῶ ‖ ~**r** *n* ὑποστηρικτής, ὑποκινητής, διοργανωτής.

promotion [prə'məuʃən] n (of sales etc) διαφήμισις, προαγωγή ‖ (in rank) προαγωγή, προβιβασμός.

prompt [prɔmpt] a ἄμεσος, σύντομος, πρόθυμος, ταχύς ‖ ad (punctually) στήν ὥρα ‖ vt παρακινῶ, ἐμπνέω ‖ (remind) ὑποβάλλω ‖ ~er n (theat) ὑποβολεύς ‖ ~ly ad ταχέως, γρήγορα, γοργά ‖ ~ness n ταχύτης, ἑτοιμότης, προθυμία.

prone [prəun] a πρηνής, μπρουμιτισμένος ‖ (inclined) (+ to) ἐπιρρεπής, ἔχων κλίσιν.

prong [prɔŋ] n δόντι πηρουνιοῦ, πηρούνα, διχάλα.

pronoun ['prəunaun] n ἀντωνυμία.

pronounce [prə'nauns] vt (gram) προφέρω ‖ (law) ἐκδίδω, ἐπιβάλλω, ἀπαγγέλλω, γνωματεύω ‖ ~d a (marked) ἔντονος, ζωηρός ‖ ~ment n δήλωσις, διακήρυξις.

pronto ['prɔntəu] ad (col) ἀμέσως, γρήγορα.

pronunciation [prənʌnsi'eiʃən] n προφορά.

proof [pru:f] n ἀπόδειξις, τεκμήριον ‖ (test) δοκιμή, δοκιμασία ‖ (copy) δοκίμιον ‖ a ἀδιαπέραστος, στεγανός, ἀνθιστάμενος εἰς.

prop [prɔp] n στήριγμα, ἔρεισμα, ὑποστήριγμα ‖ (theat) βοηθητικά, ἀξεσουάρ ‖ vt (also ~ up) (ὑπο)στηρίζω, στηλώνω.

propaganda [prɔpə'gændə] n προπαγάνδα.

propagation [prɔpə'geiʃən] n (of plants) ἀναπαραγωγή, πολλαπλασιασμός ‖ (of knowledge) διάδοσις.

propel [prə'pel] vt προωθῶ, δίδω ὤθησιν εἰς ‖ ~ler n ἕλιξ, προπέλλα.

proper ['prɔpə*] a πρέπων, ἁρμόζων ‖ ~ly ad πρεπόντως, δεόντως, καταλλήλως, σωστά ‖ ~ noun n κύριον ὄνομα.

property ['prɔpəti] n ἰδιοκτησία, περιουσία ‖ (quality) ἰδιότης, χαρακτηριστικόν ‖ (theat) βοηθητικόν, ἀξεσουάρ ‖ (land) κτῆμα, ἀκίνητον ‖ ~ owner n ἰδιοκτήτης.

prophecy ['prɔfisi] n (prediction) προφητεία.

prophesy ['prɔfisai] vt προφητεύω, προλέγω.

prophet ['prɔfit] n προφήτης ‖ ~ic a προφητικός.

proportion [prə'pɔ:ʃən] n σχέσις, ἀναλογία ‖ (share) μέρος, τμῆμα ‖ vt ρυθμίζω, μοιράζω κατ' ἀναλογίαν ‖ ~al a ἀνάλογος, συμμετρικός, ἀναλογικός ‖ ~ate a ἀνάλογος, σύμμετρος, ρυθμισμένος ‖ ~ed a μέ καλές ἀναλογίες.

proposal [prə'pəuzl] n πρότασις, σχέδιον, εἰσήγησις ‖ (of marriage) πρότασις γάμου.

propose [prə'pəuz] vt προτείνω, σκοπεύω ‖ vi (marriage) κάνω πρότασιν γάμου ‖ ~r n ὁ προτείνων, ὁ ὑποβάλλων (πρότασιν).

proposition [prɔpə'ziʃən] n πρότασις, σχέδιον, ὑπόθεσις.

propound [prə'paund] vt (theory) προτείνω, ἀναπτύσσω.

proprietary [prə'praiətəri] a τῆς ἰδιοκτησίας, τῆς κυριότητος.

proprietor [prə'praiətə*] n ἰδιοκτήτης.

propulsion [prə'pʌlʃən] n (προ)ὤθησις.

pro-rata ['prəu'ra:tə] ad κατ' ἀναλογίαν.

prosaic [prəu'zeiik] a (ordinary) πεζός.

prose [prəuz] n πεζός λόγος, πεζογραφία, πρόζα.

prosecute ['prɔsikju:t] vt ὑποβάλλω μήνυσιν.

prosecution [prɔsi'kju:ʃən] n (ποινική) δίωξις ‖ (people bringing action) κατηγορία, μηνυτής.

prosecutor ['prɔsikju:tə*] n εἰσαγγελεύς.

prospect [n 'prɔspekt] n (expectation) προσδοκία, ἐλπίς ‖ ~ing n (for minerals) ἀναζήτησις (μεταλλευμάτων) ‖ ~ive a προσδοκόμενος, μελλοντικός ‖ ~or n μεταλλοδίφης ‖ (for gold) χρυσοθήρας ‖ ~us n ἀγγελία, πρόγραμμα.

prosper ['prɔspə*] vi εὐδοκιμῶ, ἀκμάζω, προκόπτω ‖ ~ity n εὐημερία, εὐδαιμονία ‖ ~ous a εὐημερῶν, ἀκμάζων, ἐπιτυχής.

prostitute ['prɔstitju:t] n πόρνη, πουτάνα.

prostrate ['prɔstreit] a (lying flat) πρηνής, μπρούμυτος.

protagonist [prəu'tægənist] n πρωταγωνιστής.

protect [prə'tekt] vt προστατεύω, προφυλάσσω, ὑπερασπίζω, καλύπτω ‖ ~ion n προστασία, ὑπεράσπισις, ἄμυνα ‖ (shelter) σκέπαστρον, προστατευτικόν μέσον ‖ ~ive a προστατευτικός ‖ ~or n προστάτης, προφυλακτήρ.

protégé ['prɔtezei] n προστατευόμενος.

protein ['prəuti:n] n πρωτεΐνη.

protest [n 'prəutest] n διαμαρτυρία, διαμαρτύρησις ‖ [prə'test] vi (+ against) διαμαρτύρομαι ‖ P~ant a,n διαμαρτυρόμενος, προτεστάνης.

protocol ['prəutəkɔl] n πρωτόκολλον.

prototype ['prəutəutaip] n πρωτότυπον, μοντέλλο.

protracted [prə'træktid] a παρατεταμένος.

protractor [prə'træktə*] n μοιρογνωμόνιον.

protrude [prə'tru:d] vi προεξέχω, ξεβγαίνω.

protuberance [prə'tju:bərəns] n (ἐξ)όγκωμα, πρήξιμο.

proud [praud] a περήφανος ‖ φαντασμένος ‖ ἀκατάδεκτος.

prove [pru:v] vt (show) ἀποδεικνύω, ἐπαληθεύω ‖ (turn out) δείχνομαι.

proverb ['prɔvə:b] n παροιμία.

provide [prə'vaid] vt προμηθεύω ‖ χορηγῶ ‖ ~d cj ἐφ' ὅσον, ἀρκεῖ νά.

province ['prɔvins] n ἐπαρχία ‖ ἁρμοδιότης.

provincial [prə'vinʃəl] a ἐπαρχιακός, τοπικιστικός.

provision [prə'viʒən] n (supply) προμήθεια ‖ (condition) ὅρος ‖ ~s npl (food) τρόφιμα, ἐφόδια ‖ ~al a προσωρινός.

provocation [prɔvə'keiʃən] n πρόκλησις.

provocative [prə'vɔkətiv] a προκλητικός, ἐρεθιστικός.

provoke [prə'vəuk] vt προκαλῶ, διεγείρω, ἐξερεθίζω.

prow [prau] n πρώρα, πλώρη ‖ ~ess n ἐπιδεξιότης ‖ (bravery) ἀνδρεία, παληκαριά.

prowl [praul] vt (streets) περιφέρομαι, τριγυρίζω ‖ n: on the ~ ψάχνω διαρκῶς ‖ ~er n νυχτοπάτης, τριγυριστής, σουρτούκης.

proximity [prɔk'simiti] n ἐγγύτης, γειτνίασις.

proxy ['prɔksi] n πληρεξούσιος, πληρεξούσιον, ἀντιπρόσωπος ‖ by ~ δι' ἀντιπροσώπου.

prudence ['pru:dəns] n φρόνησις, σύνεσις, φροντίς.

prudent ['pru:dənt] a συνετός, φρόνιμος ‖ ~ly ad σωφρόνως, συνετά, φρόνιμα.

prudish ['pru:diʃ] a σεμνότυφος ‖ ~ness n σεμνοτυφία.

prune [pru:n] n ξερό δαμάσκηνο ‖ vt κλαδεύω.

pry [prai] vi (+ into) ψάχνω, χώνω τή μύτη (σέ).

psalm [sa:m] n ψαλμός.

pseudo ['sju:dəu] a ψεύτικος, κίβδηλος ‖ (in compds) ψευδο- ‖ ~nym n ψευδώνυμον.

psyche ['saiki] n (soul, mind, intelligence) ψυχή.

psychiatric [saiki'ætrik] a ψυχιατρικός.

psychiatrist [sai'kaiətrist] n ψυχίατρος.

psychiatry [sai'kaiətri] n ψυχιατρική.

psychic(al) ['saikik(əl)] a ψυχικός.

psychoanalyse [saikəu'ænəlaiz] vt ψυχαναλύω (κάποιον).

psychoanalysis [saikəuə'nælisis] n ψυχανάλυσις.

psychoanalyst [saikəu'ænəlist] n ψυχαναλυτής.

psychoanalyze [saikəu'ænəlaiz] vt (US) = psychoanalyse.

psychological [saikə'lɔdʒikəl] a ψυχολογικός ‖ ~ly ad ψυχολογικῶς.

psychologist [sai'kɔlədʒist] n ψυχολόγος.

psychology [sai'kɔlədʒi] n ψυχολογία.

psychopath ['saikəupæθ] n ψυχοπαθής.

psychosomatic ['saikəusəu'mætik] a ψυχοσωματικός.

psychotherapy ['saikəu'θerəpi] n ψυχοθεραπεία.

psychotic [sai'kɔtik] a,n ψυχοπαθής.

pub [pʌb] n (Brit) = public house ‖ see public.

puberty ['pju:bəti] n ἥβη, ἐφηβεία.

public ['pʌblik] a δημόσιος ‖ n (also the general ~) κοινόν ‖ ~an n (innkeeper) ταβερνιάρης, κάπελλας ‖ ~ation n (something

published) δημοσίευσις, ἔκδοσις ‖ (making known) κοινοποίησις, δημοσίευσις ‖ ~ house n ταβέρνα ‖ ~ity n δημοσιότης, διαφήμισις ‖ ~ly ad δημοσία, ὁλοφάνερα ‖ ~ opinion n κοινή γνώμη ‖ ~ relations n δημόσιες σχέσεις, διαφήμισις ‖ ~ school n (Brit) ἰδιωτικόν σχολεῖον (Ἀγγλίας) ‖ ~-spirited a ἐνδιαφερόμενος γιά τό κοινόν καλόν, φιλόπατρις.

publish ['pʌbliʃ] vt ἐκδίδω, δημοσιεύω ‖ (figures etc) ἀναγγέλλω, δημοσιεύω ‖ ~er n ἐκδότης ‖ ~ing n ἔκδοσις, δημοσίευσις.

pucker ['pʌkə*] vt ζαρώνω.

pudding ['pudiŋ] n πουτίγγα.

puddle ['pʌdl] n (pool) νερόλακκος, λιμνούλα.

puerile ['pjuərail] a παιδαριώδης.

puff [pʌf] n ξεφύσημα, φύσημα, ρουφηξιά ‖ (pad) πομπόν ‖ vt ξεφυσῶ, βγάζω, ἐκπέμπω ‖ vi φυσῶ, τραβῶ, λαχανιάζω ‖ ~ed a (col: out of breath) λαχανιασμένος.

puff pastry ['pʌf'peistri] n, (US) **puff paste** ['pʌf'peist] n πάτ-φεγιετέ.

puffy ['pʌfi] a φουσκωμένος, φουσκωτός.

pull [pul] n (tug) ἕλξις, τράβηγμα ‖ (fig) ἐπιρροή, μέσον ‖ vt (trolley) σύρω, ἕλκω, τραβῶ, σέρνω ‖ (hair) τραβῶ ‖ (trigger) πατῶ, τραβῶ ‖ vi (on rope etc) τραβῶ, σύρω ‖ '~' (sign) 'τράβηξε', 'ἀφήρεσε' ‖ to ~ a face κάνω μούτρα, μορφάζω ‖ to ~ to pieces τραβῶ καί κομματιάζω, κριτικάρω δυσμενῶς ‖ to ~ o.s. together συνέρχομαι ‖ to ~ apart vt (break) σχίζω στά δύο, ἀποχωρίζω ‖ (dismantle) λυώνω ‖ to ~ down vt (house) κατεδαφίζω, γκρεμίζω ‖ to ~ in vi (rail) εἰσέρχομαι (στό σταθμό) ‖ to ~ off vt (deal etc) ἐπιτυγχάνω (κάτι) ‖ to ~ out vi ἐξέρχομαι, ξεκινῶ, ἀναχωρῶ ‖ (vehicle) βγαίνω ἀπό τήν λωρίδα ‖ vt ἀφαιρῶ, βγάζω, τραβῶ ‖ to ~ round or through vi συνέρχομαι, γλυτώνω, ἀναρρωνύω ‖ to ~ up vi σταματῶ.

pulley ['puli] n τροχαλία.

pullover ['puləuvə*] n πουλόβερ.

pulp [pʌlp] n πολτός, σάρκωμα.

pulpit ['pulpit] n ἄμβων.

pulsate [pʌl'seit] vi πάλλομαι, πάλλω, σφύζω.

pulse [pʌls] n σφυγμός, παλμός ‖ (vegetable) ὄσπρια.

pulverize ['pʌlvəraiz] vt λειοτριβῶ, κονιοποιῶ.

pummel ['pʌml] vt γρονθοκοπῶ.

pump [pʌmp] n ἀντλία, τρούμπα, πόμπα ‖ vt ἀντλῶ ‖ to ~ up vt (tyre) φουσκώνω (λάστιχο).

pumpkin ['pʌmpkin] n κολοκύθα.

pun [pʌn] n λογοπαίγνιον.

punch ['pʌntʃ] *n* τρυπητήρι, ζουμπάς ‖ (*blow*) γροθιά ‖ (*drink*) πώντς, πόντσ ‖ *vt* γρονθοκοπῶ, δίνω μία γροθιά ‖ (*a hole*) τρυπῶ, ἀνοίγω ‖ ~-**drunk** *a* τύφλα στὸ μεθύσι.

punctual ['pʌŋktjuəl] *a* ἀκριβής, τακτικός ‖ ~**ity** *n* ἀκρίβεια, τάξις.

punctuate ['pʌŋktjueit] *vt* στίζω ‖ (*fig*) τονίζω, ὑπογραμμίζω.

punctuation [pʌŋktju'eiʃən] *n* στίξις.

puncture ['pʌŋktʃə*] *n* (παρα)κέντησις, τρύπα ‖ *vt* παρακεντῶ, τρυπῶ, σπάζω.

pundit ['pʌndit] *n* (σοφο)λογιώτατος.

pungent ['pʌndʒənt] *a* δριμύς, σουβλερός, ὀξύς.

punish ['pʌniʃ] *vt* τιμωρῶ, δέρνω ‖ (*in boxing etc*) τρώγω ἄγριο ξύλο, μαστιγώνω ‖ ~**able** *a* ἀξιόποινος, τιμωρητέος ‖ ~**ment** *n* τιμωρία ‖ κτυπήματα.

punitive ['pju:nitiv] *a* ποινικός ‖ (*mil*) ἀντιποίνων.

punt [pʌnt] *n* πλοιάρι, ρηχή λέμβος.

punter ['pʌntə*] *n* (*gambler*) παίκτης.

puny ['pju:ni] *a* μικροκαμωμένος, ἀδύνατος, ἀσήμαντος.

pup [pʌp] *n* σκυλάκι, κουτάβι.

pupil ['pju:pl] *n* μαθητής ‖ (*of eye*) κόρη (ὀφθαλμοῦ).

puppet ['pʌpit] *n* μαριονέττα ‖ (*person*) ἀνδρείκελον.

puppy ['pʌpi] *n* σκυλάκι.

purchase ['pɜ:tʃis] *n* ψώνισμα, ψώνιο ‖ (*buying*) ἀγορά, ψώνισμα ‖ *vt* ἀγοράζω, ψωνίζω ‖ ~**r** *n* ἀγοραστής.

pure [pjuə*] *a* καθαρός ‖ (*innocent*) ἄδολος, ἁγνός ‖ (*unmixed*) ἀμιγής, ἄκρατος, ἀνόθευτος.

purée ['pjuərei] *n* πουρέ(ς).

purely ['pjuəli] *ad* καθαρά.

purge [pɜ:dʒ] *n* καθάρσιον ‖ (*pol*) ἐκκαθάρισις ‖ *vt* (ἐκ)καθαρίζω.

purification [pjuərifi'keiʃən] *n* καθαρισμός, ἐξύγιανσις.

purify ['pjuərifai] *vt* καθαρίζω, ἐξαγνίζω.

purist ['pjuərist] *n* καθαρευουσιάνος.

puritan ['pjuəritən] *n* πουριτανός ‖ ~**ical** *a* πουριτανικός.

purity ['pjuəriti] *n* καθαρότης ‖ (*unmixed*) καθαρότης, γνησιότης.

purl [pɜ:l] *n* ἀνάποδη βελονιά ‖ *vt* πλέκω ἀνάποδες.

purple ['pɜ:pl] (*colour*) *a* πορφυροῦς ‖ *n* πορφύρα, πορφυροῦν (χρῶμα).

purpose ['pɜ:pəs] *n* σκοπός, πρόθεσις ‖ **on** ~ σκόπιμα ‖ ~**ful** *a* (προ)ἐσκεμμένος, σκόπιμος ‖ ~**ly** *ad* ἐπίτηδες, σκόπιμα.

purr [pɜ:*] *vi* (*of cat*) ρουθουνίζω, κάνω ρονρόν ‖ *n* χουρχούρισμα, ροχάλισμα.

purse [pɜ:s] *n* πορτοφόλι ‖ *vt* ζαρώνω.

purser ['pɜ:sə*] *n* λογιστής (πλοίου).

pursue [pə'sju:] *vt* (κατα)διώκω, κυνηγῶ ‖ (*carry on*) συνεχίζω, ἀκολουθῶ, τραβῶ ‖ ~**r** *n* διώκτης.

pursuit [pə'sju:t] *n* (κατα)δίωξις, κυνήγημα ‖ (*occupation*) ἐπιδίωξις, ἐπάγγελμα.

purveyor [pə:'veiə*] *n* προμηθευτής (τροφίμων).

pus [pʌs] *n* πύον.

push [puʃ] *n* ὤθησις, σκούντημα, σπρωξιά ‖ (*mil*) προώθησις ‖ *vt* σπρώχνω, σκουντῶ ‖ (*forward*) προχωρῶ, προοδεύω ‖ *vi* σπρώχνω, ὠθῶ, ἀσκῶ πίεσιν ‖ (*make one's way*) προχωρῶ (μὲ δυσκολίαν) ‖ '~' (*sign*) 'ὠθήσετε' ‖ **at a** ~ (*if necessary*) ἐν ἀνάγκη, στὴν ἀνάγκη ‖ **to** ~ **aside** *vt* ἀπωθῶ, παραμερίζω ‖ **to** ~ **off** *vi* (*col*) φεύγω, ξεκινῶ ‖ **to** ~ **on** *vi* (*continue*) προχωρῶ, συνεχίζω, ἐπισπεύδω ‖ **to** ~ **through** *vt* (*measure*) περνῶ (νομοσχέδιον κτλ) ‖ ~ **chair** *n* καρροτσάκι ‖ παιδικό ἁμαξάκι ‖ ~**ing** *a* ἐνεργητικός, ρέκτης ‖ ~**over** *n* (*col*) εὔκολο πρᾶμα, εὔκολη κατάκτησι.

puss [pus] *n* γατάκι, ψιψίνα.

put [put] (*irreg v*) *vt* θέτω, τοποθετῶ, βάζω ‖ (*express*) ἐκφράζω, ἐξηγῶ, ὑποβάλλω ‖ **to** ~ **about** *vi* στρέφομαι, ἀναστρέφω ‖ *vt* διαδίδω, θέτω εἰς κυκλοφορίαν ‖ **to** ~ **across** *vt* (*succeed*) ἐπιτυγχάνω, βγάζω πέρα ‖ (*meaning*) δίνω νά καταλάβη ‖ **to** ~ **away** *vt* (*store*) βάζω κατά μέρος, φυλάσσω ‖ **to** ~ **back** *vt* (*replace*) βάζω πίσω ‖ (*postpone*) ἐπιβραδύνω, ἀναβάλλω ‖ **to** ~ **by** *vt* (*money*) ἀποταμιεύω ‖ **to** ~ **down** *vt* (*lit*) κατεβάζω ‖ (*in writing*) γράφω, σημειώνω ‖ **to** ~ **forward** *vt* (*idea*) ἀναπτύσσω, εἰσηγοῦμαι, προτείνω ‖ (*date*) ἀναβάλλω ‖ **to** ~ **off** *vt* (*postpone*) ἀναβάλλω ‖ (*discourage*) μεταπείθω, ἐμποδίζω, ἀποθαρρύνω ‖ **to** ~ **on** *vt* (*clothes etc*) φορῶ ‖ (*light etc*) ἀνάβω ‖ (*play etc*) ἀνεβάζω ‖ (*brake*) φρενάρω ‖ (*false air*) προσποιοῦμαι ‖ **to** ~ **out** *vt* (*hand etc*) ἐκτείνω, ἁπλώνω ‖ (*news, rumour*) διαδίδω ‖ (*light etc*) σβήνω ‖ (*person: inconvenience*) στενοχωρῶ, ἐνοχλῶ ‖ **to** ~ **up** *vt* (*raise*) σηκώνω, ὑψώνω, ἀνεγείρω ‖ (*guest*) παρέχω τροφή καί κατάλυμα, φιλοξενῶ ‖ **to** ~ **up with** *vt* ἀνέχομαι.

putrid ['pju:trid] *a* σαπρός, σάπιος.

putt [pʌt] *vt* σέρνω (τή μπάλλα) ‖ *n* συρτό χτύπημα, πάτυκς.

putty ['pʌti] *n* στόκος.

put-up ['putʌp] *a:* ~ **job** δουλειά σκαρωμένη, στημένη μηχανή.

puzzle ['pʌzl] *n* αἴνιγμα, δύσλυτον πρόβλημα, μπέρδεμα ‖ (*toy*) παιχνίδι συναρμολογήσεως, γρίφος ‖ *vt* (*perplex*) περιπλέκω, συγχίζω, ζαλίζω ‖ *vi* σπάζω τό κεφάλι μου.

puzzling ['pʌzliŋ] *a* πολύπλοκος, δύσλυτος, μπλεγμένος.

pygmy ['pigmi] *n* πυγμαῖος.

pyjamas [pi'dʒɑ:məz] *npl* πυζάμες.

pylon ['pailən] *n* στύλος.

pyramid ['pirəmid] *n* πυραμις.
python ['paiθən] *n* πύθων.

Q, q

quack [kwæk] *n* κραυγή πάπιας ‖ (*dishonest person*) κομπογιαννίτης, τσαρλατᾶνος.
quad [kwɔd] *n* abbr of quadrangle, quadruple, quadruplet.
quadrangle ['kwɔdræŋgl] *n* (*court*) τετράγωνος αὐλή.
quadruped ['kwɔdruped] *n* τετράποδον.
quadruple ['kwɔdrupl] *a* τετραπλός, τετραπλάσιος, τετράδιπλος ‖ ['kwɔ'dru:pl] *vti* τετραπλασιάζω, τετραπλασιάζομαι.
quadruplet [kwɔ'dru:plit] *n* τετράδυμο.
quagmire ['kwægmaiə*] *n* ἕλος, τέλμα, βάλτος.
quaint [kweint] *a* παράξενος, ἀλλόκοτος ‖ ~ly ad παράξενα, ἀλλόκοτα, πρωτότυπα ‖ ~ness *n* πρωτοτυπία, ἰδιοτροπία, παραξενιά.
quake [kweik] *vi* τρέμω, σείομαι ‖ Q~r *n* Κουάκερος.
qualification [kwɔlifi'keiʃən] *n* ἱκανότης, προσόν ‖ (*reservation*) ἐπιφύλαξις, ὅρος, περιορισμός.
qualified ['kwɔlifaid] *a* ἔχων τά προσόντα, κατάλληλος ‖ (*reserved*) ἐπιφυλακτικός, περιωρισμένος, μετριασμένος.
qualify ['kwɔlifai] *vt* καθιστῶ κατάλληλον, ἀποκτῶ τά προσόντα ‖ (*limit*) τροποποιῶ, προσδιορίζω ‖ *vi* (*acquire degree*) λαμβάνω δίπλωμα.
qualitative ['kwɔlitətiv] *a* ποιοτικός.
quality ['kwɔliti] *n* (*kind*) ποιότης ‖ (*of person*) ἰδιότης, χαρακτηριστικόν, ἱκανότης ‖ *a* καλῆς ποιότητος.
qualm [kwa:m] *n* (*misgiving*) τύψις, ἐνδοιασμός.
quandary ['kwɔndəri] *n* ἀμηχανία, δίλημμα.
quantitative ['kwɔntitətiv] *a* ποσοτικός.
quantity ['kwɔntiti] *n* ποσότης ‖ (*large amount*) μεγάλη ποσότης, πολύ, μέ τό σωρό.
quarantine ['kwɔrənti:n] *n* κάθαρσις, καραντίνα.
quarrel ['kwɔrəl] *n* (*argument*) φιλονεικία, διένεξις, καυγᾶς, τσακωμός ‖ *vi* (*argue*) φιλονεικῶ, τσακώνομαι ‖ ~some *a* εὐέξαπτος, καυγαντζῆς.
quarry ['kwɔri] *n* (*of stone*) λατομεῖον ‖ (*animal*) θήραμα, κυνήγι.
quart [kwɔ:t] *n* τέταρτον τοῦ γαλλονιοῦ.
quarter ['kwɔ:tə*] *n* τέταρτον ‖ (*of year*) τριμηνία ‖ *vt* κόβω εἰς τά τέσσερα ‖ (*mil*) στρατωνίζω ‖ ~s *npl* (*esp mil*) κατάλυμα, στρατῶν ‖ στέγασις ‖ ~ of an hour ἕνα τέταρτον (τῆς ὥρας) ‖ ~ past three τρεῖς καί τέταρτον ‖ ~ to three τρεῖς παρά τέταρτο ‖ ~-deck *n*

πρυμναῖον κατάστρωμα, κάσαρο ‖ ~ly *a* τριμηνιαῖος ‖ ~master *n* (*naut*) ὑποναύκληρος ‖ (*mil*) ἐπιμελητής.
quartet(te) [kwɔː'tet] *n* τετραφωνία, κουαρτέτο.
quartz [kwɔːts] *n* χαλαζίας.
quash [kwɔʃ] *vt* (*verdict*) ἀναιρῶ, ἀκυρώνω.
quasi ['kwaːzi] *a* σάν, σχεδόν, τρόπον τινά.
quaver ['kweivə*] *n* (*mus*) ὄγδοον ‖ *vi* τρέμω, κάνω τρίλιες.
quay [ki:] *n* ἀποβάθρα, προκυμαία.
queasiness ['kwi:zinis] *n* εὐαισθησία, ἀηδία, δισταγμοί.
queasy ['kwi:zi] *a* εὐαίσθητος, ἀηδής, δύσκολος.
queen [kwi:n] *n* βασίλισσα ‖ (*cards*) ντάμα ‖ ~ mother *n* βασιλομήτωρ.
queer [kwiə*] *a* ἀλλόκοτος, παράξενος ‖ *n* (*col: homosexual*) 'τοιοῦτος'.
quell [kwel] *vt* καταπνίγω, καταβάλλω, κατευνάζω.
quench [kwentʃ] *vt* κόβω (τήν δίψα μου), κατευνάζω ‖ (*fire etc*) σβήνω.
query ['kwiəri] *n* ἐρώτησις, ἐρώτημα ‖ *vt* ἐρωτῶ, ἐρευνῶ.
quest [kwest] *n* ἀναζήτησις, ἔρευνα.
question ['kwestʃən] *n* ἐρώτησις, ἐρώτημα ‖ (*problem*) ζήτημα, θέμα ‖ (*doubt*) ἀμφιβολία, ἀμφισβήτησις ‖ *vt* ἐρωτῶ, ἐξετάζω ‖ (*doubt*) ἀμφισβητῶ ‖ beyond ~ ἀναμφισβητήτως ‖ out of the ~ ἐκτός συζητήσεως, ἀπαράδεκτος ‖ ~able *a* ἀμφίβολος, ἀμφισβητήσιμος ‖ ~er *n* ἐξεταστής, ἀνακριτής ‖ ~ing *a* ἐρώτησις, ἀνάκρισις ‖ ~ mark *n* ἐρωτηματολογικόν ‖ ~naire *n* ἐρωτηματολόγιον.
queue [kju:] *n* (*line*) οὐρά ‖ *vi* μπαίνω στήν οὐρά, σχηματίζω οὐρά.
quibble ['kwibl] *n* (*petty objection*) ὑπεκφυγή.
quick [kwik] *a* (*fast*) ταχύς, γρήγορος, γοργός ‖ (*impatient*) βιαστικός, εὐέξαπτος ‖ (*keen*) ζωηρός, ζωντανός, ἔξυπνος ‖ *ad* γρήγορα, ταχέως ‖ *n* (*anat*) εὐαίσθητον σημεῖον, σάρκα, κρέας ‖ (*old: the living*) οἱ ζῶντες ‖ ~en *vt* (*hasten*) ἐπιταχύνω ‖ (*rouse*) (ἀνα)ζωογονῶ, ζωντανεύω ‖ *vi* (ξανα)ζωντανεύω, ἀναζωπυροῦμαι ‖ ~ly ad ταχέως, γρήγορα ‖ ~ness *n* ταχύτης, ὀξύτης, σβελτάδα ‖ ~sand *n* κινητή ἄμμος ‖ ~step *n* (*music*) ταχύς ρυθμός ‖ ~-witted *a* ἀγχίνους, ξύπνιος, ἀτσίδα.
quid [kwid] *n* (*Brit col*: £1) λίρα ('Αγγλίας).
quiet ['kwaiət] *a* (*without noise*) σιωπηλός, σιγαλός, ἀθόρυβος ‖ (*still*) ἥρεμος, γαλήνιος, ἥσυχος ‖ (*peaceful*) ἥρεμος, ἀτάραχος ‖ *n* ἡσυχία, ἠρεμία ‖ ~en *vti* (*also* ~en down) (καθ)ἡσυχάζω, καλμάρω ‖ ~ly ad ἥρεμα, ἀπαλά, σιγαλά, σιωπηλά ‖ ~ness *n* ἠρεμία, γαλήνη, κάλμα.
quill [kwil] *n* (*pen*) πέννα ἀπό φτερό.

quilt [kwilt] *n* πάπλωμα, ἐφάπλωμα || ~**ing** *n* φοδράρισμα, καπιτονάρισμα.
quin [kwin] *n abbr of* quintuplet.
quince [kwins] *n* κυδώνι.
quinine [kwi'ni:n] *n* κινίνη.
quinquennial [kwiŋ'kweniəl] *a* πενταετής.
quinquennium [kwiŋ'kweniəm] *n* πενταετία.
quinsy ['kwinzi] *n* πυώδης ἀμυγδαλῖτις, πονόλαιμος.
quintet(te) [kwin'tet] *n* κουϊντέτο.
quintuplet [kwin'tju:plit] *n* πεντάδυμον.
quip [kwip] *n* εὐφυολόγημα, σκῶμα, σαρκασμός || *vi* εὐφυολογῶ.
quit [kwit] (*irreg v*) *vt* ἐγκαταλείπω, ἀναχωρῶ, φεύγω || *vi* (*give up*) παραιτοῦμαι, ἐγκαταλείπω.
quite [kwait] *ad* τελείως, ἐξ ὁλοκλήρου, ἐντελῶς || (*fairly*) μᾶλλον, πολύ || ~ (**so**)! σωστά!, σύμφωνοι!
quits [kwits] *ad* στά ἴσια, πάτσι.
quiver ['kwivə*] *vi* τρέμω, τρεμουλιάζω, πάλλομαι || *n* (*for arrows*) φαρέτρα, σαϊτοθήκη.
quiz [kwiz] *n* στραβοκοίταγμα || (*test*) προφορική ἐξέτασις || *vt* (*question*) ἐξετάζω || ~**zical** *a* αἰνιγματώδης, πειραχτικός, ἐρωτηματικός.
quoit [kwoit] *n* ἀμάδα.
quorum ['kwɔ:rəm] *n* ἀπαρτία.
quota ['kwəutə] *n* ἀνάλογον μερίδιον, μερίδα.
quotation [kwəu'teiʃən] *n* (*marks*) εἰσαγωγικά || (*from book*) χωρίον, ἀπόσπασμα || (*price*) τιμή, τιμολόγιον.
quote [kwəut] *n* (*quotation*) ἀπόσπασμα || *vti* (*price*) καθορίζω, δίνω τιμήν, προσφέρω τιμήν || (*cite*) παραθέτω, ἀναφέρω.
quotient ['kwəuʃənt] *n* πηλίκον.

R, r

rabbi ['ræbai] *n* ραββῖνος.
rabbit ['ræbit] *n* κουνέλι || ~ **hole** *n* φωλιά κουνελιοῦ, τρύπα || ~ **hutch** *n* κλουβί κουνελιοῦ.
rabble ['ræbl] *n* ὄχλος.
rabid ['ræbid] *a* (*fig*) μανιασμένος, ἀδιάλλακτος.
rabies ['reibi:z] *n* λύσσα.
race [reis] *n* (*people*) ράτσα, φυλή, γενιά || (*animals*) ράτσα || (*competition*) δρόμος, ἀγών δρόμου || (*rush*) βία, γρηγοράδα || *vt* κάνω ἀγών δρόμου || *vi* τρέχω || (*compete*) συναγωνίζομαι || ~**course** *n* (*for horses*) ἱππόδρομος || ~**horse** *n* ἵππος ἀγώνων || ~ **meeting** *n* (*for horses*) ἱπποδρομία || ~ **relations** *npl* φυλετικές σχέσεις || ~**track** *n* (*for cars etc*) πίστα (ἀγώνων).
racial ['reiʃəl] *a* φυλετικός || ~ **discrimination** *n* φυλετική διάκρισις || ~**ism** *n* φυλετισμός, ρα(τ)σισμός || ~**ist** *a* ρα(τ)σιστικός || *n* ὀπαδός τοῦ ρα(τ)σισμοῦ.
racing ['reisiŋ] *n* ἀγῶνες, συμμετοχή εἰς ἀγῶνες || ~ **car** *n* αὐτοκίνητον ἀγώνων || ~ **driver** *n* ὀδηγός αὐτοκινήτου ἀγώνων.
racist ['reisist] *a* ρατσιστής.
rack [ræk] *n* (*clothes etc*) κρεμάστρα || *vt* βασανίζω || ~ **and ruin** καταστροφή, κατά διαβόλου.
racket ['rækit] *n* θόρυβος, φασαρία, πατιρντί || (*dishonest scheme*) κομπίνα || λοβιτούρα || (*for tennis*) ρακέττα.
racquet ['rækit] *n* ρακέττα.
racy ['reisi] *a* (*spirited*) ζωηρός, κεφάτος.
radar ['reidə:*] *n* ραδιοεντοπισμός, ραντάρ.
radiance ['reidiəns] *n* ἀκτινοβολία, λάμψις.
radiant ['reidiənt] *a* λαμπερός || (*giving out rays*) ἀκτινοβόλος.
radiate ['reidieit] *vt* (*of heat*) ἀκτινοβολῶ, ἐκπέμπω || *vi* (*lines*) ἐκτείνω ἀκτινοειδῶς.
radiation [reidi'eiʃən] *n* ἀκτινοβολία.
radiator ['reidieitə*] *n* σῶμα καλοριφέρ || (*aut*) ψυγεῖον || ~ **cap** *n* πῶμα τοῦ ψυγείου.
radical ['rædikəl] *a* ριζικός || (*pol*) ριζοσπαστικός || ~**ly** *ad* ριζικῶς.
radio ['reidiəu] *n* ἀσύρματος || (*set*) ραδιόφωνον || ~**active** *a* ραδιενεργός || ~**activity** *n* ραδιενέργεια || ~**grapher** *n* ἀκτινογράφος || ~**graphy** *n* ραδιογραφία, ἀκτινογραφία || ~ **station** *n* σταθμός ραδιοφώνου || ~**telephone** *n* ἀσύρματον τηλέφωνον || ~ **telescope** *n* ἀσύρματον τηλεσκόπιον || ~**therapist** *n* ἀκτινολόγος ἰατρός.
radish ['rædiʃ] *n* ρεπανάκι.
radium ['reidiəm] *n* ράδιον.
radius ['reidiəs] *n* ἀκτίς.
raffia ['ræfiə] *n* ραφία.
raffish ['ræfiʃ] *a* (ψευτο)παλληκαράς, ἀνυπόληπτος.
raffle ['ræfl] *n* λαχεῖον, λοταρία.
raft [ra:ft] *n* σχεδία, σάλι.
rafter ['ra:ftə*] *n* δοκάρι, καδρόνι.
rag [ræg] *n* (*of cloth*) ράκος, κουρέλι || (*col: newspaper*) ἐφημερίδα || *vt* κάνω φάρσα, κάνω καζούρα || ~**bag** *n* (*fig*) κακοντυμένη γυναίκα.
rage [reidʒ] *n* (*fury*) λύσσα, μανία, ἔξαψις || (*fashion*) μανία, τῆς μόδας || *vi* (*person*) μαίνομαι, εἶμαι ἔξω φρενῶν || (*storm*) μαίνομαι, εἶμαι ἀγριεμένος.
ragged ['rægid] *a* (*edge*) τραχύς, ἀπότομος.
raging ['reidʒiŋ] *a* μαινόμενος, ἀγριεμένος.
raid [reid] *n* (*mil*) ἐπιδρομή, εἰσβολή, αἰφνιδιασμός || (*criminal*) ἐπιδρομή, γιουρούσι || (*by police*) ἐπιδρομή, μπλόκος || *vt* εἰσβάλλω εἰς, κάνω μπλόκο || ~**er** *n* ἐπιδρομεύς.
rail [reil] *n* (*on stair*) κάγκελο, κιγκλίδωμα || (*of ship*) σταθμίς, δρύφρακτον || (*rail*)

σιδηροτροχιά, γραμμή || ~s npl (rail) τροχιά, γραμμές || by ~ σιδηροδρομικῶς, μέ τραῖνο || ~ing(s) n(pl) κάγκελλα, φράχτης || ~road n (US), ~way n (Brit) σιδηρόδρομος, σιδηροδρομική γραμμή || ~road or ~way station n σιδηροδρομικός σταθμός.

rain [rein] n βροχή || vti βρέχω || πέφτω σάν βροχή || **the ~s** npl (ἐποχή) τῶν βροχῶν || ~bow n οὐράνιον τόξον || ~coat n ἀδιάβροχο || ~drop n σταγόνα βροχῆς, σταλαματιά || ~fall n βροχόπτωσις || ~storm n καταιγίδα, κατακλυσμός || ~y a (region) βροχερή (περιοχή) || (day) βροχερή (ἡμέρα) || (fig) ὥρα ἀνάγκης || (season) ἐποχή τῶν βροχῶν.

raise [reiz] n (esp US: increase) αὔξησις (μισθοῦ) || vt (build) (ἀν)ἐγείρω, στήνω || (lift) σηκώνω, ὑψώνω, ἀνεβάζω || (a question) προβάλλω, θέτω || (doubts) ἐγείρω, προκαλῶ, γεννῶ || (collect) ἐξευρίσκω, μαζεύω, συλλέγω || (bring up) ἀνατρέφω, τρέφω.

raisin ['reizn] n σταφίδα.

rake [reik] n τσουγκράνα || (dissolute person) ἔκλυτος, ἀκόλαστος || vt (agr) μαζεύω μέ τσουγκράνα, σκαλίζω || (with shot) καταπυροβολῶ, πλευροκοπῶ || (search keenly) ἐξετάζω, ἐρευνῶ || to ~ in, together etc vt μαζεύω.

rakish ['reikiʃ] a κομψός, ἐπιδεικτικός.

rally ['ræli] n (pol etc) συγκέντρωσις, συναγερμός || (aut) ράλλυ || (improvement) ἀνάκτησις, βελτίωσις || vt συναθροίζω, συγκεντρώνω, συνάζω || vi (health) συνέρχομαι, ἀναρρωνύω || to ~ round vti συσπειρόμαι.

ram [ræm] n κριάρι || (beam) ἔμβολον, κριός || vt ἐμβολίζω, μπήζω, κτυπῶ || (stuff) παραγεμίζω, χώνω.

ramble ['ræmbl] n περίπατος, περιπλάνησις || vi κάνω βόλτες, περιφέρομαι || (be delirious) μιλῶ ἀσυνάρτητα || ~r n πλάνης, σουλατσαδόρος || (plant) ἀναρριχόμενη τριανταφυλλιά.

rambling ['ræmbliŋ] a (plant) ἀναρρηχιτικός, ἕρπων || (speech) ἀσύνδετος, ἀσυνάρτητος.

ramification [ræmifi'keiʃən] n διακλάδωσις.

ramp [ræmp] n (incline) κλιτύς, πρανές, ἀνωφέρεια.

rampage [ræm'peidʒ] n: to be on the ~ vi (also ~) τά βάζω μέ ὅλο τόν κόσμο.

rampant ['ræmpənt] a (unchecked) ἀχαλίνωτος, ἐξαπλωμένος || (on hind legs) ὄρθιος, συσπειρώμενος.

rampart ['ræmpɑ:t] n ἔπαλξις, προμαχών, ντάπια.

ramshackle ['ræmʃækl] a ἑτοιμόρροπος, ἐρειπωμένος, ρημάδι.

ran [ræn] pt of run.

ranch [rɑ:ntʃ] n ἀγρόκτημα, ράντσο || ~er n κτηματίας || ἐργάτης σέ ράντσο.

rancid ['rænsid] a ταγγός, τσαγγός.

rancour, (US) **rancor** ['ræŋkə*] n μνησικακία, ἔχθρα.

random ['rændəm] a τυχαῖος || n: at ~ στήν τύχη, στά κουτουροῦ.

randy ['rændi] a (lustful) ἀσελγής, λάγνος.

rang [ræŋ] pt of ring.

range [reindʒ] n (row, line) σειρά, ὀροσειρά || (extent, series) ἔκτασις, σειρά, περιοχή || (of gun) βεληνεκές, ἐμβέλεια || (for shooting) πεδίον βολῆς, σκοπευτήριον || (cooking stove) κουζίνα, μαγειρική συσκευή || vt παρατάσσω, βάζω στή σειρά || (roam) περιπλανῶμαι, περιφέρομαι || vi (extend) ἐκτείνομαι, ἁπλώνομαι || ~r n (of forest) δασάρχης, δασονόμος.

rank [ræŋk] n (row, line) στοῖχος, γραμμή || (social position) (κοινωνική) τάξις || (high position) ἀνωτέρα θέσις, βαθμός || vi (of place) κατατάσσομαι, ἔρχομαι || a (strong-smelling) κάκοσμος, τσαγγός || (extreme) πλήρης, τέλειος, ἀπόλυτος || **the ~** npl (mil) οἱ στρατιῶτες, φαντάροι || **the ~ and file** (fig) ὁ ἁπλός λαός.

rankle ['ræŋkl] vi (cause pain) μένω στό μυαλό, μένω στήν καρδιά.

ransack ['rænsæk] vt λεηλατῶ, κάνω ἄνω κάτω, ψάχνω καλά.

ransom ['rænsəm] n λύτρα || **to hold s.o. to ~** ζητῶ λύτρα, χαρατσώνω (κάποιον).

rant [rænt] vi φωνασκῶ, οὐρλιάζω || ~ing n στόμφος, φωνασκία.

rap [ræp] n κτύπημα, κτύπος, κρότος || vt κρούω, κτυπῶ.

rape [reip] n (lit) βιασμός || (fig) ἀπαγωγή, κλέψιμο || vt (woman) βιάζω.

rapid ['ræpid] a ταχύς, γρήγορος || ~s npl μικροί καταρράκτης || ~ity n ταχύτης || ~ly ad ταχέως, γρήγορα, γοργά.

rapist ['reipist] n (esp US) βιαστής.

rapport [ræ'pɔ:*] n (sympathy) συμπάθεια.

rapprochement [ræ'prɔʃmɑ̃:ŋ] n προσέγγισις.

rapt [ræpt] a ἐκστατικός, ἀπορροφημένος.

rapture ['ræptʃə*] n ἔκστασις, μεγάλη χαρά.

rapturous ['ræptʃərəs] a ἐκστατικός, ἐνθουσιώδης.

rare [rɛə*] a σπάνιος, ἀσυνήθης, ἀραιός || (especially good) θαυμάσιος, σπουδαῖος || (in cooking) μισοψημένος, σαινιάν || ~fied a (air, atmosphere) ἀραιός, ἀραιωμένος || ~ly ad σπάνια, σπανίως.

rarity ['rɛəriti] n σπάνιον πρᾶγμα || (scarcity) σπανιότης.

rascal ['rɑ:skəl] n παλιάνθρωπος, μασκαράς, μαγκάκι.

rash [ræʃ] a παράτολμος, ἀπερίσκεπτος || n ἐξάνθημα.

rasher ['ræʃə*] n ψιλή φέτα μπέϊκον.

rashly ['ræʃli] ad ἀπερίσκεπτα, ἀσυλλόγιστα.

R

rashness ['ræʃnis] *n* ἀπερισκεψία, ἀμυαλιά.

raspberry ['ra:zbəri] *n* σμέουρο, φραμπουάζ, βατόμουρο.

rasping ['ra:spiŋ] *a* (*noise*) (ἠχος) λίμας, ὀξύς, στριγγιά.

rat [ræt] *n* (*animal*) ἀρουραῖος, ποντικός.

ratable ['reitəbl] *a*: ~ **value** φορολογήσιμον τεκμαρτὸν ἐνοίκιον (ἀκινήτου).

ratchet ['rætʃit] *n* ὄνυξ, ἀναστολεύς, καστάνια.

rate [reit] *n* (*proportion*) ἀναλογία, ἀνάλογον ποσόν, ἀνάλογος ἀριθμός ‖ (*price*) ποσοστόν, τόκος, ὕψος, τιμή ‖ (*speed*) ρυθμός, ταχύτης ‖ *vt* ἐκτιμῶ, ταξινομῶ ‖ ~**s** *npl* (*Brit*) τοπικός φόρος, εἰσφορά ‖ **at any** ~ ὁπωσδήποτε, ἐν πάσει περιπτώσει ‖ **at this** ~ ἔτσι ‖ ~ **of exchange** *n* τιμή συναλλάγματος ‖ ~**payer** *n* φορολογούμενος ‖ *see* **first**.

rather ['ra:ðə*] *ad* μᾶλλον (ἤ), καλύτερα (παρά) ‖ (*somewhat*) λίγο, κάπως, μᾶλλον, σχετικά.

ratification [rætifi'keiʃən] *n* (ἐπι)κύρωσις.

ratify ['rætifai] *vt* (ἐπι)κυρῶ, ἐγκρίνω.

rating ['reitiŋ] *n* (*classification*) ἐκτίμησις, τάξις ‖ (*naut*) μέλος πληρώματος, εἰδικότης.

ratio ['reiʃiəu] *n* λόγος, ἀναλογία.

ration ['ræʃən] *n* (*usually pl*) μερίς, σιτηρέσιον, τροφή ‖ *vt* περιορίζω, ἐπιβάλλω μερίδες.

rational ['ræʃənl] *a* λογικός ‖ ~**e** [ræʃə'na:l] *n* λογική ἐξήγησις, λογικὴ βάσις ‖ ~**ization** *n* ὀρθολογισμός ‖ ~**ize** *vt* ὀρθολογίζομαι, ὀργανώνω ὀρθολογικῶς ‖ ~**ly** *ad* λογικῶς, λογικά.

rationing ['ræʃəniŋ] *n* καθορισμός μερίδων, διανομή διὰ δελτίου.

rattle ['rætl] *n* κρότος, κροταλισμός ‖ (*toy*) ροκάνα, κρόταλον ‖ *vi* κροταλίζω, κροτῶ ‖ ~**snake** *n* κροταλίας.

raucous ['rɔ:kəs] *a* βραχνός ‖ ~**ly** *ad* βραχνά.

ravage ['rævidʒ] *vt* ἐρημώνω, ἀφανίζω, ρημάζω ‖ ~**s** *npl* (*of time etc*) φθορά τοῦ χρόνου.

rave [reiv] *vi* παραληρῶ, παραμιλῶ ‖ (*rage*) μαίνομαι, οὐρλιάζω.

raven ['reivn] *n* κόρακι, κόρακας.

ravenous ['rævənəs] *a* (*hungry*) πεινασμένος, λιμασμένος.

ravine [rə'vi:n] *n* φαράγγι.

raving ['reiviŋ] *a*: ~ **lunatic** μανιακός, παράφρων.

ravioli [rævi'əuli] *n* ραβιόλια.

ravish ['ræviʃ] *vt* ἀπάγω, κλέβω, βιάζω ‖ ~**ing** *a* γοητευτικός, μαγευτικός.

raw [rɔ:] *a* (*uncooked*) ὠμός, ἄψητος ‖ (*not manufactured*) ἀκατέργαστος ‖ (*tender*) εὐαίσθητος, ματωμένος ‖ (*inexperienced*) ἄξεστος, ἀτζαμής ‖ ~ **material** *n* πρῶτες ὕλες.

ray [rei] *n* ἀκτίς, ἀχτίδα.

rayon ['reiɔn] *n* ρεγιόν, τεχνητή μέταξα.

raze [reiz] *vt* ἰσοπεδώνω, κατεδαφίζω, γκρεμίζω.

razor ['reizə*] *n* ξυράφι ‖ ~ **blade** *n* ξυριστικὴ λεπίδα.

re- [ri:] *prefix* ἀντι-, ἀνά-, ξανά-.

reach [ri:tʃ] *n* ἔκτασις, ἅπλωμα, τέντωμα (χειρός) ‖ (*distance*) ἐντὸς βολῆς, κοντά, πλησίον ‖ *vt* (ἐκ)τείνω, ἀπλώνω, τεντώνω ‖ φθάνω, ἐγγίζω ‖ *vi* (ἐπ)ἐκτείνομαι ‖ **to** ~ **out** *vi* ἀπλώνω (τό χέρι).

react [ri:'ækt] *vi* ἀντιδρῶ ‖ ~**ion** *n* ἀντίδρασις ‖ ~**ionary** *a* ἀντιδραστικός ‖ ~**or** *n* ἀντιδραστήρ.

read [ri:d] (*irreg v*) *n* ἀνάγνωσις, διάβασμα ‖ *vti* διαβάζω, ἀναγιγνώσκω ‖ (*aloud*) διαβάζω δυνατά ‖ (*understand*) ἑρμηνεύω, δεικνύω ‖ (*find in book*) διαβάζεται ‖ ~**able** *a* ἀναγνώσιμος, ποὺ διαβάζεται ‖ ~**er** *n* ἀναγνώστης ‖ (*book*) ἀναγνωστικόν ‖ ~**ership** *n* (*of newspaper etc*) σύνολον ἀναγνωστῶν.

readily ['redili] *ad* πρόθυμα, ἀδίστακτα, εὔκολα.

readiness ['redinis] *n* προθυμία ‖ (*being ready*) ἑτοιμότης.

reading ['ri:diŋ] *n* ἀνάγνωσις, διάβασμα ‖ ~ **lamp** *n* λάμπα τοῦ τραπεζιοῦ ‖ ~ **room** *n* ἀναγνωστήριον.

readjust ['ri:ə'dʒʌst] *vt* ἀναπροσαρμόζω, διορθώνω, σιάζω ‖ ~**ment** *n* διόρθωσις, σιάξιμο.

ready ['redi] *a* ἕτοιμος ‖ (*willing*) πρόθυμος, διατεθειμένος ‖ (*condition*) ἕτοιμος, γινόμενος ‖ (*quick, facile*) ταχύς, γρήγορος, εὔκολος ‖ (*available*) πρόχειρος ‖ *ad* τελείως ‖ *n*: **at the** ~ ἕτοιμος νά ‖ ~**-made** *a* ἕτοιμος ‖ ~ **reckoner** *n* πίνακες λογιστικῶν ὑπολογισμῶν.

real [riəl] *a* πραγματικός, ἀληθινός ‖ ~ **estate** *n* ἀκίνητος περιουσία, οἰκόπεδα ‖ ~**ism** *n* πραγματισμός, ρεαλισμός ‖ ~**ist** *n* πραγματιστής, ρεαλιστής ‖ ~**istic** *a* ρεαλιστικός ‖ ~**istically** *ad* ρεαλιστικά ‖ ~**ity** [ri:'æliti] *n* πραγματικότης, ἀλήθεια ‖ **in** ~**ity** πράγματι, πραγματικά ‖ ~**ization** *n* κατανόησις, σαφὴς ἀντίληψις ‖ (*fulfilment*) πραγματοποίησις ‖ ~**ize** *vt* (*understand*) κατανοῶ, ἀνιλαμβάνομαι, καταλαβαίνω ‖ (*bring about*) πραγματοποιῶ ‖ ~**ly** *ad* πραγματικά, ἀληθινά, ὄχι δά.

realm [relm] *n* σφαίρα, δικαιοδοσία ‖ (*kingdom*) βασίλειον.

ream [ri:m] *n* δεσμίς χάρτου γραφῆς.

reap [ri:p] *vt* θερίζω ‖ (*harvest*) συγκομίζω, μαζεύω ‖ ~**er** *n* (*machine*) θεριστικὴ μηχανή.

reappear ['ri:ə'piə*] *vi* ἐπανεμφανίζομαι, ξαναφαίνομαι ‖ ~**ance** *n* ἐπανεμφάνισις, ἐπάνοδος.

reapply ['ri:ə'plai] *vi* (+ **to**, **for**) ξαναϋποβάλλω (αἴτησιν).

reappoint ['ri:ə'point] *vt* ἐπαναδιορίζω.

reappraisal ['ri:ə'preizəl] *n* ἐπανεκτίμησις.

rear [riə*] *a* ὀπίσθιος, πισινός ‖ *n* νῶτα, ὀπίσθια, ὀπισθοφυλακή ‖ *vt* (*bring up*) (ἀνα)τρέφω ‖ *vi* ἀνορθοῦμαι, σηκώνομαι σούζα ‖ **~-engined** *a* (*aut*) μέ μηχανή πίσω ‖ **~guard** *n* ὀπισθοφυλακή.

rearm ['ri'ɑ:m] *vti* ἐπανεξοπλίζω, ἐπανεξοπλίζομαι ‖ **~ament** *n* ἐπανεξοπλισμός.

rearrange ['ri:ə'reindʒ] *vt* τακτοποιῶ πάλιν, ξανασιάζω.

rear-view ['riəvju:] *a*: **~ mirror** κάτοπτρον ὁδηγήσεως.

reason ['ri:zn] *n* (*cause*) λόγος, αἰτία ‖ (*ability to think*) λογική, λογική ‖ (*judgment*) κρίσις ‖ *vi* σκέπτομαι, συλλογίζομαι, συμπεραίνω ‖ **~able** *a* λογικός, δίκαιος ‖ (*fair*) μετριοπαθής, μέτριος ‖ **~ably** *ad* λογικά ‖ **~ed** *a* (*argument*) αἰτιολογημένος, δικαιολογημένος ‖ **~ing** *n* συλλογισμός, ἐπιχειρήματα.

reassemble ['ri:ə'sembl] *vt* ξανασυγκεντρώνω, συγκαλῶ ἐκ νέου ‖ (*engine*) ξαναμοντάρω.

reassert ['ri:ə'sə:t] *vt* βεβαιῶ ἐκ νέου, ἐπιβεβαιῶ.

reassurance ['ri:ə'ʃuərəns] *n* ἐξασφάλισις, καθησύχασις, ἐνθάρρυνσις.

reassure ['ri:ə'ʃuə*] *vt* διαβεβαιώνω, ἀναθαρρύνω, καθησυχάζω.

reassuring ['ri:ə'ʃuəriŋ] *a* καθησυχαστικός, ἐνθαρρυντικός.

reawakening ['ri:ə'weikniŋ] *n* ἀφύπνισις, ξαναζωντάνεμα.

rebate ['ri:beit] *n* ἔκπτωσις.

rebel ['rebl] *n* ἀντάρτης, ἐπαναστάτης ‖ *a* ἐπαναστατημένος, ἀνταρτικός ‖ **~lion** [ri'beliən] *n* ἀνταρσία, ρεμπελιό ‖ **~lious** *a* ἀνταρτικός, ἀνυπότακτος.

rebirth ['ri:'bə:θ] *n* ἀναγέννησις.

rebound [ri'baund] *vi* ἀναπηδῶ ‖ ['ri:baund] *n* ἀναπήδησις.

rebuff [ri'bʌf] *n* ἀπόκρουσις, ἄρνησις ‖ *vt* ἀποκρούω, ἀρνοῦμαι.

rebuild ['ri:'bild] *vt* ἀνοικοδομῶ ‖ **~ing** *n* ἀνοικοδόμησις.

rebuke [ri'bju:k] *n* ἐπίπληξις, μομφή ‖ *vt* ἐπιπλήττω, ἐπιτιμῶ.

recalcitrant [ri'kælsitrənt] *a* ἀνυπάκουος, δυστροπῶν.

recall [ri'kɔ:l] *vt* (*call back*) ἀνακαλῶ ‖ (*remember*) ξαναθυμίζω, ξαναθυμᾶμε ‖ (*withdraw*) ἀνακαλῶ.

recant [ri'kænt] *vi* ἀνακαλῶ, ἀναιρῶ, ἀναθεωρῶ.

recap ['ri:kæp] *vti* ξαναβουλώνω.

recapture ['ri:'kæptʃə*] *vt* ἀνακτῶ, ἀνακαταλαμβάνω, ξαναπαίρνω.

recede [ri'si:d] *vi* ἀποσύρομαι, ὑποχωρῶ, τραβιέμαι.

receipt [ri'si:t] *n* ἀπόδειξις παραλαβῆς ‖

(*receiving*) λῆψις, παραλαβή ‖ **~s** *npl* εἰσπράξεις, ἔσοδα.

receive [ri'si:v] *vt* λαμβάνω ‖ (*welcome*) (ὑπο)δέχομαι ‖ **~r** *n* (*tel*) ἀκουστικόν.

recent ['ri:snt] *a* πρόσφατος, νέος ‖ **~ly** *ad* προσφάτως, πρόσφατα.

receptacle [ri'septəkl] *n* δοχεῖον.

reception [ri'sepʃən] *n* (*welcome*) ὑποδοχή ‖ (*party*) δεξίωσις ‖ (*at hotel etc*) γραφεῖον ὑποδοχῆς ‖ **~ist** *n* ὑπάλληλος ἐπί τῆς ὑποδοχῆς.

receptive [ri'septiv] *a* (ἐπι)δεικτικός.

recess [ri'ses] *n* (*interval*) διακοπή, διάλειμμα ‖ (*in wall*) κοίλωμα, ἐσοχή, βαθούλωμα ‖ (*inner place*) μυχός, μυστικόν μέρος.

recharge ['ri:'tʃɑ:dʒ] *vt* (*battery*) ἀναφορτίζω, ξαναγεμίζω.

recipe ['resipi] *n* συνταγή.

recipient [ri'sipiənt] *n* δέκτης, λήπτης, παραλήπτης.

reciprocal [ri'siprəkəl] *a* ἀμοιβαῖος, ἀντίστροφος.

reciprocate [ri'siprəkeit] *vt* ἀνταποδίδω, ἐναλλάσσω.

recital [ri'saitl] *n* (*mus*) ρεσιτάλ.

recitation [resi'teiʃən] *n* ἀπαγγελία.

recite [ri'sait] *vt* ἀπαγγέλλω, ἀποστηθίζω ‖ (*tell one by one*) ἐξιστορῶ, ἀπαριθμῶ.

reckless ['reklis] *a* ἀδιάφορος, ἀπρόσεκτος, ἀπερίσκεπτος ‖ **~ly** *ad* ἀπερισκέπτως, παράτολμα ‖ **~ness** *n* τολμηρότης, ἀπερισκεψία.

reckon ['rekən] *vt* (*count*) ὑπολογίζω, λογαριάζω, μετρῶ ‖ (*consider*) ἐκτιμῶ, λογαριάζω ‖ *vi* στηρίζομαι, ὑπολογίζω **to ~ on** *vt* στηρίζομαι σέ, ὑπολογίζω ‖ **~ing** *n* ὑπολογισμός.

reclaim [ri'kleim] *vt* (*land*) ἐκχερσώνω, ἀποξηραίνω.

reclamation [reklə'meiʃən] *n* ἐγγειοβελτίωσις, ἀποξήρανσις.

recline [ri'klain] *vi* ξαπλώνω, πλαγιάζω, ἀκουμπῶ.

reclining [ri'klainiŋ] *a* πλαγιαστός, ξαπλωμένος, κεκλιμένος.

recluse [ri'klu:s] *n* ἐρημίτης.

recognition [rekəg'niʃən] *n* ἀναγνώρισις.

recognizable ['rekəgnaizəbl] *a* ἀναγνωρίσιμος.

recognize ['rekəgnaiz] *vt* ἀναγνωρίζω ‖ (*admit*) ὁμολογῶ, παραδέχομαι.

recoil [ri'kɔil] *n* ἀναπήδησις, ὀπισθοδρόμησις ‖ *vi* ἀποστρέφομαι, μαζεύομαι, ἐξανίσταμαι ‖ ἀναπηδῶ, ὀπισθοδρομῶ, κλωτσῶ.

recollect [rekə'lekt] *vt* ἐνθυμοῦμαι, ἀναπολῶ ‖ **~ion** *n* ἀνάμνησις, μνημονικόν.

recommend [rekə'mend] *vt* συνιστῶ, ἐμπιστεύομαι ‖ **~ation** *n* (*advice*) σύστασις ‖ προσόν.

recompense ['rekəmpens] *n* (ἀντ)ἀμοιβή,

ἀποζημίωσις ‖ *vt* ἀνταμείβω, ἀποζημιώνω.

reconcilable ['rekənsailəbl] *a* εὐσυμβίβαστος, διαλλακτικός.

reconcile ['rekənsail] *vt* (*make agree*) συμβιβάζω ‖ (*make friendly*) συμφιλιώνω.

reconciliation [rekənsili'eiʃən] *n* συμφιλίωσις, συμβιβασμός.

reconditioned ['ri:kən'diʃənd] *a* ἐπισκευασμένος, ἀνακαινισθείς.

reconnaissance [ri'kɔnisəns] *n* κατόπτευσις, ἀναγνώρισις, ἐξερεύνησις.

reconnoitre, (*US*) **reconnoiter** [rekə'nɔitə*] *vti* κατοπτεύω, ἀναγνωρίζω, ἐξερευνῶ.

reconsider ['ri:kən'sidə*] *vti* ἀναθεωρῶ, ἐπανεξετάζω.

reconstitute ['ri:'kɔnstitju:t] *vt* ἀναπαριστῶ.

reconstruct ['ri:kən'strʌkt] *vt* ἀνοικοδομῶ, ἀνασυγκροτῶ ‖ **~ion** *n* ἀνοικοδόμησις, ἀνασυγκρότησις.

record ['rekɔːd] *n* ἀναγραφή, καταγραφή, σημείωσις ‖ (*disc*) δίσκος, πλάκα ‖ (*best performance*) πρωτάθλημα, ρεκόρ, ἐπίδοσις ‖ *a* (*time*) μέ μεγάλη ταχύτητα, σημειώνουσα ρεκόρ ‖ [ri'kɔːd] *vt* (*set down*) καταγράφω, ἀναγράφω ‖ (*music etc*) ἠχογραφῶ, ἐγγράφω ‖ **~ed** *a* (*music*) ἠχογραφημένος ‖ **~er** *n* μηχάνημα ἐγγραφῆς, μαγνητόγραφο ‖ **~ holder** *n* (*sport*) πρωταθλητής ‖ **~ing** *n* (*music*) ἠχογράφησις ‖ **~ player** *n* πικάπ.

recount ['ri:kaunt] *n* νέα καταμέτρησις ‖ [ri'kaunt] *vt* ξαναμετρῶ ‖ (*tell in detail*) ἀφηγοῦμαι, ἐξιστορῶ.

recoup [ri'ku:p] *vt* ἀποζημιώνω, ξαναπέρνω.

recourse [ri'kɔːs] *n* καταφύγιον, ἔκκλησις.

recover [ri'kʌvə*] *vt* (ἐπ)ανακτῶ, ξαναβρίσκω ‖ *vi* ἀνακτῶ (τήν ὑγείαν μου), θεραπεύομαι ‖ **~y** *n* ἀνάκτησις, ἀνεύρεσις, βρέσιμο ‖ ἀνάρρωσις.

recreate ['ri:krieit] *vt* διασκεδάζω.

recreation [rekri'eiʃən] *n* ἀναψυχή, διασκέδασις ‖ **~al** *a* διασκεδαστικός.

recrimination [rikrimi'neiʃən] *n* ἀντέγκλησις, ἀντικατηγορία.

recruit [ri'kru:t] *n* νεοσύλλεκτος ‖ *vt* στρατολογῶ ‖ **~ing office** *n* γραφεῖον στρατολογικόν ‖ **~ment** *n* στρατολογία.

rectangle ['rektæŋgl] *n* ὀρθογώνιον.

rectangular [rek'tæŋgjulə*] *a* ὀρθογώνιος.

rectify ['rektifai] *vt* ἐπανορθώνω, διορθώνω.

rectory ['rektəri] *n* (*eccl*) πρεσβυτέριον, ἐφημερεῖον.

recuperate [ri'ku:pəreit] *vi* ἀναλαμβάνω, ἀναρρωνύω.

recur [ri'kə:*] *vi* ἐπανέρχομαι, συμβαίνω πάλιν ‖ **~ rence** *n* ἐπανάληψις ‖ **~ rent** *a* περιοδικός, ἐπαναλαμβανόμενος.

red [red] *n* (*colour*) κόκκινο ‖ (*Communist*) κομμουνιστής, ἀριστερός ‖ *a* κόκκινος, ἐρυθρός ‖ **in the ~** ἔλλειμα ‖ **R~ Cross**

n 'Ερυθρός Σταυρός ‖ **~den** *vti* κοκκινίζω ‖ **~dish** *a* κοκκινωπός.

redecorate ['ri:'dekəreit] *vt* κάνω καινούργια διακόσμησι.

redecoration ['ri:dekə'reiʃən] *n* καινούργια διακόσμησις.

redeeming [ri'di:miŋ] *a* (*virtue, feature*) ἀντισταθμίζων, καλύπτων.

red-haired ['red'hεəd] *a* κοκκινομάλλης.

red-handed ['red'hændid] *a* ἐπ' αὐτοφώρω, στά πράσα.

redhead ['redhed] *n* κοκκινομάλλα.

red herring ['red'heriŋ] *n* (*fig*) ξεγέλασμα, ἀλλαγή κουβέντας.

red-hot ['red'hɔt] *a* ἐρυθροπυρωμένος ‖ (*fig*) φανατικός, ἔνθερμος.

redirect ['ri:dai'rekt] *vt* (*mail*) ἀπευθύνω εἰς νέαν διεύθυνσιν.

rediscovery ['ri:dis'kʌvəri] *n* ἐκ νέου ἀνακάλυψις.

redistribute ['ri:dis'tribju:t] *vt* ἀνακατανέμω.

red-letter ['red'letə*] *a:* **~ day** ἡμέρα εὐτυχῶν γεγονότων, ἀξιομνημόνευτος ἡμέρα.

redness ['rednis] *n* κοκκινίλα ‖ κοκκινάδα.

redo ['ri:'du:] *vt* ξανακάνω.

redouble [ri:'dʌbl] *vt* (ἀνα)διπλασιάζω.

red tape ['red'teip] *n* γραφειοκρατία.

reduce [ri'dju:s] *vt* (*decrease*) ἐλαττώνω, μικραίνω, περιορίζω, ἀδυνατίζω ‖ (*lower*) ὑποβιβάζω, κατεβάζω ‖ (*change state*) μεταβάλλω, σχηματίζω, ἁπλοποιῶ ‖ **~d** *a* (*price*) μειωμένη (τιμή).

reduction [ri'dʌkʃən] *n* ἐλάττωσις, σμίκρυνσις ‖ (*in price*) ἔκπτωσις.

redundancy [ri'dʌndənsi] *n* περίσσεια, πλεόνασμα.

redundant [ri'dʌndənt] *a* πλεονάζων, περιττός.

reed [ri:d] *n* καλάμι ‖ (*of clarinet etc*) γλωττίς, γλωσσίδι.

reef [ri:f] *n* (*at sea*) ὕφαλος, ξέρα.

reek [ri:k] *vi* ἀναδίδω κακήν ὀσμήν, βρωμάω.

reel [ri:l] *n* (*for rope*) ἀνέμη ‖ (*for cotton, film etc*) πηνίον, καρούλι, μασούρι ‖ (*dance*) ζωηρός (σκωτικός) χορός ‖ *vt* τυλίγω ‖ (*stagger*) τρικλίζω, ζαλίζομαι.

re-election ['ri:i'lekʃən] *n* ἐπανεκλογή.

re-engage ['ri:in'geidʒ] *vt* ξανασυμπλέκω ‖ ἀναπροσλαμβάνω.

re-enter ['ri:'entə*] *vi* ξαναμπαίνω.

re-entry ['ri:'entri] *n* ἐπάνοδος, ξαναμπάσιμο.

re-examine ['ri:ig'zæmin] *vt* ἐπανεξετάζω.

re-export ['ri:'ekspɔ:t] *vt* ἐπανεξάγω.

ref [ref] *n* (*col: abbr of* referee) διαιτητής.

refectory [ri'fektəri] *n* τραπεζαρία (μοναστηρίου).

refer [ri'fə:*] *vt* παραπέμπω ‖ **to ~ to** *vt* ἀναφέρομαι εἰς ‖ συμβουλεύομαι.

referee [refə'ri:] *n* διαιτητής ‖ (*for job*

application) ὑπέγγυος, ἐγγυητής ‖ *vt* (*sport*) διαιτητεύω.

reference ['refrəns] *n* ἀναφορά ‖ (*in book etc*) παραπομπή ‖ (*of character*) πιστοποιητικόν, σύστασις ‖ (*person referred to*) ὁ δίδων τήν σύστασιν, ὁ ἐγγυητής ‖ (*allusion*) μνεία, ὑπαινιγμός ‖ ~ **book** *n* βιβλίον ὁδηγός, σύμβουλος.

referendum [refə'rendəm] *n* δημοψήφισμα.

refill ['ri:fil] *n* (*for pen etc*) ἀνταλλακτικόν.

refine [ri'fain] *vt* καθαρίζω, διυλίζω, ραφινάρω ‖ (*make finer*) ἐκλεπτύνω, ἐξευγενίζω ‖ ~**d** *a* (*person*) λεπτός, καλλιεργημένος ‖ ~**ment** *n* ἐξευγενισμός, λεπτή διάκρισις ‖ ~**ry** *n* διϋλιστήριον.

reflect [ri'flekt] *vt* ἀντανακλῶ ‖ *vi* (*meditate*) σκέπτομαι, συλλογίζομαι, μελετῶ ‖ ~**ion** *n* (ἀντ)ανάκλασις ‖ (*thought*) σκέψις ‖ ~**or** *n* ἀνακλαστήρ, ἀνταυγαστής, κάτοπτρον.

reflex ['ri:fleks] *a* (*involuntary*) (ἀντ)ανακλαστικός ‖ ~**ive** *a* (*gram*) αὐτοπαθής.

reform [ri'fɔ:m] *n* μεταρρύθμισις, ἀποκατάστασις, ἀνασχηματισμός ‖ *vt* μεταρρυθμίζω, σχηματίζω ἐκ νέου, ἀποκαθιστῶ, ἀναμορφώνω ‖ **the R~ation** *n* ἡ Μεταρρύθμισις ‖ ~**er** *n* ἀναμορφωτής, μεταρρυθμιστής.

refrain [ri'frein] *vi* (+ *from*) ἀπέχω, συγκρατοῦμαι.

refresh [ri'freʃ] *vt* ἀναζωογονῶ, δροσίζω, ἐνθυμίζω ‖ ~**er course** *n* ἐπανάληψις, μετεκπαίδευσις ‖ ~**ing** *a* ἀναψυκτικός, ἀναζωογονητικός, δροσιστικός ‖ ~**ments** *npl* (*food, drink*) ἀναψυκτικά.

refrigeration [rifridʒə'reiʃən] *n* (κατά)ψυξις.

refrigerator [ri'fridʒəreitə*] *n* ψυγεῖον.

refuel [ri:'fjuəl] *vti* ἀνεφοδιάζομαι (μέ καύσιμα) ‖ ~**ling** *n* ἀνεφοδιασμός εἰς καύσιμα.

refuge ['refju:dʒ] *n* καταφύγιον, καταφυγή, προστασία ‖ ~**e** [refju'dʒi:] *n* πρόσφυγας.

refund ['ri:fʌnd] *n* ἐπιστροφή, ἀπόδοσις ‖ [ri'fʌnd] *vt* ἐπιστρέφω (χρήματα).

refurbish ['ri:'fə:biʃ] *vt* (*decorate*) ἀνακαινίζω, φρεσκάρω.

refurnish ['ri:'fə:niʃ] *vt* ἐπιπλώνω ἐκ νέου.

refusal [ri'fju:zəl] *n* ἄρνησις, ἀποποίησις.

refuse ['refju:s] *n* ἀπορρίματα, σκουπίδια ‖ [ri'fju:z] *vti* ἀρνοῦμαι, ἀποποιοῦμαι, ἀπορρίπτω.

refute [ri'fju:t] *vt* ἀνασκευάζω, ἀνατρέπω.

regain [ri'gein] *vt* ἐπανακτῶ.

regal ['ri:gəl] *a* βασιλικός ‖ ~**ia** [ri'geiliə] *n* (*royal*) βασιλικά κειμήλια.

regard [ri'ga:d] *n* (*respect*) ἐκτίμησις, σεβασμός ‖ *vt* (*consider*) θεωρῶ ‖ ~**s** *npl* (*greetings*) χαιρετισμοί, χαιρετίσματα ‖ ~**ing, as** ~**s** ὅσον ἀφορᾶ, σχετικῶς μέ ‖ **as** ~**s, with** ~ **to** ὡς πρός, ὅσο γιά ‖

~**less** *a* (+ *of*) ἀδιάφορος, ἀψήφῶν ‖ *ad* ἀδιάφορος, ἀδιαφορόντας.

regatta [ri'gætə] *n* λεμβοδρομία.

regency ['ri:dʒənsi] *n* ἀντιβασιλεία.

regent ['ri:dʒənt] *n* ἀντιβασιλεύς.

régime [rei'ʒi:m] *n* καθεστώς.

regiment ['redʒimənt] *n* σύνταγμα ‖ ~**al** *a* τοῦ συντάγματος ‖ ~**ation** *n* ὀργάνωσις εἰς πειθαρχημένα τμήματα.

region ['ri:dʒən] *n* περιοχή ‖ ~**al** *a* τοπικός, περιφερειακός ‖ ~**al development** *n* περιφερειακή ἀνάπτυξις.

register ['redʒistə*] *n* κατάλογος, ληξιαρχικόν βιβλίον, μητρῶον ‖ *vt* καταγράφω, ἐγγράφω ‖ (*write down*) σημειώνω ‖ *vi* (*at hotel*) ἐγγράφομαι ‖ (*make impression*) δεικνύω ‖ ~**ed** *a* (*design*) κατατεθειμένον ‖ (*letter*) συστημένον γράμμα.

registrar [redʒis'tra:*] *n* ληξίαρχος, γραμματεύς.

registration [redʒis'treiʃən] *n* (*act*) καταγραφή, ἐγγραφή ‖ (*number*) ἀριθμός ἐγγραφῆς.

registry ['redʒistri] *n* ληξιαρχεῖον ‖ ~ **office** *n* (*for civil marriage*) ληξιαρχεῖον.

regret [ri'gret] *n* λύπη, μετάνοια ‖ *vt* λυποῦμαι, μετανοῶ ‖ ~**fully** *ad* μέ λύπη, μέ πόνον ‖ ~**table** *a* ἀξιοθρήνητος, ἀξιολύπητος, λυπηρός.

regroup ['ri:'gru:p] *vti* ἀνασυγκροτῶ, ἀνακατατάσσω.

regular ['regjulə*] *a* τακτικός, κανονικός, συνήθης ‖ (*not varying*) ὁμαλός ‖ *n* (*client etc*) τακτικός (πελάτης) ‖ ~**ity** *n* κανονικότης, ὁμαλότης ‖ ~**ly** *ad* τακτικά, κανονικά.

regulate ['regjuleit] *vt* κανονίζω, τακτοποιῶ, ρυθμίζω.

regulation [regju'leiʃən] *n* (δια)κανονισμός ‖ (*control*) ρύθμισις.

rehabilitation ['ri:əbili'teiʃən] *n* ἀποκατάστασις, παλινόρθωσις.

rehash ['ri:'hæʃ] *vt* (*col*) ξαναδουλεύω, διασκευάζω.

rehearsal [ri'hə:səl] *n* δοκιμή, πρόβα.

rehearse [ri'hə:s] *vt* (*practise*) κάνω δοκιμές, προβάρω.

reign [rein] *n* (*period*) βασιλεία ‖ *vi* βασιλεύω, ἄρχω ‖ ~**ing** *a* (*monarch*) βασιλεύων ‖ (*champion*) ἐπικρατῶν.

reimburse [ri:im'bə:s] *vt* ἐπιστρέφω (χρήματα), ἀποζημιώνω.

rein [rein] *n* ἡνία, χαλινός.

reindeer ['reindiə*] *n* τάρανδος.

reinforce [ri:in'fɔ:s] *vt* ἐνισχύω, δυναμώνω ‖ ~**d** *a* (*concrete*) ὡπλισμένον σκυροκονίαμα, μπετόν ἁρμέ ‖ ~**ment** *n* ἐνίσχυσις ‖ ~**ments** *npl* (*mil*) ἐνισχύσεις.

reinstate ['ri:in'steit] *vt* παλινορθῶ, ἀποκαθιστῶ, ἐπανεγκαθιστῶ.

reissue ['ri:'iʃju:] *vt* ἐπανεκδίδω.

reiterate [ri:'itəreit] *vt* ἐπαναλαμβάνω.

reject [ri'dʒekt] *vt* ἀπορρίπτω, ἀποκρούω ‖ ['riːdʒekt] *n* ἀπόρριμα, σκάρτο ‖ ~**ion** *n* ἀπόρριψις.

rejoice [ri'dʒɔis] *vi* χαίρομαι, χαίρω.

relapse [ri'læps] *n* ὑποτροπή.

relate [ri'leit] *vt* διηγοῦμαι, ἐξιστορῶ ‖ (*connect*) συσχετίζω ‖ ~**d** *a* (*subjects*) σχετιζόμενος, σχετικῶς μέ ‖ (*people*) (+ *to*) συγγενής.

relating [ri'leitiŋ] *prep*: ~ **to** σχετικός μέ, ἀφορῶν (εἰς).

relation [ri'leiʃən] *n* (*of family*) συγγενής ‖ (*connection*) σχέσις, συγγένεια ‖ ~**ship** *n* συγγένεια, σχέσις.

relative ['relətiv] *n* συγγενής ‖ *a* ἀναφορικός, σχετικός ‖ ~**ly** *ad* σχετικά ‖ ~ **pronoun** *n* ἀναφορική ἀντωνυμία.

relax [ri'læks] *vi* χαλαρώνω, λασκάρω ‖ (*rest*) ἀνακουφίζω ‖ *vt* χαλαρούμαι, ἀναπαύομαι, ξεκουράζομαι ‖ ~**ation** *n* ἀναψυχή, διασκέδασις ‖ ~**ed** *a* χαλαρός, λάσκος ‖ ~**ing** *a* ξεκουραστικός. .

relay ['riːlei] *n* (*sport*) σκυταλοδρομία ‖ *vt* (*message*) ἀναμεταδίδω.

release [ri'liːs] *n* (*relief*) ἀπαλλαγή, ἀπόλυσις, ἀποφυλάκισις ‖ (*device*) διακόπτης ‖ *vt* ἀπελευθερώνω ‖ (*prisoner*) ἀπολύω, ἀποφυλακίζω ‖ (*grip*) χαλαρῶ, λασκάρω, ἀπεμπλέκω ‖ (*report*, *news*) θέτω εἰς κυκλοφορίαν, ἐπιτρέπω δημοσίευσιν.

relegate ['religeit] *vt* (*put down*) ὑποβιβάζω.

relent [ri'lent] *vi* κάμπτομαι, μαλακώνω ‖ ~**less** *a* ἀδιάλλακτος, ἀμείλικτος, ἀνηλεής ‖ ~**lessly** *ad* ἀλύπητα, σκληρά, ἀδιάκοπα.

relevance ['relɘvəns] *n* σχετικότης, ὀρθότης, καταλληλότης.

relevant ['relɘvənt] *a* σχετικός, ἔχων σχέσιν.

reliability [rilaiə'biliti] *n* ἀξιοπιστία.

reliable [ri'laiəbl] *a* ἀξιόπιστος.

reliably [ri'laiəbli] *ad* ἀσφαλῶς, σίγουρα.

reliance [ri'laiɘns] *n* ἐμπιστοσύνη, πεποίθησις.

relic ['relik] *n* ἀπομεινάρι, ἐνθύμιον ‖ (*of saint*) λείψανον.

relief [ri'liːf] *n* (*from pain etc*) ἀνακούφισις, ξελάφρωμα ‖ (*help*) περίθαλψις, βοήθεια, ἐνίσχυσις ‖ (*from duty*) ἀντικατάστασις, ἀλλαγή ‖ (*design*) ἀνάγλυφον ‖ (*distinctness*) προβολή, εὐδιακρισία.

relieve [ri'liːv] *vt* (*pain etc*) ἀνακουφίζω, ξελαφρώνω ‖ (*bring help*) βοηθῶ, περιθάλπω ‖ (*take place of*) ἀντικαθιστῶ, ἀπαλλάσσω ‖ **to** ~ **s.o. of sth** παίρνω, ἀπαλλάσσω.

religion [ri'lidʒən] *n* θρησκεία, θρήσκευμα.

religious [ri'lidʒəs] *a* θρησκευτικός, εὐσεβής ‖ ~**ly** *ad* μέ εὐσέβειαν ‖ μέ ἀκρίβειαν.

reline ['riː'lain] *vt* (*brakes*) ἐπενδύω ἐκ νέου.

relinquish [ri'liŋkwiʃ] *vt* παραιτοῦμαι, ἐγκαταλείπω.

relish ['reliʃ] *n* (*sauce*) καρύκευμα, σάλτσα ‖ *vt* ἀπολαμβάνω, τρώγω εὐχάριστα.

relive ['riː'liv] *vt* ξαναζῶ.

reload ['riː'ləud] *vt* ξαναγεμίζω.

reluctance [ri'lʌktəns] *n* ἀπροθυμία, ἀκουσιότης.

reluctant [ri'lʌktənt] *a* ἀπρόθυμος ‖ ~**ly** *ad* μέ τό ζόρι, μέ τό στανιό.

rely [ri'lai] **to** ~ **on** *vt* βασίζομαι, στηρίζομαι, ἐμπιστεύομαι.

remain [ri'mein] *vi* (*be left*) ἀπομένω, ἀπολείπομαι ‖ (*stay*) παραμένω, (δια)μένω ‖ ~**der** *n* ὑπόλοιπον ‖ ~**ing** *a* (ἀπο)μένων, ὑπόλοιπος ‖ ~**s** *npl* ὑπολείμματα, ἐρείπια, λείψανα.

remand [ri'maːnd] *n*: **on** ~ παραπομπή (κατηγορουμένου) ‖ *vt*: **to** ~ **in custody** προφυλακίζω.

remark [ri'maːk] *n* παρατήρησις, σημείωσις ‖ *vt* (*say*) λέγω ‖ (*notice*) παρατηρῶ ‖ ~**able** *a* ἀξιοσημείωτος, ἀσυνήθης ‖ ~**ably** *ad* ἀξιόλογα, ἐξαιρετικά.

remarry ['riː'mæri] *vi* ξαναπαντρεύομαι.

remedial [ri'miːdiəl] *a* θεραπευτικός.

remedy ['remədi] *n* θεραπεία, φάρμακον, γιατρικό ‖ *vt* θεραπεύω, διορθώνω.

remember [ri'membə*] *vt* ἐνθυμοῦμαι, θυμᾶμαι ‖ (*give regards*) δίνω χαιρετισμούς εἰς.

remembrance [ri'membrəns] *n* ἀνάμνησις, μνήμη.

remind [ri'maind] *vt* ὑπενθυμίζω, θυμίζω ‖ ~**er** *n* κάτι πού θυμίζει, ἐνθύμημα.

reminisce [remi'nis] *vi* ἀναπολῶ, ξαναθυμᾶμαι ‖ ~**nces** *npl* ἀναμνήσεις, ἀπομνημονεύματα ‖ ~**nt** *a* (+ *of*) πού θυμίζει κάτι, ἐνθυμίζων.

remission [ri'miʃən] *n* ἄφεσις, ἐλάττωσις ‖ (*release*) χάρις, μείωσις (ποινῆς).

remit [ri'mit] *vt* (*send money*) ἐμβάζω, μεταβιβάζω ‖ ~**tance** *n* ἔμβασμα (χρηματικόν).

remnant ['remnənt] *n* ὑπόλειμμα, λείψανον.

remorse [ri'mɔːs] *n* τύψις, μεταμέλεια ‖ ~**ful** *a* γεμάτος τύψεις, μετανοιωμένος ‖ ~**less** *a* ἄσπλαγχνος, ἀνηλεής ‖ ~**lessly** *ad* ἀλύπητα, ἄσπλαγχνα.

remote [ri'məut] *a* μακρυνός, ἀπομονωμένος, ἀπόμερος ‖ (*slight*) ἀμυδρός, ἐλαφρός, ἀόριστος ‖ ~ **control** *n* τηλερρυθμιστής ‖ ~**ly** *ad* ἀορίστως, μακρυά.

remould ['riː'məuld] *vt* (*tyre*) ξαναφορμάρω.

removable [ri'muːvəbl] *a* μεταθέσιμος, κινητός, φορητός.

removal [ri'muːvəl] *n* ἀφαίρεσις, βγάλσιμο, μετακόμισις, μετακίνησις ‖ (*from office*) ἀπόλυσις, ἀνάκλησις, ἔκπτωσις ‖ ~ **van** *n* φορτηγόν μετακομίσεως.

remove [ri'muːv] *vt* ἀφαιρῶ, βγάζω, μεταφέρω ‖ (*dismiss*) ἀπολύω, ἀπομακρύνω ‖

~r (*for paint etc*) ἐξαλειπτικόν μέσον ‖
~rs npl (*company*) ἑταιρεία μεταφορῶν οἰκοσκευῶν.
remuneration [rimju:nə'reiʃən] n ἀμοιβή, πληρωμή.
Renaissance [rə'nesā:ns] the ~ n ἡ 'Αναγέννησις.
rename ['ri:'neim] vt μετονομάζω.
rend [rend] (*irreg v*) vt σχίζω, ἀποσπῶ.
render ['rendə*] vt (*make*) καθιστῶ, κάνω ‖ (*translate*) μεταφράζω ‖ ~ing n (*mus*) ἑρμηνεία, ἀπόδοσις.
rendezvous ['rɔndivu:] n συνάντησις, ραντεβού.
renew [ri'nju:] vt (*make new*) ἀνανεώνω ‖ (*begin again*) ἀνασυνδέω, ξαναπιάνω ‖ (*negotiations*) ἐπαναλαμβάνω ‖ ~al n ἀνανέωσις, ἀνασύνδεσις.
renounce [ri'nauns] vt (*give up*) ἐγκαταλείπω, ἀποκηρύσσω ‖ (*disown*) ἀρνοῦμαι, ἀποποιοῦμαι.
renovate ['renəuveit] vt ἀνακαινίζω, ἐπισκευάζω.
renovation [renəu'veiʃən] n ἀνακαίνισις, ἐπισκευή.
renown [ri'naun] n φήμη ‖ ~ed a φημισμένος, ὀνομαστός.
rent [rent] n (*of dwelling*) ἐνοίκιον, μίσθωμα, νοίκι ‖ vt μισθώνω, ἐνοικιάζω ‖ (*aut etc*) ἐνοικιάζω (αὐτοκίνητον) ‖ ~al n μίσθωμα, νοίκι.
renunciation [rinʌnsi'eiʃən] n ἀπάρνησις.
reopen ['ri:'əupən] vt ξανανοίγω.
reorder ['ri:'ɔ:də*] vt κάνω νέαν παραγγελίαν.
reorganization ['ri:ɔ:gənai'zeiʃən] n ἀναδιοργάνωσις.
reorganize ['ri:'ɔ:gənaiz] vt ἀναδιοργανώνω.
rep [rep] n (*comm: representative*) ἀντιπρόσωπος ‖ (*theat: repertory*) ρεπερτόριο.
repair [ri'peə*] n ἐπισκευή, ἐπιδιόρθωσις ‖ (*good condition*) σὲ καλὴ κατάστασι ‖ vt ἐπισκευάζω, (ἐπι)διορθώνω ‖ ~ kit n σύνεργα ἐπισκευῆς ‖ ~man n ἐπισκευαστής, ἐπιδιορθωτής ‖ ~ shop n (*aut etc*) συνεργεῖον (αὐτοκινήτου).
repartee [repa:'ti:] n ἑτοιμολογία, (εὔστοχος) ἀπάντησις.
repay [ri:'pei] vt (*pay back*) ἀνταποδίδω ‖ (*money*) ξεπληρώνω ‖ ~ment n ἀνταπόδοσις.
repeal [ri'pi:l] n ἀνάκλησις, ἀκύρωσις ‖ vt ἀνακαλῶ, ἀκυρώνω.
repeat [ri'pi:t] n (*rad, TV*) ἐπανάληψις ‖ vt ἐπαναλαμβάνω ‖ ~edly ad ἐπανειλημμένως, πολλές φορές.
repel [ri'pel] vt ἀποκρούω, ἀπωθῶ ‖ ~lent a ἀποκρουστικός, ἀπωθητικός ‖ n: insect ~lent ἀπωθητικόν ἐντόμων.
repent [ri'pent] vi μετανοιώνω, μεταμελοῦμαι ‖ ~ance n μετάνοια, μεταμέλεια.

repercussion [ri:pə'kʌʃən] n (*effect*) ἀντίδρασις, ἀντίκτυπος.
repertoire ['repətwa:*] n δραματολόγιον, ρεπερτόριον.
repertory ['repətəri] n (*theat*) ρεπερτόριον.
repetition [repi'tiʃən] n ἐπανάληψις.
repetitive [ri'petitiv] a ἐπαναληπτικός.
replace [ri'pleis] vt ἀντικαθιστῶ ‖ (*put back*) ἐπαναθέτω ‖ ~ment n ἀντικατάστασις ‖ (*person*) ἀντικαταστάτης.
replenish [ri'pleniʃ] vt ξαναγεμίζω, συμπληρώνω.
replete [ri'pli:t] a γεμᾶτος, πλήρης, παραγεμισμένος.
replica ['replikə] n πανομοιότυπον, ἀντίγραφον ἔργου τέχνης.
reply [ri'plai] n ἀπάντησις ‖ vi ἀπαντῶ, ἀποκρίνομαι.
report [ri'pɔ:t] n (*account*) ἔκθεσις, ἐξιστόρησις, ἀναφορά ‖ (*bang*) κρότος, πυροβολισμός ‖ vt ἀναφέρω ‖ (*give account of*) ἐξιστορῶ ‖ (*news*) κάνω ρεπορτάζ ‖ vi (*make a report*) ἐκθέτω, ἀναφέρω, κάνω ἀναφορά ‖ (*present o.s.*) παρουσιάζομαι ‖ ~er n δημοσιογράφος.
reprehensible [repri'hensibl] a ἀξιόμεμπτος.
represent [repri'zent] vt (*describe*) παριστάνω, παρουσιάζω ‖ (*act*) ἀντιπροσωπεύω ‖ ~ation n παράστασις, ἀναπαράστασις ‖ (*in parliament*) ἀντιπροσώπευσις, ἀντιπροσωπεία ‖ ~ative n ἀντιπρόσωπος ‖ a ἀντιπροσωπευτικός, παραστατικός.
repress [ri'pres] vt καταβάλλω, καταστέλλω, καταπνίγω ‖ ~ion n καταστολή, κατάπνιξις ‖ ~ive a κατασταλτικός, καταθλιπτικός.
reprieve [ri'pri:v] n ἀναστολή (θανατικῆς ποινῆς), ἀναβολή ‖ vt ἀναστέλλω, ἀνακουφίζω.
reprimand ['reprima:nd] n ἐπιτίμησις, ἐπίπληξις ‖ vt ἐπιτιμῶ, ἐπιπλήττω.
reprint ['ri:print] n ἀνατύπωσις ‖ ['ri:'print] vt ἀνατυπώνω.
reprisal [ri'praizəl] n ἀντεκδίκησις, ἀντίποινον.
reproach [ri'prəutʃ] n ἐπίπληξις, μομφή ‖ (*disgrace*) ὄνειδος ‖ vt ἐπιπλήττω, μέμφομαι, ψέγω ‖ ~ful a ἐπιπληκτικός, ὑβριστικός, ἐπονείδιστος.
reproduce [ri:prə'dju:s] vt ἀναπαράγω (*make copy*) ἀνατυπώνω ‖ vi ἀναπαράγομαι, πολλαπλασιάζομαι.
reproduction [ri:prə'dʌkʃən] n (*copy*) ἀναπαράστασις, ἀντίγραφον ‖ (*breeding*) γένεσις, πολλαπλασιασμός.
reproductive [ri:prə'dʌktiv] a ἀναπαραγωγικός.
reprove [ri'pru:v] vt ἐπιπλήττω.
reproving [ri'pru:viŋ] a ἐπικριτικός, ὕφος ἐπικρίσεως.
reptile ['reptail] n ἑρπετόν.
republic [ri'pʌblik] n δημοκρατία ‖ ~an a

δημοκρατικός ‖ (party: US) ρεπουμπλικανικός ‖ n δημοκράτης, ρεπουμπλικάνος.

repudiate [ri'pju:dieit] vt (ἀπ)ἀρνοῦμαι, ἀποκρούω, ἀπορρίπτω.

repugnance [ri'pʌgnəns] n ἀπέχθεια, ἀποστροφή.

repugnant [ri'pʌgnənt] a ἀπεχθής, ἀηδής, σιχαμερός.

repulse [ri'pʌls] vt ἀπωθῶ, ἀποκρούω ‖ (reject) ἀποκρούω, ἀπορρίπτω.

repulsion [ri'pʌlʃən] n ἀποστροφή, ἄπωσις.

repulsive [ri'pʌlsiv] a ἀποκρουστικός, ἀντιπαθής, ἀηδής.

repurchase ['ri:'pə:tʃis] vt ξαναγοραζω ‖ n ἀγορά ἐκ νέου.

reputable ['repjutəbl] a ἔντιμος, ἀξιοπρεπής.

reputation [repju'teiʃən] n φήμη, ὑπόληψις, ὄνομα.

repute [ri'pju:t] n ἐκτίμησις, ὑπόληψις ‖ ~d a φημισμένος, ὑποτιθέμενος ‖ ~dly ad κατά τήν κοινήν γνώμην.

request [ri'kwest] n αἴτησις, παράκλησις ‖ (demand) ζήτησις, μόδα ‖ vt ζητῶ, παρακαλῶ.

requiem ['rekwiem] n μνημόσυνον.

require [ri'kwaiə*] vt ζητῶ, ἀπαιτῶ ‖ (oblige) χρειάζομαι ‖ ~ment n ἀπαίτησις, ἀνάγκη.

requisite ['rekwizit] n ἀπαιτούμενον πρᾶγμα, χρειῶδες ‖ a ἀπαιτούμενος.

requisition [rekwi'ziʃən] n ἐπίταξις, ἀπαίτησις ‖ vt ἀπαιτῶ, ἐπιτάσσω.

reroute ['ri:'ru:t] vt χαράσσω νέα πορεία, κάνω ἄλλο δρόμο.

resale ['ri:'seil] n μεταπώλησις, ξαναπούλημα.

rescind [ri'sind] vt ἀκυρῶ, καταργῶ, ἀνακαλῶ.

rescue ['reskju:] n διάσωσις, ἀπολύτρωσις ‖ vt (save) σώζω, λυτρώνω ‖ ~r n σωτήρας, λυτρωτής.

research [ri'sə:tʃ] n ἔρευνα ‖ vi (+ into) ἐνεργῶ ἔρευνας ‖ vt ἐρευνῶ ‖ ~er n ἐρευνητής ‖ ~ work n ἔρευνες, μελέτες ‖ ~ worker n ἐρευνητής.

resell ['ri:'sel] vt ξαναπουλῶ.

resemblance [ri'zembləns] n ὁμοιότης.

resemble [ri'zembl] vt ὁμοιάζω, μοιάζω.

resent [ri'zent] vt φέρω βαρέως, θίγομαι ἀπό ‖ ~ful a μνησίκακος, πειραγμένος ‖ ~ment n μνησικακία, ἔχθρα, πίκα.

reservation [rezə'veiʃən] n ἐπιφύλαξις, περιορισμός ‖ (place) ἐξασφάλισις, κλείσιμο ‖ (doubt) ἐπιφύλαξις.

reserve [ri'zə:v] n ἀπόθεμα, ἀποθεματικόν ‖ (self-restraint) ἐπιφύλαξις, συντηρητικότης ‖ (area of land) ἐπιφυλασσομένη περιοχή ‖ (sport) ἐφεδρικός παίκτης ‖ vt (seats etc) κρατῶ, ἀγκαζάρω, κλείνω ‖ ~s npl (mil) ἐφεδρεῖες ‖ in ~ κατά μέρος, ρεζέρβα ‖ ~d a ἐπιφυλακτικός,

συγκρατημένος ‖ '~d' (notice) 'κλεισμένος', 'κρατημένος'.

reservist [ri'zə:vist] n ἔφεδρος.

reservoir ['rezəvwa:*] n δεξαμενή, ντεπόζιτο, ρεζερβουάρ ‖ (store) ἀπόθεμα.

reshape ['ri:'ʃeip] vt μεταπλάθω, τροποποιῶ, ἀναπλάθω.

reshuffle ['ri:'ʃʌfl] n (pol) ἀνασχηματισμός.

reside [ri'zaid] vi διαμένω, ἐνυπάρχω ‖ ~nce ['rezidəns] n κατοικία, σπίτι ‖ (living) διαμονή, παραμονή ‖ ~nt n κάτοικος ‖ a ἐγκατεστημένος ‖ ~ntial a τῆς μονίμου διαμονῆς, μέ ἰδιωτικές κατοικίες.

residue ['rezidju:] n ὑπόλοιπον, ὑπόλειμμα, κατάλοιπον.

resign [ri'zain] vt παραιτοῦμαι ‖ (submit) ὑποτάσσομαι, ἐγκαταλείπομαι ‖ ~ation [rezig'neiʃən] n παραίτησις ‖ (submission) ὑποταγή, ὑπομονή ‖ ~ed a ἀνεχόμενος, ὑποτακτικός.

resilience [ri'ziliəns] n ἐλαστικότης, ἀναπήδησις.

resilient [ri'ziliənt] a ἐλαστικός.

resin ['rezin] n ρητίνη, ρετσίνι.

resist [ri'zist] vt ἀνθίσταμαι εἰς, ἀντιδρῶ κατά ‖ ~ance n ἀντίστασις ‖ ~ant a (to stains etc) ἀνθεκτικός, ἀντέχων.

resolute ['rezəlu:t] a ἀποφασιστικός, σταθερός ‖ ~ly ad ἀποφασιστικά, μέ ἀπόφασιν.

resolution [rezə'lu:ʃən] n ἀποφασιστικότης ‖ (decision) ἀπόφασις.

resolve [ri'zɔlv] n ἀπόφασις ‖ vt ἀναλύω, διαλύω, λύω ‖ vi διαλύομαι, ἀναλύομαι ‖ (decide) ἀποφασίζω ‖ ~d a ἀποφασισμένος.

resonant ['rezənənt] a ἀντηχῶν, ἀντηχητικός.

resort [ri'zɔ:t] n τόπος διαμονῆς, θέρετρον ‖ (help) καταφυγή, μέσον, βοήθεια ‖ vi (+ to) προσφεύγω, καταφεύγω (εἰς) ‖ in the last ~ σάν τελευταία λύση.

resound [ri'zaund] vi ἀντηχῶ, ἀπηχῶ ‖ ~ing a (ἀπ)ἠχῶν, ἠχηρός.

resource [ri'sɔ:s] n καταφύγιον, μέσον, βοήθημα ‖ ~s npl (of fuel) πλοῦτος (εἰς καύσιμα) ‖ (of a country etc) οἱ πόροι, πλοῦτος ‖ ~ful a ἐφευρετικός ‖ ~fulness n ἐφευρετικότης, (τό) πολυμήχανον.

respect [ris'pekt] n σεβασμός ‖ (way) ἀναφορά ‖ vt σέβομαι ‖ (treat with consideration) προσέχω ‖ ~s npl (greetings) σέβη, χαιρετίσματα ‖ with ~ to ὅσον ἀφορᾶ ‖ in ~ of ἐν σχέσει πρός ‖ in this ~ ὡς πρός αὐτό τό σημεῖον ‖ ~ability n ἐντιμότης ‖ ~able a ἔντιμος, εὐυπόληπτος ‖ (fairly good) ὑποφερτός, ἀρκετά καλός ‖ ~ed a σεβαστός ‖ ~ful a γεμάτος σεβασμόν ‖ ~fully ad εὐσεβάστως ‖ ~ing prep σχετικά μέ, ὅσον ἀφορᾶ εἰς ‖ ~ive a σχετικός, ἀμοιβαῖος, ἀντίστοιχος ‖ ~ively ad ἀντιστοίχως.

respiration [respi'reiʃən] n ἀναπνοή.

respiratory [res'paiərətəri] a ἀναπνευστικός.

respite ['respait] n ἀνάπαυλα, διακοπή.

resplendent [ris'plendənt] a λαμπρός, λάμπων || μεγαλοπρεπής.

respond [ris'pɔnd] vi ἀπαντῶ, ἀποκρίνομαι || (act in answer) ἀνταποκρίνομαι, ἀνταποδίδω.

response [ris'pɔns] n ἀπάντησις, ἀνταπόκρισις.

responsibility [rispɔnsə'biliti] n εὐθύνη.

responsible [ris'pɔnsəbl] a ὑπεύθυνος, ὑπόλογος || (reliable) ἀξιόπιστος.

responsibly [ris'pɔnsəbli] ad ὑπευθύνως.

responsive [ris'pɔnsiv] a εὐσυγκίνητος, εὐαίσθητος.

rest [rest] n ἀνάπαυσις, ξεκούρασις || (pause) πτῶσις, ἀνάπαυλα || (remainder) ὑπόλοιπον || vi ἀναπαύομαι, ξεκουράζομαι || (be supported) στηρίζομαι, ἀκουμπῶ || (remain) στηρίζομαι, βασίζομαι || the ~ of them οἱ ὑπόλοιποι.

restaurant ['restərɔːŋ] n ἐστιατόριον || ~ car n βαγκόν-ρεστωράν.

rest cure ['restkjuə*] n θεραπεία ἀναπαύσεως.

restful ['restful] a ξεκούραστος, ἥσυχος, ἀναπαυτικός.

rest home ['resthəum] n πρεβαντόριο, ἀναρρωτήριον.

restitution [resti'tjuːʃən] n ἀποκατάστασις, ἀπόδοσις.

restive ['restiv] a ἀτίθασος, ἀνήσυχος.

restless ['restlis] a ἀνήσυχος, ἀεικίνητος, ἄϋπνος || ~ly ad ἀνήσυχα, νευρικά, ταραγμένα || ~ness n ἀνησυχία, νευρικότης.

restock ['riː'stɔk] vt ἀνεφοδιάζω.

restoration [restə'reiʃən] n ἀποκατάστασις, παλινόρθωσις || (of building etc) ἐπισκευή, ἀναστήλωσις.

restore [ris'tɔː*] vt ἐπιστρέφω, ἀποκαθιστῶ || (repair) ἐπισκευάζω, ἀναστηλώνω.

restrain [ris'trein] vt ἀναχαιτίζω, συγκρατῶ || ~ed a (style etc) ἤρεμος, συγκρατημένος, μετρημένος || ~t n περιορισμός, περιστολή || (self-control) συγκράτησις.

restrict [ris'trikt] vt περιορίζω || ~ed a περιωρισμένος || ~ion n περιορισμός || ~ive a περιοριστικός.

rest room ['restrum] n (US) ἀποχωρητήριον, τουαλέτα.

result [ri'zʌlt] n ἀποτέλεσμα, συνέπεια || (of test) ἀποτελέσματα || vi (+ in) καταλήγω, ἀπολήγω || ~ant a προκύπτων.

resume [ri'zjuːm] vt ἐπαναρχίζω, ξαναρχίζω.

résumé ['reizjuːmei] n περίληψις.

resumption [ri'zʌmpʃən] n (ἐπ)ανάληψις, συνέχισις.

resurgence [ri'səːdʒəns] n ἀναζωογόνησις, ἀνανέωσις, ξεσήκωμα.

resurrection [rezə'rekʃən] n ἀνάστασις, ἀνανέωσις.

resuscitate [ri'sʌsiteit] vt ἀνασταίνω, ἐπαναφέρω εἰς τήν ζωήν.

resuscitation [risʌsi'teiʃən] n ἀναζωογόνησις, ἀνάστασις.

retail ['riːteil] n λιανική πώλησις || a λιανικός || [riː'teil] vt πωλῶ λιανικῶς || ~er n μεταπωλητής, λιανέμπορος || ~ price n τιμή λιανικῆς πωλήσεως.

retain [ri'tein] vt διατηρῶ, συγκρατῶ, κρατῶ || ~er n ὑπηρέτης || (fee) προκαταβολή δικηγόρου.

retaliate [ri'tælieit] vi ἀντεκδικοῦμαι, ἀνταποδίδω.

retaliation [ritæli'eiʃən] n ἀντεκδίκησις, ἀνταπόδοσις, ἀντίποινα.

retarded [ri'taːdid] a καθυστερημένος.

retention [ri'tenʃən] n διατήρησις, συγκράτησις.

retentive [ri'tentiv] a συνεκτικός, ἰσχυρός.

rethink ['riː'θiŋk] vt ξανασκέπτομαι.

reticence ['retisəns] n παρασιώπησις, ἀποσιώπησις.

reticent ['retisənt] a σιωπηλός, λιγομίλητος, κλειστός.

retina ['retinə] n ἀμφιβληστροειδής (χιτών).

retinue ['retinjuː] n ἀκολουθία, συνοδεία.

retire [ri'taiə*] vi ἀποχωρῶ, γίνομαι συνταξιοῦχος || (withdraw, retreat) ὑποχωρῶ, ἀποσύρομαι || (go to bed) πάω γιά ὕπνο || ~d a (person) συνταξιοῦχος || ~ment n ἀποχώρησις, σύνταξις.

retiring [ri'taiəriŋ] a ἐπιφυλακτικός, ἀκοινώνητος, ντροπαλός.

retort [ri'tɔːt] n (reply) ὀξεῖα ἀπάντησις, ξύπνηα ἀπάντησις || vi ἀνταπαντῶ, ἀποκρίνομαι.

retrace [ri'treis] vt ἀνατρέχω, ξαναγυρίζω.

retract [ri'trækt] vti ἀνακαλῶ, μαζεύω, παίρνω πίσω (κάτι) || ~able a (aerial) εἰσελκόμενος.

retread [ri'riːtred] vt (aut: tyre) ἀνεπιστρώνω, ξαναφορμάρω.

retreat [ri'triːt] n ὑποχώρησις, ὀπισθοχώρησις || (escape) καταφύγιον || vi ὑποχωρῶ, ὀπισθοχωρῶ.

retrial ['riː'traiəl] n νέα δίκη.

retribution [retri'bjuːʃən] n τιμωρία, ἀνταπόδοσις, ἐκδίκησις.

retrieval [ri'triːvəl] n ἐπανάκτησις, ἐπανόρθωσις.

retrieve [ri'triːv] vt ἐπανακτῶ, ἀποδίδω || (rescue) ἐπανορθώνω, σώζω || ~r n κυνηγετικός κύων, ριτρίβερ.

retrograde ['retrəugreid] a (step, action) ὀπισθοδρομικός, παλινδρομικός.

retrospect ['retrəuspekt] n: in ~ σέ ἀνασκόπηση, ὅταν τό σκέπτομαι || ~ive a (law) ἀναδρομικός.

return [ri'təːn] n ἐπιστροφή, ἐπάνοδος, γύρισμα, ἐρχομός || (profits) κέρδος, εἰσπράξεις ‖ (official report) ἔκθεσις, στατιστική, ἀπογραφή ‖ (rail ticket etc) εἰσιτήριον μετ' ἐπιστροφῆς ‖ (journey) ταξίδιον ἐπιστροφῆς ‖ (match) ἀγών ἀνταποδόσεως, ρεβάνς ‖ vi ἐπιστρέφω, γυρίζω, ἐπανέρχομαι ‖ vt (give back) ἐπιστρέφω, δίνω πίσω, γυρίζω ‖ (pay back) ἐπιστρέφω, πληρώνω ‖ (elect) ἐκλέγω ‖ ~able a (bottle etc) ἐπιστρεφόμενον, ἐπιστρεπτός.

reunion [riːˈjuːnjən] n συνάντησις, συγκέντρωσις.

reunite [ˈriːjuːˈnait] vt ἑνώνω πάλιν, συναντῶμαι.

rev [rev] n (aut) στροφές ‖ vti (also ~ up) φουλάρω.

revamp [ˈriːˈvæmp] vt ἐπιδιορθώνω, ἀνορθώνω.

reveal [riˈviːl] vt ἀποκαλύπτω, φανερώνω ‖ ~ing a ἀποκαλυπτικός.

reveille [riˈvæli] n ἐγερτήριον σάλπισμα.

revel [ˈrevl] vi (+ in) ἐντρυφῶ εἰς, γλεντῶ.

revelation [revəˈleiʃən] n ἀποκάλυψις.

reveller [ˈrevlə*] n γλεντζές.

revelry [ˈrevlri] n διασκέδασις, γλέντι.

revenge [riˈvendʒ] n ἐκδίκησις ‖ vt ἐκδικοῦμαι ‖ ~ful a ἐκδικητικός.

revenue [ˈrevənjuː] n πρόσοδος, ἔσοδα, εἰσόδημα.

reverberate [riˈvəːbəreit] vi ἀντηχῶ, ἀντανακλῶμαι.

reverberation [rivəːbəˈreiʃən] n ἀντήχησις, ἀντανάκλασις.

revere [riˈviə*] vt σέβομαι, εὐλαβοῦμαι ‖ ~nce [ˈrevərəns] n σέβας, σεβασμός ‖ the R~nd Smith ὁ αἰδεσιμώτατος Σμίθ ‖ ~nt a εὐσεβής.

reverie [ˈrevəri] n ὀνειροπόλησις, ρεμβασμός.

reversal [riˈvəːsəl] n ἀντιστροφή, ἀναστροφή.

reverse [riˈvəːs] n ἀντίστροφον ‖ (defeat) ἧττα, ἀτυχία ‖ (aut: gear) ὄπισθεν ‖ a (order, direction) ἀντίθετος, ἀντίστροφος ‖ vt (put upside down) ἀναστρέφω ‖ (change) ἀντιστρέφω ‖ vi βάζω τήν ὄπισθεν.

reversion [riˈvəːʃən] n ἐπιστροφή, ἐπάνοδος.

revert [riˈvəːt] vi ἐπανέρχομαι, ἐπιστρέφω.

review [riˈvjuː] n ἐπιθεώρησις ‖ (of critic) κριτική (βιβλίου) ‖ (magazine) ἐπιθεώρησις, περιοδικόν ‖ vt (look back on) ἀνασκοπῶ, ἐξετάζω ‖ (troops) ἐπιθεωρῶ ‖ (a book) γράφω κριτικήν ‖ ~er n (critic) κριτικογράφος, κριτικός.

revise [riˈvaiz] vt ἀναθεωρῶ, ξανακοιτάζω, διορθώνω.

revision [riˈviʒən] n ἀναθεώρησις, ἐπανεξέτασις.

revisit [ˈriːˈvizit] vt ξαναεπισκέπτομαι.

revitalize [ˈriːˈvaitəlaiz] vt ἀναζωογονῶ.

revival [riˈvaivəl] n ἀναγέννησις ‖ (of play) ἐπανάληψις.

revive [riˈvaiv] vt ἀναζωογονῶ, ἀνασταίνω, ξαναζωνταντανεύω ‖ vi ἀναζωογονοῦμαι, ξαναζωνταντανεύω, ἀναζωπυροῦμαι.

revoke [riˈvəuk] vt ἀνακαλῶ, ἀκυρώνω.

revolt [riˈvəult] n στάσις, ἐπανάστασις ‖ vi ἐπαναστατῶ ‖ ~ing a ἀηδιαστικόν, σκανδαλώδης.

revolution [revəˈluːʃən] n (of wheel) περιστροφή ‖ (change) ἐπανάστασις ‖ ~ary a ἐπαναστατικός, ἀνατρεπτικός ‖ n ἐπαναστάτης, περιστροφή ‖ ~ize vt ἀνατρέπω ἄρδην, ἀλλάζω τελείως.

revolve [riˈvɔlv] vi περιστρέφομαι ‖ ~r n περίστροφον.

revue [riˈvjuː] n ἐπιθεώρησις (θεατρική).

revulsion [riˈvʌlʃən] n μεταστροφή.

reward [riˈwɔːd] n (ἀντ)ἀμοιβή ‖ vt ἀνταμείβω ‖ ~ing a ἀνταμειπτικός ‖ (fig) πού ἀξίζει τόν κόπο.

rewind [ˈriːˈwaind] vt ξανατυλίγω, ξανακουρδίζω.

rewire [ˈriːˈwaiə*] vt (house) ἀλλάζω τά σύρματα (σπιτιοῦ).

reword [ˈriːˈwəːd] vt ἀνασυντάσσω, ξαναγράφω μέ ἄλλες λέξεις.

rewrite [ˈriːˈrait] vt ξαναγράφω.

rhapsody [ˈræpsədi] n ραψωδία.

rhetoric [ˈretərik] n ρητορική, ρητορία ‖ ~al a ρητορικός.

rheumatic [ruːˈmætik] a ρευματικός.

rheumatism [ˈruːmətizəm] n ρευματισμός.

rhinoceros [raiˈnɔsərəs] n ρινόκερως.

Rhodesia [rəuˈdiːʒə] n Ροδεσία ‖ ~n a ἐκ Ροδεσίας ‖ n (person) ἐκ Ροδεσίας.

rhododendron [rəudəˈdendrən] n ροδόδενδρον.

rhubarb [ˈruːbɑːb] n ραβέντι, ρουμπάρμπαρο.

rhyme [raim] n ὁμοιοκαταληξία, ρίμα.

rhythm [ˈriðəm] n ρυθμός, μέτρον ‖ ~ic(al) a ρυθμικός ‖ ~ically ad ρυθμικά, μέ ρυθμό.

rib [rib] n πλευρά, πλευρό ‖ vt (mock) ἐμπαίζω, κοροϊδεύω.

ribald [ˈribəld] a αἰσχρός, πρόστυχος, σόκιν.

ribbed [ribd] a ραβδωτός, μέ νευρώσεις.

ribbon [ˈribən] n ταινία, κορδέλλα.

rice [rais] n ρύζι ‖ ~ pudding n ρυζόγαλο.

rich [ritʃ] a πλούσιος ‖ (fertile) εὔφορος, πλούσιος, γόνιμος ‖ (splendid) πολυτελής, λαμπρός, ὑπέροχος ‖ (of food) παχύς, ἀπό ἐκλεκτά συστατικά ‖ the ~ οἱ πλούσιοι ‖ ~es npl πλούτη, ἀφθονία ‖ ~ly ad πλούσια ‖ ~ness n πλοῦτος, ἀφθονία.

rick [rik] n θημωνιά.

rickety [ˈrikiti] a (unsteady) πού τρέμει, σαθρός, σαραβαλιασμένος.

rickshaw [ˈrikʃɔː] n δίτροχος ἅμαξα συρομένη ἀπό ἄνθρωπον.

ricochet ['rikəʃei] *n* ἐποστρακισμός ‖ *vi* ἐποστρακίζω, ἀναπηδῶ.

rid [rid] (*irreg v*) *vt* ἀπαλλάσσω, ἐλευθερώνω ‖ **to get ~ of** ἀπαλλάσσομαι ἀπό ‖ **good ~dance!** καλά ξεκουμπίδια!, ἅς πάη στό καλό!

riddle ['ridl] *n* (*puzzle*) αἴνιγμα ‖ *vt* (*esp passive*) κάνω κόσκινο.

ride [raid] (*irreg v*) *n* διαδρομή, περίπατος, ταξίδι ‖ *vt* τρέχω, διασχίζω ‖ (*horse, bicycle*) καβαλικεύω ‖ *vi* πάω καβάλα, καβαλικεύω, πηγαίνω μέ ἀμάξι ‖ (*naut*) εἶμαι ἀγκυροβολημένος ‖ **~ r** *n* ἱππεύς, καβαλάρης ‖ (*in contract etc*) προσθήκη, παράρτημα, συμπληρωματική διάταξις.

ridge [ridʒ] *n* (*hill*) κορυφογραμμή, ράχη ‖ (*of roof*) κολοφών, καβελαριά, κορφιάς ‖ (*narrow raised strip*) πτυχή, ζάρα, προεξοχή.

ridicule ['ridikju:l] *n* περίγελως, ἐμπαιγμός, κοροϊδία ‖ *vt* κοροϊδεύω, γελοποιῶ.

ridiculous [ri'dikjuləs] *a* γελοῖος ‖ **~ly** *ad* γελοῖα.

riding ['raidiŋ] *n*: **to go ~** πηγαίνω ἱππασία ‖ **~ habit** *n* ἀμαζών ‖ **~ school** *n* σχολή ἱππασίας.

rife [raif] *a*: **~ with** μεστός, γεμάτος ἀπό.

riffraff ['rifræf] *n* ἀλητεία, σκυλολόϊ.

rifle ['raifl] *n* ὅπλον, τουφέκι ‖ *vt* (*rob*) ἀδειάζω, διαρπάζω ‖ **~ range** *n* πεδίον βολῆς, σκοπευτήριον.

rift [rift] *n* σχισμή, ρωγμή.

rig [rig] *n* (*outfit*) φορεσιά, στόλισμα ‖ (*oil rig*) γεωτρύπανον ‖ *vt* (*election etc*) νοθεύω τάς ἐκλογάς ‖ **~ging** *n* ξάρτια ‖ **to ~ out** *vt* ντύνω, στολίζω ‖ **to ~ up** *vt* στήνω, μαντάρω.

right [rait] *a* (*correct, proper*) ὀρθός, σωστός, κανονικός ‖ (*just, good*) εὐθύς, δίκαιος, ἔντιμος ‖ (*on right side*) δεξιός, δεξιά ‖ *n* (*what is just, true*) τό δίκαιον, ἡ δικαιοσύνη, τό καλόν ‖ (*title, claim*) δικαίωμα, προνόμιον ‖ (*not left*) δεξιά (πλευρά), τό δεξιόν ‖ (*pol*) ἡ Δεξιά ‖ *ad* (*straight*) εὐθέως, ἴσια, ντρίτα ‖ (*completely, thoroughly*) ἀκριβῶς, κατ' εὐθείαν, τελείως, δεξιά ‖ *vt* ἀνορθῶ, ἰσορροπῶ, ξαναφέρνω στά ἴσια ‖ *excl* σωστά!, σύμφωνοι!, ἔχεις δίκιο! ‖ **to be ~** ἔχω δίκαιον ‖ **all ~!** ἐν τάξει! ‖ **~ now** ἀμέσως ‖ **by ~s** δικαιωματικῶς, νομίμως ‖ **on the ~** στά δεξιά ‖ **~ angle** *n* ὀρθή γωνία ‖ **~eous** *a* εὐθύς, ἠθικός, δίκαιος ‖ **~eousness** *n* δικαιοσύνη, ὀρθότης, τιμιότης ‖ **~ful** *a* νόμιμος, δίκαιος` ‖ **~fully** *ad* δικαίως, νομίμως ‖ **~-hand drive** *a* μέ δεξιό τιμόνι ‖ **~-handed** *a* δεξιόχειρ, δεξιόστροφος ‖ **~-hand man** *n* τό δεξί χέρι ‖ **~-hand side** *n* (πρός) τά δεξιά ‖ **~ly** *ad* δικαίως, ὀρθῶς ‖ **~-minded** *a* λογικός, ὀρθοφρονῶν ‖ **~ of way** *n* ἡ προτεραιότης ‖ **~-winger** *n* δεξιός.

rigid ['ridʒid] *a* ἄκαμπτος, ἀλύγιστος ‖ (*strict*) αὐστηρός ‖ **~ity** *n* ἀκαμψία, ἀλυγισία ‖ **~ly** *ad* ἄκαμπτα, ἀλύγιστα, αὐστηρά.

rigmarole ['rigmərəul] *n* ἀσυναρτησίες, κουραφέξαλα.

rigor ['rigə*] *n* (*US*) = **rigour.**

rigor mortis ['rigə'mɔ:tis] *n* πτωματική ἀκαμψία.

rigorous ['rigərəs] *a* αὐστηρός, δριμύς, τραχύς ‖ **~ly** *ad* αὐστηρά, σκληρά.

rigour ['rigə*] *n* αὐστηρότης, δριμύτης.

rig-out ['rigaut] *n* (*col*) ντύσιμο, στόλισμα.

rile [rail] *vt* (*annoy, infuriate*) ἐκνευρίζω, ἐξαγριώνω.

rim [rim] *n* στεφάνη, χεῖλος ‖ (*of wheel*) σῶτρον, στεφάνη, ζάντα ‖ **~less** *a* χωρίς σκελετό, χωρίς γεῖσον ‖ **~med** *a* μέ στεφάνην, μέ σκελετόν.

rind [raind] *n* φλοιός, φλούδα.

ring [riŋ] (*irreg v*) *n* δακτύλιος, δακτυλίδι ‖ (*of people*) συντροφιά, φατρία, συμμορία ‖ (*arena*) παλαίστρα, στῖβος, πίστα, ἀρένα, ρίγκ ‖ (*tel*) τηλεφώνημα, κτύπημα τηλεφώνου ‖ *vt* κτυπῶ τό κουδούνι ‖ *vi* (*tel*) (*also ~ up*) τηλεφωνῶ ‖ (*resound*) ἀντηχῶ, κτυπῶ, κουδουνίζω ‖ **to ~ off** *vi* διακόπτω τήν συνομιλίαν, κλείνω τηλέφωνον ‖ **~ binder** *n* κλασέρ ‖ **~leader** *n* (*of gang*) ἀρχηγός συμμορίας ‖ **~lets** *npl* (*hair*) μπούκλες ‖ **~ road** *n* περιφερειακή ὁδός.

rink [riŋk] *n* πίστα πατινάζ.

rinse [rins] *n* ξέπλυμα ‖ *vt* ξεπλένω, ξεβγάζω.

riot ['raiət] *n* στάσις, ὀχλαγωγία ‖ *vi* ὀχλαγωγῶ, θορυβῶ ‖ **~er** *n* ταραξίας, ὀχλαγωγός ‖ **~ous** *a* ταραχώδης, ὀχλαγωγικός, ὀργιαστικός ‖ **~ously** *ad* στασιαστικῶς, ἐκλύτως.

rip [rip] *n* σχισμή, σχίσιμο ‖ *vti* (δια)σχίζω, ξεσχίζω.

ripcord ['ripkɔ:d] *n* σχοινίον ἀνοίγματος.

ripe [raip] *a* ὥριμος, γενομένο ‖ **~n** *vti* ὡριμάζω, γίνομαι ‖ **~ness** *n* ὡριμότης.

ripple ['ripl] *n* κυμάτιον, κυματιστός, ρυτίδα ‖ *vti* κυματίζω, ρυτιδώνω.

rise [raiz] (*irreg v*) *n* ὕψωμα, ἀνήφορος, κλίσις ‖ (*esp in wages*) αὔξησις, ἀνύψωσις ‖ ἄνοδος ‖ ἀνέβασμα, αὔξησις, σήκωμα (ἀέρος) ‖ *vi* (*from chair*) σηκώνομαι ὄρθιος ‖ (*from bed*) ξυπνῶ, σηκώνομαι ‖ (*sun*) ἀνατέλλω, βγαίνω ‖ (*smoke*) ὑψοῦμαι, ἀνεβαίνω ‖ (*mountain*) ὑψοῦμαι ‖ (*ground*) ἀνηφορίζω, ὑψοῦμαι ‖ (*prices*) ἀνέρχομαι, ὑψοῦμαι, ἀνεβαίνω ‖ (*revolt*) ἐξεγείρομαι, ξεσηκώνομαι, ἐπαναστατῶ ‖ **to give ~ to** προκαλῶ ‖ **to ~ to the occasion** αἴρομαι εἰς τό ὕψος τῶν περιστάσεων.

risk [risk] *n* κίνδυνος, ριψοκινδύνευσις ‖ *vt* ριψοκινδυνεύω ‖ **~y** *a* ἐπικίνδυνος, ριψοκίνδυνος.

risqué ['ri:skei] *a* τολμηρό.

rissole ['risəul] *n* κεφτές, κροκέττα.

rite [rait] *n* ἱεροτελεστία, ἐκκλησιαστική τελετή.

ritual ['ritjuəl] *n* τυπικόν, λειτουργικόν ‖ *a* τυπικός, καθιερωμένος.

rival ['raivəl] *n,a* ἀντίπαλος, ἀντίζηλος, ἀνταγωνιστής ‖ *vt* ἀνταγωνίζομαι, συναγωνίζομαι ‖ ~ry *n* ἀνταγωνισμός, συναγωνισμός.

river ['rivə*] *n* ποταμός, ποτάμι ‖ ~bank *n* ὄχθη (ποταμοῦ) ‖ ~bed *n* κοίτη ποταμοῦ ‖ ~side *n* ὄχθη ‖ *a* τῆς ὄχθης.

rivet ['rivit] *n* ἥλος, κοινωμάτιον, καρφί ‖ *vt* καθηλώνω, καρφώνω, πριτσιλίζω (*fix*) προσηλώνω, καρφώνω.

Riviera [rivi'eərə] *n*: the ~ ἡ Ριβιέρα.

road [rəud] *n* ὁδός, δρόμος ‖ ~block *n* ὁδόφραγμα ‖ ~hog *n* κακός ὁδηγός ‖ ~map *n* ὁδικός χάρτης ‖ ~side *n* παρυφή δρόμου, δίπλα στό δρόμο ‖ *a* στό δρόμο, τοῦ δρόμου ‖ ~sign *n* ταμπέλα δρόμου ‖ ~way *n* ἁμαξιτή ὁδός ‖ ~worthy *a* κατάλληλος γιά τόν δρόμο.

roam [rəum] *vi* περιπλανῶμαι, περιφέρομαι ‖ *vt* διασχίζω, διατρέχω, τριγυρίζω.

roar [rɔ:*] *n* βρυχηθμός, μουγγρητό ‖ *vi* βρυχῶμαι, ὠρύομαι ‖ ~ing *a* (*fire*) γερή (φωτιά), δυνατή (φωτιά) ‖ (*trade*) ἀκμάζον (ἐμπόριον), καλές (δουλειές).

roast [rəust] *n* ψητόν κρέας, ψητό ‖ *vt* ψήνω, καβουρντίζω.

rob [rɔb] *vt* κλέβω, ληστεύω, ἀποστερῶ ‖ ~ber *n* ληστής, κλέφτης ‖ ~bery *n* ληστεία.

robe [rəub] *n* ρόμπα, φόρεμα ‖ (*of office*) στολή, τήβεννος ‖ *vt* ἐνδύω, περιβάλλω, ντύνω.

robin ['rɔbin] *n* κοκκινολαίμης, κομπογιάννης.

robot ['rəubɔt] *n* αὐτόματον, ρομπότ.

robust [rəu'bʌst] *a* εὔρωστος, ρωμαλέος.

rock [rɔk] *n* βράχος ‖ (*geol*) πέτρωμα ‖ (*candy*) εἶδος καραμέλλας ‖ *vti* λικνίζω, κουνῶ, κουνιέμαι ‖ on the ~s (*drink*) μέ πάγο χωρίς νερό ‖ (*ship*) (πέφτω) στά βράχια ‖ (*marriage etc*) ὑπό διάλυσιν, σέ δύσκολη θέση ‖ ~-bottom *n* (*fig*) κατώτερον σημεῖον ‖ ~ climber *n* ὀρειβάτης (βράχων) ‖ to go ~ climbing πηγαίνω ὀρειβασία σέ βράχους ‖ ~ery *n* τεχνητοί βράχοι.

rocket ['rɔkit] *n* ρουκέττα, πύραυλος, βολίς.

rock fall ['rɔkfɔ:l] *n* πτῶσις βράχων.

rocking chair ['rɔkiŋtʃeə*] *n* κουνιστή πολυθρόνα.

rocking horse ['rɔkiŋhɔ:s] *n* ἀλογάκι (παιδικό).

rocky ['rɔki] *a* βραχώδης.

rococo [rəu'kəukəu] *a,n* ροκοκό.

rod [rɔd] *n* (*bar*) ράβδος, βέργα.

rode [rəud] *pt of* ride.

rodent ['rəudənt] *n* τρωκτικόν.

rodeo ['rəudiəu] *n* διαγωνισμός (καουμπόηδων).

roe [rəu] *n* (*deer*) δορκάς, ζαρκάδι ‖ (*of fish*) αὐγά ψαριῶν.

rogue [rəug] *n* παλιάνθρωπος ‖ (*mischievous*) κατεργάρης, πειραχτήριο, πονηρός.

roguish ['rəugiʃ] *a* (*playful*) κατεργάρικος, τσαχπίνικος ‖ (*cheating*) δόλιος, πανοῦργος.

rôle [rəul] *n* ρόλος.

roll [rəul] *n* (*paper, meat etc*) κύλινδρος, ρολό, τόπι ‖ (*bread*) φραντζολάκι, κουλουράκι ‖ (*list*) κατάλογος, λίστα ‖ (*of drum*) συνεχής τυμπανοκρουσία ‖ *vt* (*over*) κυλινδρῶ, κυλίω, τσουλάω ‖ (*wind round*) τυλίγω, κάνω ρολό ‖ (*smooth out*) ἰσοπεδώνω, πατῶ, στρώνω ‖ *vi* (*swing*) στριφογυρίζω, διατοιχίζομαι, μποτζάρω ‖ (*make deep sound*) ἠχῶ, βροντῶ ‖ to ~ by *vi* (*time*) περνῶ (κυλώντας) ‖ to ~ in *vi* (*mail*) μπαίνω κυλώντας, συρρέω ‖ to ~ over *vi* ἀνατρέπομαι, κυλιέμαι ‖ to ~ up *vi* (*arrive*) φθάνω, κουβαλιέμαι ‖ *vt* (*carpet*) τυλίγω, διπλώνω ‖ ~ call *n* ὀνομαστική κλήσις, προσκλητήριον ‖ ~ed *a* (*umbrella*) τυλιγμένος ‖ ~er *n* κύλινδρος, τροχός ‖ ~er skates *npl* πατίνια μέ ρόδες.

rollicking ['rɔlikiŋ] *a* εὔθυμος, γλεντζέδικος, χαρούμενος.

rolling ['rəuliŋ] *a* (*landscape*) ἀνώμαλον ἔδαφος ‖ ~ pin *n* πλάστης (γιά ἄνοιγμα φύλλου) ‖ ~ stock *n* τροχαῖον ὑλικόν.

roly-poly ['rəuli'pəuli] *n* (*pudding*) πουτίγγα ρολό μέ φροῦτα.

Roman ['rəumən] *a* ρωμαϊκός ‖ *n* Ρωμαῖος ‖ ~ Catholic *a,n* ρωμαιοκαθολικός.

romance [rəu'mæns] *n* ρομάντζο ‖ ρομαντική ἱστορία, μῦθος, θρῦλος ‖ *vi* ὑπερβάλλω, φαντασιολογῶ ‖ ~r *n* παραμυθᾶς, μυθοπλάστης.

Romanesque [rəumə'nesk] *a* ρωμανικός (ρυθμός).

Roman numerals ['rəumən'nju:mərəlz] *npl* λατινικοί ἀριθμοί.

romantic [rəu'mæntik] *a* ρομαντικός.

romp [rɔmp] *n* εὔθυμον παιχνίδι, φασαρία ‖ *vi* (*also ~ about*) θορυβῶ, κάνω φασαρία, ἀτακτῶ ‖ ~ers *npl* μπλούζα, ποδιά παιδιῶν, φουφούλια.

rondo ['rɔndəu] *n* (*mus*) ροντώ, ρόντο.

roof [ru:f] *n* στέγη, σκεπή ‖ (*of car etc*) σκεπή ‖ (*of mouth*) οὐρανίσκος ‖ *vt* στεγάζω, σκεπάζω ‖ ~ garden *n* κῆπος μέ ταράτσα ‖ ~ing *n* στέγασις, ταβάνωμα.

rook [ruk] *n* (*bird*) κορώνη, κουρούνα, χαβαρώνι ‖ (*thief*) κλέφτης, λωποδύτης ‖ *vt* (*cheat*) κλέβω, χαρτοκλέβω.

room [rum] *n* (*in house*) δωμάτιον, κάμαρα ‖ (*space*) χῶρος, τόπος ‖ (*opportunity*) περιθώριον, λόγος ‖ ~s npl (flat) δωμάτια, διαμέρισμα ‖ (lodgings) δωμάτια μετά φαγητοῦ ‖ ~iness n εὐρυχωρία ‖ ~ing house n οἰκία ἐνοικιάζουσα ἐπιπλωμένα δωμάτια ‖ ~mate n συγκάτοικος, σύνοικος ‖ ~ service n ὑπηρεσία ‖ ~y a εὐρύχωρος.

roost [ru:st] n κούρνια, κοτέτσι ‖ vi κουρνιάζω.

root [ru:t] n ρίζα ‖ (source) πηγή, αἰτία, ρίζα ‖ vt ριζώνω ‖ to ~ about vi (fig) ψάχνω ‖ to ~ for vt ὑποστηρίζω, ἐνθαρρύνω ‖ to ~ out vt ἐκριζώνω.

rope [rəup] n σχοινί ‖ vt δένω μέ σχοινί ‖ to ~ in περικλείω, προσηλυτίζω, παρασύρω ‖ to know the ~s ξαίρω τήν δουλειά μου, εἶμαι μπασμένος ‖ ~ ladder n ἀνεμόσκαλα.

rosary ['rəuzəri] n κομβολόγι.

rose [rəuz] pt of rise ‖ (flower) n τριαντάφυλλον, ρόδον ‖ a ροδόχρους, ρόζ.

rosé ['rəuzei] n (wine) κοκκινέλι.

rosebed ['rəuzbed] n ροδωνιά, συστάδα ρόδων.

rosebud ['rəuzbʌd] n μπουμπούκι τριανταφύλλου.

rosebush ['rəuzbuʃ] n τριανταφυλλιά.

rosemary ['rəuzməri] n δενδρολίβανον.

rosette [rəu'zet] n ροζέττα.

roster ['rɒstə*] n κατάλογος, κατάστασις.

rostrum ['rɒstrəm] n ἄμβων, βῆμα.

rosy ['rəuzi] a (colour) ροδόχρους, ρόδινος, ρόζ ‖ (hopeful) ρόδινα.

rot [rɒt] n σῆψις, σαπίλα, σάπισμα ‖ (nonsense) ἀνοησία, μπούρδα ‖ vti σήπομαι, ἀποσυντίθεμαι, σαπίζω.

rota ['rəutə] n κατάλογος, πίναξ.

rotary ['rəutəri] a περιστροφικός.

rotate [rəu'teit] vt (two or more things in order) ἐναλλάσσω, ἐκτελῶ ἐκ περιτροπῆς ‖ vi περιστρέφομαι, γυρίζω (γύρω ἀπό).

rotating [rəu'teitiŋ] a περιστρεφόμενος, περιστροφικός.

rotation [rəu'teiʃən] n περιστροφή ‖ in ~ ἐκ περιτροπῆς.

rotor ['rəutə*] n στροφεῖον, ρώτωρ, ρότορ.

rotten ['rɒtn] a σαθρός, σάπιος, σαπισμένος ‖ (dishonest) πρόστυχος, κακῆς ποιότητος.

rotting ['rɒtiŋ] a πού σαπίζει.

rotund [rəu'tʌnd] a στρογγυλός, παχουλός.

rouble ['ru:bl] n ρούβλι(ον).

rouge [ru:ʒ] n κοκκινάδι, βαφή.

rough [rʌf] a (uneven) ἀνώμαλος, τραχύς ‖ (violent, coarse) χονδροειδής, πρόστυχος, τραχύς, ἀπότομος ‖ (stormy, wild) ἄγριος, σφοδρός, τρικυμιώδης ‖ (without comforts) πρόχειρος, στοιχειώδης ‖ (unfinished) πρόχειρο (σκίτσο), τοῦ προσχεδίου, ἀκατέργαστος ‖ (make-shift) βιαστικό, πρόχειρος ‖ (approximate) κατά προσέγγισιν, χονδρικός ‖ n

(uncut grass) ψηλό χορτάρι ‖ (violent person) μάγκας, κουτσαβάκης ‖ vt: to ~ it στεροῦμαι τίς ἀνέσεις, ἀντιμετωπίζω δυσκολίες ‖ to play ~ παίζω σκληρό παιχνίδι ‖ to ~ out vt (draft) προσχεδιάζω, κάνω πρόχειρα ‖ ~en vt τραχύνω ‖ ~ly ad χονδροειδῶς, πρόχειρα ‖ κατά προσέγγισιν, περίπου, γενικά ‖ ~ness n τραχύτης, σκληρότης.

roulette [ru:'let] n ρουλέττα.

Roumania [ru:'meiniə] n Ρουμανία ‖ ~n n (person) Ρουμάνος ‖ a ρουμανικός.

round [raund] a στρογγυλός, σφαιρικός, κυκλικός ‖ (rough) στρογγυλός ‖ ad πέριξ, γύρω, τριγύρω ‖ prep γύρο ἀπό, περί ‖ n κύκλος, γῦρος ‖ (duty) γῦρος, βόλτα, περιοδεία, καθημερινή δουλειά ‖ (sport) γῦρος ‖ vt (corner) κάμπτω, στρίβω, κάνω στροφήν, παίρνω τήν στροφήν ‖ to ~ off vt στρογγυλεύω, τελειώνω ‖ to ~ up vt συγκεντρώνω, μαζεύω, πιάνω, περικυκλώνω ‖ ~ of ammunition n φυσίγγιον ‖ ~ of applause n ὁμοβροντία χειροκροτημάτων ‖ ~ of drinks n ἕνα γῦρο ποτῶν, μιά βόλτα ‖ ~about n παρακαμπτήριος ὁδός ‖ στρογγυλή μάντρα ‖ (merry-go-round) περιστρεφόμενα ξύλινα ἀλογάκια ‖ a κυκλικός, περιφερειακός ‖ ~ed a στρογγυλευμένος ‖ ~ers n (game) μπάλλα (εἶδος παιγνιδιοῦ) ‖ ~ly ad (fig) τέλεια, ὁλοσχερῶς, πλήρως ‖ ~-shouldered a μέ κυρτούς ὤμους, σκυφτός ‖ ~sman n περιοδεύων μεταφορεύς, διανομεύς ‖ ~up n περιμάζεμα, μπλόκο.

rouse [rauz] vt σηκώνω ‖ (stir up) προκαλῶ, διεγείρω, ξεσηκώνω.

rousing ['rauziŋ] a (welcome) θορυβώδης, ζωηρός.

rout [raut] n φυγή, ἥττα, ἄτακτος φυγή ‖ vt κατατροπώνω, τρέπω εἰς φυγήν.

route [ru:t] n δρομολόγιον, δρόμος, πορεία ‖ ~ map n ὁδικός χάρτης.

routine [ru:'ti:n] n ρουτίνα, στερεότυπος πορεία ‖ a τρέχων, κανονικός, τακτικός.

rover ['rəuvə*] n πλάνης, ἀλήτης, σουρτούκης.

roving ['rəuviŋ] a διατρέχων, περιπλανώμενος, πλάνης.

row [rəu] n (line) σειρά, στοῖχος, γραμμή, ἀράδα ‖ vt (boat) κινῶ μέ κουπί, μεταφέρω μέ τά κουπιά ‖ vi (in boat) κωπηλατῶ, τραβῶ κουπί.

row [rau] n (noise) θόρυβος, φασαρία, σαματᾶς ‖ (dispute) φιλονεικία, καυγᾶς, σκηνή ‖ (scolding) ἐπίπληξις, κατσάδα, λούσιμο ‖ vi φιλονεικῶ, καυγαδίζω, ἁρπάζομαι.

rowboat ['rəubəut] n (US) λέμβος κωπηλασίας, βάρκα μέ κουπιά.

rowdiness ['raudinis] n θόρυβος, φασαρία.

rowdy ['raudi] a θορυβώδης, πού κάνει

σαματά ‖ n (person) θορυβοποιός, καυγαντζῆς, νταῆς.

rowing ['rəuiŋ] n κωπηλασία, κουπί ‖ ~ **boat** n βάρκα μέ κουπιά.

rowlock ['rɔlək] n σκαλμοί.

royal ['rɔiəl] a βασιλικός ‖ ~**ist** n βασιλόφρων, βασιλικός ‖ a βασιλικός ‖ ~**ty** n (family) βασιλική οἰκογένεια ‖ (payment) (to inventor) δικαιώματα ἐφευρέτου ‖ (to author) συγγραφικά δικαιώματα.

rub n (polish, with cloth) τρίψιμο, σφούγγισμα ‖ vt τρίβω, ἐπαλείφω, προστρίβω ‖ (clean) στεγνώνω, σκουπίζω ‖ **to** ~ **off** vi ἀφαιρῶ διά τριβῆς, φεύγω.

rubber ['rʌbə*] n (substance) καουτσούκ, κόμμι ‖ (Brit) γομμολάστιχα ‖ ~ **band** n λάστιχο ‖ ~ **plant** n ἐβέα, δένδρον καουτσούκ ‖ ~ **stamp** n (lit) σφραγίδα ‖ (fig) ὁ ἐγκρίνων τυφλῶς ‖ ~**y** a κομμιώδης.

rubbish ['rʌbiʃ] n σκουπίδια, ἀπορρίμματα ‖ (nonsense) ἀνοησίες, κολοκύθια ‖ ~ **dump** n τόπος ἀπορρίψεως σκουπιδιῶν ‖ ~**y** a τιποτένιος, τῆς πεντάρας.

rubble ['rʌbl] n χαλίκι, σκύρα.

ruble ['ru:bl] n (US) = **rouble.**

ruby ['ru:bi] n ρουμπίνι ‖ a κόκκινο, ρουμπινί.

rucksack ['rʌksæk] n σακκίδιον.

ructions ['rʌkʃənz] npl (old) καυγᾶς, κατσάδα.

rudder ['rʌdə*] n πηδάλιον, τιμόνι.

ruddy ['rʌdi] a (colour) ροδοκόκκινος, ἐρυθρωπός ‖ (col: bloody) τρομερός, βρωμο-, παλιο-.

rude [ru:d] a (vulgar) πρόστυχος ‖ (impolite) βάναυσος, ἀπολίτιστος, ἀγενής ‖ (rough) τραχύς, πρωτόγονος ‖ ~**ly** ad πρωτόγονα, ἀπότομα, ἀπρεπῶς ‖ ~**ness** n χοντροκοπιά, ἀποτομότης.

rudiment ['ru:dimənt] n στοιχεῖον, ὑποτυπώδης ἀρχή ‖ ~**ary** a στοιχειώδης.

ruff [rʌf] n τραχηλιά.

ruffian ['rʌfiən] n παλιάνθρωπος, μαχαιροβγάλτης.

ruffle ['rʌfl] vt ρυτιδώνω, τσαλακώνω, ἀνακατεύω.

rug [rʌg] n τάπης, χαλί ‖ (for knees) σάλι, χράμι.

rugby ['rʌgbi] n ράγκμπυ.

rugged ['rʌgid] a τραχύς, ἀνώμαλος.

rugger ['rʌgə*] n ράγκμπυ.

ruin ['ru:in] n καταστροφή, συμφορά, ἀφανισμός ‖ vt καταστρέφω, ἀφανίζω ‖ ~**s** npl ἐρείπια ‖ ~**ation** n καταστροφή, ὄλεθρος, ρήμαγμα.

rule [ru:l] n (guide) κανόνας ‖ (what is usual) τό σύνηθες, τό κανονικόν ‖ (government) ἐξουσία, ἀρχή, κυριαρχία ‖ (stick) κανόνας, χάρακας, ρίγα, μέτρον ‖ vt κυβερνῶ, διοικῶ ‖ (pervade) διέπω ‖ (lines) χαρακώνω ‖ **as a** ~ κατά κανόνα,

συνήθως ‖ ~**d** a (paper) ριγωτός, χαρακωμένος ‖ ~**r** n κυβερνήτης, ἄρχων ‖ (straight edge) χάρακας.

ruling ['ru:liŋ] a (party) ἄρχων, διευθύνων, κρατῶν ‖ (class) ἄρχουσα (τάξις).

rum [rʌm] n ροῦμι ‖ a (col) παράξενος, ἀλλόκοτος.

rumble ['rʌmbl] n ὑπόκωφος βοή, βροντή ‖ vi μυκῶμαι, βροντῶ, βουΐζω, γουργουρίζω.

ruminate ['ru:mineit] vi (think over) διαλογίζομαι, σκέπτομαι διά, μελετῶ.

rummage ['rʌmidʒ] n ἔρευνα, ψάξιμο ‖ vt ἐρευνῶ, ψάχνω.

rumour (US) **rumor** ['ru:mə*] n φήμη, διάδοσις ‖ vt: **it is** ~**ed that** λέγεται ὅτι, διαδίδεται ὅτι, ψημολογεῖται ὅτι.

rump [rʌmp] n γλουτός, ὀπίσθια ‖ ~**steak** n κόντρα φιλέτο.

rumpus ['rʌmpəs] n θόρυβος, ταραχή ‖ (col) καυγάς, σαματᾶς.

run [rʌn] (irreg v) n (running) δρόμος, τρέξιμο ‖ (aut) διαδρομή, βόλτα ‖ (series) σειρά, ἀλληλουχία, συνέχεια ‖ (sudden demand) συρροή, ζήτησις ‖ (enclosed space) βοσκότοπος, χῶρος κλειστός ‖ (ski run) πίστα τοῦ σκί, κατήφορος γιά σκί ‖ vt (cause to run) κατευθύνω, λειτουργῶ, γυρίζω ‖ (train, bus) κυκλοφορῶ, κινῶ, λειτουργῶ, κάνω διαδρομή ‖ (manage) διευθύνω ‖ (compete in race) τρέχω εἰς ἀγῶνα, βάζω ὑποψηφιότητα ‖ (force) περνῶ, κάνω νά περάση, καρφώνω ‖ (pass: hand, eye) περνῶ ‖ vi (move quickly) τρέχω, τό βάζω στό πόδι, στρίβω ‖ (compete) θέτω ὑποψηφιότητα, τρέχω εἰς ἀγῶνας ‖ (machine) λειτουργῶ, κινοῦμαι, δουλεύω ‖ (flow) ρέω, κυλῶ, τρέχω ‖ (colours) ξεβάφω, βγαίνω, τρέχω ‖ **on the** ~ εἰς φυγήν, πολυάσχολος ‖ **to** ~ **riot** ὀργιάζω, ἀπειθαρχῶ ‖ **to** ~ **a risk** ριψοκινδυνεύω ‖ **to** ~ **about** vi (children) τρέχω ἐδῶ καί κεῖ ‖ **to** ~ **across** vt (find) συναντῶ τυχαία ‖ **to** ~ **away** vi δραπετεύω, διαφεύγω ‖ **to** ~ **down** vi (clock) ξεκουρδίζω ‖ vt (run over) κτυπῶ, πατῶ (κάποιον), πλακώνω ‖ (talk against) δυσφημῶ, κατηγορῶ, ἐξυβρίζω ‖ **to be** ~**-down** εἶμαι ἐξηντλημένος, εἶμαι τσακισμένος ‖ **to** ~ **off** vi φεύγω, τρέπομαι εἰς φυγήν, τό σκάω ‖ **to** ~ **out** vi (person) βγαίνω τρέχοντας ‖ (liquid) χύνομαι, τρέχω, στάζω ‖ (lease) παρέρχομαι, λήγω, περνῶ, ἐκπνέω ‖ (money) τελειώνω, ἐξαντλοῦμαι ‖ **to** ~ **out of** vt ἐξαντλῶ, τελειώνω, μένω ἀπό ‖ **to** ~ **over** vi κτυπῶ, πλακώνω, πολτοποιῶ ‖ (read) ρίχνω μιά ματιά ‖ **to** ~ **through** vt (instructions) διαβάζω γρήγορα, ἐξετάζω βιαστικά ‖ **to** ~ **up** vt (debt) ἀφήνω νά ἀνεβῆ, χρεώνομαι περισσότερα ‖ (dress) ράβω γρήγορα-γρήγορα ‖ **to** ~ **up against** vt *(difficulties)* συναντῶ, ἀντιμετωπίζω ‖ **~about** *n (small car)* αὐτοκίνητο δύο θέσεων ‖ **~away** *a (horse)* ἀφηνιασμένο (ἄλογο) ‖ *(truck)* ἀποσπασθέν (ὄχημα).

rung [rʌŋ] *pp of* **ring** ‖ *n* βαθμίς, σκαλί ἀνεμόσκαλας.

runner ['rʌnə*] *n (messenger)* ἀγγελιαφόρος ‖ *(of sleigh)* πατίνι ‖ **~-up** *n* ὁ ἐπιλαχών, ὁ δεύτερος (νικητής).

running ['rʌnɪŋ] *n (of business)* διεύθυνσις, ἐκμετάλλευσις ‖ *(of machine)* λειτουργία, κίνησις ‖ *a (water)* ῥέων, τρεχούμενος ‖ **~** *commentary n* σχολιασμένη ἔκδοσις, (ραδιο)ρεπορτάζ.

run-of-the-mill ['rʌnənðə'mil] *a* κοινός, συνηθισμένος.

runt [rʌnt] *n* κοντοστούμπης.

run-through ['rʌnθruː] *n* γρήγορο διάβασμα, γρήγορη ἐπανάληψις.

runway ['rʌnwei] *n* διάδρομος ἀπογειώσεως.

rupture ['rʌptʃə*] *n (med)* ῥῆξις, διάρρηξις ‖ *vt:* **to ~ o.s.** πάσχω ἐκ κήλης.

rural ['ruərəl] *a* ἀγροτικός, ὑπαίθριος.

ruse [ruːz] *n* τέχνασμα, πανουργία, κόλπο.

rush [rʌʃ] *n (dash)* σπουδή, τρέξιμο, βιασύνη ‖ *(sudden demand)* μεγάλη ζήτησις ‖ *(current)* ἐκτόξευσις, εἴσροή ‖ *vt* ὁρμῶ, τρέχω ἐπειγόντως, φέρω ἐπειγόντως ‖ *(attack)* ἐνεργῶ ἔφοδον ‖ *(col: overcharge)* γδέρνω ‖ *vi (dash)* (ἐξ)ὁρμῶ, ἐφορμῶ, σπεύδω, τρέχω ‖ **~es** *npl (bot)* βούρλον, σπάρτο ‖ **~ hour** *n* ὥρα συνωστισμοῦ, ὥρα πολλῆς δουλειᾶς.

rusk [rʌsk] *n* παξιμάδι.

Russia ['rʌʃə] *n* Ρωσία ‖ **~n** *n* Ρῶσος ‖ *a* ρωσικός, ρούσικος.

rust [rʌst] *n* σκωρία, σκουριά ‖ *vi* σκουριάζω.

rustic ['rʌstik] *a (of the country)* ἀγροτικός, χωριάτικος ‖ *(roughly made)* χοντροκαμωμένο.

rustle ['rʌsl] *n* ψίθυρος, τρίξιμο, μουρμούρισμα ‖ *vi* θροΐζω, μουρμουρίζω ‖ *vt (US)* κλέβω, εἶμαι ζωοκλέπτης.

rustproof ['rʌstpruːf] *a* ἀνοξείδωτος.

rusty ['rʌsti] *a* σκουριασμένος.

rut [rʌt] *n (track)* αὐλάκι, τροχιά, ροδιά ‖ *(routine)* ρουτίνα, μονοτονία.

ruthless ['ruːθlis] *a* ἀνηλεής, ἄσπλαγχνος, ὠμός ‖ **~ly** *ad* ἄνευ οἴκτου, ἀλύπητα ‖ **~ness** *n* ἀσπλαγχνία, σκληρότης.

rye [rai] *n* σίκαλις ‖ **~ bread** *n* ψωμί ἀπό σίκαλη.

S, s

sabbath ['sæbəθ] *n (Jewish)* Σάββατον ‖ *(Christian)* Κυριακή.

sabbatical [sə'bætikəl] *a:* **~ year** ἄδεια ἑνός ἔτους (καθηγητοῦ).

saber ['seibə*] *n (US)* = **sabre**.

sabotage ['sæbətɑːʒ] *n* δολιοφθορά.

sabre ['seibə*] *n* σπαθί.

saccharin(e) ['sækərin] *n* σακχαρίνη.

sachet ['sæʃei] *n* σακκουλάκι (μέ ἀρώματα).

sack [sæk] *n* σάκκος, τσουβάλι ‖ *(dismissal)* ἀπόλυσις ‖ *vt* ἀπολύω ‖ *(town)* λεηλατῶ ‖ **~ful** *n* σακκιά, τσουβάλι ‖ **~ing** *n (material)* σακκόπανον ‖ *(dismissal)* ἀπόλυσις, παῦσις.

sacrament ['sækrəmənt] *n* μυστήριον, μετάληψις.

sacred ['seikrid] *a* ἱερός, ἅγιος ‖ *(duty etc)* ἀπαραβίαστος.

sacrifice ['sækrifais] *n* θυσία ‖ *vt* θυσιάζω.

sacrilege ['sækrilidʒ] *n* ἱεροσυλία, βεβήλωσις.

sacrosanct ['sækrəusæŋkt] *a* ἱερός καί ἀπαραβίαστος.

sad [sæd] *a* λυπημένος, θλιμένος ‖ *(dull)* θλιβερός, ἐλεεινός ‖ **~den** *vt* λυπῶ, θλίβω.

saddle ['sædl] *n* σέλλα ‖ *vt (burden)* φορτώνω ‖ **~bag** *n* δισάκκι.

sadism ['seidizəm] *n* σαδισμός.

sadist ['seidist] *n* σαδιστής ‖ **~ic** [sə'distik] *a* σαδιστικός.

sadly ['sædli] *ad* λυπηρά, θλιβερά ‖ *(much)* πολύ.

sadness ['sædnis] *n* θλῖψις, μελαγχολία.

safari [sə'fɑːri] *n* σαφάρι.

safe [seif] *a* ἀσφαλής, σῶος ‖ *(cautious)* προσεκτικός, σίγουρος ‖ *(sure)* ἀσφαλής, ἀκίνδυνος ‖ *n* χρηματοκιβώτιον ‖ **~guard** *n* ἐξασφάλισις, προστασία ‖ *vt* προστατεύω ‖ **~keeping** *n* ἀσφάλεια ‖ **~ly** *ad* ἀσφαλῶς, σίγουρα ‖ **~ness** *n* ἀσφάλεια, σιγουριά ‖ **~ty** *n* ἀσφάλεια, σιγουριά ‖ **~ty belt** *n* ζώνη ἀσφαλείας ‖ **~ty curtain** *n* αὐλαία ἀσφαλείας ‖ **~ty pin** *n* παραμάνα.

sag [sæg] *vi* κάμπτομαι, βουλιάζω.

saga ['sɑːgə] *n* ἔπος, σάγκα.

sage [seidʒ] *n (herb)* φασκομηλιά, ἀλιφασκιά ‖ *(man)* σοφός.

sago ['seigəu] *n (food)* σάγος, σαγοῦ.

said [sed] *pt,pp of* **say** ‖ *a* λεγόμενος, λεχθείς.

sail [seil] *n* ἱστίον, πανί ‖ *(trip)* πλοῦς, ταξίδι, ἀπόπλους ‖ *vt* κυβερνῶ (πλοῖον) ‖ *vi* πλέω, πάω μέ τό πανί ‖ *(depart)* ἀποπλέω ‖ *(fig: cloud etc)* τρέχω, περνῶ ‖ **~boat** *n (US)* βάρκα μέ πανί ‖ **~ing** *n (sport)* ἱστιοδρομία ‖ **to go ~ing** κάνω ἱστιοδρομίες ‖ **~ing ship** *n* ἱστιοφόρον (πλοῖον) ‖ **~or** *n* ναύτης, ναυτικός.

saint [seint] *n* ἅγιος ‖ **~liness** *n* ἁγιότης ‖ **~ly** *a* ἁγίου.

sake [seik] *n:* **for the ~ of** πρός χάριν τοῦ ‖ **for your ~** γιά τό καλό σου.

salad ['sæləd] *n* σαλάτα ‖ **~ dressing** *n* εἶδος μαγιονέζας ‖ **~ oil** *n* λάδι γιά σαλάτα.

S

salami [sə'lɑːmi] *n* σαλάμι.

salaried ['sælərid] *a* (*staff*) ἔμμισθος, μισθωτός.

salary ['sæləri] *n* μισθός.

sale [seil] *n* πώλησις, πούλημα ‖ (*for short periods*) ξεπούλημα, ἐκπτώσεις ‖ ~ **room** *n* δημοπρατήριον ‖ ~ **sman** *n* πωλητής ‖ ~ **smanship** *n* τέχνη τοῦ πωλεῖν ‖ ~ **swoman** *n* πωλήτρια.

salient ['seiliənt] *a* προεξέχων, περίοπτος.

saliva [sə'laivə] *n* σάλιο.

sallow ['sæləu] *a* ὠχρός, χλωμός.

salmon ['sæmən] *n* σολομός.

salon ['sælɔ̃ŋ] *n* κομμωτήριον.

saloon [sə'luːn] *n* (*aut*) κλειστόν (αὐτοκίνητον) ‖ (*ship's lounge*) σαλόνι.

salt [sɔːlt] *n* ἅλας, ἁλάτι ‖ (*chem*) ἅλας ‖ *vt* (*cure*) ἁλατίζω, παστώνω ‖ (*flavour*) ἁλατίζω ‖ ~ **cellar** *n* ἁλατιέρα ‖ ~ **mine** *n* ἁλατορυχεῖον ‖ ~ *y a* ἁλμυρός.

salutary ['sæljutəri] *a* σωστικός, σωτήριος.

salute [sə'luːt] *n* (*mil*) χαιρετισμός ‖ *vt* (*mil*) χαιρετίζω, ἀποδίδωχαιρετισμόν.

salvage ['sælvidʒ] *n* διάσωσις ‖ (*property saved*) ὑλικόν ἐκ περισυλλογῆς ‖ *vt* διασῴζω.

salvation [sæl'veiʃən] *n* σωτηρία ‖ **S~ Army** *n* ὁ Στρατός τῆς Σωτηρίας.

salver ['sælvə*] *n* δίσκος.

salvo ['sælvəu] *n* κανονιοβολισμός, ὁμοβροντία.

same [seim] *a* ἴδιος ‖ **all the** ~ παρ' ὅλα ταῦτα.

sample ['sɑːmpl] *n* δεῖγμα ‖ *vt* (*test*) δοκιμάζω.

sanatorium [sænə'tɔːriəm] *n* σανατόριον.

sanctify ['sæŋktifai] *vt* ἁγιάζω, καθαγιάζω ‖ (*establish*) καθιερώνω.

sanctimonious [sæŋkti'məuniəs] *a* ψευτοθεοφοβούμενος, ὑποκριτής.

sanction ['sæŋkʃən] *n* (*pol, econ*) (ἐπι)κύρωσις.

sanctity ['sæŋktiti] *n* ἁγιότης, ἁγιοσύνη ‖ (*sacredness*) ἱερότης, ἀπαραβίαστον.

sanctuary ['sæŋktjuəri] *n* ἱερόν, ἄδυτον ‖ (*for fugitive*) ἄσυλον ‖ (*refuge*) καταφύγιον.

sand [sænd] *n* ἄμμος ‖ *vt* στρώνω μέ ἄμμο ‖ ~ **s** *npl* ἀμμουδιά.

sandal ['sændl] *n* σανδάλι, πέδιλον.

sandbag ['sændbæg] *n* σάκκος ἄμμου.

sand dune ['sænddjuːn] *n* ἀμμόλοφος.

sandpaper ['sændpeipə*] *n* γυαλόχαρτο.

sandpit ['sændpit] *n* (*for children*) ἀμμόκουτο.

sandstone ['sændstəun] *n* ψαμμίτης, ψαμμόλιθος.

sandwich ['sænwidʒ] *n* σάντουϊτς ‖ *vt* παρεμβάλλω, στριμώχνω.

sandy ['sændi] *a* (*with sand*) ἀμμώδης, ἀμμουδερός ‖ (*colour*) πυρόξανθος.

sane [sein] *a* ἐχέφρων, σώφρων ‖ (*sensible*) λογικός.

sang [sæŋ] *pt of* **sing**.

sanguine ['sæŋgwin] *a* (*hopeful*) αἰσιόδοξος.

sanitarium [sæni'tɛəriəm] *n* (*US*) = **sanatorium**.

sanitary ['sænitəri] *a* ὑγιεινός ‖ (*protective*) ὑγιειονομικός ‖ ~ **napkin** (*US*), ~ **towel** *n* πετσέτα ὑγιεινῆς.

sanitation [sæni'teiʃən] *n* ὑγιεινή, καθαριότης.

sanity ['sæniti] *n* πνευματική ὑγεία, ὑγιής ‖ *o* νοῦς ‖ (*good sense*) μετριοπάθεια, λογική.

sank [sæŋk] *pt of* **sink**.

Santa Claus [sæntə'klɔːz] *n* Ἅη Βασίλης.

sap [sæp] *n* (*of plants*) χυμός, ὀπός ‖ *vt* (*wear away*) ὑπονομεύω, ὑποσκάπτω.

sapling ['sæplin] *n* δενδρύλιον.

sapphire ['sæfaiə*] *n* σάπφειρος.

sarcasm ['sɑːkæzəm] *n* σαρκασμός.

sarcastic [sɑː'kæstik] *a* σαρκαστικός.

sarcophagus [sɑː'kɔfəgəs] *n* σαρκοφάγος.

sardine [sɑː'diːn] *n* σαρδέλλα.

sardonic [sɑː'dɔnik] *a* σαρδόνιος, κοροϊδευτικός.

sartorial [sɑː'tɔːriəl] *a* τοῦ ῥάφτη, τῶν ῥαφτικῶν.

sash [sæʃ] *n* (*mil*) ζώνη ἀξιωματικῶν.

sat [sæt] *pt,pp of* **sit**.

Satan ['seitn] *n* Σατανᾶς ‖ ~ **ic** [sə'tænik] *a* σατανικός.

satchel ['sætʃəl] *n* (*sch*) τσάντα, σάκκα.

satellite ['sætəlait] *n* δορυφόρος ‖ *a* δορυφορικός, ὑπόκεντρος.

satin ['sætin] *n* σατέν ‖ *a* σατινέ, ἀπό σατέν.

satire ['sætaiə*] *n* σάτυρα.

satirical [sə'tirikəl] *a* σατυρικός.

satirize ['sætəraiz] *vt* σατυρίζω, διακωμῳδῶ.

satisfaction [sætis'fækʃən] *n* ἱκανοποίησις, εὐχαρίστησις.

satisfactorily [sætis'fæktərili] *ad* ἱκανοποιητικά.

satisfactory [sætis'fæktəri] *a* 'ἱκανοποιητικός.

satisfy ['sætisfai] *vt* ἱκανοποιῶ ‖ (*convince*) πείθω, διαβεβαιῶ ‖ ~ **ing** *a* ἱκανοποιητικός.

saturate ['sætʃəreit] *vt* διαβρέχω, διαποτίζω, μουσκεύω.

saturation [sætʃə'reiʃən] *n* διάβρεξις, κορεσμός.

Saturday ['sætədi] *n* Σάββατον.

sauce [sɔːs] *n* σάλτσα ‖ ~ **pan** *n* κατσαρόλα, τέντζερες ‖ ~ **r** *n* πιατάκι.

saucily ['sɔːsili] *ad* ἀναιδῶς, μόρτικα, τσαχπίνικα.

sauciness ['sɔːsinis] *n* ἀναίδεια, ἀδιαντροπιά.

saucy ['sɔːsi] *a* ἀναιδής, αὐθάδης.

saunter ['sɔːntə*] *vi* σουλατσάρω, περπατῶ ἄσκοπα ‖ *n* βόλτα, χάζεμα.

sausage ['sɔsidʒ] *n* λουκάνικο ‖ ~ **roll** *n* λουκάνικο μέ ζύμη.

savage ['sævidʒ] *a* ἄγριος, θηριώδης ‖ (*uncivilized*) ἀπολίτιστος, βάρβαρος ‖ *n* ἄγριος ‖ *vt* δαγκώνω, ἐπιτίθεμαι ἀγρίως ‖ ~**ly** *ad* μέ ἀγριότητα ‖ ~**ry** *n* ἀγριότης, βαρβαρότης.

save [seiv] *vt* σώζω, γλυτώνω ‖ (*store up*) (ἐξ)οἰκονομῶ, ἀποταμιεύω, μαζεύω ‖ (*avoid using up*) φειδωλεύομαι, ἀποφεύγω ‖ *n* οἰκονομία ‖ *prep,cj* πλήν, ἐκτός, ἐξαιρουμένου.

saving ['seiviŋ] *a* (*redeeming*) σωτήριος ‖ *n* οἰκονομία ‖ ~**s** *npl* ἀποταμιεύσεις, καταθέσεις, οἰκονομίες ‖ ~**s bank** *n* ταμιευτήριον.

saviour ['seivjə*] *n* σωτήρας.

savoir-faire ['sævwa:'fɛə*] *n* ἐπιδεξιότης, τάκτ.

savour, (*US*) **savor** ['seivə*] *n* οὐσία, γεῦσις, γοῦστο ‖ *vt* γεύομαι ‖ (+ *of*) ὄζω, μυρίζω ἀπό ‖ ~**y** *a* γευστικός, νόστιμος, ὀρεκτικός.

savvy ['sævi] *n* (*col*) καταλαβαίνω.

saw [sɔ:] (*irreg v*) *n* (*tool*) πριόνι ‖ *vt* πριονίζω ‖ *pt of* **see** ‖ ~**dust** *n* πριονίδια ‖ ~**mill** *n* πριονιστήριον.

Saxon ['sæksn] *n* Σάξων.

saxophone ['sæksəfəun] *n* σαξόφωνον.

say [sei] (*irreg v*) *n* λόγος, κουβέντα ‖ *vt* (*tell*) λέγω ‖ (*repeat*) (ξαναλέγω ‖ (*suppose*) ὑποθέτω ‖ ~**ing** *n* ρητόν.

scab [skæb] *n* κάρκαδο ‖ (*pej: industry*) ἀπεργοσπάστης.

scabby ['skæbi] *a* καρκαδιασμένος.

scaffold ['skæfəld] *n* ἰκρίωμα ‖ ~**ing** *n* σκαλωσιά.

scald [skɔ:ld] *n* ζεμάτισμα ‖ *vt* ζεματίζω ‖ ~**ing** *a* (*hot*) ζεματιστός.

scale [skeil] *n* (*of fish*) λέπι ‖ (*mus*) κλῖμαξ, σκάλα ‖ (*for measuring*) κλῖμαξ, διαβάθμισις ‖ (*on map*) κλῖμαξ ‖ (*size*) κλίμακα ‖ *vt* (*climb*) ἀναρριχῶμαι, σκαρφαλώνω ‖ ~**s** *npl* (*balance*) ζυγός, ζυγαριά ‖ **on a large** ~ σέ μεγάλη κλίμακα ‖ ~ **drawing** *n* σχέδιον ὑπό κλίμακα.

scallop ['skɔləp] *n* (*shellfish*) χτένι.

scalp [skælp] *n* τριχωτόν δέρμα κεφαλῆς ‖ *vt* γδέρνω τό κρανίον.

scalpel ['skælpəl] *n* νυστέρι.

scamp [skæmp] *n* κακοφτιάνω, πασαλείβω.

scamper ['skæmpə*] *vi* τρέχω τρελλά, τό στρίβω.

scan [skæn] *vt* ἐξονυχίζω, διερευνῶ ‖ (*poet*) διαβάζω ἐμμέτρως.

scandal ['skændl] *n* σκάνδαλον ‖ (*gossip*) κακολογία, κουτσομπολιό ‖ ~**ize** *vt* σκανδαλίζω, ταράσσω ‖ ~**ous** *a* σκανδαλώδης.

Scandinavia [skændi'neiviə] *n* Σκανδιναβία ‖ ~**n** *a,n* Σκανδιναβικός.

scant [skænt] *a* πενιχρός, ἀνεπαρκής, λιγοστός ‖ ~**ily** *ad* ἀνεπαρκῶς, ἐλαφρά, λιγοστά ‖ ~**iness** *n* σπάνις, ἀνεπάρκεια, ἀραιότης ‖ ~**y** *a* ἀνεπαρκής, λιγοστός, πρόχειρος.

scapegoat ['skeipgəut] *n* ἀποδιοπομπαῖος τράγος.

scar [ska:*] *n* οὐλή, σημάδι ‖ *vt* ἀφήνω σημάδι.

scarce [skɛəs] *a* σπάνιος, σπανίζων ‖ ~**ly** *ad* μόλις, σχεδόν καθόλου ‖ ~**ness** *n* σπανιότης, ἔλλειψις.

scarcity ['skɛəsiti] *n* σπάνις, ἔλλειψις.

scare [skɛə*] *n* ἐκφόβισις, τρομάρα ‖ *vt* φοβίζω, τρομάζω ‖ ~**crow** *n* φόβητρον, σκιάχτρο.

scarf [ska:f] *n* σάρπα, κασκόλ.

scarlet ['ska:lit] *a* (*colour*) κατακόκκινος ‖ *n* κτυπητό κόκκινο ‖ ~ **fever** *n* ὀστρακιά, σκαρλατίνα.

scarves [ska:vz] *npl of* **scarf**.

scary ['skɛəri] *a* (*col*) τρομακτικός, τρομερός.

scathing ['skeiðiŋ] *a* καυστικός, δηκτικός.

scatter ['skætə*] *n* διασπορά, σκόρπισμα ‖ *vt* (*sprinkle*) σκορπίζω ‖ (*an enemy*) διασκορπίζω ‖ *vi* διαλύομαι, σκορπίζω ‖ ~**brained** *a* ἄμυαλος, ξεμυαλισμένος ‖ ~**ing** *n* μικρά ποσότης, σκόρπισμα.

scavenger ['skævindʒə*] *n* (ὁδο)καθαριστής, σκουπιδιάρης.

scene [si:n] *n* (*of accident etc*) τόπος, θέατρον ‖ (*of play*) σκηνή ‖ (*division of play*) σκηνή ‖ (*view*) τοπεῖον, ἄποψις, θέα ‖ (*fuss*) σκηνή, φασαρία, ἐπεισόδιον ‖ (*incident*) σκηνή, συμβάν ‖ **on the** ~ ἐπί τόπω, ἐπί σκηνῆς ‖ ~**ry** *n* σκηνικόν, σκηνογραφία, σκηνή ‖ (*view*) τοπίον, θέα, ἄποψις.

scenic ['si:nik] *a* σκηνικός, θεαματικός.

scent [sent] *n* ὀσμή, ἄρωμα, μυρουδιά ‖ (*sense of smell*) ὄσφρησις ‖ *vt* (*make fragrant*) ἀρωματίζω, μοσχοβολῶ.

scepter ['septə*] *n* (*US*) = **sceptre**.

sceptic ['skeptik] *n* σκεπτικιστής ‖ ~**al** *a* σκεπτικός, δύσπιστος ‖ ~**ism** *n* σκεπτικισμός.

sceptre ['septə*] *n* σκῆπτρον.

schedule ['ʃedju:l, (*US*) 'skedju:l] *n* κατάλογος, πρόγραμμα, δρομολόγιον ‖ *vt* καταγράφω, προγραμματίζω ‖ **on** ~ στήν ὥρα ‖ σύμφωνα μέ τό πρόγραμμα ‖ **behind** ~ καθυστερημένος.

scheme [ski:m] *n* διάταξις, συνδυασμός ‖ (*plan*) σχέδιον ‖ (*plot*) μηχανορραφία, δολοπλοκία ‖ *vti* μηχανορραφῶ, σχεδιάζω.

scheming ['ski:miŋ] *a* δολοπλόκος, κομπιναδόρος.

schism ['sizəm] *n* σχίσμα.

schizophrenic [skitsəu'frenik] *a* σχιζοφρενικός.

scholar ['skɔlə*] *n* μελετητής, μορφωμένος ‖ (*with scholarship*) ὑπότροφος ‖ ~**ly** *ad* μορφωμένος ‖ ~ship n ὑποτροφία ‖ (learning) μόρφωσις.

school [sku:l] n σχολεῖον, σκολειό ‖ (group) σχολή ‖ (department) σχολή ‖ attr a σχολικό, τοῦ σχολείου ‖ vt διδάσκω, γυμνάζω, μορφώνω ‖ ~book n σχολικόν βιβλίον ‖ ~boy n μαθητής ‖ ~days npl σχολικά χρόνια ‖ ~girl n μαθήτρια ‖ ~ing n ἐκπαίδευσις, μόρφωσις ‖ ~master n (δι)δάσκαλος, καθηγητής ‖ διευθυντής ‖ ~mistress n δασκάλα, καθηγήτρια ‖ ~room n αἴθουσα διδασκαλίας ‖ ~teacher n δημοδιδάσκαλος.

schooner [sku:nə*] n (ship) σκούνα ‖ (glass for sherry etc) ποτηράκι.

sciatica [sai'ætikə] n ἰσχιαλγία.

science ['saiəns] n ἐπιστήμη.

scientific [saiən'tifik] a ἐπιστημονικός.

scientist ['saiəntist] n ἐπιστήμων.

scintillating ['sintileitiŋ] a σπινθοβόλος, ἀστραφτερός.

scissors ['sizəz] npl ψαλίδι ‖ a pair of ~ ψαλίδι.

scoff [skɔf] vt (eat) τρώγω, καταβροχθίζω ‖ vi (mock) (+ at) σκόπτω, κοροϊδεύω.

scold [skəuld] vt ἐπιπλήττω, μαλώνω.

scone [skɔn] n εἶδος κέϊκ.

scoop [sku:p] n φτυάρι, σέσουλα ‖ vt (also ~ out or up) ἀδειάζω ‖ ἀνασκάπτω.

scooter ['sku:tə*] n (motorcycle) βέσπα ‖ (child's toy) πατίνι.

scope [skəup] n ἀντίληψις, γνῶσις ‖ (opportunity) ὁρίζων, εὐκαιρία, περιθώριον.

scorch [skɔ:tʃ] n καψάλισμα, κάψιμο ‖ vt καψαλίζω, τσουρουφλίζω ‖ (wither) ψήνω, ξεραίνω ‖ ~er n (col: hot day) πολύ ζεστή ἡμέρα, κάψα ‖ ~ing a καφτερός, καυστική.

score [skɔ:*] n (points) σκόρ ‖ (mus) παρτιτούρα ‖ (reason) θέμα, σημεῖον, ζήτημα ‖ (twenty) εἰκοσάς, εἰκοσαριά ‖ vt (win points) σημειώνω, κάνω (πόντους) ‖ (mark) χαράσσω, χαρακώνω ‖ vi (keep record) κρατῶ σκόρ ‖ ~board n πίνακα τῶν σκόρ ‖ ~r n (player) ὁ ἐπιτυχών τέρμα ‖ (recorder) μαρκαδόρος.

scorn ['skɔ:n] n περιφρόνησις ‖ vt περιφρονῶ ‖ ~ful a περιφρονητικός ‖ ~fully ad περιφρονητικά.

scorpion ['skɔ:piən] n σκορπιός.

Scot [skɔt] n Σκῶτος, Σκωτσέζος ‖ ~ch n (whisky) σκώτς (σκωτσέζικο) οὐΐσκυ.

scotch [skɔtʃ] vt (terminate) ἀποτρέπω, καταπνίγω.

Scotland ['skɔtlənd] n Σκωτία.

Scots [skɔts] npl Σκωτσέζοι ‖ a σκωτσέζος ‖ ~man n Σκωτσέζος ‖ ~woman n Σκωτς, Σκωτσέζα.

Scottish ['skɔtiʃ] a σκωτικός, σκωτσέζικος.

scoundrel ['skaundrəl] n παλιάνθρωπος.

scour ['skauə*] vt (search) διατρέχω, ἐρευνῶ ‖ (clean) καθαρίζω, παστρέβω,

γυαλίζω, τρίβω ‖ ~er n (for pans) σύρμα, μπρίλλο.

scourge [skə:dʒ] n (plague) πληγή.

scout [skaut] n ἀνιχνευτής ‖ (boy scout) πρόσκοπος ‖ vi (reconnoitre) ἀνιχνεύω, κατοπτεύω.

scowl [skaul] n συνοφρύωσις, σκυθρωπότης ‖ vi συνοφρυοῦμαι, κατσουφιάζω.

scraggy ['skrægi] a ἰσχνός, κοκκαλιάρης.

scram [skræm] vi (col) στρίβω, τό βάζω στά πόδια ‖ ~! στρίβε!, δίνε του!

scramble ['skræmbl] n σκαρφάλωμα ‖ ἀγών, πάλη ‖ vi ἀνεβαίνω, κατεβαίνω, μπουρσουλῶ ‖ συνωστίζομαι, σπρώχνομαι ‖ ~d eggs npl (αὐγά) σφουγγάτο.

scrap [skræp] n κομματάκι, ἀπόρριμμα, ψίχουλο ‖ (fight) συμπλοκή, καυγᾶς ‖ (scrap iron) παλιοσίδερα ‖ a γιά πέταμα, ἄχρηστος ‖ vt πετῶ ὡς ἄχρηστον, ἀπορρίπτω ‖ vi (fight) πιάνομαι στά χέρια ‖ ~s npl (waste) ἀπομεινάρια, ἀπορρίμματα ‖ ~book n λεύκωμα ἀποκομμάτων.

scrape [skreip] n (ἀπό)ξέσις, ξύσιμο ‖ (awkward position) ἀμηχανία, μπελάς ‖ vt (ἀπο)ξέω, ξύνω, ξεγδέρνω ‖ (clean) ξύνω, τρίβω ‖ vi τρίζω, στριγγλίζω, ξύνω ‖ ~r n ξύστρα, ξέστρα.

scrap heap ['skræphi:p] n σωρός παλιοσιδερικῶν.

scrap merchant ['skræpmə:tʃənt] n ἔμπορος παλιοσιδερικῶν.

scrappy ['skræpi] a ἀσύνδετος, ἀσυνάρτητος, ἀνακατεμένος.

scratch ['skrætʃ] n νυχιά, ἀμυχή, γρατσουνιά ‖ (itch) ξύσιμο ‖ ἐκ τοῦ προχείρου ‖ vt ξύνω, τρίβω ‖ (wound) γρατσουνίζω, ξεγδέρνω ‖ vi (rub) ξύνομαι.

scrawl [skrɔ:l] n ὀρνιθοσκαλίσματα ‖ vti κακογραφῶ, ὀρνιθοσκαλίζω.

scream [skri:m] n κραυγή, ξεφωνητό, στριγγλιά ‖ vi ξεφωνάζω ‖ (speak loudly) στριγγλίζω.

scree [skri:] n λιθών.

screech [skri:tʃ] n κραυγή, σκούξιμο, στριγγλιά ‖ vi σκούζω, στριγγλίζω, οὐρλιάζω.

screen [skri:n] n παραπέτασμα, προπέτασμα, παραβάν ‖ (for films) ὀθόνη, πανί ‖ (church) κιγκλίδωμα ‖ vt προφυλάσσω, προστατεύω ‖ (film) κινηματογραφῶ, γυρίζω.

screw [skru:] n κοχλίας, βίδα ‖ (naut) ἕλιξ, προπέλλα ‖ vt βιδώνω, σφίγγω ‖ (col) καταπιέζω, ξεζουμίζω ‖ ~driver n κατσαβίδι ‖ ~y a (col) μουρλός, ξεβιδωμένος.

scribble ['skribl] n κακογραφία ‖ vt γράφω βιαστικά, ὀρνιθοσκαλίζω.

scribe [skraib] n γραφεύς, γραφιάς.

script [skript] n χειρόγραφον ‖ (of play) κείμενον, σενάριο.

Scripture ['skriptʃə*] n Ἁγία Γραφή.

scriptwriter ['skriptraitə*] n σεναριογράφος.

scroll [skrəul] n κύλινδρος, ρόλλος (περγαμηνής).

scrounge [skraundʒ] vt (col) βουτῶ, τρακάρω, σελεμίζω ‖ n: on the ~ πάω τσάρκα.

scrub [skrʌb] n (clean) τριβή, τρίψιμο, βούρτσισμα ‖ (countryside) χαμόκλαδα, αγριμιά ‖ vt πλένω, βουρτσίζω, τρίβω ‖ (erase) απορρίπτω, σβήνω.

scruff [skrʌf] n σβέρκο.

scrum(mage) ['skrʌm(idʒ)] n συμπλοκή, συνωστισμός.

scruple ['skru:pl] n συνείδησις, ενδοιασμός, δισταγμός.

scrupulous ['skru:pjuləs] a ευσυνείδητος ‖ ~ly ad ευσυνείδητα.

scrutinize ['skru:tinaiz] vt εξετάζω προσεκτικά, διερευνώ.

scrutiny ['skru:tini] n (αυστηρός) έλεγχος, διερεύνησις.

scuff [skʌf] vt (shoes) σέρνω τά πόδια, τρίβω, φθείρω.

scuffle ['skʌfl] n συμπλοκή, καυγάς.

scull [skʌl] vi κωπηλατῶ.

scullery ['skʌləri] n πλυντήριον μαγειρίου, λάντσα.

sculptor ['skʌlptə*] n γλύπτης.

sculpture ['skʌlptʃə*] n γλυπτική ‖ (statue) γλυπτόν.

scum [skʌm] n αφρός, βρωμιά ‖ (people) κατακάθια, αποβράσματα.

scurrilous ['skʌriləs] a υβριστικός, αχρείος, βρώμικος.

scurry ['skʌri] vi τρέχα, σπεύδω.

scurvy ['skə:vi] n σκορβοῦτον.

scuttle ['skʌtl] vt (plans) εγκαταλείπω, υποχωρῶ ‖ vi (scamper) τρέχω βιαστικά, τό στρίβω.

scythe [saið] n δρεπάνι.

sea [si:] n θάλασσα ‖ (broad stretch) ωκεανός, θάλασσα ‖ a θαλασσινός, τῆς θάλασσας ‖ ~ bird n θαλασσοπούλι ‖ ~board n ακτή, παραλία ‖ ~ breeze n θαλασσία αύρα, μπάτης ‖ ~farer n θαλασσινός, θαλασσοπόρος ‖ ~faring a θαλασσοπόρος, θαλασσινός ‖ ~food n θαλασσινά ‖ ~ front n παραλία, προκυμαία ‖ ~going a ποντοπόρος ‖ ~gull n γλάρος.

seal [si:l] n (animal) φώκια ‖ (stamp) σφραγίδα, βούλα ‖ (impression) σφραγίδα ‖ vt σφραγίζω ‖ (close) κλείνω, σφραγίζω, βουλώνω.

sea level ['si:levl] n επιφάνεια θαλάσσης.

sealing wax ['si:liŋwæks] n βουλοκέρι.

sea lion ['si:laiən] n είδος φώκιας.

seam [si:m] n ραφή ‖ (joining) ένωσις, ραφή ‖ (of coal etc) φλέβα.

seaman ['si:mən] n ναυτικός, ναύτης.

seamless ['si:mlis] a χωρίς ραφήν.

seamy ['si:mi] a ανάποδος, άσχημος.

seaport ['si:pɔ:t] n λιμάνι.

search [sə:tʃ] n έρευνα, αναζήτησις ‖ vt ερευνῶ, αναζητῶ, ψάχνω ‖ κάνω έρευνες ‖ ~ing a ερευνητικός, προσεκτικός ‖ ~light n προβολεύς ‖ ~ party n απόσπασμα έρευνης.

seashore ['si:ʃɔ:*] n ακτή, παραλία.

seasick ['si:sik] a ναυτιῶν ‖ ~ness n ναυτία.

seaside ['si:said] n παραλία, γιαλό.

season ['si:zn] n εποχή ‖ vt αρτύω, καρυκεύω, ωριμάζω ‖ ~al a εποχιακός ‖ ~ed a (food) καρυκευμένος, πικάντικο ‖ ~ing n καρύκευσις, άρτυμα, μπαχαρικό ‖ ~ ticket n διαρκές εισιτήριον.

seat [si:t] n κάθισμα, καρέκλα ‖ (parl etc) έδρα ‖ (manner of sitting) κάθισμα, θέσις ‖ (bottom) πισινός, οπίσθια ‖ vt καθίζω ‖ (accommodate) (τόσων) θέσεων ‖ ~ belt n ζώνη ασφαλείας ‖ ~ing n διάταξις θέσεων, καθισμάτων.

sea water ['si:wɔ:tə*] n θαλασσινό νερό.

seaweed ['si:wi:d] n φύκι, φύκια.

seaworthy ['si:wə:ði] a πλόιμος, ικανός νά πλεύση.

secede [si'si:d] vi αποχωρῶ, αποσπῶμαι.

secluded [si'klu:did] a παράμερος, απομονωμένος, μονήρης.

seclusion [si'klu:ʒən] n απομόνωσις.

second ['sekənd] a δεύτερος ‖ ad (in second position) δεύτερος ‖ (rail) δευτέρα (θέσι) ‖ n (of time) δευτερόλεπτο ‖ ο δεύτερος ‖ (comm: imperfect) δεύτερο (χέρι) ‖ vt υποστηρίζω, βοηθῶ ‖ ~ary a δευτερεύων, ασήμαντος ‖ (education) μέση (εκπαίδευσις) ‖ ~ary school n γυμνάσιον ‖ ~er n υποστηρικτής ‖ ~hand a μεταχειρισμένος, δεύτερο χέρι ‖ (not original) μή πρωτότυπος, εμμέσως ‖ ~ly ad κατά δεύτερον λόγον ‖ ~ nature n δευτέρα φύσις ‖ ~-rate a μέτριος, δευτέρας ποιότητος ‖ ~ thoughts npl δεύτερες σκέψεις.

secrecy ['si:krəsi] n μυστικότης, εχεμύθεια.

secret ['si:krit] n μυστικόν ‖ a μυστικός, κρυφός, απόρρητος.

secretarial [sekrə'teəriəl] a τοῦ γραμματέως.

secretariat [sekrə'teəriət] n γραμματεία.

secretary ['sekrətri] n γραμματεύς ‖ (minister etc) υπουργός.

secretive ['si:krətiv] a κρυψίνους.

secretly ['si:kritli] ad μυστικά, κρυφά.

sect [sekt] n αίρεσις ‖ ~arian a αιρετικός, στενοκέφαλος, κομματικός.

section ['sekʃən] n χωρισμός, τμήσις, κόψιμο ‖ (piece) τμήμα, μέρος, τομή ‖ ~al a τμηματικός, τοπικός.

sector ['sektə*] n (private or public sector) τομεύς.

secular ['sekjulə*] a λαϊκός, κοσμικός ‖ μακροχρόνιος.

secure [si'kjuə*] a βέβαιος, ήσυχος,

ἀκίνδυνος ‖ (*fixed*) ἀσφαλής ‖ *vt* (*fix*) στερεώνω, σφίγγω ‖ (*obtain*) ἐξασφαλίζω ‖ ~**ly** *ad* ἀσφαλῶς, σίγουρα ‖ στερεά.

security [si'kjuəriti] *n* ἀσφάλεια, σιγουριά ‖ (*bond*) ἐγγύησις, χρεώγραφον ‖ (*national security*) ἀσφάλεια ‖ *see* **social**.

sedate [si'deit] *a* ἀτάραχος, ἤρεμος.

sedation [si'deiʃən] *n* (*med*) καταπράϋνσις.

sedative ['sedətiv] *n* καταπραϋντικόν ‖ *a* καταπραϋντικός.

sedentary ['sedntri] *a* ἀδρανής, καθιστικός.

sediment ['sedimənt] *n* ὑποστάθμη, κατακάθι, ἴζημα ‖ ~**ary** *a* (*geol*) ἰζηματογενής.

seduce [si'dju:s] *vt* (*general*) δελεάζω, παρασύρω ‖ (*sexually*) διαφθείρω, ἀποπλανῶ.

seduction [si'dʌkʃən] *n* ἀποπλάνησις, δελεασμός.

seductive [si'dʌktiv] *a* . γοητευτικός, ἀποπλανητικός.

see [si:] (*irreg v*) *vt* βλέπω ‖ (*find out*) φροντίζω, κοιτάζω ‖ (*understand*) καταλαβαίνω ‖ (*make sure*) φροντίζω ‖ (*accompany*) συνοδεύω ‖ (*visit*) πηγαίνω, βλέπω, ἐπισκέπτομαι ‖ *vi* ἀντιλαμβάνομαι, συλλαμβάνω ‖ φροντίζω, ἐξετάζω ‖ *n* (*bishop's*) ἐπισκοπή ‖ **to ~ through** φροντίζω μέχρι τέλους, παρακολουθῶ ‖ **to ~ to** φροντίζω γιά ‖ **to ~ off** προπέμπω, ξεπροβοδίζω.

seed [si:d] *n* σπόρος ‖ (*grain*) κόκκος, σπειρί ‖ ~**ling** *n* δενδρύλλιον, νεαρόν φυτόν ‖ ~**y** *a* (*ill*) ἀδιάθετος, τσακισμένος ‖ (*shabby*) κουρελιασμένος.

seeing ['si:iŋ] *cj* ἐφόσον, ἀφοῦ, δεδομένου ὅτι.

seek [si:k] (*irreg v*) *vt* ἀναζητῶ, ψάχνω, ζητῶ.

seem [si:m] *vi* φαίνομαι, μοιάζω ‖ ~**ingly** *ad* φαινομενικά, κατά τά φαινόμενα ‖ ~**ly** *a* κόσμιος, καθώς πρέπει.

seen [si:n] *pp of* **see**.

seep [si:p] *vi* διαρρέω, περνῶ ἀπό.

seer [siə*] *n* προφήτης.

seesaw ['si:sɔ:] *n* (*plank*) τραμπάλα.

seethe [si:ð] *vi* (*be agitated*) ἀναταράσσομαι, βράζω.

see-through ['si:θru:] *a* (*dress*) διαφανής, ση-θρού.

segment ['segmənt] *n* τμῆμα.

segregate ['segrigeit] *vt* ἀπομονώνω, χωρίζω.

segregation [segri'geiʃən] *n* ἀπομόνωσις, χωρισμός.

seismic ['saizmik] *a* σεισμικός.

seize [si:z] *vt* ἁρπάζω, πιάνω ‖ (*take possession*) κατάσχω ‖ καταλαμβάνω ‖ (*understand*) ἀντιλαμβάνω, συλλαμβάνω ‖ **to ~ up** *vi* (*mech*) σφηνώνομαι, μαγκώνω, κολλῶ.

seizure ['si:ʒə*] *n* (*illness*) ἀπότομη προσβολή.

seldom ['seldəm] *ad* σπανίως, σπάνια.

select [si'lekt] *a* ἐκλεκτός, διαλεχτός ‖ *vt* ἐκλέγω, διαλέγω ‖ ~**ion** *n* ἐκλογή, διαλογή, ἐπιλογή ‖ ~**ive** *a* ἐκλεκτικός ‖ ~**or** *n* (*person*) ἐκλέγων, ἐκλέκτωρ ‖ (*tech*) ἐπιλογεύς.

self [self] *n* ἑαυτός, τό πρόσωπον, τό ἄτομον ‖ ~**-appointed** *a* αὐτοδιορισμένος ‖ ~**-assurance** *n* αὐτοπεποίθησις ‖ ~**-assured** *a* ἐπηρμένος, φαντασμένος ‖ ~**-confidence** *n* αὐτοπεποίθησις ‖ ~**-confident** *a* γεμᾶτος αὐτοπεποίθησιν ‖ ~**-conscious** *a* δειλός, ἔχων τράκ ‖ ~**-contained** *a* αὐτοτελής, ἀνεξάρτητος ‖ (*reserved*) ἐπιφυλακτικός ‖ ~**-defence** *n* αὐτοάμυνα ‖ ~**-evident** *a* αὐταπόδεικτος ‖ ~**-explanatory** *a* αὐτεξήγητος ‖ ~**-indulgent** *a* αὐτεντρύφητος, συβαρίτης ‖ ~**-interest** *n* ἰδιοτέλεια ‖ ~**ish** *a* ἐγωϊστικός, ἰδιοτελής ‖ ~**ishly** *ad* ἐγωϊστικά ‖ ~**ishness** *n* ἐγωϊσμός, ἰδιοτέλεια ‖ ~**lessly** *ad* ἀλτρουϊστικά ‖ ~**-made** *a* αὐτοδημιούργητος ‖ ~**-portrait** *n* αὐτοπροσωπογραφία ‖ ~**-propelled** *a* αὐτοκινούμενος ‖ ~**-reliant** *a* ἀνεξάρτητος ‖ ~**-respect** *n* αὐτοσεβασμός ‖ ~**-respecting** *a* σεβόμενος τόν ἑαυτόν του ‖ ~**-righteous** *a* ὑποκριτικός ‖ ~**-satisfied** *a* ἔχων αὐταρέσκειαν, καμαρωτός ‖ ~**-service** *a* αὐτοσερβίρισμα ‖ ~**-sufficient** *a* αὐτάρκης ‖ ~**-supporting** *a* (*fin*) αὐτοσυντήρητος, αὐτάρκης.

sell [sel] (*irreg v*) *vt* πωλῶ, πουλῶ ‖ *vi* (*comm*) πωλοῦμαι ‖ ~**er** *n* πωλητής ‖ ~**ing price** *n* τιμή πωλήσεως.

selves [selvz] *pl of* **self**.

semantic [si'mæntik] *a* σημασιολογικός ‖ ~**s** *n* σημασιολογία.

semaphore ['seməfɔ:*] *n* (*system*) σηματοφόρος.

semi ['semi] *prefix* ἡμι- ‖ ~**circle** *n* ἡμικύκλιον ‖ ~**colon** *n* ἄνω τελεία ‖ ~**conscious** *a* ἡμιαναίσθητος ‖ ~**detached house** *n* ὁριζόντιος διπλοκατοικία ‖ ~**final** *n* ἡμιτελικός.

seminar ['seminɑ:*] *n* σεμινάριον.

semiquaver ['semikweivə*] *n* (*mus*) δέκατον ἕκτον.

semiskilled ['semi'skild] *a* ἡμιεκπαιδευμένος.

semitone ['semitəun] *n* (*mus*) ἡμιτόνιον.

semolina [semə'li:nə] *n* σιμιγδάλι.

senate ['senit] *n* σύγκλητος ‖ (*US*) γερουσία.

senator ['senitə*] *n* γερουσιαστής.

send [send] (*irreg v*) *vt* πέμπω, στέλνω, ἀποστέλλω ‖ (*col: inspire*) ἐνθουσιάζω, τρελλαίνω ‖ **to ~ away** *vt* ἀπολύω, διώχνω ‖ **to ~ back** *vt* στέλνω πίσω, ἐπιστρέφω ‖ **to ~ for** *vt* στέλνω νά φωνάξω, καλῶ ‖ **to ~ off** *vt* (*goods*) ἀποστέλνω, στέλνω ‖ *(player)* ἀποβάλλω ‖ **to ~ out** *vt (invitation)* στέλνω ‖ **to ~ up** *vt (general)* ἀνεβάζω, στέλνω, ἀνυψώνω ‖ **~er** *n* ἀποστολεύς ‖ **~-off** *n* ἀποχαιρετισμός.

senile ['si:nail] *a* γεροντικός.

senility [si'niliti] *n* γεράματα, ξεμωράματα.

senior ['si:niə*] *a* μεγαλύτερος, πρεσβύτερος ‖ *(rank)* ἀρχαιότερος, ἀνώτερος ‖ *n* πρεσβύτερος, γηραιότερος, μεγαλύτερος ‖ *(US)* τελειόφοιτος ‖ **~ity** *n* ἀρχαιότης (βαθμοῦ).

sensation [sen'seiʃən] *n* αἴσθησις, αἴσθημα ‖ *(state of excitement)* αἴσθησις, ἐντύπωσις ‖ **~al** *a* ἐντυπωσιακός.

sense [sens] *n* αἴσθησις ‖ *(understanding)* λογική, λογικόν ‖ *(meaning)* ἔννοια, νόημα ‖ *(feeling)* (συν)αἴσθημα ‖ *vt* (δι)αἰσθάνομαι ‖ **~less** *a* ἀνόητος, παράλογος ‖ *(unconscious)* ἀναίσθητος ‖ **~lessly** *ad (stupidly)* ἀνόητα, βλακωδῶς.

sensibility [sensi'biliti] *n* εὐαισθησία, εὐπάθεια.

sensible ['sensəbl] *a* λογικός, αἰσθητός, συνειδώς.

sensibly ['sensəbli] *ad* αἰσθητά ‖ συνετά.

sensitive ['sensitiv] *a* (+ *to*) εὐαίσθητος, εὐπαθής ‖ *(easily hurt)* εὐσυγκίνητος, εὔθικτος.

sensitivity [sensi'tiviti] *n* εὐαισθησία, εὐπάθεια.

sensual ['sensjuəl] *a* αἰσθησιακός, σαρκικός, φιλήδονος.

sensuous ['sensjuəs] *a* ἡδονοπαθής, τέρπων τάς αἰσθήσεις.

sent [sent] *pt,pp of* **send**.

sentence ['sentəns] *n (gram)* πρότασις ‖ *(law)* ἀπόφασις, ποινή.

sentiment ['sentimənt] *n* αἴσθημα, αἰσθηματικότης ‖ *(thought)* γνώμη, ἄποψις ‖ **~al** *a* αἰσθηματικός ‖ **~ality** *n* αἰσθηματισμός.

sentinel ['sentinl] *n* σκοπός, φρουρός.

sentry ['sentri] *n* σκοπός, φρουρός.

separable ['sepərəbl] *a* διαιρετός, διαχωριστός.

separate ['seprit] *a* χωριστός ‖ ['sepəreit] *vt* χωρίζω, ξεχωρίζω ‖ *vi* χωρίζομαι, ἀπομακρύνομαι ‖ **~ly** *ad* ξεχωριστά.

separation [sepə'reiʃən] *n* χωρισμός, διαχώρισις.

September [sep'tembə*] *n* Σεπτέμβρης.

septic ['septik] *a* σηπτικός.

sequel ['si:kwəl] *n* συνέπεια, ἀποτέλεσμα ‖ *(continuation)* συνέχεια.

sequence ['si:kwəns] *n* διαδοχή, συνέχεια, ἀκολουθία.

sequin ['si:kwin] *n* πούλι(α).

serenade [serə'neid] *n* σερενάτα ‖ *vt* κάνω σερενάτα.

serene [sə'ri:n] *a* γαλήνιος, ἀτάραχος ‖ **~ly** *ad* ἤρεμα, γαλήνια.

serenity [si'reniti] *n* γαλήνη, ἠρεμία.

serf [sə:f] *n* δουλοπάροικος, κολλήγος.

serge [sə:dʒ] *n* σέρζ.

sergeant ['sa:dʒənt] *n* λοχίας ‖ *(police)* ἐνωμοτάρχης.

serial ['siəriəl] *n* ἱστορία σέ συνέχειες ‖ *a (number)* τεῦχος, αὔξων (ἀριθμός) ‖ **~ize** *vt* δημοσιεύω εἰς συνεχείας.

series ['siəriz] *n* σειρά.

serious ['siəriəs] *a* σοβαρός ‖ **~ly** *ad* σοβαρά ‖ **~ness** *n* σοβαρότης.

sermon ['sə:mən] *n* κήρυγμα, ὁμιλία.

serpent ['sə:pənt] *n* ὄφις, φίδι.

serrated [se'reitid] *a* ὀδοντωτός, πριονωτός.

serum ['siərəm] *n* ὀρός.

servant ['sə:vənt] *n* ὑπηρέτης ‖ *see* **civil**.

serve [sə:v] *vt* ὑπηρετῶ ‖ *(do work of)* ἐξυπηρετῶ, ἐκτελῶ ‖ *(supply)* προμηθεύω ‖ *vi (be useful)* χρησιμεύω γιά ‖ *(in army)* ὑπηρετῶ ‖ *(wait at table)* σερβίρω ‖ *(tennis)* σερβίρω ‖ *n (tennis)* σερβίρισμα ‖ **it ~s him right** καλά νά πάθη ‖ **to ~ out** *or* **up** *vt (food)* σερβίρω, διανέμω.

service ['sə:vis] *n* ὑπηρεσία ‖ *(work done)* ἐξυπηρέτησις ‖ *(government department)* ὑπηρεσία ‖ *(civil etc)* ὑπηρεσία, ἐργασία ‖ *(help)* διάθεσις, χρησιμότης ‖ *(rel)* λειτουργία ‖ *(set of dishes)* σερβίτσιο ‖ *(tennis)* σερβίς ‖ *(aut: maintenance)* συντήρησις, ἐπισκευή ‖ *vt (aut, mech)* συντηρῶ, ἐπισκευάζω ‖ **the S~s** *npl (armed forces)* τά ὅπλα, στρατός ‖ **~able** *a* εὔχρηστος, ἀνθεκτικός, χρήσιμος ‖ **~man** *n (soldier etc)* στρατιώτης ‖ **~ station** *n* γκαράζ.

serviette [sə:vi'et] *n* πετσέτα (φαγητοῦ).

servile ['sə:vail] *a* δουλικός, δουλοπρεπής.

session ['seʃən] *n* συνεδρίασις, συνεδρία.

set [set] *(irreg v) n (of things)* σειρά, συλλογή, τακίμι ‖ *(rad, TV)* συσκευή ‖ *(tennis)* γύρος, σέτ ‖ *(group of people)* ὁμάς, κατηγορία, συντροφιά, κόσμος ‖ *(cine)* συσκευή ‖ *(theat)* διάκοσμος, σκηνικόν ‖ *a* καθωρισμένος, ἄκαμπτος ‖ *a (subject)* ὑποχρεωτικός ‖ *(ready)* ἀποφασισμένος ‖ καθωρισμένος ‖ *vt* θέτω, τοποθετῶ, βάζω ‖ *(arrange)* κανονίζω ‖ *(adjust)* ρυθμίζω, βάζω, κανονίζω ‖ *(exam)* δίδω τά θέματα ‖ *vi (of sun)* δύω, βασιλεύω ‖ *(fix)* σκληρύνομαι, σφίγγω, πιάνω ‖ **to ~ on fire** καίω, πυρπολῶ, βάζω φωτιά ‖ **to ~ free** ἐλευθερώνω ‖ **to ~ sth going** ξεκινῶ ‖ **to ~ sail** ἀποπλέω ‖ **to ~ about** *vt (task)* ἀρχίζω ‖ **to ~ aside** *vt* ξεχωρίζω, βάζω κατά μέρος, ἀπορρίπτω ‖ **to ~ back** *vt (in time)* ἐπιβραδύνω, καθυστερῶ ‖ *(cost)* κοστίζω ‖ **to ~ off** *vi* ξεκινῶ, φεύγω ‖ *vt (explode)* ἐκτοξεύω, ρίχνω, ἐκρηγνύω ‖ *(show up well)* ἐξαίρω, ἀναδεικνύω, τονίζω, ὑπογραμμίζω ‖ **to ~ out** *vi* ξεκινῶ, φεύγω ‖ *vt (arrange)* ρυθμίζω, κανονίζω, σιάζω ‖ *(state)* (καθ)ὀρίζω ‖ **to ~ up** *vt* (*organization*) ίδρύω, όργανώνω ‖ ~ **back** n (*reverse*) άποτυχία, άτυχία, άναποδιά.

settee [se'ti:] n καναπές.

setting ['setiŋ] n (*scenery*) τοποθεσία, πλαίσιον ‖ (*mus*) μελοποίησις, μουσική τραγουδιού.

settle ['setl] vt (*med: calm*) καθησυχάζω, καταπραΰνω ‖ (*pay*) έξοφλῶ, πληρώνω ‖ (*agree*) ρυθμίζω, κανονίζω ‖ vi (*also* ~ **down**) έγκαθίσταμαι ‖ καθίζω ‖ σοβαρεύω ‖ (*come to rest*) έγκαθίσταμαι ‖ ~**ment** n (*payment*) έξόφλησις ‖ (*colony*) έποικισμός ‖ άποκατάστασις ‖ ~**r** n άποικος, μετανάστης.

setup ['setʌp] n (*arrangement*) τοποθέτησις, όργάνωσις ‖ (*situation*) κατάστασις.

seven ['sevn] num έπτά ‖ ~**teen** num δεκαεπτά ‖ ~**th** a έβδομος ‖ ~**ty** num έβδομήκοντα.

sever ['sevə*] vt κόβω, διακόπτω.

several ['sevrəl] a διάφορος, ξεχωριστός ‖ pron μερικοί.

severance ['sevərəns] n διαχωρισμός, (δια)κοπή.

severe [si'viə*] a αύστηρός, σκληρός ‖ (*serious*) σοβαρός ‖ (*hard, rigorous*) δριμύς, σκληρός, άγριος ‖ (*unadorned*) αύστηρός, άπέριττος, λιτός ‖ ~**ly** ad αύστηρά, σκληρά.

severity [si'veriti] n αύστηρότης, σκληρότης, δριμύτης.

sew [səu] (*irreg v*) vti ράβω ‖ **to** ~ **up** vt έπιρράπτω, ράβω.

sewage ['sju:idʒ] n άκαθαρσίες ύπονόμων, βρωμόνερα.

sewer ['sjuə*] n όχετός, ύπόνομος.

sewing ['səuiŋ] n ράψιμο ‖ ~ **machine** n ραπτομηχανή.

sewn [səun] pp of sew.

sex [seks] n φῦλον, σέξ ‖ (*activity*) γενετήσιος όρμή ‖ ~ **act** n συνουσία, γαμήσι.

sextant ['sekstənt] n έξάς.

sexual ['seksjuəl] a γενετήσιος, σεξουαλικός ‖ ~**ly** ad σεξουαλικά.

sexy ['seksi] a έλκυστικός, σεξουαλικός.

shabbily ['ʃæbili] ad άθλια, φτωχικά.

shabbiness ['ʃæbinis] n κουρέλιασμα πενιχρότης, φτήνεια.

shabby ['ʃæbi] a κουρελιασμένος, σαραβαλιασμένο ‖ (*mean*) μικροπρεπής, τσιγγούνης.

shack [ʃæk] n καλύβα.

shackle ['ʃækl] vt δεσμεύω, βάζω τά σίδερα σέ ‖ ~**s** npl δεσμά, χειροπέδες.

shade [ʃeid] n σκιά, ίσκιος ‖ (*for lamp*) άμπαζούρ ‖ (*of colour*) άπόχρωσις ‖ (*small quantity*) ίχνος, μικρά ποσότης ‖ vt σκιάζω.

shadow ['ʃædəu] n σκιά, σκοτάδι ‖ vt (*follow*) παρακολουθῶ ‖ ~**y** a σκιερός, σκιασμένος ‖ (*dim*) άσαφής, θαμπός.

shady ['ʃeidi] a σκιερός ‖ (*dubious*) ύποπτος.

shaft [ʃɑ:ft] n κοντάρι, στέλεχος, λαβή ‖ (*of mine*) φρέαρ ‖ (*of machine*) άξων, άτρακτος ‖ (*of light*) άχτίδα.

shaggy ['ʃægi] a τραχύς, τριχωτός.

shake [ʃeik] (*irreg v*) vt σείω, κουνῶ, τινάζω ‖ (*fist etc*) άπειλῶ μέ τή γροθιά μου ‖ (*rock*) (συγ)κλονίζω, κουνῶ, τραντάζω ‖ (*weaken*) κλονίζω ‖ (*alarm*) συγκλονίζω, άναστατώνω ‖ vi τρέμω, κλονίζομαι, τραντάζομαι ‖ n τίναγμα, κούνημα, δόνησις ‖ **to** ~ **off** vt τινάζω, άπαλλάσσομαι άπό ‖ **to** ~ **up** vt (*lit*) ταράζω, κουνῶ, κουρταλῶ ‖ (*fig*) ξυπνῶ, τονώνω, κουνῶ ‖ ~-**up** n πρόχειρο πρᾶμα ‖ μεγάλη μεταβολή.

shakily ['ʃeikili] ad άσταθῶς, τρέμοντας.

shakiness ['ʃeikinis] n άστάθεια, τρεμούλιασμα.

shaky ['ʃeiki] a άσταθής, τρεμουλιαστός ‖ (*weak*) κλονισμένος, άδύνατος.

shale [ʃeil] n σχιστόλιθος.

shall [ʃæl] auxiliary v: **I** ~ **go** θά φύγω, θά πάω ‖ **you** ~ **do it!** θά τό κάμης!

shallot [ʃə'lɔt] n κρόμμυον τό άσκαλωνικόν.

shallow ['ʃæləu] a (*lit*) ρηχός ‖ (*fig*) έπιπόλαιος.

sham [ʃæm] n προσποίησις, άπομίμησις, ψευτιά ‖ a προσποιητός, ψεύτικος, πλαστός.

shambles ['ʃæmblz] n sing μακελιό, σφαγεῖον.

shame [ʃeim] n έντροπή, ντροπή ‖ (*disgrace*) (κατ)αισχύνη, αίσχος ‖ (*pity*) ντροπή, άμαρτία, κρῖμα ‖ vt (*humiliate*) ντροπιάζω ‖ **what a** ~! τί κρῖμα! ‖ ~-**faced** a κατησχυμένος, ντροπιασμένος ‖ ~**ful** a έπαίσχυντος, ντροπιασμένος ‖ ~**fully** ad αίσχρά, άπαίσια, πρόστυχα ‖ ~**less** a άναίσχυντος, ξετσίπωτος.

shampoo [ʃæm'pu:] n λούσιμο, σαμπουάν ‖ vt λούζω (τά μαλλιά μου) ‖ ~ **and set** n λούσιμο καί κτένισμα.

shamrock ['ʃæmrɔk] n τριφύλλι.

shandy ['ʃændi] n (*beer and lemonade*) μπύρα μέ λεμονάδα.

shan't [ʃɑ:nt] = shall not ‖ see shall.

shanty ['ʃænti] n καλύβα, παράγγα ‖ ~-**town** n παραγγούπολις.

shape [ʃeip] n σχῆμα, μορφή, φόρμα, καλούπι ‖ vt σχηματίζω, διαμορφώνω, διαπλάθω ‖ **to take** ~ διαμορφοῦμαι, παίρνω μορφήν ‖ ~**less** a άμορφος, άκανόνιστος ‖ ~**ly** a καλοσχηματισμένος, όμορφος.

share [ʃεə*] n (*thing received*) μερίδιον, μερδικό ‖ (*contribution*) μετοχή, μερίδιον ‖ (*fin*) μετοχή, τίτλος, άξία ‖ vt μοιράζω, διανέμω ‖ (*in common*) (συμ)μετέχω ‖ ~**holder** n μέτοχος.

shark [ʃɑ:k] n (*fish*) σκυλόψαρο, καρχαρίας.

sharp [ʃɑ:p] a όξύς, αίχμηρός, μυτερός,

κοφτερός ‖ (distinct) ξεχωριστός, ἔντονος, καθαρός ‖ (biting) δριμύς, διαπεραστικός ‖ (quick-witted) ὀξύνους, ἔξυπνος, πού κόβει ‖ (unscrupulous) πονηρός, κατεργάρης ‖ n δίεσις ‖ ad ἀκριβῶς, ἔντονα, καθαρά ‖ look ~! κάνε γρήγορα. ‖ κουνήσου! ‖ ~en vt ἀκονίζω, τροχίζω, ξεμυτίζω ‖ ~ener n ξύστρα ‖ ~-eyed a πού κόβει τό μάτι του ‖ ~ness n κόψη, ὀξύτης, μυτεράδα ‖ ξινίλα ‖ ❦-witted a ὀξύνους, εὐφυής.

shatter ['ʃætə*] vt θρυμματίζω, θραύω, κάνω κομμάτια ‖ (fig) συντρίβω, κλονίζω ‖ vi συντρίβομαι, σπάω ‖ ~ing a (experience) συντριπτικός.

shave [ʃeiv] (irreg v) n ξύρισμα ‖ vt ξυρίζω ‖ περνῶ ξυστά ‖ vi ξυρίζομαι ‖ ~n a (head) ξυρισμένος ‖ ~r n (elec) ξυριστική μηχανή.

shaving ['ʃeiviŋ] n (action) ξύρισμα, πλανιάρισμα ‖ ~s npl (of wood etc) ροκανίδια, ρινίσματα ‖ ~ brush n πινέλο τοῦ ξυρίσματος ‖ ~ cream n κρέμα ξυρίσματος ‖ ~ soap n σαπούνι ξυρίσματος.

shawl [ʃɔːl] n σάλι.

she [ʃiː] pron αὐτή ‖ a θήλυς, θηλυκός.

sheaf [ʃiːf] n δέσμη, δεμάτι.

shear [ʃiə*] (irreg v) vt (sheep etc) κείρω, κουρεύω ‖ to ~ off vt κόβω ‖ ~s npl (for hedge) ψαλίδα.

sheath [ʃiːθ] n θήκη, κολεός, θηκάρι ‖ ~e [ʃiːð] vt βάζω σέ θήκη, περικαλύπτω, ἐπενδύω.

shed [ʃed] (irreg v) n ὑπόστεγον ‖ vt ἀποβάλλω, βγάζω, ρίχνω ‖ (pour out) χύνω.

she'd [ʃiːd] = she had, she would ‖ see have, would.

sheep [ʃiːp] n πρόβατον ‖ ~dog n τσοπανόσκυλο ‖ ~ish a δειλός, ντροπαλός ‖ ~skin n προβιά.

sheer [ʃiə*] a καθαρός, πραγματικός, γνήσιος ‖ (steep) κατακόρυφος, ἀπότομος ‖ (almost transparent) διαφανής, λεπτός ‖ ad τελείως, πλήρως, ἀπολύτως.

sheet [ʃiːt] n σεντόνι ‖ (thin piece) ἔλασμα, φύλλον, λαμαρίνα ‖ (paper) φύλλον, κόλλα ‖ ~ing n ὕφασμα γιά σεντόνια ‖ (metal etc) θωράκισις, λαμαρίνα ‖ ~ lightning n διάχυτες ἀστραπές.

sheik(h) [ʃeik] n σεϊχης.

shelf [ʃelf] n ράφι.

she'll [ʃiːl] = she will, she shall ‖ see will, shall.

shell [ʃel] n κέλυφος, τσόφλι, φλοιός ‖ (explosive) ὀβίδα, βλῆμα ‖ (of building) σκελετός, καραγιαπί ‖ vt ξεφλουδίζω ‖ (mil) βομβαρδίζω ‖ ~fish n (zool) ὀστρακοειδές ‖ (as food) θαλασσινά.

shelter ['ʃeltə*] n σκέπαστρον, καταφύγιον ‖ (protection) προστασία ‖ vt προφυλάσσω, προστατεύω, στεγάζω ‖ vi προφυλάσσομαι, φυλάγομαι ‖ ~ed a

(life) ἀποτραβηγμένος, περιωρισμένος ‖ (spot) προφυλαγμένος, προστατευμένος.

shelve [ʃelv] vt (put aside) βάζω στό ράφι ‖ ~s npl of shelf.

shelving ['ʃelviŋ] n (shelves etc) ράφια.

shepherd ['ʃepəd] n ποιμήν, βοσκός ‖ vt (guide) ὁδηγῶ, συνοδεύω ‖ ~ess n βοσκοπούλα ‖ ~'s pie n κρέας ἀ-λαχασάπα.

sheriff ['ʃerif] n σερίφης.

sherry ['ʃeri] n σέρι.

she's [ʃiːz] = she is, she has ‖ see be, have.

shield [ʃiːld] n ἀσπίδα, σκουτάρι ‖ (protection) προστατευτικόν κάλυμμα ‖ vt προασπίζω, προστατεύω ‖ καλύπτω.

shift [ʃift] n (time) βάρδια ‖ συνεργετόν, ὁμάδα, βάρδια ‖ vt μετατοπίζω, μετα-θέτω, μετακινῶ ‖ (remove) ἀλλάζω, μεταβάλλω ‖ vi μετακινοῦμαι, μετατοπίζομαι ‖ ~y a πολυμήχανος, πονηρός, ὕπουλος.

shilling ['ʃiliŋ] n (old) σελλίνι.

shilly-shally ['ʃiliʃæli] vi διστάζω, κοντοστέκω, δέν ἀποφασίζω.

shimmer ['ʃimə*] n ἀνταύγεια, μαρμαρυγή, γυάλισμα ‖ vi ἀπαστράπτω, λαμποκοπῶ, γυαλίζω.

shin [ʃin] n ἀντικνήμιον, καλάμι (ποδιοῦ).

shine [ʃain] (irreg v) n (gleam) γυάλισμα, στιλπνότης, γυαλάδα ‖ vt (polish) στίλβω, λουστράρω, γυαλίζω ‖ (torch) ἀκτινοβολῶ, λάμπω ‖ vi λάμπω, ἀστράφτω, γυαλίζω ‖ (excel) διακρίνομαι, ξεπροβάλλω.

shingle ['ʃiŋgl] n ξυλοκέραμος, ταβανο-σάνιδο ‖ (on beach) βότσαλα, κροκάλαι ‖ ~s npl (med) ἔρπης, ζωστήρ.

shining ['ʃainiŋ] a (light) ἀπαστράπτων, λαμπερός, γυαλιστερός.

shiny ['ʃaini] a λαμπερός, γυαλιστερός.

ship [ʃip] n πλοῖον, σκάφος ‖ vt ἐπιβιβάζω, μπαρκάρω ‖ (transport as cargo) φορτώνω, ἀποστέλλω ‖ ~building n ναυπηγική ‖ ~ canal n πλωτή διῶρυξ ‖ ~ment n φόρτωσις ‖ (goods) φορτίον, ἐμπόρευμα ‖ ~per n (sender) ἀποστολεύς ‖ ~ping n (act) φόρτωσις ‖ (ships) πλοῖα, ναυτιλία ‖ (ships of country) ἐμπορική ναυτιλία ‖ ~shape a τακτικός, ἐξαιρετικός ‖ ~wreck n ναυάγιον ‖ ~yard n ναυπηγεῖον.

shire ['ʃaiə*] n κομητεία.

shirk [ʃɜːk] vt ὑπεκφεύγω, ἀποφεύγω, ξεφεύγω, φυγοπονῶ.

shirt [ʃɜːt] n (man's shirt) πουκάμισο ‖ ~y a (col) εὐερέθιστος, εὐέξαπτος.

shiver ['ʃivə*] n θραῦσμα, θρύμμα ‖ ρίγος, τρεμούλα ‖ vi (with cold) τρέμω, τουρτουρίζω.

shoal [ʃəul] n (of fish) κοπάδι (ψαριῶν).

shock [ʃɔk] n δόνησις, σύγκρουσις, τίναγμα ‖ (elec) ἠλεκτρικόν σόκ, ἠλεκτροπληξία ‖ (emotional) συγκλονισμός,

ταραχή ‖ (med) κατάπληξία, σόκ ‖ vt
σκανδαλίζω, σοκάρω ‖ ~ absorber n
ἀποσβεστήρ κρούσεων, ἀμορτισσέρ ‖
~ing a σκανδαλώδης ‖ συγκλονιστικός
‖ ~proof a (watch) προφυλαγμένος ἀπό
δονήσεις.
shod [ʃɔd] pt,pp of shoe.
shoddiness ['ʃɔdinis] n κακή ποιότης.
shoddy ['ʃɔdi] a κακῆς ποιότητος, τῆς
πεντάρας.
shoe [ʃuː] (irreg v) n ὑπόδημα, παπούτσι ‖
(of horse) πέταλον ‖ vt ὑποδέω, πεταλώνω (ἄλογον) ‖ ~brush n βούρτσα τῶν
παπουτσιῶν ‖ ~horn n κόκκαλο τῶν
παπουτσιῶν ‖ ~lace n κορδόνι ‖ ~shop
n παπουτσάδικο.
shone [ʃɔn] pt,pp of shine.
shook [ʃuk] pt of shake.
shoot [ʃuːt] (irreg v) n (branch) βλαστός,
βλαστάρι ‖ vt (gun) πυροβολῶ, ἐκκενῶ ‖
(kill) σκοτώνω ‖ (film) τραβῶ, γυρίζω
(ταινία) ‖ vi (move swiftly) (ἐξ)ὁρμῶ,
τρέχω, πετῶ ‖ (let off gun) πυροβολῶ,
κτυπῶ ‖ don't ~! μή ρίχνετε!, μή βαράτε!
‖ to ~ down vt (plane) καταρρίπτω ‖
~ing n (shots) πυροβολισμός, πόλεμος ‖
(hunting) κυνήγι ‖ ~ing star n διάττων
ἀστήρ.
shop [ʃɔp] n κατάστημα, μαγαζί ‖ (workshop) ἐργαστήριον, μαγαζί ‖ vi (also go
~ping) ψωνίζω ‖ ~assistant n ὑπάλληλος
καταστήματος ‖ ~keeper n καταστη-
μάταρχης, μικρέμπορος ‖ ~lifter n
κλέπτης καταστημάτων ‖ ~lifting n
κλοπή καταστημάτων ‖ ~per n πελάτης,
ἀγοραστής ‖ ~ping n ἀγοραί, ψώνια ‖
~ping bag n τσάντα γιά τά ψώνια ‖
~ping centre, (US) ~ping center n ἀγορά,
ἐμπορικόν κέντρον ‖ ~soiled a στραπα-
τσαρισμένο ‖ ~ steward n (industry)
ἀντιπρόσωπος τοῦ συνδικάτου ‖ ~
window n προθήκη, βιτρίνα ‖ see talk.
shore [ʃɔː*] n (of sea, lake) ἀκτή, παραλία
‖ ὄχθη ‖ vt: to ~ up ὑποστηρίζω,
(ἀντι)στηρίζω.
shorn [ʃɔːn] pp of shear.
short [ʃɔːt] a βραχύς, κοντός ‖ (not tall)
κοντός ‖ (soon finished) βραχύς, σύντομος ‖ (curt) ἀπότομος, ξηρός, κοφτός ‖
(in measure) λιποβαρής, ἐλλειπής,
λειψός ‖ (elec: short-circuit) βραχύς
(βραχυκύκλωμα) ‖ ad ἀποτόμως, ἀπότομα ‖ ἐντεῦθεν τοῦ στόχου, κοντά ‖ vti
(elec) βραχυκυκλώνω, βραχυκυκλοῦμαι ‖
to cut ~ τερματίζω ἀπότομως, συντομεύω, διακόπτω ‖ to fall ~ πέφτω κοντά,
δέν πετυχαίνω ‖ to stop ~ σταματῶ
ξαφνικά ‖ ~age n ἀνεπάρκεια, ἔλλειψις,
στενότης ‖ ~bread n εἶδος κέϊκ ‖
~-circuit n βραχυκύκλωμα ‖ vi βραχυκυκλοῦμαι ‖ ~coming n ἐλάττωμα,
ἀτέλεια, μειονέκτημα ‖ ~ cut n συντο-
μώτερος δρόμος, κοφτό ‖ ~en vt

βραχύνω, κοντ̄αίνω ‖ ~hand n στενογραφία ‖ ~hand typist n στενοδακτυλογράφος ‖ ~lived a βραχύβιος, ἐφήμερος
‖ ~ly ad (soon) προσεχῶς, σύντομα, σέ
λίγο ‖ ~ness n βραχύτης, συντομία ‖
~sighted a (lit) μύωψ ‖ (fig) μή προνοητικός, κοντόφθαλμος ‖ ~-sightedness n
μυωπία ‖ (fig) ἀπερισκεψία ‖ ~ story
n διήγημα ‖ ~-tempered a ἀπότομος,
εὐέξαπτος ‖ ~-term a (fin) βραχυπρόθεσμος ‖ ~wave n (rad) βραχύ κῦμα.
shot [ʃɔt] pt,pp of shoot ‖ n (firing etc)
πυροβολισμός, τουφεκιά ‖ (person)
σκοπευτής ‖ (attempt) δοκιμή, προσπάθεια, ἀπόπειρα ‖ (injection) ἔνεσις ‖
(phot) λῆψις φωτογραφίας ‖ like a ~
(very readily) ἀμέσως, πρόθυμα ‖ ~gun
n κυνηγετικόν ὅπλον.
should [ʃud] auxiliary v: I ~ go now πρέπει
νά φύγω (τώρα) ‖ he ~ be there now
πρέπει νά ἔχη φθάση (τώρα) ‖ I ~ like
to θά ἤθελα.
shoulder ['ʃəuldə*] n ὦμος ‖ vt ἐπωμίζομαι
‖ ~ blade n ὠμοπλάτη, κουτάλα.
shouldn't ['ʃudnt] = should not ‖ see should.
shout [ʃaut] n κραυγή, φωνή ‖ vt κραυγάζω
‖ vi κραυγάζω, φωνάζω ‖ ~ing n φωνές,
κραυγές.
shove [ʃʌv] n ὤθησις, σπρωξιά, σπρώξιμο
‖ vt σπρώχνω ‖ to ~ off vi (naut) ἀπωθῶ,
ἀβαράρω ‖ (fig, col) φεύγω, ξεκινῶ.
shovel ['ʃʌvl] n φτυάρι ‖ vt φτυαρίζω.
show [ʃəu] (irreg v) n ἐπίδειξις, προβολή ‖
(appearance) ἐμφάνισις, ὄψις, προσποίησις ‖ (exhibition) ἔκθεσις, θέαμα ‖
(theat, cine) θέατρον, σινεμά, παράστασις ‖ vt δεικνύω, δείχνω, ὁδηγῶ ‖
(demonstrate) παρουσιάζω, ἀποδεικνύω ‖
(explain) δεικνύω, ἐξηγῶ ‖ (give) δεικνύω ‖
vi (be visible) δεικνύομαι, φαίνομαι,
ξεπροβάλλω ‖ to ~ in πές νά μπῆ ‖
to ~ out συνοδεύω ὡς τήν ἔξοδο ‖
to ~ off vi (pej) ἐπιδεικνύομαι, κορδώνομαι, καμαρώνω ‖ vt (display) ἀποδεικνύω, δείχνω, διαφημίζω ‖ to ~ up vi
(stand out) διακρίνομαι, ξεχωρίζω ‖ vt
ἐμφανίζω, παρουσιάζομαι ‖ ἀποκα-
λύπτομαι, βγαίνω στήν φόρα ‖ ~down n
ἀναμέτρησις, διακήρυξις προθέσεων.
shower ['ʃauə*] n μπόρα ‖ (stones etc)
βροχή ἀπό πέτρες κτλ ‖ (shower bath)
ντούς ‖ vt (fig only) δίδω ἄφθονα ‖ ~y a
(weather) βροχερός.
showground ['ʃəugraund] n χῶρος ἐκθέσεως.
showing ['ʃəuiŋ] n (of film) ἐμφάνισις,
προβολή.
showmanship ['ʃəumənʃip] n ἱκανότης
ἐπιδείξεως.
shown [ʃəun] pp of show.
show-off ['ʃəuɔf] n (col: person) κορδωμένος.
showroom ['ʃəurum] n αἴθουσα ἐκθέσεως,

shrank [ʃræŋk] *pt of* shrink.

shrapnel ['ʃræpnl] *n* βολιδοφόρον βλῆμα.

shred [ʃred] *n* (*generally pl*) κομμάτι, λουρίδα, κουρέλι ‖ *vt* κομματιάζω, σχίζω σέ λουρίδες ‖ **in** ~**s** ξεσχισμένος, κουρελιασμένος.

shrewd [ʃruːd] *a* ἀγχίνους, διορατικός, ἐπιδέξιος ‖ ~**ly** *ad* μέ ἐξυπνάδα, ἔξυπνα ‖ ~**ness** *n* εὐφυΐα, ἐξυπνάδα.

shriek [ʃriːk] *n* ξεφωνητό, στριγγλιά ‖ *vti* ξεφωνίζω, στριγγλίζω.

shrill [ʃril] *a* ὀξύς, διαπεραστικός.

shrimp [ʃrimp] *n* γαρίδα.

shrine [ʃrain] *n* λειψανοθήκη, βωμός, ἱερός τόπος.

shrink [ʃriŋk] (*irreg v*) *vi* συστέλλομαι, μαζεύομαι ‖ *vt* (*make smaller*) ρικνῶ, συστέλλω, κάνω νά μαζέψη ‖ ~**age** *n* συστολή, μπάσιμο, μάζεμα.

shrivel ['ʃrivl] *vti* (*also* ~ **up**) συρρικνώνω, ζαρώνω, ξεραίνομαι.

shroud [ʃraud] *n* σάβανον ‖ *vt* σαβανώνω ‖ σκεπάζω, καλύπτω.

Shrove Tuesday ['ʃrouv'tjuːzdi] *n* Καθαρά Τρίτη.

shrub [ʃrʌb] *n* θάμνος, χαμόκλαδο ‖ ~**bery** *n* θαμνῶνι, λόγγος.

shrug [ʃrʌg] *n* σήκωμα τῶν ὤμων ‖ **to** ~ **off** *vt* ἀνασηκώνω τούς ὤμους.

shrunk [ʃrʌŋk] *pp of* shrink ‖ ~**en** *a* πού μπῆκε, πού μάζεψε ‖ ζαρωμένος.

shudder ['ʃʌdə*] *n* ῥῖγος, φρικίασις, τρεμούλα ‖ *vi* τρέμω.

shuffle ['ʃʌfl] *n* (*cards*) ἀνακάτεμα (τράπουλας) ‖ *vt* ἀνακατεύω ‖ *vi* σέρνω τά πόδια.

shun [ʃʌn] *vt* ἀποφεύγω.

shush [ʃuʃ] *excl* (*col*) σούτ! ¹

shut [ʃʌt] (*irreg v*) *vt* κλείνω ‖ *vi* κλείομαι, κλείνω ‖ **to** ~ **down** *vti* κλείνω, σταματῶ ἐργασίες ‖ **to** ~ **off** *vt* (*supply*) διακόπτω, ἀποκόπτω, ἀποκλείω ‖ **to** ~ **up** *vi* (*keep quiet*) σωπαίνω, βουλώνω ‖ *vt* (*close*) κλείνω καλά, κλειδώνω ‖ (*silence*) ἀποστομώνω, κλείνω τό στόμα ‖ ~ **up!** σκασμός! ‖ ~**ter** *n* παραθυρόφυλλον, παντζούρι ‖ (*of camera*) φωτοφράκτης.

shuttlecock ['ʃʌtlkɔk] *n* φτερωτή σφαίρα, βολάν.

shy [ʃai] *a* ντροπαλός, δειλός ‖ ~**ly** *ad* ντροπαλά, δειλά ‖ ~**ness** *n* δειλία, ντροπαλότητα.

Siamese [saiə'miːz] *a*: ~ **cat** Σιαμαία γάτα.

sick [sik] *a* ἀσθενής, ἄρρωστος ‖ (*inclined to vomit*) ἔχω τάσιν πρός ἐμετόν ‖ (*disgusting*) ἀηδιαστικός, σιχαμερός ‖ ~**bay** *n* νοσοκομεῖον πλοίου ‖ ~**bed** *n* κλίνη ἀσθενοῦς ‖ ~**en** *vt* ἀρρωσταίνω, ἀηδιάζω ‖ *vi* ἀηδιάζω ‖ ~**ening** *a* (*fig*) ἀηδιαστικός.

sickle ['sikl] *n* δρεπάνι.

sick leave ['sikliːv] *n* ἀναρρωτική ἄδεια.

sick list ['siklist] *n* κατάλογος ἀσθενῶν.

sickly ['sikli] *a* ἀρρωστιάρης, ὠχρός,

ἀσθενικός ‖ (*nauseating*) πού προκαλεῖ ἀναγούλα.

sickness ['siknis] *n* ἀσθένεια, ἀρρώστεια, νόσος ‖ (*vomiting*) ναυτία, ἀναγούλα, ἐμμετός.

sick pay ['sikpei] *n* ἐπίδομα ἀσθενείας.

side [said] *n* πλευρά, πλευρόν, μέρος, μεριά ‖ (*of body*) πλευρά, μεριά ‖ (*of lake*) ὄχθη ‖ (*aspect*) πλευρά, ὄψι, ἄποψις ‖ *a* (*door, entrance*) πλαγία (εἴσοδος), πλαϊνή (εἴσοδος) ‖ *vi*: **to** ~ **with** πάω μέ, παίρνω τό μέρος τοῦ ‖ **by the** ~ **of** στό πλευρό τοῦ, ἐν συγκρίσει μέ ‖ **on all** ~**s** ἀπό παντοῦ ‖ **to take** ~**s** (**with**) ὑποστηρίζω, μεροληπτῶ ‖ ~**board** *n* μπουφές ‖ ~**boards**, ~**burns** *npl* (*whiskers*) φαβορίτες ‖ ~ **effect** *n* (*med*) παρενέργεια ‖ ~**light** *n* (*aut*) πλευρικός φανός ‖ ~**line** *n* (*rail*) δευτερεύουσα γραμμή ‖ (*fig: hobby*) πάρεργον ‖ ~**road** *n* πάροδος ‖ ~**show** *n* δευτερεῦον θέαμα ‖ ~**track** *vt* (*fig*) περισπῶ ‖ ~**walk** *n* (*US*) πεζοδρόμιον ‖ ~**ways** *ad* πλαγίως, πλάγια, λοξά.

siding ['saidiŋ] *n* πλευρική διακλάδωσις.

sidle ['saidl] *vi*: **to** ~ **up** πλησιάζω δειλά καί πλάγια.

siege [siːdʒ] *n* πολιορκία.

siesta [si'estə] *n* μεσημβρινός ὕπνος.

sieve [siv] *n* κόσκινο ‖ *vt* κοσκινίζω.

sift [sift] *vt* κοσκινίζω ‖ (*examine*) ξεχωρίζω, ἐξονυχίζω.

sigh [sai] *n* ἀναστεναγμός ‖ *vi* (ἀνα)στενάζω.

sight [sait] *n* ὅρασις ‖ (*scene*) θέα, θέαμα ‖ (*of rifle*) κλισιοσκόπιον ‖ στόχαστρον ‖ *vt* ἀντικρύζω, βλέπω, παρατηρῶ ‖ **in** ~ φαίνομαι, γίνομαι ὁρατός ‖ **out of** ~ δέν φαίνομαι ‖ ~**seeing** *n* ἐπίσκεψις ἀξιοθεάτων ‖ **to go** ~**seeing** περιέρχομαι τά ἀξιοθέατα ‖ ~**seer** *n* περιηγητής, τουρίστας.

sign [sain] *n* (*with hand*) νεῦμα, νόημα ‖ (*indication*) ἔνδειξις, σημάδι ‖ (*notice, road etc*) σῆμα, ταμπέλα, πινακίς ‖ (*written symbol*) σημεῖον, σημάδι ‖ *vt* ὑπογράφω ‖ **to** ~ **off** *vi* ξεμπαρκάρω ‖ **to** ~ **up** *vti* (*mil*) κατατάσσομαι.

signal ['signl] *n* σύνθημα, σημεῖον, σῆμα ‖ *vt* σηματοδοτῶ, στέλνω μέ σήματα.

signature ['signətʃə*] *n* ὑπογραφή ‖ ~ **tune** *n* μουσικόν χαρακτηριστικόν (σταθμοῦ).

significance [sig'nifikəns] *n* σημασία, ἔννοια, νόημα ‖ (*importance*) σπουδαιότης, σημαντικότης.

significant [sig'nifikənt] *a* μέ σημασίαν, σημαντικός ‖ (*important*) σημαντικός, σπουδαῖος, σημαίνων ‖ ~**ly** *ad* μέ ἔννοιαν, μέ σημασίαν.

signify ['signifai] *vt* σημαίνω, ἐννοῶ ‖ (*express*) εἶμαι ἔνδειξις, (ἐκ)δηλώνω.

sign language ['sainlæŋgwidʒ] *n* δακτυλολογία.

signpost ['sainpəust] n σήμα κυκλοφορίας, όδοδείκτης.

silence ['sailəns] n σιγή, σιωπή, ήσυχία ‖ vt σωπαίνω, ήσυχάζω ‖ καταπνίγω ‖ ~r n σιγαστήρ, σιλανσιέ.

silent ['sailənt] a σιωπηλός, αθόρυβος, σιγαλός ‖ (saying nothing) άφωνος, αμίλητος ‖ ~ly ad σιωπηλά, σιγαλά, αθόρυβα.

silhouette [silu:'et] n (outline) σιλουέττα ‖ vt διαγράφομαι σάν σιλουέττα.

silk [silk] n μετάξι ‖ a μεταξωτός ‖ ~y a μεταξένιος, απαλός, προσποιητός.

silliness ['silinis] n μωρία, ανοησία, χαζομάρα.

silly ['sili] a ανόητος, μωρός.

silo ['sailəu] n σιλό.

silt [silt] n ιλύς, λάσπη.

silver ['silvə*] n άργυρος, ασήμι ‖ (coins) αργυρά νομίσματα n (objects) ασημικά ‖ a αργυρούς, ασημένιος ‖ ~ paper n ασημόχαρτο ‖ ~-plate n ασημικά ‖ ~smith n αργυροχόος ‖ ~ware n ασημικά ‖ ~y a ασημένιος.

similar ['similə*] a (+ to) όμοιος (μέ) ‖ ~ity n ομοιότης ‖ ~ly ad ομοίως, όμοια.

simile ['simili] n παρομοίωσις.

simmer ['simə*] vi σιγοβράζω.

simple ['simpl] a (easy) απλός, εύκολος ‖ (natural) απλός, απλοϊκός ‖ (plain) απλός, απλοϊκός ‖ (of one kind) απλός ‖ (weak-minded) αφελής, μωρόπιστος ‖ ~-minded a αφελής, απλοϊκός.

simplicity [sim'plisiti] n απλότης, λιτότης, ειλικρίνεια.

simplification [simplifi'keiʃən] n απλοποίησις, απλούστευσις.

simplify ['simplifai] vt απλουστεύω, απλοποιώ.

simply ['simpli] ad απλώς, απλά, μόνον.

simulation [simju'leiʃən] n (imitation) απομίμησις, προσποίησις.

simultaneous [siməl'teiniəs] a ταυτόχρονος ‖ ~ly ad ταυτόχρονα, σύγχρονα μέ.

sin [sin] n αμάρτημα, αμαρτία ‖ vi αμαρτάνω.

since [sins] ad έκτοτε, από τότε ‖ prep από ‖ cj (time) αφ' ότου, από τότε πού ‖ (because) αφού, εφ' όσον.

sincere [sin'siə*] a ειλικρινής ‖ ~ly ad ειλικρινώς.

sincerity [sin'seriti] n ειλικρίνεια.

sinecure ['sainikjuə*] n αργομισθία.

sinew ['sinju:] n τένων, νεύρο.

sinful ['sinful] a αμαρτωλός.

sing [siŋ] (irreg v) vt (song) τραγουδώ ‖ vi σφυρίζω, βουΐζω.

singe [sindʒ] vt τσουρουφλίζω, καψαλίζω.

singer ['siŋə*] n αοιδός, τραγουδιστής.

singing ['siŋiŋ] n τραγούδι.

single ['siŋgl] a μόνος, μοναδικός ‖ (bed, room) μονό (κρεββάτι, δωμάτιο) ‖ (unmarried) άγαμος ‖ (ticket) απλούν

(εισητήριον) ‖ (one part) απλός, ένας ‖ n (ticket) απλούν εισητήριον ‖ ~s npl (tennis) απλό παιχνίδι, σίγκλ ‖ to ~ out vt διαλέγω, επιλέγω, ξεχωρίζω ‖ ~-breasted a μονός, μονόπετος ‖ in ~ file κατ' άνδρα, στήν αράδα, ένας-ένας ‖ ~-handed a ολομόναχος, αβοήθητος, μόνος ‖ ~-minded a πού έχει ένα μόνον σκοπόν.

singlet ['siŋglit] n φανελλίτσα.

singly ['siŋgli] ad ξεχωριστά, ένα-ένα ‖ χωρίς βοήθειαν.

singular ['siŋgjulə*] a ενικός ‖ (odd) παράξενος, σπάνιος, μοναδικός ‖ n (gram) ενικός αριθμός ‖ ~ly ad μοναδικά, εξαιρετικά.

sinister ['sinistə*] a απαίσιος, κακός.

sink [siŋk] (irreg v) n νεροχύτης ‖ vt (put under) καταβυθίζω, βουλιάζω ‖ (dig) σκάπτω, ανοίγω ‖ vi (fall slowly) καταβυθίζομαι, βουλιάζω, καθίζω ‖ to ~ in vi (news etc) χαράσσομαι στό μυαλό ‖ ~ing a (feeling) απογοητευτικός ‖ with ~ing heart μέ σφιγμένη καρδιά.

sinner ['sinə*] n αμαρτωλός.

Sino- ['sainəu] prefix Σινο-, Κινεζο-.

sinuous ['sinjuəs] a ελικοειδής, κυματοειδής, στριφτός.

sinus ['sainəs] n (anat) κόλπος.

sip [sip] n ρουφηξιά, γουλιά ‖ vt πίνω γουλιά-γουλιά, ρουφώ.

siphon ['saifən] n σιφόνι(ον) ‖ to ~ off vt αναρροφώ, σιφωνίζω.

sir [sə:*] n κύριος, κύριε ‖ σέρ, τίτλος ευγενείας ‖ yes S~ μάλιστα, κύριε.

siren ['saiərən] n σειρήνα.

sirloin ['sə:lɔin] n κόντρα φιλέττο.

sirocco [si'rɔkəu] n σιρόκκος.

sissy ['sisi] n (col: coward) δειλός.

sister ['sistə*] n αδελφή ‖ προϊσταμένη, αρχινοσοκόμος ‖ (nun) μοναχή, καλόγρηά, αδελφή ‖ ~-in-law n κουνιάδα, νύφη.

sit [sit] (irreg v) vi κάθομαι ‖ (at session) συνεδριάζω ‖ vt (exam) δίδω εξετάσεις, εξετάζομαι ‖ to ~ tight δέν τό κουνώ, βάζω τά δυνατά μου ‖ to ~ down vi κάθομαι ‖ to ~ up vi (after lying) ανασηκώνομαι ‖ (at night) αγρυπνώ, ξενυχτώ.

site [sait] n τοποθεσία, θέσις ‖ vt τοποθετώ, εγκαθιστώ.

sit-in ['sitin] n (demonstration) διαδήλωσις.

siting ['saitiŋ] n (location) τοποθέτησις.

sitting ['sitiŋ] n συνεδρίασις ‖ ~ room n αίθουσα διαμονής.

situated ['sitjueitid] a κείμενος, ευρισκόμενος.

situation [sitju'eiʃən] n (state of affairs) κατάστασις ‖ (place) τοποθεσία, θέσις ‖ (post) θέσις, εργασία, δουλειά.

six [siks] num έξ(η) ‖ ~teen num δεκαέξ ‖ ~th a έκτος ‖ ~ty num εξήντα.

size [saiz] n μέγεθος, διάστασις, έκτασις,

δγκος ‖ (glue) κόλλα ‖ (of clothing) νούμερο ‖ to ~ up vt (assess) ἐκτιμῶ (τό μέγεθος), σχηματίζω γνώμην γιά ‖ ~able a εὐμεγέθης, μεγαλούτσικος.

sizzle ['sizl] n τριγμός, σφύριγμα, τσιγάρισμα ‖ vi τσιτσιρίζω, σφυρίζω, τσιγαρίζω.

skate [skeit] n πέδιλον, πατίνι ‖ vi πατινάρω, παγοδρομῶ ‖ ~r n πατινέρ, παγοδρόμος.

skating ['skeitiŋ] n: to go ~ πηγαίνω γιά πατινάζ ‖ ~ rink n παγοδρόμιον, πατινάζ.

skeleton ['skelitn] n σκελετός.

skeptic ['skeptik] n (US) = sceptic.

sketch [sketʃ] n σκαρίφημα, σκιαγραφία ‖ (play) σκίτσο, σκέτς ‖ vt σκιαγραφῶ, σκιτσάρω ‖ ~book n συλλογή σκίτσων ‖ σημειωματάριον ‖ ~ing n σκιτσάρισμα ‖ ~ pad n καρνέ γιά σκίτσα ‖ ~y a ἀτελής, ἀσαφής, ἀκαθόριστος.

skew [skju:] n: on the ~ λοξά.

skewer ['skjuə*] n σούβλα.

ski [ski:] n σκί ‖ vi κάνω σκί ‖ ~ boot n παπούτσι τοῦ σκί.

skid [skid] n (skid-pan) τροχοπεδωτικόν πέδιλον ‖ vi γλυστρῶ πλαγίως, ντεραπάρω.

skidmark ['skidma:k] n ἴχνη ντεραπαρίσματος.

skier ['ski:ə*] n σκιέρ.

skiing ['ski:iŋ] n: to go ~ πάω γιά σκί.

skijump ['ski:dʒʌmp] n πήδημα μέ σκί.

skilful ['skilful] a ἱκανός, ἐπιδέξιος, ἐπιτήδειος ‖ ~ly ad μέ ἐπιδεξιότητα.

skill [skil] n ἱκανότης, ἐπιδεξιότης ‖ ~ed a ἐπιδέξιος, εἰδικευμένος.

skim [skim] vt ξαφρίζω, βγάζω ‖ (read) ξεφυλλίζω ‖ (glide over) ψαύω, περνῶ ξυστά.

skimp [skimp] vt (do carelessly) ψευτοφτιάνω, τσαπατσουλεύω ‖ ~y a (work, dress) ἀνεπαρκής, στενό.

skin [skin] n δέρμα, πετσί, τομάρι ‖ (peel, rind) φλοιός, φλούδα ‖ (on milk) πέτσα ‖ vt γδέρνω, ξεφλουδίζω ‖ ~-deep a ἐπιπόλαιος, ἐπιφανειακός ‖ ~ diving n ὑποβρύχιον κολύμπι ‖ ~ny a ἀδύνατος, κοκκαλιάρης, τσίρος ‖ ~ tight a (dress etc) (ἔνδυμα) ἐφαρμοστό.

skip [skip] n (ἀνα)πήδημα, σκίρτημα ‖ vi σκιρτῶ, πηδῶ, πετάγομαι ‖ vt παραλείπω, πηδῶ.

ski pants ['ski:'pænts] npl παντανόλι τοῦ σκί.

skipper ['skipə*] n (naut, sport) πλοιοκτήτης ‖ καπετάνιος ‖ ἀρχηγός (ὁμάδος).

skipping rope ['skipiŋrəup] n σχοινάκι.

skirmish ['skə:miʃ] n ἀψιμαχία.

skirt [skə:t] n φούστα ‖ vt περιτρέχω, φέρνω βόλτα.

ski run ['ski:rʌn] n διάδρομος τοῦ σκί.

skit [skit] n εὐθυμογράφημα, παρωδία, νούμερο.

ski tow ['ski:'təu] n κρεμαστός σιδηρόδρομος γιά σκί.

skittle ['skitl] n (one pin) τσούνι ‖ ~s n (game) τσούνια.

skulk [skʌlk] vi κρύβομαι, φυγοπονῶ.

skull [skʌl] n κρανίον.

skunk [skʌŋk] n μεφῖτις, εἶδος ἀσβοῦ.

sky [skai] n οὐρανός ‖ ~-blue a ἀνοιχτό μπλέ ‖ ~ blue n οὐρανί (χρῶμα) ‖ ~light n φεγγίτις, ἀναφωτίς ‖ ~scraper n οὐρανοξύστης.

slab [slæb] n πλάξ, πλάκα.

slack [slæk] a χαλαρός, λάσκος ‖ (slow, dull) πεσμένος, νεκρά (ἐποχή) ‖ (careless) ἀμελής, ἀδρανής, πλαδαρός ‖ vi ἀτονῶ, τεμπελιάζω ‖ n (in rope etc) χαλαρότης, τά μπόσικα ‖ ~s npl (ναυτικό) παντανόλι, φαρδύ παντανόλι ‖ ~en (also ~en off) vi χαλαρώνομαι, μειοῦμαι, πέφτω ‖ vt χαλαρώνω, μετριάζω, ἐπιβραδύνω, λασκάρω ‖ ~ness n νωθρότης, ἀτονία ‖ κάμψις.

slag [slæg] n σκωρία, ἐκβολάς μετάλλου ‖ ~ heap n σωρός σκωριῶν.

slam [slæm] n κρότος, κτύπημα πόρτας ‖ vt (door) κλείνω ἀπότομα, κτυπῶ ‖ (throw down) πετάω μέ δύναμιν ‖ vi κλείνω μέ κρότον.

slander ['sla:ndə*] n κακολογία, διαβολή, συκοφαντία ‖ vt συκοφαντῶ, κακολογῶ, διαβάλλω ‖ ~ous a συκοφαντικός.

slang [slæŋ] n μάγκικη γλῶσσα, ἀργκό, σλάγκ.

slant [sla:nt] n (lit) κλίσις, γέρσιμο ‖ (fig) ἄποψις, ἀντίληψις ‖ vti κλίνω, γέρνω ‖ ~ing a κεκλιμένος, πλάγιος.

slap [slæp] n κτύπημα, ράπισμα, μπάτσο, φάπα ‖ vt ραπίζω, μπατσίζω, καρπαζώνω ‖ ad (directly) κατ᾽ εὐθεῖαν ‖ ~dash ad ξέννοιαστα, ἀπρόσεκτα ‖ ~stick n (comedy) φάρσα ‖ ~-up a (meal) ἐξαίσιος, φίνος.

slash [slæʃ] n δυνατό κτύπημα, σχίσιμο ‖ vt κόβω, σχίζω, πετσοκόβω.

slate [sleit] n σχιστόλιθος ‖ (piece of slate) ἀβάκιον, πλάκα ‖ vt (criticize) ἐπικρίνω, κουρελιάζω.

slaughter ['slɔ:tə*] n σφαγή, σφάξιμο ‖ vt σφάζω.

Slav [sla:v] n (person) Σλαῦος ‖ a Σλαυικός.

slave [sleiv] n σκλάβος, δοῦλος ‖ vi δουλεύω σκληρά, μοχθῶ ‖ ~ry n δουλεία, σκλαβιά.

slavish ['sleiviʃ] a δουλικός ‖ ~ly ad δουλικά.

sledge [sledʒ] n ἕλκηθρον ‖ ~hammer n βαρειά, μεγάλο σφυρί.

sleek [sli:k] a λεῖος, ἁπαλός, προσποιητός.

sleep [sli:p] (irreg v) n ὕπνος ‖ vi κοιμοῦμαι, πλαγιάζω ‖ to go to ~ ἀποκοιμοῦμαι ‖ to ~ in vi (late) ξυπνῶ ἀργά ‖ ~er n ὑπναράς ‖ (beam) δοκός, τραβέρσα ‖ κλινάμαξα ‖ ~ily ad κοιμισμένα

~iness n ὑπνηλία, νυσταγμός, νύστα ‖
~ing attr a κοιμώμενος, κοιμισμένος ‖
~ing bag n σάκκος ὕπνου ‖ ~ing car n
κλινάμαξα, βαγκόν-λί ‖ ~ing pill n
ὑπνωτικό χάπι ‖ ~less a (night) ἄϋπνος,
ἄγρυπνος ‖ ~lessness n ἀϋπνία, ἀγρυπνία ‖ ~walker n ὑπνοβάτης ‖ ~y a
νυσταλέος, νυστάζων.

sleet [sli:t] n χιονόνερο.

sleeve [sli:v] n μανίκι ‖ ~less a (garment)
χωρίς μανίκια.

sleigh [slei] n ἕλκηθρον.

sleight [slait] n: ~ of hand ταχυδακτυλουργία.

slender ['slendə*] a λεπτός, λιγνός ‖
(small) ἰσχνός, ἀσθενής.

slept [slept] pt,pp of sleep.

slice [slais] n κομμάτι, μερίς, φέτα ‖ vt
τεμαχίζω, κόβω σέ φέτες.

slick [slik] a (smart) γλυστερός, δόλιος,
προσποιητός.

slid [slid] pt,pp of slide.

slide [slaid] (irreg v) n τσουλήθρα, ὀλισθη-
τήριον, στίβος ‖ (phot: transparency)
διαφανής φωτογραφία, σλάϊντ ‖ (brooch)
τσιμπιδάκι ‖ (fall in prices) πτῶσις
τιμῶν ‖ vt παρακάμπτω, ξεφεύγω ‖ vi
ὀλισθαίνω, γλυστρῶ, τσουλῶ ‖ to let
~ ἀδιαφορῶ, ἀφήνω στήν τύχη ‖ ~ rule
n λογαριθμικός κανών, ρέγουλα.

sliding ['slaidiŋ] a (door) συρτή (πόρτα).

slight [slait] a λεπτός, ἰσχνός ‖ (trivial)
ἐλαφρός, μικρός ‖ (small) μικροκαμωμένος, μικρούλης ‖ n ὑποτίμησις,
περιφρόνησις ‖ vt (offend) προσβάλλω,
θίγω ‖ ~ly ad ἐλαφρά, κάπως, λιγάκι.

slim [slim] a λεπτός, ἀνεπαρκής, μικρός ‖
vi ἀδυνατίζω, λεπτύνω, κάνω δίαιτα.

slime [slaim] n λάσπη, βούρκος, ἰλύς.

slimming ['slimiŋ] n ἀδυνάτισμα.

slimness ['slimnis] n λεπτότης, λυγεράδα,
σβελτάδα.

slimy ['slaimi] a βορβορώδης, γλοιώδης.

sling [sliŋ] (irreg v) n (bandage) ἀνωμίτης,
κρεμαστάρι ‖ vt ἐκσφενδονίζω, ρίχνω,
κρεμῶ.

slip [slip] n (slipping) ὀλίσθημα, γλύστρημα
‖ (petticoat) μισοφόρι ‖ (of paper)
φύλλο χαρτί ‖ vt γλυστρῶ ἀθορύβως,
εἰσέρχομαι, μπαίνω ‖ (escape from)
ξεφεύγω ἀπό ‖ vi (lose balance) ὀλισθαίνω, γλυστρῶ ‖ (move smoothly)
κινοῦμαι ἀθορύβως ‖ (make mistake)
κάνω γκάφα, σφάλλω ‖ (decline) παρεκ-
τρέπομαι, παραστρατῶ ‖ to ~ away vi
στρίβω, τό σκάω στή ζούλα ‖ to ~ in vt
βάζω, χώνω ‖ to ~ out vi ἐξέρχομαι,
βγαίνω (κρυφά) ‖ ~ per n παντούφλα ‖
~pery a ὀλισθηρός, γλυστερός ‖ (tricky)
πανοῦργος, πονηρός ‖ ~shod a ἀκατάστατος, ἀπρόσεκτος ‖ ~-up n (mistake)
σφάλμα, γκάφα ‖ ~way n ναυπηγική
κλίνη.

slit [slit] (irreg v) n σχίσιμο, σχισμή ‖ vt
κόβω, σχίζω, σχίζομαι.

slither ['sliðə*] vi ὀλισθαίνω, γλυστρῶ.

slob [slɔb] n (col: unpleasant person) ἀντιπαθής, ἀτζαμής.

slog [slɔg] n (great effort) ἀγγαρεία,
βαρειά δουλειά ‖ vi (work hard) δουλεύω
σκληρά.

slogan ['slaugən] n (catchword) σύνθημα.

slop [slɔp] vi ξεχειλίζω, χύνομαι ‖ vt χύνω.

slope [slaup] n κλιτύς, πλαγιά ‖ (slant)
κλίσις ‖ vi: to ~ down κατηφορίζω ‖
to ~ up vi ἀνηφορίζω.

sloping ['slaupiŋ] a λοξός, ἐπικλινής,
κεκλιμένος.

sloppily ['slɔpili] ad ἀκατάστατα, τσαπατσούλικα.

sloppiness ['slɔpinis] n τσαπατσουλιά.

sloppy ['slɔpi] a λασπωμένος, λασπώδης ‖
(untidy) μπατάλικος, ἀκατάστατος ‖
(weak, silly) ἄνοστος, σαχλός.

slot [slɔt] n σχισμή, χαραμάδα, τρύπα ‖
vt: to ~ in αὐλακώνω, χαράσσω (κάτι)
‖ ~ machine n αὐτόματος πωλητής
‖ μηχάνημα τυχερῶν παιχνιδιῶν.

slouch [slautʃ] vi κινοῦμαι ἀδέξια.

slovenly ['slʌvnli] a ἀκατάστατος, ἀπρόσεκτος.

slow [slau] a βραδύς, ἀργός ‖ (of clock) ἐν
καθυστερήσει, πίσω ‖ (stupid) βραδύνους, χοντροκέφαλος ‖ ad σιγά, ἀργά ‖
'~' (roadsign) 'ἀργά' ‖ to ~ down vi
ἐπιβραδύνω, μειώνω, κόβω (ταχύτητα) ‖
vi ἐπιβραδύνω ‖ to ~ up vi σταματῶ,
φρενάρω ‖ vt ἐπιβραδύνω ‖ ~ly ad
βραδέως, ἀργά ‖ in ~ motion εἰς ἀργόν
ρυθμόν, ραλαντί.

sludge [slʌdʒ] n λάσπη, βοῦρκος.

slug [slʌg] n γυμνοσάλιαγκας ‖ (bullet)
μικρή σφαῖρα ‖ ~gish a ἀδρανής, τεμπέλης, νωθρός ‖ ~gishly ad νωθρά, ὀκνά,
τεμπέλικα ‖ ~gishness n νωθρότης,
τεμπελιά ‖ βραδύτης.

sluice [slu:s] n ὑδροφράκτης, φράγμα ‖
βάνα.

slum [slʌm] n πτωχογειτονιά, χαμόσπιτο.

slumber ['slʌmbə*] n γαλήνιος ὕπνος.

slump [slʌmp] n πτῶσις, ἐλάττωσις
ζητήσεως ‖ vi πέφτω ἀπότομα.

slung [slʌŋ] pt,pp of sling.

slur [slɜ:*] n βιαστική προφορά, τραύλισμα
‖ (insult) ὕβρις, προσβολή ‖ vt (also ~
over) κακοπροφέρω, τραυλίζω ‖ ~red a
(pronunciation) κακῆς ἀρθρώσεως.

slush [slʌʃ] n λασπωμένο χιόνι ‖ ~y a
(lit) λασπωμένος ‖ (fig: sentimental)
σαχλός, γλυκανάλατος.

slut [slʌt] n τσούλα, παλιοθήλυκο.

sly [slai] a πονηρός, πανοῦργος, ὕπουλος
‖ ~ly ad ὕπουλα, πονηρά, μπαμπέσικα ‖
~ness n πανουργία, πονηριά, κατεργαριά.

smack [smæk] n (slap) κτύπημα, ράπισμα,

μπάτσος ‖ *vt* (*slap*) ραπίζω, καρπαζώνω ‖ **to ~ one's lips** κτυπῶ τά χείλη.

small [smɔːl] *a* μικρός, ὀλίγος ‖ **~ change** *n* ψιλά ‖ **~holding** *n* μικρό κτῆμα ‖ **~ hours** *npl* πολύ πρωϊνές ὥρες ‖ **~ish** *a* μᾶλλον μικρός, μικρούτσικος ‖ **~ness** *n* μικρότης, στενότης ‖ **~pox** *n* εὐλογία, βλογιά ‖ **~-scale** *a* μικρᾶς κλίμακος ‖ **~ talk** *n* φλυαρία.

smarmy ['smɑːmi] *a* (*col*) γλοιώδης, κωλογλείφτης.

smart [smɑːt] *a* (*well-dressed*) κομψός, μοντέρνος ‖ (*clever*) ἔξυπνος, ἐπιδέξιος ‖ (*sharp, quick*) δριμύς, ταχύς, ζωηρός ‖ *vi* πονῶ, τσούζω, ὑποφέρω ‖ **to ~en up** *vi* ζωηρεύω, κάνω κέφι ‖ ξυπνῶ ‖ *vt* ἐπισπεύδω, ἐπιταχύνω ‖ **~ly** *ad* ζωηρά, σβέλτα ‖ κομψά ‖ **~ness** *n* εὐφυΐα, καπατσοσύνη ‖ κομψότης.

smash [smæʃ] *n* (*collision*) σύγκρουσις ‖ *vt* τσακίζω, θρυμματίζω, κομματιάζω ‖ (*destroy*) καταστρέφω, συντρίβω ‖ *vi* θραύομαι, κομματιάζομαι ‖ **~ing** *a* (*col*) σπουδαῖος, περίφημος.

smattering ['smætəriŋ] *n* ἐπιπολαία γνῶσις, πασάλειμμα.

smear [smiə*] *n* κηλίς, λεκές ‖ ἐπίχρισμα ‖ *vt* ἀλείφω, πασαλείφω ‖ λερώνω, μουντζουρώνω.

smell [smel] (*irreg v*) *n* ὄσφρησις ‖ (*odour*) ὀσμή, μυρουδιά ‖ *vt* (*breathe in*) ὀσφραίνομαι, μυρίζω ‖ *vi* μυρίζω, παίρνω μυρωδιά ‖ (*give out smell*) μυρίζω, βρωμάω ‖ **~y** *a* (*unpleasant*) κάκοσμος, βρωμερός.

smile [smail] *n* χαμόγελο ‖ *vi* χαμογελῶ.

smiling ['smailiŋ] *a* χαμογελαστός, γελαστός.

smirk [smɜːk] *n* ψεύτικο χαμόγελο ‖ *vi* χαμογελῶ ψεύτικα.

smith [smiθ] *n* σιδηρουργός, σιδεράς ‖ **~y** ['smiði] *n* σιδηρουργεῖον, σιδεράδικο.

smock [smɔk] *n* μπλούζα, φόρμα.

smog [smɔg] *n* μολυσμένη ὁμίχλη.

smoke [sməuk] *n* καπνός, καπνίλα ‖ (*tobacco*) κάπνισμα, τσιγάρο ‖ *vt* (*puff*) καπνίζω ‖ (*dry food*) καπνίζω ‖ *vi* ἀναδίδω καπνούς, καπνίζω ‖ (*of cigarette*) καπνίζω ‖ **~d** *a* (*bacon etc*) καπνιστός ‖ **~r** *n* (*person*) καπνιστής ‖ (*rail*) ὄχημα καπνιστῶν ‖ **~room** *n* (*in pub*) καπνιστήριον.

smoking ['sməukiŋ] *n* κάπνισμα ‖ **'no ~'** (*sign*) 'ἀπαγορεύεται τό κάπνισμα'.

smoky ['sməuki] *a* γεμάτος καπνό, καπνισμένος.

smolder ['sməuldə*] *vi* (*US*) = smoulder.

smooth [smuːð] *a* (*in consistency*) ἀπαλός, γλυκόπιοτο ‖ (*movement*) ὁμαλός, μαλακός, ἀθόρυβος ‖ (*person*) γλυκομίλητος, γαλίφης ‖ *vt* (*also ~ out*) λειαίνω, ἐξομαλύνω, ἰσιάζω ‖ **~ly** *ad* ὁμαλά,

ἤρεμα, στρωτά ‖ **~ness** *n* ὁμαλότης, ἀπαλότης.

smother ['smʌðə*] *vt* πνίγω, σβήνω ‖ καταπνίγω, σκεπάζω.

smoulder ['sməuldə*] *vi* ὑποβόσκω, σιγοκαίω.

smudge [smʌdʒ] *n* κηλίς, λεκές, βρωμιά ‖ *vt* λεκιάζω, λερώνω, βρωμίζω.

smug [smʌg] *a* αὐτάρεσκος, καμαρωτός, ἐπηρμένος.

smuggle ['smʌgl] *vt* κάνω λαθρεμπόριο, περνῶ λαθραία ‖ **~r** *n* λαθρέμπορος, κοντραμπαντζῆς.

smuggling ['smʌgliŋ] *n* λαθρεμπόριο, κοντραμπάντο.

smugly ['smʌgli] *ad* ἐπηρμένα, καμαρωτά.

smugness ['smʌgnis] *n* ὑπεροψία, ἔπαρσις, αὐταρέσκεια.

smutty ['smʌti] *a* (*fig: obscene*) αἰσχρός, βρώμικος, πρόστυχος.

snack [snæk] *n* ἐλαφρό φαγητό, κολατσό ‖ **~ bar** *n* σνάκ-μπάρ.

snag [snæg] *n* (*obstacle*) ἐμπόδιο, κώλυμα ‖ (*in stocking*) τράβηγμα κλωστῆς.

snail [sneil] *n* σαλιγκάρι.

snake [sneik] *n* ὄφις, φίδι.

snap [snæp] *n* δάγκωμα, ἅρπαγμα, δαγκωματιά ‖ (*sound*) ψαλιδιά, κράκ, στράκα, ξηρός κρότος ‖ (*photograph*) στιγμιότυπον, ἐνσταντανέ, φωτογραφία ‖ *a* βιαστικός, ἀπροσδόκητος ‖ *vt* (*make sound*) κροταλίζω, κάνω στράκα ‖ (*break*) θραύω, σπάζω, τσακίζω ‖ (*photograph*) φωτογραφίζω, τραβῶ, πέρνω ‖ *vi* (*break*) σπάω ‖ **to ~ off** *vt* (*break*) σπάω ‖ **to ~ up** *vt* ἁρπάζω, βουτάω, χάφτω ‖ **~py** *a* δηκτικός, ἀπότομος, ζωηρός ‖ **~shot** *n* φωτογραφία ἐνσταντανέ.

snare [snεə*] *n* παγίδα ‖ *vt* παγιδεύω, πιάνω.

snarl [snɑːl] *n* γρυλισμός, μούγγρισμα ‖ *vi* (*also person*) γρυλίζω ‖ βρίζω.

snatch [snætʃ] *n* ἅρπαγμα ‖ (*small amount*) τεμάχιον, κομμάτι ‖ *vt* ἁρπάζω, τσακώνω.

sneak [sniːk] *vi* κινοῦμαι κρυφά.

sneakers ['sniːkəz] *npl* παπούτσια γυμναστικῆς.

sneer [sniə*] *n* καγχασμός, σαρκασμός ‖ *vi* κοροϊδεύω, σαρκάζω, περιφρονῶ.

sneeze [sniːz] *n* φτέρνισμα ‖ *vi* φτερνίζομαι.

snide [snaid] *a* ψεύτικος, σαρκαστικός.

sniff [snif] *n* εἰσπνοή, ρούφηγμα, μύρισμα ‖ *vi* ξεφυσῶ, εἶμαι συναχωμένος ‖ *vt* (*smell*) ὀσφραίνομαι, μυρίζω, ρουφῶ.

snigger ['snigə*] *n* πνιχτό γέλιο, πονηρό γέλιο ‖ *vi* κρυφογελῶ, ξερογελῶ.

snip [snip] *n* ψαλιδιά, κομματάκι ‖ (*bargain*) εὐκαιρία, καλή δουλειά ‖ *vt* ψαλιδίζω, ἀποκόβω.

snipe [snaip] *n* μπεκάτσα.

sniper ['snaipə*] *n* (*marksman*) ἐλεύθερος σκοπευτής.

snippet ['snipit] *n* κομματάκι, ἀπόσπασμα.
snivelling ['snivliŋ] *a* (*whimpering*) κλαψιάρικος.
snob [snɔb] *n* σνόμπ, ψωροπερήφανος, κορδωμένος ‖ ~**bery** *n* σνομπισμός ‖ ~**bish** *a* σνόμπ, φαντασμένος, ποζάτος ‖ ~**bishness** *n* σνομπισμός, πόζα.
snooker ['snu:kə*] *n* εἶδος μπιλλιάρδο.
snoop [snu:p] *vi*: **to ~ about** χώνω τήν μύτη, ψαχουλεύω.
snooty ['snu:ti] *a* (*col*: *snobbish*) ὑπερόπτης, ψηλομύτης.
snooze [snu:z] *n* ὑπνάκος ‖ *vi* παίρνω ἕνα ὑπνάκο, μισοκοιμᾶμαι.
snore [snɔ:*] *vi* ροχαλίζω.
snoring ['snɔ:riŋ] *n* ροχαλητό.
snorkel ['snɔ:kl] *n* ἀναπνευστήρας.
snort [snɔ:t] *n* φρίμασμα, ξεφύσημα, ρουθούνισμα ‖ *vi* ρουθουνίζω, φριμάζω, ξεφυσῶ.
snotty ['snɔti] *a* (*col*: *snobbish*) ψηλομύτης.
snout [snaut] *n* ρύγχος, μουσούδα, μύτη.
snow [snəu] *n* χιόνι ‖ *vi* χιονίζω, ρίχνω χιόνι ‖ ~**ball** *n* μπάλλα χιόνι, χιονόσφαιρα ‖ ~**bound** *a* (ἀπο)κλεισμένος ἀπό τά χιόνια ‖ ~**drift** *n* χιονοστιβάς ‖ ~**drop** *n* γάλανθος ὁ χιονώδης ‖ ~**fall** *n* χιονόπτωσις ‖ ~**flake** *n* νιφάς ‖ ~**man** *n* χιονάνθρωπος ‖ ~**plough**, (*US*) ~ **plow** *n* ἄροτρον γιά τά χιόνια ‖ ~**storm** *n* χιονοθύελλα.
snub [snʌb] *vt* ἀποκρούω, προσβάλλω, κόβω ‖ *n* ἐπίπληξις, προσβολή, κατσάδα ‖ ~-**nosed** *a* μέ ἀνασηκωμένη μύτη.
snuff [snʌf] *n* ταμπάκο, πρέζα ‖ ~**box** *n* ταμπακέρα.
snug [snʌg] *a* ἄνετος, βολικός, ζεστός, ἀναπαυτικός.
so [səu] *ad* (*extent*) τόσο(ν) ‖ (*in such manner*) ἔτσι ‖ (*thus*) οὕτω(ς), τοιουτοτρόπως ‖ (*to such an extent*) τόσο ‖ *cj* ἑπομένως, γι' αὐτό, ἔτσι λοιπόν ‖ **or ~** περίπου, πάνω κάτω ‖ ~ **long!** (*goodbye*) γειά σου!, ἀντίο! ‖ ~ **many**, ~ **much** τόσος ‖ ~ **that** οὕτως ὥστε.
soak [səuk] *vt* διαβρέχω, μουσκεύω ‖ (*leave in liquid*) διαποτίζω, μουσκεύω ‖ **to ~ in** *vi* διεισδύω, διαποτίζω, ποτίζω ‖ ~**ing** *n* διάβρεξις, ἐμποτισμός, κατάβρεγμα.
soap [səup] *n* σαπούνι ‖ ~-**flakes** *npl* τριμμένο σαπούνι ‖ ~ **powder** *n* σαπούνι σέ σκόνη ‖ ~**y** *a* γεμᾶτος σαπούνι.
soar [sɔ:*] *vi* πετῶ ψηλά, ἀνυψοῦμαι.
sob [sɔb] *n* λυγμός, ἀναφυλλητό ‖ *vi* κλαίω μέ ἀναφυλλητά.
sober ['səubə*] *a* νηφάλιος, ξεμέθυστος ‖ (*calm*) σοβαρός, ἐγκρατής, ἥρεμος ‖ **to ~ up** *vi* συνέρχομαι, ξεμεθάω ‖ ~**ly** *ad* σοβαρά, μετρημένα, λιτά.
so-called ['səu'kɔ:ld] *a* δῆθεν, λεγόμενος.
soccer ['sɔkə*] *n* ποδόσφαιρον.
sociability [səuʃə'biliti] *n* κοινωνικότης.

sociable ['səuʃəbl] *a* κοινωνικός, φιλικός, ὁμιλητικός.
social ['səuʃəl] *a* κοινωνικός ‖ ~**ism** *n* σοσιαλισμός ‖ ~**ist** *n* σοσιαλιστής ‖ *a* σοσιαλιστικός ‖ ~**ly** *ad* κοινωνικῶς ‖ ~ **science** *n* κοινωνική ἐπιστήμη ‖ ~ **security** *n* κοινωνική ἀσφάλεια ‖ ~ **welfare** *n* κοινωνική πρόνοια ‖ ~ **work** *n* κοινωνική ἐργασία ‖ ~ **worker** *n* κοινωνικός λειτουργός.
society [sə'saiəti] *n* (*people and customs*) κοινωνία ‖ (*club*) ἑταιρεία ‖ (*fashionable life*) κοσμική ζωή, καλός κόσμος.
sociological [səusiə'lɔdʒikəl] *a* κοινωνιολογικός.
sociologist [səusi'ɔlədʒist] *n* κοινωνιολόγος.
sociology [səusi'ɔlədʒi] *n* κοινωνιολογία.
sock [sɔk] *n* (κοντή) κάλτσα ‖ *vt* (*hit*) δίνω γροθιά.
socket ['sɔkit] *n* ντουΐ, μπρίζα.
sod [sɔd] *n* (*of earth*) χορταριασμένος βῶλος ‖ (*col*: *term of abuse*) παλιάνθρωπος.
soda ['səudə] *n* (*chem*) νάτριον, σόδα ‖ (*drink*) σόδα ‖ ~ **water** *n* ἀεριοῦχον ὕδωρ, σόδα.
sodden ['sɔdn] *a* διάβροχος, μουσκεμένος ‖ (*moist and heavy*) λασπωμένος.
sofa ['səufə] *n* σοφᾶς, καναπές.
soft [sɔft] *a* μαλακός, ἁπαλός ‖ (*not loud*) ἁπαλός, γλυκός, ἐλαφρός ‖ (*kind*) τρυφερός, καλός ‖ (*weak*, *silly*) ἀνόητος, χαζός ‖ ~ **drink** *n* ἀναψυκτικόν ‖ ~**en** *vt* μαλακώνω ‖ *vi* μαλακώνω, γίνομαι μαλακός ‖ ~-**hearted** *a* εὐαίσθητος, μέ τρυφερή καρδιά ‖ ~**ly** *ad* ἁπαλά, μαλακά, ἀθόρυβα ‖ ~**ness** *n* μαλακότης, ἁπαλότης.
soggy ['sɔgi] *a* ὑδαρής, μουσκεμένος.
soil [sɔil] *n* (*earth*) ἔδαφος, χῶμα ‖ *vt* λερώνω ‖ ~**ed** *a* λερωμένος, ἀκάθαρτος.
solar ['səulə*] *a* ἡλιακός ‖ ~ **system** *n* ἡλιακόν σύστημα.
sold [səuld] *pt,pp* of **sell**.
solder ['səuldə*] *vt* (συγ)κολλῶ ‖ *n* καλάΐ, κόλλησι.
soldier ['səuldʒə*] *n* στρατιώτης.
sole [səul] *n* πέλμα, πατούσα ‖ πέλμα, σόλα ‖ (*fish*) γλῶσσα ‖ *a* μόνος, μοναδικός ‖ ~**ly** *ad* (*only*) μόνον, μοναδικά.
solemn ['sɔləm] *a* σοβαρός ‖ (*formal*) ἐπίσημος, σεμνός.
solicitor [sə'lisitə*] *n* δικηγόρος, σύμβουλος, συνήγορος.
solid ['sɔlid] *a* στερεός, συμπαγής ‖ (*hard*) στερεός, γερός, σκληρός ‖ (*reliable*) σοβαρός, βάσιμος ‖ (*meal*) γερός, ὁλόκληρος ‖ *n* στερεόν ‖ ~**arity** *n* ἑνότης, ἀλληλεγγύη ‖ ~**ify** [sə'lidifai] *vi* στερεοποιοῦμαι, πήζω ‖ *vt* στερεοποιῶ, πήζω, παγιώνω ‖ ~**ity** *n* στερεότης ‖ ~**ly** *ad* στερεά, γερά.

soliloquy [sə'liləkwi] *n* μονόλογος, μονολογία.

solitaire [sɔli'tɛə*] *n* (*game*) πασιέντσα ‖ (*gem*) μονό διαμάντι, μονόπετρο.

solitary ['sɔlitəri] *a* μόνος ‖ (*lonely*) ὁλομόναχος, μοναχικός.

solitude ['sɔlitjuːd] *n* μοναξιά, ἐρημιά, ἀπομόνωσις.

solo ['səuləu] *n* σόλο ‖ ~**ist** *n* σολίστας.

solstice ['sɔlstis] *n* ἡλιοστάσιον.

soluble ['sɔljubl] *a* διαλυτός, εὐδιάλυτος ‖ (*able to be solved*) ἐπιδεικτικός λύσεως.

solution [sə'luːʃən] *n* λύσις, λύσιμο ‖ (*explanation*) λύσις, ἐξήγησις ‖ (*in liquid*) διάλυσις, διάλυμα.

solve [sɔlv] *vt* λύω, ἐξηγῶ.

solvent ['sɔlvənt] *a* ἀξιόχρεος.

sombre, (*US*) **somber** ['sɔmbə*] *a* σκοτεινός, μελαγχολικός ‖ ~**ly** *ad* σκοτεινά ‖ μελαγχολικά.

some [sʌm] *a* (*uncertain number*) ὀλίγος, ὀλίγοι, μερικοί ‖ (*indefinite*) κάποιος, τίς ‖ (*remarkable*) σπουδαῖος, περίφημος ‖ (*partitive*) μερικός, τι ‖ *pron* μερικοί, κάτι ‖ *ad* περίπου ‖ ~**body** *pron* κάποιος ‖ *n* κάποιος, προσωπικότης ‖ ~**day** *ad* (μιά) κάποια μέρα ‖ ~**how** *ad* κάπως, κατά κάποιον τρόπον ‖ ~**one** *pron* = **somebody** ‖ ~**place** *ad* (*US*) = **somewhere**.

somersault ['sʌməsɔːlt] *n* τούμπα, κουτρουβάλα ‖ *vi* κάνω τούμπα.

something ['sʌmθiŋ] *pron* κάτι, ὁτιδήποτε.

sometime ['sʌmtaim] *ad* κάποτε ‖ ~**s** *ad* ἐνίοτε, κάπου-κάπου.

somewhat ['sʌmwɔt] *ad* κάπως.

somewhere ['sʌmwɛə*] *ad* κάπου.

son [sʌn] *n* υἱός, γιός.

sonata [sə'nɑːtə] *n* σονάτα.

song [sɔŋ] *n* τραγούδι ‖ ~ **writer** *n* (μουσικο)συνθέτης.

sonic ['sɔnik] *a* ἠχητικός.

son-in-law ['sʌninlɔː] *n* γαμβρός.

sonnet ['sɔnit] *n* σονέττο.

sonny ['sʌni] *n* (*col*) μικρέ μου, ἀγόρι μου.

soon [suːn] *ad* ταχέως, γρήγορα ‖ (*early*) σύντομα, ἐνωρίς ‖ **as** ~ **as possible** τό συντομώτερο ‖ ~**er** *ad* (*time*) γρηγορώτερα ‖ (*of preference*) καλύτερα, κάλιο.

soot [sut] *n* αἰθάλη, φοῦμο, καπνιά.

soothe [suːð] *vt* καταπραΰνω, παρηγορῶ.

soothing ['suːðiŋ] *a* καταπραϋντικός.

sop [sɔp] *n* (*bribe*) δωροδοκία, φιλοδώρημα.

sophisticated [sə'fistikeitid] *a* (*person*) κοσμικός, μοντέρνος ‖ (*machinery*) πιό σύγχρονος, τελευταίας λέξεως.

sophistication [səfisti'keiʃən] *n* ἐξεζητημένα γοῦστα.

sophomore ['sɔfəmɔː*] *n* (*US*) δευτεροετής φοιτητής.

soporific [sɔpə'rifik] *a* ὑπνωτικός, ναρκωτικός.

sopping ['sɔpiŋ] *a* (*very wet*) καταβρεγμένος, μουσκεμένος.

soppy ['sɔpi] *a* (*col: sentimental*) δακρύβρεκτος, σαχλός.

soprano [sə'prɑːnəu] *n* ὑψίφωνος, σοπράνο.

sordid ['sɔːdid] *a* ἀκάθαρτος, ρυπαρός ‖ (*mean*) ἄθλιος, χυδαῖος, τσιγγούνης.

sore [sɔː*] *a* πονῶν, πού πονεῖ, ἐρεθισμένος ‖ (*offended*) πειραγμένος, θυμωμένος ‖ *n* πληγή, τραῦμα ‖ ~**ly** *ad* (*tempted*) βαθειά, σφοδρῶς ‖ ~**ness** *n* πόνος, ἐρεθισμός, ὀδυνηρότης.

sorrow ['sɔrəu] *n* λύπη, θλίψις, μετάνοια ‖ ~**ful** *a* θλιμμένος, λυπημένος ‖ ~**fully** *ad* θλιβερά, θλιμμένα.

sorry ['sɔri] *a* λυπημένος, πονεμένος ‖ (*pitiable*) ἄθλιος, φτωχικός, κακός.

sort [sɔːt] *n* εἶδος, τάξις, λογή ‖ *vt* (*also* ~ **out**) (*papers*) ταξινομῶ, ξεκαθαρίζω ‖ (*problems*) τακτοποιῶ, (ξε)χωρίζω.

so-so ['səusəu] *ad* ἔτσι καί ἔτσι, μετρίως, ὑποφερτά.

soufflé ['suːflei] *n* σουφλέ.

sought [sɔːt] *pt,pp* of **seek**.

soul [səul] *n* ψυχή ‖ ~**-destroying** *a* ψυχοφθόρος, ἀποκτηνωτικός ‖ ~**ful** *a* αἰσθηματικός, συγκινητικός ‖ ~**less** *a* ἄψυχος, ἄκαρδος.

sound [saund] *a* (*healthy*) ὑγιής, γερός ‖ (*safe*) στερεός, ἀσφαλής, σίγουρος ‖ (*reasonable*) ὀρθός, ἰσχυρός, λογικός ‖ (*deep, hearty*) γερός, ἄγριος ‖ *n* (*noise*) ἦχος, θόρυβος ‖ (*geog*) στενόν, πορθμός ‖ *vt* (*alarm*) κτυπῶ ‖ *vi* (*find depth*) βυθομετρῶ ‖ (*seem*) φαίνομαι, μοιάζω ‖ **to** ~ **out** *vt* (*opinions*) βολιδοσκοπῶ ‖ ~ **barrier** *n* φράγμα τοῦ ἤχου ‖ ~**ing** *n* (*naut etc*) βυθομέτρησις, βολιδοσκόπησις ‖ ~**ly** *ad* (*sleep*) βαθειά, καλά, ἥσυχα ‖ (*beat*) γερά, τελείως ‖ ~**ness** *n* βασιμότης, ὀρθότης ‖ ~**proof** *a* (*room*) ἠχομονωτικός ‖ *vt* κάνω ἀδιαπέραστο ἀπό ἦχον ‖ ~ **track** *n* (*of film*) ἠχητική ζώνη (ταινίας).

soup [suːp] *n* σούπα, ζωμός ‖ **in the** ~ στή λούμπα ‖ ~**spoon** *n* κουτάλι τῆς σούπας.

sour ['sauə*] *a* ξυνός, ἄγουρος, πράσινος ‖ (*milk*) ξυνός ‖ (*bad-tempered*) στριφνός, γκρινιάρης.

source [sɔːs] *n* πηγή, προέλευσις.

sourness ['sauənis] *n* ὀξύτης, ξινίλα.

south [sauθ] *n* νότος ‖ *a* νότιος ‖ *ad* πρός νότον, νοτίως ‖ ~**-east** *n* τό νοτιοανατολικόν ‖ ~**-easterly** *a* νοτιοανατολικός ‖ ~**ern** *a* νότιος, μεσημβρινός ‖ **S ~ Pole** *n* Νότιος Πόλος ‖ ~**ward(s)** *ad* πρός νότον ‖ ~**ern** *n* τό νοτιοδυτικόν.

souvenir [suːvə'niə*] *n* ἐνθύμιον, σουβενίρ.

sovereign ['sɔvrin] *n* ἡγεμών, βασιλεύς ‖ *a* (*independent*) κυρίαρχος ‖ ~**ty** *n* ἡγεμονία, κυριαρχία, ἀνεξαρτησία.

soviet ['səuviət] *a* σοβιετικός.

sow [sau] *n* γουρούνα ‖ [səu] (*irreg v*) *vt* σπείρω, σπέρνω ‖ (*spread abroad*) (ἐν)σπείρω.

soya bean ['sɔiə'biːn] *n* σόγια.
spa [spaː] *n* ἰαματική πηγή ‖ (*place*) λουτρόπολις.
space [speis] *n* χῶρος, θέσις, τόπος ‖ (*distance*) ἀπόστασις ‖ (*length of time*) διάστημα ‖ (*universe*) διάστημα ‖ **to ~ out** *vt* ἀραιώνω, τοποθετῶ κατ' ἀποστάσεις ‖ **~craft** *n* διαστημόπλοιον ‖ **~man** *n* κοσμοναύτης.
spacing ['speisiŋ] *n* ἀραίωσις, κλιμάκωσις.
spacious ['speiʃəs] *a* εὐρύς, εὐρύχωρος, ἀπλόχωρος.
spade [speid] *n* (*tool*) φτυάρι, τσάπα, τσαπί ‖ **~s** *npl* (*cards*) μπαστούνι, πίκα ‖ **~work** *n* (*preliminary work*) προκαταρκτική ἐργασία.
spaghetti [spə'geti] *n* σπαγέτο, μακαρονάδα.
Spain [spein] *n* Ἱσπανία.
span [spæn] *n* (*of arch*) ἄνοιγμα, ἀπόστασις ‖ (*of time*) διάρκεια (ζωῆς) ‖ *vt* ζευγνύω, καλύπτω ‖ *pt of* **spin**.
Spaniard ['spænjəd] *n* Ἱσπανός.
spaniel ['spænjəl] *n* σπάνιελ.
Spanish ['spæniʃ] *n* (*ling*) ἱσπανικά ‖ *a* ἱσπανικός.
spank [spæŋk] *vt* δέρνω (στόν πισινό).
spanner ['spænə*] *n* κλειδί (ὑδραυλικοῦ).
spare [spɛə*] *a* περίσσιος, λιτός, ἰσχνός ‖ *n* = **~ part** ‖ *see below* ‖ *vt* (*do without*) οἰκονομῶ, φυλάγω, κάνω δίχως ‖ (*save from hurt*) λυποῦμαι, χαρίζω, φείδομαι ‖ (*lend, give*) περισσεύω, δίνω, παραχωρῶ, διαθέτω ‖ **to ~** περισσεύω ‖ **~ part** *n* ἀνταλλακτικόν, ἐξάρτημα, ρεζέρβα ‖ **~ time** *n* ἐλεύθερες ὧρες.
spark [spɑːk] *n* σπινθήρ, σπίθα ‖ (*fig*) ἴχνος, σπίθα ‖ **~ plug** *n* σπινθηριστής, μπουζί.
sparkle ['spɑːkl] *n* σπινθήρ, σπίθα, λάμψις ‖ (*gaiety*) σπιρτάδα ‖ *vi* σπινθηρίζω, σπιθοβολῶ, ἀστράφτω.
sparkling ['spɑːkliŋ] *a* (*lit*) ἀστραφτερός, λάμπων ‖ (*wine*) ἀφρώδης ‖ (*conversation*) πνευματώδης (ὁμιλία).
sparrow ['spærəu] *n* σπουργίτης.
sparse [spɑːs] *a* ἀραιός, σποραδικός ‖ **~ly** *ad* ἀραιά.
spasm ['spæzəm] *n* σπασμός, σπαρτάρισμα ‖ (*short spell*) κρίσις, ἔξαψις, μικρῆς διαρκείας ‖ **~odic** *a* σπασμωδικός, σπαστικός.
spastic ['spæstik] *n* σπαστικός.
spat [spæt] *pt,pp of* **spit**.
spate [speit] *n* (*fig*) πλημμύρα, πλημμύρισμα ‖ **in ~** (*river*) φουσκωμένος, πλημμυρισμένος.
spatter ['spætə*] *n* πιτσίλισμα, ράντισμα ‖ *vt* πιτσιλίζω, ραντίζω ‖ *vi* ἀναπηδῶ, (ξε)πετιέμαι, στάζω.
spatula ['spætjulə] *n* σπάτουλα.
spawn [spɔːn] *vt* ἀφήνω αὐγά ‖ γεννῶ.
speak [spiːk] (*irreg v*) *vt* λέγω, προφέρω,

ἐκφράζω ‖ (*truth*) λέγω, λέω ‖ (*language*) ὁμιλῶ, μιλῶ ‖ *vi* (+ *to*) ὁμιλῶ, μιλῶ στόν ‖ μιλῶ, συζητῶ ‖ (*make speech*) ἀγορεύω, μιλῶ ‖ **to ~ for** *vt* συνηγορῶ, μιλῶ γιά κάποιον ‖ **to ~ up** *vi* ὑψώνω τήν φωνήν, μιλῶ γιά κάποιον ‖ **~er** *n* ὁμιλητής, συνομιλητής ‖ (*chairman*) πρόεδρος ‖ (*loudspeaker: on record player*) μεγάφωνον ‖ **on ~ing terms** γνώριμοι, πού μιλιοῦνται.
spear [spiə*] *n* ἀκόντιον, δόρυ, κοντάρι ‖ *vt* τρυπῶ μέ κοντάρι, πιάνω μέ κοντάρι.
spec [spek] *n* (*col*) τύχη, κερδοσκοπία ‖ **on ~** στήν τύχη, γιά σπέκουλα.
special ['spreʃəl] *a* εἰδικός, ἴδιος ‖ (*particular kind*) ἐξαιρετικός, ἀσυνήθης ‖ (*particular purpose*) ἰδιαίτερος, ξεχωριστός ‖ *n* (*rail*) εἰδική ἁμαξοστοιχία ‖ (*cooking*) εἰδικός, ἰδιαίτερος ‖ **~ist** *n* εἰδικός ‖ **~ity** *n* εἰδικότης ‖ σπεσιαλιτέ ‖ **~ize** *vi* (+ *in*) εἰδικεύομαι εἰς ‖ **~ly** *ad* εἰδικά, ἰδιαίτερα, πρό παντός, πάνω ἀπ' ὅλα.
species ['spiːʃiːz] *n* εἶδος.
specific [spə'sifik] *a* εἰδικός, ὡρισμένος, ἀκριβής, σαφής ‖ **~ally** *ad* εἰδικά, συγκεκριμένως ‖ **~ation** [spesifi'keiʃən] *n* περιγραφή, καθορισμός, προδιαγραφή.
specify ['spesifai] *vt* καθορίζω, προσδιορίζω, διευκρινίζω.
specimen ['spesimin] *n* δεῖγμα, τύπος.
speck [spek] *n* κηλίς, λεκές, σταγόνα ‖ (*particle*) κόκκος, ψῆγμα, μόριον ‖ **~led** *a* διάστικτος, πιτσιλισμένος.
specs [speks] *npl* (*col*) γυαλιά.
spectacle ['spektəkl] *n* θέαμα ‖ **~s** *npl* ματογυάλια, γυαλιά.
spectacular [spek'tækjulə*] *a* θεαματικός.
spectator [spek'teitə*] *n* θεατής.
spectre, (*US*) **specter** ['spektə*] *n* φάντασμα, σκιάχτρο.
spectrum ['spektrəm] *n* φάσμα.
speculate ['spekjuleit] *vi* σκέπτομαι, διαλογίζομαι ‖ (*fin*) κερδοσκοπῶ, σπεκουλάρω.
speculation [spekju'leiʃən] *n* (*fin*) κερδοσκοπία, σπέκουλα.
speculative ['spekjulətiv] *a* (*fin*) κερδοσκοπικός.
sped [sped] *pt,pp of* **speed**.
speech [spiːtʃ] *n* λόγος, λαλιά ‖ (*talk*) λόγος, ἀγόρευσις, ὁμιλία ‖ (*manner*) ἄρθρωσις, εὐγλωττία, γλῶσσα ‖ **~ day** *n* (*sch*) ἀπονομή τῶν πτυχίων ‖ **~less** *a* ἄλαλος, βουβός, ἄφωνος ‖ **~ therapy** *n* θεραπευτική ἀγωγή λόγου.
speed [spiːd] (*irreg v*) *n* ταχύτης, σπουδή ‖ (*gear*) ταχύτης ‖ *vi* σπεύδω, κάνω γρήγορα, τρέχω ‖ **to ~ up** *vi* ἐπιταχύνω ‖ *vt* ἐπισπεύδω, ἐπιταχύνω ‖ **~boat** *n* ἐξωλέμβιος ‖ **~ily** *ad* ταχέως, ἐσπευσμένα, βιαστικά ‖ **~ing** *n* ὑπερβολική ταχύτης ‖ **~ limit** *n* ὅριον ταχύτητος ‖

~ometer n ἐνδείκτης ταχύτητος, κοντέρ ‖ ~way n αὐτοκινητόδρομος ‖ ~y a ταχύς, γρήγορος.

spell [spel] (irreg v) n (magic) γοητεία, μαγεία, μάγια ‖ (period of time) διάστημα, χρονική περίοδος ‖ vt ὀρθογραφῶ, γραμματίζω ‖ συλλαβίζω ‖ (mean) σημαίνω ‖ ~bound a γοητευμένος, μαγεμένος ‖ ~ing n συλλαβισμός, ὀρθογραφία.

spelt [spelt] pt,pp of spell.

spend [spend] (irreg v) vt ξοδεύω, καταναλίσκω, δαπανῶ ‖ (use up) ἐξαντλῶ, περνῶ, χρησιμοποιῶ ‖ ~ing money n χαρτζιλίκι.

spent [spent] pt,pp of spend ‖ a (patience) ἐξηντλημένος.

sperm [spə:m] n (biol) σπέρμα.

spew [spju:] vi ξερνῶ, κάνω ἐμετό.

sphere [sfiə*] n σφαῖρα, ὑδρόγειος.

spherical ['sferikəl] a σφαιρικός.

sphinx [sfiŋks] n σφίγξ, σφίγγα.

spice [spais] n καρύκευμα, μπαχαρικό, ἄρωμα ‖ vt καρυκεύω, ἀρτύω, ἀρωματίζω.

spiciness ['spaisinis] n πικάντικη γεῦσις, νοστιμιά.

spick-and-span ['spikən'spæn] a φρέσκος, καθαρός, κομψός.

spicy ['spaisi] a ἀρωματισμένος, πικάντικος.

spider ['spaidə*] n ἀράχνη ‖ ~y a ἀράχνινος.

spike [spaik] n αἰχμή, καρφί, στάχυ, πάσσαλος.

spill [spil] (irreg v) vt (upset) ἀνατρέπω, ἀναποδογυρίζω ‖ (pour out) χύνω ‖ vi (flow over) χύνομαι.

spin [spin] (irreg v) n (revolution of wheel) περιστροφή, συστροφή ‖ (trip in car) περίπατος, βόλτα ‖ (aviat) περιδίνησις, σπινάρισμα ‖ vt (wool etc) κλώθω, νέθω ‖ γυρίζω, παίζω σβούρα ‖ vi περιστρέφομαι, (στριφο)γυρίζω ‖ to ~ out vi (of money etc) οἰκονομῶ (τά λεφτά μου) ‖ vt παρατείνω, παρατραβῶ, ξεντώνω.

spinach ['spinidʒ] n σπανάκι.

spinal ['spainl] a νωτιαῖος, ραχιαῖος, σπονδυλικός ‖ ~ cord n νωτιαῖος μυελός.

spindly ['spindli] a λιγνός.

spin-drier ['spin'draiə*] n στεγνωτήριον.

spine [spain] n σπονδυλική στήλη, ραχοκοκκαλιά ‖ (thorn) ἀγκάθι ‖ ~less a δειλός, λαπάς.

spinner ['spinə*] n (of thread) κλώστης, κλώστρια.

spinning ['spiniŋ] n (of thread) κλώσιμο, στρίψιμο ‖ ~ wheel n ροδάνι, ἀνέμη.

spinster ['spinstə*] n γεροντοκόρη.

spiral ['spaiərəl] n σπείρα, ἕλιξ ‖ a ἑλικοειδής, σπειροειδής ‖ vi κινοῦμαι σπειροειδῶς ‖ ~ staircase n γυριστή σκάλα, στριφτή σκάλα.

spire ['spaiə*] n κορυφή κωδωνοστασίου.

spirit ['spirit] n πνεῦμα, ψυχή ‖ (ghost) φάντασμα ‖ (humour, mood) διάθεσις, κέφι ‖ (courage) σθένος, κουράγιο, θάρρος ‖ (alcoholic) οἰνοπνευματῶδες ποτό, σπίρτο ‖ in good ~s κεφάτος, καλόκεφος ‖ ~ed a ζωηρός, ἔντονος, θαρραλέος ‖ ~ level n ἀλφάδι ‖ ~ual a πνευματικός, ψυχικός ‖ n θρησκευτικό τραγούδι ‖ ~ualism n πνευματισμός.

spit [spit] (irreg v) n (for roasting) σούβλα ‖ (saliva) πτύελον, σάλιο ‖ vi φτύνω ‖ (of motor) ρετάρω.

spite [spait] n μῖσος, ἔχθρα, κακία ‖ vt ἐνοχλῶ, πεισμώνω, φουρκίζω ‖ in ~ of παρά τό, παρ' ὅλα ‖ ~ful a μοχθηρός, ἐκδικητικός.

splash [splæʃ] n πιτσίλισμα, πλατσούλισμα, λεκές ‖ (of colour) πολυχρωμία ‖ vti πλατσουλίζω, πιτσιλίζω ‖ ~down n προσθαλάσσωσις.

spleen [spli:n] n σπλήνα.

splendid ['splendid] a λαμπρός, μεγαλοπρεπής ‖ (fine) ἐξαίσιος, περίφημος ‖ ~ly ad λαμπρά, ὑπέροχα, περίφημα.

splendour, (US) splendor ['splendə*] n λαμπρότης, λάμψις ‖ (glory) μεγαλοπρέπεια.

splice [splais] vt ἁματίζω, συνδέω.

splint [splint] n νάρθηξ.

splinter ['splintə*] n θραῦσμα, σχίζα ‖ vi θραύομαι, σπάζω.

split [split] (irreg v) n σχισμή, σχίσιμο, ρωγμή, διαίρεσις ‖ vt σχίζω, θραύω, σπάζω ‖ vi (divide) διασπῶ ‖ (col: depart) ἀναχωρῶ ‖ to ~ up vi διαιρούμαι ‖ vt διαιρῶ, χωρίζω, διασπῶ ‖ ~ting a (headache) πού πονάει, πού σπάει.

splutter ['splʌtə*] vi λειτουργῶ κακῶς, ρετάρω.

spoil [spoil] (irreg v) vt χαλῶ ‖ ~s npl λεία, λάφυρα ‖ ~sport n αὐτός πού χαλάει τό κέφι.

spoke [spəuk] n ἀκτίνα (τροχοῦ) ‖ pt of speak ‖ ~n pp of speak ‖ ~sman n ἐκπρόσωπος.

sponge [spʌndʒ] n σφουγγάρι ‖ vt πλένω, σφουγγίζω ‖ vi (+ on) σελεμίζω, τρακάρω ‖ ~ bag n σάκκος γιά σφουγγάρι ‖ ~ cake n παντεσπάνι ‖ ~r n (col) σελέμης, τρακαδόρος.

spongy ['spʌndʒi] a σπογγώδης.

sponsor ['sponsə*] n ἀνάδοχος, ἐγγυητής, εἰσηγητής ‖ vt ὑποστηρίζω, εἰσηγοῦμαι ‖ ~ship n ὑποστήριξις.

spontaneity [spontə'neiiti] n αὐθορμητισμός.

spontaneous [spon'teiniəs] a αὐτόματος ‖ (natural) αὐθόρμητος ‖ ~ly ad αὐθόρμητα.

spooky ['spu:ki] a (col) μέ φαντάσματα, στοιχειωμένος.

spool [spu:l] n καρούλα, μασούρι.

spoon [spu:n] *n* κουτάλι ‖ ~**-feed** *vt* (*lit*) ταΐζω μέ τό κουτάλι ‖ (*fig*) ἐπιχορηγῶ ‖ ~**ful** *n* κουταλιά.

sporadic [spə'rædik] *a* σποραδικός.

sport [spɔ:t] *n* (*games*) ἀθλητισμός, σπόρ ‖ (*fun*) διασκέδασις, παιδιά ‖ (*good-humoured person*) καλός ἄνθρωπος ‖ ~**ing** *a* (*fair*) τίμιος ‖ ~**s car** *n* αὐτοκίνητον σπόρ ‖ ~**(s) coat** *n*, ~**(s) jacket** *n* σακκάκι σπόρ ‖ ~**sman** *n* φίλαθλος, τίμιος παίκτης ‖ ~**smanship** *n* τιμιότης στό σπόρ ‖ ~**s page** *n* σελίδα ἀθλητικῶν νέων ‖ ~**swear** *n* εἴδη ἀθλητισμοῦ ‖ ~**swoman** *n* ἀθλήτρια ‖ ~**y** *a* εὐγενικό, πολύ λεπτό.

spot [spɔt] *n* στίγμα, κηλίδα, λεκές ‖ (*place*) τόπος, μέρος, τοποθεσία ‖ (*small amount*) σταλιά, λίγο ‖ *vt* (*notice*) διακρίνω, σημειώνω ‖ (*make spots on*) λεκιάζω ‖ (*med*) κηλιδῶ, γεμίζω σπειριά, ἔχω πανάδες ‖ ~ **check** *n* ταχύς ἔλεγχος ‖ ~**less** *a* ἄσπιλος, ἀκηλίδωτος, καθαρός ‖ ~**lessly** *ad* (κατ)ἄσπρο, (πεντα)κάθαρα ‖ ~**light** *n* προβολεύς θεάτρου ‖ (*position*) περίοπτος θέσις, κέντρον ‖ ~**ted** *a* διάστικτος, πιτσιλωτός ‖ ~**ty** *a* (*face*) μέ πανάδες, μέ σπειριά.

spouse [spauz] *n* σύζυγος.

spout [spaut] *n* στόμιον, σωλήν, λούκι ‖ (*jet*) ἐκροή, πίδαξ ‖ *vi* ξεπηδῶ, ἀναπηδῶ, ξεχύνομαι.

sprain [sprein] *n* διάστρεμμα, στραμπούλισμα ‖ *vt* στραμπουλίζω.

sprang [spræŋ] *pt of* **spring**.

sprawl [sprɔ:l] *vi* ἐκτείνομαι, ξαπλώνομαι.

spray [sprei] *n* (*sprinkle*) ψεκάδες, πιτσιλίσματα ‖ (*instrument*) ψεκαστήρ, βαπορι-ζατέρ ‖ (*branch*) κλωνάρι ‖ *vt* ψεκάζω, καταβρέχω.

spread [spred] (*irreg v*) *n* (*extent*) ἐπέκτασις, διάδοσις ‖ (*col*) τραπέζι, πλούσιο γεῦμα ‖ *vt* ἁπλώνω, στρώνω ‖ (*scatter*) σκορπίζω, στρώνω, διαδίδω ‖ (*smear*) ἀλείφω, χύνω.

spree [spri:] *n* διασκέδασις, ξεφάντωμα, γλέντι.

sprig [sprig] *n* κλωνάρι, βλαστός.

sprightly ['spraitli] *a* ζωηρός, κεφάτος.

spring [spriŋ] (*irreg v*) *n* (*leap*) πήδημα ‖ (*of water*) πηγή ‖ (*coil*) ἐλατήριον ‖ (*season*) ἄνοιξις ‖ *vi* (ἀνα)πηδῶ, ξεπετάγομαι ‖ **to** ~ **up** *vi* (*problem*) δημιουργοῦμαι, ἐμφανίζομαι ‖ ~**board** *n* βατήρ, τραμπλέν ‖ ~**-clean** *n* γενικός καθαρισμός ‖ *vt* κάνω γενικόν καθαρισμόν ‖ ~**-cleaning** *n* γενικός καθαρισμός (ἀνοιξιάτικος) ‖ ~**iness** *n* ἐλαστικότης ‖ ~**time** *n* ἄνοιξη ‖ ~**y** *a* ἐλαστικός, εὔκαμπτος.

sprinkle ['spriŋkl] *n* ράντισμα ‖ *vt* ραντίζω, ραίνω.

sprinkling ['spriŋkliŋ] *n* μικρά ποσότης.

sprint [sprint] *n* δρόμος ταχύτητος ‖ *vi* τρέχω δρόμον ταχύτητος ‖ ~**er** *n* δρομεύς ταχύτητος.

sprite [sprait] *n* νεράϊδα.

sprout [spraut] *vi* βλαστάνω, φυτρώνω ‖ *see* **Brussels sprout**.

spruce [spru:s] *n* ἔλατο ‖ *a* κομψός, τακτικός.

sprung [sprʌŋ] *pp of* **spring**.

spry [sprai] *a* ζωηρός, ἐνεργητικός.

spud [spʌd] *n* (*col: potato*) πατάτα.

spun [spʌn] *pt,pp of* **spin**.

spur [spə:*] *n* πτερνιστήρ, σπηρούνι ‖ (*fig*) κίνητρον, ἐλατήριον ‖ *vt* (*also* ~ **on**) κεντρίζω, παρακινῶ ‖ **on the** ~ **of the moment** χωρίς σκέψι, αὐθόρμητα.

spurious ['spjuəriəs] *a* κίβδηλος, ψεύτικος.

spurn [spə:n] *vt* περιφρονῶ, ἀποκρούω.

spurt [spə:t] *n* (*effort*) σφίξιμο, φουλάρισμα, ξέσπασμα ‖ (*jet*) ἀνάβλυσις, πίδαξ ‖ *vi* ξεχύνομαι, φουλάρω.

spy [spai] *n* κατάσκοπος ‖ *vi* κατασκοπεύω ‖ *vt* διακρίνω, βλέπω, παρατηρῶ ‖ ~**ing** *n* (*espionage*) κατασκοπεία.

squabble ['skwɔbl] *n* φιλονεικία, καυγᾶς ‖ *vi* φιλονεικῶ, καυγαδίζω, πιάνομαι (μέ).

squabbling ['skwɔbliŋ] *n* φιλονεικία, καυγᾶς.

squad [skwɔd] *n* (*mil*) ἀπόσπασμα, οὐλαμός ‖ (*police*) ὑπηρεσία διώξεως.

squadron ['skwɔdrən] *n* μοίρα.

squalid ['skwɔlid] *a* βρώμικος, βρωμερός, ἄθλιος.

squall [skwɔ:l] *n* (*scream*) κραυγή, στριγγλιά ‖ ~**y** *a* (*weather*) μέ μπόρες.

squalor ['skwɔlə*] *n* ἀκαθαρσία, βρώμα, ἀθλιότης.

squander ['skwɔndə*] *vt* σπαταλῶ.

square [skwɛə*] *n* (*figure*) τετράγωνον ‖ (*of town*) πλατεῖα ‖ (*instrument*) γωνία, γνώμων ‖ (*product*) τετράγωνον ‖ (*col: person*) ἀνιαρός, ἀταίριαστος ‖ *a* τετραγωνικός ‖ (*honest*) τίμιος, καθαρός, δίκαιος ‖ (*ample*) ἱκανοποιητικός, ἄφθονος ‖ (*even*) πάτσι ‖ *ad* (*exactly*) ἀκριβῶς, καθέτως ‖ *vt* (*arrange*) ρυθμίζω, κανονίζω, τακτοποιῶ ‖ (*math*) τετραγωνίζω ‖ *vi* (*agree*) (+ *with*) συμφωνῶ, συμβιβάζομαι ‖ **all** ~ στά ἴσια, πάτσι ‖ **2 metres** ~ 4 τετραγωνικά μέτρα ‖ **1** ~ **metre** 1 τετραγωνικόν μέτρον ‖ ~**ly** *ad* γερά ‖ τίμια, ντόμπρα.

squash [skwɔʃ] *n*•(*drink*) χυμός (φρούτων) ‖ *vt* συνθλίβω, ζουλῶ, στίβω.

squat [skwɔt] *a* κοντόχοντρος ‖ *vi* κάθομαι σταυροπόδι ‖ ~**ter** *n* σφετεριστής γῆς.

squawk [skwɔ:k] *n* κράξιμο, βραχνή κραυγή ‖ *vi* κράζω, φωνάζω, κραυγάζω.

squeak [skwi:k] *n* ὀξεῖα κραυγή, σκούξιμο ‖ *vi* σκούζω, τσιρίζω, τρίζω ‖ ~**y** *a* πού σκούζει.

squeal [skwi:l] *n* ὀξεῖα κραυγή, στριγγλιά ‖ *vi* στριγγλίζω, σκούζω.

squeamish ['skwi:miʃ] *a* εὐαίσθητος, ἔχων

άναγούλες || (easily shocked) σιχασιάρης, δύστροπος || ~ness n δύσκολα γούστα, ύπερβολική λεπτότης.

squeeze [skwi:z] n (lit) σύνθλιψις, σφίξιμο, στρίμωγμα || (econ) πίεσις || vt συνθλίβω, σφίγγω, στύβω || to ~ out vt στύβω, έκθλίβω.

squid [skwid] n σουπιά.

squint [skwint] n άλλοιθωρισμός, στραβισμός || vi άλλοιθωρίζω, στραβοκοιτάζω.

squire ['skwaiə*] n πυργοδεσπότης, προύχων.

squirm [skwə:m] vi συστρέφω τό σῶμα, στενοχωριέμαι, ντρέπομαι.

squirrel ['skwirəl] n σκίουρος.

squirt [skwə:t] n έκτόξευσις, πιτσίλισμα, ριπή || vi άναβλύζω, πετάγομαι, έκτοξεύω.

stab [stæb] n (blow) κτύπημα, μπαμπεσιά || (col: try) δοκιμάζω || ~bing n (incident) μαχαίρωμα.

stability [stə'biliti] n σταθερότης.

stabilization [steibəlai'zeiʃən] n σταθεροποίησις.

stabilize ['steibəlaiz] vt σταθεροποιῶ || ~r n ζυγοσταθμιστής, σταθεροποιητής.

stable ['steibl] n στάβλος || vt σταβλίζω || a σταθερός, μόνιμος.

staccato [stə'ka:təu] a κοφτό, νευρικό, στακκάτο.

stack [stæk] n θημωνιά, σωρός || vt συσσωρεύω, στοιβάζω.

stadium ['steidiəm] n στάδιον.

staff [sta:f] n (stick) ράβδος, μπαστούνι, κοντάκι || (people) προσωπικόν, έπιτελεῖον || vt (with people) καταρτίζω προσωπικόν.

stag [stæg] n έλάφι.

stage [steidʒ] n (theatre) σκηνή || (actors) θέατρον || (degree) στάδιον || vt (play) άνεβάζω, σκηνοθετῶ || (demonstration) όργανώνω, σκηνοθετῶ || in ~s βαθμηδόν, κατά στάδια || ~coach n ταχυδρομική άμαξα || ~ door n εἴσοδος ἠθοποιῶν || ~ manager n σκηνοθέτης.

stagger ['stægə*] vi κλονίζομαι, τρικλίζω, παραπατῶ || vt (person) ζαλίζω, συγκλονίζω, κάνω νά χάση || (hours) κλιμακώνω (τίς ὥρες) || ~ing a (amazing) καταπληκτικός, συγκλονιστικός.

stagnant ['stægnənt] a στάσιμος, λιμνάζων || (dull) άδρανής, άγονος.

stagnate [stæg'neit] vi εἶμαι στάσιμος, άδρανῶ.

stagnation [stæg'neiʃən] n στασιμότης, νέκρωσις.

staid [steid] a θετικός, σοβαρός.

stain [stein] n λεκές, μουντζούρα || (colouring) χρῶμα, βαφή, μπογιά vt λεκιάζω, λερώνω || ~ed glass n καθεδρική ὕαλος || ~less (a steel) άνοξείδωτος || ~ remover n καθαριστικόν λεκέδων.

stair [stεə*] n κλῖμαξ, σκάλα || (one step)

σκαλοπάτι, σκαλί || ~case n κλῖμαξ, σκάλα || ~s npl σκάλα || ~way n σκάλα.

stake [steik] n πάσσαλος, παλούκι || (gambling) στοίχημα, μίζα, ποντάρισμα || vt ποντάρω, παίζω, διακυβεύω.

stalactite ['stæləktait] n σταλακτίτης.

stalagmite ['stæləgmait] n σταλαγμίτης.

stale [steil] a μπαγιάτικος || ~mate n άδιέξοδον.

stalk [stɔ:k] n κοτσάνι, στέλεχος, μίσχος || vt παρακολουθῶ άθέατος || (walk stiffly) βαδίζω μέ μεγάλα βήματα.

stall [stɔ:l] n παράπηγμα στάβλου, παχνί || (stand) μπάγκος, περίπτερον || vt (aut) κολλῶ, μπλοκάρω || vi (aut) κολλῶ || (delay) άναβάλλω, χρονοτριβῶ || ~s npl (theat) κάθισμα (όρχήστρας).

stallion ['stæliən] n έπιβήτωρ, κήλων.

stalwart ['stɔ:lwət] a ρωμαλέος, σθεναρός || n πρωτοπαλλήκαρο, ἡρακλῆς.

stamina ['stæminə] n σφρῖγος, ζωτική δύναμις.

stammer ['stæmə*] n τραύλισμα, τσέββδισμα || vi τραυλίζω, ψευδίζω, ψελλίζω.

stamp [stæmp] n (postage) γραμματόσημον || ένσημον || (of foot) κτήπημα ποδός, ποδοβολητό || n (document) σφραγίδα, βούλλα, στάμπα || vi χτυπῶ τό πόδι, περπατῶ βαρειά || vt (make mark) σφραγίζω, μαρκάρω, σταμπάρω || (fix postage) κολλῶ γραμματόσημο || ~ album n συλλογή γραμματοσήμων || ~ collecting n φιλοτελισμός.

stampede [stæm'pi:d] n έσπευσμένη φυγή, πανικός.

stance [stæns] n (posture) στάσις.

stand [stænd] (irreg v) n (position) στάσις || (mil) άντίστασις || (rest) ὑποστήριγμα, πόδι, στήριγμα || (seats) έξέδρα || vi (erect) ἵσταμαι, στέκομαι || (rise) σηκώνομαι || (place, set) κεῖμαι, βρίσκομαι, εἶμαι || (halt, stop) σταματῶ, στέκομαι || vt (place) τοποθετῶ, βάζω, κουμπῶ (ὄρθιο) || (endure) ὑπομένω, ὑποφέρω, ἀντέχω || ὑπομένω εἰς || to make a ~ άνθίσταμαι, κρατῶ τίς θέσεις μου || it ~s to reason εἶναι λογικόν || to ~ by vi (be ready) (εἶμαι) ἕτοιμος, εἶμαι εἰς έπιφυλακήν || vt (opinion) μένω πιστός εἰς || to ~ for vt (defend) ὑπερασπίζομαι, ὑποστηρίζω || (signify) άντιπροσωπεύω || (permit, tolerate) ὑπομένω, άνέχομαι || to ~ in for vt άντικαθιστῶ || to ~ out vi (be prominent) (προ)έξέχω, ξεχωρίζω || to ~ up vi (rise) έγείρομαι, σηκώνομαι || to ~ up for vt ὑποστηρίζω.

standard ['stændəd] n (measure) ὑπόδειγμα, κανών, μέτρον || (flag) σημαία, λάβαρον || a (size etc) πρότυπος, κανονικός, συνήθης || ~ization n τυποποίησις, καθιέρωσις, όμοιοποίησις || ~ize vt τυποποιῶ, καθιερῶ || ~ of living n έπίπεδον ζωῆς.

stand-by ['stændbai] *n* στήριγμα.

stand-in ['stændin] *n* ἀντικαταστάτης, ἀναπληρωτής.

standing ['stændiŋ] *a* ὄρθιος ‖ (*lasting*) μόνιμος, διαρκής ‖ *n* διάρκεια ‖ (*reputation*) κοινωνική θέσις, ὑπόληψις ‖ ~ **orders** *npl* (*mil*) μόνιμαι διατάξεις, κανονισμοί ‖ ~ **room only** μόνον ὄρθιοι.

stand-offish ['stænd'ɔfiʃ] *a* ὑπεροπτικός.

standpoint ['stændpɔint] *n* ἄποψις, σκοπιά.

standstill ['stændstil] *n*: **at a** ~ στασιμότης, νεκρόν σημεῖον ‖ **to come to a** ~ καταλήγω εἰς ἀδιέξοδον, σταματῶ.

stank [stæŋk] *pt of* **stink**.

stanza ['stænzə] *n* στροφή, στάντσα.

staple ['steipl] *n* ἄγκιστρον, συνδετήρας ‖ (*product*) κύριον προϊόν ‖ *a* κύριος, πρωτεύων ‖ *vt* στερεώνω, συνδέω ‖ ~**r** *n* συνδετήρας.

star [sta:*] *n* ἀστήρ, ἄστρο, ἀστέρι ‖ (*actor*) ἀστήρ, πρωταγωνιστής, στάρ ‖ (*shape*) ἀστέρι ‖ *vi* (*in film*) πρωταγωνιστῶ, παίζω σέ ταινία ‖ *vt* (*to star an actor*) παρουσιάζω ὡς πρωταγωνιστή.

starboard ['sta:bəd] *n* δεξιά πλευρά, δεξιόν ‖ *a* δεξιά.

starch [sta:tʃ] *n* ἄμυλον ‖ ~**ed** *a* (*collar*) κολλαριστός ‖ ~**y** *a* ἀμυλώδης, ἀμυλοῦχος ‖ (*formal*) ὑπεροπτικός, ποζάτος.

stardom ['sta:dəm] *n* θέσις ἀστέρος.

stare [stɛə*] *n* ἀτενές βλέμμα, καρφωτή ματιά ‖ *vi* (+ *at*) ἀτενίζω, καρφώνω μέ τό μάτι.

starfish ['sta:fiʃ] *n* ἀστερίας.

staring ['stɛəriŋ] *a* (*eyes*) ἀπλανή (ματιά), γουρλωμένα (μάτια).

stark [sta:k] *a* ψυχρός, σκληρός, γυμνός ‖ *ad*: ~ **naked** ὁλόγυμνος, θεόγυμνος, τσίτσιδος.

starless ['sta:lis] *a* (*night*) ἄναστρος, χωρίς ἄστρα.

starlight ['sta:lait] *n* ἀστροφεγγιά.

starling ['sta:liŋ] *n* ψαρώνι, καραβέλι.

starlit ['sta:lit] *a* ἀστροφέγγιος.

starry ['sta:ri] *a* ἔναστρος, ἀστερόφεγγος, λάμπων ‖ ~-**eyed** *a* (*innocent*) λάμπων, ἀθῶος.

start [sta:t] *n* ἀρχή, σημεῖον ἐκκινήσεως, ἐκκίνησις ‖ (*beginning*) ἀρχή, ἀρχίνισμα ‖ (*sudden movement*) ξάφνιασμα, ἀνατίναγμα ‖ *vt* (*set going*) ἀρχίζω, ἀνοίγω, βγάζω ‖ *vi* (*begin journey*) ἀρχίζω, ξεκινῶ ‖ (*make sudden movement*) ἀναπηδῶ, ξαφνίζομαι ‖ **to ~ doing sth** ἀρχίζω μέ, πιάνομαι μέ ‖ **to ~ off** *vi* (*begin*) ἀρχίζω, ξεκινῶ ‖ **to ~ over** *vi* (*begin again*) ξαναρχίζω ‖ **to ~ up** *vi* βάζω μπρός ‖ ~**er** *n* (*aut*) ἐκκινητήρ, στάρτερ ‖ (*for race*) ἀφέτης, στάρτερ ‖ ~**ing handle** *n* μανιβέλλα ‖ ~**ing point** *n* ἀφετηρία, σημεῖον ἐκκινήσεως.

startle ['sta:tl] *vt* ξαφνιάζω, φοβίζω, ἐκπλήσσω.

startling ['sta:tliŋ] *a* καταπληκτικός, ἐντυπωσιακός, χτυπητός.

starvation [sta:'veiʃən] *n* λιμός, λιμοκτονία, ἀσιτία, πεῖνα.

starve [sta:v] *vi* (*die of hunger*) πεθαίνω ἀπό πεῖνα ‖ (*suffer from hunger*) ψοφῶ τῆς πείνας, πεινῶ ‖ *vt* (*keep without food*) στερῶ τῆς τροφῆς.

starving ['sta:viŋ] *a* πεινῶν, λιμασμένος, ψόφιος τῆς πείνας.

state [steit] *n* κατάστασις, θέσις ‖ (*government*) κράτος, πολιτεία ‖ ὑπουργεῖον ‖ (*anxiety*) ἀναστατωμένος ‖ *vt* δηλώνω, λέγω, ἀνακοινῶ ‖ ~ **control** *n* κρατικός ἔλεγχος ‖ ~**d** *a* λεχθείς, ὡρισμένος, τακτός ‖ ~**liness** *n* μεγαλοπρέπεια, ἐπιβλητικότης ‖ ~**ly** *a* μεγαλοπρεπής, ἀξιοπρεπής ‖ ~**ment** *n* δήλωσις, ἔκθεσις ‖ ~ **secret** *n* κρατικόν μυστικόν, ἀπόρρητον ‖ ~**sman** *n* πολιτικός.

static ['stætik] *n* στατική, διαταραχή ‖ *a* ἀκίνητος, ἀδρανής ‖ (*phys*) στατικός ‖ ~ **electricity** *n* στατικός ἠλεκτρισμός.

station ['steiʃən] *n* (*rail*) σταθμός ‖ (*post*) σταθμός, θέσις ‖ (*position in life*) κοινωνική θέσις, βαθμός ‖ *vt* (τοπο)θετῶ, βάζω.

stationary ['steiʃənəri] *a* στάσιμος, ἀκίνητος.

stationer ['steiʃənə*] *n* χαρτοπώλης ‖ ~'**s** (**shop**) *n* χαρτοπωλεῖον ‖ ~**y** *n* χαρτικά εἴδη.

station master ['steiʃnma:stə*] *n* σταθμάρχης.

station wagon ['steiʃənwægən] *n* (*US aut*) στέϊσον-βάγκον.

statistic [stə'tistik] *n* στατιστικόν (στοιχεῖον) ‖ ~**al** *a* στατιστικός ‖ ~**s** *npl* στατιστική.

statue ['stætju:] *n* ἄγαλμα.

stature ['stætʃə*] *n* ἀνάστημα, ὕψος, μέγεθος.

status ['steitəs] *n* θέσις, κατάστασις ‖ **the ~ quo** *n* καθεστώς, στάτους κβό.

statute ['stætju:t] *n* νόμος, θέσπισμα.

statutory ['stætjutəri] *a* νομοθετημένος, θεσπισμένος.

staunch [stɔ:ntʃ] *a* ἀξιόπιστος, πιστός, δυνατός ‖ ~**ly** *ad* σταθερῶς, πιστῶς.

stave [steiv] *vt* ~ **off** *vt* (*attack*) ἀποκρούω, ἀπωθῶ ‖ (*threat*) ἀποτρέπω, ἀποφεύγω.

stay [stei] *n* διαμονή, παραμονή ‖ ἀναβολή ‖ *vi* (*παρα*μένω) ‖ (*at place*) μένω ‖ **to ~ put** μένω ἀδιάβλητος, δέν ἀλλάζω πιά ‖ **to ~ with friends** μένω μέ φίλους ‖ **to ~ the night** μένω τό βράδυ ‖ **to ~ behind** *vi* παρακολουθῶ ἀπό πίσω παραμένω ‖ **to ~ in** *vi* (*at home*) μένω (στό σπίτι) ‖ **to ~ on** *vi* (*continue*) παραμένω ‖ **to ~ out** *vi* (*of house*) μένω ἔξω, δέν ἐπιστρέφω ‖ **to ~ up** *vi* (*at night*) ἀγρυπνῶ, ξενυχτῶ.

steadfast ['stedfəst] *a* σταθερός.

steadily ['stedili] *ad* σταθερά, στέρεα ‖ συνεχῶς, ἐπίμονα.

steadiness ['stedinis] *n* σταθερότης.

steady ['stedi] *a* σταθερός, στερεός ‖ (*regular*) κανονικός, συνεχής, σταθερός ‖ (*reliable*) σταθερός, συνεπής, τακτικός ‖ *vt* σταθεροποιῶ, στερεώνω ‖ **to ~** *o.s.* σταθεροποιοῦμαι, καθησυχάζω.

steak [steik] *n* (*meat*) μπριζόλα, μπιφτέκι ‖ (*fish*) φέτα.

steal [sti:l] (*irreg v*) *vt* κλέβω, βουτῶ, σουφρώνω ‖ *vi* φεύγω κλεφτά, βγαίνω στήν ζούλα ‖ **~th** ['stelθ] *n*: **by ~** κρυφά, κλεφτά, στή ζούλα ‖ **~thy** *a* κρυφός, φευγαλέος, προσεκτικός.

steam [sti:m] *n* ἀτμός ‖ *vt* βράζω στόν ἀτμό ‖ *vi* ἀναδίδω ἀτμόν, ἀχνίζω ‖ (*ship*) κινοῦμαι, πλέω (δι' ἀτμοῦ) ‖ **~ engine** *n* ἀτμομηχανή ‖ **~er** *n* ἀτμόπλοιον, βαπόρι ‖ **~roller** *n* ὁδοστρωτήρ ‖ **~y** *a* ἀτμώδης, γεμᾶτος ἀτμούς.

steel [sti:l] *n* χάλυψ, ἀτσάλι ‖ *a* χαλύβδινος, ἀτσάλινος ‖ **~works** *n* χαλυβδουργεῖον.

steep [sti:p] *a* ἀπότομος, ἀπόκρημνος ‖ (*price*) ἐξωφρενική τιμή ‖ *vt* ἐμβαπτίζω, μουσκεύω, βουτῶ.

steeple ['sti:pl] *n* κωδωνοστάσιον ‖ **~chase** *n* ἱπποδρομία μετ' ἐμποδίων ‖ **~jack** *n* ἐπιδιορθωτής καπνοδόχων.

steeply ['sti:pli] *ad* ἀπότομα, κατηφορικά.

steepness ['sti:pnis] *n* τό ἀπότομον, τό ἀπόκρημνον.

steer [stiə*] *n* μικρό βώδι ‖ *vt* κυβερνῶ, ὁδηγῶ, πηδαλιουχῶ ‖ *vi* κατευθύνομαι, βάζω πλώρη γιά ‖ **~ing** *n* (*aut*) ὁδήγησις ‖ **~ing column** *n* κίων στηρίξεως τιμονιοῦ ‖ **~ing wheel** *n* βολάν, τιμόνι.

stem [stem] *n* στέλεχος, κορμός ‖ *vt* σταματῶ, ἀνακόπτω ‖ **to ~ from** *vt* προέρχομαι ἀπό.

stench [stentʃ] *n* δυσοσμία, μπόχας.

stencil ['stensl] *n* μεμβράνη ‖ *vt* γράφω μεμβράνες, πολυγραφῶ.

stenographer [ste'nɔgrəfə*] *n* στενογράφος.

step [step] *n* βῆμα, πάτημα ‖ (*stair*) βαθμίς, σκαλοπάτι, σκαλί ‖ (*action*) διάβημα, ἐνέργεια ‖ (*sound*) βῆμα, βάδισμα ‖ *vi* βηματίζω, βαδίζω ‖ **~s** *npl* = **stepladder** ‖ *see below* ‖ **to ~ down** *vi* (*fig*) παραιτοῦμαι ‖ **to ~ up** *vt* αὐξάνω, ἀνεβάζω ‖ **~brother** *n* ἐτεροθαλής ἀδελφός ‖ **~child** *n* προγονός, προγονή ‖ **~father** *n* πατριός ‖ **~ladder** *n* σκάλα (φορητή) ‖ **~mother** *n* μητρυιά.

steppe [step] *n* στέππα.

stepping stone ['stepiŋstəun] *n* σκαλοπάτι, ἐνδιάμεσος σταθμός.

stereo ['stiəriəu] *n* (*rad*) στερεοφωνικό ραδιόφωνο ‖ **~phonic** *a* στερεοφωνικό ‖ **~type** *n* στερεοτυπία ‖ *vt* τυπώνω διά στερεοτυπίας.

sterile ['sterail] *a* στεῖρος, ἄγονος, ἄκαρπος ‖ (*free from germs*) ἀποστειρωμένος.

sterility [ste'riliti] *n* στειρότης, ἀγονία.

sterilization [sterilai'zeiʃən] *n* ἀποστείρωσις.

sterilize ['sterilaiz] *vt* στειρώνω ‖ (*from germs*) ἀποστειρώνω.

sterling ['stə:liŋ] *a* στερλίνας ‖ ἀμιγής, καλῆς ποιότητος ‖ (*silver*) ἀσημικά ‖ (*service*) ἐξαιρετικῆς ἐξυπηρετήσεως ‖ **~ area** *n* περιοχή στερλίνας.

stern [stə:n] *a* αὐστηρός, βλοσυρός ‖ *n* πρύμνη, πρύμη ‖ **~ly** *ad* αὐστηρά, σκληρά ‖ **~ness** *n* αὐστηρότης, σκληρότης.

stethoscope ['steθəskəup] *n* στηθοσκόπιον.

stevedore ['sti:vidɔ:*] *n* φορτοεκφορτωτής.

stew [stju:] *n* κρέας μέ χορταρικά ‖ *vt* κάνω κρέας στή κατσαρόλα ‖ *vi* σιγοβράζω.

steward ['stju:əd] *n* (*aviat, naut, rail, in club etc*) φροντιστής, οἰκονόμος, καμαρότος ‖ **~ess** *n* (*aviat*) ἀεροσυνοδός.

stick [stik] (*irreg v*) *n* βέργα, ράβδος ‖ (*cane*) μπαστούνι ‖ *vt* ἐμπηγνύω, μπήγω, χώνω, καρφώνω ‖ (*gum*) κολλῶ ‖ (*col: tolerate*) ἀνέχομαι, ὑποφέρω ‖ *vi* (*stop*) πιάνομαι, κολλῶ, φρακάρω ‖ (*hold fast*) κολλιέμαι, κολλῶ ‖ **to ~ out** *vi* (*project*) κρατῶ μέχρι τέλους, ἐπιμένω ‖ **to ~ up** *vi* (*project*) ὑψοῦμαι, στήνω ‖ **to ~ up for** *vt* (*defend*) ὑπερασπίζομαι, παίρνω τό μέρος ‖ **~er** *n* ἐτικέττα.

stickler ['stiklə*] *n* (+ *for*) ἄκαμπτος, στενοκέφαλος (εἰς).

stick-up ['stikʌp] *n* (*col: robbery*) ληστεία.

sticky ['stiki] *a* κολλώδης, γλοιώδης.

stiff [stif] *a* δύσκαμπτος, σκληρός, ντοῦρος ‖ (*examination etc*) δύσκολος ‖ (*paste*) σκληρός, σφιχτός ‖ (*formal*) ἐπιτηδευμένος, τυπικός, ψυχρός ‖ (*strong*) ἰσχυρός, δυνατός ‖ **~en** *vt* σκληρύνω, δυναμώνω ‖ *vi* σκληρύνομαι, γίνομαι ἄκαμπτος ‖ **~ness** *n* σκληρότης, πιάσιμο.

stifle ['staifl] *vt* (*keep back*) καταπνίγω, συγκρατῶ.

stifling ['staifliŋ] *a* (*atmosphere*) ἀποπνικτικός, ἀσφυκτικός.

stigma ['stigmə] *n* στίγμα, κηλίς.

stile [stail] *n* σκαλιά, σκάλα.

still [stil] *a* ἀκίνητος, ἀθόρυβος, σιωπηλός ‖ *ad* (*yet*) ἀκόμη ‖ (*even*) ἀκόμη (περισσότερα) ‖ **~born** *a* θνησιγενής ‖ **~ life** *n* νεκρά φύσις ‖ **~ness** *n* ἠρεμία, γαλήνη, κάλμα.

stilt [stilt] *n* ξυλοπόδαρο.

stilted ['stiltid] *a* ἄκαμπτος, τυπικός, τεχνητός.

stimulant ['stimjulənt] *n* διεγερτικόν, τονωτικόν.

stimulate ['stimjuleit] *vt* διεγείρω, ἐξάπτω.

stimulating ['stimjuleitiŋ] a διεγερτικός, τονωτικός.

stimulation [stimju'leiʃən] n διέγερσις, ὑποκίνησις, τόνωσις.

stimulus ['stimjuləs] n κίνητρον.

sting [stiŋ] (irreg v) n δῆγμα, κέντρισμα ‖ vt κεντρίζω, τσιμπῶ.

stingily ['stindʒili] ad φιλάργυρα, τσιγγούνικα, σφιχτά.

stinginess ['stindʒinis] n φιλαργυρία, τσιγγουνιά.

stingy ['stindʒi] a φιλάργυρος, τσιγγούνης, σφιχτοχέρης.

stink [stiŋk] (irreg v) n δυσοσμία, βρῶμα ‖ vi βρωμῶ, βρωμάω ‖ ~er n (col) (person) ἀντιπαθής, παλιάνθρωπος ‖ (problem) δύσκολο, τρομερό ‖ ~ing a (fig) τρομερός.

stint [stint] n ὅριον, καθῆκον ‖ vt στερῶ, περιορίζω.

stipend ['staipend] n (to vicar etc) μισθός, ἐπίδομα.

stipulate ['stipjuleit] vt ἀποφαίνομαι διά, συμφωνῶ, συνομολογῶ.

stipulation [stipju'leiʃən] n ὅρος, διάταξις, συμφωνία.

stir [stɜː*] n ταραχή, σάλεμα, κούνημα, κίνησις ‖ vt (mix) ἀνακατώνω, ἀναδεύω ‖ vi (move) κουνιέμαι, σαλεύω ‖ to ~ up vt ὑποκινῶ, ὑποδαυλίζω ‖ ~ring a συγκλονιστικός, συγκινητικός.

stirrup ['stirəp] n ἀναβολεύς, σκάλα, ζεγκί.

stitch [stitʃ] n βελονιά, ραφή ‖ (sudden pain) δριμύς πόνος, σουβλιά ‖ vt ράβω, κάνω βελονιές.

stock [stɔk] n (supply) ἀπόθεμα, στόκ, προμήθεια ‖ (trader's goods) ἐμπορεύματα, στόκ ‖ (farm animals) κτήνη, ζῶα ‖ (liquid) ζωμός, κονσομέ ‖ (econ) χρεώγραφον, τίτλος, ἀξία ‖ a τῆς σειρᾶς, κανονικός, συνήθης ‖ vt ἐφοδιάζω, ἔχω παρακαταθήκην ἀπό ‖ to take ~ κάνω ἀπογραφήν ‖ (+ of) κρίνω, ἐκτιμῶ ‖ to ~ up with vt ἀποθηκεύω ‖ ~ade n πασσαλόπηγμα, φράκτης ‖ ~broker n χρηματομεσίτης, χρηματιστής ‖ ~ exchange n χρηματιστήριον.

stocking ['stɔkiŋ] n κάλτσα.

stockist ['stɔkist] n (comm: supplier, distributor) χονδρέμπορος.

stock market ['stɔkmɑːkit] n ἀγορά χρεωγράφων.

stockpile ['stɔkpail] n ἀποθέματα ‖ vt δημιουργῶ ἀποθέματα.

stocktaking ['stɔkteikiŋ] n (comm) ἀπογραφή.

stocky ['stɔki] a κοντόχοντρος.

stodgy ['stɔdʒi] a βαρύς, ἀνιαρός.

stoic ['stəuik] n στωϊκός ‖ ~al a στωϊκός ‖ ~ism ['stəuisizəm] n στωϊκισμός.

stoke [stəuk] vt τροφοδοτῶ φωτιάν, διατηρῶ φωτιάν ‖ ~r n θερμαστής.

stole [stəul] pt of steal ‖ n (fur) γούνα,

σάρπα ‖ ~n pp of steal ‖ a κλεμμένος.

stolid ['stɔlid] a ἀπαθής, βαρύς, φλεγματικός.

stomach ['stʌmək] n στομάχι ‖ (inclination) ὅρεξις, διάθεσις ‖ vt ἀνέχομαι, χωνεύω ‖ ~ ache n κοιλόπονος, στομαχόπονος.

stone [stəun] n λίθος, πέτρα ‖ (gem) πολύτιμος λίθος, πετράδι, κόσμημα ‖ (of fruit) πυρήν, κουκούτσι ‖ (weight) βάρος 14 λιβρῶν ‖ a ἀπό λίθους, πέτρινος ‖ vt βγάζω κουκούτσια ἀπό ‖ ~-cold a κρύος σάν μάρμαρο ‖ ~-deaf a θεόκουφος ‖ ~mason n κτίστης, λιθοξόος ‖ ~work n λιθοδομή.

stony ['stəuni] a πετρώδης, γεμάτος πέτρες.

stood [stud] pt,pp of stand.

stool [stuːl] n σκαμνί.

stoop [stuːp] vi σκύβω.

stop [stɔp] n στάσις, τέρμα ‖ (punctuation) σημεῖον στίξεως ‖ vt (prevent) σταματῶ ‖ (bring to end) διακόπτω, σταματῶ ‖ vi (cease) παύω, σταματῶ, διακόπτομαι ‖ (remain) παραμένω, πηγαίνω ‖ to ~ doing sth παύω νά κάνω κάτι, σταματῶ ‖ ~ it! σταμάτα!, φθάνει! ‖ to ~ dead vi σταματῶ ἀπότομα ‖ to ~ in vi (at home) περνῶ ἀπό, ἐπισκέπτομαι ‖ to ~ off vi κατεβαίνω, διακόπτω τό ταξίδι μου ‖ vt (hole) φράζω, βουλώνω, κλείνω ‖ ~lights npl (aut) κόκκινα φανάρια, κόκκινα φῶτα ‖ ~over n (on journey) σταθμός, στάθμευσις ‖ ~page n σταμάτημα, παῦσις, διακοπή ‖ ~per n πῶμα, βούλωμα ‖ ~-press n τελευταῖα νέα ‖ ~watch n χρονόμετρον.

storage ['stɔːridʒ] n (ἐν)ἀποθήκευσις, ἀποθήκη.

store [stɔː*] n παρακαταθήκη, ἐφόδιον ‖ (place) ἀποθήκη ‖ (large shop) κατάστημα, μαγαζί ‖ vt ἀποθηκεύω, ἀποθηκεύω ‖ to ~ up vt συσσωρεύω, συγκεντρώνω, μαζεύω ‖ ~room n ἀποθήκη, κελάρι.

storey ['stɔːri] n (Brit) ὄροφος, πάτωμα.

stork [stɔːk] n πελαργός, λελέκι.

storm [stɔːm] n θύελλα, καταιγίδα, φουρτούνα ‖ (disturbance) θύελλα, καταιγισμός ‖ vi μαίνομαι ‖ vt (attack) ἐξαπολύω ἔφοδον ‖ to take by ~ (lit) καταλαμβάνω ἐξ ἐφόδου ‖ (fig) κατακτῶ, παρασύρω ‖ ~ cloud n μαῦρο σύννεφο ‖ ~y a (weather) θυελλώδης.

story ['stɔːri] n (account) ἱστορία, ἀφήγησις, διήγημα ‖ (lie) παραμύθι, ψέμα ‖ (US: storey) ὄροφος, πάτωμα ‖ ~book n βιβλίον διηγημάτων ‖ ~teller n ἀφηγητής, παραμυθᾶς.

stout [staut] a (bold) δυνατός, γερός, θαρραλέος ‖ (too fat) χονδρός, σωματώδης, παχύς ‖ n εἶδος μπύρας ‖ ~ness n παχύτης, πάχος.

stove [stəuv] n (for cooking) κουζίνα,

συσκευή μαγειρεύματος ‖ (for heating) θερμάστρα, σόμπα.

stow [stəu] vt στοιβάζω, ἀποθηκεύω ‖ ~**away** n λαθρεπιβάτης.

straddle ['strædl] vt κάθομαι καβαλικευτά, καβαλικεύω.

strafe [stra:f] vt πολυβολῶ.

straggle ['strægl] vi σκορπίζω, βραδυπορῶ ‖ ~**r** n παραπλανημένος, ὁ βραδυπορῶν.

straight [streit] a εὐθύς, εὐθύγραμμος, ἴσιος ‖ (honest) δίκαιος, εὐθύς, τίμιος, ντόμπρος ‖ (in order) τακτικός, τακτοποιημένος, σιαγμένος ‖ ad ἴσια, κατ' εὐθεῖαν, ἀμέσως ‖ (drink) σχέτο ‖ n εὐθεῖα ‖ ~**away** ad (at once) ἀμέσως ‖ ~ **off** ad (without stopping) στή στιγμή, αὐτοστιγμεί ‖ ~**en** vt (also ~ out) ἰσιώνω, σιάζω, τακτοποιῶ ‖ ~**forward** a (simple) χωρίς περιστροφές, ντόμπρα, εἰλικρινής.

strain [strein] n (mental) ἔντασις, κούρασις ‖ (streak, trace) φυσικὴ διάθεσις, κλίσις, τάσις ‖ vt (stretch) ἐντείνω, τεντώνω, τεζάρω ‖ (filter) διυλίζω, φιλτράρω, στραγγίζω ‖ vi (make effort) μοχθῶ, κοπιάζω, ἐντείνω ‖ ~**s** npl (mus) τόνος, ὕφος ‖ ~**ed** a (laugh) βιασμένο γέλιο, ψεύτικο γέλιο ‖ (relations) τεταμένος ‖ ~**er** n σουρωτήρι, φίλτρον, τρυπητό.

strait [streit] n (geog) στενόν, πορθμός ‖ ~**ened** a (circumstances) σέ οἰκονομικές δυσχέρειες ‖ ~ **jacket** n ζουρλομανδύας ‖ ~**-laced** a ἠθικολόγος, σεμνότυφος.

strand [strænd] n (thread) κλῶνος, κλωνί, σπάγγος, κλωστὴ ‖ vt ἐξοκέλλω ‖ ~**ed** a ἐγκαταλειφθείς, ἀφισμένος πίσω.

strange [streindʒ] a ξένος ‖ (unusual) ἀσυνήθης, ἀσυνήθιστος, παράξενος ‖ ~**ly** ad περίεργος, παράξενα ‖ (new to a place) τό περίεργον, παράξενον ‖ ~**r** n ξένος, ἄγνωστος ‖ (new to a place) νεοαφιχθείς, καινούργιος.

strangle ['stræŋgl] vt στραγγαλίζω, πνίγω, καταπνίγω.

strangulation [stræŋgju'leiʃən] n στραγγαλισμός.

strap [stræp] n λωρίς, λουρί ‖ vt δένω μέ λουρί ‖ (beat) δέρνω μέ λουρί ‖ ~**less** a (dress) ἔξωμον ‖ ~**ping** a γεροδεμένος.

strata ['stra:tə] npl of **stratum**.

stratagem ['strætidʒəm] n στρατήγημα, κόλπο.

strategic [strə'ti:dʒik] a στρατηγικός ‖ ~**ally** ad στρατηγικῶς.

strategist ['strætidʒist] n στρατηγικός, εἰδικός στὴν στρατηγικήν.

strategy ['strætidʒi] n στρατηγική, τέχνασμα.

stratosphere ['strætəusfiə*] n στρατόσφαιρα.

stratum ['stra:təm] n στρῶμα.

straw [strɔ:] n (agr) ἄχυρον, ψάθα ‖ (drinking straw) καλάμι, καλαμάκι ‖ a (hat,

basket) ψάθινος, ἀχυρόχρους ‖ ~**berry** n φράουλα.

stray [strei] n χαμένος, περιπλανηθέν ζῶον ‖ vi περιπλανῶμαι, ἀπομακρύνομαι ‖ a (animal) περιπλανώμενος, ἀδέσποτος ‖ (thought) ξεκάρφωτος, σκόρπιος, ξεκόλλητος.

streak [stri:k] n γραμμή, λωρίδα, ρίγα ‖ (strain) δόσις ‖ vt χαράσσω, ριγώνω, σχηματίζω ραβδώσεις ‖ ~**y** a ραβδωτός, γραμμωτός, ριγωτός.

stream [stri:m] n ποτάμι, ρυάκι, ρέμα ‖ (flow) ροή, ροῦς, χείμαρρος ‖ (crowd) κύματα, ἀδιάκοπος σειρά ‖ vi ρέω, τρέχω, κυλῶ ‖ ~**er** n ἐπισείων, ταινία, σημαία ‖ ~**lined** a ἀεροδυναμικός.

street [stri:t] n ὁδός, δρόμος ‖ ~**car** n (US: tram) τράμ ‖ ~ **lamp** n φανοστάτης.

strength [streŋθ] n (lit) δύναμις, ἰσχύς ‖ (fig) βασιζόμενος εἰς, στηριζόμενος στό ‖ ~**en** vt ἐνισχύω, δυναμώνω.

strenuous ['strenjuəs] a σθεναρός, δραστήριος ‖ (requiring effort) ἐπίπονος, σκληρός ‖ ~**ly** ad ἐπιπόνως, σκληρά.

stress [stres] n (force, pressure) πίεσις, καταναγκασμός ‖ (mental strain) ἔντασις ‖ (accent) τόνος ‖ vt τονίζω.

stretch [stretʃ] n τέντωμα, ἔκτασις, ἄπλωμα ‖ vt τεντώνω, ἀπλώνω ‖ vi ἐκτείνομαι, πλαταίνω ‖ at a ~ (continuously) χωρίς διακοπή ‖ to ~ out vi ἐπεκτείνομαι, ἀραιώνω ‖ vt τείνω, ἀπλώνω ‖ ~**er** n φορεῖον.

stricken ['strikən] a (person) προσβεβλημένος, θλιμμένος ‖ (city, country) πληγεῖσα.

strict [strikt] a ἀκριβής, αὐστηρός ‖ δριμύς ‖ ~**ly** ad αὐστηρῶς, ἀκριβῶς ‖ ~**ly speaking** κυριολεκτικῶς, γιά νά ποῦμε τήν ἀλήθεια ‖ ~**ness** n αὐστηρότης.

stride [straid] (irreg v) n μεγάλο βῆμα, δρασκελιά ‖ vi δρασκελίζω, βηματίζω.

strident ['straidənt] a ὀξύς, στριγγός, στρίγγλικος.

strife [straif] n ἀγών, πάλη, σύγκρουσις.

strike [straik] (irreg v) n ἀπεργία ‖ (discovery) εὕρησις, συνάντησις ‖ (attack) ἐπιχείρησις, πλῆγμα ‖ vt κτυπῶ, προσκρούω, σκουντῶ ‖ (come into mind) μ' ἔρχεται (στό μυαλό), μοῦ φαίνεται ‖ (find gold) ἀνακαλύπτω, βρίσκω ‖ vi (stop work) κηρύσσω ἀπεργίαν, ἀπεργῶ ‖ (attack) χτυπῶ ‖ (clock) ἠχῶ, χτυπῶ, σημαίνω ‖ to ~ down vt (lay low) ρίχνω χάμω ‖ to ~ out vt (cross out) ἐξαλείφω, διαγράφω, σβήνω ‖ to ~ up vt (music) ἀρχίζω (νά παίζω) ‖ (friendship) πιάνω φιλίαν ‖ ~ **pay** n ἐπίδομα ἀπεργίας ‖ ~**r** n ἀπεργός.

striking ['straikiŋ] a κτυπητός, ἑλκυστικός, ἐνδιαφέρων ‖ ~**ly** ad ἐντυπωσιακῶς, χτυπητά.

string [striŋ] *n* σπάγγος, κορδόνι ‖ (*series*) σειρά, άλυσος ‖ (*mus*) χορδή ‖ ~ **bean** *n* φρέσκο φασολάκι.

stringency ['strindʒənsi] *n* αὐστηρότης, στενότης.

stringent ['strindʒənt] *a* αὐστηρός, στενός.

strip [strip] *n* λουρίδα, ταινία ‖ *vt* γυμνώνω, γδύνω, βγάζω ‖ (*machine etc*) ἀποσυνδέω, ξεμαρτώνω ‖ *vi* γδύνομαι, γυμνώνομαι ‖ ~ **cartoon** *n* σειρά εὐθύμων σκίτσων.

stripe [straip] *n* γραμμή, λουρίδα, ράβδωσις ‖ ~**d** *a* ραβδωτός, ριγωτός.

stripper ['stripə*] *n* στριπτηζοῦ.

striptease ['stripti:z] *n* στριπτήζ.

strive [straiv] (*irreg v*) *vi* (+ *for*) ἀγωνίζομαι (γιά), προσπαθῶ ‖ ~**n** ['strivn] *pp of* **strive**.

strode [strəud] *pt,pp of* **stride**.

stroke [strəuk] *n* κτύπημα, πλῆγμα ‖ (*tech*) κίνησις, διαδρομή, ρυθμός ‖ (*sudden attack*) προσβολή ‖ (*caress*) θωπεία, χάδι, χάϊδεμα ‖ *vt* χαϊδεύω, τρίβω, σιάζω ‖ **at a** ~ μ' ἕνα κτύπημα, μέ μιᾶς ‖ **on the** ~ **of 5** στίς 5 ἀκριβῶς.

stroll [strəul] *n* περίπατος, βόλτα ‖ *vi* κάνω περίπατο, κάνω βόλτες.

strong [strɔŋ] *a* δυνατός, ἰσχυρός, γερός ‖ (*firm*) στερεός, γερός ‖ (*flavour*) δυνατός, ἔντονος ‖ (*protest*) ἔντονος ‖ (*wind*) ἰσχυρός, δυνατός ‖ **they are 50** ~ δυνάμεως 50 ἀνδρῶν ‖ ~**hold** *n* φρούριον, ὀχυρόν, προπύργιον ‖ ~**ly** *ad* ἰσχυρῶς, δυνατά, γερά ‖ ~**room** *n* αἴθουσα χρηματοκιβωτίων.

strove [strəuv] *pt of* **strive**.

struck [strʌk] *pt,pp of* **strike**.

structural ['strʌktʃərəl] *a* οἰκοδομικός, κατασκευαστικός, δομικός ‖ ~**ly** *ad* δομικῶς.

structure ['strʌktʃə*] *n* κατασκευή, δομή ‖ (*building*) οἰκοδόμημα, κτίριον, κτίσμα.

struggle ['strʌgl] *n* ἀγών, πάλη, σκληρή προσπάθεια ‖ *vi* (+ *to*) ἀγωνίζομαι, παλεύω.

strum [strʌm] *vt* (*guitar*) παίζω ἀδέξια, παίζω ἄτεχνα.

strung [strʌŋ] **highly** ~ *a see* **high**.

strut [strʌt] *n* (*support*) στήριγμα, ἀντέρεισμα ‖ *vi* περιφέρομαι καμαρωτός, κορδώνομαι.

strychnine ['strikni:n] *n* στρυχνίνη.

stub [stʌb] *n* (*cigarette etc*) ὑπόλειμμα, γόπα.

stubble ['stʌbl] *n* καλαμιά, ρίζες ‖ (*on face*) γένια ἡμερῶν, ἀγριωρισία.

stubbly ['stʌbli] *a* γεμᾶτο καλάμια, κοντοκομμένα (γένια).

stubborn ['stʌbən] *a* ἐπίμονος, πείσμων, ξεροκέφαλος ‖ ~**ly** *ad* πεισματικά, ἐπιμόνως ‖ ~**ness** *n* πεῖσμα, ξεροκεφαλιά.

stubby ['stʌbi] *a* κοντόχοντρος.

stuck [stʌk] *pt,pp of* **stick** ‖ ~-**up** *a* ὑπεροπτικός, ἀλαζών.

stud [stʌd] *n* πλατυκέφαλο, καρφί ‖ (*of shirt*) κουμπί, ξενόκουμπο ‖ (*of horses*) σταῦλος ἵππων, ἱπποστάσιον ‖ *vt* διαστίζω, κοσμῶ μέ καρφιά.

student ['stju:dənt] *n* φοιτητής, σπουδαστής, μελετητής.

studied ['stʌdid] *a* μελετημένος, ἐσκεμμένος, θελητικός.

studio ['stju:diəu] *n* ἐργαστήριον, ἀτελιέ ‖ (*also TV*) στούντιο.

studious ['stju:diəs] *a* μελετηρός, φιλομαθής ‖ (*careful*) προσεκτικός ‖ ~**ly** *ad* (*carefully*) ἐπιμελῶς.

study ['stʌdi] *n* σπουδή, μελέτη ‖ (*something studied*) μελέτη, ἔρευνα ‖ (*room*) σπουδαστήριον, ἀναγνωστήριον, γραφεῖον ‖ *vt* σπουδάζω, μελετῶ ‖ (*examine*) μελετῶ, παρατηρῶ ‖ *vi* ἐπιμελοῦμαι, μελετῶ.

stuff [stʌf] *n* ὕλη, ὑλικόν, οὐσία ‖ *vt* (παραγεμίζω ‖ ~**iness** *n* ἔλλειψις ἀέρος, κλεισοῦρα ‖ ~**ing** *n* παραγέμισμα, γέμισι ‖ (*of fowl etc*) γέμισμα ‖ ~**y** *a* (*room*) πνιγηρός, χωρίς ἀέρα ‖ (*ideas: old-fashioned*) σεμνότυφος.

stumble ['stʌmbl] *vi* σκοντάφτω, προσκρούω ‖ **to** ~ **on** *vt* ἀνακαλύπτω ἀναπάντεχα.

stumbling block ['stʌmbliŋblɔk] *n* ἐμπόδιον.

stump [stʌmp] *n* κούτσουρο, στέλεχος ‖ *vt* (*puzzle*) μπερδεύω, τά χάνω.

stun [stʌn] *vt* ζαλίζω, ταράζω.

stung [stʌŋ] *pt,pp of* **sting**.

stunk [stʌŋk] *pp of* **stink**.

stunning ['stʌniŋ] *a* ἐξαίσιος, ὡραῖος.

stunt [stʌnt] *n* ἐκπληκτική παράστασις, ἄθλος ‖ *vt* περιστέλλω, ἐμποδίζω, κολοβώνω ‖ ~**ed** *a* κατσιασμένος.

stupefy ['stju:pifai] *vt* καταπλήσσω, ναρκώνω, ζαλίζω ‖ ~**ing** *a* ναρκωτικός.

stupendous [stju:'pendəs] *a* τεράστιος, πελώριος, καταπληκτικός ‖ ~**ly** *ad* καταπληκτικά.

stupid ['stju:pid] *a* ἠλίθιος, βλάκας, κουτός ‖ ~**ity** *n* βλακεία, κουταμάρα ‖ ~**ly** *ad* ἠλίθια, βλακωδῶς.

stupor ['stju:pə*] *n* νάρκη, λήθαργος, ζάλισμα.

sturdily ['stə:dili] *ad* μέ δύναμιν, γερά, θαρραλέα.

sturdiness ['stə:dinis] *n* ρώμη, δύναμις, λεβεντιά.

sturdy ['stə:di] *a* δυνατός, σθεναρός, γεροδεμένος.

stutter ['stʌtə*] *n* ψέλλισμα, τραύλισμα ‖ *vi* τραυλίζω, τσεβδίζω.

sty [stai] *n* χοιροστάσιον, γουρνοστάσι.

stye [stai] *n* χαλάζιον, κριθαράκι.

style [stail] *n* στύλ, τεχνοτροπία, ὕφος ‖ (*fashion*) ρυθμός, στύλ, μόδα ‖ (*distinction*) ἐπιδεξιότης, μεγαλοπρέπεια.

styling ['stailiŋ] n (of car etc) πλαίσιον, καλούπι.
stylish ['stailiʃ] a μοντέρνος, κομψός ‖ ~ly ad κομψά, μέ σίκ.
stylized ['stailaizd] a στυλιζαρισμένος.
stylus ['stailəs] n στύλος, γραφίς.
styptic ['stiptik] a: ~ pencil στυπτικόν.
suave [swɑ:v] a εὐγενής, ἀπαλός, γλυκανάλατος.
sub- [sʌb] prefix ὑπο-.
subconscious ['sʌb'kɔnʃəs] a ὑποσυνείδητος ‖ n: the ~ τό ὑποσυνείδητον.
subdivide ['sʌbdi'vaid] vt ὑποδιαιρῶ.
subdivision ['sʌbdiviʒən] n ὑποδιαίρεσις.
subdue [səb'dju:] vt κατακτῶ, ὑποτάσσω, μαλακώνω ‖ ~d a συντετριμένος, μαλακωμένος.
subject ['sʌbdʒikt] n ὑπήκοος ‖ (theme) θέμα, ἀντικείμενον ‖ (gram) ὑποκείμενον ‖ [səb'dʒekt] vt ὑποτάσσω, ὑποδουλώνω ‖ ὑποβάλλω, ἐκθέτω ‖ to be ~ to ὑπόκειμαι εἰς, ἐξαρτῶμαι ἀπό ‖ ~ion n καθυπόταξις, ὑποταγή ‖ ὑποτέλεια ‖ ~ive a ὑποκειμενικός ‖ ~ively ad ὑποκειμενικῶς ‖ ~ matter n θέμα, περιεχόμενον.
sub judice [sʌb'ju:disi] a ἐκκρεμής, μή ἐκδικασθείς.
subjunctive [səb'dʒʌŋktiv] n ὑποτακτική (ἔγκλισις) ‖ a ὑποτακτικός.
sublet ['sʌb'let] vt ὑπεκμισθῶ, ὑπενοικιάζω.
sublime [sə'blaim] a ὑψηλός, ἀνώτερος, ὑπέροχος, ἔξοχος ‖ ~ly ad ὑπερόχως, ἐξαιρετικά.
submarine [sʌbmə'ri:n] n ὑποβρύχιον.
submerge [səb'mə:dʒ] vt ἐμβαπτίζω, βυθίζω, χώνω στό νερό ‖ vi καταδύομαι, βυθίζομαι, βουλιάζω.
submission [səb'miʃən] n ὑποταγή, ὑπακοή ‖ (presentation) ὑποβολή.
submit [səb'mit] vt ὑποβάλλω ‖ vi ὑποτάσσομαι, ὑποβάλλομαι.
subnormal ['sʌb'nɔ:məl] a κάτω τοῦ κανονικοῦ.
subordinate [sə'bɔ:dnit] a κατώτερος, ἐξηρτημένος, δευτερεύων ‖ n ὑφιστάμενος.
subpoena [səb'pi:nə] n κλῆσις (μαρτύρων) ‖ vt καλῶ, ἀποστέλλω κλῆσιν.
subscribe [səb'skraib] vi (pay contribution) ἐγγράφομαι, συνεισφέρω ‖ (+ to) ἐπιδοκιμάζω, ἀποδέχομαι, παραδέχομαι ‖ ~r n (to periodical) συνδρομητής ‖ (tel) συνδρομητής.
subscription [səb'skripʃən] n συνεισφορά, συνδρομή.
subsequent ['sʌbsikwənt] a ἐπακόλουθος, μεταγενέστερος ‖ ~ly ad ἔπειτα, ἀργότερα.
subside [səb'said] vi κατακαθίζω, καθιζάνω, κοπάζω ‖ ~nce n καθίζησις, κόπασις.

subsidiary [səb'sidiəri] a βοηθητικός, δευτερεύων ‖ n θυγάτηρ ἑταιρεία.
subsidize ['sʌbsidaiz] vt ἐπιχορηγῶ, ἐπιδοτῶ.
subsidy ['sʌbsidi] n ἐπιχορήγησις, βοήθημα, ἐπίδομα.
subsistence [səb'sistəns] n ὕπαρξις, διατήρησις, τά πρός τό ζῆν.
substance ['sʌbstəns] n οὐσία ‖ (matter) περιεχόμενον, οὐσία, ἔννοια ‖ (wealth) περιουσία, ἀξία.
substandard ['sʌb'stændəd] a κάτω τοῦ μέσου ὅρου, κακῆς ποιότητος.
substantial [səb'stænʃəl] a (strong) στερεός, γερός ‖ (important) σημαντικός, οὐσιώδης ‖ ~ly ad οὐσιαστικά, πραγματικά.
substantiate [səb'stænʃieit] vt ἐπαληθεύω, ἀποδεικνύω, αἰτιολογῶ.
substation ['sʌbsteiʃən] n (elec) ὑποσταθμός.
substitute ['sʌbstitju:t] n ἀντικαταστάτης, ὑποκατάστατον ‖ vt ὑποκαθιστῶ, ἀντικαθιστῶ.
substitution [sʌbsti'tju:ʃən] n ἀντικατάστασις, ὑποκατάστασις.
subterfuge ['sʌbtəfju:dʒ] n ὑπεκφυγή, τέχνασμα, πρόφασις.
subterranean [sʌbtə'reiniən] a ὑπόγειος.
subtitle ['sʌbtaitl] n (cine) ὑπότιτλος.
subtle ['sʌtl] a (faint) λεπτός, ραφινάτος ‖ (clever, sly) ἔξυπνος, πανοῦργος ‖ ~ty n λεπτότης, λεπτολογία, πονηρία.
subtly ['sʌtli] ad λεπτῶς, μέ λεπτότητα.
subtract [səb'trækt] vt ἀφαιρῶ ‖ ~ion n ἀφαίρεσις.
subtropical ['sʌb'trɔpikəl] a ὑποτροπικός.
suburb ['sʌbə:b] n προάστειον ‖ ~an a τῶν προαστείων ‖ ~ia n προάστεια.
subversive [səb'və:siv] a ἀνατρεπτικός.
subway ['sʌbwei] n (US) ὑπόγειος σιδηρόδρομος.
sub-zero ['sʌb'ziərəu] a κάτω τοῦ μηδενός.
succeed [sək'si:d] vi ἐπιτυγχάνω, πετυχαίνω ‖ vt διαδέχομαι ‖ ~ing a (following) ἐπόμενος, μελλοντικός.
success [sək'ses] n ἐπιτυχία, εὐτυχία, ἔκβασις ‖ ἐπιτυχημένος ἄνθρωπος ‖ ~ful a ἐπιτυχής, ἐπιτυχημένος ‖ ~fully ad ἐπιτυχῶς, μέ ἐπιτυχίαν ‖ ~ion n συνέπεια, διαδοχή ‖ (to throne) διαδοχή ‖ ~ive a διαδοχικός, συνεχής, ἀλλεπάλληλος ‖ ~or n διάδοχος, ἐπόμενος.
succinct [sək'siŋkt] a σύντομος καί σαφής.
succulent ['sʌkjulənt] a εὔχυμος, ζουμερός, νόστιμος.
succumb [sə'kʌm] vi (+ to) ὑποκύπτω, ὑποτάσσομαι, ἐνδίδω.
such [sʌtʃ] a (of that kind) τέτοιος, τοιούτου εἴδους ‖ (so great etc) τόσος ‖ pron αὐτός, αὐτοί, τοιοῦτος ‖ ~like a παρόμοιος, τέτοιος ‖ pron παρόμοιος, τοῦ ἰδίου εἴδους.

suck [sʌk] vt (ice cream) γλείφω ‖ (toffee) πιπιλίζω ‖ ~ **er** n (col) κορόϊδο.

suction ['sʌkʃən] n ἀναρρόφησις, ἐκμύζησις, τράβηγμα.

Sudan [su'dɑ:n] n Σουδάν ‖ ~**ese** a σουδανικός ‖ n Σουδανέζος.

sudden ['sʌdn] a ξαφνικός, αἰφνίδιος ‖ **all of a** ~ αἰφνιδίως, ξαφνικά ‖ ~**ly** ad ξαφνικά ‖ ~**ness** n (τό) αἰφνίδιον, (τό) ἀπότομον.

sue [su:] vt ἐνάγω, κάνω ἀγωγή σέ.

suède [sweid] n καστόρι, σουέντ.

suet [suit] n λίπος, ξύγγι.

Suez Canal ['su:izkə'næl] n διῶρυξ τοῦ Σουέζ.

suffer ['sʌfə*] vt (death) θανατοῦμαι, ἐκτελοῦμαι ‖ (permit) ὑποφέρω, ἀνέχομαι, δέχομαι ‖ vi ὑποφέρω, πάσχω ‖ ~**er** n ὑποφέρων, παθών ‖ ~**ing** n πόνος, βάσανα, πάθη.

suffice [sə'fais] vi (ἐπ)ἀρκῶ, φθάνω.

sufficient [sə'fiʃənt] a ἐπαρκής, ἀρκετός ‖ ~**ly** ad ἐπαρκῶς, ἀρκετά.

suffix ['sʌfiks] n κατάληξις, πρόσφυμα.

suffocate ['sʌfəkeit] vi πνίγομαι, ἀσφυκτιῶ.

suffocation [sʌfə'keiʃən] n ἀσφυξία, πνιγμονή, πνίξιμο.

sugar ['ʃugə*] n σάκχαρις, ζάχαρη ‖ vt ζαχαρώνω, βάζω ζάχαρη σέ ‖ ~ **beet** n τεῦτλον ζαχαροποιίας ‖ ~ **cane** n ζαχαροκάλαμο ‖ ~**y** a ζαχαρένιος, ζαχαρωμένος, γλυκύτατος.

suggest [sə'dʒest] vt εἰσηγοῦμαι, προτείνω ‖ (show indirectly) ὑπαινίσσομαι, ὑπονοῶ ‖ (propose) προτείνω, ὑποβάλλω, ὑποδεικνύω ‖ ~**ion** n πρότασις, ὑποβολή ‖ ~**ive** a ὑπενθυμίζων, ὑποβλητικός, μέ ὑπονοούμενα.

suicidal [sui'saidl] a τῆς αὐτοκτονίας.

suicide ['suisaid] n αὐτοκτονία, αὐτόχειρ.

suit [su:t] n (of clothes) κοστούμι ‖ (in cards) τά τέσσαρα χρώματα ‖ vt ταιριάζω, πηγαίνω ‖ (satisfy) ἱκανοποιῶ, βολεύω ‖ (adapt) προσαρμόζω ‖ ~**ability** n καταλληλότης ‖ ~**able** a κατάλληλος, ἁρμόζων, ταιριαστός ‖ ~**ably** ad καταλλήλως, πρεπόντως, ὅπως πρέπει ‖ ~**case** n βαλίτσα.

suite [swi:t] n (of rooms) διαμέρισμα, ἀπαρτία ‖ (mus) σουΐτα.

sulfur ['sʌlfə*] n (US) = **sulphur**.

sulk [sʌlk] vi σκυθρωπιάζω, κατσουφιάζω ‖ ~**y** a κακόκεφος, κατσούφης.

sullen ['sʌlən] a (gloomy) κατηφής, μελαγχολικός ‖ (bad-tempered) κακόκεφος, κατσούφης.

sulphur ['sʌlfə*] n θεῖον, θειάφι.

sulphuric [sʌl'fjuərik] a: ~ **acid** θειϊκόν ὀξύ, βιτριόλι.

sultan ['sʌltən] n σουλτᾶνος ‖ ~**a** n σουλτάνα ‖ (raisin) σουλτανίνα.

sultry ['sʌltri] a ἀσφυκτικός, πνιγηρός.

sum [sʌm] n ἄθροισμα, σύνολον, ποσόν,

σοῦμα ‖ (problem) ἄθροισμα ‖ (of money) ποσόν (χρημάτων) ‖ to ~ **up** vi συνοψίζω, ἀνακεφαλαιώνω ‖ vi κρίνω, ἐκτιμῶ ‖ ~**marize** vt συνοψίζω, συγκεφαλαιώνω ‖ ~**mary** n (συνοπτική) περίληψις, σύνοψις.

summer ['sʌmə*] n θέρος, καλοκαίρι ‖ attr a (clothing) καλοκαιρινός ‖ ~**house** n (in garden) περίπτερον κήπου ‖ ~**time** n καλοκαίρι, θερινή ὥρα.

summing-up ['sʌmiŋ'ʌp] n ἀνακεφαλαίωσις, ἐκτίμησις.

summit ['sʌmit] n κορυφή ‖ ~ **conference** n συνεδρίασις κορυφῆς.

summon ['sʌmən] vt (συγ)καλῶ, προσκαλῶ ‖ (gather up) συγκεντρώνω, μαζεύω ‖ ~**s** n κλῆσις ‖ vt κλητεύω, καλῶ.

sump [sʌmp] n φρεάτιον ἀποστραγγίσεως ‖ κάρτερ.

sumptuous ['sʌmptjuəs] a πολυτελής, πολυδάπανος ‖ ~**ly** ad πολυτελῶς, μεγαλοπρεπῶς ‖ ~**ness** n μεγαλοπρέπεια, πλοῦτος.

sun [sʌn] n ἥλιος ‖ (rays) λιακάδα ‖ ~**bathe** vi κάνω ἡλιοθεραπείαν ‖ ~**bathing** n ἡλιοθεραπεία ‖ ~**burn** n μαύρισμα ἀπό τόν ἥλιο ‖ ~**burnt** a ἡλιοκαμμένος, μαυρισμένος.

Sunday ['sʌndi] n Κυριακή.

sundial ['sʌndaiəl] n ἡλιακόν ὡρολόγιον.

sundown ['sʌndaun] n (sunset) ἡλιοβασίλεμα.

sundry ['sʌndri] a διάφορος ‖ **sundries** npl διάφορα εἴδη.

sunflower ['sʌnflauə*] n ἥλιος, ἡλίανθος.

sung [sʌŋ] pp of **sing**.

sunglasses ['sʌnglɑ:siz] npl γυαλιά τοῦ ἡλίου.

sunk [sʌŋk] pp of **sink** ‖ ~**en** a βυθισμένος, βαθουλωμένος.

sunlight ['sʌnlait] n ἡλιακόν φῶς, λιακάδα.

sunlit ['sʌnlit] a ἡλιόλουστος.

sunny ['sʌni] a εὔηλιος, ἡλιόλουστος ‖ (cheerful) χαρωπός, γελαστός.

sunrise ['sʌnraiz] n ἀνατολή τοῦ ἡλίου.

sunset ['sʌnset] n ἡλιοβασίλεμα.

sunshade ['sʌnʃeid] n (over table) ἀλεξήλιον, ὀμπρέλλα ἡλίου.

sunshine ['sʌnʃain] n λιακάδα.

sunspot ['sʌnspɔt] n ἡλιακή κηλίδα.

sunstroke ['sʌnstrəuk] n ἡλίασις.

suntan ['sʌntæn] n μαύρισμα ἀπό τόν ἥλιο.

sunup ['sʌnʌp] n (sunrise) ἀνατολή τοῦ ἡλίου.

super ['su:pə*] a (col) ὑπέροχος, περίφημος, σπουδαῖος ‖ prefix ὑπερ-.

superannuation [su:pərænju'eiʃən] n (employers' contribution) εἰσφορά ἐργοδότου.

superb [su:'pə:b] a ὑπέροχος, ἔξοχος, ἐξαίσιος ‖ ~**ly** ad ὑπέροχα, ἔξοχα, λαμπρά.

supercilious [su:pə'siliəs] *a* ἀγέρωχος, ὑπεροπτικός.

superficial [su:pə'fiʃəl] *a* ἐπιφανειακός ‖ (*shallow*) ἐπιπόλαιος, ἐπιφανειακός ‖ ~**ly** *ad* ἐπιφανειακά, ἐπιπολαίως.

superfluous [su'pə:fluəs] *a* περιττός.

superhuman [su:pə'hju:mən] *a* (*effort*) ὑπεράνθρωπος.

superimpose ['su:pərim'pəuz] *vt* ὑπερεπιθέτω, ὑπερθέτω.

superintendent [su:pərin'tendənt] *n* (*police*) ἀξιωματικός τῆς ἀστυνομίας.

superior [su'piəriə*] *a* ἀνώτερος, ὑπέρτερος, ἐξαιρετικός ‖ (*proud*) ὑπεροπτικός, ἀκατάδεχτος ‖ *n* προϊστάμενος, ἀνώτερος ‖ ~**ity** *n* ὑπεροχή, ἀνωτερότης.

superlative [su'pə:lətiv] *a* ἀνώτατος, ὑπερθετικός ‖ *n* (τό) ὑπερθετικόν.

superman ['su:pəmæn] *n* ὑπεράνθρωπος.

supermarket ['su:pəma:kit] *n* σουπερμάρκετ.

supernatural [su:pə'nætʃərəl] *a* ὑπερφυσικός.

superpower ['su:pəpauə*] *n* (*eg USA, USSR*) ὑπερδύναμις.

supersede [su:pə'si:d] *vt* ἀντικαθιστῶ, παραμερίζω.

supersonic ['su:pə'sɔnik] *a* ὑπερηχητικός.

superstition [su:pə'stiʃən] *n* δεισιδαιμονία, πρόληψις.

superstitious [su:pə'stiʃəs] *a* δεισιδαίμων, προληπτικός.

supertanker ['su:pətæŋkə*] *n* ὑπερδεξαμενόπλοιον.

supervise [su:pə'vaiz] *vt* ἐπιβλέπω, ἐποπτεύω, διευθύνω.

supervision [su:pə'viʒən] *n* ἐποπτεία, ἐπιθεώρησις, διεύθυνσις.

supervisor ['su:pəvaizə*] *n* ἐπιθεωρητής, ἐπόπτης, ἐπιστάτης ‖ ~**y** *a* τῆς ἐποπτείας, ἐποπτικός.

supper ['sʌpə*] *n* δεῖπνον.

supple ['sʌpl] *a* εὐέλικτος, εὐλύγιστος, λυγερός.

supplement ['sʌplimənt] *n* συμπλήρωμα, παράρτημα ‖ [sʌpli'ment] *vt* συμπληρώνω ‖ ~**ary** *a* συμπληρωματικός, πρόσθετος.

supplier [sə'plaiə*] *n* προμηθευτής.

supply [sə'plai] *vt* παρέχω, ἐφοδιάζω, προμηθεύω ‖ *n* ἐφόδιον, ἀπόθεμα, προμήθεια ‖ (*supplying*) ἐφοδιασμός, τροφοδότησις ‖ **supplies** *npl* (*food*) τρόφιμα ‖ (*mil*) ἐφόδια ‖ ~ **and demand** προσφορά καί ζήτησις.

support [sə'pɔ:t] *n* (*moral, financial etc*) ὑποστήριξις, ἐνίσχυσις ‖ (*tech*) στήριγμα, ὑποστήριγμα, ἔρεισμα ‖ *vt* (ὑπο)στηρίζω, ἐνισχύω ‖ (*provide for*) συντηρῶ, κρατῶ ‖ (*speak for*) ὑποστηρίζω, ἐνισχύω ‖ (*endure*) ὑπομένω, ὑποφέρω ‖ ~**er** *n* (*pol etc*) ὀπαδός, ὑπερασπιστής ‖ (*sport*) ὀπαδός, ὑποστη-

ρικτής ‖ ~**ing** *a* (*programme, role*) βοηθητικός, δευτερεύων.

suppose [sə'pəuz] *vti* ὑποθέτω, προϋποθέτω ‖ (*think, imagine*) φαντάζομαι, νομίζω ‖ ~ **he comes** . . . ἄν ἔρθη . . . ‖ ~**dly** *ad* ὑποθετικῶς, δῆθεν.

supposing [sə'pəuziŋ] *cj* ἐάν, ἄς ὑποθέσουμε ὅτι.

supposition [sʌpə'ziʃən] *n* ὑπόθεσις, γνώμη.

suppress [sə'pres] *vt* καταπνίγω, καταστέλλω ‖ (*hold back*) συγκρατῶ, σκεπάζω ‖ ~**ion** *n* κατάπνιξις, συγκράτησις, ἀπόκρυψις ‖ ~**or** *n* (*mech*) καταστολεύς, ἀναστολεύς.

supra- ['su:prə] *prefix* ὑπερ-.

supremacy [su'preməsi] *n* ὑπεροχή, ἀνωτάτη ἐξουσία.

supreme [su'pri:m] *a* ὑπέρτατος, ἀνώτατος, ὕψιστος ‖ ~**ly** *ad* στόν ὑπέρτατον βαθμόν, ἐξαιρετικά.

surcharge ['sə:tʃa:dʒ] *n* ἐπιβάρυνσις, πρόσθετος φόρος.

sure [ʃuə*] *a* βέβαιος, ἀσφαλής, σίγουρος ‖ *ad* βεβαίως, ἀσφαλῶς ‖ ~! (*of course*) βέβαια!, ἀσφαλῶς! ‖ **to make** ~ **of** βεβαιώνω ‖ ~**-footed** *a* μέ σίγουρο πόδι ‖ ~**ly** *ad* ἀσφαλῶς, βεβαίως ‖ (*firmly*) ἀναμφιβόλως ‖ (*gladly*) βεβαίως, μετά χαρᾶς.

surf [sə:f] *n* κῦμα, ἀφρός.

surface ['sə:fis] *n* (*top side*) ἐπιφάνεια ‖ (*outward appearance*) ἐξωτερικόν, ἐμφάνισις ‖ *vt* (*roadway*) ἐπιστρώνω, στρώνω ‖ *vi* βγαίνω στήν ἐπιφάνεια ‖ ~ **mail** *n* τακτικόν ταχυδρομεῖον.

surfboard ['sə:fbɔ:d] *n* σανίδα κολυμβήσεως.

surfeit ['sə:fit] *n* ὑπεραφθονία, πληθώρα, κόρος.

surge [sə:dʒ] *n* μεγάλο κῦμα, σάλος, ἀνύψωσις ‖ *vi* ὁρμῶ, ξεχύνομαι, κυμαίνομαι.

surgeon ['sə:dʒən] *n* χειρουργός.

surgery ['sə:dʒəri] *n* χειρουργική ‖ (*room*) ἰατρεῖον, χειρουργεῖον.

surgical ['sə:dʒikəl] *a* χειρουργικός.

surly ['sə:li] *a* ἀγροῖκος, κατσούφης, ἄγενής.

surmise [sə:'maiz] *vt* εἰκάζω, ὑποθέτω, μαντεύω.

surmount [sə:'maunt] *vt* (*difficulty*) ὑπερνικῶ, ξεπερνῶ.

surname ['sə:neim] *n* ἐπώνυμον.

surpass [sə:'pa:s] *vt* ὑπερτερῶ, ὑπερβαίνω, ξεπερνῶ.

surplus ['sə:pləs] *n* περίσσευμα, πλεόνασμα ‖ *a* πλεονάζων, ὑπεράριθμος.

surprise [sə'praiz] *n* ἔκπληξις, κατάπληξις, ξάφνισμα ‖ *vt* αἰφνιδιάζω ‖ (*astonish*) ἐκπλήσσω, καταπλήσσω, ξαφνίζω.

surprising [sə'praiziŋ] *a* ἐκπληκτικός, καταπληκτικός ‖ ~**ly** *ad* καταπληκτικά, ἐκπληκτικῶς.

surrealism [sə'riəlizəm] *n* σουρρεαλισμός.

surrealist [sə'riəlist] *a* σουρρεαλιστικός ‖ *n* σουρρεαλιστής.

surrender [sə'rendə*] *n* παράδοσις, ἐγκατάλειψις, ἐκχώρησις ‖ *vi* παραδίδομαι, παραδίδω, ἐκχωρῶ.

surreptitious [sʌrəp'tiʃəs] *a* λαθραῖος, κρυφός ‖ ~ly *ad* λαθραία, στή ζούλα.

surround [sə'raund] *vt* περιβάλλω, περικυκλώνω ‖ ~ing *a* (*countryside*) περιβάλλων, ἐξοχικός ‖ ~ings *npl* περιβάλλον, πλαίσιον.

surveillance [sə:'veiləns] *n* (*observation*) ἐπιτήρησις, ἐποπτεία.

survey ['sə:vei] *n* ἐπισκόπησις ‖ χωρογράφησις, τοπογράφησις ‖ [sə:'vei] *vt* ἐπισκοπῶ, ἐξετάζω ‖ (*measure land*) χωρογραφῶ, τοπογραφῶ ‖ ~ing *n* (*of land*) χωρογράφησις, τοπογραφία ‖ ~or *n* (*of land*) τοπογράφος.

survival [sə'vaivəl] *n* ἐπιβίωσις ‖ (*from past*) ὑπόλειμμα, ἐπιβίωμα.

survive [sə'vaiv] *vi* ἐπιζῶ ‖ *vt* ἐπιζῶ ‖ (*a shipwreck etc*) σώζομαι, γλυτώνω.

survivor [sə'vaivə*] *n* ἐπιζῶν, διασωθείς.

susceptible [sə'septəbl] *a* (+ *to*) ἐπιδεκτικός, εὐεπηρέαστος.

suspect ['sʌspekt] *n* ὕποπτος ‖ *a* ὕποπτος ‖ [səs'pekt] *vt* ὑποπτεύομαι, ὑποψιάζομαι ‖ (*think likely*) ὑποψιάζομαι, φαντάζομαι.

suspend [səs'pend] *vt* ἀναστέλλω, διακόπτω ‖ (*hang up*) ἀναρτῶ, κρεμῶ ‖ ~ers *npl* καλτσοδέτες ‖ (*US*) τιράντες.

suspense [səs'pens] *n* ἐκκρεμότης, ἀνησυχία, ἀβεβαιότης.

suspension [səs'penʃən] *n* ἀναστολή, ἀνακοπή ‖ (*being suspended*) ἀπόλυσις ‖ (*aut*) ἀνάρτησις ‖ ~ bridge *n* κρεμαστή γέφυρα.

suspicion [səs'piʃən] *n* ὑποψία, ὑπόνοια ‖ (*small amount*) μικρή δόσις.

suspicious [səs'piʃəs] *a* ὕποπτος, καχύποπτος ‖ ~ly *ad* ὕποπτα, δύσπιστα.

sustain [səs'tein] *vt* ὑποστηρίζω, στηρίζω, βαστάζω ‖ (*confirm*) ἀποδέχομαι ‖ (*injury*) ὑφίσταμαι, ζημιοῦμαι, δέχομαι ‖ ~ed *a* (*effort*) ἐπίμονος, συνεχής.

sustenance ['sʌstinəns] *n* συντήρησις, τροφή.

swab [swɔb] *n* (*pad*) ξέστρον.

swagger ['swægə*] *vi* κομπάζω, ἐπιδεικνύομαι, καμαρώνω.

swallow ['swɔləu] *n* (*bird*) χελιδών, χελιδόνι ‖ (*of food etc*) μπουκιά, ρωγιά, γουλιά ‖ *vt* καταπίνω, χάφτω ‖ to ~ up *vt* καταπίνω, καλύπτω, χάνομαι.

swam [swæm] *pt of* swim.

swamp [swɔmp] *n* ἕλος, βάλτος ‖ *vt* (*overwhelm*) συντρίβω, σαρώνω ‖ ~y *a* ἑλώδης, βαλτώδης.

swan [swɔn] *n* κύκνος ‖ ~ song *n* κύκνειον ἄσμα.

swap [swɔp] *n* (*exchange*) ἀνταλλαγή ‖ *vt* (+ *for*) ἀνταλλάσσω, ἀλλάζω.

swarm [swɔ:m] *n* (*of bees*) σμῆνος, σμάρι ‖ (*of insects*) σύννεφο ‖ (*people*) μπουλούκι, τσούρμο ‖ *vi* (*crowd*) συρρέω, συγκεντρώνομαι, γέμω.

swarthy ['swɔ:ði] *a* μελαψός, μελαχροινός.

swastika ['swɔstikə] *n* ἀγκυλωτός σταυρός.

swat [swɔt] *vt* κτυπῶ, βαρῶ.

sway [swei] *vi* ταλαντεύομαι, κουνιέμαι, τρικλίζω ‖ *vi* ταλαντεύω, κουνῶ ‖ (*influence*) διευθύνω, ἐπηρεάζω, παρασύρω.

swear [sweə*] (*irreg v*) *vi* ὁρκίζομαι, ὁμνύω ‖ (*curse*) βλαστημῶ, βλασφημῶ, ὑβρίζω ‖ to ~ to sth ὁρκίζομαι στό, βεβαιῶ ‖ ~word *n* βλαστήμια, χοντροκουβέντα.

sweat [swet] *n* ἱδρώτας ‖ (*med*) ἱδρωσιά, ἵδρωμα ‖ *vi* ἱδρώνω ‖ (*toil*) μοχθῶ, σπάω στή δουλειά ‖ ~er *n* πουλόβερ, φανέλλα ‖ ~y *a* ἱδρωμένος.

Swede [swi:d] *n* Σουηδός.

swede [swi:d] *n* (*turnip*) ραπίτσα.

Sweden ['swi:dn] *n* Σουηδία.

Swedish ['swi:diʃ] *a* σουηδικός ‖ *n* (*ling*) σουηδικά.

sweep [swi:p] (*irreg v*) *n* σκούπισμα, σάρωμα ‖ (*wide curve*) κυκλική κίνησις, καμπή ‖ (*range*) ἄνοιγμα, εὐρύτης, ἐμβέλεια ‖ (*of chimney*) καπνοδοχοκαθαριστής ‖ *vt* σκουπίζω, καθαρίζω, σαρώνω ‖ *vi* (*move in curve*) ἐκτείνομαι, ἁπλώνομαι ‖ προχωρῶ μεγαλοπρεπῶς ‖ to ~ away *vt* σκουπίζω, σαρώνω ‖ to ~ past *vi* περνῶ γρήγορα, ἀντιπαρέρχομαι ‖ to ~ up *vi* φθάνω, ἀνεβαίνω ‖ *vt* σκουπίζω, μαζεύω ‖ ~ing *a* (*gesture*) πλατεία (χειρονομία) ‖ (*statement*) γενικός, ριζικός, πλήρης ‖ ~stake *n* σουηπστέϊκ.

sweet [swi:t] *n* γλυκό ‖ (*candy*) ζαχαρωτό, καραμέλα ‖ *a* γλυκός ‖ (*fresh*) δροσερός, φρέσκος ‖ (*gentle, pretty*) χαριτωμένος, γλυκός, συμπαθητικός ‖ ~breads *npl* γλυκάδια ‖ ~en *vt* γλυκαίνω ‖ ~heart *n* ἀγαπητικός, ἀγαπημένος, ἀγάπη μου ‖ ~ly *ad* γλυκά, μελωδικά, εὐχάριστα ‖ ~ness *n* γλυκότης, γλύκα ‖ ~ pea *n* λάθυρος, μοσχομπίζελο ‖ ~ tooth *n* ἀδυναμία γιά γλυκά.

swell [swel] (*irreg v*) *n* (*wave*) μεγάλο κῦμα ‖ *a* (*col: excellent*) ἐξαιρετικός, πρώτης τάξεως ‖ *vt* (*numbers*) ἐξογκώνω, αὐξάνω ‖ *vi* (*also ~ up*) ἐξογκοῦμαι, φουσκώνω ‖ (*become louder*) δυναμώνω ‖ (*med*) πρήσκομαι, πρήζομαι ‖ ~ing *n* ἐξόγκωσις, πρήξιμο.

sweltering ['sweltəriŋ] *a* ἱδρωμένος, ἀποπνυκτικός.

swept [swept] *pt,pp of* sweep.

swerve [swə:v] *n* παρέκκλισις, παρατιμονιά ‖ *vti* παρεκκλίνω, παρατρατίζω, στρίβω.

swift [swift] *n* κλαδευτήρα, σταχτάρα ‖ *a* ταχύς, γρήγορος, ἄμεσος ‖ ~ly *ad* ταχέως, γρήγορα, γοργά ‖ **~ness** *n* ταχύτης, γοργότης, γρηγοράδα.

swig [swig] *n* (*col: of drink*) μεγάλη ρουφηξιά.

swill [swil] *n* (*for pigs*) τροφή χοίρων ‖ *vt* (*pour liquid*) ξεπλένω.

swim [swim] (*irreg v*) *n* κολύμπι ‖ *vi* (*person*) κολυμπῶ ‖ (*be flooded*) πλημμυρίζω, εἶμαι πλημμυρισμένος ‖ (*feel dizzy*) ἰλιγγιῶ, γυρίζω, ζαλίζω ‖ *vt* (*cross by swimming*) περνῶ κολυμπῶντας ‖ **~mer** *n* κολυμβητής ‖ **~ming** *n* κολύμπι ‖ **to go ~ming** πάω κολύμπι ‖ **~ming baths** *npl* κολυμβητικές δεξαμενές ‖ **~ming cap** *n* σκουφί ‖ **~ming costume** *n* μαγιό ‖ **~ming pool** *n* πισίνα ‖ **~suit** *n* μαγιό.

swindle ['swindl] *n* ἀπάτη ‖ *vt* (ἐξ)ἀπατῶ ‖ **~r** *n* ἀπατεών, κατεργάρης.

swine [swain] *n* χοῖρος, γουρούνι ‖ (*person*) γουρούνι, παλιάνθρωπος.

swing [swiŋ] (*irreg v*) *n* κούνια ‖ (*swinging*) αἰώρησις, ταλάντευσις ‖ (*music*) ρυθμός, σουΐγκ ‖ *vt* ταλαντεύω, κουνῶ ‖ (*move round*) περιστρέφω, στρέφω ‖ *vi* αἰωροῦμαι, κουνιέμαι ‖ (*move round*) περιστρέφομαι, στρέφομαι, κάνω μεταβολήν ‖ **in full ~** ἐν πλήρει ὀργασμῷ ‖ **~ bridge** *n* περιστρεφόμενη γέφυρα ‖ **~ door** *n* πτερυγωτή θύρα.

swipe [swaip] *n* δυνατόν κτύπημα ‖ *vt* (*hit*) κτυπῶ δυνατά ‖ (*col: steal*) κλέβω, βουτῶ.

swish [swiʃ] *a* (*col: smart*) κομψός, μοντέρνος ‖ *vt* θροΐζω, συρίζω, μαστιγώνω.

Swiss [swis] *a* ἑλβετικός ‖ *n* (*person*) Ἑλβετός.

switch [switʃ] *n* (*for light, radio etc*) διακόπτης ‖ (*change*) ἀλλαγή ‖ *vti* διακόπτω ‖ (*turn*) γυρίζω ἀπότομα ‖ **to ~ off** *vt* διακόπτω, σβήνω ‖ **to ~ on** *vt* ἀνάβω, ἀνοίγω ‖ **~back** *n* (*at fair*) ρωσικά βουνά ‖ **~board** *n* πίναξ διανομῆς, ταμπλό.

Switzerland ['switsələnd] *n* Ἑλβετία.

swivel ['swivl] *vti* (*also* **~ round**) (περι)στρέφομαι, στρέφω.

swollen ['swəulən] *pp* of **swell** ‖ *a* (*ankle etc*) πρησμένος, διογκωμένος.

swoon [swu:n] *vi* λιγοθυμῶ, λαγγεύω.

swoop [swu:p] *n* (*esp by police*) ξαφνική ἐπίθεσις, ἐφόρμησις ‖ *vi* (*also* **~ down**) ἐφορμῶ, ἐπιπίπτω, πέφτω.

swop [swɔp] = **swap**.

sword [sɔ:d] *n* ξίφος, σπαθί ‖ **~fish** *n* ξιφίας ‖ **~sman** *n* ξιφομάχος.

swore [swɔ:*] *pt* of **swear**.

sworn [swɔ:n] *pp* of **swear**.

swum [swʌm] *pp* of **swim**.

swung [swʌŋ] *pt,pp* of **swing**.

sycamore ['sikəmɔ:*] *n* συκομουριά.

sycophantic [sikə'fæntik] *a* συκοφαντικός.

syllable ['siləbl] *n* συλλαβή.

syllabus ['siləbəs] *n* πρόγραμμα.

symbol ['simbəl] *n* σύμβολον, σημεῖον ‖

~ic(al) [sim'bɔlik(əl)] *a* συμβολικός ‖ **~ism** *n* συμβολισμός ‖ **~ize** *vt* συμβολίζω, παριστάνω.

symmetrical [si'metrikəl] *a* συμμετρικός ‖ **~ly** *ad* συμμετρικῶς.

symmetry ['simitri] *n* συμμετρία.

sympathetic [simpə'θetik] *a* συμπαθητικός ‖ (*agreeing*) συμπαθής, εὐνοϊκός ‖ **~ally** *ad* ἐκ συμπαθείας, συμπονετικά.

sympathize ['simpəθaiz] *vi* (+ *with*) συμπάσχω μέ, συμπονῶ, συμπαθῶ ‖ **~r** *n* συμπαθῶν, ὀπαδός.

sympathy ['simpəθi] *n* συμπάθεια, συμπόνια, οἶκτος.

symphonic [sim'fɔnik] *a* συμφωνικός.

symphony ['simfəni] *n* (*composition*) συμφωνία ‖ **~ orchestra** *n* συμφωνική ὀρχήστρα.

symposium [sim'pəuziəm] *n* (*meeting for discussion*) συμπόσιον, συμπόσιον.

symptom ['simptəm] *n* σύμπτωμα ‖ **~atic** *a* συμπτωματικός.

synagogue ['sinəgɔg] *n* συναγωγή.

synchromesh ['siŋkrəu'meʃ] *n* συγχρονισμένη ἐμπλοκή.

synchronize ['siŋkrənaiz] *vt* συγχρονίζω ‖ *vi* (+ *with*) γίνομαι ταυτοχρόνως, συμφωνῶ.

syndicate ['sindikit] *n* συνδικάτον.

syndrome ['sindrəum] *n* (*med*) σύνδρομον.

synonym ['sinənim] *n* συνώνυμον ‖ **~ous** [si'nɔniməs] *a* συνώνυμος.

synopsis [si'nɔpsis] *n* σύνοψις, περίληψις.

syntax ['sintæks] *n* σύνταξις, συντακτικόν.

synthesis [sin'θəsis] *n* σύνθεσις.

synthetic [sin'θetik] *a* (*artificial*) συνθετικός ‖ **~ally** *ad* συνθετικῶς.

syphilis ['sifilis] *n* σύφιλις.

syphon ['saifən] = **siphon**.

syringe [si'rindʒ] *n* σύριγγα.

syrup ['sirəp] *n* σιρόπι ‖ **~y** *a* σιροπώδης.

system ['sistəm] *n* σύστημα ‖ (*railway etc*) δίκτυον ‖ (*method*) σύστημα, μέθοδος ‖ **~atic** *a* συστηματικός, μεθοδικός ‖ **~atically** *ad* συστηματικῶς, μέ μέθοδον.

T, t

tab [tæb] *n* θηλίτσα, πάτ, αὐτί.

tabby ['tæbi] *n* (*cat*) γάτα ‖ *a* μουαρέ.

tabernacle ['tæbənækl] *n* (*in R.C. Church*) ἱεροφυλάκειον, ἀρτοφόριον.

table ['teibl] *n* τραπέζι ‖ (*list*) πίνακας.

tableau ['tæbləu] *n* (*representation*) ταμπλώ, δραματικὴ σκηνή.

tablecloth ['teiblklɔθ] *n* τραπεζομάντηλο.

table d'hote ['ta:bl'dəut] *a* τάμπλ-ντότ.

table lamp ['teibllæmp] *n* πορτατίφ.

tablemat ['teiblmæt] *n* καρέ, σεμέν.

tablespoon ['teiblspu:n] *n* κουτάλι τῆς σούπας ‖ **~ful** *n* κουταλιά τῆς σούπας.

T

tablet ['tæblit] *n* πλάκα, σημειωματάριον ‖ (*pellet*) δισκίον, ταμπλέττα, χάπι.

table tennis ['teibltenis] *n* πίγκ-πόγκ.

table wine ['teiblwain] *n* ἐπιτραπέζιο κρασί.

taboo [tə'bu:] *n* ταμπού ‖ *a* ἀπηγορευμένος, ταμπού.

tacit ['tæsit] *a* σιωπηρός, ὑπονοούμενος ‖ ~ly *ad* σιωπηρῶς ‖ ~urn *a* σιωπηλός, λιγόλογος.

tack [tæk] *n* πινέζα ‖ (*stitch*) μεγάλη βελονιά, τρύπωμα ‖ (*naut*) ἀναστροφή, διαδρομή ‖ (*course*) πορεία.

tackle ['tækl] *n* (*for lifting*) σύσπαστον, παλάγκο ‖ (*sport*) τάκελ ‖ *vt* ἀντιμετωπίζω, καταπιάνομαι μέ ‖ (*a player*) κάνω τάκελ.

tacky ['tæki] *a* κολλώδης.

tact [tækt] *n* τάκτ, λεπτότης ‖ ~ful *a* μέ τάκτ, λεπτότης ‖ ~fully *ad* μέ λεπτότητα, λεπτά.

tactical ['tæktikəl] *a* τακτικός.

tactics ['tæktiks] *npl* τακτική.

tactless ['tæktlis] *a* στερούμενος τάκτ, ἀδέξιος ‖ ~ly *ad* χωρίς τάκτ, ἀδιάκριτα.

tadpole ['tædpəul] *n* γυρῖνος, γύρινος.

taffeta ['tæfitə] *n* ταφτᾶς.

tag [tæg] *n* (*label*) ἐτικέττα.

tail [teil] *n* οὐρά ‖ *to* ~ **off** *vi* (*in size, quality etc*) ἐλαττώνομαι, λεπτύνω ‖ ~ **end** *n* ὀπίσθιον ἄκρον, οὐρά, τέλος.

tailor ['teilə*] *n* ράπτης ‖ ~**ing** *n* ραπτική ‖ ~-**made** *a* καμωμένο εἰδικῶς.

tailwind ['teilwind] *n* οὔριος ἄνεμος.

tainted ['teintid] *a* μολυσμένος, χαλασμένος.

take [teik] (*irreg v*) *vt* παίρνω, βγάζω ‖ (*seize*) πιάνω, παίρνω, καταλαμβάνω ‖ (*require*) ἀπαιτῶ, χρειάζομαι ‖ (*hire*) παίρνω, νοικιάζω ‖ (*understand*) δέχομαι, παραδέχομαι, συμπεραίνω ‖ (*choose*) διαλέγω ‖ (*phot*) φωτογραφίζω, φωτογραφίζομαι ‖ *to* ~ **part in** συμμετέχω ‖ *to* ~ **place** συμβαίνω ‖ *to* ~ **after** *vt* μοιάζω ‖ *to* ~ **back** *vt* (*return*) φέρνω πίσω, παίρνω πίσω ‖ *to* ~ **down** *vt* κατεβάζω, ξεκρεμῶ, κατεδαφίζω ‖ (*write*) σημειώνω, καταγράφω ‖ *to* ~ **in** *vt* (*deceive*) ἐξαπατῶ, ξεγελῶ ‖ (*understand*) καταλαβαίνω, ἀντιλαμβάνομαι ‖ (*include*) περιλαμβάνω ‖ *to* ~ **off** *vi* (*aeroplane*) ἀπογειοῦμαι, ξεκινῶ ‖ *vt* (*remove*) ἀφαιρῶ, βγάζω, παίρνω ‖ (*imitate*) μιμοῦμαι, παρῳδῶ ‖ *to* ~ **on** *vt* (*undertake*) ἀναλαμβάνω ‖ (*engage*) μισθώνω, προσλαμβάνω ‖ (*accept as opponent*) δέχομαι τήν πρόσκλησιν ‖ *to* ~ **out** *vt* (*licence etc*) λαμβάνω, παίρνω ‖ (*stain*) βγάζω ‖ *to* ~ **over** *vt* ἀναλαμβάνω, διαδέχομαι ‖ *to* ~ **to** *vt* συμπαθῶ, ἐπιδίδομαι εἰς, μ' ἀρέσει καί ‖ *to* ~ **up** *vt* (*raise*) σηκώνω, μαζεύω ‖ (*occupy*) καταλαμβάνω, πιάνω ‖ (*absorb*) ἀπορροφῶ, τραβῶ ‖ (*engage in*) ἀπασχολοῦμαι

εἰς ‖ ~**off** *n* (*aviat*) ἀπογείωσις ‖ (*imitation*) μίμησις ‖ ~**over** *n* (*comm*) ἀνάληψις ἐπιχειρήσεως, κτῆσις.

takings ['teikiŋz] *npl* (*comm*) εἰσπράξεις.

talc [tælk] *n* (*also* ~**um powder**) τάλκ.

tale [teil] *n* ἀφήγησις, παραμύθι, ἱστορία.

talent ['tælənt] *n* ταλέντο ‖ ~**ed** *a* μέ ταλέντο.

talk [tɔ:k] *n* συζήτησις, συνομιλία, κουβέντα ‖ (*rumour*) φλυαρία, διάδοσις ‖ (*speech*) λόγος, ὁμιλία ‖ *to* ~ **shop** συζητῶ γιά τήν ἐργασία μου ‖ *to* ~ **over** *vt* συζητῶ ‖ ~**ative** *a* φλύαρος ‖ ~**er** *n* ὁμιλητής, συζητητής, λογᾶς.

tall [tɔ:l] *a* ὑψηλός, ψηλός ‖ ~**boy** *n* (*furniture*) ψηλό κομμό, ψηλός καθρέπτης ‖ ~**ness** *n* ἀνάστημα, ὕψος ‖ ~ **story** *n* μπούρδα, ἀρλούμπα.

tally ['tæli] *n* (*account*) λογαριασμός, ὑπολογισμός.

tambourine [tæmbə'ri:n] *n* ντέφι.

tame [teim] *a* ἥμερος ‖ (*dull*) ἄτονος, πλαδαρός ‖ ~**ness** *n* ἡμερότης.

tamper ['tæmpə*] *to* ~ **with** *vt* μαστορεύω, ἀνακατεύομαι μέ.

tan [tæn] *n* (*colour*) χρῶμα πίτυκα-καφέ, φαιοκίτρινον ‖ (*of sun*) μελαχρινόν χρῶμα, μαύρισμα ‖ *a* (*colour*) φαιοκίτρινος, καφέ.

tandem ['tændəm] *n* (*ποδήλατο*) τάντεμ.

tang [tæŋ] *n* ὀξεῖα γεῦσις, δυνατή ὀσμή.

tangent ['tændʒənt] *n* ἐφαπτομένη.

tangerine [tændʒə'ri:n] *n* μανταρίνι.

tangible ['tændʒəbl] *a* ἁπτός, ψηλαφητός ‖ (*real*) πραγματικός, αἰσθητός.

tangle ['tæŋgl] *n* μπέρδεμα, ἀνακάτωμα, περιπλοκή ‖ *vti* περιπλέκω, μπερδεύομαι.

tango ['tæŋgəu] *n* ταγκό.

tank [tæŋk] *n* δεξαμενή, ντεπόζιτο ‖ (*mil*) τάνκ, ἅρμα.

tankard ['tæŋkəd] *n* κύπελλον, μαστραπᾶς, κούπα.

tanker ['tæŋkə*] *n* (*ship*) δεξαμενόπλοιον, τάνκερ ‖ (*truck for carrying bulk liquids*) βυτιοφόρον.

tankful ['tæŋkful] *n* γεμᾶτο δοχεῖο.

tanned [tænd] *a* (*skin*) κατειργασμένος, ἀργασμένος.

tantalizing ['tæntəlaiziŋ] *a* προκλητικός, βασανιστικός.

tantrum ['tæntrəm] *n* ἔκρηξις ὀργῆς, ξέσπασμα, παραφορά.

tap [tæp] *n* κάνουλα, βρύση, στρόφιγξ ‖ (*gentle blow*) ἐλαφρόν κτύπημα ‖ *vt* (*strike*) κτυπῶ ἐλαφρά ‖ (*supply*) παίρνω, τροφοδοτῶ, ἀντλῶ.

tap-dance ['tæpdɑ:ns] *vi* χορεύω μέ κλακέτες.

tape [teip] *n* (*also* **magnetic** ~) ταινία, μαγνητοταινία ‖ *vt* (*to record*) μαγνητογραφῶ, ἠχογραφῶ ‖ ~ **measure** *n* μετρική ταινία.

taper ['teipǝ*] n λαμπάς, κερί ‖ vi λεπτύνομαι, μειοῦμαι, μπαίνω.

tape recorder ['teiprikɔːdǝ*] n μαγνητόφωνον.

tapered ['teipǝd] a, **tapering** ['teipǝriŋ] a κωνικός, μυτερός, μειουμένος.

tapestry ['tæpistri] n τάπης, ταπέτο, ταπετσαρία.

tappet ['tæpit] n ὠστήριον, πλῆκτρον.

taproom ['tæprum] n καπελιό.

tar [taː*] n πίσσα.

tardy ['taːdi] a βραδύς, ἀργός.

target ['taːgit] n στόχος.

tariff ['tærif] n (list of charges) τιμολόγιον ‖ (duty) δασμός, δασμολόγιον.

tarmac ['taːmæk] n (aviat) διάδρομος ἀπογειώσεως.

tarn [taːn] n λιμνούλα (τῶν βουνῶν).

tarnish ['taːniʃ] vt (lit) θαμπώνω, σκοτεινιάζω ‖ (fig) ἀμαυρῶ, κηλιδώνω.

tarpaulin [taː'pɔːlin] n κηρόπανον, μουσαμᾶς.

tarragon ['tærǝgǝn] n τράχος, τραχούρι.

tart [taːt] n (pie) τούρτα, τάρτα ‖ (col: low woman) τσούλα ‖ a ξυνός, ὀξύς, δριμύς.

tartan ['taːtǝn] n σκωτσέζικο ὕφασμα.

tartar ['taːtǝ*] n τρύξ, πουρί.

tartly ['taːtli] ad δηκτικά, ἀπότομα.

task [taːsk] n καθῆκον, ἔργον, δουλειά, ἀποστολή.

tassel ['tæsǝl] n θύσανος, φούντα.

taste [teist] n γεῦσις, γοῦστο, προτίμησις ‖ vti γεύομαι, δοκιμάζω ‖ ~ful a κομψός, μέ γοῦστο, καλαίσθητος ‖ ~fully ad νόστιμα, κομψά, μέ γοῦστο ‖ ~less a ἄγευστος, ἄνοστος ‖ (bad taste) χωρίς γοῦστο, κακόγουστος ‖ ~lessly ad χωρίς γοῦστο.

tastily ['teistili] ad κομψά, μέ γοῦστο.

tastiness ['teistinis] n γευστικότης, νοστιμιά.

tasty ['teisti] a γευστικός, νόστιμος.

tata ['tæ'taː] excl (Brit col: goodbye) γειά, ἀντίο, ὡρεβουάρ.

tattered ['tætǝd] a κουρελιασμένος, κουρελής.

tatters ['tætǝz] npl: **in** ~ κουρελιασμένος.

tattoo [tǝ'tuː] n (νυκτερινή) στρατιωτική ἐπίδειξις ‖ (on skin) δερματοστιξία, τατουάζ ‖ vt διαστίζω, τατουάρω.

tatty ['tæti] a (col: cheap, of poor quality) φτηνός, πρόστυχος.

taught [tɔːt] pt, pp of **teach**.

taunt [tɔːnt] n χλευασμός, λοιδορία, κοροΐδία ‖ vt χλευάζω, κοροΐδεύω.

taut [tɔːt] a τεντωμένος, τεταμένος.

tavern ['tævǝn] n ταβέρνα.

tawdry ['tɔːdri] a φανταχτερός, φτηνός, τιποτένιος.

tawny ['tɔːni] a φαιοκίτρινος.

tax [tæks] n φόρος ‖ vt φορολογῶ ‖ (burden) ἐξαντλῶ, θέτω ὑπό δοκιμασίαν ‖ ~ation n φορολογία ‖ ~ collector n εἰσπράκτωρ

φόρων ‖ ~-free a ἀτελής, ἀφορολόγητος.

taxi ['tæksi] n ταξί ‖ vi (aviat) τροχοδρομῶ.

taxidermist ['tæksidǝːmist] n ταριχευτής, βαλσαμωτής.

taxi driver ['tæksidraivǝ*] n ὁδηγός ταξί, ταξιτζῆς.

taxi rank ['tæksiræŋk] n, **taxi stand** ['tæksistænd] n στάσις ταξί, πιάτσα.

taxpayer ['tækspeiǝ*] n φορολογούμενος.

tea [tiː] n τέϊον, τσάϊ ‖ (drink) τσάϊ ‖ (meal) ἀπογευματικό τσάϊ, γεῦμα μέ τσάϊ ‖ ~ **bag** n σακκουλάκι τσαγιοῦ ‖ ~ **break** n διάλειμμα γιά τσάϊ ‖ ~**cake** n (small bun) εἶδος κουλουράκι.

teach [tiːtʃ] (irreg v) vti διδάσκω, μαθαίνω ‖ ~**er** n διδάσκαλος, δασκάλα ‖ ~**ing** n διδασκαλία ‖ (what is taught) δίδαγμα, μάθημα.

tea cosy ['tiːkǝuzi] n σκέπασμα τσαγιέρας.

teacup ['tiːkʌp] n φλυτζάνι τσαγιοῦ.

teak [tiːk] n τίκ, τέκ ‖ a ἀπό τίκ.

tea leaves ['tiːliːvz] npl φύλλα τσαγιοῦ.

team [tiːm] n ὁμάδα, συνεργεῖον ‖ (of animals) ζευγάρι ‖ ~ **spirit** n πνεῦμα συνεργασίας ‖ ~**work** n ὁμαδικό παίξιμο, συνεργασία.

tea party ['tiːpaːti] n δεξίωσις μέ τσάϊ.

teapot ['tiːpɔt] n τσαγιέρα.

tear [tɛǝ*] (irreg v) n σχίσιμο, σχισμή ‖ vt ἀνοίγω τρύπα ‖ (pull apart) σχίζω, σπαράσσω ‖ vi (become torn) σχίζομαι ‖ (rush) τρέχω, ὁρμῶ.

tear [tiǝ*] n δάκρυ ‖ **in** ~**s** δακρυσμένος, βουτηγμένος στά δάκρυα ‖ ~**ful** a δακρυσμένος, κλαμμένος ‖ ~**gas** n δακρυγόνον ἀέριον.

tearing ['tɛǝriŋ] a (hurry) μέ ἐξωφρενική ταχύτητα.

tearoom ['tiːrum] n αἴθουσα τείου.

tease [tiːz] n πειραχτήριο, πείραγμα ‖ vt πειράζω, κοροΐδεύω.

tea set ['tiːset] n σερβίτσιο τσαγιοῦ.

teashop ['tiːʃɔp] n τεϊοπωλεῖον.

teaspoon ['tiːspuːn] n κουταλάκι τοῦ τσαγιοῦ ‖ ~**ful** n κουταλιά τοῦ τσαγιοῦ.

tea strainer ['tiːstreinǝ*] n σουρωτήρι τοῦ τσαγιοῦ.

teat [tiːt] n θηλή, ρώγα.

teatime ['tiːtaim] n ὥρα τοῦ τσαγιοῦ.

technical ['teknikǝl] a τεχνικός ‖ ~**ity** n τεχνικός χαρακτήρ, τεχνική λεπτομέρεια ‖ ~**ly** ad τεχνικῶς.

technician [tek'niʃǝn] n τεχνίτης, τεχνικός, εἰδικός.

technique [tek'niːk] n τεχνική, εἰδική μέθοδος.

technological [teknǝ'lɔdʒikǝl] a τεχνολογικός.

technologist [tek'nɔlǝdʒist] n τεχνικός, τεχνολόγος.

technology [tek'nɔlǝdʒi] n τεχνολογία.

teddy (bear) ['tedi(beə*)] *n* ἀρκουδάκι (παιχνίδι).

tedious ['ti:diəs] *a* ἀνιαρός, βαρετός ‖ **~ly** *ad* ἀνιαρά, πληκτικά, βαρετά.

tedium ['ti:diəm] *n* ἀνιαρότης, μονοτονία, ἀνία.

tee [ti:] *n* ὑψωματάκι, σωρός (ἄμμου).

teem [ti:m] *vi* βρίθω, ἀφθονῶ ‖ (*pour*) πέφτω καταρρακτωδῶς.

teenage ['ti:neidʒ] *a* ἐφηβικός, μεταξύ 13 καί 20 ‖ **~r** *n* ἔφηβος.

teens [ti:nz] *npl* ἡλικία μεταξύ 13 καί 20 ἐτῶν.

teeth [ti:θ] *npl of* tooth.

teethe [ti:ð] *vi* βγάζω δόντια.

teething ring ['ti:ðiŋriŋ] *n* ροδέλα μωροῦ (διά ὀδοντοφυΐαν).

teetotal ['ti:'təutl] *a* ἀντιαλκοολικός ‖ **~ler**, (*US*) **~er** *n* ἀπέχων ἀπό οἰνοπνευματώδη ποτά.

telecommunication ['telikəmju:ni'keiʃən] *n* τηλεπικοινωνία.

telegram ['teligræm] *n* τηλεγράφημα.

telegraph ['teligra:f] *n* τηλέγραφος ‖ **~ic** *a* (*address*) τηλεγραφική (διεύθυνσις) ‖ **~ pole** *n* τηλεγραφικός στύλος.

telepathic [teli'pæθik] *a* τηλεπαθητικός.

telepathy [ti'lepəθi] *n* τηλεπάθεια.

telephone ['telifəun] *n* τηλέφωνον ‖ *vt* τηλεφωνῶ ‖ **~ booth**, **~ box** *n* τηλεφωνικός θάλαμος ‖ **~ call** *n* τηλεφώνημα, κλῆσις ‖ **~ directory** *n* τηλεφωνικός κατάλογος ‖ **~ exchange** *n* κέντρον ‖ **~ number** *n* ἀριθμός τηλεφώνου.

telephonist [ti'lefənist] *n* τηλεφωνήτρια.

telephoto ['teli'fəutəu] *a*: **~ lens** τηλεφακός.

teleprinter ['teliprintə*] *n* τηλέτυπον.

telescope ['teliskəup] *n* τηλεσκόπιον ‖ *vt* (*compress*) συμπτύσσω.

telescopic [telis'kɔpik] *a* τηλεσκοπικός.

televiewer ['telivju:ə*] *n* θεατής τηλεοράσεως.

televise ['telivaiz] *vt* μεταβιβάζω διά τῆς τηλεοράσεως.

television ['televiʒən] *n* τηλεόρασις ‖ **~ set** *n* δέκτης τηλεοράσεως.

tell [tel] (*irreg v*) *vt* λέγω, λέω ‖ (*make known*) ἀφηγοῦμαι, γνωστοποιῶ ‖ (*order*) διατάσσω, παραγγέλλω, λέω σέ ‖ (*person of sth*) λέω κάτι, ἀνακοινώνω ‖ *vi* (*have effect*) ἀποφέρω, συνεπάγομαι, ἔχω ‖ **to ~ on** *vt* (*inform against*) καταδίδω, προδίδω ‖ **to ~ off** *vt* μαλώνω, κατσαδιάζω, περιλούζω ‖ **~er** *n* (*in bank*) ταμίας ‖ **~ing** *a* ἀποτελεσματικός ‖ **~tale** *a* μαρτυριάρης, κουτσομπόλης.

telly ['teli] *n* (*col*) τηλεόρασις.

temerity [ti'meriti] *n* θάρρος, τόλμη.

temper ['tempə*] *n* (*disposition*) διάθεσις, τεμπεραμέντο ‖ (*burst of anger*) ὀργή, θυμός ‖ *vt* (*moderate*) ἀπαλύνω, μαλακώνω, συγκρατῶ ‖ **~ament** *n* διάθε-

σις, ἰδιοσυγκρασία, τεμπεραμέντο ‖ **~amental** *a* (*moody*) ἰδιότροπος, γεμάτος βίδες.

temperance ['tempərəns] *n* (*in drinking*) ἀποφυγή οἰνοπνευματωδῶν ποτῶν ‖ (*moderation*) ἐγκράτεια, μετριοπάθεια ‖ **~ hotel** *n* ξενοδοχεῖον ὅπου ἀπαγορεύεται πώλησις τῶν οἰνοπνευματωδῶν ποτῶν.

temperate ['tempərit] *a* μετριοπαθής, εὔκρατος.

temperature ['tempritʃə*] *n* θερμοκρασία.

tempered ['tempəd] *a* (*steel*) ἐσκληρυμένος, βαμμένος.

tempest ['tempist] *n* θύελλα, τρικυμία, φουρτούνα ‖ **~uous** *a* φουρτουνιασμένος.

template ['templit] *n* πρότυπον, ἰχνάριον, φόρμα.

temple ['templ] *n* (*building*) ναός ‖ (*anat*) κρόταφος, μηλίγγι.

tempo ['tempəu] *n* ρυθμός, τέμπο ‖ (*of movement*) ρυθμός, μέτρον.

temporal ['tempərəl] *a* (*of time*) χρονικός, τοῦ χρόνου ‖ (*worldly*) ἐγκόσμιος, κοσμικός.

temporarily ['tempərərili] *ad* προσωρινῶς, γιά λίγο.

temporary ['tempərəri] *a* προσωρινός, πρόσκαιρος.

tempt [tempt] *vt* (*persuade*) παροτρύνω, προτρέπω ‖ (*attract*) δελεάζω ‖ **~ation** *n* πειρασμός, δελεασμός ‖ **~ing** *a* δελεαστικός.

ten [ten] *num* δέκα.

tenable ['tenəbl] *a* ὑπερασπίσιμος, ὑποστηρίξιμος, λογικός.

tenacious [ti'neiʃəs] *a* ἐμμένων, ἐπιμένων ‖ **~ly** *ad* ἐπίμονα, μέ ἐπιμονήν.

tenacity [ti'næsiti] *n* ἐμμονή, ἐπιμονή.

tenancy ['tenənsi] *n* ἐνοίκιασις, μίσθωσις.

tenant ['tenənt] *n* ἐνοικιαστής, μισθωτής, νοικάτορας.

tend [tend] *vt* (*look after*) περιποιοῦμαι ‖ *vi* τείνω, ρέπω, κλίνω ‖ **~ency** *n* τάσις, κλίσις, ροπή.

tender ['tendə*] *a* τρυφερός, μαλακός ‖ (*delicate*) λεπτός, εὐπαθής, τρυφερός ‖ (*loving*) στοργικός, εὐαίσθητος, πονετικός ‖ *n* (*comm: offer*) προσφορά ‖ **~ly** *ad* ἁπαλά, τρυφερά, μέ στοργή ‖ **~ness** *n* τρυφερότης, λεπτότης, στοργικότης.

tendon ['tendən] *n* τένων.

tenement ['tenimənt] *n* λαϊκή πολυκατοικία.

tenet ['tenət] *n* ἀρχή, ἀξίωμα, γνώμη.

tennis ['tenis] *n* τέννις, ἀντισφαίρισις ‖ **~ ball** *n* μπάλλα τοῦ τέννις ‖ **~ court** *n* γήπεδον τοῦ τέννις ‖ **~ racket** *n* ρακέτα τοῦ τέννις.

tenor ['tenə*] *n* (*male voice*) ὀξύφωνος, τενόρος ‖ (*singer*) τενόρος ‖ (*general meaning*) νόημα, ἔννοια, σημασία.

tense [tens] *a* (*fig*) εἰς ὑπερέντασιν, τεταμένος ‖ (*taut*) τεντωμένος ‖ *n* χρόνος ‖ ~ly *ad* τεταμένως, τέζα, εἰς ὑπερέντασιν ‖ ~ness *n* ἔντασις, τεταμένη κατάστασις.

tension ['tenʃən] *n* ἔντασις ‖ (*stretching*) τάσις, τέντωμα, τεζάρισμα.

tent [tent] *n* σκηνή, τέντα.

tentacle ['tentəkl] *n* κεραία, πλόκαμος.

tentative ['tentətiv] *a* δοκιμαστικός, προσωρινός ‖ ~ly *ad* πειραματικῶς, δοκιμαστικῶς.

tenterhooks ['tentəhuks] *npl*: **on** ~ ἀνήσυχος, ἀνυπομονῶν.

tenth [tenθ] *a* δέκατος, δέκατον.

tent peg ['tentpeg] *n* πάσσαλος σκηνῆς.

tent pole ['tentpəul] *n* ὀρθοστάτης σκηνῆς.

tenuous ['tenjuəs] *a* λεπτός, ἀραιός, ἐλαφρός.

tenure ['tenjuə*] *n* κατοχή, κτῆσις.

tepid ['tepid] *a* χλιαρός.

term [tə:m] *n* τέρμα, ὅριον, τέλος ‖ (*fixed time*) περίοδος, διάρκεια, χρόνος ‖ (*word*) ὅρος, ἔκφρασις, λέξις ‖ *vt* ὀνομάζω, καλῶ ‖ ~s *npl* ὅροι, διατάξεις ‖ (*relationship*) σχέσεις ‖ ~inal *a* τελικός, ἄκρος, τριμηνιαῖος ‖ *n* (*elec*) ἀκροδέκτης, πόλος ‖ (*for oil, ore etc*) ἀκραῖος σταθμός ‖ ~inate *vi* (+*in*) (καταλήγω, τελειώνω, τερματίζομαι ‖ ~ination *n* τερματισμός, περάτωσις, κατάληξις ‖ ~inology *n* ὁρολογία ‖ ~inus *n* ἀκραῖος σταθμός, τέρμα.

termite ['tə:mait] *n* τερμίτης.

terrace ['terəs] *n* σειρά οἰκιῶν ‖ (*in garden etc*) ἐπιπέδωμα, ταράτσα ‖ ~d *a* (*garden*) εἰς βαθμίδας, κλιμακωτός ‖ (*house*) ὁμοίου ρυθμοῦ.

terracotta ['terə'kɔtə] *n* ὀπτή γῆ, τερρακότα.

terrain [te'rain] *n* ἔδαφος, πεδίον, ἔκτασις.

terrible ['terəbl] *a* (*causing fear*) τρομερός, τρομακτικός, φοβερός ‖ (*inferior*) φοβερός, κατώτερος ‖ (*very great*) ἀπερίγραπτος, ὑπερβολικός.

terribly ['terəbli] *ad* τρομερά, φρικτά, τρομακτικά.

terrier ['teriə*] *n* τερριέ.

terrific [tə'rifik] *a* τρομερός, πελώριος ‖ ~ally *ad* τρομακτικά, τρομερά.

terrify ['terifai] *vt* τρομάζω, τρομοκρατῶ ‖ ~ing *a* τρομακτικός, τρομερός.

territorial [teri'tɔ:riəl] *a* ἐδαφικός, τοπικός, κτηματικός ‖ ~ **waters** *npl* χωρικά ὕδατα.

territory ['teritəri] *n* γῆ, χώρα, περιοχή, ἔδαφος.

terror ['terə*] *n* τρόμος, φρίκη, φόβος, τρομάρα ‖ ~ism *n* τρομοκρατία ‖ ~ist *n* τρομοκράτης ‖ ~ize *vt* τρομοκρατῶ.

terse [tə:s] *a* σύντομος, βραχύς, περιληπτικός.

Terylene ['terəli:n] *n* Ⓡ τερυλήνη.

test [test] *n* δοκιμή, δοκιμασία, ἐξέτασις, ἀνάλυσις ‖ *vt* δοκιμάζω, ἐξετάζω.

testament ['testəmənt] *n* διαθήκη.

test flight ['testflait] *n* δοκιμαστική πτῆσις.

testicle ['testikl] *n* ὄρχις, ἀρχίδι.

testify ['testifai] *vi* καταθέτω (ἐνόρκως).

testimonial [testi'məuniəl] *n* πιστοποιητικόν, βεβαίωσις ‖ (*gift*) δῶρον εὐγνωμοσύνης.

testimony ['testiməni] *n* μαρτυρία, κατάθεσις, ἀπόδειξις.

test match ['testmætʃ] *n* (*cricket, rugby*) μεγάλη διεθνής συνάντησις.

test paper ['testpeipə*] *n* (*in exam*) ἐρωτήσεις, δοκιμαστική ἐξέτασις.

test pilot ['testpailət] *n* πιλότος δοκιμῶν.

test tube ['testtju:b] *n* δοκιμαστικός σωλήν.

testy ['testi] *a* (*short-tempered*) εὐέξαπτος, δύστροπος.

tetanus ['tetənəs] *n* τέτανος.

tether ['teðə*] *vt* δένω.

text [tekst] *n* κείμενον ‖ ~**book** *n* ἐγχειρίδιον, διδακτικόν βιβλίον.

textile ['tekstail] *n* ὑφαντόν, ὕφασμα ‖ ~**s** *npl* ὑφαντά, ὑφάσματα.

texture ['tekstʃə*] *n* (*of surface*) ὑφή.

than [ðæn] *prep*,*cj* ἤ, παρά, ἀπό.

thank [θæŋk] *vt* εὐχαριστῶ ‖ ~**ful** *a* εὐγνώμων ‖ ~**fully** *ad* μέ εὐγνωμοσύνην, εὐγνωμόνως ‖ ~**less** *a* ἀγνώμων, ἀχάριστος, ἄχαρις ‖ ~**s** *excl* εὐχαριστῶ ‖ (*gratitude*) εὐγνωμοσύνη, εὐχαριστίαι ‖ T~**sgiving** *n* (*US: festival*) Ἡμέρα τῶν Εὐχαριστιῶν.

that [ðæt] *a* αὐτός, ἐκεῖνος ‖ *pron* ἐκεῖνος, ὁ ὁποῖος, πού ‖ *cj* ὅτι, ὥστε, διότι, νά ‖ *ad* τόσον, ἔτσι.

thatched [θætʃt] *a* (*cottage*) ἀχυροστρωμένος.

thaw [θɔ:] *n* τῆξις, λυώσιμο ‖ *vi* τήκομαι, λυώνω.

the [ði:, ðə] *definite article* ὁ, ἡ, τό, οἱ, αἱ, τά.

theater (*US*), **theatre** ['θiətə*] *n* θέατρον ‖ (*cinema*) σινεμά ‖ (*drama*) θεατρική τέχνη, δραματική τέχνη ‖ (*med*) ἀμφιθέατρον ‖ ~**goer** *n* θεατρόφιλος.

theatrical [θi'ætrikəl] *a* θεατρικός, θεαματικός ‖ (*showy*) θεατρινίστικος, προσποιητός.

theft [θeft] *n* κλοπή, κλεψιά.

their [ðɛə*] *poss a* δικός τους, δική τους ‖ ~**s** *poss pron* ἰδικός τους, δικοί τους.

them [ðem, ðəm] *pron* αὐτούς, αὐτές, αὐτά.

theme [θi:m] *n* θέμα, ὑπόθεσις ‖ (*melody*) θέμα, μοτίβο ‖ ~ **song** *n* (*of film etc*) κυρία μελωδία.

themselves [ðəm'selvz] *pl pron* τούς ἑαυτούς των ‖ αὐτοί οἱ ἴδιοι.

then [ðen] *ad* τότε, ἐκείνην τήν στιγμήν ‖ (*next*) κατόπιν, ἔπειτα, ἀκολούθως ‖ *cj* λήπόν, τότε, στήν περίπτωσιν αὐτήν ‖ ἐπί πλέον ‖ *n* ἐκείνη ἡ ἐποχή, ἐκεῖ.

theologian [θiə'ləudʒiən] *n* θεολόγος.

theological [θiə'lɔdʒikəl] *a* θεολογικός.

theology [θi'ɔlədʒi] n θεολογία.

theorem ['θiərəm] n θεώρημα.

theoretical [θiə'retikəl] a θεωρητικός ‖ ~**ly** ad θεωρητικῶς.

theorize ['θiəraiz] vi κάνω θεωρίες.

theory ['θiəri] n θεωρία ‖ (idea) ἰδέα.

therapeutic(al) [θerə'pju:tik(əl)] a θεραπευτικός.

therapist ['θerəpist] n θεραπευτής.

therapy ['θerəpi] n θεραπεία.

there [δεə*] ad ἐκεῖ, νά, ἕλα ‖ n ἐκεῖνος ἐκεῖ ‖ (interj) ἰδού, νά ‖ (never mind) ἕλα, ἕλα ‖ ~ is ὑπάρχει ‖ ~ are ὑπάρχουν ‖ ~**abouts** ad ἐκεῖ κοντά, περίπου ‖ ~**after** ad μετά ταῦτα, κατόπιν ‖ ~**fore** ad γι'αὐτό τό λόγο, ἐπομένως ‖ ~**'s** = **there is** ‖ see above.

thermal ['θə:məl] a θερμικός.

thermodynamics ['θə:məudai'næmiks] n θερμοδυναμική.

thermonuclear ['θə:məu'nju:kliə*] a θερμοπυρηνικός.

Thermos ['θə:məs] n ® (flask) θέρμο(ς).

thermostat ['θə:məstæt] n θερμοστάτης.

thesaurus [θi'sɔ:rəs] n θησαυρός, συλλογή λέξεων.

these [δi:z] pl pron αὐτοί, αὐτές, αὐτά.

thesis ['θi:sis] n θέμα, θέσις ‖ (univ) διατριβή.

they [δei] pl pron αὐτοί, αὐτές, αὐτά ‖ ~**'d** = **they had, they would**, see **have, would** ‖ ~**'ll** = **they shall, they will**, see **shall, will** ‖ ~**'re** = **they are**, see **be** ‖ ~**'ve** = **they have**, see **have**.

thick [θik] a χονδρός, παχύς, πυκνός, πηχτός ‖ (person: slow, stupid) κουτός, χονδροκέφαλος ‖ n: **in the** ~ **of** στή φούρια, στό δξύτερο σημεῖον ‖ ~**en** vi (fog) πυκνώνω, γίνομαι πυκνότερον ‖ vt (sauce etc) πήζω, πηχτώνω, δένω ‖ ~**ness** n (of object) πάχος, πυκνότης ‖ (of voice) βραχνάδα ‖ ~**set** a κοντόχοντρος ‖ ~**skinned** a παχύδερμος, χοντρόπετσος.

thief [θi:f] n κλέφτης, λωποδύτης.

thieves [θi:vz] npl of **thief**.

thieving ['θi:viŋ] n κλοπή, κλεψιά.

thigh [θai] n μηρός, μπούτι ‖ ~**bone** n μηριαῖον ὀστοῦν.

thimble ['θimbl] n δακτυλήθρα.

thin [θin] a λεπτός, ψηλός, ἀδύνατος ‖ (not abundant) ἀραιός, διεσπαρμένος ‖ (person) ἰσχνός, λιγνός, ἀδύνατος ‖ (crowd) ἀραιός, λιγοστός.

thing [θiŋ] n πρᾶγμα, ἀντικείμενον.

think [θiŋk] (irreg v) vi σκέπτομαι ‖ (believe) νομίζω ‖ (have in mind) σκοπεύω ‖ **to** ~ **over** vt σκέπτομαι, συλλογίζομαι ‖ **to** ~ **up** vt σκέπτομαι, καταστρώνω.

thinly ['θinli] ad (disguised) μόλις.

thinness ['θinnis] n λεπτότης, ἀδυναμία, ἀραιότης, ρευστότης.

third [θə:d] a τρίτος ‖ n τρίτος, τρίτον ‖ ~**ly** ad κατά τρίτον λόγον, τρίτον ‖

~-**party insurance** n ἀσφάλισις τρίτων ‖ ~-**rate** a τρίτης τάξεως, κακῆς ποιότητος.

thirst [θə:st] n δίψα ‖ (strong desire) δυνατή ἐπιθυμία, πόθος ‖ ~**y** a διψασμένος.

thirteen ['θə:'ti:n] num δεκατρία.

thirty ['θə:ti] num τριάντα.

this [δis] pron,a αὐτός, αὐτή, αὐτό ‖ τόσος.

thistle ['θisl] n γαϊδουράγκαθο.

thorn [θɔ:n] n ἀγκάθι ‖ (plant) ἀκανθώδης θάμνος, ἀγκάθι ‖ ~**y** a ἀγκαθωτός ‖ (problem) ἀκανθώδης.

thorough ['θʌrə] a πλήρης, τέλειος ‖ (accurate) λεπτομερής, ἐξονυχιστικός ‖ ~**bred** n καθαρόαιμος, ἀπό ράτσα ‖ a καθαρόαιμος ‖ ~**fare** n ὀδός, διάβασις, ἀρτηρία ‖ (main street) κεντρικός λεωφόρος, ἀρτηριακός ‖ ~**ly** ad τελείως, πλήρως, κατά βάθος ‖ ~**ness** n ἐπιμέλεια, τελειότης.

those [δəuz] pl pron αὐτές, αὐτοί, αὐτά ‖ a τοῦτοι, ἐκεῖνοι.

though [δəu] cj καίτοι, ἄν καί, μολονότι, ἀγκαλά καί ‖ ad παρά ταῦτα, μολοντούτο, κι'ὅμως.

thought [θɔ:t] n ἰδέα, σκέψις ‖ (thinking) σκέψις, συλλογισμός ‖ pt, pp of **think** ‖ ~**ful** a σοβαρός, σκεπτικός ‖ (also kind) διακριτικός, εὐγενικός ‖ ~**less** a ἀπερίσκεπτος, ἀπρόσεκτος, ἀδιάκριτος.

thousand ['θauzənd] num χίλιοι, χίλια ‖ ~**th** a χιλιοστόν.

thrash [θræʃ] vt (lit) κτυπῶ, δέρνω, ξυλοφορτώνω ‖ (fig) νικῶ.

thread [θred] n (of cotton, silk etc) νήμα, κλωστή ‖ (of screw) σπείρωμα, βῆμα, πάσο ‖ (of story) συνέχεια, εἰρμός ‖ vt (needle) βάζω κλωστή σέ, περνῶ ‖ vi (pick one's way) περνῶ μέ δυσκολία ‖ ~**bare** a ξεφτισμένος, παλιός.

threat [θret] n φοβέρα, φοβέρισμα ‖ (sign of danger) ἀπειλή ‖ ~**en** vti (person) ἀπειλῶ, φοβερίζω ‖ (storm) ἀπειλεῖται ‖ ~**ening** a ἀπειλητικός.

three [θri:] num τρεῖς, τρία ‖ ~-**dimensional** a τρισδιάστατος ‖ ~**fold** a τριπλός, τρίδιπλος ‖ ~-**piece suit** n (clothes) τρουαπιές ‖ ~-**ply** a (wool) τρίκλωνος ‖ ~-**wheeler** n (car) τρίτροχον (αὐτοκίνητον).

thresh [θreʃ] vt ἁλωνίζω ‖ ~**ing machine** n ἁλωνιστική μηχανή.

threshold ['θreʃhəuld] n (beginning) κατώφλι, ἀρχή ‖ (doorway) κατώφλι.

threw [θru:] pt of **throw**.

thrift [θrift] n (economy) οἰκονομία, ἀποταμίευσις ‖ ~**y** a οἰκονόμος, μετρημένος.

thrill [θril] n ρίγος, ἀνατριχίλα, σύγκρυο, τρεμούλα ‖ vt προκαλῶ ρίγος εἰς, συγκινῶ, ἠλεκτρίζω ‖ vi φρικιῶ, ριγῶ, τρέμω, ἀγωνιῶ ‖ ~**er** n μυθιστόρημα ἀγωνίας ‖ ~ing a συναρπαστικός, συγκλονιστικός, συγκινητικός.

thrive [θraiv] vi (+ on) εὐδοκιμῶ, εὐημερῶ, ἀναπτύσσομαι.

thriving [ˈθraiviŋ] a ἀκμαῖος, ρωμαλέος, ἀκμάζων, ἐπιτυχής.

throat [θrəut] n λαιμός ‖ (internal passages) φάρυγξ, λάρυγξ, λαρύγγι.

throb [θrɔb] n κτύπημα, παλμός, δόνησις ‖ vi κτυπῶ, πάλλομαι.

throes [θrəuz] npl: **in the ~ of** ἀγωνιζόμενος μέ, παλαιῶν μέ.

thrombosis [θrɔmˈbəusis] n θρόμβωσις.

throne [θrəun] n θρόνος.

throttle [ˈθrɔtl] n ρυθμιστική βαλβίς μηχανῆς, δικλείδα ‖ vt (choke) στραγγαλίζω.

through [θru:] prep διά μέσου, καθ'ὅλην τήν διάρκειαν τοῦ ‖ (because of) λόγω τοῦ, ἐξ αἰτίας τοῦ ‖ ad ἐξ ὁλοκλήρου, κατ'εὐθεῖαν, ἀπό τήν ἀρχήν μέχρι τό τέλος ‖ a (without a stop) κατ'εὐθεῖαν ‖ (end to end) πέρα γιά πέρα ‖ (ticket) ὁλοκλήρου διαδρομῆς (εἰσητήριον) ‖ (finished) τελειωμένος ‖ ~out prep εἰς ὁλόκληρον, εἰς ὅλον, παντοῦ εἰς ‖ ad παντοῦ, ὁλόκληρα.

throw [θrəu] (irreg v) n ρίξις, ρίξιμο, πέταγμα, βολή ‖ vt ρίπτω, πετῶ ‖ **to ~ out** vt (lit) ρίπτω, ρίχνω, πετῶ ἔξω ‖ (reject) ἀπορρίπτω, ἀποκρούω ‖ **to ~ up** vi (vomit) ἐξεμῶ, ξερνῶ, κάνω ἐμετό ‖ ~-in n (sport) ἐπανάληψις τοῦ παιγνιδιοῦ.

thru [θru:] (US) = through.

thrush [θrʌʃ] n κίχλη, τσίχλα.

thrust [θrʌst] (irreg v) n (tech) ὤθησις, ὤσις ‖ vti σπρώχνω, μπήγω ‖ (push one's way) διαπερνῶ, διασχίζω, περνῶ.

thud [θʌd] n γδοῦπος.

thug [θʌg] n γκάγκστερ, μπράβος.

thumb [θʌm] n ἀντίχειρ ‖ vt φυλλομετρῶ (βιβλίον), χειρίζομαι ἀδεξίως ‖ **to ~ a lift** κάνω ὦτο-στόπ ‖ ~ **index** n (on book) εὑρετήριον ‖ ~**nail** n νύχι τοῦ ἀντίχειρος ‖ ~**tack** n (US) πινέζα.

thump [θʌmp] n βαρύ κτύπημα, γροθιά ‖ vti κτυπῶ δυνατά, γρονθοκοπῶ.

thunder [ˈθʌndə*] n βροντή ‖ vi βροντῶ, βροντοφωνῶ ‖ ~**ous** a βροντώδης, θυελλώδης ‖ ~**storm** n καταιγίδα, θύελλα ‖ ~**struck** a ἐμβρόντητος, κατάπληκτος ‖ ~**y** a (weather, sky) θυελλώδης.

Thursday [ˈθə:zdi] n Πέμπτη.

thus [δʌs] ad οὕτω, τοιουτοτρόπως, ἔτσι ‖ (therefore) ἔτσι, λοιπόν.

thwart [θwɔ:t] vt ματαιώνω, ἀνατρέπω, ἐμποδίζω.

thyme [taim] n θυμάρι.

thyroid [ˈθaiɾɔid] n θυρεοειδής (ἀδήν).

tiara [tiˈɑ:rə] n διάδημα, τιάρα.

tic [tik] n (nervous) τίκ, σπάσμα, σπασμός.

tick [tik] n τίκ (ὡρολογιοῦ), λεπτόν ‖ (small mark) σημεῖον ἐλέγχου, τσεκάρισμα ‖ vi κτυπῶ, κάνω τίκ ‖ vt σημειώνω, τσεκάρω.

ticket [ˈtikit] n (for travel etc) εἰσητήριον, δελτίον ‖ (label) σημείωσις, ἐτικέττα ‖ ~ **collector** n ἐλεγκτής, εἰσπράκτωρ ‖ ~ **holder** n κάτοχος εἰσητηρίου ‖ ~ **office** n γραφεῖον ἐκδόσεως εἰσητηρίων.

ticking-off [ˈtikiŋˈɔf] n (col) ἐπίπληξις, κατσάδα.

tickle [ˈtikl] n γαργάλισμα ‖ vt γαργαλίζω, γαργαλῶ ‖ (amuse) διασκεδάζω.

ticklish [ˈtikliʃ] a πού γαργαλιέται εὔκολα ‖ (difficult) λεπτός, δύσκολος.

tidal [ˈtaidl] a παλιρροιακός.

tidbit [ˈtidbit] n (US) μεζές.

tide [taid] n παλίρροια, ρεῦμα ‖ (season) ἐποχή.

tidily [ˈtaidili] ad μέ τάξιν, καθαρά, τακτικά.

tidiness [ˈtaidinis] n τάξις, εὐπρέπεια.

tidy [ˈtaidi] a συγυρισμένος, τακτοποιημένος, σιαγμένος ‖ vt τακτοποιῶ, σιάζω, συγυρίζω.

tie [tai] n λαιμοδέτης, γραβάτα ‖ (connection) δεσμός, δέσιμο ‖ (sport) ἰσοπαλία ‖ vt προσδένω, δένω ‖ (into knot) δένω, κάνω κόμπο ‖ vi Ἔρχομαι ἰσόπαλος, ἰσοψηφῶ ‖ **to ~ down** vt (lit) στερεώνω, δένω καλά ‖ (fig) δεσμεύω ‖ **to ~ up** vt (dog) προσδένω, δένω ‖ (boat) δένω.

tier [tiə*] n στοῖχος, σειρά.

tiff [tif] n μικροτσακωμός, καυγαδάκι.

tiger [ˈtaigə*] n τίγρις.

tight [tait] a σφικτός, στερεός ‖ (stretched) τεντωμένος, τεζαρισμένος ‖ (close) στεγανός, ἑρμητικός ‖ (col) πιωμένος, σκνίπα ‖ (miserly) τσιγγούνης ‖ ~s npl ἐφαρμοστή κυλότα, μαγιό ‖ ~en vti σφίγγω, σφίγγομαι, τεζάρω ‖ ~-**fisted** a σφιχτοχέρης, σπαγγοραμμένος ‖ ~**ly** ad σφιχτοκλεισμένα, σφιχτά, γερά ‖ ~**ness** n στεγανότης, τέντωμα, στενότης ‖ ~**rope** n τεντωμένο σχοινί.

tile [tail] n (in roof) κεραμίδι ‖ (on wall or floor) πλακάκι ‖ ~**d** a (roof) μέ κεραμίδια.

till [til] n συρτάρι ταμείου ‖ vt καλλιεργῶ ‖ prep ἕως, ὡς, μέχρι ‖ cj ἕως ὅτου, ὡς πού.

tilt [tilt] vti γέρνω, κλίνω.

timber [ˈtimbə*] n ξυλεία ‖ (trees) δάσος, ὑψηλά δένδρα.

time [taim] n χρόνος ‖ (period) καιρός ‖ (hour) ὥρα ‖ (point in time) στιγμή, ὀλίγος, φορά ‖ (occasion) καιρός, ἐποχή ‖ (rhythm, speed) χρόνος, ρυθμός ‖ vt ρυθμίζω, χρονομετρῶ ‖ **in ~** ἐγκαίρως, ἐν καιρῷ ‖ (mus) μέτρον, χρόνος ‖ **on ~** στήν ὥρα ‖ **five ~s** πέντε φορές ‖ **local ~** τοπική ὥρα ‖ **what ~ is it?** τί ὥρα εἶναι; ‖ ~**keeper** n (sport) χρονομετρητής ‖ ~-**lag** n (in travel) διαφορά ὥρας ‖ ~**less** a (beauty) αἰώνιος, ἄφθαρτος ‖ ~ **limit** n χρονικόν ὅριον, προθεσμία ‖ ~ly *a* ἔγκαιρος, ἐπίκαιρος ‖ ~-saving *a* πού γλυτώνει χρόνον ‖ ~ switch *n* χρονοδιακόπτης ‖ ~table *n* δρομολόγιον, ὡρολόγιον πρόγραμμα ‖ ~ zone *n* ἄτρακτος χρόνου, ὡριαία ζώνη.

timid ['timid] *a* δειλός, φοβιτσιάρης ‖ ~ity *n* δειλία, ντροπαλότης ‖ ~ly *ad* δειλά, ντροπαλά.

timing ['taimiŋ] *n* ῥύθμισις, χρονισμός, χρονομέτρησις.

timpani ['timpəni] *npl* τύμπανα.

tin [tin] *n* κασσίτερος, καλάϊ ‖ (*container*) τενεκές, κουτί κονσέρβας ‖ ~foil *n* ἀσημόχαρτο, ἀλουμινόχαρτο, χρυσόχαρτο.

tinge [tindʒ] *n* χροιά, ἀπόχρωσις, δόσις ‖ *vt* χρωματίζω, βάφω.

tingle ['tiŋgl] *n* τσούξιμο, ἔξαψις, διέγερσις ‖ *vi* τσούζω, διεγείρομαι, τσιμπῶ.

tinker ['tiŋkə*] *n* γανωματᾶς ‖ to ~ with *vt* σκαλίζω, φτιάχνω ἀδέξια.

tinkle ['tiŋkl] *n* κουδούνισμα ‖ (*col: phone call*) τηλεφώνημα ‖ *vi* κουδουνίζω, ἠχῶ.

tinned [tind] *a* (*food*) κονσέρβα, τοῦ κουτιοῦ.

tin opener ['tinəupnə*] *n* ἀνοιχτήρι.

tinsel ['tinsəl] *n* γυαλιστερές κορδέλλες μετάλλου, ἀσημένια βροχή.

tint [tint] *n* χροιά, ἀπόχρωσις.

tiny ['taini] *a* μικροσκοπικός, μικρούτσικο.

tip [tip] *n* ἄκρη, ἄκρον, μύτη ‖ (*for protection*) σιδηρά ἄκρα, σίδερο, πετσάκι ‖ (*of money*) φιλοδώρημα, πουρμπουάρ ‖ (*useful hint*) ὑπαινιγμός, μυστική πληροφορία ‖ *vt* (*put end on*) προσθέτω ἄκρην εἰς ‖ γέρνω, ἀναποδογυρίζω ‖ (*waiter*) φιλοδωρῶ, δίνω πουρμπουάρ ‖ ~-off *n* (*hint*) πληροφορία, ὑπαινιγμός ‖ ~ped *a* (*cigarette*) μέ φίλτρο.

tipple ['tipl] *n* (*drink*) ποτόν.

tipsy ['tipsi] *a* μεθυσμένος, πιωμένος.

tiptoe ['tiptəu] *n*: on ~ ἀκροποδητί, στά νύχια.

tiptop ['tip'tɔp] *a*: in ~ condition σέ καλή φόρμα, πρώτης τάξεως.

tire ['taiə*] *n* (*US*) = tyre ‖ *vti* κουράζω, ἐξαντλῶ, κουράζομαι, βαριέμαι ‖ ~d *a* κουρασμένος, μπουχτισμένος, ἐξηντλημένος ‖ ~d of βαριέμαι, βαρέθηκα ἀπό ‖ ~dness *n* κόπωσις, κούραση ‖ ~less *a* ἀκούραστος, ἀκαταπόνητος ‖ ~lessly *ad* ἀκαταπόνητα, δραστήρια ‖ ~some *a* κουρασ τικός, βαρετός, ἐνοχλητικός.

tiring ['taiəriŋ] *a* κουραστικός, πληκτικός, ἀνιαρός.

tissue ['tiʃu:] *n* (*biol*) ἱστός, ὑφή ‖ (*collection*) σύμπλεγμα, δίκτυον ‖ (*paper handkerchief*) χαρτομάντηλο ‖ ~ paper *n* τσιγαρόχαρτο.

tit [tit] *n* (*bird*) αἰγίθαλος, καλόγηρο ‖ (*col: breast*) βυζί, μαστός ‖ ~ for tat ὀφθαλμόν ἀντί ὀφθαλμοῦ.

titbit ['titbit] *n* μεζές.

title ['taitl] *n* τίτλος, ἐπικεφαλίς ‖ (*rank etc*) τίτλος ‖ (*legal*) τίτλος, δικαίωμα ‖ (*sport*) (παγκόσμιος) τίτλος ‖ ~ deed *n* τίτλος κυριότητος, τίτλος ἰδιοκτησίας ‖ ~ rôle *n* πρῶτος ρόλος, ρόλος πού δίνει τόν τίτλον τοῦ ἔργου.

titter ['titə*] *vi* γελῶ ἀνόητα, κρυφογελῶ.

titular ['titjulə*] *a* ἐπίτιμος.

tizzy ['tizi] *n*: in a ~ χαμένα, σέ ἔξαψι, θυμωμένος.

to [tu:, tə] *prep* (*towards*) πρός, στό, σ' ‖ (*as far as*) μέχρι ‖ (*comparison*) πρός τό, ἔναντι ‖ (*for infin*) ἵνα, διά νά, γιά νά ‖ ~ and fro πάνω κάτω, πηγαινοέλα, ἀνεβοκατέβασμα.

toad [təud] *n* φρῦνος, βάτραχος, μπούφος ‖ ~stool *n* βωλήτης ὁ δηλητηριώδης (μανιτάρι) ‖ ~y *n* κωλογλείφτης, γαλίφης.

toast [təust] *n* φρυγανιά ‖ (*drink*) πρόποσις ‖ *vt* (*drink*) κάνω πρόποσιν ‖ (*brown*) ψήνω, φρυγανίζω ‖ (*warm*) ζεσταίνω ‖ ~er *n* φρυγανιέρα ‖ ~master *n* προϊστάμενος τῶν προπόσεων ‖ ~ rack *n* δίσκος γιά τίς φρυγανιές.

tobacco [tə'bækəu] *n* καπνός ‖ ~nist *n* καπνοπώλης ‖ ~nist's (shop) *n* καπνοπωλεῖον.

toboggan [tə'bɔgən] *n* ἔλκηθρον, τόμπογκαν.

today [tə'dei] *n* (ἡ) σήμερον, (τό) σήμερα ‖ *ad* σήμερα ‖ (*present time*) σήμερα, τώρα.

toddle ['tɔdl] *vi* στρατουλίζω.

toddy ['tɔdi] *n* (*warm, alcoholic drink*) ζεστό γκρόγκ.

to-do [tə'du:] *n* (*fuss*) φασαρία, σαματάς.

toe [təu] *n* δάκτυλος τοῦ ποδός ‖ *vt*: to ~ the line (*fig*) ὑπακούω, ὑποτάσσομαι ‖ ~nail *n* νύχι τοῦ ποδιοῦ.

toffee ['tɔfi] *n* καραμέλλα μέ βούτυρο ‖ ~ apple *n* ζαχαρωμένο μῆλο.

together [tə'geðə*] *ad* μαζί, μόνοι, ὁ ἕνας μέ τόν ἄλλον ‖ (*at the same time*) ὁμοῦ, μαζί, συγχρόνως ‖ ~ness *n* πνεῦμα συνεργασίας.

toil [tɔil] *n* μόχθος, κόπος, σκληρή δουλειά ‖ *vi* μοχθῶ, ἐργάζομαι σκληρά.

toilet ['tɔilit] *n* (*lavatory*) ἀποχωρητήριον, μέρος ‖ *a* τῆς τουαλέττας ‖ ~ paper *n* χαρτί καμπινέτου, χάρτης ὑγείας ‖ ~ries *npl* εἴδη τουαλέττας ‖ ~ roll *n* ρολλό χαρτιοῦ καμπινέτου ‖ ~ soap *n* σαπούνι τουαλέττας ‖ ~ water *n* κολώνια, ὀ-ντέ-κολόν.

token ['təukən] *n* ἔνδειξις, τεκμήριον, σημεῖον.

told [təuld] *pt, pp* of **tell**.

tolerable ['tɔlərəbl] *a* ἀνεκτός, ὑποφερτός ‖ (*moderate*) καλούτσικος.

tolerably ['tɔlərəbli] *ad* ἀνεκτά, ὑποφερτά.

tolerance ['tɔlərəns] *n* ἀνοχή, ἀνεκτικότης ‖ (*engineering*) ἀνοχή.

tolerant ['tɔlərənt] *a* ἀνεκτικός ‖ ~**ly** *ad* ἀνεκτικά.

tolerate ['tɔləreit] *vt* ἀνέχομαι, ὑποφέρω.

toleration [tɔlə'reiʃən] *n* ἀνοχή, ἀνεκτικότης.

toll [tɔul] *n* (*tax, charge*) διόδια, φόρος ‖ *vi* (*bell*) κτυπῶ (καμπάνα), καμπανίζω ‖ ~**bridge** *n* γέφυρα μέ διόδια ‖ ~ **road** *n* ὁδός μέ διόδια.

tomato [tə'mɑːtəu] *n* ντομάτα.

tomb [tuːm] *n* τύμβος, τάφος.

tomboy ['tɔmbɔi] *n* ἀγορακόριτσο.

tombstone ['tuːmstəun] *n* ἐπιτύμβιος λίθος.

tomcat ['tɔmkæt] *n* γάτος.

tomorrow [tə'mɔrəu] *n* αὔριον, αὐριανή ἡμέρα ‖ *ad* αὔριον.

ton [tʌn] *n* τόννος (2240 λίμπρες) ‖ (*US*) τόννος (2000 λίμπρες) ‖ ~**s of** (*col*) μεγάλη ποσότης, πολλές φορές.

tonal ['təunl] *a* τονικός.

tone [təun] *n* τόνος, ἦχος ‖ (*character*) τόνος, πνεῦμα, τάσις ‖ (*colour*) τόνος, ἀπόχρωσις ‖ *vi* συντονίζομαι, ταιριάζω ‖ *vt* τονίζω, τονώνω, ρυθμίζω ‖ **to ~ down** *vt* ἀπαλύνω, μαλακώνω, μετριάζω.

tongs [tɔŋz] *npl* λαβίδα, τσιμπίδα, μασιά.

tongue [tʌŋ] *n* γλῶσσα ‖ (*ox tongue: food*) βοδινή γλῶσσα ‖ **with ~ in cheek** εἰρωνικά ‖ ~**-tied** *a* σιωπῶν, βωβός (ἀπό κατάπληξιν) ‖ ~ **twister** *n* γλωσσοδέτης.

tonic ['tɔnik] *n* τονωτικόν, δυναμωτικόν ‖ (*mus*) τονική, βασική νότα ‖ ~ **water** *n* τόνικ (σόδα).

tonight [tə'nait] *n* σήμερα τό βράδυ ‖ *ad* ἀπόψε.

tonnage ['tʌnidʒ] *n* χωρητικότης, τοννάζ.

tonne [tʌn] *n* (*metric ton*) μετρικός τόννος.

tonsil ['tɔnsl] *n* ἀμυγδαλῆ ‖ ~**itis** *n* ἀμυγδαλῖτις.

too [tuː] *ad* πολύ, πάρα πολύ, ὑπερβολικά ‖ (*also*) ἐπίσης, ὡσαύτως, ὁμοίως.

took [tuk] *pt of* **take.**

tool [tuːl] *n* ἐργαλεῖον ‖ ~**box** *n* κιβώτιον ἐργαλείων ‖ ~**kit** *n* ἐργαλειοθήκη, κιβώτιον ἐργαλείων.

toot [tuːt] *n* κορνάρισμα ‖ *vi* κορνάρω.

tooth [tuːθ] *n* δόντι ‖ (*on gearwheel*) δόντι, δόντι ‖ ~**ache** *n* πονόδοντος, ὀδοντόπονος ‖ ~**brush** *n* ὀδοντόβουρτσα ‖ ~**paste** *n* ὀδοντόπαστα ‖ ~**pick** *n* ὀδοντογλυφίδα ‖ ~**powder** *n* σκόνη γιά τά δόντια.

top [tɔp] *n* κορυφή, κορφή, ἀπάνω (μέρος) ‖ (*at school*) πρῶτος, καλύτερος ‖ (*spinning toy*) σβούρα ‖ *a* ἀνώτερος, ψηλότερος ‖ *vt* (*list*) εἶμαι ἐπί κεφαλῆς, εἶμαι πρῶτος ‖ **from ~ to toe** ἀπό κορυφῆς μέχρις ὀνύχων ‖ ~**coat** *n* παλτό ‖ ~**flight** *a* (*first-class*) ἀνώτερος, κορυφαῖος ‖ ~**hat** *n* ὑψηλό καπέλλο ‖ ~**-heavy** *a* ἀσταθής, βαρύς στήν κορυφήν.

topic ['tɔpik] *n* θέμα, ζήτημα ‖ ~**al** *a* ἐπίκαιρος.

top-level ['tɔp'levl] *a* ὑψηλοῦ ἐπιπέδου.

topmost ['tɔpməust] *a* ὑψηλότατος, κορυφαῖος, ὕψιστος.

topple ['tɔpl] *vti* κλονίζομαι, πέφτω, ἀναποδογυρίζω.

top-secret ['tɔp'siːkrit] *a* αὐστηρῶς ἀπόρρητον.

topsy-turvy ['tɔpsi'təːvi] *a,ad* ἄνω-κάτω, κουλουβάχατα.

torch [tɔːtʃ] *n* (*electric*) φακός, φανάρι ‖ (*Olympic*) πυρσός, λαμπάδα, δαυλί.

tore ['tɔː*] *pt of* **tear.**

torment ['tɔːment] *n* βασανιστήριον, μαρτύριον ‖ [tɔː'ment] *vt* ἐνοχλῶ, πειράζω ‖ (*distress*) βασανίζω, τυραννῶ.

torn [tɔːn] *pp of* **tear** ‖ *a* (*undecided*) (+ *between*) ταλαντευόμενος, ἀναποφάσιστος.

tornado [tɔː'neidəu] *n* ἀνεμοστρόβιλος, λαῖλαψ.

torpedo [tɔː'piːdəu] *n* τορπίλλη.

torpor ['tɔːpə*] *n* νάρκη, νωθρότης, ἀδράνεια.

torrent ['tɔrənt] *n* χείμαρρος ‖ ~**ial** *a* χειμαρρώδης.

torso ['tɔːsəu] *n* κορμός, τόρσο.

tortoise ['tɔːtəs] *n* χελώνα.

tortuous ['tɔːtjuəs] *a* ἑλικοειδής, στρεβλός ‖ (*deceitful*) ἀνέντιμος, δόλιος.

torture ['tɔːtʃə*] *n* βασανιστήριον, βασανισμός, μαρτύριον ‖ *vt* βασανίζω.

Tory ['tɔːri] *n* συντηρητικός ‖ *a* συντηρητικός, δεξιός.

toss [tɔs] *vt* πετῶ, τραντάζω ‖ (*in the air*) ρίχνω, πετῶ ‖ *n* (*of coin to decide*) στρίψιμο ‖ **to ~ a coin, to ~ up for sth** ρίχνω κορώνα-γράμματα.

tot [tɔt] *n* ποτηράκι, γουλιά ‖ (*child*) παιδάκι, μωρό, μπέμπης.

total ['təutl] *n* σύνολον, ὅλον, ἄθροισμα, σοῦμα ‖ *a* (συν)ὁλικός, ὁλόκληρος, τέλειος ‖ *vt* προσθέτω, ἀθροίζω ‖ (*amount to*) συμποσοῦμαι εἰς, φθάνω ‖ ~**ity** *n* σύνολον, ὁλότης ‖ ~**ly** *ad* συνολικῶς, πλήρως, τελείως.

totem pole ['təutəmpəul] *n* στήλη τοῦ τότεμ.

totter ['tɔtə*] *vi* παραπαίω, τρικλίζω.

touch [tʌtʃ] *n* ἁφή, ἐπαφή, ἄγγισμα, γγίξιμο ‖ (*sense*) ἐπαφή, ἁφή ‖ (*small amount*) μικρά δόσις, ἴχνος, ὑποψία ‖ (*style*) πινελιά, μολυβιά, ὕφος ‖ *vt* ἅπτομαι, ψαύω, ἀγγίζω ‖ (*come against*) ἐφάπτομαι, ἀκουμπῶ ‖ (*move*) θίγω, συγκινῶ ‖ **in ~ with** σ'ἐπαφή μέ, (διατηρῶ) ἐπαφήν, παρακολούθησις ‖ **to ~ on** *vt* (*topic*) θίγω (θέμα) ‖ **to ~ up** *vt* (*paint*) ρετουσάρω, τονίζω ‖ ~**-and-go** *a* ἐπικίνδυνος, ἀβέβαιος, ἐπισφαλής ‖ ~**down** *n* προσγείωσις ‖ ~**iness** *n* εὐθιξία ‖ ~**ing** *a* συγκινητικός, παθητικός ‖ ~**line** *n* γραμμή τοῦ τέρματος ‖ ~**y** *a* (ὑπερ)ευαίσθητος, εὔθικτος.

tough [tʌf] *a* σκληρός, στερεός, ἀλύγιστος ‖ *(difficult)* δυσχερής, σκληρός, δύσκολος ‖ *(meat)* σκληρός ‖ *n (gangster etc)* κακοποιός, μπράβος ‖ ~**en** *vti* σκληραίνω, σκληρύνομαι ‖ ~**ness** *n* σκληρότης, ἀντοχή.

toupée [ˈtuːpeɪ] *n (wig)* περούκα.

tour [ˈtuə*] *n* περιοδεία, περιήγησις ‖ *vi* περιηγοῦμαι, περιοδεύω ‖ ~**ing** *n* τουρισμός, περιοδεία ‖ ~**ism** *n* τουρισμός ‖ ~**ist** *n* τουρίστας, περιηγητής ‖ ~**ist office** *n* τουριστικῶν γραφεῖον.

tournament [ˈtuənəmənt] *n* πρωτάθλημα, τουρνουά.

tousled [ˈtauzld] *a (hair)* ἀναστατωμένα, ξεχτένιστα.

tow [təu] *n (pull)* ρυμούλκησις ‖ *vt (pull)* ρυμουλκῶ.

toward(s) [təˈwɔːd(z)] *prep* πρός, κατά, διά, γιά.

towel [ˈtauəl] *n* πρόσοψι, πετσέτα.

tower [ˈtauə*] *n* πύργος ‖ ~**ing** *a* πανύψηλος ‖ *(rage)* βίαιος, ἄγριος.

towline [ˈtəulain] *n* ρυμούλκιον, γεντέκι.

town [taun] *n* πόλις, πολιτεία, χώρα ‖ ~ **clerk** *n* γραμματεύς δημαρχίας ‖ ~ **hall** *n* δημαρχεῖον ‖ ~ **planner** *n* πολεοδόμος ‖ ~ **planning** *n* πολεοδομία.

towpath [ˈtəupaːθ] *n (along canal)* δρομάκος ρυμουλκήσεως ποταμοπλοίων.

towrope [ˈtəurəup] *n* ρυμούλκιον, γεντέκι.

toxic [ˈtɔksik] *a* τοξικός.

toy [tɔi] *n* παιχνίδι, παιχνιδάκι ‖ **to** ~ **with** *vt* παίζω μέ ‖ σκέπτομαι νά.

trace [treis] *n* ἴχνος ‖ *(small amount)* ἴχνος, ὑπόλειμμα, ‖ *vt* παρακολουθῶ ‖ *(find out)* ἀνιχνεύω, διακρίνω ‖ *(copy)* χαράσσω, ἀντιγράφω, ξεσηκώνω.

track [træk] *n* ἴχνη, πέρασμα, πατημασιές ‖ *(road, path)* ἀτραπός, μονοπάτι, δρομάκος ‖ *(racing)* διάδρομος ἀγώνων, στίβος, πίστα ‖ *(rail)* (σιδηροδρομική) γραμμή ‖ *vt* παρακολουθῶ, καταδιώκω ‖ **to keep** ~ **of** παρακολουθῶ, βρίσκομαι εἰς ἐπαφήν μέ ‖ **to make** ~**s for** κατευθύνομαι, πηγαίνω βιαστικά ‖ **to** ~ **down** *vt* ἀνακαλύπτω, βρίσκω ‖ ~**er dog** *n* κυνηγόσκυλο ‖ ~**less** *a* ἀδιάβατος, χωρίς μονοπάτια.

tract [trækt] *n* περιοχή, ἔκτασις ‖ *(book)* φυλλάδιον.

tractor [ˈtræktə*] *n* ἑλκυστήρ, τρακτέρ.

trade [treid] *n* ἐμπόριον ‖ *(business)* ἐπάγγελμα, δουλειά ‖ *(people)* συντεχνία, κλάδος, συνάφι ‖ *vi (+in)* ἐμπορεύομαι, συναλλάσσομαι, κάνω δουλειές ‖ ~**mark** *n* σῆμα (κατατεθέν) ‖ ~ **name** *n* ἐμπορική ἐπωνυμία, φίρμα ‖ ~**r** *n* ἔμπορος ‖ ~**sman** *n* καταστηματάρχης, προμηθευτής, ἐπαγγελματίας ‖ *(skilled workman)* τεχνίτης ‖ ~ **union** *n* ἐργατική ἕνωσις, συνδικάτον ‖ ~ **unionist** *n* συνδικαλιστής.

trading [ˈtreidiŋ] *n* ἐμπόριον ‖ ~ **stamp** *n* δελτίον ἐκπτώσεως.

tradition [trəˈdiʃən] *n* παράδοσις ‖ ~**s** *npl* παραδόσεις ‖ ~**al** *a* ἐκ παραδόσεως, πατροπαράδοτος ‖ ~**ally** *ad* κατά παράδοσιν.

traffic [ˈtræfik] *n* κίνησις, κυκλοφορία ‖ *(esp in drugs)* ἐμπόριον, συναλλαγή, δοσοληψία ‖ *vt (esp drugs)* ἐμπορεύομαι (κάτι) ‖ ~ **circle** *n (US: roundabout)* κυκλοφοριακός δρόμος ‖ ~ **jam** *n* συνωστισμός ‖ ~ **lights** *npl* φανάρια, φῶτα κυκλοφορίας.

tragedy [ˈtrædʒidi] *n* τραγωδία, δράμα.

tragic [ˈtrædʒik] *a* τραγικός ‖ ~**ally** *ad* τραγικά.

trail [treil] *n* ἴχνος, πατήματα ‖ *(something trailing)* γραμμή (καπνοῦ), οὐρά ‖ *(rough road)* μονοπάτι ‖ *vi (follow)* σέρνομαι πίσω ‖ *(hang loosely)* σέρνομαι, σέρνω ‖ **on the** ~ ἐπί τά ἴχνη ‖ **to** ~ **behind** *vi* σέρνομαι πίσω ‖ ~**er** *n (truck)* ρυμουλκούμενον ὄχημα ‖ *(film)* ἀπόσπασμα ταινίας ‖ *(US: caravan)* τροχόσπιτο.

train [trein] *n* συρμός ἁμαξοστοιχίας, τραῖνο ‖ *(of gown)* οὐρά ‖ *(series)* σειρά, ἀλληλουχία, εἱρμός ‖ *vt* ἐκπαιδεύω, διδάσκω, μαθαίνω ‖ *(plant)* κατευθύνω, ὁδηγῶ ‖ *(point gun)* σκοπεύω, διευθύνω ‖ *vi (exercise)* προπονῶ, προγυμνάζω ‖ ~**ed** *a* ἐκγυμνασμένος, ἐξησκημένος ‖ ~**ee** *n* ἀσκούμενος μαθητής ‖ ~**er** *n* ἐκπαιδευτής, προπονητής, γυμναστής ‖ ~**ing** *n* ἐκπαίδευσις, ἐξάσκησις, προπόνησις ‖ **in** ~**ing** σέ φόρμα ‖ ~**ing college** *n* ἐπαγγελματική σχολή, διδασκαλεῖον.

traipse [treips] *vi (wander)* σέρνομαι ἐδῶ καί κεῖ, σουρτουκεύω.

trait [treit] *n* χαρακτηριστικόν.

traitor [ˈtreitə*] *n* προδότης.

tram(car) [ˈtræm(kaː*)] *n* τράμ ‖ ~ **line** *n* τροχιοδρομική γραμμή, γραμμή τράμ.

tramp [træmp] *n (vagabond)* ἀλήτης ‖ *vi* περπατῶ βαρειά, βηματίζω βαρειά ‖ *(by foot)* πεζοπορῶ, πηγαίνω πεζῆ ‖ ~ **le** *vt* (ποδο)πατῶ, καταπατῶ ‖ ~**oline** *n* τραμπολῖνο.

trance [traːns] *n* ἔκστασις, ὕπνωσις, δράμα.

tranquil [ˈtræŋkwil] *a* ἤρεμος, ἥσυχος ‖ ~**ity** *n* ἠρεμία ‖ ~**lizer** *n (drug)* καταπραϋντικόν.

trans- [trænz] *prefix* διά μέσου, πέραν, στήν ἄλλη πλευράν.

transact [trænˈzækt] *vt* ἐκτελῶ, διεξάγω, διεκπεραιώνω ‖ ~**ion** *n* διεκπεραίωσις, διεξαγωγή, συναλλαγή.

transatlantic [ˈtrænzətˈlæntik] *a* ὑπερατλαντικός.

transcend [trænˈsend] *vt* ὑπερέχω, ὑπερβαίνω.

transcript [ˈtrænskript] *n* ἀντίγραφον, ἀντιγραφή ‖ ~**ion** *n* ἀντιγραφή, ἀντίγραφον.

transept ['trænsept] n πτέρυξ ναοῦ, ἐγκάρσιον κλίτος.

transfer ['trænsfə*] n μεταφορά, μετάθεσις ‖ (legal) μεταβίβασις, ἐκχώρησις, μεταγραφή ‖ (design) χαλκομανία, στάμπα, ἀντιγραφή ‖ (sport) μεταβίβασις, μεταφορά ‖ [træns'fə:*] vt μεταφέρω, μεταθέτω, ἀλλάζω ‖ ~able a μεταβιβάσιμος, μεταφερτός ‖ 'not ~able' (on ticket) 'προσωπικόν'.

transform [træns'fɔːm] vt μετασχηματίζω, μεταβάλλω, μεταμορφώνω ‖ ~ation n μετασχηματισμός, μεταβολή, μεταμόρφωσις ‖ ~er n (elec) μετασχηματιστής.

transfusion [træns'fjuːʒən] n μετάγγισις.

transient ['trænziənt] a παροδικός.

transistor [træn'zistə*] n κρυσταλλικός πολλαπλασιαστής ‖ (radio) τρανσίστορ, φορητό ραδιόφωνο.

transit ['trænzit] n: in ~ (κατά) τήν μεταφοράν, ὑπό μεταφοράν.

transition [træn'ziʃən] n μετάβασις, μεταβολή, ἀλλαγή ‖ ~al a μεταβατικός.

transitive ['trænzitiv] a μεταβατικόν (ρῆμα) ‖ ~ly ad μεταβατικῶς.

transitory ['trænzitəri] a παροδικός, βραχύς, ἐφήμερος.

translate [trænz'leit] vt μεταφράζω.

translation [trænz'leiʃən] n μετάφρασις.

translator [trænz'leitə*] n μεταφραστής.

transmission [trænz'miʃən] n (of information) μεταβίβασις, διαβίβασις, μετάδοσις ‖ (aut) μετάδοσις ‖ (rad) ἐκπομπή, μετάδοσις, διάδοσις.

transmit [trænz'mit] vt μεταδίδω, μεταβιβάζω, διαβιβάζω ‖ ~ter n πομπός.

transparency [træns'peərənsi] n (phot: slide) πλάξ προβολῆς, σλάϊντ.

transparent [træns'peərənt] a διαφανής, διαυγής, καθαρός.

transplant [træns'plaːnt] vt μεταφυτεύω, μεταφέρω ‖ ['trænsplaːnt] n (also med) μεταφύτευσις, μεταμόσχευσις.

transport ['trænspɔːt] n μεταφορά ‖ [træns'pɔːt] vt μεταφέρω ‖ means of ~ μέσα συγκοινωνίας ‖ ~able a μετακομιστός, φορητός ‖ ~ation n μεταφορά, συγκοινωνία.

transverse ['trænzvəːs] a ἐγκάρσιος.

trap [træp] n (trick) παγίδα, ἀπάτη ‖ (snare) παγίδα, φάκα ‖ (carriage) δίτροχος ἅμαξα, σούστα ‖ (col: mouth) στόμα ‖ vt παγιδεύω, πιάνω στήν παγίδα ‖ ~door n καταπακτή.

trapeze [trə'piːz] n τραπέζιον.

trapper ['træpə*] n κυνηγός, παγιδευτής.

trappings ['træpiŋz] npl διακόσμησις, στολίδια.

trash [træʃ] n σκουπίδια, φτηνολόϊ ‖ (nonsense) μπούρδες, τρίχες ‖ ~ can n (US) σκουπιδοτενεκές ‖ ~y a μηδαμινός, τῆς πεντάρας.

trauma ['trɔːmə] n τραῦμα ‖ ~tic a τραυματικός.

travel ['trævl] n ταξίδι, περιήγησις ‖ vi ταξιδεύω, κάνω ταξίδια ‖ vt (distance) πηγαίνω, βαδίζω, προχωρῶ, μετακινοῦμαι ‖ ~ler, (US) ~er n ταξιδιώτης ‖ (salesman) πλασιέ, ἀντιπρόσωπος ‖ ~ler's cheque, (US) ~er's check n ταξιδιωτική ἐπιταγή, τράβελλερς τσέκ ‖ ~ling, (US) ~ing n τά ταξίδια ‖ attr a ταξιδιωτικός, τοῦ ταξιδίου ‖ ~ sickness n ναυτία, ἀναγούλα.

traverse ['trævəs] vt διασχίζω, διαβαίνω, περνῶ.

travesty ['trævisti] n διακωμώδησις, παρωδία.

trawler ['trɔːlə*] n ἁλιευτικόν, τράτα.

tray [trei] n δίσκος.

treacherous ['tretʃərəs] a (person) δόλιος, ὕπουλος ‖ (road: dangerous, icy etc) ἐπικίνδυνος, ἄστατος.

treachery ['tretʃəri] n δολιότης, προδοσία, ἀπιστία.

treacle ['triːkl] n μελάσσα, πετιμέζι.

tread [tred] (irreg v) n περπάτημα ‖ (way of walking) βῆμα, βηματισμός ‖ (stair, tyre) βαθμίς, πάτημα, πέλμα ἐλαστικοῦ ‖ vi βαδίζω, περπατῶ ‖ to ~ on vt (ποδο)πατῶ.

treason ['triːzn] n προδοσία.

treasure ['treʒə*] n θησαυρός, χρῆμα, πλούτη ‖ vt ἀποθησαυρίζω ‖ (value highly) ἐκτιμῶ, θεωρῶ πολύτιμον ‖ ~ hunt n θησαυροθηρία ‖ ~r n ταμίας.

treasury ['treʒəri] n θησαυροφυλάκειον, ταμεῖον.

treat [triːt] n εὐχαρίστησις, ἀπόλαυσις ‖ vt μεταχειρίζομαι, φέρομαι ‖ (entertain) κερνῶ, προσφέρω.

treatise ['triːtiz] n πραγματεία, διατριβή.

treatment ['triːtmənt] n μεταχείρησις, περιποίησις, κούρα, θεραπεία.

treaty ['triːti] n συνθήκη.

treble ['trebl] a τριπλός, τριπλάσιος ‖ vt τριπλασιάζω ‖ n πρίμο ‖ (voice) ὑψίφωνος, σοπράνο ‖ ~ clef n κλειδί τοῦ σόλ.

tree [triː] n δένδρον, δέντρο ‖ ~ trunk n κορμός δένδρου.

trek [trek] n ταξίδι, μετανάστευσις ‖ vi (migrate) μετοικῶ, μεταναστεύω.

trellis ['trelis] n δικτυωτόν πλέγμα, καφασωτόν πλαίσιον.

tremble ['trembl] vi τρέμω, δονοῦμαι.

trembling ['trembliŋ] n τρόμος, τρεμούλα ‖ a τρέμων, τρεμουλιάρης.

tremendous [trə'mendəs] a (vast) πελώριος, τρομερός ‖ ~ly ad τρομερά, ὑπερβολικά, ἀφάνταστα.

tremor ['tremə*] n τρεμούλιασμα.

trench [trentʃ] n τάφρος, αὐλάκι, χαντάκι ‖ (of war) χαράκωμα.

trend [trend] n τάσις, πορεία ‖ vi τείνω.

trepidation [trepi'deiʃən] n φόβος, τρόμος, τρεμούλα.

trespass ['trespəs] *vi* καταπατῶ ‖ '~ers will be prosecuted' 'ἀπαγορεύεται ἡ εἴσοδος'.

tress [tres] *n* βόστρυχος, πλεξούδα, κοτσίδα, μπούκλα.

trestle ['tresl] *n* ὑποβάτης, βάσταξ, καβαλέτο ‖ ~ **table** *n* τραπέζι σέ καβαλέτο.

tri- [trai] *prefix* τρι-.

trial ['traiəl] *n* (*in court*) δίκη, κρίσις ‖ (*test*) δοκιμή ‖ (*hardship*) δοκιμασία, βάσανο ‖ **by ~ and error** διά δοκιμῆς καί πλάνης, ψαχτά.

triangle ['traiæŋgl] *n* τρίγωνον.

triangular [trai'æŋgjulə*] *a* τριγωνικός.

tribal ['traibəl] *a* φυλετικός.

tribe [traib] *n* φυλή ‖ ~**sman** *n* μέλος φυλῆς.

tribulation [tribju'leiʃən] *n* δοκιμασία, συμφορά, πάθημα.

tribunal [trai'bju:nl] *n* δικαστήριον.

tributary ['tribjutəri] *n* παραπόταμος.

tribute ['tribju:t] *n* (*respect*) φόρος τιμῆς.

trice [trais] *n*: **in a ~** στή στιγμή.

trick [trik] *n* τέχνασμα, κόλπο, κατεργαριά ‖ (*clever act*) δεξιοτεχνία, ταχυδακτυλουργία ‖ (*habit*) συνήθεια ‖ (*cards*) κόλπο, πιάσιμο, λεβέ ‖ *vt* ἐξαπατῶ ‖ ~**ery** *n* ἀπάτη, κοροϊδία.

trickle ['trikl] *n* λεπτή ροή, στάξιμο, στάλα (νεροῦ) ‖ *vi* σταλάζω, στάζω.

tricky ['triki] *a* (*problem, situation*) περίπλοκος, δύσκολος.

tricycle ['traisikl] *n* τρίκυκλον.

tried [traid] *pt, pp of* **try** ‖ *a* δοκιμασμένος, ἀξιόπιστος.

trier ['traiə*] *n* (*person who tries hard*) ὁ δοκιμάζων ἐπίμονα.

trifle ['traifl] *n* εἶδος τούρτας ‖ (*of little importance*) μικροπρᾶγμα, ἀσήμαντον γεγονός, μηδαμινόν ποσόν.

trifling ['traifliŋ] *a* ἀσήμαντος, τιποτένιος.

trigger ['trigə*] *n* σκανδάλη.

trigonometry [trigə'nɔmitri] *n* τριγωνομετρία.

trilby ['trilbi] *n* μαλακό καπέλλο, ρεπούμπλικα.

trim [trim] *a* τακτικός, κομψός, εὐπρεπής ‖ *n* τάξις, φόρμα, εὐπρεπής κατάστασις ‖ (*haircut etc*) κόψιμο, φρεσκάρισμα (μαλλιῶν) ‖ *vt* κόβω, κουρεύω, κλαδεύω ‖ (*decorate*) γαρνίρω ‖ ~**mings** *npl* γαρνιτούρες.

Trinity ['triniti] *n*: **the ~** (*rel*) Ἁγία Τριάς.

trinket ['triŋkit] *n* μικρόν κόσμημα, μπρελόκ, μπιμπελό.

trio ['triəu] *n* τριάδα ‖ (*mus*) τρίο.

trip [trip] *n* ἐκδρομή, ταξίδι ‖ (*stumble*) παραπάτημα, τρικλοποδιά ‖ *vi* περπατῶ ἐλαφρά, ἀλαφροπατῶ ‖ (*stumble*) σκοντάφτω, παραπατῶ ‖ **to ~ over** *vt* σκοντάφτω σέ ‖ **to ~ up** *vi* ἀναβαίνω ἐλαφροπατόντας ‖ *vt* βάζω τρικλοποδιά σέ.

tripe [traip] *n* (*food*) πατσᾶς ‖ (*rubbish*) ἀνοησίες, μπούρδες.

triple ['tripl] *a* τριπλός, τρίδιπλος ‖ ~**ts** *npl* τρίδυμα.

triplicate ['triplikit] *n*: **in ~** εἰς τριπλοῦν.

tripod ['traipɔd] *n* τρίπους, τρίποδο.

tripper ['tripə*] *n* ἐκδρομεύς.

trite [trait] *a* τετριμμένος, κοινός, κοινοτοπικός.

triumph ['traiʌmf] *n* θρίαμβος ‖ *vi* θριαμβεύω ‖ ~**al** *a* θριαμβικός ‖ ~**ant** *a* θριαμβευτικός ‖ ~**antly** *ad* θριαμβευτικά.

trivial ['triviəl] *a* ἀσήμαντος, τιποτένιος ‖ ~**ity** *n* ἀσημαντότης, κοινοτοπία.

trod [trɔd] *pt of* **tread** ‖ ~**den** *pp of* **tread**.

trolley ['trɔli] *n* (*small truck*) καρροτσάκι ‖ ~ **bus** *n* τρόλλεϋ.

trombone [trɔm'bəun] *n* τρομπόνι.

troop [tru:p] *n* ὁμάς, ἴλη, παρέα ‖ ~**s** *npl* στρατεύματα ‖ **to ~ in, out** *vi* εἰσέρχομαι, ἐξέρχομαι ὁμαδικῶς ‖ ~**er** *n* ἱππεύς, ἔφιππος ἀστυνομικός ‖ **T~** of Capri-**corn** *n* Τροπικὸς τοῦ Αἰγόκερω ‖ ~**al** *a* τροπικός.

trophy ['trəufi] *n* τρόπαιον, ἔπαθλον.

tropic ['trɔpik] *n* τροπικός ‖ **the ~s** *npl* τροπικαί (χῶραι) ‖ **T~** of Cancer *n* Τροπικὸς τοῦ Καρκίνου ‖ **T~** of Capri-**corn** *n* Τροπικὸς τοῦ Αἰγόκερω ‖ ~**al** *a* τροπικός.

trot [trɔt] *n* τριποδισμός, ἐλαφρό τρέξιμο ‖ *vi* τρέχω σιγά.

trouble ['trʌbl] *n* στενοχώρια, ἀνησυχία, σκοτούρα ‖ (*effort, care*) κόπος ‖ *vt* ἐνοχλῶ, ἀνησυχῶ ‖ ~**d** *a* ἀνήσυχος, ταραγμένος ‖ ~**-free** *a* χωρίς σκοτούρες ‖ ~**maker** *n* ταραχοποιός, ταραξίας ‖ ~**some** *a* ὀχληρός, ἀνιαρός, δύσκολος.

trough [trɔf] *n* σκάφη, ποτίστρα ‖ (*channel*) αὐλών, τάφρος ‖ (*meteorology*) σφήν ὑφέσεως.

trounce [trauns] *vt* (*esp sport*) συντρίβω, τσακίζω.

troupe [tru:p] *n* θίασος.

trousers ['trauzəz] *npl* πανταλόνι.

trousseau ['tru:səu] *n* προῖκα (ἀσπρόρουχα καί φορέματα).

trout [traut] *n* πέστροφα.

trowel ['trauəl] *n* μυστρί.

truant ['truənt] *n*: **to play ~** τό σκάω, ἀπουσιάζω ἀδικαιολογητα.

truce [tru:s] *n* ἀνακωχή.

truck [trʌk] *n* φορτηγό ἁμάξι, καμιόνι ‖ (*rail*) φορεῖον ‖ (*barrow*) χειράμαξα ἀχθοφόρου ‖ ~**driver** *n* ὁδηγός φορτηγοῦ ‖ ~ **farm** *n* (*US*) ἀγρόκτημα λαχανικῶν, περιβόλι.

truculent ['trʌkjulənt] *a* βίαιος, ἄγριος, ἐπιθετικός.

trudge [trʌdʒ] *vi* βαδίζω μέ δυσκολίαν, σέρνομαι.

true [tru:] *a* ἀληθής, ἀληθινός, ἀκριβής ‖ (*genuine*) πραγματικός, αὐθεντικός, γνήσιος ‖ (*friend*) πιστός, τίμιος, ἀληθινός.

truffle ['trʌfl] *n* ὕχνο, τερφεζία.

truly ['tru:li] *ad* εἰλικρινά, πιστά, γνήσια,

άληθῶς ‖ (exactly) μέ ἀκρίβειαν, ἀκριβῶς, ὀρθῶς ‖ yours ~ ὅλως ὑμέτερος.

trump [trʌmp] n (cards) ἀτοῦ ‖ ~**ed-up** a ψευδής, σκαρωμένο.

trumpet ['trʌmpit] n σάλπιγξ, τρουμπέτα.

truncated [trʌŋ'keitid] a κολοβωμένος, κόλουρος.

truncheon ['trʌntʃən] n ρόπαλον, ἀστυνομικόν γκλόμπ.

trundle ['trʌndl] vti: **to** ~ **along** κυλῶ, τρέχω, τσουλῶ.

trunk [trʌŋk] n κορμός, κούτσουρο ‖ (body) κορμός, τόρσο ‖ (box) κιβώτιον, μπαοῦλο ‖ (of elephant) προβοσκίς ‖ ~**s** npl μαγιό, κυλοτίτσα ‖ ~ **call** n ὑπεραστική κλῆσις.

truss [trʌs] n (med) κοιλεπίδεσμος, ζώνη.

trust [trʌst] n πίστις, ἐμπιστοσύνη ‖ (property) καταπίστευμα ‖ vt ἐμπιστεύομαι εἰς ‖ ~**ed** a ἔμπιστος, τῆς ἐμπιστοσύνης ‖ ~**ee** n ἐπίτροπος, κηδεμών, ἔφορος ‖ ~**ful** a γεμᾶτος ἐμπιστοσύνην, εὐκολόπιστος ‖ ~**ing** a πλήρης ἐμπιστοσύνης ‖ ~**worthy** a ἀξιόπιστος. ‖ ~**y** a πιστός, ἀξιόπιστος.

truth [tru:θ] n ἀλήθεια ‖ ~**ful** a φιλαλήθης, ἀληθής ‖ ~**fully** ad ἀληθινά, εἰλικρινῶς, πιστά ‖ ~**fulness** n φιλαλήθεια, εἰλικρίνεια.

try [trai] (irreg v) n προσπάθεια ‖ (test) δοκιμή, ἀπόπειρα ‖ vt δοκιμάζω, κάνω δοκιμήν ‖ (in court) δικάζω ‖ (strain) κουράζω ‖ vi (attempt) προσπαθῶ, ζητῶ νά ‖ **to** ~ **on** vt δοκιμάζω, προβάρω ‖ **to** ~ **out** vt δοκιμάζω (πλήρως) ‖ ~**ing** a δυσχερής, κουραστικός, σκληρός, ἐντατικός.

tsar [za:*] n Τσάρος.

T-shirt ['ti:ʃə:t] n φανέλλα (ἀθλητική).

T-square ['ti:skwεə*] n Ταῦ.σχεδιάσεως.

tub [tʌb] n μεγάλη λεκάνη, σκάφη, κάδος, μαστέλο, μπάνιο.

tuba ['tju:bə] n μεγάλη κορνέτα, κοντραμπάσο.

tubby ['tʌbi] a (fat) στρογγυλός σάν βαρέλι, κοντόχονδρος.

tube [tju:b] n σωλήν, ἀγωγός, αὐλός ‖ (also for toothpaste etc) σωληνάριον ‖ (in London) ὑπόγειος σιδηρόδρομος ‖ (aut: for tyre) σαμπρέλλα ‖ ~**less** a (aut) χωρίς σαμπρέλλα.

tuber ['tju:bə*] n βολβός, γογγύλι.

tuberculosis [tjubə:kju'ləusis] n φυματίωσις.

tube station ['tju:bsteiʃən] n σταθμός τοῦ ὑπογείου τραίνου.

tubing ['tju:biŋ] n σωλήν(ωσις).

tubular ['tju:bjulə*] a (steel, furniture) σωληνοειδής, σωληνωτός.

tuck [tʌk] n πιέτα ‖ γλυκά ‖ vt (gather) διπλώνω, μαζεύω ‖ **to** ~ **away** vt χώνω ‖ **to** ~ **in** vt μαζεύω, χώνω ‖ vi (food) πέφτω μέ τά μοῦτρα στό φαΐ ‖ **to** ~ **up** vt (child) σκεπάζω, τακτοποιῶ ‖ ~-**shop** n ζαχαροπλαστεῖον.

Tuesday ['tʃu:zdi] n Τρίτη.

tuft [tʌft] n θύσανος, φούντα.

tug [tʌg] n ἀπότομο τράβηγμα ‖ (steamship) ρυμουλκόν (πλοῖον) ‖ vti σύρω, τραβῶ δυνατά ‖ ~-**of-war** n διελκυστίνδα.

tuition [tju'iʃən] n διδασκαλία, δίδακτρα.

tulip ['tju:lip] n τουλίπα.

tumble ['tʌmbl] n πέσιμο, τούμπα, κουτρουβάλα ‖ vi πέφτω, τουμπάρω ‖ (somersault) κάνω τούμπες, ἀναποδογυρίζω ‖ vt (toss about) κατρακυλῶ, σωριάζομαι ‖ **to** ~ **to** vt συλλαμβάνω, ἀντιλαμβάνομαι ‖ ~**down** a ἑτοιμόρροπος, σαραβαλιασμένος ‖ ~**r** n (acrobat) ἀκροβάτης ‖ (glass) ποτήρι.

tummy ['tʌmi] n (col: stomach, belly) στομάχι, κοιλιά.

tumour ['tju:mə*] n ὄγκος.

tumult ['tju:mʌlt] n θόρυβος, σαματᾶς, φασαρία ‖ ~**uous** a θορυβώδης, ταραχώδης, θυελλώδης.

tumulus ['tju:mjuləs] n τύμβος.

tuna ['tju:nə] n τόννος.

tundra ['tʌndrə] n τούντρα.

tune [tju:n] n μελωδία, σκοπός ‖ (pitch) τόνος, συντονισμός ‖ vt κουρδίζω, συντονίζω ‖ (motorcar) ρυθμίζω, ἐναρμονίζω, συντονίζω ‖ **in** ~ ἐν ἁρμονία, συντονισμένος ‖ **out of** ~ παραφωνή, ἔξω ἀπό τόν τόνο ‖ **to** ~ **in** vi πιάνω σταθμό ‖ **to** ~ **up** vi (mus) συντονίζομαι, βρίσκω τόν τόνο ‖ ~**ful** a μελωδικός, ἁρμονικός.

tungsten ['tʌŋstən] n βολφράμιον, τουγκστένιον.

tunic ['tju:nik] n χιτώνιον, ἀμπέχονο.

tuning ['tju:niŋ] n (rad) συντονισμός ‖ (aut) ρύθμισις.

tunnel ['tʌnl] n σήραγξ, τουνέλι ‖ vi ἀνοίγω σήραγγα.

tunny ['tʌni] n τόννος.

turban ['tə:bən] n σαρίκι, τουρμπάνι.

turbid ['tə:bid] a θολός, λασπώδης, βρώμικος.

turbine ['tə:bain] n στρόβιλος, τουρμπίνα.

turbulence ['tə:bjuləns] n (aviat) στροβιλισμός, ρεμού.

turbulent ['tə:bjulənt] a ταραχώδης, βίαιος, ἄτακτος.

turf [tə:f] n χλόη, γρασίδι ‖ (sod) χορταριασμένος βῶλος ‖ **the T**~ n ὁ ἱππόδρομος.

turgid ['tə:dʒid] a (pompous) στομφώδης, πομπώδης.

Turk [tə:k] n Τοῦρκος.

turkey ['tə:ki] n γαλλοπούλα, ἰνδιάνος ‖ **T**~ n Τουρκία.

Turkish ['tə:kiʃ] a τουρκικός ‖ n (ling) τουρκική ‖ ~ **bath** n χαμάμ ‖ ~ **delight** n λουκούμι.

turmoil ['tə:moil] n ἀναταραχή, ἀναστάτωσις, πατιρντί.

turn [tə:n] *n* περιστροφή, γύρισμα ‖ *(turning)* στροφή ‖ *(performance)* σειρά ‖ *(shape, manner)* νοοτροπία, διάθεσις ‖ *(chance)* σειρά ‖ *(med)* κρίσις ‖ *vt (περι)-στρέφω, γυρίζω, στρίβω ‖ *(change position)* ἀλλάζω, γυρίζω ‖ *(of colour)* ἀλλάζω χρῶμα ‖ *vi* περιστρέφομαι, γυρίζω ‖ *(change direction)* στρέφομαι, κατευθύνομαι, στρίβω ‖ *(become sour)* ξυνίζω ‖ to ~ back *vti* γυρίζω πίσω ‖ to ~ down *vt (refuse)* ἀπορρίπτω ‖ *(fold down)* διπλώνω, τσακίζω ‖ to ~ in *vi (go to bed)* πάω γιά ὕπνο ‖ *vt (fold)* γυρίζω (μέσα), στριφώνω ‖ to ~ off *vi (from road)* ἀλλάζω δρόμο, στρίβω ‖ *vt (light)* κλείνω, σβήνω ‖ *(rad)* κλείνω, σβήνω ‖ to ~ on *vt (light)* ἀνοίγω, ἀνάβω ‖ *(rad)* ἀνοίγω ‖ to ~ out *vt* ἐξελίσσομαι, πάω ‖ *(extinguish)* κλείνω, σβήνω ‖ to ~ up *vi (person)* ἐμφανίζομαι, φθάνω αἰφνιδίως ‖ *(lost object)* ξαναβρίσκω ‖ *vt (collar)* σηκώνω, ἀνασηκώνω ‖ *(rad: increase volume)* ἀνεβάζω, δυναμώνω ‖ ~around *n (reversal)* γύρισμα, μεταβολή ‖ ~ed-up *a (nose)* ἀνασηκωτή (μύτη) ‖ ~ing *n (in road)* καμπή, στροφή ‖ ~ing point *n* κρίσιμον σημεῖον, ἀποφασιστικόν σημεῖον.

turnip ['tə:nip] *n* γογγύλι.

turnout ['tə:naut] *n* συνάθροισις, ἀκροατήριον.

turnover ['tə:nəuvə*] *n* κεφάλαιον, τζίρος.

turnpike ['tə:npaik] *n (US: toll highway)* ὁδός μέ διόδια.

turnstile ['tə:nstail] *n* περιστροφική εἴσοδος.

turntable ['tə:nteibl] *n* περιστροφική ἐξέδρα, περιστροφική βάσις.

turn-up ['tə:nʌp] *n (on trousers)* ρεβέρ.

turpentine ['tə:pəntain] *n* νέφτι.

turquoise ['tə:kwɔiz] *n* τουρκουάζ ‖ *a (colour)* κυανοπράσινος.

turret ['tʌrit] *n* πυργίσκος.

turtle ['tə:tl] *n* χελώνα.

tusk [tʌsk] *n* χαυλιόδους.

tussle ['tʌsl] *n* τσακωμός, καυγᾶς.

tutor ['tju:tə*] *n* ἰδιαίτερος καθηγητής, οἰκοδιδάσκαλος ‖ *(at college)* ὑφηγητής ‖ ~ial *n (univ)* ἰδιαίτερον μάθημα ἀπό καθηγητήν.

tuxedo [tʌk'si:dəu] *n (US)* σμόκιν.

twaddle ['twɔdl] *n (col)* μωρολογία, φλυαρία, μπούρδες.

twang [twæŋ] *n* ὀξύς ἦχος χορδής, ἔνρινος τόνος, σβούρισμα ‖ *vti* ἀφήνω τεταμένην χορδήν, ἀντηχῶ, σβουρίζω.

tweed [twi:d] *n* τουήντ.

tweezers ['twi:zəz] *npl* τσιμπίδα.

twelfth [twelfθ] *a* δωδέκατος ‖ **T ~ Night** *n* παραμονή τῶν Φώτων.

twelve [twelv] *num* δώδεκα.

twentieth ['twentiiθ] *a* εἰκοστός.

twenty ['twenti] *num* εἴκοσι.

twerp [twə:p] *n (col: fool)* βλάκας.

twice [twais] *ad* δίς, δύο φορές, διπλάσιος.

twig [twig] *n* κλαδί, κλωνάρι ‖ *vt (understand, realize)* ἀντιλαμβάνομαι, μπαίνω, πιάνω.

twilight ['twailait] *n* λυκόφως, λυκαυγές.

twill [twil] *n* (ὕφασμα) καρρωτό.

twin [twin] *n* δίδυμος ‖ *a* δίδυμος.

twine [twain] *n* σπάγγος, χονδρή κλωστή ‖ *vi* τυλίγομαι.

twinge [twindʒ] *n* δυνατός πόνος, σουβλιά.

twinkle ['twiŋkl] *n* σπινθηρισμός, σπίθισμα ‖ *vi* σπινθηροβολῶ, σπιθίζω, τρεμοσβήνω.

twin town ['twin'taun] *n* δίδυμη πόλις.

twirl [twə:l] *n* περιστροφή, στρίψιμο ‖ *vti* περιστρέφω, στρίβω.

twist [twist] *n* συστροφή, στρίψιμο, στραμπούληγμα ‖ *vt* συστρέφω, πλέκω, στρίβω ‖ *(distort)* στρεβλώνω, στραβώνω ‖ *(cheat)* ἐξαπατῶ ‖ *vi* συστρέφομαι, στρίβομαι ‖ *(curve)* στρίβω.

twit [twit] *n (col: fool)* κορόϊδο, βλάκας.

twitch [twitʃ] *n* σύσπασις, τίναγμα ‖ *vi* συσπῶμαι νευρικά.

two [tu:] *num* δύο ‖ ~-door *a (aut)* μέ δύο πόρτες ‖ ~-faced *a (pej: person)* διπρόσωπος ‖ ~fold *ad* δίς, δύο φορές, διπλά ‖ *a* διπλός ‖ ~-piece *a (suit)* ντεπιές ‖ *(swimsuit)* κοστούμι μπάνιου ντεπιές ‖ ~-seater *n (plane)* διθέσιον ‖ *(car)* διθέσιον ‖ ~some *n* ζευγάρι ‖ ~-way *a (traffic)* διπλής κυκλοφορίας.

tycoon [tai'ku:n] *n* μεγιστάν τῶν ἐπιχειρήσεων.

type [taip] *n* τύπος ‖ *(example)* εἶδος, τάξις ‖ *(printing)* χαρακτῆρες, στοιχεῖα ‖ *vt* δακτυλογραφῶ ‖ ~script *n* δακτυλογραφημένον κείμενον ‖ ~writer *n* γραφομηχανή ‖ ~written *a* δακτυλογραφημένον.

typhoid ['taifɔid] *n* τυφοειδής.

typhoon [tai'fu:n] *n* τυφών.

typhus ['taifəs] *n* τύφος.

typical ['tipikəl] *a* τυπικός, χαρακτηριστικός ‖ ~ly *ad* τυπικῶς.

typify ['tipifai] *vt* ἀντιπροσωπεύω, συμβολίζω.

typing ['taipiŋ] *n* δακτυλογράφησις.

typist ['taipist] *n* δακτυλογράφος.

tyranny ['tirəni] *n* τυραννία.

tyrant ['tairənt] *n* τύραννος.

tyre ['taiə*] *n (aut)* ρόδα, λάστιχο.

U, u

udder ['ʌdə*] *n* μαστός, μαστάρι.

ugh [ə:h] *excl* πφ!, οὐφ!

ugliness ['ʌglinis] *n* ἀσχήμια.

ugly ['ʌgli] *a* ἄσχημος, ἄσκημος ‖ *(bad)* ἄσχημος, κακός ‖ *(dangerous)* δυσάρεστος, ἐπικίνδυνος, ἄσχημος.

ukulele [ju:kə'leili] *n* οὐκελελέ.

ulcer ['ʌlsə*] *n* (*in mouth, stomach*) ἕλκος.

ulterior [ʌl'tiəriə*] *a* (*hidden*) ὑστερόβουλος, κρυφός.

ultimate ['ʌltimit] *a* τελευταῖος, τελικός, ὕστατος, βασικός ‖ ~**ly** *ad* τελικῶς, τελικά, βασικῶς.

ultimatum [ʌlti'meitəm] *n* τελεσίγραφον.

ultra- ['ʌltrə] *prefix* ὑπερ-.

ultraviolet ['ʌltrə'vaiəlit] *a*: ~ **light** ὑπεριῶδες φῶς.

umbilical [ʌmbi'laikəl] *a*: ~ **cord** ὀμφάλιος λῶρος, ὀμφαλίς.

umbrage ['ʌmbridʒ] *n* : **to take** ~ πειράζομαι ἀπό, δυσφορῶ.

umbrella [ʌm'brelə] *n* ὀμπρέλλα.

umpire ['ʌmpaiə*] *n* διαιτητής ‖ *vti* διαιτητεύω.

umpteen ['ʌmpti:n] *num* (*col*) ἕνα σωρό, δέν ξέρω πόσοι.

un- [ʌn] *prefix* ἀ-, ἐκ-, ξε-, ἀντι-, μή-.

unabashed ['ʌnə'bæʃt] *a* ἀτάραχος, ἀκλόνητος.

unabated ['ʌnə'beitid] *a* ἀμείωτος, ἀδιάπτωτος.

unable ['ʌn'eibl] *a* ἀνίκανος, μή δυνάμενος.

unaccompanied ['ʌnə'kʌmpənid] *a* (*child, lady*) ἀσυνόδευτος, μόνος.

unaccountably ['ʌnə'kauntəbli] *ad* ἀνεξηγήτως.

unaccustomed ['ʌnə'kʌstəmd] *a* ἀσυνήθης ‖ (+ *to*) ἀσυνήθιστος (σέ, νά).

unadulterated ['ʌnə'dʌltəreitid] *a* ἀνόθευτος, ἀγνός.

unaided ['ʌn'eidid] *a* χωρίς βοήθειαν, ἀβοήθητος.

unanimity [ju:nə'nimiti] *n* ὁμοφωνία.

unanimous [ju:'næniməs] *a* ὁμόθυμος, ὁμόφωνος ‖ ~**ly** *ad* ὁμοφώνως, παμψηφεί.

unattached ['ʌnə'tætʃt] *a* (*single*) ἐλεύθερος, ἐργένης.

unattended ['ʌnə'tendid] *a* χωρίς συνοδείαν, ἀπεριποίητος.

unattractive ['ʌnə'træktiv] *a* μή συμπαθητικός.

unauthorized ['ʌn'ɔ:θəraizd] *a* ἄνευ ἀδείας, μή ἐξουσιοδοτημένος.

unavoidable [ʌnə'vɔidəbl] *a* ἀναπόφευκτος.

unavoidably [ʌnə'vɔidəbli] *ad* ἀναποφεύκτως.

unaware ['ʌnə'wεə*] *a* ἀνίδεος, μή γνωρίζων, ἀγνοῶν ‖ ~**s** *ad* ἐξ ἀπίνης, χωρίς προειδοποίησιν.

unbalanced ['ʌn'bælənst] *a* μή ἰσορροπημένος, ἀνισόρροπος.

unbearable ['ʌn'bεərəbl] *a* ἀνυπόφορος, ἀφόρητος.

unbeatable ['ʌn'bi:təbl] *a* (*team*) ἀήττητος, ἀκατανίκητος.

unbeaten ['ʌn'bi:tn] *a* (*team, record*) ἀήττητος, οὐδέποτε καταριφθέν.

unbecoming ['ʌnbi'kʌmiŋ] *a* ἀνάρμοστος, ἀπρεπής, πού δέν πηγαίνει.

unbeknown ['ʌnbi'nəun] *ad* (+ *to*) ἐν ἀγνοίᾳ τοῦ.

unbelief ['ʌnbi'li:f] *n* ἀπιστία, δυσπιστία.

unbelievable [ʌnbi'li:vəbl] *a* ἀπίστευτος.

unbend ['ʌn'bend] *vi* εὐθυγραμμίζομαι, σιάζω ‖ *vt* χαλαρώνω, ξετεντώνω.

unbounded [ʌn'baundid] *a* ἀπεριόριστος, ἀπέραντος.

unbreakable ['ʌn'breikəbl] *a* ἄθραυστος.

unbridled [ʌn'braidld] *a* ἀχαλίνωτος, ἀσυγκράτητος.

unbroken ['ʌn'brəukən] *a* ἄθραυστος, ἄσπαστος, ἀπαράβατος, ἀδιατάρακτος.

unburden [ʌn'bə:dn] *vt*: **to** ~ **o.s.** ἀνακουφίζω, ξαλαφρώνω.

unbutton [ʌn'bʌtn] *vt* ξεκουμπώνω.

uncalled-for [ʌn'kɔ:ldfɔ:*] *a* ἄκαιρος, ἀδικαιολόγητος.

uncanny [ʌn'kæni] *a* παράξενος, ἀφύσικος, μυστηριώδης.

unceasing [ʌn'si:siŋ] *a* ἀκατάπαυστος.

uncertain [ʌn'sə:tn] *a* ἀβέβαιος, ἀμφίβολος ‖ (*weather etc*) ἀσταθής ‖ (*vague*) ἀκαθόριστος ‖ ~**ty** *n* ἀβεβαιότης, ἀμφιβολία, ἀστάθεια.

unchanged ['ʌn'tʃeindʒd] *a* ἀμετάβλητος.

uncharitable [ʌn'tʃæritəbl] *a* ἄσπλαγχνος, αὐστηρός, ἀφιλάνθρωπος.

uncharted ['ʌn'tʃɑ:tid] *a* ἀνεξερεύνητος.

unchecked ['ʌn'tʃekt] *a* ἀνεμπόδιστος, ἀσταμάτητος, ἀνεξέλεγκτος.

uncivil [ʌn'sivil] *a* ἀγενής, ἄξεστος, κακότροπος.

uncle ['ʌŋkl] *n* θεῖος, μπάρμπας.

uncomfortable [ʌn'kʌmfətəbl] *a* (*uneasy*) ἀνήσυχος, δυσάρεστος.

uncompromising [ʌn'kɔmprəmaiziŋ] *a* ἀδιάλλακτος, ἄκαμπτος.

uncongenial ['ʌnkən'dʒi:niəl] *a* δυσάρεστος, μή εὐνοϊκός, ἀσυμπαθής.

unconscious [ʌn'kɔnʃəs] *a* ἀσυνείδητος ‖ (*not aware*) μή ἔχων συνείδησιν τοῦ, ἀγνοῶν ‖ *n*: **the** ~ τό ἀσυνείδητον ‖ ~**ly** *ad* ἀσυνειδήτως, χωρίς νά τό καταλάβω ‖ ~**ness** *n* (τό) ἀσυνείδητον, ἀναισθησία.

uncontrollable ['ʌnkən'trəuləbl] *a* ἀχαλίνωτος, ἀκατάσχετος, ἀσυγκράτητος.

uncork ['ʌn'kɔ:k] *vt* ἐκπωματίζω, ξεβουλώνω.

uncouth [ʌn'ku:θ] *a* ἀδέξιος, ἄξεστος.

uncover [ʌn'kʌvə*] *vt* ξεσκεπάζω ‖ (*expose*) ἀποκαλύπτω, ἐκθέτω.

unctuous ['ʌŋktjuəs] *a* (*too smooth*) ἀνειλικρινής, γλυκανάλατος.

undaunted ['ʌn'dɔ:ntid] *a* ἀτρόμητος, ἀπτόητος, ἄφοβος.

undecided ['ʌndi'saidid] *a* ἀναποφάσιστος, ἐκκρεμῶν.

undeniable [ʌndi'naiəbl] *a* ἀναμφισβήτητος.

undeniably [ʌndi'naiəbli] *ad* ἀναντιρρήτως, ἀναμφισβητήτως.

under ['ʌndə*] *prep* ὑπό, κάτω ἀπό ‖ (*in time*

of) ἐπί, στήν ἐποχή τοῦ ‖ *ad* κάτω, ὑποκάτω ‖ ~ **age** *a* ἀνήλιξ ‖ ~ **repair** ὑπὸ ἐπισκευήν.

undercarriage ['ʌndəkærɪdʒ] *n*, **undercart** ['ʌndəkɑ:t] *n* σύστημα προσγειώσεως.

underclothes ['ʌndəkləuðz] *npl* ἐσώρρουχα.

underclothing ['ʌndəkləuðiŋ] *n* ἐσώρρουχα.

undercoat ['ʌndəkəut] *n* (*paint*) βασικόν χρῶμα.

undercover ['ʌndəkʌnvə*] *a* μυστικός, κρυφός.

undercurrent ['ʌndəkʌrənt] *n* ρεῦμα κάτω ἀπό τήν ἐπιφάνειαν.

undercut ['ʌndəkʌt] *n* (*cooking*) φιλέττο κρέατος ‖ *vt* πουλῶ φθηνότερα ἀπό.

underdeveloped ['ʌndədɪ'veləpt] *a* (*country*) ὑποανάπτυκτος.

underdog ['ʌndədɔg] *n* ὁ ἡττημένος, ὁ πιό ἀδύνατος.

underdone ['ʌndə'dʌn] *a* (*cooking*) ἄψητος, σαινιάν.

underestimate ['ʌndər'estimeit] *vt* ὑποτιμῶ.

underexpose ['ʌndəriks'pəuz] *vt* ἐκθέτω ὀλιγώτερον τοῦ δέοντος.

underfed ['ʌndə'fed] *a* ὑποσιτιζόμενος.

underfoot ['ʌndə'fut] *ad* κάτω ἀπό τά πόδια.

undergo ['ʌndə'gəu] *vt* ὑφίσταμαι, παθαίνω.

undergraduate ['ʌndə'grædjuit] *n* φοιτητής.

underground ['ʌndəgraund] *n* ὑπόγειος σιδηρόδρομος ‖ *a* (*press etc*) μυστικός, κρυφός, τῆς ἀντιστάσεως.

undergrowth ['ʌndəgrəuθ] *n* θάμνοι, χαμόκλαδα.

underhand ['ʌndəhænd] *a* πανοῦργος, ὕπουλος.

underlie [ʌndə'lai] *vt* ὑπόκειμαι, εἶμαι ἡ βάσις τοῦ.

underline [ʌndə'lain] *vt* ὑπογραμμίζω ‖ (*draw attention to*) ὑπογραμμίζω, τονίζω.

underling ['ʌndəliŋ] *n* ὑφιστάμενος, παραγιός, κολαοῦζος.

undermine [ʌndə'main] *vt* ὑπονομεύω, ὑποσκάπτω, τρώγω.

underneath ['ʌndə'ni:θ] *ad* κάτωθεν, ἀπό κάτω ‖ *prep* κάτωθεν, (ὑπο)κάτω ἀπό, ὑπό.

underpaid ['ʌndə'peid] *a* κακῶς ἀμειβόμενος.

underpass ['ʌndəpɑ:s] *n* ὑπόγειος διάβασις.

underprivileged ['ʌndə'privilidʒd] *a* μέ μειωμένα προνόμοια, πτωχός.

underrate [ʌndə'reit] *vt* ὑποτιμῶ.

underside ['ʌndəsaid] *n* κάτω πλευρά, τό ἀποκάτω.

underskirt ['ʌndəskə:t] *n* κομπιναιζόν, μεσοφόρι.

understand [ʌndə'stænd] *vt* ἀντιλαμβάνομαι ‖ (*know*) γνωρίζω, καταλαβαίνω ‖ (*hear, believe*) μαθαίνω, πιστεύω, νομίζω ‖ (*gram*) ὑπονοῶ ‖ ~**able** *a* (κατα)νοητός, καταληπτός, εὐνόητος ‖ ~**ing** *n* συνεννόησις, συμφωνία, κατανόησις.

understatement ['ʌndəsteitmənt] *n* δήλωσις κάτω τῆς πραγματικότητος.

understudy ['ʌndəstʌdi] *n* ἀντικαταστάτης.

undertake [ʌndə'teik] *vt* ἀναλαμβάνω ‖ ~**r** *n* ἐργολάβος κηδειῶν.

undertaking [ʌndə'teikiŋ] *n* ἐπιχείρησις ‖ (*promise*)·δέσμευσις, ὑποχρέωσις.

underwater ['ʌndə'wɔ:tə*] *ad* ὑποβρυχίως ‖ *a* ὑποβρύχιος.

underwear ['ʌndəweə*] *n* ἐσώρρουχα.

underweight [ʌndə'weit] *a* λιποβαρής, ἀδύνατος.

underworld ['ʌndəwə:ld] *n* (*of crime*) ὑπόκοσμος.

underwriter ['ʌndəraitə*] *n* (*insurance*) ἀσφαλιστής.

undesirable ['ʌndi'zaiərəbl] *a* ἀνεπιθύμητος.

undies ['ʌndiz] *npl* (*col*) ἐσώρρουχα (γυναικεῖα).

undiscovered ['ʌndis'kʌvəd] *a* μή ἀνακαλυφθείς.

undisputed ['ʌndis'pju:tid] *a* ἀδιαφιλονίκητος, ἀδιαμφισβήτητος.

undistinguished ['ʌndis'tiŋgwiʃt] *a* μέτριος, κοινός, ἀσήμαντος.

undo [ʌn'du:] *vt* λύνω, ξεκουμπώνω, ἀνοίγω ‖ (*work*) καταστρέφω, χαλνῶ ‖ ~**ing** *n* καταστροφή, ἀφανισμός.

undoubted [ʌn'dautid] *a* ἀναμφισβήτητος, ἀναμφίβολος ‖ ~**ly** *ad* ἀναμφισβητήτως.

undress ['ʌn'dres] *vti* γδύνομαι, γδύνω.

undue ['ʌn'dju:] *a* ὑπερβολικός, ἀδικαιολόγητος.

undulating ['ʌndjuleitiŋ] *a* κυμαινόμενος, ταλαντευόμενος.

unduly ['ʌn'dju:li] *ad* ὑπερβολικά, ἀπρεπῶς.

unearth ['ʌn'ə:θ] *vt* ἀνασκάπτω, ἀνακαλύπτω ‖ ~**ly** *a* ὑπερφυσικός, ἀπίθανος.

unease ['ʌn'i:z] *n* ἀνησυχία, στενοχώρια, ταραχή.

uneasy [ʌn'i:zi] *a* ἀνήσυχος, στενοχωρημένος.

uneconomic(al) ['ʌni:kə'nɔmik(əl)] *a* ἀνοικονομικός, σπάταλος, ἀσύμφορος.

uneducated ['ʌn'edjukeitid] *a* ἀπαίδευτος, ἀσπούδαστος, ἀμόρφωτος.

unemployed ['ʌnim'plɔid] *a* ἄνεργος, ἀχρησιμοποίητος ‖ *npl*: **the** ~ οἱ ἄνεργοι.

unemployment ['ʌnim'plɔimənt] *n* ἀνεργία.

unending [ʌn'endiŋ] *a* ἀτελείωτος, διαρκής.

unenviable ['ʌn'enviəbl] *a* ἀζήλευτος, ἀνεπιθύμητος.

unerring ['ʌn'ə:riŋ] *a* ἀλάνθαστος, ἀκριβής.

uneven ['ʌn'i:vən] *a* (*surface*) ἀνώμαλος, ὀρεινός ‖ (*quality*) ἄνισος, ἀνώμαλος.

unexploded ['ʌniks'pləudid] *a* (*bomb*) μή ἐκραγείς.

unfailing [ʌn'feiliŋ] *a* ἀλάνθαστος, ἀτελείωτος, διαρκής, πιστός.

unfair ['ʌn'feə*] *a* (*unkind, unreasonable*) ἄδικος, μή ὀρθός, ἄνισος ‖ ~**ly** *ad* ἄδικα, ἄτιμα, πρόστυχα.

unfaithful [ʌn'feiθful] a (to spouse) ἄπιστος.

unfasten ['ʌn'fɑːsn] vt λύνω, ξεκουμπώνω, ξεκλειδώνω.

unfavourable, (US) **unfavorable** ['ʌn'feivərəbl] a δυσμενής, δυσοίωνος.

unfeeling [ʌn'fiːliŋ] a σκληρόκαρδος, ἀναίσθητος.

unfinished ['ʌn'finiʃt] a ἡμιτελής, ἀτελής.

unfit ['ʌn'fit] a (in health) ἀνίκανος, ἀδιάθετος ‖ (+for) ἀκατάλληλος (γιά).

unflagging [ʌn'flægiŋ] a ἀκλόνητος, ἀκατάπαυστος, ἀλύγιστος.

unflinching [ʌn'flintʃiŋ] a σταθερός, ἀποφασιστικός.

unfold [ʌn'fəuld] vt ξεδιπλώνω, ξετυλίγω, ἁπλώνω ‖ (reveal) ἀποκαλύπτω, ἀναπτύσσω, ἐξηγῶ ‖ vi (develop) ἀναπτύσσομαι, ἐκτυλίσσομαι.

unforeseen ['ʌnfɔː'siːn] a ἀπρόβλεπτος, ἀπροσδόκητος.

unforgivable ['ʌnfə'givəbl] a ἀσυγχώρητος.

unfortunate [ʌn'fɔːtʃnit] a ἀτυχής, δυστυχής, ἄστοχος ‖ ~ly ad δυστυχῶς, ἀτυχῶς.

unfounded ['ʌn'faundid] a (rumour) ἀβάσιμος, ψευδής.

unfriendly ['ʌn'frendli] a ἀφιλόφρων, ἐχθρικός.

unfurnished ['ʌn'fəːniʃt] a (flat) ἄνευ ἐπίπλων.

ungainly [ʌn'geinli] a ἀδέξιος.

ungodly [ʌn'gɔdli] a (col: hour) ἀθεόφοβος, ἀκατάλληλος, παράλογος.

unguarded ['ʌn'gɑːdid] a (moment) ἀπρόσεκτος, ἀπερίσκεπτος.

unhappiness [ʌn'hæpinis] n θλῖψις, στενοχώρια.

unhappy [ʌn'hæpi] a δυστυχής, δυστυχισμένος, στενοχωρημένος.

unharmed ['ʌn'hɑːmd] a σῶος, ἀβλαβής, ἀπείραχτος.

unhealthy [ʌn'helθi] a (lit) ἀνθυγιεινός, ἀρρωστιάρης ‖ (fig) νοσηρός.

unheard-of [ʌn'həːdɔv] a πρωτάκουστος, ἀνήκουστος.

unhurt ['ʌn'həːt] a χωρίς τραῦμα, σῶος καί ἀβλαβής.

unicorn ['juːnikɔːn] n μονόκερως.

unidentified ['ʌnai'dentifaid] a μή ἀναγνωρισθείς, ἄγνωστος.

unification [juːnifi'keiʃən] n ἑνοποίησις.

uniform ['juːnifɔːm] n στολή ‖ a ὁμοιόμορφος, ἴδιος ‖ ~ity n ὁμοιομορφία.

unify ['juːnifai] vt ἑνοποιῶ.

unilateral ['juːni'lætərəl] a μονόπλευρος.

unimaginable [ʌni'mædʒinəbl] a ἀδιανόητος, ἀφάνταστος.

uninjured ['ʌn'indʒəd] a σῶος καί ἀβλαβής, ἄθικτος.

unintentional ['ʌnin'tenʃənl] a ἀκούσιος, ἀθέλητος.

union ['juːnjən] n ἕνωσις, συγκόλλησις ‖ (alliance) ἕνωσις, συμφωνία ‖ (of workers) ἐργατικόν σωματεῖον, συνδικᾶτον ‖ U~ Jack n Ἀγγλική σημαία.

unique [juː'niːk] a μοναδικός, ἰδιόρρυθμος, ἀσυνήθης.

unison ['juːnisn] n: in ~ ἐν ὁμοφωνία, ἐν συμφωνία ‖ (mus) ἁρμονία, μονοφωνία, ὁμηχία.

unit ['juːnit] n μονάς ‖ (team, squad) ὁμάδα, συγκρότημα.

unite [juː'nait] vt ἑνώνω ‖ vi ἑνώνομαι (μέ) ‖ ~d a ἡνωμένος, ἑνωμένος, συνδεδυασμένος ‖ U~d Kingdom n Ἡνωμένον Βασίλειον ‖ U~d Nations npl Ἡνωμένα Ἔθνη ‖ U~d States (of America) npl Ἡνωμέναι Πολιτεῖαι.

unit trust ['juːnit'trʌst] n (Brit) σύστημα ἐπενδύσεων εἰς μετοχάς.

unity ['juːniti] n ἑνότης, ἁρμονία, σύμπνοια, μονάς.

universal [juːni'vəːsəl] a γενικός, καθολικός, πάγκοινος ‖ (of the world) παγκόσμιος ‖ ~ly ad καθολικῶς, παγκοσμίως.

universe ['juːnivəːs] n σύμπαν, οἰκουμένη.

university [juːni'vəːsiti] n πανεπιστήμιον.

unjust ['ʌn'dʒʌst] a ἄδικος.

unjustifiable [ʌn'dʒʌstifaiəbl] a ἀδικαιολόγητος.

unkempt ['ʌn'kempt] a ἀκατάστατος, ἀκτένιστος.

unkind [ʌn'kaind] a ἀφιλόφρων, ἄστοργος, σκληρός.

unknown ['ʌn'nəun] a (+to) ἄγνωστος (εἰς), ἀγνοούμενος ἀπό.

unladen ['ʌn'leidn] a (col: weight) ἄνευ φορτίου, κενός.

unleash ['ʌn'liːʃ] vt λύνω, ἐλευθερώνω.

unleavened ['ʌn'levnd] a ἄζυμος.

unless [ən'les] cj ἐκτός ἐάν, ἐκτός ἄν.

unlicensed ['ʌn'laisənst] a (to sell alcohol) ἄνευ ἀδείας, μή ἐπιτρεπόμενος.

unlike ['ʌn'laik] a ἀνόμοιος, διάφορος ἀπό.

unlimited [ʌn'limitid] a ἀπεριόριστος.

unload ['ʌn'ləud] vt ἐκφορτώνω, ξεφορτώνω.

unlock ['ʌn'lɔk] vt ξεκλειδώνω.

unmarried ['ʌn'mærid] a ἄγαμος.

unmask ['ʌn'mɑːsk] vt (expose) ἀποκαλύπτω ‖ ἀφαιρῶ προσωπεῖον ἀπό.

unmistakable ['ʌnmis'teikəbl] a προφανής, καταφανής, σαφής.

unmistakably ['ʌnmis'teikəbli] ad σαφῶς, καταφανῶς, καθαρά.

unmitigated [ʌn'mitigeitid] a ἀμετρίαστος, ἄκρος, ἀπόλυτος.

unnecessary [ʌn'nesisəri] a περιττός, ἄσκοπος, μάταιος.

unobtainable ['ʌnəb'teinəbl] a ἀνεπίτευκτος.

unoccupied ['ʌn'ɔkjupaid] a (seat etc) ἐλεύθερος, διαθέσιμος.

unopened ['ʌn'əupənd] a (letter etc) κλειστός, πού δέν ἀνοίχθηκε.

unorthodox ['ʌn'ɔ:θədɔks] a ἀνορθόδοξος.

unpack ['ʌn'pæk] vti ἀδειάζω ἀποσκευές, βγάζω ἀπό βαλίτσες.

unparalleled [ʌn'pærəleld] a ἀπαράμιλλος.

unpleasant ['ʌn'pleznt] a δυσάρεστος.

unplug ['ʌn'plʌg] vt ξεβουλώνω, βγάζω τήν πρίζα.

unpopular ['ʌn'pɔpjulə*] a ἀντιδημοτικός.

unprecedented [ʌn'presidəntid] a ἄνευ προηγουμένου.

unqualified ['ʌn'kwɔlifaid] a ἀναρμόδιος, ἀκατάλληλος || (success) ἀμετρίαστος, ἀπόλυτος.

unravel [ʌn'rævəl] vt ξεφτώ, ξηλώνω, ξετυλίγω || (solve) διευκρινίζω, λύνω, διαλύω.

unreal ['ʌn'riəl] a ἀπατηλός, φανταστικός.

unreasonable [ʌn'ri:znəbl] a (unfair) παράλογος.

unrelenting ['ʌnri'lentiŋ] a ἀδυσώπητος, ἀνηλεής.

unrelieved ['ʌnri'li:vd] a (monotony) χωρίς ποικιλίαν, μονότονος.

unrepeatable ['ʌnri'pi:təbl] a (offer) πού δέν ἐπαναλαμβάνεται.

unreserved ['ʌnri'zə:vd] a (seat) θέσις ὄχι κρατημένη, ἐλεύθερη θέσι.

unrest [ʌn'rest] n (discontent, trouble) ἀνησυχία, ταραχή.

unroll ['ʌn'rəul] vt ξετυλίγω.

unruly ['ʌn'ru:li] a ἀνυπότακτος, ταραχώδης, ἄτακτος.

unsafe ['ʌn'seif] a ἐπικίνδυνος, ἀνασφαλής.

unsaid ['ʌn'sed] a: to leave sth ~ ἀποσιωπῶ κάτι.

unsatisfactory ['ʌnsætis'fæktəri] a μή ἱκανοποιητικός, ἀνεπαρκής.

unsavoury, (US) unsavory ['ʌn'seivəri] a (of bad character) ὕποπτος, σκοτεινός.

unscrew ['ʌn'skru:] vt ξεβιδώνω.

unscrupulous [ʌn'skru:pjuləs] a ἀσυνείδητος, ἀνενδοίαστος.

unselfish ['ʌn'selfiʃ] a ἀφιλοκερδής, ἀλτρουΐστικός.

unsettled ['ʌn'setld] a ἀνήσυχος, ἀβέβαιος, ἀσταθής || (weather) εὐμετάβλητος, ἀβέβαιος.

unshaven ['ʌn'ʃeivn] a ἀξύριστος, ἀξούριστος.

unsightly [ʌn'saitli] a ἄσχημος, δυσειδής.

unskilled ['ʌn'skild] a (workman) ἀνειδίκευτος.

unsophisticated ['ʌnsə'fistikeitid] a ἀφελής, ἁπλός, ἀδ῀θος, ἀγνός.

unsound ['ʌn'saund] a (ideas) ἐπισφαλής, ἐσφαλμένος.

unspeakable [ʌn'spi:kəbl] a ἀπερίγραπτος, ἀνείπωτος, ἀνέκφραστος || (very bad) ἀποκρουστικός, ἀηδής, σιχαμερός.

unstuck ['ʌn'stʌk] a: to come ~ ξεκολλᾶ || (lit) ξεκολλᾶ, ξεκολλιέμαι || (fig) καταρρέω, γκρεμίζομαι.

unsuccessful ['ʌnsək'sesful] a ἀνεπιτυχής.

unsuitable ['ʌn'su:təbl] a ἀκατάλληλος.

unsuspecting ['ʌnsəs'pektiŋ] a πού δέν ὑποπτεύεται.

unswerving [ʌn'swə:viŋ] a (loyalty) σταθερός, πιστός.

untangle ['ʌn'tæŋgl] vt ξεχωρίζω, ξεμπλέκω.

untapped ['ʌn'tæpt] a (resources) μή χρησιμοποιηθείς, ἀνεκμετάλλευτος.

unthinkable [ʌn'θiŋkəbl] a ἀσύλληπτος, πολύ ἀπίθανος.

untidy [ʌn'taidi] a ἀκατάστατος.

untie ['ʌn'tai] vt λύνω, ξεκουμπώνω.

until [ən'til] prep μέχρις, ἕως || cj μέχρις ὅτου, ἕως ὅτου.

untimely [ʌn'taimli] a (death) πρόωρος.

untold ['ʌn'təuld] a (countless) ἀμέτρητος, ἀνυπολόγιστος.

untoward [ʌntə'wɔ:d] a δυσάρεστος, ἀτυχής.

untranslatable ['ʌntræns'leitəbl] a ἀμετάφραστος.

untried ['ʌn'traid] a (plan) ἀδοκίμαστος.

unused ['ʌn'ju:zd] a ἀσυνήθιστος, μή συνηθισμένος (εἰς).

unusual [ʌn'ju:ʒuəl] a ἀσυνήθης, σπάνιος, ἀξιοσημείωτος || ~ly ad ἐξαιρετικά, ἀφάνταστα, ἀσυνήθιστα.

unveil [ʌn'veil] vt ἀποκαλύπτω, ξεσκεπάζω.

unwary [ʌn'weəri] a ἀπρόσεκτος, ἀμέριμνος.

unwavering [ʌn'weivəriŋ] a ἀσάλευτος, σταθερός.

unwell ['ʌn'wel] a ἀδιάθετος, ἄρρωστος.

unwieldy [ʌn'wi:ldi] a δυσκίνητος, βαρύς, ἀδέξιος.

unwilling ['ʌn'wiliŋ] a ἀπρόθυμος, ἀκούσιος.

unwind [ʌn'waind] vt (lit) ἐκτυλίσσω, ξεκουρδίζω || vi (relax) χαλαρώνομαι.

unwitting [ʌn'witiŋ] a ἀγνοῶν, ἀκούσιος.

unwrap ['ʌn'ræp] vt ξετυλίγω.

unwritten ['ʌn'ritn] a (law) ἄγραφος, πατροπαράδοτος, προφορικός.

up [ʌp] prep πρός τά ἄνω, ἀντίθετα μέ τό ρεῦμα || ad ἐπάνω, ἄνω, τελείως || it is ~ to you ἐξαρτᾶται ἀπό σένα || what is he ~ to? τί ἐπιδιώκει; τί θέλει; || he is not ~ to it δέν ἔχει τήν ἱκανότητα (νά) || ~-and-coming a ἐξαιρετικά δραστήριος, ἀναπτυσσόμενος || n: the ~s and downs of διακυμάνσεις, μεταβολές τῆς τύχης.

upbringing ['ʌpbriŋiŋ] n ἀνατροφή.

update [ʌp'deit] vt συντομεύω ἡμερομηνίαν (συναντήσεως).

upend [ʌp'end] vt (lift up) σηκώνω.

upheaval [ʌp'hi:vəl] n (violent disturbance) ἀναστάτωσις, ἀναταραχή.

uphill ['ʌp'hil] a ἀνηφορικός || ad πρός τά ἄνω.

uphold [ʌp'həuld] vt (maintain) ὑποστηρίζω.

upholstery [ʌp'həulstəri] n ταπετσαρία.

upkeep ['ʌpki:p] n συντήρησις, ἔξοδα συντηρήσεως.

upon [ə'pɔn] *prep* ἐπί, εἰς.

upper ['ʌpə*] *a* ἀνώτερος, ἄνω, ἀπό πάνω ‖ the ~ class *n* ἡ ἀνωτέρα τάξις, ἡ καλή κοινωνία ‖ ~-class *a* τῆς ἀνωτέρας τάξεως ‖ ~most *a* ὑψηλότερος, πιό πάνω, πάνω-πάνω, ἀνώτατος.

upright ['ʌprait] *a* ὄρθιος, κατακόρυφος, κάθετος ‖ (*honest*) εὐθύς, δίκαιος, τίμιος ‖ *n* ὀρθοστάτης.

uprising [ʌp'raiziŋ] *n* ἐξέγερσις, ξεσήκωμα.

uproar ['ʌprɔ:*] *n* θόρυβος, πάταγος, φασαρία, ἀναστάτωσις.

uproot [ʌp'ru:t] *vt* ξερριζώνω.

upset ['ʌpset] *n* ἀναστάτωσις, ἀνατροπή, ἀναποδογύρισμα ‖ [ʌp'set] *vt* ἀνατρέπω, ἀναποδογυρίζω ‖ (*distress*) ταράσσω, ἀναστατώνω, συγκινῶ ‖ ~ting *a* συνταρακτικός, ἀνησυχητικός.

upshot ['ʌpʃɔt] *n* ἀποτέλεσμα, ἔκβασις, κατάληξις.

upside ['ʌpsaid] ~ down *ad* ἄνω-κάτω, ἀνάποδα, φύρδην-μύγδην.

upstairs ['ʌp'stɛəz] *ad* στό ἐπάνω πάτωμα ‖ *a* (*room*) ἐπάνω, τοῦ ἄνω ὀρόφου ‖ *n* ἐπάνω.

upstart ['ʌpsta:t] *n* νεόπλουτος, ἀναιδής ἄνθρωπος.

upstream ['ʌp'stri:m] *ad* ἀντίθετα μέ τό ρεῦμα.

uptake ['ʌpteik] *n*: quick, (slow) on the ~ (δέν) παίρνω, (δέν) ἁρπάζω.

up-to-date ['ʌptə'deit] *a* σύγχρονος, μοντέρνος, τῆς μόδας.

upturn ['ʌptə:n] *n* (*in luck*) βελτίωσις, ἄνοδος.

upward ['ʌpwəd] *a* πρός τά ἄνω ‖ ~(s) *ad* πρός τά ἄνω.

uranium [juə'reiniəm] *n* οὐράνιον.

urban ['ə:bən] *a* ἀστικός.

urbane [ə:'bein] *a* εὐγενής, ἀβρόφρων, ραφιναρισμένος.

urchin ['ə:tʃin] *n* (*boy*) ἀλητάκι ‖ (*also* sea ~) ἐχίνος, ἀχινός.

urge [ə:dʒ] *n* (*desire*) ἐπίμονος ἐπιθυμία, ὤθησις ‖ *vt* (*entreat*) παροτρύνω, συνιστῶ ‖ to ~ on *vt* παρορμῶ, παρακινῶ, ἐνθαρρύνω.

urgency ['ə:dʒənsi] *n* ἐπείγουσα ἀνάγκη, ἐπιμονή, πίεσις.

urgent ['ə:dʒənt] *a* ἐπείγων, πιεστικός, ἄμεσος ‖ ~ly *ad* ἐπειγόντως.

urinal ['juərinl] *n* οὐρητήριον, οὐροδοχεῖον.

urinate ['juərineit] *vi* (κατ)οὐρῶ.

urine ['juərin] *n* οὖρα.

urn [ə:n] *n* ὑδρία, δοχεῖον, ἀγγεῖον ‖ (*teapot*) σαμοβάρι.

us [ʌs] *pron* ἡμᾶς, ἐμᾶς, μας.

usage [ju:zidʒ] *n* μεταχείρησις, ἔθιμον, συνήθειο ‖ (*esp ling*) χρῆσις.

use [ju:s] *n* χρῆσις ‖ (*custom*) συνήθεια, ἔθιμον ‖ (*employment*) χρῆσις, χρησιμο-

ποίησις ‖ (*value*) χρησιμότης ‖ [ju:z] *vt* χρησιμοποιῶ, μεταχειρίζομαι ‖ (*make most of*) χρησιμεύω ‖ in ~ ἐν χρήσει ‖ out of ~ ἄχρηστος ‖ ~d to συνηθίζω νά ‖ she ~d to do it συνήθιζε νά τό κάνει ‖ to ~ up *vt* καταναλίσκω, ἐξαντλῶ ‖ ~d *a* (*car*) μεταχειρισμένο, δεύτερου χεριοῦ ‖ ~ful *a* χρήσιμος, πρακτικός ‖ ~fulness *n* χρησιμότης, ὠφελιμότης ‖ ~less *a* ἄχρηστος, μάταιος, ἄκαρπος ‖ ~lessly *ad* ματαίως, ἀνωφελῶς, μάταια ‖ ~lessness *n* ἔλλειψι; ὠφελιμότητος ‖ ~r *n* χρησιμοποιῶν.

usher ['ʌʃə*] *n* (*at wedding*) παράνυμφος ‖ ~ette *n* (*at cinema*) ταξιθέτρια.

usual ['ju:ʒuəl] *a* συνήθης, συνηθισμένος ‖ ~ly *ad* συνήθως.

usurp [ju:'zə:p] *vt* σφετερίζομαι, ἁρπάζω ‖ ~er *n* σφετεριστής.

usury ['ju:zuri] *n* τοκογλυφία.

utensil [ju:'tensl] *n* σκεῦος, ἐργαλεῖον.

uterus ['ju:tərəs] *n* μήτρα.

utilitarian [ju:tili'teəriən] *a* κοινωφελής, ὠφελιμιστικός.

utility [ju:'tiliti] *n* χρησιμότης, εὐχρηστία ‖ (*useful thing*) χρήσιμον πρᾶγμα ‖ (*also public utility: electricity supply industry*) δημοσία ὑπηρεσία, κοινωφελής ἐπιχείρησις.

utilization [ju:tilai'zeiʃən] *n* χρησιμοποίησις.

utilize ['ju:tilaiz] *vt* χρησιμοποιῶ, ἐκμεταλλεύομαι.

utmost ['ʌtməust] *a* ἀκρότατος, ἀπώτατος, ἔσχατος ‖ *n*: to do one's ~ κάνω ὅ,τι μπορῶ.

utter ['ʌtə*] *a* πλήρης, ὁλοσχερής ‖ *vt* ἀρθρώνω, ἐκστομίζω, προφέρω, λέω ‖ ~ance *n* ἔκφρασις, γνώμη ‖ ~ly *ad* τελείως, ἐξ ὁλοκλήρου.

U-turn ['ju:'tə:n] *n* (*aut*) στροφή 180 μοιρῶν.

V, v

vacancy ['veikənsi] *n* κενόν, κενή θέσις, δωμάτιον.

vacant ['veikənt] *a* κενός ‖ (*not occupied*) ἄδειος, χηρεύων ‖ (*stupid*) ἀφηρημένος, ἀνέκφραστος ‖ '~' (*on door*) 'δωμάτια'.

vacate [və'keit] *vt* ἐκκενώνω, ἀδειάζω, ἐγκαταλείπω.

vacation [və'keiʃən] *n* διακοπή, .ἀργία ‖ ~ist *n* (*US*) ἀδειοῦχος, παραθεριστής.

vaccinate ['væksineit] *vt* ἐμβολιάζω, μπολιάζω.

vaccination [væksi'neiʃən] *n* δαμαλισμός, μπόλιασμα.

vaccine ['væksi:n] *n* δαμαλίς, ἐμβόλιον, βατσίνα.

vacuum ['vækjum] *n* κενόν ‖ ~ bottle *n* (*US*) φιάλη κενοῦ, θερμός ‖ ~ cleaner *n* ήλεκτρική σκούπα ‖ ~ flask n (Brit) φιάλη κενοῦ, θερμός.

vagary ['veigəri] n ἰδιοτροπία, φαντασιοπληξία, βίδα.

vagina [və'dʒainə] n κόλπος (γυναικός).

vagrant ['veigrənt] n τυχωδιώκτης, ἀλήτης.

vague [veig] a ἀσαφής, ἀμυδρός, ἀκαθόριστος ‖ ~ly ad ἀορίστως, ἀσαφῶς ‖ ~ness n ἀσάφεια, ἀοριστία.

vain [vein] a μάταιος, ἄκαρπος, κενός ‖ (conceited) ματαιόδοξος, καμαρωτός ‖ in ~ ματαίως, μάταια ‖ ~ly ad μάταια, ἀνωφελῶς, ἄσκοπα.

vale [veil] n κοιλάδα, λαγκαδιά.

valeting ['vælitiŋ] a: ~ service ὑπηρεσία σιδηρώματος ἀνδρικῶν ἐνδυμάτων.

valiant ['væliənt] a γενναῖος ‖ ~ly ad ἀνδρείως, παληκαρίσια.

valid ['vælid] a ἔγκυρος, βάσιμος, νόμιμος, λογικός ‖ ~ity n ἐγκυρότης, ἰσχύς.

valise [və'li:z] n (suitcase) βαλίτσα.

valley ['væli] n κοιλάδα, λαγκάδι.

valuable ['væljuəbl] a πολύτιμος ‖ ~s npl ἀντικείμενα ἀξίας.

valuation [vælju'eiʃən] n ἐκτίμησις, ἀξία.

value ['vælju:] n ἀξία, τιμή, σημασία, ἔννοια ‖ vt ἐκτιμῶ ‖ ~d a (appreciated) ἐκτιμώμενος ‖ ~less a ἄνευ ἀξίας, εὐτελής ‖ ~r n ἐκτιμητής.

valve [vælv] n βαλβίς, βαλβίδα, δικλείς, λυχνία.

vampire ['væmpaiə*] n βρυκόλακας.

van [væn] n φορτηγόν, σκευοφόρος.

vandal ['vændəl] n βάνδαλος ‖ ~ism n βανδαλισμός.

vanilla [və'nilə] n βανίλλη, βανίλλια ‖ attr a (ice cream) κρέμα.

vanish ['væniʃ] vi ἐξαφανίζομαι, ἐκλείπω, χάνομαι.

vanity ['væniti] n ματαιοδοξία, ἐγωϊσμός ‖ (worthless display) ματαιότης, τὸ μάταιον ‖ ~ case n πουντριέρα.

vantage ['va:ntidʒ] n: ~ point (good viewpoint) πλεονεκτική θέσις.

vapour, (US) vapor ['veipə*] n ἀχνός, πάχνη ‖ (gas) ἀτμός, ὑδρατμός.

variable ['vεəriəbl] a μεταβλητός, εὐμετάβλητος.

variance ['vεəriəns] n: at ~ εἰς διάστασιν, εἰς διαφωνίαν.

variant ['vεəriənt] n διάφορος μορφή, μεταβλητή.

variation [vεəri'eiʃən] n παραλλαγή, παρέκκλισις, μεταβολή.

varicose ['værikous] a: ~ veins κιρσώδεις φλέβες.

varied ['vεərid] a διάφορος, ποικίλος, μεταβαλλόμενος.

variety [və'raiəti] n ποικιλία, διαφορά ‖ (varied collection) ποικιλία, πολλά καί διάφορα ‖ (kind) ποικιλία ‖ ~ show n (theat) παράστασις ποικιλιῶν, ἐπιθεώρησις.

various ['vεəriəs] a ποικίλος, πολυειδής.

varnish ['va:niʃ] n βερνίκι, στιλβωμένη ἐπιφάνεια ‖ vt βερνικώνω, στιλβώνω.

vary ['vεəri] vt διαφοροποιῶ, ποικίλω ‖ vi ἀλλάζω, μεταβάλλομαι, παρεκκλίνω ‖ ~ing a μεταβαλλόμενος, μεταβλητός, ποικίλος.

vase [va:z] n βάζο, ἀγγεῖον.

vast [va:st] a πελώριος, ἐκτεταμένος, μεγάλος, ἀπέραντος ‖ ~ly ad ἀπεράντως, ἀπέραντα ‖ ~ness n ἀπεραντοσύνη, ἀπέραντος ἔκτασις.

vat [væt] n κάδος, βούτα, ξυλοβάρελον.

Vatican ['vætikən] n: the ~ τό Βατικανόν.

vault [vɔ:lt] n θόλος, καμάρα ‖ (cellar) ὑπόγειον, θολωτός τάφος ‖ (leap) πήδημα, ἅλμα ‖ vt πηδῶ, κάνω ἅλμα ἐπί κοντῶ.

veal [vi:l] n μοσχάρι.

veer [viə*] vi στρέφω, μεταπίπτω, γυρίζω.

vegetable ['vedʒitəbl] n φυτόν, λαχανικόν, χορταρικό.

vegetarian [vedʒi'tεəriən] a,n χορτοφάγος, φυτοφάγος.

vegetate ['vedʒiteit] vi φυτοζωῶ.

vegetation [vedʒi'teiʃən] n βλάστησις.

vehemence ['vi:iməns] n βιαιότης, βία, ὁρμή.

vehement ['vi:imənt] a βίαιος, ὁρμητικός, σφοδρός.

vehicle ['vi:ikl] n ὄχημα, ἁμάξι.

vehicular [vi'hikjulə*] a (traffic) τοῦ ὀχήματος.

veil [veil] n πέπλος, βέλο ‖ (fig) κάλυμμα, συγκάλυψις ‖ vt καλύπτω, ἀποκρύπτω.

vein [vein] n φλέψ, φλέβα ‖ (of ore) φλέβα, στρῶμα ‖ (streak) φλέβα, διάθεσις, ταλέντο ‖ (mood) πνεῦμα, διάθεσις, κέφι.

velocity [vi'lɔsiti] n ταχύτης.

velvet ['velvit] n βελοῦδο.

vendetta [ven'detə] n βεντέττα, ἐκδίκησις.

vending machine ['vendiŋməʃi:n] n μηχάνημα πωλήσεως.

vendor ['vendɔ:*] n πωλητής.

veneer [və'niə*] n (lit) καπλαμᾶς, ἐπίστρωσις, ἐπένδυσις ‖ (fig) ἐπίχρισμα, ἐπίστρωμα, λοῦστρο.

venerable ['venərəbl] a ἀξιοσέβαστος, σεβάσμιος.

venereal [vi'niəriəl] a (disease) ἀφροδίσιος.

venetian [vi'ni:ʃən] a: ~ blind περσίδες.

vengeance ['vendʒəns] n ἐκδίκησις.

venison ['venisn] n κρέας ἐλαφιοῦ, κρέας ἀγρίου ζώου.

venom ['venəm] n δηλητήριον, φαρμάκι ‖ ~ous a φαρμακερός ‖ ~ously ad φαρμακερά.

vent [vent] n ὀπή ἐξαερισμοῦ, διέξοδος, ἄνοιγμα ‖ vt ξεσπῶ, ξεθυμαίνω.

ventilate ['ventileit] vt ἀερίζω.

ventilation [venti'leiʃən] n (ἐξ)ἀερισμός.

ventilator ['ventileitə*] n ἐξαεριστήρ, ἀνεμιστήρ.

ventriloquist [ven'trilǝkwist] *n* ἐγγαστρίμυθος.

venture ['ventʃǝ*] *n* τόλμημα, ἐγχείρημα, ἐπιχείρησις ‖ *vt* ριψοκινδυνεύω, ρισκάρω ‖ *vi* ἀποτολμῶ, τολμῶ.

venue ['venjuː] *n* τόπος συναντήσεως, τόπος δίκης.

veranda(h) [vǝ'rændǝ] *n* βεράντα.

verb [vǝːb] *n* ῥῆμα ‖ ~al *a* λεκτικός, προφορικός ‖ *(of a verb)* ῥηματικός ‖ ~ally *ad* προφορικῶς ‖ ~atim *ad* κατά λέξιν, καταλεκτικῶς.

verbose [vǝː'bǝus] *a* πολύλογος, μακροσκελής.

verdict ['vǝːdikt] *n* κρίσις, γνώμη ‖ *(of jury)* ἐτυμηγορία, ἀπόφασις.

verge [vǝːdʒ] *n* *(of road)* ἄκρη (τοῦ δρόμου) ‖ **on the ~** *a (of doing* ἕτοιμος νά ‖ *vi:* **to ~ on** πλησιάζω, τείνω πρός, γγίζω μέ.

verger ['vǝːdʒǝ*] *n* νεωκόρος.

verification [verifi'keiʃǝn] *n* ἐπιβεβαίωσις, ἐπικύρωσις, ἀπόδειξις.

verify ['verifai] *vt* ἐπιβεβαιώνω, ἐλέγχω, ἀποδεικνύω.

vermin ['vǝːmin] *npl* βλαβερά ζωύφια.

vermouth ['vǝːmǝθ] *n* βερμούτ.

vernacular [vǝ'nækjulǝ*] *n* τοπική διάλεκτος, ντοπολαλιά, κοινή γλῶσσα.

versatile ['vǝːsǝtail] *a* πολύπλευρος, εὔστροφος.

versatility [vǝːsǝ'tiliti] *n* τό πολύπλευρον, εὐστροφία.

verse [vǝːs] *n* ποίησις, ποιήματα ‖ *(line)* στίχος ‖ *(of poem, song)* στροφή ‖ *(of Bible)* ἐδάφιον ‖ ~d *a* (+*in*) ἐπιδέξιος, πεπειραμένος, μορφωμένος.

version ['vǝːʃǝn] *n (account)* ἔκδοσις, ἑρμηνεία.

versus ['vǝːsǝs] *prep* κατά, ἐναντίον.

vertebra ['vǝːtibrǝ] *n* σπόνδυλος, ραχοκόκκαλο.

vertebrate ['vǝːtibrit] *a* σπονδυλωτός.

vertical ['vǝːtikǝl] *a* κάθετος, κατακόρυφος, τῆς κορυφῆς ‖ *n:* **the ~** κάθετος ‖ ~**ly** *ad* καθέτως, κατακορύφως.

vertigo ['vǝːtigǝu] *n* ἴλιγγος, ζάλη.

verve [vǝːv] *n* ἔμπνευσις, ἐνθουσιασμός, κέφι.

very ['veri] *ad* πολύ, ἀκριβῶς ‖ *a (identical)* ἴδιος, αὐτός οὗτος ‖ *(mere)* καί μόνη, καί πού.

vespers ['vespǝz] *npl* ἑσπερινός.

vessel ['vesl] *n* πλοῖον, σκάφος ‖ *(container)* ἀγγεῖον, σκεῦος.

vest [vest] *n* φανελλάκι ‖ *(US: waistcoat)* γιαλέκο ‖ *vt* περιβάλλω, παραχωρῶ, παρέχω, ἐνδύω ‖ ~**ed** *a (interest)* κεκτημένος, ἐπενδεδυμένος.

vestibule ['vestibjuːl] *n (of house)* προθάλαμος, χώλ, ἀντρέ.

vestige ['vestidʒ] *n* ὑπόλειμμα, ἴχνος.

vestry ['vestri] *n* ἱεροφυλάκειον, σκευοφυλάκιον, βεστιάριον.

vet [vet] *n* κτηνίατρος ‖ *vt* ἐξετάζω.

veteran ['vetǝrǝn] *n* παλαίμαχος, βετεράνος ‖ *a* τοῦ παλαιμάχου, πεπειραμένος.

veterinary ['vetǝrinǝri] *a* κτηνιατρικός ‖ ~ **surgeon** *n* κτηνίατρος.

veto ['viːtǝu] *n* δικαίωμα ἀρνησικυρίας, βέτο ‖ *(prohibition)* ἀπαγόρευσις ‖ *vt* προβάλλω βέτο (είς).

vex [veks] *vt* ἐνοχλῶ, ἐρεθίζω, ταράσσω ‖ ~**ed** *a* θυμωμένος, πειραγμένος.

via ['vaiǝ] *prep* διά, διά μέσου.

viability [vaiǝ'biliti] *n* βιωσιμότης.

viable ['vaiǝbl] *a* βιώσιμος, βατός.

viaduct ['vaiǝdʌkt] *n* ὁδογέφυρα, κοιλαδογέφυρα, ἁψιδωτή γέφυρα.

vibrate [vai'breit] *vi* πάλλομαι, δονοῦμαι, ταλαντεύομαι ‖ *(resound)* ἠχῶ.

vibration [vai'breiʃǝn] *n* ταλάντευσις, δόνησις, κούνημα.

vicar ['vikǝ*] *n* ἐφημέριος, βικάριος ‖ ~**age** *n* πρεσβυτέριον, οἰκία ἐφημερίου.

vice [vais] *n (evil)* ἐκφυλισμός, ἀκολασία, ἁμάρτημα ‖ *(tech)* συνδήκτωρ, μέγγενη ‖ **vice-** *prefix* ἀντί-, ὑπό ‖ ~**-chairman** *n* ἀντιπρόεδρος ‖ ~**-president** *n* ἀντιπρόεδρος ‖ ~ **versa** *ad* τανάπαλιν.

vicinity [vi'siniti] *n* γειτονιά, ἐγγύτης, περιοχή.

vicious ['viʃǝs] *a (also cruel)* κακός, κακοήθης, στρυφνός ‖ ~**ness** *n* κακία.

vicissitudes [vi'sisitjuːdz] *npl* περιπέτειες, μεταβολές, γυρίσματα τῆς τύχης.

victim ['viktim] *n* θῦμα ‖ ~**ization** *n* καταπίεσις, ἀντίποινα ‖ ~**ize** *vt* λαμβάνω ὡς θῦμα, θυσιάζω.

victor ['viktǝ*] *n* νικητής.

Victorian [vik'tɔːriǝn] *a* βικτωριανός.

victorious [vik'tɔːriǝs] *a* νικηφόρος, θριαμβευτής.

victory ['viktǝri] *n* νίκη.

video ['vidiǝu] *a* τῆς εἰκόνος.

vie [vai] *vi (compete)* (+*with*) ἁμιλλῶμαι, ἀνταγωνίζομαι.

view [vjuː] *n* ὄψις, ματιά, βλέμμα ‖ *(scene)* θέα, προοπτική, ὄψις ‖ *(opinion)* ἄποψις, ἔποψις, ἔκθεσις ‖ *(intention)* πρόθεσις, βλέψις, σκοπός ‖ *vt (situation)* κυττάζω, ἐπιθεωρῶ, ἐξετάζω ‖ ~**er** *n (viewfinder)* σκόπευτρον ‖ *(phot: small projector)* μικρό μηχάνημα προβολῆς ‖ *(TV)* θεατής ‖ ~**finder** *n* στόχαστρον, εἰκονοσκόπιον ‖ ~**point** *n* σημεῖον μέ καλήν θέαν ‖ *(attitude)* ἄποψις.

vigil ['vidʒil] *n* ἀγρυπνία, ξενύχτι, ὁλονυχτία ‖ ~**ance** *n* ἀγρυπνία, προσοχή ‖ ~**ant** *a* ἄγρυπνος, προσεκτικός ‖ ~**antly** *ad* ἀγρύπνως.

vigor ['vigǝ*] *n (US)* = **vigour**.

vigorous ['vigǝrǝs] *a* ρωμαλέος, σθεναρός, ζωηρός ‖ ~**ly** *ad* γερά, δυνατά.

vigour ['vigǝ*] *n* σθένος, σφρῖγος, ζωτικότης, ζωηρότης.

vile [vail] *a* ἀνήθικος, ἀχρεῖος, αἰσχρός ‖

(*foul*) ἀκάθαρτος, βρωμερός, σιχαμερός.

villa ['vilə] *n* ἔπαυλις, βίλλα.

village ['vilidʒ] *n* χωριό ‖ ~**r** *n* χωριάτης.

villain ['vilən] *n* ὁ κακός, παλιάνθρωπος.

vindicate ['vindikeit] *vt* δικαιώνω, ὑπερ-ασπίζω, δικαιολογῶ.

vindication [vindi'keiʃən] *n* δικαίωσις, ὑπεράσπισις.

vindictive [vin'diktiv] *a* ἐκδικητικός.

vine [vain] *n* ἄμπελος, κλῆμα.

vinegar ['vinigə*] *n* ὄξος, ξύδι.

vineyard ['vinjəd] *n* ἀμπελών, ἀμπέλι.

vintage ['vintidʒ] *n* (*wine*) κρασί ὡρισμένου ἔτους ‖ (*gathering*) τρυγητός, τρύγος.

vinyl ['vainl] *n* βινύλιον.

viola [vi'əulə] *n* (*mus*) βιόλα.

violate ['vaiəleit] *vt* (*break promise*) ἀθετῶ, καταπατῶ ‖ (*disturb*) παραβιάζω ‖ (*desecrate*) βεβηλώνω.

violation [vaiə'leiʃən] *n* παραβίασις, παράβασις, ἀθέτησις.

violence ['vaiələns] *n* σφοδρότης, ἔντασις ‖ (*rough treatment*) βία, βιαιότης.

violent ['vaiələnt] *a* βίαιος, σφοδρός, ὁρμητικός ‖ (*extreme*) ζωηρός, ἔντονος, ὀξύς, ἰσχυρός ‖ ~**ly** *ad* βίαια, ἀπότομα, ἐξαιρετικά, πολύ.

violet ['vaiəlit] *n* βιολέττα, μενεξές ‖ *a* ἰώδης, μώβ.

violin [vaiə'lin] *n* βιολί.

viper ['vaipə*] *n* ἔχιδνα, ὀχιά.

virgin ['və:dʒin] *n* παρθένος ‖ *a* παρθένος, παρθενικός, καθαρός ‖ ~**ity** *n* παρθενία.

virile ['virail] *a* ἀνδρικός, δυνατός, σθεναρός.

virility [vi'riliti] *n* ἀνδρισμός, ἀνδροπρέπεια, δύναμις.

virtual ['və:tjuəl] *a* οὐσιαστικός, πραγματικός ‖ ~**ly** *ad* (*in fact*) κατ'οὐσίαν, οὐσιαστικῶς ‖ (*almost*) σχεδόν.

virtue ['və:tju:] *n* ἀρετή ‖ (*good quality*) ἱκανότης, δραστικότης ‖ **by** ~ *of* δυνάμει, συνεπεία, λόγω, ἐξ αἰτίας τοῦ.

virtuoso [və:tju'əuzəu] *n* δεξιοτέχνης μουσικός, βιρτουόζος.

virtuous ['və:tjuəs] *a* ἐνάρετος.

virulence ['viruləns] *n* φαρμακερότης ‖ (*hatred*) κακεντρέχεια.

virulent ['virulənt] *a* δηλητηριώδης, θανατηφόρος ‖ (*bitter*) ἐχθρικός, κακεντρεχής, φαρμακερός.

virus ['vaiərəs] *n* ἰός, μικρόβιον.

visa ['vi:zə] *n* θεώρησις, βίζα.

vis-à-vis ['vi:zəvi:] *prep* ἀπέναντι, ἀντίκρυ, καρσί.

viscount ['vaikaunt] *n* ὑποκόμης.

visibility [vizi'biliti] *n* ὁρατότης.

visible ['vizəbl] *a* ὁρατός, ἐμφανής, προφανής.

visibly ['vizəbli] *ad* καταφανῶς, προφανῶς, ὁλοφάνερα.

vision ['viʒən] *n* ὅρασις ‖ (*imagination*) διορατικότης ‖ (*dream*) ὅραμα, ὀπτασία

‖ ~**ary** *n* φαντασιοκόπος, οὐτοπιστής, ὀνειροπόλος ‖ *a* (*unpractical*) οὐτοπικός, φανταστικός.

visit ['vizit] *n* ἐπίσκεψις ‖ *vt* ἐπισκέπτομαι ‖ (*stay with*) κάνω βίζιτα, φιλοξενοῦμαι ‖ ~**ing** *a* (*professor*) ἐπισκέπτης καθηγητής ‖ ~**ing card** *n* ἐπισκεπτήριον, μπιλιέτο ‖ ~**or** *n* ἐπισκέπτης ‖ ~**ors' book** *n* βιβλίον ἐπισκεπτῶν.

visor ['vaizə*] *n* προσωπίς.

vista ['vistə] *n* θέα, ἄνοιγμα, προοπτική, ἄποψις.

visual ['vizjuəl] *a* ὀπτικός, ὁρατός, πραγματικός ‖ ~ **aid** *n* ὀπτικό βοήθημα ‖ ~**ize** *vt* κάνω ὁρατόν, ὁραματίζομαι ‖ ~**ly** *ad* ὀπτικῶς.

vital ['vaitl] *a* οὐσιώδης, κεφαλαιώδης, ζωτικός ‖ (*necessary to life*) ζωτικός, οὐσιώδης ‖ ~**ity** *n* ζωτικότης, ἀνθεκτικότης, ζωή ‖ ~**ly** *ad* ζωτικῶς.

vitamin ['vitəmin] *n* βιταμίνη.

vitiate ['viʃieit] *vt* (*make ineffective*) φθείρω, διαστρέφω.

vivacious [vi'veiʃəs] *a* ζωηρός, εὔθυμος, κεφάτος.

vivacity [vi'væsiti] *n* ζωηρότης, εὐθυμία.

vivid ['vivid] *a* ζωντανός, ζωηρός, σαφής ‖ (*bright, clear*) ζωηρός, λαμπρός ‖ ~**ly** *ad* ζωηρά, λαμπρά.

vivisection [vivi'sekʃən] *n* ζωοτομία.

vocabulary [vəu'kæbjuləri] *n* λεξιλόγιον.

vocal ['vəukəl] *a* φωνητικός, ἠχητικός ‖ ~ **cord** *n* φωνητική χορδή ‖ ~**ist** *n* ἀοιδός, τραγουδιστής.

vocation [vəu'keiʃən] *n* (*calling*) προορισμός, κλῆσις ‖ (*profession*) ἐπάγγελμα, τέχνη.

vociferous [vəu'sifərəs] *a* κραυγαλέος, κραυγάζων, φωνακλάς ‖ ~**ly** *ad* φωνάζοντας, φωνακλάδικα.

vodka ['vɔdkə] *n* βότκα.

vogue [vəug] *n* μόδα, δημοτικότης.

voice [vɔis] *n* φωνή ‖ (*right of opinion*) ψῆφος, γνώμη ‖ (*gram*) φωνή (τοῦ ρήματος) ‖ *vt* ἐκφράζω ‖ **with one** ~ ὁμοφώνως.

void [vɔid] *n* κενόν ‖ *a* (*of meaning*) παράλογος, στερούμενος.

volatile ['vɔlətail] *a* κέφατος, εὐμετάβολος, παιχνιδιάρικος ‖ (*evaporating quickly*) πτητικός.

volcanic [vɔl'kænik] *a* ἡφαιστειώδης, ἐκρηκτικός.

volcano [vɔl'keinəu] *n* ἡφαίστειον.

volition [və'liʃən] *n*: **of one's own** ~ μέ τήν θελήσί μου.

volley ['vɔli] *n* ὁμοβροντία ‖ (*shower*) χείμαρρος, καταιγισμός, θύελλα ‖ (*tennis*) βολλέ, κατ'εὐθείαν κτύπημα ‖ ~**ball** *n* χειροσφαίρησις, βόλλεϋ-μπώλ.

volt [vəult] *n* βόλτ ‖ ~**age** *n* τάσις, βολτάζ.

volte-face ['vɔlt'fɑːs] *n* πλήρης στροφή, ἀλλαγή γνώμης.

voluble ['vɔljubl] *a* εὐφραδής, εὔγλωττος.

volume ['vɔlju:m] *n* τόμος βιβλίων ‖ *(amount)* μεγάλη ποσότης ‖ *(space)* ὄγκος ‖ *(loudness of sound)* ἔντασις, ὄγκος.

voluntarily ['vɔləntərili] *ad* ἑκουσίως, αὐθορμήτως, ἐθελοντικῶς.

voluntary ['vɔləntəri] *a* ἐθελοντικός, ἑκούσιος, ἐθελοντής.

volunteer [vɔlən'tiə*] *n* ἐθελοντής ‖ *vi* προσφέρομαι.

voluptuous [və'lʌptjuəs] *a* φιλήδονος, ἡδυπαθής.

vomit ['vɔmit] *n* ἐμετός, ξέρασμα ‖ *vti* ἐξεμῶ, ξερνῶ.

vote [vəut] *n* ψηφοφορία, ψῆφος ‖ *(right)* δικαίωμα ψήφου ‖ *(result)* ἀποτέλεσμα ψηφοφορίας ‖ *vt* ψηφίζω, ἐγκρίνω ‖ *vi* ψηφίζω ‖ ~**r** *n* ψηφοφόρος, ἐκλογεύς.

voting ['vəutiŋ] *n* ψηφοφορία.

vouch [vautʃ] **to** ~ **for** *vt* ὑποστηρίζω, ἐγγυῶμαι γιά.

voucher ['vautʃə*] *n* ἀπόδειξις πληρωμῆς, δικαιολογητικόν.

vow [vau] *n* εὐχή, ὅρκος, τάξιμο, τάμα ‖ *vt* ὁρκίζομαι, διακηρύττω.

vowel ['vauəl] *n* φωνῆεν.

voyage ['vɔiidʒ] *n* ταξίδι.

vulgar ['vʌlgə*] *a* χυδαῖος, πρόστυχος, ἄξεστος ‖ *(of common people)* κοινός, λαϊκός ‖ ~**ity** *n* χυδαιότης, προστυχιά.

vulnerability [vʌlnərə'biliti] *n* τό τρωτόν, τρωτότης, εὐπάθεια.

vulnerable ['vʌlnərəbl] *a* τρωτός, εὔτρωτος, εὐπρόσβλητος.

vulture ['vʌltʃə*] *n* γύψ, ὄρνιο.

W, w

wad [wɔd] *n* *(bundle)* δέσμη, μάτσο.

wade [weid] *vi* βαδίζω στό νερό, περνῶ πεζῆ.

wafer ['weifə*] *n* γκωφρέτα, λεπτό μπισκότο.

waffle ['wɔfl] *n* *(food)* εἶδος τηγανίτα ‖ *(col: empty talk)* φλυαρία, μπούρδες ‖ *vi* *(col)* φλυαρῶ.

waft [wa:ft] *vti* μεταφέρω, σκορπίζω.

wag [wæg] *vti* κινῶ, κουνῶ, κινοῦμαι.

wage [weidʒ] *n* ἡμερομίσθιον, μισθός, ἀμοιβή, μεροκάματο ‖ *vt* διεξάγω, διενεργῶ ‖ ~**s** *npl* μισθός ‖ ~ **earner** *n* μισθωτός ‖ ~ **freeze** *n* παγίωσις μισθῶν.

wager ['weidʒə*] *n* στοίχημα.

waggle ['wægl] *vti* *(tail)* κουνῶ, ταλαντεύομαι.

wag(g)on ['wægən] *n* *(road, rail)* ἄμαξα, βαγόνι.

wail [weil] *n* θρῆνος, ὀλοφυρμός ‖ *vi* θρηνῶ, κλαίω, ὀλοφύρομαι.

waist [weist] *n* ὀσφύς, μέση, ζώνη ‖ ~**coat** *n* γιλέκο ‖ ~**line** *n* μέση, τάγια.

wait [weit] *n* ἀναμονή, στάσις ‖ *vi* περι-

μένω, ἀναμμένω, σερβίρω ‖ **to** ~ **for** *vt* περιμένω, ἀναμένω, καρτερῶ ‖ ~**er** *n* σερβιτόρος, γκαρσόνι ‖ ~**ing room** *n* αἴθουσα ἀναμονῆς, προθάλαμος ‖ ~**ress** *n* σερβιτόρα.

wake [weik] *(irreg v)* *vt* ἐξυπνῶ ‖ *vi* ἀγρυπνῶ, εἶμαι ἄϋπνος ‖ *n* ξενύχτι νεκροῦ ‖ ~**n** *vt* ἀφυπνίζω, ξυπνῶ.

Wales [weilz] *n* Οὐαλλία.

walk [wɔ:k] *n* πορεία, περπάτημα, βόλτα, περίπατος ‖ *(way of walking)* βάδισμα, περπατησιά ‖ *(path, route)* περίπατος, λεωφόρος, δρόμος, πεζοδρόμιον ‖ *(occupation)* ἐπάγγελμα ‖ *vi* περπατῶ, βαδίζω ‖ ~**er** *n* πεζοπόρος, περπατητής ‖ ~**ie-talkie** *n* πομποδέκτης, φορητός ἀσύρματος ‖ ~**ing** *n* πεζοπορία, περπάτημα ‖ *attr* *a* *(holiday)* μέ τά πόδια, βαδίζων ‖ *(shoes)* *(παπούτσια)* πεζοπορίας ‖ ~**ing stick** *n* μπαστούνι ‖ ~**out** *n* *(of workers)* ἀπεργία ‖ ~**over** *n* *(col)* εὔκολος νίκη, εὔκολη δουλειά.

wall [wɔ:l] *n* τοῖχος, τεῖχος ‖ ~**ed** *a* *(city)* περιτειχισμένος.

wallet ['wɔlit] *n* πορτοφόλι.

wallop ['wɔləp] *vt* *(col: thrash)* σπάω στό ξύλο.

wallow ['wɔləu] *vi* (+ *in*) κυλίομαι (εἰς), πλέω (εἰς), κολυμπῶ (στό).

wallpaper ['wɔ:lpeipə*] *n* τοιχόχαρτον, χαρτί ταπετσαρίας.

walnut ['wɔ:lnʌt] *n* καρύδι ‖ *(tree)* καρυδιά.

walrus ['wɔ:lrəs] *n* θαλάσσιος ἵππος.

waltz [wɔ:lts] *n* βάλς ‖ *vi* χορεύω βάλς.

wand [wɔnd] *n* ράβδος, ραβδί.

wander ['wɔndə*] *vi* περιπλανῶμαι, περιφέρομαι, τριγυρίζω ‖ ~**er** *n* περιπλανώμενος, σουρτούκης ‖ ~**ing** *a* πλανόδιος, περιπλανώμενος.

want [wɔnt] *vt* θέλω, ἐπιθυμῶ ‖ *(need)* χρειάζομαι, ἔχω ἀνάγκη, ἐλλείπω ‖ *n*: **for** ~ **of** ἐλλείψει ‖ ~**s** *npl* *(needs)* ἀνάγκες.

wanton ['wɔntən] *a* ἀχαλίνωτος, ἀκόλαστος, ἐσκεμμένος.

war [wɔ:*] *n* πόλεμος.

ward [wɔ:d] *n* *(division)* περιφέρεια, συνοικία ‖ *(hospital)* θάλαμος ‖ *vt*: **to** ~ **off** ἀποκρούω, ἀποφεύγω.

warden ['wɔ:dn] *n* διευθυντής, φύλακας.

warder ['wɔ:də*] *n* φύλαξ, δεσμοφύλαξ.

wardrobe ['wɔ:drəub] *n* ντουλάπα ‖ *(clothing)* γκαρταρόμπα, τά ροῦχα.

ware [wɛə*] *n* κατασκευασμένα εἴδη ‖ ~**s** *npl* ἐμπορεύματα ‖ ~**house** *n* ἀποθήκη.

warfare ['wɔ:fɛə*] *n* πόλεμος.

warhead ['wɔ:hed] *n* κῶνος βλήματος.

warily ['wɛərili] *ad* προσεκτικά, ἐπιφυλακτικά.

warlike ['wɔ:laik] *a* πολεμικός, πολεμοχαρής, φιλοπόλεμος.

warm [wɔ:m] *a* θερμός ‖ *(fire)* ζεστός ‖ *(welcome)* ἔνθερμος, ζωηρός ‖ **to** ~ **up**

vti ζεσταίνω ‖ ζωηρεύω, ἐνθουσιάζομαι ‖ ~-hearted *a* μέ ζεστή καρδιά, συμπονετικός ‖ ~ly *ad* θερμά, ἐνθουσιωδῶς ‖ ~th *n* θερμότης, ζεστασιά, ἐνθουσιασμός.

warn [wɔ:n] *vt* προειδοποιῶ ‖ ~ing *n* προειδοποίησις ‖ (*caution*) εἰδοποίησις ‖ ~ing light *n* προειδοποιητικόν φῶς.

warp [wɔ:p] *vt* στήμων, στημόνι.

warrant ['wɔrənt] *n* (*police*) ἔνταλμα.

warranty ['wɔrənti] *n* ἐξουσιοδότησις, δικαιολογία, ἐγγύησις.

warrior ['wɔriə*] *n* πολεμιστής.

warship ['wɔ:ʃip] *n* πολεμικόν (πλοῖον).

wart [wɔ:t] *n* κρεατοελιά.

wartime ['wɔ:taim] *n* πολεμική ἐποχή, πολεμική περίοδος.

wary ['wɛəri] *a* προσεκτικός, πονηρός, ἐπιφυλακτικός.

was [wɔz, wəz] *pt* of be.

wash [wɔʃ] *n* πλύσις, πλύσιμο, νίψιμο ‖ (*clothes*) ροῦχα, μπουγάδα ‖ *vt* πλένω, πλύνω ‖ *vi* πλένομαι, πλένομαι ‖ to ~ away *vt* παρασύρω, παίρνω ‖ ~able *a* πού πλένεται ‖ ~basin *n* λεκάνη (νιπτήρος) ‖ ~er *n* παράκυκλος, ροδέλλα ‖ (*person, machine*) πλύστρα, πλυντήριον ‖ ~ing *n* (*linen etc*) ροῦχα γιά πλύσιμο, πλύση, πλύσιμο ‖ ~ing machine *n* πλυντήριον ‖ ~ing powder *n* σκόνη πλυσίματος ‖ ~ing-up *n* πλύσιμο τῶν πιάτων ‖ ~out *n* (*col*) ἀποτυχία, φιάσκο ‖ ~room *n* τουαλέττα.

wasn't ['wɔznt] = was not ‖ *see* be.

wasp [wɔsp] *n* σφήκα.

wastage ['weistidʒ] *n* σπατάλη.

waste [weist] *n* σπατάλη ‖ (*what is wasted*) ἄχρηστα ὑλικά, σκουπίδια ‖ ἀπορρίμματα, σκάρτα ‖ (*wilderness*) ἔρημος, λόγγος ‖ *a* ἄχρηστος ‖ (*land*) χέρσος, ἐρημωμένος ‖ *vt* (*object*) καταναλίσκω, καταστρέφω, φθείρω ‖ (*time*) σπαταλῶ, χάνω ‖ *vi*: to ~ away φθίνω, ἀδυνατίζω ‖ ~ful *a* σπάταλος, ἄσωτος, σκορποχέρης ‖ ~fully *ad* σπάταλα, ἀπερίσκεπτα, ἄσκοπα ‖ ~paper basket *n* κάλαθος ἀχρήστων.

watch [wɔtʃ] *n* ἐπίβλεψις, ἐπιτήρησις, ἐπαγρύπνησις ‖ (*guard*) φυλακή, φρουρός ‖ (*naut*) φυλακή, βάρδια ‖ (*timepiece*) ὡρολόγιον, ρολόϊ ‖ *vt* παρατηρῶ, παρακολουθῶ ‖ *vi* ἀγρυπνῶ, προσέχω, φυλάσσω ‖ ~dog *n* (*fig*) ἐπιστάτης, φύλακας ‖ ~ful *a* ἄγρυπνος, προσεκτικός ‖ ~maker *n* ὡρολογοποιός, ρολογάς ‖ ~man *n* (νυκτο)φύλαξ ‖ ~ strap *n* λουρίδα ὡρολογίου.

water ['wɔ:tə*] *n* ὕδωρ, νερό ‖ *vt* ποτίζω, βρέχω, καταβρέχω, διαβρέχω ‖ to ~ down *vt* ἀπαλύνω (ἔκφρασιν), ἐξασθενίζω, συγκαλύπτω ‖ ~ closet *n* ἀποχωρητήριον, ἀπόπατος, μέρος ‖ ~colour, (*US*) ~color *n* πίναξ μέ νερομπογιά,

ἀκουαρέλα ‖ (*paint*) ὑδρόχρωμα, νερομπογιά ‖ ~cress *n* νεροκάρδαμο ‖ ~fall *n* ὑδατόπτωσις, καταρράκτης ‖ ~ hole *n* νερόλακκος ‖ ~ing can *n* ποτιστήρι ‖ ~ level *n* (*in radiator*) ὑδροστάτης ‖ ~lily *n* νούφαρο ‖ ~line *n* ἴσαλος (γραμμή) ‖ ~logged *a* πλημμυρισμένος, διάβροχος, μουσκεμμένος ‖ ~melon *n* καρπούζι ‖ ~ polo *n* ὑδρόσφαιρον ‖ ~proof *a* ἀδιάβροχος, ὑδατοστεγής ‖ ~shed *n* γραμμή διαχωρισμοῦ ὑδάτων ‖ ~-skiing *n* θαλάσσιον σκί ‖ to go ~skiing κάνω θαλάσσιο σκί ‖ ~tight *a* ὑδατοστεγής, στεγανός, ἀδιάβροχος ‖ ~works *npl* μηχανοστάσιον ὑδρεύσεως ‖ ~y *a* (*colour*) ὠχρός, ἄτονος.

watt [wɔt] *n* βάτ(τ).

wave [weiv] *n* κῦμα ‖ (*of hand*) κούνημα τοῦ χεριοῦ ‖ (*rad*) κῦμα ‖ (*in hair*) κυμάτωσις, κατσάρωμα ‖ *vt* (*hand*) χαιρετῶ μέ τό χέρι, κουνῶ τό χέρι ‖ (*shape in curves*) κατσαρώνω, ὀντουλάρω ‖ *vi* (*flag*) κυματίζω, ἀνεμίζω ‖ ~length *n* μῆκος κύματος.

waver ['weivə*] *vi* ταλαντεύομαι, κυμαίνομαι ‖ (*weaken*) κλονίζομαι, ἀμφιρρέπω.

wavy ['weivi] *a* κυματώδης, κυματιστός.

wax [wæks] *n* κηρός, κερί ‖ *vt* (*floors*) κερώνω, παρκετάρω ‖ *vi* (*moon*) μεγαλώνω, γίνομαι.

way [wei] *n* ὁδός, δρόμος ‖ (*manner*) τρόπος ‖ (*direction*) κατεύθυνσις, μεριά, δρόμος ‖ (*habit*) τρόπος, συνήθεια, ἔθιμο ‖ in the ~ φράζω, ἐμποδίζω, κόβω (τόν δρόμο) ‖ by the ~ παρεμπιπτόντως, καθ' ὁδόν, μέ τήν εὐκαιρία ‖ '~ in' 'εἴσοδος' ‖ '~ out' 'ἔξοδος' ‖ ~lay *vt* ἐνεδρεύω, καιροφυλακτῶ ‖ ~ward *a* δύστροπος, διεστραμμένος.

we [wi:] *pl pron* ἡμεῖς, ἐμεῖς.

weak [wi:k] *a* ἀδύνατος, ἀσθενής ‖ (*not powerful*) ἀνίσχυρος ‖ (*diluted*) ἀδύνατος, ἐλαφρός ‖ ~en *vti* ἐξασθενίζω, ἀδυνατίζω, ἐξασθενῶ ‖ ~ling *n* ἀδύνατος ἄνθρωπος, ἀσθενής πλάσμα ‖ ~ly *ad* ἀδύνατα ‖ ~ness *n* ἀδυναμία ‖ (*fault*) ἐλάττωμα ‖ (*fondness*) προτίμησις, ἀδυναμία.

wealth [welθ] *n* πλοῦτος ‖ (*abundance*) ἀφθονία ‖ (*things having value*) περιουσία ‖ ~y *a* πλούσιος.

wean [wi:n] *vt* ἀπογαλακτίζω, ἀποκόβω.

weapon ['wepən] *n* ὅπλον.

wear [wɛə*] (*irreg v*) *n* ροῦχα, ρουχισμός, φόρεμα ‖ (*use*) χρῆσις, φθορά ‖ *vt* φέρω, φορῶ ‖ (*show*) δείχνω, κρατιέμαι ‖ (*use*) φθείρω, τρώω, τρίβω, λυώνω ‖ *vi* (*last long*) ἀντέχω, διατηροῦμαι ‖ ~ and tear φθορά ‖ to ~ away *vti* φθείρω, φθείρομαι, τρώγομαι, τρίβω ‖ to ~ down *vt* φθείρω, τρώγω ‖ to ~ off *vi* ἐξαλείφομαι, σβήνομαι, σβήνω ‖ *vt* φθείρω, τρίβω, λυώνω ‖ to ~ out *vt* φθείρω, τρίβω, λυώνω ‖ ~er *n* φορῶν.

wearily ['wiərili] *ad* κουρασμένα, κοπιαστικά.

weariness ['wiərinis] *n* κόπωσις, κούρασι.

weary ['wiəri] *a* κουρασμένος, ἀποκαμωμένος ‖ (*tiring*) κουραστικός, πληκτικός, ἀνιαρός ‖ *vti* κοπιῶ, κουράζω, κουράζομαι.

weasel ['wi:zl] *n* νυφίτσα, κουνάβι.

weather ['weðə*] *n* καιρός ‖ *vt* διέρχομαι, περνῶ ἐπιτυχῶς ‖ (*season*) ἐκθέτω στόν καιρό ‖ ~-**beaten** *a* ἀνεμοδαρμένος, ἡλιοκαμμένος, μαυρισμένος ‖ ~**cock** *n* ἀνεμοδείκτης ‖ ~ **forecast** *n* πρόβλεψις καιροῦ.

weave [wi:v] (*irreg v*) *vt* ὑφαίνω, πλέκω, συνθέτω ‖ ~**r** *n* ὑφαντής.

weaving ['wi:viŋ] *n* ὕφανσις, πλέξιμο.

web [web] *n* ὕφασμα, μεμβράνη ‖ (*of spider*) ἱστός ἀράχνης, ἀράχνη ‖ ~**bed** *a* μεμβρανώδης ‖ ~**bing** *n* ὕφασμα λωρίδων, ἐνισχυτική ταινία.

wed [wed] *vt* νυμφεύω, νυμφεύομαι, παντρεύομαι.

we'd [wi:d] = **we had, we would** ‖ *see* **have, would.**

wedding ['wediŋ] *n* γάμος, παντρειά, στεφάνωμα ‖ ~ **day** *n* ἡμέρα τῶν γάμων, ἐπέτειος τῶν γάμων ‖ ~ **present** *n* γαμήλιον δῶρον ‖ ~ **ring** *n* ἀρραβῶνος, βέρα.

wedge [wedʒ] *n* σφήν(α) ‖ *vt* ἐνσφηνώνω, χώνω, μπήγω ‖ (*pack tightly*) σφηνώνω, στριμώχνω.

Wednesday ['wenzdi] *n* Τετάρτη.

wee [wi:] *a* (*Scottish col*) μικρούλης, λιγάκι, τόσο δά.

weed [wi:d] *n* ζιζάνιον, ἀγριόχορτο ‖ *vt* ξεχορταριάζω, σκαλίζω, βγάζω, καθαρίζω ‖ ~**killer** *n* ζιζανιοκτόνον.

week [wi:k] *n* ἐβδομάς, βδομάδα ‖ ~**day** *n* καθημερινή ‖ ~**end** *n* Σαββατοκύριακο ‖ ~**ly** *ad* ἐβδομαδιαίως, καθ' ἐβδομάδα ‖ *a* ἐβδομαδιαῖος.

weep [wi:p] (*irreg v*) *vi* κλαίω, χύνω δάκρυα, δακρύζω.

weigh [wei] *vt* σταθμίζω, ζυγίζω ‖ (*have weight*) ζυγίζω ‖ *vi* (*be important*) βαραίνω, ζυγίζω ‖ **to ~ down** *vt* (ὑπερ)φορτώνω, βαραίνω, πιέζω ‖ **to ~ up** *vt* ἐκτιμῶ, ζυγίζω ‖ ~**bridge** *n* γεφυροπλάστιγξ.

weight [weit] *n* βαρύτης ‖ (*something used on scales*) σταθμόν, μέτρον, ζύγι ‖ (*load*) βάρος, φορτίον ‖ (*importance*) κύρος, ἐπιρροή, ἀξία ‖ ~**lessness** *n* τό ἀβαρές ‖ ~ **lifting** *n* ἄρσις βαρῶν ‖ ~**y** *a* βαρύς, σπουδαῖος, πειστικός.

weir [wiə*] *n* κλεισιάς, ὑδατοφράκτης.

weird [wiəd] *a* ὑπερφυσικός, παράξενος.

welcome ['welkəm] *n* ὑποδοχή, δεξίωσις ‖ *vt* καλωσορίζω, (ὑπο)δέχομαι.

welcoming ['welkəmiŋ] *a* καλῆς ὑποδοχῆς.

weld [weld] *n* συγκόλλησις, κόλλησι ‖ *vt* (συγ)κολλῶ, ἐνώνω ‖ ~**er** *n* συγκολλητής ‖ ~**ing** *n* συγκόλλησις, κόλλησι.

welfare ['welfeə*] *n* εὐημερία, κοινωνική πρόνοια ‖ ~ **state** *n* κράτος προνοίας, κράτος σοσιαλιστικό.

well [wel] *n* φρέαρ, πηγάδι, πηγή, πετρελαιοπηγή ‖ *ad* καλῶς, καλά ‖ (*to considerable extent*) ἀρκετά, σχεδόν ‖ (*thoroughly*) καλά, τελείως ‖ *a* ὑγιής, καλά ‖ (*satisfactory*) καλόν, καλά ‖ *interj* (*beginning conversation*) λοιπόν, ἴσως, καλά ‖ (*surprise*) ἀδύνατον, μπά ‖ **as** ~ (*also*) ἐπίσης, ὁμοίως.

we'll [wi:l] = **we will, we shall** ‖ *see* **will, shall.**

well-behaved ['welbi'heivd] *a* φρόνιμος, πειθαρχημένος.

well-being ['welbi:iŋ] *n* εὐημερία.

well-built ['wel'bilt] *a* καλοφτιαγμένος.

well-developed ['weldi'veləpt] *a* (*girl*) ἀναπτυγμένη, γεμάτη.

well-earned ['wel'ə:nd] *a* (*rest*) δίκαιος, καλοκερδισμένος.

well-heeled ['wel'hi:ld] *a* (*col: wealthy*) πλούσιος, εὔπορος.

wellingtons ['weliŋtənz] *npl* ψιλές μπότες.

well-known ['wel'nəun] *a* (*person*) πασίγνωστος, φημισμένος.

well-meaning ['wel'mi:niŋ] *a* καλοπροαίρετος.

well-off ['wel'ɔf] *a* εὔπορος, πλούσιος, τυχερός.

well-read ['wel'red] *a* μορφωμένος, πολυδιαβασμένος.

well-to-do ['weltə'du:] *a* εὔπορος.

well-wisher ['welwiʃə*] *n* καλοθελητής.

Welsh [welʃ] *a* οὐαλλικός ‖ *n* (*ling*) οὐαλλικά ‖ ~**man** *n* Οὐαλλός.

wench [wentʃ] *n* (*old*) κορίτσι, κοκότα, τσούλα.

went [went] *pt of* **go.**

wept [wept] *pt,pp of* **weep.**

were [wə:*] *pt pl of* **be.**

we're [wiə*] = **we are** ‖ *see* **be.**

weren't ['wə:nt] = **were not** ‖ *see* **be.**

west [west] *n* δύσις ‖ (*country*) δυσμαί, δύσις, δυτικά ‖ *a* δυτικός ‖ *ad* δυτικά, πρός δυσμάς ‖ **the W~** *n* ἡ Δύσις ‖ ~**erly** *a* δυτικός (ἄνεμος), πρός δυσμάς ‖ ~**ern** *a* δυτικός ‖ *n* (*cine*) ταινία μέ κάου-μπόϋς ‖ **W~ Indies** *npl* Οἱ Ἀντίλλες ‖ ~**ward(s)** *ad* πρός δυσμάς, δυτικῶς.

wet [wet] *a* ὑγρός, βρε(γ)μένος, μουσκεμένος ‖ (*rainy*) βροχερός ‖ '~ **paint**' 'προσοχή χρῶμα' ‖ ~ **blanket** *n* (*fig*) ἄνθρωπος πού χαλάει τό κέφι, κρύος ‖ ~**ness** *n* ὑγρότης, ὑγρασία.

we've [wi:v] = **we have** ‖ *see* **have.**

whack [wæk] *n* μπάτσος, γερό κτύπημα ‖ *vt* κτυπῶ, δέρνω στά ψαχνά, συντρίβω.

whale [weil] *n* φάλαινα.

wharf [wɔ:f] *n* ἀποβάθρα, προκυμαία.

what [wɔt] *a* (*relative*) ὅτι, ὅσος ‖ (*quantity*) ὅσος, πόσον ‖ (*interrogative*) τί; πῶς;

ποιός; ‖ *interj* τί, πῶς ‖ ~**ever** *a* ὁποιος ...
καί, ὅ, τι ... καί, ὁποιοσδήποτε.

wheat [wi:t] *n* σῖτος, σιτάρι, στάρι.

wheel [wi:l] *n* τροχός, ρόδα ‖ *vt* (περι)-
στρέφω, σπρώχνω ‖ *vi* περιστρέφομαι,
γυρίζω γύρω-γύρω ‖ ~**barrow** *n* χειράμαξα ‖ ~**chair** *n* ἀναπηρική καρέκλα.

wheeze [wiz] *n* φύσημα, σφύριγμα, λαχά-
νιασμα ‖ *vi* ἀναπνέω δύσκολα, ἀσθμαίνω,
σφυρίζω.

when [wen] *ad* πότε ‖ (*relative*) ὅταν ‖ *cj*
ὅταν, ὅτε, πού ‖ ~**ever** *ad* ὁποτεδήποτε.

where [wεə*] *ad* ποῦ ‖ (*relative*) (ἐκεῖ) πού,
ὅπου ‖ ~**abouts** *ad* ποῦ ‖ (λοιπόν) ‖ ποῦ
περίπου ‖ *n* θέσις, διαμονή, κατατόπια ‖
~**as** *cj* ἐφ' ὅσον, ἐνῶ ‖ ~**ver** *ad* ὁπουδήποτε, ἀπ'ὅπου.

whet [wet] *vt* (*appetite*) διεγείρω, ἀνοίγω
(τήν ὄρεξι).

whether ['weðə*] *cj* ἐάν, ἄν, εἴτε.

which [witʃ] *a* ποῖος ‖ *pron* (*interrogative*)
ποῖον; ‖ (*relative*) ὁ ὁποῖος, στόν ὁποῖον,
τοῦ ὁποίου ‖ ~**ever** *a* ὁποιος, ἀπ'ὅπου ‖
pron οἰοσδήποτε.

whiff [wif] *n* πνοή, φύσημα, ρουφηξιά.

while [wail] *n* χρονική περίοδος, καιρός,
χρόνος ‖ *cj* ἐνῶ ‖ **for a ~** γιά λίγη ὥρα,
κάμποσο, γιά λίγο καιρό.

whim [wim] *n* παραξενιά, ἰδιοτροπία,
καπρίτσιο.

whimper ['wimpə*] *n* κλαυθμηρισμός,
κλάψα ‖ *vi* κλαυθμηρίζω, βογγῶ.

whimsical ['wimzikəl] *a* ἰδιότροπος,
παράξενος, βιδάτος.

whine [wain] *n* κλάψιμο, κλάμα, τσίριγμα ‖
vi κλαυθμηρίζω, μεμψιμοιρῶ.

whip [wip] *n* μαστίγιον, καμτσίκι ‖ (*parl*)
κοινοβουλευτικός ἡγέτης ‖ *vt* μαστιγώνω, δέρνω, κτυπῶ ‖ (*snatch*) κινῶ
ἀπότομα, ἀρπάζω ‖ ~**-round** *n* ἔρανος,
συνεισφορά.

whirl [wə:l] *n* στροβιλισμός, στριφογύρι-
σμα, γύρισμα ‖ *vti* στροβιλίζω, στριφογυρίζω, περιστρέφομαι ‖ ~**pool** *n* δίνη,
ρουφήχτρα ‖ ~**wind** *n* ἀνεμοστρόβιλος.

whirr [wə:*] *vi* βουίζω, σβουρίζω.

whisk [wisk] *n* (*for eggs*) χτυπητήρι ‖ *vt*
(*cream etc*) κτυπῶ, ἀνακατεύω.

whisker ['wiskə*] *n* φαβορίτες ‖ (*of cat*)
μουστάκι.

whisk(e)y ['wiski] *n* οὐίσκυ.

whisper ['wispə*] *n* ψίθυρος, θρόϊσμα,
ψιθύρισμα ‖ *vi* ψιθυρίζω, μουρμουρίζω ‖
(*leaves*) θροΐζω, ψιθυρίζω ‖ *vt* (*secretly*)
ψιθυρίζω, λέγω, σφυρίζω.

whist [wist] *n* οὐίστ.

whistle ['wisl] *n* σφύριγμα ‖ (*instrument*)
σφυρίχτρα ‖ *vi* συρίζω, σφυρίζω.

white [wait] *n* λευκόν, ἄσπρον ‖ (*of egg,
eye*) λεύκωμα, ἀσπράδι ‖ *a* λευκός,
ἄσπρος ‖ (*with fear*) ἄσπρος, κίτρινος,
χλωμός ‖ ~**collar worker** *n* δημόσιος
ὑπάλληλος ‖ ~ **lie** *n* ἀθῶο ψέμμα ‖

~**ness** *n* ἀσπρίλα, ἀσπράδα, χλωμάδα ‖
~**wash** *n* (*paint*) ἀσβεστόνερο, ἀσβεστόχρωμα ‖ *vt* ἀσβεστώνω, ἀσπρίζω ‖ (*fig*)
ἀποκαθιστῶ, δικαιολογῶ.

Whitsun ['witsn] *n* (*also Whit Sunday*)
Πεντηκοστή.

whittle ['witl] *vt*: **to ~ away, down** ἐλαττώνω, περιορίζω, λεπταίνω.

whizz [wiz] *vi* συρίζω, σφυρίζω, περνῶ
ὁλοταχῶς ‖ ~ **kid** *n* (*col*) σπουδαῖο
παιδί.

who [hu:] *pron* ποῖος, ποιός ‖ (*relative*)
ὁποῖος, ὅστις, πού ‖ ~**ever** *pron* ὁποιοσδήποτε, οἰοσδήποτε.

whole [houl] *a* (*complete*) ὁλόκληρος, ὅλος,
πλήρης ‖ (*uninjured*) ἀβλαβής, σῶος ‖ *n*
(τό) ὅλον, σύνολον ‖ (*not broken*)
σύνολον, ἀκέραιον ‖ ~**hearted** *a* ὁλόψυχος ‖ ~**heartedly** *ad* ὁλοψύχως ‖
~**sale** *n* χονδρική πώλησις, χονδρεμπό-
ριον ‖ *attr a* (*trade*) χονδρικός ‖ (*destruction*) ὁλοκληρωτικός ‖ ~**saler** *n* χονδρέμπορος, κατάστημα χονδρικῆς πωλή-
σεως ‖ ~**some** *a* ὑγιεινός, ὑγιής.

wholly ['houli] *ad* πλήρως, τελείως.

whom [hu:m] *pron* (*object*) ποῖον ‖ ποιόν.

whooping cough ['hu:piŋkɔf] *n* κοκκύτης.

whore ['hɔ:*] *n* πόρνη, πουτάνα.

whose [huz] *pron* ποίου ‖ τίνος ‖ ποιανοῦ ‖
τοῦ ὁποίου.

why [wai] *ad* διατί; ‖ γιατί; ‖ (*relative*) πού,
γιατί ‖ *interj* μπά ‖ ἒ ‖ ἄς.

wick [wik] *n* θρυαλλίς, φυτίλι.

wicked ['wikid] *a* κακός, διεστραμμένος,
κακοήθης ‖ (*mischievous*) πειρακτικός,
κατεργάρης ‖ ~**ly** *ad* μέ κακίαν,
αἰσχρῶς, πονηρά ‖ ~**ness** *n* κακία,
ἀχρειότης, κακοήθεια.

wicker ['wikə*] *n* λυγαριά, πλέγμα.

wicket ['wikit] *n* (*cricket*) φράκτης, στυλί-
σκοι τοῦ κρίκετ.

wide [waid] *a* εὐρύς, πλατύς, φαρδύς,
ἐκτενής ‖ (*mouth*) ὀρθάνοικτος ‖ (*in
firing*) ἔξω (τοῦ στόχου), ἄστοχος ‖ *ad*
(*opening*) διάπλατα ‖ ~**-angle** *a* (*lens*)
εὐρυγώνιος φακός ‖ ~**-awake** *a* ἐντελῶς
ξύπνιος, ἄγρυπνος ‖ ~**ly** *ad* εὐρέως,
πλατειά, κατά πολύ ‖ ~**n** *vt* (*road*)
εὐρύνω, πλαταίνω, διευρύνω ‖ ~**ness** *n*
εὐρύτης ‖ ~ **open** *a* (*lit*) ὀρθάνοιχτος,
ἀκάλυπτος ‖ ~**-spread** *a* ἐκτεταμένος,
πλατύς ‖ (*rumour etc*) διαδεδομένος,
γενικός.

widow ['widəu] *n* χήρα ‖ ~**ed** *a* χηρεύσας,
χηρεύσασα ‖ ~**er** *n* χῆρος, χηρευάμενος.

width [widθ] *n* εὖρος, πλάτος, φάρδος.

wield [wi:ld] *vt* χειρίζομαι, ἐλέγχω,
ἐξασκῶ.

wife [waif] *n* ἡ σύζυγος, γυναίκα.

wig [wig] *n* περούκα.

wiggle ['wigl] *vti* κινῶ νευρικά, κινῶ
παλινδρομικά.

wild [waild] *a* ἄγριος ‖ (*not cultivated*) εἰς

άγρίαν κατάστασιν ‖ (excited) άχαλίνωτος, ξετρελλαμένος, τρελλός ‖ the ~s npl άκαλλιέργητος έκτασις, ζούγκλα ‖ ~erness ['wildənis] n έρημος, άγριότοπος ‖ ~-goose chase n ματαία άναζήτησις, άσκοπος έπιχείρησις ‖ ~life n άγρια ζῶα ‖ ~ly ad παράξενα, σάν τρελλός, μανιωδῶς, άπερίσκεπτα.

wilful ['wilful] a έσκεμμένος, έκ προμελέτης ‖ (obstinate) πείσμων, ίσχυρογνώμων.

will [wil] auxiliary v: he ~ come θά έρθη ‖ I ~ do it! θά τό κάνω! ‖ n βούλησις, θέλησις ‖ (purpose) άπόφασις, βούλησις, θέλημα ‖ (inheritance) διαθήκη ‖ vt θέλω, άποφασίζω ‖ ~ing a πρόθυμος ‖ ~ingly ad πρόθυμα, εύχαρίστως ‖ ~ingness n προθυμία.

willow ['wiləu] n ίτέα, ίτιά.

will power ['wilpauə*] n θέλησις, αύτοέλεγχος.

wilt [wilt] vi μαραίνομαι.

wily ['waili] a πανούργος.

win [win] (irreg v) n νίκη, έπιτυχία ‖ vt νικῶ, κερδίζω ‖ vi έπιτυγχάνω ‖ to ~ over vt κατακτῶ, άποκτῶ.

wince [wins] n σύσπασις, τρεμούλιασμα ‖ vi μορφάζω, σφίγγομαι.

winch [wintʃ] n βαρούλκον, βίντσι.

wind [waind] (irreg v) vt (wrap) περιελίσσω, τυλίγω ‖ (tighten) σφίγγω, κουρδίζω ‖ vi στρέφω, στρέφομαι, έλίσσομαι, τυλίγομαι ‖ to ~ up vt (clock) κουρδίζω ‖ (debate) κλείνω, τερματίζω, διαλύω.

wind [wind] n άνεμος, άέρας ‖ (med) άέρια, τυμπανισμός ‖ ~fall n (good luck) κελεπούρι.

winding ['waindiŋ] a (road) έλισσόμενος, φιδίσιος, μέ κορδέλλες, στριφτός.

wind instrument ['windinstrumənt] n (mus) πνευστόν (όργανον).

windmill [windmil] n άνεμόμυλος.

window ['windəu] n παράθυρον, βιτρίνα ‖ ~ box n κιβώτιον λουλουδιῶν, γάστρα ‖ ~ cleaner n (man) καθαριστής παραθύρων ‖ ~ frame n πλαίσιον παραθύρου, κούφωμα ‖ ~ ledge n περβάζι παραθύρου ‖ ~ pane n τζάμι ‖ ~sill n περβάζι παραθύρου.

windpipe ['windpaip] n τραχεῖα, λαρύγγι.

windscreen ['windskri:n], (US) **windshield** ['windʃi:ld] n άλεξήνεμον, παρμπρίζ ‖ ~ wiper n ύαλοκαθαριστήρ.

windswept ['windswept] a άνεμοδαρμένος.

windy ['windi] a άνεμώδης, έκτεθειμένος στούς άνέμους.

wine [wain] n οίνος, κρασί ‖ ~ cellar n κάβα ‖ ~glass n ποτήρι τοῦ κρασιοῦ ‖ ~ list n κατάλογος κρασιῶν ‖ ~ merchant n κρασέμπορος ‖ ~ tasting n δοκιμή κρασιῶν ‖ ~ waiter n σερβιτόρος γιά τά κρασιά.

wing [wiŋ] n πτέρυξ, φτερούγα, φτερό ‖

(of building) πτέρυξ (κτιρίου) ‖ (mil) πτέρυξ ‖ ~s npl (theat) παρασκήνια ‖ ~er n (sport) (ό) έξω.

wink [wiŋk] n άνοιγοκλείσιμο τοῦ ματιοῦ, νεῦμα ‖ vi κλείνω τό μάτι, νεύω ‖ forty ~s ύπνάκο.

winner ['winə*] n κερδίσας, νικητής.

winning ['winiŋ] a (team) κερδίζων, νικήτρια (όμάδα) ‖ (goal) κερδίζων γκόλ ‖ ~s npl κέρδη ‖ ~ post n άφιξις, τέρμα.

winter ['wintə*] n χειμών, χειμώνας ‖ attr a (clothes) χειμωνιάτικα ‖ vi περνῶ τό χειμώνα (είς) ‖ ~ sports npl χειμωνιάτικα σπόρ.

wintry ['wintri] a χειμωνιάτικος, ψυχρός, θυελλώδης.

wipe [waip] n σκούπισμα, στέγνωμα, σφούγγισμα ‖ vt σκουπίζω, στεγνώνω, σφουγγίζω ‖ to ~ out vt (debt) άποσβενύω, έξοφλῶ ‖ (destroy) έξολοθρεύω, σαρώνω.

wire ['waiə*] n σύρμα ‖ (cable) τηλεγράφημα ‖ vt ένώνω μέ σύρμα, τοποθετῶ τά καλώδια ‖ ~less n άσύρματος ‖ (radio) ραδιόφωνον.

wiry ['waiəri] a σάν σύρμα, νευρώδης, δυνατός.

wisdom ['wizdəm] n σοφία, φρόνησις ‖ (good judgment) σωφροσύνη ‖ (prudence) φρονιμάδα, γνώση ‖ ~ tooth n φρονιμίτης.

wise [waiz] a σοφός, φρόνιμος, συνετός ‖ -wise suffix κατά κάποιον τρόπο, σάν ‖ ~crack n εύφυολόγημα, καλαμπούρι ‖ ~ly ad σοφῶς, φρόνημα, γνωστικά.

wish [wiʃ] n (desire) έπιθυμία, εύχή ‖ vt (desire) εύχομαι, έπιθυμῶ ‖ with best ~es μέ τίς καλύτερες εύχές ‖ to ~ s.o. goodbye εύχομαι καλό ταξίδι ‖ to ~ to do έπιθυμῶ, θέλω νά ‖ ~ful thinking n εύσεβεῖς πόθοι.

wisp [wisp] n (of hair) τσουλούφι, τολύπη.

wistful ['wistful] a ποθῶν, λαχταρῶν, πικραμένος.

wit [wit] n (sense) άντίληψις, κατανόησις, νοῦς, μυαλό ‖ (cleverness) πνεῦμα, εύφυΐα ‖ (person) πνευματώδης άνθρωπος, εύφυής, σπίρτο ‖ ~s npl μυαλό, σκέψι.

witch [witʃ] n μάγισσα ‖ ~craft n μαγεία.

with [wið, wiθ] prep μετά, σύν, μαζί, μέ ‖ (by means of) μέ, άπό ‖ (concerning) μαζί μέ, μετά ‖ (notwithstanding) παρά, παρ' όλον.

withdraw [wiθ'drɔ:] vt άποσύρω, σύρω, τραβῶ, σύρνω ‖ vi άποσύρομαι, άποτραβιέμαι, τραβιέμαι ‖ ~al n άποχώρησις, άνάκλησις.

wither ['wiðə*] vi μαραίνομαι, ξεραίνομαι ‖ ~ed a μαραμένος.

withhold [wiθ'həuld] vt άναστέλλω, κατακρατῶ.

within [wið'in] prep έντός, μέσα σέ, έν.

without [wiðˈaut] *prep* ἐκτός, ἄνευ, χωρίς, δίχως.

withstand [wiðˈstænd] *vt* ἀνθίσταμαι εἰς, ἀντέχω εἰς.

witness [ˈwitnis] *n* μαρτυρία ‖ (*law*) μάρτυς, μάρτυρας ‖ *vt* (*see*) παρίσταμαι μάρτυς, βλέπω ‖ (*sign documents*) ἐπικυρώνω, βεβαιῶ, ὑπογράφω ‖ ~ **box**, (*US*) ~ **stand** *n* θέσις τοῦ ἐξεταζομένου μάρτυρος.

witticism [ˈwitisizəm] *n* εὐφυολογία, εὐφυολόγημα, ἐξυπνάδα, ἀστεῖον.

wittily [ˈwitili] *ad* πνευματωδῶς, ἔξυπνα, σπιρτόζικα.

witty [ˈwiti] *a* πνευματώδης, σπιρτόζικος, ἔξυπνος.

wives [waivz] *npl of* **wife**.

wizard [ˈwizəd] *n* μάγος.

wobble [ˈwɔbl] *vi* παραπατῶ, ταλαντεύομαι, τρέμω.

woe [wəu] *n* συμφορά, δυστυχία, λύπη, θλίψις.

woke [wəuk] *pt,pp of* **wake**.

wolf [wulf] *n* λύκος.

wolves [wulvz] *npl of* **wolf**.

woman [ˈwumən] *n* γυνή, γυναίκα ‖ *attr a* (*doctor*) (ἡ) ἰατρός, γιατρίνα.

womb [wuːm] *n* μήτρα.

women [ˈwimin] *npl of* **woman**.

won [wʌn] *pt,pp of* **win**.

wonder [ˈwʌndə*] *n* θαῦμα ‖ (*feeling*) θαυμασμός, κατάπληξις ‖ *vi* (*want to know*) ἀπορῶ, διερωτῶμαι, μήπως ‖ ~**ful** *a* θαυμάσιος, ἐκπληκτικός ‖ ~**fully** *ad* θαυμάσια, ὑπέροχα, περίφημα.

won't [wəunt] = **will not** ‖ *see* **will**.

wood [wud] *n* ξύλον, ξυλεία ‖ (*forest*) δάσος, δρυμός, ἄλσος ‖ ~ **carving** *n* ξυλογλυπτική ‖ ~**ed** *a* δασώδης, δασωμένος ‖ ~**en** *a* ξύλινος ‖ (*stiff*) ἀδέξιος, ἄκαμπτος ‖ ~**pecker** *n* δρυοκολάπτης ‖ ~**wind** *n* ξύλινα πνευστά ‖ ~**work** *n* ξυλουργική ‖ ~**worm** *n* σκουλήκι τοῦ ξύλου.

wool [wul] *n* ἔριον, μαλλί ‖ (*material*) μάλλινον ὕφασμα ‖ ~**len**, (*US*) ~**en** *a* μάλλινος ‖ (*industry*) ὑφαντουργική ‖ ~**ly**, (*US*) ~**y** *a* σάν μαλλί, σκεπασμένος μέ μαλλί.

word [wəːd] *n* λέξις ‖ (*talk, speech*) λόγος, παρατήρησις ‖ (*news*) εἰδήσεις, εἰδοποίησις, μήνυμα, νέο ‖ (*promise*) λόγος ‖ *vt* διατυπώνω, ἐκφράζω μέ λέξεις ‖ ~**ing** *n* διατύπωσις, φρασεολογία.

wore [wɔː*] *pt of* **wear**.

work [wəːk] *n* ἔργον ‖ (*task*) ἐργασία, δουλειά, ἀπασχόλησις ‖ (*art, liter*) ἔργον, προϊόν ἐργασίας ‖ *vi* ἐργάζομαι, δουλεύω ‖ (*have occupation*) ἐργάζομαι, ἀσχολοῦμαι μέ, δουλεύω ‖ *vt* (*cause to act*) λειτουργῶ, ἐπιτυγχάνω ‖ ~**s** *n* (*factory*) ἐργοστάσιον ‖ **to** ~ **on** *vt* συνεχίζω ‖ ἐπηρεάζω ‖ **to** ~ **out** *vi* (*sum*)

ὑπολογίζομαι, ἀνέρχομαι εἰς ‖ *vt* (*problem*) λύνω, ἀναπτύσσω ‖ (*plan*) ἐπεξεργάζομαι ‖ **to** ~ **up to** *vt* ἀνέρχομαι, παράγω ‖ **to get** ~**ed up** ἐξάπτομαι, θυμώνω ‖ ~**able** *a* ἐπεξεργάσιμος, ἐκμεταλλεύσιμος, ἐφαρμόσιμος ‖ ~**er** *n* ἐργάτης, ἐργαζόμενος ‖ ~**ing class** *n* ἐργατική τάξις, ἐργαζόμενοι ‖ ~**ing-class** *a* τῆς ἐργατικῆς τάξεως ‖ ~**ing man** *n* ἐργάτης, δουλευτής ‖ ~**man** *n* ἐργάτης, τεχνίτης ‖ ~**manship** *n* ἐκτέλεσις, δούλεμα, ἐπεξεργασία ‖ ~**shop** *n* ἐργαστήριον.

world [wəːld] *n* σύμπαν, ὑφήλιος, κόσμος ‖ (*the earth*) γῆ, κόσμος ‖ (*mankind*) κόσμος, ἀνθρωπότης ‖ (*society*) κοινωνία, κόσμος ‖ (*sphere*) κόσμος ‖ *attr a* (*champion*) παγκόσμιος, διεθνής ‖ **out of this** ~ ἀπίστευτος, περίφημος ‖ ~**-famous** *a* παγκοσμίου φήμης ‖ ~**ly** *a* ἐγκόσμιος, τοῦ κόσμου ‖ ~**-wide** *a* παγκόσμιος, διεθνής.

worm [wəːm] *n* σκουλήκι.

worn [wɔːn] *pp of* **wear** ‖ *a* ἐφθαρμένος, φορεμένος ‖ ~**-out** *a* (*object*) τριμμένος, φαγωμένος ‖ (*person*) ἐξηντλημένος, τσακισμένος.

worried [ˈwʌrid] *a* στενοχωρημένος, ἀνήσυχος.

worrier [ˈwʌriə*] *n* (*person who worries*) ὁ πάντα στενοχωρημένος, ἀνήσυχος.

worry [ˈwʌri] *n* ἀνησυχία, σκοτούρα, μπελᾶς, βάσανο ‖ *vt* (*trouble*) βασανίζω, στενοχωρῶ ‖ *vi* (*feel uneasy*) ἀνησυχῶ, στενοχωροῦμαι ‖ ~**ing** *a* ἐνοχλητικός, βασανιστικός, πληκτικός.

worse [wəːs] *a comparative of* **bad** ‖ *ad comparative of* **badly** ‖ *n* κάτι χειρότερο, πιό κακό ‖ ~**n** *vt* ἐπιδεινώνω, χειροτερεύω ‖ *vi* ἐπιδεινοῦμαι.

worship [ˈwəːʃip] *n* λατρεία, προσκύνησις ‖ (*religious service*) λατρεία, ἐκκλησίασμα ‖ (*title*) ἡ αὐτοῦ ἐντιμότης ‖ *vt* λατρεύω ‖ (*adore*) ἀγαπῶ, λατρεύω ‖ ~**per** *n* πιστός.

worst [wəːst] *a superlative of* **bad** ‖ *ad superlative of* **badly** ‖ *n* ὁ χειρότερος, ὁ πιό κακός, χείριστον.

worsted [ˈwustid] *n* ὑφάσματα πενιέ, μαλλί πενιέ.

worth [wəːθ] *n* ἀξία ‖ *a* ἀξίζων ‖ ~**less** *a* χωρίς ἀξίαν, ἄχρηστος ‖ ~**while** *a* ἀξίζων τόν κόπον ‖ ~**y** [ˈwəːði] *a* ἀξίζων, ἄξιος ‖ (+ *of*) ἀντάξιος.

would [wud] *auxiliary v*: she ~ come ἐρχόταν ‖ **if you asked he** ~ **come** ἄν παρακαλοῦσες θ' ἐρχόταν ‖ **you like a drink?** θέλεις κανένα ποτό; ‖ ~**-be** *a* δῆθεν ‖ ~**n't** = ~ **not**.

wound [waund] *pt,pp of* **wind** ‖ [wuːnd] *n* τραῦμα, πληγή ‖ *vt* τραυματίζω, πληγώνω.

wove [wəuv] *pt of* **weave** ‖ ~**n** *pp of* **weave**.

wrangle ['ræŋgl] *n* διαπληκτισμός, τσακωμός, λογομαχία ‖ *vi* διαπληκτίζομαι, λογομαχῶ, τσακώνομαι.

wrap [ræp] *n* πανωφόρι, σάλι ‖ *vt* (*also* ~ **up**) τυλίσσω, περιβάλλω, καλύπτω ‖ ~**per** *n* περιτύλιγμα, κάλυμμα, ρόμπα ‖ ~**ping paper** *n* χαρτί περιτυλίγματος.

wreath [ri:θ] *n* στέφανος.

wreck [rek] *n* ἐρείπιον, καταστροφή ‖ (*naut*) ναυάγιον ‖ (*ruin*) καταστροφή ‖ *vt* καταστρέφω, προκαλῶ ναυάγιον ‖ ~**age** *n* ναυάγιον, συντρίμματα.

wren [ren] *n* τρόχιλος, τρυποκαρύδα.

wrench [rentʃ] *n* (γαλλικό) κλειδί ‖ (*violent twist*) .βιαία κίνησις στρέψεως, στρέβλωσις ‖ *vt* στρεβλώνω, στραμπουλίζω.

wrestle ['resl] *vi* (+ *with*) ἀγωνίζομαι ‖ (*sport*) παλαίω, παλεύω.

wrestling ['resliŋ] *n* πάλη, πάλεμα ‖ ~ **match** *n* ἀγώνισμα πάλης.

wretched ['retʃid] *a* πολύ δυστυχής, ἄθλιος, δυστυχής ‖ (*bad, poor*) ἄθλιος, θλιβερός, ἀξιοθρήνητος.

wriggle ['rigl] *n* συστροφή, σκωληκοειδής κίνησις ‖ *vi* συστρέφομαι, σπαρταρῶ, περνῶ συρτά, γλιστρῶ.

wring [riŋ] (*irreg v*) *vt* συστρέφω, στρίβω.

wrinkle ['riŋkl] *n* ρυτίδα, πτυχή ‖ *vt* ρυτιδώνω, ζαρώνω ‖ *vi* ρυτιδοῦμαι, ζαρώνω.

wrist [rist] *n* καρπός (τοῦ χεριοῦ) ‖ ~ **watch** *n* ρολόι τοῦ χεριοῦ.

writ [rit] *n* (*law*) δικαστική πρᾶξις, ἔνταλμα.

write [rait] (*irreg v*) *vt* γράφω ‖ (*book*) συντάσσω, γράφω ‖ *vi* (*send letter*) γράφω, στέλνω γράμμα ‖ **to** ~ **down** *vt* διατυπώνω, (κατα)γράφω, σημειώνω, περιγράφω ‖ **to** ~ **off** *vt* (*dismiss*) ἀκυρώνω, διαγράφω, ξεγράφω ‖ **to** ~ **out** *vt* καθαρογράφω, γράφω ἐν ἐκτάσει, συντάσσω ‖ **to** ~ **up** *vt* (*report*) συντάσσω, γράφω ‖ ~**-off** *n* (*smashed car*) τελείως κατεστραμμένο ‖ ~**r** *n* συγγραφεύς, συντάκτης, γράψας.

writing ['raitiŋ] *n* γράψιμο, γραφή ‖ (*books etc*) λογοτεχνικόν ἔργον ‖ ~ **paper** *n* κόλλα, χαρτί γραψίματος.

written ['ritn] *pp of* **write**.

wrong [rɔŋ] *a* κακός, ἄδικος ‖ (*incorrect*) ἐσφαλμένος, ἀνακριβής, λαθεμένος ‖ (*mistaken*) λάθος ‖ ~**ful** *a* ἄδικος, ἀδικαιολόγητος ‖ , ~**ly** *ad* ἀδίκως, ἐσφαλμένως, λαθεμένα.

wrote [rəut] *pt of* **write**.

wrought [rɔ:t] *a*: ~ **iron** κατειργασμένος σίδηρος.

wrung [rʌŋ] *pt,pp of* **wring**.

wry [rai] *a* στρεβλός, στριμμένος, στραβός.

X, x

Xmas ['eksməs] *n* (*col: Christmas*) Χριστούγεννα.

X-ray ['eks'rei] *n* ἀκτινογραφία, ἀκτινοσκόπησις.

xylophone ['zailəfəun] *n* ξυλόφωνον.

Y, y

yacht [jɔt] *n* θαλαμηγός, γιώτ, κότερο ‖ ~ **club** *n* ἱστιοπλοϊκός ὅμιλος ‖ ~**ing** *n* ἐνασχόλησις μέ γιώτ, γιώτιγκ ‖ ~**sman** *n* ἄνθρωπος ἀσχολούμενος μέ γιώτ.

Yank [jæŋk] *n* (*col: American*) 'Αμερικανός, Γιάγκης.

yap [jæp] *vi* (*dog*) γαυγίζω.

yard [jɑ:d] *n* (*of house etc*) αὐλή, προαύλιον, μάνδρα ‖ (*measure*) ὑάρδα (0.914 μ) ‖ ~**stick** *n* (*for comparing*) μέτρον συγκρίσεως.

yarn [jɑ:n] *n* νῆμα, κλωστή ‖ (*tale*) ἱστορία φανταστική.

yawn [jɔ:n] *n* χασμούρημα, χασμουρητό ‖ *vi* χασμουριέμαι ‖ ~**ing** *a* (*gap*) χάσκων, ἀνοικτός.

year ['jiə*] *n* ἔτος, χρόνος ‖ ~**ly** *a* ἐτήσιος ‖ *ad* ἐτησίως, κάθε χρόνο.

yearn [jə:n] *vi* (+ *for*) ποθῶ, λαχταρῶ ‖ ~**ing** *n* πόθος, λαχτάρα.

yeast [ji:st] *n* ζύμη, προζύμι, μαγιά.

yell [jel] *n* ὠρυγή, κραυγή, σκούξιμο ‖ *vi* ὠρύομαι, φωνάζω δυνατά, σκούζω.

yellow ['jeləu] (*colour*) *a* κίτρινος ‖ *n* κίτρινον ‖ ~ **fever** *n* κίτρινος πυρετός.

yelp [jelp] *n* ὑλακή, γαύγισμα, οὐρλιασμα ‖ *vi* γαυγίζω, ὑλακτῶ.

yes [jes] *ad* ναί, μάλιστα, ἀσφαλῶς ‖ *n* καταφατική ἀπάντησις, ναί ‖ ~ **man** *n* τυφλός ὀπαδός, δουλοπρεπής.

yesterday ['jestədei] *n* χθές, ψές ‖ *ad* χθές, χτές, ψές.

yet [jet] *ad* (*by now*) ἀκόμη, τώρα ‖ (*still*) ἀκόμη ‖ (*by that time*) κι ὅμως, παρ' ὅλα ταῦτα ‖ *cj* παρά ταῦτα, κι ὅμως, ἐν τούτοις.

yew [ju:] *n* σμίλαξ.

Yiddish ['jidiʃ] *n* (*ling*) γερμανοεβραϊκά.

yield [ji:ld] *n* παραγωγή, ἀπόδοσις ‖ *vt* ἀποδίδω, ἀποφέρω, παράγω, δίνω ‖ (*surrender*) παραδίδω, παραχωρῶ ‖ *vi* (*surrender*) ὑποτάσσομαι, παραδίδομαι, ὑποκύπτω.

yodel ['jəudl] *vi* τραγουδῶ (τυρολέζικα).

yoga ['jəugə] *n* γιόγκα.

yogourt ['jəugət] *n* γιαούρτι.

yoke [jəuk] *n* ζυγός, ζευγάρι ‖ (*servitude*) ζυγός.

yolk [jəuk] *n* κρόκος, κροκάδι.

you [ju:] *pron* (ἐ)σεῖς, (ἐ)σύ.

Z, z

you'd [ju:d] = you had, you would ‖ *see* have, would.

you'll [ju:l] = you will, you shall ‖ *see* will, shall.

young [jʌŋ] *a* νέος, νεαρός, μικρός ‖ *npl* οἱ νέοι, ἡ νεολαία ‖ ~**ish** *a* μᾶλλον νέος, νεούτσικος ‖ ~**ster** *n* νεαρός, νέος, ἀγόρι, παιδάκι.

your ['juə*] *poss a* σου, σας, ὑμέτερος.

you're ['juə*] = you are ‖ *see* be.

yours ['juəz] *poss pron* (δικός) σου, (δικός) σας, ὑμέτερος ‖ ~ **faithfully** ὑμέτερος ‖ ~ **sincerely** ὅλως ὑμέτερος.

yourself [jə'self] *pron* σύ (ὁ ἴδιος), τόν ἑαυτόν σας, χωρίς βοήθειαν.

yourselves [jə'selvz] *pron pl* σεῖς (οἱ ἴδιοι), μόνοι σας.

youth [ju:θ] *n* νεότης, νειᾶτα, νειότη ‖ (*young man*) νέος, νεαρός, ἔφηβος ‖ (*young people*) νέοι, νεολαία ‖ ~**ful** *a* νέος, νεανικός, νεαρός ‖ ~ **hostel** *n* πανδοχεῖον νεότητος.

you've [ju:v] = you have ‖ *see* have.

Yugoslav ['ju:gəu'slɑ:v] *a* γιουγκοσλαβικός ‖ *n* (*person*) Γιουγκοσλάβος ‖ (*ling*) γιουγκοσλαβικά ‖ ~**ia** *n* Γιουγκοσλαβία.

zany ['zeini] *a* ἠλίθιος, βλάκας.

zeal [zi:l] *n* ζῆλος ‖ ~**ous** *a* γεμᾶτος ζῆλον, ἔνθερμος, φλογερός.

zebra ['zi:brə] *n* ζέβρα ‖ ~ **crossing** *n* διάβασις (πεζῶν).

zenith ['zeniθ] *n* ζενίθ.

zero ['ziərəu] *n* μηδέν, μηδενικόν ‖ ~ **hour** *n* ὥρα μηδέν, ὥρα (ἐπιθέσεως).

zest [zest] *n* ζέσις, ἐνθουσιασμός, ὄρεξι.

zigzag ['zigzæg] *n* ζίγκ-ζάγκ ‖ *vi* κάνω ζίγκ-ζάγκ.

zinc [ziŋk] *n* ψευδάργυρος, τσίγκος.

Zionism ['zaiənizəm] *n* σιωνισμός.

zip [zip] *n* (*also* ~ **fastener**, ~**per**) φερμουάρ, ἐκλαίρ ‖ *vt* (*also* ~ **up**) κλείνω (μέ φερμουάρ).

zither ['ziðə*] *n* σαντούρι.

zodiac ['zəudiæk] *n* ζωδιακός κύκλος.

zone [zəun] *n* ζώνη.

zoo [zu:] *n* ζωολογικός κῆπος ‖ ~**logical** *a* ζωολογικός ‖ ~**logist** *n* ζωολόγος ‖ ~**logy** *n* ζωολογία.

zoom [zu:m] *vi* βομβῶ, βουΐζω ‖ (*rise sharply*) ἀνυψοῦμαι κατακορύφως ‖ ~ **lens** *n* φακός μεταβλητῆς ἑστιακῆς ἀποστάσεως ζούμ.

English Strong and Irregular Verbs
Ἰσχυρά καί Ἀνώμαλα Ρήματα

Ἐνεστώς	Ἀόριστος	Παθ. Μετοχή
abide	abode	abode
arise	arose	arisen
awake	awoke, awaked	awakened, awoke
be	was	been
bear	bore	born(e)
beat	beat	beaten
begin	began	begun
bend	bent	bent
beseech	besought	besought
bet	bet	bet
bid	bade, bid	bidden
bid	bid	bid
bind	bound	bound
bite	bit	bitten
bleed	bled	bled
blow	blew	blown
break	broke	broken
breed	bred	bred
bring	brought	brought
build	built	built
burn	burned, burnt	burned, burnt
burst	burst	burst
buy	bought	bought
cast	cast	cast
catch	caught	caught
choose	chose	chosen
cling	clung	clung
come	came	come
cost	cost	cost
creep	crept	crept
cut	cut	cut
deal	dealt	dealt
dig	dug	dug
do	did	done
draw	drew	drawn
dream	dreamed, dreamt	dreamed, dreamt
drink	drank	drunk
drive	drove	driven
dwell	dwelt, dwelled	dwelt, dwelled
eat	ate	eaten

Z

fall	fell	fallen
feed	fed	fed
feel	felt	felt
fight	fought	fought
find	found	found
flee, fly	fled	fled
fling	flung	flung
fly	flew	flown
forbid	forbade	forbidden
forsake	forsook	forsaken
freeze	froze	frozen
get	got	got, gotten
gild	gilded	gilded, gilt
give	gave	given
go	went	gone
grind	ground	ground
grow	grew	grown
hang	hung	hung
have	had	had
hear	heard	heard
heave (*naut*)	hove	hove
hew	hewed	hewn
hide	hid	hid(den)
hit	hit	hit
hold	held	held
hurt	hurt	hurt
keep	kept	kept
kneel	knelt, kneeled	knelt, kneeled
know	knew	known
lay	laid	laid
lead	led	led
lean	leant, leaned	leant, leaned
leap	leaped, leapt	leaped, leapt
learn	learnt, learned	learnt, learned
leave	left	left
lend	lent	lent
let	let	let
lie	lay	lain
light	lighted, lit	lighted, lit
lose	lost	lost
make	made	made
may	might	—
mean	meant	meant
meet	met	met
mow	mowed	mown
pay	paid	paid
put	put	put
quit	quit	quit
read	read	read
rend	rent	rent
rid	rid	rid
ride	rode	ridden
ring	rang	rung
rise	rose	risen
run	ran	run

426

saw	sawed	sawn, sawed
say	said	said
see	saw	seen
seek	sought	sought
sell	sold	sold
send	sent	sent
set	set	set
sew	sewed	sewn, sewed
shake	shook	shaken
shall	should	—
shave	shaved	shaved, shaven
shear	sheared	shorn, sheared
shed	shed	shed
shine	shone	shone
shoe	shod	shod
shoot	shot	shot
show	showed	shown
shrink	shrank	shrunk
shut	shut	shut
sing	sang, sung	sung
sink	sank, sunk	sunk
sit	sat	sat
sleep	slept	slept
slide	slid	slid
sling	slung	slung
slit	slit	slit
smell	smelled, smelt	smelled, smelt
sow	sowed	sown
speak	spoke	spoken
speed	sped, speeded	sped, speeded
spell	spelt, spelled	spelt, spelled
spend	spent	spent
spill	spilt	spilt
spin	spun, span	spun
spit	spat, spit	spat, spit
split	split	split
spoil	spoiled, spoilt	spoiled, spoilt
spread	spread	spread
spring	sprang	sprung
stand	stood	stood
steal	stole	stolen
stick	stuck	stuck
sting	stung	stung
stink	stank, stunk	stunk
stride	strode	stridden, strode
strike	struck	struck
strive	strove	striven
swear	swore	sworn
sweep	swept	swept
swell	swelled	swollen
swim	swam	swum
swing	swung	swung
take	took	taken
teach	taught	taught
tear	tore	torn

427

tell	told	told
think	thought	thought
throw	threw	thrown
thrust	thrust	thrust
tread	trod	trodden
try	tried	tried
wake	woke, waked	woken, waked
wear	wore	worn
weave	wove	woven, wove
weep	wept	wept
will	would	—
win	won	won
wind	wound	wound
wring	wrung	wrung
write	wrote	written

Numerals
Ἀριθμητικά

ΑΠΟ'ΛΥΤΑ		CARDINAL NUMBERS
μηδέν	0	zero
ἕνας, μία, ἕνα	1	one
δύο	2	two
τρεῖς, τρία	3	three
τέσσερες, τέσσερα	4	four
πέντε	5	five
ἕξι	6	six
ἑπτά, ἑφτά	7	seven
ὀκτώ, ὀχτό	8	eight
ἐννιά	9	nine
δέκα	10	ten
ἕντεκα	11	eleven
δώδεκα	12	twelve
δεκατρεῖς, δεκατρία	13	thirteen
δεκατέσσερες, δεκατέσσερα	14	fourteen
δεκαπέντε	15	fifteen
δεκαέξι	16	sixteen
δεκαεφτά	17	seventeen
δεκαοχτό	18	eighteen
δεκαννιά	19	nineteen
εἴκοσι	20	twenty
εἴκοσι-ἕνα	21	twenty-one
εἴκοσι-δύο	22	twenty-two
εἴκοσι-τρία	23	twenty-three
τριάντα	30	thirty
σαράντα	40	forty
πενῆντα	50	fifty
ἐξῆντα	60	sixty
ἐβδομῆντα	70	seventy
ὀγδόντα	80	eighty
ἐνενῆντα	90	ninety
ἐνενῆντα-πέντε	95	ninety-five
ἑκατό	100	one hundred
ἑκατό-ἕνα	101	hundred and one
ἑκατό-δέκα	110	hundred and ten
διακόσια	200	two hundred

πεντακόσια σαράντα	540	five hundred and forty
χίλια	1,000	one thousand
ἑβδομῆντα χιλιάδες διακόσια ὀγδόντα	70,280	seventy thousand two hundred and eighty
πεντακόσιες χιλιάδες	500,000	five hundred thousand
ἕνα ἑκατομμύριο	1,000,000	one million
ἕνα δίσεκατομμύριο	1,000,000,000	one billion

TAKTIKA′		ORDINAL NUMBERS
πρῶτος, πρώτη, πρῶτο	1st	first
δεύτερος	2nd	second
τρίτος	3rd	third
τέταρτος	4th	fourth
πέμπτος	5th	fifth
ἕκτος	6th	sixth
ἕβδομος	7th	seventh
ὄγδοος	8th	eighth
ἕνατος	9th	ninth
δέκατος	10th	tenth
ἑνδέκατος	11th	eleventh
δωδέκατος	12th	twelfth
δέκατος τρίτος	13th	thirteenth
δέκατος τέταρτος	14th	fourteenth
δέκατος πέμπτος	15th	fifteenth
δέκατος ἕκτος	16th	sixteenth
δέκατος ἕβδομος	17th	seventeenth
δέκατος ὄγδοος	18th	eighteenth
δέκατος ἕνατος	19th	nineteenth
εἰκοστός	20th	twentieth
εἰκοστός πρῶτος	21st	twenty-first
εἰκοστός δεύτερος	22nd	twenty-second
εἰκοστός τρίτος	23rd	twenty-third
τριακοστός ′	30th	thirtieth
τεσσερακοστός	40th	fortieth
πεντηκοστός	50th	fiftieth
ἑξηκοστός	60th	sixtieth
ἑβδομηκοστός	70th	seventieth
ὀγδοηκοστός	80th	eightieth
ἐνενηκοστός	90th	ninetieth
ἐνενηκοστός πέμπτος	95th	ninety-fifth
ἑκατοστός	100th	(one) hundredth
διακοσιοστός	200th	two hundredth
χιλιοστός	1,000th	(one) thousandth
ἑκατομμυριοστός	1,000,000th	millionth